lonely planet

East Africa

**Hugh Finlay
Mary Fitzpatrick
Matthew Fletcher
Nick Ray**

LONELY PLANET PUBLICATIONS
Melbourne • Oakland • London • Paris

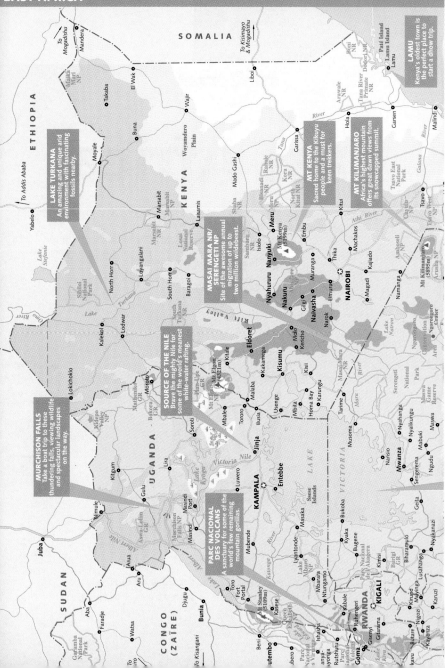

SOMALIA

To Mogadishu

To Kismayo & Mogadishu

LAMU
Kenya's oldest town is the perfect place to start a dhow trip.

ETHIOPIA

To Addis Ababa

LAKE TURKANA
An amazing and unique environment with fascinating fossils nearby.

KENYA

MT KENYA
Sacred home to the Kikuyu people and a must for keen trekkers.

MT KILIMANJARO
Africa's highest mountain offers great dawn views from its snowcapped summit.

MASAI MARA NR/ SERENGETI NP
Site of the awesome annual migration of up to two million wildebeest.

NAIROBI

SOURCE OF THE NILE
Brave the mighty Nile for some of the world's meanest white-water rafting.

MURCHISON FALLS
Take a boat trip to these thundering falls, viewing wildlife and spectacular landscapes on the way.

UGANDA

KAMPALA

LAKE VICTORIA

PARC NATIONAL DES VOLCANS
A sanctuary for some of the world's few remaining mountain gorillas.

SUDAN

CONGO (ZAÏRE)

KIGALI

RWANDA

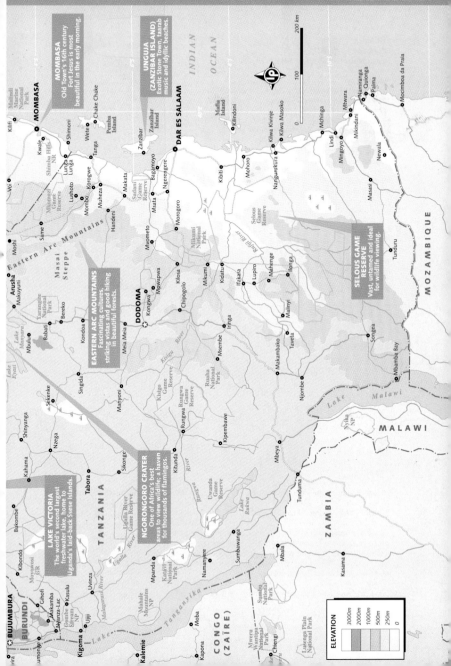

EAST AFRICA

MOMBASA
Old Town's 16th century Fort Jesus is most beautiful in the early morning.

UNGUJA
(ZANZIBAR ISLAND)
Exotic Stone Town, taarab music and idyllic beaches.

200 km

100

0

INDIAN OCEAN

EASTERN ARC MOUNTAINS
Fascinating cultures, striking vistas and good hiking in beautiful forests.

SELOUS GAME RESERVE
Vast, untamed and ideal for wildlife viewing.

LAKE VICTORIA
The world's second largest freshwater lake, home to Uganda's laid-back Ssese Islands.

NGORONGORO CRATER
One of Africa's best areas to view wildlife; a haven for thousands of flamingos.

KENYA

Malindi Marine National Park

Kilifi

MOMBASA

Kwale

Shimoni

Shimba Hills NR

Lunga Lunga

Voi

Moshi

Arusha

Makuyuni

Tarangire National Park

Babati

Mbulu

Lake Manyara

Lake Eyasi

Sekenke

Singida

Manyoni

Kisigo Game Reserve

Rungwa

Rungwa Game Reserve

Lwafi River

Ugalla River

Malagarasi River

Ugalla Game Reserve

Uvinza

Kigoma

Ujiji

Kasulu

Gombe Stream NP

Kibondo

Moyowosi GR

Gihofi

Makamba

Nyanza-Lac

BUJUMBURA

BURUNDI

Kibondo

Kigoma

Lake Tanganyika

Mahale Mountains NP

Mpanda

Katavi National Park

Sitalike

Namanyere

Sumbawanga

Mbala

Kasama

ZAMBIA

Tunduma

Moba

Kapona

Kalemie

CONGO (ZAÏRE)

Chiengi

Mweru Wantipa National Park

Sumbu National Park

Mbeya

Mbala

Lusenga Plain National Park

Lake Mweru

Lake Rukwa

Mbamba Bay

Songea

Njombe

Makambako

Taveta

Iringa

Msembe

Ruaha National Park

Kitunda

Kipembawe

Lake Malawi

MALAWI

Nyika NP

MOZAMBIQUE

Tunduru

Masasi

Newala

Mikindani

Mtwara

Namiranga

Quionga

Palma

Mocimboa da Praia

Lindi

Mingoyo

Nangwrukuru

Mchinga

Kilwa Masoko

Kilwa Kivinje

Kilwa

Mohoro

Kibiti

Kidatu

Ifakara

Mahenge

Ilonga

Lupiro

Mikumi

Selous Game Reserve

Mikumi National Park

Morogoro

Kilosa

Kidatu

Mpwapwa

Chipogolo

DODOMA

Kongwa

Mela Mela

Kondoa

Bereko

Masai Steppe

Eastern Arc Mountains

Same

Mombo

Korogwe

Muheza

Handeni

Lushoto

Tanga

Pangani

Bagamoyo

DAR ES SALAAM

Mkata

Msata

Ngerengere

Saadani Game Reserve

Zanzibar Island

Zanzibar

Mafia Island

Kilindoni

Mkomazi Game Reserve

Pemba Island

Chake Chake

Wete

Lunga Lunga

Myometo

Kongwa

TANZANIA

Tabora

Nzega

Kahama

Shinyanga

Bakombe

Kibondo

Lake Victoria

Skonge

Kiteta

ELEVATION

3000m
2000m
1000m
500m
250m
0

East Africa
5th edition – June 2000
First published – September 1987

Published by
Lonely Planet Publications Pty Ltd A.C.N. 005 607 983
192 Burwood Rd, Hawthorn, Victoria 3122, Australia

Lonely Planet Offices
Australia PO Box 617, Hawthorn, Victoria 3122
USA 150 Linden St, Oakland, CA 94607
UK 10a Spring Place, London NW5 3BH
France 1 rue du Dahomey, 75011 Paris

Photographs
Many of the images in this guide are available for licensing from
Lonely Planet Images.
email: lpi@lonelyplanet.com.au

Front cover photograph
Grevy's Zebra, Samburu NR, Kenya (Andrew van Smeerdijk)

Title page photograph
Facing page 88 (Jason Edwards)

ISBN 0 86442 676 3

Contents – Text

UGANDA 499

THE MOUNTAIN GORILLAS OF EAST AFRICA 611

RWANDA 617

BURUNDI 653

Contents – Maps

RWANDA 617

BURUNDI 653

The Authors

Hugh Finlay

Deciding there must be more to life than civil engineering, Hugh took off around Australia in the mid-1970s, working at everything from spray painting to diamond prospecting before hitting the overland trail. He joined Lonely Planet in 1985 and has written *Jordan & Syria* and *Northern Territory*, co-authored *Kenya* and *Morocco, Algeria & Tunisia*, and updated *Nepal* and the Queensland chapter of *Australia*. Hugh lives in central Victoria. Hugh was the coordinating author for this book and updated the introductory chapters.

Mary Fitzpatrick

Mary grew up in Washington, DC and has travelled extensively in Africa, Asia and Europe. Her journeys have taken her on foot through remote Malagasy rainforests, on rickety pick-ups to dusty villages in the Sahel, by dhow to palm-fringed East African islands, and on bicycle through Tibet and south-western China. For most of the past six years, she has worked in Africa, first on development projects in Mozambique, and more recently as a freelance writer in Liberia and Sierra Leone. Mary also wrote Lonely Planet's *Tanzania, Zanzibar & Pemba* and *Read This First – Africa* and has contributed to LP's *West Africa* and *Africa on a shoestring* guidebooks. Mary updated the Tanzania chapter.

Matt Fletcher

Matt's first major travels were along the northern coast of Spain in a combi-van. Hooked on travel and trekking, after leaving art college Matt traded a damp flat in England for camp sites under African skies where the Maralal International Camel Derby and northern coast of Mozambique inspired a writing career. A brief incarnation as a staff writer on an adventure sports magazine soon passed and Matt has been freelancing ever since, his travel and trekking articles appearing in a wide range of newspapers and magazines from the *Guardian* to *Feng Shui for Modern Living*. He has authored Lonely Planet's *Kenya* and contributed to Lonely Planet's *Walking in Spain* and *Bushwalking in Australia*. Matt updated the Kenya chapter.

Nick Ray

A Londoner of sorts, Nick comes from Watford, the sort of town that makes you want to travel. Nick doesn't spend much time in the big smoke now, having swapped his pint glass for a large bottle of the local brew wherever he may be working. He studied history and politics at the University of Warwick and staggered out a few years later, dazed and confused, clutching a piece of paper that said he knew stuff about things. After a stint as a journalist in London, he decided office hours were not for him and headed overseas. During this time he found himself on adventure tours in countries from Morocco to Vietnam. But Cambodia was the one country that really got under his skin and he now likes to think of it as something of a base. Nick updated the Uganda, Rwanda and Burundi chapters.

FROM THE AUTHORS

From Mary

First of all, a big thank you to my husband Rick, for his ongoing support, encouragement and patience. In Tanzania, I'd like to extend my gratitude to all those who assisted me with my research, in particular: Tim Fowler in Mtwara (who also gets belated thanks for his help on an earlier research trip); Tim Straker-Cook in Lindi; Leah Barton in Bukoba; Maryam Suleiman Omar in Zanzibar; Stefan Bekker on Pemba; and Mr. Atu Mathew in Dar es Salaam.

From Matt

As always, many people lent assistance in many ways. At the top of the Role of Honour are Tony and Susanna Irvin. Without their help and hospitality the job would have been 10 times harder and half as much fun. Big thanks to Pete & Dyreen Quinn, Clive Wells, Dave Elsworth, Dave and Lynn, and all those folks at ILRI who gave me help and advice. Thanks also to Chris & Kerstin Handelman, Kris Zachrisson, Pete Toms, Malcolm Gascoigne, Jane & Julia Barnley, Manmeet Sandhu, Liz Peacock, David Chianda, Steve Turner, Patrick Wanjohi and Alex English. Thanks also to fellow Lonely Planet author David Andrew for his assistance with the national parks information and lowdown on the inner workings of Lonely Planet. Lastly many thanks (again) to Clare Irvin, Jon 'too tall' Cummins and Angus Thompson for all the proofreading and piss taking.

From Nick

On a project of this size, many people help in many ways and it is never possible to thank everyone who helped make my work easier and more fun in Uganda, Rwanda and Burundi.

In Uganda, thank you to the staff of the UWA and particularly to Lilly B Ajarova for assistance in Kampala. Also thanks to the staff of UTB and particularly to Shaun and Ignatius. Thanks to John and Beatrice Hunwick, Niklas, Danny Ssozi, Pam, KK, Michael and Rose, Corrie Bell, Andy Roberts, Chris Zweigenthal, Chibina and of course the Kampala nightshift that included, among others, Gordon, Fiona, Sharon and Carol.

In Rwanda many thanks to my companions for the trip, Santos and Christian Mejia, Beatrice and Nick. Also many thanks to the family of Beatrice for looking after us in Kigali and brother Richard who helped introduce us to the night scene. Thanks to Beth Payne, Mwanzi Kayihura and Patrice.

In Burundi thanks to Aly Wood, Colonel Minani and friends for a night out and some background on security. Also to Andy Johnson and Mum and Dad for dipping their toes into a new part of the world – I hope you enjoyed the experience.

This Book

Geoff Crowther wrote the 1st edition of *East Africa* and then teamed with Hugh Finlay to update the next three editions. Hugh coordinated this 5th edition and updated the introductory chapters while Matt Fletcher updated Kenya, Mary Fitzpatrick took care of Tanzania and Nick Ray worked on Uganda, Rwanda and Burundi.

FROM THE PUBLISHER

This 5th edition of *East Africa* was edited in Lonely Planet's Melbourne office by Justin Flynn and his eagle-eyed team of trusty pen-pushers: Elizabeth Swan, Kerryn Burgess, Evan Jones, Michelle Coxall, Anne Mulvaney, Sarah Mathers, Susan Holtham, Dan Goldberg and Bethune Carmichael. The cartography & design was expertly coordinated by Rodney Zandbergs with assistance from the dedicated Katie Butterworth, Anna Judd, Sarah Sloane and Shahara Ahmed. Thanks to Luke Hunter for writing the East African Wildlife special section and to Adriana Mammarella for the design. Well done to Quentin Frayne for the Language chapter. Mark Germanchis took care of the climate charts, Sarah Jolly provided the illustrations and Maria Vallianos can take the credit for the brilliant cover design.

THANKS
Many thanks to the travellers who used the last edition and wrote to us with helpful hints, advice and interesting anecdotes. Your names appear on the following pages.

9

Acknowledgments

Many thanks to the travellers who used the last edition and wrote to us with helpful hints, useful advice and interesting anecdotes:

A Gage, Alexander Cisik, Alexander Niklas, Alistair Spicer, Anantrai Chatrabhuj, Anders Bjornestad, Anders Hole, Anders Jonsson, Andrea Arnold, Andrea Cervenka MD, Andrew Bracken, Andrew Hill, Andrew McNeil, Andrew Petrow, Andrew Pickett, Andrew Redfern, Andrew Thorburn, Andrew Van Smeerdijk, Andy Lepp, Andy Medwell, Angela Dale, Angela Stamm, Angela Wiens, Anita Sylte, Ann Martin, Anna Stockley, Anna Woltschenko, Anne Dethlefsen, Anne Marte Jensen, Annette Magnusson, Annika Holmberg, Anthony Abry, Anthony Solomon, Arjan Snijders, Arne RagoBnig, Audun Lundberg, B Schnell, Barbara Knopf, Barbara Konrad, Bent Olsby, Bernd Friese, Beverley Gadsdon, Bill Burt, Bouke Endtz, Brian Johnson, Brigette Reineld, Brigitte Hauselmann, Bruno Herberth, C & C Bell, C L Rutherfors, Carey Eaton, Caroline Fafflok, Cass Farrar, Catherine Willemsen, Cato & Henk Verschoor, Cerutti Thierry, Charles Lyamba, Charmaine & Ian Otto, Cheryl Robinson, Chris Chandler, Chris Kilala, Chris Mithchell, Chris Wilson, Christina Baccino, Christina Nikolaus, Christine Azzaro, Christine Holtschoppen, Christine McNeal, Claire & Edouard Tavernier, Cleo Wiesent, Colin Royed, Colin Stubley, Conrad Aalpol, Craig Bolger, Craig Lenske, Dan Kobb, Dan Taylor, Daniella Zipkin, Darren Welsh, Darryl Cloonan, Darryn McConkey, Dave Harcourt, David & Cynthia Andrewartha, David Barbour, David Heath, David Irvine, David Katz, David Kutten, David Luttig, David Marsh, David Pluth, David Thomforde, David Walter, Derek Jackson, Diallo Yassine, Diana Johnson, Dirk Barth, Doug Gage, Dr Jitka Jilemicka, Dr Pierre Dil, Duby Gurtinkel, Duncan & Alison Swallow, E L Train, Emile Baak, Emily Roberts, Emma Granville, Emmeram Rabhofer, Enrico Pozzi, Eric Johnson, Erik Veldkamp, Esther Snowden, Evert Nieuwenhais, Eyal Shaham, Fernanda Carley, Filip Bogaert, Florian Roser, Frances Laurence, Frank Bassler, Frank Hawes, Franklin Murillo, Frans van Velden, Fredric Carlson, Fredrik Esbjornsson, G Corner, Gabriela Furlotti, Gard Halvorseen, Gary Thomass, George Bogojevic, Georgina Cranston, Gerard Kohl, Gianni Fontana, Ginger Mielke, Giorgio Scala, Glenn Hori, Graham Barnes, Grahame Grover, Griselda Haz, Grith Poulstrup, Guuster Visser, Hans & Jane Bode, Hans Claessens, Hans Gysin, Hans Verhoef, Heidi Brooks, Helen & Iorwenth Jones, Helen Readdie, Helene Croon, Henk Hamminga, Henri Bemelmans, Henriette van den Elzen, Henrik Stabell, Herman Heller, Hugh Wilkins, Ian Morgan, Ian Ramsbottom, Ilona Duijs, Imke Haenen, Imke Nabben, Ingitha Borisch, J Christie, J Murphy, J Walker, Jake Lebowitz, James Howson, James Milner, James Munn, James Stubberfield, Jan Christian Igelkjoen, Jan Slapeta, Jane Bode, Jeff Wilner, Jeff Willmot, Jenny Svensson, Jenny Woodhouse, Jens Henkner, Jeremy Thornley, Jeroen Thiss, Jeroen van As, Jim Nilson, Jim Runnels, Jim Wilson, Joan Attridge, Joanna Keable, John W Dickie, Jonathon Steele, Jorg van Gent, Josef Mladek, Judy & Burgess

Williams, Julia Spargo, Julie Goulding, Julie Jeffcott, Julie Noywood, June Skodje Skaar, Justine Waddington, Jutta Christoph, Karen Gregor, Karen Lyons, Karl Mattsson-Boze, Karla Huber, Karlein Morgan, Kate Hudson, Kate McMahon, Kath & Will Staughton, Kathryn O'Neill, Katja Masjosthusmann, Katte Lee, Keiko Yamamoto, Keiran Houghton, Keith Anderson, Kerstin Schropfer, Kevin Pollock, Konstantin Joanidopoulos, Kylie Bradford, Lara Pacellini, Lars Holmgren, Laura Lenyk, Laura Ospina, Laura Wade, Leana Killough, Leanne Kaufman, Leigh Harrington, Leisha Zanardo, Lia Reedijk, Liam O'Duidhir, Line Thaudahl Jakobson, Lisa Goulet, Lori Graham, Lorraine White, Lorrie Scnurr, Louise Armitage, Luke Jackson, Lynn Anat, M Raymond, M Riley, Mads Odgaard Andersen, Magnus Seger, Malcolm Ruckledge, Manuel Guillen, Marah & Lis Rhoades, Marc Grutering, Marguerite Jackson, Mari Toyohara, Maria Klambauer, Marianne Cornila, Marianne Destoop, Marit Holen, Mark Adams, Mark Howard, Mark Ogilvie, Mark Simmeren, Mark Ssebo Ogwang, Marla Smith-Nilson, Marlies Kappers, Martin De Paepe, Martin Griffiths, Martin Marousek, Martin Romeder, Mary K Holland, Mary Tolfree, Matha Linchausen, Matilde Juul, Matt Brown, Matt Wipf, Matthew Harries, Matthias Kyhlstedt, Meghan Powell, Mel Saltzman, Melissa Carr, Michael Gatto, Michael Hauser, Michael Herfurth, Michael Maltenfort, Michael Maurer, Michael Moss, Michele Genovese, Michelle Gavin, Mike Best, Mike Cannon, Mike Matthews, Milena Holcova, Minaz Dhanani, Mirjam de Jager, Morten Broberg, Mrisho Haji Vuaa, Naomi Cummings, Naomi Stephen-Smith, Natalie Smith, Natalie Yates, Neil Stevenson, Niall Watt, Nick Meech, Nicola J Rizza, Niels Claessens, Nina Kulas, Nizam Hasham, Olaf Brodacki, Oliver Lotz, Oliver Thornton, Pal Wibe, Pam Sykes, Paronuzzi Frederick, Patricia Van Delft, Patrik Pettersson, Paul Kortenaar, Paula Hutt, Pauline Horton, Pedro Arizti, Peter Gum, Peter Keil, Peter Kelly, Peter Simpson, Petra Sachs, Phil Dunnington, R J Neate, R McSporran, Rachel Keen, Rachel Stepek, Rachel Taylor, Raimo Lonka, Rainer Kocherscheidt, Ralf Barth, Rebecca Casey, Rebecca Casson, Rebecca McGinley, Rebecca Minnit, Rebecca Winterborn, Richard A Riegels, Richard Carr, Richard Carroll, Richard Klaver, Richard Walter, Rick Chatteron, Rini Paul, Rob Kent Kalamazoo, Robert Chamberlin, Robert Crane, Robert Goldberg, Robert Lichtenstein, Robert Money, Rolf Layer, Rupert Kaul, Russ Ty, Ruth Coxall, Ryan Matthews, Said Hassan Mnkeni, Saleem Taibjee, Sally Tong, Samantha Witman, Sanche Simpson-Davis, Sandie Gustus, Sandra Mos, Sanjay Anantrai, Sarah Jane McKay, Sarah Pickup, Sarah Varnes, Sarfo Addo, Shane Ryan, Sigrun Wagner, Simon Deverell, Simon Murray, Staffan & Lotta Johnson, Stefan Burm, Stefan Gossling, Steve Fisher, Sue Jackson, Suen de Vocht, Susan Buchanan, Susie Muir, Synnove Holst, Tami Ebner, Tanya Beaumont, Tessa Mattholie, Therese Allan, Thomas Jensen, Thomas Mauhart, Thomas Nigg, Thomas V Maloney, Thorleif Etgen, Tim Jenkins, Tonia Walden, Tony Dunne, Tracey O'Higgins, Val Leichti, Venu Parameswar, Venu Thirunamachandran, Viv Molloy, Vivian Wesselingh, Wayne Levy, Wendy Pratt, William Mee, Willis Jenkins, Wouter van der Heidje, Yvonne & Albert de Haas.

Foreword

ABOUT LONELY PLANET GUIDEBOOKS

The story begins with a classic travel adventure: Tony and Maureen Wheeler's 1972 journey across Europe and Asia to Australia. Useful information about the overland trail did not exist at that time, so Tony and Maureen published the first Lonely Planet guidebook to meet a growing need.

From a kitchen table, then from a tiny office in Melbourne (Australia), Lonely Planet has become the largest independent travel publisher in the world, an international company with offices in Melbourne, Oakland (USA), London (UK) and Paris (France).

Today Lonely Planet guidebooks cover the globe. There is an ever-growing list of books and there's information in a variety of forms and media. Some things haven't changed. The main aim is still to help make it possible for adventurous travellers to get out there – to explore and better understand the world.

At Lonely Planet we believe travellers can make a positive contribution to the countries they visit – if they respect their host communities and spend their money wisely. Since 1986 a percentage of the income from each book has been donated to aid projects and human rights campaigns.

Updates Lonely Planet thoroughly updates each guidebook as often as possible. This usually means there are around two years between editions, although for more unusual or more stable destinations the gap can be longer. Check the imprint page (following the colour map at the beginning of the book) for publication dates.

Between editions up-to-date information is available in two free newsletters – the paper *Planet Talk* and email *Comet* (to subscribe, contact any Lonely Planet office) – and on our Web site at www.lonelyplanet.com. The *Upgrades* section of the Web site covers a number of important and volatile destinations and is regularly updated by Lonely Planet authors. *Scoop* covers news and current affairs relevant to travellers. And, lastly, the *Thorn Tree* bulletin board and *Postcards* section of the site carry unverified, but fascinating, reports from travellers.

Correspondence The process of creating new editions begins with the letters, postcards and emails received from travellers. This correspondence often includes suggestions, criticisms and comments about the current editions. Interesting excerpts are immediately passed on via newsletters and the Web site, and everything goes to our authors to be verified when they're researching on the road. We're keen to get more feedback from organisations or individuals who represent communities visited by travellers.

Lonely Planet gathers information for everyone who's curious about the planet – and especially for those who explore it first-hand. Through guidebooks, phrasebooks, activity guides, maps, literature, newsletters, image library, TV series and Web site we act as an information exchange for a worldwide community of travellers.

Research Authors aim to gather sufficient practical information to enable travellers to make informed choices and to make the mechanics of a journey run smoothly. They also research historical and cultural background to help enrich the travel experience and allow travellers to understand and respond appropriately to cultural and environmental issues.

Authors don't stay in every hotel because that would mean spending a couple of months in each medium-sized city and, no, they don't eat at every restaurant because that would mean stretching belts beyond capacity. They do visit hotels and restaurants to check standards and prices, but feedback based on readers' direct experiences can be very helpful.

Many of our authors work undercover, others aren't so secretive. None of them accept freebies in exchange for positive write-ups. And none of our guidebooks contain any advertising.

Production Authors submit their raw manuscripts and maps to offices in Australia, USA, UK or France. Editors and cartographers – all experienced travellers themselves – then begin the process of assembling the pieces. When the book finally hits the shops, some things are already out of date, we start getting feedback from readers and the process begins again ...

WARNING & REQUEST

Things change – prices go up, schedules change, good places go bad and bad places go bankrupt – nothing stays the same. So, if you find things better or worse, recently opened or long since closed, please tell us and help make the next edition even more accurate and useful. We genuinely value all the feedback we receive. Julie Young coordinates a well travelled team that reads and acknowledges every letter, postcard and email and ensures that every morsel of information finds its way to the appropriate authors, editors and cartographers for verification.

Everyone who writes to us will find their name in the next edition of the appropriate guidebook. They will also receive the latest issue of *Planet Talk*, our quarterly printed newsletter, or *Comet*, our monthly email newsletter. Subscriptions to both newsletters are free. The very best contributions will be rewarded with a free guidebook.

Excerpts from your correspondence may appear in new editions of Lonely Planet guidebooks, the Lonely Planet Web site, *Planet Talk* or *Comet*, so please let us know if you *don't* want your letter published or your name acknowledged.

Send all correspondence to the Lonely Planet office closest to you:

Australia: PO Box 617, Hawthorn, Victoria 3122
USA: 150 Linden St, Oakland, CA 94607
UK: 10A Spring Place, London NW5 3BH
France: 1 rue du Dahomey, 75011 Paris

Or email us at: talk2us@lonelyplanet.com.au

For news, views and updates see our Web site: www.lonelyplanet.com

HOW TO USE A LONELY PLANET GUIDEBOOK

The best way to use a Lonely Planet guidebook is any way you choose. At Lonely Planet we believe the most memorable travel experiences are often those that are unexpected, and the finest discoveries are those you make yourself. Guidebooks are not intended to be used as if they provide a detailed set of infallible instructions!

Contents All Lonely Planet guidebooks follow roughly the same format. The Facts about the Destination chapters or sections give background information ranging from history to weather. Facts for the Visitor gives practical information on issues like visas and health. Getting There & Away gives a brief starting point for researching travel to and from the destination. Getting Around gives an overview of the transport options when you arrive.

The peculiar demands of each destination determine how subsequent chapters are broken up, but some things remain constant. We always start with background, then proceed to sights, places to stay, places to eat, entertainment, getting there and away, and getting around information – in that order.

Heading Hierarchy Lonely Planet headings are used in a strict hierarchical structure that can be visualised as a set of Russian dolls. Each heading (and its following text) is encompassed by any preceding heading that is higher on the hierarchical ladder.

Entry Points We do not assume guidebooks will be read from beginning to end, but that people will dip into them. The traditional entry points are the list of contents and the index. In addition, however, some books have a complete list of maps and an index map illustrating map coverage.

There may also be a colour map that shows highlights. These highlights are dealt with in greater detail in the Facts for the Visitor chapter, along with planning questions and suggested itineraries. Each chapter covering a geographical region usually begins with a locator map and another list of highlights. Once you find something of interest in a list of highlights, turn to the index.

Maps Maps play a crucial role in Lonely Planet guidebooks and include a huge amount of information. A legend is printed on the back page. We seek to have complete consistency between maps and text, and to have every important place in the text captured on a map. Map key numbers usually start in the top left corner.

Although inclusion in a guidebook usually implies a recommendation we cannot list every good place. Exclusion does not necessarily imply criticism. In fact there are a number of reasons why we might exclude a place – sometimes it is simply inappropriate to encourage an influx of travellers.

Introduction

If your vision of Africa is of elephants crossing the plain below snowcapped Mt Kilimanjaro, an Arab dhow sailing into the stone town of Zanzibar, a million pink flamingos on a glistening lake and/or Maasai tribespeople guarding their cattle, then East Africa is where this vision becomes reality.

This book covers a small group of countries of absorbing interest and diversity.

Whatever your interests, East Africa has plenty to see, experience and consider.

Kenya and Tanzania are the heart of African safariland. Some of the most famous game reserves are found here, and in a trip to these countries you will probably see everything from rhinos to lions, hippos to baboons, wildebeest to flamingos. Safaris are an experience in themselves but the reserves, such as Ngorongoro in Tanzania,

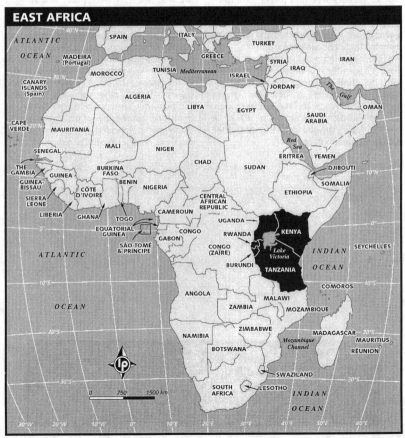

EAST AFRICA

which is in the crater of a colossal extinct volcano, or Amboseli in Kenya, which has Mt Kilimanjaro as a spectacular backdrop, are also spectacular.

The reserves of Kenya and Tanzania are the region's best-known natural attractions, but they are certainly not the only ones. Murchison Falls is just one of a number of spectacular national parks in Uganda, and Bwindi in the country's rugged south-west offers the region's premier gorilla-viewing opportunities. Gorillas are also the highlight of Rwanda, where the Parc Nacional des Volcans has recently reopened. Scuba divers and snorkellers will find plenty to interest them along the coast and around the offshore islands, while other visitors may find lazing on the pristine beaches and collecting a suntan quite enough exercise.

If lazing isn't a word in your vocabulary, East Africa offers some wonderful mountains to climb or trek. If you're fit, an assault on Mt Kenya or, best of all, snow-capped Mt Kilimanjaro, the highest mountain in Africa, is within your reach, or there's less crowded Mt Elgon on the Kenya-Uganda border.

East Africa isn't just wildlife and scenery – there are also people, cultures and politics. Politically the region offers as wide a span of Africa's problems and aspirations as you could ask for. At one extreme there's Kenya, where Africa really works and where stability and progress have been the norm, a situation very different from so many other African nations. Tanzania illustrates where the best of African intentions can go disastrously awry, while Rwanda and Burundi are painful examples of the horrors of tribal animosity. Uganda is the shining light in the area – the bad old days are well and truly over, peace and stability have returned and there's a new feeling of optimism.

The cultures and peoples of the region are equally interesting. Along the coast, and particularly on islands such as Zanzibar and Lamu, you can observe the strong influence of the Arabs, who came first as traders and later as slavers and remained in the region for centuries. Everywhere you'll see the many and varied tribes of the region, particularly the strong-minded Maasai of Kenya. Go there – it's a wonderful region.

Facts about East Africa

HISTORY
The Birthplace of Humanity

The Rift Valley, which cuts a swathe through East Africa, has been established as the 'cradle of humanity' as a result of the now famous digs of the Leakey family in Olduvai Gorge (Tanzania) and around Lake Turkana (Kenya). Their discoveries of several hominoid skulls, one of which is estimated to be 2½ million years old, radically altered the accepted theories on the origin of humans.

Before the East African digs, the generally accepted theory was that the ancestors of modern humans were of two different species: the ape-like *Australopithecus africanus* and the *Australopithecus robustus*. It was believed one of these died out while the other gave rise to *Homo sapiens*. The Leakey discoveries suggest that there was a third contemporary species, *Homo habilis*, and that it was this one which gave rise to modern humans while both the Australopithecus species died out, leaving no descendants.

Early Settlement

This area of Africa has a large diversity of peoples – it is home to almost every major language stock in Africa. Even Khoisan, the 'click' language spoken by the San and Hottentots in Southern Africa, has its representatives, although these days they are only tiny communities in Kenya and Tanzania. This diversity is clear evidence that East Africa has been a major migratory pathway over the centuries.

The first wave of immigrants were the tall, nomadic, Cushitic-speaking peoples from Ethiopia who began to move south about 2000 BC. They were pastoralists and depended on good grazing land for their cattle and goats, so when the climate began to change and the area around Lake Turkana became more arid, they were forced to resume their migration south. They were to reach as far as central Tanzania. Their advance was only stopped by the Gogo people, who occupied an area west of the Rift Valley, and the Hehe to the south of Dodoma.

A second group of pastoralists, the Eastern Cushitics, followed them in about 1000 BC and occupied much of central Kenya. The rest of the ancestors of the region's medley of tribes arrived from all over Africa between 500 BC and 500 AD, though there was still much movement and rivalry for land right up to the beginning of the 20th century.

Further west, in the Great Lakes region which encompasses what is now Rwanda and Burundi, the original inhabitants were the Twa Pygmies, who now comprise only 1% of the population of this area. They were gradually displaced from about 1000 AD onwards by Hutu, mostly farmers of Bantu stock, who now make up 85% of the population of Rwanda and Burundi.

In the 16th and 17th centuries, the western region experienced another wave of migration. This time it was the tall, pastoralist Watutsi from Ethiopia, who now make up around 14% of the population. The Watutsi gradually subjugated the Hutu into a type of feudal system, similar to that which operated in medieval Europe. The Watutsi became a loosely organised aristocracy with a *mwami* (king), at the top of each social pyramid. Under this system the Hutu relinquished their land and mortgaged their services to the nobility in return for cattle – the symbol of wealth and status.

Arab & Persian Traders

While migrations were going on in the interior, Muslims from the Arabian peninsula and Shirazis from Persia (now Iran) began to visit the East African coast from the 8th century AD onwards. They came to trade, convert and settle rather than conquer as they had done in North Africa and Spain. Their dhows would head down on the north-east monsoon bringing with them glassware, ironware, textiles, wheat and wine, returning with ivory, slaves, tortoise-shell and rhino horn.

It was Arab traders and slavers who first penetrated the interior as far as Lake Tanganyika in the middle of the 18th century. Their main depots were at Ujiji on the shores of Lake Tanganyika and at Tabora on the central plain. Their captives, generally acquired by commerce rather than force, were taken first to Bagamoyo and then to Zanzibar, where they were either put to work on plantations or shipped to the Arabian Peninsula for sale as domestic servants.

Trade with East Africa soon extended right across the Indian Ocean to India and beyond. (Even China entered the fray at one point early in the 15th century, with a fleet of 62 ships and an escort of some 37,000 men, after the king of Malindi had sent the Chinese emperor a gift of a giraffe!) Many of the traders stayed to settle and intermarry with the Africans. As a result, a string of relatively affluent and Islamic-influenced coastal towns sprang up along the East African coast from Somalia to Mozambique, acting as entrepots for the cross-Indian Ocean trade. Though there was naturally rivalry between these towns from time to time, up until the 16th century life was relatively peaceful. All this was to be rudely shattered with the arrival of the Portuguese.

Portuguese Invaders

While the Spanish Crown was busy backing expeditions to the Americas, the Portuguese were determined to circumvent the Ottoman Turks' grip on trade with the Far East, particularly the trade in spices, which were worth more than their weight in gold in Europe. Throughout the 15th century, the Portuguese had been exploring further and further down the western coast of Africa until, in 1498, they finally rounded the Cape of Good Hope and headed up the east coast under the command of Vasco da Gama.

The Portuguese were given a hostile reception both at Sofala on the Mozambique coast and at Mombasa but were lucky to find a friendly sultan at Malindi who provided them with a pilot who knew the route to India. Da Gama was back again with another expedition in 1502, after selling the first expedition's cargo of spices in Portugal and reaping a small fortune.

The main Portuguese onslaught began with Dom Francisco de Almeida's armada of 23 ships and some 1500 men in 1505. Sofala was burned to the ground and looted, while further north Kilwa was occupied and garrisoned, and Mombasa was taken after a naval bombardment and fierce street fighting. Mombasa was sacked again by Nuña da Cunha in 1528. The Arab monopoly of Indian Ocean trade had been broken and, though the Ottoman Turks attempted to wrest it back from the Portuguese in 1585 and again in 1589, they were unsuccessful.

After the original onslaught, there followed two centuries of harsh colonial rule. Tribute was demanded and levies were imposed on all non-Portuguese ships visiting the coastal towns. Severe retribution was the reward for the slightest offence. Economic exploitation came hand in hand with a drive to convert the local population to Catholicism but they never had much success at this, and whenever they abandoned an outpost, those who had been 'converted' reverted to Islam. Mombasa came to be the principle Portuguese outpost following the construction of Fort Jesus there in 1593.

The Portuguese task was made easier as they were able to play one sultan off against another. However, their grip over the East African coast was always tenuous since their outposts had to be supplied from Goa in India, where the viceroy had his headquarters. Delays were inevitable. The colonial bureaucracy also became moribund because of the sale of offices to the highest bidder. And, in the final analysis, Portugal lacked sufficient resources to effectively hold onto a worldwide empire.

The beginning of the end came in 1698 when Fort Jesus fell to the Arabs after a siege lasting 33 months. By 1720 the Portuguese had packed up and left the East African coast for good.

Omani Dynasties

The Arabs were to remain in control of the East African coast until the arrival of the

British and Germans in the late 19th century. The depredations of the Portuguese period had exacted a heavy price and the constant quarrelling among the Arab governors who succeeded them led to a decline in the trade and prosperity that the East African coast had once enjoyed. Political and economic recovery had to wait until the beginning of the 19th century.

Throughout the 18th century, Omani dynasties from the Persian Gulf entrenched themselves along the East African coast. They were nominally under the control of the sultan of Oman but this control was largely ineffective until Seyyid Said came to the Omani throne in 1805.

The Omanis had built up a relatively powerful navy during the latter part of the 18th century and Seyyid Said decided to use this to bring the East African dynasties into line. In 1822 he sent an army to subdue Mombasa and the islands of Paté and Pemba, which were then ruled by the Mazrui people.

The Mazruis appealed to Britain for help, which it provided the following year in the form of two warships on a survey mission. The commander of one of these ships, Captain Owen, decided to act first and ask questions later, so the British flag was raised over Fort Jesus and a protectorate was declared. A small garrison was left in charge but three years later the British government repudiated the protectorate and the flag was hauled down. Seyyid Said reasserted his control the following year, garrisoned Fort Jesus and began to lay out clove plantations on Zanzibar. In 1832 he moved his court there.

19th Century Colonialism

By the mid-19th century, several European nations, including Britain and Germany, were showing an interest in the East African coast. The British were interested in the suppression of the slave trade and when Seyyid Said moved to Zanzibar they set up a consulate on the island. Later an agreement was reached between the British and the Germans which gave the Germans Tanganyika, Rwanda and Burundi, while the

British took Kenya and Uganda. Part of the deal was that the sultan of Zanzibar would be allowed to retain a 16km-wide strip of the coastline under a British protectorate. It remained as such right up until independence when the last sultan of Zanzibar, Seyyid Khalifa, ceded the territory to the new government.

Towards the end of the century the region was explored by people including Gustav Fischer (a German whose party was virtually annihilated by Maasai at Hell's Gate on Lake Naivasha in 1882), Joseph Thomson (a Scot who reached Lake Victoria via the Rift Valley lakes and the Aberdare Highlands in 1883), and Count Teleki von Szek (an Austrian who explored the Lake Turkana region and Mt Kenya in 1887). James Hannington, an Anglican bishop who set out in 1885 to set up a diocese in Uganda, discovered Lake Bogoria (known as Lake Hannington during colonial days), but was killed when he reached the Nile. Other explorers included Burton and Speke, who were sent to Lake Tanganyika in 1858 by the Royal Geographical Society. The most famous explorers were Stanley and Livingstone. Stanley's famous phrase, 'Dr Livingstone, I presume', stems from their meeting at Ujiji on Lake Tanganyika.

At the turn of the 20th century, both the British and German colonial powers set about building railways and roads to open their colony to commerce, building hospitals and schools and encouraging the influx of Christian missionaries. Kenya's fertile and climatically pleasant highlands were eminently suitable for European farmers to colonise, unlike much of Tanganyika, which was unsuitable for agriculture. Also, in large areas of central and southern Tanganyika, the tsetse fly made cattle grazing or dairying impossible. Most farming in Tanganyika occurred along the coast and around Mt Kilimanjaro and Mt Meru. A few descendants of the original German settlers still live in these areas.

The German occupation of Tanzania continued until the end of WWI, after which the League of Nations mandated Tanganyika to the British and Rwanda and Burundi to the

Belgians. Because of the tsetse flies, the British tended to neglect development of Tanganyika in favour of the more lucrative and fertile options available in Kenya and Uganda. Nevertheless, political consciousness gradually coalesced in the form of farmers' unions and cooperatives through which popular demands were expressed. By the early 1950s, there were over 400 such cooperatives, which were shortly to amalgamate with the Tanganyika Africa Association (TAA), based in Dar es Salaam.

In Uganda the British tended to favour the recruitment of the powerful Buganda people for the civil service. Other tribespeople, unable to acquire responsible jobs in the colonial administration or to make inroads into the Buganda-dominated commercial sector, were forced to seek other ways of joining the mainstream. The Acholi and Lango, for example, chose the army and became the tribal majority in the military. Thus were planted the seeds for the intertribal conflicts which were to tear Uganda apart following independence.

The Belgian period of rule in Rwanda and Burundi was characterised by the increase in power and privilege of the Tutsi, as the Belgians found it convenient to rule indirectly through the mwami and his princes. They were not only trained to run the bureaucracy but had a monopoly on the educational system operated by the Catholic missionaries.

African Nationalism & Independence

The 1950s and early 1960s resulted in the rise of nationalist movements across East Africa. These culminated in the granting of independence to Tanzania (1961); Uganda, Rwanda and Burundi (all in 1962); and Kenya (1963).

The ultimate paths to independence were varied: in Kenya it was violent and protracted; in Tanzania and Uganda it was relatively peaceful and painless; while in Rwanda and Burundi the tribal rivalries, which had existed for centuries and led to the 1994 genocide in Rwanda, were a major impediment.

For details of these various independence movements, and the history of each country since independence, see the individual Facts about the Country chapters.

GEOGRAPHY

East Africa straddles the equator and encompasses a variety of geographical zones. The region is bordered on the western side by the Congo (Zaïre) border, which largely follows the lakes and mountains of the western branch of the Great Rift Valley (see the following Geology section), on the north by Sudan, Ethiopia and Somalia, and on the south by Zambia, Malawi and Mozambique.

The coastal belt, which varies from about 15 to 65km in width, covers littoral coastal forest; coral reefs and beaches; the Lamu and Zanzibar archipelagos; various river estuaries; and a narrow, low-lying and fertile strip of land suitable for agriculture. Beyond this, the terrain rises, steeply at times, towards the central plateau and gives way to arid scrub.

The lake-studded eastern arm of the Great Rift Valley runs through the region from Lake Turkana through Lake Magadi before opening out into the vastness of the Serengeti and is peppered with the cones of extinct volcanoes. This is one of the most fertile areas of the region and the lower slopes of the mountains are intensively cultivated.

An undulating plateau stretches from the Sudanese border south through Uganda, western Kenya and Tanzania. Mt Elgon (4321m) is here. Further south, the shores of Lake Victoria are particularly fertile, and intensively cultivated, while south and east of the lake the land merges into scrub and savanna. It's here that the region's most popular wildlife sanctuaries are situated: Masai Mara, Serengeti and Amboseli. To the south of Amboseli rises the spectacular massif of Mt Kilimanjaro – Africa's highest mountain (5895m).

The north-eastern region of Kenya is a vast mountainous area of bushland, scrub and desert, where rainfall is sparse and the land is suitable only for cattle grazing.

GEOLOGY

The major geological feature in East Africa is the Great Rift Valley, a huge depression which extends nearly 5000km from the Middle East south through to Mozambique in south-eastern Africa.

The valley system consists of a series of troughs and areas of uplift known as swells. The troughs, generally 40 to 55km wide, are along parallel fault lines and are formed by blocks dropping down in relation to the rest of the land. They account for most of the lakes and escarpments in East Africa. The swells are the land on either side of the troughs, and it's on these that you find two of Africa's mightiest peaks: Mt Kilimanjaro (5895m) and Mt Kenya (5199m). These peaks and lesser peaks such as Mt Elgon (4321m) are all extinct volcanoes. The floor of the Rift Valley is still dropping, although at the rate of only a few millimetres each year so therefore you are hardly likely to notice anything.

The Great Rift Valley is certainly not one long well-formed valley with huge escarpments either side, although this does occur in places (the Rift Valley Province in Kenya is one such place). Sometimes there is just a single scarp on one side (such as the Nkuruman Escarpment east of Masai Mara) or just a series of small scarps. In some cases uplift has occurred between parallel fault lines and this has led to the formation of often spectacular mountain ranges such as the Ruwenzoris on the Uganda-Congo (Zaïre) border.

CLIMATE

The climate in East Africa varies with each region because of the varied topography. Broadly speaking, the climate is hot and humid on the coast, and becomes less humid as you move inland. The heat is moderated largely by altitude, and so the cooler areas are found in the highlands. In general, the coolest months are from June to October, and the warmest from December to March.

Rainfall generally comes in two seasons, the 'long' rains from mid-March through May, and the 'short' rains during November and December, but again there are regional variations. Rainfall varies from less than 250mm per year in the semi-arid areas of Kenya's north-east to about 1500mm along the coast and over 3000mm in mountainous areas such as Uganda's south-west.

ECOLOGY & ENVIRONMENT
Pressure for Land

The pressure for land in many parts of East Africa is enormous due to high population growth. This particularly applies to people who live in the immediate vicinity of national parks and reserves, where they face a dual problem: not only is the land reserved for animals but these same animals wander outside the parks, often doing tremendous amounts of damage in the process.

The lack of available grazing land for the tribespeoples' own livestock is a source of tension. Tribe members are often arrested by park wardens and face fines for trespassing in the conservation areas. In Tanzania, they pay a stiff fee of US$13 if they are caught looking for their wayward animals within parks and a fine of US$130 if the animal is found there.

On Maasai land between Amboseli and Tsavo national parks in Kenya the local people have tried a new approach and established their own wildlife sanctuary. This is one of the very few options left open to people who have had much of their land gazetted as parks or reserves and placed off limits. Another is to start some other sort of tourism project, such as a lodge, but this requires investment capital and so is only an option for the well-off few. Still another is to plough up the land and grow wheat, something governments are keen to do in their drive for self-sufficiency. This then creates more conflicts between the people and the animals, as wildlife corridors disappear and animals have to cross previously unfenced land.

What can be done about the conflict between the people and the animals is anyone's guess but the solution will not be easy. Compensating local people out of the tourist receipts from national parks and reserves is one approach which has gained favour recently, as is the case at Bwindi National Park in Uganda. But even here, the amount which finds its way back to the people is very small indeed. One answer may lie in raising the entrance fees into the national parks (as has already been done with gorilla-tracking visits), and making seeing these superb wildlife spectacles a privilege rather than the relatively cheap experience it has been. Of course this is hardly likely to encourage the tourist trade but unless the local people are properly compensated for their land (so that they are financially capable of not turning to crops), it's not inconceivable that the great wildlife reserves of East Africa will become little more than large 'safari parks' not unlike those found in the west.

Environmental Problems

Again it is the tourist industry which is the cause of some of East Africa's major environmental problems. Parks such as Masai Mara (in Kenya) are criss-crossed with tracks and crawling with tourist minibuses. The problem is particularly bad in the Mara, where minibuses seem to go pretty much where they please as regulations are not policed by the local council which administers the reserve. The lodges within the parks themselves also create problems. Foremost among these is in their use of firewood, a valuable and scarce resource – a recent survey found that each of the lodges and tented camps around Masai Mara used, on average, 100 tonnes of firewood in a year.

Other environmental problems include desertification (a particular problem in northern Kenya), erosion, soil degradation and deforestation. Much of the damage being done in these areas is linked directly back to population pressures and insufficient funds put towards the promotion of environmentally sound agricultural practices. While governments are strapped for cash, priority is given to other issues, which require more immediate solutions. Fortunately there are some organisations working for environmental conservation in East Africa, although lack of resources and poor infrastructure are significant hindrances.

Water Hyacinth

Lake Victoria is being choked by water hyacinth. This exotic ornamental pond plant, imported to Kenya from East Asia, was first reported here in 1986 and in 10 years reached plague proportions. Uganda's economy has been the hardest hit by the emerald weed.

The hyacinth's long runners intertwine, forming large impenetrable mats. Cargo ships are often stranded for days because landing sites have become blocked and local people are unable to fish because their boats cannot move through the weed. The hyacinth also provides a great habitat for mosquitoes and snails and cases of malaria and bilharzia around the lake have increased. And it's not just the nonsensical introduction of an exotic plant without any natural predators that humans are responsible for. Fertiliser run-off from surrounding farmland and the dumping of raw sewage into Lake Victoria have increased algal growth, thus reducing oxygen levels in the water and creating conditions intolerable for most of the lake's unique invertebrates.

The cost of trying to control the weed is enormous. In 1996 the World Bank set aside US$77.6 million to help the three countries bordering the lake. Booms are being used to stop the weed spreading into rivers that run into and from the lake, and machines and people clear the weed daily. Herbicide is also used on the hyacinth, though this initiative is controversial due to potential pollution of the lake.

There have been some encouraging signs in recent years, however. An ongoing research project has introduced two species of weevils into the lake that feed exclusively on the hyacinth. Initial findings suggest that the experiment is a success and researchers are also confident that the weevils will not attack crops.

Some of these organisations are listed on the following page.

As a visitor you have the obligation to act responsibly when it comes to environmental matters, and there are a number of ways in which you can help in promoting environmentally friendly practices. See the Responsible Tourism section in the Regional Facts for the Visitor chapter for details.

African Wildlife Foundation PO Box 48177, Nairobi, Kenya 1717 Massachusetts Ave NW, Washington, DC 20036, USA

Laikipia Wildlife Forum, Kenya (☎ 0176-22156, email nicky@swiftkenya.com)

World Wildlife Fund (☎ 1-800-CALL-WWF) 1250 Twenty-forth St, Washington, DC 20077-7180, USA
Web site: www.worldwildlife.org/

FLORA & FAUNA
Flora

The types of vegetation found throughout East Africa are largely dictated by rainfall.

The arid areas of the north-east support little more than the ubiquitous thorn trees, although after rains there is a burst of activity as annual grasses and other shrubs make the most of the moist conditions.

Savanna country is typical where the rainfall is between 300 and 1200mm, and where there is a pronounced dry season. At the drier end of the scale the vegetation is largely a medium-to-thick cover of small

The root-like branches of the baobab tree give it the impression of being 'upside down'.

trees. As rainfall increases, so does the tree size, and a light canopy is formed, which gives protection to a floor layer of grasses and smaller shrubs. This type of vegetation is typical of large areas of Tanzania.

Areas of real forest are rare across East Africa as much has been cleared for agriculture. The rainforests of south-west Uganda and those in Rwanda are the most extensive these days.

Montane forests exist throughout the highlands of Kenya and in western Uganda, and high-altitude heather and moorlands are found above the treeline in these areas.

Grasslands, such as the Serengeti and Masai Mara, are not all that common, and are only found where drainage is poor or where there is a high water table.

The coastline is broken by large areas of mangrove swamps, particularly around the mouths of rivers.

Field Guide to Flowers of East Africa by Michael Blundell is a good reference.

Fauna

East Africa is a naturalist's dream, with abundant animal and birdlife, especially in the many national parks and reserves. All of the Big Five (black rhino, buffalo, elephant, leopard and lion) can be seen in a number of parks, and there's a huge variety of less famous but equally impressive animals to be seen.

A good field guide is an essential companion for anyone seriously interested in getting to grips with the wildlife. Some suggestions include: Lonely Planet's *Watching Wildlife East Africa*; *The Kingdon Field Guide to African Mammals* by Jonathan Kingdon; and *Birds of Kenya & Northern Tanzania* by Dale Zimmerman and Don Turner.

NATIONAL PARKS & RESERVES

The national parks and game reserves of East Africa are among the best in the world. A visit to at least one is virtually a mandatory part of any visit to the region.

The parks with the biggest reputations are those which have the highest concentrations of wildlife – Masai Mara and Amboseli in

The National Parks & Reserves of East Africa

KENYA	location	features
Amboseli National Park	Nairobi	Viewing wildlife with the captivating backdrop of snow-capped Mt Kilimanjaro – the highest peak in Africa. Concentrations of wildlife are small but easy to spot.
Hell's Gate National Park	Rift Valley	Offers the rare chance to walk through a national park. Walking trails and camp sites.
Kagamega Forest Reserve	Western Kenya	Virgin forest with walking trails, camping and forest resthouses.
Lake Baringo National Park	Rift Valley	Superb birdwatching – more than 450 of Kenya's 1200 species have been sighted here.
Lake Nakuru National Park	Rift Valley	One of a number of shallow soda lakes famous for huge concentrations of pink flamingos. Camping and luxury lodge options.
Malindi & Watamu Marine National Parks	The Coast	Marine parks which offer excellent diving or glass-bottomed boats for those who'd rather stay dry.
Masai Mara Game Reserve	Rift Valley	Some of the greatest wildlife concentrations in the world; contiguous with the Serengeti. The highlight is the annual wildebeest migration.
Mt Elgon National Park	Western Kenya	Similar to Mt Kenya, but without the crowds. A great opportunity for trekking off the beaten track.
Mt Kenya National Park	Central Highlands	Africa's second highest peak and a magnet for trekkers, particularly from mid-January to late February. Unique montane vegetation and stunning views.
Nairobi National Park	Nairobi	For those with little time or just as a taste of what's around, this park on the outskirts of Nairobi is filled with a surprisingly diverse range of wildlife. An easy half-day excursion.

TANZANIA	location	features
Lake Manyara National Park	Northern Tanzania	Guaranteed sightings of giraffe, wildebeest, baboon and hippo, and a chance of spotting elephant and the famous tree-climbing lion.
Mt Kilimanjaro National Park	Northern Tanzania	Trekking to the roof of Africa is the main attraction. The rainforest supports a varied wildlife population.
Gombe Stream National Park	Western Tanzania	The journey here by Lake Tanganyika is an experience in itself, but the chimpanzee sanctuary remains the major highlight.
Mikumi National Park	Southern Highlands	Crawling with wildlife year round and a lush vegetation area called Mkata River floodplain.

The National Parks & Reserves of East Africa

Ngorongoro Conservation Area	Northern Tanzania	Views from the rim are unsurpassed and the abundance of wildlife on the crater floor is equally impressive.
Selous Game Reserve	Sth-Eastern Tanzania	Huge, wild and largely untouched by humans, this reserve is teeming with wildlife. It's said to contain 100,000 elephants so there's every chance of spotting herds containing several hundred.
Serengeti	Northern Tanzania	Tanzania's most famous park where it's possible to see millions of hoofed animals, including up to two million wildebeest, on the annual migration – an awesome sight.
Tarangire National Park	Northern Tanzania	During the dry season the park fills up with herds of zebra, wildebeest and kongoni.
UGANDA	**location**	**features**
Budongo Central Forest Reserve	Northern Uganda	A superb place for viewing chimpanzees; dense virgin tropical forest with massive mahogany trees and a wealth of birdlife.
Bwindi National Park	Sth-Western Uganda	Encompasses one of the last remaining habitats of mountain gorillas in the world; one of Africa's richest areas for flora and fauna.
Kibale National Park	Sth-Western Uganda	Believed to have the highest concentrations of primates in the world, including about 500 chimpanzees and has Uganda's third largest elephant population.
Mgahinga National Park	Sth-Western Uganda	Habitat of some of the rarest creatures on earth, the mountain gorilla, deep in lush tropical rainforest.
Mt Elgon National Park	Sth-Eastern Uganda	Views from the higher reaches across wide plains are some of the most spectacular in Uganda; there's also unique montane vegetation such as giant groundsels and giant lobelias.
Murchison Falls National Park	Northern Uganda	Take a boat ride up the Victoria Nile to the breathtaking Murchison Falls, spotting crocodile, elephant and thousands of birds.
Queen Elizabeth National Park	Sth-Western Uganda	See hundreds of hippos and perhaps a rare shoebill stork, go chimpanzee viewing or enjoy a walking safari of Kyambura Gorge.
Ruwenzori National Park	Sth-Western Uganda	For the well prepared, these mist-covered mountains probably offer the best trekking in East Africa. (Currently closed.)
RWANDA	**location**	**features**
Parc Nacional des Volcans		The original gorilla-viewing park and the most spectacular. Open once again after the horrors of 1994, and still stunning.

Kenya and the Serengeti and Ngorongoro in Tanzania are among them. Some other parks are famous for just one type of animal, such as the parks of Rwanda (Parc National des Volcans) and Uganda (Bwindi and Mgahinga) set aside for the protection of the endangered mountain gorilla, or Gombe Stream (western Tanzania) or Kibale (southwestern Uganda), where chimpanzees are the focus.

Other inland parks offer the opportunity for adventure trekking, with Mt Kenya, Mt Kilimanjaro and Mt Elgon among the most accessible.

The coastal marine parks offer still more options; this time it's the chance to get under water – either snorkelling or scuba diving.

GOVERNMENT & POLITICS

Until 1977, Kenya, Uganda and Tanzania were members of the East African Community (EAC), an economic union which linked the currencies of the three countries and provided for freedom of movement and shared telecommunications and postal facilities. Following the break-up of the EAC due to political differences, Tanzania and Kenya entered into a long dispute, during which then border was closed for six years. Since then relations have improved.

In 1996 the presidents of Tanzania, Kenya and Uganda agreed to establish the Tripartite Commission for East African Cooperation with the goal of re-establishing the old economic and customs union. The actual treaty was signed on 30 November 1999.

Unlike the East African Community, which sought to impose supranational control over a variety of areas, the new EAC seeks harmonisation of fiscal and other policies. Agreement in principle has been achieved on various measures towards these ends, and targets for tariff reductions have been set, although it will likely be some time before these reductions are implemented.

POPULATION & PEOPLE

The population of East Africa is close to 100 million. The most populous nation is Tanzania (31 million), followed closely by Kenya (30 million), then Uganda (22 mil-

lion), Rwanda (8.5 million) and Burundi (seven million).

The rate of population growth is high across the region, averaging around 3%, putting great strain on the ability of the countries to expand economically and to provide reasonable educational facilities and other urban services. It has also resulted in tremendous pressure to increase the area of land under cultivation or for grazing with its associated environmental problems.

Africans

There are literally hundreds of tribal groups among the Africans, although the distinctions between many of them are blurred and are becoming more so as western cultural values become more ingrained. Traditional values are also disintegrating as more and more people move to the larger towns, family and tribal groups become scattered and the tribal elders gradually die off.

Yet even though the average African may have outwardly drifted away from tribal traditions, the tribe is still the single most important part of a person's identity. When two Africans meet and introduce themselves they will almost always say right at the outset what tribe they are from. Although nominally Christian for the most part, a surprising number of people still practice traditional customs. Though some of the more inhumane customs, such as clitoridectomy (female circumcision), were outlawed by the British, usually with the aid of the local missionaries, circumcision still remains the principal rite of passage from childhood to adulthood for boys.

The most important distinguishing feature between the tribes is language. The majority of the region's Africans fall into one of two major groups: the Bantu speakers and the Nilotic speakers. The Bantu-speaking peoples arrived in East Africa in waves from West Africa over a period of time from around 500 BC. Among the Bantu the largest tribal groups are the Kikuyu, Meru, Gusii, Embu, Akamba, Luyha and Mijikenda in Kenya; the Sukuma, Nyamwezi, Makonde, Haya, Zaramo, Pare and Chagga in Tanzania; and the Buganda and Busoga in Uganda.

The Nilotic speakers migrated to the area from the Nile Valley some time earlier but then had to make room for the migrations of Bantu-speaking peoples. Nilotic-speaking groups include the Maasai and Samburu in Kenya and Tanzania; the Turkana, Pokot, Luo and Kalenjin in Kenya; and the Lango, Acholi, Teso and Karamajong in Uganda.

Together these tribal groups account for more than 90% of the total African population in East Africa.

A third language group, and in fact the first migrants into the region, are the Cushitic speakers, who include such tribes as the El-Molo, Somali, Rendille and the Galla in Kenya; and the Iraqw, Gorowa and Burungi in Tanzania.

On the coast, Swahili is the name given to the local people who, while having various tribal ancestries, have in common the fact that they have been mixing, trading and intermarrying both among themselves and with overseas immigrants for hundreds of years.

See the special section 'Tribal Groups & Cultures' for more details.

Asians

The economically important Asian minority is made up largely of people of Indian descent whose ancestors originated from the western state of Gujarat and from the Punjab. In Uganda the Asians were thrown into exile during the Amin years, although sense prevailed in Kenya and Tanzania, largely because their influence was too great.

India's connections with East Africa go back centuries to the days when hundreds of dhows used to make the trip between the west coast of India or the Persian Gulf and the coastal towns of East Africa every year. In those days, though, the Indians came as traders and only a very few stayed to settle. This all changed with the building of the Mombasa-Uganda railway at the turn of the century. In order to construct it, the British colonial authorities brought in some 32,000 indentured labourers from Gujarat and Punjab. When their contracts expired many of them decided to stay and set up businesses. Their numbers were augmented after WWII with the encouragement of the British.

As they were an industrious and economically aggressive community, the Indians quickly ended up controlling large parts of the economies of Kenya, Tanzania and Uganda as merchants, artisans and financiers. Not only that but they kept very much to themselves, regarding the Africans as culturally inferior and lazy. Few gave their active support to the black nationalist movements in the run-up to independence despite being urged to do so by Nehru, India's prime minister. And when independence came, like many of the white settlers, they were very hesitant to accept local citizenship, preferring to wait and see what would happen. To the Africans, therefore, it seemed they were not willing to throw their lot in with the newly independent nations and were there simply as exploiters.

As is well known, Uganda's Idi Amin used this suspicion and resentment as a convenient ruse to enrich himself and his cronies. Uganda's economy collapsed shortly after the Asians were forced to leave the country, their assets confiscated, since Amin's henchmen were incapable of running the industries and businesses they had siezed.

For a time in the 1970s it seemed that there was little future for Asians in Africa. Governments were under heavy pressure to 'Africanise' their economies and job markets. Even in Kenya thousands of shops owned by Asians who had not taken out Kenyan nationality were confiscated in the early 1970s and Asians were forbidden to trade in the rural areas. Those days appear to have passed and African attitudes towards them have mellowed. What seemed like a widespread demand that they should go 'home' has been quietly dropped and the Asians are there to stay. The lesson of what happened to the economy of Uganda when the Asians were thrown out is one reason for this.

ARTS
Indigenous Arts

Though there is some superb craftwork produced in East Africa, most craft produced in the region is for the mass tourist market and so is of dubious quality. However, if you shop carefully you can pick up some good quality pieces at reasonable prices.

Fabrics & Batik Made in Kenya but also found in Tanzania and Uganda, *kangas* and *kikois* are the local sarongs and serve many purposes. Kangas are colourful prints on thin cotton. Each bears a Swahili proverb and they are sold in pairs, one to wrap around your waist and one to use to carry a baby on your back.

Kikois, traditionally worn by men, are made of a thicker cotton and feature stripes only. They are originally from the coast.

Batik cloth is another good buy and there's a tremendous range. The cheapest batik is printed on cotton and you can expect to pay about US$10 for 1 sq metre. Batiks printed on silk are of superior quality and the prices are much higher.

Makonde *Makonde* carvings, which are made from ebony, a very black and very heavy wood, are widely available in Kenya and Tanzania, although the style originates from the Makonde tribe who live around the Ruvuma River in southern Tanzania. Unfortunately, much of what is passed off as ebony is actually lighter (and cheaper) wood blackened with Kiwi boot polish; it's further degraded by the often slapdash quality of the carving. A quality piece of makonde carving is always superbly finished and it's best to buy it in Tanzania, though the more expensive shops in Nairobi also stock originals.

Sisal Baskets Sisal baskets, or *kiondos*, are probably the most distinctive East African souvenir and are popular and widely available in the west. They are still an excellent buy and the range is staggering – take a look in the market in Nairobi (although prices there are expensive). They come in a variety of sizes, colours and configurations with many different straps and clasps. Some of the finer baskets have the bark of the baobab tree woven into them and this bumps up the price considerably.

Soapstone Soapstone carvings from western Kenya are the main sculptural offering

on sale. The soft, lightly coloured soapstone is carved into dozens of different shapes, from ashtrays to elephants. The best place for buying Kisii soapstone carvings is not in Kisii, as you might expect, but in Kisumu on Lake Victoria. The only problem for the traveller is its weight.

Jewellery & Tribal Souvenirs Most of the jewellery on sale is of tribal origin, although very little of it is the genuine article. The colourful Maasai beaded jewellery is the most striking and the most popular, and other Maasai items include the decorated calabash (dried gourds used to store a mixture of blood and milk). As you might imagine, these gourds often smell a bit but are quite strikingly decorated with Maasai beads. Spears and shields are also popular, although these days they are made specifically for the tourist trade.

One of the best places to pick up Maasai souvenirs is at Namanga on the Tanzanian border. This is where most minibuses headed for Amboseli National Park stop for a few minutes, so starting prices are outrageous. However, with some persistent bargaining you can reduce the prices to realistic levels. Tribal souvenirs are bought cheaper out in the bush away from the tourist circuits, though buying still demands judicious haggling.

Elephant Hair Bracelets On the streets of Nairobi and Arusha you'll undoubtedly be approached by hawkers trying to sell you 'elephant hair' bracelets. Despite all the protestations to the contrary, these bracelets are made from reed grass (which is then covered in boot polish), from slivers of cow horn, or simply from plastic. You can safely assume that none of them are the real McCoy.

Painting
Tingatinga Painting Tanzania's most well-known style of painting was begun in the 1960s by Edward Saidi Tingatinga. In the 1950s, while working in Dar es Salaam, he began to seek creative outlets and additional income, first as a member of a musical group, and then later as a self-taught artist,

painting fanciful and colourful animals on small shingles.

His work soon became popular with European tourists, and he began to attract a small circle of students. These students organised themselves into the Tingatinga Partnership (now the Tingatinga Arts Co-operative Society) following the artist's accidental shooting in 1972. The society now numbers about 50 artists and is still based near Morogoro Stores in Dar es Salaam, where Tingatinga's work was originally sold.

Dance
Sigana This traditional African performance form contains elements of all the major traditional African cultural forms – narration, song, music, dance, chant, ritual, mask, movement, banter and praise poetry – blending into one long wonderful story-telling performance. It's not something you'll see very often on the tourist trail, but one place where you have a good chance of seeing a performance is in Nairobi. The Nyungu Cultural Club at the Mzizi Arts Centre (see Nairobi section) puts on Sigana performances once a month and will also be able to recommend other shows and other African performance.

Music
The music scene in East Africa is rich and diverse. So many contrasting styles and types of music get played in the country that it's difficult to work out what comes from where. Indigenous pop music does exist and with a little digging around you'll find it but you may have to wade through a lot of foreign imports first.

Congolese bands were playing in Nairobi in the early 1960s and have been the single greatest influence on music in East Africa ever since. The Congolese styles of *rumba* and *soukous* were tremendously popular in the 1980s when artists such as Samba Mapangalal (still playing today) made their names.

Benga is the contemporary dance music of Kenya. It originated among the Luo people of western Kenya and became popular in the 1950s. Since then it has spread throughout the country and been taken up by Akamba and Kikuyu musicians. The music is characterised by clear electric guitar licks and a bass rhythm. The guitar takes the place of the traditional *nyatiti* (folk lyre), while the bass guitar replaces the drum, which originally was played by the nyatiti player with a toe ring. Some well-known exponents of benga include DO Misiani (a Kikuyu). He and his group Shirati Jazz have been around since the 1960s and are still churning out the hits. You should also look out for Victoria Kings and Ambira Boys.

Music from Tanzania was influential in the early 1970s. The ground-breaking band Simba Wanyika, influenced by Congolese styles, helped build Swahili rumba, which was taken up by bands like the Maroon Commandos and Les Wanyika and remains popular today.

Popular bands today play a mix of music, heavily influenced by benga, soukous and western music, with lyrics generally in Swahili. These include bands such as Them Mushrooms and Safari Sound.

Taarab is the music of the East African coast (see Traditional Music & Dance in the Zanzibar Archipelago chapter). It combines African, Arabic and Indian influences, and is traditionally played by an orchestra of several dozen musicians. Themes usually centre around love, with many puns and double meanings. Taarab is generally played without written music and traditions are passed down from musician to musician.

Literature
Swahili Literature While Swahili only became entrenched as a major regional language in the second half of the 20th century, written Swahili poetry, in Arabic script, dates back to at least the early 18th century. It wasn't until the mid-19th century that Latin script was used in favour of Arabic.

Early this century Swahili fiction drew heavily from local oral traditions and Arabic tales. It was only in the 1950s and 1960s that Swahili writing emerged which told of the East African experience of a changing society struggling for independence.

Swahili literature has also been hindered by the lack of local Swahili-language publishers – the best place to find Swahili poetry or short stories is in local newspapers. The major author writing in Swahili has been Tanzania's Shaaban Robert, best known for his poetry. Other contemporary Swahili authors include Kenyans Ahmad Nassir, Abdilatif Abdalla, Ali Jemaadar Amir, Katama Mkangi and PM Kareithi; and Tanzanian novelists Euphrase Kezilahabi and Mohammed S Mohammed and dramatists Ebrahim Hussein and Penina O Mlama.

English Literature English has largely been the language of contemporary East African writers, and Heinemann's African Writers Series has arguably the best range (see the list of writers included in the series inside each African Writers Series book).

Major writers include Peter Palangyo, William Kamera and Tolowa Marti Mollel from Tanzania; Ngugi wa Thiong'o and Meja Mwangi of Kenya; and Moses Isegawa from Uganda.

For writing by women in Africa, try *Unwinding Threads*, a collection of short stories by many different authors from all over the continent.

SOCIETY & CONDUCT
Dress
Despite their often exuberant and casual approach to life, Africans are generally quite conservative in dress, and foremost here is modesty in dress. They go to great lengths to make sure they are well dressed even if they do not necessarily have the money to spare on such luxuries. It is extremely important that visitors also take care about their appearance, as to see tourists scruffily dressed when they can clearly afford to dress well understandably upsets a lot of Africans. While you hardly have to bring a suit and tie or an evening dress, it is the little things like ripped shorts or filthy T-shirts that are easy to do something about. Travellers on overland trucks need to be particularly aware of this, as all too often it is easy to forget that you are crossing borders into different cultures.

Many travellers get around in T-shirts and shorts, which is acceptable (only just) in most areas, but you should be much more circumspect in isolated areas and on the Muslim-dominated coast, particularly at Lamu and Zanzibar. Here women should wear tops that keep the shoulders covered and skirts or pants that reach at least to the knees. Shorts on men are likewise not particularly appreciated.

When doing official business with people such as civil servants, embassy staff and border officials, your position will be much enhanced if you're smartly dressed and don't look like you've just spent five weeks on the back of a truck without a wash (even if you have!).

Social Etiquette
Basics As in any part of the world, the best way to learn about a society's conduct is to watch or listen to the locals. The first thing to remember is not to worry: Africans are generally very easy-going towards foreigners, and any social errors that you might make are unlikely to cause offence (although they may cause confusion or merriment). Having said that, there are a few things that are frowned upon wherever you go. These include public nudity, open displays of anger, open displays of affection (between people of same or opposite sex) and vocal criticism of the government or country.

Common Courtesies A few straightforward courtesies may also greatly improve your chances of acceptance by the local community, especially in rural areas. Pleasantries are taken quite seriously, and it's *essential* to greet someone before going any further, even if you're just shopping in the local market or asking directions. Learn the local words for hello, goodbye and how are you, and use them unsparingly.

Great emphasis is also placed on handshakes. There are various local variations, involving linked thumbs or fingers, or the left hand touching the right elbow, which you'll pick up by observation, but these are reserved for informal occasions (not greeting officials). A 'normal' western handshake will do fine in most situations. Sometimes, people who know each other continue to hold hands right through their conversation, or at least for a few minutes.

Dealing with Officials & Elders As in most traditional societies, older people are treated with deference. Teachers, doctors and other professionals (usually men) often receive similar treatment. Likewise, people holding positions of authority – immigration officers, government officials, police, village chiefs and so on (also usually men) – should be dealt with politely.

Officials are normally courteous and fairly efficient, although there are always exceptions, and in some places inefficiency, corruption and unpleasantness are the rule. On your side, manners, patience and cooperation will get you through most situations. Even if you meet somebody awkward or unpleasant, the same rules apply. It is one thing to stand up for your rights but undermining an official's authority or insulting an ego may only serve to waste time, tie you up in red tape and inspire closer scrutiny of future travellers.

Women & Children At the other end of the spectrum, children rate very low on the social scale. They are expected to do as they're told without complaint and defer to adults in all situations. Unfortunately for half the region's population, the status of women is only slightly higher than for children. For example, an African man on a bus might give his seat to an older man but not normally to a woman, never mind that she is carrying a baby and luggage and minding two toddlers. In traditional rural areas, women are expected to dress and behave modestly, especially in the presence of chiefs or other esteemed persons. Visitors should act in the same way.

Visiting Villages When visiting rural settlements, especially when away from areas normally reached by tourists, it is a good idea to request to see the chief to announce your presence and request permission before setting up a tent or wandering through a village. You will rarely be refused permission. Visitors should also ask permission before drawing water from a community well. Avoid letting water spill on the ground, especially in dry areas. If you want to wash your body or your clothing, fill a container with water and carry it elsewhere. Always try to minimise your water use.

Meals Most travellers will have the opportunity to share an African meal sometime during their stay and will normally be given royal treatment and a seat of honour. Although concessions are sometimes made for foreigners, table manners are probably different from what you're accustomed to.

Before eating, a member of the family may pass around a bowl of water, or jug and bowl, for washing hands. If it comes to you first as honoured guest and you're not sure of the routine, indicate that the bowl should be taken to the head of the family, then do what they do when it comes to you.

The African staple – maize or sorghum meal – is the centre of nearly every meal. It is normally taken with the right hand from a communal pot, rolled into balls, dipped in some sort of sauce (meat gravy or vegetables) and eaten. As in most societies, it is considered impolite to scoff food; if you do, your hosts may feel that they haven't provided enough. In fact, for the same reason, it may be polite *not* to be the one who takes the last handful from the communal bowl. If your food is served on separate plates, and you can't finish your food, don't worry; again this shows your hosts that you have been satisfied. Though containers of water or home-brew beer are often passed around from person to person, it is not customary to share coffee, tea or bottled soft drinks.

Giving & Receiving Gifts If you do visit a remote community, tread lightly and leave as little lasting evidence of your visit as possible. In some societies it isn't considered impolite for people to ask others for items they may desire; but likewise it isn't rude to refuse. So if a local asks for your watch or camera, say 'no' politely, explaining it's the only one you've got, and all will be fine. If you start feeling guilty about your relative wealth and hand out all your belongings, you may be regarded as strange. Reciprocation of kindness is OK but indiscriminate distribution of gifts from outside, however well intentioned, tends to create a taste for items not locally available, diminishes well-established values, robs people of their pride and, in extreme cases, creates villages of dependent beggars.

On the other hand, when you're offered a gift, don't feel guilty about accepting it; to refuse it would bring shame on the giver. To politely receive a gift, local people may accept it with both hands and perhaps bow slightly, or they may receive it with the right hand while touching the left hand to their right elbow; this is the equivalent of saying 'thanks'. You can try this if you think it's appropriate. Spoken thanks aren't common and local people tend to think westerners say 'thank you' too often and too casually, so don't be upset if you aren't verbally thanked for a gift.

Dos & Don'ts

The following are some tips on avoiding offence while travelling in East Africa:

- Dress modestly, particularly in more traditional Muslim areas along the coast.
- Treat locals with respect, and honour local customs and culture in your behaviour and speech. Elders, chiefs and other authority figures warrant particular politeness.
- Always greet people (preferably in Swahili or their local language) before attempting to transact business or otherwise engage them in conversation.
- Don't lose your temper, or do anything to insult an official or undermine their authority. Even in trying situations when dealing with officialdom, patience and humour will get you further than frustrated outbursts.
- Be conservative when using your camera, especially in seldom-visited areas, and always ask permission when photographing people.
- Always ask permission before camping near a village, or before drawing water from a community well.
- Avoid public displays of affection with persons of both the same or opposite sex.

- Show respect for places of worship. In some areas, particularly on the coast, mosques in active use are off limits to non-Muslims. If you do arrange to enter one, dress appropriately, with most or all of your arms and legs covered (whether you are a man or a woman). In some places, women are also expected to cover their head and shoulders with a scarf.
- Don't use your left hand for eating (according to ancient tradition, the left hand is reserved for personal toiletries), and always try to give things with your right hand.
- When hitching, motion by moving your hand up and down (with arm outstretched) at about waist level. The western gesture with the thumb is not used in East Africa.
- Wherever you are, and especially in remote areas, try to tread lightly and leave as little lasting evidence of your visit as possible.

RELIGION

The dominant religion in the area is Christianity, although along the coast Islam is the major religion. There are also still communities, especially in Uganda, that practice traditional religions.

Christianity

As a result of intense missionary activity from colonial times to the present, just about every Christian sect is represented in East Africa, from Lutherans to Catholics to Seventh Day Adventists and Wesleyans. The success which all these sects have enjoyed would be quite mind-boggling if it were not for the fact that they have always judiciously combined Jesus with education and medicine – two commodities in short supply until recently. Indeed, there are still many remote areas where the only place you can get an education or medical help is at a mission station. There's no doubt those who volunteer to staff these missions are dedicated people.

On the other hand, the situation is often not as simple as it might at first appear. As with Catholicism in Central and South America, which found it necessary to incorporate native deities and saints into the Roman Catholic pantheon in order to placate local sensibilities, African Christianity is frequently syncretic. This is especially so where a tribe has strong ancestral beliefs.

There are also many pure home-grown African Christian sects which owe no allegiance to any of the major western cults. The only thing they have in common is *The Bible*, though their interpretation of it is often radically different. It's worth checking out a few churches while you're in the area if only to get an understanding of where the religion is headed and even if you can't understand the language that is being used, you'll certainly be captivated by what only Africans can do with such beauty and precision – unaccompanied choral singing.

The upsurge of home-grown Christian sects has much to do with cultural resurgence, the continuing struggle against neo-colonialism, and the alienation brought about by migration to urban centres far from tribal homelands in search of work. Some of these sects are distinctly radical and viewed with alarm by the government.

Islam
Most Muslims belong to the Sunni branch of the faith and, as a result, the Sunni communities have been able to attract quite substantial Saudi Arabian funding for schools and hospitals along the coast and elsewhere.

Only a small minority belong to the Shia branch of Islam and most are to be found among the Asian community. On the other hand, Shiites have been coming to East Africa from all over the eastern Islamic world for centuries, partially to escape persecution but mainly for trading purposes. They didn't come here to convert souls, and there was a high degree of cooperation between the schismatic sects and the Sunnis, which is why there's a total absence of Shiite customs in Swahili culture today.

Among the Asian community, there are representatives of several Shiite sects but the most influential are the Ismailis – followers of the Aga Khan. As with all Ismailis, they represent a very liberal version of Islam and are perhaps the only branch of the faith that is strongly committed to the education of women at all levels and their participation in commerce and business. Going by all the

schools and hospitals dedicated to the Aga Khan which you will come across in most urban centres, it's obvious that the sect has prospered in Kenya.

Hinduism
Hinduism, as is the case in India, remains a self-contained religion which concerns only those born into it. You'll come across a considerable number of temples in the larger urban areas where most people of Indian origin live. There are literally scores of different sects of Hinduism to be found in East Africa, far too many in this book, but many are economically quite influential.

Traditional Religions
Traditional religions of East Africa centre on a supreme deity, ancestor worship, spirits, the land and various ritual objects. Rituals and sacrifices of domestic animals were common in order to appease unpredictable spirits.

In the communities of western Uganda and Tanzania there were, in addition to the supreme deity, a number of lesser gods who also received sacrifices.

Among the Maasai and other tribes of the north-east there is no tradition of ancestor or spirit worship; the supreme deity is the sole focus of devotion.

LANGUAGE
Swahili and English are the dominant – and official – languages in Kenya and Tanzania. In Uganda it is English that predominates, while Luganda is the other major language. While it is easy to get by speaking only English in these countries, as always, any attempt (no matter how inept) to speak the local language will be hugely appreciated and will gain you much respect.

In Rwanda the official languages are French and Kinyarwanda; in Burundi it's French and Kirundi. Travel in this area is much easier if you can speak at least some French, although it is still possible to get by in English.

See the Language chapter at the back of this book for a useful introduction to speaking Swahili.

Heart of Darkness

Congo (Zaïre) is the dark heart of Africa, a vast and rich country that remains one of the poorest, un-stable places on the continent. It is a land of failed reputations which is often considered as ungovern-able. Today it is a country that is destabilising and diverting the attention of much of the continent, as intrigues and rivalries as far apart as Zimbabwe and Sudan unravel on its stage. As many as nine coun-tries are at war in Congo (Zaïre), none of them really on behalf of the Congolese (Zaïrean) people who have already suffered so much. They are all there for their own reasons. This latest round of trouble is linked to the overthrow of President Mobutu in early 1997, but its roots go further back in time.

In pre-colonial times a Tutsi clan, the Banyarwanda, quarrelled with their *mwami* (king) and migrated from Rwanda to the Uvira region, where they became assimilated into the local community.

Another wave of Tutsi migrants, the Banyamulenge, arrived from Rwanda in 1959 after the Hutu revolution and settled in both North and South Kivu provinces. Both groups were soon treated as Con-golese (Zaïrean) citizens until a new nationality law came into force in 1972 that denied citizenship to the Banyamulenge. Another nationality law was enacted in 1981 that deprived both groups of obtain-ing Congolese (Zaïrean) citizenship and prohibited them from acquiring land and property. By 1993 the conflict between the ethnic Tutsi and other tribes, who were supported by the Congolese (Zaïrean) army, had left some 7000 people dead and 250,000 homeless. Worse calamities were to follow.

In 1994 about two million Hutu fled Rwanda into Congo (Zaïre) following the genocide there and the victory of the Tutsi-led Rwandan Patriotic Front (RPF). The refugees found themselves virtually held hostage in camps controlled by the *Interahamwe*, Hutu extremists who had perpetrated the genocide. The extremists were joined in 1995 by Hutu militias from eastern Congo (Zaïre) and to-gether with the encouragement of the Congo (Zaïre) army chief of staff, began an 'ethnic cleans-ing' of Tutsi from eastern Congo (Zaïre) as well as mounting cross-border raids into Rwanda.

In late October 1996, the RPF army attacked four refugee camps in North Kivu, precipitating the return of Hutu refugees to Rwanda (and from elsewhere), as well as forcing the retreat of the Intera-hamwe and the Congolese (Zaïrean) army further west towards Kisangani. In support of the initiative, the Banyamulenge joined the Alliance of Democratic Forces for the Liberation of Congo (Zaïre) led by Laurent Kabila. Though not a specifically a Tutsi force, the ADFL drew its principal support from the Banyamulenge, who had been essentially dispossessed and threatened with annihilation.

In less than six months, the ADFL had swept across the country taking city after city until they en-tered Kinshasa virtually unopposed. Mobutu and his henchmen fled into exile. The Congolese (Zaïrean) army and their Interahamwe allies scattered throughout the country in complete disarray and indisci-pline, bringing fear into every city and village they passed through by raping, looting and killing.

Events soon changed dramatically. The governments of Rwanda and Uganda had bankrolled Kabila's rebellion and provided troops and training on the basis that Kabila flushed out the remaining Rwandan and Ugandan rebels on his soil. President Mobutu had run Congo (Zaïre) like a medieval fiefdom, and as long as he received his generous cut, provincial governors were pretty much allowed to get away with whatever they wanted. It was this climate that helped the Rwandan militias re-establish themselves and launch attacks on their homeland in the immediate years after the genocide there. Rwanda and its ally Uganda were not prepared to see their security violated by the inaction of their larger neighbour.

But the Rwandans and Ugandans didn't realise that Congo (Zaïre) is a massive country and it is a long way from Kivu to Kinshasa, in ideology as well as geography. Kabila came to power on a wave of popular euphoria and promised sweeping changes, as well as an end to the culture of cronyism and corruption. He also changed the name of the country to the Democratic Republic of Congo. However, the new dawn was soon to darken once again. Kabila soon found himself in the clutches of the Kin-shasa clique that successfully drove a wedge between him and his eastern allies. This they did with consummate skill, calling him a foreign lackey and playing on his ego. As early as the start of 1998, it

Heart of Darkness

was becoming clear to Rwanda and Uganda that they had not got the action man they had hoped for; if anything, rebels were finding it easier to attack Rwanda and Uganda than ever before.

This situation was unacceptable. Rwanda and Uganda backed a new rebel group, the Rally for Congolese Democracy (RCD). History was repeating itself town by town as the RCD swept from Kivu to Kisangani and the gates of the capital itself. By October 1998, Kinshasa was poised to fall for the second time in less than two years. At this time, Kabila accused his former allies Rwanda and Uganda of mounting an invasion of Congo (Zaïre). He made an appeal for assistance and soon found himself overwhelmed with African allies, principally Zimbabwe, Namibia and Angola, and to a lesser extent Chad and Sudan (the latter always keen to put one over on Uganda). The capital was saved and the rebels halted. Africa's first great war had begun. The war rapidly reached a stalemate in late 1998 with none of the sides in the conflict having sufficient resources to do much damage to each other. The people of Congo (Zaïre) continue to suffer because they cannot get on with their lives while the country is at war.

Although war weariness produced a push for peace around the region, this has proved difficult to achieve as even the allies are divided as to why they are there. Rwanda wants to guarantee its security in the face of cross-border attacks from the militias based in Congo (Zaïre), and Uganda claims to be involved for similar reasons, due to attacks from the Allied Democratic Front (ADF), a rebel group raising hell in the west of the country. Both justifications look a little lame when Rwandan and Ugandan troops are holed up in Kisangani, at least 700km from their nearest border. More likely, once the Rwandans and the Ugandans were in the country, and plundering its vast resources, it has proved hard to get the armies out. Robert Mugabe's case looks more pathetic still. Zimbabwe doesn't even share borders with Congo (Zaïre) but soon after Kabila came to power, Mugabe signed contracts with Kabila for mineral prospecting thought to be worth more than US$100 million. If Kabila had fallen, Mugabe's bank balance would have followed.

In contrast to the Ugandans, the Rwandans don't want or need peace in Congo (Zaïre) as their security back home has been better than ever since the second war in 1998. The rebels are divided as their main objectives have not been achieved, and their divisions have sent shock waves up and down the Great Rift Valley, provoking a fallout between long-time allies Rwanda and Uganda in mid-1999. The international community seems prepared to forgive Rwanda its sins because of those committed against it back in 1994. On the other hand, Uganda is finding itself rapped on the knuckles by everyone from the World Bank to governments in Europe, and investors are feeling shaky. The Ugandan government needed out and a split with Rwanda was imminent. The Rwandans and the Ugandans nominated different rebel leaders of the rebellion and, by July 1999, soldiers from the two countries were killing each other in the streets of Kisangani. It was just another pointless chapter in another pointless war which has seen yet more Africans lose their lives due to the egos of their politicians.

Peace talks have involved politicians from both extremes, including Colonel Gadaffi and Nelson Mandela. However, a solution has remained elusive. Even if those at the top sign, it's no certainty that those at the bottom will, as war has become the norm. No settlement will be worth the paper it is written on unless the issues that brought Rwanda and Uganda to the war are addressed and the militias disarmed.

Congo (Zaïre) is a mess, but its problems are those of Africa. Artificial borders and playground politics have cost the continent years in development. Over the years, many an African leader has blamed his country's problems on the legacy of colonialism and there is much truth in such statements; however the worst legacy of all has yet to be addressed maturely, that of lines on a map. Unless the politicians are prepared to put people before politics, Africans will continue to suffer the belligerent whims of their politicians. Colonel Gadaffi may have been far off the mark in the past, but his recent call for a United States of Africa is arguably the way to go. It may be utopian and it may be a long way off, but everywhere needs a light to strive for, especially a Heart of Darkness.

TRIBAL GROUPS & CULTURES

The tribal groups of East Africa possess rich and diverse traditions, languages and heritages. The following guide to the major tribal groups in the region gives a rudimentary outline of the histories and cultures of these groups, as well as an indication of their place in the societies of present-day Kenya, Tanzania, Uganda, Rwanda and Burundi.

KENYA

Akamba

The region east of Nairobi towards Tsavo National Park is known as the *Ukambani* and is the traditional homeland of the Akamba people.

The Akamba migrated here from the south several centuries ago in search of food. Great traders, they ranged all the way from the coast to Lake Victoria and up to Lake Turkana. Ivory was one of their main barter items, but so too were locally made products such as beer, honey, iron weapons and ornaments. The Akamba traded to obtain food stocks from the neighbouring Maasai and Kikuyu, as their own low-altitude land was relatively poor.

In colonial times the Akamba were highly regarded by the British for their intelligence and fighting ability and were drafted in large numbers into the British army. Thousands lost their lives in WWI. When it came to land, the British were not quite so respectful; they tried to limit the number of cattle the Akamba could own (by confiscating them) and also settled more Europeans in Ukambani. The Akamba response was the formation of the Ukamba Members Association, which marched en masse to Nairobi and squatted peacefully at Kariokor Market in protest. After three weeks, the administration gave way and the cattle were eventually returned to the people.

All adolescents go through initiation rites to adulthood at around the age of 12, and have the same *riiko* (age-set) groups common to many of Kenya's peoples. The various age-set rituals involve the men, and to a lesser extent the women, gaining seniority as they get older.

Young parents are known as *mwanake/mwiitu* or 'junior elders' (men/women) and are responsible for the maintenance and upkeep of the village. Once his children are old enough to become junior elders themselves, the mwanake goes through a ceremony to become a *nthele* (medium elder), and later in life a *atumia ma kivalo* (full elder) with the responsibility for death ceremonies and administering the law. The last stage of a person's life is that of *atumia ma kisuka* (senior elder) with responsibility for the holy places.

Akamba subgroups include Kitui, Masaku and Mumoni.

Kalenjin

'Kalenjin' is a name formulated in the 1950s to describe the group of peoples previously called the Nandi by the British. The Nandi tag was

Top: Young Maasai woman. (Photo: Mitch Reardon)

erroneous as the people were all Nandi-speakers (one of many dialects) but were not all Nandis; the other groups included Kipsigis, Eleyo, Marakwet, Pokot and Tugen (arap Moi's people). The word *kalenjin* means 'I say to you' in Nandi.

The Kalenjin people occupy the western edge of the central Rift Valley area, which includes Kericho, Eldoret, Kitale, Baringo and the Mt Elgon area. They first migrated to the area west of Lake Turkana from southern Sudan around 2000 years ago and gradually filtered south as the climate changed and the forests dwindled.

Although originally pastoralists, most Kalenjin groups took up agriculture. A few, such as the Okiek, stuck to the forests and to a hunter-gatherer existence. Beekeeping was a common activity and the honey was used in trade and for brewing beer. The Kipsigis, on the other hand, have always had a passionate love for cattle, and cattle rustling by them continues to cause friction with their neighbours.

The Nandi, the second largest of the Kalenjin communities, settled in the Nandi Hills between the 16th and 17th centuries, where they prospered after learning agricultural techniques from the Luo and Luyha. They had a formidable military reputation and between 1895

and 1905 they clashed with the British over the construction of the Mombasa-Uganda Railway. They managed to delay the 'Lunatic Line' for more than a decade until Koitalel, their chief, was killed.

As with most tribes, Kalenjin have age-sets into which a man is initiated after circumcision and remains for the rest of his life. Polygamy was widely practised in the past. Administration of the law is carried out at the *kok* – an informal gathering of the clan's elders and other interested parties in the dispute. Kalenjin doctors are mainly (and unusually) women and they use herbal remedies in their work. Other specialist doctors practised trepanning – taking out pieces of the skull to cure certain ailments from mental illness to headaches – which is also practised by the Bantu-speaking Gusii of the Kisii district.

The Kalenjin, especially the Nandi and Kipsigis, are renowned athletes.

Right: The Pokot people of Kenya are one of a number of groups that together comprise the Kalenjin. (Photo: Mitch Reardon)

Kikuyu

The Kikuyu are Kenya's largest ethnic group and their heartland surrounds Mt Kenya. The original Kikuyu are thought to have migrated to the area from the east and north-east over a period of a couple of hundred years from the 16th century, and were actually part of the group known as Meru. Basically they overran the original occupants of the area such as the Athi and the Gumba, although intermarriage and trading did take place.

The Kikuyu's new land was bordered by the Maasai and although there were periods of calm between the two groups, there were also times when raids were carried out against each other's property and cattle. Both groups placed a high value on cattle. Intermarriage was not uncommon between them and today they share a number of similarities – particularly in dress, weaponry, and dancing – as a result of their intermingling. Early in the 20th century, European settlers seized large tracts of their homeland – the Kikuyu responded by forming an opposition political association in 1920 and subsequently instigated the Mau Mau rebellion in the 1950s.

The administration of the *mwaki* (clans), made up of many *nyumba* (family groups), was originally taken care of by a council of elders, with a good deal of importance being placed on the role of the witch doctor, the medicine man and the blacksmith. Traditionally, the Kikuyu god (Ngai) is believed to reside on Mt Kenya *(Kirinyaga* – the 'mountain of brightness', 'mountain of whiteness' or 'black and white peak spotted like ostrich feathers') and this accounts for the practice of orientating Kikuyu homes with the door facing Mt Kenya.

Initiation rites for both boys and girls are important ceremonies and consist of circumcision in boys and clitoridectomy in girls (the latter now rarely practised), accompanied by elaborate preparations and rituals. Each group of youths of the same age belong to a riika and pass through the various stages of life (with associated rituals) together.

Subgroups of the Kikuyu include Embu, Ndia and Mbeere.

Luo

The Luo people, Kenya's second largest ethnic group, make up approximately 15% of the population. They live in the west of the

Top: Kikuyu society places huge importance on the role of the witch doctor. (Photo: David Wall)

country on the shores of Lake Victoria. Along with the Maasai, they migrated south from the Nile region of Sudan around the 15th century. Although they clashed heavily with the existing Bantu-speaking peoples of the area, intermarriage and cultural mixing occurred. During the struggle for *Uhuru* (independence) many of the country's leading Kenyan politicians and trade unionists were Luos, including Tom Mboya (assassinated in 1969) and the former vice-president, Jaramogi Oginga Odinga.

The Luo are unusual among Kenya's ethnic groups in that circumcision is not practised in either sex. The tradition was replaced by something that one can imagine being almost as painful: the extraction of four or six teeth from the bottom jaw. Although uncommon these days, you still see many middle-aged and older people of the region who are minus a few bottom pegs.

Although originally cattle herders, the devastating effects of rinderpest in the 1890s forced the Luo to adopt fishing and subsistence agriculture. The family group consists of the man, his wife (or wives) and their sons and daughters-in-law. The house compound is enclosed by a fence, and includes separate huts for the man and for each wife and son. (There is a good reconstruction of a Luo homestead in the grounds of the Kisumu Museum.)

The family group is a member of a *dhoot* (clan), several of which in turn make up a group of *ogandi* (a grouping of several clans) each led by a *ruoth* (chief). Collectively the ogandi constitute the Luo tribe. As is the case with many tribes, great importance is placed on the role of the medicine man and the spirits.

The Luo, like the Luyha, have two major recreational passions: music and soccer.

Luyha

The Luyha are of Bantu origin and are made up of 17 different groups. They are the third largest group after the Kikuyu and Luo. They occupy a relatively small area in western Kenya centred on Kakamega, where they settled in around the 14th century. Population densities here are the highest in rural Kenya, with more than 700 people per sq km, and the birth rate of the Luyha is one of the highest in the world.

In times past, the Luyha were skilled metal workers forging knives and tools for working the land which were traded with other groups. While pottery and basket-making are still common crafts, the Luyha are now agriculturists and have taken to farming groundnuts, sesame and maize. Small holders also grow large amounts of cash crops such as cotton and sugar-cane but the pressure for land is quickly becoming an increasing problem as plot sizes begin to shrink with each passing generation.

Many Luyha still have a strong and powerful belief in witchcraft and superstition, though to the passing traveller this is rarely obvious.

TRIBAL GROUPS & CULTURES

Maasai

It is the Maasai more than anyone who have become a symbol of 'tribal' Kenya and, to a lesser extent, Tanzania. With a reputation (often exaggerated) as fierce warriors and a supercilious demeanour, the Maasai have largely managed to stay outside the mainstream of development in Kenya and still maintain their cattle herds in the area south of Nairobi straddling the Tanzania border.

They first came to the region from Sudan and eventually came to dominate a large area of central Kenya until, in the late 19th century, they were decimated by famine and disease, and their cattle herds were routed by rinderpest. Up until the Masai Mara National Reserve was created in the early 1960s, the Maasai had plenty of space for their cattle grazing, but at a stroke much of this land was put off-limits. As their population increased (both the cattle and the Maasai) pressure for land became intense and conflict with the authorities was constant. Settlement programs have only been reluctantly accepted as Maasai traditions scorn agriculture, and land ownership is a foreign concept.

Another consequence of the competition for land is that many of the ceremonial traditions can no longer be fulfilled. Part of the cere-

mony where a man becomes a *moran* (warrior), involves a group of young men around the age of 14 going out and building a *manyatta* (village) after their circumcision ceremony. Here they should spend as long as eight years alone. Today, while the tradition and will survives, the land is just not available.

Tourism provides an income to some, either through selling everyday items (gourds, necklaces, clubs and spears), dancing or acting as guides. While a few can make a lot of money from these activities, the benefits are not widespread.

Top: A Maasai girl displays the unique beadwork that Maasai women are renowned for. (Photo: Mitch Reardon)

Left: Maasai wedding celebrants prepare for a traditional ceremony. (Photo: Mitch Reardon)

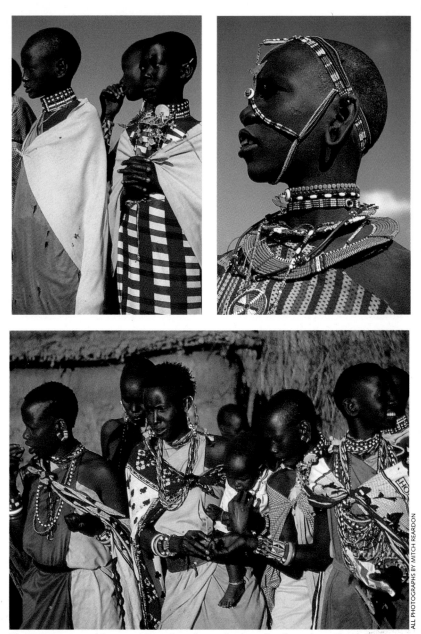

The Maasai women of Kenya and Tanzania are known for decorating themselves with colourful beadwork. The handmade beads are also a source of income for tribespeople, who sell their crafts to tourists.

The infectious smiles of the children of East Africa: Pokot girls (top left); Turkana girl (top right); Turkana children (bottom).

Faces of East Africa: Kenyan girls (top left); Ugandan boy (top right); Rwandan drummers (bottom).

Hanging out with your brothers and sisters (top) or smoking the gourd pipe (bottom) are two ways to pass time in rural Tanzania.

Meru

The Meru arrived in the area north-east of Mt Kenya from the coast sometime around the 14th century following invasions of that area by Somalis from the north. The group was led by a chief known as the *mogwe* up until 1974, when the incumbent converted to Christianity and denied his son from inheriting the role. A group of *njuuri* (tribal elders) were all-powerful and, along with the mogwe and witch doctor, would administer justice as they saw fit. This justice often consisted of giving poison-laced beer to an accused person. Other curious practices included holding a newly born child to face Mt Kenya and then blessing it by spitting on it, while witch doctors sometimes eliminated one of their rival's sons by putting poison on the circumcision blade. The Meru now live on some of the most fertile farmland in Kenya and grow numerous cash crops, including *miraa*, the stems of which contain a mild stimulant.

Subgroups of the Meru include the Chuka, Igembe, Igoji, Tharaka, Muthambi, Tigania and Imenti.

Samburu

Closely related to the Maasai, and in fact speaking the same language, the Samburu occupy an arid area directly north of Mt Kenya. It seems that when the Maasai migrated to the area from Sudan, some headed east (and became the Samburu) while most continued south to the area they occupy today.

As is often the case, age-sets are an integral part of the society and the men pass through various stages before becoming powerful elders

at the top of the ladder. Circumcision is practised in both sexes; with the girls it is only done on the day of marriage, which is usually when she is around 16 years old. Men are often in their 30s by the time they pass out of warriorhood and become elders qualified to marry.

Swahili Peoples

Although the people of the coast do not have a common heritage, they do have a linguistic link – Kiswahili (commonly referred to as Swahili), a Bantu-based language which evolved as a means of communication between Africans and foreign traders such as Arabs, Persians and the Portuguese. As might be expected with such a diverse input, Swahili language borrows

Right: Samburu males pass through various stages before becoming powerful elders. (Photo: Lee Foster)

words from Arabic, Hindi, Portuguese and even English. The word *swahili* is a derivative of the Arabic word *sahel*, meaning 'coast'.

Arab traders first started plying the coast in their sailing dhows sometime before the 7th century, arriving with the north-east monsoon and sailing home on the south-west monsoon. The main exports were ivory, tortoiseshell and leopard skins, while items such as glass beads from India and porcelain from as far afield as China found their way here.

After the 7th century, Islam became a strong influence as traders began settling along the coast. Today the majority of the coastal people are Muslims, although their lifestyles are a world away from the more traditional forms of Islam that prevail in some places in the Middle East.

Swahili subgroups include Bajun, Siyu, Pate, Mvita, Fundi, Shela, Ozi, Vumba and Amu (residents of Lamu).

Turkana

The Turkana are another of Kenya's more colourful (and warlike) people. Originally from the Karamajong district of north-eastern Uganda, the Turkana number around 250,000 and live in the virtual desert country of Kenya's north-west. Due to their isolation, the Turkana were probably the least affected by the 20th century of all Kenya's people.

Like the Samburu and the Maasai (with whom they are linguistically linked), the Turkana are cattle herders first and foremost, although more recently some have taken up fishing the waters of Lake

Below: The Turkana women of Kenya wear beads around their necks to indicate significant events in each woman's life. (Photo: Eric Wheater)

Turkana and even growing the occasional crops, weather permitting. But unlike the other two tribes, the Turkana have discontinued the practice of circumcision.

The traditional dress of the Turkana people is amazing, as is the number of people who still wear it – catching a bus up in the north-west is a real eye-opener for the first-time visitor. The men cover part of their hair with mud, which is then painted blue and decorated with ostrich and other feathers. The main garment they wear, despite the blast-furnace heat of the region, is a woollen blanket (usually a garish modern checked one), which is worn around the shoulder.

Traditional accessories include a small wooden stool carved out of a single piece of wood (used either as a pillow or stool), a wooden stick with a distinctive shape and a wrist knife. Both the men and the women wear with great flourish the lip plug through the lower lip. The women wear a variety of beaded and metal adornments, much of it indicating to the trained eye events in the woman's life. A half skirt of animal skins and a piece of black cloth are the only garments worn, al-though these days pieces of colourful cloth are not uncommon for use as baby slings.

Tattooing is also common and usually has special meaning. Men are tattooed on the shoulders and upper arm each time they kill an enemy – the right shoulder for killing a man, the left for a women; it's sur-prising the number of men you still see with these markings. Witch doctors and prophets are held in high regard and tattooing on someone's lower stomach is usually a sign of attempts by witch doctors to cast out an undesirable spirit rather than any sort of decoration.

TANZANIA

Chagga
The Chagga people, who live on the slopes of Mt Kilimanjaro in and around Moshi, are one of Tanzania's largest ethnic groups. For much of their early history they were subdivided into numerous small, inde-pendent chiefdoms, which were often at war with each other and with their neighbours over control over caravan trade with the coast. In the early 20th century, the Germans succeeded in overpowering the Chagga and ruling them, largely through a system of deposing resisters and appointing more pliable chiefs in their stead. It was during this time that a common Chagga cultural identity began to develop.

The Chagga, who are patrilineal, were traditionally small-scale banana farmers, and even today are known for their *mbege* (banana beer). Together with the British colonial administrators, the Chagga formed a successful sales cooperative early in the 20th century for mar-keting the coffee crop. With the increased revenues earned in the coffee industry, more and more Chagga were able to receive formal ed-ucation, and today the Chagga are one of the most modernised and prosperous ethnic groups in Tanzania.

While most Chagga are Christian, animistic beliefs continue to play an important role in everyday life. The Chagga maintain close links with the spirit world, and rituals and traditional practices are also very common.

Sukuma & Nyamwezi

The Sukuma (people of the north), who live around Mwanza and in the southern Lake Victoria region, comprise close to 15% of Tanzania's total population. For much of their history they were loosely organised into numerous Bantu-speaking subgroups; it is only recently that they have come to view themselves as a single entity. The Sukuma are closely related to the Nyamwezi, Tanzania's second largest ethnic group, centred in the Tabora region.

Most Sukuma are farmers and their lands comprise one of Tanzania's most important agricultural areas, producing the majority of the country's cotton as well as other crops. Cattle are also an important source of livelihood. The Sukuma have traditionally had a highly developed and structured form of village organisation in which each settlement is subdivided into chiefdoms ruled by a *ntemi* (chief) in collaboration with a council of elders.

Divisions of land and labour are made by village committees consisting of similarly aged members from each family in the village. These age-based groups, each with their own leader, perform numerous roles ranging from assisting with the building of new houses to farming and other community-oriented work. As a result of this system – which gives most families at least a representational role in many village activities – houses and land are often viewed as communal property among the Sukuma.

Haya

The Haya, who live in the region west of Lake Victoria around Bukoba, are another of Tanzania's larger ethnic groups. They are related linguistically to both the Bantu and Nilotic families.

The Haya had one of the most highly developed early societies on the continent. By the 18th or 19th century they were organised into eight different states or kingdoms, each headed by a powerful and often despotic *mukama*, who ruled in part by divine right. It was the mukama who controlled all trade, and at least nominally owned all property, while land usage was shared among small, patrilineal communities. Order was maintained through a system of appointed chiefs and officials, assisted by an age-group based army. With the arrival of the colonial authorities, this political organisation began to disintegrate. The various Haya groups splintered and many chiefs were replaced by persons considered more malleable and more sympathetic to colonial interests.

In the 1920s, in the wake of growing resentment towards these propped-up leaders and the colonial government, the Haya began to regroup and in 1924 founded the Bukoba Buhaya Union. This association was initially directed towards local political reform but soon developed into the more influential and broad-based African Association. Together with similar groups established elsewhere in the country – notably in the Kilimanjaro region and in Dar es Salaam – it constituted one of Tanzania's earliest political movements and was an important force in the drive towards independence.

Makonde

The Makonde, known throughout East Africa for their ebony woodcarvings, are one of Tanzania's largest ethnic groups. They originated in northern Mozambique, where many of them still live. In Tanzania, apart from a significant carving community in Dar es Salaam, the Makonde have settled primarily in the Mtwara region in the south-east of the country, with the largest concentration inhabiting the Makonde plateau.

The Makonde, like many tribes in the south-east, are matrilineal. Although customs are gradually changing, children and inheritances normally belong to the woman, and it is quite common for the husbands to pack up and move to the villages of their wives after they are married.

Due to their isolated location, the Makonde have remained largely insulated from colonial and postcolonial influences, and are considered to be one of Tanzania's most traditional groups. Most still adhere to traditional religions, although there are small pockets of Muslims and Christians.

Pare

The Pare people, who inhabit the northern and southern Pare mountains, originally came from the Taita Hills area of southern Kenya, where they were herdsmen, hunters and farmers.

According to tradition, the Pare were pursued into the mountains by the Maasai, who began to capture and steal their cattle. Over the years, they adapted their lifestyle to the more rugged mountain terrain. Today they are known principally as farmers, cultivating vegetables, maize, bananas, cassava and cardamom.

Traditional Pare society is patrilineal. Fathers are considered to have enormous authority during their lifetime as well as after death. Because of the great powers which deceased persons are believed to possess, the Pare have developed elaborate rituals which centre around the dead.

Around most villages are sacred areas in which skulls of tribal chiefs are kept. When people die, they are believed to inhabit a netherworld between the land of the living and the spirit world. If they are allowed to remain in this state, ill fate will befall their descendants. The prescribed rituals allowing the deceased to pass into the world of the ancestors are therefore of great importance.

UGANDA

Buganda

The Buganda are the largest ethnic group in Uganda, and they account for around 17% of the population. Their traditional land is the area to the north and north-west of Lake Victoria, which includes Kampala. While most Buganda these days are Christian, their traditional religion was based around spirits, ancestors and gods, accessed through spirit mediums.

The Buganda were the most well-organised of the tribes in the region, and had a political system based around the absolute power of the *kabaka*, or king, who ruled through district chiefs. The Buganda became even more powerful with the arrival of the British, as the British favoured the recruitment of Buganda to the civil service.

During the chaotic Obote/Amin years the Bugandan monarchy was abolished. It was restored in 1993, though with no political power.

Iteso

The Nilotic-language-speaking Iteso people are the second largest tribal group in Uganda, accounting for around 8% of the population. They occupy the area between Karamoja and Lake Kyoga in the north and are predominantly crop growers, with coffee and cotton being important cash crops.

The greater part of their traditional culture was lost when they were defeated by the Buganda in the 19th century, and they are now largely Christians.

Basoga

The Basoga make up about 8% of the population. Before the arrival of the Europeans, they were subsistence farmers who also kept cattle, sheep and goats.

Bagisu

The Bagisu, subsistence farmers occupying the east of the country around Mt Elgon, make up around 5% of the population.

Karamajong

The Karamajong, who comprise only about 2% of the Ugandan population, live in the north-eastern region, north of Mt Elgon. They are closely related to the Turkana of Kenya and, like the Turkana, are predominantly cattle herders. Cattle are their most valued possession.

The Karamajong also have a reputation as cattle raiders, and have long been involved in disputes with the Turkana across the border in Kenya. Although many tribal traditions have slowly been lost or forgotten as Uganda walks the path to modernity, the Karamajong have retained their identity. These hardy cattle-raising fighters have resisted outside domination for years and still uphold many of their traditions.

RWANDA & BURUNDI

Hutu

The Hutu were the original Bantu-speaking farmers who inhabited the area that is today Rwanda and Burundi. Prior to the colonial period, many Hutu lived under Tutsi domination; theirs was a harsh life which in many ways resembled the situation in feudal Europe. Their fortunes have risen and fallen over the years in both Rwanda and Burundi.

The Hutu will be forever associated with the genocide of 1994 carried out against the Tutsi and against Hutu moderates, although to give a fuller picture, large numbers of Hutu have also been massacred in neighbouring Burundi over the years. While reconciliation may be working in Rwanda, Hutu remain outside the political spectrum in Burundi and extremist elements remain a force for instability in the Great Lakes region.

Tutsi

The Tutsi are a tall, warrior-like people and were most likely nomadic pastoralists that migrated to the region of Rwanda and Burundi during the 16th and 17th Centuries, probably from Ethiopia or southern Sudan. They soon established control over the local Hutu population and have maintained a presence in the region until the present day. While hundreds of thousands of Tutsi were massacred during the Rwandan genocide of 1994, in Burundi the Tutsi-dominated regime has also been responsible for the deaths of many Hutu in the period since independence. Relations between the Tutsi and neighbouring tribes of the region remain fraught with mistrust.

Right: Rwandan drummers (Photo: Nick Ray)

Regional Facts for the Visitor

SUGGESTED ITINERARIES

A multicountry visit to East Africa usually involves a visit to Kenya combined with either or both Tanzania and Uganda. It is far less practical to combine only Tanzania and Uganda as the land (and lake) connections are difficult, and the flight options into and out of the region from the two capitals are much more limited than at Nairobi.

The suggested itineraries below assume that you want to visit more than just one country in the region.

One Month

With a month to spend in East Africa, you could spend two weeks in Kenya, before slotting in another couple of weeks in either Uganda or northern Tanzania.

With a couple of weeks in Kenya, you could take in Nairobi and then visit the major wildlife parks of Masai Mara and Amboseli on a week-long organised safari, before heading off overland to Tanzania or Uganda.

Two weeks in Uganda would give you time to track gorillas in Bwindi National Park (in the stunning south-west of the country) and, leaving the tourists behind, visit Murchison Falls National Park.

Northern Tanzania has a lot packed into a compact area, so choices need to be made. Arusha makes a good base from which to organise trips to Mt Kilimanjaro and the mighty Serengeti National Park.

Two Months

Kenya & Tanzania Two months gives you a lot more scope. From Nairobi you could head for the beaches and snorkelling off the Kenyan coast for a week or so, before heading south to Tanzania, either overland or with a flight from Mombasa to Dar es Salaam. A week or more on the Zanzibar archipelago would be time well spent, and you could then head for the Mt Kilimanjaro/Arusha/Moshi region, with a pause in the Usambara Mountains region for a few days of hiking. After tackling Kilimanjaro

and the Serengeti, you could then re-enter Kenya at Namanga and return to Nairobi. Any remaining time could easily be spent in Kenya, exploring the lakes of the Rift Valley or perhaps climbing Mt Kenya.

Kenya, Uganda & Rwanda Two months in Kenya and Uganda gives you time to enjoy the major highlights of both countries. These include the national parks along the western border of Uganda (Bwindi, Ruwenzori and Murchison Falls); and in Kenya the major wildlife reserves, Mt Kenya and the coast. It would also be possible while in Uganda to include a brief visit to the mountain gorillas in Rwanda.

Three Months

With three months at your disposal, you could combine a visit to all the three major countries of the region (see the one and two month itineraries earlier), including a visit the mountain gorillas in Rwanda. For those after a real taste of adventure, there is the option of entering western Tanzania direct from Rwanda, making a full circuit of the region.

PLANNING
When to Go

The main tourist season in East Africa is January and February, as the weather at this time of year is generally considered to be the best – hot and dry. It's also when you'll find the largest concentrations of birdlife on the Rift Valley lakes, and when the animals in the wildlife parks tend to congregate more around the watercourses as other sources dry up, making them easier to spot.

From July to September could be called the 'shoulder season' as the weather is still dry and it's the time of the visual extravaganza – the annual wildebeest migration into the Masai Mara National Reserve (Kenya) from the Serengeti National Park (Tanzania).

During the long rains (from March to May) and the short rains (from October to December) things are much quieter – places tend to be less full and accommodation prices come down. The rains generally don't affect your ability to move around and see things, it's just that you will probably get rained on in a big way, especially in the late afternoon.

What Kind of Trip

East Africa is a compact region, which is relatively easy to get around. For this reason many travellers choose to travel independently, using a combination of public transport, organised safaris and occasional vehicle hire. For anyone on a budget, organised safaris are the best option for getting to the wildlife parks, although in Uganda the opportunities are limited and safaris are expensive. The main bases from which to take a safari are Nairobi (Kenya) and Arusha (in northern Tanzania). See the Organised Vehicle Safaris sections in the Kenya and Tanzania chapters for full details on the pros and cons of taking a safari of this kind.

Maps

There are a number of maps that cover the region. The Hallwag 1:2,000,000 *Kenya & Tanzania* also includes Uganda, Rwanda, Burundi and eastern Congo (Zaïre).

Michelin's 1:4,000,000 *Africa – Central & South* also gives good regional coverage, although on a smaller scale.

The best map you can buy is probably the recent Bartholomew's 1:2,500,000 *Kenya & Tanzania*.

Lonely Planet's *Kenya travel atlas* provides handy, accurate maps and is a great companion to this guidebook.

What to Bring

Bring the minimum. Many travellers in East Africa find that once they actually get there they have far too much gear. This is not only an uncomfortable inconvenience, it also means that instead of taking back some special reminders of the region, you'll be taking back the same extra pullover and jeans that you set off with. Unless it's absolutely essential, *leave it at home!*

A rucksack (backpack) is far more practical than an overnight bag, and is essential

if you plan to do any trekking or walking. It is worth buying a good-quality bag right at the start – African travel soon sorts out the good stuff from the junk, and if it's the latter you've opted for, you'll be cursing it the whole way.

A day pack is a worthwhile item, if only for keeping your camera dry and out of the incredible dust which seems to permeate every crack and crevice when you're on safari. For these reasons and for security, it needs to be one that zips shut.

A sleeping bag is more or less essential if you are travelling overland beyond East Africa, taking a safari or planning to climb mountains; however, within the region itself there are enough hotels for you not to need one. On the other hand, carrying a sleeping bag and closed-cell foam mat does give you a greater degree of flexibility. Sleeping bags are the one thing that all camping safari companies require you to provide.

There's always much discussion about the pros and cons of carrying a tent, and basically it boils down to what sort of travelling you want to do, and how much weight you're prepared to carry. As with a sleeping bag, a tent is not necessary if you're just travelling from town to town, but carrying your own portable shelter opens up a stack of exciting possibilities. The full range of camping equipment can be hired from various places in Kenya but not in Tanzania or Uganda.

Quite a few travellers carry a mosquito net, and with the risk of malaria there is no doubt that this is a good idea, although with judicious use of insect repellent and mosquito coils, you should have few problems. On the topic of insect repellent, bring a good supply and make sure that whatever you bring contains the active ingredient diethyl toluamide, commonly known as DEET. This has been found to be the most effective against mosquitoes. Mosquito coils are what the locals use (when they use anything at all, that is) to keep the mosquitos at bay, and local brands such as Doom are available in even the smallest stores.

Clothes need to be both practical and to take into account local sensibilities. Although this region straddles the equator, the large variations in altitude lead to equally large variations in climate. A windproof and waterproof jacket also comes in handy, particularly during the rainy seasons. Most travellers seem to get around in T-shirts and shorts, which is fine in most areas, but you should be more circumspect on the Muslim-dominated coast, particularly on Lamu and Unguja (Zanzibar Island). Neither do civil servants, officials and embassy staff appreciate scantily dressed travellers; they will treat you with disdain.

Overlooked by many people but absolutely indispensable is a good pair of sunglasses. The huge amount of glare you will experience in the bright tropical light is not only uncomfortable but can also damage your eyes. A hat that shades your face and neck is also well worth considering, and a water bottle is worth any slight inconvenience it may cause. It needs to be unbreakable, have a good seal and be able to hold at least 1L.

Most toiletries – soap, shaving cream, shampoo, toothpaste, toilet paper, tampons – are available throughout the region.

The one thing that you're really going to appreciate is a pair of binoculars, whether they be pocket ones or larger field binoculars. When out in the wildlife parks you can put them to constant use and they are essential for identifying the dozens of species of mammal and bird that you'll come across. If you don't plan on going to the wildlife parks, they are still handy just for the scenery, or perhaps for trying to spot that potential lift coming over the horizon when you're stuck out in the middle of nowhere.

Also important are those little things that can often make your life just that bit more comfortable:

- Swiss Army pocketknife
- small sewing kit (including a few metres of fishing line and a large needle for emergency rucksack surgery)
- 10m length of light nylon cord for a washing line
- handful of clothes pegs
- half a tennis ball makes a good fits-all wash basin plug

RESPONSIBLE TOURISM

Tourism generally is having a big environmental and social impact in East Africa, and this largely comes through the safari business. National parks and reserves have suffered seriously from the sheer weight of visitor numbers, and in many cases there hasn't been the necessary will or resources (or both) to enforce regulations. The local communities which live in or around the parks have also been hugely affected – both by the reduction of their traditional grazing lands and in becoming tourist attractions in themselves. Some communities have also been forced off their land, inevitably ending up in the shanty settlements of the capital cities.

A few tour operators are making conscious efforts to diversify in an effort to address these problems but progress is slow. The best companies are those that have a serious commitment to protecting the fragile ecosystems in these and other areas, and that put some of the profits back into local communities. Although these companies won't always be the cheapest, the extra money you spend is an important way of contributing to the future well-being of the areas that you visit.

When evaluating a company based on these criteria, try to distinguish between mere lip service and real action. You can contact the various country National Parks or Wildlife Conservation boards or similar agencies (see the individual country chapters for details) to learn about environmental- and tourism-related issues in the areas you wish to visit. Avoiding souvenir shops that stock items made from shells, coral, ivory and turtle shells – the export of which is illegal – is also an important way to contribute to the preservation of East Africa's ecosystems.

Another dimension of responsible tourism, especially in countries such as Kenya and Tanzania (which see so many foreign visitors), is the manner and attitude that visitors assume towards local people. Respect is of the utmost importance, both in personal dealings as well as in your overall behaviour and your style of dress.

A good source of information on sustainable tourism is the UK-based Tourism Concern (Stapledon House, 277-281 Holloway Rd, London N7 8HN).
Web site: www.gn.apc.org/tourismconcern

VISAS & DOCUMENTS
Passport
If you already have a passport, make sure it's valid for a reasonably long period of time and has plenty of blank pages on which stamp-happy immigration officials can do their stuff. If it's more than half full and you're going to need a lot of visas, get a new passport before you set off. This way you won't have to waste time hanging around in a capital city somewhere while your embassy issues you with a new one. In some countries there is the option of getting a normal-sized passport or a 'jumbo' passport. Get the larger one. US nationals can have extension pages stapled into full passports at any of their embassies.

Visas
Visas are obtained from the embassy or consulate of the appropriate country, either before you set off or along the way. It's best to get them along the way, especially if your travel plans are not fixed, but keep your ear to the ground regarding the best places to get them. Two different consulates of the same country may have completely different requirements – the fee may be different (one consulate might want to see how much money you have whereas another won't); one might demand an onward ticket while another won't even mention it; one might issue visas while you wait and another might insist on referring the application back to the capital (which can take weeks).

Whatever you do, don't turn up at a border without a visa unless you're absolutely sure that visas aren't necessary or you can get one at the border. If you get this wrong, you'll find yourself tramping back to the nearest consulate, and in some countries this can be a long way.

Another important fact to bear in mind about visas is their sheer cost. None are free and some are expensive. Unless you carry a passport from one of the Commonwealth or European Community (EC) countries, you'll need visas, and if you're on a tight budget, the cost can make a hole in your pocket. It's a good idea to make a rough calculation of what the visa fees are going to amount to before you set off, and allow for it. Make sure you have plenty of passport-size photographs for visa applications – 12 should be sufficient.

Some countries demand that you have a ticket out of the country before they will issue you with a visa or let you into the country. As long as you intend to leave from the same place you arrived, there is no problem, but if you want to enter at one point and leave from another, this can be a headache. Fortunately, having to show an onward ticket seems to be rare in East Africa, and usually only happens when arriving by air. If they do insist on you having an onward ticket but you want to spend the minimum amount possible (and have it refunded without problems), try buying a Miscellaneous Charges Order (MCO) from an international airline for, say, US$100.

The other way to get around the onward ticket requirement is to buy the cheapest ticket available out of the country and then get it refunded later on. If you do this, make sure you can get a refund without having to wait months. Don't forget to ask specifically where it can be refunded, since some airlines will only refund tickets at the office where you bought them, and some only at their head office.

See individual country chapters for details on visa requirements and the addresses of embassies.

Travel Insurance
A travel insurance policy to cover theft, loss and medical problems is a wise idea. See under Predeparture Planning in the Health section of this chapter for details about health insurance.

Driving Licence & Permits
If you're taking your own transport or are thinking of hiring a vehicle to tour certain national parks, get hold of an International

Driving Permit (IDP) before you set off. Any national motoring organisation will fix you up with this, provided you have a valid driving licence for your own country. The cost of these permits is generally about US$5. On the other hand, a national driving licence seems to suffice for hiring a vehicle in most countries.

Student Card

An International Student Identity Card (ISIC) or the graduate equivalent is useful in many places and can save you a bit of money, although its usefulness diminishes with each passing year. Possible concessions include airline tickets, train fares and reduced entry charges to museums and to archaeological sites.

Vaccination Certificates

Whoever supplies you with your vaccinations will provide an International Health Certificate with the necessary stamps. In most places you won't be asked to present it but border officials often see it as a good way of catching people out. The Kenyan/ Ethiopian border at Moyale and Unguja (Zanzibar Island) has been a problem in this way.

Other Documents

For information on a *carnet de passage*, a document needed if you want to bring a foreign-registered vehicle into East Africa, see the Regional Getting Around chapter.

Copies

Before beginning your trip, make copies of your passport, your international health card, airline tickets, travellers cheque serial numbers and any other essential documents. Leave one set of copies with family or friends and bring a second set with you, stored separately from the originals. Doing this will make replacement much easier should your documents be lost or stolen.

EMBASSIES & CONSULATES

As a tourist, it's important to realise what your own embassy – the embassy of the country of which you are a citizen – can and can't do.

Generally speaking, it won't be much help in emergencies if the trouble you're in is remotely your own fault. Remember that you are bound by the laws of the country you are in. Your embassy will not be sympathetic if you end up in jail after committing a crime locally, even if such actions are legal in your own country.

In genuine emergencies you might get some assistance but only if other channels have been exhausted. For example, if you need to get home urgently, a free ticket home is exceedingly unlikely – the embassy would expect you to have insurance. If you have all your money and documents stolen, it might assist with getting a new passport, but a loan for onward travel is out of the question.

For lists of embassies and consulates, see the individual country chapters.

CUSTOMS

See Customs in the individual country Facts for the Visitor chapters for details.

MONEY
Currency

Be careful which currency you take with you, as some are difficult or even impossible to change. US dollars, Canadian dollars, UK pounds, French francs, German marks, Swiss francs and Italian lire are all readily accepted. Australian and New Zealand dollars can be difficult to change, except in Nairobi, as the exchange rate may not be known. You don't get this problem with North American and European currencies.

See individual country Facts for the Visitor chapters for exchange rates.

Exchanging Money

Travellers Cheques & Cash For maximum flexibility, take the larger slice of your money in travellers cheques and the rest in cash – say up to US$500. American Express (Amex), Thomas Cook and Citibank cheques are the most widely used and their offices generally offer instant replacement in the event of loss or theft. Keep a record of the cheque numbers and the original bill of sale for the cheques in a safe place, in case you lose your cheques. Replacement is a lot quicker if you can produce this information. Even so, if you don't look clean and tidy, or if they don't believe your story for some reason or another, replacement can take time, since quite a few travellers have sold their cheques on the black market, or simply pretended to lose them, and then demanded a replacement set. This is particularly so with Amex cheques. You should avoid bringing cheques from small banks which only have a few overseas branches, as you'll find them very difficult, if not impossible, to change in many places.

Make sure that you buy a good range of cheque denominations so that you don't get stuck changing large denomination bills for short stays or for final expenses. Small cheques are advisable for Tanzania since officially all mid-range and top end accommodation and all national park fees have to be paid in hard currency, although this is not always enforced. See the Money section of the Tanzania Facts for the Visitor chapter for more details.

Credit Cards Amex, Diner's Club, Visa and MasterCard are all widely recognised credit cards which can be used to pay for accommodation, food, airline tickets, books, clothing and other services in most large towns, especially in Kenya (though less so in neighbouring countries).

Cash advances on a credit card are also an excellent way of getting funds as you go but don't expect to make use of this service outside the capital cities. Visa, Amex and MasterCard are the main cards. There are Amex offices or agents in Nairobi, Mombasa, Kampala and Dar es Salaam.

Credit cards also have their uses when 'sufficient funds' are demanded by immigration officials before they will allow you to enter a country. It's generally accepted that you have 'sufficient funds' if you have a credit card.

International Transfers If you run out of money while you're abroad and need more, ask your bank back home to send a draft to you (assuming you have money back home to send). Make sure you specify the city and the bank branch. Transferred by cable or telex, money should reach you within a few days. Western Union has branches in all countries of the region and offers quick and reliable service. Remember that some countries will only give you your money in local currency; others will let you have it in US dollars or another hard currency. Find out what's possible before you request a transfer; you could lose a fair amount of money if there's an appreciable difference between the official and unofficial exchange rates. Kenya is probably the best place to transact this sort of business.

Black Market You cannot always change travellers cheques in small places or, of course, when the banks are closed. You should bring some cash with you, however, because it allows you to take advantage of any street rate of exchange (black market), although this is minimal these days and barely worth the hassle (the exception is Burundi).

The black market is a thorny issue. Some people regard it as morally reprehensible, even economic sabotage. You'll have to make up your own mind about which side of the moral fence you stand on, but one thing is for sure – you won't meet many budget travellers who don't use the black market where there's a significant difference between the bank and street rates. And you'll meet plenty of officials – some of them in remarkable positions of authority and in full view of everyone around – who will make it plain that they're interested in swapping local currency for hard cash.

This doesn't mean that you should be blasé and incautious. Quite the opposite. Discretion is the name of the game.

When changing on the black market, have the exact amount you want to change available – avoid pulling out large wads of notes. Be very wary about sleight of hand tricks. Insist on personally counting out the notes that are handed to you. Don't allow yourself to be distracted by supposed alarms such as 'police' and 'danger'. Whatever else you do, *don't* actually change on the street, as you may be set up by a police undercover agent.

Costs

It's very difficult to predict what a trip to East Africa is going to cost, since so many factors are involved: how fast you want to travel, what degree of comfort you consider to be acceptable, how much sightseeing you want to do, whether you intend to hire a vehicle to explore a wildlife park or go on an organised safari, whether you're travelling alone or in a group and a host of other things.

There's only one thing that remains the same in Africa, and that's the pace of change – it's fast. Inflation and devaluations can wreak havoc with your travel plans if you're on a very tight budget. You should budget for at least US$20 per day in this region. This should cover the cost of basic but reasonable accommodation, food in local cafes and public transport. It won't include the cost of getting to Africa, safaris in wildlife parks or major purchases in markets. On the other hand, if you stay in one place for a while and cook your own food, you can reduce daily costs considerably.

Bargaining

Many purchases involve some degree of bargaining. This is always the case with things bought from a market, street stall or craft shop. Bargaining may also be necessary for hotels and transport in some places, though these are often fairly standard and you won't be paying any more than the local people. Food and drink bought at restaurants don't usually involve any bargaining – the prices will be written on the menu.

Where bargaining is the name of the game, commodities are looked on as being worth what their owners can get for them. The concept of a fixed price would invoke laughter. If you cop out and pay the first price asked, you'll not only be considered a halfwit but you'll be doing your fellow travellers a disservice, since this will create the impression that all travellers are equally stupid and are willing to pay outrageous prices. You are expected to bargain – it's part of the fun of going to Africa. All the same, no matter how good you are at it, you'll never get things as cheaply as local people do. To traders and hotel and cafe owners, you represent wealth – whatever your appearance.

In most cases bargaining is conducted in a friendly, sometimes exaggeratedly extroverted manner, though there are occasions when it degenerates into a bleak exchange of numbers and leaden handshakes. Decide what you want to pay or what others have told you they've paid, and start off at a price at least 50% lower than this. The seller will inevitably start off at a higher price, sometimes up to 100% higher, than they are prepared to accept. This way you can both end up appearing to be generous.

There will be times when you simply cannot get a shopkeeper to lower the prices to anywhere near what you know the product should be selling for. This probably means that a lot of tourists are passing through and if you don't pay those outrageous prices, some mug will. Don't lose your temper while bargaining. There's no need to. You can always walk away and come back another day or go to a different shop. It's just theatre.

POST & COMMUNICATIONS

Have letters sent to you at Poste Restante, GPO, in whatever city or town you will be passing through. Alternatively, you can use the mail-holding service operated by Amex offices and their agents if you have their cheques or one of their credit cards. Plan ahead – it can take up to two weeks for a letter to arrive even in capital cities, and sometimes much longer in smaller places.

The poste restante services in most of East Africa are pretty reliable. Mail is generally held for four weeks – sometimes more, sometimes less – after which it is returned to the sender. The service is free in most places but in Tanzania there is a small charge for each letter that you collect. As a rule you need your passport as proof of identity.

If you have not received expected letters, ask them to check under every conceivable combination of your given name, surname, any other initials and even under 'M' (for Mr, Ms, Miss, Mrs). This sort of confusion isn't as widespread as many people believe, though most travellers will have an improbable story to tell about it. If there is confusion, it's generally because of bad handwriting on the envelope or language difficulties. If you want to make absolutely sure that the fault won't be yours, have your friends address letters with your surname in block letters and underlined.

Avoid sending currency notes through the post. They'll often be stolen by post office employees no matter how cleverly you disguise the contents.

For more Post & Communications information, see that section in each individual country Facts for the Visitor chapter.

INTERNET RESOURCES

The World Wide Web is a rich resource for travellers. You can research your trip, hunt down bargain air fares, book hotels, check on weather conditions or chat with locals and other travellers about the best places to visit (or avoid!).

There's no better place to start your Web explorations than the Lonely Planet Web site, found at www.lonelyplanet.com. Here you'll find succinct summaries on travelling to most places on earth, postcards from other travellers and the Thorn Tree bulletin board, where you can ask questions before you go or dispense advice when you get back. You can also find travel news and updates to many of our most popular guidebooks, and the subWWWay section links you to the most useful travel resources elsewhere on the Web.

Some American universities have comprehensive Web sites associated with their African Studies departments. Web sites to try include:

University of Pennsylvania's African Studies
  www.sas.upenn.edu/African_Studies/NEH/afr_
  encyclo.html
Stanford University's South of the Sahara
  www.sul.stanford.edu/depts/ssrg/africa/east.html
Columbia University's African Studies
  www.cc.columbia.edu/cu/libraries/indiv/area/A
  frica/East.html
Regional Information Network
  For news stories, the UN Integrated has daily regional bulletins on humanitarian issues.
  www.re lief web.int/IRIN/cea/ceafp.htm
Moja
  www.moja.com/

Kamusi Project
  For complete Swahili-English and English-Swahili dictionaries, try this site, which comes under the auspices of Yale University
  www.yale.edu/swahili/
Africa News Online
  The East Africa section is a wonderful source of news articles taken from both local and international news sources
  www.africanews.org/east/

BOOKS

You can walk into any decent bookshop in Europe, America or Australasia and find countless books on western and eastern history, culture, politics, economics, religion, philosophy, craft and anything else you care to name. Finding the same thing in and about Africa is somewhat more difficult.

What you will be hard-pressed to find is a good selection of novels, plays and biographies by contemporary African authors, even though many are published by the African branches of major western publishers. Heinemann's African Writers Series, for instance, offers a major collection of such works.

In East Africa, the bookshops of Nairobi carry an excellent selection but the choice is considerably more limited in Tanzania and Uganda. In western countries, they're to be found only in specialist bookshops.

Most books are published in different editions by different publishers in different countries. As a result, a book might be a hardcover rarity in one country while it's readily available in paperback in another. Fortunately, bookshops and libraries search by title or author, so your local bookshop or library is best placed to advise you on the availability of the recommendations that follow.

See also the Books sections for each individual country.

Lonely Planet

Lonely Planet's *Africa on a shoestring* covers 48 African countries, concentrating on practical information for budget travellers. *Kenya* and *Tanzania, Zanzibar & Pemba* are both available as separate guidebooks, and are just the thing if you plan to explore either of those two countries in depth.

Lonely Planet's *Trekking in East Africa* by David Else covers a selection of treks and expeditions in the mountains and wilderness areas of Kenya, Tanzania, Uganda and Malawi, and has plenty of advice and general information about trekking in this part of the world.

Those with an interest in the wildlife of the region can get a copy of Lonely Planet's *Watching Wildlife East Africa*.

For coverage of Kenya and northern Tanzania you can't go past Lonely Planet's *Kenya travel atlas*. And Lonely Planet's *Swahili phrasebook* will help you solve most of your language problems in East Africa.

Travel

Dian Fossey's research with the mountain gorillas of Rwanda is recounted in her book *Gorillas in the Mist*. *The White Nile* by Alan Moorehead is a superbly evocative account of the exploration of the upper Nile and the rivalry between the European powers. *Journey to the Jade Sea* by John Hillaby recounts this prolific travel writer's epic trek to Lake Turkana in northern Kenya in the days before the safari trucks began travelling this route. Other books to look for include *Initiation* by JS Fontaine, *A Bend in the River* by VS Naipaul and *Travels in the Congo* by Andre Gide.

Two women's accounts of life in East Africa earlier this century are worth a read: *Out of Africa* by Karen Blixen (also made into a hugely popular movie) and *West with the Night* by Beryl Markham.

Last of the Free by Gareth Patterson is the story of the raising and ultimate release into the wild of three lion cubs left by George Adamson.

Inveterate traveller, Dervla Murphy, recounts her bicycle trip from Kenya to Zimbabwe in *The Ukimwi Road*, a book equally revealing about the impact of HIV/AIDS on the people of Africa.

Unhappy Valley by Bruce Berman & John Lonsdale takes a fresh look at the colonial history of Kenya, while Nigel Pavitt's *Kenya: The First Explorers* has some excellent photographs and it extracts from the early European explorers to visit the area.

Safari: A Chronicle of Adventure by Bartle Bull tells the tale of the whole safari business from the early days to today.

History, Politics & Economics

There are numerous books on the history of Africa including *The Penguin Atlas of African History* by Colin McEvedy and *A Short History of Africa* by Roland Oliver & JD Fage. Also excellent reading is *The Africans – A Triple Heritage* by Ali A Mazrui, which was published in conjunction with a BBC TV series of the same name.

For the origins and development of the coastal Swahili culture and how it has been affected by the arrival of the Portuguese in the Indian Ocean, the standard work is *The Portuguese Period in East Africa* by Justus Strandes. For a radical African viewpoint of the effects of colonialism in general, Walter Rodney's *How Europe Underdeveloped Africa* is well worth a read.

Worthwhile contemporary accounts include the readable but rather discouraging *The Africans* by David Lamb. Or there's *The Making of Contemporary Africa* by Bill Freund, and *A Year in the Death of Africa* by Peter Gill. On contemporary Kenyan politics, it's worth reading Oginga Odinga's *Not Yet Uhuru*, and *Detained – A Writer's Prison Diary* by Ngugi wa Thiong'o, for a view radically different from that put out by the Kenyatta and Moi regimes.

Not exclusively about Africa, but very relevant to bilateral and multilateral aid issues, is the *Lords of Poverty* by Graham Hancock, an exposé of the bungling and waste perpetrated by the UN, IMF, World Bank and others.

Flora & Fauna

A Field Guide to the Larger Mammals of Africa by Jean Dorst & Pierre Dandelot, with *The Collins Field Guide to the Birds of East Africa* by JG Williams & N Arlott, should suffice for most people's purposes in East Africa's national parks and wildlife reserves.

General

There are some excellent but quite expensive photo-essay hardbacks which you may prefer to look for in a library, such as *Journey though Kenya* by Mohammed Amin, Duncan Willets & Brian Tetley. There is a companion volume entitled *Journey through Tanzania* by the same authors.

Other colourful books on the region include *Africa Adorned* by Angela Fisher; *Ivory Crisis* by Ian Parker & Mohammed Amin; *Isak Dinesen's Africa* by various authors; *Africa: A History of a Continent* by Basil Davidson; and *Through Open Doors: A View of Asian Cultures in Kenya* by Cynthia Salvadori. Salvadori also co-authored with Andrew Fedders *Peoples & Cultures of Kenya*.

In addition to the above, there has been a flurry of large-format, hardback books on the various tribal societies of Kenya, especially the Maasai and Samburu, which you'll see in the bookshops of Nairobi and Mombasa.

NEWSPAPERS & MAGAZINES

Locally produced regional publications are pretty thin on the ground. The *East African* is a weekly newspaper published in Kenya and covers regional issues. It is also available online at its Web site: www.nationaudio .com/News/EastAfrican/Current.

Magazines with a broader African focus include the monthly *New African* and *South*.

Well known international news publications such as the *International Herald Tribune, Time* and *Newsweek* are available in the capital cities.

RADIO & TV

Kenya, Uganda and Tanzania all have government-run national broadcasters which have radio and TV transmissions in English, although the political bias is usually pretty heavy. For international coverage, you'll need a shortwave radio to catch foreign services such as the BBC World Service, Deutsche Welle and Voice of America. The BBC has particularly good coverage of East African affairs, and its daily *Focus on Africa* current affairs program is one of the best sources of current news.

Cable TV is available but you'll usually only come across it in upmarket hotels.

BBC World Service 17640 kHz (6 am to 7 pm), 17885 kHz (8 am to 5 pm) 15420 kHz (6.30 to 9.30 am) and 9630 kHz (8 pm to midnight), plus 93.7 FM (Nairobi) and 93.9 FM (Mombasa)
Deutsche Welle 6130 to 6145 kHz (morning), 9565 and 15410 kHz (day) and 9735 and 1195 kHz (evening)
Voice of America 6035 kHz (morning), 17725 kHz (day) and 15410 kHz (evening)

PHOTOGRAPHY & VIDEO
Film & Equipment

The availability of film varies, with a wide range available in Nairobi to virtually nothing in small towns. Kampala and Dar es Salaam have a decent range but it's best to bring what you need with you. Processing (slides and colour negatives) is reliable in Nairobi; elsewhere it's probably best to hang on to your film until you return home.

Technical Tips

For serious wildlife photography an SLR (single lens reflex) camera which can take long focal length lenses is necessary. If all you have is a little generic 'snapomatic', you may as well leave it behind; although they are becoming more sophisticated these days, the maximum focal length is around 110mm – still too small for getting decent shots.

Zoom lenses are best for wildlife photography as you can frame your shot easily to get the best composition. This is important as the animals are constantly (and often quickly) on the move. The 70 to 210mm zoom lenses are popular and the 200mm is really the minimum you need to get good close-up shots. The only problem with zoom lenses is that with all the glass (lenses) inside them, they absorb about 1½ 'f' stops of light, which is where the 200 and 400 ASA film starts to become useful.

Telephoto (fixed focal length) lenses give better results than zoom lenses but you're limited by having to carry a separate lens for every focal length. A 400 or 500mm lens brings the action right up close but again you need the 200 or 400 ASA film to make the most of them. You certainly need a 400 or 500mm lens if you're keen on photographing birdlife.

When using long lenses a tripod can be extremely useful, and with anything greater than about 300mm it's a necessity. The problem here is that in the confined space of the hatch of a minibus (assuming you'll be taking an organised safari) it is impossible to set up the tripod, especially when you are sharing the space with at least three or four other people. Miniature tripods are available and these are very useful for setting up on the roof of the van, although you can also rest the lens itself on the roof, provided that the van engine is switched off to kill any vibration.

Whatever combination of camera, lenses and accessories you decide to carry, make sure they are kept in a decent bag which will protect them from the elements, the dust and the knocks they are bound to receive. It's also vital to make sure that your travel insurance policy includes your camera gear if it is stolen.

Photographing People

Ask permission before taking shots of people. Respect their right to privacy. Respect them as individuals. Many of these people have customs which are at odds with your own.

Most Muslim women strongly resent having their photographs taken by strangers, and you could get yourself into a lot of trouble by doing so without permission. The same goes for many tribal people, especially the Maasai of Kenya and Tanzania. There are, however, some tribes who have been exposed to tourism for a long time and will allow you to photograph them – it's generally a question of negotiating a price.

This might strike you as nonsense or as an example of a people spoiled by tourism. Yet who is exploiting whom? You come

Africa Wins Again (or AWA)

Welcome to Africa! Leave your comfortable, Aristotelian logic at home and embrace lateral thinking – African style. These people have their own centuries-old thought patterns and ways of making sense of the world; it takes time to tune in to what you might think is a malevolent miasma but which makes perfect sense to them.

'Is this the way to Morogoro?' you might ask. 'Yes', comes the answer. You later discover, after wasting several hours, that it's in the exact opposite direction.

'Is there a bus to Dar es Salaam tomorrow?' 'Yes, in the morning.' You wait in vain and discover two days later that you just missed it.

You arrange to meet someone at a certain time at a certain place. You're there on time but they're not. But they'll be there eventually, and possibly at the agreed time, even if it's the day after.

The attitude is benevolent. They don't want to disappoint you by giving you a negative or ambivalent answer. The response to 'Habari' (How are you) is always, 'Nzuri' (Good). Likewise, time is flexible and the present always takes precedent over the future. You could be forgiven for thinking that Africans only wear watches so they can tell you *exactly* how late they are for an appointment.

In the same vein, buses which are going 'now' never leave until they're full regardless of how much engine revving and horn hooting takes place in the meantime. A place that is further than a day's walk is 'far'. Don't bother asking how far. It's 'far' – many people might never have actually been that far if you're out in the sticks.

Too many visitors to Africa work themselves up into a rage of frustration when things don't go like clockwork. They pop the veins on their brows, scream and shout, abuse all and sundry and generally make a complete and utter spectacle of themselves. All this does is create embarrassment and inaction.

If you want something done in Africa then treat the person you're dealing with as a *person*. Ask how their family is going, how their children are doing at school – something personal – and have the patience to listen to the answer. Time means nothing and remember that you're a long time pushing up daisies. And don't forget the handshake. Relax. There's no hurry in Africa.

through briefly with your expensive camera gear and an (apparently) endless supply of leisure time in search of local colour, and then you're gone, having contributed nothing to the local economy and, sometimes, not even having spoken to anyone. They go back to their humble lifestyle; you jump on a 747 and go back to the land of plenty. How would you feel if you were an extra on a film project and didn't get paid?

TIME

Time in Kenya, Uganda and Tanzania is GMT/UTC plus three hours year-round; in Rwanda and Burundi it's GMT/UTC plus two hours.

ELECTRICITY

The countries of the region use the 240V system. The power supply varies – from reliable in Kenya to widely fluctuating in Tanzania and most of Uganda.

Power sockets also vary but are usually of the three-square-pin variety as used in the UK, although some older buildings have two-round-pin sockets. Bring a universal adaptor if a power supply is important to you.

TOILETS

These vary from pits (quite literally) to full-flush luxury conveniences that can spring up in the most unlikely places. Nearly all hotels sport flushable sit-down types but toilet seats are a rare commodity. You'll be riding bareback most of the time.

Cleanliness levels vary; if you go in expecting the worst, you will often be surprised that they're not all that bad. Toilets with running water are a rarity outside major hotels.

In the more upmarket bush camps you'll be confronted with a long drop covered with some sort of seating arrangement. The best of these is located in Tusk Camp high in the Aberdare National Park – you'll have a view across the forest to Mt Kenya. Things are less pleasant when camping in the wildlife parks. Squatting on crumbling concrete is common. When trekking it's good practice to burn your toilet paper before burying it.

HEALTH

Travel health depends on your predeparture preparations, your daily health care while travelling and how you handle any medical problem that does develop. While the potential dangers can seem quite frightening, in reality few travellers experience anything more serious than an upset stomach.

Predeparture Planning

Immunisations Plan ahead for getting your vaccinations: some of them require more than one injection, while some vaccinations should not be given together. Note that some vaccinations should not be given during pregnancy or to people with allergies – discuss this with your doctor.

It is highly recommended that you seek medical advice at least six weeks before travel. Be aware that there is often a greater risk of disease among children and to women during pregnancy.

Discuss your requirements with your doctor but vaccinations you should consider for this trip include those listed below (for more details about the diseases themselves, see the individual disease entries later in this section). Carry proof of your vaccinations, especially yellow fever, as this is sometimes needed to enter some countries.

Diphtheria & Tetanus Vaccinations for these two diseases are usually combined and are recommended for everyone. After an initial course of three injections (usually given in childhood), boosters are necessary every 10 years.

Polio Everyone should keep up-to-date with this vaccination, which is normally given in childhood. A booster every 10 years maintains immunity.

Hepatitis A Hepatitis A vaccine (eg Avaxim, Havrix 1440 or VAQTA) provides long-term immunity (possibly more than 10 years) after an initial injection and a booster at six to 12 months. Alternatively, an injection of gamma globulin can provide short-term protection against hepatitis A – two to six months, depending on the dose given. It is not a vaccine but is ready-made antibody collected from blood donations. It is reasonably effective and, unlike the vaccine, it is protective immediately, but because it is a blood product, there are current concerns about its long-term safety. Hepatitis A vaccine is also available in a combined form, Twinrix, with hepatitis B vaccine. Three injections over a six-month period are required, the first two providing substantial protection against hepatitis A.

Typhoid Vaccination against typhoid may be required if you are travelling for more than a couple of weeks in most parts of Africa. It is available either as an injection or as capsules to be taken orally.

Cholera The current injectable vaccine against cholera is poorly protective and has many side effects, so it is not generally recommended for travellers. However, in some situations it may be necessary to have a certificate as travellers are very occasionally asked by immigration officials to present one, even though all countries and the World Health Organisation (WHO) have dropped cholera immunisation as a health requirement for entry.

Meningococcal Meningitis Vaccination is recommended for travellers to East Africa. A single injection gives good protection against the major epidemic forms of the disease for three years. Protection may be less effective in children under two years.

Hepatitis B Travellers who should consider vaccination against hepatitis B include those on a long trip, as well as those visiting countries where there are high levels of hepatitis B infection, where blood transfusions may not be adequately screened or where sexual contact or needle sharing is a possibility. Vaccination involves three injections, with a booster at 12 months. More rapid courses are available if necessary.

Yellow Fever A yellow fever vaccine is now the only vaccine that is a legal requirement for entry into certain countries, usually only enforced when coming from an infected area. Vaccination is recommended for travel in areas where the disease is endemic (this includes East Africa). You may have to go to a special yellow fever vaccination centre.

Rabies Vaccination should be considered by those who will spend a month or longer in a country where rabies is common, especially if they are cycling, handling animals, caving or travelling to remote areas, and for children (who may not report a bite). Pretravel rabies vaccination involves having three injections over 21 to 28 days. If someone who has been vaccinated is bitten or scratched by an animal, they will require two booster injections of vaccine; those not vaccinated require more.

Tuberculosis The risk of TB to travellers is usually very low, unless you will be living with or closely associated with local people in village areas. Vaccination against TB (BCG) is recommended for children and young adults living in these areas for three months or more.

Malaria Medication Antimalarial drugs do not prevent you from being infected but kill the malaria parasites during a stage in their development and significantly reduce the risk of becoming very ill or dying. Expert advice on medication should be sought, as there are many factors to consider, including the area to be visited, the risk of exposure to malaria-carrying mosquitoes, the side effects of medication, your medical history and whether you are a child or an adult or pregnant. Travellers to isolated areas in high-risk countries may like to carry a treatment dose of medication for use if symptoms occur.

Health Insurance It is very important to make sure that you have adequate health insurance.

If you find yourself travelling through Africa for quite some time or heading for the more remote corners of the region, it may be worth signing up with either the Flying Doctors or the AAR. These two organisations can come and get you even should you become ill in a *lugga* (dry river bed) west of North Horr.

The Flying Doctor's Society of Africa (☎/fax 02-502699) is part of the African Medical & Research Foundation (AMREF) and operates a 24 hour air ambulance service out of Nairobi's Wilson Airport. They will get you from wherever you fall to the nearest decent hospital (often Nairobi). The emergency numbers are ☎ 02-501280 and ☎ 02-602492. A Tourist Membership is available where you are covered for two months within a 500km radius of Nairobi. This will cost you US$25 and two-months cover within a 1000km radius of Nairobi will set you back US$50.

In the UK, AMREF (☎ 020-7233 0066) can be contacted at 11 Old Queen St, London SW1H 9JA.

AAR (☎ 02-715319, email aar@users.africaonline.co.ke) offers a more comprehensive road and local service as well as emergency air evacuation. Tourist cover is US$65 per month. An extra KSh 5400 a year pays for a 'white card' that will get you back to the hospital of your choice anywhere in the world. Their emergency number in Nairobi is ☎ 02-717376.

Travel Health Guides Lonely Planet's *Healthy Travel: Africa* is a handy pocket size and is packed with useful information including pretrip planning, emergency first aid, immunisation and disease information and what to do if you get sick on the road. *Travel with Children* from Lonely Planet also includes advice on travel health for younger children.

If you are planning to be away or if you are travelling through remote areas for a lengthy period of time, you may like to consider taking a more detailed health guide with you.

CDC's Complete Guide to Healthy Travel, Open Road Publishing, 1997. The US Centers for Disease Control & Prevention recommendations for international travel.
Staying Healthy in Asia, Africa & Latin America, Dirk Schroeder, Moon Publications, 1994. Probably the best all-round guide to carry; it's detailed and well organised.
Travellers' Health, Dr Richard Dawood, Oxford University Press, 1995. Comprehensive, easy to read, authoritative and highly recommended, although it's rather large to lug around.
Where There Is No Doctor, David Werner, Macmillan, 1994. A very detailed guide intended for someone, such as a Peace Corps worker, going to work in an underdeveloped country.

There are also a number of excellent travel health sites on the Internet. From the Lonely Planet home page there are links to the World Health Organization and the US Centers for Disease Control & Prevention.

Other Preparations Make sure you're healthy before you start travelling. If you are going on a long trip, make sure your teeth are OK. If you wear glasses, take a spare pair and your prescription.

Medical Kit Check List

Following is a list of items you should consider including in your medical kit – consult your pharmacist for brands available in your country.

☐ **Aspirin or paracetamol (acetaminophen in the USA)** – for pain or fever
☐ **Antihistamine** – for allergies, eg, hay fever; to ease the itch from insect bites or stings; and to prevent motion sickness
☐ **Cold and flu tablets, throat lozenges and nasal decongestant**
☐ **Multivitamins** – consider for long trips, when dietary vitamin intake may be inadequate
☐ **Antibiotics** – consider including these if you're travelling well off the beaten track; see your doctor, as they must be prescribed, and carry the prescription with you
☐ **Loperamide or diphenoxylate** –'blockers' for diarrhoea
☐ **Prochlorperazine or metaclopramide** – for nausea and vomiting
☐ **Rehydration mixture** – to prevent dehydration, which may occur, for example, during bouts of diarrhoea; particularly important when travelling with children
☐ **Insect repellent, sunscreen, lip balm and eye drops**
☐ **Calamine lotion, sting relief spray or aloe vera** – to ease irritation from sunburn and insect bites or stings
☐ **Antifungal cream or powder** – for fungal skin infections and thrush
☐ **Antiseptic (such as povidone-iodine)** – for cuts and grazes
☐ **Bandages, Band-Aids (plasters) and other wound dressings**
☐ **Water purification tablets or iodine**
☐ **Scissors, tweezers and a thermometer** – note that mercury thermometers are prohibited by airlines
☐ **Sterile kit (sealed medical kit containing syringes and needles)** – in case you need injections in a country with medical hygiene problems; discuss with your doctor

Everyday Health

Normal body temperature is up to 37°C (98.6°F); more than 2°C (4°F) higher indicates a high fever. The normal adult pulse rate is 60 to 100 per minute (children 80 to 100, babies 100 to 140). As a general rule the pulse increases about 20 beats per minute for each 1°C (2°F) rise in fever.

Respiration (breathing) rate is also an indicator of illness. Count the number of breaths per minute: between 12 and 20 is normal for adults and older children (up to 30 for younger children, 40 for babies). People with a high fever or serious respiratory illness breathe more quickly than normal. More than 40 shallow breaths a minute may indicate pneumonia.

If you require a particular medication, take an adequate supply, as it may not be available locally. Take part of the packaging showing the generic name rather than the brand, which will make getting replacements easier.

It's a good idea to have a legible prescription or letter from your doctor to show that you legally use the medication to avoid any problems.

Basic Rules

Food There is an old colonial adage which says: 'If you can cook it, boil it or peel it you can eat it...otherwise forget it'. Vegetables and fruit should be washed with purified water or peeled where possible. Beware of ice cream as it might have been melted and refrozen; if there's any doubt (eg, a power cut in the last day or two), steer well clear.

Shellfish such as mussels, oysters and clams should be avoided as well as undercooked meat, particularly in the form of mince. Steaming does not make shellfish safe for eating.

If a place looks clean and well run and the vendor also looks clean and healthy, then the food is probably safe. In general, places that are packed with travellers or locals will be fine, while empty restaurants are questionable. The food in busy restaurants is cooked and eaten quite quickly with little standing around and is probably not reheated.

Water The number one rule is *be careful of the water* and especially of ice. If you don't know for certain that the water is safe, assume the worst. Reputable brands of bottled water or soft drinks are generally fine, although in some places bottles may be refilled with tap water. Only use water from containers with a serrated seal – not tops or corks. Take care with fruit juice, particularly if water may have been added. Milk should be treated with suspicion as it is often unpasteurised, though boiled milk is fine if it is kept hygienically. Tea or coffee should also be OK, since the water should have been boiled.

Water Purification The simplest way of purifying water is to boil it thoroughly. Vigorous boiling should be satisfactory, though at high altitude water boils at a lower temperature, so germs are less likely to be killed. Boil it for longer in these environments.

Consider purchasing a water filter for a long trip. There are two main kinds of filter. Total filters take out all parasites, bacteria and viruses and make water safe to drink. They are often expensive but they can be more cost effective than buying bottled water. Simple filters (which can even be a nylon mesh bag) take out dirt and larger foreign bodies from the water so that chemical solutions work much more effectively; if water is dirty, chemical solutions may not work at all.

It's very important when buying a filter to read the specifications so that you know exactly what it removes from the water and what it doesn't. Simple filtering will not remove all dangerous organisms, so if you cannot boil water it should be treated chemically. Chlorine tablets will kill many pathogens but not some parasites like giardia and amoebic cysts. Iodine is more effective in purifying water and is available in tablet form. Follow the directions carefully and remember that too much iodine can be harmful.

Medical Problems & Treatment

Self-diagnosis and treatment can be risky, so you should always seek medical help. An embassy, consulate or five star hotel can usually recommend a local doctor or clinic. Although we give drug dosages in this section, they are for emergency use only. Correct diagnosis is vital. In this section we have used the generic names for medications – check with a pharmacist for brands available locally.

Note that antibiotics should ideally be administered only under medical supervision. Take only the recommended dose at the prescribed intervals and use the whole course, even if the illness seems to be cured earlier. Stop immediately if there are any serious reactions and don't use the antibiotic at all if you are unsure that you have the correct one. Some people are allergic to commonly prescribed antibiotics such as penicillin; if this applies to you, carry this information (eg, on a bracelet) when travelling.

Environmental Hazards

Altitude Sickness Lack of oxygen at high altitudes (over 2500m) affects most people to some extent. The effect may be mild or severe and occurs because less oxygen reaches the muscles and the brain at high altitude, requiring the heart and lungs to compensate by working harder. Symptoms of Acute Mountain Sickness (AMS) usually develop during the first 24 hours at altitude but may be delayed up to three weeks. Mild symptoms include headache, lethargy, dizziness, difficulty sleeping and loss of appetite. AMS may become more severe without warning and can be fatal. Severe symptoms include breathlessness, a dry, irritative cough (which may progress to the production of pink, frothy sputum), severe headache, lack of coordination and balance, confusion, irrational behaviour, vomiting, drowsiness and unconsciousness. There is no hard-and-fast rule as to what is too high: AMS has been fatal at 3000m, although 3500 to 4500m is the usual range.

Treat mild symptoms by resting at the same altitude until recovery, usually a day or two. Paracetamol or aspirin can be taken for headaches. If symptoms persist or become worse, *immediate descent is necessary*; even 500m can help. Drug treatments should never be used to avoid descent or to enable further ascent.

The drugs acetazolamide and dexamethasone are recommended by some doctors for the prevention of AMS, though their use is controversial. They can reduce the symptoms but they may also mask warning signs; severe and fatal AMS has occurred in people taking these drugs. In general we do not recommend them for travellers.

The prevention of acute mountain sickness includes the following measures:

- Ascend slowly – have frequent rest days, spending two to three nights at each rise of 1000m. If you reach a high altitude by trekking, acclimatisation takes place gradually and you are less likely to be affected than if you fly directly to high altitude.
- It is always wise to sleep at a lower altitude than the greatest height reached during the day if possible. Also, once above 3000m, care should be taken not to increase the sleeping altitude by more than 300m per day.
- Drink extra fluids. The mountain air is dry and cold and moisture is lost as you breathe. Evaporation of sweat may occur unnoticed and result in dehydration.
- Eat light, high-carbohydrate meals for increased energy.
- Avoid alcohol as it may increase the risk of dehydration.
- Avoid sedatives.

Heat Exhaustion Dehydration and salt deficiency can cause heat exhaustion. Take time to acclimatise to high temperatures, drink sufficient liquids and do not do anything too physically demanding.

Salt deficiency is characterised by fatigue, lethargy, headaches, giddiness and muscle cramps; salt tablets may help but adding extra salt to your food is better.

Anhidrotic heat exhaustion is a rare form of heat exhaustion that is caused by an inability to sweat. It tends to affect people who have been in a hot climate for some time, rather than newcomers. It can progress to heatstroke (see following). Treatment involves removal to a cooler climate.

Heatstroke This serious, and occasionally fatal, condition can occur if the body's heat-regulating mechanism breaks down and the body temperature rises to dangerous levels. Long, continuous periods of exposure to high temperatures and insufficient fluids can leave you vulnerable to heatstroke.

The symptoms are feeling unwell, not sweating very much (or at all) and having a high body temperature (39° to 41°C or 102° to 106°F). Where sweating has ceased, the skin becomes flushed and red. Severe, throbbing headaches and lack of coordination will also occur, and the sufferer may be confused or aggressive. Eventually the victim will become delirious or convulse. Hospitalisation is essential but in the interim get victims out of the sun, remove their clothing, cover them with a wet sheet or towel and then fan continually. Give fluids if they are conscious.

Hypothermia Too much cold can be just as dangerous as too much heat. If you are trekking at high altitudes or simply taking a long bus trip over mountains, particularly at night, be prepared.

Hypothermia occurs when the body loses heat faster than it can produce it and the core temperature of the body falls. It is surprisingly easy to progress from very cold to dangerously cold due to a combination of wind, wet clothing, fatigue and hunger, even if the air temperature is above freezing. It is best to dress in layers; silk, wool and some of the new artificial fibres are all good insulating materials. A hat is important, as a lot of heat is lost through the head. A strong, waterproof outer layer (and a 'space' blanket for emergencies) is essential. Carry basic supplies, including food containing simple sugars to generate heat quickly and fluid to drink.

Symptoms of hypothermia are exhaustion, numb skin (particularly toes and fingers), shivering, slurred speech, irrational or violent behaviour, lethargy, stumbling, dizzy spells, muscle cramps and violent bursts of energy. Irrationality may take the form of sufferers claiming they are warm and trying to take off their clothes.

To treat mild hypothermia, first get the person out of the wind and/or rain, remove their clothing if it's wet and replace it with dry, warm clothing. Give them hot liquids – not alcohol – and some high-kilojoule, easily digestible food. Do not rub victims: instead, allow them to slowly warm themselves. This should be enough to treat the early stages of hypothermia. The early recognition and treatment of mild hypothermia is the only way to prevent severe hypothermia, which is a critical condition.

Motion Sickness Eating lightly before and during a trip will reduce the chances of motion sickness. If you are prone to motion sickness, try to find a place that minimises movement – near the wing on aircraft, close to midships on boats, near the centre on buses. Fresh air usually helps; reading and cigarette smoke don't. Commercial motion-sickness preparations, which can cause drowsiness, have to be taken before the trip commences. Ginger (available in capsule form) and peppermint (including mint-flavoured sweets) are natural preventatives.

Prickly Heat Prickly heat is an itchy rash caused by excessive perspiration trapped under the skin. It usually strikes people who have just arrived in a hot climate. Keeping cool, bathing often, drying the skin and using a mild talcum or prickly heat powder or resorting to air-conditioning may help.

Sunburn In the tropics, the desert or at high altitude you can get sunburnt surprisingly quickly, even through cloud or when it's not particularly hot. Use a sunscreen, a hat, and a barrier cream for your nose and lips.

Calamine lotion or a commercial after-sun preparation are good for mild sunburn. Protect your eyes with good quality sunglasses, particularly if you will be near water, sand or snow.

Infectious Diseases
Diarrhoea Simple things like a change of water, food or climate can all cause a mild

bout of diarrhoea but a few rushed toilet trips with no other symptoms is not indicative of a major problem.

Dehydration is the main danger with any diarrhoea, particularly in children or the elderly as dehydration can occur quite quickly. Under all circumstances *fluid replacement* (at least equal to the volume being lost) is the most important thing to remember. Weak black tea with a little sugar, soda water, or soft drinks allowed to go flat and diluted 50% with clean water are all good. With severe diarrhoea a rehydrating solution is preferable to replace minerals and salts lost. Commercially available oral rehydration salts (ORS) are very useful; add them to boiled or bottled water. In an emergency you can make up a solution of six teaspoons of sugar and a half teaspoon of salt to a litre of boiled or bottled water. You need to drink at least the same volume of fluid that you are losing in bowel movements and vomiting. Urine is the best guide to the adequacy of replacement – if you have small amounts of concentrated urine, you need to drink more. Keep drinking small amounts often. Stick to a bland diet and avoid fatty foods as you recover.

Gut-paralysing drugs such as loperamide or diphenoxylate can be used to bring relief from the symptoms, although they do not actually cure the problem. Only use these drugs if you do not have access to toilets, for example, if you *must* travel. Note that these drugs are not recommended for children under 12 years.

In certain situations antibiotics may be required: diarrhoea with blood or mucus (dysentery), any diarrhoea with fever, profuse watery diarrhoea, persistent diarrhoea not improving after 48 hours and severe diarrhoea. These suggest a more serious cause of diarrhoea and in these situations gut-paralysing drugs should be avoided.

In these situations a stool test may be necessary to diagnose what bug is causing your diarrhoea, so you should seek medical help urgently. Where this is not possible the recommended drugs for bacterial diarrhoea (the most likely cause of severe diarrhoea in travellers) are norfloxacin 400mg twice daily for three days or ciprofloxacin 500mg twice daily for five days. These are not recommended for children or pregnant women. The drug of choice for children would be co-trimoxazole with dosage dependent on weight. A five day course is given. Ampicillin or amoxycillin may be given in pregnancy but medical care is necessary.

Two other causes of persistent diarrhoea in travellers are giardiasis and amoebic dysentery.

Giardiasis is caused by a common parasite, *Giardia lamblia*. Symptoms include stomach cramps, nausea, a bloated stomach, watery, foul-smelling diarrhoea and frequent gas. Giardiasis can appear several weeks after you have been exposed to the parasite. The symptoms may disappear for a few days and then return; this can go on for several weeks.

Amoebic dysentery, caused by the protozoan *Entamoeba histolytica*, is characterised by a gradual onset of low-grade diarrhoea, often with blood and mucus. Cramping abdominal pain and vomiting are less likely than in other types of diarrhoea, and fever may not be present. It will persist until treated and can recur and cause other health problems.

You should seek medical advice if you think you have giardiasis or amoebic dysentery but where this is not possible, tinidazole or metronidazole are the recommended drugs. Treatment is a 2gm single dose of tinidazole or 250mg of metronidazole three times daily for five to 10 days.

Fungal Infections Fungal infections occur more commonly in hot weather and are usually found on the scalp, between the toes (athlete's foot) or fingers, in the groin and on the body (ringworm). You get ringworm (which is a fungal infection, not a worm) from infected animals or other people. Moisture encourages these infections.

To prevent fungal infections wear loose, comfortable clothes, avoid artificial fibres, wash frequently and dry yourself carefully. If you do get an infection, wash the infected area at least daily with a disinfectant or medicated soap and water, and rinse and dry well. Apply an antifungal cream or powder such as tolnaftate. Try to expose the infected area to air or sunlight as much as possible and wash all towels and underwear in hot water, change them often and let them dry in the sun.

Hepatitis Hepatitis is a general term for inflammation of the liver. It is a common disease worldwide. There are several different viruses that cause hepatitis, and they differ in the way that they are transmitted. The symptoms are similar in all forms of the illness, and include fever, chills, headache, fatigue, feelings of weakness and aches and pains, followed by loss of appetite, nausea, vomiting, abdominal pain, dark urine, light-coloured faeces, jaundiced (yellow) skin and yellowing of the whites of the eyes. People who have had hepatitis should avoid alcohol for some time after the illness, as the liver needs time to recover.

Hepatitis A is transmitted by contaminated food and drinking water. You should seek medical advice but there is not much you can do apart from resting, drinking lots of fluids, eating lightly and avoiding fatty foods. **Hepatitis E** is transmitted in the same way as hepatitis A; it can be particularly serious in pregnant women.

There are almost 300 million chronic carriers of **hepatitis B** in the world. It is spread through contact with infected blood, blood products or body fluids, for example through sexual contact, unsterilised needles and blood transfusions, or contact with blood via small breaks in the skin. Other risk situations include having a shave, tattoo or body pierce with contaminated equipment. The symptoms of hepatitis B may be more severe than type A and the disease can lead to long-term problems such as chronic liver damage, liver cancer or a long-term carrier state. **Hepatitis C** and **hepatitis D** are spread in the same way as hepatitis B and can also lead to long-term complications.

There are vaccines against hepatitis A and B but there are currently no vaccines against the other types of hepatitis. Following the basic rules about food and water (hepatitis A and E) and avoiding risk situations (hepatitis B, C and D) are important preventative measures.

HIV & AIDS Infection with the human immunodeficiency virus (HIV) may lead to acquired immune deficiency syndrome (AIDS), which is a fatal disease. Any exposure to blood, blood products or body fluids may put the individual at risk. The disease is often transmitted through sexual contact or dirty needles – vaccinations, acupuncture, tattooing and body piercing can be potentially as dangerous as intravenous drug use. HIV/AIDS can also be spread through infected blood transfusions; some developing countries cannot afford to screen blood used for transfusions.

If you do need an injection, ask to see the syringe unwrapped in front of you, or take a needle and syringe pack with you.

Fear of HIV infection should never preclude treatment for more serious medical conditions.

Intestinal Worms These parasites are most common in rural, tropical areas. The different worms have different ways of infecting people. Some may be ingested on food such as undercooked meat (eg, tapeworms) and some enter through your skin (eg, hookworms). Infestations may not show up for some time, and although they are generally not serious, if left untreated some can cause severe health problems later. Consider having a stool test when you return home to check for these and determine the appropriate treatment.

Meningococcal Meningitis This serious disease can be fatal. There are recurring epidemics in sub-Saharan Africa.

A fever, severe headache, sensitivity to light and neck stiffness which prevents you bending your head forward are the first symptoms of this disease. There may also be purple patches on the skin. Death can occur within a few hours, so urgent medical treatment is required.

Treatment involves large doses of penicillin given intravenously, or with chloramphenicol injections.

Schistosomiasis (bilharzia) This disease is transmitted by minute worms. They infect certain varieties of freshwater snails found in rivers, streams, lakes and particularly behind dams. The worms multiply and are eventually discharged into the water.

The worm enters through the skin and attaches itself to your intestines or bladder. The first symptom may be a general feeling of being unwell, or a tingling and sometimes a light rash around the area where it entered. Weeks later a high fever may develop. Once the disease is established, abdominal pain and blood in the urine are other signs. The infection often causes no symptoms until the disease is well established (several months to years after exposure) and damage to internal organs irreversible.

Avoiding swimming or bathing in fresh water where bilharzia is present is the main method of preventing the disease. Even deep water can be infected. If you do get wet, dry off quickly and dry your clothes as well.

A blood test is the most reliable way to diagnose the disease but the test will not show positive until a number of weeks after exposure.

Sexually Transmitted Diseases HIV/ AIDS and hepatitis B can be transmitted through sexual contact – see the relevant sections earlier for more details. Other STDs include gonorrhoea, herpes and syphilis; sores, blisters or rashes around the genitals and discharges or pain when urinating are common symptoms. In some STDs, such as wart virus or chlamydia, symptoms may be less marked or not observed at all, especially in women. Chlamydia infection can cause infertility in men and women before any symptoms have been noticed. Syphilis symptoms eventually disappear completely but the disease continues and can cause severe problems in later years. While abstinence from sexual contact is the only 100% effective prevention, using condoms is also effective. The treatment of gonorrhoea and syphilis is with antibiotics. The different sexually transmitted diseases each require specific antibiotics.

Typhoid Typhoid fever is a dangerous gut infection caused by contaminated water and food. Medical help must be sought.

In its early stages sufferers may feel they have a bad cold or flu on the way, as early symptoms are a headache, body aches and a fever which rises a little each day until it is around 40°C (104°F) or more. The victim's pulse is often slow, relative to the degree of fever present – unlike a normal fever where the pulse increases. There may also be vomiting, abdominal pain, diarrhoea or constipation.

In the second week the high fever and slow pulse continue and a few pink spots may appear on the body; trembling, delirium, weakness, weight loss and dehydration may occur. Complications such as pneumonia, perforated bowel or meningitis may occur.

Insect-Borne Diseases
Chagas' disease, filariasis, leishmaniasis, Lyme disease, sleeping sickness, typhus and yellow fever are all insect-borne diseases but they do not pose a great risk to travellers. For more information on them, see Less Common Diseases at the end of this Health section.

Malaria This serious and potentially fatal disease is spread by mosquito bites. If you are travelling in areas where malaria is endemic, it is extremely important to avoid mosquito bites and to take tablets to prevent this disease. Symptoms range from fever, chills and sweating, headache, diarrhoea and abdominal pains to a vague feeling of ill-health. Seek medical help immediately if malaria is suspected. Without treatment malaria can rapidly become more serious and can be fatal.

If medical care is not available, malaria tablets can be used for treatment. You need to use a malaria tablet that is different from the one you were taking when you contracted malaria. The standard treatment dose of mefloquine is two 250mg tablets and a further two six hours later. For Fansidar, it's a single dose of three tablets. If you were previously taking mefloquine and cannot obtain Fansidar, then other alternatives are

Malarone (atovaquone-proguanil; four tablets once daily for three days), halofantrine (three doses of two 250mg tablets every six hours) or quinine sulphate (600mg every six hours). There is a greater risk of side effects with these dosages than in normal use if used with mefloquine, so medical advice is preferable. Be aware also that halofantrine is no longer recommended by the WHO as emergency standby treatment because of side effects, and should only be used if no other drugs are available.

Travellers are advised to prevent mosquito bites at all times. The main messages are:

- Wear light-coloured clothing
- Wear long trousers and long-sleeved shirts
- Use mosquito repellents containing the compound DEET on exposed areas (prolonged overuse of DEET may be harmful, especially to children but its use is considered preferable to being bitten by disease-transmitting mosquitoes)
- Avoid perfumes or aftershave
- Ase a mosquito net that is impregnated with mosquito repellent (permethrin) – it may be worth taking your own

Dengue Fever This viral disease is transmitted by mosquitoes and is fast becoming one of the top public health problems in the tropical world. Unlike the malaria mosquito, the *Aedes aegypti* mosquito, which transmits the dengue virus, is most active during the day and is found mainly in urban areas, in and around human dwellings.

Signs and symptoms of dengue fever include a sudden onset of high fever, headache, joint and muscle pains (hence its old name, 'breakbone fever') and nausea and vomiting. A rash of small red spots sometimes appears three to four days after the onset of fever. In the early phase of illness, dengue may be mistaken for other infectious diseases, including malaria and influenza. Minor bleeding such as nose bleeds may occur in the course of the illness but this does not necessarily mean that you have progressed to the potentially fatal dengue haemorrhagic fever (DHF). This is a severe illness, characterised by heavy bleeding, which is thought to be a result of second infection due to a different strain (there

are four major strains) and usually affects residents of the country rather than travellers. Recovery even from simple dengue fever may be prolonged, with tiredness lasting for several weeks.

You should seek medical attention as soon as possible if you think you may be infected. A blood test can exclude malaria and indicate the possibility of dengue fever. There is no specific treatment for dengue. Aspirin should be avoided, as it increases the risk of haemorrhaging. There is no vaccine against dengue fever. The best prevention is to avoid mosquito bites at all times by covering up, using insect repellents containing the compound DEET and mosquito nets – see the Malaria section earlier for more advice on avoiding mosquito bites.

Cuts, Bites & Stings
See Less Common Diseases (following) for details of rabies, which is passed through animal bites.

Cuts & Scratches Wash and treat any cut with an antiseptic such as povidone-iodine. Where possible avoid bandages and Band-Aids, which can keep wounds wet. Coral cuts are notoriously slow to heal and if they are not adequately cleaned, small pieces of coral can become embedded in the wound.

Bedbugs & Lice Bedbugs live in various places but particularly in dirty mattresses and bedding, evidenced by spots of blood on bedclothes or on the wall. Bedbugs leave itchy bites in neat rows. Calamine lotion or a sting relief spray may help.

All lice cause itching and discomfort. They make themselves at home in your hair (head lice), your clothing (body lice) or in your pubic hair (crabs). You catch lice through direct contact with infected people or by sharing combs, clothing and the like. Powder or shampoo treatment will kill the lice and infected clothing should then be washed in very hot, soapy water and left in the sun to dry.

Bites & Stings Bee and wasp stings are usually painful rather than dangerous. However, in people who are allergic to them, severe breathing difficulties may occur and require urgent medical care. Calamine lotion or a sting relief spray will give relief and ice packs will reduce the pain and swelling. There are some spiders with dangerous bites but antivenins are usually available. Scorpion stings are notoriously painful. Scorpions often shelter in shoes or clothing.

There are various fish and other sea creatures, that can sting or bite dangerously or that are dangerous to eat – seek the advice of locals.

Jellyfish Avoid contact with these sea creatures, which have stinging tentacles – seek local advice.

Leeches & Ticks Leeches may be present in damp rainforest conditions; they attach themselves to your skin to suck your blood. Trekkers often get them on their legs or in their boots. Salt or a lighted cigarette end will make them fall off. Do not pull them off, as the bite is then more likely to become infected. Clean and apply pressure if the point of attachment is bleeding. An insect repellent may keep them away.

You should always check all over your body if you have been walking through a potentially tick-infested area, as ticks can cause skin infections and other more serious diseases. If a tick is found attached, press down around the tick's head with tweezers, grab the head and gently pull upwards. Avoid pulling the rear of the body as this may squeeze the tick's gut contents through the attached mouth parts into the skin, increasing the risk of infection and disease. Smearing chemicals on the tick will not make it let go and is not recommended.

Snakes To minimise your chances of being bitten, always wear boots, socks and long trousers when walking through undergrowth where snakes may be present. Don't put your hands into holes and crevices, and be careful when collecting firewood.

Snake bites do not cause instantaneous death and antivenins are usually available.

Immediately wrap the bitten limb tightly, as you would for a sprained ankle, and then attach a splint to immobilise it. Keep the victim still and seek medical help. Tourniquets and sucking out the poison are comprehensively discredited.

Women's Health
Gynaecological Problems Antibiotic use, synthetic underwear, sweating and contraceptive pills can lead to fungal vaginal infections, especially when travelling in hot climates. Fungal infections are characterised by a rash, itch and discharge and can be treated with a vinegar or lemon-juice douche, or with yoghurt. Nystatin, miconazole or clotrimazole pessaries or vaginal cream are the usual treatment. Maintaining good personal hygiene and wearing loose-fitting clothes and cotton underwear may help prevent these infections.

Sexually transmitted diseases are a major cause of vaginal problems. Symptoms include a smelly discharge, painful intercourse and sometimes a burning sensation when urinating. Medical attention should be sought and male sexual partners must also be treated. For more details, see the section on Sexually Transmitted Diseases earlier. Besides abstinence, the best thing is to practise safer sex using condoms.

Pregnancy It is not advisable to travel to some places while pregnant, as some vaccinations normally used to prevent serious diseases are not advisable during pregnancy (eg, yellow fever). In addition, some diseases are much more serious for the mother (and may increase the risk of a stillborn child) in pregnancy (eg, malaria).

Most miscarriages occur during the first three months of pregnancy. Miscarriage is not uncommon and can occasionally lead to severe bleeding. The last three months should also be spent within reasonable distance of good medical care. A baby born as early as 24 weeks stands a chance of survival but only in a good modern hospital. Pregnant women should avoid all unnecessary medication, although vaccinations and malarial prophylactics should still be taken where needed. Additional care should be taken to prevent illness and particular attention should be paid to diet and nutrition. Alcohol and nicotine, for example, should be avoided.

Less Common Diseases

The following diseases pose a small risk to travellers, and so are only mentioned in passing. Seek professional medical advice if you think you may have been infected with any of these diseases.

Cholera This is the worst of the watery diarrhoeas and medical help should be sought. Outbreaks of cholera are generally widely reported, so you can avoid such problem areas. *Fluid replacement is the most vital treatment* – the risk of dehydration is severe, as you may lose up to 20L a day. If there is a delay in getting to hospital, then begin taking tetracycline. The adult dose is 250mg four times daily. It is not recommended for children under nine years nor for pregnant women. Tetracycline may help shorten the illness but adequate fluids are required to save lives.

Filariasis This is a mosquito-transmitted parasitic infection found in many parts of Africa. Possible symptoms include fever, pain and swelling of the lymph glands; inflammation of lymph drainage areas; swelling of a limb or the scrotum; skin rashes; and blindness. Treatment is available to eliminate the parasites from the body but some of the damage already caused may not be reversible. Medical advice should be obtained immediately if the infection is suspected.

Leishmaniasis This is a group of parasitic diseases transmitted by sandflies, which are found in many parts of Africa. Cutaneous leishmaniasis affects the skin tissue, causing ulceration and disfigurement; and visceral leishmaniasis affects the internal organs. Seek medical advice, as laboratory testing is required for diagnosis and correct treatment. Avoiding sandfly bites is the best precaution.

Rabies This fatal viral infection is found in many countries. Many animals can be infected (such as dogs, cats, bats and monkeys) and it is their saliva which is infectious. Any bite, scratch or even lick from an animal should be cleaned immediately and thoroughly. Scrub with soap and running water, and then apply alcohol or iodine solution. Medical help should be sought promptly to receive a course of injections to prevent the onset of symptoms and death.

Sleeping Sickness In parts of tropical Africa, tsetse flies can carry trypanosomiasis, or sleeping sickness. The tsetse fly is about twice the size of a housefly and is recognisable by the scissor-like way it folds its wings when at rest. Only a small proportion of tsetse flies carry the disease but it is a serious disease, which can be fatal without treatment. No protection is available except avoiding the tsetse fly bites. The flies are attracted to large moving objects such as safari buses, to perfume and aftershave and to colours such as dark blue. Swelling at the site of the bite five or more days later is the first sign of infection; this is followed within two to three weeks by fever.

Tetanus This disease is caused by a germ which lives in soil and in the faeces of horses and other animals. It enters the body via breaks in the skin. The first symptom may be discomfort in swallowing, or stiffening of the jaw and neck; this is followed by painful convulsions of the jaw and whole body. The disease can be fatal. It can be prevented by vaccination.

Tuberculosis (TB) TB is a bacterial infection usually transmitted from person to person by coughing but which may be transmitted through consumption of unpasteurised milk. Milk that has been boiled is safe to drink, and the souring of milk to make yoghurt or cheese also kills the bacilli. Travellers are usually not at great risk as close household contact with the infected person is usually required before the disease is passed on. You may need to have a TB test before you travel, as this can help diagnose the disease later if you become ill.

Typhus This disease is spread by ticks, mites or lice. It begins with fever, chills, headache and muscle pains, followed a few days later by a body rash. There is often a large painful sore at the site of the bite and nearby lymph nodes are swollen and painful. Typhus can be treated under medical supervision. Seek local advice on areas where ticks pose a danger and always check your skin carefully for ticks after walking in a danger area such as a tropical forest. An insect repellent can provide some help, and walkers in tick-infested areas should consider having their boots and trousers impregnated with benzyl benzoate and dibutylphthalate.

Yellow Fever This viral disease is endemic in East African countries and is transmitted by mosquitoes. The initial symptoms are fever, headache, abdominal pain and vomiting. Seek medical care urgently and drink lots of fluids.

WOMEN TRAVELLERS
Women travelling alone are often viewed as a curiosity, particularly in rural areas. There is little comprehension of the reasons why you might not have a husband or children, or if you have them, why they are not with you. Otherwise, there are no particular travel hassles unique to the area that are worth noting.

Sexual harassment is far less prevalent in East Africa than in many countries. White women come under the category of 'tourists' and enjoy a somewhat dubious, though privileged, status. If you're a white woman, you may get the occasional hassle but it's rarely persistent if treated with the cold shoulder. There are, nonetheless, certain areas in Nairobi where you wouldn't want to walk alone at night.

However, if you're a black woman you could face other problems. If you're in the company of a white man, most East Africans will assume that you're a prostitute and often ask you to participate in scams to rip off the white male. Take a taxi at night to avoid this situation.

In country areas women need to exercise caution and not place themselves in situations where if a problem arose they would not be able to alert someone. Attacks on foreign women (and indeed, men) are not unknown, especially in Kenya. As with travelling anywhere, avoid isolated or rough places, particularly at night.

In general, you'll have an easier time if you are conservatively dressed – wear long pants or skirt, and a modest top with sleeves.

As a foreign woman your best chance of making contact with local women is in the villages and countryside where people have more time and are generally less wary of strangers. A global organisation called Women Welcome Women (☎ 01494-465441), 88 Easton St, High Wycombe, Bucks HP11, UK, fosters international friendship by enabling women of different countries to visit one another. They may be worth contacting in advance of a trip to the region, and have members in Tanzania and Kenya. Check out the Web site at easy web.easynet.co.uk/~nicolag

GAY & LESBIAN TRAVELLERS
African society is generally conservative, and public displays of affection, whether between people of the same or opposite sex, are frowned upon. Such displays show insensitivity to local feelings. Gay sexual relationships are culturally taboo, although some homosexual activity – especially among younger men – does occur.

From an official point of view the attitude towards homosexual activities is one of disdain, if not outright hostility. In practice, it's a different matter but discretion is the key, as homosexual acts are officially illegal and penalties are harsh, although prosecutions are rare. In general, gay travellers should anticipate no particular difficulties.

DISABLED TRAVELLERS
People with limited mobility will find travel in East Africa difficult; people in wheelchairs will find the challenge is even greater – the almost complete lack of ramps and

lifts, inaccessible and crowded public transport, and the poor state of pavements (where they exist) are among the greatest problems.

The only hotels and lodges that provide any sort of facilities for the disabled are those at the top end of the range, and even then they are far from comprehensive; however, you're likely to get assistance where and when you need it.

Public transport is also difficult, although it is easy enough to hire a car and drive reasonably cheaply, at least in the main towns and cities. Minibuses and 4WDs are also available for hire but none have modified access for those with disabilities.

There aren't many tour companies that specifically cater for travellers with disabilities, making an organised safari extremely difficult. Hopefully the increasing competition for clients in the region will give impetus to expanded offerings in this area. One company to try is Jofra Twende Safaris (☎ 02-746841), PO Box 41558, Nairobi, which has been organising safaris for disabled people for a number of years. They'll meet you at the airport and vehicles can be fitted with ramps if requested.

For information about disabled travel in the UK, contact the Holiday Care Service (☎ 01293-774535, fax 771500, minicom 01293-776943), 2nd floor, Imperial Bldgs, Victoria Rd, Horley, Surrey RH6 7PZ. In the USA, try Access-able Travel Source (☎ 303-232 2979, fax 239 8486, email carol@access-able.com), PO Box 1796, Wheatridge Co, USA. Its Web site at www .access-able.com is worth checking. In Australia, Wheelchair Travel (☎ 1800-674 468, fax 03-9787 9454, email sales@travelability.com), 29 Ranelagh Drive, Mount Eliza, Vic 3930, has a Web site at www.travelab ility.com which is useful. The Association for the Physically Disabled in Kenya (☎ 02-219541), on Lagos Rd, Nairobi, may also be able to help disabled visitors.

See also Travellers with Special Needs in the Regional Getting There & Away chapter.

SENIOR TRAVELLERS

East Africa poses no particular difficulties for senior travellers in the major tourist areas. Places such as Nairobi, Mombasa, Dar es Salaam, Unguja (Zanzibar Island) and Kampala have a good selection of comfortable, upmarket accommodation (on the assumption that you don't want to rough it), western dining options and direct airport access, as well as offering a variety of activities (eg, wildlife-viewing safaris) that do not require excessive physical exertion.

In other areas of the region, in addition to limited lodging and dining options, one of the major considerations is likely to be transport. Road journeys can be long and taxing even for the most fit travellers. Unless you are on an organised tour, or will be met at all your destinations by friends with vehicles, luggage can be another problem for seniors travelling independently; backpacks are in many cases the only practical option.

Although there are no tour companies set up specifically for senior travellers, the more expensive tours cater well to seniors' requests and requirements. Ask the operator before you book what they can do to help make your trip possible and comfortable.

Despite these considerations, there are many elderly and retired people who have travelled extensively in the region and had a wonderful time, coping with deprivations that may have younger travellers looking for the first flight home.

TRAVEL WITH CHILDREN

This presents few problems other than those you would encounter anywhere else in the world. Africans in general are very friendly, helpful and protective towards children and their mothers.

Most hotels will not charge children under two years of age. For those between two and 12 years sharing their parents' room, it's usually 50% of the adult rate. You'll also get a cot thrown in for this price. If you want reasonable toilet and bathroom facilities, you'd be advised to stay in a mid-range hotel.

Camping is really enjoyed by small children and should be considered, but be alert for potential hazards such as mosquitoes, wandering fauna and campfires.

Most reasonable restaurants will cater for children by serving smaller portions at a suitably adjusted price, but avoid feeding your children street food.

Travelling between towns in East Africa is not always easy with children. The roads are bad, which means some long journeys are inevitable. Break journeys into four-to-five-hour stretches, avoiding the hottest time of day, with an overnight stay if possible. It's not advisable to travel at night when the children are asleep because of the poor state of roads, bad security and general (drunk) driving standards.

Travelling by matatu and bus can be a real squeeze with young children who don't count as passengers in their own right, but as wriggling luggage – kids have to sit on your lap. Keep in mind the fact that the safety record of buses and matatus is poor.

Safari and hire car companies rarely have child seats so bring your own and check that they clip into the seat belts. Young children tend to be more prone to air sickness, especially in smaller planes, so carry sick bags, wipes and changes of clothes. The journey to and from the Kenyan coast by train is highly enjoyable for all ages.

Canned baby foods, powdered milk, disposable nappies and the like are available in most large supermarkets, but are expensive. Bring as much as possible from home, together with child-friendly insect repellent.

Avoid malarial areas (such as the Kenyan coast and around Lake Victoria) until the child is old enough to take prophylactics and ensure that you are doubly careful by using mosquito nets and covering up at dawn and dusk. Letting your children run around in bare feet is usually entirely safe, however you should be aware of thorns, bees and scorpions and snakes hiding under rocks. If your children are walking barefoot around areas of habitation, there may be a risk of hookworm infestation. The same applies to lakeshores, where bilharzia is often contracted. On the coast look out for sea urchins and be aware of a painful but treatable infection known as coral ear.

For further invaluable advice see Lonely Planet's *Travel with Children* by Maureen Wheeler.

DANGERS & ANNOYANCES

Travel in this area is relatively trouble free if you stay clear of certain areas warned about in parts of this book – in particular areas of Rwanda, Burundi and northern Uganda. There is the risk of petty theft, and this mainly occurs in Nairobi and other tourist areas of Kenya, notably the coastal resort areas. However, elsewhere also keep your wits about you. See the individual country Facts for the Visitor for more details on specific trouble spots.

As is so often the case in the developing world, the police will usually be of little help in the event of trouble.

LEGAL MATTERS

For visitors from western countries, it comes as something of a surprise to find that the local police forces are not seen by the local people as protectors and upholders of the law.

Any encounter between police and civilians is likely to end with money changing hands, regardless of the situation. Basically, they are a major cause of hassle to be avoided at all cost. As a foreigner you are probably less of a target than a local person but it still pays to keep your head down and keep your contact with the authorities to the necessary minimum.

If you do run into trouble and are asked for a bribe, be firm but insistent, and don't pay the bribe unless there is absolutely no choice. Generally, the police (or bogus police) will be bluffing as to the consequences for you of not greasing their palm, and they usually give up and go in search of easier prey when it becomes clear you are not prepared to be intimidated.

If you have had something stolen and need to get a police statement for insurance purposes, this is generally straightforward, although it does take time.

BUSINESS HOURS

Government offices are open from 8 or 8.30 am to 1 pm, and 2 to 5 pm Monday to Friday. Some private businesses also open their doors from about 8.30 am to 12.30 pm on Saturdays.

Banking hours are from 9 am to 2 pm Monday to Friday. Banks are also open on the first and last Saturday of the month from 9 to 11 am. Foreign exchange bureaus are open much longer hours but only open on weekdays.

ACTIVITIES

East Africa offers the visitor a few special-interest activities. Following is a summary of these activities; for more details, see the Activities section in the individual country chapters.

Cycling

Touring the region by bicycle is gaining in popularity, and while it has its hazards, it also gives you the opportunity to get to grips with East Africa on a very intimate level. The International Bicycle Fund maintains a comprehensive Web site at www.ibike.org /africaguide, with plenty of details on preparation and planning for a trip in East Africa, as well as a country by country guide to local conditions and what to expect.

If you would prefer to let someone else take care of the logistics, it's possible to take an organised trip with Bicycle Africa Tours (☎/fax 206-7670848, email ibike@ibike.org, 4887) Columbia Drive, South Seattle, WA 98108-1919, USA. The company operates in Kenya, Tanzania and Uganda. For more information check out the Web site at www .ibike.org/bikeafrica/index.htm

Gorilla Tracking

Right up there in popularity with safaris are gorilla-tracking trips. The focus for this activity is Bwindi National Park in Uganda. Although things took a real dive in early 1999, when Hutu rebels killed a number of tourists and park staff, the park is generally safe to visit. Check in Kampala about the current situation before setting off.

Rwanda is safe enough to travel around at the moment and a steady trickle of visitors are once again visiting the gorillas there.

Safaris

This is probably the number one attraction of a visit to East Africa. Kenya has tradi-tionally been the base for budget safaris but these days there is also a good range of options in Tanzania, especially in Arusha, and to a lesser extent in Uganda.

Snorkelling & Scuba Diving

In both Kenya and Tanzania you can don a mask and snorkel, or the full scuba gear, and dive on the reefs. There are operators in both countries offering scuba courses. In recent years Unguja (Zanzibar Island) has become a major dive centre; in Kenya the main diving centre is in or around Malindi. See those sections in the relevant chapters for details of what is on offer.

Trekking & Mountain Climbing

Again, there are excellent opportunities for trekkers, the main ones being Mt Kilimanjaro and the Usambara Mountains in northern Tanzania, and Mt Kenya and Mt Elgon in western Kenya (although Elgon can also be approached from the Ugandan side).

The Ruwenzori Mountains, on the western Ugandan border with Congo (Zaïre), once a famed trekking region, have been closed for a number of years due to security problems, and look likely to stay that way for the foreseeable future.

White-Water Rafting

There are a couple of options available: one operating out of Nairobi (see the Activities section in the Kenya Facts for the Visitor chapter), the other out of Kampala to the source of the Nile (see the Jinja section in the South-Eastern Uganda chapter).

WORK

The most likely areas for employment are the safari industry, tourism, dive masters and teaching. Work and residency permits must generally be arranged through the potential employer or sponsoring organisation, and residency permits must normally be applied for from outside the region.

While Kenya and Tanzania have a large safari industry, there are many operators, competition is stiff and positions are few and far between. The best way to identify openings within existing organisations is to get to know someone already working in the business. If you are contemplating establishing your own operation, you will first need to get a good feel for the country and find an open market niche in order to survive, plus arrange all the necessary permits and paperwork.

At resort diving areas, the number of available positions is also limited, and you'll most likely need both connections and experience to land a good job. The best places to inquire are at coastal resorts, and with dive shops operating in the country.

Most teaching positions are voluntary, and are best arranged through voluntary agencies or mission organisations at home.

There are numerous aid organisations operating in East Africa. As most positions for international staff are arranged through headquarters offices in the west, it's best to start your inquiries at home before heading to East Africa.

There are numerous opportunities for volunteer work, although here, too, it's best to research the options thoroughly from home before setting off for East Africa as many organisations require applicants to go through their headquarters office (usually in the west). If you are already in the region, inquire at local churches or charitable organisations for information about volunteering.

ACCOMMODATION

Except in Burundi and Rwanda, where options for cheap accommodation are very limited, you can usually find somewhere cheap to stay, even in the smallest towns. Options include a wide choice of hotels, youth hostels (Kenya only) and camp sites.

Camping

There are camping grounds all over East Africa but the facilities vary tremendously – some are nothing more than a patch of dirt without even a tap, while others are purpose-built. Where there's nothing, religious missions will often allow you to camp in their compounds – usually for a small fee. Don't simply camp out in the bush or on a patch of wasteland in a town or city, as this is asking for problems; if you leave your tent unattended, there'll be nothing left in it when you get back. In small villages off the beaten track, ask permission first from someone in authority before setting up your tent.

Hotels

In budget hotels, what you get depends largely on what you pay for, though in general, they're good value. You can certainly expect clean sheets and shared showers but you don't always get a fan or mosquito net and, if you're paying rock-bottom prices, the showers will be cold.

Very cheap hotels often double as brothels but so do many other more expensive hotels. Theft from hotel rooms generally isn't a problem, though only a fool would tempt fate by leaving money and other valuables lying around unattended for hours at a time. Check the door locks and the design of keys. Many cheap hotels also have a full-time doorman or even a locked grille and they won't let anyone in who is not staying there.

Obviously, you need to take care in dorm accommodation, since you can't lock anything up (unless there are lockers). All in all, the chances of being mugged in a dark alley at night in a dubious part of a city or along a deserted stretch of beach are far greater than having your gear stolen from a hotel room.

Top end hotels such as the Hilton are only really found in the major cities, and prices and facilities are as you would expect for this type of place. Other large towns usually have at least one mid-range or better place to stay, and at these you can expect to pay from US$15/20 for a single/double room with private facilities.

FOOD
Local Food

For the main part, East African cuisine consists largely of stodge filler with beans or a (tough) meat sauce and is really just subsistence food for the local people – maximum filling-up potential at minimum cost. It is still possible to eat cheaply and well, although the lack of variety becomes tedious after a while. People with carnivorous habits are far better served by the local food than vegetarians (see under Vegetarian following).

The most basic local eateries (usually known as *hotelis*) hardly warrant being called restaurants. These places usually have a limited menu and are open only for lunch – the main meal of the day. If you find yourself on a tight budget, you'll also find yourself eating in these places most of the time. If you have the resources, even in the smaller towns it's usually possible to find a restaurant that offers more variety and better-quality food at a higher price. Often these restaurants are connected in some way with the mid-range and top end hotels.

The only place where any sort of distinctive African cuisine (other than Kenya's *nyama choma*, or roasted goat's meat) has developed is on the coast, where the Swahili dishes reflect the history of contact with Arabs and other Indian Ocean traders. Coconut and spices are used heavily and the results are generally excellent.

As might be expected with the large number of Asians in the region, there are also large numbers of Indian restaurants. In addition, many hotels are owned by Indians and the choice of food available on their menus reflects this. If you like Indian cuisine, you're in luck even in small towns. Indian food also offers the best choice for vegetarians.

Throughout East Africa there are markets teeming with vendors selling their produce.

Sambusas are probably the most common snack and are obvious descendants of the Indian samosa. They are deep-fried pastry triangles stuffed with spiced mince meat. Occasionally you come across sambusas with vegetable fillings but this is usually only in the Indian restaurants. If you can find them freshly made and still warm, sambusas can be excellent. Unfortunately, it is more common for them to be several hours old, cold and limp and greasy from the oil saturation.

Another item that fits into the pure starch category is that curious beast known as the *mandazi*. These are semisweet, flat doughnut and, once again, when they're fresh they can be very good. They are usually cooked and eaten at breakfast time – often dunked in tea. Should you decide to eat one later in the day, chances are it will be stale and hard.

Something that you don't come across very often, but which makes an excellent snack meal, is *mkate wa mayai* (literally 'bread eggs'). This was originally an Arab dish and is now found in countries as far ranging as Kenya and Singapore. Basically it's a wheat dough which is spread into a thin pancake, filled with minced meat and raw egg and then folded into a neat parcel and fried on a hotplate.

Seemingly on every second street corner someone is trying to make a few bob selling corn cobs roasted on a wire grille over a bed of hot coals. Another street-corner snack is deep-fried yams, eaten hot with a squeeze of lemon juice and a sprinkling of chilli powder.

Main Dishes Basically it's meat, meat and more meat, accompanied by starch of some sort. The meat is usually in a stew with perhaps some potato or other vegetables thrown in, and is often as tough as an old boot. Beef, goat and mutton are the most commonly eaten meats.

The starch comes in four major forms: potatoes, rice, *matoke* (mashed plantains) and maize meal *(ugali* in Kenya, *posho* in Uganda). The maize meal is cooked up into a thick porridge until it sets hard. It's then served up in flat bricks. Incredibly stodgy and almost totally devoid of any flavour, it

Nutrition

If your diet is poor or limited in variety, if you're travelling hard and fast and therefore missing meals or if you simply lose your appetite, you can soon start to lose weight and place your health at risk.

Make sure your diet is well balanced. Cooked eggs, tofu, beans, lentils (dhal in India) and nuts are all safe ways to get protein. Fruit you can peel (bananas, oranges or mandarins for example) is usually safe (melons can harbour bacteria in their flesh and are best avoided) and a good source of vitamins. Try to eat plenty of grains (including rice) and bread. Remember that although food is generally safer if it is cooked well, overcooked food loses much of its nutritional value. If your diet isn't well balanced or if your food intake is insufficient, it's a good idea to take vitamin and iron pills.

In hot climates make sure you drink enough – don't rely on feeling thirsty to indicate when you should drink. Not needing to urinate or small amounts of very dark yellow urine is a danger sign. Always carry a water bottle with you on long trips. Excessive sweating can lead to loss of salt and therefore muscle cramping. Salt tablets are not a good idea as a preventative, but in places where salt is not used much, adding salt to food can help.

tends to sit on the stomach like a royal corgi, but most local people swear by it. Naturally, you must try it at least once – some travellers actually get to like it, but don't hold your breath. The main thing it has going for it is that it's cheap.

Roast chicken and steak are popular dishes in the more upmarket restaurants of the bigger towns. Food in this sort of place differs little from what you might get at home. Cooked red kidney beans are always an alternative to meat and are widely available in local eateries.

Menus, where they exist in the cheaper places, are usually just a chalked list on a board on the wall. In better restaurants they are usually just in English.

For a useful list of food terms, see the Language chapter.

Fast Food

Fast food has taken off in a big way in Kenya (less so elsewhere) and virtually every town has a place serving food that rates high in grease and low in price. Fried chips with lashings of lurid tomato sauce are a basic filler but fried sausages, eggs, fish and chicken are also popular. In Nairobi there are literally dozens of these places, and they can be handy places to pick up a snack.

Vegetarian

Vegetarians are not well catered for. Away from the main cities, there are virtually no vegetarian dishes to accompany the starch. Beans are going to figure prominently in any vegetarian's culinary encounters in East Africa. Buying fresh fruit and vegetables at a market can help relieve the tedium.

Self-Catering

Preparing your own food is a viable option if you are camping and carrying cooking gear. Every town has a market and there's usually an excellent range of fresh produce available.

DRINKS
Nonalcoholic Drinks

Locally produced sodas (soft drinks) are widely available and pretty cheap. Also good are the excellent fresh fruit juices, which are more refreshing, better for you and also inexpensive.

Alcoholic Drinks

Beer If you like beer, you'll love East Africa. Beer is probably the most widely available commodity in the entire region. The locally produced product varies from country to country but is generally pretty good. The only problem is that in Kenya most Kenyan beer drinkers prefer to take it warm, so getting a cold beer can be a task.

The most widely available import is Castle Lager from South Africa but its availability depends on local import laws.

Local Brews Locally produced alcohol is available throughout the region. The *pombe* (fermented banana or millet beer) is usually fine; distilled liquors can be lethal.

Getting There & Away

AIR

Unless you are coming overland from the south, flying is the most convenient – and just about the only – way of getting to East Africa.

Airports

Nairobi (Kenya) is the main hub for flights to the region and the route on which you are most likely to get a relatively cheap ticket; however, it's also worth checking out cheap charter flights to Mombasa (Kenya) from Europe. The other main international airports in the region are Dar es Salaam (Tanzania) and Entebbe (Uganda).

Buying Tickets

The plane ticket will probably be the single most expensive item in your budget, and buying it can be an intimidating business. There is likely to be a multitude of airlines and travel agencies hoping to separate you from your money, and it is always worth putting aside a few hours to research the current state of the market.

Start early: some of the cheapest tickets have to be bought months in advance, and some popular flights sell out early. Look at the ads in newspapers and watch for special offers, then phone around travel agencies for bargains. Find out the fare, the route, the duration of the journey and any restrictions on the ticket.

Use the fares quoted in this book as a guide only. They are approximate and based on the rates advertised by travel agencies at the time of going to press. Quoted air fares do not necessarily constitute a recommendation for the carrier. If you are travelling from the UK or the USA, you will probably find that the cheapest flights are being advertised by obscure bucket shops whose names haven't yet reached the telephone directory. Many such firms are honest and solvent but there are a few rogues who will take your money and disappear, to reopen elsewhere a month or two later under a new name. If you

Warning

The information in this chapter is particularly vulnerable to change: prices for international travel are volatile, routes are introduced and cancelled, schedules change, special deals come and go, and rules and visa requirements are amended. Airlines and governments often seem to take a perverse pleasure in making price structures and regulations as complicated as possible. You should check directly with the airline or a travel agent to make sure you understand how a fare (and ticket you may buy) works. In addition, the travel industry is highly competitive and there are many lurks and perks.

The upshot of this is that you should get opinions, quotes and advice from as many airlines and travel agents as possible before you part with your hard-earned cash. The details given in this chapter should be regarded as pointers and are not a substitute for your own careful, up-to-date research.

feel suspicious about a firm, don't give them all the money at once – leave a deposit of 20% or so and pay the balance when you get the ticket. If they insist on cash in advance, go somewhere else. And once you have the ticket, phone the airline to confirm that you are actually booked on the flight.

You may decide to pay more than the rock-bottom fare by opting for the safety of a better-known travel agency. Firms such as STA Travel, which has offices worldwide, Council Travel in the USA or Travel CUTS in Canada are highly unlikely to disappear overnight, leaving you clutching a receipt for a nonexistent ticket; however, they do offer good prices to most destinations.

Once you have your ticket, write down its number, together with the flight number and other details, and keep the information somewhere separate. If the ticket is lost or stolen, this will help you get a replacement. It's sensible to buy travel insurance as early as possible. If you buy it the week before

Air Travel Glossary

Apex An Apex or 'advance purchase excursion' ticket is a discounted ticket that must be paid for in advance. There are penalties if you wish to change it; see Cancellation Penalties.

Baggage Allowance This will be written on your ticket: usually one 20kg item to go in the hold, plus one item of hand luggage.

Bucket Shop An unbonded travel agency specialising in discounted airline tickets.

Bumped Just because you have a confirmed seat doesn't mean you're going to get on the plane.

Cancellation Penalties If you have to cancel or change an Apex ticket there are often heavy penalties involved. Insurance can sometimes be taken out against these penalties. Some airlines impose cancellation penalties on regular tickets as well, particularly against 'no show' passengers.

Check In Airlines ask you to check in a certain time ahead of the flight departure (usually two hours on international flights). If you fail to check in on time and the flight is overbooked the airline can cancel your booking and give your seat to somebody else.

Confirmation Having a ticket written out with the flight and date you want doesn't mean you have a seat until the agent has checked with the airline that your status is 'OK' or confirmed. Meanwhile you could just be 'on request'.

Lost Tickets If you lose your airline ticket an airline will usually treat it like a travellers cheque and, after inquiries, issue you with another one. Legally, however, an airline is entitled to treat it like cash and say that if you lose it then it's gone forever. Take good care of your tickets.

On Request An unconfirmed booking for a flight; see Confirmation.

Open Jaws A return ticket where you fly out to one place but return from another. If available this can save you backtracking to your arrival point.

Reconfirmation At least 72 hours prior to departure time of an onward or return flight you must contact the airline and 'reconfirm' that you intend to be on the flight. If you don't do this the airline can delete your name from the passenger list and you could lose your seat. You don't have to reconfirm the first flight on your itinerary or if your stopover is less than 72 hours. It doesn't hurt to reconfirm more than once.

Standby A discounted ticket where you only fly if there is a seat available at the last moment. Standby fares are usually only available on domestic routes.

Transferred Tickets Airline tickets cannot be transferred from one person to another. Travellers sometimes try to sell the return half of their ticket, but officials can ask you to prove that you are the person named on the ticket. This is unlikely to happen on domestic flights, but on international flights, tickets may be compared with passports.

you fly, you may find, for example, that you're not covered for delays to your flight caused by industrial action.

Travellers with Special Needs

If you have special needs of any sort – you've broken a leg or you're vegetarian, travelling in a wheelchair, taking the baby, terrified of flying – you should let the airline know as soon as possible so that it can make arrangements accordingly. You should remind the airline when you reconfirm your booking (at least 72 hours before departure) and again when you check in at the airport. It may also be worth ringing around the airlines before you make your booking to find out how they can handle your particular needs.

Airports and airlines can be surprisingly helpful but they do need advance warning. Although most international airports will provide escorts from the check-in desk to the plane where needed, and there should be ramps, lifts, wheelchair-accessible toilets and reachable phones, African airports are generally not well equipped in this regard. Aircraft toilets are likely to present a problem to travellers in wheelchairs; discuss this with the airline at an early stage and, if necessary, with your doctor.

The USA
Most flights from North America are via Europe; there are few bargain deals. Expect to pay anywhere between US$1500 and US$2500 for a return ticket depending on the season. Good places to look for whatever deals there may be around include the Sunday travel sections in the major newspapers, such as the *Los Angeles Times* or *San Francisco Examiner-Chronicle* on the west coast and the *New York Times* on the east coast. Student travel bureaus, such as STA Travel or Council Travel, are also worth trying. If you are really interested in cutting costs, your best option is to buy an inexpensive ticket to London and from there purchase an onward ticket to Africa.

The following is a list of travel agents that handle flights to East Africa. Please remember that they are only suggestions, and not necessarily recommended. Before booking, shop around and gather as much information as you can. If possible, talk with others who have used the services of the agent you plan to use.

AdventureWomen Inc (☎ 800-804 8686, 406-587 3883, fax 406-587 9449) 15033 Kelly Canyon Rd, Bozeman, MT 59715

African Adventures (☎ 800-927 4641, 803-559 2300, fax 803-559 2325, email warthogs@charleston.net) 1618 Regimental Lane, Johns Island, SC 29455

Baobab Safari Company (☎ 800-835 3692, email info@baobabsaf aris.com) 210 Post St, Suite 911, San Francisco, CA 94108

Himalayan Travel Inc (☎ 800-225 2380, 203-359 3711, fax 203-359 3669, email world adv@netaxis.com) 110 Prospect St, Stamford, CT 06901

Legendary Adventure Company (☎ 800-324 9081, 713-744 5244, fax 713-895 8753, email legendary@tfcomp.com) 13201 NW Freeway, Suite 800, Houston, TX 77040

Rafiki Safaris (☎ 207-236 4244, fax 236 6253, email rafiki@midcoast.com) 45 Rawson Ave, Camden, ME 04843

Thomson Family Adventures (☎ 800-262 6255, 617-864 4803, fax 617-497 3911, email info@familyadventures. com) 347 Broadway, Cambridge, MA 02139

Voyagers International (☎ 607-273 4321, fax 273 3873, email explore@voyagers.com) PO Box 915, Ithaca, NY 14851

The UK
Return tickets between London and East Africa cost about UK£580 during the high season (January and February). The British Airways and SA Alliance Air direct flights between London and Entebbe are among the cheapest options. It is sometimes possible to pick these up for UK£400 return in the low season (March to May).

UK and Ireland-based travel agencies specialising in East Africa include:

Africa Travel Centre (☎ 020-7387 1211) 21 Leigh St, London WC1H 9QX

African Travel Specialists (☎ 020-7630 5434) Glen House, Stag Place, Victoria, London SW1E 5AG

Council Travel (☎ 020-7437 7767) 28A Poland St, London W1V 3DB

Footloose Adventure Travel (☎ 019-4360 4030) 105 Leeds Rd, Ilkley, West Yorkshire LS29 8EG

STA Travel (☎ 020-7581 4132) 86 Old Brompton Rd, London SW7 3LQ (also in Manchester, Bristol and elsewhere)

Trailfinders (☎ 020-7938 3939) 42-50 Earls Court Rd, London W8 6FT (also in Manchester, Bristol and elsewhere)

USIT Travel (☎ 01-679 8833) 19 Aston Quay, Dublin, Ireland

Continental Europe
Fares from continental Europe are similar to or slightly higher than those from London. Flights from Europe are often heavily booked between June and August, so try to reserve well in advance. There are often better deals to Nairobi than to Dar es Salaam, so it's worth checking these out.

Aeroflot flies between Moscow and Nairobi once weekly or twice monthly depending on the season for about US$650 return.

Sabena (Belgium's national airline) flies between Brussels and Entebbe. Sabena's promotional returns to European cities can be found for around US$900 but standard fares are high, with one-way fares at US$1042.

Iran Air flies between Tehran and Entebbe. A return to Entebbe costs US$570. While Uganda to Iran may not be an obvious tourist route, Iran Air has an extensive worldwide network of destinations at reasonable prices, which makes the possibility of a stopover on the way to Europe, India or the Far East a very attractive prospect. Entebbe-London return costs as little as US$700.

KLM and Kenya Airways have a partnership that serves a number of African destinations including Entebbe and Nairobi, and KLM's European network ensures most gateways are served. Ticket prices start as low as US$700 return, off-season, rising to more than US$1000 in the summer months.

Australia & New Zealand

There are no direct flights from Australia or New Zealand to anywhere in East Africa. Qantas and South African Airways have flights to Harare (Zimbabwe) and Johannesburg (South Africa), from where you can connect direct to Dar es Salaam, Entebbe and Nairobi. Expect to pay between A$1700 and A$2000 for the intercontinental leg of the trip. Other options would be routings via Cairo, via Singapore and the United Arab Emirates, via Mumbai (Bombay), or a round-the-world ticket, all of which usually cost between A$1700 and A$2500. A good place to search for a ticket is the travel section of the Saturday issue of either the *Sydney Morning Herald* or the *Age;* alternatively, visit a student travel bureau.

African flight specialists include:

Africa Travel Centre (☎ 02-9267 3048) Level 11, 456 Kent St, Sydney, NSW 2000, Australia
Africa Travel Shop (☎ 09-520 2000) 21 Remuera Rd, Newmarket, Auckland, New Zealand
African Wildlife Safaris (☎ 03-9696 2889) 1st floor, 259 Coventry St, South Melbourne, Victoria 3205, Australia

Asia

You may safely assume that flying is the only feasible way of getting between the Indian subcontinent and Kenya. There are

plenty of flights between East Africa and Mumbai for around US$420 because of the large Indian population in the region. There are bucket shops of a sort in New Delhi and Mumbai, and most of the discounted tickets will be with Air India.

Typical return fares from Mumbai to Nairobi are about US$506/890 one way/return with Air India, Ethiopian Airlines, Kenya Airways, or Pakistan International Airlines (PIA; via Karachi).

In Nairobi there are travel agencies offering tickets to Karachi, Islamabad, New Delhi, Mumbai and Calcutta. Most flights will be with Air India or PIA.

Elsewhere in Africa

African airlines serving East Africa include Air Burundi, Air Madagascar, Air Malawi, Air Mauritius, Air Tanzania, Air Zimbabwe, Cameroon Airlines, City Connexion Airlines, EgyptAir, Ethiopian Airways, Kenya Airways, Rwanda Airlines, SA Airways, SA Alliance Air, SA Alliance Express, Sudan Airways and Uganda Airlines.

For information on flying between the countries of East Africa, see Getting There & Away in individual country chapters.

Congo (Zaïre) City Connexion Airlines flies to Bujumbura in Burundi from cities in Congo (Zaïre) including Beni, Bunia and Goma. Ethiopian Airways flies to Nairobi and Dar es Salaam from Brazzaville and Kinshasa; Rwanda Airlines flies between Gisenyi and Kigali.

Egypt EgyptAir has flights from Cairo to Entebbe (Uganda) and Nairobi.

Ethiopia From Addis Ababa there are flights to Kigali (Rwanda), Dar es Salaam (Tanzania), Bujumbura, Entebbe and Nairobi with Ethiopian Airways. Kenya Airways also flies from Addis Ababa to Nairobi.

Ghana Ethiopian Airways flies between Accra and Nairobi.

Madagascar Air Madagascar flies between Antananarivo and Nairobi.

Malawi Kenya Airways and Air Malawi both fly between Lilongwe and Nairobi. Air Zimbabwe and Air Malawi connect Lilongwe with Dar es Salaam.

Mauritius Air Mauritius flies between Mauritius and Nairobi.

Nigeria Ethiopian Airways flies between Lagos and Nairobi.

South Africa From Johannesburg there are flights to Entebbe with SA Alliance Air, SA Alliance Express and Uganda Airlines. A popular route for travellers arriving in Africa from Australia and New Zealand is the one from Johannesburg to Nairobi with SA Airways or Kenya Airways. SA Alliance Express flies between Johannesburg and Kigali. Air Tanzania flies between Dar es Salaam and Johannesburg.

Sudan Kenya Airways and Sudan Airways fly between Khartoum and Nairobi. Sudan Airways also flies between Khartoum and Entebbe.

Zambia Uganda Airlines flies between Lusaka and Entebbe.

Zimbabwe Air Zimbabwe and Kenya Airways fly between Harare and Nairobi, while Uganda Airlines flies between Harare and Entebbe, and Air Zimbabwe and Air Tanzania connect Harare and Dar es Salaam.

LAND

Many travellers get to East Africa overland as part of a much lengthier journey through the continent. Unfortunately the overland routes through Sudan to the north and Congo (Zaïre) to the west are currently out of the question because of ongoing problems in these countries. There are no problems coming up from the south from Zambia, Mozambique and Malawi.

For information on travelling overland between the countries of East Africa, see Getting There and Away in individual country chapters.

For information on taking your own vehicle into East Africa, see Car & Motorcycle in the Getting Around the Region chapter.

WARNING

We strongly advise against crossing by land into Congo (Zaïre) from East Africa as there is a civil war going on there at the time of writing involving troops from as many as nine countries. There are also armed members of the *Interahamwe* roaming this part of Congo (Zaïre) and they have been known to target tourists. However, because of the possibility that peace will eventually return to this region, we include the following information.

Congo (Zaïre)

Burundi There are two possible routes between Congo (Zaïre) and Burundi but you're seriously advised to avoid the route that passes through Bugarama in northwestern Burundi as it's dangerous (there's fighting going on).

Uvira in Congo (Zaïre) is just across the top of Lake Tanganyika from Bujumbura and it is straightforward enough to take a minibus from Bujumbura to the border for about BFr 500.

To get to Bukavu in Congo (Zaïre), you could cross into Uvira and head north, but the roads are pretty poor in Congo (Zaïre). Faster and more comfortable is the route via Cyangugu in Rwanda, but you will need to factor in the cost of a Rwandan transit visa to go this way. See Cyangugu to Bukavu later in this section for details.

Rwanda The two main crossing points between Rwanda and Congo (Zaïre) are between Gisenyi and Goma (at the northern end of Lake Kivu) and between Cyangugu and Bukavu (at the southern end of Lake Kivu). These borders are open from 6 am to 6 pm for non-Africans and until midnight for Africans.

Gisenyi to Goma The two crossing points are the Poids Lourds crossing along the main road (a rough one) north of the ritzy part of Gisenyi; and there's a sealed road along the lakeshore. It's only 2 to 3km from Gisenyi to the border either way. From either post it's a couple of kilometres to Goma.

The easier of the two routes is along the lakeshore, but from the border, you'll have to take a taxi or a taxi-motor into Goma. There are minibuses from Gisenyi to the Poids Lourds post.

Cyangugu to Bukavu On the Rwandan side, Cyangugu is the actual border crossing but Kamembe is the town and transport centre. From Kamembe, minibuses make the 15 minute ride to the border for RFr 100. It is an easy border crossing in that you can walk between the two posts. From the Ruzizi border crossing, it's a 3km walk or a taxi ride to Bukavu.

Uganda The two main crossing points are on the border with Uganda: between Rutshuru and Kisoro via Bunagana; and between Beni and Kasese via Katwe and Kasindi. The Ishasha crossing between Rutshuru and Kasese is another possibility. There are less-used border crossings further north, between Mahagi and Pakwach, and between Aru and Arua.

Ethiopia
The border crossing with Kenya at Moyale is open but the area is unstable, mainly due to conflict between the Oromo Liberation Front and the Ethiopian army which is spilling across the Kenyan border. In 1999 there were skirmishes in the area which led to periodic border closures. Before planning to use this crossing, seek reliable advice as to the current state of play.

Be aware that when crossing into Kenya you will be asked for a vaccination card here with valid cholera and yellow-fever stamps. Those without cards are refused entry into Kenya.

Malawi
The only land crossing into East Africa from Malawi is at the Songwe River bridge, south-east of Mbeya in Tanzania.

Between Dar es Salaam (Tanzania) and Lilongwe (Malawi) there is a direct weekly service on the Twiga bus line (Sunday) and the Matema Beach line (Tuesday and Friday), departing Dar es Salaam's Mnazi Mmoja station at 5 am and arriving in Lilongwe about 27 hours later. The cost is TSh 25,000 on Twiga, TSh 20,000 on Matema Beach. Twiga is the more reliable of the two companies. The fare between Dar es Salaam and Mzuzu (Malawi) is about TSh 16,000.

The same companies run buses several times weekly direct from Mbeya to Mzuzu (TSh 10,000) and Lilongwe (TSh 17,000). Buses leave Mbeya in the afternoon, arriving in Lilongwe the next day.

There are minibuses from Mbeya to the border, but you'll need to verify that they really go all the way to the border, as many that say they do only go to Ibanda junction, 5km before Kyela and 7km before the border. If you get dropped off at Ibanda, you'll have to either hitch to the border, walk, or get a ride on a bicycle (there will be boys there waiting for you; they'll charge about TSh 500). Unless you don't mind a lot of walking, don't attempt to cross the border this way on a Sunday, when there's hardly any traffic. Once at the border, you'll need to walk a few hundred metres across the bridge. On the Malawian side, several minibuses a day run between the border and Karonga (about US$1).

Many trucks use the route between Mbeya and Karonga so it is usually easy to find a direct lift between the two towns.

Going in the other direction, you can sometimes find minibuses direct from the border all the way to Dar es Salaam (TSh 10,000), although it's far more comfortable to go just to Mbeya and get an express bus from there.

The border closes at 6 pm; remember that there's a one hour time difference between Tanzania and Malawi. Malawi time is GMT plus two hours, one hour behind Tanzania. The border crossing is hassle free. If you are coming from Malawi into Tanzania, have your visa arranged in advance. There's no Tanzanian embassy in Malawi, and visas are not issued at the border.

Mozambique
The main crossing between East Africa and Mozambique is at Kilambo, south of

Mtwara (Tanzania). There is a rarely used border crossing further west between Masuguru (Tanzania) and Negomane (Mozambique), but this puts you in the middle of nowhere on the Mozambique side.

There's usually at least one pick-up daily between Mtwara and the border crossing at Kilambo (TSh 2000, about one hour). From Kilambo, vehicles continue on to within about 2km of the Ruvuma River during the dry season; otherwise you'll need to walk (about 5km). The river is bridged only by dugout canoe (TSh 1500), although a ferry is planned for the near future. The crossing takes from 10 minutes in the dry season to about an hour in the rainy season when water levels are high. Once on the Mozambique side of the river, there are pick-ups (usually two daily) going to Palma and on to Moçimboa da Praia. During the rainy season, you may have to walk about 45 minutes to Namoto (the Mozambique customs post) and get onward transport from there. The last vehicle to Palma leaves Namoto between 1 and 4 pm. If you get stuck, there are some basic huts for sleeping. The foreigners price for transport from the Ruvuma to Palma is Mtc 100,000. Locals pay Mtc 50,000 but attempts to bargain are generally futile, especially if it's the last car of the day. Going in the other direction, there are usually two pick-ups daily from Moçimboa da Praia to Palma and on to the Ruvuma, leaving Moçimboa da Praia between 3 and 5 am. There's one basic hotel in Palma and several accommodation options in Moçimboa da Praia.

If you are coming from Mozambique, entry permits for Tanzania are issued at Kilambo. They cost US$20 if you can persuade the officials you want one for transit only; otherwise the cost is US$50 for most nationalities. From the river you may have to walk into Kilambo (5km), from where there is usually one pick-up a day to Mtwara.

The other Tanzania-Mozambique border crossing at Masuguru is reached via Masasi and Mangomba. There's only sporadic transport on the Tanzanian side and on the Mozambique side, you'll find yourself in the middle of nowhere. The nearest major town is Mueda, 150km away. We've heard reports

that there's also a border crossing by Nangade (on the Mozambique side). However, this crossing likely entails a walk of up to 40km on the Tanzania side and at least 10km on the Mozambique side to reach Nangade, from where there's a vehicle daily to Mueda.

Somalia

There's no way you can travel overland between Kenya and Somalia (unless you're part of a refugee aid convoy). Even if you attempted it, the Kenyan police or the army would turn you back. Moreover, the entire border area is infested with well-armed Somali *shiftas*, making any attempt to cross it a dangerous and foolhardy venture.

Sudan

As with Somalia, there's no way you can travel overland between Kenya and Sudan at present. The furthest north you're going to get is Lokichokio, and you'll be lucky to get that far unless you're with a refugee aid convoy.

Similarly, the route through northern Uganda is out of the question, as it is effectively closed to traffic. The governments of Uganda and Sudan have been engaged in proxy wars within each other's territory for years and relations are terrible. Most of southern Sudan is controlled by a Christian rebel group opposed to Khartoum's Islamic rule, and fighting flares up occasionally. You would be wise to stay away from this border until some sort of peace accord emerges.

Zambia

The main crossing between East Africa and Zambia is at Tunduma (Tanzania), southwest of Mbeya. There is another crossing between Isopa (Tanzania) and Mbala.

Bus Minibuses go daily between Mbeya and Tunduma (TSh 1500, two hours), where you can change to Zambian transport. To travel between the border and Lusaka costs between ZK40,000 and ZK45,000. There's also a direct bus three or four times weekly between Mbeya and Lusaka (TSh 17,500).

Twiga bus line runs twice weekly (usually Monday and Wednesday) between Dar es

Salaam and Lusaka (TSh 25,000 or US$40, 24 hours). Buses depart from Dar es Salaam's Mnazi Mmoja station at about 5 am. The border closes at 6 pm, so if your bus hasn't left Dar es Salaam by about 5 am, you'll likely wind up sleeping in Tunduma.

Train The Tanzania-Zambia (TAZARA) rail line links Dar es Salaam with Kapiri Mposhi (Zambia) via Mbeya and Tunduma. There are express and ordinary trains, but only express trains cross the border into Zambia. Express trains depart Dar es Salaam on Tuesday and Friday at 5.34 pm, and Mbeya at 1.30 pm on Wednesday and Saturday, arriving in New Kapiri Mposhi at 8.40 am on Thursday and Sunday (TSh 42,400/27,700/16,600 in 1st/2nd/3rd class).

Departures from Kapiri Mposhi are on Thursday and Sunday at 2.27 pm, arriving in Mbeya at 11.51 am on Friday and Monday, and in Dar es Salaam at 8.30 am on Saturday and Tuesday. You'll need a Tanzanian visa before boarding the train in Zambia. Prices on the TAZARA line are scheduled to increase by about 15% in the near future.

Ordinary trains between Kapiri Mposhi and Nakonde on the Zambian border are less expensive, but slower.

SEA & LAKE
Congo (Zaïre)
There is currently no regular passenger service on Lake Tanganyika between Congo (Zaïre) and Tanzania. Previously, the MV Liemba connected Kigoma with Kalemie weekly (US$25/20/15 for 1st/2nd/3rd class).

Malawi
Nkhata Bay in Malawi is connected with Mbamba Bay in Tanzania via the Tanzanian ferry Iringa and the Malawian boat Ilala. The other Tanzanian ferry, MV Songea, is currently out of service.

The Iringa departs Nkhata Bay weekly on Friday in the late afternoon or evening, arriving at Mbamba Bay about four or five hours later – sometime in the middle of the night. From Mbamba Bay, it continues up to Itungi port. Going in the other direction, the Iringa departs Itungi on Thursday morning,

arriving in Mbamba Bay around noon on Friday and in Nkhata Bay by late Friday afternoon. Tickets between Nkhata Bay and Mbamba Bay cost TSh 1340 (deck seating).

The Ilala connects Nkhata Bay with Mbamba Bay once or twice weekly, usually on Tuesday and/or Sunday though the schedule is very erratic. Tickets cost US$16/10/2 for cabin/1st class deck/3rd class deck.

There is a Malawi immigration office at Nkhata Bay.

Mozambique
There's a small motorboat that sails sporadically between Mtwara (Tanzania) and Moçimboa da Praia (Mozambique). Inquire at the ports for details. Otherwise, the only option is local boats (dhows). Only take these when there are favourable winds (the monsoon blows north to south from about November to February and south to north from about April to September), and bring plenty of water. Depending on wind and weather, the trip can take anywhere between 12 and 30 hours.

Zambia
The MV Liemba connects Kigoma (Tanzania) with Mpulungu (Zambia) weekly. Departures from Kigoma are on Wednesday at 4 pm, arriving in Mpulungu on Friday morning. From Mpulungu, departures are on Friday at 4 pm, arriving in Kigoma on Sunday any time between 10 am and 6 pm. Fares are US$55/45/40 for 1st/2nd/3rd class. Food is available on board, but it's best to bring some supplements, as well as your own water. First class is relatively comfortable, with two reasonably clean bunks and a window. Second class cabins (four bunks) and 3rd class seating, however, are both poorly ventilated and uncomfortable. If you're going to travel 3rd class, it's more comfortable to find yourself deck space than to sit in the 3rd class seating section.

For information on the MV Liemba's route between Kigoma and Bujumbura (Burundi), see the Getting There & Away sections of the Tanzania and Burundi chapters.

Tickets bought in Mpulungu and Bujumbura must be paid for in US dollars.

Getting Around East Africa

AIR

There's a good network of internal flights within Kenya but fewer flights in Tanzania, Uganda, Rwanda and Burundi. Most of the internal sectors are serviced by the national carriers (see the individual country Getting Around chapters for details) but in Kenya and Tanzania there are also quite a few private companies that operate light aircraft, usually six to eight-seater twin-propeller planes.

BUS, MINIBUS & TAXI

Buses are usually quicker than trains or trucks. In Kenya, where there's a fairly good network of sealed roads, you may have the choice of going by so-called 'luxury' bus or by ordinary bus over certain routes. The luxury buses are more comfortable and hence cost more but are not always quicker than the ordinary buses.

In Tanzania there's also a choice of luxury and ordinary buses, but only on the main routes: Arusha to Moshi and Dar es Salaam, and Dar es Salaam to Mombasa. Uganda has ordinary buses only, except on the international Kampala-Nairobi run. There are very few full-size buses in Burundi and Rwanda – minibuses are often the rule.

Most East African countries rely heavily on minibuses (known as *matatus* in Kenya, *taxis* in Uganda, *dalla-dallas* in Tanzania) for transport. They're generally more expensive than ordinary buses, but quicker. In Kenya and Tanzania, you can expect them to be packed to bursting point. Because of overloading, excessive speed, poor maintenance and driver recklessness, matatus in Kenya and Tanzania are not the safest way of getting around. In fact, they can be downright dangerous, and newspaper reports of matatu crashes are a regular feature. In Uganda, Rwanda and Burundi, however, travelling in minibuses is much safer.

Kenya, Tanzania and Uganda also have share-taxis (which take up to five or six pas-

A ride in a matatu or dalla-dalla is often a hair-raising experience.

sengers and leave when full) and private taxis. Except for short trips, you can forget about private taxis if you're on a budget, but share-taxis should definitely be considered. They can cost up to twice as much as the corresponding bus fare but in some places are only slightly more expensive than matatus, and they're certainly quicker and more comfortable. They're also considerably safer than matatus.

TRAIN

In Kenya these days, the only route on which the train is the preferred method of transport is the one between Nairobi and Mombasa. Tanzanian trains are considerably slower but they are the best way to get around, since many roads are in such bad shape that going by bus is generally an uncomfortable experience. Ugandan passenger services, including the service between Kampala and Nairobi in Kenya, are currently suspended and look likely to remain that way.

Third class train travel is usually very crowded and uncomfortable and you may have thieves to contend with, so it's not generally recommended. Second class is preferable and will cost you about the same as a bus over the same distance. Travelling 1st class will cost you about double what a bus would cost but does give you a considerable measure of privacy and comfort. See the individual country Getting Around chapters for more information.

TRUCK

For many travellers, trucks are the favoured means of transport, and they may be the *only* form of transport in some areas. They're not only the cheapest way of getting from A to B as a rule, but you also get an excellent view from the top of the load.

For most regular runs there will be a 'fare', which is more or less fixed and is what the locals pay – but check this out before you agree to a price. Sometimes it's possible to get the truckie to lower the price if there's a group of you. You can sometimes travel in the cab for about twice what it costs to travel on top of the load.

There are trucks on main routes to most places every day, but in more remote areas they may run only once or twice a week. Many lifts are arranged the night before departure at the 'truck park' – a compound/dust patch that you'll find in almost every African town. Just go there and ask around for a truck that is going your way. If the journey is going to take more than one night or one day, ask what to do about food and drink.

CAR & MOTORCYCLE

For detailed information on car, 4WD and motorcycle rental, road rules and road conditions, see the individual country Getting Around chapters.

Road Conditions

The main roads of Kenya, Uganda, Rwanda and Burundi are sealed and generally in a good state of repair, though you'll occasionally encounter the odd rough patch. However, the main roads of Tanzania are often in an appalling state (with the exceptions of the roads from Namanga to Moshi, Moshi to Dar es Salaam and Dar es Salaam to Morogoro).

Roads in far-flung rural areas of all East African countries may well be in a bad state of repair, so breakdowns and getting stuck, especially in the wet season, are a regular feature of any journey. Desert roads in north and north-east Kenya may be just a set of tyre tracks left in the sand or dust by previous trucks. Don't pay too much attention to lines drawn on maps in places like this. Many roads are impassable in the wet season, and on some of them a convoy system may be in operation, so it's only possible to travel at certain times of the day.

Carnet

A foreign-registered vehicle being brought into East Africa must be covered by a *carnet de passage*. The purpose of a carnet is to allow an individual to take a vehicle into a country where duties would normally be payable, without having to pay those duties. It's a document that guarantees that if a vehicle is taken into a country but not exported, then the organisation that issued it will accept responsibility for payment of import duties. Carnets can only be issued by national motoring organisations. Before they will issue such a document they have to be absolutely sure that if the need to pay duties ever arose they would be reimbursed by the individual to whom the document was issued.

The amount of import duty can vary quite a lot but generally it's between 100 and 150% of the new value of the vehicle.

The motoring organisation will calculate the duty payable in all the countries you intend to visit and use the highest figure to arrive at what is known as an 'indemnity figure'. This amount must be guaranteed to the motoring organisation by the individual before carnet documents are issued.

If duties ever become payable – for example, if you take the vehicle into a country but don't export it again – the authorities of that country will demand payment of duties from the motoring organisation. It, in turn, will surrender the indemnity it was holding.

To get a carnet you first need to apply to a motoring organisation. It will issue you with an indemnity form for completion by either a bank or an insurance company. Once you have deposited a bond with a bank or paid a premium to an insurance company, the motoring organisation issues a carnet. The cost of the carnet itself is minimal. The whole process generally takes about a week to complete.

HITCHING

In Kenya, but less so in the other countries of East Africa, resident expats and aid workers with their own vehicles seem to be reasonably generous about offering free lifts. Remember that in many African countries, sticking out your thumb is the equivalent of an obscene gesture, though allowances are generally made for foreigners. Wave your hand up and down instead.

A word of warning about taking lifts in private cars. Smuggling across borders does go on, and if whatever is being smuggled is

Hitching

Hitching is never entirely safe in any country in the world, and we don't recommend it. Travellers who decide to hitch should understand that they are taking a small but potentially serious risk. People who do choose to hitch will be safer if they travel in pairs and let someone know where they are planning to go.

found, you may be arrested even though you knew nothing about it. Most travellers manage to convince police that they were merely hitching a ride (passport stamps are a good indication of this), but the convincing can take days.

Free lifts on trucks are the exception rather than the rule, though it depends on the driver. You may have to wait a long time until a free lift comes along, so it's often not worth bothering to try for one.

BOAT

There are quite a few possibilities for travelling by boat, either inland on the lakes or along the coast. In particular, there are some amazingly venerable old steamships operating on the lakes. If it starts running again, a trip on the MV *Liemba* on Lake Tanganyika is quite an experience.

WILDLIFE GUIDE

PRIMATES

Bushbabies Greater or thick-tailed bushbaby *Otolemur crassicaudatus* (pictured); East African lesser bushbaby *Galago senegalensis*; Zanzibar lesser bushbaby *Galagoides zanibaricus*

Named for their plaintive wailing call, bushbabies are actually primitive primates. Heightened night vision and extremely sensitive hearing makes them ideally adapted to their nocturnal way of life. Fruit and tree-sap is the mainstay of their diet, supplemented by insects and, in the case of the greater bushbaby, lizards, nestlings and eggs. Locally very common, they are difficult to see because they are strictly nocturnal.

Size: greater bushbaby: up to 80cm long, half of which is its bushy tail; mass 1.5kg. Lesser bushbabies: 40cm long; mass, around 150 to 200g. **Distribution:** lightly wooded savannah to thickly forested areas. Greater and lesser bushbabies occur throughout the region. **Status:** common, but strictly nocturnal.

Vervet monkey *Cercopithecus aethiops*

The most common monkey of the savannah and woodlands, the vervet is easily recognisable by its grizzled grey hair and black face fringed with white. The male has a distinctive bright blue scrotum, an important signal of status in the troop. Troops may number up to 30. They are diurnal and forage for fruits, seeds, leaves, flowers, invertebrates and the occasional lizard or nestling. They rapidly learn where easy-pickings can be found around lodges and camp sites but become pests when they grow habituated to being fed. Most park authorities destroy such individuals so avoid feeding them.

Size: up to 130cm long including the 60cm-long tail; mass 3.5 to 8kg. **Distribution:** present in all woodland-savannah habitats in the region. **Status:** very common in parks; easy to see due to their diurnal habits and boldness in protected areas.

Blue monkey (Syke's monkey) *Cercopithecus mitis*

Similar to the vervet monkey but slightly larger and much darker. Blue monkeys have a grey-to-black face; black shoulders, limbs and tail; and a reddish-brown or olive-brown back. They are more arboreal than vervet monkeys and generally prefer dense forest and woodland rather than savannah. More vegetarian than the vervet, they feed largely on foliage, fruits, bark, gum and leaves. Social groups may be as large as 30 but generally number between four and 12. Predators include leopards and eagles.

Size: 140cm long, 80cm of which is tail; mass 8 to 10kg. **Distribution:** widely distributed in most evergreen forests and forest patches in the region. **Status:** locally common; active during the day, but often difficult to see among foliage. Easy to see in Uganda's Kibale Forest.

Baboon *Papio cynocephalus*

Known by different sub-species names, the baboon is unmistakable and races differ only in superficial appearance. The yellow baboon *(P. c. cynocephalus)* is a yellow-brown colour whereas the olive baboon *(P. c. anubis*; pictured) has olive-brown hair. Baboons live in complex troops numbering between eight and 200 and there is no single dominant male. They forage mostly in open woodland-savannah for grasses, tubers, fruits, insects and spiders, and occasionally for small vertebrates. Baboons may become pests when visiting camp sites for hand-outs. Such individuals can be dangerous and are destroyed, so don't feed them.

MITCH REARDON

Size: a large monkey, up to 160cm long and 75cm at the shoulder; mass 25 to 45kg. **Distribution:** throughout the region. **Status:** extremely common in all conservation areas; active during the day. Tanzania's Manyara National Park probably has the highest baboon density of any park in Africa.

Chimpanzee *Pan troglodytes*

The chimpanzee is Man's closest living relative. Though requiring a rich year-round food supply and prefering productive, moist forests, the chimp is adaptable and can be found in habitats ranging from dry woodland to dry savannah. They are highly sociable, living in communities numbering up to 120, however all individuals in a social group almost never all congregate and typical group size is much smaller. Individuals may also spend considerable time alone. Primarily vegetarians, chimps consume fruit, bark, stems and leaves with the occasional meal of insects, nestling birds, eggs and larger prey.

JASON EDWARDS

Size: up to 1.7m; mass 40 to 55kg. **Distribution:** equatorial forest in western Tanzania, Rwanda, Burundi and western Uganda. Best seen in Tanzania's Gombe National Park. **Status:** threatened by habitat destruction, civil unrest and hunting. Chimpanzees are endangered and occur in small isolated populations.

Gorilla *Gorilla gorilla*

Two races occur in the region: the eastern lowland gorilla *(G. g. graueri;* pictured*)*, numbering 4000 in eastern Congo (Zaïre) and Rwanda; and the mountain gorilla *(G. g. beringei)*, of which there are only 600 to 700 left in the Congo (Zaïre)/Rwanda/Uganda border region. Gorillas inhabit humid equatorial rainforest up to 4000m. Groups number between two and 20, usually with a single adult male (silverback), though large groups of the eastern race may contain up to four silverbacks. Males make all decisions regarding movements, foraging and where and when to rest. They are vegetarians.

JASON EDWARDS

Size: up to 1.8m; mass up to 210kg in males and 70 to 100kg in females. **Distribution:** equatorial forest in western Tanzania, Rwanda, Burundi and south-western Uganda. **Status:** threatened by poaching, habitat destruction and civil unrest; highly endangered.

CARNIVORES

WILDLIFE GUIDE

LUKE HUNTER

Genets Small-spotted or common genet *Genetta genetta* (pictured); large-spotted or rusty-spotted genet *Genetta tigrina*

Relatives of mongooses, genets resemble long, slender domestic cats and have a pointed fox-like face. The two species in the region are very similar but can be differentiated by the tail tips (white in the small-spotted genet and black in the large spotted). They are solitary, sleeping by day in abandoned burrows, rock crevices or hollow trees and emerging at night to forage. Very agile, they hunt equally well on land or in trees, feeding on small rodents, birds, reptiles, nestlings, eggs, insects and fruits.

Size: both species very similar: length 85 to 110cm; mass: 1.5 to 3.2kg. **Distribution:** widely distributed throughout the region. **Status:** very common, but largely nocturnal. Often the most common small carnivore seen on night safaris.

RICHARD I'ANSON

Mongooses

Though common, most mongooses are solitary and are usually seen fleetingly. The slender mongoose *(Galerella sanguinea)* is recognisable by its black-tipped tail, which it holds aloft like a flag when running. A few species, including the dwarf mongoose *(Helogale parvula)*, weighing only 400g, and the 1.5kg banded mongoose *(Mungos mungo*; pictured), are intensely sociable. Close family groups are better at spotting danger and raising kittens. Social behaviour also helps when confronting a threat: collectively, they intimidate larger enemies. Insects and other invertebrates are their most important prey.

Size: ranging from the dwarf mongoose at 40cm/400g to the 150cm-long/5.5kg white-tailed mongoose *(Ichneumia albicauda)*. **Distribution:** widely distributed and common. **Status:** many species are common; sociable species are active during the day, solitary species may be nocturnal or diurnal.

MITCH REARDON

Aardwolf *Proteles cristatus*

The smallest of the hyaena family, the aardwolf subsists almost entirely on harvester termites and almost never consumes meat. Aardwolves resemble the striped hyaena but are considerably smaller. Rather than forming clans or denning communally, they form loose associations between pairs and forage alone. The male assists the female raising the cubs, mostly by baby-sitting at the den while the mother forages.

Size: height at shoulder 40 to 50cm; mass 8 to 12kg but often looks larger due to the extensive cape it erects when threatened. **Distribution:** widespread in savannah-woodland habitats from central Tanzania into the arid north of Kenya. **Status:** uncommon; nocturnal, though occasionally seen at dawn and dusk.

Striped hyaena *Hyaena hyaena*

A lean long-legged hyaena whose overall appearance is of a more robust animal due to its long shaggy mane and 'cape' along the back. Striped hyaenas subsist largely by scavenging from the kills of other predators and carrying off large parts to cache. They also catch insects and small vertebrates but are poor hunters of larger prey. Striped hyaenas forage alone, but groups of up to seven may congregate on large carcasses.

D MASON/WINDRUSH PHOTOS

Size: height at shoulder 65 to 80cm; mass: 25 to 45kg. **Distribution:** central Tanzania into arid zones of northern Kenya. **Status:** uncommon; strictly nocturnal.

Spotted hyaena *Crocuta crocuta*

Widely reviled as a cowardly scavenger, the spotted hyaena is actually a highly efficient predator with a fascinating social system. Females are larger and dominant to males and even have male physical characteristics, the most remarkable of which is an erectile clitoris rendering the sexes virtually indistinguishable at a distance. Spotted hyaenas are massively built and appear distinctly canine, though they are more closely related to cats than to dogs. They can reach speeds of up to 60km/h and a pack can easily dispatch adult wildebeests and zebras.

JASON EDWARDS

Size: shoulder height 85cm; length 120 to 180cm; mass up to 80kg. **Distribution:** throughout the region. **Status:** very common in protected areas; mainly nocturnal, but also seen during the day.

Cheetah *Acinonyx jubatus*

The world's fastest land mammal, the cheetah reaches speeds of at least 105km/h but is exhausted after a few hundred metres, causing it to stalk prey to within 60m before unleashing its tremendous acceleration. Cheetahs prey on antelopes up to 60kg as well as hares and young wildebeests and zebras. Litters may be as large as nine but in open savannah habitats, most cubs are killed by predators. The young disperse from the mother at around 18 months. Males form coalitions, while females are solitary for life.

ALEX DISSANAYAKE

Size: shoulder height 85cm; length 180 to 220cm; mass up to 65kg. **Distribution:** largely restricted to protected areas or the regions surrounding them. Shuns densely forested areas. **Status:** usually occurs at low density, with individuals moving over large areas. Active by day, and frequently seen in national parks.

Leopard *Panthera pardus*

Leopards are supreme ambush hunters, using infinite patience to stalk prey within metres before an explosive attack. They eat everything from insects to zebras, but antelopes such as impalas and gazelles are their primary prey. Leopards are highly agile and hoist their kills into trees to avoid losing them to lions and hyaenas. They are solitary animals, except during the mating season, when the male and female stay in close association for the female's week- long oestrus. A litter of up to three cubs is born after a gestation of three months and the females raises them without any assistance from the male.

Size: shoulder height 70 to 80cm; length 160 to 210cm; mass up to 90kg. **Distribution:** throughout the region; abundant in parks, they also persist in human-altered habitat due to their great adaptability. **Status:** common, but mainly nocturnal and very secretive, making them the most difficult of the large cats to see.

Lion *Panthera leo*

Lions spend much of the night hunting, patrolling territories and playing. They live in prides of up to about 30, with the the core comprising between four and 12 related females who remain in the pride for life. Males form coalitions and defend the female groups from foreign males. Lions are strictly territorial, defending ranges of between 50 and 400 sq km. Young males are ousted from the pride at two or three, entering a period of nomadism ending at around five years old when they are able to take over a pride of their own. Though lions hunt virtually anything, wildebeest, zebras and buffaloes are the mainstay of their diet.

Size: shoulder height 120cm; length 250 to 300cm; mass up to 240kg (males), 160kg (females). **Distribution:** largely confined to protected areas and present in all woodland-savannah parks in the region. **Status:** common in many of the larger parks; largely nocturnal but conspicuous during the day.

Caracal *Felis caracal*

Sometimes also called the African lynx due to its long tufted ears, the caracal is a robust, powerful cat which preys predominantly on small antelopes, birds and rodents but is capable of taking down animals many times larger than itself. Like most cats, they are largely solitary. Females give birth to one to three kittens after a 79 or 80 day gestation and raise the kittens alone. They are territorial, marking their home-range with urine sprays and faeces. Caracals have a wide habitat tolerance but prefer semi-arid regions, dry savannahs and hilly country. They are absent from dense forest.

Size: shoulder height 40 to 45cm; length 70 to 110cm; mass up to 20kg. **Distribution:** throughout the region. **Status:** not common; mostly nocturnal and difficult to see.

African wild cat *Felis lybica*

The progenitor of the household tabby, the African wild cat was originally domesticated by the Egyptians. African wild cats differ from domestic cats in having reddish backs to their ears, proportionally longer legs and a generally leaner appearance. They cross freely with domestic cats close to human habitation where the two meet, and this is probably the greatest threat to the integrity of the wild species. They subsist mainly on small rodents, but also prey on birds and insects and species up to the size of hares. They are solitary except when females have kittens.

ANDREW MacCOLL

Size: shoulder height 35cm; length 85 to 100cm; mass up to 6kg. **Distribution:** throughout the region.
Status: common; nocturnal, although sometimes spotted at dawn and dusk.

Serval *Felis serval*

A tall, slender, long-legged cat, the serval has very large upright ears, a long neck and a relatively short tail. The tawny to russet-yellow coat is dotted with large black spots, forming long bars and blotches on the neck and shoulders. All-black individuals occasionally occur, particularly in Kenya's mountainous regions. The serval favours floodplains, wetlands and woodlands near streams where favoured prey – mice, vlei rats, cane rats, hares and frogs – is abundant.

MITCH REARDON

Size: shoulder height 60cm; length 95 to 120cm; mass up to 13kg. **Distribution:** throughout the region.
Status: relatively common; active in the early morning and late afternoon.

Bat-eared fox *Otocyon megalotis*

The huge ears of this little fox detect the faint sounds of invertebrates below ground before unearthing them in a burst of frantic digging. As well as insects (especially termites), they take small vertebrates and wild fruit. They are monogamous, and apparently pair for life: groups comprising a mated pair and their offspring are often seen. Their natural enemies include large birds of prey, caracals and the larger cats.

JASON EDWARDS

Size: shoulder height 35cm; length 75 to 90cm; mass up to 5kg. **Distribution:** throughout the region.
Status: locally very common, especially in parks; mainly nocturnal, but often seen in the late afternoon and early morning.

ANDREW MacCOLL

Jackals
The most common is the golden jackal *(Canis aureus)*, normally a golden to silvery-grey colour. The black-backed or silver-backed jackal *(Canis mesomelas;* pictured) has a distinctive mantle of silver-grey hair along the back on a rufoustan ground colour and a black-tipped tail. The side-striped jackal *(Canis adustus)* is least common and has a grey appearance with a light stripe along each side and a white tail tip. All species form enduring pairs which defend a territory around 1 to 3 sq km. The young stay with the parents and help in raising new pups. Jackals scavenge their food from kills of larger predators but are also efficient hunters.

Size: Shoulder height 38 to 50cm; length 95 to 120cm; mass up to 15kg. **Distribution:** widespread with a wide habitat tolerance. All species are present in open plains and woodlands; side-striped jackals prefer well-watered wooded areas. **Status:** generally abundant in protected areas.

RICHARD I'ANSON

Wild dog *Lycaon pictus*
The wild dog's blotched black, yellow and white coat, together with its large, round ears, makes it unmistakable. Wild dogs are highly sociable, living in packs numbering up to 40, though 12 to 20 is typical. Marvellous endurance hunters, they chase prey relentlessly to the point of exhaustion, then the pack cooperates to pull down the quarry. Though they are widely reviled for killing prey by disembowelling and eating it alive, this is in fact probably as fast as any of the 'cleaner' methods used by carnivores. Mid-sized antelopes are preferred, but they can kill animals as large as buffaloes. The wild dog requires enormous areas in which to range.

Size: shoulder height 65 to 80cm; length 105 to 150cm; mass up to 30kg. **Distribution:** reduced by persecution, disease and destruction of habitat; now restricted to the largest protected areas in the region. **Status:** highly threatened and now absent from many areas of their former distribution.

LORNA STANTON/ABPL

Honey badger or ratel *Mellivora capensis*
Africa's equivalent of the European badger, the ratel has a reputation for a vile temper and ferocity. While stories of them attacking animals the size of buffaloes are probably folklore, they are pugnacious and astonishingly powerful for their size. They have few natural enemies and even feed alongside lions on their kills, though they are occasionally killed by the larger carnivores. Normally active between dusk and dawn, they are highly omnivorous, feeding on meat, fish, frogs, scorpions, spiders, reptiles, small mammals, roots, honey, berries and eggs.

Size: length 90 to 100cm; mass up to 15kg. **Distribution:** widespread in the region, occupying most habitats. **Status:** generally occurs in low densities though is nowhere threatened; mainly nocturnal.

UNGULATES (HOOFED ANIMALS)

African elephant *Loxodonta africana*

Elephants usually live in small family groups of between 10 and 20 which frequently congregate with much larger herds at a common water source or food resource. Their society is matriarchal and herds are dominated by old females. Bulls live alone or in bachelor groups, joining the herds when females are in season. A cow may mate with many bulls during her oestrus. An adult's average daily food intake is about 250kg of grass, leaves, bark and other vegetation. They usually live for about 60 to 70 years.

ALEX DISSANAYAKE

Size: shoulder height up to 4m in males; mass 5000 to 6300kg. **Distribution:** widely distributed in the region though large populations only occur in protected areas. **Status:** very common in parks (which may become overpopulated due in part to immigration from areas where elephants are persecuted).

Hyraxes (dassies)

Although hyraxes resemble large, robust guinea-pigs, they are most closely related to elephants and dugongs. Three species occur, the most common being the rock hyrax *(Procavia capensis)* found on mountains or rocky outcrops. They form colonies of up to 60, often with the yellow-spotted hyrax (or bush hyrax: *Heterohyrax brucei),* which is slightly smaller with distinctive white underparts. 'Kopjes' (rock outcrops) in the Serengeti National Park are excellent sites for observing the two species together. The third species, the tree hyrax *(Dendrohyrax arboreus),* prefers thick forest rather than rocks. All three species are herbivorous.

LUKE HUNTER

Size: length 60cm; mass up to 5.5kg. **Distribution:** bush and rock species very widely distributed; tree hyrax restricted to lowland rain forest and best seen in forest reserves such as Aberdare, Mt Kenya and Ruwenzoris. **Status:** common, and easy to see where they occur; a regular inhabitant of lodges, where they become tame.

Black or hook-lipped rhinoceros *Diceros bicornis*

Poaching for rhino horn used in traditional Chinese medicine and for dagger handles by Yemeni tribesmen has made the rhino Africa's most endangered large mammal. White rhinos are extinct in East Africa; the black rhino still occurs, though it is vary rare. The black rhino (the smaller species) is actually more unpredictable and is prone to charging when alarmed. They are browsers and use their pointed, prehensile lip to selectively feed on branches, foliage and leaves. Black rhinos are solitary and territorial, only socialising during the mating season, though females are relatively tolerant of each other.

DAVID WALL

Size: shoulder height 1.6m; mass 800 to 1100kg; record horn length 1.2m. **Distribution:** now restricted to relict populations in a few reserves; best seen in Ngorongoro Crater (Tanzania) and Nairobi National Park (Kenya). **Status:** highly endangered in the region (much more numerous in Southern Africa).

WILDLIFE GUIDE

RICHARD I'ANSON

Zebras Common or Burchell's zebra *Equus burchelli* (pictured); Grevy's zebra *Equus grevyi*

Two species occur in the region, the most common being Burchell's zebra, famous for its huge migrating herds. Burchell's zebras are marked with broad alternating black and white stripes, interspersed with faint 'shadow stripes'. Grevy's zebras are marked all over with much finer stripes and lack shadow stripes. Both species are grazers but occasionally browse on leaves and scrub. The social system centres around small groups of related mares over which stallions fight fiercely. Stallions may hold a harem for 15 years but single mares are often lost to younger males.

Size: Burchell's zebra shoulder height 1.4m; Grevy's 1.6m. Mass Burchell's up to 360kg; Grevy's up to 390kg. **Distribution:** Burchell's zebras occur throughout the region. Grevy's zebras restricted to northern Kenya. **Status:** Burchell's zebras common. Grevy's zebras only common in Kenya's Northern Frontier District.

TONY WHEELER

Warthog *Phacochoerus aethiopicus*

Warthogs are abundant in all savannah-woodland habitats in East Africa. They live in families comprising up to four related females accompanied by their young. Males form bachelor groups and only associate with the sows during the breeding season. The distinctive facial warts can be used to determine sex. Females have a single pair of warts under the eyes whereas males have a second set further down the snout. Warthogs feed mainly on grass, but also eat fruit and bark; they grub for roots and bulbs when other food is scarce. Warthogs shelter and give birth in abandoned aardvark burrows or excavate cavities in termite mounds.

Size: shoulder height 70cm; mass up to 105kg, though averaging between 50 to 60kg. **Distribution:** in all areas in East Africa except for dense rainforest and mountains above 3000m. **Status:** very common; diurnal and easy to see.

RICHARD I'ANSON

Hippopotamus *Hippopotamus amphibius*

Hippos are found close to fresh water, spending most of the day submerged and emerging at night to graze on land. They can consume about 40kg of vegetable matter each evening. They live in large herds, tolerating close contact in the water, but forage singly when on land. Cows with young babies are aggressive to other individuals. Adult bulls defend territories against each other aggressively and most males bear the scars of conflicts, often a convenient method of sexing hippos. Hippos are extremely dangerous on land and kill many people each year, usually when someone inadvertently blocks the animal's retreat to the water.

Size: shoulder height 1.5m; mass up to 2000kg, males larger than females. **Distribution:** occur widely in the region, but are restricted to large bodies of fresh water. **Status:** common and easy to see.

Giraffe *Giraffa camelopardalis*

Three different races occur in the region. Most common is the Masai giraffe (*G.c. tippelskirchi*; pictured), with its large leaf-like markings, while the reticulated giraffe *(G. c. reticulata)* of northern Kenya has fine white lines separating large reddish patches. A third race, Rothschild's giraffe *(G.c. rothschildi),* is pale in colour and occurs from western Kenya into Uganda. Both sexes have knob-like 'horns. Males have bald tips to the horns and females have a covering of hair. Giraffes browse on trees, the only herbivores other than elephants which can do so. Juveniles are prone to predation and lions will even take down fully grown adults.

JOHN HAY

Size: up to 5.2m tall; mass 900 to 1400kg. **Distribution:** Masai giraffe very widespread in region south and west of Nairobi into Tanzania. Rothschild's giraffe restricted to Uganda and western Kenya near Lake Barigo. Reticulated giraffe occurs in northern Kenya. **Status:** common and easy to see.

Klipspringer *Oreotragus oreotragus*

A small and sturdy antelope, the klipspringer is easily recognised by its curious tip-toe stance – the hooves are adapted for balance and grip on rocky surfaces. The widely spaced 10cm-long horns are present only on the male. Klipspringers normally inhabit rocky outcrops; they also venture into adjacent grasslands, but when alarmed they retreat into the rocks for safety. These amazingly agile and sure-footed creatures are capable of bounding up impossibly rough rockfaces.

RICHARD I'ANSON

Size: shoulder height 60cm; mass up to 13kg. **Distribution:** on rocky outcrops and mountainous areas throughout the region. Absent from dense forests. **Status:** common.

Kirk's dik-dik *Madoqua kirkii*

Dik-diks are best identified by their miniature size, their pointed mobile snout and a tuft of dark hair on their forehead. Only the males have short horns. Dik-diks are monogamous, and the pairs are territorial. They are usually seen singly, in pairs or in family parties of three. Mainly found in fairly dense vegetation, they feed exclusively on browse and are completely water-independent.

MITCH REARDON

Size: shoulder height 43cm; mass up to 5.1kg. **Distribution:** throughout the region. **Status:** common, but shy and easy to miss. Active in the morning and afternoon.

MITCH REARDON

Steenbok *Raphicerus campestris*

A very pretty and slender small antelope, the steenbok has distinctive strawberry-reddish brown fur with pale underparts. The upper surface of their nose bears a black, wedge-shaped 'blaze' useful for identification. Males have small, straight and widely separated horns. They are solitary animals and only have contact with others during the mating season.

Size: shoulder height 50cm; mass up to 11kg. **Distribution:** restricted to central and southern Kenya, into Tanzania. **Status:** common where they occur.

RICHARD I'ANSON

Impala *Aepyceros melampus*

Often dismissed because they are so abundant, impalas are unique antelopes with no close relatives. Males have long, lyre-shaped horns averaging 75cm in length. They are gregarious, and males defend female herds during the rut. Outside the breeding season, males congregate in bachelor groups. Impalas are extremely fast, agile antelopes able to cover 10m in a single bound, which may be 3m high. Extremely common, impalas are readily preyed upon by all large carnivores.

Size: shoulder height 90cm; mass up to 70kg. **Distribution:** savannah regions from central Kenya south into Tanzania. **Status:** very common and easy to see.

MITCH REARDON

Gazelles

Often the most common medium-sized antelope where they occur, gazelles form the main prey item of many predators in East Africa. Three species are common in the region. Thomson's gazelle (*Gazella thomsonii*; pictured) is the smallest. It is often found in with the impala-sized Grant's gazelle (*G. granti*), which lacks the 'Thommy's' black side stripe. The gerenuk (*Litocranius walleri*) has uniquely long limbs and neck, allowing it to reach otherwise inaccessible parts of trees. All three species are sociable but the gerenuk forms small herds rarely numbering more than 12.

Size: Grant's shoulder height 90cm; Thomson's 70cm; gerenuk 105cm. Mass Grant's 65kg; Thomson's 29kg; gerenuk 45kg. **Distribution:** Grant's/Thomson's common in savannah and woodland; gerenuks from north-western Tanzania through central Kenya. **Status:** Grant's/Thomson's common; gerenuk less so.

Blue wildebeest (brindled gnu) *Connochaetes taurinus*

Blue wildebeest are very gregarious, sometimes forming herds tens of thousands strong, often in association with zebras and other herbivores. Males are territorial, and attempt to herd groups of females. Wildebeest are grazers, and move constantly in search of short green grass and water. Because they prefer to drink daily and can survive only five days without water, wildebeest will migrate large distances to find it. Major predators include lions, hyaenas and wild dogs.

RICHARD I'ANSON

Size: shoulder height 1.5m; mass 250kg. **Distribution:** widely distributed. Most parks in the region have a population. **Status:** extremely common; 1.5 million occur in the Serengeti-Masai Mara complex.

Hartebeest *Alcelaphus buselaphus*

The hartebeest is a red-to-tan coloured, medium-sized antelope characterised by a long, narrow face and short, stout horns present in both sexes. Hartebeest feed exclusively on grass and prefer open plains but are also found in sparsely forested woodlands. They often associate with other herbivores such as zebras and wildebeests.

ANDREW MacCOLL

Size: shoulder height 1.25m; mass 120 to 150kg. **Distribution:** wide ranging. Coke's hartebeest is common in south Kenya and north Tanzania, while Jackson's hartebeest occurs in Uganda. **Status:** common where they occur.

Topi (tsessebe) *Damaliscus lunatus*

Resembling the hartebeest, topis have dark, almost violet patches on the rear thighs, front legs and face. Both sexes have horns. Highly gregarious antelopes, topis live in herds, often with other grazers. Although they can live on dry grasses spurned by other antelope, topis prefer flood plains and moist areas that support lush pasture. They have a characteristic habit of standing on high vantage points such as termite mounds to observe their surroundings.

LUKE HUNTER

Size: shoulder height 1.2m; mass 120 to 150kg. **Distribution:** widespread, occurring in all medium length grasslands in the region. **Status:** common; abundant in the Serengeti ecosystem.

WILDLIFE GUIDE

LUKE HUNTER

Sable antelope *Hippotragus niger*

Sables are often considered the most magnificent of Africa's antelopes. Their colouring is dark-brown-to-black, with a white belly and face markings; the male's coat is a rich glossy black when adult. Both sexes have long sweeping horns, but those of the male are longer and more curved. Sables feed mainly on grass, but foliage accounts for around 10% of their diet. Females and the young live in herds while males are territorial, or form bachelor groups. The sable is a fierce fighter and there are occasional records of males killing lions when attacked. Other predators include leopards, hyaenas and wild dogs.

Size: shoulder height 135cm; mass up to 270kg. **Distribution:** in East Africa, restricted to south-eastern Kenya and Tanzania. **Status:** uncommon; in Kenya, they occur only in Shimba Hills National Reserve. They are more widely distributed in Tanzania.

MATT FLETCHER

Oryx *Oryx gazella*

Adapted for arid zones, the oryx can tolerate areas uninhabitable for most antelopes. Two races occur in the region: the beisa oryx *(O. g. beisa)* of northern Kenya; and the slightly smaller fringe-eared oryx *(O. g callotis)* of southern Kenya and northern Tanzania. The oryx is a solid and powerful animal with long, straight horns, which are present in both sexes. Oryx are principally grazers but also browse on thorny shrubs unpalatable to many species. They can survive for long periods without water. Herds vary from five to 40 individuals.

Size: shoulder height 150cm; mass up to 300kg. **Distribution:** northern Kenya (beisa oryx); southern Kenya and northern Tanzania (fringe-eared oryx). **Status:** relatively common where it occurs, and easy to see. It is, however, often shy, and flees from humans at great distances.

LUKE HUNTER

Kudus Greater kudu *Tragelaphus strepsiceros* (pictured); lesser kudu *Tragelaphus imberbis*

The two kudus in the region are similar, but the greater kudu is by far the more spectacular. It is Africa's second tallest antelope and the males carry massive spiralling horns much sought after by trophy hunters. Both species are light grey in colour with between six and 10 white stripes down the sides and a white chevron between the eyes. Kudus live in small herds of females and their young, periodically joined by the normally solitary males during the breeding season. They eat a variety of browse. Kudus prefer woodland-savanna with fairly dense cover.

Size: greater kudu shoulder height 150cm; lesser kudu shoulder height 105cm. Mass greater kudu up to 310kg; lesser kudu up to 105kg. **Distribution:** greater kudu throughout the region, except in the driest areas. Lesser kudus prefer the arid regions of Tanzania and northern Kenya. **Status:** common.

Eland *Taurotragus oryx*

Africa's largest antelope, the eland is a massive animal. Both sexes have horns about 65cm long which spiral at the base and sweep straight back. The male has a distinctive hairy tuft on the head and stouter horns than the female. Elands prefer savanna scrub, and feed on grass and tree foliage. They usually live in groups of around six to 12, normally comprising several females and one male. Larger aggregations (up to 1000) sometimes form at localised 'flushes' of new grass growth.

DAVID WALL

Size: shoulder height 170cm; mass up to 900kg in males. **Distribution:** patchily distributed, mostly in woodlands. Common in Nairobi National Park and Tsavo National Park (Kenya). **Status:** naturally low density but relatively common in their range and easy to see.

Waterbuck *Kobus ellipsiprymnus*

This very solid antelope has a thick, shaggy, dark brown coat with a distinctive bull's-eye ring around its rump and white markings on the face and throat. Only the males have horns, which reach a length of about 75cm. Feeding primarily on grasses, reeds and rushes, they are usually found close to water and sometimes flee into water to escape predators. Herds are small and consist of cows, calves and one mature bull; while younger bulls live in small groups apart from the herd.

MITCH REARDON

Size: shoulder height 130cm; mass up to 270kg. **Distribution:** wet areas throughout the region. **Status:** common and easy to see.

African buffalo *Syncerus caffer*

The only native wild cow of Africa. Both sexes have distinctive curving horns that meet over the forehead in a massive 'boss', though those of the female are usually smaller. They have a fairly wide habitat tolerance but require areas with abundant grass, water and cover. African buffaloes are gregarious and may form herds numbering thousands. Group composition is fluid and smaller herds often break away, sometimes rejoining later. Although they're generally docile, buffaloes can be very dangerous and should be treated with caution.

RICHARD I'ANSON

Size: shoulder height 1.4m; mass up to 820kg in males. **Distribution:** widespread, but these days large populations only occur in parks. **Status:** common and can be approachable where they are protected.

ANOTHINY BANNISTER/ABPL

Aardvark (antbear) *Orycteropus afer*

Vaguely pig-like (its Afrikaans name translates as 'earth-pig') with a long tubular snout, powerful kangaroo-like tail and large rabbit-like ears, the aardvark is unique and has no close relatives. Protected by thick wrinkled pink-grey skin, aardvarks forage at night by sniffing for termite and ant nests which they rip open with their astonishingly powerful front legs and large spade-like nails. They dig deep, complex burrows for shelter which are also used by many other animals such as warthogs and mongooses. Normally nocturnal, they occasionally spend cold winter mornings basking in the sun before retiring underground.

Size: length 140 to 180cm; mass 40 to 70kg. **Distribution:** widely distributed throughout the region; rare or absent in rainforest. **Status:** uncommon; nocturnal and rarely seen.

DEANNA SWANEY

RODENTS

Porcupine *Hystrix africaeaustralis*

This is by far the largest rodent in Africa, and with its long black and white banded quills cannot be mistaken for any other species. It erects its crest of long coarse hair and its quills when alarmed. Porcupines are mainly nocturnal and shelter in caves, burrows or dense vegetation during the day, emerging at night to forage. They are occasionally seen in daylight hours during winter. Their diet consists mainly of bark, tubers, seeds and a variety of plants and ground-level foliage.

Size: 75 to 100cm; mass 10 to 24kg. **Distribution:** widely distributed throughout the region, favouring savannah-woodland mosaics. **Status:** common; reasonably frequently observed on night safaris.

ANTHONY BANNISTER/ABPL

Springhare *Pedetes capensis*

In spite of its name and large ears, the springhare is not a hare, but a rodent. With is powerful, outsized hind feet and small forelegs, it most resembles a small kangaroo and shares a similar hopping motion. Springhares dig extensive burrows from which they emerge at night to feed on grass and grass roots. Reflections of spotlights from their large, bright eyes often give them away on night safaris. Although swift, everything from jackals to lions prey upon them.

Size: 75 to 85 cm long; mass 2.5 to 3.8kg. **Distribution:** Kenya southwards into mid-Tanzania. Generally restricted to grassland habitats with sandy soils. **Status:** common, but strictly nocturnal.

Organised Safaris

CHOOSING A SAFARI

Many travellers to East Africa use tour companies for assistance with all or some of their travel arrangements. While this often makes things easier and can be the best option if your time is limited, it usually works out to be more expensive than if you arrange things yourself.

One variable which significantly affects the overall tour price is accommodation. Camping safaris will be the least expensive, while those including accommodation in luxury lodges or luxury tented camps will cost much more. Group size is another important variable; the larger your group, the lower will be your per person vehicle and catering costs. In addition, almost all operators charge a supplement for single-occupancy accommodation, ranging from 20 to 50% of the shared-occupancy rate. Prices provided in this chapter are based on the cost per person for shared occupancy.

If you're travelling alone or with just a few others, be aware that budget companies will often combine groups. While this may save you money, you may not know the people who will be on your safari with you. Be sure you still get what you paid for.

Camping Safaris

Camping safaris cater for budget travellers, for the young (or young at heart) and for those who are prepared to put up with a little discomfort. On the other hand, you're in for an authentic adventure in the African bush with nothing between you and the animals at night except a sheet of canvas and the embers of a dying fire.

The amount of baggage you can bring is limited and don't forget to bring a torch (flashlight) and pocket-knife – the company will provide kerosene lanterns for the camp but it's unlikely they'll be left on all night.

For camping safaris, it's common practice to tip drivers, guides and porters if service has been good. For vehicle safaris, a rough guideline is to give an additional day's wage for every five days worked (with a similar

proportion for a shorter trip). Exceptional service deserves a higher than average tip. Wages are low and these people will have made a lot of effort to make your trip memorable, so be generous.

Lodge & Luxury Tented Camp Safaris

Lodge safaris will cost you up to four times what a camping safari costs, sometimes considerably more. Often guests in the lodges are on package deals and happy to keep the African bush at arm's length, but some lodges are well worth staying in as they are designed and conceived to bring the bush close to their clients, yet with all the trimmings of a luxury hotel.

Luxury tented camps are often more expensive than lodges and are for rich people who want to experience what it must have been like in the days of the big-game hunters.

Choosing a Company

The general rule with safari companies is that you get what you pay for. There are of course exceptions where you will get very good service from a budget or mid-range company, and mediocre service from a top end outfit, but as a rule, price is a good gauge. Many of the top end companies have branches or agents abroad and larger companies often have Web sites or email addresses which can assist in arranging all or part of your trip before you arrive.

Before you make a booking, try to find out whether companies actually operate their own safaris with their own vehicles or whether they are just agents for other safari companies; it's often, although not always, cheaper to deal directly with the operating company. But more importantly, if anything goes wrong or the itinerary is changed without your agreement, you have very little comeback with an agent and you'll be pushing it to get a refund.

It's important before finalising your arrangements to verify exactly what will be included in the price, and what costs you

Warning

At Lonely Planet we receive letters extolling the virtues of some companies and lamenting the lack of them in others. Unfortunately, in such a changing industry, the practices of tour operators can vary widely in a relatively short period of time. In particular, tourism in Tanzania and Uganda has developed rapidly in recent years. With this development has come competition among tour operators for clients, and the resultant shortcuts and cost-cutting associated with this.

Companies recommended in this chapter enjoyed a good reputation at the time of research. However, we cannot emphasise enough the need to check on the current situation with all of the listed companies and any others you may hear about.

Another excellent source of advice is other travellers, as those you meet on the road will always be the most reliable means of up to date information.

The following organisations are another source of information or assistance. The Kenyan Association of Tour Operators (KATO; 02-225570, fax 218402), PO Box 4861, Nairobi, is a regulatory body which gives you some recourse in case of conflict with an affiliated company.

Tanzania Tourist Board's Tourist Information Centre (☎ 3842, fax 8628, email ttb-info@yako.habari.co.tz) in Arusha maintains a blacklist of tour operators, as well as a listing of all registered companies.

The government-run Uganda Tourist Board (UTB; ☎ 041-342196, fax 342188, email utb@starcom.co.ug) keeps detailed information on tour operators as does the self-administered Association of Ugandan Tour Operators (AUTO).

If you do have problems with a tour company, do tell us what the problem was and what was done about it (if anything). Also tell us about your good experiences.

must pay separately during your trip. If you are booking with a shoestring company, quoted prices will often not include park fees or – in the case of camping safaris – equipment rental. With top end companies, prices are frequently all-inclusive – often covering accommodation costs before and after your trip, airfield transfers (if applicable) and all meals and park fees.

Safaris in Kenya

ORGANISED VEHICLE SAFARIS
Routes

Whether you take a camping safari or a lodge safari, there's a plethora of options available ranging from two days to 15 days and, in some cases, up to six weeks. Safaris of five to seven days are often best. At least one whole day will be taken up with travel and, after seven, you may well feel like a rest.

The shorter safaris concentrate on Amboseli National Park and the Masai Mara National Reserve, while short Amboseli and the Tsavo national parks safaris are also common. You need a little more time to head north to the other popular parks of Samburu and Buffalo Springs national reserves, while a week gives you time to tag on visits to lakes Nakuru, Bogoria and Baringo to either a Masai Mara, Amboseli or northern parks itinerary.

Most of the safari companies cover the standard routes described in the previous paragraph, but some also specialise in different routes designed to take you off the beaten track. Meru, Mt Elgon, Saiwa Swamp and the Aberdare national parks are all possible.

Some companies also offer safaris to Lake Turkana which range from six to 10 days. The shorter trips take one or other of the standard routes – Nairobi, Nakuru, Nyahururu, Maralal, Baragoi, South Horr and Loyangalani or alternatively Nairobi, Isiolo, Maralal, Baragoi, South Horr and Loyangalani. The longer trips detour from this route and take you to either or both of Samburu and Buffalo Springs and either Meru National Park or Shaba National Reserve and then up to Marsabit National Park before crossing the Chalbi Desert to Lake Turkana. There are also combination safaris which include a vehicle safari to

Lake Turkana and a camel safari in the Matthews Range or the Ndoto Mountains. A full description of the options available can be found under Lake Turkana Safaris in the Other Safaris section later in this chapter.

Costs

There's a lot of competition for the tourist dollar and for camping safaris with no frills you are looking at an all-inclusive price of between US$65 to US$80 per day on a share basis. This price is on a reducing scale the longer the safari. The more popular parks (Amboseli and Masai Mara) are cheaper as competition is strongest. The price per day for safaris more than 11 days and to remote areas tend to rise somewhat because of the extra logistics involved.

The price generally includes transport, two wildlife drives per day (on average), food (three meals per day), park entry and for camping safaris, camping fees, tents and cooking equipment. Sleeping bags are not included in the price and mosquito nets are generally not provided.

On a camping safari, meals will be cooked by camp staff. The tents provided sleep two people as a rule; there are some mobile safaris where the camp is broken and moved for you, while some companies have permanent tented camps on site.

Prices that involve staying in lodges or luxury tented camps are considerably higher. You're looking at a minimum of US$180 per person per night in the lodges and up to US$350 in the luxury tented camps (although prices drop in the low season).

Departure Frequency

Most companies have regular departures (one every two or three days) to the Masai Mara and Amboseli, but with the slump in tourism things are becoming more demand oriented. Most companies will leave for any of the most popular wildlife parks at any time so long as you have a minimum number of people wanting to go – usually four. However, due to the slump in tourism you may have to wait around for a vehicle to fill up before heading off. This is more common in the low season.

It makes a lot of sense to book ahead, especially for the Lake Turkana safaris since they're heavily subscribed in the high season. It's also essential to book ahead for any of the less-visited parks (such as Meru or Shaba) and the more exotic options described in the Other Safaris section.

Choosing a Company in Kenya

During the 1980s and early 1990s tourism in Kenya developed at an amazing rate. However, now that the number of tourists has tumbled, competition among the camping safari companies has become intense and corners have been cut. Some companies enter wildlife parks through side entrances to avoid park fees, while others use glorified matatu drivers as guides, offer sub-standard food and poorly maintained vehicles.

Do some legwork (the Internet is a good start, see the boxed text 'Web Directory' in the Kenya Facts for the Visitor chapter). Spending a morning in Nairobi talking to companies and fellow travellers is worth it.

If you are looking for a real budget safari, you are likely to get a better price by shopping around as negotiation is then possible. If you find shopping around too daunting you might consider going to a travel agent (see the Travel Agencies section in the Nairobi chapter).

Quite a lot of genuine safari companies put out leaflets giving the impression that they do every conceivable safari under the sun. They don't, they simply sell-on to other companies the occasional specialist bookings that comes their way. This doesn't mean they're out to rip you off. If a popular company operates its own safaris, it has a reputation to look after and it will only be on-selling to companies that it trusts.

Another aspect of Kenya's safari business is that there's a good deal of client swapping between companies whose vehicles are full and those which aren't. You can easily find yourself on a certain company's safari which is not the one you booked through, especially if you are booking from abroad. The reputable companies won't do this without informing you but the agents certainly will. Getting swapped onto another company's safari isn't necessarily a bad thing but make sure that the safari you booked and paid for is what you get. See also the boxed text 'Warning' earlier in this chapter.

KATO, the Kenyan Association of Tour Operators (☎ 02-225570, fax 218402), PO Box 48461, Nairobi, may not be the most powerful of regulatory bodies, but the most reputable safari companies are members and going with a KATO member will give you *some* recourse to appeal in case of conflict. Their Web site is a good reference (www.safariweb.com/kato) though links have yet to be added.

Despite the potential pitfalls mentioned here, there are many reliable companies offering safaris that have their own vehicles and an excellent track record. The following companies had a good reputation at the time of writing, but we cannot emphasise enough the need to check on the current situation on the ground – often the best source of information are other travellers. Companies are listed alphabetically and are not in any order of preference, reliability or cost.

This is by no means an exhaustive list, nor is there necessarily any implication that others are unreliable – though some certainly are. For instance, we receive regular letters from readers complaining about an outfit called Come to Africa Safaris. Readers allege that Come to Africa's vehicles are poorly maintained, that they often unex-

pectedly cut their safaris short, and that the company's camp in the Mara is not a place for women on their own. Touts selling their safaris are a constant hassle in Nairobi.

Budget and Mid-Range Companies

Some of the companies listed here also offer safaris using lodge accommodation.

Best Camping Tours (☎ 02-229667, fax 217923) PO Box 40223, Norwich Union House (opposite Hilton Hotel), Mama Ngina Street, Nairobi. This is a popular and reliable company that offers budget camping safaris on all the main routes plus other more unusual options. Average cost is about US$80 per person per day. Recommended by numerous readers.
Web site: www.kenyaweb.com/bestcampingtours

Flight Centres (☎ 02-210024, fax 332407, email fcswwat@form-net.com) PO Box 70181, 2nd floor, Lakhamshi House, Biashara St, Nairobi. As well as running its own overland trips across Africa, Flight Centres acts as an informal broker for camping safaris in Kenya and is a good barometer of quality.

Gametrackers Camping Safaris (☎ 02-338927, fax 330903, email game@africaonline.co.ke) PO Box 62042, 1st floor, Kenya Cinema Plaza, Moi Ave, Nairobi. Also long established and reliable, this company offers a wide range of both camping and lodge safaris. It also offers longer safaris such as a four-week Mountain Gorilla Safari (US$890 plus kitty US$320), a five-week Southern Africa Safari (US$855 plus kitty costing US$224), and a nine-week Africa in Depth Safari (US$1425 plus kitty US$544). It also covers the national parks of Tanzania, Mt Kenya treks, Lake Turkana and a camel safari (see Other Safaris section following for more details of the last two). Departures for the shorter trips vary between once a week and 10 times a month. For the longer trips it's usually once a week and for the four and five-week safaris it's once a month.
Web site: www.gametrackers.com

Kenia Tours & Safaris (☎ 02-223699, fax 217671, email kenia@africaonline.co.ke) PO Box 19730, 4th floor, Jubilee Insurance Bldg, Wabera St, Nairobi. Using minibuses and 4WD vehicles Kenia offers basic camping, comfortable camping and lodge-based safaris to the major wildlife parks, including Aberdare National Park. It has a good reputation within the industry and also offers tailor-made packages elsewhere in Kenya. The basic camping safaris cost between US$55 to US$65 per person per day, though it has been known to swap clients with Savuka. The 12 Days Adventurers Delight

---

A Good Guide

The Kenya Professional Safari Guides Association (☎ 02-609355, fax 609365) has recently been set up with the help of Kenya Wildlife Society. Aimed at everyone from safari drivers/guides to lodge in-house experts, it's hoped that certification will weed out the cowboys and glorified matatu drivers, raise standards and give customers a good idea of the quality they can expect before parting with any money. Guides can apply to take the bronze award after one year's experience, the silver three years later and the gold award (aimed at real specialists) after a further three years. It's another point of reference when choosing a safari company.

package covering many of Kenya's wildlife highlights costs between US$75 and US$80 per day. Comfortable camping costs between US$90 and US$95 per day.
Web site: www.gorp.com/kenia

Ketty Tours (☎ 011-315178, fax 311355, email ketty@africaonline.co.ke) PO Box 82391, Diamond Trust House, Moi Ave, Mombasa. This company specialises partly in short tours of the coastal region (Wasini Island, Shimba Hills, Gedi ruins etc) and into Tsavo. However, it also offers camping safaris to all the usual parks ranging from two to 10 days. Prices range between US$70 and US$100 per person per day for a camping safari and between US$120 and US$180 for a luxury trip.

Planet Safari Adventure (☎ 02-229799, fax 211899, email Planet@africaonline.co.ke) PO Box 79347, 9th floor, Sonalux House, Moi Ave, Nairobi. A new company offering camping tours to the major parks. Its great advantage over other budget operations is the use of Land Cruiser 4WDs, though it also operates minibus tours. If you book with this company you get a couple of nights dormitory accommodation in rooms (with kitchen attached) adjacent to its office. Camping safaris cost US$60 per person per day while luxury, lodge-based safaris cost US$135 per day. It also organises trekking trips to Mt Kenya (US$60 per day).

Safari Camp Services (☎ 02-330130, fax 212160, email safaricamp@form-net.com) PO Box 44801, Barclays Plaza, Loita St, Nairobi. This company was one of the first camping safari companies in Kenya and has been operating successfully for 20 years. You'll hear nothing but praise. Safari Camp Services is concerned with authenticity, good organisation and value for money. Its legendary Turkana Bus is one of the best (see Other Safaris section following) and its Wildlife Bus, which visits Samburu, Lake Nakuru and Masai Mara is just as good (US$636, seven days, departures once a fortnight on Saturday). Safari Camp Services also does camel safaris (see Other Safaris section following) and luxury and tailor-made safaris.
Web site: www.kenyaweb/com/safari/camp/

Safari Seekers (☎ 02-226206, fax 334585) PO Box 9165, 5th floor, Jubilee Insurance Exchange Bldg, Kaunda St, Nairobi; (☎ 220122, fax 228277) PO Box 88275, Ground floor, Diamond Trust Arcade, Moi Ave, Mombasa. This company has been operating for some years and consistently gets good reports. It also has its own permanent camp sites in Amboseli, Samburu and Masai Mara. Safari Seekers offers both camping and lodge safaris (ex-Nairobi and Mombasa) as well as mountain climbing in Kenya. Camping safaris cost US$80 to US$105

per person per day all-inclusive except for sleeping bags (US$10 per trip). Departures are at least once a week or any time assuming a minimum of four people. It also offers flying safaris and a choice of 10 lodge/luxury tented camp safaris which will depart any day assuming there's a minimum of two people at an average cost of US$250 per person per day all-inclusive.
Web site: www.kenyaweb.com/safari-seekers

Special Camping Safaris Ltd (☎/fax 02-350720, email speccampsaf@thorntree.com) PO Box 51512, Nairobi, Whistling Thorns, Isinya/Kiserian Pipeline Rd, near Kiserian. This small company offers trips of varying length around Kenya's national parks. It also has a 10-day Turkana expedition. Departures are once a week for the shorter trips and once a fortnight for the longer ones. As a guide of price, four days in the Masai Mara costs US$350.
Web site: www.africaonline.co.ke/campingsafaris

Top End Companies

If you don't want to camp but prefer to stay in a lodge each night, then check out the following:

Abercrombie & Kent Ltd (☎ 02-334955, fax 215752, email Marketing@abercrombiekent .co.ke) PO Box 59749, 6th & 7th floor, Bruce House, Standard St, Nairobi; (☎ 011-223307, fax 314734) PO Box 90747, 3rd floor, Palli House, Nyerere Ave, Mombasa

Inside Africa Safaris (☎ 02-223304, fax 215448) PO Box 59767, Ground floor, Jubilee Insurance Bldg, Wabera St, Nairobi

Kuldip's Touring Company (☎ 011-223780, fax 313347) PO Box 82662, Moi Ave, Mombasa

Pollman's Tours & Safaris (☎ 02-500386, fax 544639) PO Box 45895, Pollman's House, Mombasa Rd, Nairobi; (☎ 011-312565, fax 314502) PO Box 84198, Taveta Rd, Mombasa

Private Safaris (☎ 02-337115, fax 212238, email psafari@form-net.com) PO Box 45205, 3rd floor, Caxton House, Kenyatta Ave, Nairobi; (☎ 011-316684) Ambalal House, Nkrumah Rd, Mombasa

Southern Cross Safaris (☎ 02-225255, fax 216553, email sxsnbo@africaonline.co.ke) PO Box 56707, New Stanley Hotel, Standard St, Nairobi; (☎ 475074, fax 473533, email scross@swiftmombasa.com) PO Box 99456, The Kanstan Centre (near Nyali Bridge), Malindi Rd, Mombasa
Web site: www.kenya-direct.com/southerncross

Somak Travel (☎ 02-535500, fax 535175, email somak@form-net.com) PO Box 48495, Somak House, Mombasa Rd, Nairobi; (☎ 011-313871, fax 315514) PO Box 90738, Somak House, Nyerere Ave, Mombasa

United Touring Company (☎ 02-331960, fax 331422, email utcn@africaonline.co.ke) PO Box

42196, Fedha Towers, corner of Muindi Mbingu and Kaunda Sts, Nairobi; (☎ 011-316333, fax 314549, email utcmba@africaonline.co.ke) PO Box 84782, Moi Ave, Mombasa

Vacational Tours & Travel Ltd (☎ 02-220256, fax 210530) PO Box 44401, Hilton Hotel, Nairobi

Within this category, Inside Africa Safaris is the cheapest company; Pollman's prices are about intermediate; and UTC, along with Abercrombie & Kent, are the most expensive.

Departure frequency is another factor to take into consideration. UTC and Abercrombie & Kent have daily departures on their shorter safaris and guaranteed weekly departures on their longer trips whereas Inside Africa Safaris, which is a much smaller company, will not guarantee regular departures unless your group is large enough (or willing to pay a higher price for a smaller group).

OTHER SAFARIS

The following lists, which contain recommended safari companies offering Lake Turkana trips, camel safaris or walking and cycling treks in the more remote corners of Kenya, are presented alphabetically and not in any order of preference or price.

Lake Turkana Safaris

There can be few travellers who come to Kenya who do not relish the idea of what amounts to a pilgrimage through the semi-arid wilds of Samburu and up to the legendary Lake Turkana (The Jade Sea). To get an idea of the sort of country you will pass through on this journey, see the East of Lake Turkana section in the Northern Kenya chapter.

East African Anthropological Tours (☎ 02-229650, fax 250787, email Anthrotours@thorntree.com) PO Box 38941, 2nd floor, Embassy House, Harambee Ave, Nairobi. This company tries to give its trips a more in-depth cultural and anthropological basis. The eight-day trip via Lake Baringo costs US$555 and leaves every Thursday. A longer nine-day trip heads through the Chalbi Desert, costs US$640 and leaves every Sunday. Web site: at www.thorntree.net/anthro

Gametrackers Camping Safaris (see details under Budget & Mid-Range Companies). This company offers camel treks, walking safaris and Lake Turkana trips. There are 10-day and eight-day options to Lake Turkana. The first 10-day option takes in Mt Kenya, Samburu, Marsabit, Chalbi Desert, Lake Turkana, Maralal and Lake Baringo. It is the only company which goes to Marsabit National Park. It costs US$550 (plus a local payment of US$95 per person) and departs every Wednesday. The eight-day option takes in Lake Baringo, South Horr, Lake Turkana, the Nabuyotom volcano on the southern shore of the lake, Maralal and Samburu National Reserve. It costs US$415 (plus a local payment of US$54 per person) and there are regular departures every month. Both safaris have the use of a powerboat for a short excursion on Lake Turkana and traditional Turkana huts make up Gametrackers' camp beside the lake 10km south of Loyangalani. There's also a 10-day combined camel safari and vehicle safari which starts and finishes in Nairobi, but the camels are used exclusively for transporting baggage: you have to walk alongside them. The trip takes in the Ndoto Mountains and Lake Turkana (reached by vehicle). There are departures twice a month (on a Monday) except during April, May and November and the cost is about US$600 per person which includes all transport, food and camping equipment (except sleeping bags). A four-day walking safari into the Aberdare National Park is available on request (expect to pay about US$350).
Web site: www.gametrackers

Jade Sea Journeys (☎ 02-218336, fax 224212, email jadesea@africaonline.co.ke) PO Box 39439, 4th floor, Arrow House, Koinange St, Nairobi. This company offers boat safaris on Lake Turkana. All trips leave from Kalekol on the western shore of the lake and then head north up to the mouth of the Omo River before heading south to Sibiloi National Park, Central Island and South Island and Loyangalani. This eight-day safari costs US$1200, with the option to add on a 4WD tour of the Omo Valley in Ethiopia and Chalbi desert in northern Kenya. Cheaper no-frills boat trips to Sibiloi and Central Island national parks may also be possible. For a two-day trip this costs US$540 and US$220 respectively, including a boat (eight people maximum) and crew.

Safari Camp Services (see details under Budget & Mid-Range Companies). This is the group that blazed the trail 20 years ago. There are two options: the Turkana Bus and the Vanishing Africa safari. The Turkana Bus is the economy option and takes in Maralal, Lake Turkana, Wamba and Samburu National Reserve. It takes seven days, costs US$495, and departs Nairobi every alternate Saturday in low season and every Saturday in high season. Camel trekking is possible as part of the Turkana Bus tour (see Lake Turkana Safaris). The Short Camel Train Walk includes

the first and last parts of the Turkana Bus tour with a four-day camel trek in and around the Ndoto Mountains in the middle. This trip lasts nine days, costs US$555 and does not include Lake Turkana. The Full Camel Train Walk lasts 14 days and includes all of the Turkana Bus tour with six days trekking beginning after Lake Turkana. It costs US$868.
Web site: www.kenyaweb.com/safari/camp

Camel Safaris

This is a superb way of getting right off the beaten track and into areas where vehicle safaris don't or cannot go. Camel safaris offer maximum involvement in areas of Kenya which the 20th century has hardly touched, if at all. Most of them take place in the Samburu and Turkana tribal areas between Isiolo and Lake Turkana and, escorted by Samburu *morani* (warriors), you'll have plenty of opportunity to become accustomed to the pace of nomadic life and to mingle with the indigenous people.

You have the choice of riding the camels or walking alongside them (you don't have to be super fit on these safaris) and most travelling is done in the cool parts of the day and a camp site is established around noon.

All the companies provide a full range of camping equipment (two-person tents, as a rule) and ablution facilities, but they vary in what they require you to bring along – no two safaris are exactly alike.

Bobong Camp Site (☎ 035-61413, email kembu@net2000ke.com) PO Box 5, Rumuruti or contact Kembu Camp Site for details. Bobong Camp Site 18km north of Rumuruti offers some of the cheapest camel safaris in Kenya – KSh 750 per day for basic hire of one camel and a handler, no other equipment included. For KSh 1900 they will provide equipment as well. After that you can go in for varying degrees of luxury. Most trips run across the land of Ol Maisor Ranch, but it is up to you where you choose to roam. Real do-it-yourself stuff.
Camel Trek Ltd (☎ 02-891079, fax 891716) PO Box 15076, Nairobi. Camel Trek is a small, reliable company which has camel treks starting from 1½ hours west of Isiolo. Departures are weekly from mid-December to March, and from July to mid-October, and the cost is about US$650 for a five-day safari and US$500 for three nights. Return transport from Nairobi is available for US$55.

Desert Rose Camels (☎ 02-228936, fax 212160, email safaricamp@form-net.com) PO Box 44801, Nairobi. Camel treks cover the Matthews Range, Ndoto Mountains and Oldoinyo Nyiru between Wamba and South Horr. The exact route depends on the season, the number of days you have available and personal interests. You will be accompanied by experienced Samburu camel handlers and guides. All baggage, camping equipment and food and drink are transported by camels. There are, of course, camels for riding, too. Desert Rose prefers a minimum of six days for a safari and for this the rates are about US$250 per person per day though this price is cheaper for large groups. The rates include all food and drink (including wine and beer), camping equipment, and a medical kit. They will also supply camels and handlers for a flat fee of US$70 per person per day, but you'll need to get up to their base camp which is approximately 17km north of Baragoi to start the trip. Book in advance.
Gametrackers Camping Safaris (see details under Budget & Mid-Range Companies)
Safari Camp Services (see details under Budget & Mid-Range Companies)
Yare Safaris Ltd (☎/fax 02-214099, 0368-2295, email travelkenya@iconnect.co.ke) PO Box 63006, 1st floor, Union Towers, Mama Ngina St, Nairobi. Yare offers a seven-day camel safari although the first and last days involve transfer from and to Nairobi. Overnight accommodation the night before and after the trek is in double self-contained *bandas* (thatched huts) at Yare's Maralal club and camp site. The actual trek starts at Barsalinga on the Ewaso Ngiro River and a support vehicle carrying the bulk of your luggage, the tents and supplies plus any personal needs such as beer, spirits and soft drinks will go ahead of the camels to the next camp site. This is not an arduous safari but neither is it luxury. The cost is US$495 per person which includes everything except a sleeping bag, items of a personal nature and alcoholic drinks. Other options are available and there is a great deal of flexibility. For instance, it's possible to hire a camel and guide only, and then set out on your own. This costs US$30 per camel per day and US$15 per person accompanying per day.

Walking & Cycling Safaris

For keen walkers and those who don't want to spend all their time in a safari minibus, there are a number of options.

Bike Treks (☎ 02-446371, fax 442439, email bike treks@form-net.co.ke) PO Box 14237, Nairobi.

This company offers walking and cycling as well as combined walking/cycling safaris. Its shortest safari is a three-day Masai Mara combined trip which costs US$285 and includes transport to and from Nairobi, all camping equipment, food and bicycles but excludes park fees and tips. A more substantial safari is the six-day walking trip (US$720) in the Loita plains and hills of Maasai land west and south of Narok which includes a full-day wildlife viewing drive in the Masai Mara National Reserve. There's a six-day safari for cyclists which has a similar itinerary to the walking trip and costs US$720 including everything except park entry and public camp site fees and tips. A minimum of three people guarantees departure on any safari.

Web site: www.angelfire.com/sk/biketreks

Gametrackers Camping Safaris (see details under Budget & Mid-Range Companies)

Hiking & Cycling Kenya (☎ 02-218336, fax 228107, email jadesea@africaonline.co.ke) PO Box 39439, 4th floor, Arrow House, Koinange St, Nairobi. This company specialises in hiking and cycling safaris involving camping all over Kenya. Its 10-day safari takes you to Lake Turkana in the footsteps of Count Teleki. On the way back to Nairobi, by vehicle, you visit Maralal and Samburu National Reserve.

Samburu Trails Trekking Safaris (☎/fax 0365-32379) PO Box 40, Maralal. Based on Samburu land at Poror, just north of Maralal this company offers two great trekking safaris. The first explores the trails of the legendary hunter AH Newman east of Maralal, while the second drops down the escarpment at World's View and heads to Laiteruk, the so called Mountain of Birds on the edge of the Suguta Valley. These are comfortable safaris with everything provided including tents, camp beds and bedding, safari showers, tables and chairs. All the equipment is transported by donkeys so it's a good idea to keep your personal baggage down to a minimum. The cost is US$160 per person per day. Set aside a minimum of five days (not including travel) for either trek. The company is also prepared to hire donkeys and guides for a rate of US$40 per person per day to those wishing to strike out on their own (see Maralal in the Northern Kenya chapter). Lonely Planet's *Trekking in East Africa* also covers the area in depth.

Sirikwa Safaris (☎/fax 0325-20061) PO Box 332, Kitale. This outfit is run by Jane and Julia Barnley from their farmhouse/guesthouse and camping site about 20km outside Kitale on the Lodwar road. They have considerable knowledge of all the routes and camp sites in the Cherangani Hills and can provide guides (KSh 600 per day) and porters (KSh 300) for extended treks in the area. They can also arrange birdwatching trips into the

Hills (along with a very capable guide) as well as trips to Saiwa Swamp National Park, Marich Pass, Mt Elgon and the Kongelai Escarpment.

Birdwatching

East African Ornithological Safaris (☎ 02-331191, fax 330698, email eaos@africaonline.co.ke) PO Box 48019, 11th floor, Fedha Towers, Standard St, Nairobi. This is a specialist birdwatching safari outfit, based around all the ornithological sites of Kenya. Mt Kenya, Lakes Baringo, Bogoria and Elmenteita, the Tugen Hills and Kerio Valley, Kakamega Forest and the Masai Mara National Reserve are all visited during a two-week trip. First class lodges are used throughout this trip and other itineraries are available and the cost, based on two people sharing, works out at US$3000 per person in the high season and US$2250 in low season. There are departures every second Monday of every month throughout the year. This company was set up by one of the best ornithologists in Kenya.

Sirikwa Safaris (see details under Walking & Cycling Safaris)

Conservation Research

Taita Discovery Centre (☎ 02-331191, fax 330698, email eaos@africaonline.co.ke) PO Box 48019, 11th floor, Fedha Towers, Standard St, Nairobi. An off-shoot from Savannah Camps and Lodges, this is a purpose-built conservation research centre in the 170,000 acres of the Taita/Rukinga Ranches which forms part of a vital corridor for elephants and other animals migrating between the Galana River in Tsavo East south to the foothills of Mt Kilimanjaro. Courses on a huge range of conservation topics are run along with a bush adventure course. Costs range from US$95 per person per night for stays of between one and 30 days down to US$49 for those intending to stay for 91 days or more.

The Wakuluzu Trust, at Colobus Cottage in Diani and the Elsamere Conservation Centre on Lake Naivasha also takes paying volunteers. See The Coast and The Rift Valley chapters for details.

Miscellaneous

Fredlink Co Ltd (☎ 011-230484, email fred link@swiftmombasa.com) PO Box 85976, Shimanzi Road, High Level Area, Mombasa. Fredlink runs motorcycle safaris out of Mombasa. A set route through the Rift Valley and up to Samburu has been worked out, but itineraries are flexible. All tours are supported by a Land Rover and Yamaha TT600cc motorcycles are used. The company also rents 600cc and 350cc motorcycles plus modern 50cc scooters from its

Mombasa base. The hire rates are KSh 2100/2100/1200 respectively and Fredlink will deliver these machines as far north as Mtwapa (24km from Mombasa – KSh 500 extra) and as far south as Diani (KSh 600 extra).

Tropic Air Ltd (☎ 0176-32890, fax 32787, email tropicair@kenyaonline.com) PO Box 161, Nanyuki. This company runs a fishing camp in Mt Kenya National Park overlooking Lake Rutundu north-east of the main peaks. Accommodation consists of two log cabins, with open log fires, en suite bathrooms. Lakes Rutundu and Lake Alice, a two-hour drive to the south are well stocked with rainbow trout, while the Kazita Munyi River flowing through a gorge below the camp is stocked with brown trout. Rods, flies, boats and guides are all available and full-board (US$215 per person) or self-catering (US$150) options are available. Resident rates are much, much cheaper. Return flights from around Mt Kenya are US$225.

White-Water Rafting

Savage Wilderness Safaris Ltd (☎/fax 02-521590, email whitewater@thorntree.org) PO Box 44827, Nairobi. This is the only outfit of its kind in Kenya. Depending on water levels, rafting trips of up to 450km and of three weeks duration can be arranged, though most trips last between one and four days during which you cover up to 80km. One of the most popular short trips (one day's duration) is on the Tana River, north-east of Nairobi though another popular short trip is the three-day adventure on the Athi River, south-east of Nairobi between Tsavo East and West national parks. These trips leave any day of the week subject to a minimum of four passengers and cost US$380 per person with additional days at US$95. The other rafting possibility is along the Ewaso Ngiro River, north-west of Isiolo. This trip takes a minimum of three days. It's a scenic river all the way and there's plenty of wild game to be seen. This trip costs US$420 per person with additional days at US$105. The above prices are inclusive of transport, high quality food, soft drinks, beer, and, where applicable, tents, airbeds and sleeping bags. You are also provided with all necessary equipment – life jackets, helmets etc. National park entry and camping fees are not included but the usual itineraries do not enter parks. The most exciting times to go on these white-water rafts are from late October to mid-January and from early April to late July when water levels are at their highest. The Tana River generally maintains a higher water level longer than the Athi. Be aware that rafting on both rivers is less predictable than say on the Zambezi at Victoria Falls. There have been a number of fatalities in recent years. Web site: www.kilimanjaro.com

Safaris in Tanzania

ORGANISED VEHICLE SAFARIS

There are close to 200 registered tour companies in Tanzania. Almost half of these are based in Arusha, with many in Dar es Salaam and Moshi. Most of the less expensive companies are generalist outfits which simply put together standard packages for the most common sites of interest. Specialist companies are usually more expensive, but will customise your itinerary. The best operators are experts themselves in a particular area or activity, such as trekking, birdwatching, cycling etc.

If you are already in Tanzania and decide to book through a tour operator, especially one you don't know, it's usually best (not to mention cheaper) to just do local bookings with them. For example, don't book your itinerary on Unguja with a tour operator in Moshi, unless you are sure they are reliable. Rather, wait until you get to Unguja to book. That way if something goes wrong, you'll be able to track the company down and attempt to find a resolution – not so easy if they are in a distant city. In general, it's probably best to book treks on Mt Kilimanjaro or Mt Meru, and visits to the northern parks, in Arusha or Moshi, and visits to the Selous Game Reserve, Mikumi National Park, or Mafia Island in Dar es Salaam. Unless you book in Kigoma itself, excursions to Gombe Stream and Mahale Mountains national parks will more than likely be subcontracted to a local agent anyway.

Costs

Companies in this section have been classed into three categories: budget, mid-range and top end:

Budget Safaris For budget companies, expect to pay between US$85 and US$120 per person per day for organised vehicle safaris. These prices will often not be all-inclusive. If camping is involved, you can expect barely adequate equipment; meals will be no-frills and chances are that the vehicle will break down at least once.

Mid-Range Safaris Mid-range companies average between US$120 and US$200 per person per day. Standards at these prices should be higher, including better equipment, better vehicles, and more specialised knowledge. Prices are often all-inclusive, though you should always verify this at the outset.

Top End Safaris Top end companies aim to offer comfortable, luxury tours, generally individually tailored; prices are from US$200 per person per day (often much more than this) and are generally all-inclusive although, again, it's best to confirm this.

Departure Frequency

Most Tanzanian-based companies can organise safaris extremely quickly – you should not have to wait more than two or three days at most, and can often leave the next day.

Choosing a Company in Tanzania

A selection of safari and tour operators have been listed here. For a more complete list check Travel Agencies in the regional Tanzania chapters. There are many other reputable companies which could not be listed in this book due to space limitations, and many companies based abroad in places like London or New York.

When choosing a company, try to talk with others who have used the same operator before finalising your arrangements. Some issues to be aware of are highlighted in the boxed text 'Warning' earlier in this chapter and also under the boxed text 'Warning' in the Arusha section of the Northern Tanzania chapter.

Travel agencies and safari operators in Tanzania include:

Coastal Travels (☎ 051-117959, fax 118647, email coastal@twiga.com) PO Box 3052, Upanga Rd, Dar es Salaam
Easy Travel & Tours (☎ 051-123526, fax 113842, email easytravel@raha.com) Avalon House, Zanaki St, near Sokoine Drive, Dar es Salaam
Gogo Safaris (☎ 051-114719, fax 113619) PO Box 7064, Mkwepu St, near Samora Ave, Dar es Salaam

Hippotours & Safaris (☎ 051-75164, 0811-320849, fax 71610, email hippo@twiga.com) PO Box 13894, off Old Bagamoyo Rd, Mikocheni, Dar es Salaam
Key's Hotel (☎ 055-52250, 51875, fax 50073, email keys@form-net.com) PO Box 933, Moshi. Mid-range; reliable Kilimanjaro packages.
Mauly Tours & Safaris (☎ 055-50730, fax 53330, email mauly@africaonline.co.tz) PO Box 1315, on Mawenzi Rd between the clock tower and the bus station, Moshi. Budget to mid-range; standard Kilimanjaro packages.
Samjoe Tours & Travels (☎ 055-51468, fax 52136) PO Box 1467, ground floor, KNCU Bldg, Moshi. Budget to mid-range; standard Kilimanjaro packages and safaris to Tanzania's northern parks.
Shah Tours (☎ 055-52370, fax 51449, email kilimanjaro@eoltz.com) PO Box 1812, Mawenzi Rd, Moshi. Mid-range to top end; specialises in quality standard and customised packages for Kilimanjaro and Mt Meru and wildlife safaris Web site: www.kilimanjaro_shah.com
Zara Tanzania Adventures (☎ 055-54240, fax 53105, email zara@form-net.com) PO Box 1990, on Rindi Lane behind New Livingstone Hotel, Moshi. Budget to mid-range; standard Kilimanjaro packages.
Adventure Tours & Safaris (☎ 057-7600, fax 8195) PO Box 1014, Goliondoi Rd, Arusha. Mid-range; offers standard treks and safaris.
Bobby Tours & Safaris (☎ 057-3490, fax 8176, email bobbytours@yako.habari.co.tz) PO Box 2169, Goliondoi Rd, Arusha. Mid-range to top end; offers standard treks and northern circuit safaris.
Hoopoe Adventure Tours (☎ 057-7011, fax 8226, email hoopoesafari@cybernet.co.tz) PO Box 2047, India St, Arusha. Top end; a well established operator organising wildlife safaris in all the northern parks, and specialised treks on Mt Kilimanjaro, Mt Meru and in other areas.
Let's Go Travel (☎ 057-7111, fax 4199, email letsgotravel@habari.co.tz) PO Box 12799, at the Adventure Centre on Goliondoi Rd, Arusha. Mid-range to top end; offers standard and customised safaris to the northern parks, and treks on Mt Meru and Mt Kilimanjaro.
Web site: www.eastafricansafari.com
Nature Discovery (☎ 057-4063, fax 8406, email naturediscovery@eoltz.com) PO Box 10574, Sakina, about 5km from the clock tower. Mid-range to top end; focusing on ecologically sound safaris in the northern circuit.
Roy Safaris (☎ 057-2115, fax 8892, email roysafaris@habari.co.tz) PO Box 50, Just off Sokoine

Rd, with a branch office (Safari Destinations) at the YMCA, Arusha. Well established, reliable and efficiently managed tour operator offering mid-range wildlife safaris and Kilimanjaro trekking packages
Web site: www.intafrica.com/roysafaris

Sunny Safaris (☎ 057-7145, fax 8094, email sunny@arusha.com) PO Box 7267, Colonel Middleton Rd north-west of the stadium, Arusha. Budget to mid-range Kilimanjaro and Meru treks; popular with shoestring travellers.

Tropical Trails (☎/fax 057-8299, email mike@ tropicaltrails.com) PO Box 6130, at Masai Camp, Arusha. Mid-range to top end, though will also cater to budget travellers. Specialises in treks and walking safaris on Kilimanjaro, Meru and the Crater Highlands.
Web site: www.tropicaltrails.com

OTHER SAFARIS

There are a variety of options for those who do not want to tour the country in an organised vehicle tour. An increasing number of mid-range and top end companies are offering **walking safaris**, both within some of the national parks and wildlife reserves, as well as in bordering areas.

North of Arusha, you can go on **camel safaris**, organised within the framework of the SNV (Netherlands Development Organisation) Cultural Tourism Program. See Around Arusha in the Northern Tanzania section for further details. There are also SNV-sponsored Cultural Tourism Program tours encompassing half-day to multi-day hikes and walks in numerous areas in northern and north-eastern Tanzania. See the Northern Tanzania chapter for further information, or contact either SNV or the Tanzania Tourist Board's Tourist Information Centre based in Arusha.

A good contact for those interested in organised **cycling trips** is Bicycle Africa Tours. For more information take a look at the Web site: www.ibike.org/bikeafrica

Safaris in Uganda

ORGANISED VEHICLE SAFARIS

As tourism in Uganda slowly gains momentum, so do the number of safari operators and the options open to punters.

Currently there are quite a few reliable companies that offer safaris to the national parks and other places of interest, including trips to the gorillas of Bwindi and Mgahinga in the extreme south-west of the country. National parks that are covered by these companies include Murchison Falls, Queen Elizabeth, Kibale Forest, Bwindi, Mgahinga, Lake Mburo, Kidepo Valley and Semliki Valley (hot springs, Pygmies).

Other places of interest that are covered include Lake Bunyonyi (Kabale) and the Source of the Nile (Jinja).

Costs

Unlike Kenya, where budget travellers are well catered for with no-frills camping safaris, Ugandan companies rely heavily on lodge and hotel accommodation while on safari, so they're proportionally much more expensive. Even where camping is involved, it's usually the luxury tented camp variety and thus no cheaper.

Since none of the Ugandan companies offer genuine budget camping safaris such as those in Kenya, it's worth considering going with a Kenyan company that covers Uganda. Check out the Safaris in Kenya section earlier in this chapter.

Costs vary from one company to another, but are consistently high, and depend considerably on how many people are in the group – the more there are of you, the less you pay individually. As an example, the per person cost of a three-day safari to Murchison Falls National Park can vary from US$990 (one person) to US$435 (four people).

In general, if you budget for US$150 to US$250 per day you won't be too far off the mark. This should include all transport, three meals a day, accommodation (including all camping equipment where appropriate) and park entry fees (though some companies exclude park entry fees).

Departure Frequency

Most companies have weekly departures (some more frequent) for all the safaris they offer. Even where departures are not so frequent, there are usually departures two or three times per month. As in Kenya, any safari company will lay on a trip almost immediately if you have a group of at least three (sometimes four) people.

Choosing a Company

Tourism in Uganda has developed rapidly in recent years. With this development has come increasing competition among safari companies for clients and the resultant shortcuts and cost cutting associated with this. See the boxed text 'Warning' earlier in this chapter.

The government-run Uganda Tourist Board (UTB; ☎ 041-342196, fax 342188, email utb@starcom.co.ug) keeps detailed information on tour operators as does the self-administered Association of Ugandan Tour Operators (AUTO). Another excellent source of advice is other travellers, as those you meet on the road will always be the most reliable means of up to date information.

Following (in alphabetical order) is a selected list of companies of good repute that could be recommended at the time of writing. However, we can not emphasise enough the need to check on the current situation with all these companies and any others that you hear about. Remember to ask as many questions as possible to find out exactly what you are going to get for your money.

Most of the companies listed below offer the same sort of itineraries to Uganda's national parks, the main difference being where you stay. However, one thing that is important to note is that there is a difference between a tour company and a safari company, as safari companies specialise in wildlife viewing.

African Pearl Safaris (☎ 041-233566, fax 235770) Lower Ground floor, Embassy House, Kampala. African Pearl offers a variety of short trips to national parks around the country, including Bwindi where it operates the comfortable Buhoma Homestead.

Afri Tours & Travel (☎ 041-233596, fax 344855, email afritour@swiftuganda.com) 30 Lumumba Ave, Kampala. Afri Tours has a limited range of short safaris, specialising in Murchison Falls, as it runs the Sambiya River Lodge in the park. It also operates as a reliable travel agent.

Belex Tours (☎ 041-244105, fax 234180) Sheraton Hotel, Kampala. Belex offers a selection of short tours, but is not really specialised enough to consider for a safari as half its tour program covers towns.

Blacklines Tours (☎ 041-255520) PO Box 6968, 2 Colville St, Kampala. Blacklines offers tours covering most of Uganda's national parks, including a 12-day highlights tour.

Lake Kitandara Tours & Travels (☎ 041-348243, fax 345580, email kitanda@infocom.co.ug) Blacklines House, Plot 2 Colville St, Kampala. Lake Kitandara has an extensive tour program throughout Uganda including birdwatching trips. They also offer cheaper camping safaris for US$80 per person per day, including transport, food and park fees, but not park activities.

Nile Safaris Ltd (☎ 041-244331, fax 245967) PO Box 12135, Farmers House, Parliament Ave, Kampala. Nile Safaris offers a range of short visits to Uganda's most popular national parks, and can arrange visits to places further afield such as Kidepo Valley.

Semliki Safaris (☎/fax 041-259700, email gwg@swiftuganda.com) Acacia Avenue, Kololo, Kampala. Semliki Safaris is a specialist safari operator offering luxury trips to Murchison Falls and Kidepo Valley in the remote northeast. It also operates a luxury lodge in the remote Semliki Valley Game Reserve.

Volcanoes (☎ 041-346464, fax 341718, email volcano@swiftuganda.com) 27 Lumumba Avenue, Nakasero Hill, Kampala. Volcanoes has an extensive brochure offering trips that cover every aspect of Uganda, from a few days to a few weeks. It also operates small camps at Mgahinga and Sipi Falls, and a guesthouse in Kisoro.

OTHER SAFARIS

The possibilities of a do-it-yourself safari without your own transport are limited in Uganda, as there's so little traffic into the national parks. That doesn't mean you can't do it – travellers do – but it involves a fair amount of hitching and waiting around for a ride, or the hire of a vehicle and driver.

Climbing the Ruwenzoris when the park reopens is much easier in this respect, as it's all very well organised and caters to walkers. All you have to do is get yourself to Kasese and contact the Ruwenzori Mountaineering Services office there. They'll get you fixed up and arrange everything. See the Ruwenzori National Park section in the South-Western Uganda chapter for details.

Kenya

In past centuries, the main visitors to Kenya were the Arab traders who plied their *dhows* along the eastern coast of Africa. These days it's tourists and adventurers who come to Kenya in large numbers – little wonder as it has an amazing variety of attractions.

Kenya is the heart of safari country and a trip through a few of Kenya's spectacular parks and reserves is a memorable experience. Breathtaking sights include millions of wildebeest on their annual migration and equally large numbers of pink flamingo massing on the shores of the Rift Valley soda lakes. For sheer majesty it's hard to beat the sight of a herd of elephant crossing the plains with Africa's most famous mountain, the evocative snow-capped Kilimanjaro, rising in the background.

If relaxation is on your mind then head for the coast. Mombasa is a town with a

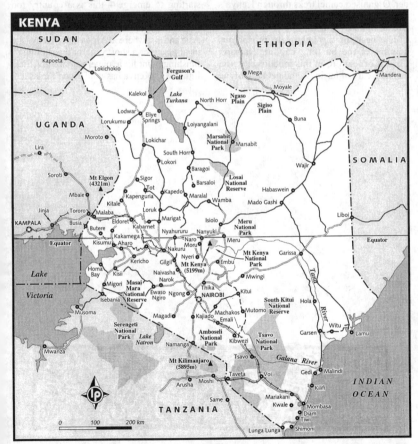

KENYA

history, and from here any of the superb picture-postcard beaches are easily accessible. But without doubt the highlight of the coast is the island of Lamu, where the Arab influence is evident and the pace of life definitely a few steps behind the rest of the country – the perfect place to unwind for a week, or two.

Those seeking more energetic pursuits will find no shortage of challenges – Kenya has some excellent mountains to climb, especially the popular Mt Kenya with its unusual alpine flora, and the much less visited Mt Elgon in the west on the Ugandan border. Organised camel treks through Kenya's semi-desert north also attract a steady stream of hardy souls.

The heart of this relatively prosperous country is the bustling capital, Nairobi. Love it or loath it, in this modern city you can take care of business and get hold of the goods you may have expected only to see in the shops of Europe or North America – quite a shock if you've come from Uganda.

Kenya has had its fair share of problems in recent years. The political violence surrounding the general election in 1997, the disastrous El Niño rains that destroyed infrastructure and caused disease have all been major setbacks. These factors, coupled with a number of unfortunate attacks on tourists and the tragic bombing of the US embassy led to a massive drop in tourists, which resulted in a marked downturn in the economy. However, signs of recovery are starting to emerge – this is a country too good to ignore for long.

Excellent air connections with Europe, Asia and elsewhere in Africa make Kenya the ideal place for a short visit, or the starting or finishing point for a longer sojourn in Africa. Either way Kenya has it all – don't miss it.

Facts about Kenya

HISTORY
The history (and pre-history) of Kenya up until independence is covered in the Facts about East Africa chapter.

Mau Mau Rebellion
After WWII Kenyans increasingly began to resent the shackles placed on them by their colonial masters. Kenyan troops who had fought for Britain returned with new aspirations for themselves and their country and the Kenya African Union (KAU), with Jomo Kenyatta at its head, began to argue strongly for change.

As the demands of the KAU became more and more strident and the colonial authorities less willing to make concessions, oath-taking ceremonies where participants of a secret society pledged to kill Europeans and African collaborators began to spread among various tribes like the Kikuyu, Maasai and Luo. The Mau Mau was one such secret political society. Formed in 1952, it consisted mainly of Kikuyu tribespeople, and its aim was to drive white settlers out of Kenya.

By the time the rebellion came to an end in 1956 with the defeat of the Mau Mau, the death toll stood at more than 13,500 Africans – Mau Mau guerrillas, civilians and troops – and just over 100 Europeans, 37 of whom were settlers. In the process, an additional 20,000 Kikuyu had been thrown into detention camps where many died. The end of the Mau Mau rebellion marked the beginning of the process of change that would bring independence in December 1963.

Independence
The two parties, Kenyan African National Union (KANU) and Kenya African Democratic Union (KADU), formed a coalition government in 1962, but after the May 1963 elections, KANU and Kenyatta came to power. Independence came on 12 December 1963 with Kenyatta as the first presi-

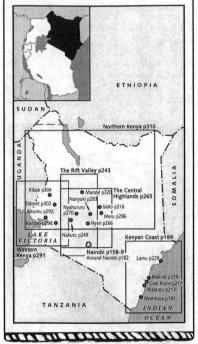

KENYA AT A GLANCE
Area: 583,000 sq km
Population: 30 million
Population Growth Rate: 3.3%
Capital: Nairobi
Head of State: President Daniel Arap Moi
Official Languages: English & Swahili
Currency: Kenyan shilling (KSh)
When to Go: January & February

dent. He ruled Kenya until his death in 1978. Under Kenyatta's presidency, Kenya developed into one of Africa's most stable and prosperous nations. By the time he died, there were enough Kenyans with a stake in their country's continued progress to ensure a relatively smooth succession to the presidency – violence and instability would have benefited few people. Kenyatta's main failings were that he was excessively biased in favour of his own tribe and that he often regarded honest criticism as tantamount to treason. Opponents of his regime who became too vocal for comfort frequently 'disappeared'.

Control of the government and large sectors of the economy still remain in the hands of the Kikuyu, to the social and financial detriment of other ethnic groups. Corruption in high places remains a problem and once prompted JM Kariuki, a former Mau Mau fighter and later an assistant minister in the government, to remark that Kenya had become a nation of '10 millionaires and 10 million beggars'.

In 1964, Kenya became a one-party state following the voluntary dissolution of the opposition KADU party. However, when Oginga Odinga, a Luo, was purged from the KANU hierarchy in 1966, due to allegations that he was plotting against the government, he formed his own opposition party, the Kenya People's Union. The party was later banned and Odinga was frequently imprisoned.

Tom Mboya, an intelligent young Luo who was widely regarded as future presidential material, was murdered by a Kikuyu gunman in 1969. JM Kariuki, a very popular Kikuyu who spoke out stridently about the new black elite and their corrupt practices, met a similar fate: he was assassinated in 1975. Other politicians who opposed Kenyatta – however mildly – found themselves arrested and held for long periods, often without trial.

The 1980s

Kenyatta was succeeded by his vice president, Daniel Arap Moi. A member of the Tugen tribe, Moi was regarded by Kikuyu power brokers as a suitable front man for their interests. He lacked the charisma and cult following of Kenyatta, and was even less willing to tolerate criticism of his regime. The early years of his regime were marked by the arrest of dissidents, the disbanding of tribal societies and the closure of universities. There were allegations of conspiracies to overthrow the government, the details of which were often so labyrinthine that they could have come straight out of a spy novel. Whether these conspiracies were real or just a convenient facade to justify Moi's consolidation of power is hard to tell, since names and details were rarely released.

What certainly was real was the attempted coup by the Kenyan air force in August 1982. It was put down by forces loyal to the government, but at least 120 people died and there was widespread looting. Twelve ringleaders were subsequently sentenced to death and 900 others received jail sentences. The entire Kenyan air force was disbanded and replaced by a new unit.

After winning the 'election' in 1988, Moi expanded his cabinet to 33 ministers – many on the basis of political patronage. As a result, the government's (and therefore Moi's) position seemed totally secure. With the fall of a couple of outspoken politicians

SARAH JOLLY

Jomo Kenyatta ruled Kenya from 1963 until his death in 1978.

KENYA

in the 1987 elections (amid allegations of vote rigging) it seemed unlikely that parliamentary opposition to Moi on major issues in the immediate future would be anything more than a whisper. Changes to the constitution were rushed through parliament unopposed in late 1987, giving Moi increased presidential powers, including the right to dismiss senior judges and public servants without redress.

From this point on there ceased to be any effective political opposition within the parliamentary system and the party strengthened its hold by augmenting the ranks of the KANU youth wing, which pretty much served as pro-government vigilantes. They were frequently unleashed to disrupt demonstrations, harass opposition figures and maintain a climate of intimidation. Many opposition political leaders were detained without trial during this period, including Kenneth Matiba who had two strokes while in prison.

But times were changing. Multiparty politics was sweeping Africa and Kenya was not to escape.

The 1990s

With the collapse of communism in Eastern Europe and the break up of the Soviet Union, the west's attention was abruptly refocused. It was no longer necessary to prop up corrupt African regimes in the name of containing communism.

The Kenyan government quickly found itself under intense pressure from western donor countries to introduce a multiparty system and to name a date for elections if it wanted aid to be maintained. Though it continued to act evasively, the suspension of aid forced the government to give in.

Meanwhile, KANU was doing its best to silence any credible contenders for the Statehouse other than the present incumbent. In 1990 the erudite former minister for foreign affairs, Dr Robert Ouko, was murdered shortly after returning from the USA, and the inquiry into his death has dragged on inconclusively ever since (witnesses and evidence have had an alarming habit of disappearing over the years).

By 1991 everyone was freely talking politics and there emerged a clear consensus that Forum for the Restoration of Democracy (FORD) would sweep to victory in any election, assuming that the elections were reasonably free and fair.

In the meantime, Moi, according to the IMF/World Bank, authorised the printing of KSh 9 billion in bank notes (more than US$250 million), unsupported by foreign currency or gold reserves. He used these to line the pockets of his supporters and blatantly buy votes (KSh 500 a throw) for the ruling party (KANU). Moi knew that full stomachs would buy votes even if the economy collapsed shortly after the elections – which it virtually did.

Moi would certainly have lost if the opposition, namely Oginga Odinga, Kenneth Matiba and Mwai Kibaki could decide which one of them would be the opposition presidential candidate. Instead egos got in the way and the opposition was split into three: FORD-Kenya (Oginga Odinga), FORD-Asili (Kenneth Matiba) and the Democratic Party or DP (Mwai Kibaki). Moi strolled home to win the election in December 1992.

The lead up to the 1997 election was highly fractious which culminated in the infamous Saba Saba opposition rally in Nairobi on 7 July that eventually turned into a riot. Television pictures of opposition MPs and church leaders being badly beaten by police in All Saint's Cathedral stunned the entire nation. To cool the political temperature KANU and the opposition entered negotiations on constitutional reform. Some limited measures were in place in time for the election and it was agreed that a comprehensive constitutional review, in which all stakeholders and political parties could have their say, would take place soon after the election.

Despite this small collective victory the opposition was again unable to unite behind a single candidate and remained divided along tribal lines. Once again Moi had the presidential election in the bag well before polling day, strolling home with 40% of the vote.

When the dust settled KANU had 113 seats and the combined opposition 109. The scene was set for a highly confrontational parliament, but in a smooth move KANU immediately engaged in an era of cooperation with the two biggest opposition parties, the Democratic Party (Kikuyu, 39 seats) and the National Democratic Party (NDP) (Luo, 21 seats).

After much publicity (much of it in the western press) Safina, a party that aimed to unite the opposition formed by Dr Richard Leaky, turned out to be a nonevent. Without countrywide grassroots support it managed to pick up only three parliamentary seats. Leakey was given back his old job at the Kenya Wildlife Service (KWS) (thus removing him from politics) where his tough style plugged some of the holes in the bucket, balanced the budget and got World Bank funding.

The 1997 election was an organisational shambles more than anything else, though the violence on the coast before the elections was certainly instigated by local KANU politicians. They feared that anti-KANU Kikuyu and Luo people (who'd moved to the area for work) would swing the coastal elections away from them. Already resentful local people attacked Kikuyu and Luo businesses and homes. Hundreds died and the coast was ethnically cleansed (temporarily) of the Kikuyu and Luo people in time for polling day. To his credit Moi did move to stamp out this violence, but he did so slowly and the damage was already done. As soon as the media coverage hit TV screens in Europe and North America tour companies cancelled bookings en mass. Around 60,000 people lost their jobs and Kenya's economy was seriously weakened.

Bad weather added to the country's problems: following a harsh drought the country was battered by torrential El Niño rains between March 1997 and June 1998. These caused widespread flooding and destroyed infrastructure. Mombasa and the Rift Valley were practically cut off from the rest of the country and the extremely wet conditions caused Rift Valley fever, cholera and malaria epidemics.

Thanks to the influx of weapons from conflicts in Somalia and southern Sudan there is a growing feeling of insecurity, especially in the north of the country, where traditional tribal conflicts are now settled with AK-47s. But the most dramatic act of violence to take place in the country in living memory had nothing to do with Kenya at all. In August 1998 a terrorist organisation linked to Saudi Arabian terrorist Osama bin Laden bombed the US embassy, which stood in the very heart of Nairobi. The embassy was destroyed and more than 200 people (mostly Kenyans) were killed and hundreds more injured. On the same day the US embassy in Dar es Salaam was also hit. It's no surprise that there has been a drop in tourism of around 50% since 1996.

Into the next Millennium

To many the sight of KANU and opposition figures such as Ralia Odinga of the NDP, once sworn enemies, cosying up to each other is frankly bizarre. Some maintain that this is one big fat sell-out by the opposition, who have traded principle for power, and in part it may be (the jury is still out). However, the situation is probably more subtle. Politically Kenya is divided almost totally along tribal lines. By restraining the bully-boy tactics and starting cooperative politics not only has KANU taken the sting out of the opposition but importantly, has made considerable concessions to two of the biggest and most successful tribal groups in the country. Both the Luo (12% of the population) and the Kikuyu people (21% of the population) never vote for KANU and have long complained of being marginalised.

The big test will be the long-awaited constitutional review. By appearing to accept reform in 1997 Moi outflanked his opponents and carried a huge political advantage into the elections. However, in May 1999 he announced that the whole constitutional review should be given back to parliament (which he controls) to sort out. Suddenly the future of reform doesn't look so rosy.

The constitutional review is a major factor in the most important political decision that Kenya faces in the next couple of years. Who will be the next president? The current constitution states that Moi must step down in 2002, but there are no obvious candidates to replace him, at least none willing to show their hand. If the old man dies in office you'll need a super-slow motion video to watch all of the ensuing fast political footwork.

However, there are some encouraging signs. At the end of July 1999 Dr Richard Leakey was appointed as secretary to the cabinet, head of the civil service and governor of the Central Bank by Moi (who'd once described Leakey as the anti-Christ and as an 'atheistic colonial'). Several prominent sackings were announced on the same day and several young, capable Kenyan technocrats were appointed to very senior positions in government and the civil service. Leakey then promptly sacked the head of the Kenya Tourism Board for corruption and incompetence, then began to prise out corrupt characters in government and the judiciary. Leakey ordered investigations into all the land deals of the past five years in response to a dramatic rise in the dubious acquisition of public land by those with political influence. All sales of public land were halted and some sales were revoked.

Just how long Leakey survives (both politically and physically) remains to be seen. There's a huge backlog of corruption and embezzlement cases to work through and the most prominent of these cases, the Goldenberg Scandal (which alone amounts to almost KSh 20 billion) involves the vice president Professor George Saitoti.

With high population growth the strain on health and educational facilities is already showing, and the economy is in sharp decline. Hundreds of thousands of people are unable to find work, infrastructure is crumbling, corruption is endemic and there's a failure of the rule of law. Foreign aid organisations (governmental and nongovernmental) are so fed up with the government that they are redirecting aid money elsewhere. This is a recipe for increased social turmoil and political instability.

Many believe that patronage politics, which for so long has built corruption into the system, must be confronted and contained. There are bright, young politicians who know the system needs to be totally changed, but it remains to be seen if the old guard will let it happen.

GEOGRAPHY

Kenya straddles the equator and covers 583,000 sq km, which includes around 13,600 sq km of inland water in the form of part of Lake Victoria. It is bordered to the north by the arid bushlands and deserts of Ethiopia and Sudan, to the east by Somalia and the Indian Ocean, to the west by Uganda and Lake Victoria and to the south by Tanzania. The main rivers in Kenya are the Athi/Galana and the Tana.

CLIMATE

Because of Kenya's diverse geography, temperature, rainfall and humidity vary widely, but there are effectively four zones.

The undulating plateau of western Kenya is generally hot and fairly humid with rainfall spread throughout the year, which falls mostly in the evenings. The greatest rainfall is usually during April when a maximum of 200mm may be recorded, while the lowest falls are in January with an average of 40mm. Temperatures range from a minimum of 14 or 18°C to a maximum of 30 to 34°C.

The central highlands and Rift Valley enjoy perhaps the most agreeable climate in the country, though there's quite a variation between the hot and dry floor of the central Rift Valley and the snow-covered peaks of Mt Kenya. Rainfall varies from a minimum of 20mm in July to 200mm in April and falls essentially in two seasons: March to May (the 'long rains') and October to December (the 'short rains'). The Aberdare Range and Mt Kenya are the country's main water catchment areas, and falls of up to 3000mm per year are often recorded. Average temperatures vary from a minimum of 10 or 14°C to a maximum of 22 to 26°C.

The vast semi-arid bushlands, deserts and lava flows of northern and eastern Kenya

KENYA

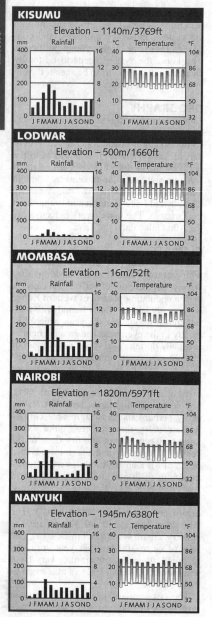

are where the most extreme variations in temperature are to be found, ranging from highs of up to 40°C during the day in the deserts, dropping down to 20°C or less at night. Rainfall in this area is sparse and when it does fall it's as violent storms. July is generally the driest month and November the wettest. The average annual rainfall varies between 250 and 500mm.

The fourth climatic zone is the coastal belt, which is hot and humid all year round, though it's tempered by coastal sea breezes. Rainfall ranges from a minimum of 20mm in February to a maximum of 300mm in May. The annual average rainfall is anywhere between 1000 and 1250mm. Average temperatures vary little throughout the year, ranging from a minimum of 22°C to a maximum of 30°C.

ECOLOGY & ENVIRONMENT
Wildlife Conservation

After the return of Dr Richard Leakey to the Kenya Wildlife Service (KWS) more funds were raised from overseas and a course of consolidation was set. There is now discussion of abandoning the more remote parks to concentrate resources on the parks that actually receive visitors. Privately officials admit that some lesser-known and isolated species may be lost, but realise that given the money available hard choices need to be made.

At the same time the organisation strongly encourages local community conservation projects.

It has been claimed that more than 75% of Kenya's wildlife lies outside the national parks and reserves and it is often the private game reserves that have the resources to work intensively on specific conservation issues. It's no accident that some of the largest concentrations of rhino are to be found within these areas – Lewa Downs is the prime example. Many private conservation initiatives take place in Laikipia, a large slab of ranch land north-west of Mt Kenya. The Laikipia Wildlife Forum (☎ 0176-22156, email nicky@swiftkenya.com) can provide more information on conservation projects and accommodation in the area.

The Green Belt Movement

On Earth Day in 1977 Professor Wangari Maathai founded the Green Belt Movement by planting seven trees in her backyard. Since then, 15 million trees have been planted in Kenya and the movement has expanded to over 30 African countries.

At its core the movement remains a grass roots organisation that encourages individuals to protect their own environment and helps rural communities by educating women about the link between soil erosion, undernourishment and poor health. Farmers (70% of whom are women) are encouraged to plant 'green belts' of trees to prevent erosion and to set up tree nurseries. Seedlings are distributed free to groups and individuals wanting to improve their environment.

It's estimated that half of Africa's forests have been felled this century and Professor Maathai believes that only 2.9% of Kenya's original forest still exists. Since the movement started Maathai has become a major force in Kenyan conversation; through her work with the UN and other NGOs and her high profile abroad she has been able to influence the government to some degree. It's probably not a coincidence that since 1977 the Kenyan government has increased spending on tree planting by 2000%.

In December 1984 Maathai received international recognition for her work and was awarded Sweden's Right Livelihood Award (the alternative Nobel Prize) and spoke at Earth Summits in 1992 and 1998, as well as at the Fourth World Congress on Women in Beijing in 1995. Unfortunately not everyone appreciates her work and she has been beaten up and jailed for her environmental activism.

NATIONAL PARKS & RESERVES

Kenya's national parks and reserves rate among the best in Africa. The tremendous variety of birds and animals is the main attraction, and the more popular parks such as Masai Mara National Reserve and Amboseli National Park receive huge numbers of visitors – from budget campers to hundreds-of-dollars-a-day Hilton hoppers. On a game drive in the peak season (January and February), you can observe at close quarters the daily habits of the prolific Nissan Urvan. Smaller parks, such as Saiwa Swamp National Park, near Kitale in the country's western highlands, see a handful of visitors a day at any time of year.

In addition to protecting wildlife, some parks have been created to preserve the landscape and these can be extremely exciting and rewarding places to visit: Mt Kenya, Mt Elgon, Hell's Gate, Mt Longonot and the Kakamega Forest are all worth investigating.

The marine national parks of Malindi and Watamu off the central coast offer excellent diving possibilities. Shimoni and Wasini islands in the extreme south are even better, but are much less accessible and developed.

What makes Kenyan parks such a drawcard for the budget traveller is that the competition among safari companies for the

Park Entry Prices

category	parks	nonresident (US$) children/adults	resident (KSh) children/adults
A	Aberdares, Amboseli, Lake Nakuru	10/27	50/250
B	Tsavo East & West	8/23	50/200
C	Nairobi, Shimba Hills, Meru	5/20	50/150
D	All other parks	5/15	50/100
Others	Mountaineering	5/10	50/100

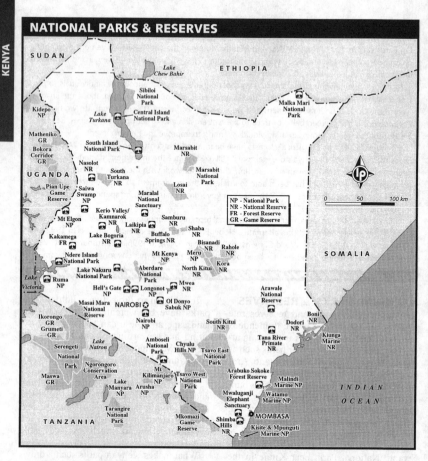

NATIONAL PARKS & RESERVES

NP - National Park
NR - National Reserve
FR - Forest Reserve
GR - Game Reserve

traveller's dollar is so fierce that a safari of at least a few days is within the reach of the vast majority of travellers. For those at the other end of the scale the competition is equally brisk and there are lodges and tented camps within the major parks that have superb facilities and are a real experience – if you can afford them.

Information

Entry Fees Entry fees to national parks are controlled by KWS. National reserves, such as Masai Mara, are administered by the local council, and within these areas local people are allowed to graze their animals, while this is totally prohibited in the national parks.

KWS has set four different price levels with the aim of encouraging visitation to less popular parks and easing pressure on the major parks. The fees cover visitors for a 24 hour period.

The entry fee to Masai Mara National Reserve is the same as for the Category A parks.

Books & Maps If you are driving your own vehicle it's a good idea to equip yourself with maps of the parks before you set

Animal Spotting

When you visit Kenya's parks and reserves, you'll be spending a lot of time craning your neck and keeping a watchful eye out for the animals and birds you've come so far to see. There are a few telltale signs to note, as well as a few things you can do, to maximise your chances of success. Most of them are just common sense, but it's amazing the number of people who go belting around noisily expecting everything to come to them:

• The best time to see game is between 6.30 and 9.30 am and then from 3.30 to 6.30 pm. Make sure your safari company takes you out during these times. Game drives in the middle of the day are largely pointless, though there are signs that in the popular parks (such as Amboseli and Masai Mara), animals are actually changing their normal hunting habits to fit in with the tourists. When the tourists head back to the lodges for lunch the carnivores go out hunting – in peace.

• Drive slowly and, wherever possible, quietly. Keep your eyes not only on the ground ahead but also out the sides of the car and in the branches above.

• Vultures circling are not necessarily an indication of a kill below, but if they are gathering in trees and seem to be waiting you can reasonably assume they are waiting their turn for a go at the carcass.

• In wooded country, agitated and noisy monkeys or baboons are often a sign that there's a big cat (probably a leopard) around.

out. The best maps are published by the Survey of Kenya, but are getting rarer and rarer.

As you'll see in the bookshops of Nairobi hundreds of glossy coffee-table tomes have been produced about almost all the national parks in Kenya. KWS sponsors and sells some more factual books and a number of maps from its shop at the main entrance to Nairobi National Park.

Accommodation

Camping out in the bush is the authentic African safari experience. There's nothing quite like having just a sheet of canvas between you and what you would normally see on the residents' side of a zoo cage, but you'll feel pretty close to the action staying in KWS *bandas*. These simple wooden or stone huts vary in quality, but in the Shimba Hills, Meru, Mt Elgon and Aberdares national parks you'll find some real gems. Unless otherwise stated you won't need a reservation (unless it's a holiday weekend), just book and pay at the gate (US$10 per person).

There are also 'special camp sites' in many national parks. They cost a little extra and have few if any facilities, but exclusive use is guaranteed. They're often in wonderful locations and worth considering for large groups.

There are some beautifully conceived and constructed game lodges and if you have the money, it's worth spending a night or two in one of them. The smaller lodges tend to be the most sensitively designed and you'll still get a real feeling of being in the bush. Just as the practice of baiting leopards and crocodiles is falling out of favour, so lodges and tented camps are trying to become more eco-friendly and in tune with the people and wildlife close by.

GOVERNMENT & POLITICS

Kenya is a multiparty state, with the KANU being the ruling party. The major opposition parties (in order of numbers of seats held) are the NDP, the DP and FORD-Kenya. The government consists of the president, who holds executive power, and a single legislative assembly that consists of 210 members, the attorney general, the speaker, and 12 members who are nominated by the major parties in parliament in proportion to the number of seats won. At the moment the president can only serve two terms in office. There's a very high degree of political patronage. For the political history of Kenya see the History section earlier in this chapter.

Until 1987 the judiciary was independent of government pressure and free to interpret both the constitution and the laws passed by the legislative assembly. In that year, however, parliament rushed through a bill giving the president the right to dismiss judges without recourse to a tribunal, thus effectively silencing them as a source of opposition. This unpopular measure has yet to be repealed.

As far as the independence and freedom of action of government ministers is concerned, it would be fair to say that it's very limited. Indeed, it would not be inappropriate to slightly misquote Louis XIV's classic statement: *'L'état? C'est Moi!'* (the state? It's me!).

ECONOMY

The cornerstone of Kenya's capitalist economy is agriculture, which employs around 80% of the population, contributes some 29% of the GDP and accounts for more than 50% of the country's export earnings. The main cash crops are coffee, tea, cotton, sisal, pyrethrum and tobacco. The bulk of food crops (maize, sorghum, cassava, beans and fruit) are grown by subsistence farmers on small plots of land, whereas most of the cash crops originate from large, privately owned plantations employing contract labour. Tea and coffee crops (the largest agricultural export earners) are the exceptions. The production of processed tea came to a staggering 290 million tonnes in 1998 (see the boxed text 'Picking Tea' in the Western Kenya chapter).

In recent years tourism has replaced coffee as the country's largest export earner, although arrivals have dropped off since the mid-1990s. Each year around 400,000 people visit Kenya, contributing more than US$200 million to the country's economy.

Kenya has a relatively well developed industrial base, which accounts for some 16% of GDP. However, poor infrastructure (including power, water and roads), high taxation and rampant corruption are strangling the vital industrial base that is concentrated around Nairobi and Mombasa. Principal products include processed food, beer, vehicles and accessories, construction materials, engineering, textiles, glass and chemicals.

Kenya's external debt of around US$6.5 billion (in 1997) is still considered to be low, but a worrying aspect is the high proportion of the country's foreign exchange earnings that go into servicing foreign debt – currently around 22%.

Another worrying trend is the drop in foreign aid, which has declined from US$921 million in 1991 to US$457 million in 1997. Increasing conditions (namely good governance and a reduction in corruption) are being placed on aid and unless the government goes some way to meet these demands the figure is likely to keep falling.

Mining is a relatively small contributor to GNP and is centred around the extraction of soda and fluorspar for export. Other minerals, which include silver, gold, lead and limestone have yet to be developed commercially.

Kenya's major export trading partners are the EU (45%), the UK (17%), Germany (12%) and the USA (about 5%). Kenya's major sources of imports are the EU (39%), the UK (about 18%), Japan (9%), Germany (8%) and the USA (5%).

Some 70% of domestic energy requirements are imported, but geothermal projects are being developed: there are four hydroelectric plants in operation along the Tana River and a hydroelectric plant was recently completed in the Turkwel Gorge.

Inflation is currently running at about 12%, GNP is around US$9.7 billion and GDP per capita is US$372. Kenya is the 22nd poorest country in the world with the third-largest gap between rich and poor. Perversely, while the economy gets worse and worse, the more shopping centres seem to be built and the more *wabenzi* (people who drive Mercedes Benz cars on, it's implied, the proceeds of corruption) are seen on the roads.

POPULATION & PEOPLE

Kenya's population stands at around 30 million and is made up almost entirely of Africans, with small (although influential) minorities of Asians (about 80,000), Arabs (about 40,000) and Europeans (about 40,000).

The are more than 70 tribal groups among the Africans, although the distinctions between many of them are already blurred and are becoming more so as western cultural values become more ingrained. The first major influx of Asians occurred at the turn of the 20th century when the Mombasa-Uganda railway was built. In order to construct it, the British colonial authorities brought in some 32,000 indentured labourers from Gujarat and Punjab. When their contracts expired many of them decided to stay and set up businesses. Their numbers were augmented after WWII with the encouragement of the British. The Asian community now controls large sections of the economy.

The population growth rate is around 3.3%, this is one of the highest in the world and is putting great strain on the country's ability to expand economically. It has also resulted in tremendous pressure to increase the area of land under cultivation. However, AIDS seems likely to have a major impact on the population growth rate in future years.

Taking 1997 UN figures, life expectancy in Kenya is estimated at 52, while 47% of the population has access to clean drinking water and 23% have adequate sanitation. The infant mortality rate is 57 per 1000 births (roughly half of what it was in 1970) and 46% of the population is under 15 years. Around 27% of all Kenyans live in urban areas.

EDUCATION

School education is not free in Kenya, nor is it compulsory. Around 65% of all eligible children attend the 15,000 or so primary schools, while the country's 2500 secondary schools cater for around 700,000 students and competition for places is fierce.

There are four universities, with a total enrolment of around 35,000 students: the University of Nairobi (established in 1956) and Kenyatta University (1972), both in Nairobi; Egerton University (1939) in Nakuru; and Moi University (1984) in Eldoret.

Literacy rates runs at around 79%, which is markedly higher than neighbouring African states.

ARTS
Music

Despite imports, Kenyan music has retained its own identity, though local musicians find it hard to make a living. *Benga* is the contemporary dance music of Kenya. Kikuyu music often borrows from benga. Stars include Sam Chege, Francis Rugwati and Daniel 'Councillor' Kamau who was popular in the 1970s and is still going strong. Joseph Kamaru, the popular musician and notorious nightclub owner of the late 1960s, converted to Christianity in 1993 and now dominates the gospel scene.

The live-music scene in Nairobi is quite fluid, but is always vibrant and a variety of clubs cater for traditional and contemporary musical tastes. Outside the capital live-music venues are not difficult to find. You'll see posters and adverts flagging gigs well in advance.

A good reference is the *Daily Nation*, which publishes weekly top 10 African, international and gospel charts and countrywide gig listings on Saturdays. Live music venues are listed throughout this book.

For cassettes and CDs of Kenyan and African artists try the Nairobi Music Centre on Luthuli Ave, Musicrama on Moi Ave and Assanand's and Melodica on Tom Mboya St (all in Nairobi).

Literature

Two of Kenya's best authors are Ngugi wa Thiong'o and Meja Mwangi, whose books are a good introduction to what's happening in East African literature.

Ngugi is uncompromisingly (but somewhat dogmatically) radical, and his harrowing criticism of the neocolonialist politics of the Kenyan establishment landed him in jail for a year, lost him his job at Nairobi University and forced him into exile. His books, surprisingly, are not banned in Kenya. Meja Mwangi sticks more to social issues and themes of urban dislocation but has a brilliant sense of humour that threads its way through his books.

Titles worth reading by Ngugi wa Thiong'o include *Petals of Blood*, *A Grain of Wheat*, *Devil on the Cross* and *Weep Not*

Child. Titles by Meja Mwangi include *Going Down River Road, Kill me Quick* and *Carcass for Hounds*. All these titles are published by Heinemann.

SOCIETY & CONDUCT

See this section in the Facts about East Africa chapter for more information on cultural dos and don'ts in the region.

Conflicts in southern Sudan, southern Ethiopia and Somalia have led to a massive influx of refugees into Kenya. There are many big camps in northern Kenya, especially around Loikichokio, and plenty of refugees have moved further south setting up home in the central highlands, Nairobi, Mombasa and to a lesser degree, the coastal resort towns. As Kenya is a relatively stable country, with opportunities to make a living or at least receive hand-outs from tourists, you'll come across plenty of refugees on your travels.

Kenya's wildly photogenic tribal people are generally less than wildly enthusiastic about being photographed, and with good reason. Always ask permission before photographing anyone.

RELIGION

It's probably true to say that most Kenyans outside the coastal and eastern provinces are Christians of one sort or another, while most of those on the coast and in the eastern part of the country are Muslim. Muslims make up some 30% of the population. In the more remote tribal areas you'll find a mixture of Muslims, Christians and those who follow their ancestral tribal beliefs.

LANGUAGE

English and Swahili (correctly known as Kiswahili) are the official languages and are taught in schools throughout Kenya, but there are many other major tribal languages, including Kikuyu, Luo, Kikamba, Maasai and Samburu as well as a plethora of minor tribal languages. Most urban Kenyans and even tribal people involved in the tourist industry speak English so you shouldn't experience many problems making yourself understood. Italian and German are also spoken by many Kenyans but usually only among those associated with the tourist trade on the coast.

It's extremely useful to have a working knowledge of Swahili, especially outside urban areas and in remote parts of the country, since this will open doors and enable you to communicate with people who don't speak English. It's also the most common language which speakers of different tribal languages use to communicate with each other. Even tribespeople who haven't been to school will usually be able to speak *some* Swahili. If you're planning on visiting Tanzania you'll find it extremely useful, as it's now the official language there (though English is still used extensively).

Another language you'll come across in Kenya, one which is spoken almost exclusively by the younger members of society, is Sheng. Essentially a patois, it's a fairly recent development and, like Swahili, is still evolving. It's composed of a mixture of Swahili and English along with a fair sprinkling of Hindi, Gujarati, Kikuyu and several other Kenyan tribal languages. It originated in the colonial days as a result of the employment of African nannies by whites to look after their children.

Unless you can speak Swahili reasonably well, you probably won't realise Sheng is being spoken since it does sound quite similar to Swahili. One of the indications that it's being spoken is the initial greeting between friends. The greeting will be *'Sassa'*. The response to this can be, *'Besht'*, *'Mambo'* or *'Fit'* (pronounced almost like 'feet'). There is then an option to continue in Sheng or any other mutually intelligible language.

See the Language chapter at the back of this book for a brief guide to Swahili and some useful words and phrases.

Facts for the Visitor

HIGHLIGHTS

Without doubt it is the national parks and reserves that attract most people to Kenya – the wildlife viewing here is still probably the best (and most easily accessible) in Africa. The Masai Mara National Reserve is the number one attraction but other parks and reserves such as Amboseli, Tsavo and Samburu also provide great vantage points. Getting off the beaten track and into parks such as Meru and Aberdare is also a fantastic experience. Birdwatchers will also be impressed by a visit to Kakamega Forest Reserve, Saiwa Swamp National Park and Arabuko Sokoke Forest, though all the Rift Valley lakes (especially Bogoria, Naivasha and Nakuru) are excellent birdwatching spots, while Nairobi National Park hosts more than 550 species.

For the more intrepid traveller, Kenya offers some exciting prospects. Scaling the snowy heights of Mt Kenya, the second highest peak in Africa, is a thrilling experience and one that doesn't require specialised equipment. The Central Highlands has some excellent trout fishing, there are good rocks for technical climbing in various locations (not least Hell's Gate National Park) and some of the longest lava cave systems in the world are to be found in the Chyulu Hills National Park. Other options include camel (or even donkey) safaris with Samburu tribespeople in the semidesert regions of the north, white-water rafting, hiking, safaris, sailing, ballooning, diving and snorkelling plus some of the best deep-sea fishing in the world.

People looking for activities requiring slightly less energy will find the beaches the perfect place to chill out for a while. And this doesn't have to be a purely hedonistic experience either, as there is a rich history and strong Swahili culture to delve into along the coast.

SUGGESTED ITINERARIES
One Week

Rather than trying to cram as much as possible into seven days, you're better off making a choice between the coast or wildlife parks. If you're desperate to see the 'Big Five' join a trip to the Masai Mara and Lake Nakuru. If you want a laid-back spot on the coast, head to Tiwi Beach, Watamu or Lamu.

Two Weeks

Two weeks gives you much more scope for exploration. An excellent option is a Lake Turkana truck safari. In the remaining time you could head down to the coast or go to the Masai Mara.

One Month

One month is ideal. You can fly straight to Lamu and go on a four day dhow trip, explore the coast and then take a safari into Tsavo. There's time for a Lake Turkana trip as well as a safari into the Masai Mara and a trek up Mt Kenya.

PLANNING
When to Go

The main tourist season (high season) is January and February, when the weather is considered to be the best – hot and dry. It's also when you'll find the animals in the national parks and reserves congregating around the watercourses as other sources dry up.

From June to September could be called the 'shoulder season' as the weather is still dry and the annual wildebeest migration into the Masai Mara from the Serengeti occurs.

During the long rains between March and the end of May (low season), you can get some great deals in the parks and on the coast. To a lesser extent this is true during the short rains from October to December. The rains don't affect your ability to get around and see things unless you are right out in the sticks.

What Kind of Trip?

Most travellers arriving in Kenya go on safari, and a week-long trip is just about right – it's not being in a minibus that's the problem, but the state of Kenyan roads and the transfer times between destinations that takes its toll.

Many budget safaris to the Masai Mara last three or four days, but if you want to see as many wildlife parks as possible in, say, two weeks, you should take the time to relax for a day or two in the middle of your safari.

You can do most of the popular traveller activities in Kenya without going on organised tours, but if you want to tour the national parks and reserves unaccompanied, you'll have to hire a car.

Maps

Lonely Planet's *Kenya travel atlas* provides the handiest, most accurate maps available and is a great companion to this guidebook. *Tourist Map of Kenya*, printed and published in Kenya, offers good detail, as does *Kenya Route Map*. Both maps cost KSh 250. Marco Polo's 1:1,000,000 *Shell Euro Karte Kenya* is widely available in Europe. The scale and clarity are very good but the location of some minor features are totally inaccurate.

Macmillan publishes a series of maps to the national parks and reserves and these are not bad value at KSh 250 each. Three areas are available: Amboseli, Masai Mara and Tsavo East and West.

Tourist Maps also publish a *National Park* series priced roughly the same, but the best national park maps are the original Survey of Kenya sheets available from the Public Map Office (☎ 02-799679) on Thika Rd, PO Box 30046, Nairobi. Take a matatu from the KBS bus station (Nos 44 or 145). Asked to be dropped at the Survey of Kenya – it's behind a Shell petrol station, opposite the Kenya School of Monetary Studies. You can't buy more general maps without security clearance. It can take weeks.

TOURIST OFFICES
Local Tourist Offices

The only tourist offices in the entire country are in Mombasa (☎ 011-311231) on Moi Ave, in Malindi on Lamu Rd (largely ineffectual) and in Diani in the Private Safaris building.

Tourist Offices Abroad

The Ministry of Tourism maintains a number of overseas offices including:

France
    (☎ 01 42 60 66 88, fax 01 42 61 18 84) 5 Rue Volney, Paris 75002
Germany
    (☎ 069-232017/8, fax 239239) Neue Mainzer Strasse 22, 60311 Frankfurt
UK
    (☎ 020-7355 3144, fax 7495 8656) 25 Brook's Mews (off Davies St) Mayfair, London
USA
    Los Angeles: (☎ 213-274 6635, fax 859 7010) 9150 Wiltshire Blvd, Suite 160, Beverly Hills, CA 90212
    New York: (☎ 212-486 1300, fax 688 0911) 424 Madison Ave, New York, NY 10017

VISAS & DOCUMENTS
Visas

For stays of under 30 days, visas are no longer required by nationals of Australia, Austria, Belgium, Canada, France, Japan, Luxembourg, Netherlands, New Zealand, Switzerland, USA and UK. The following nationalities do not require visas for stays of up to six months: Bangladesh, Denmark, Finland, Germany, Ireland, Italy, Jamaica, Norway, Singapore, Spain, Sweden, Trinidad & Tobago, Turkey and Uruguay. For these people a Visitor's Pass, valid for a stay of up to six months, is issued upon entry.

The cost of a three-month, single-entry visa is UK£35. A multiple-entry visa costs UK£70. Two photos (sometimes three) are required if you go through a Kenyan embassy, but you normally do not have to show an onward ticket. Check the current visa exemptions before you go, as more nations may be added.

Visas remain valid for a period of three months from the date of issue. Apply well in advance for your visa especially if doing it by mail – they can take up to two weeks in some countries (eg, Australia). In Tanzania and Uganda, Kenyan visa applications are simple and straightforward and payment is accepted in local currency. Visas are also available at Jomo Kenyatta international airport. Transit visas issued at the airport are valid for three days only and are definitely not extendable.

If you enter Kenya through a land border no-one will ever ask you for an onward ticket or 'sufficient funds'. This isn't always the case if you enter by air. A lot depends on what you look like, whether you're male or female, what you write on your immigration card and which immigration officer you deal with. If it's fairly obvious that you aren't intending to stay and work then you'll generally be given the benefit of the doubt. Put yourself in a strong position before you arrive: look smart and write the name of an expensive hotel on your immigration card in the appropriate section.

So long as your visa remains valid, you can visit either Tanzania or Uganda and return without having to apply for another visa. This does not apply to visiting any other countries.

Visa Extensions Visas can be renewed in Nairobi at the immigration office (☎ 02-332110), Nyayo House (ground floor), on the corner of Kenyatta Ave and Uhuru Highway, at the office in Mombasa (☎ 011-311745) or at immigration on the 1st floor of Reinsurance Plaza, corner of Jomo Kenyatta Highway and Oginga Odinga Rd in Kisumu during normal office hours. Staff at the immigration offices are generally friendly and helpful, but it takes a while.

Other Visas The following African countries offer visa services in Nairobi:

Burundi Everyone needs a visa to enter Burundi; it takes at least 24 hours and costs US$20. Applications are made on Mondays and Wednesdays for collection Tuesdays and Thursdays respectively.

Congo (Zaïre) Visa fees are the same for all nationalities. A standard single-entry visa costs US$40. Other visa prices vary, and some long-stay multi-entry visas cost well over US$100. Two photos and a yellow fever vaccination certificate are required. A letter of introduction from your embassy may also be necessary. Remember this is a country at war.

Ethiopia In theory, the embassy here only issues visas to people who have no Ethiopian embassy in their own country. In practice, anyone can get one, although you may have to come up with a reason why you didn't get one before leaving home. One-month visas cost US$63, require one photo, a yellow fever vaccination certificate and take 48 hours to issue. Visas can be extended in Addis Ababa. Applications must be submitted before noon.

Rwanda It costs US$50 for a single-entry one-month visa. You'll need a yellow fever vaccination certificate and possibly a letter of invitation. Two photos are also required. Transit visas valid for 15 days are available at the border (US$20).

Sudan Visas are difficult to get because of the civil war and all applications have to be referred to Khartoum. It can take three or four weeks and costs US$83. Cholera and yellow fever vaccination certificates, an onward ticket and three photographs are required.

Tanzania The cost of a visa depends on your nationality and ranges from US$50 for British and Canadian nationals, US$25 for French to US$10 for Italians. One photo is required and visas take 30 minutes to issue. Visas are also available on arrival at Namanga, Kilimanjaro airport (Arusha), Dar es Salaam airport and at Zanzibar. Nationals of the Republic of Ireland, Norway, Sweden, Denmark and Finland are exempt from obtaining a visa.

Uganda Most non-African nationalities require visas. A three-month single-entry visa costs US$30 and multi-entry visa valid for six months costs US$80. One photo is required and processing takes 24 hours. The visa office closes at noon. Visas are also available at the border.

Driving Licence
If you plan on doing any driving, your licence from home is sufficient. However, it may be wise to bring an international driving licence with you as well. This way if you are stopped by the police and your international licence is confiscated pending a large and dubious 'fine' you will still have your national licence.

EMBASSIES
Kenya has diplomatic representation in many countries. Where there is no Kenyan embassy or high commission, visas can be obtained from the British embassy or high commission.

KENYA

Kenyan Embassies

Kenya maintains the following embassies and consulates abroad:

Australia (☎ 02-6247 4788, fax 6257 6613) QBE Bldg, 33-35 Ainslie Ave, Canberra, ACT 2601

Canada (☎ 613-563 1773, fax 233 6599) 415 Laurier Ave East, Ottawa, Ontario, KIN 6R4

Congo (Zaïre) (☎ 012-372 3641) 4002 Ave de l'Ouganda, BP 9667, Zone Degombe, Kinshasa

Ethiopia (☎ 01-610033, fax 611433) Fikre Miriam Rd, PO Box 3301, Addis Ababa

France (☎ 01 56 62 25 25, fax 01 47 20 44 41) 3 Rue Freycinet, 75116 Paris

Germany (☎ 0228-935800, fax 935805) Villichgasse 17, 5300 Bonn-Bad Godesburg 2, Michael Plaza

Netherlands (☎ 070-350 4215, fax 355 3594) Niewe Parklaan 21, 2597 La Hague

Rwanda (☎ 070-82774, fax 86234) Rue Kadyiro, near Hôtel Umubano, Kacyiru, Kigali

South Africa (☎ 012-362 2249, fax 362 2252) 302 Brooke St, Menlo Park, 0811, Pretoria

Sudan (☎ 011-460386, fax 472264) Street 3 Amarat, PO Box 8242, Khartoum

Tanzania (☎ 051-112811, fax 113098) NIC Life House, Samora Ave, PO Box 5231, Dar es Salaam

Uganda (☎ 041-258235, fax 267369) Nakasero Rd, PO Box 5220, Kampala

UK (☎ 020-7636 2371, fax 7323 6717) 45 Portland Place, London W1N 4AS

USA (☎ 202-387 6101, fax 462 3829) 2249 R Street NW, Washington DC 20008

Embassies in Kenya

Countries which maintain diplomatic missions in Kenya include:

Australia (☎ 02-445034, fax 444617) Riverside Drive, PO Box 39341, Nairobi. Open from 8 am to 4.30 pm Monday to Thursday and 7.45 am to 12.30 pm Friday.

Burundi (☎ 02-575113, fax 219005) Development House, Moi Ave, PO Box 44439, Nairobi. Open from 8.30 am to 12.30 pm and 2 to 5 pm Monday to Friday.

Canada (☎ 02-214804, fax 226987) Comcraft House, Haile Selassie Ave, PO Box 30481, Nairobi. Open from 7.30 am to 4 pm Monday to Friday.

Congo (Zaïre) (☎ 02-229771, fax 334539) Electricity House, Harambee Ave, PO Box 48106, Nairobi. Open from 8.30 am to 12.30 pm and 2 to 5 pm Monday to Friday.

Ethiopia (☎ 02-723027, fax 723401) State House Ave, PO Box 45198, Nairobi. Open from 8.30 am to 12.30 pm and 2 to 5 pm Monday to Friday.

France (☎ 02-339783, fax 217013) Barclays Plaza, Loita St, PO Box 41784, Nairobi. Open from 8.30 am to noon Monday to Friday.

Germany (☎ 02-712527, fax 714886, email ger-emb@form-net.com) Williamson House, 4th Ngong Ave, PO Box 30180, Nairobi. Open from 8.30 am to 12.30 pm Monday to Friday. (☎ 011-228781, fax 314504) Palli House, Nyerere Rd, PO Box 86779 Mombasa. Open from 9 am to noon Monday to Friday.

Netherlands (☎ 02-227111, fax 339155) Uchumi House, Aga Khan Walk, PO Box 41537, Nairobi. Open from 9 am to 12.30 pm Monday to Friday. (☎ 011-311043) ABN Bank Bldg, Nkrumah Rd, Mombasa

Rwanda (☎ 02-240563, fax 336365) International House, Mama Ngina St, PO Box 48579, Nairobi. Open from 9 am to 12.30 pm and 2 to 5 pm daily.

South Africa (☎ 02-215616, fax 223687) Lonrho House, Standard St, PO Box 42441, Nairobi. Open from 8.30 am to 12.30 pm and 1.30 to 4.30 pm Monday to Friday.

Sudan (☎ 02-720853, fax 710612) Minet-ICDC House, Mamlaka Rd, PO Box 48784, Nairobi. Open from 8.30 am to 3.30 pm Monday to Friday.

Tanzania (☎ 02-721742, fax 218269) Continental House, corner of Uhuru Highway and Harambee Ave, PO Box 47790, Nairobi. Open from 8.30 am to noon Monday to Friday. (☎ 011-229595, fax 227077) Palli House, Nyerere Ave, Mombasa. Open from 8.30 am to 12.30 pm and 2.30 to 5 pm Monday to Friday.

Uganda (☎ 02-330801, fax 330970, email ugahinrb@users.africaonline.co.ke) Uganda House, Baring Arcade, 4th floor, Kenyatta Ave, Nairobi. Open from 9 am to 12.30 pm and 2 to 5 pm Monday to Friday.

UK (☎ 02-714699, fax 719082, email bhcinfo @africaonline.co.ke) Visa & Immigration Section, Upper Hill Rd, PO Box 30465, Nairobi. Open from 7.45 am to 12.30 pm and 1.30 to 4.30 pm Monday to Friday.

USA (☎ 02-751613, fax 749590) The Crescent, Parklands, PO Box 30137, Nairobi. (Temporary address until the completion of the new embassy on the Mombasa Rd near the airport. Opening hours are from 7.30 am to 12.30 pm and 1.15 to 4.15 pm Monday to Friday.)

CUSTOMS

There are strict laws about taking wildlife products out of Kenya. The export of products made from elephant, rhino and sea turtle are prohibited. The collection of coral is also not allowed.

Always check to see what permits are required, especially for the export of any plants, insects and shells.

The other usual regulations apply – 250g of cigarettes, 1L of alcohol and other personal items (such as cameras, laptop computers and binoculars) can all be brought in.

MONEY
Currency

The unit of currency is the Kenyan shilling (KSh), which is made up of 100 cents. Notes in circulation are KSh 1000, 500, 200, 100, 50 and 20, there are new ('copper') coins of KSh 1, 5, 10 and 20 also in circulation.

Exchange Rates

After a period of instability in the early 1990s, the Kenyan shilling stabilised for a while, but went through something of a slide against the dollar and pound in 1999. At the time of writing it was around the US$1 = KSh 74 mark.

country	unit		shilling
Australia	A$1	=	KSh 47
Canada	C$1	=	KSh 51
euro	€1	=	KSh 73
France	10FF	=	KSh 111
Germany	DM1	=	KSh 37
Japan	¥100	=	KSh 68
New Zealand	NZ$1	=	KSh 37
Tanzania	TSh1	=	KSh 9
Uganda	USh1	=	KSh 49
UK	UK£1	=	KSh 119
USA	US$1	=	KSh 74

Exchanging Money

While most major currencies are accepted in Nairobi and Mombasa, once away from these two centres you'll run into problems with currencies other than US dollars, pounds sterling, French francs and German marks.

If you are going to be travelling elsewhere in East Africa, play it safe and carry dollars – it makes life much simpler.

Use banks and foreign exchange bureaus (forex) to change money. The rates for both are published in the *Daily Nation* newspaper. Watch out for differing small bill (US$10) and large bill (US$100) rates in forex bureaus. Commission, charged by banks, is sometimes very high. Always check first. Normal banking hours in Kenya are 9 am to 3 pm Monday to Friday and 9 to 11 am Saturday.

American Express (Amex) offices are confined to Mombasa and Nairobi.

ATMs & Credit Cards Barclays Bank has a huge network of ATMs covering most major Kenyan towns. They support Master-Card, Visa, Plus and Cirrus international networks. Standard Chartered Bank ATMs are not so widespread, but do take Visa cards. The only problem is Kenya's data link with the outside world, which is unreliable. There is about a one in eight chance your card won't work. The same basic rule applies to using credit cards as new electronic swipe machines are common.

MasterCard is the most popular card in Kenya, but Visa is gaining in popularity.

International Transfers Pos Bank, a branch of the Kenyan Post Office, is the agent for the Western Money Union, the global money transfer company. Using them is an easy way of receiving money in Kenya (as long as the phones are working). Handily, the sender pays all the charges and there's a branch of Pos Bank in most towns, often within the post office itself or close by.

Costs

The cost of budget accommodation in Kenya is very reasonable so long as you're happy with communal showers and toilets. At the budget end of the scale you're looking at KSh 150/300 for singles/doubles. If you want your own bathroom, budget for KSh 300/500.

There are plenty of small cafes in every town. They cater to local people and you can get a meal for between KSh 80 and KSh 200. Indian restaurants are terrific value. Some offer all-you-can-eat lunches for around KSh 300. It's not too difficult to spend in excess of US$50 in Nairobi's top restaurants.

On average a 500ml bottle of beer costs KSh 70 in a bar and soft drinks cost around KSh 17.

Public transport is very reasonable (budget for around KSh 1 per kilometre) though imported western goods are more expensive here than back home (with the exception of camera film).

In certain circumstances tipping is expected in Kenya. Expect to leave 5 to 10% when eating in half-decent restaurants and around KSh 200 per day per employee at the end of a safari.

POST & COMMUNICATIONS
Post
The Kenyan postal system is run by the government Kenya Posts & Telecommunications Corporation (KPTC, known disparagingly as 'kaput'). Letters sent from Kenya rarely go astray but do take up to two weeks to reach Australia or the USA. Incoming letters to Kenya take around a week to reach Nairobi. Be aware that credit card companies will not post cards to Kenya. You will have to arrange a courier.

Postal Rates The airmail rates (in KSh) for items posted from Kenya are:

item	Africa	Europe	USA & Australia
letter	40	47	59
postcard	20	27	35
aerogram	34	34	34

Sending Mail Kenya is a good place from which to send home parcels of goodies, or excess gear. In theory, parcels sent by surface mail take up to 4½ months to arrive, but there *is* a problem with theft – most of the magazines on sale along the Uhuru Highway are ex-pats' long-lost subscriptions. Curios, clothes, textiles and crafts will be OK, but send anything of obvious value by courier.

Receiving Mail Letters can be sent care of poste restante in any town. The majority of it finds its way into the correct pigeonholes though there's naturally some mistakes – Nairobi is the worst place due to the volume of mail.

Some travellers use the American Express Clients Mail Service and this can be a useful, and more reliable, alternative to poste restante. Officially you are supposed to have an Amex card or be using their travellers cheques to avail yourself of this service but no check of this is made at the office in Nairobi. The postal addresses in Nairobi and Mombasa are:

American Express Clients Mail Service
  Express Kenya Ltd, PO Box 40433, Nairobi
  Express Kenya Ltd, PO Box 90631, Mombasa

The Nairobi office (☎ 02-334722, email ex pressk@africaonline.co.ke) is found in Bruce House on Standard St, while the Mombasa office (☎ 011-312461) is on Nkrumah Rd.

Telephone
The phone system works, just. It can take a number of attempts to get a local or international connection depending on the time of day. Card phones are common all across Kenya (except up north) and have a better success rate.

Local & Long Distance Calls Local calls cost KSh 3, while long distance call rates vary depending on the distance. When making a local call, make sure you put a coin into the slot first (regardless of what you insert after that). If you don't, you may have problems making your call.

Calls to Tanzania and Uganda are considered long distance calls, not international calls.

International Calls To Europe or the USA the rate is US$3 per minute, to Australia and New Zealand it's US$4 per minute. From a private phone it's marginally cheaper.

From smaller towns you may have no choice other than go through an operator either from a private phone or a post office. A three-minute minimum call charge applies to these calls. You can always dial direct through a card phone. They take KSh 300, KSh 500 and KSh 1000 denomination cards available from post offices. Check the card's expiry date before leaving the post office (at the time of writing all cards were due to expire on 31 December 1999). All phones can receive incoming calls.

Reverse-charge (collect) calls are possible, but only from card phones and only to the following countries with direct dial freephone numbers: the UK (☎ 0800-44), Italy (☎ 0800-47) and the USA (☎ 0800-10-12).

Calls put through a hotel operator from your room will be loaded at between 25 and 50%, so make certain you check what they're going to charge you before making a call.

Email & Internet Access
Email is well established in Kenya. Many towns have email bureaus and computer training centres where you can surf the Internet or send and receive email. Costs vary from KSh 100 to KSh 200 for 15 minutes surfing and KSh 80 to KSh 120 to send an email, KSh 20 to 60 to receive. Receiving is often cheaper if you don't want to print it out.

With no local call rate for Internet access, email costs increase away from the big cities.

BOOKS
Large-format, hardback, photo-essay books on Africa are becoming easier to find in western bookshops, and are readily available in Mombasa and Nairobi – the more photogenic Kenyan tribes are covered in greatest detail. Some of these are well worth picking up. Literature by Kenyan writers is more difficult to find out of the country (see Literature under Arts in the Facts about Kenya chapter).

Guidebooks
Fielding's Kenya is a popular guide to Kenya's more exclusive (and often more expensive) safaris, hotels, lodges, camps and homestays throughout Kenya. Very useful if you have your own transport.

Mountains of Kenya, a Walkers Guide by Paul Clarke will guide you through some of the more remote and less visited mountain ranges, although having your own transport some or all of the time would be a tremendous advantage.

Travel
Journey to the Jade Sea by John Hillaby recounts this prolific travel writer's epic trek to Lake Turkana in northern Kenya in the days before the safari trucks began pounding up the dirt. Other books to look for include *A Bend in the River* by VS Naipaul, *The Snows of Kilimanjaro* and *Green Hills of Africa* by Ernest Hemingway and *The Life of My Choice* and *My Kenya Days* by Wilfred Thesiger. *No Picnic on Mt Kenya* by Felice Benuzzi is a classic mountaineering account of two Italians who escape from a British prisoner of war camp to climb Mt Kenya.

General
Numerous books have been written about African history and they are covered in the Regional Facts for the Visitor chapter, though there are a few specific titles that are of interest.

It's well worth reading Oginga Odinga's *Not Yet Uhuru* and *Detained – A Prison Writer's Diary* by Ngugi wa Thiong'o, for a radically different view from that put out by the Kenyatta and Moi regimes. Left-field and excellent reading is *Rogue Ambassador* by Smith Hempstone the outspoken former American ambassador.

Lastly, if you want a background on the famous Leakey dynasty, read *Ancestral Passions: The Leakey family and the quest for humankind's beginnings* by Virginia Morell.

FILMS
With its wide, sweeping landscapes and superb scenery, Kenya has been the location for many feature films. Unfortunately the quality of the films does not always match the quality of the backdrop.

Films shot in Kenya include the 1950s Tarzan movies, *King Solomon's Mines* in

Web Directory

Let's Go Travel
A brilliant site that lists almost every major hotel, camp and lodge in Kenya. Many smaller camp sites, bandas in national parks and cottages are also featured and prices given.
www.letsgosafari.com

The Kenya Wildlife Service
An overview of Kenya's parks and reserves with educational material on indigenous flora and fauna.
www.kenya-wildlife-service.org

Kenya Association of Tour Operators
Get the low down on who are members and who are not.
www.kato.com

The Kenya Beach Site
An extensive site covering many of the hotels and businesses on Diani and Tiwi beaches.
www.kenyabeach.com

Kenyaweb
Self-proclaimed as Kenya's 'definitive Internet resource', this site has links to virtually anything Kenya-related.
www.kenyaweb.com

The National Museums of Kenya Web Site
Galleries, exhibitions, museums. This one is for those with a penchant for culture.
www.museums.or.ke

African Wildlife Update
A good site for independent news on African wildlife.
www.africanwildlife.org

The Mountain Club of Kenya
Good advice on trekking to Mt Kenya as well as technical climbing and trekking throughout the country.
www.geocities.com/~mckenya

Kilimanjaro Adventure Travel
Mountaineering, trekking and adventure travel Web site for Tanzania and Kenya.
www.kilimanjaro.com

The _Daily Nation_
The Web site of the _Daily Nation_, Kenya's best daily newspaper.
www.nationaudio.com

1950, the pretty awful _White Mischief_, featuring Sarah Miles and John Hurt, and the 1985 film depiction of the life of Karen Blixen, _Out of Africa_, which starred Robert Redford and Meryl Streep.

A slightly more recent offering is the 1990 _Mountains of the Moon_, which dramatised the historic journey of Burton and Speke in their search for the source of the Nile.

INTERNET RESOURCES
Your best bet for pre-trip information about Kenya is the Internet (see the boxed text 'Web Directory'). Many tourist businesses, from the cheapest camping safari company to the most exclusive lodge, have Web sites and email addresses.

NEWSPAPERS & MAGAZINES
Kenya's best paper is the _Daily Nation_, which has both local and overseas coverage. It criticises both government and opposition vigorously and is constantly exposing corruption. The others are the _Kenya Times_ (the KANU party rag) and the _Standard_, which is not bad.

The _Weekly Review_ is the Kenyan equivalent of _Time/Newsweek_, though a little too pro-KANU for some people, while the _East African_ is a decent weekly paper, covering important stories in depth. The _Economic Review_ has in-depth articles which pulls no punches.

Foreign newspapers and magazines are available in Nairobi and Mombasa.

RADIO & TV
The Kenyan Broadcasting Corporation (KBC) has radio transmissions in English, Swahili and more specialised languages such as Hindi and African.

The BBC World Service (www.bbc.co.uk /worldservice), Voice of America and Deutsche Welle all transmit in Kenya. Most of the output is in English (or German), but considerable output is in Swahili. Program listings are published in the _Daily Nation_. All stations broadcast on shortwave frequencies, although the BBC World Service is also broadcasted on FM in Nairobi and Mombasa.

There are four TV channels – KBC, KBC2, KTN and STV. The latter two are better for both news and programs, while late in the evening STV broadcasts news programs from BBC World and Sky TV. KBC shows some good programs, but it is painfully dated. Many programs are imported from Europe, the USA and Australia.

Satellite TV is widely shown in the more expensive bars and hotels.

PHOTOGRAPHY
Film
You'll find Kodak and Fuji 64, 100, 200 and 400 ASA slide film readily available in Nairobi and Mombasa, but 800 ASA is harder to find. The same is true for colour-negative film.

Shops and booths offering film processing are popping up in small towns all over Kenya. In addition there are plenty of one-hour film processing labs in Nairobi, and at least one in all other major towns. They can handle any film speeds, but results can vary.

Three good places are Expo Camera Centre, Camera Experts and the lab next to the Coffee House, all on Mama Ngina St.

As an indication of price, 36 exposure colour print film is KSh 300 to KSh 400 (watch out for out-of-date film). Developing and mounting of slide film is cheap, however, and it saves you the worry of taking exposed film through dodgy airport X-ray machines. It costs KSh 400 for a roll of 36 and takes four hours, but can only be done in Nairobi.

Camera Hire & Repair
If you don't have the inclination or the resources to buy expensive equipment but you know a bit about photography, it is possible to hire SLR cameras and lenses in Nairobi. The best place to do this is Expo Camera Centre (☎ 02-221797, piocom@ form-net.com), Jubilee Exchange, Mama Ngina St. It's well used by local businesses and tourists, the service is reliable and prices are competitive.

Expo also has a well-equipped repair shop where you can leave an ailing camera to be repaired with confidence. They do an excel-lent job but they're not cheap (neither is anyone else). A new Expo shop was also due to open in Westlands at the time of writing.

TIME
Time in Kenya is GMT/UTC plus three hours all year round.

BUSINESS HOURS
Banking hours are Monday to Friday from 9 am to 2 pm. Banks are also open on the first and last Saturday of the month from 9 to 11 am. Nairobi and Mombasa have branches of Barclays Bank which stay open until 4.30 or 5 pm Monday to Saturday. The branch at Nairobi airport is open 24 hours. Foreign exchange bureaus are open much longer hours, but still only on weekdays.

ELECTRICITY
Kenya uses the 240-volt system. The power supply is usually reliable and uninterrupted in most places though there are occasional failures. Power sockets are of the three-square-pin variety as used in the UK, although some older buildings have round-pin sockets.

WEIGHTS & MEASURES
Kenya is a metric country by and large. Kenyans drive on the left side of the road (most of the time), and distances are measured in kilometres.

DANGERS & ANNOYANCES
It is a sad fact that crime is rife in Kenya. It ranges from petty theft and mugging right on up through violent armed robbery and car-jacking and even goes into the white-collar ranks and above. Rarely does one come across a country where such lawlessness is so ingrained that it's accepted as part of life. It certainly doesn't help that the authorities are not only unable but also seem unwilling to do anything to clean the place up. Indeed it could be argued that the authorities are among the worst offenders.

From a visitor's point of view, the situation is worst in the areas with the highest concentration of tourists, namely Nairobi, Mombasa and the coast. Simple snatch thefts

KENYA

and robbery with minimal force are the most common problems, and many, many people are relieved of their valuables on a daily basis. The worst instances involve armed robbery or other violence which has ended in the death of some tourists. The problem is certainly not limited to attacks on tourists, but obviously they make pretty juicy targets.

If someone approaches you on the street and engages you in conversation, be suspicious. Confidence tricks are very common in the major towns (see the boxed text 'Confidence Tricks').

Banditry is a problem in some parts of North Kenya (see the relevant chapters for details).

PUBLIC HOLIDAYS

Kenya observes the following public holidays:

New Year's Day 1 January
Easter March/April – Good Friday, Holy Saturday and Easter Monday
Labour Day 1 May
Madaraka Day 1 June
Moi Day 10 October
Kenyata Day October 20
Independence Day 12 December
Christmas Day 25 December
Boxing Day 26 December

ACTIVITIES
Cycling
See Bicycle in the Getting Around chapter for information.

Trekking & Walking
Mt Kenya is the obvious area, but other promising territory includes Mt Elgon, the Cherangani Hills and Kerio Valley east of Kitale, the Matthews Range and Ndoto Mountains north of Isiolo, the Loroghi Hills north of Maralal, the Mau Forest near Nakuru and even the Ngong Hills close to Nairobi.

For more information refer to the relevant chapters in this book, get hold of a copy of *Trekking in East Africa* by David Else and contact the Mountaineering Club of Kenya (☎ 02-501747). For more information take a look at its Web site at www.geocities.com/~mckenya.

Confidence Tricks

In Nairobi the chances are you'll come across confidence tricksters who play on the emotions and gullibility of foreigners. Policeman, desperate refugees, the receptionist from your hotel (you remember the guy who showed you to your room yesterday) and car mechanics, among others, all improvise with the purpose of extracting large sums of money from you.

A good tale currently doing the rounds involves a well-dressed young guy who, by some fantastic coincidence, turns out to be going to a university in the town/city/tiny island off the Baltic coast that you come from. After a convincing and friendly chat, it turns out he's a bit short of cash (his sponsor has not sent over the money for the plane ticket/his mother has died/his dog has VD) and he could use a loan. And why not? After all, you'll almost be neighbours next year.

Windsurfing & Sailing
Most of the resort hotels south and north of Mombasa have sailboards for hire, and the conditions are ideal. The going rate at most places seems to be about KSh 400 per hour, more if you need instruction.

Sailing clubs are dotted up and down the coast and at Lake Naivasha and Lake Victoria, where the windsurfing and sailing are excellent, but water hyacinth is a real problem. You may pick up some crewing or even be able to hitch a ride up or down the coast.

Diving & Snorkelling
Malindi, Watamu and Wasini Island are the spots for scuba diving. October to March is the best time; during June, July and August it's often impossible due to rough weather. Visibility is variable due to plankton in the water.

There was a huge coral die-off in 1997 (see the boxed text 'Kenyan Reefs' in The Coast chapter), but thousands of colourful marine species remain.

For more traditional sailing, head to Lamu and go on a *dhow* trip.

Beaches

Kenya's beaches are picture postcard stuff – coconut palms, dazzling white sand and clear blue water.

The beach at Diani is one of the best although it's lined solidly with resort hotels. Tiwi Beach is much more low-key and there are similar possibilities north of Mombasa, although at certain times of year seaweed accumulates on the beach in huge quantities. Lamu doesn't suffer this problem and has some of the best beaches on the coast.

Desert Exploring

There's the opportunity to experience this on either side of Lake Turkana and, on the eastern side of the lake, it is possible to explore for a considerable distance south. For most travellers, this is one of the highlights of their trip to Kenya.

On the western side, access to the lake is easy with a bitumen road all the way from Kitale, and there's plenty of transport every day in each direction. On the eastern side your best bet is to join an organised safari.

Gliding & Flying

The Gliding Club of Kenya has its headquarters in Mweiga near Nyeri in the Aberdares, and there are flights every day except Monday. For more information contact the Gliding Club of Kenya (☎ 0171-55261, email gliding@africaonline.co.ke), PO Box 926, Nyeri – see the Nyeri section in the Central Highlands chapter. Also check out the Web site at www.innowebtive.de/kenya.htm.

Flying lessons are reasonably priced and easily arranged in Nairobi. Contact the Aero Club of East Africa (☎ 02-500693) and Ninety-Nines Flying Club (☎ 02-500277, email gary@insightkneya.com) both at Wilson airport.

Balloon Safaris

Balloon safaris in the nature parks and reserves are a superb way of seeing the savannah plains and wildlife. The most popular of these trips is in the Masai Mara Game Reserve and costs US$385. Bookings can be made through Adventures Aloft (☎ 02-221439, fax 332170, email madahold@form-net.com), Eagle House, Kimathi St, PO Box 40683, Nairobi; the Fig Tree Lodge, Block Hotels (☎ 02-540780), PO Box 40075, Nairobi; or directly at Keekorok Lodge.

Fishing

The Kenya Fisheries Department operates a number of fishing camps in various parts of the country, but they're difficult to reach without your own vehicle. For full details see the Fisheries Department in Nairobi (the office is near the Nairobi National Museum). You'll also need a fishing licence, also available from the Fisheries Department.

The deep-sea fishing on the coast is some of the best in the world (see the boxed text 'Deep-Sea Fishing' in The Coast chapter). Fishing on Lake Victoria and Lake Turkana could land you a Nile perch as big as a person, while some of the trout fishing around the Aberdares and Mt Kenya is exceptional.

Fishing licenses for Mt Kenya, Mt Elgon and Aberdares are obtained from the respective park gates for KSh 200 per day.

White-Water Rafting

Rafting is still in its infancy in Kenya, perhaps because of the limited possibilities – there are only two major rivers in Kenya, the Athi/Galana and Tana. The Tana flows through relatively flat country so it's sluggish and unsuitable for rafting. The Athi/Galana, on the other hand, has substantial rapids, chutes and waterfalls. The only outfit which can fix you up with a trip down this river is operated by Mark Savage (☎ 02-521590, email whitewater@thorntree.org), PO Box 44827, Nairobi.

White-water rafting in Kenya is a little more unpredictable than on the Zambezi and there have been a number of deaths in recent years.

COURSES
Language

Speaking KiSwahili is a tremendous practical advantage in Kenya and taking a language course (or indeed any course) also entitles you to a Pupils' Pass, an immigration permit allowing continuous stays of up to 12 months. Expect to pay around KSh 2500 for a one-year pass with your school sorting out the paperwork. Many missionaries often start off their stays in Kenya on Pupils' Passes.

ACK Language & Orientation School (☎ 02-721893, fax 714750, email ackenya@insightkenya .com) PO Box 47429, Bishops Rd, Upper Hill, Nairobi. Full-time group courses (six hours per day, three days per week) last from anywhere between one and 14 weeks (KSh 1550/21700 respectively). Part-time courses are KSh 170 per hour. Individual tuition is KSh 230 per hour. Other booking fees, course materials and field trips amount to a further KSh 9000. Around 350 hours of tuition brings you up to level one. It's highly recommended.

Trans Africa Language Services (☎ 02-561160, fax 566231) PO Box 72061, Joseph Kang'ethe Rd off Ngong Rd, Nairobi. A full-time four-week course (four hours per day, five days per week) cost KSh 16000. Unfortunately staff lack motivation and teaching materials are few and far between.

Codelink Training Services (☎ 02-252092, fax 211701) PO Box 60713, 2nd floor, Gilfillan House, Kenyatta Ave, Nairobi. Flexible courses charged between KSh 200 and KSh 250 per hour and tuition is available at their offices opposite Norfolk Hotel or at a venue of your choice (you pay extra for this).

WORK

It's difficult for foreigners to find jobs. The 'disaster business' is booming in Nairobi as the UN and other aid agencies deal with the victims of conflict and famine in Somalia and southern Sudan. But remember that the work is tough, often dangerous and the pay low.

Freelance work in the fields of journalism, literature and the film industry is also possible, but make sure you have a cast-iron contract for the work which you do.

Teaching and nursing are the easiest fields to break into (at least some jobs may be advertised), though you'll need previous experience.

Work permits and resident visas are not easy to arrange either. A prospective employer may be able to pull some strings, but usually you'll spend a lot of money and time at Nyayo House (immigration).

For those interested in volunteer work, Voluntary Service Overseas (☎ 020-8780 2266, fax 8780 1326), 317 Putney Bridge Rd, London SW15 2PN, can provide placements for professionals.

ACCOMMODATION

Kenya has a good range of accommodation from the very basic KSh 150 a night budget hotels to luxury tented camps in the national parks for up to US$500 a night. However, budget accommodation within national parks and reserves is restricted to camp sites, simple bandas and cottages.

Most places have separate, cheaper rates for residents.

Camping

There are huge opportunities for camping in Kenya. There are camp sites in every national park and reserve, though private sites are few and far between. Where they do exist, facilities are usually good. Often it's possible to camp in the grounds of a hotel.

Camping in the bush is also possible though you would be advised to ask permission from locals first. Small amounts of money will usually have to change hands. Sleeping on the beaches is asking for trouble.

Bandas

Bandas are basic wooden huts and stone cottages, often only one or two rooms, but offer an excellent alternative to camping if you are on a budget and visiting national parks and reserves. Facilities usually include a bed, mattress and mosquito net. Others are set up as dormitories, some have kitchens and a few even have en suite bathrooms. Let's Go Travel (☎ 02-340331, email info@letsgosafari.com), in Nairobi are the agents for an increasing number of banda-based resorts. There's also a Web site at www.letsgosafari.com.

If you choose to stay in a banda you'll need to bring all your food, bedding and firewood.

Hostels

The only youth hostels affiliated with Hostelling International (HI) are in Nairobi and Malindi. They are fine, but not so cheap and there are better options available.

There are other places which call themselves youth hostels but are not members of HI. Some are good, others less so.

Hotels

Hotel accommodation ranges from brothels/board and lodgings at KSh 150/250 for a single/double up to US$500 a night luxury camps in the Masai Mara. At the former you'll have to share showers and toilets, it might not be too clean and you'll hear comings and goings all night. For US$500 a night you get all the luxuries you could desire, safari drives and a personal butler to boot.

Compared to Europe and the USA, plenty of mid-range and top end hotels in Kenya are really bad value. With the downturn in tourism, some hotels have increased their prices while ceasing investment. Prime examples are hotels from the AT&H (now defunct) and Msafari Inns chains. Homestays and small, family-run hotels tend to be better value.

Great deals during the low season can make luxury (be it brief) travel possible for those on a budget. Bargain hunters should head into Westlands in Nairobi at the end of March for the Sarit Centre Travel Show (☎ 02-747408, email info@saritcentre.com).

FOOD

The food in Kenya is the same as that found across the region. The one major dish that is unique to the country is the national obsession known as *nyama choma* (barbecued goat's meat). Sometimes it's good; sometimes it's tough as old leather. What you get is what you choose from a refrigerated selection of various cuts which you buy by the kilogram. Once it's barbecued, it's brought to your table by a waiter and sliced into bite-sized pieces along with a vegetable mash (often *matoke*, which are plantains). It's not a cheap option but not expensive either and the Kenyan middle class regard an invitation to nyama choma (and copious quantities of Tusker lager) as a special night out.

DRINKS

Nonalcoholic Drinks

Despite the fact that Kenya grows some of the finest tea and coffee in the world, getting a decent cup of either can be difficult. *Chai* (tea) is made the same way in Kenya as it is in India: all the ingredients (tea, milk and masses of sugar) are put into cold water and the whole lot is brought to the boil and stewed. Coffee is similarly disappointing. For tea without milk ask for *chai kavu*, and for delicious spiced tea ask for *chai masala*.

Coke, Sprite and Fanta are widely available and go under the generic term of soda. Try Stoney's ginger ale, it's excellent.

Passionfruit juice is also popular, though other fruit juices are not so common (KSh 30 to KSh 150 per glass).

Alcoholic Drinks

Kenya has a thriving local brewing industry and formidable quantities of beer are consumed. Warm and cold beer are available just about everywhere.

White Cap, Tusker and Pilsner (all manufactured by Kenya Breweries Ltd) are sold in 500ml bottles (KSh 45 from a supermarket, KSh 70 from a bar). Tusker is also available on draught and you can get bottled Guinness, but it tastes nothing like the genuine article.

South African brewer Castle has recently set up shop in Kenya triggering some fierce competition. Both companies have been offering sweeteners such as fridges to bars who promise product allegiance.

Kenya has a fledgling wine industry and the Lake Naivasha colombard wines are said to be quite good. Papaya wine on the other hand tastes foul and smells worse. You can also get cheap imported South African, European and even Australian wine by the glass for around KSh 150 in Nairobi restaurants.

Although it is strictly illegal to brew or distil liquor, it still goes on. *Pombe* is the local beer and shouldn't do you any harm. The same cannot be said for *chang'a*, a distilled fire water and effective poison. This methyl alcohol could blind you if you're lucky and do worse if you're not. Leave it alone!

KENYA

ENTERTAINMENT
Pubs/Bars
Kenyans love to party and you'll find numerous bars (from flash five star places to roadside *dukas*) and at least one disco in the main towns; Nairobi has six nightclubs. Single men may find that in some places they attract an unusual amount of attention from very keen single women. Alas, prostitution is widespread in Kenya and this unwanted attention can be a real pain. Entry to discos is cheap, and women often get in free.

Live Music
Saturday's *Daily Nation* will give you some idea of the popular venues – concerts of note are usually advertised well in advance. Flyers are also a good source of information, though you can't beat word of mouth.

The really big gigs are often sponsored by tobacco or drinks companies and take place in the Carnivore Restaurant or at the horse racing track on the outskirts of Nairobi. They're quite an experience.

Cinemas
There are cinemas in Nairobi, Mombasa and other major towns. Options vary from Indian masala to trashy Hollywood ultra-violence. The Nairobi cinemas usually have fairly recent Hollywood releases. The price is a bargain, usually around KSh 180 or less.

Small video theatres are very common throughout Kenya. Cheap enough for just about anyone (KSh 15), they play a heady mix of Hong Kong martial art movies and Hollywood violence/soft porn flicks. Some places even show live European soccer matches via satellite.

Dance, Theatre & Performance
There are a number of contemporary Kenyan dance and theatre groups in Kenya, though the vast majority of performances take place in Nairobi. The Phoenix and Mijuiza Players, Mbalamwezi Theatre Group, plus the La Campagnie Gaara and Bakututu dance groups, and Sigana Troupe are all names to look out for.

Plays and performances are often held in the various foreign cultural centres in Nairobi,

Mombasa and Kisumu. However you could stumble across events almost anywhere.

For a greater background to the current Kenyan scene, contact the Mzizi Arts Centre (☎ 02-245364, fax 245366), 6th floor, Sonalux House, Moi Ave, Nairobi, and above all check in Saturday's *Daily Nation*.

SPECTATOR SPORTS
Soccer is a big deal in Kenya. Harambee Stars, AFC Leopards and Mathare United are among the best teams in the Kenyan Premiership. The grounds and pitches are not on a European scale, but the action is fast, furious and passionate. Tickets to a game cost between KSh 300 and KSh 600. Check in the *Daily Nation* for fixtures.

Kenyan long-distance runners are the best in the world, though much of their run-

---

The East African Safari Rally

Known originally as the Coronation Rally (in honour of Queen Elizabeth II) the first event was held in 1953 when 57 expat drivers took off around East Africa with a 'can do' attitude and a couple of spare tyres in the back. It wasn't until 1957 that it became international, changing its name to the East African Safari Rally, but the local bush attitude remained. In the 1960s Eric Carlson got his Saab stuck in some mud in the middle of nowhere. Not one to be deterred, he and his co-driver simply rolled it over out of the mud back onto its wheels and carried on. He then demonstrated his technique at the prize-winning ceremony.

Those days are gone and the event now attracts drivers and major teams from all over the world. The last local to win the race was Ian Duncan in 1994, but local outfits cannot compete with the professional foreign teams who follow their drivers in helicopters and change all their tyres at every opportunity.

The race is surely unique, and one of the toughest rallies in the world. Where else is a 3000km rally held on public roads (that are still open), attracting the best drivers who have to dodge potholes, matatus and antelope in the pursuit of the laurel?

ning takes place outside the country. Even trials and national events sometimes fail to attract these stars, though these events are flagged in the press well in advance. Moi Stadium outside Nairobi on Thika Rd is a popular venue.

The Safari Rally hits Kenya in March, usually over the Easter weekend; it's worth seeking out. Exact times and routes are best obtained from the Nation or from the AA of Kenya (☎ 02-720383) in the Hurlingham Shopping Centre in Nairobi.

SHOPPING
Kenya is an excellent place for souvenirs, although much of the cheap stuff available is just pure junk mass-produced for the tourist trade. Look carefully at what's avail-

able before parting with your money. It's illegal to export some wildlife products.

Nairobi and Mombasa are the main centres but many of the items come from the various regions, so it's often possible to pick up the same at source, although you then have the problem of transporting your wares.

It's certainly possible to pick up something which will look good in your living room without spending a fortune but, these days, something of genuine quality and artistry is going to cost real money. In some cases, you can be talking about thousands of US dollars.

If you're interested in quality artwork, spend time doing the rounds of the shops and galleries which deal in it.

Getting There & Away

For information on getting to Kenya from outside East Africa, see the regional Getting There & Away chapter.

AIR
Airports

Wilson airport handles most internal flights, both charters and scheduled Air Kenya Aviation departures, with the notable exception of Kenya Airways, which flies from Jomo Kenyatta international airport. Jomo Kenyatta international airport handles almost all the international traffic, though Mombasa receives a large number of charter flights from Europe during peak season.

Departure Tax

The airport departure tax for international flights is US$20. This is payable in cash, in either Kenyan shillings or a major foreign currency.

Burundi

Air Burundi, Kenya Airways and SA Alliance Express all fly between Nairobi and Bujumbura. Flights cost US$200 one way and US$275 for a 21-day return with Air Burundi.

Rwanda

SA Alliance Express and Kenya Airways both fly between Nairobi and Kigali three times a week. Promotional fares cost about US$150/250 one way/return. Rwanda Airlines flies the same route via Bujumbura (Burundi) once a week (US$175/250).

Tanzania

The cheapest regular flights between Kenya and Tanzania are between Nairobi and Dar es Salaam on Kenya Airways (☎ 02-210771) or Air Tanzania (☎ 02-336224). Both offer flights for US$150/300 one way/return. They also offer daily flights between Unguja (Zanzibar Island) and Nairobi (US$145/290) via Mombasa. However, it may be cheaper to pick up a good deal from Nairobi to Mombasa (sometimes as little as KSh 3500 one way) and then get a flight to Unguja from there (US$66/132). All these flights are very popular and you'll need to book ahead if you want to be sure of getting a seat.

Air Kenya Aviation (☎ 02-501601, email resvns@airkenya.com) flies between Kilimanjaro international airport and Nairobi daily (US$135 one way) and occasionally runs special deals to Unguja.

Air Tanzania has flights twice weekly between Mombasa and Dar es Salaam (US$75). Precision Air offers a service between Mombasa and Kilimanjaro (US$127) if there is sufficient demand, which is infrequent.

Skylink (☎ 02-606852, fax 606508) has offices at Wilson airport and flies between Nairobi and Mwanza on Tuesdays and Thursdays (US$195 one way).

Uganda

Uganda Airlines (☎ 02-221354, fax 214744) and Kenya Airways both have two flights a day to Entebbe for US$138/200 one way/return.

LAND
Tanzania

Mombasa to Dar es Salaam Tawfiq has departures twice daily to Dar es Salaam (KSh 600) via Tanga. Buses leave at 9 am and 6 pm. You'll get lunch on the 9 am departure and you have to sleep in the bus at the border on the 6 pm departure. Tawfiq also offers a minibus service to Tanga at 1.30 pm (KSh 300). Officially, the journey from Mombasa to Tanga takes about 4½ hours, and to Dar es Salaam about 11 hours, but delays at the border can lengthen these times considerably.

The bus office in Mombasa is on Kenyatta Ave opposite the Kobil station. Tawfiq also has an office in Ukunda, south of Mombasa.

The minibus services offered by Takrim and Al-Yumeiny are a good option. Both offer shuttle minibus services to Dar es

Salaam for KSh 800 including lunch, and both leave at around 9 am from near the Kobil station on Kenyatta Ave. Al-Yumeiny (☎ 011-490281) is the better operator and can be persuaded to pick you up south of Mombasa, in Ukunda or on the main road above Tiwi Beach.

No one but a masochist would do this journey the hard way by taking public buses in stages. For a start, there's a 3km walk between the two border crossings and hitching is well-nigh impossible. Doing it this way could take you the best part of two days.

Nairobi to Arusha & Moshi Between Nairobi and Arusha there's a choice of normal buses and minibus shuttles. All of them go through the border crossings without a change of vehicle.

Minibus shuttles vary slightly in price (cheap rates have to be requested) but all take the same amount of time (five hours).

Riverside Shuttle (☎ 02-335561) 5th floor, Consolidated Bank House, Koinange St, Nairobi. One of the cheapest shuttle companies. It departs Nairobi for Arusha at 8.30 am and 2 pm from opposite Norfolk Hotel on Harry Thuku Rd. The fare is KSh 1000 and the shuttle should drop you at any downtown hotel; just ask the driver. Be careful regarding fares – Riverside may initially attempt to charge you US$25 (US$30 to Moshi) if you're a nonresident. Simply telling them you're going to check our prices with their rivals usually does the trick.

Davanu Shuttle (☎ 02-217178) 4th floor, Windsor House, University Way, Nairobi. It departs Nairobi for Arusha daily at 8.30 am and 2 pm. The fare is KSh 1000. Davanu services continue to Dar es Salaam. Like Riverside, Davanu will drop you at any downtown hotel at either end on request. Services leave from outside New Stanley Hotel, which is where you can book your ticket. The warning on nonresident fares applies to Davanu as well as Riverside.

Arusha Express Much cheaper is Arusha Express, which operates full-sized buses. The office is in among the cluster of bus companies down Accra Rd in Nairobi. It operates a daily service from Nairobi to Arusha departing at 8.30 am (KSh 600, about four hours).

Tawfiq & Akamba Also on Accra Rd in Nairobi, Tawfiq offers similar services (leaving at 7 am and 7 pm) and Akamba is preparing its own 7 am service (KSh 600).

Getting through customs and immigration on all the above buses is straightforward. The only snag you might encounter is being approached by touts who claim they are employed by the bus company to get you through the border crossing. This they will do (unnecessarily), claiming in the process that officially you have to change US$50 to enter Tanzania and offering a ridiculous exchange rate. Don't fall for it.

It's easy, but less convenient, to do this journey in stages, and since the Kenyan and Tanzanian border crossings are next to each other at Namanga, there's no long walk involved. From Nairobi there are frequent matatus (KSh 240, three hours) and share-taxis (KSh 350, two hours) to the border, which go when full. Both have depots outside the petrol station on Ronald Ngala St in Nairobi, close to the junction with River Rd.

Nairobi to Dar es Salaam Tawfiq, Taqwa and Hoodliner all operate daily services to Dar es Salaam leaving at 7 pm (KSh 1200, 10 to 12 hours). There are also occasional departures at 7 am with other companies. In Nairobi the buses park outside the Arusha Express office in Accra Rd. A sign on the bus door displays the departure time. Tickets can be booked with the bus crew – they hang out on the bus.

Voi to Moshi The crossing between Voi and Moshi via Taveta is reliable as far as transport goes (buses, matatus and share-taxis), especially if you go on Wednesday or Saturday (market days in Taveta).

A matatu between Voi and Taveta (along a bumpy road) takes 2½ hours and costs KSh 220. It's a 3km walk from Taveta to Holili (the Tanzanian border), but there are boda-boda (bicycle taxis) for TSh 300. From Holili there are plenty of matatus and share-taxis to Moshi.

There are no trains between Kenya and Tanzania. There *may* be an occasional train from Voi to Taveta, but that is it. Allegedly, it leaves at 5 am every day and costs KSh 180 in 2nd class (which is all that is on offer). The journey takes about five hours and the train returns to Voi the same day.

KENYA

Kisumu/Kisii to Musoma/Mwanza The road is sealed all the way between Kisumu and Mwanza; this is a fine route to travel. Rumours persist of a Tawfiq and Trans-African Roadways bus service between the two; however, in reality the direct transport is an occasional bus from Kisii to Musoma and Mwanza and vice versa. There are also frequent matatus from Kisii to the border, and it is only a short walk between border crossings. There is plenty of transport on the other side.

Alternatively, you can take the Nyambongo bus from Kisumu to Serara, which is just before the border or just after the border depending on who you talk to – check locally. It leaves at 8.30 am and costs KSh 300. Not much traffic uses this route but travelling it poses no great problems.

At the time of writing Akamba were preparing to start a service from Nairobi to Mwanza leaving at 4 pm (KSh 1000).

Masai Mara to Serengeti There is no public transport along this route. If you look at any detailed map of Masai Mara Game Reserve and Serengeti National Park, you'll see that there's a border crossing between Sand River and Bologonya. It's straightforward to use, although you'll need to pay park fees. See the Serengeti National Park section in the Northern Tanzania chapter and the Masai Mara Game Reserve section in The Rift Valley chapter for details of fees.

Officially, to cross into Tanzania here you need to be a resident of East Africa, and as there is no customs post, officially you should have a customs clearance from Nairobi. However, with a little polite haggling it's usually possible to cross.

Uganda

The main border crossing for overland travellers is Malaba, with Busia being an alternative if you are coming from Kisumu.

Nairobi to Kampala Akamba (☎ 02-225488) operates four direct buses between Kampala and Nairobi daily. The executive class buses cost KSh 900 and depart at 7 am and 7 pm. The journey takes around 12 to

14 hours. Akamba also has its daily Royal service, which is real luxury with large seats similar to 1st-class in an aircraft. There are only three in each row! Tickets cost KSh 1600 and the price includes a meal at the halfway point (Eldoret). The Akamba office in Nairobi is on Lagos Rd.

Mawingo, Takwa, Tawfiq and Coastline also operate daily buses to Kampala, leaving at around 8 pm from the bottom of Accra Rd in Nairobi. These are marginally cheaper than Akamba (Ksh 700), but are more crowded and take up to 15 hours.

A more comfortable option is the door-to-door shuttle minibus service offered by Jaguar Tours & Camping Safaris (☎ 02-335156, email jaguar@nbnet.co.ke), based at Gilfilan House, Kenyatta Ave, Nairobi. Minibus shuttles depart Nairobi on Monday and Thursday at 8 am. The bus is fully air-conditioned and lunch in Eldoret is thrown in. The cost is KSh 2000. At the border tell the driver exactly the length of visa you require and it will be taken care of.

You can also do the journey in stages: several companies run daily buses between Nairobi and Malaba (KSh 500). Akamba departs at around 8 pm and arrives at about 6 am the following day. There are frequent matatus until the late afternoon between the border and Kampala.

The Ugandan and Kenyan border crossings are about 1km from each other at Malaba and you can walk or take a boda-boda.

Kisumu to Kampala The other border crossing between Kenya and Uganda is via Busia further south. There are frequent matatus between Kisumu and Busia, and frequent share-taxis between Busia and Jinja. Akamba has direct buses between Kisumu and Kampala. Buses leave Kisumu daily at noon, and cost KSh 700 (KSh 1000 for the Royal service). Tawfiq operates on the same route and charges KSh 500.

Train All Ugandan passenger train services were suspended at the time of writing, but they may someday resume. For this reason, the following information may be useful. Departure from Kampala was at 4 pm on

Wednesday, arriving in Nairobi at 2.40 pm on Thursday, and the fare was USh 57,850/35,300 in 1st/2nd class.

SEA & LAKE
Tanzania

It's possible to go by dhow between Unguja and Pemba islands and Mombasa but sailings are very infrequent these days. You could try at Shimoni, where a new customs house is being built, but you may have to return to Mombasa for an exit stamp.

The ferry MS *Sepideh* operated by Zanzibar Sea Ferries Ltd (☎ 011-311486) is not much more reliable. It sometimes connects Mombasa with Pemba and Unguja islands, Tanga and Dar es Salaam, but at the time of writing was not operating in Kenya. Luxurious cruise liners still ply the route, but they are very expensive. Inquire locally before deciding on anything.

At the time of writing there were no ferry services on Lake Victoria, though if newspaper stories are to be believed some are planned. Dhows do sail between small Kenyan and Tanzanian ports on the lake, but many are smuggling (fruit mostly!) and cannot be recommended.

Getting Around

AIR

Domestic Air Services

Kenya Airways (☎ 02-229291) connects Nairobi, Mombasa, Kisumu, Malindi and Lamu. It's advisable to book in advance and essential to reconfirm 48 hours before departure if you're coming from Malindi or Kisumu and have to connect with an international flight from Nairobi or Mombasa airports. See the relevant city entries in the Kenya chapters for flight schedules and fares.

The main Kenya Airways booking office in Nairobi is located with the KLM offices at Barclays Plaza on Loita St.

Air Kenya Aviation (☎ 02-501601, email resvns@airkenya.com) is the only other scheduled airline in the country. Using large and small prop aircraft it has scheduled services connecting Lamu, Kiwayu, Mombasa, Malindi, Nanyuki and the national parks/reserves of Amboseli, Masai Mara, Samburu, Tsavo and Lewa Downs. It is an efficient, well-run organisation and operates out of Nairobi's Wilson airport and Mombasa's Moi airport.

A much smaller operation, African Express Airways (☎ 02-823497) flies from Nairobi to Eldoret (daily) and Nairobi to Mombasa (twice daily). It operates from Jomo Kenyatta international airport.

Private Charter Airlines

Chartering a small plane saves you time and is the only realistic way to get to some parts of Kenya. It is expensive, but not prohibitively so. For a three-day trip up to Sibiloi National Park on the west of Lake Turkana expect to pay around US$350 per person if five people are sharing.

With the growth in the humanitarian relief business in Sudan and Somalia many charter companies have sprung up at Wilson airport. Excel Aviation (☎/fax 02-501751) has an excellent reputation, while Boskovic Air Charters (☎ 02-501210, fax 505964) can also be recommended. The members of the Aero Club at Wilson airport may be able to steer you in the direction of a cheap charter.

Domestic Departure Tax

There is a KSh 100 departure tax on all domestic flights.

BUS

Bus fares are generally very cheap, about KSh 1 per kilometre at a rough estimate. Seats are preassigned and when you purchase a ticket you'll be given a choice of available seats. Don't sit at the back (you'll be thrown around) and sitting at the front gives you a great view of oncoming traffic, often a frightening experience. Unlike the trains, which travel at night, many buses travel during the day so you may prefer to take a bus if you want to see the countryside.

Akamba has the most comprehensive network, and it has a pretty good safety record. The government bus line, KBS Stagecoach, runs rather tired buses around Mombasa and Nairobi and between the main towns. They tend to be slower, but they are reliable and safe. The new KBS buses on the coast are very good. Of the other private companies, Coastline, Goldline, Eldoret Express and Kensilver are all OK, but the drivers employed by Shaggy Home Boyz are speed-crazed fanatics.

Some Kenyan towns have a designated bus station (often just a spare patch of ground) while some bus companies have their own terminus (Akamba always has its own separate terminus). Matatu and share-taxi ranks sometimes use the same stations as buses but this isn't always the case, especially in Nairobi.

A number of private 'shuttle buses' connect Nairobi with Mombasa. They're more comfortable than ordinary buses and take around 18 passengers, but they are more expensive than ordinary buses. Their schedules can be found in the Getting Around section in the Nairobi chapter and the Mombasa section in the Coast chapter.

A number of passengers have been drugged on buses recently. After accepting food or drink from strangers they fell asleep, waking much later to find all their possessions missing.

MATATU

Most local people travel in matatus. These can be anything from small, dilapidated Peugeot 504 pick-ups with a cab on the back, to shiny, brightly painted 20-seat minibuses complete with mega-decibel stereos, as found in Nairobi. The majority of those tackling the long-distance runs, however, are white Nissan minibuses that should take 18 passengers, but often take many, many more. Most matatu drivers are under a lot of pressure to maximise profits

---

How to Survive a Matatu

Matatus are more than just transport. They are Kenya's contribution to world culture. These gaudily painted minibuses with 200-decibel stereo systems have a crew of three: the driver, who normally hasn't slept for three days, keeping himself going by chewing miraa shoots; the conductor, who extracts fares from reluctant passengers; and the tout, a veritable Daddy Cool whose aerial gymnastics on the outside of the minibus ought to be an Olympic event. Governmental efforts to regulate the matatu industry have reduced decibel levels, but not much more.

Matatu travel is not exactly a bed of roses. In fact, as one look at the *Daily Nation* will tell you, the beds most often associated with matatus are the ones in hospitals, so there are a few rules and principles you should be aware of:

- Under no circumstances allow yourself to be placed in the 'Death Seat' next to the driver – extra leg-room and the occasional shoot of miraa do not outweigh the disadvantage of certain death in the event of a head-on collision.
- Just which are the best seats in a matatu is debatable. The two rows behind the driver should be avoided for safety reasons, while the back seat is a pain in the neck for tall people. Sitting next to the window is OK, but you'll bang your head when crossing rough ground. Wedged in like a sardine on the middle two seats in the second row from the back you'll be better protected in the event of a head-on collision, overturning on a sharp corner or any end-over-end Evil Knevel-type stunts. Fight for these seats.
- Don't voluntarily get into a matatu named 'Death or Glory', 'White Lightning', 'Get in & Die', 'Velocity' or 'Beat the Reaper' for obvious reasons.
- Valium is available over the counter in Kenya.
- Avoid night journeys because of drunk drivers and the lack of adequate/any lights on many vehicles. However, it's been suggested that matatu standard operating procedure (overtaking on blind bends, below the crest of steep hills etc) makes travelling at night a safer option. At least headlights warn of an oncoming vehicle, if it has any headlights ...
- If the locals look nervous you have a problem.
- Engine ignition can occur 45 minutes before you leave and is simply a method of attracting passing trade. The same goes for a sudden, but slow, departure (often just a tour of the bus station). Up to five changes of driver may occur during this stage.
- There is always room for one more.
- Getting into a passing half-empty matatu is not always a good idea if the crew is just trawling the streets in an effort to fill the vehicle. At the bus station numerous touts will try and fill the vehicle which will speed up your journey. Not that it'll require much speeding up.
- A pot-holed road is a good road. It slows you down.

so they tend to drive recklessly and overload their vehicles. Of course, many travellers use them and, in some cases, there is no alternative, but if there is (such as a bus or train) then take that in preference. The Mombasa-Nairobi and Nairobi-Meru roads are notorious for smashes.

You can always find a matatu that is going to the next town or further afield so long as it's not too late in the day. Simply ask around among the drivers at the park. Matatus leave when full and the fares are fixed. It's unlikely you will be asked for more money than other passengers.

SHARE-TAXI

Share-taxis are usually Peugeot 505 station wagons that take seven to nine passengers and leave when full. They are much quicker than the matatus as they go from point to point without stopping, and of course are more expensive. They are probably slightly more common in western Kenya, but numerous destinations are serviced from Nairobi. Like matatus, most of the share-taxi companies have offices around the Accra, Cross and River Rds area in Nairobi.

TRAIN

Travelling by train in Kenya is becoming a rare experience. The train compartments, tracks and other essential works have been allowed to deteriorate and at the time of writing the only remaining 1st and 2nd class service was from Nairobi to Mombasa. A 3rd class service between Kisumu and Nairobi still runs, and there is, allegedly, a train from Voi to Taveta, but passenger services to Eldoret, Malaba, Tanzania and Uganda have all stopped. Much safer than taking the bus, the Mombasa train generally departs on time, but usually arrives around an hour late.

Classes

First class consists of two-berth compartments with a washbasin, drinking water, a wardrobe and a drinks service. There's a lockable door between one compartment and the adjacent one, so if there are four of you travelling together, you can make one compartment out of two. They're usually very clean, but you can't lock the door of your compartment from the outside when you go for meals.

Second class consists of four-berth compartments with a washbasin and drinking water. Third class is seats only. All the compartments have fans. Sexes are separated in 1st and 2nd class unless you book the whole compartment. Again, compartments aren't lockable from the outside, so don't leave any valuables lying around and maybe padlock your backpack to something.

Travelling overnight in uncomfortable 3rd class cannot be recommended for security reasons.

Reservations are required for 1st and 2nd class. This can be done over the phone. Compartment and berth numbers are posted on a noticeboard on the platform about 30 minutes before departure.

Meals & Bedding

Most trains have a dining car for dinner and breakfast. Meals on the trains used to be something special, but as the quality of the trains has deteriorated, so has the quality of food. However, cold beer is available. Bedding is provided in 1st and 2nd class.

CAR & 4WD

If you are bringing your own vehicle to Kenya you can get a free three-month permit at the border on entry, so long as you have a valid *carnet de passage* (see Carnet under Car & Motorcycle in the Getting Around East Africa chapter). If you don't have a carnet you should be able to get a free one-week permit at the border, after which you must get an 'authorisation permit for a foreign private vehicle' at Nyayo House, Kenyatta Ave, Nairobi. It costs only a few dollars but involves a lot of time queuing. Before you do this, however, get in touch with the Automobile Association of Kenya (☎ 02-720341) in the Hurlingham shopping centre (signposted) in Nairobi.

Foreign-registered vehicles with a seating capacity of more than six people are not allowed to enter Kenyan wildlife parks and reserves.

Road Conditions

There are some good roads in Kenya but to a degree it depends on which party the local member of parliament belongs to. If it's KANU (the ruling party) the roads will be good; elsewhere, watch out for potholes. The best road in the country is from Marigat to Kabarnet – President Moi is the local MP.

The torrential El Niño rains of 1997 and 1998 had a particularly devastating effect on the Kenyan road network and on the Mombasa-Nairobi road (A104) in particular. Drive very carefully along here as it's dangerously narrow in places, and at all costs avoid driving at night (good advice for all Kenyan roads).

The roads in the north and north-east and in the national parks are all gravel, in varying states of repair and long sections are badly corrugated. Naturally, there are washouts on some of these gravel roads during the rainy seasons and journey times can be considerably longer. If a bridge gets washed out, you'll have to either turn back or wait. You need a 4WD for venturing into these areas.

After rain, many roads in the region, particularly on the flat parts of the deserts, turn into treacherous seas of mud. Only a complete fool would attempt to drive in these circumstances without 4WD, sand ladders, adequate jacking equipment, shovels, a tow rope or wire, drinking water and spare metal cans of fuel. This is particularly true of the stretches of track between North Horr and Maikona and on any of the tracks leading off the Marsabit to Isiolo road through the Losai National Reserve.

Little transport travels these roads and you can sometimes drive for hours only to find that it's impossible to cross a river, which may not even exist in the dry season. Fuel is also very difficult to find in this region and is usually only available at mission stations for up to three times what you would pay for it in Nairobi.

Fuel Costs

In Nairobi, petrol costs KSh 45 per litre. Diesel is somewhat cheaper at KSh 39.

Rental

Hiring a vehicle to tour Kenya (or at least the national parks) is a relatively expensive way of seeing the country but it does give you freedom of movement and is sometimes the only way of getting to the more remote parts of the country. If you can share the costs it can be a feasible option, and is highly recommended.

Of all the world's tourist destinations, Kenya must be one of the most expensive when it comes to vehicle hire. Every element seems to carry its own cost. The costs range between KSh 1200 and KSh 6500 for the standard daily charge, plus KSh 12 to KSh 25 for every kilometre travelled, then KSh 600 to KSh 1100 per day for CDW insurance (Collision Damage Waiver) and around KSh 600 per day for TPW insurance (Theft Protection Waiver).

At the bottom end of the scale are the tiny 2WD runabouts and at the top end the Land Rovers. Most people end up with a small 4WD vehicle such as a Suzuki Sierra which costs roughly KSh 1500 per day plus KSh 15 per kilometre, plus CDW and TPW of KSh 600 each.

You'll get a better day rate the longer you hire, and some unlimited mileage deals are available though invariably there is a maximum weekly mileage (often 1200km). There could also be a minimum mileage rate of 50 or 100km which you would pay regardless.

The most important thing to look out for is the statutory excess which you'll be left to pay in the event of an accident or theft. Almost all companies levy an excess of around KSh 40,000 (Glory has an excess of KSh 150,000) and this is in addition to the insurance costs. Some companies offer an optional excess waiver charge of around KSh 400 that protects you from paying any excess in the event of an accident or theft.

You'll also need to add 16% value added tax (VAT) to the total cost plus an extra 1 to 4% on top of this if you pay by credit card.

Deposit A large deposit will always be required but the amount varies. The most convenient way to pay is by credit card.

Driving Licence An international driving licence or your own national driving licence is standard. Some companies stipulate a minimum age of 23 years but with others it is 25. Some companies require that you have a clear driving record and that you have been driving for at least two years. You will also need acceptable ID such as a passport.

Maintenance Although it's not always the case, you usually get what you pay for. However, check the vehicle thoroughly wherever you hire it from before handing over any money.

Also find out what the company will do for you in the event of an accident. Some companies will come out and get the vehicle fixed; others will tell you to get it fixed, promising to refund the money when you return (you'll need receipts to prove what you spent). Some companies will make you pay for repairs to punctures or new tyres if they're needed.

Rental Agencies At the top end of the market are a number of international companies:

Avis (☎ 02-822186) Jomo Kenyatta international airport, Nairobi; (☎ 02-336794) Koinange St, Nairobi; (☎ 011-223048) Moi Ave, Mombasa; (☎ 0123-20513) Sitawi House, Malindi; (☎ 011-485721) Serena Beach Hotel, Mombasa

Budget Rent-a-Car (☎ 02-822370) Jomo Kenyatta international airport, Nairobi; (☎ 02-440333, email payless@kenyaonline.com) Hilton Hotel, Simba St, Nairobi; (☎ 011-434759) Moi international airport, Mombasa; (☎ 011-221281) Saroya House, Moi Ave, Mombasa

Hertz (☎ 02-822339) Jomo Kenyatta international airport, Nairobi; (☎ 02-331960, email utcn@attmail.com) Muindi Mbingu St, Nairobi; (☎ 011-433211) Moi international airport, Mombasa; (☎ 011-316333) Moi Ave, Mombasa; (☎ 0123-20040) Moi Ave, Malindi

National Car Rental (☎ 02-440333, email natcarnb@africaonline.co.ke) Woodvale Grove, Westlands, Nairobi; (☎ 011-221358, email natcarnbma@africaonline.co.ke) Harbour House, Moi Ave, Mombasa; (☎ 035-41747) Jovena Service Station, Kisumu

Somewhat cheaper but very reliable companies with well maintained vehicles include:

Central Rent-a-Car (☎ 02-222888, fax 339666, email cars@carhire.kenya.com) Fedha Towers, Standard St, Nairobi Web site: www.carhirekenya.com

Concorde Car Hire (☎ 02-743304, fax 748628, email Concorde@swiftkenya.com) 2nd floor, Sarit Centre, Westlands, PO Box 25053, Nairobi

Glory Car Hire (☎ 02-2250224, fax 331533) Diamond Bldg, Tubman Rd, Nairobi; (☎ 011-313561, fax 221196) Moi Ave, Mombasa; (☎/fax 0123-20065) Ngala Bldg, Lamu Rd, Malindi

Habib's Tours & Travel (☎ 02-220463, fax 220985, email habibtours@attmail.com) Haile Selassie Ave, PO Box 48095, Nairobi

Market Car Hire (☎ 02-225797, email market@net2000ke.com) Market Service Station, on the corner of Koinange & Banda Sts, Nairobi

Central Rent-a-Car is the best in this category with a well maintained fleet of fairly new vehicles and a good back-up service. Its excess liability on CDW is also the lowest (KSh 2000), and its insurance rates include *both* TPW and CDW. Habib's is also a reliable company.

Market and Payless are run by the same people and their excess liability on CDW would leave you penniless if you had an accident (KSh 40,000), although this is nothing compared to Glory which levies KSh 150,000 in excess.

BICYCLE

Anyone foolish enough to risk cycling along main roads in Kenya must be considered suicidal. Always assume that the vehicle approaching you from behind is going to knock you off the road. In the countryside off the main roads things are a little better. Popular locations for cycling include the edge of the Masai Mara, Central and Western Highlands, the Kerio Valley, Arabuko Sokoke Forest and Hell's Gate National Park. Expect to cover around 80km per day in the hills. Be especially wary of cycling off-road, where punctures from thorn trees are a major problem.

It's possible to hire mountain bikes in an increasing number of places for between KSh 300 and KSh 500 per day. Several tour operators now offer cycling safaris. See the Organised Safaris chapter for details.

HITCHING

Hitching is usually good on the main roads and may be better than travelling by matatu, but if you are picked up by an African driver and you expect a free lift, then make this clear from the outset. Most will expect a contribution at least.

Hitching to the national parks, on the other hand, can be very difficult since most people either go on a tour or hire their own vehicle. Apart from that, once you get to the park lodges or camping areas, you will be entirely dependent on persuading other tourists with their own transport to take you out with them to view game since walking in the parks is generally forbidden.

Although many travellers hitch (it's the only way to get to some places), it is not a totally safe way of getting around. Just because we explain how hitching works does not mean we recommend it.

BOAT
Lake Victoria

The collapse of the ferry system on Lake Victoria means that taxi boats (10m-long motorised canoes) are the only way to get to Mfangano, Rusinga and Takawiri Islands from the lakeshore. The best place to pick them up is Mbita Point.

There is no reliable boat transport connecting Kisumu, Kendu Bay and Homa Bay, despite speculation that a new ferry service may start. It's best to inquire locally.

Nairobi

☎ 02

Until the late 19th century, what is now a bustling city was just a boggy watering hole for the Maasai. Then came the Mombasa to Uganda railway, with its 32,000 indentured Indian labourers from Gujarat and the Punjab, along with their British colonial overlords intent on beating the German colonial push for the Ugandan heartland. Being approximately halfway between Mombasa and Uganda and a convenient place to pause before the arduous climb into the highlands, Nairobi became a tent city.

Much of the area was still a foul-smelling swamp and wildlife roamed freely over the surrounding plains, yet by 1900 it had become a town of substantial buildings and five years later succeeded Mombasa as the capital of the British East Africa protectorate. With a population of over 1.5 million it's now the largest city between Cairo and Johannesburg.

Nairobi is a city of contrasts. It's a place of smart office workers, huge mansions and expensive shopping centres as well as shameful overcrowded slums and the most basic of manual labour that pays less than US$1 per day. Sooner or later you'll find yourself in River Rd, the matatu centre of Kenya. It's an area full of energy, aspiration and opportunism where manual workers, exhausted matatu drivers, the unemployed, the devious, the down-and-out and the disoriented mingle with budget travellers, whores, shopkeepers, high-school students, food-stall vendors, drowsy security guards and those with life's little illicit goodies for sale.

Elsewhere in Nairobi are all the things you won't have seen for months if you've been making do with the shortages in other parts of Africa. You can take care of business here in offices where you can get things done with minimum fuss. It's a cosmopolitan place with the latest films on big screens, bookshops, cafes and bars full of travellers from all over the world. There are a huge number of restaurants (everything

Highlights

- Taking a guided tour through the National Museum of Kenya
- Becoming a kid again at Langata Giraffe Centre
- Listening to live Kenyan music at the City Cabanas or the African Heritage Hotel
- Partying long into the night at La Papa Loca and the Klub House
- Splashing out on some seriously good food at Alan Bobbe's Bistro, Haandi or Akasaka
- Birdwatching with the East Africa Natural History Society

from Lebanese to Japanese) and there are also excellent photographic shops, express mail and fax services and numerous places where you can send and receive email. It's a great place to stay for a while and party hard, but stay too long and you'll spend a fortune.

On the downside, Nairobi is becoming increasingly lawless and you'll have to be on your guard. Partly because of the crime rate in the city centre and partly because of the traffic problems, many restaurants, bars, shops and other businesses are moving to Westlands and the other suburbs.

ORIENTATION

The compact city centre is bounded by Uhuru Hwy, Haile Selassie Ave, Tom Mboya St and University Way. The main bus and train stations are within a few minutes walk of this area, while the main budget travellers' accommodation area is centred on Latema Rd, just east of Tom Mboya St on the fringe of the bustling and somewhat sleazy River Rd area.

North of the centre are the University of Nairobi, the National Museum, the International Casino and one of Nairobi's original colonial hotels, the Norfolk. Beyond here is

Westlands. South-east of the centre is Jomo Kenyatta international airport and south are Wilson airport and Nairobi National Park.

Maps
Of the many available maps of Nairobi, the best is probably the *City of Nairobi: Map & Guide* (produced by the Survey of Kenya) which is in English, French and German. It covers the suburbs as well as having a detailed map of the central area, but it's now difficult to get. Also good, with all the hotels and places of interest marked, is the 1:25000 *Map of Greater Nairobi* (KSh 250) published by Tourist Maps.

If you're staying for a while, *Nairobi A to Z* (Kenway Publications, KSh 375), by RW Moss, is worth buying.

INFORMATION
Tourist Office
Remarkably there is no tourist office in Nairobi and you'll have to glean what you can from two average (but free) booklets: *Tourist's Kenya* and *What's On?* You can occasionally pick these up at the better hotels, car hire companies, travel agents etc. They both contain considerable advertising, but there are some good listings for Nairobi, Mombasa and the major wildlife parks.

Money
Barclays Bank at Jomo Kenyatta international airport is open 24 hours a day, seven days a week. In Nairobi, there are numerous branches with ATMs. A central branch is on the corner of Kenyatta Ave and Moi Ave and is open Monday to Saturday from 9 am to 4.30 pm.

Foreign exchange bureaus are found on virtually every street in the city centre including Mama Ngina St (Crown), Standard St (Finerate), Kenyatta Ave (Taipan and Chase), Muindi Mbingu St (Nairobi) and Utalii St. Up in Westlands there are two choices – the Travellers Forex Bureau in the basement of the Mall shopping centre and the Union Forex Bureau in the Sarit Centre. All display the day's rates for European and North American currencies and some will also take Australian and New Zealand currencies.

American Express (☎ 334722), at Express Travel Kenya, Bruce House, Standard St, is open Monday to Friday from 8.30 am to 4.30 pm. It can issue travellers cheques but cannot cash them. It also has a client mail service.

Post & Communications
Post The main post office is on Haile Selassie Ave. A new post office on Kenyatta Ave has been under construction for many years now and will probably remain in that condition for some time to come. The office on Haile Selassie is open Monday to Friday from 8 am to 5 pm and Saturday from 9 am to noon. At the poste restante you are allowed to look through as many piles as you like, which is just as well as letters can get misfiled. As a favour to other travellers, pull out any letters you come across that are misfiled so the clerk can put them into the right pile. There's no charge for letters collected. The only trouble is that the poste restante counter is also one of the few that sells stamps, so the queues are often long.

This post office is also the best one for posting parcels. You have to take the parcel *unwrapped* to be inspected by customs at the post office not later than 3.30 pm. One of the cheapest places to buy good packing materials is the supermarket on Koinange St opposite the new post office. Otherwise, try Biba on Kenyatta Ave at the Muindi Mbingu St intersection.

If you just want stamps, the small post office on Moi Ave just north of Kenyatta Ave is much more central. There's also a post office on the ground floor of the Kenyatta Conference Centre overlooking the city square and another in the Sarit Centre in Westlands.

Private couriers DHL (☎ 223063, email booking@nbo-co.kedhl.com) are found in Longonot Place, Kijabe St, and on the ground floor of the Sarit Centre.

See Post & Communications in the Kenya Facts for the Visitor chapter for more details.

Telephone The introduction of cardphones throughout central Nairobi makes operator-assisted calls unnecessary, but should you get stuck the Extelcoms office is on Haile Selassie Ave, almost opposite the post office. It is open from 8 am to midnight. You can also make calls at the post office on the ground floor of the Kenyatta Conference Centre. As long as there's not a conference in progress it's much quieter than the Extelcoms office.

A number of private agencies in the centre of town offer international telephone services but their charges are higher than at the Extelcoms office. Count on about KSh 300 per minute to anywhere in Europe, North America and Africa and KSh 400 per minute to anywhere in South America, Asia and Australasia.

In Westlands, two good places to make international calls are CopyCat on the ground floor of the Sarit Centre, and Finance & General (☎ 443864) in the basement of the Mall shopping centre (credit cards accepted).

Fax The Extelcoms office offers cheap telex and fax services, but be prepared to queue.

As with telephone calls, there are numerous private agencies offering fax services, but prices vary wildly. Major Secretarial Services (☎ 218595, email masese@insightkenya .com) in Uniafric House on Koinange St is among the cheapest (KSh 180 for a one-page fax to Europe).

In Westlands you can send faxes through Finance & General (cheaper) in the basement of the Mall shopping centre or at CopyCat (more expensive) in the Sarit Centre.

Internet & Email Competition between Internet Service Providers (ISPs) is fierce in Nairobi meaning that it's the cheapest place in Kenya to send email. Browsing prices vary, but simply to send/receive an email costs KSh 100/40.

Major Secretarial Services (☎ 218595, email masese@insightkenya.com) is among the cheapest for browsing (KSh 100 for 15 minutes). Try Bazaar Business Centre (☎ 250602) on the corner of Muindi Mbingu and Biashara Sts for the same rate. Cyberc@fe Services (email cybercom@ africaonline.co.ke) on Kaunda St charges KSh 150 for 15 minutes access, but rates are

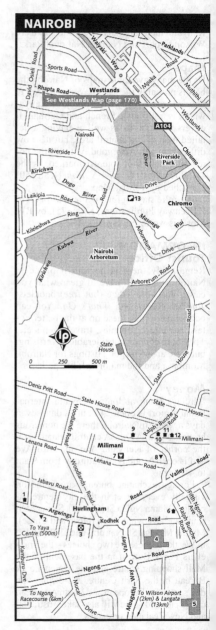

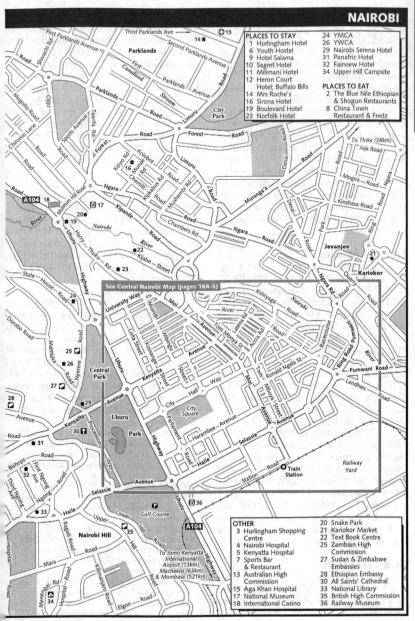

KENYA

NAIROBI

PLACES TO STAY
1 Hurlingham Hotel
6 Youth Hostel
9 Hotel Salama
10 Sagret Hotel
11 Milimani Hotel
12 Heron Court
   Hotel; Buffalo Bills
14 Mrs Roche's
16 Sirona Hotel
19 Boulevard Hotel
23 Norfolk Hotel
24 YMCA
26 YWCA
29 Nairobi Serena Hotel
31 Panafric Hotel
32 Fairview Hotel
34 Upper Hill Campsite

PLACES TO EAT
2 The Blue Nile Ethiopian
   & Shogun Restaurants
8 China Town
   Restaurant & Fredz

OTHER
3 Hurlingham Shopping
   Centre
4 Nairobi Hospital
5 Kenyatta Hospital
7 Sports Bar
   & Restaurant
13 Australian High
   Commission
15 Aga Khan Hospital
17 National Museum
18 International Casino
20 Snake Park
21 Kariokor Market
22 Text Book Centre
25 Zambian High
   Commission
27 Sudan & Zimbabwe
   Embassies
28 Ethiopian Embassy
30 All Saints' Cathedral
33 National Library
35 British High Commission
36 Railway Museum

See Central Nairobi Map (pages 164-5)

discounted between 8.30 and 9.30 am. The Hard Rock Cafe charges KSh 300 for 30 minutes, but there's only one machine.

Cyber Cafe in the Mall in Westlands charges KSh 150 for 15 minutes, though CopyCat on the ground floor of the Sarit Centre is better set up. Prices are the same and there are three machines.

In the Yaya Centre in Hurlingham, Millenium Cyber Cafe (email yayaguest@hotmail .com) has 14 machines and charges KSh 350 per hour for browsing. Rates are cheaper between 8.30 and 10.30 am.

As for the ISPs themselves, Africaonline (☎ 243775, email sales@africaonline) is the biggest and the best, followed by Net2000 (☎ 213000, email info@net2000ke.com) and Form Net (☎ 245630, email sales@ form-net.com).

Travel Agencies

One of the best agencies (and the best for budget travellers) is Flight Centres (☎ 210024, fax 332407, email fcswwat@arcc.or.ke) on the 2nd floor, Lakhamshi House, Biashara St. This company has been doing discounted airline tickets for years and is totally switched on to the backpacker market. It also offers a visa service, acts as a broker for camping safaris and runs overland trips across east and southern Africa.

Also highly recommended is Let's Go Travel (☎ 340331, fax 336890, email info@ letsgosafari.com), on Standard St, close to the intersection with Koinange St. A second branch is in the Mall at Westlands. It can deal with all your travel requirements and publishes an excellent price list of hotels, lodges, camps and bandas in Kenya. Visit its Web site at www.letsgosafari.com for online information.

Dream Travel Africa (☎ 572139, fax 577489, email dreamtravel@form-net.com) on Galana Rd, just off Argwings Kodhek Rd, Hurlingham, is also very sharp.

Visa Extensions

Visas can be renewed at the immigration office (☎ 332110) in Nyayo House (ground floor) on the corner of Kenyatta Ave and Uhuru Hwy.

Bookshops

Text Book Centre (☎ 747405, email info@ tbc.co.ke) on the ground floor of the Sarit Centre in Westlands must be the best bookshop in East Africa. The selection is enormous, including not only imported western books and glossy coffee table tomes, but also books by Kenyan and other African writers. It's a good place to pick up maps. There is a sister shop on Kijabe St.

Another place to try is the Westland Bookshop on Kenyatta Ave, around the corner from New Stanley Hotel.

Libraries

The main public library in Nairobi is the Kenya National Library (☎ 725550), Ngong Rd. It's open from 9.30 am to 6 pm Monday to Friday. The other library is the McMillan Memorial Library (☎ 221844) on Banda St. It's open from 9 am to 5 pm Monday to Friday and from 9.30 am to 1 pm Saturday.

Cultural Centres

All the foreign cultural organisations have libraries which are open to the public and are free, except for the American Cultural Center and the British Council, which are for members only (temporary membership costs around KSh 100). Maison Française is particularly good at showcasing Kenyan and African dance, music, art and performance. Its *Le Jardin Cafe* serves some of the best coffee in Nairobi. The addresses are:

American Cultural Center (☎ 334141 ext 343) National Bank Bldg, Harambee Ave. Open from 9 am to 5 pm Monday, Tuesday and Thursday, from 9 am to noon Wednesday and from 9 am to 4 pm Friday.
British Council (☎ 334855) ICEA Bldg, 1st floor, Kenyatta Ave. Open from 10 am to 6 pm Tuesday to Friday and from 10 am to 1 pm Saturday.
Goethe Institute (☎ 224640) Maendeleo House, corner Monrovia and Loita Sts. Open from 10 am to 5 pm Monday to Friday.
Maison Française (☎ 336263, fax 336253, email maisonfrance@form-net.com) Maison Française Bldg, Loita St. Open from 8.30 am to 5.30 pm Monday to Friday and 8.30 am to 1 pm Saturday.
Web site: www.frenchembassykenya.org

Nairobi Cultural Institute (☎ 569205) Ngong Rd. Has lectures and other functions of local cultural interest.

Camping Equipment

If you want to hire camping equipment (anything from a sleeping bag to a folding toilet seat) the only place to go is Atul's (☎ 225935) on Biashara St. The gear available is by no means mountaineering quality, but it will see you through a lightweight camping trip. Rates are not cheap and you'll have to leave a deposit.

Before paying to hire have a scoot around the big Uchumi supermarket in the Sarit Centre in Westlands. You may be able to buy waterproofs, blankets, cooking equipment etc, for the same price it costs to hire them.

Photography

Shops selling and developing film are common across Nairobi, as are booths taking passport-size photographs. You can also get passport photos from the photography shops all over the city, though they are more expensive; try the shop in Kimathi House opposite New Stanley Hotel or the camera shops on Mama Ngina St. For more information, see Photography in the Kenya Facts for the Visitor chapter.

Laundry

Lavage Laundrett & Dry Cleaners will wash and dry your clothes for KSh 80 per kilogram. Dry cleaning here is also reasonably priced. There are branches on Mpaka Rd in Westlands and in Norfolk Towers on Kijabe St (behind Norfolk Hotel). There's another laundrette in Hurlingham Shopping Centre, just outside the city centre towards the Yaya Centre.

For dry cleaning, try the outlets of White Rose Drycleaners on Kenyatta Ave between Loita and Koinange Sts and on Aga Khan Walk.

Medical Services

The surgery on the 3rd floor of Bruce House on Standard St (☎ 333977) is used to travellers turning up convinced they have ebola or the like. For a consultation before

and after blood tests you'll pay around KSh 1800. Laboratory tests are extra (expect to pay KSh 1500 for the works). There's a dentist on the same floor.

KAM Pharmacy (☎ 221825, fax 214076) on the corner of Standard and Kimathi Sts is a one-stop shop for medical treatment. There's a pharmacy on the ground floor, a doctor's surgery on the 1st floor and a laboratory on the 2nd.

Otherwise go to outpatients at either Nairobi Hospital (☎ 722160), off Valley Rd, or the Aga Khan Hospital (☎ 740000) on Third Parklands Ave. Avoid the Kenyatta National Hospital because, although it's free, stretched resources may cause you more problems than you have when you arrive.

Get all your immunisations done before arriving in Kenya.

Emergency

In case of emergency you could try the police (☎ 717777), or simply dial (☎ 999) but don't rely on their prompt arrival.

In a medical emergency call the Aga Khan Hospital (☎ 740000). It's reliable and has a 24-hour casualty section.

Accident Air Rescue (☎ 717376 in an emergency) is probably the best of a number of private ambulance and emergency air evacuation companies (see Health Insurance in the regional Facts for the Visitor chapter for more information).

Dangers & Annoyances

You'll often hear Nairobi referred to as 'Nairobbery.' by residents, both Kenyan and expatriate, and you'll certainly read about robberies and muggings, some of them violent, in the newspapers almost daily. See Dangers & Annoyances in the Kenya Facts for the Visitor chapter for more information.

Other specific precautions you should take are:

- Do not walk from the city centre to any of the hotels on Milimani Rd or to the youth hostel, YMCA or YWCA after dark. Uhuru Park is infamous for its muggers. Take a taxi.
- Touts selling cheap safaris (Come to Africa and Savuka are commonly hawked) are a real pain

in central Nairobi. Try not to look like a tourist, not only because of touts.

• If you think you are being followed through town, dive into a shop or bank and get someone to help you. Shopkeepers hate thieves and most have security guards.

NATIONAL MUSEUM

The Kenya National Museum (☎ 742131, fax 741424, email nmk@africaonline.co.ke) is on Museum Rd off Museum Hill Rd, and is well worth an afternoon's look.

One of the museum's major exhibits is the Peoples of Kenya portraits by Joy Adamson (of *Born Free* fame) which record the traditional cultures of the local people. They are a fantastic record and an amazing achievement. The Ethnography Gallery also houses exhibits on the material culture of the various Kenyan tribal groups.

There are displays of rock art, fossils, Swahili culture and the origins of humans plus a bird gallery with more than 900 stuffed and mounted specimens. Local artists exhibit in the Gallery of Contemporary East African Art and there's a snake park opposite the main museum.

The volunteer guides are highly knowledgeable and it's worth booking with them in advance. They do not charge for their services, but a donation to the museum is appropriate.

The museum is open from 9.30 am to 6 pm daily and admission is KSh 400 (KSh 100 for children). Take a look at the Web site at www.museums.or.ke.

NATIONAL ARCHIVES

Near the Hilton Hotel on Moi Ave is the National Archives. Along with the usual documents you'll see photographs of former presidents Kenyatta and Moi visiting different countries, and exhibitions of handicrafts and paintings.

It's open from 8.30 am to 4.30 pm Monday to Friday and from 8.30 am to 1 pm on Saturday. There is no charge, but a donation is appropriate.

The Kima Killer

Early this century when the railway line was being pushed through from Mombasa to Kampala and beyond, a remarkable incident occurred at Kima, a small siding about 110km along the track southwest of Nairobi.

A rogue lion had been terrorising the track gangs and had in fact claimed a few victims. In an attempt to eradicate this menace, a superintendent of Uganda Railways stationed in Mombasa, Charles Ryall, decided to mount a night vigil in a railway carriage specially positioned at the Kima siding. The station staff wanted nothing to do with the escapade and locked themselves firmly in the station buildings.

Ryall left the carriage door open, in the hope that the lion would be lured in, sat back with rifle at the ready and waited. Inevitably he fell asleep and just as inevitably the lion showed up. The struggle that ensued caused the sliding door on the compartment to shut and the lion was trapped inside with a firm grip on Ryall's neck. Accompanying Ryall in the carriage were two European merchants who had hitched a ride to Nairobi with Ryall, agreeing to the overnight stop in Kima. So petrified were they that one of them ducked into the toilet and bolted the door, while the other watched transfixed as the lion wrested the body out the train window!

Ryall's mother offered a reward for the capture of the offending lion but it was only when a trap, baited with a live calf, was devised that the human-eater was snared. It seems there was no reason for the lion to have turned human-eater as it was a healthy beast and there was an abundance of game animals in the vicinity – supposedly it just developed a liking for human flesh.

The railway carriage involved in this incident is today preserved in the Nairobi Railway Museum, while Ryall's tombstone is in the Hill Cemetery, also in Nairobi. It bears the inscription 'He was attacked whilst sleeping and killed by a man-eating lion at Kima'.

RAILWAY MUSEUM

The Railway Museum is on Station Rd – follow the railway tracks until you are almost at the bridge under Uhuru Hwy or walk across the small piece of vacant land next to the Haile Selassie Ave roundabout on Uhuru Hwy.

Although it looks more than a little sad these days, the museum will give you a good idea of Kenya's history since the beginning of the colonial period. As well as old steam engines and rolling stock, there's also a scale model of the venerable MV *Liemba* which plies the waters of Lake Tanganyika between Mpulungu (Zambia) and Bujumbura (Burundi).

The museum is open from 8.30 am to 5 pm daily; entry is KSh 200.

PARLIAMENT HOUSE

Like to take a look at how democracy works in Kenya? You can get a permit for a seat in the public gallery at parliament house (☎ 221291) on Parliament Rd or, if parliament is out of session, you can tour the buildings by arrangement with the sergeant-at-arms.

MZIZI ARTS CENTRE

Mzizi Arts Centre (☎ 245364, fax 245366) on the 6th Floor, Sonalux House, Moi Ave (PO Box 48955) is a good place to view contemporary Kenyan art, craft, dance, literature and performance art. 'Cultural Personality Evenings' (when Kenyan cultural stars give lectures) and Sigana performances are held here.

ART GALLERIES

There's not much in Nairobi in the way of art galleries. At the National Museum, the Gallery of Contemporary East African Art is worth a look. Of the private galleries, the Gallery Watatu in Lonrho House, Standard St, is the longest established and has fairly regular exhibitions and a permanent display.

Work by contemporary Kenyan and other African artists are often displayed in the foreign cultural centres.

KENYATTA CONFERENCE CENTRE

The centre is on the City Square. There is a viewing level on the 28th floor of the centre but the revolving restaurant hasn't operated for years. If you'd like to go up there, it costs KSh 100. You're allowed to take photographs from the viewing level. Access is sometimes restricted when there's a conference in progress.

ACTIVITIES
Clubs & Societies

There are lots of specialist clubs and societies in Nairobi, many of which welcome visitors.

East African Wildlife Society (☎ 748170) PO Box 20110, Hilton Hotel. This society is at the forefront of conservation efforts in East Africa and publishes an interesting bimonthly magazine, *Swara*. Membership costs US$35 which includes subscription to *Swara* (US$70 if you want the magazine sent by airmail rather than surface mail).

Friends of Nairobi National Park (☎ 500622, fax 505866) PO Box 42076, Kenya Wildlife Service Headquarters, Langata Rd. Meetings are held on the first Sunday of every month at 11.30 am in a hall close to the main gate of Nairobi National Park. There is usually a speaker and entry is free, though a donation is appropriate. The organisation's aim is to maintain the park and protect the migration routes to the Masai Mara.

Mountain Club of Kenya (MCK; ☎ 501747) PO Box 45741. The club meets every Tuesday at 8 pm at the clubhouse at Wilson airport. Members organise frequent climbing and trekking weekends around the country and have a huge pool of technical knowledge about climbing in East Africa (Mt Kenya in particular). A number of trekking and climbing books are available from the club.

Web site: www.geocities.com/~mckenya

Nairobi Sailing and Sub Aqua Club (☎ 501250) Nairobi Dam, Langata Rd. Though no sailing currently takes place on the lake because of the high level of pollution, the club offers British Sub Aqua Club diver training and runs diving trips to the coast between September and April.

East Africa Natural History Society (☎ 746090) PO Box 40658, National Museum of Kenya, Museum Hill Rd. Members meet outside Nairobi Museum at 8.45 am every Wednesday for enjoyable half-day birdwatching outings close to town. Other trips and lectures are held regularly.

KENYA

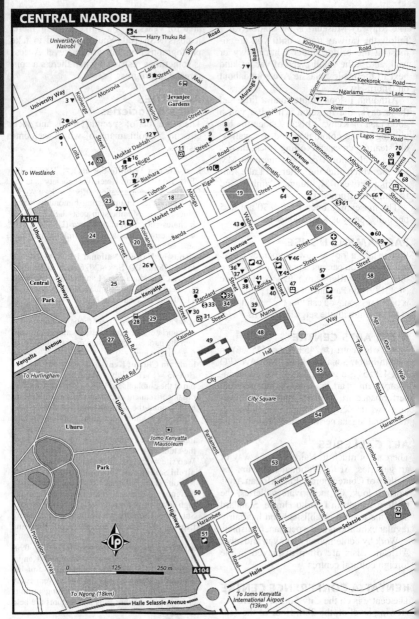

CENTRAL NAIROBI

CENTRAL NAIROBI

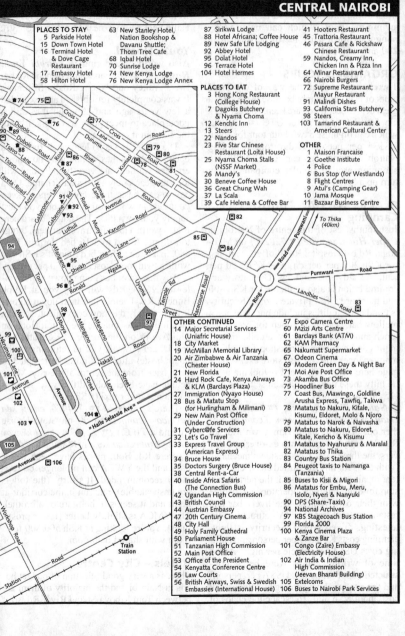

PLACES TO STAY
5 Parkside Hotel
15 Down Town Hotel
16 Terminal Hotel & Dove Cage Restaurant
17 Embassy Hotel
58 Hilton Hotel
63 New Stanley Hotel, Nation Bookshop & Davanu Shuttle; Thorn Tree Cafe
68 Iqbal Hotel
70 Sunrise Lodge
74 New Kenya Lodge
76 New Kenya Lodge Annex
87 Sirikwa Lodge
88 Hotel Africana; Coffee House
89 New Safe Life Lodging
92 Abbey Hotel
95 Dolat Hotel
96 Terrace Hotel
104 Hotel Hermes

PLACES TO EAT
3 Hong Kong Restaurant (College House)
7 Dagokis Butchery & Nyama Choma
12 Kenchic Inn
13 Steers
22 Nandos
23 Five Star Chinese Restaurant (Loita House)
25 Nyama Choma Stalls (NSSF Market)
26 Mandy's
30 Beneve Coffee House
36 Great Chung Wah
37 La Scala
39 Cafe Helena & Coffee Bar
41 Hooters Restaurant
45 Trattoria Restaurant
46 Pasara Cafe & Rickshaw Chinese Restaurant
59 Nandos, Creamy Inn, Chicken Inn & Pizza Inn
64 Minar Restaurant
66 Nairobi Burgers
72 Supreme Restaurant; Mayur Restaurant
91 Malindi Dishes
93 California Stars Butchery
98 Steers
103 Tamarind Restaurant & American Cultural Center

OTHER
1 Maison Francaise
2 Goethe Institute
4 Police
6 Bus Stop (for Westlands)
8 Flight Centres
9 Atul's (Camping Gear)
10 Jama Mosque
11 Bazaar Business Centre

To Thika (40km)

Pumwani Road

Ring Road

Pumwani Road

Landhies Road

OTHER CONTINUED
14 Major Secretarial Services (Uniafric House)
18 City Market
19 McMillan Memorial Library
20 Air Zimbabwe & Air Tanzania (Chester House)
21 New Florida
24 Hard Rock Cafe, Kenya Airways & KLM (Barclays Plaza)
27 Immigration (Nyayo House)
28 Bus & Matatu Stop (for Hurlingham & Milimani)
29 New Main Post Office (Under Construction)
31 Cyberc@fe Services
32 Let's Go Travel
33 Express Travel Group (American Express)
34 Bruce House
35 Doctors Surgery (Bruce House)
40 Inside Africa Safaris (The Connection Bus)
42 Ugandan High Commission
43 British Council
44 Austrian Embassy
47 20th Century Cinema
48 City Hall
49 Holy Family Cathedral
50 Parliament House
51 Tanzanian High Commission
52 Main Post Office
53 Office of the President
54 Kenyatta Conference Centre
55 Law Courts
56 British Airways, Swiss & Swedish Embassies (International House)
57 Expo Camera Centre
60 Mzizi Arts Centre
61 Barclays Bank (ATM)
62 KAM Pharmacy
65 Nakumatt Supermarket
67 Odeon Cinema
69 Modern Green Day & Night Bar
71 Moi Ave Post Office
73 Akamba Bus Office
75 Hoodliner Bus
77 Coast Bus, Mawingo, Goldline Arusha Express, Tawfiq, Takwa
78 Matatus to Nakuru, Kitale, Kisumu, Eldoret, Molo & Njoro
79 Matatus to Narok & Naivasha
80 Matatus to Nakuru, Eldoret, Kitale, Kericho & Kisumu
81 Matatus to Nyahururu & Maralal
82 Matatus to Thika
83 Country Bus Station
84 Peugeot taxis to Namanga (Tanzania)
85 Buses to Kisii & Migori
86 Matatus for Embu, Meru, Isiolo, Nyeri & Nanyuki
90 DPS (Share-Taxis)
94 National Archives
97 KBS Stagecoach Bus Station
99 Florida 2000
100 Kenya Cinema Plaza & Zanze Bar
101 Congo (Zaïre) Embassy (Electricity House)
102 Air India & Indian High Commission (Jeevan Bharati Building)
105 Extelcoms
106 Buses to Nairobi Park Services

Train Station

KENYA

Swimming Pools

Most of the international tourist hotels have swimming pools which can be used by nonguests for a daily fee of between KSh 200 and KSh 500.

ORGANISED TOURS

There's not much in the way of organised tours of Nairobi, simply because there's not a great deal to see. If you are keen, contact Let's Go Travel (☎ 340331) or UTC (☎ 225842) which can organise a two-hour tour for about US$35 per person. A day tour including Nairobi National Park can cost US$130, but shopping around smaller companies may turn up a bargain.

PLACES TO STAY – BUDGET
Camping

Just south-west of the centre of Nairobi is *Upper Hill Campsite* (☎ 720290) on Menengai Rd off Hospital Rd. It offers camping for KSh 200 per person, plus KSh 150 per tent, in shady surroundings. Dormitory accommodation is also available for KSh 300 and there are a few private rooms. Security is good and facilities include hot showers, a mellow bar, restaurant (open for breakfast, lunch and dinner), a library, a collection of games and a covered workshop for vehicle maintenance. You can also store excess baggage here safely. The yard is looking a little tatty these days, but it's close to the city (15 minutes walk).

Nairobi Park Services (☎/fax 890325, email brendan-black@hotmail.com) is further out of town, about 1km down Magadi Rd. Recently set up by two ex-overland drivers, the three work bays, resident mechanic (with tools for hire), qualified electrician and tent repair workshop make it the perfect pitstop for overland truck operators and people with their own vehicle. The lively bar and restaurant (with satellite TV) attracts an interesting, mixed crowd. Security is tight, camping costs KSh 200 per person and parking costs US$2 per vehicle per night. At the time of writing cabins were being constructed (approximately US$7 per person) and the site was being enlarged. Dinner will cost about KSh 300. To escape the chaos of

Nairobi take a No 125 or 126 bus or matatu from Kenya Commercial Bank House on Haile Selassie Ave, near Moi Ave (KSh 30).

Youth Hostel

Also worth considering is *Nairobi Youth Hostel* (☎ 721765) on Ralph Bunche Rd between Valley and Ngong Rds in Milimani. It was completely refurbished and extended a few years ago and although it is still a good place to meet other travellers, it's not the bargain it once was.

The hostel is very clean, well run, stays open all day and has wonderfully hot showers. The wardens are very friendly and will lock up gear safely for a small charge. On a day-to-day basis there are lockers to keep your gear in when you go out, but you must supply your own lock. The notice board here is also worth a look for travel partners, things to sell etc. A bed in a 16 bed dorm is KSh 380, in a three or four bed room it's KSh 420 while a twin room costs KSh 480 per person.

Any matatu or bus going down either Valley or Ngong Rds will drop you at Ralph Bunche Rd. The No 8 matatu down Ngong Rd is probably the most convenient. You can pick it up either outside the Hilton Hotel on Moi Ave or on the corner of Kenyatta Ave and Uhuru Hwy. If you're returning to the youth hostel after dark don't be tempted to walk back from the centre of the city. Many people have been robbed this way. Always take a matatu or taxi (KSh 300).

There's a *YMCA* (☎ 724070, email ken yaymca@iconnect.co.ke) on State House Rd and a *YWCA* (☎ 724699, email kenyay wca@iconnect.co.ke) on Mamlaka Rd off Nyerere Rd. Both places have seen better days and the YWCA can no longer be seriously recommended. It's dirty (the toilets are unspeakable), rats run in the corridor at night and it seems to be more of a brothel. The YMCA is slightly better (fewer prostitutes). You're looking at KSh 500/800 for a room with shared bathroom.

Hotels – City Centre

There is a very good selection of budget hotels in Nairobi and the majority of them are between Tom Mboya St and River Rd, so if one is full it's only a short walk to another. Virtually all the hotels in the city centre suffer from chronic water shortages. Often there is water for only a couple of hours a day, so getting a shower at some of these places can be a bit of an ordeal. The area also has a bad reputation for theft and muggings, especially at night. Be careful around here.

Many of the cheaper hotels, such as the Iqbal and New Kenya Lodge, will store baggage for you, usually for a small daily charge. However, don't leave anything valuable in your left luggage.

New Kenya Lodge (☎ 222202) on River Rd at the Latema Rd intersection is a bit of a legend among budget travellers and still one of the cheapest places, though many people feel it's well past it these days. There's always an interesting bunch of people from all over the world staying there and the notice board is good. Accommodation is basic but clean and there's supposedly hot water in the evenings. A bed in a dormitory costs KSh 200 while a double room costs KSh 500. All rooms have a shared bathroom. New Kenya Lodge also runs its own safaris, but we've had mixed reports of these.

The nearby *Iqbal Hotel* (☎ 220914) on Latema Rd has been equally popular for years and is now probably the best of the cheapies. There's supposedly hot water available in the morning but you have to be up early to get it. Singles/doubles cost KSh 210/420 with shared bathroom. The Iqbal's notice board is always a good place to look for just about anything and security is very good – the security guard is something of a Mr Fix It, and happy to arrange taxis at reasonable prices.

Also on Latema Rd, *Sunrise Lodge* is clean, secure and friendly and there's usually hot water in the morning and evening. It costs KSh 320/440 with shared bathroom including a simple breakfast. The front two rooms overlooking the street are the largest but they're right next to the Modern Green Day & Night Bar which rages 24 hours a day, 365 days a year, so if you want a quiet room take one at the back. If you're looking for material for a novel, on the other hand, take one of the front rooms.

Two other places on Dubois Rd, just off Latema Rd, are *New Safe Life Lodging* (☎ 221578) and *Nyandarua Lodging*. They are much cheaper, but the single rooms are just glorified closets. Ask what the checkout time is as it's often very early.

None of the other rock-bottom hotels in this area can seriously be recommended. They're just brothels or somewhere for drunks with a few shillings left to sleep off their hangovers.

Moving up the scale is *Terrace Hotel* (☎ 221636) on Ronald Ngala St which has rooms with bath and hot water for KSh 350/450. It doesn't win any prizes for friendliness and some of the rooms are noisy, but overall it's not a bad place.

Dolat Hotel (☎ 222797) on Mfangano St is one of the best places in the budget category. It's quiet and costs KSh 590/710. You'll have to forgo such luxuries as toilet seats, but the sheets are changed daily, the rooms are spotless and there's usually 24-hour water. It's a good, secure place with friendly management and quite a few travellers stay here. Get a room at the back.

PLACES TO STAY – MID-RANGE
City Centre

A good place in the centre of town is *Abbey Hotel* (☎ 243256) opposite Malindi Dishes on Gaberone Rd. It's well run and has a good atmosphere despite being in the thick of the action. The tidy rooms come with a bath (you even get a toilet seat). Singles/doubles are KSh 720/1040 with breakfast. There's a good bar and restaurant in the building.

Sirikwa Lodge (☎ 333838) on the corner of Munyu and Accra Rds is also a good place, although perhaps overpriced. For KSh 700/1000 you get a clean room with bath, hot water, a phone and breakfast. Security is good and there's a TV room, but no mosquito nets. Accra Rd is quieter than Tom Mboya St.

Hotel Africana (☎ 220654, fax 331886) on Dubois Rd is showing its age, but it's clean and really not bad. Rooms with bath are KSh 650/900 including breakfast. The Coffee House downstairs specialises in Indian vegetarian food.

Right at the bottom of Moi Ave at the junction with Haile Selassie Ave is *Hotel Hermes*. The staff here are friendly and laid back and huge rooms with bath cost KSh 800/1000 including breakfast.

Across the other side of the city centre, west of Moi Ave, there are four reasonably priced hotels which are popular with travellers. Best value is the recently redecorated *Terminal Hotel* (☎ 228817, fax 220075) on Moktar Daddah St, near Koinange St. It's clean and there's hot water around the clock. Security is excellent, the rooms are generally quiet and there's a notice board downstairs. Rooms with bath cost KSh 900/1200/1500. Children sharing with their parents are charged KSh 50 per day. You can also store excess baggage here for KSh 30 per article per day.

Down Town Hotel (☎ 332360, fax 338581) next door to the Terminal is even smarter, though a little more expensive at KSh 990/1200. It's well recommended.

Nearby is *Embassy Hotel* (☎ 224087, fax 224534) a somewhat older place on Biashara St. All rooms have baths and hot water. Small singles here cost KSh 900. Standard rooms are KSh 1000/1200/1400. Breakfast is available for KSh 150. The hotel has its own bar and restaurant.

Parkside Hotel (☎ 214154, fax 334681) is on Monrovia St which runs alongside Jevanjee Gardens. The staff are very friendly and the hotel has its own restaurant. It's a little more expensive but still very good value at KSh 1100/1500/2000 including breakfast. All rooms have hot showers. It's very popular with foreign volunteer workers.

Milimani/Hurlingham

Most of the other mid-range hotels are along Milimani, Ralph Bunche and Bishops Rds but there are others scattered around the fringes of the city centre with a few in Westlands. Many are popular with travellers as well as United Nations and nongovernment organisation (NGO) staff.

Perched behind the infamous Buffalo Bills on Milimani Rd is *Heron Court Hotel* (☎ 720740, fax 721698, email herco@iconnect .co.ke). It's a large place where all the rooms have baths with hot water, and there's a swimming pool, sauna, massage parlour and guarded car park. The cheapest singles/doubles are KSh 750/890. There are also apartments with a double bedroom, separate lounge with balcony, bathroom and fully equipped kitchen for KSh 1190/1400. On the face of it, Heron Court with Buffalo Bills seems to be primarily a whore house and a pick-up joint. However, if you're in a group, the apartments are great value, and Buffalo Bills – well, it's an experience.

Sagret Hotel (☎ 720933, PO Box 18324) at the top of Milimani Rd at the Ralph Bunche Rd intersection is of a somewhat higher standard than the Heron Court. It offers rooms with bath for KSh 1925/2750/ 3500 including breakfast. If you stay for one week there's a 10% discount on these rates. The hotel has its own bar and restaurant (very popular for *nyama choma*) and accepts Visa and MasterCard. There's also guarded parking.

Further up the road is *Hotel Salama* (☎ 721858, email hotel_salama@hotmail .com) which is a quieter place with a nyama choma restaurant. It's possible to camp here for KSh 150, with rooms going for KSh 1000/1400 with breakfast.

Fairview Hotel (☎ 711321, fax 721320, email reserv@fairviewkenya.com, PO Box 40842) is on Bishops Rd at the back of the Panafric Hotel. Billed as 'the country hotel in the city', it is surrounded by pleasant gardens, catering mainly for businesspeople and families, but it makes a good first port of call when arriving in the country. There are a number of different classes of room with private bathrooms, satellite TV, video, telephone and voice mail. Rooms start at KSh 4300/6000/6400. All prices include breakfast, with the lunch buffet costing KSh 800 and the authentic African buffet (every Tuesday and Friday) KSh 900. Guests are entitled to use the swimming pool at Panafric Hotel.

Parklands

A popular place is *Sirona Hotel* (☎ 742730) Kolobot Rd off Forest Rd, on the fringes of Parklands. It's sometimes used by safari companies to accommodate their clients. It's a quiet place and costs KSh 1050/1500 for 'executive' singles/doubles and KSh 1400/1950 for 'VIP' singles/doubles including breakfast. There's a large restaurant and bar area (decorated with some excellent prints of Ernest Watson's paintings – check out 'Night Life at the Studio'), a beer garden, a pool table and ample safe parking. Most major credit cards are accepted.

Westlands

Considering the number of bars, restaurants, and shopping and entertainment centres springing up in Westlands, as well as the overall trend for businesses to relocate here, it's surprising that no backpackers places have opened up yet. It's probably a matter of time.

Hillcrest Hotel (☎ 448046) is set back from Waiyaki Way on the outskirts of Westlands. Though getting on a bit, the rooms are clean and well maintained and this is a pleasant little hotel. There's a restaurant and safe parking. Singles/doubles with bath go for KSh 1300/1700. The rooms at the front are noisy.

PLACES TO STAY – TOP END

In a city the size of Nairobi there are naturally many top-of-the-range hotels. Booking through a travel agent in the low season *may* get you a slightly better deal.

City Centre

In a nice garden setting is *Boulevard Hotel* (☎ 227567, fax 334071, email hotelboulevard@form-net.com, PO Box 42831) is on Harry Thuku Rd. It offers singles/doubles/triples with bathroom, balcony, telephone and radio for KSh 4450/5300/5900 including taxes. Facilities include a swimming pool, tennis court, restaurant, barbecue, bar and beer garden. If you hear stories about the swimming pool being dangerous on account of out-of-control matatus plunging into it off adjacent Chiromo Rd, you can put your mind at rest. It did happen twice, but now a fence that you'd need a tank to get through has been erected. For more information check out the Web site at www.kenyaweb.com/hotelboulevar.

Near the centre is *New Stanley Hotel* (☎ 333233, fax 229388, PO Box 30680) on the corner of Kimathi St and Kenyatta Ave. Built in 1907, it still has a touch of colonial charm despite numerous renovations. Rooms cost US$160/175 including breakfast and taxes. There are also more-expensive suites. All the rooms have air-con, colour TV (including cable) and direct-dial telephones. Facilities include a rooftop swimming pool, two restaurants, a ballroom, bar, health club and shops. The popular Thorn Tree Cafe at street level has been renovated and lost a lot of its charm, but remains popular.

Hilton Hotel (☎ 334000, fax 339462, email info_nairobi@hilton.com, PO Box 30624) on Mama Ngina St near Moi Ave has all the usual Hilton facilities including a rooftop swimming pool, business centre (with email) and well appointed rooms. Singles/doubles here go for US$138/173, while executive rooms with breakfast and complimentary bar are US$210/245, but you must add 29% in taxes!

Norfolk Hotel (☎ 335422, fax 336742, PO Box 40064) on Harry Thuku Rd is Nairobi's oldest hotel – built in 1904 – and it was *the* place to stay in the old days. It's still extremely popular among those with a taste for nostalgia and money to spend. All the old-world charm has been retained despite facilities having been brought up to international standards and a large expansion is currently going on. Rooms in the main block cost US$250/280 and suites are US$275 to US$460. A double room in the 1937 block costs US$330 for nonresidents, while residents are charged KSh 6720 for singles or doubles. Breakfast costs US$16; lunch and dinner are US$21. The Ibis Grill Restaurant is one of the best in Kenya and the Lord Delamere terrace bar and restaurant is always popular.

Nairobi Serena Hotel (☎ 725111, fax 725184, email nairobi@serena.co.ke, PO Box 46302) is on the edge of Central Park between Kenyatta Ave and Nyerere Rd. It is a recent creation and imaginatively designed. It's owned by the Serena Lodges group and has rooms for US$180/216, with suites for US$252 to US$468 excluding a 10% service

KENYA

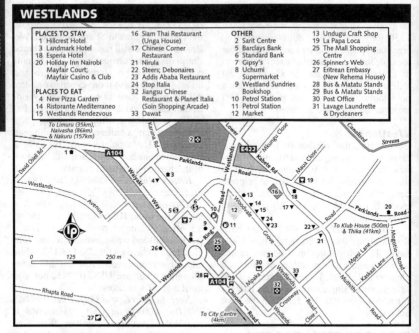

WESTLANDS

PLACES TO STAY
1 Hillcrest Hotel
3 Landmark Hotel
18 Esperia Hotel
20 Holiday Inn Nairobi
   Mayfair Court;
   Mayfair Casino & Club

PLACES TO EAT
4 New Pizza Garden
14 Ristorante Mediterraneo
15 Westlands Rendezvous

16 Siam Thai Restaurant
   (Unga House)
17 Chinese Corner
   Restaurant
21 Nirula
22 Steers; Debonaires
23 Addis Ababa Restaurant
24 Stop Italia
32 Jiangsu Chinese
   Restaurant & Planet Italia
   (Soin Shopping Arcade)
33 Dawat

OTHER
2 Sarit Centre
5 Barclays Bank
6 Standard Bank
7 Gipsy's
8 Uchumi
   Supermarket
9 Westland Sundries
   Bookshop
10 Petrol Station
11 Petrol Station
12 Market

13 Undugu Craft Shop
19 La Papa Loca
25 The Mall Shopping
   Centre
26 Spinner's Web
27 Eritrean Embassy
   (New Rehema House)
28 Bus & Matatu Stands
29 Bus & Matatu Stands
30 Post Office
31 Lavage Laundrette
   & Drycleaners

charge, 2% training levy and 16% VAT. It has all the facilities you'd expect from a five-star hotel. Even Jimmy Carter stays here. Meals cost US$14 (breakfast), US$20 (lunch) and US$22 (dinner) plus taxes.

Langata
Some exclusive little hotels can be found in this high-class area of Nairobi. *Macushla House* (☎ 891987, fax 891971) is more like a private house, catering for just 10 guests. Located about 300m from the Giraffe Centre on Gogo Falls Rd, there's a swimming pool, beautiful gardens and an excellent restaurant. The rates are very reasonable all things considered; singles/doubles cost US$95/170 with breakfast.

Also a short walk from the Giraffe Centre, *Ngong House* (☎ 890840, fax 890674, email ngonghouse@form-net.com) is an altogether different sort of hotel. The four treehouse 'rooms' are raised 4m high on stilts, with views out across the Ngong

Hills. You dine with the owners and a number of small excursions are provided free of charge. It's a magical place, but you pay for it: US$250 per person for full board, including transfers and all drinks.

Contact Langata Link (☎ 891314, email the_link@swiftkenya.com) for more information about hotels and restaurants in Langata and Karen.

Milimani
A little outside of the city centre where Kenyatta Ave turns into Valley Rd is *Panafric Hotel* (☎ 720822, fax 726356, email gm@panafric.sarova.co.ke, PO Box 30486). Part of the Sarova Hotels chain, it's a large, multi-storey modern hotel with all the facilities you'd expect. Singles/doubles cost US$71/94 and there are more-expensive suites.

Westlands
Situated on the 'border' of Westlands and Parklands is *Holiday Inn Nairobi Mayfair*

Court (☎ 740920, fax 748823, email may fair@africaonline.co.ke, PO Box 66807) on Parklands Rd. A large, colonial-style hotel situated in beautifully maintained grounds, it offers standard singles/doubles costing US$150/196 including breakfast. A few executive rooms are also available. There are two swimming pools, a health club and boutiques, while the Mayfair Casino & Club is just next door. It's a rather good place to stay, though unfortunately the infamous Mischiefs Bar has been replaced by a Spur Steak Ranch, part of the sanitised South African steak house chain.

PLACES TO EAT

Lunch is the main meal of the day for many Kenyans and this is what the cheaper restaurants cater for. If you want a full meal in the evening it generally involves eating from a mid-range (or better) restaurant, or from a barbecue attached to a bar.

Nairobi is replete with restaurants offering cuisine from all over the world and at many places the prices are surprisingly reasonable. For about KSh 500 per person you can eat well.

There's a good selection of restaurants in the city centre and an increasing number of places in the suburbs, especially Westlands. To get to these places after dark you'll need to take a taxi.

The big Uchumi supermarkets on Waiyaki Way in Westlands and near the Yaya Centre on Ngong Rd, Hurlingham are excellent for self-caterers.

Restaurants

Most of the pricier restaurants are licensed and offer beer, wine and spirits but the major exceptions are the Indian vegetarian restaurants which usually offer only fruit juices and tea or coffee. Virtually all these restaurants accept credit cards.

Chinese Nairobi has a reasonable selection of Chinese restaurants although none of them are particularly cheap. Probably the cheapest is *Great Chung Wah* on Muindi Mbingu St. The lunch-time platter is good value and a la carte dishes cost from KSh 200 to KSh 350.

Hong Kong Restaurant (☎ 228612) in College House on Koinange St is very popular at lunch-time. The food is much better than the restaurant interior. Main dishes cost about KSh 220 to KSh 490.

On Loita St in Loita House, *Five Star Chinese Restaurant* (☎ 244816) is also recommended. Mains cost around KSh 350 to KSh 400, more for seafood. Soups are roughly KSh 120.

Dragon Pearl (☎ 340451), in Bruce House on Standard St, also has good Chinese food at prices comparable to the other places. It's open daily for lunch and dinner.

Rated as the best Chinese restaurant in town by some residents is *Rickshaw Chinese Restaurant* (☎ 223604) in Fedha Towers on Standard St. It has an extensive menu and the food is delicious. Expect to spend at least KSh 700 per person.

Up in Westlands are a number of Chinese restaurants. Top of the line, but expensive, is probably *Jiangsu Chinese Restaurant* on the 2nd floor of Soin shopping arcade. *Chinese Corner Restaurant* on Muthithi Rd is cheaper but still good.

Ethiopian The decor at *Daas* includes many Ethiopian artefacts and there's often live music in the evenings. Meals based around excellent unleavened bread are eaten with the fingers. Expect to pay about KSh 400 to KSh 500 per person for a full meal including drinks. This place is in an old house some distance from the centre, off Ngong Rd (signposted) about halfway between the Kenyatta Hospital roundabout and Dagoretti Corner.

On Argwings Kodhek Rd the *Blue Nile Ethiopian Restaurant* (☎ 716080) in Hurlingham is also good though Daas probably has the edge. Also try the new *Addis Ababa* (☎ 447321) on Woodvale Grove out in Westlands.

Greek & Middle Eastern At Yaya Centre in Hurlingham is *Sugar & Spice* (☎ 562876) a modest place serving a wide variety of snacks. In the same centre is *Patra Bakery* an informal eatery serving Middle Eastern favourites such as felafel (KSh 150) and doner kebabs (KSh 180).

KENYA

Indian The excellent *Mayur Restaurant* (☎ 331586) above Supreme Restaurant on River Rd at the roundabout, has been famous for superb Indian vegetarian food for years. It's not bad value at KSh 260/280 for a buffet lunch or dinner, but the hushed atmosphere can be a bit daunting.

Minar Restaurant (☎ 229999) specialises in Mughlai dishes and offers buffet lunches and a la carte dinners. Expect to pay about KSh 750 for a three course dinner and KSh 540 for a buffet lunch. It also has branches at the Yaya Centre (☎ 577874) on Argwings Kodhek Rd in Hurlingham; and a cafe in Barclays Plaza.

Out at Westlands are two excellent Indian restaurants. The best of the lot, according to local residents, is *Haandi* (☎ 448294) on the 1st floor of the Mall shopping centre. It's open from 12.30 to 2.30 pm and 7.30 to 10.30 pm daily including public holidays. Judge it for yourself. Also highly recommended by locals is *Dawat* (☎ 749337) on Westlands Rd.

International Arguably one of the best restaurants in Kenya, *Alan Bobbe's Bistro* (☎ 224945) on Koinange St, serves expensive, predominantly French cuisine to very discerning Kenyans and expats. Reservations are recommended and wear something other than a t-shirt and shorts.

Ibis Grill (☎ 250900) at Norfolk Hotel, which specialises in nouvelle cuisine, is in the same league.

Italian The long-running and very popular *Trattoria* (☎ 340855) on the corner of Wabera and Kaunda Sts is open daily from 8.30 am to 11.30 pm. Both food and atmosphere are excellent. Three courses and some house chianti will relieve you of about KSh 1000 per person. The ice cream is superb.

Probably just as good, but lacking the same reputation (and therefore prices), is *La Scala* (☎ 332130) on Standard St near Muindi Mbingu St. This place specialises in Italian food but also has dishes such as steaks and burgers. It's open daily from 7 am to midnight and is very popular with Kenyans looking for a modestly priced decent meal in pleasant surroundings.

La Cucina (☎ 562871) in the Yaya Centre, Hurlingham, is an excellent place. Main pasta dishes are between KSh 550 and KSh 650, though seafood is double that.

Up in Westlands, *Stop Italia* (☎ 445234) and *Ristorante Mediterraneo* (☎ 447494) almost each other on Woodvale Grove slug it out for the expat Italian trade. Both are excellent. Pasta dishes and pizza cost between KSh 350 and KSh 550.

Japanese In the city centre is the excellent *Akasaka* (☎ 333948) on Standard St between Koinange and Muindi Mbingu Sts. It's done out in traditional Japanese style and there's a tatami room (reserve in advance). It offers the full range of Japanese cuisine including tempura, teriyaki and sukiyaki as well as soups and appetisers. The lunch-time menu can be very reasonable, but you can easily spend a couple of thousand over dinner.

Shogun (☎ 716080) on Argwings Kodhek Rd in Hurlingham is cheaper, with a very nice atmosphere, and the food is almost as good.

Korean The only Korean restaurant in Nairobi is *Restaurant Koreana* in the Yaya Centre, Hurlingham. The food is excellent and authentic but expensive. A full meal costs about KSh 800 to KSh 1000 and the restaurant is licensed. It's open from noon to 2.30 pm and 6 to 10.30 pm Monday to Saturday.

Nyama Choma For steak eaters who haven't seen a decent doorstep since they left Argentina, Australia, Uruguay or the USA and who are looking for a gut-busting extravaganza, there are a couple of excellent places.

Very popular with tourists is *Carnivore* (☎ 501709) out at Langata just past Wilson airport. Apart from the usual meats, at least three game meats are offered daily (ostrich, eland, hartebeest, crocodile, wildebeest or zebra). For KSh 1290 you get as much food as you can eat. To get there take bus No 14, 24 or 124 and tell the conductor where you are going; the restaurant is a 1km walk (signposted) from where you are dropped off. It's easy to hitch back into the town centre when you're ready to go. Otherwise, negotiate for a taxi (about KSh 600).

The Horseman (☎ 882033) at Karen Shopping Centre on Langata Rd is a similar meat eaters' paradise (with game meat) set in a leafy compound complete with its own pond and croaking frogs. It's straight out of rural Surrey, England and recommended by locals.

For something a little less extravagant there's *Dagokis Butchery & Nyama Choma* at the top end of Tom Mboya St at the intersection of Muranga'a Rd.

Opposite Malindi Dishes on Gaberone Rd and also cheap is *California Stars Butchery* a very popular, full-on bar and nyama choma joint. For meat eaters and beer drinkers only.

Highly rated by residents, particularly Africans, is the nyama choma at *Sagret Hotel* on Milimani Rd, Milimani. It's best to come here with a group because you have to choose a hunk of meat from the refrigerated display and there'll be enough to feed at least four people. Count on about KSh 400 to KSh 600 per person plus drinks. It's open for lunch and dinner daily.

For authentic, no-frills Nairobi nyama choma head to the suburb of Kilmichael, some distance from the town centre, out past Pangani and Eastleigh. It's certainly not for the squeamish as the goats are slaughtered only a few metres away from where you eat and barbecued right in front of you; there's no doubting the freshness of the meat! This is not a place to go to alone, as the people here are not used to seeing *wazungu* and while it's not threatening, it's best to be in the company of a reliable Kenyan. You probably wouldn't find it on your own anyway. African prices apply here so it's cheaper than anywhere else you'll find. Even Smith Hempstone, a former American ambassador to Kenya, once came here, much to the displeasure of the government – Kilmichael isn't exactly ambassadorial territory.

Similar places can be found past Dagoretti Corner on Ngong Rd.

Seafood The best seafood restaurant is *Tamarind (☎ 338959)* in the National Bank building on Nkrumah Lane, between Harambee and Haile Selassie Aves. It offers a wide selection of exotic seafood dishes, and culinary influences range from European to Asian to coastal Swahili. Eating here is a major night out as most main courses are priced well over KSh 800, with crab and prawn dishes costing much more. There's a special vegetarian menu. It's open for lunch from 12.30 to 1.45 pm Monday to Saturday and for dinner from 6.30 to 9.45 pm daily.

Thai For authentic Thai food, try *Bangkok Restaurant (☎ 751311)* in Rank Xerox House, Parklands Rd, Westlands, which has been in business for a number of years and has a good reputation. It's open from 12.30 to 2.30 pm and 6 to 10.30 pm daily.

Siam Thai (☎ 751727) in Unga House on the corner of Muthithi and Parklands Rds also has a very good reputation. Expect to pay KSh 1200 for a real feast with drinks.

Western A good restaurant for plain meat and vegie dishes (eg, sausages and mashed potato) is *Zanze Bar (☎ 222532)* on the top floor of the Kenya Cinema Plaza, Moi Ave, though a range of other dishes are available. It's open for lunch and dinner daily but is not strictly a restaurant alone – more a combination of bar, live music venue and restaurant. You *may* have to pay an entry charge in the evenings.

Tusks Restaurant (☎ 522565, email tusks@insightkenya.com) looks down the wooded slope to the Ruaka River north of Nairobi along the Limuru Rd, 2km past the Village Market (take taxi or matatu No 106 and ask to be dropped off at Tusks). A nature trail leads down to the river and there are weekend pony rides, a children's playground, an animal nursery and pool tables. Main courses *(fajitas, pastas, steaks and vegetarian dishes) cost between KSh 600 and KSh 800.

Steaks, burgers and the like at *Hard Rock Cafe (☎ 220802)* on the mezzanine floor of Barclays Plaza on Loita St are good but cost around KSh 450. The food at *Buffalo Bills* is not too bad.

The food at *La Papa Loca* on Parklands Rd, Westlands is good, particularly the fajitas.

Cafes

Growers Cafe on Tom Mboya St is deservedly popular with both locals and travellers and prices are reasonable. Food on offer includes eggs, sausages and other hot foods, fruit salads, yoghurt and good coffee.

Upstairs from Growers is *Swara Restaurant* which does a decent traditional African breakfast of *mandazi* (a semisweet donut) and tea, as well as good-value buffet lunches featuring Kenyan food.

If you're staying in the Koinange St area, *Dove Cage Restaurant* on Moktar Daddah St next to the Terminal Hotel is an excellent little place. A full breakfast with juice and coffee sets you back about KSh 200, and the service is fast and friendly. Very similar is *Calypso* in the basement of Bruce House on Standard St, where you can get an English-style breakfast for KSh 150.

For a breakfast splurge, try a buffet at a major hotel. The best value is offered by *New Stanley Hotel* where a continental buffet breakfast costs KSh 450, or a full English breakfast is KSh 650.

There are a lot of very cheap cafes and small restaurants in the Latema Rd and River Rd area and at the top end of Tom Mboya St where you can pick up a breakfast of mandazi and tea or coffee. Most of these places offer eggs and since many are Indian-run, they have traditional Indian breakfast menus including foods like samosa and *idli* (rice dumplings) with a sauce.

Several of Nairobi's budget hotels have good budget restaurants nearby. Around the corner from New Kenya Lodge is *Sunsweet Restaurant* which serves Indian and Thai food for about KSh 300 for as much as you can eat. Around the corner from the Iqbal on Taveta Rd is the *Taj* which is much the same but concentrates on good Indian food.

Malindi Dishes restaurant on Gaberone Rd is well worth checking out. As the name suggests, food here has the Swahili influence of the coast, so coconut and spices are used to rev up otherwise pretty ordinary cuisine. You'll get a grand feed for about KSh 150 and the usual snacks and burgers are also available (with a Swahili twist).

For a good solid meal mixing western and local cuisine such as steak and *matoke* (mashed plantains and maize) or *maharagwe* (kidney beans), try the self-service *Cafe Helena* on Mama Ngina St opposite the city hall. It's open only at lunch-time and is popular with businesspeople. Meals cost around KSh 140 and are excellent value. *Beneve Coffee House* on the corner of Standard and Koinange Sts has a tasty selection of self-service food ranging from stews to curries, fish and chips, samosas, pasties and a host of other choices.

The western-style *Pasara* cafe in the Lonrho building on Standard St is an excellent place for breakfast sandwiches, cakes and decent coffee. There's an open-air patio, newspapers and magazines.

Kenya is the home of all-you-can-eat lunches at a set price and Nairobi has a wide choice of them, most offering Indian food. One of the best is *Supreme Restaurant* on River Rd at the roundabout, which offers an excellent Indian (Punjabi) vegetarian *thali* for KSh 230. It also has superb fruit juices. *Coffee House* below Hotel Africana on Dubois Rd has similar fare for similar prices though it's not as good.

Hooters on Kaunda St is a good place for lunch, though the western menu of burgers, steaks and pizza makes it a little expensive. The bar is well stocked and apparently the owners will give you a free drink if you can down their bizarre house cocktail in one.

Mandy's on Koinange St just before Kenyatta Ave is another good place for lunch. Chicken Kiev and steak go for about KSh 200. Breakfast is about KSh 150.

In Westlands, the stalls in the Sarit Centre's *Food Court* cater for most tastes. Indian, Chinese, Italian and African food, and western fast food are all available.

Westlands Rendezvous on Woodvale Grove offers good African and European-style meals in its open-air cafe for KSh 120 to KSh 220. It's open until 8 pm and beer is available.

If you don't mind spending a little over the odds, the pizzas in the Landmark Hotel's *New Pizza Garden* (just off Waiyaki Way) are excellent and cost around KSh 250. It also has a range of other dishes at about the same price and there's live music on Sunday afternoon.

Up in Hurlingham **Motherland Restaurant** on Ngong Rd is worth a try for reasonably priced Kenyan food while **Kwality Hotel** next to the Hurlingham Hotel on Argwings Kodhek Rd does an all-you-can-eat Indian buffet for about KSh 400.

Fast Food

Things look set to change on Nairobi's fast food scene. Some huge North American chains may have passed Kenya by, but the South African chains have missed no such opportunity. **Nandos** (spicy fried chicken), **Steers** (hamburgers), **Chicken Inn**, **Creamy Inn** (milkshakes), **Pizza Inn** and **Debonaires** (pizza) have all arrived. Branches are opening all over greater Nairobi, but at present the main branches in the city centre are on Moi Ave close to the Hilton (Nandos, Chicken Inn, Pizza Inn and Creamy Inn), Koinange St (Nandos), Muindi Mbingu St (Steers) and Tom Mboya St (Steers). In Westlands Steers and Debonaires are on Muthithi Rd.

Wimpy has branches on Kenyatta Ave, Tom Mboya St and Mondlane St. These places have the usual range of snacks and meals (burgers, sausages, eggs, fish, chicken, milk shakes etc) costing up to KSh 250. They are open from 7.30 am to 9.30 pm.

Another good cafe for burgers, fish or chicken with a mountain of chips and salad for about KSh 200 is **Nairobi Burgers** on Tom Mboya St opposite the end of Latema Rd. Sweets, soups and ice cream are also served – it's a very popular place.

Supermac on Kimathi St (directly opposite the Thorn Tree Cafe) is very popular at lunch-time for fish and chips. It is on the mezzanine floor of the shopping centre.

For takeaway chicken and chips, go to the very popular **Kenchic Inn** on the corner of Moktar Daddah and Muindi Mbingu Sts. It sells a phenomenal number of roast chickens every day (full chicken KSh 300, half chicken KSh 150, quarter chicken KSh 75).

ENTERTAINMENT

For entertainment in Nairobi and for big music venues in the rest of the country get hold of the *Saturday Nation* which lists everything from cinema releases to live music venues.

Pubs & Bars

Thorn Tree Cafe in the New Stanley Hotel on the corner of Kimathi St and Kenyatta Ave, once a legendary meeting place with a message board for travellers, has been renovated along with the New Stanley. The big acacia that stood in the middle of the terrace was diseased and has been felled, replaced with a tiny sapling, there is no message board and the new interior looks to have been supplied by *Plastic Identi-kit Cafes 'R Us*. However, the cafe remains a fine meeting place and the juices are good (if expensive).

A very rough and ready Nairobi institution is **Modern Green Day & Night Bar** on Latema Rd. It's open 24 hours a day, 365 days a year and the front door has never been closed since 1968, partly because there isn't one.

Friendship Corner bar across the road is much livelier than the Modern Green. This tiny 24 hour place really kicks on. **Dawas Bar & Restaurant** across from New Kenya Lodge on River Rd at the Latema Rd intersection, attracts a younger crowd and serves cheap food (KSh 150) and cheap cold beer.

Outside the city centre is the legendary **Buffalo Bill's**. In front of Heron Court Hotel on Milimani Rd, the bar attracts a different sort of crowd – namely all of Nairobi's eccentrics, adventurers, entrepreneurs, safari operators, NGO employees, dodgy politicians, disco queens, hookers and bullshit artistes. At any time of the night or day hookers will try and pick up any single man in the place, but once you've accepted that you've walked into the wild west it's a fun place. Beers cost KSh 80, warm or cold. There's disco music most nights of the week but nowhere to dance.

Further up Milimani Rd on the right-hand side is **Hotel Salama**. This bar and restaurant occupies an old colonial-style house. It's a friendly place and gets very lively most evenings. Beers are cheaper here than at Buffalo Bill's and the music (and clientele) are not as intrusive.

Ngong Races

Every second Sunday for most of the year there's horse racing at the Ngong Racecourse. It's a very genteel day out, and with an entry fee of KSh 50 for the members' enclosure or just KSh 20 in the public area, it's hardly going to break the bank. There's betting with the bookies or the tote, and while the odds you get are hardly going to set the world on fire, it's great fun to have a punt. You can bet as little as KSh 20, so even the most impecunious should be able to afford a flutter.

Local cynics will tell you that all the races, like everything else in the country, are rigged. It may well be true, but it hardly seems to matter. There's a good restaurant on the ground floor of the grandstand and two bars with beer at regular bar prices. If you don't have transport back to town it's easy enough to find a lift by talking to people in the members' enclosure. Bus or matatu No 24 from Haile Selassie Ave in the city centre goes right past the racecourse.

Those looking for more genteel surroundings in which to sip their beer could try *Ngong Hills Hotel* on Ngong Rd, the beer gardens at the *Boulevard* or *Landmark* hotels, or the *Lord Delamere* bar at *Norfolk Hotel*.

Some of the most popular bars among foreigners and expats are in Westlands. *Gipsy's* at the back of Ring Rd opposite Barclays Bank was, until the opening of *La Papa Loca* on Parklands Rd, the most popular bar in Westlands. Thanks to good food and decent music it still holds a crowd (Tuesday is an informal gay night), but La Papa Loca with live music, a disco, pool and more space has stolen much of its thunder. *Klub House* further down Parklands Rd past Holiday Inn has more pool tables than anyone else and seems a good place to party until late.

Sports Bar & Restaurant (☎ 717591) on Lenana Rd in Milimani, 15 minutes walk from the Sagret Hotel, is *the* place to head to for big sporting events, with its large TV screens and satellite dish.

Discos

There's a good selection of discos in the centre of Nairobi and there are no dress codes, though there's an unspoken assumption that you'll turn up looking half-decent.

The most popular discos in the centre of town are *Florida 2000* on Moi Ave near City Hall Way, and *New Florida* (known locally as the 'Mad House'). The entry fee depends on the night but is between KSh 100 and KSh 200 for men and half that for women. Both places are open to 6 am and are an experience: steamy, frantic and filled with prostitutes, both clubs have a loyal if incoherent following. Respite from the mayhem can be found in bars and restaurants at both places. The best thing about the New Florida is the architecture; it's a mushroom-shaped building above a petrol station.

Further out of town is *Mamba* at the International Casino, just off Uhuru Highway. This disco is favoured by young Asians and not quite as gutsy as the Floridas.

If you're in the Milimani Rd area, check out *Fredz* next door to China Town Restaurant on Ralph Bunche Rd. It's open from around 6 pm but the disco doesn't fire up until later. If you get there early there's no cover charge.

There's a live band or disco every Wednesday night at the *Simba Saloon* at the Carnivore in Langata but entry costs KSh 200 per person. It's known locally as wazungu night and the music is unashamedly western, but there's usually a good crowd and it makes a refreshing change from the more enclosed and crowded spaces of the discos in town.

Beer in all these places is reasonably priced, but other drinks, especially imported liquors, are more expensive. Snacks and meals are available at all of them.

Live Music

City Cabanas (☎ 820992) out on Mombasa Rd before the turn-off to the airport is a good venue. The clientele are mainly middle-class Kenyans looking for a good time and a variety of bands play out here.

La Papa Loca on Parklands Rd in Westlands also has live bands, Kenyan and

African groups, and local expats are regular features on Friday and Saturday nights.

African Heritage Hotel on Kenyatta Ave is a serious little venue with some good bands, a lively atmosphere, and beer for KSh 80. Entry is KSh 100. *Ngong Hills Hotel* on Ngong Rd may not look like a swinging live music venue (more like a uninspired mid-range hotel next to an Uchumi supermarket), but some very good Kenyan and Tanzanian bands play here.

Also try *Cantina Club* close to the entrance of Wilson airport. It has something of a reputation for never closing. Don't mistake it for the Dam Busters Club nearby.

For a classy night out try *Jazz Cafe* at the Yaya Centre in Hurlingham. It's both a restaurant and live music venue and is well worth a look.

Cinema

Nairobi is a good place to take in a few films at a price substantially lower than what you'd pay back home, but if you don't want scratched films go to one of the better cinemas such as *Kenya Cinema Plaza* on Moi Ave, or *20th Century Cinema* on Mama Ngina St. The new *Nairobi Cinema* near City Hall Way and Aga Khan Walk can also be recommended. Expect to pay KSh 160 to KSh 250 (VIP seats) to see a film.

The cheaper cinemas are on Latema Rd and include *Odeon* and *Embassy*. *Cameo* on Kenyatta Ave is also relatively cheap, and at the time of writing two cinema screens were being added to the Sarit Centre complex in Westlands.

There are also two good drive-ins (remember them?) if you have the transport: both have snack bars and bars. The best is the *Belle-Vue* on Mombasa Rd.

Theatre

Phoenix Players put on regular performances at the Professional Centre (☎ 336146) on Parliament Rd. Many of the plays are by foreign playwrights, but a good proportion are Kenyan. Tickets cost KSh 840.

Kenya National Theatre (☎ 220536) on Harry Thuku Rd opposite the Norfolk Hotel also puts on performances.

For African theatre the numerous foreign cultural centres are often the places to head for (see Cultural Centres listed earlier in this chapter). Above all, check the *Daily Nation* to see what's on.

SHOPPING

Nairobi is a good place to pick up souvenirs, but shop around. There are many small stall-holders in Westlands at the crossroads of Ring and Parklands Rds. In central Nairobi there are hundreds of stalls selling the same sorts of wares along just about every tiny alley that branches off from Biashara St between Muindi Mbingu and Tom Mboya Sts.

There are plenty of 'fixed-price' souvenir shops around the Hilton Hotel (the gift shop of the East African Wildlife Society is in the hotel itself), though the best place to head is the Spinners Web off Waiyaki Way near Viking House in Westlands. It describes itself as a 'consignment handicraft shop' and sells goods made in workshops and by self-help groups around the country. It has some superb items, including hand-knitted jumpers, all sorts of fabrics and huge Turkana baskets – well recommended.

If you want fine art, and there are some good artists around, a good place to check out what's happening is the Gallery Watatu on the 1st floor of Lonhro House on Standard St. There's a permanent display here, much of which is for sale, and there are regular auctions. Bring your credit card. Almost nothing goes for less than KSh 15,000 and prices can be as high as KSh 100,000. It is also worth checking out the Gallery of East African Contemporary Art at the National Museum, and the Mzizi Arts Centre on Moi Ave. See Mzizi Arts Centre earlier in this chapter for contact information. The staff at the latter will be able to put you in touch with the artists they display, or whose work interests you.

For a much less touristy atmosphere try the Kariokor Market east of the centre on Racecourse Rd in Eastleigh. It's a few minutes ride by bus or taxi. Another place out of the centre is the Undugu Crafts Shop in Woodvale Grove, Westlands, opposite the market. This nonprofit organisation supports community projects in Nairobi.

The Maasai Market is an informal market where Maasai women sell beaded jewellery, gourds, baskets and other Maasai crafts. It takes place only on Fridays at the Village Market (☎ 522488), an upmarket shopping centre on Limuru Rd past Muthaiga, from around 9 am to mid-afternoon. It's changed location a couple of times in recent years so check before heading out there.

GETTING THERE & AWAY
Air
Airlines with offices in Nairobi include:

Aeroflot (☎ 220746) Corner House, Mama Ngina St
Air France (☎ 216954) International House, Mama Ngina St
Air India (☎ 334788) Jeevan Bharati House, Harambee Ave
Air Madagascar (☎ 225286, email mdnbo@ africaonline.co.ke) Hilton Hotel, City Hall Way
Air Mauritius (☎ 229166) International House, Mama Ngina St
Air Tanzania (☎ 336224) Chester House, Koinange St
Air Zimbabwe (☎ 339522, email airzim@ swiftglobal.com) Chester House, Koinange St
British Airways (☎ 244430) International House, 8th floor, Mama Ngina St
EgyptAir (☎ 226821) Hilton Arcade, City Hall Way
El Al Israel Airlines (☎ 228123) KCS House, Mama Ngina St
Ethiopian Airlines (☎ 330837) Bruce House, Muindi Mbingu St
Japan Airlines (☎ 244084) c/o Flying Rickshaw Ltd, 20th Century Plaza, Mama Ngina St
Kenya Airways (☎ 210771) Barclays Plaza, 1st floor, Loita St
KLM (☎ 210771, email reservations@klm.co.ke) Barclays Plaza, 1st floor, Loita St
Pakistan International Airlines (☎ 333900) ICEA Bldg, Kenyatta Ave
South African Airways (☎ 229663) Lonrho House, Standard St

Kenya Airways is the main domestic carrier and operates from Nairobi's Jomo Kenyatta international airport. It has three flights daily to Kisumu (KSh 3500 one way) and Eldoret (KSh 3500), five flights weekly to Malindi (KSh 5650), daily flights to Lamu (KSh 8490) and flights roughly

every two hours to Mombasa (KSh 5650). It often offers special deals to Mombasa (for as little as KSh 7200 return) and occasionally on its other routes. Standby fares to Mombasa are also available and fares vary with the flexibility of the ticket. Pay in either US dollars or local currency, but find out the absolutely cheapest fare first. It is usually best to go through a travel agent.

A much smaller operation, African Express Airways (☎ 823497) flies from Nairobi to Eldoret (KSh 5200 return) once a day, and Nairobi to Mombasa (KSh 8400 return) twice a day. Flights leave from Jomo Kenyatta international airport.

The privately owned Air Kenya Aviation (☎ 501601) located at Wilson airport connects Nairobi with a number of centres. All the following fares are one way/return:

destination	fare	frequency
Amboseli	US$80/140	daily
Lamu	US$135/270	daily
Malindi	KSh 5385/10770	twice weekly
Masai Mara	US$87/150	twice daily
Mombasa	KSh 5385/10770	nine times weekly
Nanyuki	US$80/130	daily
Samburu	US$115/200	daily

The check-in time for all domestic flights is 30 minutes before departure and the baggage allowance is 15kg. All flights are non-smoking. Make sure you reconfirm flights 48 hours before departure.

Bus
In Nairobi, most long-distance bus offices are along Accra Rd near the River Rd junction. For Mombasa there are numerous companies (such as Coast Bus, Crossline, Akamba, Mawingo, Malindi Bus, Takrim and Tawfiq) doing the route by day and night. The fare is about KSh 500 and the trip takes between eight and 10 hours with a meal break on the way. Buses leave from outside each company's office.

Akamba (☎ 225488) is the biggest private bus company in the country and has an extensive network. It's not the cheapest, but it's probably the safest and most reliable company. Its office is conveniently located on Lagos Rd just off Latema Rd and very close to Tom Mboya St. Apart from the Mombasa service (KSh 500), it also has daily connections to Eldoret (KSh 350), Homa Bay (KSh 450), Isiolo (KSh 320), Kakamega (KSh 500), Kitale (KSh 480), Kisii (KSh 400), Kisumu (KSh 420), Magadi (KSh 170) Malaba (KSh 500) and Nanyuki (KSh 160). Buses to Isiolo travel around the western side of Mt Kenya via Nanyuki, thus missing out Embu, Meru and Chogoria.

The government-owned KBS Stagecoach company is another large, reliable operator and is cheaper than Akamba, but the buses are much slower. They leave from the central bus station.

Apart from the companies listed above, a huge number of small companies leave from the main country bus station just off Landhies Rd, about 15 minutes walk south-east of the budget hotel area around Latema Rd. It's a huge but reasonably well organised place and all the buses have their destinations displayed in the window. There is at least one daily departure and often more to virtually every main town in the country; the buses leave when full (see Getting There & Away in the relevant chapters for more details).

For details on travelling to Uganda or Tanzania, see the Kenya Getting There & Away chapter.

Shuttle Minibus
A good option for travel to or from Mombasa, but more expensive than the large buses, is the shuttle service run by The Connection. The company offers air-con, 18-seater minibuses for KSh 1000 one way which will drop you off anywhere in the centre of Nairobi or Mombasa. Book at Inside Africa Safaris (☎ 223304) on Wabera St in Nairobi, or at Vogue Tours & Travel (☎ 011-223613) in the Jubilee Arcade buildings, Moi Ave, Mombasa. Check-in is at 9.30 am in Nairobi and 8.30 am in Mombasa. Shuttle minibuses to Kampala (Uganda), Arusha and Moshi (both in Tanzania) are also available (see the Kenya Getting There & Away chapter for details).

Matatu
Most matatus leave from the area around Latema, Accra, River and Cross Rds.

For Embu (KSh 150), Meru (KSh 270), Isiolo (KSh 300), Nyeri (KSh 150) and Nanyuki (KSh 200), head for the junction of River and Accra Rds (also try the central reservation area of Accra Rd). Molo Line (☎ 336363) and Cross Road Travellers (☎ 245377) have their offices on Cross Rd.

Matatus (and some Peugeot share-taxis) to Eldoret (KSh 300), Kericho (KSh 290), Kisumu (KSh 500) Kitale (KSh 400), Naivasha (KSh 90), Nakuru (KSh 150) and Narok (KSh 150) can be found on Cross Rd east of the junction with Kumasi Rd. Some destinations require a change in Nakuru, but you buy only one ticket.

A little further down Cross Rd is Nuclear Investments (☎ 214398) which runs matatus to Nyahururu (KSh 220) and Maralal (KSh 470).

Matatus to Nakuru, Kitale, Kisumu, Eldoret, Molo and Njoro can be found close to the corner of Kumasi and Duruma Rds.

Share-Taxi
Like matatus, most of the share-taxi companies have their offices around the Accra and River Rds area.

Daily Peugeot Service (DPS; ☎ 210866) on Dubois Rd is typical of these companies and has daily Peugeots to Kisumu (KSh 550, four hours), Nakuru (KSh 280, two hours), Malaba on the Ugandan border, Kitale (KSh 600), and Kericho. On any of these services you can pay an extra KSh 20 for the front seat. These services depart only in the mornings so you need to be at the office by around 7 am, and it's a good idea to book one day in advance.

Cross Road Travellers (☎ 245377) on Cross Rd has numerous departures to western Kenya, while other companies in the area service destinations in the Central Highlands, with departures all day.

Tanzania Share-taxis for the Tanzanian border at Namanga leave from the service station on the corner of Ronald Ngala St and River Rd. Most people prefer to take either a bus or a shuttle minibus direct from Nairobi to Arusha. See the Kenya Getting There & Away chapter for details.

Train

The booking office at Nairobi train station (☎ 335160) is open from 8 am to 7 pm daily. The evening train to Mombasa is the only 1st and 2nd class service available (see the Kenya Getting Around chapter for further information). Trains between Nairobi and Mombasa leave daily in both directions at 7 pm and the journey takes about 13 hours, though services are often an hour or so late. Fares for nonresidents are KSh 2100/3000 in 2nd/1st class. It's advisable to book two days in advance.

Nairobi train station also has a left-luggage office open daily from 8 am to noon and 2 to 6 pm. It costs KSh 200 per item per day.

Car & Motorcycle

Comprehensive information on car hire and a list of companies can be found in the Kenya Getting Around chapter.

Hitching

For Mombasa, take bus No 13, 34 or 109 as far as the airport turn-off and hitch a ride from there. For Nakuru and Kisumu, take bus No 23 from the Hilton to the end of its route and hitch from there. Otherwise start from the junction of Chiromo Rd and Waiyaki Way (the extension of Uhuru Hwy) in Westlands.

For Nanyuki and Nyeri take bus No 45 or 145 from the central bus station up Thika Rd to the entrance of Kenyatta National University and hitch from there. Make sure you get off the bus at the university entrance and not the exit. It's very difficult to hitch from the latter. You could also start from the roundabout where Forest and Muranga'a Rds meet Thika Rd.

GETTING AROUND
To/From the Airport

Jomo Kenyatta international airport is 15km out of town off the road to Mombasa. The cheapest way of getting into town is the city bus No 34 *but* (and this is a big but) a large number of travellers have been ripped off on this bus. Take a taxi into town (about KSh 1000, or KSh 800 from town). When leaving Kenya there is generally no problem catching the No 34 city bus *to* the airport when your money is spent. The fare from the bottom of Moi Ave is KSh 20 and the trip takes about 45 minutes, longer at peak times.

If you have a problem at the airport the staff at the 'Jambo Office' are reportedly very helpful in a crisis. The Airport Business Center (☎ 824536, email abcenter@nbnet .co.ke) offers telephone, fax and Internet services. The staff are very clued up and located in the British Airways check-in hall.

To get to Wilson airport (for light aircraft services to Malindi, Lamu etc) you can take bus or matatu No 15, 31, 34, 125 or 126 from Moi Ave for KSh 20. A taxi from the centre of town will cost KSh 500 to KSh 700 depending on the driver. The entrance to the airport is easy to miss; get off at the BP station.

Bus

Buses are the cheapest way of getting around Nairobi, but hopefully you won't need to use them much. Forget about them in rush hour if you have a backpack – you'll never get on and if by some Herculean feat you manage it, you'll never get off.

Useful buses include No 46 from outside the new post office on Kenyatta Ave for the Yaya Centre in Hurlingham (KSh 10), or No 23 from Moi Ave at Jevanjee Gardens for Westlands (KSh 10). You need to be super-vigilant though because they're a pickpocket's paradise. Never take your hand off your valuables and have small change handy for the fare.

Matatu

Matatus are also packed during peak hour, but not bad at other times. The main disadvantage is that the drivers are downright crazy. Matatus are frequent and only slightly more expensive than the buses. They follow the same routes as buses, and can be caught in the same places. Keep an eye on your valuables.

Taxi

Other than the fleet of London cabs, Nairobi taxis rate as some of the most dilapidated and generally unroadworthy buckets of bolts ever to have graced a city street. Despite this they are expensive. Taxis cannot usually be hailed on the street (they don't cruise for passengers) but you can find them parked in just about every second street corner in the city centre. At night, they're found outside bars and nightclubs.

The cabs are not metered but the fares are remarkably standard: KSh 200 to KSh 300 gets you just about anywhere within the city centre. The same is true from Ralph Bunche Rd or Milimani Rd to the main post office though they sometimes ask for a bit more as the trip involves backtracking down the other side of Haile Selassie Ave. From the city centre to anywhere in Westlands is about KSh 400 (for locals it's KSh 300).

Around Nairobi

The attractions listed below are easily accessible from central Nairobi.

THE BOMAS OF KENYA

The Bomas of Kenya (☎ 891801) is a cultural centre at Langata – a short way past the main entrance to Nairobi National Park, on the right as you head out from Nairobi. Here you can see traditional dances and hear songs from the country's 16 ethnic groups. There's a performance daily at 2.30 pm (3.30 pm at weekends). Entry will set you back KSh 600 for adults and KSh 300 for children.

Bus or matatu No 15, 125 or 126 from outside Development House on Moi Ave will get you there in about 30 minutes. Get off at Magadi Rd, from where it's about a 1km walk; follow the signposts.

OSTRICH PARK

The Ostrich Park (☎ 891051) is about 1km further along Langata Rd, well signposted right opposite the turn-off for Langata itself. This makes a good family excursion where you can feed ostriches and see artisans at work making handicrafts. There's also a good kids' playground.

The park is open daily and entry is KSh 200 (KSh 100 for children).

LANGATA GIRAFFE CENTRE

The Langata Giraffe Centre (☎ 891658) is on Gogo Falls Rd about 1km from the Hardy Estate shopping centre in Langata, about 18km from central Nairobi. Here you can observe and hand-feed Rothschild giraffes from a raised circular wooden structure which also houses a display of information about giraffes.

Across the road but still part of the centre is a small patch of forest through which you can take a 1km, self-guided forest walk. Booklets (KSh 20) are available from the ticket office.

The centre is open from 9 am to 5.30 pm daily. Admission costs KSh 500 (KSh 100 for children). From Nairobi take matatu No 24 to the Hardy Estate shopping centre in Langata and walk from there.

KAREN BLIXEN MUSEUM

This is the farmhouse where Karen Blixen, author of *Out of Africa*, lived between 1914 and 1931 until she left Kenya after a series of personal tragedies. The property was presented to the Kenyan government at Independence by the Danish government along with the adjacent agricultural college.

The museum is open daily from 9.30 am to 6 pm and entry costs KSh 200. It's next door to the Karen College on Karen Rd about 2km from Langata Rd.

Karen Blixen Coffee Garden (☎ 882138) is 500m back towards town. It has a bar, restaurant and gift shop. The food is not bad (expect to pay about KSh 400 for a main course) and the bar attracts a good mixed crowd in the evenings.

The No 111 bus or matatu from Moi Ave will get you here in about 40 minutes (KSh 30). Alternatively, take bus No 27 from Kenyatta Ave or from the corner of Ralph Bunche and Ngong Rds to Karen village (the shopping centre) and change to a No 24 matatu. A taxi will cost you about KSh 850 one way.

KENYA

AROUND NAIROBI

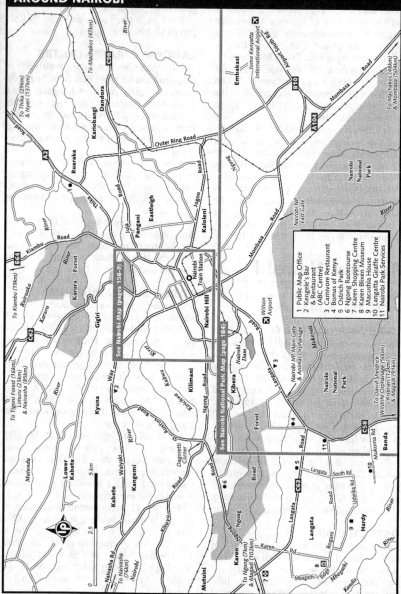

To Thika (29km)
& Nyeri (137km)

To Machakos (47km)

River

C58

Dandora

Kariobangi

Ruaraka

River

Outer Ring Road

Road

Thika

A2

Jomo Kenyatta
International Airport

Embakasi

Airport South Rd

B10

Mombasa Road

A104

To Machakos (48km)
& Mombasa (504km)

Kiambu
Road

E434

To Kiambu (19km)

River

Karura
Forest

Karura

River

Gigiri

Kyuna

Way

To Tigoni Forest (16km),
Limuru (23km)
& Naivasha (85km)

C62

River

Karura

Juja Road

Eastleigh

Pangani

Kaloleni

Jogoo Road

Nairobi
Train Station

See Nairobi Map (pages 158-9)

Nairobi Hill

Nairobi NP
East Gate

River

Nairobi
National
Park

Ngong Road

Mombasa Road

Wilson
Airport

Nairobi
Dam

Kibera

See Nairobi National Park Map (page 184)

Kilimani

Kirichwa River

Kuwua

St Austin's Road

Dagoretti
Corner

Kyuna

Wayaki

Kangemi

Kabete

Lower
Kabete

Matundu

Kirichwa
River

River

Ngong Road

Kikuyu
Road

5 km

2.5

0

To Naivasha Rd
To Naivasha
(76km)
Nairobi

Mutuini

Ngong

Ngong Road

Karen

Karen Rd

To Ngong (7km)
& Magadi (102km)

Mbagathi

7

Ngong

Langata Road

Langata

Langata South Rd

C63

Bogani

Uhuru Rd

Hardy

9

8

Mbagathi

Mbagathi

River

Kandis River

Mokoyeti

Nairobi NP Main Gate
& Animal Orphanage

Langata

▼3

Nairobi
National
Park

▼2

▼6

C58

Mukoma Rd

Banda

To David Sheldrick
Wildlife Orphanage (500m)
Kiserian (12km)
& Magadi (91km)

Forest

4

11

5

10

1 Public Map Office
2 Kengele's Bar
   & Restaurant
   (ABC Centre)
3 Carnivore Restaurant
4 Bomas of Kenya
5 Ostrich Park
6 Ngong Racecourse
7 Karen Shopping Centre
8 Karen Blixen Museum
9 Macushla House
10 Langatta Giraffe Centre
11 Nairobi Park Services

KENYA

NAIROBI NATIONAL PARK

Nairobi National Park is the oldest park in the country, having been created in 1946. It's an underrated park and you should certainly set aside a morning or an afternoon to see it. For a park so close to the city centre there is an amazing variety of animals; only elephants are missing from the big five, though over 50 black rhinos are present in this small park.

The terrain is classic African savannah with steep river valley and hippo pools set against a backdrop of Nairobi's skyscrapers and jumbo jets approaching Jomo Kenyatta international airport. Over 550 species of bird have been recorded here and it's also possible to see some of the less common antelopes, such as Klipspringer, Suni, Steinbock and Chandler's mountain reedbuck.

The national park is not fenced and wildlife is still able (for the time being) to migrate along a narrow wildlife corridor to the Rift Valley.

Entry to the park costs US$20 (KSh 150 for residents) and US$5 for children (KSh 50 for residents) plus KSh 200 for a vehicle.

Sebastian's Cafe by the entrance is a good place for a drink and a meal. The gift shop has a good selection of maps and books about other parks and reserves and the Friends of Nairobi National Park are based here (see Activities earlier in this chapter).

Rhino Rescue

Many of Africa's animals are threatened by the loss of their habitat due to human overpopulation or poachers, and it's the poor rhino that is in the greatest danger. The rhino's horn, its trademark, causes the problem – plenty of people covet it and this pushes the price up as it becomes increasingly rare.

The stark statistics are horrific. It is estimated that in 1970, Kenya had about 20,000 black rhinos. By 1985, that number had dwindled to just 425, and rhinos were so few and so scattered that it was becoming increasingly difficult for a lady rhino to meet a compatible gentleman rhino, with the aim of creating baby rhinos. With this huge fall in numbers, the price of rhino horn on the black market soared from US$35 per kg to over US$30,000 per kg – and it's still rising. Elsewhere in Africa, the fall in rhino numbers has been equally dramatic.

Rhino horn is a popular ingredient in many Chinese traditional medicines. However the major market for rhino horn is Yemen, where Jambiya daggers with rhino horn handles are worth over US$15,000. These massive prices are inspiring ruthless tactics from poachers who tote modern weapons and are as likely to shoot as run when confronted by rangers. In 1990, their brazenness reached new heights when they shot Kenya's only five white rhinos (in Meru National Park) and the rhinos' armed guards.

The only solution to the carnage is thought to be the creation of small parks where rhinos can be carefully watched and protected. Funded by Rhino Rescue, an organisation set up in 1986 specifically to save the rhinos, the Nakuru National Park was selected as the first manageable rhino sanctuary. The park is now protected by a 74km electric fence with guard posts at 15km intervals. The construction involved more than 11,000 fence posts and 880km of high-tensile wire. There are currently 26 white rhinos (imports from Southern Africa) in the park, which you'll see grazing at the water's edge, and a smaller number of the more shy black rhino.

Additional sanctuaries enclosed by electric fences and protected by highly trained rangers have been established in Tsavo East and West national parks and more are planned. Aberdare National Park is almost totally enclosed by an electric fence that helps protect an estimated 70 black rhino. However a 52km stretch remains to be completed, and at UK£18,581 per kilometre, saving the rhino isn't going to be cheap. If you want to help this scheme send your donation to Rhino Ark (☎ 020-8944 6688, email rhinoark@globalnet.co.uk), Thornton House, Thornton Rd, Wimbledon, London SW19 4NG. The Web site is www.rhinoark.org.uk.

The population of black rhino in Kenya now stands at 424 with possibly another 34 wandering in the wild. This represents an increase of 11% in the population since 1987.

KENYA

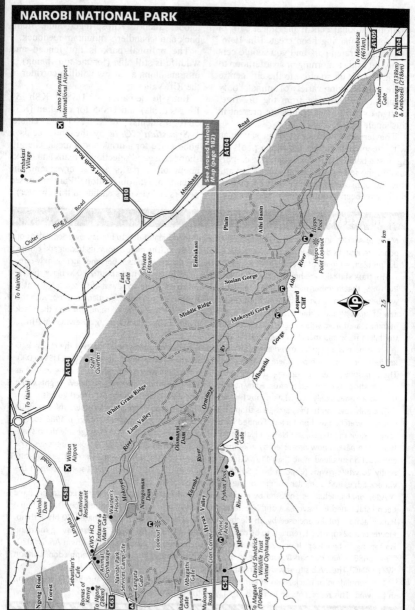

NAIROBI NATIONAL PARK

See Around Nairobi Map (page 182)

To Mombasa (461km)

To Namanga (138km) & Amboseli (218km)

Cheetah Gate

Jomo Kenyatta International Airport

Embakasi Village

Airport South Road

Mombasa Road

Outer Ring Road

Ring Road

To Nairobi

Private Entrance

East Gate

Wilson Airport

To Nairobi

Staff Quarters

White Grass Ridge

Lion Valley

Mokoyeti River

Warden's House

Carnivore Restaurant

KWS HQ

Entrance & Main Gate

Animal Orphanage

Sebastian's Cafe

Bomas of Kenya

To Ngong (28km)

Ngong Road Forest

Nairobi Dam

Langata Road

Langata Gate

Nairobi Park Services Camp Site

Mbagathi Gate

Banda Gate

Mukoma Road

David Sheldrick Wildlife Trust Animal Orphanage

To Magadi (104km)

Lion Corner

Hyrax Valley

Picnic Area

Python Pool

Mbagathi River

Masai Gate

Ksembe River

Narogoman Dam

Olomunyi Dam

Ormonye

Lookout

Kv

Middle Ridge

Embakasi

Plain

Athi Basin

Athi River

Hippo Pool

Leopard Cliff

Point Lookout

Sosian Gorge

Mokoyeti Gorge

Gorge

Mbagathi

5 km

2.5

0

Getting There & Away

This is the most accessible of Kenya's national parks. If you want to hitch a ride through the park, city bus No 24 from Moi Ave will get you to the main gate.

There are many companies offering tours of Nairobi National Park and there's probably not much between them. The four-hour tours usually depart twice a day at 9.30 am and 2 pm and cost about US$50. It may be cheaper to hire a 2WD car or negotiate with a taxi driver (roads in the park are very good).

DAVID SHELDRICK WILDLIFE TRUST

The trust was established shortly after the death of David Sheldrick in 1977. David and his wife Daphne pioneered techniques of raising orphaned black rhino and elephant and reintroducing them to the wild. Rhino and elephant are still reared on-site and can be viewed between 11 am and noon daily. Admission is free, but it's reasonable to donate at least KSh 200. There's a gift shop and information centre (☎ 891996, fax 890053) and there's someone around to answer questions.

From outside Development House on Moi Ave take bus or matatu No 125 or 126 and ask the driver to drop you off at the Kenya Wildlife Service (KWS) central workshop opposite the Kenya College of Communication and Training on Magadi Rd (the journey takes about 50 minutes). Walk through the KWS gate and stay on the dirt road that leads past the central workshop and winds up to the top of the hill. Staff will take care of you from then on.

NGONG HILLS

Ngong and Karen to the west of Nairobi, along with Limuru to the north, were where many white settlers set up farms and built their houses in the early colonial days. The transformation they wrought was quite remarkable so that even today, as you catch a glimpse of a half-timbered house through woodland or landscaped gardens full of flowering trees, you could imagine yourself to be in the Home Counties of England.

The hills provide some excellent walking, but the risk of being mugged is high, so go on an organised tour or pick up an escort from either Ngong police station or the KWS office in Ngong. The hills still contain plenty of wildlife (antelope and buffalo are common).

Close to the summit of the range is the grave of Denys George Finch-Hatton, the famous lover of Karen Blixen. A large obelisk east of the summit on the lower ridges marks his grave. There are a number of stories about a lion and lioness standing guard at Denys' graveside.

One excellent place to stay in the Maasai land foothills of the Ngong is *Whistling Thorns* (*☎/fax 350720, email speccampsaf@ thorntree.com, PO Box 51512, Nairobi*). You can camp here for KSh 250, or KSh 450 if you don't have a tent. Self-contained cottages cost KSh 3500 for a double room including breakfast. There's a swimming pool, pool table and restaurant. There are also horses for riding (KSh 1000 per hour) and numerous walking trails in the area.

To get here take bus No 111 via Ngong or No 126 via Ongata Rongai from Moi Ave to Kiserian. From the Total petrol station in Kiserian, pick up a matatu for Isinya/Kajiado. Ask to be dropped at Whistling Thorns, which is 200m from the roadside. Count on a two hour trip from door to door.

LIMURU
☎ 0154

Limuru has possibly even more of a European feel than the Ngong Hills, except there are vast coffee and tea plantations blanketing the rolling hills, cut by swathes of conifer and eucalypt forest. It's up here that you'll find *Kentmere Club* (*☎ 41053, fax 40692, Limuru Rd, Tigoni*). This is the quintessential white settlers' club – even more so than the Norfolk Hotel in Nairobi.

About 10km beyond Kentmere Club, and well signposted, is *Waterfalls Inn* (*☎ 40672*) with its picnic site, waterfall, viewing point and restaurant. Admission costs KSh 600 per car (with up to five passengers) on Saturday and Sunday and KSh 250 on weekdays. Although used mainly by day-tripping picnickers, the extensive grounds can also be used for camping (KSh 300 per person).

It's a very relaxing place during the week, although you really need your own transport as there are no public transport routes close by. Pony riding and horse riding are also available.

Kiambethu Tea Farm (☎ 40756) offers tours of its tea estate at Tigoni, about 35km north-east of Nairobi. Trips start daily at 11 am and finish at 2.30 pm. The cost is KSh 1500 including food, but you must book in advance.

KBS bus No 116 will take you within a few kilometres of the tea farm. If you have your own transport, take Limuru Rd (C62) past City Park and turn left at Muthaiga round-about. About 7km further on you reach Ruaka village where you turn right at the signpost for Nazareth Hospital and onto Limuru Rd (D407, otherwise known as Banana Rd). This takes you past Kentmere Club and the signposted turn-off to Waterfall Inn. Alternatively, for tours from Nairobi (US$55), contact Let's Go Travel (☎ 02-340331).

AMBOSELI NATIONAL PARK

Amboseli is the next most popular park after Masai Mara, mainly because of the spectacular backdrop of Africa's highest peak, Mt Kilimanjaro, which broods over the southern boundary of the park.

At 392 sq km Amboseli is not a large park, but the wildlife on the plains are easy to spot. Buffalo, lion, gazelle, cheetah, wildebeest, hyena, jackal, warthog, zebra and baboon are all present. The last rhinos were translocated to Tsavo West in 1995 after a sustained period of vicious poaching. Elephants suffered a great deal, but large herds can still be seen grazing in the permanent swamps of Enkongo Narok and Ol Okenya.

Most visitors approach Amboseli through **Namanga** which has a couple of reasonable hotels. The petrol station is a good place to ask around for lifts.

Entry to the national park costs US$27 per person (US$10 children) per day.

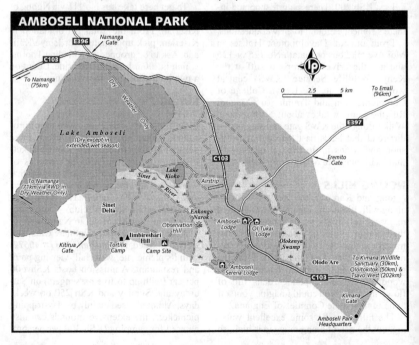

Places to Stay – Budget & Mid-Range

The only *camp site* is right on the southern boundary of the park (US$8). There are a couple of long-drop toilets, an unreliable water supply (bring your own) and a small *duka*. Elephants can be a real problem here so *don't* keep food in your tent.

Very close to the settlement of Oloitokitok, and accessible by matatu from Emali, is *Kibo Slope Cottages* (☎ 0302-22091, fax 22427) where B&B accommodation costs US$20/35 dropping to KSh 600/1000 in low season.

Places to Stay – Top End

Amboseli Lodge is run by the Kilimanjaro Safari Club in Nairobi (☎ 02-227136, fax 219982). The lodge consists of a number of comfortable cottages dotted around an expansive lawn and garden, with sweeping views of Kilimanjaro (weather permitting, of course). There's also a swimming pool. Rooms cost US$70 per person for full board during the low season and US$168/210 for singles/doubles in the high season.

Close by is the modern *Ol Tukai Lodge*, belonging to Block Hotels (☎ 02-540780, fax 540821). This lodge has a beautiful central building and the guest cottages are spread around a lawn (two have wheelchair access). This is a very comfortable hotel, complete with swimming pool. Rooms cost US$107/165 in the high season and about 20% less in the low season.

Close to the southern perimeter of the park is *Amboseli Serena Lodge* (☎ 02-711077, fax 725184). Sensitively designed and constructed, it blends in well with the landscape. The nearby Enkongo Narok Swamp ensures constant bird and animal activity. Rooms cost US$55/110 (full board) during the low season, rising to US$128/166 in the high season.

Also on the southern edge of the park, at the western end, is the secluded *Tortilis Camp* (☎ 02-748307, fax 750225, email chelipeacock@form-net.com). The open-air, makuti-roofed lounge and dining areas are elevated to make the most of the views of Kilimanjaro, while the permanent luxury tents, each with veranda, nestle in among a stand of *Acacia tortilis* trees. The whole place has been designed to be eco-friendly, making use of solar power for heating water, and no wood is used for fires. The food is excellent, and reflects the Kenyan owners' Italian background. Because it's on the park boundary, they can offer activities such as guided nature walks, which are not possible within the park. The cost is US$120/240 for full board in the low season, rising to US$210/326 in the high season.

About 30km or so east of the park, and close to the private Kimana Wildlife Sanctuary (entry US$10) is *Kilimanjaro Buffalo Lodge*, operated by the Kilimanjaro Safari Club in Nairobi (☎ 02-227136, fax 219982, email ksc@africaonline.co.ke). There are excellent views of Kilimanjaro and the Chyulu Hills. Room rates are US$70/140 in the low season, up to US$160/200 in the high season. There's Maasai dance every evening, and a swimming pool.

Getting There & Away

Air Air Kenya Aviation has daily flights between Wilson airport (Nairobi) and Amboseli. These leave Nairobi at 7.30 am and the trip takes about an hour (US$70 one way). The return flight leaves Amboseli at 8.30 am.

Car & 4WD The usual approach to Amboseli is through Namanga, 165km south of Nairobi on the A104 and the last fuel stop before the park. The road is in excellent condition from Nairobi to Namanga, however the 75km dirt road from Namanga to the Namanga Gate can be fiercely corrugated (allow four hours for the whole trip).

When the seasonal lakes are dry it is also possible to enter through Kitirua Gate by forking right onto a well used dirt road 15km out of Namanga, although 4WD recommended.

It's also possible to enter Amboseli from the east via Tsavo. There have been bandit attacks in the past, so all vehicles travel in a convoy accompanied by armed policemen. The convoys leave the Kimana Gate of Amboseli at 8.30 and 10.30 am, and 2.30 pm. Fortunately, incidents are very rare (just one in the last eight years). The trip to Chyulu Gate and Kilaguni Lodge in Tsavo East takes about three hours.

The Coast

This cannot be less than natural beauty, the end-less sand, the reefs, the lot, are completely un-matched in the world.

Ernest Hemingway

The coast of Kenya is one of the country's main attractions. It offers a combination of historical sites, trading ports with a strong Arab-Muslim influence, superb beaches and diving opportunities – an area not to be missed.

Mombasa is the coast's capital and is the first port of call for many people after leaving Nairobi. It's an old trading port with a history going back at least to the 12th century; the city's old quarter shows heavy Portuguese, Arabic and Indian influences. It has a steamy humid climate but is a pleasant place nonetheless and definitely worth exploring.

South and north of Mombasa are some of the finest beaches in Africa. South of Mombasa, Tiwi and Diani beaches are the great draw while a strip of hotels stretches up the coast north of the city. The coral reefs of Watamu and Kisite-Mpunguti marine national parks provide some excellent diving, while the historical sites at Gedi and Kilifi, the birdlife of Arabuko-Sokoke Forest Reserve and the elephants in Shimba Hills National Reserve are all a short distance from the nearest 'sunlounger'. Further inland are the Tsavo national parks; the largest in Kenya. For the more sporting, the Indian Ocean offers some of the greatest game fishing in the world.

Head further north and you come to the island of Lamu – a beautiful Arab-influenced town that has been something of a travellers mecca for years; its unique culture and laid-back atmosphere attract thousands of visitors.

The people of the coast are the Swahili and it's here that Kiswahili (Swahili), the lingua franca of the modern nation, evolved as the means of communication between the local inhabitants and the Arab traders.

Highlights

- Staying at the edge of the forested escarpment of the Shimba Hills National Reserve overlooking the Indian Ocean
- Swimming and diving in the deep lagoon just off Tiwi Beach
- Walking through Arabuko Sokoke Forest Reserve on the trail of the golden-rumped elephant shrew
- Wandering at dawn through the magnificent Swahili ruins at Gedi
- Taking a dhow trip along the Lamu Archipelago and swimming under the stars in the calm bay off Kiwayu Island
- Eating seafood in Mambrui
- Snorkelling among the coral and brightly coloured fish at Watamu and Kisite-Mpunguti marine national parks

If you are planning to hit the coast in the low season, it's worth contacting a travel agent to see what kind of cheap flight-and-accommodation deal they can put together. Good deals do come along now and again, both within Kenya and from Europe.

History

The first traders here appear to have been Arabs from the Persian Gulf in the 7th century who sailed south along the coast during the north-east monsoon, sailing home north with the south-west monsoon. By the 12th century some substantial settlements had developed, mainly on islands such as Lamu, Manda, Pemba and Unguja (Zanzibar Island).

From the 12th to the 15th centuries settlements grew and a dynasty was established at Kilwa (in present-day Tanzania). By the end of this period Mombasa, Malindi and Paté (in the Lamu archipelago), all substantial Arabic towns, were vying for supremacy. So preoccupied were they with their own internal struggles that the coastal centres

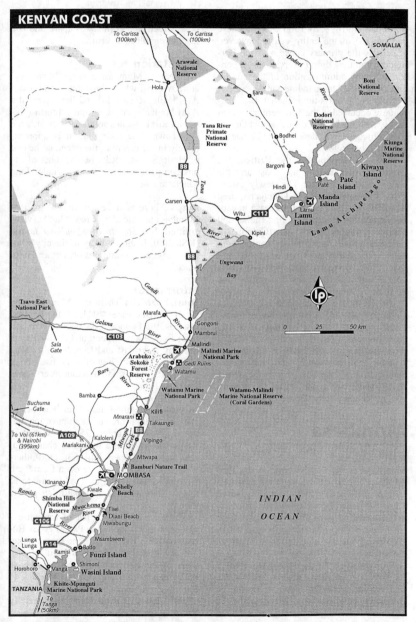

KENYAN COAST

To Garissa (100km)
To Garissa (100km)

SOMALIA

Arawale National Reserve

Hola

Ijara

Dodori River

Boni National Reserve

Tana River Primate National Reserve

Bodhei

Dodori National Reserve

Kiunga Marine National Reserve

B8

Bargoni

Hindi

Paté Paté Island

Kiwayu Island

Garsen

Witu

C112

Manda Island

Lamu Lamu Island

Lamu Archipelago

Kipini

B8

Tana River

Ungwana Bay

Gandi

IP

0   25   50 km

Tsavo East National Park

Galana River

Marafa

Gongoni

Mambrui

C103

Malindi

Sala Gate

Arabuko Sokoke Forest Reserve

Gedi

Malindi Marine National Park

Gedi Ruins

Watamu

Rare River

Watamu Marine National Park

Watamu-Malindi Marine National Reserve (Coral Gardens)

Bamba

Kilifi

Mnarani

Buchuma Gate

Takaungu

B8

To Voi (61km) & Nairobi (395km)

A109

Kaloleni

Vipingo

Mariakani

Mwapa Creek

Mtwapa

Bamburi Nature Trail

Kinango

MOMBASA

Kwale

Shelly Beach

Shimba Hills National Reserve

Mwachema River

Tiwi

Diani Beach

Ramisi

C106

River

Mwabungu

Msambweni

INDIAN

OCEAN

Lunga Lunga

A14

Ramisi

Bodo

Horohoro

Vanga

Shimoni

Funzi Island

Wasini Island

TANZANIA

Kisite-Mpunguti Marine National Park

To Tanga (50km)

were quite unprepared for the arrival of the Portuguese in 1498. By 1506 the Portuguese had control of the entire coast. However, trade was the primary concern of the Portuguese and they didn't exercise direct control over the administration of the coastal cities – just kept them in line and dependent.

Numerous uprisings against the Portuguese occurred in the 17th century; eventually, with the help of the sultans of Oman, the Portuguese were defeated and Fort Jesus occupied by 1698.

With the support of the British, the Omani's prospered on the coast and the slave trade flourished. The newly established clove plantations on Unguja required labourers and the resulting increase in economic activity brought the first Indian and European traders into the area. Omani Sultan Seyyid Said transferred his capital from Muscat to Zanzibar Town in 1840, and thanks to a strong economy was eventually able to side with the British when they took up their fight against slavery.

Despite the fact that the British East Africa Company took over administration of the interior of the country, a 16km-wide coastal strip was recognised as the sultan's patch and it was leased by the British from him in 1887, first for a 50-year period and then permanently. In 1920 the coastal strip became a British protectorate, the rest of the country having become a fully fledged British colony.

Mombasa

☎ 011

Mombasa is the largest port on the East African coast. It has a population of nearly half a million. Its docks not only serve Kenya, but also Uganda, Rwanda, Burundi and eastern Congo (Zaïre). The bulk of the town sprawls over Mombasa Island, which is connected to the mainland by an artificial causeway.

Mombasa may be large but it has retained its character and it's a more relaxed place than Nairobi. The Old Town, between the massive Portuguese-built Fort Jesus and the old dhow careening dock, remains much the same as it was in the mid-19th century, asphalt streets and craft shops apart, and is a fascinating place to visit.

Orientation

The heart of Mombasa is Digo Rd and Nyerere Ave, off which three main roads (Moi Ave, Haile Selassie Rd and Jomo Kenyatta Ave) branch north-west and a fourth (Nkrumah Rd) branches south-east towards the Old Town. The train station is approximately in the centre of the island at the end of Haile Selassie Rd whereas most of the bus companies have their terminals along Kenyatta Ave.

Maps There is a new 1:10,000 map of Mombasa produced by Coast Map Services entitled *The Streets of Mombasa Island* (KSh 200). It shows many of the city's hotels, banks and restaurants plus other useful places.

Information

Tourist Offices There is a Mombasa and Coast Tourist Office (☎ 311231, fax 228208) just past the famous tusks on Moi Ave. It's open from 9 am to noon and 2 to 4.30 pm Monday to Friday, and from 9 am to noon Saturday. The office is of *some* use – they will make flight, safari and tour reservations for you.

Money There are at least four branches of Barclays Bank; three of them have international ATMs. The branch 250m west of Digo Rd on Moi Ave has a foreign exchange bureau that stays open until 4.30 pm. Otherwise all banks in town are open from 9 am to 3 pm Monday to Friday and from 9 to 11 am on the first and last Saturday of the month.

There are also a number of foreign exchange bureaus including Pwani Forex Bureau on Digo Rd opposite the main market and the Fort Jesus Forex Bureau right in front of the entrance to the fort. They're both open from 8 am to 5 pm Monday to Saturday. The exchange rates are generally slightly lower than in Nairobi, especially for travellers cheques.

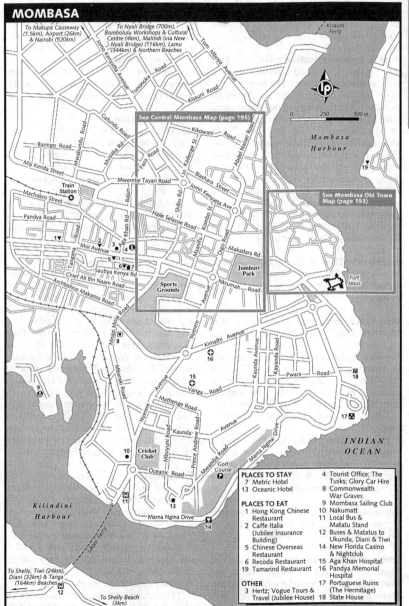

MOMBASA

To Makupa Causeway (1.5km), Airport (26km) & Nairobi (520km)

To Nyali Bridge (700m), Bombolulu Workshops & Cultural Centre (4km), Malindi (via New Nyali Bridge) (116km), Lamu (344km) & Northern Beaches

Kisauni Ferry

Jomo Kenyatta Avenue
Tononoka Road
Tom Mboya Avenue
Kisauni Road
Gatundu Road
Mwabundu Road
Baringo Road
Muyaka Rd
Faza Road
Miji Kenda Street
Machakos Street
Train Station
Pandya Road
Bajuni
Tangana Road
Moi Avenue
Aga Khan Rd
Haile Selassie Road
Sautiya Kenya Rd
Chief Ali Bin Naam Road
Archbishop Makarios Road

See Central Mombasa Map (page 195)
Kikowani Road
Kadenge St
Jo
Biashara Street
Abdel Nasser Road
Shibu Rd
Mwembe Tayari Road
Jomo Kenyatta Ave
Kombo St
Msanifu
Digo Road
Makadara Rd
Msanifu

Mombasa Harbour

0   250   500 m

See Mombasa Old Town Map (page 193)

Jumhuri Park

Sports Grounds

Nkrumah Road

Fort Jesus

Mnazi Moja Road
Mharaki Road
Nyerere Avenue
Kimathi Avenue
Kaunda Avenue
Kayanda Road
Pwani Road
Vanga Road
Mathenge Road
Kaunda Avenue
Mbuyuni Road
Prince Andrew Road
Mwamba Road
Mama Ngina Drive

INDIAN OCEAN

Cricket Club
Golf Course
Oceanic Road
Mama Ngina Drive

Kilindini Harbour

Likoni Ferry

To Shelly, Tiwi (24km), Diani (32km) & Tanga (164km) Beaches

To Shelly Beach (3km)

State House

PLACES TO STAY
7   Metric Hotel
13 Oceanic Hotel

PLACES TO EAT
1   Hong Kong Chinese Restaurant
2   Caffe Italia (Jubilee Insurance Building)
5   Chinese Overseas Restaurant
6   Recoda Restaurant
19 Tamarind Restaurant

OTHER
3   Hertz; Vogue Tours & Travel (Jubilee House)

4   Tourist Office; The Tusks; Glory Car Hire
8   Commonwealth War Graves
9   Mombasa Sailing Club
10 Nakumatt
11 Local Bus & Matatu Stand
12 Buses & Matatus to Ukunda, Diani & Tiwi
14 New Florida Casino & Nightclub
15 Aga Khan Hospital
16 Pandya Memorial Hospital
17 Portuguese Ruins (The Hermitage)
18 State House

American Express (Amex) is represented by Express Kenya (☎ 312461), PO Box 90631, Nkrumah Rd.

Post & Communications The main post office is on Digo Rd and is open from 8 am to 6 pm Monday to Friday and from 9 am to noon Saturday. Cardphones are dotted all over town, but for more reliable phone communications head to Post Global Services (☎ 314496, fax 314942, email inglobal@africaonline.co.ke) on Maungano Rd opposite the Polana Hotel. It's open from 7.30 am to 11 pm; rates are reasonable and it's the cheapest place in town to surf the Web (KSh 100 for 15 minutes). The owner Rashmi is a source of much useful tourist information and a capable 'can do' person. You can also surf the Web in the Hard Rock Cafe on Nkrumah Rd (KSh 300 per hour).

Bookshops There are few good bookshops in Mombasa. The Bahati Book Centre and Bahari Bookshop on Moi Ave are the pick of the crop.

Visa Extensions Visas can be extended at Mombasa immigration office (☎ 311745).

Medical Services The two best hospitals in Mombasa are the Aga Khan Hospital (☎ 312953) on Vanga Rd, and the Pandya Memorial Hospital (☎ 314140) on Kimathi Ave. You must pay for all services and medication at both, so have that travel insurance handy.

If you're going to be scuba diving, the only decompression chamber in the region is in Mombasa and is run by the Kenyan Navy (☎ 451201). Ask for the officer in charge of recompression.

Emergency The police hotline is reached by phoning ☎ 222121 and for Africa Air Rescue call ☎ 12405, 24 hours.

Dangers & Annoyances A few years ago Mombasa acquired a bad reputation for snatch-and-run thieves and muggers. That era appears to have passed and if you take precautions you're far less likely to be mugged

walking around here than in Nairobi. However, do not walk along the beaches to the north and south of town. Another thieves' paradise is the Likoni ferry where a number of tourists have had their cameras snatched.

A more immediate risk is malaria; for information see the Health section in the Regional Facts for the Visitor chapter.

The Old Town

The Old Town isn't as immediately interesting as the fort, but it's still a fascinating area to wander around in. Early morning or late afternoon is the best time to walk around as there's more activity than in the middle of the day.

The buildings in the area are a mixture of Swahili, late 19th century Indian and British colonial architecture. Some gentrification has occurred but the fine balconies and lattice work and wonderful Swahili carved doors can still be found.

In later years, as Mombasa expanded along what are today the main roads, many of the businesses that had shops and offices in the Old Town gradually moved out, leaving behind ornate signs, etched glass windows and other relics of former times. Their exact location is described in *The Old Town Mombasa: A Historical Guide*, by Judy Aldrick & Rosemary Macdonald. It can be bought from the tourist office, Fort Jesus, or one of the bookshops on Moi Ave.

The Mombasa Old Town Conservation Society (☎ 312246, fax 226302) is currently trying to encourage the renovation of many dilapidated buildings in the old town. The have an office on Mbarak Hinawy Rd.

Fort Jesus

The Old Town's biggest attraction dominates the harbour entrance. Begun in 1593 by the Portuguese, Fort Jesus changed hands nine times between 1631 and 1875. These days it's a museum and is open from 8.30 am to 6 pm daily. Entry costs KSh 200 for nonresidents and KSh 50 for residents (KSh 100 and KSh 20, respectively, for children under 12 years old).

The fort was designed by an Italian architect, Joao Batista Cairato, who had done

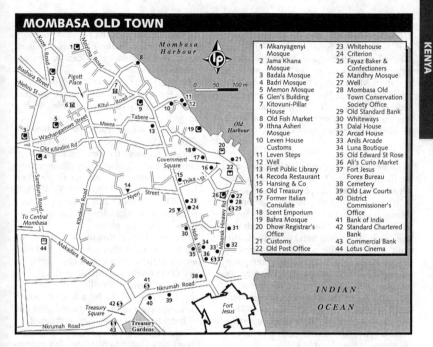

MOMBASA OLD TOWN

1	Mkanyagenyi Mosque	23	Whitehouse
2	Jama Khana Mosque	24	Criterion
3	Badala Mosque	25	Fayaz Baker & Confectioners
4	Badri Mosque	26	Mandhry Mosque
5	Memon Mosque	27	Well
6	Glen's Building	28	Mombasa Old Town Conservation Society Office
7	Kitovuni-Pillar House	29	Old Standard Bank
8	Old Fish Market	30	Whiteways
9	Ithna Asheri Mosque	31	Dalal House
10	Leven House	32	Arcad House
11	Leven Steps	33	Anils Arcade
12	Well	34	Luna Boutique
13	First Public Library	35	Old Edward St Rose
14	Recoda Restaurant	36	Ali's Curio Market
15	Hansing & Co	37	Fort Jesus Forex Bureau
16	Old Treasury	38	Cemetery
17	Former Italian Consulate	39	Old Law Courts
18	Scent Emporium	40	District Commissioner's Office
19	Bahra Mosque	41	Bank of India
20	Dhow Registrar's Office	42	Standard Chartered Bank
21	Customs	43	Commercial Bank
22	Old Post Office	44	Lotus Cinema

a lot of work for the Portuguese in Goa. He incorporated some ingenious elements into the design, such as the angular configuration of the walls, making it impossible for would-be invaders to lay siege to one wall without being sitting ducks for soldiers in one of the other walls.

The most interesting features today include the **Omani house** in the San Felipe bastion in the north-western corner of the fort. Built in the late 18th century it has served different functions as the purpose of the fort changed – it was the chief warder's house when the fort was a prison in the early 20th century. The view of the Old Town from the roof here is excellent.

The **museum** along the southern wall is built over what was the barracks rooms for the garrison. The exhibits are mostly ceramics but include other interesting odds and ends donated from private collections or dug up from various sites along the coast and reflect the variety of cultures that have influenced the coastal culture: Chinese, Indian, Portuguese and Persian. Also displayed are finds from the Portuguese frigate *Santo Antônio de Tanná*, which sank off the fort during the siege in 1697.

The **western wall** of the fort is probably the most interesting and includes an Omani audience hall (now covered by a second storey but still complete with official inscriptions – and unofficial graffiti) and the Passage of the Arches (a passage cut through the coral giving access to the outer part of the fort, although it was later blocked off).

Worth buying is *Fort Jesus* by James Kirkman, which gives a detailed account of the history of the Fort and points out the salient features.

Harbour Cruises

Luxury dhow cruises are popular in Mombasa and are a great way of seeing the harbour at night. The Tamarind Dhow, run by the Tamarind Restaurant serves fantastic food; the tour lasts four hours and costs US$75. Bookings can be made through Southern Cross Safaris (☎ 475074, fax 473533, email scross@swiftmombasa.com). Prices include transport to/from your hotel.

Jahazi Marine Ltd (☎ 472213) offers the same sort of deal, but with dinner served inside Fort Jesus itself. The full deal, including transfers to/from your hotel and nightclubbing afterwards costs US$80.

Activities

A number of tour companies have branches in Mombasa (see Safaris in Kenya in the Organised Safaris chapter for details).

If you can **sail**, it may be worth joining the Mombasa Sailing Club (☎ 313350); fees are KSh 600/2000 per week/month. Club days are Wednesday and Sunday and qualified sailors may be able to get some crewing. Bosun boats are also available to temporary members for KSh 200 per day. The members are a friendly bunch and the bar is a lovely place to be in the evening, though you'll need to take a taxi back into town. Those hoping to hitch a lift on a passing yacht will have a better (though still remote) chance at Swynford's Boat Yard in Kilifi.

Also out of town is the Mombasa **Golf** Club (☎ 222620) perched on the south-eastern edge of the island. Day membership is KSh 1500 and you can play as many holes as you like. Clubs can be rented for KSh 700 per day and taking a caddy will cost you KSh 100 per nine holes. The wonderful old club house has a bar and a grand snooker table.

Places to Stay

There's a lot of choice for budget travellers and for those who want something slightly better, both in the centre of the city and on the mainland to the north and south. Accommodation north and south of Mombasa Island is dealt with later in this chapter.

Places to Stay – Budget

In addition to the list below, there are a number of cheap, shabby fleapits dotted around the centre of town, but travellers should beware of thieves at these places. The word among travellers at the time of research was that Mvita Hotel, on the corner of Hospital and Turkana Sts, and all Glory accommodation in the city (Glory Guest House in particular) provided inadequate security.

Lucky Guest House (☎ 220895) on Shibu Rd is recently refurbished and not bad value. Self-contained doubles with a fan go for KSh 500.

Berachah Guest House (☎ 224106) opposite the Shell petrol station on Haile Selassie Rd (close to the junction of Digo Rd) is good value. Clean and tidy (though some rooms are better than others) singles/doubles with shared bath go for KSh 420/600 (KSh 480/700 with bath). All rates include breakfast. The restaurant is cheap and popular with local people.

Evening Guest House (☎ 221380) on Mnazi Moja Rd is also good value and convenient to the city centre. It has simple but very clean rooms at KSh 400 a single with shared bath and KSh 600 a double with bath. The rooms may be a little cramped, but they have mosquito nets and fans and the hotel has its own bar and restaurant.

Tana Hotel, on the corner of Mwembe Tayari and Gatundu Rds, is also recommended. It may be a little noisy being close to the transport hub of the city, but the rooms (KSh 400/500) are clean and tidy.

Try the new *Ramadhan Guest House* on Abdel Nasser Rd (near the Malindi Bus office) if you're heading to Malindi or Lamu the next day. It is bright, airy and tidy, and all the rooms face away from the main road and look directly out over Mombasa Harbour. It's cheap (KSh 250/400 with shared bath) and at the time of writing the owner was in the process of installing a restaurant and lounge on the roof. There's a fruit juice and ice-cream cafe next door. This place is highly recommended.

Metric Hotel (☎ 222155) is off Moi Ave behind Wimpy. Recently renovated, this place has clean and tidy rooms (with fans but no mosquito nets), and friendly staff. Rooms with shared bath are KSh 400/500, including breakfast. VIP doubles with bath cost KSh 700. The bar and restaurant downstairs is popular with local office workers.

CENTRAL MOMBASA

PLACES TO STAY
4 Tana Hotel
17 Excellent Hotel
19 Lucky Guest House
20 Royal Court Hotel
23 Berachah Guest House
28 Hotel Hermes
29 Polana Hotel
34 Hotel Splendid
37 Glory Guest House
43 Evening Guest House
52 New Palm Tree Hotel

PLACES TO EAT
9 Roasters Choice
16 Blue Room Restaurant

18 Kencoast Cafe
21 New Chetna Restaurant
25 Al Sultan Restaurant
26 Blue Fin Restaurant
32 Shehnai Restaurant
33 Splendid View Restaurant
38 Pistachio Ice Cream & Coffee Bar
38 Mombasa Coffee House
40 Le Bistro
47 Hard Rock Cafe
50 Afro Bar
54 Hunters' Bar; Air Kenya
     Aviation (Ambalal House)

OTHER
1 Buses & Matatus to Malindi & Lamu

2 Akamba Bus Office
3 Tawfiq Bus Office
5 Coast Bus
6 Kobil Petrol Station
     & Matatus to Voi
     & Wundanyi
7 Al-Yemeiny Bus Office
8 KBS Bus Station
10 Buses to Mawingo
11 Malindi Taxi Bus
12 Barclays Bank (ATM)
13 Pwani Forex Bureau
14 Main Market
15 Shell Petrol Station
22 City Grocers
24 Main Post Office

27 Sheikh Jundoni Mosque
30 Post Global Services
31 High Roller Casino
36 Bahari Bookshop
39 Post Bank
41 Bahati Book Centre
42 Barclays Bank (ATM)
44 Barclays Bank
45 Craft Stalls
46 Royal Casino
48 Kenya Airways
49 Toyz Disco
51 Barclays Bank (ATM)
53 Express Kenya (American
     Express) & Europcar
55 Cathedral

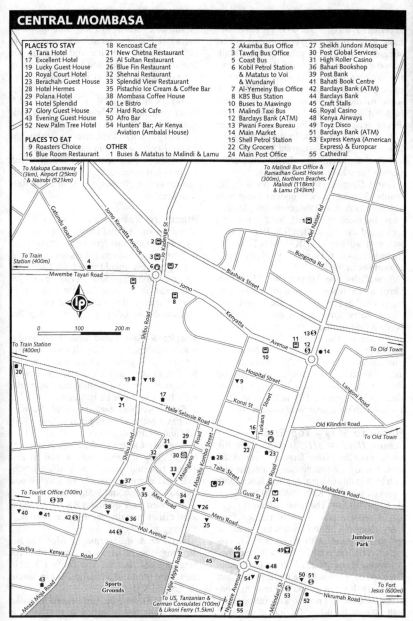

KENYA

Places to Stay – Mid-Range

Excellent Hotel (☎ 227683) on Haile Selassie Rd is at the very bottom end of this category and is good value. A short walk from the station, it offers B&B singles/doubles with bath, mosquito nets, towel, soap, toilet paper and fans for KSh 750/1050. Some of the bathrooms have seen better days but some rooms have balconies; you should book early in the day to have your pick of the best rooms. In the evening the downstairs bar and restaurant transforms itself into a pavement cafe, and there's a rooftop bar where live bands play.

Hotel Hermes (☎ 313599) on Msanifu Kombo St near Sheikh Jundoni Mosque is well maintained, and the rooms are pleasant (most overlook the street), but because it's such good value it's often full. Rooms with bath and air-con cost KSh 800/1100, including breakfast. There's a good pool table downstairs in the bar.

New Palm Tree Hotel (☎ 315272) on Nkrumah Rd is top value in this range. The reception, bar (cheap, cold beers) and restaurant (tasty food at a reasonable price) exude an air of fading grandeur and all the rooms are on the 1st and 2nd floors surrounding a spacious courtyard furnished with tables and chairs. It's a comfortable, spotlessly clean place; rooms with bath and fan cost KSh 944/1320 including breakfast. You can leave gear safely in the rooms and it's justifiably popular with travellers.

Places to Stay – Top End

Oceanic Hotel (☎ 311193) off Oceanic Rd, not far from the Likoni ferry, has seen better days. Untidy air-con singles/doubles/triples with bath in this five storey tower block (with a broken lift) cost KSh 1500/1800/2100 including breakfast. The price (which is negotiable) and the great view of the sea from every room are all that makes this place an option. Nonguests with strong immune systems can use the pool for KSh 120 per day.

Polana Hotel (☎ 222168) on Maungano Rd, close to Haile Selassie Rd, is in the heart of the city. It's a huge soulless modern construction with 140 rooms with full air-con, bath, shower, mini-bar, TV (including CNN) and international direct-dial phones. Singles/doubles cost KSh 1800/2800 including breakfast. Facilities include a restaurant, bar, casino, laundry service and parking. On Monday, Wednesday and Friday there's an eat-as-much-as-you-can buffet lunch costing KSh 420.

Royal Court Hotel (☎ 312389, fax 312398, email royalcourt@swiftmombasa) down Haile Selassie Rd towards the train station is the best place in this price range. Every room has air-con and satellite TV, and there's a great view from the restaurant on the roof terrace, which is open to nonguests, reasonably priced and recommended. Rooms cost KSh 2150/3000 with breakfast.

Places to Eat

Mombasa has a good range of restaurants; the international fast food outlets now found in Nairobi have yet to get established here.

Self-caterers should make for City Grocers on Haile Selassie Rd or the extensive Nakumatt on Nyerere Ave close to Likoni ferry. A wide variety of fruit and vegetables are available in the main market on Digo Rd.

Snacks & Fast Food *Blue Fin Restaurant* on the corner of Meru Rd and Msanifu Kombo St, is good if you are just looking for fish or chicken with chips. There is little variety but most main meals are under KSh 100 and it's not a bad place.

Blue Room Restaurant on Haile Selassie Rd has a better choice; pizza is under KSh 300 and a hamburger costs KSh 110.

Roasters Choice on Msanifu Kombo St has slightly cheaper snacks and *nyama choma* (roasted goat); it also offers lunchtime and evening specials of Swahili and Indian food for about KSh 150.

Kencoast Cafe on Shibu Rd has delicious local dishes at really cheap prices. The staff are very friendly.

Sky Bar & Restaurant on Moi Ave not far from the tusks, is recommended for breakfast and snacks. You can eat a main meal here (chicken and chips, for instance) for around KSh 140.

Recoda Restaurant, just beyond the tusks opposite the tourist office is similar. It is open daily and offers buffet lunches and fruit juices at a very reasonable price. *Al Sultan Restaurant* on Meru Rd and *Ethiopian Bar* on Haile Selassie Rd near the train station are similar.

Mombasa Coffee House on Moi Ave is a good place for fresh coffee and snacks; you can also buy coffee beans here. An excellent place for food and drink is *Afro Bar* on Nkrumah Rd.

Chinese *Chinese Overseas Restaurant* on Moi Ave, just west of the tusks on the left-hand side, has main dishes for around KSh 300 to KSh 400; a full-on feast will set you back about KSh 700. Further down Moi Ave past Tangana Rd is *Hong Kong Chinese Restaurant*, which is also recommended.

Indian *New Chetna Restaurant* on Haile Selassie Rd is popular and an excellent place for south Indian vegetarian *thali* food at lunch-time. An all-you-can-eat vegetarian lunch costs KSh 210.

Splendid View Restaurant on Maungano Rd (opposite but not part of Hotel Splendid), is also popular and has excellent tandoori specialities. It's open until 11.30 pm most nights.

Swahili *Recoda Restaurant* (another one) on Nyeri St in the Old Town, is an excellent place you should try at least once for its coastal Swahili dishes made with coconut. It's hugely popular among the locals and the tables are set up along the footpath. The atmosphere is great and the waiters are keen to explain what is available that day: usually dishes such as beans in coconut, grilled fish, meat, superb chapatis and salad. You may well find yourself coming back here each night. This is a Muslim restaurant, so there are no alcoholic drinks and it's closed all day until after sunset during Ramadan.

Other Restaurants *Hotel Splendid* has a rooftop restaurant that catches the breeze in the evenings and surprisingly moderate prices (from KSh 160 for a main meal). However, the food is only mediocre and the service is far from lightning fast.

Pistachio Ice Cream & Coffee Bar is a small cafe on Meru Rd near Hotel Splendid. Not only does it have excellent ice cream but the fruit shakes are great. The buffet lunch or dinner is KSh 390. A la carte dishes such as spaghetti are also served. It's open from 9 am to 10 pm daily.

Le Bistro (☎ 229470) on Moi Ave, close to the tusks, has cheaper main dishes. The owners of this restaurant and cocktail bar also own the Pistacchio and it's open daily from breakfast to late at night. Both the atmosphere and the food, which includes pizza, pasta, steak and seafood, are excellent. Expect to pay around KSh 100 for a starter and from KSh 210 to KSh 300 for a main dish.

Hunters' Bar in Ambalal House on Nkrumah Rd is one of Mombasa's better restaurants serving continental cuisine. In the evening, main courses cost about KSh 800. Wildlife conservationists should be aware that the walls of the bar are festooned with hunting trophies from a bygone era and the guy who shot them certainly wasn't a greenie. It's open Monday to Saturday for lunch and dinner but (closed Sunday and public holidays).

Shehnai Restaurant (☎ 312492) in the centre of town near Polana Hotel specialises in Indian Mughal cuisine and has a huge menu. The food here is excellent and the service good. Expect to pay around KSh 1000 for a big splurge, though for groups they'll prepare a mixed buffet to a set budget.

Caffe Italia (☎ 229217) in the Jubilee Insurance building on Moi Ave is a great (and recommended) Italian restaurant. The bar is well stocked; pasta goes for around KSh 330, and mains for between KSh 470 and KSh 650. The lunch-time specials are a good deal.

Tamarind Restaurant (☎ 471747) is certainly up there with the very best restaurants in Kenya. It's on the foreshore across from the Old Dhow Harbour in Nyali. The food is superb (you'd be pushed to find better seafood anywhere in Kenya), the service impeccable and the restaurant is open daily for lunch and dinner. Expect to part with at least KSh 2500 per person and considerably more if you drink wine with your meal.

Entertainment

Casablanca Restaurant & Bar, on Mnazi Moja Rd, attracts much the same clientele as Buffalo Bill's in Nairobi but the food is better. It's very popular and consists of a double-storey, *makuti*-roofed (thatched with palm leaves) open-air bar and restaurant, which is open all day until very late. There's a disco each evening.

Royal Casino, on the corner of Moi Ave and Digo Rd, has a number of pool tables and a bar, as well as the slots and gaming tables. Beers are cheap (KSh 60).

For live music, try *Hotel Splendid*, *Club Zaituni* or *Excellent Hotel*, which has bands playing on the rooftop terrace.

New Florida Casino & Nightclub on Mama Ngina Drive is the most lively nightclub. Built right on the seashore and enclosing its own swimming pool, it's owned by the same people who run the Florida clubs in Nairobi. The atmosphere (and clientele) are much the same here but there are three open-air bars as well as an enclosed dancing area. Entry costs KSh 150 for men and KSh 70 for women (slightly more on Friday and Saturday nights) or KSh 50 per person on Sunday afternoon until 8 pm.

Toyz Disco, on Baluchi St off Nkrumah Rd, is good if you're looking for a slightly quieter night without the endless booming rap music of the New Florida. Entry is free, there's a main bar downstairs and a dance floor upstairs.

For information on entertainment north of Mombasa Island see Mombasa to Kilifi under North of Mombasa later in this chapter.

Shopping

While Mombasa isn't the craft centre you might expect it to be, it's still not too bad and the Bombolulu Workshops & Cultural Centre (☎ 471764, email kbom@africaonline .co.ke) more than makes up for the tourist tat that can be found in town. Examples of traditional homesteads sit in the grounds and there's a good Kenyan restaurant, The Ziga (meaning 'cooking pot') on site. However, the real reason that the centre exists is to give vocational training to the physically disabled people who make everything from jewellery, dresses and baskets through to furniture. The turn-off for the centre is on the left about 3km north of Nyali Bridge. Though signs point the way, the exact turn-off is often obscured by traffic. The show rooms and cultural centre are open 8 am to 5 pm Monday to Saturday. The Web site is www.africaonline.co.ke/bombolulu.

Biashara St, which runs west of the Digo Rd intersection, is the centre for *kikoi* and *kangas*. Kikois are woven pieces of cloth traditionally worn by men and kangas are beautifully patterned, wraparound skirts complete with Swahili proverbs, which most (non-Asian) East African women wear even if they wear it under a *bui-bui* (black wraparound skirt). You may need to bargain a little over the price; they cost around KSh 300 a pair (they are not sold singly). Buy them in Mombasa if possible. You can sometimes get them as cheaply in Nairobi, but elsewhere prices escalate.

Getting There & Away

Air Kenya Airways (☎ 221251, fax 313815) on Nkrumah Rd fly between Nairobi and Mombasa every couple of hours during the day. Most flights are nonstop but some go via Malindi. The fare from Mombasa (or Malindi) to Nairobi is KSh 5650 one way. Special deals between Mombasa and Nairobi (for as little as KSh 7200 return) are sometimes available. If you're relying on these flights to get back to Nairobi to connect with an international flight, then make absolutely sure you have a confirmed booking or, preferably, go back a day before. Standby fares to Mombasa are also available and fares can vary on the flexibility of the ticket.

A much smaller operation, African Express Airways (☎ 02-823497), also flies from Mombasa to Nairobi (KSh 8400 return) twice daily. Air Kenya Aviation (☎ 229777, email resvns@airkenya.com) at Ambalal House, Nkrumah Rd, has nine flights per week (KSh 5385/10770 one way/return), arriving at Nairobi's Wilson airport.

Only Air Kenya Aviation has scheduled flights to Lamu. There's a flight (also stopping at Malindi) every morning at 8.15 or 9.30 am. The fare costs US$85/170 one way/return. In theory you could fly to Lamu with Kenya Airways, but you'd have to fly back to Nairobi first. Kenya Airways has daily direct flights to/from Malindi.

Bus & Matatu Bus offices are mainly concentrated along Jomo Kenyatta Ave except for some buses to Malindi and Lamu, which leave from Abdel Nasser Rd. For buses and matatus to the beaches south of Mombasa, you first need to get off the island via the Likoni ferry (see Boat under Getting Around later in this section).

Nairobi For Nairobi, there are many departures daily in either direction (mostly in the early morning and late evening) by, among others, Coast, Coastline, Mawingo, Takrim, Tawfiq, Malindi Bus and Akamba. The most expensive is Coastline (KSh 600) and the cheapest Malindi Bus (KSh 400). You get what you pay for, and Malindi Bus' vehicles don't look good. Akamba are reliable. The trip takes anywhere from eight to 10 hours including a meal break about halfway. Most of these companies have at least four departures daily.

Safer and more comfortable (but more expensive) is the shuttle bus service run by The Connection. They offer air-con, 18-seater minibuses for KSh 1000 per person one way, which will drop you off anywhere in the two city centres. Bookings with The Connection can be made at Vogue Tours & Travel (☎ 223613) at Jubilee House, Moi Ave, or at Inside Africa Safaris (☎ 02-223304), on Wabera St, Nairobi. Check-in is at 8.30 am in Mombasa and at 9.30 am in Nairobi.

Heading North There are numerous daily departures to/from Malindi. Most bus companies and matatus operate from Abdel Nasser Rd. Buses take up to 2½ hours, matatus about two hours (KSh 70/100). In 1999 KBS took delivery of some fine new buses (some are 100 seaters!) and these are currently the safest and easiest transport heading north. Frequent departures leave from the central KBS bus station.

It's possible to go straight through from Mombasa to Lamu departing at 8 am (KSh 350), but most travellers stop en route at Malindi.

Tanzania For Tanga, Dar es Salaam and Morogoro in Tanzania, Tawfiq, Takwa and Al-Yemeiny have daily departures. Other dubious looking vehicles heading to Moshi leave from opposite the KBS bus station when full, which can take days. See Tanzania in the Land section of the Kenya Getting There & Away chapter for details.

Train Trains to/from Nairobi leave in either direction at 7 pm, arriving the next day at 8.30 am, though the train is usually an hour late. The fares are KSh 3000/2100 for 1st/2nd class and include dinner, breakfast and bedding (whether you want them or not). You should make a reservation as far in advance as possible as demand sometimes exceeds supply. The booking office (☎ 312220) at the station in Mombasa is open from 8 am to noon and 2 to 6.30 pm daily.

The left-luggage service at the train station costs KSh 200 per item per day. It's open from 8 am to noon (7.30 to 10 am Sunday) and 2 to 6.30 pm daily.

Boat In theory it's possible to get a ride on a dhow to Pemba, Unguja (Zanzibar Island) or Dar es Salaam in Tanzania, but departures from Mombasa are very infrequent and dependent on the trade winds. There was no ferry service at the time of writing. See the Sea & Lake section in the Kenya Getting There & Away chapter for details.

Getting Around

To/From the Airport Kenya Airways operates a shuttle bus from its Nkrumah Rd office at 10.20 am and 2.20 and 5.40 pm. There's also a regular public bus to the airport, which costs KSh 20. Any 'Port Reitz' matatu will take you past the airport turn-off (ask to be dropped off) from where it's about a 15 minute walk. The standard taxi fare is KSh 600, although you'll have to bargain down from KSh 1000.

Car & Motorcycle The Automobile Association (AA) of Kenya (☎ 492431) has its office on Jomo Kenyatta Ave between the Total garage and KBC Bank.

All the major hire companies and many of the smaller outfits have branch offices in Mombasa. Most (such as Avis, Hertz, Payless and Glory) are on Moi Ave; Europcar is on Nkrumah Rd. For more details of hire charges and conditions, see the Car & 4WD section in the Kenya Getting Around chapter. Also try Unik Car Hire & Safaris (☎ 314864, fax 311384) in Fatemi building, Maungano Rd. A 4WD Suzuki Samurai costs KSh 1700 plus KSh 15 per kilometre and KSh 700 insurance.

Fredlink Co Ltd rent 350cc and 600cc motorcycles plus modern 50cc scooters. The rates are KSh 2100/2100/1200 per day respectively and they will deliver these machines as far north as Mtwapa (KSh 500 extra) and as far south as Diani (KSh 600 extra). They also run motorcycle safaris (see Miscellaneous under Other Safaris in the Safaris in Kenya section of the Organised Safaris chapter for contact details).

Taxi Taxis in Mombasa are as expensive and in the same terrible state as those in Nairobi. Assume KSh 200 from the train station to the city centre and KSh 600 from the airport.

Boat The Likoni ferry connects Mombasa Island with the southern mainland and runs at frequent intervals throughout the night and day. There's a crossing every 20 minutes on average between 5 and 12.30 am, less frequently at other times. It's free to pedestrians and KSh 35 for a car.

To get to the ferry from the centre of town, take a Likoni matatu from outside the main post office on Digo Rd (KSh 20).

South of Mombasa

The real attractions of the coast south of Mombasa are the white coral beaches, the warm clear ocean and the coral reefs. There are a large number of big resort hotels in and around Diani, and some great budget options at Tiwi, though it suffers a bit from

large amounts of floating seaweed between March and December.

Do not, under any circumstances, walk along beaches carrying valuables at any time of day or night. Nine times out of 10 you'll be relieved of them (see the boxed text 'Safety on the Coast' below).

Safety on the Coast

Though Tourist Police Units have been set up specifically to protect tourists on Kenya's beaches, obeying a few simple rules will save you a whole host of problems. It's not that you'll be mugged as soon as you leave the safety of your hotel (a favourite line from many coastal hotels), you just have to be careful.

Firstly, and most importantly, don't carry anything of value when walking on the beaches. Don't wear jewellery, a watch or anything that looks like it's worth a few dollars. Don't go naked, but look poor.

Under no circumstances should you walk down any of the dirt roads to Tiwi Beach. You will most likely get mugged.

At night make sure the taxi drops you exactly where you want to go. Don't walk down any tracks, no matter how short, between the main road and beach bars or restaurants.

Don't buy drugs on the beach. It's highly likely that you'll get mugged or set up in a crude police sting operation. Either way it will cost you a lot of money.

You'll also come across 'beach boys', unemployed young men who try to make money by approaching tourists on the beach, selling them curios and offering services including guiding, shopping and sexual favours. They can be a real nuisance in some places and you'll get very little peace and quiet. They have gained a reputation for theft and mugging, but most are just poor guys trying to get by.

Considering the huge number of job losses all along the coast (thanks to the continuing slump in tourism), it is no wonder that crime remains a problem. People displaying cameras and jewellery make tempting targets for those without enough money to feed and clothe their families.

TIWI BEACH
☎ 0127

Tiwi Beach is about 3km off the main coast road 24km south of Mombasa. A gravel track down to the beach hotels and cottages is signposted from the main road (do not walk down this track – see the warning in Getting There & Away later in this section). This is the best beach to head for if you're on a budget and/or have your own camping gear. Handily for self-caterers there's a supermarket and a great vegetable *duka* (shop) just off the main road at the start of the track leading to Tiwi. Men on bicycles carrying fruit, vegetables and freshly caught fish tour around all the cottage complexes during the day and of course, you could arrange to eat at a lodge that has a restaurant and bar.

If you want a cottage during the high season, it's a very good idea to book in advance.

Activities

Next to Twiga Lodge is a small outfit called Tiwi Divers, which offers good **snorkelling** and **diving** expeditions. Snorkelling is KSh 600 and lasts about two hours. If you just want to snorkel out from the beach, gear can be hired for about KSh 250 per day. Just past Tiwi Villas a deep circular pool has formed in the coral. At low tide this becomes a beautiful swimming pool.

Traveller's Tiwi Beach Hotel (see details following) runs day trips (US$65) as well as overnight excursions (US$130) to **Mwalu-ganje Elephant Sanctuary** (see the Shimba Hills National Reserve section at the end of this chapter).

Places to Stay & Eat

First up is *Travellers Tiwi Beach Hotel* (☎ 51202, fax 51207, email travellershtl@ swiftmombasa.com) on the northern bank of the Mwachema River. Huge and imposing, large mukuti-roofed barns roost hundreds of package tourists. Singles/doubles cost US$60/120 for half board, rising to US$130/160 in the high season.

Tiwi Sea Castles (☎ 02-862026) is a combination of double rooms with bath, simple apartments and cottages sleeping

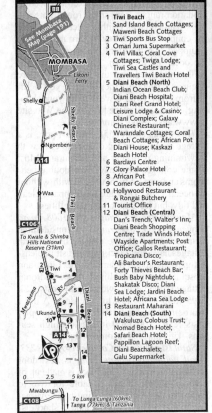

SOUTH OF MOMBASA

1. Tiwi Beach
   Sand Island Beach Cottages;
   Maweni Beach Cottages
2. Tiwi Sports Bus Stop
3. Omari Juma Supermarket
4. Tiwi Villas; Coral Cove
   Cottages; Twiga Lodge;
   Tiwi Sea Castles and
   Travellers Tiwi Beach Hotel
5. Diani Beach (North)
   Indian Ocean Beach Club;
   Diani Beach Hospital;
   Diani Reef Grand Hotel;
   Leisure Lodge & Casino;
   Diani Complex; Galaxy
   Chinese Restaurant;
   Warandale Cottages; Coral
   Beach Cottages; African Pot
   Diani House; Kaskazi
   Beach Hotel
6. Barclays Centre
7. Glory Palace Hotel
8. African Pot
9. Corner Guest House
10. Hollywood Restaurant
    & Rongai Butchery
11. Tourist Office
12. Diani Beach (Central)
    Dan's Trench; Walter's Inn;
    Diani Beach Shopping
    Centre; Three Winds Hotel;
    Wayside Apartments; Post
    Office; Gallos Restaurant;
    Tropicana Disco;
    Ali Barbour's Restaurant;
    Forty Thieves Beach Bar;
    Bush Baby Nightclub;
    Shakatak Disco; Diani
    Sea Lodge; Jardini Beach
    Hotel; Africana Sea Lodge
13. Restaurant Maharani
14. Diani Beach (South)
    Wakuluzu Colobus Trust;
    Nomad Beach Hotel;
    Safari Beach Hotel;
    Pappillon Lagoon Reef;
    Diani Beachalets;
    Galu Supermarket

0   2.5   5 km

four to five people. The rooms are nice and there's a pool, bar and restaurant. Rooms cost about KSh 500/800.

Twiga Lodge (☎ 51210/67) has long been *the* place to stay at Tiwi but at the time of writing, there was a serious problem with thefts from rooms and it can no longer be recommended. This is a shame because the camp site is the best on the coast (KSh 150) and the facilities (bar/restaurant) are good. Rooms go for KSh 600/1200, and cottages for KSh 1500. Nonguests can use the bar/restaurant where a good English breakfast goes for KSh 200.

Coral Cove Cottages (☎ *51295, fax 51062*) next door, has bags of character and accommodation ranges from small round huts and open-plan cottages (with a kitchen) suitable for couples (KSh 500/800) through to fully equipped two-bedroom places overlooking the ocean (KSh 2500). The whole place is well maintained and the management are open and friendly (they'll give you a lift to/from Diani twice a week to do your shopping). It's a great place to stay. The Web site is www.aussiemike.com/coralcove.

Tiwi Villas (☎ *51265*), further north, is a cottage complex on top of a small cliff, with a swimming pool, bar and restaurant. Most of the cottages here have two double bedrooms and cost KSh 1600/1200 with/without an ocean view. They are all compact, clean and tidy, but have no cooking facilities.

Maweni Beach Cottages (☎ *51008, email maweni@net2000ke.com*) is a considerable distance further up the coast. The well run cottages have good facilities and sit in pleasant gardens above a small cove. Linen and mosquito nets can be hired. A one bedroom cottage (suitable for two people) costs KSh 1195/1530 in the low/high seasons. A three bedroom cottage (suitable for eight people) costs KSh 2800/3400 in the low/high seasons. This place is recommended.

Sand Island Beach Cottages (☎/*fax 51233, email hatfield@form-net.com*) is next door and more upmarket. This place is made up of colonial-style cottages suitable for two to eight people on a self-catering basis. All accommodation faces Sand Island, a short distance out to sea. Prices range from KSh 2065 and KSh 2478 a double, up to KSh 3965 and KSh 5206 for six or eight people, depending on the season. Bed linen, mosquito nets and fans are provided. There's also a cook who will prepare meals for you and an orchard that provides fresh fruit; snorkelling equipment is available. There are no 'beach boys' (see the boxed text 'Safety on the Coast' earlier in this chapter) on its private beach.

If you are interested in staying with a Kenyan family, it is possible to rent a cheap room (KSh 100 per double) close to the main road. Ask for Vastic at the Omari Juma shop behind the Tiwi Sports bus stop.

Getting There & Away

The buses and matatus heading for Ukunda and beyond from Likoni drop you at the start of the gravel access road (ask for 'Sports' stage, KSh 20), from where it's 3km to the beach. Under no circumstances walk down this road; it is notorious for muggings. Wait for a lift (quite a few cars pass this way so you shouldn't have to wait too long) or catch one of the ancient waiting taxis (KSh 250).

DIANI BEACH & UKUNDA
☎ 0127

Diani is geared up for mass tourism and remains popular with package tourists from Europe. Resort hotels line the beach for the first 10km south of the Mwachema River, while shops, restaurants and bars run parallel to the hotels on the beach road. This is where you should come if you want water sports, or to play beach volleyball or lie on a sunlounger for extended periods.

Sandwiched between the swathes of giant hotels are a number of good cottage complexes, though they're not always cheap.

Unfortunately the Diani tourist industry has suffered badly since the ethnic cleansing of Likoni and Ukunda before the 1997 elections (see the Facts about Kenya chapter) and those bars and restaurants remaining have been hit hard by the hotel industry's shift to all-inclusive packages.

If you intend to stay for some time and are a big group, scan the ads beside the road and in the shopping centres to secure a cheap private lease.

Orientation

The town of Ukunda on the main Mombasa-Tanzania highway is the turn-off point for Diani Beach. There's a post office, and a number of basic lodging houses. From here, a tarmac road runs about 2km down to a T-junction with the beach road, which runs north and south. Along this beach road is everything that Diani has to offer.

Information

In the Barclays Centre just north of the Ukunda road T-junction in Diani, there is a Barclays Bank with an ATM; Disana Inter-

Colobus Climbing Frames

Once common all along the coast, habitat destruction has restricted the Angolan black and white Colobus *(Colobus angolensis palliatus)* to a few isolated pockets of forest and hotel gardens south of Mombasa. This Colobus is often mistaken for its upcountry cousin, the Guereza Colobus, but it is smaller and has distinctive white tufts of hair on its cheeks and very long white tufts on its shoulders rather than a cape of long white hair.

In Diani, the tourist industry has been the main culprit. The sprawling resort complexes have destroyed large areas of forest and a busy road divides the remaining pockets. Unlike the baboon and the Sykes and vervet monkeys, the Colobus is not a scavenger and is unable to adapt its diet to a changing environment. Its three-part stomach has evolved to digest the leaves of specific coastal trees; once the trees disappear so does the Colobus.

A survey in 1997 concluded there were 200 Angolan black and white Colobus left in the Diani area and in the previous four months 21 animals had been killed crossing the road. It seems to have much less road sense than say, the baboon, which will stroll across the road with considerable confidence and arrogance.

In an effort to protect the remaining population, the Wakuluzu Colobus Trust (☎ 0127-3517, fax 3223, email colobus@africaonline.co.ke) was formed in January 1997 by a group of Diani residents. To help the Colobus, a series of ladders spanning the road were constructed at known crossing points. There are now eight bridges in place and plans for another four. In the year after the bridges were erected only two animals were killed on the road and estimates suggest that in 1999 the population had risen to 274 Colobus in the Diani area.

Colobus Cottage, between the Two Fishes and Jardini Beach hotels, is the trust's base and has a good information centre. Research students help fund the place and there is a nature trail with guided walks and a tree nursery. Bookings are not necessary and you should pay about KSh 300 for a guided walk. The trust runs a program of wildlife education and awareness for local people and hotel staff.

---

national (☎ 2080) offer reasonable international telephone and fax rates. In the same building, email can be sent from Kenya Beach.com (☎ 2191, email webmaster@kenyabeach.com); surfing the Web costs KSh 500 per hour. This company has a Web site (www.KenyaBeach.com) that represents many of the companies, hotels and restaurants operating on Diani and Tiwi beaches.

The post office (with cardphone) is south of the Ukunda road T-junction before the Diani Plaza Shopping Complex.

There's a tourist office (☎ 2227) in the Private Safaris building on the Ukunda road – it's not amazingly useful, but they have plenty of leaflets and staff will make reservations for you.

Diani Beach Hospital (☎ 2435) is about 1km north of the Ukunda road T-junction. Ask for Dr Riki.

Diani police can be contacted on (☎ 22 29).

Dangers & Annoyances We have had reports that people have been mugged while walking along the road from Ukunda to Diani, though local people dismiss this. In any case numerous matatus (and KBS buses) run up and down this road all day so there's no reason to walk.

Walking along the beach from Diani to Tiwi can also be dicey. The place where you cross the creek that divides the two is known locally as 'Machete Point', and a number of travellers have been done over here. If you do decide to walk, take nothing of value with you and make sure it is at low tide, as the creek crossing is quite deep at high tide and you'll need to swim across (see the boxed text 'Safety on the Coast' earlier in this chapter).

Activities

If you want **water sports**, then approach one of the big hotels. Try Safari Beach Hotel, Jardini Beach Hotel and Africana Sea Lodge first. There is a dive school at Safari Beach Hotel. You can hire boats (known as 'toppers') for KSh 2000 per day or KSh 600 per hour from Forty Thieves Beach Bar (☎ 2033).

Several companies offer **dhow trips** further down the coast to either Funzi or Wasini islands. Try the Funzi Island Club (☎ 2044, fax 2346), Wasini Island Restaurant & Kisite Marine Park Dhow Tours (☎ 2331, fax 3154, email kisite@africaonline.co.ke) and Pilli-Pipa (☎ 2401). All cost about US$80 for a day trip.

Diani House (☎ 3487, fax 2412, aceltd@ africaonline.co.ke) offers day trips and overnight stays at the **Shimba Hills National Reserve** (see that section at the end of this chapter).

The Wakuluzu Colobus Trust organises **guided walks** of a nature trail in the area. See the boxed text 'Colobus Climbing Frames' earlier in this chapter for contact details.

Places to Stay – Budget

There are a number of basic lodging houses in Ukunda. Try **Corner Guest House** first; singles/doubles are KSh 250/400.

Glory Palace Hotel (☎ 3392) is halfway down the road to Diani from Ukunda. It has clean basic rooms with fans for KSh 600/ 1200 and there's a bar and swimming pool. Prices rise considerably in the high season.

Dan Trench's in front of the (closed) Trade Winds Hotel, is the only cheap place in Diani, but it's turning into a dive with questionable security. Rooms cost KSh 250/ 400 and camping is KSh 150.

Places to Stay – Mid-Range

Few places in this category are cheap, most are cottages and apartments, and some aren't even on the beach. Rates reduce dramatically for long lets. Unless indicated, all the places listed are self-catering and kitchen facilities are provided.

Diani Beachalets (☎ 2180) is a little old but probably the best bet for the backpacker.

There are some cheap (and basic) *bandas* (thatched walled huts) with shared facilities for KSh 350/460 in the low/high seasons. There are also a few small self-contained maisonettes for KSh 650/900 in the low/ high seasons. Four-bedroom seafront 'beachettes' with full facilities (including hot water) cost KSh 1600/2050 (low/high season). Add 17% tax to all prices. There is a tennis court (rackets and balls are available) and it's right on the beach.

Wayside Apartments (☎ 3119) is near the Trade Winds Hotel (closed). These open-plan apartments (suitable for two to four people) are in a modern block. They are tidy and well appointed and each has a balcony but no sea view. There's a good communal pool, bar and lounging area. The small apartments go for KSh 1400 and the larger, four person places for KSh 2400. Prices rise during the high season. Watch out for the *mbwa kali*, the fierce dog.

Coral Beach Cottages (☎ 2413) are further north past the turn-off for Ukunda. Large, well appointed two and three bedroom places go for KSh 2000/3000 in the low season, rising to KSh 4000/5000 in the high season. They are nicely located and with the excellent African Pot restaurant at the entrance gate you need not self-cater.

Warandale Cottages (☎/fax 2187) is last but by no means least. This eccentric collection of cottages packed tightly together at the edge of a small cliff features architecture that seems part Andalucian, part English Tudor and part Swahili. Despite being so close to one another, each cottage feels private and each has a veranda and barbecue area; most have en suite bathrooms. There is a swimming pool and a secluded beach that's often cut off from the beach boys by the tide. In low/high seasons two-bedroom places cost KSh 2000/4500 and three-bedroom places cost KSh 2000/5000. The smaller one-bedroom places are let through a different agent (☎ 2186) and are a little cheaper.

Places to Stay – Top End

Other accommodation along the beach is major resort complexes and flash hotels. Prices double and triple in the high season with all-inclusive packages. All the resorts offer much the same: air-con rooms, swimming pool, bars, restaurant, usually a disco, and some have water-sports equipment for hire. The better ones have been designed with the environment and local architectural styles in mind.

With the downturn in tourism at the coast, those who are staying here have usually paid a fraction of these prices as part of an all-inclusive package from Europe. If you just want to stay for a night or two, ring around as you should be able to get a significant discount.

From north to south along the strip the hotels are as follows:

Indian Ocean Beach Club (☎ 3730, 02-540780 in Nairobi) is a well designed hotel on the edge of the Mwachema River with a degree of style sadly lacking elsewhere. Rooms are well spread out, with the pool the focus of activity. Basic singles/doubles cost US$81/162 with half board in the low season and US$221/276 in the high season. Ocean views are more expensive.

Diani Reef Grand Hotel (☎ 2723, fax 2196, email dianireef@form-net.com) is one of the few Diani hotels with disabled access. However, the service is far from speedy and the standard rooms are basic. Half-board rates are US$115/170 in the low season and US$170/240 in the high season. For deluxe rooms add 25%. Guests must not wear shorts for evening meals.

Leisure Lodge & Casino (☎ 2272/3, email leisure@africaonline.co.ke) has a golf course over the road. There are two classes of rooms here: club and hotel (with average rooms). You'll pay KSh 2000 per person in the hotel and KSh 3200 in the club during the low season, rising to KSh 3000/4200 in the high season, all with full board. Suites are more expensive.

Diani House (☎ 3487, fax 2412, email aceltd@africaonline.co.ke) is a lovely place far removed from the rest of the top end accommodation in Diani. There are four doubles and one single in a beautiful colonial-style house facing the ocean. Set in 4.8 hectares of gardens, the house has 500m of beach frontage; windsurfing, deep-sea fishing and snork-

elling are all possible. It costs US$187 per person per night full board. The same people own Mukurumuji Tented Camp in the Shimba Hills (an overnight excursion is possible for US$115, see the Shimba Hills National Reserve section at the end of this chapter).

Kaskazi Beach Hotel (☎ 3170/9, email kaskazi@africaonline.co.ke) is another all-inclusive place, which caters mainly for German and Swiss package tourists. The Arab-influenced architecture is stylish, rooms have some nice touches and the restaurant, pool and bar terraces descend to the ocean. Rooms cost US$50/90 in the low season rising to US$100/150 in the high season.

Diani Sea Lodge, Jardini Beach Hotel & Africana Sea Lodge (☎ 2060/9, fax 3439) are all owned by the Alliance Hotels group (☎ 02-332825 in Nairobi) and have the same bells and whistles though Africana Sea Lodge is the best of the bunch with excellent water-sports facilities. Room rates start at US$45/70 in the low season and rise to US$85/100 in the high season.

Nomad Beach Hotel (☎ 2155, fax 2391, email nomad@swiftmombasa.com) is one of the more relaxed top end places. It's made up of simple, comfortable cottages and bandas on the edge of the beach. All are tidy and well planned. The bar on the beach is a local favourite and the restaurant does a KSh 500 curry lunch on Sunday. Prices are perhaps a little high but it's a good place to stay. It costs US$38 per person for a banda and US$50 for a cottage in the low season rising to US$55/75 in the high season, although you may be able to cut a better deal. Prices include breakfast.

Safari Beach Hotel (☎ 2726, fax 2357) has accommodation in two-storey round buildings some way from the sea. The service is efficient and friendly and it's a good place for people with kids. If the owners can't arrange an activity here, they'll pass you on to Jardini Beach Hotel or Africana Sea Lodge. Rooms cost US$62/95 in the low season, rising to US$100/135 in the high season.

Places to Eat

Diani is well supplied with shopping centres, so you needn't bring everything from

Ukunda village if you are self-catering, although fruit and vegetables are cheap there.

Rongai Butchery in Ukunda (an excellent place for nyama choma) is a good place to buy meat for beach barbecues. Also in Ukunda is *Hollywood Restaurant*, which shows movies in the evening.

North of the T-junction are *Galaxy Chinese Restaurant* (☎ 2529) next to the Quinnsworth supermarket, and *African Pot* just before the entrance to Coral Beach Cottages. The latter serves extremely fine Swahili and Kenyan food – 500g of meat either grilled, stir fried or deep fried costs about KSh 150. Side dishes such as *ugali* (maize porridge), *matoke* (cooked green bananas) or *mataha* (mashed beans, potatoes, maize and greens) cost about KSh 60. Beer here is cheap.

South of the T-junction in Diani are a cluster of restaurants and nightclubs. *Restaurant Maharani* (☎ 2439) is open from 7 to 11 pm daily as well as for lunch from 12.30 to 3 pm weekends. Mains are about KSh 500 and the food is usually very good.

In the same area but down a track on the opposite side of the road is *Ali Barbour's* (☎ 2163), an expensive seafood restaurant set in a coral cave between Trade Winds Hotel (closed) and Diani Sea Lodge. It costs KSh 1200 for a basic three course meal. It's quite a dining experience, but at night take a taxi all the way to/from the door as numerous people have been mugged walking down this track. Free transport is available to groups staying in Diani.

Closer to the junction are *Tropicana Disco* (☎ 2303) and *Gallo's Restaurant & Bar* (☎ 3150). The Tropicana is more of a bar and disco, but the pizza (KSh 350) and pasta (KSh 380) are not bad. An English breakfast is KSh 380. Gallo's is a good restaurant with an international menu. Standard main courses are between KSh 775 and KSh 1500, but some cheaper food is available. You can also use the Internet here. Free transport within Diani is provided.

If you're longing for some Austrian meat loaf or German bratwurst, head to nearby *Walter's Inn* (☎ 3522). A thoroughly European feed will cost you around KSh 700 per person.

Many of the beach hotels offer buffet lunches and dinners at weekends, which are open to nonguests. *Nomad Beach Hotel*'s curry lunch is probably the best deal in town at KSh 500.

Entertainment

Bar on the Beach at Nomad Beach Hotel and *Forty Thieves Beach Bar*, not far from Ali Barbour's Restaurant are probably the two best bars in town. Both stay open until late and the music gets gradually louder and louder. *Tropicana Disco* (see Places to Eat previously) is also worth a look.

Further south is *Bush Baby Nightclub*, an open-air restaurant and nightclub that's not bad for a bop. Close by is *Shakatak Disco*. Both are pick-up joints of the highest order, but OK for letting your hair down.

You'll find Kenyan and African music (live and recorded) in the bars of Ukunda – *African Pot* (see Places to Eat previously) is a good place to start.

Getting There & Away

Bus & Matatu Diani is the most accessible beach if you're dependent on public transport. From the Likoni ferry there are KBS buses (No 32) every 20 minutes or so from early morning until about 7 pm. The fare is minimal and the trip takes about 30 minutes.

Plenty of matatus go from Likoni to Diani. They do the journey slightly faster than the bus and cost a little more. Other matatus and buses only go as far as Ukunda from where you'll get a quick connection to Diani.

When the buses and matatus get to Diani they first head north along the Diani beach road then turn around and go to the southern end of the bitumen where they turn again and head for Likoni. Just tell the driver where you want to get off.

Car Cars can be hired from Leisure Car Hire (☎ 3225). Some of their 4WDs are bombs, but they may cut you a deal. Their office is next to the Agip petrol station just south of Kaskazi Hotel.

SHIMONI & WASINI ISLAND

Shimoni is at the end of a small peninsula 76km south of Likoni, and not far from the Tanzanian border. The main reason to come here is the coral reef of Kisite-Mpunguti Marine National Park and the ocean around Wasini Island. These habitats contain a huge amount of marine life.

Wasini Island itself is just off the coast of the Shimoni Peninsula. It's well wooded and unspoilt and is the perfect place to relax and experience a Swahili culture virtually untouched by the 20th century and tourism. There are no cars, roads or running water and the only electricity comes from generators.

On a wander around you can come across Muslim ruins, women weaving mats, men preparing for fishing by mending nets and making fish traps, huge old baobab trees and extensive 'coral gardens' with odd-shaped stands of old coral that you can walk through (except at certain times of year when the sea floods it).

Back in Shimoni you can walk around the **slave caves** (though some people dispute slaves were ever kept in them) just outside the village. Here you'll be close to the edge of the tropical coastal forest.

Kisite-Mpunguti Marine National Park

This park south of Wasini Island, is one of the best marine parks in Kenya. The 28 sq km of coral reefs south-east of Wasini Island offer some excellent diving and snorkelling.

To visit this park, you'll need to go by boat – members of the Shimoni Boat Owners Association (supported by the Kenya Wildlife Service) are the people to see; the KWS office about 200m south of the main pier, is a good place to start looking. Expect to pay about KSh 4000 for the boat but bargain hard.

Entry to the park costs US$5 for nonresidents, KSh 100 for residents and KSh 200 for boats. The best time to dive and snorkel is between October and March. Avoid June, July and August because of the likelihood of rough seas and silt. Masks and snorkels are usually available to rent.

You've a reasonable chance of seeing Indo-Pacific humpback dolphins when heading out into the Shimoni Channel, while the territory of the Pantropical spotted dolphin extends from the eastern edge of Wasini Island into the marine park. Between August and October you may even see humpback whales.

The Friends of Kenyan Dolphins have set up a Dolphin Dhow trip around Shimoni Island, which leaves from Shimoni Jetty at 9 am daily. The cost is US$75 (or US$95 including transport from the coast south of Mombasa). They also run a week-long dolphin watching package for US$1640, staying at the Pemba Channel Fishing Club (PCFC, see Places to Stay & Eat following). For

Mining, Multinationals & Marine Life

The Kenya Wildlife Service (KWS) is currently involved in a fierce battle to prevent the multinational mining company Tiomin Resources Incorporated developing Shimoni into a commercial port for the export of titanium dioxide ore.

The company already has permission to extract five million tonnes of titanium ore from a site near Kwale over a 21 year period and is intending to develop the unspoilt fishing village into its export terminal. The other possible (and seemingly more sensible) site in Mombasa is out of favour. Dr Richard Leakey (now head of the civil service and former KWS chief) and KWS are strongly opposed to the development. They maintain that increased commercial traffic of large bulk carriers will have a disastrous effect on Kisite-Mpunguti Marine National Park and the local aquatic life, including the schools of resident dolphins in the channel. In addition, the storage facility will destroy four hectares of coastal forest.

While a final decision had not been reached at the time of writing, what's certain is that new port buildings and a customs house are already under construction.

further details contact Dolphin Dhow (☎/fax 0127-2094, email dolphin@africaonline .co.ke), PO Box 85636, Mombasa. The Web site is www.dolphindhow.com.

Snorkelling & Diving

In addition to boats that can be hired in Shimoni, Masood Abdullah (who runs Mpunguti Lodge on Wasini Island, see Places to Stay & Eat following) can arrange trips to the marine park. He has his own dhow as well as masks and snorkels.

Diving safaris off Pemba Channel (spectacular!) can be arranged through the PCFC (see Places to Stay & Eat following), but they are expensive. A PADI Open Water beginners course including seven days half-board accommodation, costs UK£575 at the PCFC, while their seven-day diving safari costs between UK£550 to UK£750. Bookings should go through Don McGilchrist in the UK (☎ 01334-472504, email Pem badiver@aol.com).

Places to Stay & Eat

Camp Eden (PO Box 55, Ukunda) is behind the KWS headquarters; it consists of simple bandas (US$10 per person) and a camp site (US$2). Mosquito nets are provided and there is a big covered cooking area, pit toilets and showers.

Pemba Channel Fishing Club (☎ 011-313749, fax 316875, PO Box 86952, Mombasa) is a fantastic upmarket place, which charges US$90/100 per person in low/high season (full board) for elegant colonial-style cottages. This place is primarily concerned with fishing – the Pemba Channel itself is reckoned to have the finest fishing in all of Kenya and 70% of the country's Marlin fishing records are held by the club (see the boxed text 'Deep-Sea Fishing' under Malindi Marine National Park later in this chapter). The food here is excellent and the bar (open to nonguests) is most 'Hemingway-esque'. A meal will cost you about US$25, but the cooks need advance warning.

Mpunguti Lodge (☎ 0127-52288) is the only accommodation across the channel on Wasini Island (and can only be reached via the phone box across the road). It is run by

Masood Abdullah. At the time of writing Mr Abdullah was in the process of building a large rainwater tank and installing fresh-water showers and saltwater toilets. You can camp here for KSh 150 or rent a very clean and pleasant room for KSh 800/1000 per person (full board). Cooking facilities are available for those who prefer self-catering. Masood is a affable and well organised character, and the traditional Swahili food he turns out is delicious. He organises snorkelling trips and is also the local historian (he is trying to set up a small museum). Alcoholic drinks must be brought with you from the mainland.

You'll be able to buy basic foodstuffs in Shimoni and on Wasini (ie, fish, coconuts, maize flour and rice) but very little else.

Getting There & Away

There are a couple of direct buses and matatus daily between Shimoni and Likoni but it's best to be waiting on the main road by 6.30 am. From Shimoni matatus return at around 2 and 4 pm. There may be a KBS bus but don't count on it.

You could take a matatu towards Lunga Lunga and get off at the Shimoni turn-off, but you'd then have to hitch the remaining 14km from the main road to Shimoni. It's not that difficult – even the locals do it.

For a boat to the island, budget for about KSh 600 (return).

North of Mombasa

MOMBASA TO KILIFI

Like the coast south of Mombasa, the north coast has been well developed with resort complexes that take up much of the beach frontage almost two-thirds of the way up to Kilifi. These cater mostly for package tourists from Europe. Only Kanamai Conference Centre at Kikambala and Timeless Camping at Vipingo genuinely fall into the budget accommodation bracket.

Like Tiwi Beach south of Mombasa, the northern beaches are plagued with seaweed. The beaches are also plagued with petty crime – see the boxed text 'Safety on the

Coast' earlier in this chapter. Going north from Mombasa the names of the beaches are Nyali, Bamburi, Shanzu, Kikambala and Vipingo.

Things to See & Do
Mamba Crocodile Village (☎ 011-472709, email mamba@africaonline.co.ke) opposite Nyali Golf Club is a crocodile farm and also a nightclub complex. Entry to the farm costs KSh 400. Live music acts perform in the nightclub.

Further up the coast at **Nguuni Wildlife Sanctuary**, the Bamburi Cement Company

(☎ 011-485729, email baobabfarm@swift mombasa.com) has created the Bamburi Quarry and North Quarry **nature trails**. The transformation of these old quarry workings into a mini-wildlife park is particularly impressive. Tours of the sanctuary must be booked in advance. To get there, take a public bus to Bamburi Quarry Nature Trail stop (signposted) on the main Mombasa-Malindi road (KSh 40).

Jumba la Mtwana is a national monument just north of Mtwapa Creek. The ruins of a 15th century Swahili slaving settlement sit above a very pleasant beach. Entry is KSh 200, guides are available and it's signposted on the right about 1km north of Mtwapa Bridge (it's a 3km walk from the Malindi road).

Places to Stay – Budget
Kanamai Conference Centre (☎ 0125-32046) at Kikambala Beach is one of the few genuine cheapies. The complex of cottages, dormitories and rooms was previously a youth hostel and now has a strong Christian emphasis (there is no bar). Camping is KSh 120 per person and dormitory beds are KSh 400 (with breakfast). Double rooms are KSh 1200, one-bedroom cottages KSh 1500, two-bedroom cottages KSh 1800 (KSh 1500 in the low season), and three-bedroom places KSh 2100 (KSh 1800 in the low season). All the cottages have bathrooms. Meals are available for KSh 200 for breakfast, KSh 300 for lunch and KSh 350 for dinner – expensive for what are basically simple stews. The Whispering Palms Hotel, where nonguests can use the facilities, is a five minute walk away.

The trouble with Kanamai is getting there. First you have to take a matatu to Majengo on the Mombasa-Kilifi road (get off when you see a yellow sign for the centre), then follow the sign down a dirt track for

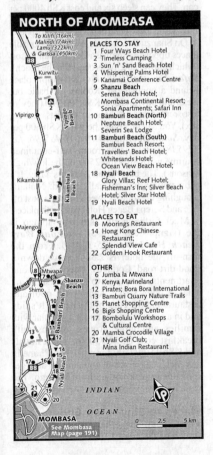

NORTH OF MOMBASA

To Kilifi (16km),
Malindi (74km),
Lamu (322km)
& Garissa (450km)

Kurwitu

Vipingo

Kikambala

Majengo

Mtwapa

Shimo

PLACES TO STAY
1 Four Ways Beach Hotel
2 Timeless Camping
3 Sun 'n' Sand Beach Hotel
4 Whispering Palms Hotel
5 Kanamai Conference Centre
9 Shanzu Beach
  Serena Beach Hotel;
  Mombasa Continental Resort;
  Sonia Apartments; Safari Inn
10 Bamburi Beach (North)
  Neptune Beach Hotel;
  Severin Sea Lodge
11 Bamburi Beach (South)
  Bamburi Beach Resort;
  Travellers' Beach Hotel;
  Whitesands Hotel;
  Ocean View Beach Hotel;
18 Nyali Beach
  Glory Villas; Reef Hotel;
  Fisherman's Inn; Silver Beach
  Hotel; Silver Star Hotel
19 Nyali Beach Hotel

PLACES TO EAT
8 Moorings Restaurant
14 Hong Kong Chinese
  Restaurant;
  Splendid View Cafe
22 Golden Hook Restaurant

OTHER
6 Jumba la Mtwana
7 Kenya Marineland
12 Pirates; Bora Bora International
13 Bamburi Quarry Nature Trails
15 Planet Shopping Centre
16 Bigis Shopping Centre
17 Bombolulu Workshops
  & Cultural Centre
20 Mamba Crocodile Village
21 Nyali Golf Club;
  Mina Indian Restaurant

INDIAN

OCEAN

MOMBASA
See Mombasa
Map (page 191)

0   2.5   5 km

about 300m then fork left. Continue for about 3km and you'll find it on the left-hand side by the beach. It's a long, hot walk and lifts are few and far between.

Further up the coast at Vipingo, about 40km north of Mombasa, is *Timeless Camping* (☎ *0125-32218, PO Box 19, Vipingo*). It's a simple place with a number of rooms in the house itself, a couple of fully equipped cottages and a large camping area. At the time of writing a bar and dining area were being added. The nearest shop or restaurant is many kilometres away, so self-caterers should bring supplies with them (although meals are always available). Allow for roughly KSh 600 per person per day half board and KSh 200 for camping. The coast here is particularly beautiful; it's unspoilt and the reef comes right up to the beach. Timeless is a simple place where travellers are made to feel more like house guests than visitors. The family can arrange various activities including reasonably priced deep-sea fishing trips.

If arriving alone by public transport, it's better to phone ahead and someone will collect you from Vipingo village (note that the public phone at Vipingo is permanently out of order). Don't walk in the area of the camp unaccompanied as there have been muggings in the past. Those in a group or with transport should look for the large sign for Fourways Beach Hotel 2km north of Vipingo. From there it's 1.5km down a good dirt road to a T-junction. Turn right (Timeless is signposted) and then right again at a stone wall. Timeless is about 200m away.

Places to Stay – Mid-Range

Fisherman's Inn (☎ *011-474738/9*) is almost at the end of Nyali Beach near Reef Hotel. This is a more intimate place than the surrounding resorts, and much cheaper. Singles/doubles with breakfast go for KSh 1800/2300 in the low season (add 20% in the high season). There's a swimming pool, a good restaurant, room service and the rooms are well appointed. Walk through Reef Hotel to get to the beach. Oasis Pizzeria next door is good.

Glory Villas (☎ *011-474758*) is just off Links Rd close to the Planet shopping cen-tre. It's not right on the beach, but near enough to the action at the Bora Bora and Pirates discos. Accommodation (with uninspired interiors) is in tall cylindrical towers surrounding a swimming pool. Doubles are KSh 1000 and cottages KSh 2000. Nyali Beach is a 15 minute walk away.

Bamburi Beach Resort (☎ *011-485632*) between Travellers Beach Hotel and Bamburi Beach Hotel, is a tidy little apartment complex with direct access to the beach. One-bedroom places without cooking facilities (but air-con) cost KSh 1800 with breakfast. Apartments have a kitchen, balcony and air-con. They can sleep six and cost KSh 4000 per night. The beach bar and restaurant has a fully vegetarian menu and a good atmosphere.

On Shanzu Beach there are two reasonable places opposite Mombasa Continental Resort (which allows nonguests access to the beach). *Safari Inn* (☎ *011-485094*) is a simple place behind a popular bar. Rooms are basic but clean and tidy, and cost KSh 500/900 (they're also rented by the hour to tourists seeking sex). You can hire bikes here for KSh 600 per day. *Sonia Apartments* (☎ *011-485196, fax 229538*) lets one-bedroom self-contained apartments (KSh 1500/2500 in the low/high seasons). The bar is open 24 hours a day. It's a bit untidy, but basically sound. Matatus ploughing the route between Mtwapa post office and Serena Beach Hotel pass both places.

Much further north, 2km past Vipingo, is the (signposted) turn-off to *Four Ways Beach Hotel* (☎ *0125-32269*). From the turn-off the hotel is 2.5km away down a good dirt road. Cottages (sleeping six) and apartments (sleeping two to three) surround a large open space, swimming pool and restaurant at the edge of the beach. It's tidy and in a great location, and it's popular with families and large groups. Rooms with breakfast cost US$28/50 for nonresidents and KSh 1500/2400 for residents. Phone in advance, negotiate a good price and get someone to pick you up from Vipingo. The restaurant is expensive.

Places to Stay – Top End

Virtually all the other hotels along this stretch of the coast before you reach Kilifi are resort complexes that cater largely for package tourists from Europe. Most of them are so self-contained that many of those staying there hardly ever see anything of Africa other than Mombasa airport, the inside of minibuses, the hotel itself and black Kenyan resort staff.

All the hotels compete furiously with each other to provide the utmost in creature comforts, mellow surroundings, day trips and sports facilities and there's little to choose between them though it's generally true to say that the more you pay the more style and luxury you get.

Nyali Beach *Nyali Beach Hotel (☎ 011-471551)* is a classy and very expensive Block Group hotel not far from Mombasa. Singles/doubles (with half board) for nonresidents cost US$63/126 in the low season; add 25% in the high season.

Silver Beach Hotel and *Silver Star Hotel (☎ 011-475114/7)* have rooms (with half board) for residents for KSh 1915/3190 in the low season, rising to KSh 2574/4290 in the high season. These aren't inspiring hotels but they're good value. Call to get rates for nonresidents.

Reef Hotel (☎ 02-214322 in Nairobi) has rooms for US$59/98 in the low season, rising to US$92/140 in the high season. It's a little more intimate than the grand Mombasa Beach Hotel but the views aren't as good.

Bamburi Beach *Ocean View Beach Hotel (☎ 011-485602)* is cheap at KSh 1300/2000 for singles/doubles with breakfast. It's close to the action at the Bora Bora and Pirates discos.

Whitesands Hotel (☎ 011-485926, 485652, email gm@whitesands.sarova.co.ke) is possibly the best resort hotel on this section of coast with good service, thoughtful design and high standards. Excellent water-sports facilities include scuba diving and windsurfing. Rooms (with half board) cost US$60/120 in the low season, rising to US$130/160 in the high season.

Travellers' Beach Hotel (☎ 011-485121, 483678, email travellershtl@swiftmombasa.com) is big but a little claustrophobic, and

caters for German and English package tourists. There's a good Indian restaurant and interesting swimming pool. Rooms (with half board) are US$60/120 in the low season, rising to US$130/160 in the high season.

Severin Sea Lodge (☎ 011-4855001, fax 485212, email severin@form-net.com) has cottage-style accommodation with air-con, a safe, piped music etc. This is a reasonable place with cheap low-season rates. Rooms (with half board) are US$45/90 in the low season, rising to US$137/172 in the high season.

Neptune Beach Hotel (☎ 011-485701/3, email neptune@users.africaonline.co.ke) is a big three storey block of a hotel but thought has gone into the bright and airy interior. Rooms (with full board) cost KSh 2400/3800 in the low season, rising to KSh 1900/2800 in the high season. All rates include breakfast and are good value.

Shanzu Beach *Mombasa Continental Resort (☎ 011-486721, email msaconti@africaonline.co.ke)* is a ridiculously grand multistorey international hotel on the coast, but the facilities and service are good. Rooms (with half board) cost KSh 1700/ 2800 in the low season, rising to US$81/105 in the high season.

Serena Beach Hotel (☎ 011-485721, fax 485453, email mombasa@serena.co.ke) is in Lamu/Arabic style and seems quite intimate despite its 166 rooms. It's well appointed but the garden rooms are much better than the standard accommodation. It's a mile better than its continental neighbour and is also more expensive: standard rooms (with half board) cost US$60/120 and garden rooms cost US$75/150 in the low season, rising to US$126/160 and US$160/220 in the high season. Add 28% tax to these rates.

Kikambala Beach *Sun 'n' Sand Beach Hotel (☎/fax 0125-32133, email sunsnd@africaonline.co.ke)* deserves its reputation as the best hotel for kids along the north coast, but it's all-inclusive so there are no casual visitors. Although showing its age in places, the hotel has good sports facilities. Rooms (with half board) cost US$52/104 in the low season, rising to US$110/130 in the high season; children are charged 50% of the adult rate.

Whispering Palms Hotel (☎ *0125-32004, fax 32029, email whispers@africaonline .co.ke*) is an ageing package holiday place with some good sports and recreational facilities. Reasonably cheap rooms (with half board) cost US$35/56 in the low season, rising to US$42/75 in the high season. The bar and restaurant are open to nonguests who can also use the pool for KSh 150 or play tennis for KSh 100 per hour. A nearby colony of Wahlberg's epauletted fruit bats make regular evening appearances.

Places to Eat

The Planet and Bigis shopping centres at the top end of Nyali Beach have a few food shops for self-caterers. The Royal Supermarket is on Kikambala Beach.

Golden Hook Restaurant, across the Nyali Bridge just out of Mombasa on the left-hand side, is something of a live music venue as well as a bar and restaurant.

Heading down Nyali Rd you come to Nyali Golf Club (where you can play a round of golf for between KSh 1000 and KSh 2000). The club is home to the well regarded *Minar Indian Restaurant* (☎ *011-471220).*

On the main Malindi road are two good restaurants. First up is *Hong Kong Chinese Restaurant* (☎ *011-485422)* followed by *Splendid View Cafe* (☎ *011-487270),* which serves Indian Mughal cuisine. Both places offer main dishes for around KSh 350, while the 'special Sunday biryani' at Splendid View is KSh 250.

Moorings Restaurant, floating off the north shore of Mtwapa Creek, is an excellent bar and restaurant and a favourite of the yachting and fishing community. If you're heading north, take the first left after the bridge then follow the sign (a surf board) down to the water's edge.

Entertainment

You can eat at *Pirates* or the infamous *Bora Bora International Night Club* by Bamburi Beach, but you're better off just dancing and drinking there. Down on the beach

front there is the small *Club Coco* attached to Bamburi Beach Resort, and *Chameleons* is another good beach bar.

KILIFI
☎ 0125

A bit of a backwater, Kilifi is inhabited by discerning white Kenyans and artists, writers and adventurers from various parts of the world who have gradually bought up most of the land overlooking the wide creek and the ocean. Without an introduction however, it's unlikely you'll meet them.

Mnarani, on the southern bank of Kilifi Creek overlooking the ferry landing, was once one of the string of Swahili city-states that dotted the East African coast. The principal ruins here include the Great Mosque with its finely carved inscription around the mihrab, a group of tombs to the north (including one pillar tomb) and a large and quite forbiddingly deep well whose shaft must go down at least as far as the low-tide level of the creek.

All the buses and matatus travelling between Mombasa and Malindi stop at Kilifi (about KSh 40 each way).

WATAMU
☎ 0122

About 24km south of Malindi, Watamu is a smaller beach resort development with its own marine national park and is in many ways a far better place to stay than its big brash neighbour. The coral reef here is more spectacular, underwater visibility is not affected by silt during the rainy season and it's more relaxed and considerably safer. The marvellous ruins at Gedi are close by and for those wanting to explore the natural wonders of the coast, Mida Creek, the coral gardens and Arabuko-Sokoke Forest Reserve all await.

Before tourist development got underway here, Watamu was a mellow little fishing village nestling beneath coconut palms and it still retains much of that atmosphere despite the intrusion of souvenir shops, bars and restaurants. In fact the contrasts are quite bizarre – it's one of the few places where you'll see package tourists in designer beach attire wandering down the dusty streets of an African village.

Between December and April the sea grass that lines the beach (and in fact protects it) disappears to reveal dazzling white coral sand.

Information

There are branches of both Barclays Bank and Kenya Commercial Bank in the village. The post office is at the start of the road to Gedi, but there's also a cardphone in the centre of the village.

Next to Barclays Bank is International Phone & Fax (☎ 32522) where you can send and receive email.

Bio Ken Snake Farm & Laboratory

James Ashe is the owner of a very well run snake farm north of Watamu village on the main beach road towards the Kalulu Caves. Geared up to produce snake antivenene, James Ashe is an expert on Kenyan reptiles and *dudus* (creepy crawlies), and has published a tourist guide to those more commonly encountered. It's open from 9 am to noon and 2 to 5 pm daily; there is a small entry charge.

Watamu Marine National Park

The actual coral reef lies between 1km and 2km offshore and to get to it you'll have to hire a glass-bottomed boat. This can be arranged at the park entrance and KWS Watumu headquarters; expect to pay between KSh 2000 and KSh 3000, excluding park fees.

All the big hotels offer snorkelling trips to nonguests for an average fee of around KSh 750. Resident zoologist Richard Bennett runs trips from Turtle Bay Beach Club (☎ 32003, email turtles@users.africaonline.co.ke); the trip costs KSh 1020. Mrs Simpson's Guest House also runs less expensive trips with an excellent local guide. Both these trips are highly recommended. The best time to dive and snorkel is between October and March. Avoid June, July and August because of rough seas and poor water visibility.

Entry to the park costs US$5 for nonresidents and KSh 100 for residents.

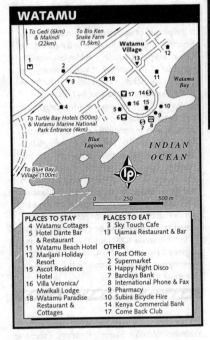

PLACES TO STAY	PLACES TO EAT
4 Watamu Cottages	3 Sky Touch Cafe
5 Hotel Dante Bar & Restaurant	13 Ujamaa Restaurant & Bar
11 Watamu Beach Hotel	
12 Marijani Holiday Resort	OTHER
15 Ascot Residence Hotel	1 Post Office
16 Villa Veronica/ Mwikali Lodge	2 Supermarket
18 Watamu Paradise Restaurant & Cottages	6 Happy Night Disco
	7 Barclays Bank
	8 International Phone & Fax
	9 Pharmacy
	10 Subira Bicycle Hire
	14 Kenya Commercial Bank
	17 Come Back Club

Activities

Mida Creek is also worth exploring. There's a popular **boat trip** to a group of caves, which are home to a school of giant rock cod (up to 2m long), while the extensive mangrove forests support a huge number of bird species. KWS have also set up a boardwalk and picnic site among the mangroves at Sudi Island. A guide is invaluable here.

Giant turtles lay eggs on Watamu's beach between January and April. Contact Watamu Turtle Conservation Group (☎ 32420, email aquav@africaonline.co.ke) for details.

Aqua Ventures (☎ 32008, fax 32266, email aquav@africaonline.co.ke) PO Box 275, Watamu, run a variety of specialist **diving** courses, dive safaris and both PADI and BSAC beginners courses from their base next to Ocean Sports Hotel. A five-day PADI Open Water beginners course costs UK£250 and includes four dives. Guided dives in the marine park are UK£16. Aqua Ventures are a well run and well respected outfit.

Tag & Brag

If the picture of you standing grinning inanely next to a huge dead fish puts you right off the idea of deep-sea fishing, a milder less terminal variation of the sport is at hand, namely the 'Tag & Brag' scheme operated by the African Billfish Foundation, PO Box 342, Watamu.

With Tag & Brag, when a fish is caught it's not removed from the water, but a data tag is inserted into the shoulder muscle before the fish is released. The tag contains information about the fish at its time of capture and the same information is collected when the fish is recaptured. This helps researchers establish the range and patterns of migration, life span and total population of game fish off the East African coast so that management and conservation strategies can be established.

In 1998 some 4000 tags were issued. Hemingway's Hotel (☎ 32624, fax 32256, email hemingways@form-net.com) is the best place for more information.

You can join a group who **run** through Arabuko-Sokoke Forest Reserve (see the Around Watamu section later in the chapter for details).

Bicycles can be hired for KSh 350 per day from Subira Bicycle Hire opposite Ascot Residence Hotel.

Places to Stay – Budget
Budget accommodation has always been something of a problem in Watamu. **Blue Lodge** and **Sam's Lodge** are total dives and can't be recommended.

Villa Veronica/Mwikali Lodge (☎ 32083) opposite the Hotel Dante Bar & Restaurant, is family run and the best value of the regular lodges. This is a very friendly and secure place; clean rooms with double bed, fan, mosquito nets, shower and toilet cost KSh 700 including breakfast. The only drawback to this place is that it's tucked into a hollow so you miss out on sea breezes and it's close to the very loud Come Back Club. Get a room as far away from the disco as possible.

Watamu Cottages (☎ 32211) is a hot 15 minute walk along the main access road to the village and is the only other place that fits this price bracket. Rooms are a good deal at KSh 750 per double with bath and breakfast but it's often full. The rooms are set in a pleasant garden, and there's also a swimming pool.

Places to Stay – Mid-Range
Watamu Paradise Restaurant & Cottages (☎ 32062) on the main road leaving the village has a number of double and triple cottages. Depending on the standard, a double with bath costs from KSh 800 to KSh 1200. All the rooms have a fan and mosquito nets. It's a very pleasant place to stay and there's a small swimming pool, a bar and restaurant, as well as a disco on the weekend.

Marijani Holiday Resort (☎/fax 32448) is probably the best place in the village. It's a big stone house tucked away behind Watamu Beach Hotel a couple of minutes from the beach. It has 10 nice rooms with balconies and verandas; singles/doubles cost KSh 1260/1400 with breakfast in the high season, and a separate self-contained one-bed apartment costs KSh 1225 – you may be able to get a better deal in the low season. Wonderful wooden furniture, stone floors and huge double four-poster beds with mosquito nets come as standard.

Ascot Residence Hotel (☎ 32326, PO Box 14, Watamu) in the centre of Watamu village is a sprawling walled complex containing numerous makuti-roofed cottages, a bar, restaurant and a swimming pool (drained in the low season). It gives the appearance of being a top end hotel but the prices don't reflect this – well equipped doubles cost from KSh 1000. Apartments with simple facilities are available for KSh 10,000 per week. The surroundings are very pleasant and the Italian restaurant serves fantastic pizza.

Mrs Simpson's Guest House (☎ 32023, email jakekh@users.africaonline.co.ke, PO Box 33, Watamu) is also highly recommended. Barbara Simpson has lived in Kenya for more than 70 years, and although her health is failing she still has many a tale to tell. A manager runs the place and accommodation and facilities are good. Accommodation only is KSh 1000 per person, rising to KSh 1750 for full board, laundry service included. You can camp here for KSh 200 or sleep on the roof or in the boat shed for KSh 400. The atmosphere is relaxed and homey and the food is good. Snorkelling trips and other excursions can be arranged and the bird and marine guides based here are really excellent. The guesthouse is a 200m walk from a beach and about 2.5km from Turtle Bay. Ask the matatu driver to drop you at Plot 28.

Places to Stay – Top End

The southern cove sports the resort hotels. *Blue Bay Village* (☎ 32626, email blue bay@africaonline.co.ke) is closest to Watamu village and caters mostly for Italians. Depending on the type of room you take (standard, deluxe or superior), full-board doubles vary from US$60 to US$120 per person including taxes and service charges. The single-room supplement is US$25. Children aged between three and 12 years are charged 25% less. It's closed between 15 April and 15 July.

Ocean Sports Hotel (☎ 32008, fax 32266) is next along and has mainly British clientele. It's much smaller than the other places and the facilities are fairly modest. However, attached to the Hotel is Aqua Ventures (see Activities earlier in this section for contact details). Singles/doubles for nonresidents (with half board) cost UK£46/62 and KSh 3200/4200 for residents in the low season, rising to UK£48/72 and KSh 3600/4800 in the high season. Children between the ages of six and 12 years can stay for UK£12/KSh 1200, and UK£14/KSh 1400 respectively. Most of the clientele are middle-aged and have children with them.

Hemingway's Hotel (☎ 32624, fax 32256, email hemingways@form-net.com) next to Ocean Sports Hotel, is a much larger place that also caters for a largely British clientele. Rates for nonresidents (including breakfast) start at UK£64/95 in the low season, rising to UK£123/176 in the high season (depending on what type of room you take). Expensive suites are also available.

Children up to the age of five years stay for free but from five to 12 years they stay for only 10% of the standard rate. Rates include free transport to/from Malindi airport (by prior arrangement) and free snorkelling trips in the marine national park, excluding national park fees.

Places to Eat

The supermarket just outside of the village is handy for self-caterers and it's possible to get simple meals at the local bars in the village – try *Ujamaa Restaurant & Bar*.

Friend's Corner is one of the best small dukas on the road between Ascot Residence Hotel and Come Back Club.

Sky Touch Cafe just outside Watamu, does some good curried dishes for around KSh 300, while the Italian food at *Ascot Residence Hotel* ranges from KSh 350 to KSh 800. The wonderful pizzas are a steal at about KSh 400.

If you fancy a splurge, then the Sunday lunch buffets at either *Ocean Sports Hotel* (KSh 700) or *Hemingway's Hotel* (KSh 900) are well worth the cash (see previous entries under Places to Stay – Top End).

Entertainment

For dancing and drinking, head to *Happy Night Disco* next to Hotel Dante and *Come Back Club* just up the road. There's a nominal entry fee. *Ujamaa Restaurant & Bar* and *Sky Touch Cafe* can get lively before the clubs open, while the *Pole-Pole Bar* opposite the Turtle Bay Beach Club is an excellent little place for a drink and a snack. There are bats that swoop over drinkers in the early evening.

Getting There & Away

Buses leave the bus station in Malindi throughout the day. You can also pick up a matatu just outside the station on the main road. They cost KSh 30 and take about 30 minutes. Most of these go down to the Turtle Bay Beach Club first then turn away and go to Watamu village. On the return journey they generally go direct from Watamu village to Malindi. For Mombasa you may need to change transport at Gedi.

AROUND WATAMU
Arabuko-Sokoke Forest Reserve

Close to the marine park at Watamu, Arabuko-Sokoke Forest is the largest remaining tract of indigenous coastal forest in East Africa. It's home to an unusually high concentration of rare species, especially birds (240 species) and butterflies (260 species). Clarke's weaver and the wonderful golden-rumped elephant-shrew are two star species, while you may even see an elephant or two trundling around the forest.

There's a visitors centre (☎ 0122-32462, email sokoke@africaonline.co.ke) at Gedi Forest Station (open 8 am to 5 pm daily) and a series of nature trails and running tracks cut through the forest. Trained bird and wildlife guides cost KSh 300 for half a day, KSh 600 for a full day and KSh 400 for a night walk (highly recommended). All guides are very knowledgeable not only about the forest, but also Mida Creek in Watamu Marine National Park. An excellent guide to Arabuko-Sokoke Forest Reserve (KSh 300) and other maps and bird lists are available from the visitors centre.

Apart from taking walks, you can join a group of runners who meet at Ocean Sports Hotel in Watamu at 5 pm on Monday, Wednesday and Friday for a 4 to 10km run through Arabuko-Sokoke Forest Reserve.

There is no charge for entry to the forest at present, and there is a basic *camp site* close to the visitors centre (KSh 200 per person). However, with permission camping is also allowed within the forest.

The forest is just off the main Malindi-Mombasa road and the entrance to the forest and visitors centre is about 1.5km after the turn-off to Gedi and Watamu. All transport from Mombasa to Watamu and from Malindi to Kilifi and Mombasa can drop you at the entrance, while transport from Malindi to Watamu will drop you at the junction.

Gedi

Some 4km from Watamu, just off the main Malindi-Mombasa road, are the famous Gedi ruins, one of the principal historical monuments on the coast. Though the ruins are extensive, this Arab-Swahili town is something of a mystery since it's not mentioned in any of the Portuguese or Arab chronicles of the time.

Excavations (which uncovered such things as Ming Chinese porcelain and glass and glazed earthenware from Persia) indicate the 13th century as the time of Gedi's foundation. It was inexplicably abandoned in the 17th or 18th century, possibly because the sea receded and left the town high and dry, or because of invasions by marauding Galla tribespeople from the north. The forest took over and the site was not rediscovered until the 1920s. Even if you have only a passing interest in archaeology it's worth a visit.

Gedi is quite large and surrounded by two walls, the inner one of which was possibly built to enclose a smaller area after the city was temporarily abandoned in the 15th to 16th centuries. In places it actually incorporates earlier houses into its structure.

The site is lush and green with numerous baobab trees. Monkeys chatter in tree tops, lizards rustle in the undergrowth and large, colourful butterflies flutter among the ruins.

The buildings were constructed of coral rag, coral lime and earth and some have pictures incised into the plaster finish of their walls, though many of these have deteriorated in recent years. The toilet facilities in the houses are particularly impressive, generally in a double-cubicle style with a squat toilet in one and a wash stand in the other where a bowl would have been used. Fancier versions even have double washbasins with a bidet between them.

The other notable feature of the site is the great number of wells, many of them remarkably deep.

Most of the interesting excavated buildings are concentrated in a dense cluster near the entrance gate. Of particular interest is the Dated Tomb (so-called because the Muslim date corresponding to 1399 has been deciphered), the Great Mosque dating from the mid-15th century and the Palace with its fine pillar tomb. Several other buildings are scattered around the site within the inner wall and even between the inner and outer walls. Outside the site, by the car park, there's a small museum with

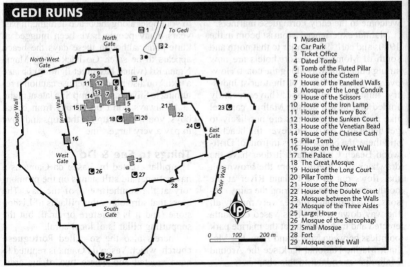

GEDI RUINS

To Gedi

North Gate

North-West Gate

Outer Wall

Inner Wall

West Gate

South Gate

East Gate

Outer Wall

0   100   200 m

1 Museum
2 Car Park
3 Ticket Office
4 Dated Tomb
5 Tomb of the Fluted Pillar
6 House of the Cistern
7 House of the Panelled Walls
8 Mosque of the Long Conduit
9 House of the Scissors
10 House of the Iron Lamp
11 House of the Ivory Box
12 House of the Sunken Court
13 House of the Venetian Bead
14 House of the Chinese Cash
15 Pillar Tomb
16 House on the West Wall
17 The Palace
18 The Great Mosque
19 House of the Long Court
20 Pillar Tomb
21 House of the Dhow
22 House of the Double Court
23 Mosque between the Walls
24 Mosque of the Three Aisles
25 Large House
26 Mosque of the Sarcophagi
27 Small Mosque
28 Fort
29 Mosque on the Wall

some items found on the site. Other items are exhibited in Fort Jesus in Mombasa.

Entry to the site costs KSh 200 for non-residents and KSh 30 for residents (less for students and children) and it's open from 7 am to 6 pm daily. A good guidebook with map is for sale at the entrance for KSh 30.

Just outside the North Gate is a 'traditional' **Giriama tribal village** and here the package tourists are entertained with 'traditional' Giriama dances. Unfortunately it's *very* contrived and the dancing girls' costumes look something like a cross between a Hawaiian skirt and a tennis outfit.

Getting There & Away Take the same matatu as you would to go to Watamu but get off at Gedi village where the matatu turns off from the main Malindi-Mombasa road. From there it's about a 1km signposted walk to the ruins along a *murram* (dirt or part-gravelled road).

It's also possible to get a taxi to take you on a round trip from Malindi for about KSh 1000 with an hour or more to look around the site. This could be worth it if your time is limited and you're in a small group that can share costs.

Kilepeo Butterfly Farm

About 1km from the Gedi ruins is the Kipepeo Butterfly Farm (☎ 32380, email kipepeo@africaonline.co.ke). Set up by a zoologist from Nairobi University, locals are paid to collect live pupae from the Arabuko-Sokoke Forest Reserve. After these hatch the butterflies are sold to foreign collectors and for live exhibits in the UK and USA. The money is then ploughed back into conservation of the forests. Between 8 am and 5 pm guides will show you the large flight cage containing examples of the forest's butterflies and the stages of the rearing process. Entry costs KSh 100 for nonresidents (KSh 50 for children).

MALINDI
☎ 0123

Malindi has a pedigree going back to the 12th century and was an important Swahili settlement as far back as the 14th century. It often rivalled Mombasa and Paté for control of this part of the East African coast. Malindi was one of the ports visited by the Chinese junks of Cheng Ho between 1417 and 1419, before the Chinese emperor prohibited further overseas voyages. It was also one of the

KENYA

few places on the coast to offer a friendly welcome to the early Portuguese mariners.

Malindi experienced a tourist boom in the 1980s and early 90s similar to that north and south of Mombasa. Resort hotels are now strung out all the way along the coast. However, with the collapse of the tourist industry numerous businesses have recently folded and in low season Malindi can feel like a ghost town. Things are not likely to get better in a hurry. However, the beach is still there; the best stretch is in front of Driftwood Beach Club though it does have the drawback of suffering from the brown silt that flows out of the Galana River at the northern end of the bay during the rainy seasons. This can make the sea very muddy all the way down to the cross Vasco da Gama erected and makes diving at the marine park pointless between March and June. For Malindi Marine National Park see the Around Malindi section later in this chapter.

Information

Tourist Information There is a tourist office next door to Kenya Airways on Harambee Rd. The staff are friendly but the place is of little use.

The best travel agent in town is based at Scorpio Villas (☎ 20194, email scorpio@ swiftmombasa.com).

Money Barclays Bank and Standard Chartered Bank are open from 9 am to 4.30 pm Monday to Friday, and from 9 to 11 am Saturday; both have ATMs.

Immigration There's an office next to the Juma Mosque and pillar tombs on Vasco da Gama Rd, but it often refers people to Mombasa.

Post & Communications You can make international phone calls through the post office or from the cardphones outside. Magictex Communication Centre (☎ 30574, fax 31837) in the Malindi Complex on Lamu Rd provides international telephone, fax and email services. The cardphones in the quiet lobby of the casino are also a good bet.

Dangers & Annoyances Don't walk back to your hotel along the beach at night. In past years many people have been mugged at knife-point, although these days the beach appears to be safer. Go back along Mama Ngina Rd (which has street lighting) or take a taxi. You also need to exercise caution if returning to Silversands Camp Site late at night.

As always don't buy drugs from beach boys; you'll be set up for the cops and have to pay a very large 'fine'.

Things to See & Do

The **pillar** erected by Vasco da Gama as a navigational aid still stands on the promontory at the southern end of the bay. The cross that surmounts this pillar is of Lisbon stone (and it is therefore original) but the supporting pillar is of local coral.

There's also the so-called **Portuguese church**, which Vasco da Gama is reputed to have erected and where two of his crew were buried. What is more plausible is that this church is the one which St Francis Xavier visited on his way to India. The rest of the compound is taken up by the graves of Catholic missionaries from the late 19th and early 20th centuries. The site is run by the Kenya Museums authority and entry is the standard KSh 200.

Not far to the north of the church are a number of pillar tombs and the remains of **Juma Mosque** and a palace. Other than this, however, little remains of the old town. The nearest substantial ruins from pre-Portuguese days are at Gedi, south of Malindi (see Gedi in the Around Watamu section earlier in this chapter).

For **excursions** from Malindi see the Around Malindi section later in this chapter. For **deep-sea fishing** charters see Malindi Sea Fishing Club under Entertainment later in this section and the boxed text 'Deep-Sea Fishing' later in this chapter.

Places to Stay – Budget

Tana Hotel (☎ 20116) is the best of the basic places; simple singles/doubles with fan and mosquito nets cost KSh 250/300.

New Wananchi Bar & Restaurant on Tana St, is even more basic with rooms for

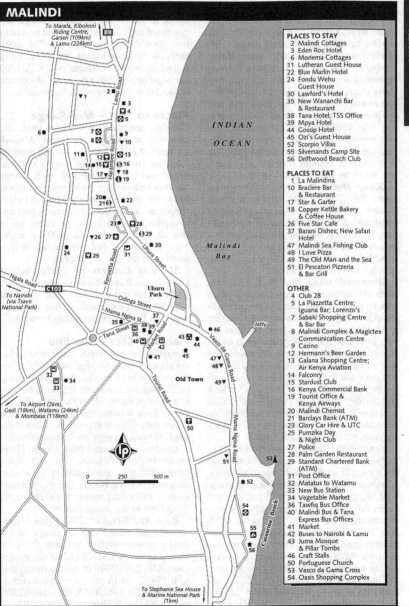

MALINDI

To Marafa, Kibokoni
Riding Centre,
Garsen (109km)
& Lamu (228km)

B8

Lamu Road

Harambee Road

Kenyatta Road

INDIAN
OCEAN

Uhuru Street

Malindi
Bay

Ngala Road

To Nairobi
(via Tsavo
National Park)

C103

Odinga Street

Uhuru
Park

Mama Ngina St

Tana Street

Market Road

Tourist Road

Vasco da Gama Road

Jetty

Old Town

Mama Ngina Road

To Airport (2km),
Gedi (18km), Watamu (24km)
& Mombasa (118km)

0   250   500 m

To Stephanie Sea House
& Marine National Park
(1km)

Casuarina Beach

PLACES TO STAY
2 Malindi Cottages
3 Eden Roc Hotel
6 Moriema Cottages
11 Lutheran Guest House
22 Blue Marlin Hotel
24 Fondu Wehu
   Guest House
30 Lawford's Hotel
35 New Wananchi Bar
   & Restaurant
38 Tana Hotel; TSS Office
39 Mpya Hotel
44 Gossip Hotel
45 Ozi's Guest House
52 Scorpio Villas
55 Silversands Camp Site
56 Driftwood Beach Club

PLACES TO EAT
1 La Malindina
10 Braciere Bar
   & Restaurant
17 Star & Garter
18 Copper Kettle Bakery
   & Coffee House
26 Five Star Cafe
37 Barani Dishes; New Safari
   Hotel
47 Malindi Sea Fishing Club
48 I Love Pizza
49 The Old Man and the Sea
51 El Pescatori Pizzeria
   & Bar Grill

OTHER
4 Club 28
5 La Piazzetta Centre;
   Iguana Bar; Lorenzo's
7 Sabaki Shopping Centre
   & Bar Bar
8 Malindi Complex & Magictex
   Communication Centre
9 Casino
12 Hermann's Beer Garden
13 Galana Shopping Centre;
   Air Kenya Aviation
14 Falconry
15 Stardust Club
16 Kenya Commercial Bank
19 Tourist Office &
   Kenya Airways
20 Malindi Chemist
21 Barclays Bank (ATM)
23 Glory Car Hire & UTC
25 Pumzika Day
   & Night Club
27 Police
28 Palm Garden Restaurant
29 Standard Chartered Bank
   (ATM)
31 Post Office
32 Matatus to Watamu
33 New Bus Station
34 Vegetable Market
36 Tawfiq Bus Office
40 Malindi Bus & Tana
   Express Bus Offices
41 Market
42 Buses to Nairobi & Lamu
43 Juma Mosque
   & Pillar Tombs
46 Craft Stalls
50 Portuguese Church
53 Vasco da Gama Cross
54 Oasis Shopping Complex

KSh 150/180. *Mpya Hotel (☎ 31658)* on Mama Ngina St in the centre of town has rooms for KSh 200/300 (KSh 300 with bath).

Most travellers prefer to stay in one of the hotels closer to the beach. *Ozi's Guest House (☎ 20218)* just off the foreshore road, is probably the best in this area. It's kept spotlessly clean, and safe lockers are available. The rooms (with shared bath) all have fans and mosquito nets. Singles/doubles/ triples cost KSh 450/700/950 with breakfast. The only problem here is that rooms on one side face the mosque, while those on the other side overlook Malindi Bus station – either way you'll be woken early.

Gossip Hotel (☎ 20307) on Vasco da Gama Rd, is a friendly well kept place, though a little expensive. Rooms (with bath) cost KSh 400/800 including breakfast. There's a restaurant downstairs with a mainly Italian menu (main courses cost up to KSh 500). It's next to the Metro Hotel, which seems to be a brothel.

Silversands Camp Site (☎ 20412) 2km south of town along the coast road, is another popular place. It costs KSh 150 per person to camp here (KSh 75 for children, KSh 20 for a mattress) and there are good facilities but very little shade. A laundry service is available and there are three types of 'tented bandas' for rent, ranging from KSh 390 to KSh 590 per night for a double (there is no tariff for singles). Bicycles can be rented for KSh 200 per day or KSh 30 by the hour. A cafe next door does simple meals at a reasonable price and there's a supermarket in the Oasis Complex nearby on the coast road.

Fondo Wehu Guest House (☎ 30017) in the western part of town, is by far the best place away from the beachfront. It's about a 15 minute walk from the bus station and is well signposted both from Kenyatta and Lamu Rds. It's a very popular place to stay, though there are only a few rooms (KSh 500/750). Rates include an excellent breakfast and free laundry service. Tasty snacks are also available. At the time of writing the rooftop terrace was being turned into a restaurant.

Lutheran Guest House (☎ 21098) off Lamu Rd at the back of the Malindi Complex, is excellent value. It's a popular place to stay and deservedly so. Clean well maintained rooms are set around a quiet garden courtyard and come with fans and mosquito nets. Doubles go for KSh 600/750 without/with bath, including breakfast. Fully furnished two-bed cottages cost KSh 1300 per night or KSh 5000 per week. Alcoholic drinks are not permitted on the premises.

Places to Stay – Mid-Range

There are few places in this price range and rates vary according to the season. *Malindi Cottages (☎ 20304)* out on Lamu Rd opposite Eden Roc Hotel, is OK but looking a bit old. Set around a swimming pool, each cottage has two bedrooms, a sitting room, kitchen, bathroom and veranda. Facilities include a fridge, gas cooker, cooking utensils, fans and mosquito nets. Each cottage sleeps up to five adults and costs KSh 2000 per night. There are also so-called single cottages with a double bed for KSh 750 per night.

Moriema Cottages (☎ 30816) behind Lutheran Guest House is a much better set up. There's a bar and restaurant; well appointed tidy cottages (with good kitchen facilities) cost KSh 1000/2000, including breakfast.

Places to Stay – Top End

Malindi's top end hotels cater mostly, but not exclusively, to package tourists from Europe on two to three-week holidays. If being by the beach is important, it's worth bearing in mind that the hotels to the north of town do not have a beach frontage as there is a wide swathe of sand dunes there; those to the south of town are right on the beachfront.

Lawford's Hotel and *Blue Marlin Hotel (☎ 20440 for both hotels)* are right in the town itself; they are owned by a German company, Kenya-Hotels GmbH. Singles/doubles (with half board) at either is KSh 2700/3700 in the low season.

Eden Roc Hotel (☎ 20480, fax 21225) north of town on Lamu Rd is one of the more pleasant resorts in Malindi. Rates for nonresidents are KSh 1804/2406 in bungalows, KSh 2060/2740 in deluxe rooms and KSh 2943/3924 in private suites. Resident rates are KSh 1465/1954, KSh 1650/2200 and KSh 1854/2472 respectively.

Scorpio Villas (☎ 20194, email scorpio@
swiftmombasa.com), south of the Vasco da
Gama cross, is spread throughout some 1.5
hectares of beautiful tropical gardens, with
three swimming pools and just 50m from the
beach. All the Lamu-style cottages are fully
furnished and you'll get your own house
steward. There's an excellent restaurant and
bar within the complex. It's Italian-owned
and Italians form the bulk of the clientele.
Doubles (with breakfast) are from KSh 2500
and from KSh 3600 (full board) in the low
season; add 20% in the high season. There
is also a well respected travel agent based
here.

Driftwood Beach Club (☎ 20155, fax
30712, email driftwood@swiftmombasa
.com) is further down the beach beyond the
Silversands Camp Site. This long-established hotel is used more by individual travellers than package groups and the clientele
is mainly, though not exclusively, British
and white Kenyan. The club offers a variety
of rooms from KSh 1200/1900 with fan and
shared bath to KSh 3200/4300 with air-con
and private bath. There are also two luxury
cottages each consisting of two air-con bedrooms, two bathrooms, living room and veranda, which will sleep up to four people for
KSh 7000. Children between the ages of
three and 11 years sharing with parents are
charged KSh 700. All prices include breakfast and full-board rates are also available.
The bar, restaurant and other facilities are
open to nonguests on payment of a temporary membership fee of KSh 200 per day or
KSh 700 per week, so there's often an interesting mix of budget travellers hanging
out beside the pool.

Stephanie Sea House (☎ 20720, fax
20613) overlooking the marine national
park is new and Italian-owned. It's also one
of the best hotels and has an excellent beach
completely free of seaweed. There are five
different 'seasons' and rates vary between
US$30 per person (including breakfast) in
the low season, through to US$50 to US$75
in the shoulder and high seasons. Transfers
can be arranged to/from both Mombasa and
Malindi airports for a fairly modest fee. The
resort has a good restaurant.

Places to Eat
Cheap African-style meals can be found in
the restaurants in or near the hotels in the
centre of town. *New Safari Hotel* and *Barani Dishes* opposite the Tana Hotel are both
local favourites but are closed during the
month of Ramadan.

Five Stars Cafe is an excellent and friendly
duka out near Fondo Wehu Guest House (see
Places to Stay earlier in this section), which
serves nyama choma, stews and *pilau*. You'll
get a meal here for under KSh 60.

Star & Garter (formerly the Trattoria) on
Harambee Rd offers something completely
different: MTV, pool tables, a king fish dinner for KSh 290 and a cold Tusker for only
KSh 60.

Braciere Bar & Restaurant on Lamu Rd
opposite the Malindi complex, is more expensive but still excellent value. The curries
here are good and cheap (KSh 230) and
they also do seafood.

El Pescatori Pizzeria & Grill Bar, not far
from the Vasco da Gama cross, is worth
checking out for lunch and dinner if you
like pizza (from KSh 250) or spaghetti
(from KSh 220). The rest of the menu, especially the seafood, is highly priced.

Gossip Hotel (see Places to Stay earlier in
this section) has good Italian food and the
prawns at *Malindi Sea Fishing Club* (KSh
300) are worth the KSh 100 entrance fee (see
Entertainment later in this section).

Driftwood Beach Club has a restaurant
that's good for a splurge (see Places to Stay –
Top End earlier in this section). You have to
pay KSh 100 for temporary membership (you
can use all the facilities including hot showers). Prices range from about KSh 200 to 500
and seafood is a speciality. The Sunday curry
lunch buffet is good value at KSh 350.

I Love Pizza in front of the fishing jetty
is also a popular place for a splurge. The
pizza is excellent (KSh 350) as are the more
expensive meals such as chicken casserole
and seafood (from KSh 600 to KSh 800).
The octopus salad (KSh 160) is also recommended. The restaurant is open from
noon to midnight daily.

The Old Man & the Sea (☎ 31106) is close
by and is arguably the best restaurant in town.

It specialises in seafood and you could easily part with KSh 1000 here given the menu – and that's before you look at the wine list. Its sister restaurant, *The Sun Also Rises* (☎ 83450), is in a beautiful old Arab building next to the old slave market in Mambrui just up the coast, is also highly regarded.

Two more Italian restaurants are found in the north of town. *Lorenzo's* (☎ 31758) in the La Piazzetta shopping centre is a full-blown Italian place, with air-con and an ever-present Italian owner. A short distance away *La Malindina* has a better reputation than Lorenzo's, but there is not much in it. Be prepared to part with at least KSh 1300 at either place.

Bar Bar in front of Sabaki shopping centre, is good for a decent cappuccino and Italian pastries. Truly a piece of Italy in Africa, by dark it's filled with local and visiting Italians. It also does good pizza and ice cream.

Copper Kettle Bakery & Coffee House next to Kenya Commercial Bank is also good for coffee and snacks.

Entertainment

Because Malindi is a holiday resort there are a number of bars and discos, some of which rock until dawn. The most infamous is *Stardust Club*, which generally doesn't get started until 11 pm and costs KSh 100 for women and KSh 400 for men (more on Saturday nights). Similar is *Club 28* next to Eden Roc Hotel. Beers at both places are about KSh 130.

Hermann's Beer Garden (featuring a makuti roof) is the liveliest tourist bar, followed closely by *Star & Garter*. MTV plays constantly at both and there are pool tables. If the presence of prostitutes makes you uncomfortable, these are probably not the places for you. The same applies to *Palm Garden Restaurant*, where you can listen to live bands. *Pumzika Day & Night Club*, back from the main strip, goes on and on just about every evening, while *Iguana Bar* has a reggae disco until 5 am on the weekend.

Malindi Sea Fishing Club, near Gossip Hotel, is a good place to sit with a beer looking out over the Indian Ocean. Snacks and meals are available, the beers are among the cheapest in town and there's satellite TV for

all those important sporting occasions. The clientele, mainly British and white Kenyans, are friendly; this is one of the best places on the coast to find a cheap private deep-sea fishing charter. These can be picked up for as little as US$250 for four people in the low season (see the boxed text 'Deep-Sea Fishing' earlier in the chapter). Daily membership for the club is KSh 100 or KSh 300 per week.

Getting There & Away

Air Two companies fly between Malindi and Lamu. Air Kenya Aviation (☎ 30808, email resvns@airkenya.com) has flights for US$85 one way and Kenya Airways (☎ 20237) has flights for KSh 3475.

Air Kenya Aviation flies between Malindi and Mombasa daily (KSh 1480 one way) and between Malindi and Nairobi on Wednesday, Friday and Sunday (KSh 5385). Kenya Airways flies between Malindi and Nairobi daily (KSh 5650 one way).

If you're relying on these flights to get back to Mombasa or Nairobi to connect with an international flight, make absolutely sure you have a confirmed booking or, preferably, go back a day before.

Bus & Matatu There's a new bus station in Malindi in the west of town. At the time of writing all buses except those going to Lamu or Mombasa were using it, but it's likely that all bus companies will move there.

Malindi to Mombasa At least five bus companies operate services between Malindi and Mombasa on a daily basis. They include Malindi Bus, TSS, Tana Express, KBS and the Faza Express. The first four have offices in Mombasa and Malindi but Faza Express only has offices in Mombasa and Lamu. The new KBS buses are smooth-running, 100-seaters, and can be recommended. There are numerous daily departures in either direction (KSh 70, 2½ hours).

Matatus also do this run (KSh 100, two hours).

Malindi to Lamu One of the biggest development plans in the region is the construction of a tarmac road from Malindi to

Thika via Garissa. At the time of writing only the Garsen to Garissa leg was incomplete. This new road has cut journey times to Lamu, but the 119km stretch of road between Garsen and Lamu remains bad.

Shifta (bandits) remain a major problem in this area. After a convoy containing the district commissioner of Baringo was attacked early in 1999 the army was called in. At the time of writing we cannot recommend taking the bus as sooner or later a tourist is going to get killed on this stretch of road. If you still want to go by bus make inquiries locally as to the current situation.

Three bus companies operate between Malindi and Lamu: Faza Express, TSS and Tawfiq. The official departure time for Lamu is 8.30 am, but this happens extremely rarely as all the buses have to come from Mombasa first. The pick-up point for Faza is outside New Safari Hotel in the centre of town. Other buses leave from outside their offices. The fare between Malindi and Lamu is KSh 250 and the journey takes about eight hours if you're lucky. The ferry to Lamu from the mainland costs KSh 70 and takes about 20 minutes.

Think seriously about flying.

Share-Taxi It's possible to find Peugeot 504 station wagons that do the journey between Malindi and Mombasa, but these are difficult to find in the opposite direction. They leave when full (seven passengers) and cost about KSh 200 per person. You'll find them at the bus station in Malindi but only in the mornings.

Train You can make advance reservations for the train from Mombasa to Nairobi at most of the large hotels in Malindi and at travel agencies, but you'll be charged for the service. You can call the station direct on (☎ 011-312220). See Getting There & Away in the Mombasa section for information on train fares and timetables.

Getting Around
You can rent bicycles from Silversands Camp Site, Ozi's Guest House (see Places to Stay – Budget earlier in this section) and

some of the mid-range or cheaper top end hotels. Charges range from KSh 200 to KSh 500 per day. This is probably the best way to get around town unless you prefer to walk.

Taxis are mainly concentrated along Lamu Rd between the post office and the Sabaki Centre. A very short journey shouldn't cost you more than KSh 150 and the fare to the airport is between KSh 300 and KSh 400.

Glory (☎ 20065), Hertz (☎ 20069), Avis and Europcar all have offices on Harambee Rd near Blue Marlin Hotel. In the high season book a car in advance to be sure of getting the class and type of vehicle you want.

AROUND MALINDI
Malindi Marine National Park
The most popular excursion from Malindi is to Malindi Marine National Park several kilometres south of town past Silversands Camp Site. Here you can rent a glass-bottomed boat to take you out to the coral reef. Masks and snorkels are provided though they're usually pretty well used. Fins can be rented for about KSh 100 from the kiosk on the beach inside the marine park gate. You'll have to negotiate at the jetty for a glass-bottom boat, but it shouldn't cost more than KSh 2000 (per boat) for a couple of hours.

There is still some amazing marine life in the park but the area is getting a little overused and there's been a lot of damage to the coral. Shell collectors have also degraded the area. Between March and June visibility is severely reduced by the silt in the water that gets washed in from the Galana River.

If you want to join a tour, Juspho Tours & Safaris (☎ 20140) is just one company that arranges trips for about KSh 900 per person.

Scuba diving can be arranged at the Driftwood Beach Club. A dive costs the equivalent of US$35, plus park entry fee. You can also complete a beginners PADI Open Water Diver course here for US$320, not including accommodation.

The marine park entry fee is US$5 for nonresidents and KSh 100 for residents. It is open daily from 7 am to 7 pm, but the boats only go out at low tide, so check the tide times in advance. The KWS Malindi

Deep-Sea Fishing

Kenya has some of the best game fishing in the world. Sailfish, swordfish, several species of shark, tuna and three species of marlin can all be caught off its shores. The hunting, fishing and drinking ghost of Hemingway lingers long at the coast and there's no reason why you can't pick up a case of beer, charter a boat and give it a go.

The nine month fishing season lasts from August to late April. August to November is best for tuna and December to March is good for billfish such as striped marlin, blue marlin, broadbill swordfish and sailfish. The best time to hook the biggest game fish on the coast, black marlin (the all-Kenyan record is 362kg), is between January and March.

You can expect to pay between US$350 and US$450 (much less in the low season) for a 10 to 12-hour trip.

The following game-fishing companies had good reputations at the time of writing:

• Hemingway's Hotel (☎ 0122-32624, fax 32256, email hemingways@form-net.com) PO Box 267, Watamu

• James Adcock (☎/fax 011-485527) PO Box 95693, Nyali, Mombasa

• Kingfisher (☎ 0123-21168, fax 30261) PO Box 29, Malindi

• Pemba Channel Fishing Club (☎ 011-313749, fax 316875) PO Box 86952, Mombasa

More informal and cheaper arrangements can sometimes be made at the Malindi Sea Fishing Club where you can pay as little as US$250 for four people in the low season; at Moorings Restaurant in Mtwapa; Swynford's Boatyard in Kilifi; and Timeless Camping in Vipingo.

office (☎ 20845), PO Box 109, Malindi, can provide information.

Excursions from Malindi

Obligingly the crocodiles at **Malindi Crocodile Farm & Snake Park** (☎ 20121) engage in a feeding frenzy at 4 pm every Wednes-

day and Friday. The park is just off the main road leading to the marine park and is open from 9 am to 5.30 pm daily. Entry is KSh 150/300 for children/adults.

The beautiful **Marafa Depression** is also called Hell's Kitchen, Devil's Kitchen or Nyari, 'the place broken by itself'. It lies about 30km directly north-east of Malindi near Marafa. Over the millennia wind and rain have eroded a ridge of sandstone into a grand geological sculpture that is at its most beautiful at dawn and dusk. It's about a 90km return trip, and you can go on a tour run by one of the big hotels or hire a taxi. Expect to pay about US$40 in either case.

The **Kibokoni Riding Centre** (☎ 21273, fax 21030), a few kilometres north of Malindi, is the place to contact for horse riding and they also have some accommodation.

The **Malindi Golf & Country Club** is a couple of kilometres north of town. It has a daily membership fee of KSh 100 (a round costs KSh 1000, but it has a range of other facilities as well).

Lamu Island

☎ 0124

In the early 1970s Lamu, Kenya's oldest living town, acquired a reputation as the Kathmandu of Africa – a place of fantasy and other-worldliness wrapped in a cloak of medieval romance. It drew all self-respecting seekers of the miraculous, the globe-trotters, and that much maligned bunch of people called hippies. The attraction was obvious. Both Kathmandu and Lamu were remote, unique and fascinating self-contained societies, which had somehow escaped the depredation of the 20th century with their culture, their centuries-old way of life and their architecture intact.

Men still wear the full length white robes known as *khanzus* and the *kofia* caps, and women cover themselves with the black wraparound *bui-bui* as they do in other Islamic cultures, although here it's a liberalised version that often hugs the body, falls short of the ankles and dispenses completely with the veil worn in front of the face.

Lamu has problems (namely a rising population, precious few resources and mass tourism) and there are signs of creeping gentrification as foreigners buy up more property on the island, but by and large little changes here.

Access is still by diesel-powered launch from the mainland (though there's an airstrip on Manda Island) and the only motor-powered vehicle on the island, other than the occasional tractor, is that owned by the district commissioner. The streets are far too narrow and winding to accommodate anything other than pedestrians or donkeys.

There are probably more dhows to be seen here than anywhere else along the East African coast and local festivals still take place with complete disregard for camera-toting tourists. The beach at Shela is still magnificent and uncluttered and nothing happens in a hurry. It's one of the most relaxing places you'll ever have the pleasure to visit.

History

The 20th century may have brought Lamu a measure of peace and tranquillity but it has not always been that way. The town was only of minor importance in the string of Swahili settlements that stretched from Somalia to Mozambique. Although it was a thriving port in it's own right by the early 1500s, it was generally politically dependent on the more important sultanate of Paté. Until the late 1700s it managed to avoid the frequent wars between the sultanates of Paté, Mombasa and Malindi following the decline of Portuguese influence in the area. There then followed many years of internecine strife between the island city-states of Lamu, Paté, Faza and Siyu.

In the early 1800s Lamu became subject to the sultanate of Zanzibar, which nominally controlled the whole of the coastal strip until Kenya became independent in 1963. Lamu had a slave-based economy (in common with the other Swahili coastal city-states) until the turn of the 20th century. The availability of cheap labour fuelled a period of economic growth for Lamu and traders grew rich by exporting ivory, cowries, tortoiseshell, mangrove poles, oil seeds and grains, and importing oriental linen, silks, spices and porcelain.

The British forced the Sultan of Zanzibar to sign an anti-slavery agreement in 1907. The economy of the island rapidly went into decline and stayed that way until very recently when increased receipts from tourism gave it a new lease of life. That decline, and its strong sense of tradition, is what has preserved the Lamu you see today. No other Swahili town, other than Zanzibar Town (on Tanzania's Unguja), can offer you such a cultural feast and an uncorrupted traditional style of architecture – if you can ignore the TV aerials.

LAMU TOWN
Information
Tourist Office There's a tourist information office just up from the waterfront near New Star Restaurant, but it's of limited use.

Money The Kenya Commercial Bank is the only bank on Lamu. It's open from 9 am to 3 pm Monday to Friday, and from 9 to 11 am Saturday. Unfortunately it will only take Visa for cash advances. Watch out for large commissions on credit cards and travellers cheques.

Post & Communications There are a couple of temperamental cardphones outside the post office.

You can send email from the Lamu Internet Spider (☎ 33107, email lamu@africa online.co.ke) based at New Mahrus Guest House. It's KSh 200/50 to send/receive a message. Surfing the Web is KSh 50 per minute!

Medical Services There is a hospital on the island, but you don't really want to visit it. Langoni Health Services is a small clinic behind New Lamu Palace Hotel. They can do malaria tests.

Bookshops The Lamu Book Centre, close to Whispers Coffee Shop, has a small but reasonable selection of English-language novels and other books. It's also the only place where you can buy local newspapers

KENYA

and international news magazines such as *Time* and *Newsweek*. It's open from 6.30 am to 12.30 pm and 2.30 to 9 pm daily.

Town Buildings

Lamu town dates back to at least the late 14th century when the Pwani Mosque was built. Most buildings date from the 18th century, but the lower parts and basements are often considerably older. The streets are narrow, cool and quiet and there are many small courtyards and intimate spaces enclosed by high walls. Traditionally, buildings were constructed from faced coral-rag blocks, wooden floors supported by mangrove poles, makuti roofs and intricately carved shutters for windows. The increasing use of imported materials is of great concern to conservationists.

One of the most outstanding features of the houses here, as in old Zanzibar Town, is the intricately **carved doors** and lintels, which have kept generations of carpenters busy. Sadly, many of them have disappeared in recent years but the skill has not been lost. Walk down to the far end of the waterfront in the opposite direction to Shela and you'll see them being made.

The numerous **mosques** in Lamu town give few outward signs of their purpose (few have minarets) and it can be hard to distinguish them from domestic buildings.

Lamu Museum

A couple of hours spent in the Lamu Museum, on the waterfront near Petley's Inn, is an excellent introduction to the culture and history of Lamu Island. It's one of the most interesting small museums in all of Kenya. There's a reconstruction of a traditional Swahili house, charts, maps, ethnological displays, models of the various types of dhows and two examples of the remarkable and ornately carved ivory *siwa* (a wind instrument peculiar to the coastal region, which is often used as a fanfare at weddings). There's a good slide show available – ask to see it. The museum is open from 8 am to 6 pm daily; entry costs KSh 200/100 for nonresident adults/children and KSh 50/10 for residents.

The museum has a good bookshop specialising in books on Lamu and Swahili culture, including *Lamu: A Study of the Swahili Town*, by Usam Ghaidan. If you're going to stay long in Lamu, the leaflet-map *Lamu: Map & Guide to the Archipelago, the Island & the Town* is worth buying.

Swahili House Museum

If the museum stokes your interest in Swahili culture then visit this museum tucked away off to the side of Yumbe House (a hotel). It's a beautifully restored traditional house with furniture and other house wares as well as a pleasant courtyard. Entry charges and opening hours are the same as the main museum.

Lamu Fort

The building of this massive structure was begun by the Sultan of Paté in 1810 and completed in 1823. From 1910 right up to 1984 it was used as a prison. It has recently undergone complete restoration and now houses an impressive and colourful illustrated walk-through display of the local environment and natural history (ideal for kids). The island's library is also housed here. Entry fees and opening times are the same as for the main museum.

German Postal Museum

In the late 1800s, the Germans regarded Lamu as an ideal base from where they could successfully and safely exploit the interior. The German East Africa Company set up a post office a short distance from New Star Restaurant and the old building is now a museum exhibiting photographs and memorabilia of that time. Entry fees and opening times are the same as for the main museum.

Donkey Sanctuary

One of the most unexpected sights on Lamu is the Donkey Sanctuary, which is run by the International Donkey Protection Trust of Sidmouth, Devon, UK. Injured, sick or worn-out donkeys (the common beast of burden) are brought here to find rest and protection. Although the free clinic has been going since 1985, land for the sanctuary wasn't purchased until 4 July 1987, a day that is celebrated by the sanctuary's manager as Donkey Independence Day (it also just happens to coincide with America's Independence Day!). There are no regular opening hours and entry is free.

Dhow Trips

Taking a dhow trip is almost obligatory, and it is a very relaxing way to pass a day. You will constantly be approached while walking along the waterfront by people wanting to take you out for a trip (by asking around you'll quickly discover who the reliable

captains are). The cost is about KSh 300 per person for four or more people and KSh 400 for less than four people. Five is a comfortable number as the boats are not very big.

The price includes fishing and snorkelling, although both can be disappointing as it's not easy to catch fish during the day, and the best snorkelling is a couple of hours away. A barbecue fish lunch on the beach at Manda is provided, supposedly with the fish you have caught but usually with fish provided by the captain. Make sure you take a hat and some sunblock as there is rarely any shade on the dhows, despite assurances to the contrary.

Day trips lasting six to eight hours usually head to Manda Toto for snorkelling and then lunch on the island. Longer trips (say three days) head to Paté and five-day trips journey to Kiwayu. As always, don't jump at the first offer, negotiate hard and find out just what will be included. Checking out the dhow before handing over any money is essential for these long trips. If you're in a group of six, the cost should work out about US$8 per person per day which includes accommodation.

As these boats rely on the wind and tide, it is easy to get becalmed out in the channels between the islands or find yourself stranded by the tide, so occasionally a three day trip can turn into a five-day trip, although this is unusual.

Peponi Hotel (see their listing in the Shela section later in this chapter) also offers full moon dhow cruises for KSh 4500 (minimum eight people), including drinks, wine and a lobster dinner.

Maulid Festival

This festival is a celebration of the birth of the Prophet Mohamed and takes place in the middle of the year. Much singing, dancing and general jollity takes place around this time and organised events include; swimming galas, poetry reading, donkey races for young boys and dhow races for all the dhow captains. Most of the celebrations are centred around Lamu's two main mosques and the festival has been celebrated on the island for over one hundred years.

KENYA

Excursions from Lamu Town

Matondoni Village You'll see many dhows anchored along the waterfront at Lamu town and at Shela in the harbour at the southern end of town; if you want to see them being built or repaired the best place is at the village of Matondoni on the west of the island.

To get there you have a choice of walking (about two hours, but you'll need to ask local people the way), hiring a donkey, or hiring a dhow. If you choose the dhow it will cost KSh 500 per person (minimum five passengers) but it usually includes a barbecue fish lunch.

Kipongani Village This place is also worth a visit. Local people make straw mats, baskets and hats. It's a friendly place; tea and snacks can be arranged plus there's a beautiful empty beach nearby with waves. You could walk there or take a dhow.

Places to Stay – Budget

Lamu has been catering for budget travellers for some two decades and there are still loads of cheap places to stay despite the downturn in the tourist industry. Running water can be a problem in many places. If you're thinking of staying for a month or more, consider renting a whole house; it's possible to find some remarkably luxurious places (especially around Shela, see that section later in this chapter).

Lamu Guest House (☎ 33338) close to the Lamu Museum is clean and simple and very good value. The best rooms here are probably those on the top floor that catch the sea breeze. Doubles with bath and fan cost KSh 500 to KSh 600 and triples are KSh 800. There are also some rooms with shared bath for about KSh 400.

New Castle Lodge is next to the fort that overlooks the main square, and since the lodge is fairly high up it picks up sea breezes. It used to be very popular with backpackers but has seen better days. A range of singles/doubles with shared bath cost KSh 200/300. The rooms have mosquito nets and fans. There's a wide choice of rooms, but privacy can be a problem as the walls partitioning some of the rooms don't reach the ceiling.

Pole Pole Guest House is north of the centre of town and back from the waterfront. One of the tallest buildings in Lamu town, it has 15 doubles with bath, fans and mosquito nets for KSh 400. There's a spacious, makuti-roofed area on top of the hotel (great views over the town and the waterfront). This is probably the best of the cheapies.

Peace Guest House is way out the back of town through a maze of sandy alleyways, about a 15-minute walk from the waterfront. It is very clean, provides mosquito nets and charges KSh 200 for a bed in a four-bed dorm including breakfast. Spacious doubles with bath and fan start at KSh 500. If you're staying more than one or two nights, you can get a 20% discount. Camping is KSh 100 per tent, including the use of kitchen facilities and a fridge. Surrounded by gardens and flowering trees, it has been popular for years, though it is quite a way from the centre of town. It's signposted from the waterfront but you can still get lost in the last 300m.

Sunshine Guesthouse is a relatively new place with four clean doubles (with bath) for about KSh 400 (you'll have to bargain but not too hard). Other rooms are available at negotiable prices. There's a rooftop terrace and a shared kitchen and fridge. It's handy if you're on a tight budget.

Bush Guest House behind Bush Gardens Restaurant has a communal kitchen, plus a lounge, cold showers, good toilets and great views from the rooftop terrace. Rooms range from bed only (KSh 200) to a 'suite' (KSh 1000). Ask at the restaurant for details of a private house for rent.

Places to Stay – Mid-Range

Casuarina Rest House (☎ 33123) is good value in this range. Formerly the police headquarters, it offers large, airy rooms with good views; it's clean and well maintained but often full. Doubles with bath start at KSh 500 in the low season; cheaper rooms with shared bath are available.

Stone House Hotel (☎ 33544, bookings on ☎ 02-226384 through Kisiwani Ltd in Nairobi, email kisiwani@swiftkenya.com) is

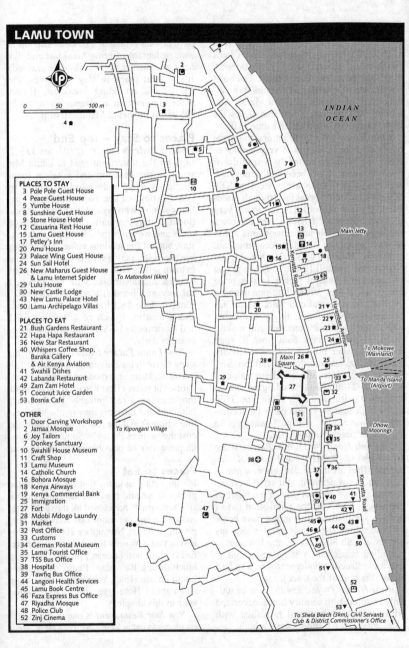

LAMU TOWN

0   50   100 m

INDIAN OCEAN

Main Jetty

To Matondoni (6km)

To Mokowe (Mainland)

To Manda Island (Airport)

Main Square

Dhow Moorings

To Kipongani Village

To Shela Beach (3km), Civil Servants Club & District Commissioner's Office

PLACES TO STAY
3 Pole Pole Guest House
4 Peace Guest House
5 Yumbe House
8 Sunshine Guest House
9 Stone House Hotel
12 Casuarina Rest House
15 Lamu Guest House
17 Petley's Inn
20 Amu House
23 Palace Wing Guest House
24 Sun Sail Hotel
26 New Maharus Guest House & Lamu Internet Spider
29 Lulu House
30 New Castle Lodge
43 New Lamu Palace Hotel
50 Lamu Archipelago Villas

PLACES TO EAT
21 Bush Gardens Restaurant
22 Hapa Hapa Restaurant
36 New Star Restaurant
40 Whispers Coffee Shop, Baraka Gallery & Air Kenya Aviation
41 Swahili Dishes
42 Labanda Restaurant
49 Zam Zam Hotel
51 Coconut Juice Garden
53 Bosnia Cafe

OTHER
1 Door Carving Workshops
2 Jamaa Mosque
6 Joy Tailors
7 Donkey Sanctuary
10 Swahili House Museum
11 Craft Shop
13 Lamu Museum
14 Catholic Church
16 Bohora Mosque
18 Kenya Airways
19 Kenya Commercial Bank
25 Immigration
27 Fort
28 Mdobi Mdogo Laundry
31 Market
32 Post Office
33 Customs
34 German Postal Museum
35 Lamu Tourist Office
37 TSS Bus Office
38 Hospital
39 Tawfiq Bus Office
44 Langoni Health Services
45 Lamu Book Centre
46 Faza Express Bus Office
47 Riyadha Mosque
48 Police Club
52 Zinj Cinema

Kenyatta Road

Harambee Avenue

more expensive but excellent value. Beautiful singles/doubles with bath cost KSh 1500/2100 which includes breakfast. Check which rooms face the sea; if yours doesn't, there may be a reduction in rates. The hotel has its own superb rooftop restaurant (no alcoholic drinks) with excellent views. Add around 30% for half board and if it's the high season, add another 10% onto that.

Lulu House (☎ 33539) among the maze of streets behind the fort is very similar in style and quality. Formerly a traditional Swahili house, it has been well renovated, and rooms with bath are a steal at KSh 600/800, including breakfast (though prices rise in the high season). The rooms are very pleasant, the staff friendly and there's a rooftop area, a table tennis room and a safe to leave valuables – highly recommended.

Yumbe House (☎ 33101, fax 33300) close to the Swahili House Museum is one of the most beautiful places in this price range. It's a four storey traditional house surrounding a central courtyard which has been superbly and sensitively converted into a hotel with airy terraces and makuti roofs. All rooms have bath (towels, soap and toilet paper provided), are spotlessly clean and have mosquito nets and fan. Singles/doubles/triples are excellent value at KSh 1100/2100/2900 (including breakfast) in the low season and KSh 1290/2700/3860 in the high season. If you can't be accommodated here, they will pass you over to their sister hotel, *Yumbe Villa*.

Sun Sail Hotel (☎ 33269), *Palace Wing Guest House* (☎ 33107) and *Lamu Archipelago Villas* are three relatively new places right on the waterfront. All have tremendous sea views and put you in the heart of the action; however, the renovation hasn't been as sympathetic as it might have been, and the rooms are a little spartan. Rooms are about KSh 800/1500 in the low season including breakfast. A large restaurant is under construction underneath the Sun Sail Hotel (the best of the three).

Amu House (☎/fax 33420) is a beautifully restored 16th century house decorated with plaster carvings and furnished with local antiques. All rooms have a bath, fan,

antique beds and mosquito nets, and some have private verandas. The hotel also has its own restaurant offering breakfast and dinner (specialising in Swahili-style seafood). It's a great place to stay and costs KSh 1500/2000, including breakfast. If you make a reservation in advance and arrive by air, you'll be met at Manda airstrip.

Places to Stay – Top End

Historic *Petley's Inn* (☎ 33107, fax 33378) right on the waterfront next to Lamu Museum, is the best top end hotel in town. Originally set up in the late 19th century by Percy Petley – a somewhat eccentric English colonist who retired to Lamu – traditional features remain, including makuti roofs and woven blinds. It's a nice place to stay, but not tremendous value. The rooftop bar and restaurant is only one of two places in town selling cold beer and there is a pool. Singles/doubles/triples with sea views, a balcony and breakfast are US$70/90/105. Rates include boat transfer to/from Manda Island airstrip. Lunch costs about US$12 and dinner costs US$15. The seafood menu changes daily.

New Lamu Palace Hotel is owned by the same German businessmen as Petley's. It is intrusive, large and modern by Lamu standards, but some effort has recently been put into creating a recognisably Lamu facade (although the interiors may not be to everyone's liking). All the rooms have a bath and cost the same as Petley's. Some negotiation on price may be possible in the low season.

Places to Eat

It's important to know that *all* of the cheap places to eat and many of the more expensive restaurants are closed all day until after sunset during the month of Ramadan (beginning 27/16/5 November 2000/1/2). This leaves you with only four choices for breakfast (if your hotel doesn't provide this) and lunch during Ramadan: Petley's Inn, New Lamu Palace Hotel, Whispers Coffee Shop and Peponi Hotel (see the Shela section later in this chapter).

New Star Restaurant is one of the cheapest places to eat in Lamu. You certainly won't beat the prices and some people recommend it highly, but service can be slow. Fish and chips/rice costs KSh 150 to KSh 180.

Swahili Dishes just off the waterfront is cheaper still but very basic. This tiny place caters purely for the locals and serves no-frills African food at rock-bottom prices (around KSh 60). **Zam Zam Hotel** close to the Lamu Book Centre and **Bosnia Cafe** close to the Zinj Cinema are two other local eateries well worth checking out. The latter, set up by an ex-soldier, serves a fine pilau and biryani (KSh 60).

Labanda Restaurant, close by the dhow moorings, serves some vegetarian dishes, *poulet yassa* (a delicious Senegalese chicken dish – KSh 280) and the usual Swahili cuisine. The quality varies at this place.

Bush Gardens on the waterfront, is a little more expensive but is arguably the best seafood restaurant in Lamu. It's run by the very personable and energetic 'Bush Baby' who personally supervises the cooking – this can sometimes make for slow service but guarantees you an excellent meal. Fish dishes (barracuda, tuna, snapper or shark) cost KSh 200, lobster in coconut sauce is KSh 650 and a seafood platter is KSh 800. All meals are served with chips or coconut rice and salad, and fruit juices are also available. Next door is **Hapa Hapa Restaurant**, which is also very good and offers a similar range of dishes as Bush Gardens (and the prices are about the same too).

Coconut Juice Garden on 'Main Street' just beyond the Lamu Book Centre should be visited at least once by juice lovers. It's still selling excellent, cheap fruit juices and coconut milk, which is just as well – a sign on the waterfront reads: 'Recommended in the Lonely Planet'.

Ali Hippy has been wandering around Lamu town offering home-cooked seafood to travellers for over 30 years. This can be a variable experience, but probably one worth trying once. You can expect to pay around KSh 200.

Whispers Coffee Shop in the same building as Baraka Gallery on 'Main Street' in Lamu town is worth trying for an upmarket snack or coffee. Main meals are less than

KSh 300 and it's open from 8.45 am to 8.45 pm. As it's European-owned, it doesn't close during Ramadan.

Stone House Hotel has surely one of the best rooftop restaurants in Lamu (see Places to Stay – Mid-Range earlier in this section). The wonderful panorama of the town and seafront is matched by the quality of the food. A good meal here costs about KSh 600.

Entertainment

Bars There are a number of places where you can get a beer in Lamu itself but only three of them have cold beers. One of them is the makuti-roofed terrace bar at **Petley's Inn**. This is a very fine place to relax and catch the sea breeze, and can get quite animated later in the evening. It's the most popular watering hole on the island and their (expensive) food is good (see under Places to Stay – Top End).

New Lamu Palace Hotel on the waterfront is another place with cold beer and an interesting place to watch the passing parade of pedestrians. Every Friday and Saturday night they organise a beach party over at their private restaurant on Manda Island. There is a restaurant and bar and the party rages until dawn. The trip over from outside the hotel costs KSh 100 return. Boats run all night. The island restaurant also opens every lunch-time and once you arrange your transport (either at the hotel or down on the waterfront) you can spend the day there.

Civil Servants' Club occasionally has a disco on Friday and Saturday nights so keep an eye out for advertising posters around town. Entry costs KSh 100 and it's a good night out.

Cinema A number of little video theatres are dotted around Lamu, but for the real thing head to Zinj Cinema at the southern end of town. It shows the usual mix of low-budget Hollywood flicks and Indian action movies, and is a great place to spend an evening. Tickets start at KSh 25.

Getting There & Away

Air Two companies operate one flight daily to Lamu. Air Kenya Aviation (☎ 33445, email resvns@airkenya.com) based at Nairobi's

Wilson airport has daily flights between Lamu and Nairobi (US$135 one way), Mombasa (US$85) and Malindi (US$65). Kenya Airways (☎ 32040) has daily flights between Lamu and Malindi (KSh 3475) and Nairobi (KSh 8490).

With Kenya Airways there is the possibility of flying to Lamu straight after your arrival in Kenya; connections with other international Kenya Airways flights are favourable, and Lamu makes a great place to start your trip. However, if you're relying on these flights to get back to Mombasa or Nairobi to connect with an international flight then make absolutely sure you have a confirmed booking or, preferably, go back a day before.

Air Kenya Aviation has an office in Baraka House, next door to Whispers Coffee Shop; Kenya Airways is based on the waterfront close to Petley's Inn.

The airport at Lamu is an airstrip on Manda Island and the ferry across the channel to Lamu costs KSh 70. You will probably be met by registered guides at the airport who will offer to carry your bags to the hotel of your choice for a small consideration (around KSh 100).

Bus & Ferry Buses travelling between Malindi and Lamu have been subject to attack by bandits in the past and there is some risk if you travel this way (see the warning under Getting There & Away in the Malindi section earlier in this chapter) – consider flying.

Three bus companies operate between Mombasa, Malindi and Lamu: Faza Express, TSS and Tawfiq. Faza has offices in Mombasa and Lamu but not in Malindi. The fare between Malindi and Lamu is KSh 250 (eight hours if you're lucky) and between Mombasa and Lamu it's KSh 300.

Buses from Lamu are more prompt and leave at 7 am. The buses to/from Lamu arrive and depart from the ferry jetty on the mainland not far from Mokowe. Motorised ferries to Lamu cost KSh 70 per person and take about 20 minutes (this means you have to get up early if travelling from Lamu to Malindi/Mombasa). Book early as demand is heavy, and be aware of the dangers of travelling overland to Malindi.

Boat Dhows can be hired for trips around the Lamu archipelago (see Dhow Trips earlier in this section), but the chances of finding a dhow sailing to Mombasa are slight (and you'll need to get permission to sail from the district commissioner). The journey takes two days on average and prices are negotiable.

Frequent motorised dhows shuttle back and forth between Lamu town and Shela (KSh 50 per person) and are a good alternative to walking (see Getting There & Away in the Shela section following).

There are frequent ferries (KSh 70) between Lamu town and the bus terminal on the mainland (near Mokowe). Ferries between the airstrip on Manda Island and Lamu also cost KSh 70.

There are also regular ferries between Lamu and Paté Island.

SHELA

Shela village, a 40-minute walk from Lamu town, is a pleasant little village well worth a wander around. The ancestors of the people here came from Takwa on Manda Island when that settlement was abandoned in the late 17th century; they still speak a dialect of Swahili that is distinct from that of Lamu. Don't miss the famous mosque with its characteristic minaret at the back of Peponi Hotel. Many of the houses in this village have been bought up and restored by foreigners in the last few years, but while it has a surprising air of affluence, the languorous atmosphere remains unspoiled. Quite a few travellers prefer to stay in Shela rather than in Lamu town.

The Beach

There's no beach on the Lamu town waterfront itself. What there is here is a muddy, garbage-strewn mess in urgent need of a major clean-up. For a white-sand beach and crystal-clear water you need to go to Shela, a 40-minute walk or 10-minute trip by dhow from Lamu town. The beach starts at Peponi Hotel, circles around the headland and continues all the way along the Indian Ocean side of the island. The best part of the beach if you want waves is well past Peponi Hotel – there's no surf at Peponi because you're still in the channel between Lamu and Manda islands.

Peponi Hotel is a water-sports centre and there are a number of activities (including water-skiing, windsurfing and scuba diving) and equipment are available to both guests and nonguests.

Places to Stay – Mid-Range & Top End

There are a number of good, reasonably priced options in Shela.

Shela Bahari Guest House (☎ 32046, fax 33029) between Peponi Hotel and Kijani House has rooms above a rather good terrace restaurant. A number of rooms open onto a wide balcony above the bay; doubles go for between KSh 1500 and KSh 3000 (including breakfast), depending on the season and how hard you bargain – aim for about KSh 500 per person – highly recommended.

Pwani Guest House (☎ 33540) at the back of Peponi Hotel is a very pleasant place with five spacious doubles. All rooms have two double beds as well as a child's cot and cost KSh 2000 (including breakfast) in the low season, rising to KSh 3500 in the high season. All have a bath, hot water and mosquito nets plus there's a beautiful rooftop lounge area overlooking the channel.

White House Guest House (☎ 33092, fax 33542) behind Pwani is a new place. There are five rooms, someone to run around after you as well as a kitchen with two fridges for self-caterers. You can also rent windsurfers. Rooms cost KSh 1200/1500 in the low season, rising to KSh 1500/2000 in the high season including breakfast.

Peponi Hotel (☎ 33421, fax 33029, email peponi@users.africaonline.co.ke) at the far end of Shela village and right on the beach is *the* top end hotel on the island. It consists of whitewashed cottages with their own verandas, which face the channel between Lamu and Manda islands, and is reckoned to be one of the best hotels in the country. Standard singles/doubles cost US$140/180 and superior rooms cost US$170/230, including breakfast. For full board, add about 30%. Advance booking is essential. Peponi Hotel is a water-sports centre and there are a number of activities and equipment available both to guests and nonguests (see The Beach earlier in this section). Other facilities open to nonguests are the bar and the lunch-time barbecue area (Barbecue Grill), which serves very tasty fish and meat dishes (open during Ramadan). The hotel is closed during May and June.

Kijani House (☎ 33235, fax 33237) is at the far end of Shela village and is right on the beach. It has beautifully furnished rooms arranged around a lush and colourful garden. There are two swimming pools, and like Peponi, a number of activities and trips can be arranged. Rooms cost US$80/120, including breakfast in the standard rooms and US$95/150 in the superior rooms. Full-board rates are US$115/190 and US$130/220 respectively. Children between the ages of three and 12 are approximately half price. Boat transfers to/from Manda airstrip are free. Kijani is closed between April and June.

Island Hotel (☎ 33290, fax 33568, book on ☎ 02-446384 through Kisiwani Ltd in Nairobi, email kisiwani@swiftkenya.com) in the centre of Shela village is a superb traditional Lamu-style house. It has the romantic rooftop Barracuda Restaurant and is only a five-minute walk from the waterfront. The hotel has 14 rooms, including three family rooms. Rooms are US$51/72 with breakfast and US$73/115 with full board. Children between the ages of three and 12 sharing their parents room are charged US$13 for bed and breakfast and US$28 for full board. Rates are the same year-round and include boat transfers to/from Manda Island airstrip.

Places to Eat

Shaniyake Tea Room on the way to Shela from Lamu town offers simple food for about KSh 70. *Ragali Cafe* is the only cheap place in the centre of Shela; the usual stew and ugali goes for KSh 60.

Stop Over Restaurant right on the beach in Shela, was being renovated at the time of writing and should be open again. Similar but offering a slightly wider range, is *Bahari Restaurant* on the foreshore between Kijani House and Peponi Hotel. Lobster here can cost as little as KSh 450.

The rooftop **Barracuda Restaurant** at Island Hotel (see their listing under Places to Stay – Top End earlier in this section) is also ideal for romantic nights out. It's open to nonguests, the food is excellent and the prices are reasonable. Starters go for KSh 120 to KSh 160 and main dishes range from KSh 290 (fish) to KSh 780 (lobster).

Barbecue Grill at Peponi Hotel in Shela (open during Ramadan, see their listing under Places to Stay – Top End earlier in this section) is good for a modest splurge. Good snacks cost around KSh 500 (but the food has been known to be rather average and not good value).

Entertainment

Peponi Hotel is a mandatory watering hole (see their listing under Places to Stay – Mid-Range & Top End earlier in this section). The beer here (KSh 140) is always ice cold and the bar overlooks the channel; it's open all day until late. The hotel certainly attracts the jetset and there are always a few characters around, but if you don't own a yacht you might not get some of their jokes.

Getting There & Away

To get to Shela, follow the waterfront road south till it ends and then follow the shore line. If the tide is out, you can walk along the beach most of the way. When it's in, you may well have to do a considerable amount of wading (up to your thighs and deeper). There is a path behind the beach but it's not easy to follow.

Between Lamu town and Shela there are plenty of motorised dhows in either direction throughout the day until around sunset (KSh 50 per person or KSh 200 for the boat). They'll take up to 10 people at a time. Expect to have to wade back to shore at the Lamu town end but not at the Shela end.

ISLANDS AROUND LAMU

The islands of Manda, Paté and Kiwayu are great to explore. In particular the settlements of Paté, Faza and Siyu (on Paté Island) have fascinating histories dating back the 7th and 8th centuries when Arab traders first sailed down these shores. Swahili ruins

Kenyan Reefs

In March 1997 unusually warm currents, caused in part by the climatic extremes of El Niño, sent much of the coral on the Kenyan coast into shock. There was a huge coral die-off; some marine parks went from 45 to 10% coral cover, while on other unprotected reefs the coral cover has dropped from 25 to 10%. The area surrounding Kiwayu and Kiunga Marine National Reserve was particularly badly affected.

Once underwater the effect of this die-off is immediately noticeable. In many places there is an obvious loss of colour and the once-vibrant reefs now look grey, dull and dead. The effects on other marine life is harder to judge. To the casual observer it may seem like business as usual with myriad colourful fish at every turn, but the Wildlife Conservation Society is currently undertaking a comprehensive survey of fish and other marine life that may show otherwise.

But it's not all doom and gloom. Coral may be easily killed by human touch, pollution and carelessly tossed anchors, but as an organism it is biologically resilient and will regenerate given time. Regeneration could be as short as five years, or may take up to 20 years. Much depends on how frequently unusually warm currents pass along the East African coast. On average they come every four years or so and are rarely devastating, but increasingly extreme global weather patterns suggest the coral may be in for a tough time in years to come.

are to be found in numerous places on Paté and Manda islands, while Kiwayu is part of the Kiunga Marine Reserve.

Almost everyone takes a half-day trip to the extensive **Takwa ruins** at the head of the creek that almost bisects Manda Island. Just off the north-eastern coast of Manda is **Manda Toto Island**, which offers some of the best snorkelling possibilities in the archipelago (probably better than at Kiunga Marine Reserve). The reefs here are excellent and there are also good beaches.

There are a number of historical sites on Paté Island including **Paté town**, **Siyu**,

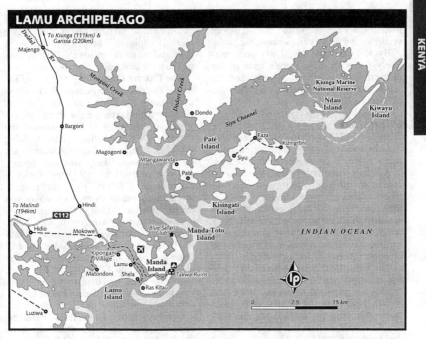

LAMU ARCHIPELAGO

To Kiunga (111km) &
Garissa (220km)

Majengo

Dudu R.

Mongani Creek

Bargoni

Dodori Creek

Dondo

Siyu Channel

Kiunga Marine
National Reserve

Ndau
Island

Kiwayu
Island

Faza

Kizingitini

Paté
Island

Magogoni

Mtangawanda

Siyu

Paté

To Malindi
(194km)

C112

Hindi

Kisingati
Island

INDIAN OCEAN

Hidio

Mokowe

Blue Safari
Club

Manda Toto
Island

Kipongani
Village

Lamu

Matondoni

Shela

Manda
Island

Takwa Ruins

Lamu
Island

Ras Kitau

Luziwa

0   7.5   15 km

Mtangawanda and **Faza**. All are still inhabited – mainly by fishermen and mangrove-pole cutters – very little effort has been put into preserving or clearing the remains of these once powerful Swahili city-states.

Places to Stay & Eat
The only place to stay on Manda Island is the *camp site* adjacent to the ruins but very few people stay here because facilities are minimal. Most people seem to sleep on the beach.

Accommodation and food on Paté Island is easy to arrange with local families. The cost is negotiable but very reasonable at around KSh 200 per person.

Getting There & Away
Both Manda and Paté islands can be reached by infrequent motorised dhows from Lamu, but the best method of exploration is to take a dhow trip from Lamu (see Dhow Trips in the Lamu Town section earlier in this chapter).

Coastal Hinterland

There are a number of national parks in the hinterland behind the coast. Shimba Hills is south of Mombasa, while Tsavo straddles the main Nairobi-Mombasa A109 road.

TSAVO NATIONAL PARK
Tsavo is the largest national park in Kenya and is split into Tsavo West National Park, with an area of 9000 sq km and Tsavo East National Park, which covers 11,700 sq km.

The northern area of Tsavo West, west of the Nairobi-Mombasa road, is the most developed and has some excellent scenery. It is particularly beautiful at the end of the wet season when things are green. At other times it tends to get very dusty in Tsavo. Tsavo East consists of vast rolling plains with scrubby vegetation. Almost the entire area north of the Galana River (and this constitutes the bulk of the park) is off limits to the general public due to the ongoing campaign against poachers. The rhino population has been decimated but happily it seems the authorities are winning the battle.

By Kenyan standards, Tsavo sees relatively few visitors so there's none of the congestion found in other parks and reserves and its size means you can get right off the beaten track.

Information

Entry is US$23 per person per day but note that the two parks are administered separately, so you'll pay separate entrance fees.

All track junctions in Tsavo West have a numbered and signposted cairn, which in theory makes navigation simple. However, the cairns are not all there (especially in the southern reaches of the park), and those which are there don't always give comprehensive directions. A map marked with the numbered intersections is a real help.

Don't attempt this park without a 4WD if you intend to get off the main routes. You can certainly get to Kilaguni Lodge and Ngulia Lodge on the main service road from Mtito Andei in a 2WD but don't attempt to enter through the Tsavo Gate further south in a 2WD.

Fuel is available at Kilaguni and Ngulia lodges in Tsavo West.

Tsavo West National Park

The main access to Tsavo West is through the Mtito Andei Gate on the Mombasa-Nairobi road near the northern end of the park. The park headquarters is here.

The focus here is the watering holes by the Kilaguni and Ngulia lodges. The one at Kilaguni is the best and attracts a huge variety of animals and birds, particularly during the dry season.

The **Mzima Springs** are not far from Kilaguni Lodge and the pools here are favourite haunts of both hippo and crocodile. The underwater viewing chamber was designed to give you a view of the hippos' submarine activities, but the hippos have retreated to the far end of the pool. There are, however, plenty of fish.

Also in the area of the lodges is the spectacular **Shetani lava flow** and **caves**. Both

are worth investigating, though for the caves you'll need to exercise caution and carry a torch (flashlight). The black lava flow is spectacular and is outside the Chyulu Gate on the track that leads to Amboseli.

The **Chaimu Crater** just south-east of Kilaguni Lodge and the **Roaring Rocks** viewpoint nearby can also be climbed. The view from the latter is stunning, with falcons, eagles and buzzards whirling around the cliffs. While there is little danger walking these trails be aware that park animals are far from tame and keep your eyes open – just ask yourself why Roaring Rocks is called Roaring Rocks. These nature trails are the only places in the park where you are permitted to get out of the vehicle.

Another attraction in Tsavo West is the **Ngulia Rhino Sanctuary**, at the base of Ngulia Hills, not far from Ngulia Lodge. Here 70 sq km has been surrounded by a metre-high electric fence, and 42 black rhinos live here in relative security. There are tracks within the enclosed area and there's a good chance of seeing one of these elusive creatures.

Climbers may be interested in **Tembo Peak** in the Ngulia Hills, which has some good technical climbing. Trekking may also be possible. Approach the warden in advance for further information (☎ 0302-22483) PO Box 71, Mtito Andei.

Places to Stay – Budget Tsavo West has a number of basic *camp sites*, namely close to each of the three main gates (Tsavo, Mtito Andei and Chyulu). The fees are US$8 per person. There are also a number of *special camp sites*.

Down on Lake Jipe are some simple *bandas* and a *camp site*.

Kitani Safari Camp and *Ngulia Safari Camp* has, by park standards, quite cheap self-contained accommodation at KSh 2500 per one bedroom banda with a bathroom and fully equipped kitchen. Kitani Camp is in the north-west of the park (not the best location), while Ngulia camp is perched on the edge of the Ngulia Hills and with its elevation has some fine views. Both camps supply bedding, towels, mosquito nets and kerosene lanterns. Take with you toilet

TSAVO EAST & WEST NATIONAL PARKS

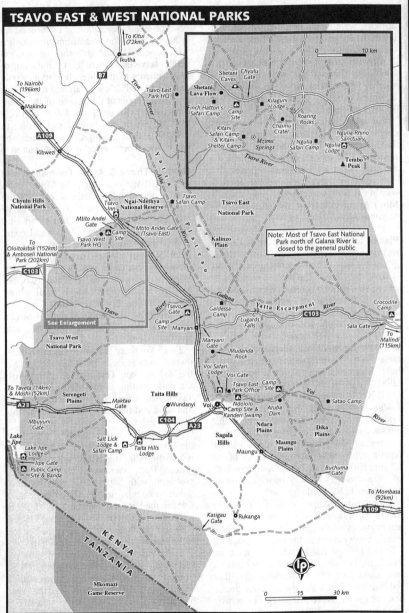

To Kitui
(72km)

Ikutha

B7

To Nairobi
(196km)

Makindu

A109

Kibwezi

Tiva

Tsavo East
Park HQ

0   10 km

Shetani   Chyulu
Caves   Gate

Shetani
Lava Flow

Finch Hatton's
Safari Camp

Camp
Site

Kilaguni
Lodge

Roaring
Rocks

Kitani
Safari Camp
& Kitani
Shelter Camp

Mzima
Springs

Chaimu
Crater

Ngulia
Safari Camp

Ngulia Rhino
Sanctuary

Ngulia
Lodge

Tsavo River

Tembo
Peak

Chyulu Hills
National Park

Athi

Yatta

River

Tsavo
Inn

Ngai-Ndethya
National Reserve

Mtito Andei
Gate

To
Oloitokitok (152km)
& Amboseli National
Park (202km)

C103

Tsavo
Safari Camp

Tsavo West
Park HQ

Mtito Andei Gate
(Tsavo East)

Camp
Site

Galana

River

Tsavo East
National Park

Kalinzo
Plain

Plateau

Note: Most of Tsavo East National
Park north of Galana River is
closed to the general public

Galana

Yatta Escarpment

River

Crocodile
Camp

Tsavo

See Enlargement

Tsavo West
National Park

River

Tsavo
Gate

Camp
Site

Manyani

Galdessa
Camp

Lugards
Falls

C103

Sala Gate

To
Malindi
(115km)

Manyani
Gate

Mudanda
Rock

To Taveta (14km)
& Moshi (52km)

A23

Serengeti
Plains

Maktau
Gate

Taita Hills

Wundanyi

C104   A23

Voi Safari
Lodge

Voi Gate

Tsavo East
Park Office

Voi

Camp
Site

Voi

Satao Camp

River

Mbuyuni
Gate

Lake
Jipe

Lake Jipe
Lodge

Jipe Gate

Public Camp
Site & Banda

Salt Lick
Lodge &
Safari Camp

Taita Hills
Lodge

Ndololo
Camp Site &
Kanderi Swamp

Sagala
Hills

Ndara
Plains

Maungu

Aruba
Dam

Maungu
Plains

Dika
Plains

Buchuma
Gate

To Mombasa
(92km)

A109

Kasigau
Gate

Rukanga

KENYA

TANZANIA

Mkomazi
Game Reserve

0   15   30 km

paper, washing-up liquid, soap, matches, drinking water and a portable ice box. Eating at the lodges is expensive (and the food unremarkable).

Kitani Shelter Camp is 500m from Kitani Safari Camp and is in better condition with a better view. It is slightly better equipped, slightly more expensive (KSh 3000), but sleeps six.

For reservations at any of these camps, contact Let's Go Travel in Nairobi (☎ 02-340331, fax 336890, email info@letsgosafari.com). For more information check out the Web site at www.letsgosafari.com.

If you don't have the money or desire to stay in the park, you can stay just outside in Mtito Andei village on the main Nairobi-Mombasa road.

Places to Stay – Top End *Ngulia Lodge* was once part of the African Tours & Hotels group but who actually runs the place now is anybody's guess. The hotel is wonderfully placed on a rocky outcrop with grassland and a water hole on one side (with a visiting leopard) and a sheer drop down to the Yatta Plateau and Ngulia Rhino Sanctuary on the other. It always has guests despite looking like a 1960s tower block. Elephants are regular evening visitors to the lodge's water hole. Singles/doubles (with full board) cost US$100/130 in the low season, rising to US$120/170 in the high season. *Kilaguni Lodge* costs exactly the same as Ngulia Lodge. The main draw is also a water hole that attracts a wide variety of game. It's a more attractive and more comfortable lodge than the Ngulia and there are excellent views of the Chyulu Hills out to the north-west. Book both of these through Let's Go Travel in Nairobi (see Places to Stay – Budget earlier).

Lake Jipe Lodge (☎ 02-227623, fax 218376) in a fairly isolated spot on the western boundary of the park almost on the Tanzanian border is one of the cheaper places at US$100/160 for full board. The views are excellent, this time it's the Pare Mountains just across the border in Tanzania. As well as wildlife drives, it's also possible for guests and nonguests to take a dhow ride on nearby Lake Jipe for KSh 750 per person.

Finch Hattons (☎ 02-604321/2, fax 604323, email finchhattons@iconnect.co.ke) is a very upmarket establishment complete with bone china and gold shower taps, excellent service and great food. All the aristocratic clients of the late Mr Hatton would have approved. It's sited around the springs and hippo pools at the source of the Looltureshi River. Rooms (with full board) cost US$200/275 in the low season, rising to US$250/350 in the high season. The Web site is www.kenya-direct.com/finchhatton.

Getting There & Away The main access to Tsavo West is through the Mtito Andei Gate on the Mombasa-Nairobi road near the northern end of the park. The park headquarters is here and there's a camp site. From the gate it's 31km to Kilaguni Lodge.

A further 48km along the main road away from Nairobi is the Tsavo Gate, where there's another camp site. This gate is 75km from the Kilaguni area, so if you're hitching, the Mtito Andei Gate is much closer and far busier. It's also worth taking into consideration the diabolical state of certain sections of the road between the Tsavo Gate and the lodges.

From Voi there is access past the Hilton-owned Taita Hills and Salt Lick lodges via the Maktau Gate. This road cuts clear across the park, exiting at the Mbuyuni Gate, to Taveta from where it's possible to cross into Tanzania and the town of Moshi at the foot of Kilimanjaro.

There's also a road running west from the Chyulu Gate that connects Tsavo West with Amboseli. This is a popular route with groups from Mombasa, but because of problems with bandits, all vehicles must travel in convoy and an armed policeman rides in the first and last vehicles. The convoys leave daily from the Chyulu Gate at 8.30 and 10.30 am, and at 2.30 pm. The trip to Amboseli takes a couple of hours.

Tsavo Park Hotel in Voi can arrange a vehicle and driver for safaris into Tsavo West (roughly KSh 8000 per minibus per day). There's no public transport into the park, but several buses could drop you off at Mtito Andei Gate.

Tsavo East National Park

The southern third of this park is open to the public and the rolling scrub-covered hills are home to large herds of elephants, usually covered in red dust.

The **Kanderi Swamp**, not far into the park from the main Voi Gate and park headquarters, is home to a profusion of wildlife and there's a camp site here. Further into the park, 30km from the gate, is the main attraction in this part of the park, the **Aruba Dam** built across the Voi River. Here too you'll encounter a wide variety of wildlife without the usual hordes of tourists. There's a camp site close to the lake.

Also of interest is the **Mudanda Rock** towering over a natural dam, which attracts elephants in the dry season. **Yatta Plateau** is the world's largest lava flow and the beautiful worn rock formations of **Lugards Falls** on the **Galana River** are worth a visit.

Until their partial translocation to Tsavo East, the sole surviving population of Hirola antelope was found near the Kenya/Somali border in the south Tana River/Garissa Districts. Intense poaching (for meat) and habitat destruction have reduced their numbers from an estimated 14,000 in 1976 to a pitiful 350 today. In addition a number of black rhino have recently been moved here from Nairobi National Park.

Places to Stay – Budget

There are *camp sites* at the Voi Gate, Kanderi Swamp (*Ndololo Campsite*) and Aruba Dam. *Mukwaju Campsite* on the Voi River is 50km in from the main gate (US$8 per person). The bandas in the park are uninhabitable.

If you don't want to camp, you can stay in Voi (see Voi in the Around Tsavo section later in this chapter).

Places to Stay – Top End

Voi Safari Lodge (☎ 02-340894) is signposted from the town of Voi and is one of the best hotels built by African Tours & Hotels (which no longer runs it). It's 5km inside the park from Voi Gate. It's more peaceful here than at the lodges in Tsavo West. Singles/doubles with full board cost US$100/130 in low season, rising to US$120/170 in high season.

Satao Camp is a very popular tented camp and very good value at US$120/170. Book through Let's Go Travel in Nairobi (☎ 02-340331, fax 336890, email info@letsgosafari .com).

Tsavo Safari Camp on the banks of the Athi River is one of the nicest places to stay. It's run by the Kilimanjaro Safari Club (☎ 02-338888, fax 219982, email ksc@ africaonline.co.ke). It's a great place to chill out for a few days; there's a swimming pool and wildlife drives can be arranged. Access to the lodge, which lies 27km off the main Nairobi-Mombasa road, is from Mtito Andei – the turn-off is well signposted, 1km out of town towards Mombasa. To stay in the well set-up permanent tents costs US$50/100 (with full board) in the low season, rising to US$104/160 in the high season.

Galdessa Camp (☎ 02-574689, fax 577851, email mellifera@swiftkenya) on the Galana River 12km from Lugards Falls, is very ecofriendly and frighteningly expensive (US$325 to US$244 per person). It's closed in May. The Web site is www .galdessa.com.

Getting There & Away

The main access point and the park headquarters is Voi Gate near Voi, off the Nairobi-Mombasa road. Further north near the Tsavo Gate entrance of Tsavo West is the Manyani Gate. The murram road from here cuts straight across to the Galana River and follows the river clear across the park, exiting at Sala Gate on the eastern side, a distance of 100km. From Sala Gate it's a further 110km to Malindi.

The Tsavo Park Hotel in Voi can arrange a vehicle and driver for safaris into Tsavo East (roughly KSh 8000 per minibus per day). See Voi in the following Around Tsavo National Park section for details on getting here by public transport.

AROUND TSAVO NATIONAL PARK

Taita Hills & Wundanyi

The Taita Hills west of the main Nairobi-Mombasa road cover a vast area and are scenically spectacular. Part of the area is gazetted as the **Taita Hills Game Reserve**.

Further into the hills the land is fertile and verdant, a far cry from the semi-arid landscape of Tsavo. The steep hillsides are heavily cultivated. Exploring on foot from the small town of **Wundanyi** in the heart of the hills is possible; other attractions include **Ngangao Forest** (a 6km matatu ride north-west to Werugha), the huge granite **Wesu Rock** overlooking Wundanyi (a long hike, but the views are stunning) and the **Cave of Skulls** where the Taita people once put the skulls of their ancestors. The original **African violets**, a favourite of gardeners everywhere, were discovered here; the UNDP East Africa Cross Border Biodiversity Project office in Wundanyi has more information about local fauna and flora.

Places to Stay & Eat *Wundanyi Lodge* (☎ 0148-2029) is the best place to stay in Wundanyi. Simple, friendly, secure, clean and tidy singles/doubles go for KSh150/250. Next door there's a video theatre (KSh 10 entry), which shows live English Premiership soccer (via satellite) to packed houses. *Tsavo Hill Cafe* just down from the matatu station is a popular place to eat.

Three *Hilton lodges* (☎ 02-250000, fax 250099) offer upmarket accommodation, as does **Rukinga Wildlife Conservancy** run by Savannah Camps & Lodges (☎ 02-331684, fax 216528, email eaos@africaonline.co.ke).

Getting There & Away Most Nairobi to Mombasa buses stop in Voi, from where there are constant matatus to Wundanyi (KSh 70). When returning, leave by around 8.30 am to ensure connection with the buses heading to Nairobi (you may need to book from Voi in advance). There are frequent matatus linking Mombasa and Wundanyi via Voi (KSh 270), leaving from the petrol station at the junction of Jomo Kenyatta Ave and Mwembe Tayari Rd in Mombasa.

Voi
☎ 0147
Voi is a pleasant small town, which is a good stepping stone to the Taita Hills or Tsavo National Park or a good an overnight stop between Mombasa and Nairobi.

Trips to Tsavo East and West national parks can be arranged through Tsavo Park Hotel.

There are a couple of cardphones in town and Barclays Bank has an ATM.

Distarr Hotel (☎/fax 30277) just down from the bus station is friendly and the best-value place in town. All rooms come with bath, mosquito nets and a fan. The cheap restaurant downstairs (most meals are under KSh 150 – try the vegetable curry) is popular and there's a cinema next door. Singles/doubles with breakfast cost KSh 350/450. Book in advance for public holidays. *Kahn Silent Guest House* (☎ 30297) on Moi Hospital Rd opposite Kenya Commercial Bank has slightly cheaper rooms for KSh 200/300.

Johaar's 24-Hour Cafe opposite Tsavo Park Hotel, serves simple, cheap Swahili dishes and good fresh juices.

Getting There & Away There are plenty of buses and matatus to Mombasa (KSh 200, three hours), but for Nairobi (KSh 500, 5½ hours), you must wait until 11 am when buses from Mombasa start to pass through town. There are at least a couple of buses a day to Taveta on the Tanzanian border (more on Tuesdays and Fridays) and regular matatus to Wundanyi (KSh 70).

Trains to Mombasa (1st/2nd class costs KSh 1410/1130) and Nairobi (1st/2nd class costs 2100/1475) depart daily at 4.36 am and 11.15 pm respectively. At the time of writing there was a train to Taveta at 5 am daily (KSh 180, five hours), returning later the same day (2nd class only). However, this service may be suspended and is notoriously unreliable.

See the Tanzania Getting There & Away chapter for details about the overland crossing into Tanzania from Voi.

Chyulu Hills National Park
Joined to the north-western corner of Tsavo West National Park are the Chyulu Hills. Gazetted as a national park in 1983, the beautiful volcanic hills offer trekking and cave exploration (the longest **Lava Tube** in the world is found here). The lack of fresh water is a big problem here.

It's best if you go on a trip organised by Savage Wilderness Safaris (☎/fax 02-521590, email whitewater@thorntree.com). The Web site is www.kilimanjaro.com. For a trekking guide, contact the warden of Tsavo West (☎ 0302-22483) PO Box 71, Mtito Andei, in advance.

There's no accommodation in the park, though fly camping is permitted. Entry is US$15 (US$5 for children).

SHIMBA HILLS NATIONAL RESERVE

This national reserve is in the hills behind the coast south of Mombasa, directly inland from Diani Beach. The wildlife is not prolific, but the steep-sided valleys, rolling hills and pockets of tropical rainforest are wonderful. Elephant are the dominant species though the headline act is the rare sable antelope: a tall and compact animal with beautifully curved horns on both the male and female. This is the only reserve in Kenya where they are still found. The area around the Marere Dam and the forest of Mwele Mdogo Hill are good for birds and the walk down to Sheldrick Falls (and swim in the cool pool) at the southern end of the park highly recommended – a ranger will escort you.

Any walking possibilities need to be addressed with the warden in advance (☎ 0127-4159) PO Box 30, Kwale.

Entry to the reserve costs US$20 for non-residents (US$5 for children).

Places to Stay

The public *camp site* and excellent round *bandas* are superbly located on the edge of an escarpment with stunning views down to Diani Beach. Each stone banda has two beds, a covered veranda and a barbecue. Monkeys, including the Colobus, sit in the trees around the camp and very tame zebra occasionally warm themselves by your camp fire. Camping here is US$8 and the bandas cost US$10 per person.

Shimba Hills Lodge (☎ 0127-4077 or 02-540780 in Nairobi) is a good Treetops-type affair with a walkway extending into the rainforest to a viewing platform and bar. Singles/doubles with shared bath (half board)

cost US$55/110 in the low season, rising to US$139/174 in the high season. Children under seven are not admitted and children seven or over pay full rates. The water hole here attracts some wildlife, including herds of elephant.

Mukurumuji Tented Camp (☎/fax 0127-2412, email aceltd@africaonline.co.ke) on the southern park boundary is more exclusive. Walking safaris are a speciality. Full board is US$94 per person. Transfers from Diani to the camp are US$10 one way.

Getting There & Away

KBS buses and matatus (No 34) to Kwale leave from Likoni. The service from Kwale to Kinango actually passes the main gate and northern part of the park, but you'll have a long wait for a vehicle into the park proper.

Diani House on Diani Beach organises day trips here for US$82 and overnight stays at Mukurumuji Tented Camp for US$115.

MWALUGANJE ELEPHANT SANCTUARY

This small community-run sanctuary is 3km north-west of the Shimba Hills main gate. Essentially focused on the valley of the Cha Shimba River, the 2500 hectares of the sanctuary are rugged and beautiful, and a single road runs through the best of it. Other than the 150 elephants, attractions include a rare cycad forest (this primitive fan-like plant species is over 300 million years old).

Entry is US$10 plus KSh 100 per vehicle. There is a good information centre close to the main gate.

Surrounding a water hole, *Traveller's Mwaluganje Elephant Camp* (☎ 011-485121, fax 485678, email travellershtl@swiftmombasa.com) is a good place to stay (US$75 per person per day), though there's a *camp site* surrounded by an electric fence (KSh 100 per night) nearby.

Traveller's Tiwi Beach Hotel on Tiwi Beach (see Places to Stay & Eat in the Tiwi Beach section earlier in this chapter) run day trips to the sanctuary (US$65) as well as overnight excursions (US$130).

See Getting There & Away earlier in this section for public transport details.

The Rift Valley

In Kenya, the Rift Valley comes down through Lake Turkana, the Cherangani Hills, Lake Baringo, Bogoria, Nakuru and Naivasha and then exits south through the plains to Tanzania. Lake Turkana (see the Northern Kenya chapter) is a huge lake in the semidesert north, home to nomadic pastoralists and a world away from the tourist minibuses and fancy hotels of the south.

The Cherangani Hills (see the Western Kenya chapter) provide some excellent walking opportunities. More accessible are the central lakes which attract literally hundreds of bird and mammal species – they're a naturalist's dream.

Kenya has several extinct volcanoes, the most prominent being Mts Kenya, Kulal and Longonot. The latter, in the heart of the Rift Valley, is an easy climb (see Longonot National Park below). Further south are vast plains, home to the Maasai and a profusion of wildlife. The spectacle of a million lesser flamingos on Lake Bogoria is amazing, as is Kenya's other soda lake, Lake Magadi. The Rift Valley is not an area to be missed.

Viewpoints

The best places to see the escarpments of the Rift Valley are from the viewpoints signposted along the Nairobi to Naivasha road, just past Limuru. The views across to Mt Longonot and the Maasai plains are stunning.

The old road to Naivasha descends dramatically into the rift, and it's the route to take if you're heading for Mt Longonot or Masai Mara. It has recently been resurfaced and is in better condition than the 'new' road.

LONGONOT NATIONAL PARK

View seekers should climb to the rim of Mt Longonot (2886m), a fairly young, dormant volcano. As this is a national park there is an entrance fee of US$15. The scramble up to the rim takes about 45 minutes from the parking area and to complete the circuit of the rim a further two to three hours is

Highlights

- Walking around Crater Lake on the western shore of Lake Naivasha
- Watching Colobus monkeys while drinking tea on the lawn of Elsamere Conservation Centre, Lake Naivasha
- Marvelling at the fantastic pink and white sci-fi landscape of Lake Magadi
- Spotting the amazing birdlife at Lake Baringo
- Taking in the views from the 'Old' Naivasha Road, near Limuru, where it descends from the escarpment into the Rift Valley

needed. If you're feeling brave there's a track leading down inside the crater, though it's worth hiring a guide if you intend to do this. In fact, due to recent muggings on the volcano it is worth taking a guide anyway, at least as far as the crater rim.

Places to Stay

There's no accommodation in the park or the immediate vicinity, but it is possible to camp at the ranger station at the foot of the mountain. If you're just on a day trip you can leave your gear at the park office or the police station.

Getting There & Away

If you don't have your own transport take a matatu from Nairobi as far as the Longonot National Park turn-off, just past a railway crossing. From here it is a 3km walk down a dirt road to the trailhead where car owners can leave their vehicles.

NAIVASHA
☎ 0311

There's little of interest in Naivasha town itself. Most travellers just pass through on the way to or from Mt Longonot, Lake Naivasha, Hell's Gate National Park and Nakuru; the main Nairobi to Nakuru road bypasses Naivasha. However, it's a good place to stock up with supplies if you're planning a sojourn by the lake.

The area around Naivasha was one of the first settled by *wazungu* (Swahili for white person) and the Delamere Estates (originally owned by Lord Delamere), and this area was one of the stamping grounds of the 'Happy Valley' set of the 1930s. Many white settlers remain.

The town consists of two main roads and a handful of other streets. Everything is within walking distance.

Information

There are branches of Barclays Bank (with ATMs) and the Kenya Commercial Bank on Moi Ave which are open during normal banking hours.

Places to Stay

Heshima Bar Boarding & Lodging and *Othaya Annexe Hotel*, both on Kariuki Chotara Rd, which runs parallel to Moi Ave, are two of the best places to stay. The Heshima is a lively place, charging KSh 150/300 for singles/doubles with shared bath, while single (no doubles) self-contained (toilet and shower) rooms at Othaya go for KSh 250. This is a bit of a find, equipped as it is with a balcony bar, butchery, bakery, cafe and hot water.

Naivasha Silver Hotel (☎ 20580) on Kenyatta Ave offers more salubrious lodgings with clean and tidy rooms – including nets and hot water – going for KSh 400/600. There's an upstairs bar and restaurant.

La Belle Inn (☎ 21007, fax 21119) on Moi Ave is the best accommodation in town. It's rustic ambience makes for a popular watering hole for locals and a meal stop for safari companies. Currently, the room rates are KSh 2000/2800 for self-contained rooms with breakfast, but all the rooms were being upgraded at the time of writing and prices may rise. There's guarded parking, and all credit cards are accepted.

Places to Eat

Naivasha has a large number of cheap eating places, of which *Jim's Corner Dishes*

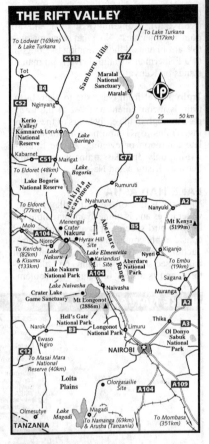

probably serves the best stews and Kenyan favourites.

La Belle Inn provides food of a different class entirely (three courses for KSh 500) and the outdoor terrace is a great place to have a beer or a meal. Open daily (all day) except Tuesday.

Getting There & Away

Bus & Matatu The main bus and matatu station is behind the corner of Kariuki Chotara and Mbaria Kanui Rds close to the municipal market. There are frequent buses and matatus to Nairobi (KSh 110), Nakuru

(KSh 100), Nyahururu (KSh 150), Narok (KSh 220), Kongoni (KSh 50) and all points further west. Note that some matatus to Nairobi and all those heading to Kongoni (via Fisherman's Camp) leave from matatu stands on Kenyatta Ave.

Train Travel from Naivasha to Nairobi by train is inconvenient as most of the trains pass through in the early hours of the morning. Trains to Kisumu pass through in the late afternoon or evening. At the time of writing only 3rd class trains were running between Kisumu and Nairobi.

LAKE NAIVASHA

Naivasha is one of the Rift Valley's freshwater lakes and is home to an incredible variety of bird species. It is also the focus of considerable conservation effort. The introduction of the dreaded water hyacinth that has caused so many problems on Lake Victoria, and is already causing big problems

here, and pesticide and herbicide run-off from the surrounding flower farms has contaminated the lake. This has had a large impact, not least on the local population of fish eagles which have stopped breeding.

Between 1937 and 1950 Lake Naivasha was Nairobi's airport. Imperial Airways and then BOAC flew Empire and Solent flying boats here on the four-day journey from Southampton. Passengers came ashore at the Lake Naivasha Hotel (now the Lake Naivasha Country Club), where buses would be waiting to shuttle them to Nairobi.

For a full account of the history of the 'Happy Valley' set in the 30s and European activity in the area generally, get hold of a copy of *Naivasha & the Lake Hotel* by Jan Hemsing, available from the Lake Naivasha Country Club.

Things to See & Do

On the western side of Lake Naivasha, past the village of Kongoni, is **Crater Lake,** at the

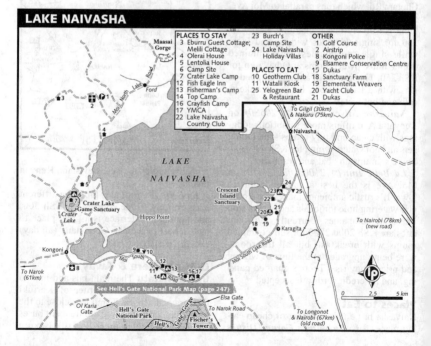

LAKE NAIVASHA

PLACES TO STAY		PLACES TO EAT	OTHER
3 Eburru Guest Cottage;	23 Burch's	10 Geotherm Club	1 Golf Course
Melili Cottage	Camp Site	11 Watalii Kiosk	2 Airstrip
4 Olerai House	24 Lake Naivasha	25 Yelogreen Bar	8 Kongoni Police
5 Lentolia House	Holiday Villas	& Restaurant	9 Elsamere Conservation Centre
6 Camp Site			15 Dukas
7 Crater Lake Camp			18 Sanctuary Farm
12 Fish Eagle Inn			19 Elementeita Weavers
13 Fisherman's Camp			20 Yacht Club
14 Top Camp			21 Dukas
16 Crayfish Camp			
17 YMCA			
22 Lake Naivasha			
Country Club			

Maasai Gorge

Moi North Lake Road

Ford

To Gilgil (30km) & Nakuru (75km)

Naivasha

LAKE NAIVASHA

Crescent Island Sanctuary

Crater Lake Game Sanctuary

Crater Lake

Hippo Point

To Nairobi (78km) (new road)

Karagita

Kongoni

Moi South Lake Road

To Narok (61km)

See Hell's Gate National Park Map (page 247)

Ol Karia Gate

Hell's Gate National Park

Elsa Gate

To Narok Road

To Longonot & Nairobi (67km) (old road)

Hell's Gate Gorge

Fischer's Tower

0   2.5   5 km

bottom of a beautiful but small volcanic crater. An excellent nature trail leads through lush vegetation around the crater (a two-hour walk). The area is full of wildlife including Colobus monkeys and over 150 species of birds have been recorded here. The crater is part of the **Crater Lake Game Sanctuary** (entry KSh 100) and there's a very pleasant bar and restaurant down by the lakeshore (see Places to Stay).

South of the lake is the Hell's Gate National Park which is one of the few national parks you're allowed to walk in (see later in this chapter). On the eastern side of the lake is **Crescent Island**, a bird sanctuary which you can visit by boat (see Getting Around later in this chapter) or car. The owner of Sanctuary Farm allows vehicles to cross his land (KSh 200) and drive across the causeway to the reserve. There is a US$10 entry fee (US$6 for children) to the island.

Elsamere

Almost opposite Hippo Point, a couple of kilometres past Fisherman's Camp, is El-samere, home of the late Joy Adamson of *Born Free* fame. It is now a conservation centre focusing on lake ecology and environmental awareness programs and is open to the public from 3 to 6 pm daily. The entrance fee of KSh 250 includes afternoon tea on the lawn (keep an eye out for the guereza or black and white Colobus), a visit to the memorial room and a film-viewing of *The Joy Adamson Story*. Occasionally they run escorted trips to Hell's Gate National Park.

The only other way to visit is to stay here (see Places to Stay) or book in for a meal – lunch costs KSh 600, dinner KSh 800. Bookings can be made through the El-samere Conservation Centre (☎ 21055; fax 21074, email elsa@africaonline.co.ke) Moi South Lake Rd, Naivasha.

Places to Stay – Budget

Fisherman's Camp (☎ 30088) is the most popular budget accommodation on the lakeshore. You can camp here for KSh 200 per person, there are tents for hire (KSh 200 per night) and there are fully self-contained four-bed *bandas* (thatched huts) for KSh 600 per

person. Dorm beds cost KSh 350 with bedding. They also have what is known as the *Top Camp* (up the hill across the other side of the road) where much quieter bandas cost between KSh 250 and KSh 1900 per person. Firewood is available at both camps. At the main camp there's a bar and restaurant that is open until late – meals are between KSh 200 and KSh 300. You can also rent a boat (see Getting Around). It's a huge and very pleasant site with grass and shady acacia trees. At weekends it gets very busy. If you just want to spend the day here you must pay KSh 100. The hippos that once wandered around the camp site at night are now restricted to certain sections of grass by an electric fence and there's a real chance of seeing one of these great beasts grazing at night.

YMCA (☎ 30396) close to the turn-off for Hell's Gate National Park has a good camp site (KSh 150 per person) and a number of somewhat spartan and run-down bandas for KSh 300 per person (children half price). Bring all your own food and drink with you.

Burch's Campsite (☎ 21010) about 1km beyond the Yelogreen Bar & Restaurant towards Fisherman's Camp offers a range of good accommodation options as well as a store selling basic provisions. Pitching your tent in the shady camp site costs KSh 200 per person, or there are basic (but adequate) twin-bed rondavels (bed and mattress only) for KSh 450. Bigger, four-bed rondavels go for KSh 600 or KSh 900 (if you want your own bathroom) – this includes bedding, cooking equipment and use of a gas stove. Campers and those in the basic rondavels have access to hot showers and a communal cooking area. This is a very good place to stay and ideal for those wanting to avoid the noise and comings and goings at Fisherman's Camp.

Crater Lake Game Sanctuary is a well equipped site with running water (hot showers on request), a barbecue, eating area and decent toilets. Camping costs KSh 150 per person. The restaurant and bar down by the lake are open all day, but if you want meals (lunch is KSh 750, dinner KSh 850) book in advance. Those walking from Kongoni are advised to ask for an escort to the sanctuary; there have been muggings in the past.

Places to Stay – Mid-Range

Fish Eagle Inn (☎ 30306) right next door to the Fisherman's Camp is a new place with a number of very expensive cottages around a spacious lawn. There are loads of facilities here (sauna, steam room, pool, satellite TV etc) and singles/doubles cost KSh 1450/2890 which is way over the odds. The dorm accommodation is more reasonably priced (KSh 360) and you can camp for KSh 200, though there's little shade.

If you have transport or are prepared to hike, there are a couple of good low-key self-catering places to stay on the slopes of Eburru Hill in the Greenpark Development off Moi North Lake Road some 30km from Naivasha town.

Eburru Guest Cottage consists of two small wooden chalets each containing two rooms, a lounge and a kitchen. As you would expect at 2133m, the views across the lake to the Aberdares are quite stunning and zebra, eland, dik-dik, Grant's and Thompson's gazelles are commonly spotted. Rooms are KSh 1500/1000. Book through Let's Go Travel (☎ 02-340331, fax 336890, email info@letsgosafari.com) in Nairobi. Its Web site address is www.lets gosafari.com.

Melili Cottage further on is a little better and offers stone cottages accommodating four people each. They are well equipped, cool and cost KSh 2500 per night. Book through Holiday Homes (☎ 02-444052, fax 444057) in Nairobi.

Places to Stay – Top End

Lake Naivasha Country Club (☎ 21004, fax 21161) has a beautiful, expansive garden with access to the lake, a kids' playground and a pool. Singles/doubles with half board in the high season cost US$138/172 (US$60/120 low season). Cottages are more expensive at US$254/169 in high season. Boat trips cost KSh 1000 per hour; the trip to Crescent Island costs KSh 800 return – with a picnic lunch it's an excellent day excursion. The hotel is part of the Block Hotels chain so bookings need to be made by contacting Nairobi (☎ 02-540780, fax 543810).

Elsamere Conservation Centre (☎ 21055, fax 21074, email elsa@africaonline.co.ke) offers rooms with full board (the only choice) for KSh 3500 per person per night. It's a very pleasant place to stay and the staff are friendly.

Crater Lake Camp (☎ 20613, 21372) is a luxury tented camp set among the trees and vegetation on the lakeshore. The food is good, the service excellent and you have the whole of the sanctuary to explore on foot (maps are provided). Night wildlife drives are available (within the sanctuary) and an excursion to Lady Delamere's grave is also possible. Full board is currently on offer for KSh 4930/8800 – but these prices are likely to rise.

Lentolia House managed by the same people who run Crater Lake is a huge Edwardian style house with 50ha of land down by the shore of Lake Naivasha. Let on a self-catering basis, it sleeps 14 and costs KSh 12,000 per night. This is just one of the expensive homestays, lodges and private houses on Moi North Lake Rd.

Places to Eat

Geotherm Club just before the Elsamere Conservation Centre is set in a beautiful spot among acacia trees overlooking the lake. This place caters to employees at the thermal power plant. The simple meals here are good and cheap (KSh 100 to KSh 200) and the beer is cold (KSh 60). Tables are laid out in a large garden and there is a pool and a jetty out onto the lake. It's about a 45 minute walk from Fisherman's Camp.

Yelogreen Bar & Restaurant another place for cheap eating and drinking is near the eastern end of Moi South Lake Rd, though it isn't really in the same class as Geotherm.

Shopping

The are a number of craft shops and galleries off the Moi South Lake Rd. Elementeita Weavers (☎ 30115) is the pick of the bunch and sells hand-woven rugs, carpets, sweaters, *kangas* and *kikois*, baskets and the like. Quality is high and the prices reflect this. It's open between 9 am and 5.30 pm daily.

Getting There & Away

The usual access to Lake Naivasha is along Moi South Lake Rd, which also goes past the turn off to Hell's Gate National Park (both the Elsa and Ol Karia Gate entrances). There are fairly frequent matatus between Naivasha town and Kongoni on the western side of the lake from where it's 5km to Crater Lake. It's 17km from the turn-off on the old Naivasha to Nairobi road to Fisherman's Camp and costs KSh 40.

For Moi North Lake Rd there is one matatu from the Total Garage in Naivasha town at around 3 pm. Returning to town you'll need to be on the road by about 7 am, otherwise it's a long, dusty walk.

Getting Around

Cheap rowing and motorised boats can be hired from Fisherman's Camp (KSh 2400 per hour) and Elsamere Conservation Centre (KSh 2500 per hour), which also offers a good birdwatching guide, but it's a long way from there to Crescent Island. Taking a boat from Burch's camp site or Lake Naivasha Country Club would be much cheaper. Rowing boats (KSh 200 per hour, maximum four people) are also available

from Fisherman's Camp. Watch out for the hippos!

For land exploration, mountain bikes can be hired from Fisherman's Camp for KSh 500 per day. Bikes can also be hired from Watalii Kiosk opposite the Fish Eagle Inn (KSh 250 for a Chinese machine and KSh 300 for the one mountain bike available). Cheap transport to Crater Lake can also be arranged from here; ask for Tom.

HELL'S GATE NATIONAL PARK

The looming cliffs and the Hell's Gate gorge, home to a wide variety of bird and animal life, are spectacular. You can walk (or cycle) through this park without a ranger/guide and it's possible to see zebra, Thomson's gazelle, baboon and even the occasional cheetah or leopard. Efforts are being made to reintroduce lammergeyer, a rare raptor not sighted here since 1984.

The usual access point is through the main **Elsa Gate**, which is 2km from Moi South Lake Rd. From here the road takes you past **Fischer's Tower**, a 25m-high column of volcanic rock named after Gustav Fischer, a German explorer who reached here in 1883.

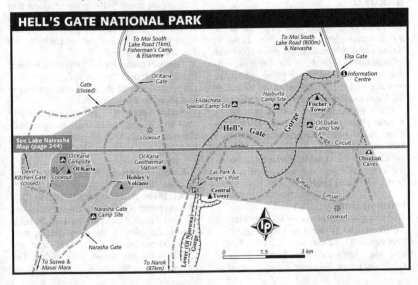

HELL'S GATE NATIONAL PARK

To Moi South Lake Road (1km), Fisherman's Camp & Elsamere

To Moi South Lake Road (800m) & Naivasha

Elsa Gate

Information Centre

Gate (closed)

Ol Karia Gate

Endachata Special Camp Site

Naiburta Camp Site

Fischer's Tower

Gorge

Ol Dubai Camp Site

Hell's Gate

Twiga Circuit

See Lake Naivasha Map (page 244)

Lookout

Ol Karia Campsite

Ol Karia

Ol Karia Geothermal Station

Obsidian Caves

Devil's Kitchen Gate (closed)

Lookout

Hobley's Volcano

Car Park & Ranger's Post

Buffalo

Circuit

Central Tower

Lookout

Narasha Gate Camp Site

Lower (Ol Njorowa) Gorge

Narasha Gate

0   1.5   3 km

To Suswa & Masai Mara

To Narok (87km)

Further south is **Central Tower**, another column of volcanic rock overlooking the beginning of the Lower Gorge. There's an excellent walk (passable in the dry season) down into the gorge. The descent is steep (and can be very slippery) but some steps have been cut. The channels cut by the water are truly beautiful and you could easily spend a couple of hours wandering around.

The main road finally emerges at the **Ol Karia Geothermal Station** – a power project which utilises one of the hottest sources of natural steam (seen all over the park) in the world.

If you intend walking the whole way through the park, allow a full day, and take plenty of water (only available at the park's camp sites) and something to eat. Alternatively hire a mountain bike from beside the lake or ask around for a lift at Fisherman's Camp.

Entry to the park costs US$15 (US$5 for children) and camping US$2 per person. Ol Dubai and Naiberta are probably the best camp sites.

A photocopied guide (KSh 100) to the park is available at the gate.

NAKURU
☎ 037

Kenya's fourth largest town is the centre of a rich farming area about halfway between Nairobi and Kisumu on the main road and railway line to Uganda. It's here that the railway forks, with one branch going to Kisumu on Lake Victoria and the other to Malaba on the Ugandan border and on to Kampala.

It's a pleasant town with a population around 80,000 and the big draw for travellers is the nearby Lake Nakuru National Park with its prolific birdlife. The Menengai Crater and Hyrax Hill Prehistoric Site in the immediate area are both worth a visit (see later in this chapter).

Information
There is a forex bureau on George Morara Rd (the highway) next to Marshalls (Peugeot dealers). The Barclays Bank (on Kenyatta Ave) has an ATM. There have been reports of excessive commission charged at

this branch, so check out the rates before handing over any money.

Crater Travel (☎/fax 215019) just off Kenyatta Ave is recommended. Email can be sent from Volcano Eight Kenya (☎ 44187, email vek@net2000ke.com) on Government Rd. Browsing costs KSh 8 per minute. You can make telephone calls from here.

The Marie Stopes Clinic on Gusii Rd offers a variety of health services as well as birth control.

Places to Stay – Budget
Amigos Guest House on Gusii Rd is a very friendly place and the best value in this price range. The rooms and bathroom facilities are passably clean, towels are provided and there's hot water. Singles/doubles with shared facilities cost KSh 150/220. Don't confuse this place with the other 'Amigos' at the junction of Kenyatta Ave and Bondoni Rd. The owner may be able to set you up with a cheap driver to the park.

Shik Parkview Hotel (☎ 212345) on the corner of Kenyatta Ave and Bondoni Rd is a large place with a loud bar and restaurant on the 1st floor. The beds are comfortable and the rooms fine, but those overlooking Kenyatta Ave are noisy. Self-contained rooms cost KSh 400/600 and those with shared facilities KSh 300/500. The best thing about this place is its central location and proximity to the bus and train stations.

Tropical Lodge (☎ 242608) is far quieter, but a little more expensive. Big, light, airy rooms and shared shower (with hot water) and toilet go for KSh 250/350.

Joska Hotel (☎ 212546) is reasonably new and another good place to stay. Self-contained single rooms with big beds go for KSh 300, or KSh 400 with breakfast. There are no doubles.

Kembu Campsite (☎ 61413, email kembu@net2000ke.com) just north-west of Njoro about 18km from Nakuru is an excellent place to camp. The owners, the Nightingales, are well switched on to the needs of the backpacker. Camping in the large garden costs KSh 300 per person on the first night, and KSh 200 for any consecutive nights. Two rather flash bandas cost KSh 1000/1200. All

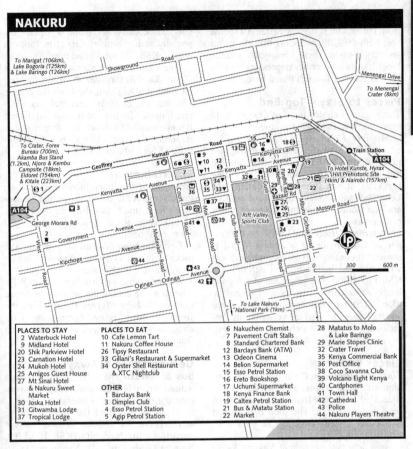

NAKURU

To Marigat (106km),
Lake Bogoria (125km)
& Lake Baringo (126km)

Showground
Road

Menengai Drive

To Menengai
Crater (8km)

To Crater, Forex
Bureau (700m),
Akamba Bus Stand
(1.2km), Njoro & Kembu
Campsite (18km),
Eldoret (154km)
& Kitale (223km)

Train Station

A104

To Hotel Kunste, Hyrax
Hill Prehistoric Site
(4km) & Nairobi (157km)

George Morara Rd

Rift Valley
Sports Club

0   300   600 m

To Lake Nakuru
National Park (1km)

PLACES TO STAY	PLACES TO EAT		
2 Waterbuck Hotel	10 Cafe Lemon Tart	6 Nakuchem Chemist	28 Matatus to Molo
9 Midland Hotel	11 Nakuru Coffee House	7 Pavement Craft Stalls	& Lake Baringo
20 Shik Parkview Hotel	26 Tipsy Restaurant	8 Standard Chartered Bank	29 Marie Stopes Clinic
23 Carnation Hotel	33 Gillani's Restaurant & Supermarket	12 Barclays Bank (ATM)	32 Crater Travel
24 Mukoh Hotel	34 Oyster Shell Restaurant	13 Odeon Cinema	35 Kenya Commercial Bank
25 Amigos Guest House	& XTC Nightclub	14 Belion Supermarket	36 Post Office
27 Mt Sinai Hotel		15 Esso Petrol Station	38 Coco Savanna Club
& Nakuru Sweet	OTHER	16 Ereto Bookshop	39 Volcano Eight Kenya
Market	1 Barclays Bank	17 Uchumi Supermarket	40 Cardphones
30 Joska Hotel	3 Dimples Club	18 Kenya Finance Bank	41 Town Hall
31 Gitwamba Lodge	4 Esso Petrol Station	19 Caltex Petrol Station	42 Cathedral
37 Tropical Lodge	5 Agip Petrol Station	21 Bus & Matatu Station	43 Police
		22 Market	44 Nakuru Players Theatre

the essentials are available behind the bar (including Alka Seltzer) and you can bed down in the large open-fronted lounge area if the bandas are full. Based here, backpackers have the freedom of 400 hectares and you can hire mountain bikes for US$15 per 24 hours. Fresh fruit, vegetables and other food stuffs are always available and you can send/receive email. One of the most exciting possibilities is the potential for trekking into the Mau Forest not far away. The Nightingales can put you in touch with a local ex-poacher who knows the forest well. Week-long treks are possible and fees very low. To get to

Kembu take a matatu from Nakuru heading to Molo (via Njoro) and ask to be dropped at the sign for Kembu Campsite (it's about 6km north-east of Njoro on the C56). It's also signposted from the A104.

Places to Stay – Mid-Range

Mukoh Hotel (☎ 213516) on the corner of Mosque and Gusil Rds is clean and comfortable and has good views of the lake from the rooftop. Singles/doubles (with private bath) cost KSh 350/500. Soap and towels are provided and there is hot water, albeit erratic. The hotel has its own bar and restaurant.

Carnation Hotel (☎ 43522) a few doors from the Mukoh is slightly better. All rooms cost KSh 450/700, including breakfast, and security is good. There's hot water and the hotel has its own rather depressing restaurant. Blackbird Tours is based here.

Places to Stay – Top End
There's some choice but don't expect gold taps and flowers on your pillow.

Midland Hotel (☎ 212155, fax 44517) on Geoffrey Kamati Rd is a rambling old place. Rooms with attached bathroom and hot water cost KSh 1800/2500 including breakfast. It has three bars (including the Long Bar) and two restaurants (one outdoor and one indoor). Easily the best place in this price range.

Waterbuck Hotel (☎ 215672) on the corner of Government Ave and West Rd is somewhat cheaper and offers shabby rooms with attached bathroom and balcony for KSh 1300/1800. The price includes a good breakfast, which is just as well given the rooms. The hotel has its own bar, restaurant and barbecue; the staff are very friendly. Vehicles can be parked safely in the hotel compound, which is guarded 24 hours a day.

Places to Eat
Tipsy Restaurant on Gusil Rd is very popular with local people, especially at lunchtime. Dishes include Indian curries, western food and fresh fish. The food is tasty and reasonably priced – around KSh 90 to KSh 130 for main dishes.

Next door is the excellent *Nakuru Sweet Mart* which specialises in Indian *thali* (vegetarian) curries and snacks as well as sweets, pastries and cakes. Highly recommended.

The restaurant on the ground floor of the *Mukoh Hotel* is a good place for breakfast. For just a coffee and a snack, try the *Nakuru Coffee House* on the corner of Moi Rd and Kenyatta Ave; you can also buy roasted coffee beans here.

Also try *Moore's Cafe* on Kenyatta Lane (another popular local place); and *Cafe Lemon Tart* and *Gillani's Restaurant* on Moi Rd (above the shop of the same name) can also be recommended.

The open-air bar at *Midland Hotel* offers good barbecued chicken and is popular, especially at lunch-time. Expect to fork out around KSh 400 for a good meal.

One of the best restaurants in town is *Oyster Shell Restaurant* (☎ 40946) upstairs on Kenyatta Ave near the Club Rd corner. The menu is extensive and includes western, Indian, Mughal and Indonesian dishes. It's open daily for lunch and dinner and is reasonably priced; main dishes range between KSh 150 and KSh 250.

Entertainment
Apart from the bars mentioned earlier, there's the *XTC* disco above the Oyster Shell Restaurant. Good bands often play here. There is no cover charge and beers sell for normal bar prices.

Coco Savanna Club on Government Ave rocks night and day, while *Dimples Club* on Kenyatta Ave is also popular.

Odeon cinema on Geoffrey Kamati Rd is a bit of a flea pit but the only movie house in town. *Nakuru Players Theatre* is on the street between Oginga Odinga and Kipchoge Aves, and Kenyan plays are put on from time to time.

Getting There & Away
Bus & Matatu The rather chaotic bus and matatu station is at the eastern edge of town, near the train station. Generally it doesn't take too long to find the vehicle you're after. There are regular matatu/Peugeot departures for Naivasha (KSh 100/120), Nairobi (KSh 150/280), Nyahururu (KSh 80/100), Nyeri (KSh 150/200), Eldoret (KSh 200/250), Kericho (KSh 150/200), Kisii (KSh 200) and Kisumu (KSh 250/300).

Akamba buses also service Nairobi and points west. The only problem is that the Akamba depot is about 1.2km west of town, at the Agip station on the main road out.

Other buses go to Eldoret (KSh 150), Nairobi (KSh 140) and Kisumu (KSh 200), among other places.

Matatus to Molo (KSh 80) and Lake Baringo (KSh 150) leave from near the Total petrol station on Bazaar Rd.

Hyrax Hill Prehistoric Site

This prehistoric site, just outside Nakuru on the Nairobi road, was first excavated in 1937, although the significance of the site had been suspected by Louis Leakey since 1926. Further excavations were conducted periodically, right up into the 1980s.

Finds at the site indicate that three settlements existed here: the earliest possibly 3000 years ago; the most recent only 200 to 300 years ago. From the museum at the northern end you can take a stroll around the site, starting with the North-East Village where 13 enclosures, or pits, were excavated. Only Pit D, excavated in 1965, is still open; the others have grown over. The North-East Village is believed to be about 400 years old, dated by comparison with the nearby Lanet site. A great number of pottery fragments were found at the site, some of which have been pieced together into complete jars and are now displayed in the museum.

From the village the trail climbs to the scant remains of the stone-walled hill fort near the top of Hyrax Hill. You can continue up to the peak, from which there is a fine view of the flamingo-lined Lake Nakuru.

Descending from the hill on the other side you come to the Iron Age settlement where the position of Hut B and Hut C is clearly visible. Just north of these huts, a series of burial pits containing 19 skeletons was found. Since they were mostly male, and a number of them had been decapitated, it's likely they were killed in some sort of fighting. Unfortunately, souvenir seekers have stolen the bones that were displayed.

Virtually underneath the Iron Age site, a Neolithic site was discovered. The Iron Age burial pits actually topped a Neolithic burial mound, and a second Neolithic burial mound was found nearby. This mound is fenced off as a display. Between the burial mound and the Nairobi road are more Iron Age pits, excavated in 1974. The large collection of items found in these pits included a real puzzle – six Indian coins, one of them 500 years old, two of them dating from 1918 and 1919!

Finally, following the path back to the museum, there's a *bau* board in a large rock. This popular game is played throughout East Africa.

You are free to walk around the site yourself but a guide is useful. He'll expect a small tip at the end.

The site is open daily from 9 am to 6 pm and admission is KSh 200. The *Visitor's Guide to the Hyrax Hill Site* is available from the museum there.

Train As is the case with Naivasha, trains often come through in the middle of the night and only 3rd class is available.

AROUND NAKURU
Menengai Crater

Rising up on the northern side of Nakuru is the Menengai Crater, an extinct 2490m-high volcano. The crater itself descends to 483m below the rim. You can drive right up to the edge, where there's one of those totally trivial and irrelevant signs telling you that you're five million kilometres from some city halfway across the world.

The walk up to the crater takes a solid couple of hours and it really is *up*. The views back over Lake Nakuru are stunning, as are the views north to Lake Bogoria once you reach the top. About three-quarters of the way along there is a small group of *dukas* (shops) where you can get fed and watered.

LAKE NAKURU NATIONAL PARK

Created in 1961, the park covers some 180 sq km. Like most of the other Rift Valley lakes, it is a shallow soda lake. For a number of years until the El Niño rains in 1997, the water level decreased steadily almost to the point where it was nearly dry during the dry season, and the flamingos, once synonymous with the lake, sought happier hunting grounds – mainly Lake Bogoria. At present the lake is 3.5m deep, the deepest for a decade and since flamingos are nomadic creatures they may return in the future. However, even without them, Lake

Nakuru remains an ornithologists' paradise with over 400 species found here.

There is much more to the park, though, than just the lake. Areas of grassland, bush, euphorbia and acacia forest and rocky cliffs support hundreds of species of birds and animals. You'll see plenty of warthogs, waterbucks and buffaloes near the lake, while further into the bush are Thomson's gazelles and reedbucks. There's a small herd of hippos and even the occasional leopard.

The park is surrounded by a high electric fence, which keeps in the few black and white rhino introduced some years ago. The southern end of the lake is the best place to see white rhino grazing; the black rhino, browsers by nature, are more difficult to spot.

In recent years pollution from Nakuru coupled with pesticide and herbicide run-off from surrounding farms and massive deforestation within the lake's water catchment area have caused concern and all visitors should be aware of the delicate nature of the environment they are driving through. World Wildlife Fund (WWF) is running a major project aimed at reducing pressures on the lake.

The national park entrance is about 6km from the centre of Nakuru. Entry costs US$27 per person (US$10 for children) plus KSh 200 per vehicle. Walking is not permitted so hitch a ride with other tourists, rent a vehicle or go on a tour.

An excellent map of Lake Nakuru National Park is available at the park gate and at KWS HQ in Nairobi (KSh 500).

Warning
Don't drive too close to the water's edge, the mud is very soft.

Places to Stay – Budget
Backparkers' Camp Site (due to a signwriter's typo), just inside the park gate, has basic facilities – but bring all your own food. Make sure tents are securely zipped up when you're away from them otherwise the vervet monkeys or baboons will steal everything.

The other *public camp site* is at the far end of the park at the (seasonal) **Makalia**

Falls. Facilities are not as good but the location is excellent. *Special camp sites* (where you get the entire camp site to yourself with the KSh 5000 fee contributing to the cost of rubbish removal, cutting of grass etc) are dotted all over the park. Camping in the public camp sites costs US$8 per person (US$2 for children) and US$15 (plus a KSh 5000 set up fee) in the special camp sites.

Naishi House Banda is another option. At the time of writing it wasn't quite finished but will cost US$10 per person.

Wildlife Club of Kenya Youth Hostel (☎ 037-212632, PO Box 33, Nakuru) is a cheaper alternative; dorm beds cost KSh 300 while self-contained, self-catering cottages go for KSh 1100/1600 for single/doubles. Half-board is KSh 1500 and KSh 2400 respectively.

Places to Stay – Top End
Sarova Lion Hill Lodge (☎ 02-713333, fax 715566, email reservations@sarova.co.ke) is the first place you come to down the eastern access road of the park. Singles/doubles in the high season will cost US$135/180, US$60/120 in the low season. There's a swimming pool and open-air bar/restaurant as well as more expensive suites. It's the best lodge in the park.

Lake Nakuru Lodge (☎ 037-850228, 02-212405, fax 230962), almost 3km beyond the southern end of the lake, is similar to the Sarova Lion Hill. It has all the usual facilities and consists of a series of shingle-roofed octagonal cottages. Full board prices are US$50/100 low season and US$150/180 high season. Children aged three to 12 are charged 50%. Horse riding outside the park is charged at KSh 850 per hour.

Outside the park, just past Lanet Gate and the rather poor Lion Hill Bar & Lodgings, is the well equipped *Eldorado Lodge* (☎ 037-85491, fax 86493) where self-contained rooms cost KSh 1000/1500.

Getting There & Away
If you don't have your own vehicle, the only way into the park from Nakuru is by taxi (unless you can persuade a tourist with a car to give you a ride), costing around KSh 1000

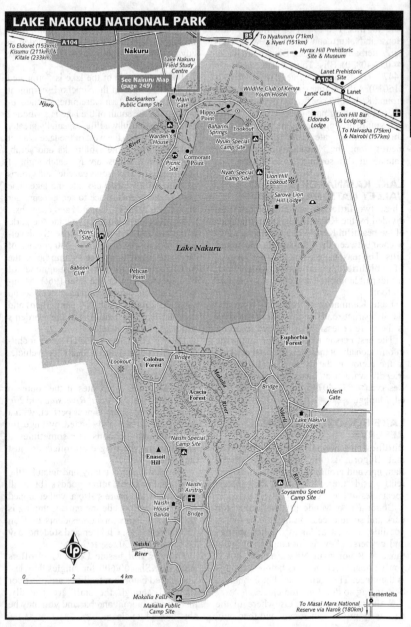

LAKE NAKURU NATIONAL PARK

To Eldoret (153km), Kisumu (211km) & Kitale (233km)

A104

Nakuru

B5 To Nyahururu (71km) & Nyeri (151km)

Hyrax Hill Prehistoric Site & Museum

Lake Nakuru Field Study Centre

Lanet Prehistoric Site

See Nakuru Map (page 249)

A104

Lanet

Njoro

Backpackers' Public Camp Site

Main Gate

Wildlife Club of Kenya Youth Hostel

Lanet Gate

Lion Hill Bar & Lodgings

Hippo Point

Eldorado Lodge

Warden's House

Baharini Springs

Lookout

To Naivasha (75km) & Nairobi (157km)

River

Nyuki Special Camp Site

Picnic Site

Cormorant Point

Nyati Special Camp Site

Lion Hill Lookout

Sarova Lion Hill Lodge

Picnic Site

Lake Nakuru

Baboon Cliff

Pelican Point

Euphorbia Forest

Lookout

Colobus Forest

Bridge

Bridge

Makalia River

Nderit Gate

Acacia Forest

Nderit River

Lake Nakuru Lodge

Naishi Special Camp Site

Enasoit Hill

Naishi Airstrip

Soysambu Special Camp Site

Naishi House Banda

Bridge

Naishi River

0   2   4 km

Makalia Falls

Makalia Public Camp Site

To Masai Mara National Reserve via Narok (180km)

Elementeita

for three hours, though you'll have to bargain hard for this. The owner of Amigo's Guest House in Nakuru can set you up with a driver. Alternatively, contact Black Bird Tours (☎ 037-40830), Bliss Tours & Travel (☎ 037-44477, fax 45739) or Crater Travel (☎ 037-215019). A three-hour trip into the park costs around KSh 4000 per Suzuki open-top vehicle, not including park fees.

If you're driving, there's access from three points: the main gate; Lanet, just a few kilometres along the Nairobi road; and Nderit gate about 4km south of Lake Nakuru.

LAKE KAMNAROK & KERIO VALLEY NATIONAL RESERVES

These two little-visited national reserves, divided by the Kerio River, lie in the heart of the beautiful Kerio Valley which is sandwiched between the **Cherangani** and **Tugen** hills. The reasons to come here are the prolific birdlife, the crocodiles, elephants, wonderful landscape and chance to explore on foot.

Lake Kamnarok (signposted from the Iten-Kabarnet road) on the east of the river is the more accessible of the two reserves.

The best person to contact for up-to-date information about these reserves and trekking in the region is the dynamic and traveller-friendly warden at Lake Bogoria National Reserve (☎ 037-40746, fax 40748) PO Box 64, Marigat.

LAKE BOGORIA NATIONAL RESERVE

Birdlife International recently announced that Bogoria is the new home of the flamingo and around 1.5 million birds currently reside there. It's one of the greatest spectacles in East Africa.

Bogoria is a wonderful, well run little park and some access on bicycle or foot is possible, at least as far as the **hot springs** and **geysers**. They're not comparable with those at Rotorua in New Zealand but if you've never seen geysers before then this is the place. The springs are hot enough to boil an egg so don't get too close.

Walking and cycling elsewhere in the park is by prior arrangement and then only

with an armed ranger; the arrival of a small buffalo population has made walking a little more hazardous. Contact the warden in advance (☎ 037-40746, fax 40748) PO Box 64, Marigat.

The eastern side of the lake is dominated by the sheer face of the Siracho Escarpment and the north-eastern extremities of the Aberdares. To the south of the lake is a wooded area with plentiful wildlife, especially greater kudu. The land to the west of the lake is a hot and barren wilderness of rocks and scrub, though you'll almost always catch sight of small herds of Thomson's gazelle, and groups of zebra and warthog close to the lake. The park is also a great place to see klipspringer and, if you're lucky, leopards and cheetahs.

North of Lake Bogoria, outside the park, is the **Kesubo Swamp**, only recently developed as a tourist area. Over 200 species of birds are resident and the swamp holds the Kenyan record for the largest number of bird species seen in one hour (96!). Members of a local youth group have been set up as guides (around KSh 250 per person) and they are learning fast. Ask at the warden's office for further details.

Entry is US$15 per person (US$5 for children and students) plus KSh 200 per vehicle.

Places to Stay

There are three camp sites at the southern end of the lake – *Acacia*, *Riverside* and *Fig Tree*. Fig Tree Camp is near perfect, with a permanent stream and shaded by huge fig trees, though baboons are sometimes a problem and the long drop toilets are just about dead.

The lake water is totally undrinkable (the stream at Fig Tree Camp is good) so bring all drinking water. There's also a well equipped camp site just outside the gate. Camping is US$8 per person for nonresidents or KSh 150 for residents. Children and students pay US$2 and KSh 50 respectively.

Papyrus Inn beside Loboi Gate offers B&B at KSh 400/600 for singles/doubles. The shared bathroom facilities are of a poor standard, though the staff are friendly, there's a restaurant and bar and you may be able hire a bicycle.

Lake Bogoria Hotel (☎ 037-40748, 02-249055, fax 249066) about 2km before the same entry gate is a huge, top end place set in well tended gardens. Rooms cost the equivalent of US$60/120 in the low season rising to US$130/160 in the high season, full board. There's a swimming pool fed from a natural spring and the place is open to nonresidents for lunch (US$13) and dinner (US$15).

Marigat Inn or the shabbier *Salama Lodge* are possibilities in Marigat town.

Getting There & Away
There are two entrance gates to Lake Bogoria – Emsos in the south and Loboi in the north. You'll see the signpost for the Emsos Gate on the B4 about 38km past Nakuru heading north but if you take it, you'll need a serious 4WD – the last 5km leading down to the southern park entrance is like a rough, dry river bed. In addition, signposting along the route from the turn-off is almost nonexistent.

The more straightforward entry to the park is from the Loboi Gate a few kilometres before you reach Marigat on the B4. It's also signposted. From the turn-off, it's 20km to the actual park entrance along a good, sealed road, which continues to the hot springs.

Three matatus leave Marigat for Loboi every day after about 4.30 pm, returning to Marigat at 8 am the following morning.

There's an Esso petrol station on the main road at Marigat.

LAKE BARINGO
☎ 0328
Some 25km north of the town of Marigat you come to the village of **Kampi ya Samaki** which is the centre for exploring Lake Baringo. Unfortunately soil erosion is so bad on the western perimeter of the lake that whenever there's a downpour the lake fills with a massive amount of mud and silt ensuring that the water is almost always muddy. It has been over-fished to such an extent that any tilapia caught these days are rarely more than 15cm long.

Despite all this, Lake Baringo, with its islands (two of them inhabited) and encircling mountains, is still a spectacular sight

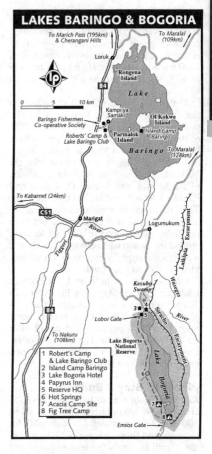

LAKES BARINGO & BOGORIA

1 Robert's Camp & Lake Baringo Club
2 Island Camp Baringo
3 Lake Bogoria Hotel
4 Papyrus Inn
5 Reserve HQ
6 Hot Springs
7 Acacia Camp Site
8 Fig Tree Camp

and a very mellow place to visit. Boating trips are a popular activity and there's even a so-called 'Devil's Island' which local people will tell you is haunted.

Tourists pay an entrance fee of KSh 200 to enter Kampi ya Samaki (there is a barrier across the road just before the Baringo Club).

Activities
Other than birdwatching, the most popular activity is **boat rides** on the lake and visits to the islands. These are best arranged through the Baringo Fishermen Co-operative Society

(☎ 51408) which has an office on the outskirts of Kampi ya Samaki. This quite well organised group of mainly out-of-work fishermen have their own boats and charge KSh 1800 per boat per hour. If you want to go to Devil's Island there is an additional charge of KSh 200 per person.

The group also runs **birdwatching trips** to the dramatic cliffs (the rock is said to be suitable for technical climbing) where 75% of Baringo's 480 recorded bird species have been seen. Cultural tours to Pokot, Tugen and Njemps villages close to the lake are also possible. The Njemps are local cousins of the Maasai who live on Ol Kokwa and Parmalok Islands and around the lakeshore. The tribe practices a mixture of pastoralism and fishing and has an arrangement with the fishermen so you're allowed to walk around freely and take photographs. There's a KSh 500 charge for entering each village, plus the cost of your guide's time.

One-hour boat trips from Lake Baringo Club (see Places to Stay – Top End) cost KSh 800 per person per hour (minimum two people), bird walks KSh 400 per person, **horse rides** KSh 1000 per hour and **camel rides** KSh 500 per half hour. The club also offers trips to Lake Bogoria for KSh 2500 per person (minimum two people), plus park fees.

Places to Stay – Budget

Robert's Camp next to Lake Baringo Club charges KSh 200 per person per night (KSh 100 for children under 12 years old) for camping and firewood costs KSh 80 a bundle. Facilities include clean showers and toilets, a store with a good selection of groceries, meat (fresh and processed) and dairy products, plus a bar which is open daily from 7 am to noon and 4 pm until midnight. There are also three double bandas available for KSh 500/1000 for singles/doubles, but you pay extra (KSh 500) for a private bathroom and cooking facilities. Demand is heavy and it's best to book in advance through Mrs E Roberts, PO Box 1051, Nakuru. The people here are very friendly and there's a huge land tortoise which ambles around the grounds and appears to be used to the attention it receives.

Campers need to exercise some common caution regarding the hippos. Although they may graze within just 1m of your tent at night, you should stay at least 20m away from them when you can, especially if they have young ones, and don't use torches (flashlights) or flash photography. They are wild animals and should be regarded with respect.

Bahari Lodge where all the drivers of safari vehicles stay is the best accommodation in Kampi ya Samaki. It's very clean and tidy and all the beds have mosquito nets though the double rooms are a little small. Rates are KSh 200/400 with shared bathrooms. All the rooms surround a bar/restaurant area and meals and cold drinks are available.

Lake View Lodge overlooks, unsurprisingly, the lake. In a simple setting, beds (with mosquito nets) cost KSh 100 per person. Bring your own padlock.

Lake Breeze Hotel is in a great position and the rooms are OK at KSh 200/400, but the noise from the bar is a problem. An extension is being built and you can camp here for KSh 150.

Places to Stay – Top End

Lake Baringo Club one of the Block Hotels chain (☎ 02-540780, fax 543810) is right next door to Robert's Camp. Singles/doubles with full board are US$56/112 in the low season and US$122/152 in the high season (July and August). Children under 12 years sharing a room with adults stay for free and pay only for meals (50% of adult meal prices). The rooms are pleasant, the cuisine excellent and the staff very friendly. Facilities at the club include a swimming pool, dart boards, table tennis table, badminton court, a library and a whole range of local excursions. You can use the facilities by paying a KSh 150 fee (KSh 200 at weekends). The useful guides *Birds of Lake Baringo* by Terry Stevenson and *Guide to Trees of Lake Baringo Club* by Hilary Garland (not as specific as you may think) are available at reception.

Island Camp Baringo is an excellent place to stay. A beautifully conceived, luxury tented lodge sited on the extreme southern tip of Ol Kokwa Island, it's the perfect hideaway.

Baringo Wildlife

Many different species of aquatic, animal and birdlife are supported by Lake Baringo. Herds of hippo invade the grassy shores every evening to browse, and you'll probably hear their characteristic grunt at night. If they decide to crop the grass right next to your tent, stay where you are. They're not aggressive animals but if you frighten or annoy them they might go for you. And, despite all appearances, they can *move!* The crocodiles are relatively small and, so far, there have been no recorded incidents of humans being attacked. They prefer goats, of which vast flocks contribute seriously to deforestation and soil erosion in this area.

Lake Baringo's main attraction is the bird life: it's the birdwatching centre of Kenya and attracts people from all over the world. Kenya has over 1200 different species of birds and more than 450 of them have been sighted at Lake Baringo. Birdwatching is a serious business and Lake Baringo Club has a resident ornithologist who leads birdwatching tours and gives advice to guests. A few years ago she set a world record for the number of species seen in a 24 hour period – over 300!

There's a constant twittering, chirping and cooing of birds in the trees around the lake, in the rushes on the lake and even on the steep face of the nearby escarpment. Even if you have no previous interest in birdwatching, it's hard to resist setting off on a dawn walk, the highlight of which is likely to be sighting hornbills or the magnificent eagles which live almost exclusively on rock hyrax.

There are 25 double tents each with their own shower and toilet and all of them have superb views over the lake. Facilities at Island Camp include two bars, a swimming pool and water sports equipment. Full board costs US$85/170 inclusive of return boat transfer. Children under 12 pay 50%. Guarded parking is available in the village between the main street and the lakeshore. The locals can all point you in the right direction. The boats leave from a jetty at the far northern end of Kampi

ya Samaki village. Book through Let's Go Travel (☎ 02-340331, fax 336890, email info@letsgosafari.com) in Nairobi. For more information, check out the Web site at www.letsgosafari.com.

Places to Eat

Campers should bring much of what they need from Nakuru or even Marigat. Vegetables and fruit are sometimes in short supply in Kampi ya Samaki.

Those who want to splurge can eat at the *Lake Baringo Club*. As you might expect, the meals here are excellent but it will cost you KSh 870 for lunch, KSh 990 for dinner. Beers are expensive at KSh 120 for a large Tusker. The club is also the only place where you can buy petrol and diesel between Marigat and Maralal.

In the village, try *Mombasa* and *Bethania* hotels for cheap stodge. The *Lake Breeze Hotel* offers a wider menu (main courses around KSh 150) and certainly picks up a breeze in the evening – it's a great place for a cold beer. *Hippo Lodge* is also not bad and you can go to the Hippo Video Show for KSh 10.

Getting There & Away

There are three buses (KSh 100) per day in either direction between Kampi ya Samaki and Nakuru as well as a number of matatus (KSh 130) and Nissan minibuses (KSh 150). The journey takes almost two hours. From Kampi ya Samaki much of the transport leaves early in the morning. If you have difficulty finding direct transport from Kampi ya Samaki to Nakuru at any time of day, first take something to Marigat from where there are more frequent connections to Nakuru.

MASAI MARA NATIONAL RESERVE

The Mara is, with good reason, the most popular national reserve in Kenya: this is the Kenyan section of the Serengeti Plains and wildlife abounds. This is also traditionally the land of the Maasai.

The Mara is 320 sq km of open grassland, dotted in the south-east corner with the distinctive flat-topped acacia trees. It is watered by the Mara River and its tributary the Talek River. The western border of the park is the spectacular Esoit Oloololo (Siria) Escarpment, where the concentration of wildlife is the highest. However, this area of swampy ground is almost impossible to get around after heavy rain. Conversely, the concentrations of tourist minibuses are highest at the eastern end of the park around the Oloolaimutiek and Talek gates as it's these areas which are the most accessible by road from Nairobi.

Minibuses wander all over the Mara making new tracks wherever they feel fit. This should not be encouraged.

Fauna

Wherever you go in the Mara you'll see an astonishing amount of wildlife. Lions are found in large prides everywhere and it's not at all uncommon to see them hunting. Cheetahs and leopards are harder to spot but are still fairly common. Elephants, buffaloes, zebras and hippos also exist in large numbers within the reserve as do the black-striped Thomson's gazelle (Tommys), the larger Grant's gazelle, impala, topi, Coke's hartebeest and of course the wildebeest. Around 37 black rhino live in the park but are rarely seen: some may have been poached from over the border in Tanzania. Other common animals include the Maasai giraffe, baboon (especially around the lodges), warthog, spotted hyena (see the boxed text 'The Sisterhood'), bat-eared foxes and grey (or side-striped) jackal.

The highlight of the Mara is without doubt the annual wildebeest migration when millions of these ungainly beasts move north from the Serengeti in July and August in search of lush grass, before turning south again around October. It is truly a staggering experience to be in the reserve at these times.

Information

Entry to the reserve is US$27 per person per day (US$10 for children). Vehicle entry is KSh 200, or KSh 500 if there are more than six seats. We've had reports from some

The Sisterhood

Hyenas get bad press. They are portrayed as the 'bad boys' of the African plains, scavengers and rogues who steal kills from poor defenceless lions, and who would eat their own mother if she stood still for long enough. Don't believe the Disney pro-lion brigade. The truth is far more complex.

Hyena society is matriarchal. Social status is hereditary and if the alpha female has a female cub she will take over leadership of the clan when her mother dies. Males only acquire status when they are sons of high-ranking females, but even they are cast out upon maturity (three years old) to join the lower ranks of a different clan.

High-ranking animals get priority at kills so those at the bottom of the pile (ie males) need to get as much meat down them before being turfed off (hence the feeding frenzy). An average hyena (50kg) can eat 15kg of food in one sitting and nothing is wasted. They feed on their own kills about 75% of the time: lions steal hyena kills, not the other way around – it takes 20 hyenas to see off one male lion.

Hyenas are not cannibals and are extremely sociable. Their whooping calls are greetings to other members of the clan and cubs are brought up in a communal den with up to 17 other youngsters. The hysterical laughter attributed to hyenas is not a gesture of merciless pleasure when closing in for the kill, rather a response to being attacked by a higher ranking animal, 'Don't hurt me. I'm only a subordinate!'

Hyenas are not hermaphrodite. Females do have phalluses, but they are for display not fornication – they become erect when greeting members of the clan. While this makes it hard for humans to tell the sexes apart, female hyenas have no problem in finding a mate (of the opposite sex) when they come into season.

Researchers have been studying one clan of spotted hyenas in the Masai Mara since 1988 and give regular lectures at Dream Camp.

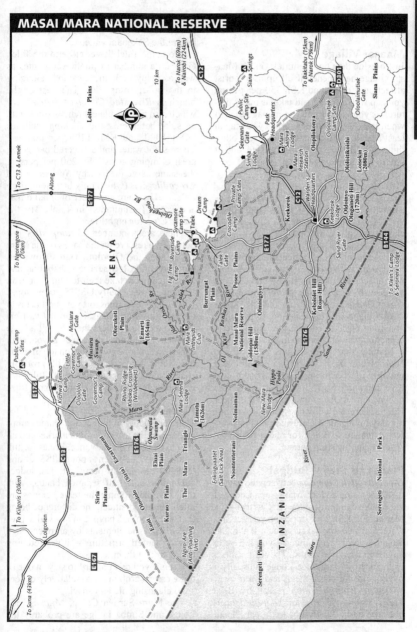

MASAI MARA NATIONAL RESERVE

KENYA

readers that park fees have been charged even when camping outside the park gates.

Maasai Village

Just outside the Ooloolaimutiek Gate a Maasai village has opened itself up as a tourist attraction. For around KSh 350 per person you can walk around and take as many pictures as you like. If you can manage to visit when there are no other tourists you may at least be able to talk to the villagers; at other times you'll have the crap hassled out of you to buy trinkets and bead work.

Narok

Narok, the main access point to the Mara, is a small provincial town a few hours drive west of Nairobi. There are branches of Barclays (with an ATM) and the Kenya Commercial banks, a post office (with a card phone) and a range of budget and mid-range hotels. *Spear Hotel* has reasonable rooms with attached bathrooms at KSh 300/600, but eat elsewhere. *Osupuko Motel* and *Kamiti Guest House* are also cheap and OK. *Kim's Dishes* diagonally opposite the Agip station, is a good place to eat and there are several basic but busy bars on the main street.

Matatus/share-taxis between Narok and Nairobi cost KSh 200/150. Less frequent matatus to Nyahururu and Naivasha cost KSh 220 and KSh 150. Matatus leave from outside Kim's Dishes and up from the Spear Hotel. There is usually one truck or staff bus per day to Sekenani Gate and one long-suffering matatu to Talek for about KSh 200. Ask around the Agip garage.

Places to Stay – Budget

Ooloolaimutiek Campsite between the gate of the same name and the Mara Sopa Lodge at the eastern extremity of the park is run by the Maasai. For KSh 200 per person you get firewood and an *askari* (security guard) at night, though water is very limited – you'll have to buy extra from the Maasai. The staff canteen of the nearby Mara Sopa Lodge is usually a lively place for cheap meals and warm beer.

Olperr Elongo Camp is run by Bike Treks (☎ 02-446371, email biktreks@formnet.com) and offers full board in permanent

tents or the well equipped camp site next door. The turn-off to the camp is about 1km before the Sekenani Gate.

Along the Talek River close to the Talek Gate are a number of public camp sites as well as many permanent camps belonging to the safari companies. The best of the bunch is *Riverside Camp* (☎ 0305-2128) which also has permanent tents – some with en suite bathrooms and cooking facilities (KSh 1000 and KSh 1200 per double). There's hot water and a covered bar/eating area. Camping costs KSh 250 per person, the same as at the nearby *Sycamore* and *Crocodile* sites (which only have long-drop toilets). There are a number of small dukas and *hoteli* (restaurants) in Talek. Try the *Sicily Club* for nightlife.

There are a number of *camp sites* just outside the reserve on the banks of the Mara River near the Oloololo Gate. However, they are none too secure – baboons and thieves can both take their toll on your gear. Camping costs a hefty US$15 per person.

If you have no transport your best bet is to go walking with Maasai *moran* (warrior) outside the park, where there is still a large amount of wildlife. This can be a wonderful experience, but be aware that on top of guide fees local Maasai groups will probably charge you for crossing their land. Talek is a good base for sorting out short walking trips.

Places to Stay – Top End

There are plenty of lodges and tented camps catering to the top end of the market and all should be booked in advance. Prices for full board vary between about US$50 and US$300 per person per night. The lodges generally consist of separate bandas with their own bathrooms; the tented camps are often almost identical, the difference being that the 'rooms' have canvas walls protected from the elements by an open-sided *makuti*-roofed structure – it's stretching things to call them tents.

Even if you can't afford to stay in one of these camps drop in for a (relatively expensive) cleansing ale and snack.

The Mara Sarova Camp, Mara Serena Lodge and Simba Lodge are probably the best places for fuel in the park, though prices are higher than in Narok or Nairobi.

You don't have to pay the high park entry fees if you're staying in any of the lodges that are actually outside the reserve.

Eastern End *Mara Sopa Lodge* (☎ 02-336088) by Oloolaimutiek Gate is an attractively designed modern place with a commanding view. Rates for singles/doubles with full board are US$81/115. Over Christmas, May and June prices double.

Keekorok Lodge part of the Block Hotels (☎ 02-540780, fax 543810) is an older but well maintained lodge on a grassy plain. Full board costs US$47/94 in the low season, US$119/183 in the high season. Keekorok also operates balloon flights.

Mara Sarova Lodge part of the Sarova Hotels chain (☎ 02-713333, fax 715566, email reservations@sarova.co.ke) is not far from the Sekenani Gate and has the works, including a swimming pool. Full board here is US$60/120 in low season, US$150/200 in high season.

Siana Springs (☎ 02-750298, fax 746826) is a tented lodge about 15km from Sekenani Gate, outside the reserve. The 'cottages' are dotted around a beautiful green clearing with shady trees and sweeping lawns. There's an open-air bar and dining room and a roaring log fire at night. Although it's not actually in the reserve, there's a lot of wildlife around the camp. There's dawn walks and night-time spotlight wildlife drives as well as a baited leopard (meat left out in front of the lodge to entice leopards into the sight of guests). The cost is US$90/180 in low season, rising to US$200/280.

Sekenani Camp (☎ 02-333285, fax 228 875), also on the north-eastern boundary outside the reserve, is a small place – well placed to make the most of the views – with just 15 tents. Accommodation costs US$64/128 in low season, US$185/247 high season for full board and including wildlife drives.

Centre *Fig Tree Camp* (☎ 02-221439, fax 332170, email madahold@form-net.com) along the northern banks of the Talek River is a tented camp with a swimming pool and singles/doubles for US$147/200 with full board in high season, US$55/110 in low season. This is the other lodge from which you can take a balloon safari; it's wise to book in advance at the Nairobi office though you can book here too. Wildlife drives are available for US$35, night drives US$30, wildlife walks cost US$17 or you can take a horse safari for US$30. The food and management have improved in recent years.

Mara Intrepids Club (☎ 02-716628, fax 716457, email prestigehotels@form-net .com) also along the banks of the river has 30 tents and is considerably more expensive at US$239/325 for full board dropping to US$107/173 in the low season. It is also the base for Night Sight (☎ 02-581676) which runs night wildlife drives using powerful nightsights and infra-red equipment. The bar overlooking the river is very pleasant and the sunset views over the plains are wonderful, but it's overpriced.

Dream Camp (☎ 02-572139, fax 577489, email dreamtravel@form-net.com) is a new kid on the block and the only eco-lodge in the Mara. All power comes from solar panels, kitchen and toilet waste is composted and all the rubbish is separated and disposed of in an environmentally friendly manner. Even the dirty washing water is saved and used to water the grounds. Every one of the 18 permanent tents has been designed individually and all have interesting views. Conservationists in the Mara come in to give informal lectures, and walking safaris with the local Maasai can be arranged. Rates are US$80 per person per night year round with full board. A three day (two night, flights included) visit will cost you US$425 all in.

Mara Serena Lodge (☎ 02-711077, fax 718103, email cro@serena.co.ke) is on a superb site overlooking the Mara River, in the centre of the reserve. It blends in beautifully with the surrounding countryside and was built to resemble a modern Maasai village. Rates with full board are US$120/160, dropping to US$50/100 in the low season.

North-Western End *Governor's Camp* (☎ 02-331871, fax 726427, email govscamp@ africaonline.co.ke) and *Little Governor's*

Camp (owned by the same people) are both beautiful little places where service is very personalised and excellent. Singles/doubles with full board plus wildlife drives at either place cost US$260/390.

Kichwa Tembo Camp (☎ *02-750298, fax 746826, email conscorp@conscorp.co.ke)* just outside the northern boundary has spectacular savanna views. The cost is US$300/400 in high season, dropping to US$150/200 in low season. This place is highly rated and supposedly serves the best food in the Mara.

Mara Safari Club (☎ *02-216940, fax 216796, email lonhotsm@form-net.com)* part of the Lonrho chain of hotels is also outside the reserve, north of Oloololo Gate. The camp is built on a bend in the Mara River, and the main building is cantilevered right out over the bank. Full board rates during the high season are US$320/430 and US$232/303 in the low season; all prices include two wildlife drives per day.

Other accommodation outside the park north of Oloololo Gate includes *Mara River Camp* (☎ *02-331684, fax 216528, email sa vannah@africaonline.co.ke)* at US$63/136 in the low season, US$223/346 in the high season, including wildlife drives and walks are possible.

Getting There & Away

Air Air Kenya Aviation (☎ 02-501601, fax 602951, email resvns@airkenya.com) has twice-daily flights between Nairobi's Wilson airport and Masai Mara, departing Nairobi at 10 am and 3 pm, and from the Mara at 11 am and 4 pm. The one-way/return fares are US$100/170, but if you are not on a package and being met by your hosts, you'll have to add the cost of airstrip transfers. When picking up from a host of airstrips in the Mara the plane does not wait around even if it arrives early.

Matatu, Car & 4WD The Mara is not a place you come to without transport. There is no public transport within the park and even if there was there's certainly no way you could do a wildlife drive in a matatu. You can get public transport of sorts to the

Sekenani and Talek gates from Narok, but then you have the problem of getting into the park. Hitching may be possible in the high season, but could take days. After Narok there is about 50km of good road before the bitumen runs out and the road becomes rough for the next 40km.

It's also possible to approach the reserve from Kisii and the west along reasonably well maintained dirt roads. You can get closer to the park by public transport but there are far fewer tourist vehicles to hitch a ride with. Matatus run as far as Kilgoris directly south of Kisii, or Suna on the main A1 route close to Isebania on the Tanzanian border.

LAKE MAGADI

Lake Magadi is the most southerly of the Rift Valley lakes in Kenya and is rarely visited by tourists. Of the soda lakes it is the most mineral-rich and supports many flamingos and other water birds. In parts the surface of the lake resembles a weird sci-fi landscape of shimmering pink and white. This soda crust is formed when the mineral-rich water, pumped up from hot springs deep underground, evaporates rapidly in the 38°C heat to leave a layer of mineral salts: a soda extraction factory 'harvests' this layer and extracts sodium chloride (common salt) and sodium carbonate ('soda').

A causeway leads across the most visually dramatic part of this strange landscape to a viewpoint on the western shore. It's worth a drive (4WD only) or alternatively head to the hot springs to the south. While the springs are nothing special, the fish swimming in the near-boiling water are rare. Wildebeest and gazelles are sometimes seen here.

The town of Magadi was built by the multinational ICI, and the soda factory is the only reason why so many people live in this extremely hot place. Facilities in town are limited, but you will find a number of small bars/restaurants, shops and a swimming pool – though a sign says 'Residents Only', they appear to be flexible. Campers are not short of space to pitch a tent, but it is best to ask at the police station as to the best location.

Olorgasailie Prehistoric Site
Important archaeological finds were made at this site, 40km before Magadi, by Louis and Mary Leakey in the 1940s. Hand axes and stone tools thought to have been made by *Homo erectus* around half a million years ago were unearthed. Fossils have also been discovered and some have been left in place, protected from the elements by shade roofs. A guided tour is available and there are numerous notice boards and displays.

Places to Stay
At Olorgasailie, there are three twin-bed bandas for rent at KSh 500 per person. You need to bring all your own food, but water

is available. This is not a bad place to stay for the night.

At Kiserian in the foothills of the Ngong Hills *Whistling Thorns* makes a good staging post for the trip down to Magadi (see Ngong Hills in the Nairobi chapter).

Getting There & Away
The C58 is a good minor road from Nairobi, along which Akamba buses run at 1 pm and 3 pm every day (KSh 170). There are other bus services from Nairobi country bus station around 10 am and 5 pm; return trips are at 6 am and 3 pm. Both buses pass the junction which leads to the archaeological site, about a 2km walk from the main road.

The Central Highlands

The Kenyan Central Highlands form the eastern wall of the Rift Valley as far as Maralal. They comprise the Aberdare Range (known to the Kikuyu as *Nyandarua*, 'drying hide') and the massif of Mt Kenya and are the heartland of the Kikuyu people (see the Facts about Kenya and Facts about East Africa chapters). Within the area are the Aberdare and Mt Kenya national parks. For ease of reference, the areas of the highlands that lie north of Nyahururu, Nanyuki and Meru are discussed in the Northern Kenya chapter.

The region is very fertile, well watered, intensively cultivated and thickly forested. The climate is excellent. No wonder the land was coveted by white settlers, who found they could make a good living growing cash crops all year round. They began arriving in ever increasing numbers once the Mombasa-Uganda railway was completed. It's also unsurprising that the Kikuyu greatly resented the loss of their land and that the Mau Mau Rebellion eventually came to pass (see the Facts about Kenya chapter).

Today the Kikuyu are a strong political and economic power in Kenya – so strong that the tribe has outgrown its homelands. The rapidly expanding population is putting the remaining highland forests under great pressure and it's unlikely that much forest will remain in 20 years.

NYERI
☎ 0171

Nyeri is one of the largest towns in the Central Highlands, the administrative headquarters of Central province and a gateway to Aberdare National Park. It's a lively place, essentially a trading centre for the surrounding farmland, with an extensive market. It also has a good choice of hotels and restaurants but little to delay you long. On a clear day you can see Mt Kenya.

Information
You can send email from Niblo Stationers (☎ 2706) and there are a number of card-

Highlights

- Trout fishing high in the Aberdare Ranges
- Taking tea on the lawn at Outspan Hotel in Nyeri
- Drinking beer by the fire at Thomson's Falls Lodge
- Sampling the fine *miraa* available in Meru

phones outside Nyeri's three post offices. Barclays Bank has an ATM machine.

Things to See & Do
Lord Baden-Powell, the founder of the Scout Association movement, spent his final years here (see the boxed text 'Baden-Powell Museum').

The **Gliding Club of Kenya** has its headquarters at Mweiga, a short distance north of Nyeri. If you are into soaring or would like to take a glide over the Aberdares get in touch with the managers, Peter & Petra Allmendinger (☎/fax 2748, email gliding@africaonline.co.ke) PO Box 926, Nyeri. Pleasure flights will cost you US$50. The Allmendingers also run **horse riding trips**, Aberdares **safaris** and an excellent homestay (see Places to Stay – Top End). Its Web site is www.innowebtive.de/kenya.htm.

Wajee Camp (☎ 60359, 02-226770 in Nairobi) is a lovely little place in the foothills of the Aberdares about 18km south of Nyeri. The 10-hectare nature reserve is criss-crossed with trails. A good bird guide will point out the rare forest birds of the area for about KSh 300 per day – you can borrow binoculars. Food is available. The sanctuary is signposted from the main road 5km south of Nyeri, and also from the road 2km north of Karatina. Coming from either direction (you can get a matatu from Karatina and Nyeri), you head to Mukurweini before turning off the main road and heading 3km south to Mihuti – the camp is a further 1km south of the village. If you want to stay here,

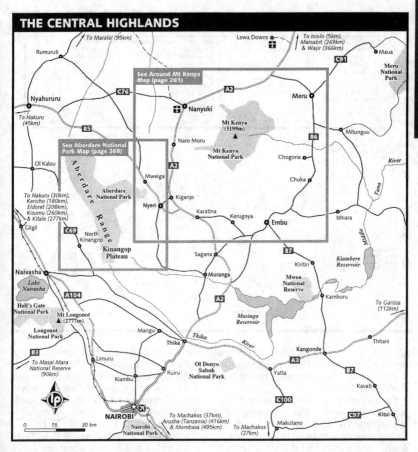

THE CENTRAL HIGHLANDS

To Maralal (95km)

Rumuruti

Lewa Downs

To Isiolo (5km),
Marsabit (269km)
& Wajir (366km)

Maua

C91

Meru
National
Park

Nyahururu

C76

See Around Mt Kenya
Map (page 281)

A2

Nanyuki

Meru

To Nakuru
(45km)

B5

Mt Kenya
(5199m)

Mitunguu

Ol Kalou

See Aberdare National
Park Map (page 268)

Naro Moru

Mt Kenya
National Park

Chogoria

B6

River

A2

Mweiga

Chuka

Aberdare
National Park

Kiganjo

Tana

To Nakuru (30km),
Kericho (180km),
Eldoret (208km),
Kisumu (260km),
& Kitale (277km)

Nyeri

Karatina

Kerugoya

Embu

Ishiara

Gilgil

C69

North
Kinangop

Middle

Kinangop
Plateau

Sagana

B7

Kiritiri

Kiambere
Reservoir

Naivasha

Muranga

Lake
Naivasha

A104

Mwea
National
Reserve

Kamburu

Hell's Gate
National Park

Mt Longonot
(2777m)

Masinga
Reservoir

To Garissa
(112km)

Longonot
National Park

Mangu

Thika

Thika

River

Kangonde

Thitani

B3

Limuru

Ruiru

A2

Yatta

A3

B7

To Masai Mara
National Reserve
(90km)

Kiambu

Ol Donyo
Sabuk
National Park

Kavati

NAIROBI

To Machakos (37km),
Arusha (Tanzania) (416km)
& Mombasa (495km)

To Machakos
(27km)

Makutano

C100

C97

Kitui

Nairobi
National Park

0   15   30 km

there are a few cheap *bandas* (KSh 180 per person) and a *camp site* (KSh 120).

Places to Stay – Budget

The reliable *Nyeri Star Restaurant and Board & Lodging* offers singles/doubles with attached bathroom for KSh 250/400. It's a big, friendly place with a popular bar and restaurant and secure parking. Despite its proximity to the bus station it's rarely full.

Cheaper, though not as good, is *Kimathi Way Motel* behind a popular bar, which is a little noisy at times. The rooms are reasonable at KSh 200/400, though only the singles

are self-contained. The *rooms* at the back of Greenleaf Restaurant (☎ 2126) are more expensive at KSh 300/450, but a little better.

At the northern end of town the new *Ibis Hotel* (☎ 4858) is also a good place. Self-contained rooms here cost KSh 300/500. There's a pleasant covered courtyard and restaurant. Ibis hotels are being opened all over the highlands.

Places to Stay – Mid-Range

One of the best places in this range is the modern *Central Hotel* (☎ 2235) where singles/doubles with their own bathroom (and

KENYA

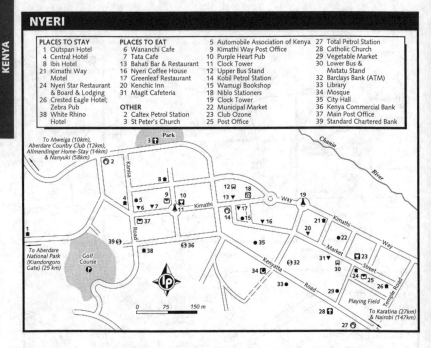

NYERI

PLACES TO STAY	PLACES TO EAT	5 Automobile Association of Kenya	27 Total Petrol Station
1 Outspan Hotel	6 Wananchi Cafe	9 Kimathi Way Post Office	28 Catholic Church
4 Central Hotel	7 Tata Cafe	10 Purple Heart Pub	29 Vegetable Market
8 Ibis Hotel	13 Bahati Bar & Restaurant	11 Clock Tower	30 Lower Bus &
21 Kimathi Way	16 Nyeri Coffee House	12 Upper Bus Stand	Matatu Stand
Motel	17 Greenleaf Restaurant	14 Kobil Petrol Station	32 Barclays Bank (ATM)
24 Nyeri Star Restaurant	20 Kenchic Inn	15 Wamugi Bookshop	33 Library
& Board & Lodging	31 Magit Cafeteria	18 Niblo Stationers	34 Mosque
26 Crested Eagle Hotel;		19 Clock Tower	35 City Hall
Zebra Pub	OTHER	22 Municipal Market	36 Kenya Commercial Bank
38 White Rhino	2 Caltex Petrol Station	23 Club Ozone	37 Main Post Office
Hotel	3 St Peter's Church	25 Post Office	39 Standard Chartered Bank

hot water) cost KSh 800/900. There are noisy suites for KSh 1000. The restaurant food is good and reasonably priced and there's guarded parking.

For a touch of old-world charm there's always the old white settlers' watering hole, *White Rhino Hotel (☎ 30934)*. However, it's shabby these days and really a better place to drink than to stay. And the self-contained rooms are expensive at KSh 700/1100.

Top of the range is the modern *Crested Eagle Hotel (☎ 30743)* which has rooms with attached bathroom for KSh 860/1020, including breakfast. The decor may be pure cheese, but the hotel is well appointed, and all the rooms have a radio and telephone. The double rooms at the front face Mt Kenya. Most credit cards are accepted and there's a guarded parking lot.

Places to Stay – Top End

On the outskirts is *Outspan Hotel (☎ 2424)* part of the Block Hotels chain. This is the check-in place for guests of Treetops Lodge in Aberdare National Park. It's sited in beautifully landscaped gardens opposite the golf course and has all the facilities you would expect from a top end country hotel (including a full-size snooker table). In the high season, half board costs US$122/152 for singles/doubles, and single/twin cottages cost US$146/200. In the low season it's KSh 2200/4400 for singles/doubles, with single/twin cottages at KSh 2950/5150. Children between the ages of two and 12 are charged about 30% of the adult rate.

Aberdare Country Club (☎ 55620, fax 55224, ark@form-net.com) situated about 17km north of Nyeri was once a watering hole and social focus for the white planters. These days it caters for the international leisure set heading to The Ark. Full board is US$138/182 in high season and US$91/144 in low season. Children aged from two to 12 are charged US$50 all year. Without a reservation you won't get through the gate.

Baden-Powell Museum

Nyeri is famous as the former home of Lord Baden-Powell, the founder of the worldwide Scout Association movement. It was here in the cottage called Paxto in the grounds of Outspan Hotel that he lived until his death. He's buried in the cemetery behind St Peter's church. The cottage was later occupied by Jim Corbett, a 'destroyer of man-eating tigers in central India during the 1920s and 1930s', according to the plaque in front of the cottage. These days, the cottage is a museum packed with scouting memorabilia. Bus loads of Scouts and Guides from all over the world tramp through every day. Just about everyone who visits leaves a memento so the place is awash with troop colours. Entry is free to members of the scouting movement and KSh 50 for anyone else (how the curator tells the difference is anyone's guess).

It's ironic that a white colonist should be honoured in this manner in Nyeri while one of Kenya's foremost independence fighters, General Dedan Kimathi, lies in an unmarked grave. Kimathi was captured by the British colonial authorities towards the end of the Mau Mau rebellion and was hanged in Kamiti prison – or so the western history books say. That, however, is not what is taught in Kenyan schools. Students are taught that he was buried alive. That's hard to believe, but who knows the truth?

SARAH JOLLY

Peter and Petra Allmendinger's *homestay* (☎/fax 2748, email gliding@africaonline .co.ke, PO Box 926, Nyeri) just north of the Aberdare Country Club is highly recommended, though the road can be difficult in the rainy season. It costs US$50 per person.

Places to Eat

The most reliable place to eat in town is the excellent *Greenleaf Restaurant* on Kimathi Way. It feels almost like an old London pub, all wood panelling and ancient fixtures and fittings. The food is good (chicken stew KSh 160) and you can sit on the balcony with a cold beer and watch street below.

Bahati Bar & Restaurant serves some good 'special chicken' (roasted) and *Magit Cafeteria* is a good place for breakfast. Other cheap cafes include *Tata Cafe* and *Wananchi Cafe*, and you can get some reasonable coffee and snacks at *Nyeri Coffee House*. A quarter fried chicken with chips at *Kenchic Inn* costs KSh 130.

The *restaurant* at the Crested Eagle isn't bad and lunch/dinner costs KSh 300/350. *Zebra Pub* downstairs is open to nonguests and serves cheap Tusker (KSh 65).

Entertainment

Purple Heart Pub is designed for drinkers who fear daylight. Or you can dance till dawn at *Club Ozone* (KSh 100 entry for men, KSh 50 for women) which plays a mixture of music and has some live acts.

The *bar* in front of Kimathi Way Motel has a balcony overlooking the street. It's good value and the jukebox is packed with Kikuyu music.

Getting There & Away

Generally speaking the upper bus stand deals with the big buses while the lower stage takes care of the matatus and local departures. There are regular buses to Nairobi (KSh 150), Nyahururu, Nakuru, Thika, and Nanyuki, and less frequently to places further on such as

Isiolo, Meru and Eldoret (KSh 350). The buses to Nairobi may involve a change at Karatina so check before buying a ticket.

Nissan minibuses and Peugeot share-taxis are more comfortable and faster than regular buses to Nairobi (KSh 180/220 for minibuses/share-taxis) and Nakuru (KSh 200/240). A Nissan minibus to Nanyuki costs KSh 80. To Mweiga and the Aberdare National Park headquarters the cost is KSh 30.

ABERDARE NATIONAL PARK

The park rarely features in the itineraries of safari companies and is even less visited by

independent travellers, mainly because vehicle entry is restricted to 4WD only. However, it is possible to take organised wildlife drives or even treks in the park.

Two different environments make up this park: the moorland, peaks and high forest of the 60km-long Kinangop plateau; and the Salient to the east where the forest slopes down to Nyeri.

Elephant and buffalo are the predominant animals, while rarer species include black rhino, bongo antelope, bush pig, giant forest hog, black serval cat and black leopard. Hundreds of bird species can be seen (look

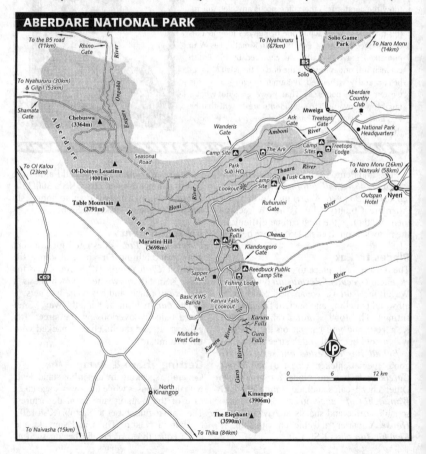

ABERDARE NATIONAL PARK

To the B5 road (11km)
Rhino Gate
River
To Nyahururu (67km)
Solio Game Park
To Naro Moru (14km)
B5
Solio
To Nyahururu (30km) & Gilgil (53km)
Aberdare Country Club
Shamata Gate
Chebuswa (3364m)
Ongobit
Ensure
Mweiga
Ark Gate
Treetops Gate
National Park Headquarters
Wanderis Gate
Amboni
River
The Ark
Camp Sites
Treetops Lodge
Aberdare Range
Camp Site
Park Sub-HQ
Seasonal Road
To Ol Kalou (23km)
Ol-Doinyo Lesatima (4001m)
River
Thaara
River
To Naro Moru (26km) & Nanyuki (58km)
Lookout
Camp Site
Tusk Camp
Table Mountain (3791m)
Honi
Ruhuruini Gate
Outspan Hotel
Nyeri
River
Maratini Hill (3698m)
Chania Falls
Chania
Chania
C69
Kiandongoro Gate
Reedbuck Public Camp Site
Gura
River
Sapper Hut
Fishing Lodge
Basic KWS Banda
Karura Falls Lookout
Karura Falls
Mutubio West Gate
Karura River
Gura River
Gura Falls
North Kinangop
Kinangop (3906m)
The Elephant (3590m)
To Naivasha (15km)
To Thika (84km)
0   6   12 km

out for the giant kingfishers) and it's worth remembering the Aberdares' small lion population when viewing the dramatic **Chania** and **Karura** falls, trout fishing or trekking.

Information

The park headquarters are in Mweiga (☎ 0171-55024, PO Box 22, Nyeri). Trekkers need advance permission from the warden and to take an obligatory armed ranger/guide (US$10 per day).

If you have no vehicle, wildlife viewing drives can be arranged through Aberdare Country Club or Outspan Hotel in Nyeri for about US$35 per person.

An excellent new 1:25,000 *Map of the Aberdare Salient & the Aberdare National Park* is available at the Mweiga headquarters (KSh 250). The 1:150,000 *The Aberdares National Park & Environs* produced by Tourist Maps is a reasonable guide to the area (KSh 250).

Entry through the Treetops or Ark gates requires permission from the park office in Mweiga. When driving from the Aberdare Salient to the Kinangop Plateau you must arrange for the road barrier below Tusk Camp to be unlocked.

Entry to the park costs US$27 per day (US$10 for children).

Places to Stay

Campers must make reservations at the park headquarters at Mweiga. The cost to stay at the *public camp sites* is US$8 per person (US$2 for children). There are also numerous *special camp sites*, with separate costs and booking procedures.

Fishing Lodge up on the high moor can be booked through the park headquarters for US$10 per person. The two large stone cottages sleep 12 people each and have bathrooms and store rooms. You can cook on the huge open fire, but bring your own wood. A black serval cat lives nearby. Bring your own bedding for all the bandas.

The excellent *Tusk Camp* close to Ruhuruini Gate, and *Sapper Hut* overlooking a waterfall on the Upper Magura River can be booked through Let's Go Travel in Nairobi (☎ 02-340331, email info@letsgosafari.com).

Tusk Camp sleeps eight and there are cooking facilities and hot water. The cost is KSh 5000 per night for the camp, plus KSh 2000 per group. Sapper hut (KSh 2000 per night) is more basic with an open fire, two beds and a hot water boiler.

Treetops Lodge with its shoebox-sized rooms and shared bathroom facilities isn't exactly a 'luxury' lodge. The words 'massively overrated' spring to mind and the constant elephant traffic to the salt lick and water hole below the lodge has destroyed much of the local vegetation. Full board (including transfer from Nyeri but excluding park entry fees) in the high season costs US$124/248 for singles/doubles, whereas in the low season it costs US$62/124. Children under seven years old are not admitted and those over seven are charged full adult rates. Book through Block Hotels (☎ 02-540780, fax 543810) in Nairobi. Having booked, turn up at Outspan Hotel in Nyeri by 12.30 pm for transfer to the park.

The Ark further into the park is better appointed and costs much more. Full board including transfers costs US$270/321 in the high season and US$147/173 in the low season. Restrictions on children are the same as at Treetops. Book through Lonrho Hotels (☎ 02-216940, fax 216796) in Nairobi. All guests are transferred from Aberdare Country Club at Mweiga, 12km north of Nyeri.

NYAHURURU (THOMSON'S FALLS)
☎ 0365

Nyahururu, or 'T Falls' as virtually everyone calls it, was one of the last white settler towns to be established in the colonial era and didn't really take off until the arrival of the railway spur from Gilgil in 1929. These days the railway carries only freight. Nyahururu is one of the highest towns in Kenya at 2360m; the climate is cool and invigorating and the surrounding undulating plateau is intensively cultivated.

The falls, on the outskirts of town, are named after Joseph Thomson, who in 1882 became the first European to walk from Mombasa to Lake Victoria. Formed by the

KENYA

waters of the Ewaso Narok River, the falls plummet over 72m into a ravine. A series of stone steps are the only safe access to the bottom of the ravine. There are also some fantastic walks downstream through the forested valley of the river or upstream a couple of kilometres to one of the highest hippo pools in Kenya. Take time to explore a little. Guides can be found, but you'll have to bargain hard.

Information

Email can be sent from Heri General Merchants (☎ 32138, email heri@net2000ke .com) on Sharpe Rd and there's a cardphone in front of the post office.

Places to Stay – Budget

Campers can stay at the *camp site* attached to the upmarket Thomson's Falls Lodge (☎ 22006, fax 32170). It's very pleasant and costs KSh 300 per person with as much firewood as you need and hot showers included.

A good value budget hotel is *Good Shepherd's Lodge* which offers self-contained singles for KSh 200 (no doubles). It's very clean and there's a popular restaurant out front.

For solo travellers (and couples) the quiet *Nyandarua County Council Guest House* behind the post office is a good bet. All the single rooms have attached bathrooms. The cost is KSh 150 per person and there is a restaurant and TV room that's well used by council workers and locals.

Going up in price, the family-run *Stadium Lodging* (☎ 32773) is OK value at KSh 300/450 for singles/doubles with attached bathroom. It's clean, the atmosphere is relaxed and the security is excellent.

Places to Stay – Mid-Range

In this category, *the* place to stay is *Thomson's Falls Lodge* (☎ 22006, fax 32170) overlooking the falls. It exudes nostalgia and old-world charm with its polished wooden floorboards and log fires. Accommodation is available either in the main building with its bar, lounge and dining room, or in separate cottages scattered over the well maintained lawns. Self-contained singles/doubles with hot water and your own

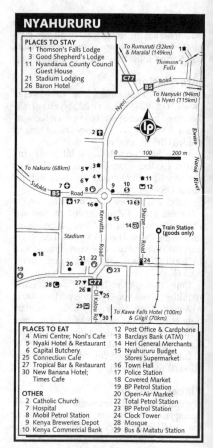

NYAHURURU

PLACES TO STAY
1 Thomson's Falls Lodge
3 Good Shepherd's Lodge
11 Nyandarua County Council
    Guest House
21 Stadium Lodging
26 Baron Hotel

PLACES TO EAT
4 Mimi Centre; Noni's Cafe
5 Nyaki Hotel & Restaurant
6 Capital Butchery
25 Connection Cafe
27 Tropical Bar & Restaurant
30 New Banana Hotel;
    Times Cafe

OTHER
2 Catholic Church
7 Hospital
8 Mobil Petrol Station
9 Kenya Breweries Depot
10 Kenya Commercial Bank
12 Post Office & Cardphone
13 Barclays Bank (ATM)
14 Heri General Merchants
15 Nyahururu Budget
    Stores Supermarket
16 Town Hall
17 Police Station
18 Covered Market
19 BP Petrol Station
20 Open-Air Market
22 Total Petrol Station
23 BP Petrol Station
24 Clock Tower
28 Mosque
29 Bus & Matatu Station

log fire cost KSh 1600/2000, with triples at KSh 2800 (all rates include breakfast).

If you prefer modernity then choose either *Baron* (☎ 32056) or *Kawa Falls* (☎ 32295) hotels. The Baron is a little more expensive at KSh 500/800, and a little tattier, but both are reasonable value.

Places to Eat

Most of the budget hotels and many of the bars have a *restaurant* where you can get standard African food. Meals at Kawa Falls Hotel, Baron Hotel and Nyaki Hotel are probably the best.

If you like beer and *nyama choma* try *Tropical Bar & Restaurant* around the corner from Baron Hotel. *Capital Butchery* next to Nyaki Hotel is also good for nyama choma.

For breakfast or a cheap lunch, *Times Cafe*, *New Banana Hotel* or *Connection Cafe* opposite the bus and matatu station are really pretty good. Or you can try *Noni's Cafe* in the new Mimi Centre at the other end of town.

For a minor splurge – or if you're staying there – eat at the *restaurant* at Thomson's Falls Lodge. A full English breakfast costs KSh 200. Three-course lunches or dinners with dessert and tea or coffee cost KSh 500. The lodge has the most interesting bars in town with deep, comfortable armchairs and blazing log fires. All facilities are open to nonguests and on-site campers.

For those who want to prepare their own meals, there's an excellent choice of fruit, vegetables and meat in the covered market, or try Nyahururu Budget Stores Supermarket.

Entertainment
There is a *disco* at Baron Hotel every Saturday night – reggae and Congolese pop are popular – and it sometimes hosts live bands. The *Kenya Breweries depot* on Subukia Rd also hosts gigs sometimes.

Getting There & Away
There are plenty of matatus until late afternoon in both directions between Nyahururu and Nakuru (KSh 80), and between Nyahururu and Nyeri (KSh 120). Other destinations served by regular matatus and buses include Nanyuki (KSh 170) and Naivasha (KSh 150). There are only two buses daily to Nairobi (KSh 250) and they leave early in the morning.

A number of matatus head to Maralal (about KSh 250), but departures dry up after about 1 pm. The Calypso bus passes through Nyahururu on its way to Maralal at about 10 am (it starts in Nairobi). Advance booking is not a bad idea. For the rest of the day, hitching is feasible but not easy. The road is surfaced as far as Rumuruti (KSh 70) after which it's gravel or *murram* (dirt).

Parts of the gravel road are in terrible shape but generally it's just very bumpy and not impassable.

THIKA
☎ 0151
Despite the fame that came with Elspeth Huxley's popular novel *Flame Trees of Thika*, the town itself comes as something of a disappointment – there are not even many flame trees! However, it's a great escape from the madness of urban Nairobi just 38km down the road. If you want to get a feel for a small Kenyan agricultural service town, Thika could be just the place.

The town's only 'attractions' as such are **Chania Falls** and **Thika Falls**, 1km from the centre of town off the busy Nairobi-Nyeri road (which thankfully bypasses Thika).

Places to Stay & Eat
If you decide to stay, there's a good choice of accommodation, particularly in the mid-range area, as it seems Thika is also a popular weekend conference venue.

Cheap is *Sky Motel* on Uhuru Rd (KSh 200). The place is really a seedy late-night drinking establishment however.

Best value in town, if not throughout all of the Central Highlands, is *New Fulilia Hotel (☎ 31286)* on the north end of Uhuru Rd – not to be confused with the other New Fulilia opposite Prismos Hotel. Single self-contained rooms, with hot water and beds big enough for a couple, go for KSh 350. It's very clean and tidy, there's a restaurant/bar downstairs and each room has a button to call room service.

More expensive is *12th December Hotel (☎ 22140)* on Commercial St near the post office. Singles/large doubles cost KSh 500/600, but the singles are not self-contained. Nevertheless it's a good place to stay.

Blue Post Hotel (☎ 22241) is a reasonable upmarket place set close to the very busy highway and the Chania River 2km north of town. Rooms cost KSh 850/1200 which is good value if you can get one with a balcony in the Chania Wing overlooking the falls. The other rooms are nowhere near as nice.

The hotel's restaurant is rather average, but the gardens and views of the falls make this a very pleasant place to stay.

For a good meal try the amazingly named **Macvast Executive Restaurant Two** on Commercial St, **Prismos Hotel** just north of the clock tower, or the wonderfully pink **David's Royal Paradise**, one block north of Commercial St, east of Uhuru St.

Getting There & Away

Matatus leave from a number of places around Thika. The main matatu stand, used mostly by local matatus, is near Sagret Hotel. Most long-distance matatus – to Nairobi (KSh 40, 45 minutes), Nakuru (KSh 180), Naivasha (KSh 170), Nyeri (KSh 150), Nyahururu (KSh 240) and Embu (KSh 120) – leave from behind Barclays Bank. Transport east towards Ol Donyo Sabuk, Kangonde and beyond can be caught from another matatu stand which is opposite White Line Hotel, or at the Garissa stage on the main road.

In Nairobi, matatus for Thika leave from around the Racecourse Rd and Ronald Ngala St junction.

OL DONYO SABUK NATIONAL PARK

Gazetted in 1967, this park contains buffalo, myriad bird species and numerous primates. The park's one road leads directly to the forested summit of **Ol Donyo Sabuk** (2146m). The Kikuyu people call the mountain *Kilimambongo*, which means 'buffalo mountain'. Accompanied by a ranger you can explore on foot, which will cost you KSh 300 for a half day and KSh 500 for a full day of guiding.

Park entry costs US$15/KSh 100 for non-residents/residents, while children pay US$5/KSh 50. Vehicle entry costs an additional KSh 200.

There's a shaded **camp site** (US$2 per person) just before the main gate, but facilities are minimal.

To get to the park, take a matatu from Thika to Kilimambongo then take another one to the village of Ol Donyo Sabuk, from where it's 2km to the park.

Mt Kenya

Mt Kenya is Africa's second-highest mountain at 5199m. Its gleaming and eroded snow-covered peaks can be seen for miles until the late-morning clouds obscure the view. Its lower slopes are intensively cultivated by the Kikuyu people and the closely related Embu and Meru peoples, along with the descendants of white settlers.

So vast is this mountain that it's not hard to understand why the Kikuyu deified it, why their houses are built with the doors facing the peak and why it was probably never scaled until the arrival of European explorers. It's the seat of *Ngai*, the Kikuyu god. You *must* climb to the top of this mountain. It's a superb experience. But take it steady otherwise Ngai will teach you a lesson.

Mt Kenya's highest peaks, Batian and Nelion, can only be reached by mountaineers with technical skills. However, Point Lenana, the third-highest peak at 4985m, can be reached by trekkers. There are superb views over the surrounding country from Point Lenana and from other high points around the main peaks, though the summit is often clothed in mist from late morning until late afternoon.

As marvellous as the summit is, a common complaint from trekkers is that they didn't allow enough time to enjoy the whole of the mountain. Walks through the foothills (particularly those to the east and north-east of the main peaks) and the circular traverse around Batian and Nelion are dramatic and tremendously rewarding. You won't regret setting aside a week or more for Mt Kenya, rather than just four days for a summit rush.

Safety

Mt Kenya's accessibility and the technical ease with which Point Lenana can be reached create problems for over-enthusiastic trekkers. The trek to Point Lenana is not easy and people die on the mountain every year. Many people ascend much too quickly and end up with altitude sickness (see the Health section of the Regional Facts for the Visitor chapter for more details). By spend-

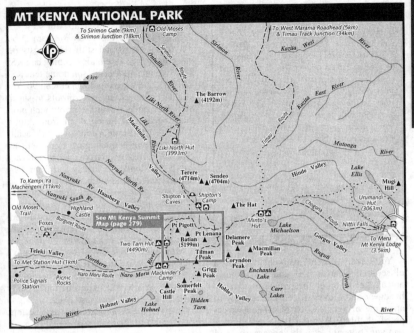

MT KENYA NATIONAL PARK

ing at least three nights on the ascent before reaching the summit you'll enjoy yourself much more.

If you're not a regular mountain walker, and don't know how to use a map and compass, trekking without a competent companion or a local guide is simply asking for trouble, particularly on routes other than the Naro Moru route. Hiring a guide is not compulsory, but it's a very good idea for all trekkers.

The best times to go, as far as fair weather is concerned, are from mid-January to late February and from late August to September. Proper clothes and equipment are essential at all times of the year.

Books & Maps

We strongly recommend that you buy a copy of *Mt Kenya 1:50,000 Map & Guide* by Mark Savage & Andrew Wielochowski, available in Nairobi. It has a detailed topographical map and is full of information on the various routes, mountain medicine, plants, animals and accommodation.

If you want to explore the park more fully, Lonely Planet's *Trekking in East Africa* by David Else is an excellent guide, while the *Guide to Mount Kenya & Kilimanjaro*, edited by Iain Allan, is essential for technical climbers or mountaineers. Both are available in Nairobi. Cameron Burns' *Kilimanjaro & Mount Kenya: a Climbing and Trekking Guide* also contains detailed climbing information.

The Mountain Club of Kenya (see the Nairobi chapter) has up-to-date mountain information posted on its Web site.

Clothing & Equipment

The summits of Mt Kenya are surrounded by glaciers and often covered by snow. At night the temperature often drops to below -10°C (it feels like it in Mackinder's Hut). Harsh cold, wet and windy weather can come from nowhere.

KENYA

Retreating Glaciers

Mt Kenya is the only mountain in the country with a permanent covering of ice. Its glaciers, just 16km south of the equator, are something of a geographical marvel. The largest is the Lewis Glacier, which you pass on the trek from Teleki Valley to Point Lenana via the Austrian Hut, and there are several others on the main peaks. Records show that Mt Kenya's glaciers are shrinking. In the last 20 years, the rate has increased noticeably, and some glaciers have completely disappeared. Maps produced in the early 1960s show the Lewis Glacier descending from the ridge between Lenana and the main peaks all the way to the Lewis Tarn at 4700m. Today, the snout of the glacier is almost 100m above the tarn.

David Else

You need a decent sleeping bag (and a closed-cell foam mat if you're camping) and a set of warm clothes, including quality headgear and gloves. It can rain heavily at any time of year so you also need waterproof clothing. Walking boots are an advantage but not strictly necessary, but carrying a spare pair of light shoes for the evening is advisable. You will really suffer without a good pair of sunglasses.

It's not a good idea to sleep in clothes that you have worn during the day, because the sweat they absorb from your skin keeps them damp at night and reduces their heat-retention capabilities.

You'll also need a stove, basic cooking equipment, eating utensils, a water container with a capacity of at least 2L per person and water-purifying tablets for use on the lower levels of the mountain. Stove fuel in the form of petrol and kerosene (paraffin) is fairly easily found in the towns. Methylated spirits is available in Nairobi; so are gas cartridges, although the availability of these is not guaranteed. Lighting fires is prohibited within the national park (except in an emergency).

If you intend to engage porters you have to supply each of them with a rucksack to carry your gear and theirs.

Clothing & Equipment Hire Some gear can be hired in Nairobi at Atul's (☎ 02-225935) PO Box 43202, on Biashara St but it's hardly expedition stuff. Hire costs per day are roughly: mountain sleeping bag KSh 220, two-person/four-person dome tent KSh 420/720, and waterproof jacket KSh 90. You might be able to buy waterproofs in supermarkets such as Uchumi for not much more than the cost of hiring them from Atul's. Atul's also has some secondhand and locally made trekking and camping equipment for sale. The store is open from 9 am to noon and 2 to 5 pm Monday to Friday and from 9 am to noon and 2.30 to 4 pm Saturday.

Rental gear is also available at Naro Moru River Lodge. It's mostly in good condition, although it can't be booked in advance and it tends to be more expensive than at Atul's. It carries plenty of stock.

Mountain Rock Hotel and Mt Kenya Hostel & Camp Site near Naro Moru have a less extensive range of equipment for hire. See the Naro Moru section of this chapter for contact details for these places.

Many of the official guiding associations also offer a limited range of rental gear.

Food

In an attempt to cut down on baggage, quite a few people forgo taking a stove and cooking equipment, and exist entirely on canned and dried foods. You can certainly do it so long as you keep up your fluid intake but it's not a good idea. Those cups of coffee in the morning and hot soup in the evening can make all the difference between enjoying the trek and hating it or at least feeling irritable.

There are, however, a few things to bear in mind about cooking at high altitudes. The main consideration is the lower boiling point of water. At 4500m, for example, water boils at 85°C. This temperature is too low to cook rice or lentils (pasta is better) and you won't be able to brew a good cup of tea from it either (instant coffee is the answer). Cooking times increase considerably at high altitude, with consequent increased use of fuel.

The best range of food suitable for trekking is to be found in the Nakumatt and Uchumi supermarkets in Nairobi. Otherwise there's a good range of food available in Nyeri, Nanyuki, Embu and Meru, but little in Naro Moru. When you're buying dehydrated foods, remember to buy the precooked variety to cut down on cooking time – two-minute noodles are the answer. You might want to bring these with you to Kenya although two-minute noodles are widely available. Fresh fruit and vegetables are available in all reasonably sized towns and villages.

Take plenty of chocolate, sweets or dried fruit to keep your blood sugar levels high on the trek.

One last thing – and this is important – remember to drink at least 3L of fluid per day to avoid severe headaches and dehydration. Bringing rehydration sachets is an excellent idea.

Park Fees

National park entry fees are US$10 per day (US$5 if you have an international student card and US$5 for children). If you take a guide or porters then you'll have to pay their entry fees too, and these are KSh 150 per person per night. Camping fees are an additional US$8 per person.

Guides, Cooks & Porters

Considerable effort has been made in recent years to regulate guides and porters operating on the mountain. Kenya Wildlife Service (KWS) now issues vouchers to all registered guides and porters, and they won't be allowed into the park without one. They must also carry proof of identity. Female guides are becoming more common and technical guides for climbing Batian and Nelion are widely available.

Reputable trekking companies, guiding organisations and hotels will be members of the Association of Mount Kenya Operators (☎ 0166-22096), which is backed by KWS and the Mountain Club of Kenya.

The charges for guides, porters and cooks vary according to the route. For the Naro Moru route, it costs about KSh 450 per day to hire a guide, about the same for a cook, and about KSh 350 to hire a porter. Costs are higher for the Chogoria and Sirimon routes. These costs exclude park entry fees

and tips at the end of the trek. If you calculate tips at KSh 500 per trip for guides and cooks and KSh 250 per trip for porters, you won't be too far off the mark.

Porters will carry up to 18kg for a three-day trip or 16kg for a longer trip, excluding the weight of their own food and equipment. If you want them to carry more you'll have to negotiate a price for the extra weight. A normal day's work is regarded as one stage of the journey – from the Met Station to Mackinder's Camp, for example. If you want to go further than this in one day then you'll have to pay the porters two days wages even if they don't do anything on the second day.

If you ascend the mountain along one route and descend along a different one, you are responsible for arranging and paying for transport back to your starting point for guides and porters. It would be a good idea to sort this out before you set off, and to agree on extra costs such as return transport, food, accommodation and extra wages (a day spent travelling home counts as a working day).

Places to Hire Guides, Cooks & Porters

Everyone likes to think they're super-fit and can deal with the altitude, but hiring a guide and porter will improve your chances of getting to the top of Mt Kenya. The difference between having a porter carry your heavy gear and doing it yourself is like the difference between a Mercedes Benz and a matatu, while a guide will help you set a sustainable pace. Both will enhance your appreciation of this mountain many times over, and at the prices they charge, even including tips, their services are a bargain.

On the western side of the mountain, Mt Kenya Guides & Porters Safari Club (☎ 0176-62015) PO Box 128, Naro Moru is a reliable body. Its office is 5km along the road from Naro Moru towards the Naro Moru park gate. The club's guides, cooks and porters can be booked directly through the club, or through Naro Moru River Lodge.

Mt Kenya Hostel & Camp Site and Mountain Rock Hotel, both in Naro Moru, can also provide guides. See the Naro Moru section later in this chapter for contact information.

Mountain Rock Hotel specialises in the Burguret route north of Naro Moru, but can provide guides for all western routes. However, like many of the hotels, it is inclined to insist that you take an expensive all-inclusive package. Guides and porters based at the hotel are affiliated with the Old Moses Guides & Porters Club and cost US$16 and US$9 per day respectively. The hotel has another office on Kenyatta Ave in Nanyuki – useful for the Sirimon route – called Out-Back Services (☎/fax 0176-31629, email outback@mountainrockkenya.com).

On the eastern side of the mountain, by far the best place to organise guides and porters is in Chogoria at Transit Motel, which is the base of the Mt Kenya Chogoria Guides & Porters Association. See the Chogoria section later in this chapter for contact information. Touts and hustlers in Chogoria village are a complete pain in the arse – they may even tell you Transit Motel has burnt down. Guides and porters are definitely not available beyond Chogoria Forest Station.

For the Sirimon route you can pick up guides in Nanyuki at Nanyuki Riverside Hotel (see the Nanyuki section later in this chapter for contact information) or at Out-Back Services, but the guiding association in Sirimon seems to be no more.

Places to Stay

There are quite a lot of huts on the mountain but not all are available to the general public. Several are owned by the Mountain Club of Kenya (MCK). A few of these huts are reserved exclusively for use by members, while others can be used by the public, although these are all basic and most are in very bad condition. The huts can be booked and paid for at either the MCK clubhouse or at Let's Go Travel in Nairobi, or at Naro Moru River Lodge. They cost about US$3, but because of their bad condition, very few trekkers use them – it's much better to camp. Officially you can camp anywhere on the mountain but it is usual to camp near one of the huts or bunkhouses, where there is often a water supply.

There are also some larger bunkhouses with more facilities. These are owned by

lodges outside the park but they can be used by independent trekkers for a fee. Bookings must be made in advance.

On the Naro Moru route, the bunkhouses are at the meteorological station (called the Met Station), and at Mackinder's Camp (occasionally called Teleki Lodge). Both can be booked through Naro Moru River Lodge (see the Naro Moru section later in this chapter), or through Let's Go Travel in Nairobi (see Travel Agencies in the Nairobi chapter). Beds cost KSh 400 at the Met Station and KSh 500 at Mackinder's Camp. MCK members are entitled to a 25% discount on these prices and at Naro Moru River Lodge.

On the Sirimon route, the bunkhouses are at Old Moses Camp and Shipton's Camp, and both can be booked through Mountain Rock Hotel in Naro Moru. Beds cost US$10 and US$12 respectively. Make sure you get a receipt, otherwise when you leave the park, the rangers will assume you've been camping and charge you US$8 per night.

On the Chogoria route, there are 12 comfortable bandas at **Meru Mt Kenya Lodge**, near the park gate, each containing a lounge/dining area with fireplace, a twin bedroom, a small extra bed and a bathroom with hot water. Electricity (KSh 50 per banda per day) is provided by generator in the morning and evening. Cooking is on single-ring electric cookers and primus stoves. Bed linen and cooking equipment are provided. There's also a central lounge/dining area with a kitchen and toilets. The bandas cost KSh 1050 per person per day (KSh 400 for children between the ages of two and 11 years). Reservations can be made through Let's Go Travel in Nairobi.

Getting to the Trekking Routes

There are at least seven different routes up the mountain, but only the most popular routes are mentioned here – Naro Moru, Sirimon and Chogoria – and we have described only the Naro Moru route in detail. For the Sirimon and Chogoria routes you must employ a guide, while the other routes not even mentioned are harder to follow and you could easily get lost without a compass, decent maps and the ability to use them.

Mt Kenya – Geology, Flora & Fauna

Mt Kenya was formed between 2½ and three million years ago as a result of successive volcanic eruptions. Its base diameter is about 120km, and it is likely that when first formed it was over 6000m in height and had a summit crater much like Kilimanjaro's. Intensive erosion, principally by glacial ice, has worn away the cone and left a series of jagged peaks, U-shaped valleys and depressions containing glacial lakes, or tarns.

In many of these valleys you will come across terminal moraines, or curved ridges of boulders and stones carried down by the glaciers. Their location – some as low as 3000m – indicates that during the Ice Ages the glaciers must have been far more extensive than they are today. The glaciers began retreating rapidly about 150,000 years ago as the climate changed and the process is still going on today.

The volcanic soil and the many rivers that radiate from the central cone have created a very fertile environment, especially on the southern and eastern sides, which receive the most rain. Small farms currently extend up to around 1900m in what used to be rainforest. However, even today, the area is still well wooded. Above this zone – except where logging occurs – is the untouched rainforest, characterised by an abundance of different species, particularly the giant camphors, along with vines, ferns, orchids and other epiphytes. This forest zone is not quite so dense on the northern and western sides, since the climate here is drier and the predominant tree species are conifers.

The forest supports a rich variety of wildlife and it's quite common to come across elephant, buffalo and various species of monkey on the forest tracks. Rhino, numerous varieties of antelope, giant forest hog and lion also live here, but are usually seen only in the clearings around lodges.

On the southern and western slopes, as altitude increases the forest gradually merges into a belt of dense bamboo which often grows to a height of 12m or more. This eventually gives way to more open woodland consisting of hagena and hypericum trees along with an undergrowth of flowering shrubs and herbs.

Further up still is a belt of giant heather which forms dense clumps up to 4m high, interspersed with tall grasses.

Open moorland forms the next zone and is often very colourful with a profusion of small flowering plants. The only large plants to be found in this region – and then only in the drier, sandier parts such as the valley sides and the ridges – are the bizarre giant lobelias and senecios. This moorland zone stretches right up to the snow line at between 4500m and 4700m, though the vegetation gets more and more sparse the higher you go. Beyond the snow line, the only plants you will find are mosses and lichens.

The open woodland and moorland supports various species of antelope, such as the duiker and eland, as well as zebra, but the most common mammal is the rock hyrax. Leopard also live in this region and have been observed as high as 4500m. The larger birds you'll undoubtedly see up here include the verreaux eagle (which preys on hyrax), the auger buzzard and the lammergeier (or bearded vulture). Smaller birds include the scarlet-tufted malachite sunbird, which feeds on nectar and small flies, and the friendly cliff chat, which often appears in search of scraps.

To reach the routes by public transport, take a bus or matatu along the Mt Kenya ring road. For the Naro Moru route, the starting point is Naro Moru village, where there's a prominent signpost pointing to the Naro Moru park gate on the right-hand side just outside the village on the way to Nanyuki.

For the Sirimon route, take a matatu to Nanyuki and then take another matatu up the main road towards Timau. The route is signposted off to the right about 13km north-east of Nanyuki.

For the Chogoria route, all matatus and buses between Embu and Meru stop at Chogoria village. If you prefer, they'll drop you at the track for Transit Motel, south of the village. From where you're dropped off, it's quite a walk to any of the park entry gates, but expensive private transport to the gates is available.

If you have your own 2WD transport, you can get up to the Naro Moru and Sirimon park entry gates if it hasn't been raining, but you will not get up to the Chogoria park entry gate in anything other than 4WD. Beyond the park entry gates, you'll probably make it up to the roadhead (Old Moses Camp) on the Sirimon route in 2WD but you certainly won't make it up to the Met Station on the Naro Moru route or the roadhead on the Chogoria route in 2WD. Both these roads are getting worse and often become impassable in very wet weather, even for 4WDs fitted with snow chains.

Naro Moru Route

The Naro Moru route is the most straightforward and popular of the routes. It's also the least scenic, although it's still a spectacular and very enjoyable trail. You should allow a minimum of four days for the trek up and down this route, or three if you have transport between Naro Moru and the Met Station, although doing it this quickly risks serious altitude sickness.

Naro Moru to the Met Station Your starting point is the village of Naro Moru. The first part of the route takes you along a relatively good gravel road through farmlands for some 13km (all the junctions are signposted) to the start of the forest where there's a wooden bridge across a small river. A further 5km brings you to the park entry gate at an altitude of 2400m. Pay your fees, then continue on another 8km to the roadhead and Met Station Hut (3000m), where you stay for the night.

If your time is limited and you're prepared to reduce your chances of acclimatising to altitude properly, you can use one of the following transport options from Naro Moru.

Naro Moru River Lodge's 4WD will take you to the park gate (US$40 per vehicle) or Met Station (US$75 per vehicle). The Mt Kenya Guides & Porters Association will take you to the gate for KSh 1500, while Mt Kenya Hostel & Camp Site's 4WD does the

trip for KSh 1200 to the gate or KSh 3000 to the Met Station.

There is also an infrequent matatu service from Naro Moru to Kiambuthi (KSh 50), which is 3km short of the park gate. This goes past Blue Line Hotel, Mt Kenya Guides & Porters Safari Club and Mt Kenya Hostel & Camp Site.

Hitching is another alternative but your chances of a lift *up* the mountain are limited – it's easier to get a ride on the way down.

Met Station to Mackinder's Camp On the second day you set off up the Teleki Valley along a well marked path, past the police signals station and up to the edge of the forest at around 3200m. From here you scale the so-called Vertical Bog and walk along a ridge from which you can see Mackinder's Camp. The route divides into two here and you have a choice between the higher path, which gives the best views but is often wet, and the lower path, which crosses the Naro Moru River and continues gently up to Mackinder's Camp (4160m). This part of the trek should take around 4½ hours. Here you can stay the night in the stark stone cabin (the bunk beds have mattresses), or camp. There are toilets and drinking water is available. The caretaker will check your bunkhouse booking receipts.

Mackinder's Camp to Point Lenana On the third day you can either rest at Mackinder's Camp to acclimatise, or aim for Point Lenana. The trek from Mackinder's Camp to Point Lenana takes four to five hours, so it's usual to leave at around 2 am to reach the summit of Lenana in time to see the sunrise. You'll need to take a torch (flashlight) with you.

From the bunkhouse, continue up the valley past the ranger station to a fork in the path. Keep right, and go across a swampy area, then a moraine and then up a very long scree slope – this is a long, hard slog. You'll reach Austrian Hut about three to four hours from Mackinder's Camp. This is about one hour below the summit of Lenana, so it's a good place to rest before the final push for the summit.

MT KENYA SUMMIT

To avoid the long slog in the dark you could head to Austrian Hut on the third day, then go for the summit of Lenana on the morning of the fourth day. However, conditions at Austrian Hut are very basic.

Alternatively, those who are camping and not staying at either Mackinder's Camp or Austrian Hut have another choice in the so-called American Camp. To reach it, branch off left along a minor track just before the swampy area above the ranger station. It's an excellent camp site on a grassy meadow.

The final section of the trek, from Austrian Hut to Point Lenana, takes you up a narrow rocky path that traverses a ridge parallel to the glacier. One last climb/scramble brings you up onto the peak. In good weather the going is fairly straightforward, but in bad weather you should not attempt to reach the summit unless you are experienced in trekking in mountain conditions, or have a guide. Plenty of inexperienced trekkers have come to grief on this section, falling off icy cliffs or even disappearing into crevasses.

Return Routes From Point Lenana most people return to the Met Station back down the same route. Assuming you get to Point Lenana early in the day, you can reach the Met Station on the same day.

Alternatively, you can return to Austrian Hut then walk along the Summit Circuit path around the base of the main peaks to reach the top of either the Sirimon or Chogoria route and go down one of those routes. The Summit Circuit path is reckoned to be one of the most exciting trekking routes in East Africa. Completely circling the mountain, you cross several major cols and get great views of the peaks and glaciers from all angles. The Summit Circuit path is also demanding and potentially dangerous. Many people have become lost on this trail and you should not attempt it unless you have plenty of time, proper equipment and mountain navigation experience.

Organised Treks

If your time is limited or if you'd like someone else to make all the arrangements for your Mt Kenya trek, there are several possibilities. The following companies were deemed to be reliable and competent at the time of writing. But as always, watch out for the sharks. Stories of trips being cut short by mystery illnesses suffered by the porters and guides are all too common.

Bike Treks (☎ 02-446371, fax 442439, email biketreks@form-net.com) PO Box 14237, Nairobi. This company offers a range of possibilities including the Naro Moru route (US$300, three days), the Sirimon/Naro Moru routes (US$400, four days) and the Sirimon/Chogoria routes (seven days, US$720). These prices include: transfers to and from Nairobi; park entry and camping fees; guide, cook and porters; food; and tents. They exclude rucksacks, clothing, boots and tips.

KG Mountain Expeditions (☎ 0176-62403, fax 62078, email kgexpd@arcc.or.ke) PO Box 199, Naro Moru. This company is run by a highly experienced mountaineer with considerable technical expertise, and offers all-inclusive packages for about US$115 per day. The company also provides climbing training sessions on the mountain with a view to getting clients to the very top.

Mountain Rock Hotels & Safaris (☎ 02-242133, fax 210051, email reservation@mountainrockkenya.com) Jubilee Insurance House, Wabera St, PO Box 50484, Nairobi. This company really specialises in Mt Kenya climbs and runs Mountain Rock Hotel near Naro Moru. 'Standard' (budget) package prices per day based on a group of four are US$80 for the Burguret route (the company's speciality), US$81 for the Chogoria route and US$71 for a trek ascending the Sirimon route and descending the Naro Moru route. Executive packages cost US$96, US$100 and US$85 respectively. You can mix the ascent and descent routes. These prices are a good benchmark. Transfers from Nairobi are available. The company has an agent in Nanyuki (see the Nanyuki section later in this chapter for contact information).

Naro Moru River Lodge (☎ 0176-62622, fax 62211, email mt.kenya@africaonline.co.ke) PO Box 18, Naro Moru. The lodge runs trips similar to Mountain Rock's, all of which include a guide/cook, porters, all meals, park entry fees, camping fees and transfers. The prices are more expensive than the competition's and the usual route is up and down Naro Moru. If you take one of these treks, you're entitled to a special accommodation deal at the lodge.

Around Mt Kenya

Mt. Kenya is circled by an excellent tarmac road along which are the area's main towns – Naro Moru, Nanyuki, Meru, Chogoria and Embu.

NARO MORU
☎ 0176
The village of Naro Moru, on the western side of the mountain, consists of little more than a string of small shops and houses, a couple of very basic hotels, a market, a post office, agricultural warehouses and nearby,

the famous Naro Moru River Lodge. However, it's the most popular starting point for climbing Mt Kenya because several of its hotels offer organised treks or can arrange accommodation on the mountain for independent trekkers. See the Mt Kenya section earlier in this chapter for trekking details.

Activities

Mountain Rock Hotel offers **horse riding** (US$13 per hour), **trout fishing** (US$6.50 per hour including rod and licence) and **birdwatching**. More interesting is the hotel's four-hour **guided walk** to a Mau Mau cave

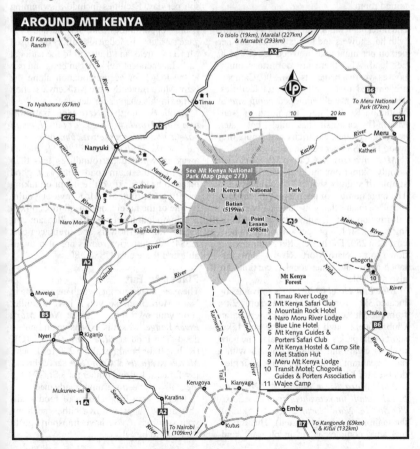

AROUND MT KENYA

1 Timau River Lodge
2 Mt Kenya Safari Club
3 Mountain Rock Hotel
4 Naro Moru River Lodge
5 Blue Line Hotel
6 Mt Kenya Guides & Porters Safari Club
7 Mt Kenya Hostel & Camp Site
8 Met Station Hut
9 Meru Mt Kenya Lodge
10 Transit Motel; Chogoria Guides & Porters Association
11 Wajee Camp

for KSh 300. The guides seem very knowledgeable about the Mau Mau rebellion and the fauna and flora of the region.

Places to Stay

There are a number of basic hotels in Naro Moru village itself, but very few travellers intent on climbing the mountain stay here. Still, if you want to stay in the village there are four options, none of them cheap: *Naro Moru 82 Lodge*, *Naro Moru Hotel 86*, *Joruna Lodge* and *Mountain View Hotel*. The best of the lot, the Mountain View, costs a hefty KSh 520 for a single self-contained room.

Naro Moru River Lodge is essentially a top end hotel but it has a well equipped *camp site* with hot showers and toilets for KSh 200 per person per night and firewood for KSh 150 per load. Also there are dormitory bunkhouses where a bed costs KSh 300. Campers are entitled to use all the hotel facilities. There's also a well equipped *camp site* at Mountain Rock Hotel 7km north of Naro Moru. The camp site has toilets, hot water, cooking facilities, electricity and ample firewood for US$5 per person per night.

Mt Kenya Hostel & Camp Site (☎ 62412) is only 6km from the park gate. It offers simple (if slightly shabby) accommodation. The large number of people moving through the place means that you can usually pick up information about the mountain here. Camping costs KSh 150 per person and dorm beds cost KSh 250. The hostel offers nature walks down to the Naro Moru River a short distance away and other local excursions are also available.

Blue Line Hotel (☎ 62217) is conveniently located 3km from Naro Moru and only 2km from the Mt Kenya Guides & Porters Safari Club office, though it does leave you 15km short of the park's Naro Moru gate. The hotel itself is clean and pleasant enough with a bar, restaurant and self-contained singles/doubles for KSh 300/600.

Naro Moru River Lodge (☎ 62622, fax 62211, email mt.kenya@africaonline.co.ke, PO Box 18, Naro Moru) is about 1.5km off the main road (it's signposted). This top-of-the-range complex is set in pleasant landscaped gardens alongside the Naro Moru River. The luxury accommodation consists of standard or superior rooms, or self-service cottages. In the low season, standard singles/doubles cost KSh 2300/3400 and superior singles/doubles cost KSh 2800/4300. All rates are for half board. In the high season, prices rise to KSh 3800/4800 and KSh 4300/5700 respectively. The self-service cottages vary in price: two-bedroom cottages cost between KSh 6000 and KSh 7800; three-bedroom cottages cost between KSh 6840 and KSh 8700. Between 22 December and 5 January there's a surcharge of US$20 per person per day. Facilities include a swimming pool, two bars, restaurant, secure parking, fishing opportunities, hire service and baggage storage. The lodge also offers organised Mt Kenya treks and transport to the national park. Independent trekkers can book and pay at the lodge for accommodation along the Naro Moru route. See the Mt Kenya section earlier in this chapter for details.

About 7km north of Naro Moru is *Mountain Rock Hotel (☎ 62625, fax 62051, email base@mountainrockkenya.com, or in Nairobi ☎ 02-210051, fax 210051)*, tucked away in wooded surroundings less than 1km from the main road. This is a good place to head for if you're intent on taking the Burguret route up Mt Kenya or you're on one of the hotel's organised treks. Fixed accommodation is expensive. Pleasant cottages with hot showers and fireplaces cost US$45/60. Superior rooms are also available and these cost US$60/80.

Places to Eat

There are no restaurants worth mentioning in Naro Moru itself so you'll have to either cook your own food or eat at *Naro Moru River Lodge*, which is expensive and not so good. The food at *Blue Line Hotel* is OK (KSh 150 for breakfast, KSh 200 for lunch). *Mt Kenya Hostel & Camp Site* serves breakfast for KSh 100 and dinner for KSh 250, but the staff will need warning in advance.

There's very little choice of food available at the shops in town either, so bring your own or, if you have transport, go to Nanyuki to buy it.

Getting There & Away

There are plenty of buses, Nissan minibuses and Peugeot share-taxis from Nairobi and Nyeri to Nanyuki and Isiolo that will drop you off in Naro Moru. The fare from Nairobi to Naro Moru is about KSh 200 (more in a share-taxi) and the journey takes about 2½ hours. From Nyeri to Naro Moru the fare is KSh 50 and the journey takes a little over 30 minutes.

The park gate is 18km from Naro Moru. You can get a matatu from the post office in Naro Moru to Kiambuthi (KSh 50), which is 3km short of the park gate. This takes you past Blue Line Hotel (3km from Naro Moru), Mt Kenya Guides & Porters Safari Club (5km from Naro Moru) and Mt Kenya Hostel & Camp Site (12km from Naro Moru).

NANYUKI
☎ 0176

Nanyuki is a typical small country town about halfway along the northern section of the Mt Kenya ring road and a popular base from which to trek up the mountain via the Burguret or Sirimon routes. It was founded by white settlers in 1907 in the days when wildlife roamed freely and in large numbers over the surrounding grassy plains. The wildlife has almost disappeared, but the descendants of the settlers remain. The town is a Kenyan airforce base, as well as a British army base for the joint manoeuvres conducted by the two armies each year. It's a fairly pleasant town that still has a faint ring of the colonial era.

Information

Email can be sent from Nanyuki Email & Internet situated next to Barclays Bank. It will cost you KSh 60 to send an email and KSh 540 to browse the Internet for 10 minutes There are a couple of cardphones next to the post office. The Imani Medical Clinic (☎ 31518) is upstairs from Sirimon Little Rock Hotel.

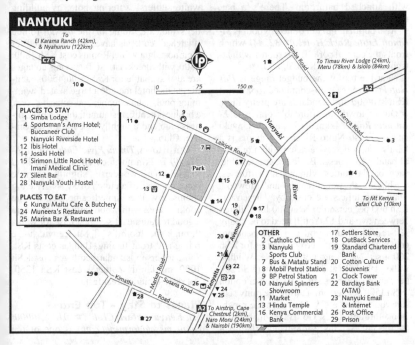

NANYUKI

To El Karama Ranch (42km), & Nyahururu (122km)

C76

To Timau River Lodge (24km), Meru (78km) & Isiolo (84km)

A2

Simba Road

Nanyuki

Mt Kenya Road

Laikipia Road

Park

River

To Mt Kenya Safari Club (10km)

0   75   150 m

Kenyatta

Avenue

Market Road

Susana Road

Kimathi Road

A2 To Airstrip, Cape Chestnut (2km), Naro Moru (24km) & Nairobi (190km)

PLACES TO STAY
1 Simba Lodge
4 Sportsman's Arms Hotel; Buccaneer Club
5 Nanyuki Riverside Hotel
12 Ibis Hotel
14 Josaki Hotel
15 Sirimon Little Rock Hotel; Imani Medical Clinic
27 Silent Bar
28 Nanyuki Youth Hostel

PLACES TO EAT
6 Kungu Maitu Cafe & Butchery
24 Muneera's Restaurant
25 Marina Bar & Restaurant

OTHER
2 Catholic Church
3 Nanyuki Sports Club
7 Bus & Matatu Stand
8 Mobil Petrol Station
9 BP Petrol Station
10 Nanyuki Spinners Showroom
11 Market
13 Hindu Temple
16 Kenya Commercial Bank
17 Settlers Store
18 OutBack Services
19 Standard Chartered Bank
20 Cotton Culture Souvenirs
21 Clock Tower
22 Barclays Bank (ATM)
23 Nanyuki Email & Internet
26 Post Office
29 Prison

For trekking information, contact OutBack Services (☎/fax 31629, email outback@ mountainrockkenya.com) on Kenyatta Ave. This well respected company is a booking agent for Mountain Rock Hotels, and also runs Mountain Rock Cafeteria on Kenyatta Ave, which stays open until 8 pm. You can book organised treks, guides and transport in both places.

Places to Stay – Budget

Campers can stay out of town at the *camp site* at Timau River Lodge for KSh 200. See Places to Stay – Mid-Range for details.

Otherwise, the cheapest place is *Nanyuki Youth Hostel* at the Emmanuel Parish Centre, Market Rd, but it's very basic. Dorm beds cost KSh 100 per person. Also cheap is the friendly *Silent Bar* at KSh 200 for single rooms only, with hot water in the mornings.

More expensive but quite popular is *Josaki Hotel* (☎ 222820) which has large, clean, singles/doubles for KSh 400/600 with attached bathroom. There's a bar, restaurant and secure parking.

Also popular, but not quite as good, is *Sirimon Little Rock Hotel* (☎ 32344) which fronts the central park. It has rooms with attached bathroom for KSh 300/500.

Near the top of the budget range is *Ibis Hotel* (☎ 31536). Self-contained rooms cost KSh 350/600 and standards are pretty high.

Out of town, an affordable option is *El Karama Ranch* 42km north-west of Nanyuki on the Ewaso Ngiro River. El Karama is a family-run, self-service ranch with a number of bandas for guests. Basic but comfortable, each banda comes with beds, mattresses, washbasin, shower, fireplace and firewood. Long-drop toilets are close by. The cost is KSh 600 per person or KSh 300 for children between two and 12. You'll need to be totally self-reliant though you can rent bedding, cooking utensils and kerosene lamps for KSh 200 a set. Meals are not available. Wildlife walks start daily at 7 am and 4 pm (KSh 200 per person) and horse riding is another option (KSh 1500 per person). During the rainy season you'll need a 4WD to reach the ranch. Book through Let's Go Travel in Nairobi (☎ 02-340331, fax 336890, email info@

letsgosafari.com), which can provide you with directions and a map. You'd need considerable determination to get here by public transport.

Places to Stay – Mid-Range

A short distance north-east of the town centre is *Simba Lodge* (☎ 22556) not far from the Catholic church. Rooms with attached bathroom in this comfortable, quiet, but slightly overpriced hotel cost KSh 600/1300 for single/doubles, including breakfast. The hotel has its own nyama choma area, restaurant, bar, pool tables, card phone and secure parking. It holds discos at the weekend.

Nanyuki Riverside Hotel (☎ 32523) beside the Nanyuki River is a large place, convenient to the centre of town. Rooms with private bathroom cost KSh 550/900 including breakfast.

Sportsman's Arms Hotel (☎ 32347, fax 22895) east of the town centre and across the river is newly refurbished. This was once the white settlers' watering hole, as building style and the four-hectare landscaped gardens indicate. Some of the *makuti*-roofed (thatched) cottages have been preserved for their nostalgia value. Rooms cost KSh 1800/2400 with breakfast. Self-catering cottages are also available for KSh 2500/4500. Facilities at the hotel include a large heated swimming pool, sauna, tennis and squash courts, a business centre, restaurant, three bars, a fitness club and a nightly disco in the Buccaneer Club.

Out of town, *Timau River Lodge* (☎ 0176-41230) is 2km north of Timau on the road to Isiolo. This wonderful, slightly eccentric place consists of a clutch of Swiss-style log cabins, a well equipped camp site, a large cooking area with wood-burning stove and a good restaurant. It's a great base for walks through the foothills of Mt Kenya, horse riding and trout fishing. Bandas costs KSh 750 per person, standard cottages cost KSh 1000 and family cottages cost KSh 1250. All rates include breakfast.

Places to Stay – Top End

Mt Kenya Safari Club (☎ 0176-30000, email mksc@form-net.com) is one of the most exclusive hotels in the country and is 10km from Nanyuki. This hotel, originally the homestead of a white Kenyan settler family, sits almost exactly on the equator and has excellent views up to Mt Kenya. Facilities include golf, tennis, croquet, snooker, heated pool, fishing and the small Sweetwaters Game Reserve. All this luxury starts at US$276/358 for singles/doubles with full board, rising to US$639 for a presidential suite and more for exclusive cottages and villas. Children aged from two to 12 years are charged US$48. Access is either from the west of Nanyuki (a distance of about 10km, paved most of the way), or from a turn-off about 2km south of Nanyuki from where it's 9km along a dirt road.

Places to Eat
Most of the restaurants in Nanyuki are attached to hotels, so take your pick of these. *Sportsman's Arms Hotel* serves the best food in town. *Marina Bar & Restaurant* and *Muneera's Restaurant*, which are next to each other on Kenyatta Ave, are reasonable. The Marina attracts a lot of expats.

Kungu Maitu Cafe & Butchery is a reasonable place for nyama choma, but if you prefer smoked trout, try *Cape Chestnut* (☎ 0176-32208) an excellent little coffee garden and snack place catering mostly for tourists, local white farmers and expats. It's a good place to pick up information about the local area and Laikipia. Follow the signs for Nanyuki Cottage Hospital and you can't go far wrong. It's closed on Sundays.

Shopping
The Cotton Culture store on the main street has some interesting craft items, but the best place to shop is Nanyuki Spinners, a women's craft cooperative that specialises in woven woollen sweaters, rugs and shawls. It has a showroom on Laikipia Rd. The quality of the pattern design and crafting is high. A good jumper will set you back KSh 2600; a big rug costs about KSh 6000.

Getting There & Away
Air Air Kenya Aviation (☎ 02-501421, email resvns@airkenya.com) flies daily from Wilson airport in Nairobi to Nanyuki, Lewa Downs (on request) and Samburu National Reserve, and then returns to Nairobi via Nanyuki. The fares from Nanyuki are US$80 to Nairobi and US$65 to Samburu.

Land There are daily buses between Nairobi and Nanyuki (KSh 180) as well as Nissan minibuses (KSh 200) and Peugeot share-taxis (KSh 300). Share-taxis to Nyahururu cost KSh 100. Matatus run from Nanyuki to Nyahururu (KSh 120), Isiolo (KSh 150) and Nyeri (KSh 80).

MERU
☎ 0164
On the north-eastern section of the ring road around Mt Kenya, Meru services the intensively cultivated and forested highlands in this part of Central province. Meru's main claim to fame is the quality of its *miraa* (see the boxed text 'Miraa'). These are the bundles of leafy twigs and shoots that you'll see being chewed by people all over Kenya (particularly Somalis and matatu drivers) as a stimulant and appetite-suppressant.

Although there's a small town centre of sorts, Meru is essentially just a built-up area along the main road, and unless you're in the middle of a long journey or stocking up before heading into Meru National Park, there's precious little reason for a traveller to stay the night here. It's certainly much too far away from Mt Kenya to be a suitable trekking base.

Information
You may be able to send email from Royal Paramount Enterprises (☎ 30289) on the main road and there are a number of card-phones outside the post office.

Meru National Museum
This small museum just off the main road is worth visiting, though some of the live animal exhibits are very depressing – the star of the show is currently a three-legged cow. The museum is open from 9.30 am to 6 pm Monday to Saturday, from 11 am to 6 pm on Sunday and from 1 to 6 pm on holidays. Entry costs KSh 200.

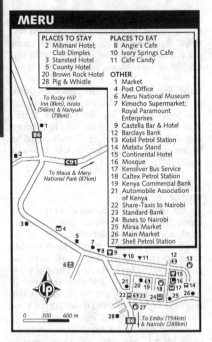

MERU

PLACES TO STAY	PLACES TO EAT
2 Milimani Hotel;	8 Angie's Cafe
Club Dimples	10 Ivory Springs Cafe
3 Stansted Hotel	11 Cafe Candy
5 County Hotel	
20 Brown Rock Hotel	**OTHER**
28 Pig & Whistle	1 Market
	4 Post Office
To Rocky Hill	6 Meru National Museum
Inn (8km), Isiolo	7 Kimocho Supermarket;
(56km) & Nanyuki	Royal Paramount
(78km)	Enterprises
	9 Castella Bar & Hotel
	12 Barclays Bank
	13 Kobil Petrol Station
	14 Matatu Stand
To Maua & Meru	15 Continental Hotel
National Park (87km)	16 Mosque
	17 Kensilver Bus Service
	18 Caltex Petrol Station
	19 Kenya Commercial Bank
	21 Automobile Association
	of Kenya
	22 Share-Taxis to Nairobi
	23 Standard Bank
	24 Buses to Nairobi
	25 Miraa Market
	26 Main Market
	27 Shell Petrol Station

0   300   600 m

To Embu (154km)
& Nairobi (288km)

Places to Stay

The best cheap place is *Brown Rock Hotel*. Clean, tidy, self-contained singles/doubles, some with balconies, will set you back KSh 250/350. You can fit an extra padlock to some of the rooms, but security seems very good anyway.

Stansted Hotel on the main road past the post office is not bad value. It is clean and quiet and offers rooms with attached bathroom at KSh 250 per person including breakfast. The hotel has its own bar and restaurant.

Milimani Hotel (☎ 20224) about 2km from the centre of town offers good rooms with attached bathroom for KSh 500/700.

With more character is *Pig & Whistle (☎ 31411)* opposite the Shell petrol station. The main building (a bar and restaurant) is a classic wooden colonial structure, beside which are a number of ageing wooden chalets. The rather austere stone cottages around the back provide the best accommodation at KSh 1000/1100, including breakfast.

County Hotel up on the main road close to the turn-off for the museum is a nice place to stay. The County is clean and comfortable with its own restaurant, lively bar and secure parking. Rooms with attached bathroom cost KSh 1000/1500, including breakfast.

If you have your own transport, you might like to check out *Rocky Hill Inn (☎ 41321)* about 8km north of town. This friendly, weird maze of a place has basic wooden chalets, a good bar, reasonable nyama choma and stunningly cheap accommodation. Rooms with shared facilities cost KSh 200/300. It gets busy on the weekend.

Places to Eat

For a good meal the best of the cheap cafes is *Cafe Candy*. It's a welcoming place where a good feed will cost you about KSh 120. The cakes and buns are particularly good.

Also worth checking out are *Angie's Cafe*, for good chicken curry, and *Ivory Springs Cafe* further up the hill on the main road.

The *restaurants* at the main hotels are OK. County Hotel has the edge but don't expect too much – a la carte meals cost from about KSh 200 or there's a three-course set meal for KSh 450.

Entertainment

Club Dimples at Milimani Hotel has the best disco in town on the weekend, but the best place for a beer is *Pig & Whistle*. *Continental Hotel* and *Castella Bar & Hotel* are always lively.

Getting There & Away

Akamba has closed its Meru office, so Kensilver Bus (☎ 02-221839) is the easiest and safest way to get to and from Nairobi. It has seven departures in each direction from 7.30 am and 3 pm (KSh 240) and can be booked in advance. They leave from outside the Kensilver offices on Dubois Rd in Nairobi and from close to the mosque in Meru. Cheaper Tawfiq and Sunbird buses (KSh 200) leave during the day in each direction. All buses travel via Chogoria, Embu and Thika.

From the matatu park in Meru there are regular departures for Maua (KSh 80), Isiolo (KSh 80), Nanyuki (KSh 100) and Nai-

Miraa

Miraa, those small twigs and leaves you see being chewed by so many people on the coast, comes from a gnarly evergreen tree native to East Africa, Southern Africa, Afghanistan, Yemen and Madagascar. Miraa is also known as *coas*, *khat*, *qat* and has more than 40 other names in different cultures. Miraa-chewing pre-dates coffee-drinking and is deeply rooted in the cultural traditions of some societies, especially in Muslim countries, where it is chewed at weddings and on holidays. Usually chewed in company, it creates feelings of confidence and contentment and a flow of ideas. It's also used to increase alertness and concentration – just like for driving a matatu. The active ingredient *cathinone* is closely related to amphetamine, and euphoric effects last up to 24 hours. However, too much can cause aggressive behaviour, nightmares and hallucinations. Reduced appetite, constipation and brown stained teeth are common side effects.

In Kenya, chewing miraa is becoming an increasingly popular pastime, but in Somalia it is ingrained in the culture. Some of the best miraa in the world is grown around Maua in the Central Highlands and exported to Somalia. The shelf-life of miraa is short (after 48 hours its potency is diminished) and so soon after picking, massively overloaded pick-up trucks driven by people who look remarkably alert race the miraa from Meru to Wilson airport in Nairobi where it's flown to Mogadishu. Rumours have it that at the height of the civil war many a bush pilot made a fortune flying miraa into Somalia.

Growing miraa is far more profitable than growing vegetables, and when traded it can fetch KSh 1500 per kilogram. But it's not without its social problems. Miraa-chewing reached such epidemic proportions in Somalia that the government tried to ban it in 1983.

Though illegal in the USA, it is legally imported into parts of Europe, including the UK, where it can be ordered over the Internet.

robi (KSh 280). Share-taxis leave from the matatu park and also from opposite the Shell petrol station in the centre of town, destined for Isiolo (KSh 100), Nanyuki (KSh 120) and Nairobi (KSh 350).

MERU NATIONAL PARK

This is one of the most geographically diverse parks in Kenya and a favourite with old safari hands. Joy and George Adamson (of *Born Free* fame) were based here and you need to stay a few days to fully appreciate what the park has to offer.

Located on the lowland plains east of Meru town, this park receives abundant rainfall. Numerous permanent watercourses flowing from the Mt Kenya massif support a luxuriant jungle of forest, bush, swamp and tall grasses which, in turn, provide fodder and shelter for a wide variety of herbivores and their predators. The vegetation is dense in places, and after years of poaching wildlife is shy. Elephant can often be found in the marshy Bisanadi Plains to the north, while lion, cheetah, lesser kudu, eland, water buck, Grant's and Thompson's gazelle and oryx can also be seen. Buffalo, reticulated giraffe, Grevy's zebra and impala are common. Monkeys, crocodiles and a plethora of bird species (including the palm nut vulture and Marshal eagle) are common in dense vegetation along the watercourses, where Ura and Tana on the southern boundary are the most dramatic.

The road to the park will soon be sealed. There's a bridge across the Tana River into Kora National Park at Adamson's Falls (worth a visit) and all the park roads are being upgraded. Kora National Park may soon become more accessible and once the new road to the coast from Thika via Garissa is completed, access to Meru National Park through Kora will be an exciting possibility for tourists heading from Nairobi or the coast. A 4WD is an advantage, but soon it won't be essential.

Entry costs US$20 (US$10 for students and US$5 for children) plus KSh 150 for vehicles with fewer than six seats. It's a good idea to have a copy of the Survey of Kenya's *Meru National Park* map, though it can't be bought at the gate – see Planning in the Kenya Facts for the Visitor chapter for details of where to purchase it.

KENYA

Places to Stay

At the turn-off to Meru National Park just outside Maua is **Kiringo Hill Lodge** (☎ *167-21081*). Self-contained singles/ doubles cost KSh 500/600, including breakfast.

In the park itself, there are numerous special camp sites but the only public one is **Bwatherongi Camp Site** (US$8 per person). It's well equipped and also has four excellent **bandas** (US$10 per person), two of which have private bathroom.

Cottages at the newly built **Leopard Rock Lodge** (☎ *02-246982, fax 212389*) are good value at US$120/200 in the high season and US$60/100 low season. There's a swimming pool and a trail to leopard rock, which, incidentally, sees more lion than leopard.

Elsa's Kopje (☎ *02-748307, fax 750225, email chelipeacock@attmail.com*) is a far more exclusive place. Open-fronted stone and wood cottages with great views are built around the rocks and trees of Mugwongo Hill, the site of George Adamson's first camp in Meru. Rooms cost US$340/560. Night wildlife drives, walking safaris and fishing and rafting trips on the Tana River can all be arranged.

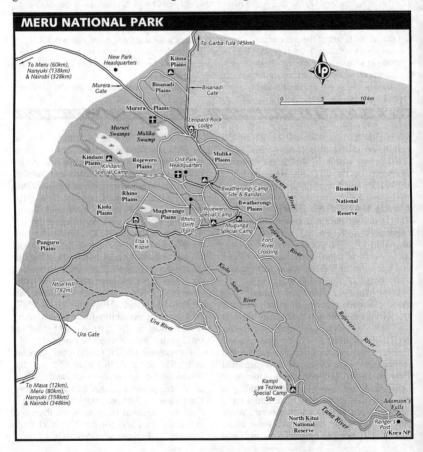

MERU NATIONAL PARK

To Garba Tula (45km)

To Meru (60km), Nanyuki (138km) & Nairobi (328km)

New Park Headquarters

Kinna Plains

Murera Gate

Bisanadi Plains

Bisanadi Gate

Murera Plains

0   5   10 km

Mururi Swamps

Mulika Swamp

Leopard Rock Lodge

Kindani Plains

Kindani Special Camp

Rojewero Plains

Old Park Headquarters

Mulika Plains

Murera River

Bisanadi National Reserve

Rhino Plains

Bwatherongi Camp Site & Bandas

Kiolu Plains

Mughwango Plains

Rojewero Special Camp

Bwatherongi Plains

Rhino Drift (Ford)

Mugunga Special Camp

Punguru Plains

Elsa's Kopje

Ford River Crossing

Rojewero River

Ntoe Hill (782m)

Kiolu Sand River

Ura River

Ura Gate

Rojewero River

To Maua (12km), Meru (80km), Nanyuki (158km) & Nairobi (348km)

Kampi ya Teziwa Special Camp Site

Tana River

Adamson's Falls

North Kitui National Reserve

Ranger's Post

Kora NP

Getting There & Away
You could probably get as far as the park headquarters at Murera Gate by public transport (given enough time), but you're very likely to get stuck there – visitor numbers are very low. Organised trips to Meru are still few and far between, but things may change after access has been improved.

CHOGORIA
☎ 0166
The only reason to come to this small town on the lower eastern slopes of Mt Kenya is that it's the access point to one of the most scenic routes up the mountain – the Chogoria route. Chogoria village itself has gained something of a reputation for hassle, with every man and his dog offering to take you up the mountain.

Transit Motel (☎ 22096, fax 22096, PO Box 190, Chogoria) can be reached by alighting from the bus on the main road just south of Chogoria village and walking about 1.5km down a dirt road (it's signposted). Self-contained clean and tidy singles/doubles go for KSh 600/900 and there's a restaurant, lounge area and cheap bar. You can *camp* here for KSh 100 per person. The motel is also the base of the Mt Kenya Chogoria Guides & Porters Association and you can hire guides and porters here for your Mt Kenya trek.

The best transport between Chogoria and Nairobi (KSh 220, seven buses daily) is with Kensilver. There are regular matatus from Chogoria to Embu (KSh 120) and Meru (KSh 40).

EMBU
☎ 0161
On the south-eastern slopes of Mt Kenya, Embu is an important provincial centre spread along the main road. Not many travellers stay here overnight because there's nothing much to see or do and it's a long way from the Chogoria route up Mt Kenya.

Places to Stay
Overlooking the BP petrol station in the town centre is *Highway Court Hotel* (☎ 20046) is very good value. Basic rooms with bathroom (and hot water) cost KSh 300/600 for sin-

gles/doubles or KSh 450/900 with breakfast. The only drawback is noise from the lively bar and restaurant. An *askari* (watchman) guards the stairs to the rooms.

New White Rembo Guest House is almost opposite the bus and matatu park above a row of shops. Safe, clean, suprisingly quiet rooms go for KSh 220/250.

Izaak Walton Inn (☎ 20128) about 2km from the town centre towards Meru on the main road is more upmarket. It is right out of the colonial era, though it seems to be losing some character after a series of renovations. The cottages are set around extensive lawns and gardens and there's a good restaurant and cosy bar, both with fireplaces. Rooms cost KSh 1500/2000 including breakfast, with suites and triples at KSh 3000.

Places to Eat
For a meal or snack at lunch-time, try *Arkland Hotel* or *New Beverly* near the main roundabout in the centre of town. *Rehana Cafe* (which serves reasonable curries), not far from the post office, and *Rose Pot Cafe*, just east of Highway Court Hotel, are also worth a try.

For breakfast it has to be *Morning Glory*, on the main road in the centre of town, which does good *samosas*, *mandazi* and *chai*. If you want the full treatment, head for the *restaurant* at Izaak Walton Inn.

Getting There & Away
Seven Kensilver buses pass through Embu in each direction every day. They stop at the BP station in the centre of town. The first departure from Nairobi is at 7.30 am (KSh 140) and the first from Meru is at 7.45 am (KSh 100).

Matatus offer the same service but the usual matatu perils apply doubly. The road between Nairobi and Meru is probably one of the best (therefore one of the fastest) in the country and accidents are common. Matatus to Nairobi (KSh 150) terminate on Accra Rd. Peugeot share-taxis will propel you to Nairobi for about KSh 170 depending on the driver and the time of day.

Matatus also run to a host of highlands destinations including Meru (KSh 160), Nyeri (KSh 100) and Chogoria (KSh 120).

Western Kenya

Western Kenya has many attractions, but is often overlooked by travellers. The countryside is, for the most part, beautiful rolling hills, often cultivated with the bright green bushes of vast tea plantations.

In the far west is Lake Victoria with the regional capital of Kisumu on its shore, and from here there are plenty of possibilities. To the south-west are the accessible islands of Rusinga and Mfangano, while a short distance to the north lies the Kakamega Forest with its lush vegetation and abundant wildlife. Close to the regional town of Kitale are the national parks of Mt Elgon and Saiwa Swamp, while further north still are the Cherangani Hills, which drop away dramatically into the Kerio Valley.

Busia and Malaba are the gateways to Uganda, while Isebania sits on the Tanzanian border.

Lake Victoria

With an area approaching 70,000 sq km, Lake Victoria is obviously the major geographical feature in this part of the continent and touches on three countries – Uganda, Tanzania and Kenya.

At present the only boat traffic between the countries is made up of large freighters and small dhow-like vessels that are often smuggling fruit. There is talk of ferry services being restarted, but don't hold your breath.

Water hyacinth is a major problem and is suffocating the fishing industry and restricting lake traffic. Various plans are in place to try to deal with this problem (see the boxed text 'Water Hyacinth' in the Facts about East Africa chapter).

Bilharzia is prevalent in Lake Victoria, but you are at far greater risk of contracting malaria. Kisumu has the highest infection rates in Kenya. See the Health section in the Regional Facts for the Visitor chapter for more information.

Highlights

- Exploring the tiny islands of Rusinga and Mfangano on Lake Victoria
- Staying at the New Lincoln Hotel and eating out at the Elcove Restaurant in Eldoret
- Trekking through the Cherangani Hills and down into the Kerio Valley
- Getting right off the beaten track and camping in Ruma National Park

KISUMU
☎ 035

Although it hardly feels like it, Kisumu is Kenya's third-largest town. It has a very easy-going, almost decaying, atmosphere. Kisumu was a busy port from early in the 20th century right up until the East African Community split up in 1977, but since then it seems to have been marking time. The water hyacinth hasn't helped either, but a recent increase in cooperation between the former East African partners and Kisumu's oil refinery give cause for optimism (oil is pumped from Mombasa then exported).

Despite its relative isolation, Kisumu is ideal to head for from the east of the country as the travel connections are excellent. There's enough to do here to make it an interesting place to stop for a few days, though the summer heat and humidity are intense.

Orientation
On the gently sloping shore of Lake Victoria, Kisumu is a fairly sprawling town, but everything you're likely to need is within five minutes walk of Oginga Odinga Rd.

The best access to the lake itself is at Dunga, a small village about 3km south of town along Nzola Rd. You can arrange boat trips at Dunga fish market, water hyacinth permitting.

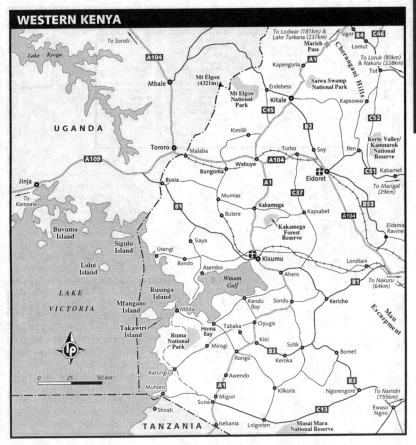

WESTERN KENYA

Information

Money Change money at Pel Forex Bureau in Al-Imran Plaza, next to Pel Travel, while Standard Chartered and Barclays have ATMs.

Post & Communications The post office is in the centre of town on Oginga Odinga Rd. It's open from 8 am to 5 pm Monday to Friday, and from 9 am to noon Saturday. For international calls there are a number of cardphones on the opposite side of the road.

Internet Resources For email and Internet access try the Passage Bureau (☎ 22109,

email user@passage.africaonline.com) in Kenya National Assurance House on Bank St. Surfing the Internet is KSh 10 per minute. The Imperial Plaza Cafe (email bhatbagar@net2000ke.com) in the Imperial Hotel is a relaxed place to surf and the cakes and drinks are good.

The British Council (☎ 45004, email bc-kisumu@africaonline.co.ke) Oginga Odinga Rd, has newspapers and magazines and quite a good library. It's open from 10 am to 6 pm Tuesday to Friday, and 9.30 am to 1 pm on Saturday. Internet access is available and 30 minutes of surfing costs KSh 400. Temporary

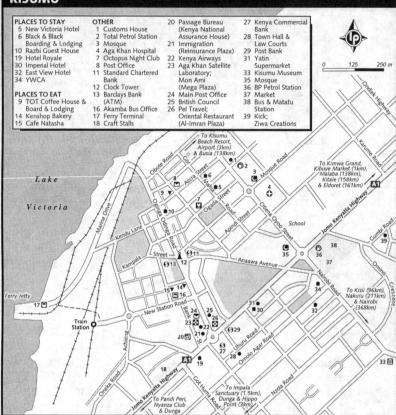

KISUMU

PLACES TO STAY
5 New Victoria Hotel
6 Black & Black
   Boarding & Lodging
10 Razbi Guest House
19 Hotel Royale
30 Imperial Hotel
32 East View Hotel
34 YWCA

PLACES TO EAT
9 TOT Coffee House &
   Board & Lodging
14 Kenshop Bakery
15 Cafe Natasha

OTHER
1 Customs House
2 Total Petrol Station
3 Mosque
4 Aga Khan Hospital
7 Octopus Night Club
8 Post Office
11 Standard Chartered
   Bank
12 Clock Tower
13 Barclays Bank
   (ATM)
16 Akamba Bus Office
17 Ferry Terminal
18 Craft Stalls

20 Passage Bureau
   (Kenya National
   Assurance House)
21 Immigration
   (Reinsurance Plaza)
22 Kenya Airways
23 Aga Khan Satellite
   Laboratory;
   Mon Ami
   (Mega Plaza)
24 Main Post Office
25 British Council
26 Pel Travel;
   Oriental Restaurant
   (Al-Imran Plaza)

27 Kenya Commercial
   Bank
28 Town Hall &
   Law Courts
29 Post Bank
31 Yatin
   Supermarket
33 Kisumu Museum
35 Mosque
36 BP Petrol Station
37 Market
38 Bus & Matatu
   Station
39 Kick;
   Ziwa Creations

membership is KSh 100; to join for a year costs KSh 850 and entitles you to cheaper Internet time (KSh 150 for 30 minutes). The centre frequently hosts Kenyan art exhibitions, poetry events and performances.

Bookshops The best bookshop is the Sarit Bookshop on Oginga Odinga Rd.

Medical Services In case of an emergency head to the Aga Khan Hospital (☎ 43516, 40372) on Otiena Oyoo St. It also has a laboratory in Mega Plaza, with a good chemist a couple of doors down.

Markets

Kisumu's main market is one of the most animated in Kenya, and one of the largest. It's worth a stroll around.

If you're in town on a Sunday don't miss the Kibuye Market, a huge outdoor affair where you can buy anything, from secondhand clothes to furniture and food. It is held on Jomo Kenyatta Hwy, about 1km north of the main intersection with Nairobi Rd.

Impala Sanctuary

About 500m before Kisumu Yacht Club is the Kenya Wildlife Service (KWS) Impala

Sanctuary. This tiny sanctuary (1 sq km) is home to a small herd of impala and provides open grazing for local hippo.

Kisumu Bird Sanctuary
Twitchers have plenty to keep them occupied around Kisumu. About 8km south-east of town on the way to Ahero is Kisumu Bird Sanctuary. Covering a large area of swampland, the sanctuary is an important breeding ground for heron, ibis, stork, cormorant and egret. The best time to visit is between April and May. Transport is easy to catch along the A1, but you'll have a 3km walk once you reach the turning.

Ndere Island National Park
Gazetted as a national park only in 1986, tourism to this 4.2 sq km island has never really taken off. Water hyacinth in Kisumu Bay makes it difficult for small tourist boats to leave with any regularity and tsetse flies are a big problem after the rains. The island, which is forested and very beautiful, is home to numerous bird species, hippo, a few impala (introduced) and a population of spotted crocodile.

There's no accommodation on the island and just about your only chance of getting there is with a boat trip from the Kisumu Beach Resort (see Places to Stay – Budget, following).

Places to Stay – Budget
Campers should head for **Kisumu Beach Resort** (☎ 44006) out on the pipeline road on the opposite side of the bay from the main town near the airport. There's a bar, restaurant, cottages (KSh 1500/2000 for singles/doubles, B&B) and a camp site (KSh 200 per person). Boat trips to Ndere Island National Park can be arranged depending on the water hyacinth (KSh 500 per person – the bay is clearest between June and December) and there are hippo (one's a real show-off). Meals here cost around KSh 500. It's about 3km from the main road so take a taxi (KSh 300) or 'Pipeline' matatu from the main stage (KSh 20). The matatu may drop you a little short so take a *boda-boda* (bicycle taxi) the rest of the way.

One of the cheapest reasonable hotel options is the *YWCA* (☎ 43192) on the corner of Omolo Agar and Nairobi Rds. It's a bit of a dive but has dorm beds (three people per room) for KSh 150. Self-contained doubles vary from KSh 200 to KSh 400 per person. The Y takes both men and women and there's a canteen where you can get basic meals.

Razbi Guest House (☎ 22408) upstairs on the corner of Oginga Odinga Rd and Kendu Lane is very secure, the rooms are clean and a towel and soap are provided. It's KSh 200/300 for singles/doubles with shared cold bath (doubles are better value).

Places to Stay – Mid-Range
In the centre of town *Black & Black Boarding & Lodging* (☎ 42571) has clean and tidy singles/doubles with shared bathrooms for KSh 400/655, all including breakfast. There's hot water.

KENYA

New Victoria Hotel (☎ 21067) on the corner of Kendu Lane and Gor Mahia Rd is close by. It's a very nice place to stay (especially if you get one of the front rooms with a balcony and views of Lake Victoria) but overpriced. The singles (KSh 550) have shared facilities while the doubles (KSh 900) and triples (KSh 1350) are self-contained. All rates include breakfast. There's a good restaurant and a popular TV lounge.

East View Hotel close to the bus station is a quiet and clean sort of place with self-contained singles/doubles for KSh 660/900. Some rooms have a shower and bath. All are bright and airy.

Joy Guest House in Dunga at the turning to Hippo Point is a nice place to stay. Self-contained singles/doubles will set you back KSh 500/700.

Places to Stay – Top End
Imperial Hotel (☎ 40345, email imperial-hotel@form-net.com) on Jomo Kenyatta Hwy has been recently refurbished, the facilities are good and the atmosphere is relaxed. The cheapest rooms with all the bells and whistles you'd expect cost KSh 3300/4200. There's a rooftop bar, a downstairs bar, two restaurants (lunch/dinner KSh 650/750) and a small swimming pool.

Hotel Royale (☎ 40924) is an old colonial hotel fronted by a huge awning that covers a popular open-air terrace bar. Unfortunately some of the colonial interior is fading to the point of no return. Rooms on the 1st floor are best and cost KSh 1250/2100 including breakfast for singles/doubles with attached bathrooms.

Nyanza Club (☎ 22433) off Jomo Kenyatta Hwy is a good option if you're looking for luxury. Though strictly it takes members only, you can rent one of its pleasant and well appointed rooms (fridge, TV, phone and hot water all day) for KSh 2050/2550. The 1st floor rooms have good lake views. Stay here and you can use the swimming pool, squash and tennis courts, bar and restaurant. Temporary membership is KSh 100, but phone in advance otherwise you may not get through the gate.

Places to Eat
TOT Coffee House and Board & Lodging in town is a good place to eat, drink and be merry. It serves good Indian food and there is a pool table, dartboard and bar. It also has some nice self-contained rooms.

Dilkhush Sweets just down from Hotel Royale has a large menu of good Indian *thali* (vegetarian) dishes, plus a range of cakes and biscuits. Main meals cost between KSh 150 and KSh 300.

Cafe Natasha just off Oginga Odinga Rd has a wide variety of good cheap meals and is a popular place for breakfast.

Expresso Coffee House nearby is also recommended.

Kenshop Bakery on Oginga Odinga Rd is an excellent place for bread and snacks.

The cafe below the *New Victoria Hotel* does a breakfast of juice, papaya, eggs, toast, butter and tea or coffee for KSh 100, served from 7 to 9 am. It also serves the standard lunch dishes, but no alcohol.

Kimwa Cafe around the corner serves cheap local dishes such as *matoke* (mashed plantains).

The terrace at *Hotel Royale* is the place to go for some good fast food. It's also a great place to meet for a drink.

Mon Ami at Mega Plaza is the most popular western-style place in town. It's a good bar with a pool table and you can eat hamburgers here for about KSh 350. Constant satellite TV can be a bit intrusive, though handy for European soccer games if you're interested.

Oriental Restaurant at Al-Imran Plaza is the place to head for Chinese food. Mains cost around KSh 400, but the food is rather average (too much salt). Nice for a change though.

Nyanza Club and *Yacht Club (☎ 22050)* are among the best places to drink and eat, though you'll need temporary membership (KSh 100 and KSh 200 respectively) and may need to make a reservation in the evening.

The food at *Imperial Hotel* is equally good and will cost you about KSh 750 per person.

Entertainment
Octopus Night Club on Ogada St is the place everyone in search of action heads to. It is an excellent disco/bar/restaurant complex, and

is a weird and wonderful place. The complex includes the Bottoms Up disco (entry KSh 90). Beers are sold at normal prices and the disco is a good rage on weekends.

Kimwa Grand out at Kimwa on the road to Kakamega may look like a cheap office block, but it's where the action is. This nightclub, restaurant and bar complex is *the* place to go at the weekend, and has some live acts. Entry is around KSh 200.

Hotel Royale holds more earthy discos on Wednesday, Friday and Saturday.

Shopping
Kisumu is about the best place to buy Kisii soapstone carvings and there are pavement stalls set up near the Hotel Royale on Jomo Kenyatta Hwy.

A good place for fabric designs and clothes is Pandi Peri, down on the ring road at the end of Jomo Kenyatta Hwy. Proceeds fund a charity for street children.

Ziwa Creations has a showroom next to the offices of KICK (☎ 22498, email kick@ net2000ke.com) on Ramogi Rise just east of the bus station. KICK has been supporting local businesses for almost 10 years and the showroom is a market place for local craftworkers.

Getting There & Away
For information on travelling from Kisumu to Tanzania and Uganda, see the Kenya Getting There & Away chapter.

Air Kenya Airways has three flights a day to Nairobi. The trip takes one hour and costs KSh 3500 one way. The office (☎ 44055) is in the Alpha building on Oginga Odinga Rd.

Bus & Matatu Buses, matatus and Peugeots leave from the large bus station just north of the market.

Akamba has the best buses to Nairobi (KSh 450), and the depot is in the centre of town. There's also the deluxe Akamba Royal service to Nairobi daily (KSh 750). Stagecoach, Tawfiq and Shaggy Home Boyz charge KSh 300 to Nairobi.

There are plenty of Nissan matatus/Peugeot share-taxis to Nairobi (KSh 400/600),

Nakuru (KSh 250/350), Busia (KSh 150/250), Eldoret (KSh 180/250), Kakamega (KSh 80/100), Kericho (KSh 150), Migori (KSh 230) and Kisii (KSh 150). There are very few direct services to Kitale; take a vehicle to Kakamega and change there.

Train At the time of writing the only trains to Nairobi were all 3rd class, which can't be recommended – and they may have stopped altogether by the time you read this.

Car For car rental try Pel Travel (☎ 41525, fax 22495, email soni@form-net.com) in Al-Imran Plaza on Oginga Odinga Rd. It has a number of 2WD vehicles, but only one expensive Toyota Surf 4WD (KSh 2500 per day plus KSh 1000 insurance per day plus KSh 25 per kilometre). No small cheap Suzuki 4WDs are available in Kisumu.

Boat At the time of writing there were no ferries operating between Kisumu and the small Kenyan ports to the south, or into Tanzania or Uganda.

Getting Around
There are a couple of useful circular matatu routes. The first loops clockwise down Jomo Kenyatta Hwy, around Oginga Odinga Rd and Anaawa Ave and back up Jomo Kenyatta to Kimwa (ideal for the Kimwa Grand entertainment complex and Kibuye Market on Sunday) and Carwash. The second starts from outside the Hotel Royale, heads south to the ring road and down to Dunga Junction before heading back into town via the Gulf Stream Hotel.

Matatus can be stopped anywhere on these routes. A short journey should cost around KSh 20; however, the presence of a *mzungu* (white person) can turn these vehicles into taxis when you'll be charged between KSh 100 and KSh 200 for journeys around town.

AROUND LAKE VICTORIA
Homa Bay
☎ 0385
Homa Bay is a nondescript busy town on a small bay in Lake Victoria containing a large number of dead and abandoned buses.

Most of the action involves transporting agricultural products from the area to Kisumu.

Nearby is the intriguing volcano-shaped **Mt Homa**, the small Ruma National Park and **Thimlich Ohinga**, possibly one of the most important archaeological discoveries in East Africa. Getting to Thimlich is difficult without transport. Head down the Homa Bay-Rongo road for 12km then turn right at Rod Kopany heading south-west through Mirogi to the village of Miranga. Signposts lead from here to the site.

In Homa Bay you can send email from Munglu Computers (☎ 22055, email munglu@africaonline.co.ke) in the maze of streets opposite the Total garage. There is a Barclays Bank (no ATM) and there are cardphones by the post office.

Places to Stay & Eat There are several budget hotels just off the main road.

Summer Bay Hotel next to Asego Stores just off the main road on the lane to the post office is probably the best. The sign simply announces 'Bed & Breakfast'. Self-contained singles/doubles cost KSh 450/500.

Bay Lodge is up the hill behind the new bus station, close to the post office. It only has singles (KSh 250, or KSh 300 with bath), but it's clean, tidy and quiet.

Neem Shade Restaurant serves reasonable Swahili dishes (it's signposted from the main road).

Tawakal Hotel down by the main road is the place to head for food and drink before dancing the night away in the romantic *Cave Inn Club*.

Getting There & Away A brand new bus station has just been completed in Homa Bay, so it's likely all departures will now leave from there.

Akamba has departures to Nairobi at 7 am and 7.30 pm (KSh 480). Numerous other companies also ply the route. There are frequent matatus to Kisii (KSh 70), Mirogi (KSh 100), Kisumu (KSh 150, three hours), Rongo (KSh 50), Kericho (KSh 200) and Mbita (KSh 100).

The main road to Kisumu is appalling.

Ruma National Park

Ruma National Park covers 120 sq km of riverine woodland and savanna grassland nestling in the Lambwe Valley and is the last Kenyan habitat of the Roan antelope. There is good potential for trekking, climbing and fishing but contact the warden in advance (☎ 0385-22656) PO Box 420, Homa Bay.

There are two basic *camp sites* and the roads within the park are good. Entry costs US$15 per person plus US$2 to camp. Access is from the Homa Bay-Mbita road.

Rusinga, Mfangano & Takawiri Islands

Mbita town is the access point for all these tiny islands – Rusinga Island is in fact linked to Mbita by a causeway. The islands are ruggedly beautiful and worth exploring, but you'll need to be totally self-sufficient unless you're staying in one of the islands' exclusive resorts.

Of immediate interest are the rock paintings of **Mt Kwitutu** (1694m) on Mfangano Island, and the mausoleum of Tom Mboya on Rusinga.

Places to Stay & Eat *Patroba Ogweno Lodge* (☎ 0385-22184) is the best place to stay in Mbita. Self-contained singles/doubles cost KSh 300/400.

New Foxton Hotel close to Mbita's tiny post office is the best cheap eating house.

Rusinga Island Fishing Club an exclusive resort on the north side of Rusinga Island will set you back US$410/700. Book through Mellifera Ltd (☎ 02-574689, fax 02-577851, email Mellifera@swiftkenya.com) in Nairobi.

Mfangano Island Camp on the neighbouring island is the same sort of deal and costs US$310/460 for singles/doubles. This is primarily a fishing resort, and fishing trips are available at US$100 per day. Contact Mutiara Ltd (☎ 02-331871, fax 726427, email govscamp@africaonline.co.ke) in Nairobi.

Takawiri Island Resort is on nearby Takawiri Island. Prices start at KSh 4000/6000, rising to KSh 7000/9000 in the high season. Transfers from Mbita Point cost

Trekking to the peak of Mt Kenya is one of the highlights of a trip to East Africa.

The coast at Vipingo, with its magnificent coral reef, is one of the least spoiled in Kenya.

Lake Baringo, in Kenya's Rift Valley, is home to abundant birdlife and is popular for boat trips.

ALL PHOTOGRAPHS BY MATT FLETCHER

Askari monument, Nairobi, Kenya

Mangoes for sale at the market, Mombasa, Kenya

Bahra Mosque, Mombasa Old Town, Kenya

A dhow trip at Lamu, off Kenya's coast, is a relaxing way to spend a sunny afternoon.

KSh 8000 per boat load, but it is quite possible to pick up a taxi-boat to the island. At the time of writing there were plans to add a *camp site* to the resort. Book through Dream Travel (☎ 02-572139, fax 577489, email dreamtravel@form-net.com) in Nairobi.

Getting There & Away There are usually three buses to and from Kisumu every day (KSh 200); they leave Mbita first thing in the morning (the last one departs at around 8 am). Matatus to Homa Bay are more frequent (KSh 100).

After the death of the ferry, 10m-long canoes are the only transport between the islands and all leave from the causeway at Mbita. There are usually three boats per day between Mfangano, Rusinga and Takawiri islands, and more on Thursday (market day in Mbita). First transport for Mbita (via Takawiri) leaves Mfangano at around 6.30 am.

Western Highlands

The Western Highlands are the agricultural heartland of Kenya, and separate Kisumu and Lake Victoria from the rest of the country. In the south around Kisii and Kericho lie vast tea plantations, while further north around Kitale and Eldoret it's all fertile farming land.

Towns here are really just small agricultural service centres and they're not very interesting. The attractions of the area lie outside these towns – the tea plantations around Kericho; Kakamega Forest near Kakamega; Mt Elgon and Saiwa Swamp national parks (both near Kitale) and the Cherangani Hills, north-east of Kitale.

KERICHO
☎ 0361
Tea – it's everywhere! Kericho's climate is perfect for growing tea and the surrounding hills are a uniform bright green mainly because of the afternoon showers that fall every day of the year. Yes, Kericho is a wet place and there's not a great deal to the town, but there are worse places to be stranded.

Information
The post office (plus cardphones) and the two main banks are all on Moi Hwy. The banks are open from 8 am to 1 pm Monday to Friday and from 8.30 to 11 am Saturday. Barclays has an ATM.

Email can be sent from Tealand Computers or Luli Comptech Services, located in the same complex next to the Mwalimu Hotel.

North of town on Moi Hwy is a laboratory of the Aga Khan Hospital.

Tea Plantations
The plantation closest to town is behind the Tea Hotel, which was once owned by the Brooke Bond company. If you walk through the hotel grounds behind what was the service station and out through the back gate, the path leads through the tea bushes to the hotel workers' huts. If you're lucky picking may be in progress.

Places to Stay – Budget
Campers have a couple of options: *Kericho Garden Lodge* (☎ 20878) where you can camp in the pleasant grounds (KSh 250 per tent per night); or the rough camp site at the *Kericho Lodge & Fish Resort* (☎ 20035) down on the Kimugi River behind the Tea

---

Picking Tea

Tea accounts for between 20 and 30% of Kenya's export income and tea picking is a great source of employment around Kericho. The bushes are picked every 17 days, and the same picker picks the same patches of the plantations each time. A good picker can collect 100kg of tea per day.

The Kenyan tea industry is unique in that it's small holders who produce 66% of the country's tea, which is then sold to the Kenya Tea Development Authority (KTDA), which guarantees farmers 70% of the sale price.

After being flagged for privatisation, the KTDA (widely seen as corrupt and inefficient) is being taken over by small-scale farmers who are gradually taking a bigger role in the production of Kenya's most important cash crop.

KENYA

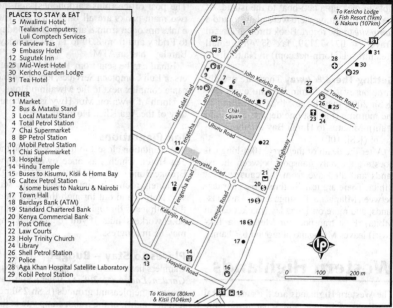

KERICHO

PLACES TO STAY & EAT
5 Mwalimu Hotel;
   Tealand Computers;
   Luli Comptech Services
6 Fairview Tas
9 Embassy Hotel
12 Sugutek Inn
25 Mid-West Hotel
30 Kericho Garden Lodge
31 Tea Hotel

OTHER
1 Market
2 Bus & Matatu Stand
3 Local Matatu Stand
4 Total Petrol Station
7 Chai Supermarket
8 BP Petrol Station
10 Mobil Petrol Station
11 Chai Supermarket
13 Hospital
14 Hindu Temple
15 Buses to Kisumu, Kisii & Homa Bay
16 Caltex Petrol Station
   & some buses to Nakuru & Nairobi
17 Town Hall
18 Barclays Bank (ATM)
19 Standard Chartered Bank
20 Kenya Commercial Bank
21 Post Office
22 Law Courts
23 Holy Trinity Church
24 Library
26 Shell Petrol Station
27 Police
28 Aga Khan Hospital Satellite Laboratory
29 Kobil Petrol Station

To Kericho Lodge & Fish Resort (1km) & Nakuru (107km)

Harambee Road
John Kericho Road
Moi Road
Chai Square
Uhuru Road
Isaac Selat Road
Tengecha Lane
Tengecha Road
Kenyatta Road
Kelenjin Road
Temple Road
Moi Highway
Tower Road

To Kisumu (80km) & Kisii (104km)

0   100   200 m

Hotel (KSh 150 per person). The former has some overpriced self-contained rooms (KSh 480/780) and a homey bar, while the latter has some very expensive *bandas* (KSh 950/1300), though guided river walks, fishing trips and hikes into the tea estates are available.

Sugetek Inn a warren-like place on Tengecha Rd offers a number of cheap rooms (KSh 150 per person), which aren't amazing.

Places to Stay – Mid-Range
Mwalimu Hotel (☎ 21777) is a reasonably modern place in the centre of town that has a popular bar and restaurant. Singles/doubles with bathroom cost KSh 470/610 including breakfast. There are no mosquito nets, but it's not a bad place.

Places to Stay – Top End
Tea Hotel (☎ 30004, fax 20576) is a grand old place that was originally built by the Brooke Bond company in the 1950s for its managers. Set in vast grounds, it exudes an atmosphere of days gone by, though nostalgia is not generally an excuse for running a place into the ground. Cottages offer the best accommodation, though at US$60/84 they're stunningly overpriced.

Places to Eat
Fairview Tas does good cheap breakfasts while *Embassy Hotel* on Isaac Selat Rd is also popular. *Mwalimu Hotel*'s restaurant is more sophisticated and good value and *Tea Hotel* has lunches (US$11) and dinners (US$12) that are a step up.

Getting There & Away
The matatu station is fairly well organised, though buses to Nairobi (KSh 300) leave from the Caltex station on the main road. Similarly, buses and matatus to Kisumu and Kisii use a lay-by south of the Caltex station. Inquire locally first.

Nissan minibuses/Peugeot share-taxis leave regularly for Kisumu (KSh 100/120), Kisii (KSh 120/140), Eldoret (KSh 200/ 250), Nakuru (KSh 140/200) and Nairobi (KSh 300/450).

If you are hitching, the turn-off to Kisumu is about 2km south of town along the Kisii road.

KAKAMEGA

If you arrive late in the day it's not a bad idea to stay here before heading for the Kakamega Forest Reserve.

There's a good market, and email can be sent from the Highland Computer College (email kakamega@africaonline.com), Kenyatta Rd. Barclays has an ATM.

Places to Stay & Eat

Bendera Hotel has self-contained twin rooms for KSh 300 above a popular bar and restaurant while *Salama Hotel* is a basic place with rooms for KSh 150/200.

Stock up with supplies at *Mama Watoto's Supermarket* and check out the West African cuisine at *Lawino 2000*.

Two great little cafes opposite Muliro Gardens are *Sparkles* and the *Chill Park Cafe*.

Getting There & Away

Akamba, Tawfiq and Coastline have offices just off Kenyatta Rd. Nairobi departures are mostly in the afternoon and evening (KSh 450 to KSh 550).

The main matatu station is behind the Total station on the northern edge of town. There are buses and matatus to Kisumu (KSh 100), Eldoret (KSh 160), Kitale (KSh 160, two hours), Bungoma (KSh 100) and Nakuru (KSh 250), where you should change for another matatu to Nairobi.

KAKAMEGA FOREST RESERVE

The Kakamega Forest Reserve is a superb slab of virgin tropical rainforest in the heart of an intensively cultivated agricultural area. It is home to a huge variety of birds and animals and is a real must see.

The forest is divided into two sections, the southern **Kakamega Forest Reserve** centred on Isecheno and maintained by the For-

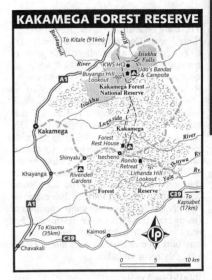

est Department, and the Buyangu northern area, the **Kakamega Forest National Reserve**, looked after by KWS.

The northern section of the forest is dense with considerable areas of primary forest and regenerating secondary forest – recently there has been a total ban of grazing, wood collection and cultivation in the KWS-controlled area. The southern section still experiences considerable farming activity and the pressure on the forest is enormous.

Further development of tourism facilities by KWS in the north is likely and only here can you find the rare De Brazza's monkey. Other forest primates include red-tailed monkey, Colobus and blue monkey. At night you may see hammer-headed fruit bats or a flying squirrel, but birds are the main wildlife draw. The best months are June and August, and then October when many migrant species arrive. More than 330 bird species have been recorded here. You are likely to see black-and-white casqued hornbill, Ross' turaco and great blue turaco. Wildflowers and butterflies are wonderful in October.

At the time of writing the bridge connecting the northern and southern sections was down.

KENYA

Information

There are no entry fees. The Kenya Indige-nous Forest Conservation Program (KIF-CON) publishes an excellent little guide to the forest. It's available from the KWS head-quarters in the north (KSh 300) and from the Rondo Retreat in the south (KSh 500), as well as from KWS headquarters in Nairobi.

It's just about essential to take a Kaka-mega Biodiversity Conservation Tour Op-erators Association (KABICOTOA) guide along when exploring the forest. Its offices are next to the Forest Rest House in the south and beside the KWS headquarters in the north. It charges KSh 100 for a short walk, but you should tip KSh 200 extra per hour. Not only can guides show you around (many trail signs have been destroyed), but most are excellent naturalists, able to recog-nise bird species by their calls alone. Caleb is highly recommended.

Walking Trails

The best way to appreciate the forest is to walk, and trail systems radiate out from the two centres north and south.

The trails vary from to 1 to 7km, the lon-gest being the Isiukhu Trail up to the in-significant Isiukhu Falls in the north. The short walk to the viewing platform on Buyangu Hill in the north or to Lirhanda Hill in the south for sunrise or sunset is highly recommended.

With a good torch (flashlight) and an ex-pert guide, night walks can be fantastic, opening your eyes to a whole different side of the forest.

Places to Stay & Eat

Rivendell Gardens (☎ 0331-41316, email gb@net2000ke.com) in the village of Shi-buye close to Shinyalu, is a nice place to stay and a good base for exploring the southern half of the forest (if you have a ve-hicle). Accommodation consists of three round bungalows with two double rooms in each (KSh 1200 per person B&B), a camp site (KSh 200 per tent) and a simple banda (KSh 300 per double). There are hot show-ers and flush toilets and guests can use the lounge and wide veranda in the main house.

Adventurous walks along the Isecheno River and night walks can be arranged here. From the main road at Khayaga follow the signs along the dirt track and then turn right down a narrow lane after Arap Moi Sec-ondary School (it's about KSh 50 by bicy-cle-taxi). Alternatively once in Shinyalu turn right heading to Khayanga then turn left upon reaching the sign 2km later.

Forest Rest House is in the forest itself and is decidedly shabby though still quite pleasant. It's an elevated wooden building with four double rooms each with semi-func-tional bathroom (no hot water). Blankets are supplied but you need your own sleeping bag. Rooms cost KSh 198 per person or you can camp for KSh 127. If the resthouse is full and you have your own sleeping gear, it is usually possible to sleep on the veranda. If you want to be sure of a room, book in advance through the Forest Ranger, PO Box 88, Kakamega.

You'll need to bring your own food and preferably something to cook it on. The al-ternative is the small kiosk just down the lane. It sells beer, tea, sodas, basic provi-sions and simple meals. Evening meals can be arranged with advance notice – the kiosk closes at 6.30 pm. You can also get basic meals and supplies from *dukas* about 2km back towards Shinyalu.

Rondo Retreat (☎ 0331-30268, email TF-RONDO@maf.org) about 3km further along the road from Isecheno is a former sawmiller's residence built in the 1920s. It is owned by a church group, primarily as a re-treat for missionaries, and offers wonderful top end accommodation in self-contained bungalows. The gardens and surrounding for-est are beautiful and KABICOTOA guides can be arranged from here. It costs KSh 2700 per person for room only, or KSh 4900 for full board. The food is very good – lunch is KSh 600 and dinner KSh 900, but they pre-fer advance warning. Transfers from Kaka-mega can be arranged for KSh 600 per vehicle (maximum five people). If you've been saving some cash for a special treat then this is an excellent place to spend it.

Buyangu KWS operates *Udo's Bandas & Campsite* a tidy and well maintained place with seven simple bandas each with two beds and mosquito nets. There's a communal cooking and dining shelter, pit toilets and bucket showers. The bandas are US$10 and camping is US$2. Advance bookings can be made through the District Warden (☎ 0331-20425) KWS, PO Box 879, Kakamega.

Getting There & Away
Isecheno The Forest Rest House lies about 12km east (as the crow flies) of the A1 Kisumu-Kitale road, about 30km from Kisumu. Access is possible either from Kakamega village on the main road when coming from the north or from Khayaga, also on the main road when coming from the south. From both places dirt roads lead east to the small market village of Shinyalu, from where it's a further 5km to the resthouse, signposted to the left. There are matatus from Kakamega to Shinyalu, and even the occasional one from Khayaga to Shinyalu. Matatus linking Isecheno with Kakamega leave in both directions at 6.30 am.

If you want to walk – and it is beautiful walking country – it's about 7km from Khayaga to Shinyalu, or about 10km from Kakamega to Shinyalu, then 5km to Isecheno. You may be able to hitch, but there are numerous bicycle-taxis along most of the route (Khayaga to Shinyalu KSh 50, Shinyalu to Isecheno KSh30). These roads become extremely treacherous after rain.

From the turn-off to the resthouse the dirt road continues on to Kapsabet, so you could also come from that direction but it is a long walk if you can't get a lift.

Buyangu Local matatus heading north on the Kakamega-Kitale road pass by the northern access road (signposted), about 18km north of Kakamega town. You'll have a 2km walk from where the matatus drop you.

ELDORET
☎ 0321
There is little to see or do here but this pleasant and affluent town makes a convenient stopover, particularly if you are heading to or from the Cherangani Hills or Kerio Valley.

The construction of a brand-new international airport outside the town has caused some controversy, but it's certainly handy for President Moi, who has a house just down the road – what a happy coincidence.

Information
The main post office is on Uganda Rd and cardphones are dotted around town. Also on the main street are Barclays (with an ATM) and Standard Chartered Bank branches.

Email can be sent from Write Image (☎ 32909, email writmage@net2000ke.com) on the corner of Elijaa Cheruhota and Oginga Odinga Sts. Surfing costs KSh 15 per minute.

The Dorinyo Lessos Creameries Cheese Factory sells excellent cheese. Phone in advance on ☎ 63308 if you want to look around.

Places to Stay – Budget
Mahindi Hotel (☎ 31520) above the Honey Drops Hotel close to the bus and matatu station is good value at KSh 300 for a single with shared bath. The hotel has a restaurant, though the noise from the Silent Night Bar downstairs can sometimes be distracting.

Top Lodge on Oginga Odinga St has rooms for KSh 200/300. *Aya Inn* (☎ 32259) on the same street charges KSh 400/600.

Naiberi River Campsite (☎ 61195) is 22km south-east of town on the C54 road to Kaptagat. It's in a beautiful spot right on the Naiberi River, and is rightly popular with overland trucks. It's an eccentric maze of a place, and its two bars stay open until the last person falls over. Meals are available and nature walks along the river with the knowledgeable local guide, Ashe, are recommended. As well as camping (KSh 200) there's a dormitory (KSh 400) and a few very comfortable double cabins with private bathrooms (KSh 1600). Getting there by local transport is a pain, but the owner, Raj Shah, works in Eldoret during the day, so if you ring ☎ 32644 before 5 pm on weekdays he can give you a lift out to the site.

Places to Stay – Mid-Range
New Lincoln Hotel (☎ 22093) is an excellent and popular quiet place with guarded parking. Rooms with bathrooms are good

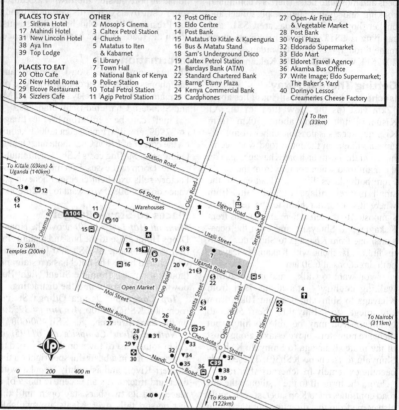

ELDORET

PLACES TO STAY	OTHER		
1 Sirikwa Hotel	2 Mosop's Cinema	12 Post Office	27 Open-Air Fruit
17 Mahindi Hotel	3 Caltex Petrol Station	13 Eldo Centre	& Vegetable Market
31 New Lincoln Hotel	4 Church	14 Post Bank	28 Post Bank
38 Aya Inn	5 Matatus to Iten	15 Matatus to Kitale & Kapenguria	30 Yogi Plaza
39 Top Lodge	& Kabarnet	16 Bus & Matatu Stand	32 Eldorado Supermarket
	6 Library	18 Sam's Underground Disco	33 Eldo Mart
PLACES TO EAT	7 Town Hall	19 Caltex Petrol Station	35 Eldoret Travel Agency
20 Otto Cafe	8 National Bank of Kenya	21 Barclays Bank (ATM)	36 Akamba Bus Office
26 New Hotel Roma	9 Police Station	22 Standard Chartered Bank	37 Write Image; Eldo Supermarket;
29 Elcove Restaurant	10 Total Petrol Station	23 Barng' Etuny Plaza	The Baker's Yard
34 Sizzlers Cafe	11 Agip Petrol Station	24 Kenya Commercial Bank	40 Dorinyo Lessos
		25 Cardphones	Creameries Cheese Factory

value at KSh 600/800, including breakfast. The staff are friendly, there's normally enough hot water for a bath and the hotel has its own bar and restaurant.

Places to Stay – Top End

Sirikwa Hotel (☎ 63433, fax 61018) a modern yet ageing place is the only top end hotel in Eldoret. It has rooms for KSh 4000/5000, including breakfast. All major credit cards are accepted and the hotel has the only swimming pool in Eldoret (nonguests can use it for KSh 100). Meals in the restaurant cost KSh 500 (lunch) and KSh 600 (dinner).

Places to Eat

Otto Cafe on Uganda Rd is a popular lunchtime spot. Check out the fiery samosas.

Sizzlers Cafe on Kenyatta St is a popular place that is slightly more upmarket. Here you'll find a whole range of burgers, curries, steaks and sandwiches.

The Baker's Yard under Write Image has some great snacks.

New Hotel Roma on Elijaa Cheruhota St is an excellent local place. It has dirt-cheap Kenyan and Swahili staples.

Elcove Restaurant on Oloo Rd opposite New Lincoln Hotel is the best restaurant in

The Fastest Men & Women in the World

Kenya produces some of the best middle-distance and long-distance runners in the world. They have dominated for the past 15 years, and in the past five years Kenyans have begun to dominate the marathon as well.

Marathon running was almost unknown in Kenya until 1987, when Kenyan Douglas Wakiihuri won the world title and Ibrahim Hussein became the first black man to win the New York Marathon. However, one of the biggest stars of Kenyan athletics is Paul Tergat, five times world cross-country champion. This is amazing progress for a country that won its first athletics Olympic gold medal only 30 years ago.

The year 1999 was particularly good. In one weekend Japhet Kosgei and Tecal Loroupe won the Rotterdam Marathon, Joseph Chebet won the Boston Marathon and Joyce Chepchumba won the London Marathon. In doing so she collected one of the biggest cheques ever awarded to a female athlete.

So why are the Kenyans so good? It's partly to do with the solid support structure provided by the Kenya Amateur Athletic Association, which has been spotting and fostering young talent since 1967, when annual school athletics championships began nationwide. US college scholarships, prize money and appearance fees all help to boost interest, and hundreds of Kenyans are making US$10,000 a year as road racers.

What is remarkable about Kenya's top distance runners is that most of them are from one tribe, the Kalenjin, who make up 10% of the country's population and live in the highlands of western Kenya. Over the last decade Kalenjin have won 31 Olympic or World Championship medals including 12 golds. Kalenjin men hold world records at five of the eight commonly run distances. It's a good bet that the next person to beat the men's marathon record will be a Kalenjin.

Nobody can quite explain this amazing talent, though genetics may hold the answer. The Kalenjin have lived for centuries at altitudes of over 2000m and traditionally kept cattle. Inconclusive research suggests the Kalenjin have an incredible capacity to increase aerobic efficiency with training, a trait that is largely hereditary. Linguistic studies have linked the Kalenjin with other pastoral tribes in East Africa that have produced world-class runners.

---

town. The Indian food is very good and you can expect to spend KSh 750 on a pig-out.

Entertainment
Sam's Underground Disco is best for a bop.

Getting There & Away
The bus and matatu station is in the centre of town, just off Uganda Rd. Matatus/share-taxis depart throughout the day for Kisumu (KSh 180/250), Nakuru (KSh 170/220), Nairobi (KSh 350/500), Kericho (KSh 200/250), Eldama Ravine (KSh 150), Kapsabet (KSh 50/60), Iten (KSh 40/60) and Kitale (KSh 90/120). There are also buses on all these routes.

Akamba buses leave from the company's office/depot on Oginga Odinga St. Executive services to Nairobi (KSh 370) leave at 10.30 am and 9 pm. There's a daily service to Kampala (KSh 670) at noon.

There are no passenger train services to Eldoret.

For car rental, check out the Eldoret Travel Agency (☎ 33351) on Kenyatta St, but no 4WDs are available here or anywhere else in town.

CHERANGANI HILLS
The beautiful Cherangani Hills are part of the Rift Valley system and extend for about 60km from the north-east of Eldoret. They form the western wall of the spectacular **Elgeyo Escarpment**. Jane or Julia Barnley of Sirikwa Safaris (PO Box 332, Kitale) can organise ornithological tours of the hills or simply provide guides and porters (see Sirikwa Safaris in the Kitale section following for details).

KENYA

KITALE
☎ 0325

Kitale is another in the string of agricultural service towns in the Western Highlands. The museum is interesting, but Kitale's main function is as a base for explorations further afield – Mt Elgon, Saiwa Swamp National Park – and as a starting point for the trip up to the western side of Lake Turkana (see West of Lake Turkana in the Northern Kenya chapter for detailed information).

Information

The post office is on (surprise, surprise) Post Office Rd. Email can be sent from Alrood Enterprises (email alro.ent@net2000ke.com) on Moi Ave. It costs KSh 30/120 to receive/send an email, and a massive KSh 180 for three minutes of Internet time. Barclays has an ATM and there's a busy market.

Things to See

The **Kitale Museum** houses some fine ethnographic displays and wildlife exhibits. It's open from 8 am to 6 pm daily; entry is KSh 200.

Next to the museum is the **Olaf Palme Agroforestry Centre**, open daily and well worth a visit if you're interested in reforestation and Kenyan trees.

Places to Stay – Budget

Kahuruko Lodge is the best of the cheapies/brothels, offering singles with clean sheets and shared bathroom for KSh 250 (upstairs) and KSh 200 (downstairs – rather noisy).

Sirikwa Safaris is 23km north of Kitale on the Kapenguria road. Jane and Julia Barnley are very friendly and know the Western Highlands like the back of their hands, plus they're great conversationalists. Stay here and feel right at home! Camping with your own tent costs KSh 300 per person including firewood, hot showers, flush toilets and electricity. There are also comfortable, furnished permanent tents for KSh 900/1200 or two very comfortable rooms with double beds in the main house for KSh 1800/2700. Add 35% tax to these prices which include breakfast. To find Sirikwa

KITALE

PLACES TO STAY
10 Kahuruko Lodge
26 Sunrise Motel;
     Lantern Restaurant
30 Alakara Hotel

PLACES TO EAT
6   Rose Cafe
13 Suncourt Cafe
19 Bongo Hotel
31 Executive Restaurant

OTHER
1   Covered Market
2   Local Matatus
3   Bus & Matatu Park
4   Open-Air Market
5   Mobil Petrol Station
7   Caltex Petrol Station
8   Krishna Bakery
9   National Bank of Kenya
     (Bureau de Change)
11 Shell Petrol Station
12 Kenya Commercial Bank
14 Town Hall
15 Law Courts
16 Crystal Medical Clinic
17 Alrood Enterprises
18 Akamba Bus Office
20 Mombasa Video Show;
     Ngecha Butchery;
     Nyama Choma
21 Soy Trading
22 Police Station
23 Barclays Bank (ATM)
24 Standard Chartered Bank
25 Suam Supermarket
27 Post Office
28 Caltex Petrol Station
29 Mwalimu Co-Op
     Bookshop
32 Kitale Museum
33 Olaf Palme
     Agroforestry Centre

To Enderbess (20km)
& Mt Elgon (25km)

0   100   200 m

Mt Elgon Road

Train Station

To Saiwa Swamp (18km),
Sirikwa Safaris (23km),
Kapenguria (34km) &
Lodwar (284km)

Askari Road

Bank Street

Kenyatta

Moi

Street

Post Office Road

A1

Kenyatta Street

A1

To Kitale Club (300m),
Eldoret (69km)
& Kisumu (160km)

Safaris, look for the sign on the right 1km after the small village of Kesagen (KSh 40). Most matatu drivers know it.

Places to Stay – Mid-Range

Alakara Hotel (☎ 20395) on Kenyatta St is good value and a little stylish. It offers spacious singles/doubles with shared bath for KSh 400/600. Rooms with phone and private bath cost KSh 600/900, including breakfast. Facilities include a good bar/restaurant and TV room. Staff are friendly and helpful. It's the best place in this range.

Bongo Hotel (☎ 20593) on Moi Ave is popular. It has rooms with shared bath for KSh 400/600, or KSh 600/800 with private bath, all including an excellent breakfast. Hot water and the usual trimmings are provided.

Sunrise Motel (☎ 31841) on Kenyatta St is upstairs next to the Lantern restaurant. Deluxe self-contained singles/doubles go for KSh 750/850, and standard rooms are KSh 600/770. The long, dark central corridor may be off-putting, but the deluxe rooms are huge and have balconies (with plants) overlooking the street. Mosquito nets are provided and prices include breakfast in the Lantern.

Places to Eat

The Lantern (☎ 30360) the sister restaurant to the Elcove in Eldoret (with the same menu) is by far the best place to eat in town. Stick to the Indian food and you can't go wrong. The bar has the right blend of potent cocktails and kitsch decor to make it an essential pit stop. Main courses are around KSh 270.

Executive Restaurant is a very popular lunch-time spot. The menu is extensive and the food is good and reasonably priced.

Suncourt Cafe and *Rose Cafe* are also worth trying.

The restaurants at the *Bongo* and *Alakara* hotels are both very popular places for an evening meal. They have (competing) lively bars and takeaway food sections.

Kitale Club has more-expensive food.

Entertainment

Mombasa Video Show puts on third-rate action movies and soft porn (sometimes combined).

Getting There & Away

For Lodwar in the Turkana district two Kenya Witness buses leave every morning at about 9 am and cost KSh 400. The Nissan matatus are more reliable and leave about five times daily (KSh 500, five hours).

On the Nairobi route there is a variety of transport – bus, matatu and share-taxi. Akamba runs daily buses to Nairobi at 9 am and 9 pm (KSh 420 day, KSh 480 night, seven hours). The Eldoret Express runs a number of times daily and costs KSh 350. The bus companies have their offices mainly around the bus station area; the exception is Akamba, which has its office on Moi Ave.

Matatus/share-taxis also run to Nairobi (KSh 380/620), Eldoret (KSh 90/120), Nakuru (KSh 230/340), Kisumu (KSh 200/ 250) and Kakamega (KSh 120/150).

Tropex Bus runs services direct to Kisii (KSh 350). For Kericho change at Eldoret.

For the village of Enderbess (the nearest place to Mt Elgon National Park), Nissan matatus cost KSh 60.

MT ELGON NATIONAL PARK

Mt Elgon sits astride the Kenya-Uganda border and while it offers similar trekking possibilities to Mt Kenya, its location makes it far less popular. It is, however, quite accessible for those without their own transport if you're prepared to walk a few kilometres. The lower altitude also means that conditions are not so cold, although rain can be more frequent here than on Mt Kenya.

The mountain is an extinct volcano and the national park extends from the lower slopes right up to the Ugandan border. The highest peak is Wagagai (4321m), on the far side of the crater in Uganda. The highest peak on the Kenyan side is Koitoboss. There are warm springs in the crater itself, the floor of which is around 3500m above sea level.

The mountain's biggest attraction is the elephants, renowned the world over for their predilection for digging salt, the major source of which is the caves on the eastern slopes. There are four main caves open to visitors – Kitum, Chepnyalil, Mackingeny and Ngwarisha. Kitum is where you are most likely to see elephants (especially if you get up there before dawn) while Mackingeny, with a waterfall cascading across the entrance, is the most spectacular. Bring a good torch (flashlight) if you want to explore the caves.

Kitum Cave has been the centre of some controversy in recent years following the deaths from Marburg's (an Ebola type virus) of two people who visited it. All is gruesomely retold in Richard Preston's book *Hot Zone*. However, tens of thousands of other people have safely visited the cave over the years and the US Army's Infectious Diseases Unit couldn't find a trace of anything. More obvious dangers are the occasional rock falls.

The mountain's fauna and flora are also great attractions. Starting with rainforest at the base, the vegetation changes as you ascend to bamboo jungle and finally alpine moorland with the bizarre giant groundsel and giant lobelia plants. The lower forests are the habitat of the impressive black-and-white Colobus, blue and De Brazza's monkeys – most likely seen near waterways – which share the canopy with noisy red-fronted parrots, Ross' turaco and black-and-white casqued hornbill. There are over 240 bird species on the mountain, and on the peaks you may even see a Lammergeier gliding through the thin air. Most commonly sighted animals include buffalo, bushbuck, olive baboon, giant forest hog and duiker. The Elephant Platform and Enderbess Bluff viewpoints are worth a visit. Some mountain streams may contain trout.

Elgon can be a wet place at any time of the year, but the driest months are December, January and February. You should bring waterproofs and warm clothes (it gets cold at altitude). Take it easy climbing the peaks; the altitude will be a problem for some people (see the Health section in the Regional Facts for the Visitor chapter).

Access to the 169 sq km park is permitted without a vehicle. Entry costs US$10 per person per day. A ranger will escort you to the camp site (1km inside the park) and on any walks you may want to do on the lower forested slopes – such as to the caves – for which a small fee may be payable. For any trekking on the higher slopes you'll

need a tent and camping gear. Andy Wielochowski's *Mt Elgon Map & Guide* is an essential purchase. It's available in Nairobi for around US$5 and from Stanford's in London for UK£6.95. Lonely Planet's *Trekking in East Africa* also has further information on the mountain.

For information on the Ugandan part of Mt Elgon National Park, see the South-Eastern Uganda chapter.

Walks

The most popular route used to be from **Kimilili**, a small village 36km south of Kitale on the main A1 road to Webuye and Kisumu. Unfortunately at the time of writing, this route was still closed after an outbreak of cross-border cattle-rustling and general banditry. This situation may change so contact the KWS headquarters in Nairobi or the assistant warden at Mt Elgon National Park (☎ 0325-31456) PO Box 753, Kitale.

The **Park Route** is a well worn trail from Chorlim gate up to **Koitoboss Peak** (requiring one or two overnight camps). If you have a vehicle you can drive up to over 3500m, but the current state of the roads means the 32km drive can take half a day, and then it's a walk of two to three hours up to the peak.

Descending to the foot of Koitoboss Peak you have several options. Firstly you could descend north-west into the crater to the **Suam warm springs**. Secondly, if security improves, you could press on east around the crater rim and descend via the **Masara Route**. Lastly you could head south-west around the rim of the crater (some very hard walking) to **Lower Elgon Tarn** (where you can camp) and then ascend **Lower Elgon Peak** (4301m). To return you could either head back the way you came or trek down the **Kimilili Route** (if open).

It is best to arrange any guiding with KWS in advance.

Places to Stay

There are no lodges in the park, but the stone bandas at *Kapkuro Camp Site* just up from the Chorlim gate are excellent and worth the US$10 per person. Camping is US$2 per person. Bring all your food as

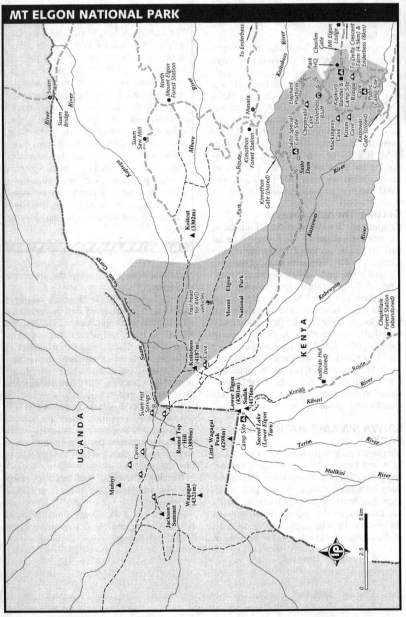

MT ELGON NATIONAL PARK

there's only one small shop, which sells beer and a few basics for the park staff and their families.

You can probably forget about *Mt Elgon Lodge* 1km before the Chorlim gate (though you can camp in the once elegant grounds for KSh 300). It's likely to have closed. However, 4.5km from Chorlim gate *Delta Crescent Farm (☎/fax 0325-31462)* makes a good stopover before heading into the park. There are simple bandas (KSh 200 per person) and a camp site with good facilities (KSh 100 per person). Organic fruit, vegetables and eggs are available. You can go horse riding for KSh 600 per hour, and 4WD tours of the park can be arranged.

Getting There & Away

Chorim gate is about 9km from Enderbess, the nearest village to Mt Elgon National Park. If you're on foot take a matatu from Kitale (KSh 60) to Enderbess. Walk down to the post office and turn left onto a dirt road. Keep walking straight, ignoring the first crossroads, and after 3.5km turn right at the second junction where there's a school and a signpost for Chorlim gate (it's 5.5km away not 4km). The entrance to Delta Cresent Farm is 200m down this road on the left.

If you're driving, the park is signposted several kilometres before Enderbess, though it's difficult to hitch this route. A 4WD is essential within the park and the dirt roads haven't been graded in years.

SAIWA SWAMP NATIONAL PARK

This small park north of Kitale is a real delight and home of the sitatunga antelope. Sadly the park is under pressure. Hardwood trees have been known to disappear overnight and fertiliser from surrounding fields has encouraged the growth of tall grasses suffocating the wild sage, the typical food of the sitatunga. However, local people are

Sitatunga Antelope

The sitatunga is fairly elusive and really the only way to spot one is to sit atop one of the observation towers armed with a pair of binoculars and a hefty dose of patience. As in most of the parks, the best time for animal-spotting is the early morning or late afternoon.

This shy antelope is not unlike a bushbuck in appearance, although larger, and it has elongated hooves that are supposed to make it easier for it to get around in swampy conditions – it's hard to see how, but no doubt nature has it all worked out. The colouring is basically grey-brown, with more red noticeable in the female, and both sexes have white spots or stripes on the upper body. The male has long twisted horns that grow up to 1m in length.

becoming more involved in the protection of the park.

Blue, vervet and De Brazza's monkeys and some 370 species of bird are crammed into 3 sq km of swamp and tropical riverine forest. The black-and-white Colobus (distinguished by its flowing 'cape' of white hair as it flies through the canopy) and the impressive crowned crane, queen of the marsh, are both very distinctive. You may also see Cape clawless and spot-throated otters.

What makes this park unique is that it is only accessible on foot. There are marked walking trails that skirt the swamp, duckboards right across the swamp, and some rickety observation towers (number four is the best placed).

Recently a beautiful, well equipped *camp site* has been built close to the river (US$2 per person).

The park is a 5km walk from the main Kitale-Kapenguria road. Day entry costs US$15 per person.

Northern Kenya

This vast area, covering thousands of square kilometres up to the borders with Sudan, Ethiopia and Somalia, is an explorer's paradise hardly touched by the 20th century. The tribes that live here – the Samburu, Turkana, Rendille, Boran, Gabra, Merille and El-Molo – contain some of the most fascinating people in the world. Many of them have little contact with the modern world, preferring their own centuries-old traditional lifestyles and customs which bind members of a tribe together and ensure that each individual has a part to play. Many have strong warrior traditions and in the past, it was the balance of power between the tribes that defined their respective areas, though cheap guns brought in from conflicts in surrounding countries have changed things considerably.

Not only are the people another world away from Nairobi and the more developed areas of the country but the landscapes are tremendous, with an incredible diversity of wildlife showcased in a number of national parks and reserves.

Geography

Much of northern Kenya is scrub desert dissected by *luggas* (dry river beds that burst into a brief but violent life whenever there is heavy rain) and peppered with acacia trees, which are often festooned with weaver birds' nests. But there are also extinct and dormant volcanoes; barren, shattered lava beds; canyons through which cool, clear streams flow; oases of lush vegetation hemmed in by craggy mountains and huge islands of forested mountains surrounded by sand deserts. And of course there's the legendary 'Jade Sea' (Lake Turkana) – Kenya's largest lake and regarded by many as the birthplace of humanity.

A long narrow body of water, Lake Turkana stretches south from the Ethiopian border for some 250km, yet it's never more than 50km wide. While it looks fairly placid most of the time, it is notorious for the vicious squalls that whip up seemingly out of

Highlights
• Joining the fun at the Maralal International Camel Derby
• Trekking down into Suguta Valley from World's View at Poror
• Taking a safari through the varied landscapes of northern Kenya to Lake Turkana
• Exploring the ever-changing fossil sites within Sibiloi National Park, the 'Cradle of Mankind'
• Camel trekking around the Ndoto Mountains and Matthews Range
• Meeting people from the culturally diverse northern tribes

nowhere and are largely responsible for fatalities among the Turkana and El-Molo people who live along the lakeshore.

The lake was first reached by Europeans in the late 19th century by two Austrian explorers, von Hehnel and Teleki, who named it Lake Rudolf; it wasn't until the early 1970s that the name was changed to Turkana. The fossil hominid skulls discovered here by the Leakeys in the 1960s are thought to be around 2½ million years old. It is believed that at that time the lake was far more extensive than it is today and supported a richer plant and animal life. Around 10,000 years ago the water level was high enough for the lake to be one of the sources of the Nile.

Climate

The contrasts here are incredible and the climate mirrors this. By noon on the plains the temperature can reach 50°C without a breath of wind. Mirages shimmer in the distance on all sides. Nothing moves. Yet in the evening, the calm can suddenly be shattered as a violent thunderstorm tears through the place, soaking all before it. And just as suddenly, it can all be over, leaving you with clear, star-studded skies.

NORTHERN KENYA

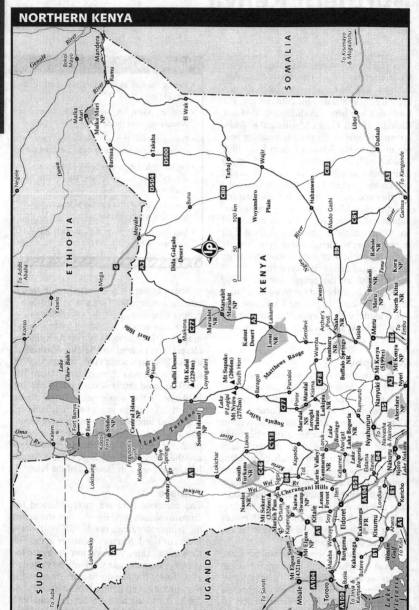

Getting Around

You could, of course, buy a camel and do a John Hillaby – he wrote *Journey to the Jade Sea*. This isn't something to approach lightly, but it is a distinct possibility, especially if you are part of a small group. You'd have the adventure of your life!

Bus & Matatu There is regular public transport on the west side of Lake Turkana as far as Kalekol. On the east side of the lake you are pretty much on your own after you pass through Marsabit or Maralal.

4WD For most travellers who want freedom of movement and to see a lot of places it comes down to hiring a 4WD or going on an organised safari (see the Organised Safaris chapter). If you're taking your own vehicle bring a high-rise jack, sand ladders, a shovel, a long, strong rope or chain (that you can hitch up to camels or other vehicles) plus enough fuel and water. The only regular petrol pumps you will find are at Isiolo, Maralal and Marsabit. Elsewhere you'll have to get it out of a plastic container from a roadside *duka* (small shop or kiosk selling household basics).

Other than the crumbling track that leads from Kitale to Lokichokio and the good tarmac that ends at Rumuruti and Isiolo, none of the roads in the region are surfaced. The main A2 route to Moyale is corrugated *murram* (dirt or part-gravelled road) which will shake the guts out of both you and your vehicle. The El Niño rains have taken their toll on all the roads in the north and each year the rains throw up more hazards. You need a 4WD and must know how to use it.

Security in the North

While in Kenya you'll hear regular reports of lawlessness and banditry in northern Kenya. The UN and your embassy will probably tell you it's unsafe to travel there and after reading the papers you could be forgiven for thinking that you're destined to be robbed at gunpoint the moment you leave a tarmac road. Locals, on the other hand (especially white Kenyans), will often laugh at your fears and argue, with some justification, that it's always been like this and tourists are very rarely targeted. As always the truth lies somewhere in the middle.

It's true that the north of Kenya has always been wild and unpredictable. Competition for grazing land and traditional cattle-rustling have always led to the occasional inter-tribal conflict, though the passing traveller will rarely see evidence of these conflicts. However, the influx of trusty AK-47s from Uganda, southern Sudan, Ethiopia and Somalia has upped the ante and a more general form of banditry is on the increase.

In recent times matatus have been held up at gunpoint on the Marich Pass-Lodwar road, while the entire region around Garsen, Garissa, Wajir and Marsabit can be bandit country. Buses heading to Lamu and between Garissa and Thika have also been attacked.

At the beginning of 1999 the conflict between the Ethiopian government and the Oromo Liberation Front, which is fighting for an independent homeland in southern Ethiopia, spilled over into Kenya around Moyale. Land mines have been found in the area, but the border remains open.

Intrepid trekkers heading up the Suguta Valley must be aware that armed gangs roam these lands. During the conflicts of 1996 the Ng'oroko (heavily armed Turkana bandits) shot down an army helicopter in the Suguta Valley, killing the district commissioner and a number of army officers. They also attacked at least one party of trekkers, and while other readers have escaped with losing only a couple of packets of cigarettes upon meeting large groups of armed men, you may not be so lucky. On the other hand, no trucks heading up to Lake Turkana have been held up, so like walking the streets of London, security here is a lottery.

As a general rule of thumb seek local advice before you travel here and don't take any unnecessary risks.

West of Lake Turkana

From Kitale the road north winds through fertile highlands, passing the turn-off for the tiny Saiwa Swamp National Park, which is well worth a visit (see the Western Kenya chapter for details) before reaching Kapenguria. It then snakes its way up along a forested ridge and through the narrow northern gorges of the Cherangani Hills, emerging on to the desert plains through the Marich Pass. The change in scenery is dramatic and there are some fantastic views of the plains.

The only town in this part of the hills is **Ortum**, just off the road. If you want to stop and explore the area, there is basic accommodation in the town but the best place to stay is undoubtedly the Marich Pass Field Studies Centre further north (see under Places to Stay & Eat in the following Marich Pass Area section).

After kilometres of endless plains and dry creek beds the town of **Lokichar** is little more than a collection of dismal dukas by the side of the road. The heat here is oppressive and the settlement seems to be gripped by a permanent torpor. The one redeeming feature of the place is that it is possible to buy basketware and other Turkana trinkets cheaper than you'll find them further north.

MARICH PASS AREA

The main reason for visiting this area is to stay at the Marich Pass Field Studies Centre and use this as a base for a number of excursions in the area. The staff have a wealth of local knowledge.

Those with their own vehicles should bring sufficient supplies of petrol. There is only one small service station between Kapenguria and Lodwar, at Sigor some 7km east of Marich Pass. If you intend walking in the vicinity then you need to be adequately prepared for a variety of weather conditions.

South of the pass are the **Cherangani Hills**, which offer some of the best hill walking in Kenya. There are numerous small **caves** dotted around the hills and most have special significance for the local Pokot. **Mt Sekerr** (3326m) to the north-west and **Elgeyo Escarpment** which rises to more than 1830m above the Kerio Valley are other enticing trekking possibilities.

Lomut at the foot of the escarpment (and accessible by matatu) holds a fascinating market every Saturday that brings together the pastoral Pokot from the northern plains and the farming Pokot from the hills to the south.

South Turkana National Reserve in the dry and rugged hills north-east of the field studies centre is the domain of Turkana herders and rarely visited by outsiders. However, the Kenya Wildlife Service (KWS) is upgrading all the roads (4WD only) within the reserve and there is a beautiful natural camp site by some hot springs on the eastern side of the reserve. The area has a large elephant population and herds of up to 150 have been seen. There was no entrance fee to the reserve at the time of research. The 40km drive to get there traverses grazing lands of the pastoral Pokot.

Lastly, **Turkwel Gorge** hydroelectric station is only 40km away along a fine tarmac road. Much of the gorge, with its towering rock walls, has not been affected by the construction, while the dam itself is spectacular. KWS levies fees at visitors and in theory you need prior permission from the Kerio Valley Development Authority in Eldoret to visit the site.

Places to Stay & Eat

The best place to stay is *Marich Pass Field Studies Centre (PO Box 564, Kapenjuria)* which occupies a beautiful site alongside the Maruni River and is surrounded by dense bush and woodland. The birdlife here is prolific, monkeys and baboons are 'in residence' and warthog, buffalo, antelope and elephant are regular visitors. Facilities include a secure camp site (KSh 200 per person per night) with drinking water, toilets, showers and firewood, as well as dorm beds for KSh 280 and simple but comfortable *bandas* (thatched-roof huts with wooden or earthen walls) which cost KSh 600/800 for singles/doubles. English-speaking Pokot and Turkana guides are available for half-day (KSh 240), full-day (KSh 360) and 24-hour (KSh 720) excursions. Bird walks with the local ornithologist cost KSh 600 for a group of five people. You can get breakfast for KSh 120 and dinner for KSh 220. Vegetarian food is also available, but all meals should be ordered in advance.

About 35km north of Marich Pass is *Amolem Elephant Camp Site* a community-based tourism project built and managed by the local Pokot. The camp is located next to an ancient elephant migration trail, so between November and May, elephants trundle past the very edge of the camp. The site has fresh water, showers and western-style toilets. A number of bandas were under construction at the time of writing. Camping is KSh 150 per person. Local KWS-trained guides are available.

Getting There & Away
To reach the field studies centre, take the main Kitale to Lodwar road and watch out for the signpost, 2km north of the Sigor to Tot road junction (signposted), at Marich Pass. The centre is about 1km down a clearly marked track. There are also a few daily matatus which cover the stretch from Kitale to Lokichar via Marich Pass.

To get to Amolem Elephant Camp Site take a matatu heading north to Lodwar and get off at Kainuk 35km north of Marich Pass. It's signposted on the right shortly after the road block and the camp is about 2km further down a dirt track.

LODWAR
☎ 0393
The hot and dusty administrative town of Lodwar is the only town of any significance in the north-west. While a crumbling bitumen road (destroyed by the convoys of aid trucks heading up to the Sudanese border) connects it with the highlands, it still lags a few steps behind the rest of the country.

Lodwar is the base for any excursion to the lake from the western side and it's convenient to spend a night here at least. There's little to do in the town itself and the

Turkana have found that tourists are a good bet when it comes to selling trinkets and crafts.

It's also worth walking into the stark volcanic hills before dawn and watching the sun rise. You are bound to be approached by a group of sharp young businessmen calling themselves the Lodwar Tour Guides Association and offering to escort you to the lake, into the hills and out to local communities. They try hard to please and are a useful source of information.

Information
Lodwar has several petrol stations, a post office and a branch of the Kenya Commercial Bank.

If you're self-catering the Stop in Rose Grocery is the best shop in town.

Places to Stay
Lodwar is one place where it's worth spending a bit more on accommodation – mainly to get a room with a mosquito net and a fan.

Probably the best of the cheapies is *New Surburb Tourist Lodge* (☎ 21027). Self-contained rooms here are KSh 200/360 for singles/doubles, though you can pay an extra KSh 50 for the upstairs room, which catches the evening breeze. All rooms have fans, but no nets. The owners have a habit of trying to charge extra for things such as baggage left in the room during the day.

A good option (the only one for campers) is *Nawoitorong Guest House* (☎ 21208). The turn-off is signposted 1km south of Lodwar on the main road, and from there it's a further 2km walk. Run by a local women's group, camping costs KSh 100 and there are a number of very pleasant bandas, some with kitchens, which accommodate between two and four people and cost KSh 1200/1500. Double/triple dormitory style accommodation costs KSh 400/600, which includes breakfast. All accommodation is thatched, making it cooler, and nets are provided, but no fans.

Turkwel Hotel (☎ 21235) offers the best accommodation in town, though the single rooms are far from great. Singles/doubles with fan and bath cost KSh 470/700, while in one of the spacious cottages, singles/doubles are KSh 950/1350. Prices include breakfast.

Places to Eat

The new **Lodwar Nature Hotel** (☎ 21218) is the best place to have a drink though the food is not up to much. There are plans for rooms, satellite TV, camel safaris and a video theatre here. It's over the road from Turkwel Hotel.

The best place to eat is probably **Hotel Salama** which does excellent chai masala and samosas, as well as more substantial Somali dishes in the evening. **Turkwel Hotel** does standard western fare such as steak and chips. The bar is a popular place.

Entertainment

Every Friday and Saturday **Vibrations Disco** kicks off close to Turkwel Hotel. Also try **Lodwar Club** out past the airstrip.

Getting There & Away

Kenya Witness operates two converted trucks from Kitale to Lodwar every day (KSh 400). Generally the first one leaves around 9 am. The Nissan matatus are more reliable and there are usually five per day which leave when full (KSh 500, six hours). There is sometimes a midnight departure in each direction – book before 6 pm.

Matatus from Lodwar to Kalekol leave when full from opposite New Towhid Stores in the centre of town (KSh 100, one hour).

KALEKOL

Most visitors to the area head on from Lodwar to Kalekol, a fairly dismal little town a few kilometres from the lakeshore. The main building in this one-street town is the fish-processing factory built with Scandinavian money and expertise and currently not operating.

The basic **Skyways Lodge** is probably the best place to stay (KSh 200/400 for singles/doubles), and **Kalekol Tourist Lodge** is the best place for a cheap feed.

To get out to the lake it's a hot 1½-hour walk. Locals will point you in the right direction or offer to be your guide.

FERGUSON'S GULF

This is the most accessible part of the lakeshore and although it's not particularly attractive, the sense of achievement in just getting there usually compensates. After receding for years the El Niño rains filled the lake to capacity and so a boat is required to get over to the thin strip where Lake Turkana Fishing Lodge is situated – for the first 15 minutes the boat weaves through a maze of dead acacia bushes.

The birdlife along the shore is prolific and particularly wonderful in March and April when thousands of European migrants stop here before their long journey north. There are also hippos and crocodiles (and bilharzia) so seek local advice before having a refreshing dip.

In the middle of the lake is the **Central Island National Park**, a barren yet scenic volcanic island. The only way to get there is to hire a boat from Jade Sea Journeys in Nairobi (see the Organised Safaris chapter) or from Lake Turkana Fishing Lodge. It's good value if you are in a group, but will take some planning.

Places to Stay

Lake Turkana Fishing Lodge is half open while improvements are made. Accommodation consists of tidy wooden beach huts with en suite toilet and shower, but considerable investment is needed before the KSh 2800/3000 price tag can be justified. You can camp here for KSh 300 per person. Solar powered fridges keep the drinks cool and the bar is an excellent place to watch the wildlife on the lake. Meals can be cobbled together. Boat trips may also be possible (KSh 6000 to Central Island, KSh 800 for a pleasure cruise/fishing trip), but contact Hill Barrett Travel (02-760226, fax 761073, email ivory@form-net.com) in Nairobi in advance.

If you follow the road you'll arrive at a jetty from where transport can easily be arranged across the channel (KSh 20, but you may get quoted a 'taxi fare'). Alternatively you can cut through the scrub to the ferry stage which is situated almost opposite the lodge.

Though local people will point you in the right direction, taking a guide is not a bad idea – it's easy to get lost.

ELIYE SPRINGS

This is a far more attractive place than Ferguson's Gulf but is inaccessible without a 4WD (the road deteriorates into heavy sand in places). The springs however do provide enough moisture for a curious variety of palm tree (the doum palm) which gives the place a very misplaced tropical island feel.

Places to Stay & Eat

The *camp site* and *lodge* have long since ceased to function as an upmarket establishment – only one banda (KSh 800) is left with a roof on it and the camp site (KSh 200) is run on an informal basis by the locals.

Getting There & Away

The turn-off for Eliye Springs is signposted halfway along the road from Lodwar to Kalekol. As there are so few vehicles, hitching is not on and it's a long, hot 35km trek.

You may be able to arrange transport in Lodwar, but it will cost around KSh 3000.

LOKICHOKIO

This frontier town is the last one on the Pan African Highway before the Sudan border and is the focus for dozens of aid agencies working in southern Sudan where a brutal civil war continues. Such is the scale of relief effort here that Kenya Airways has three flights a week from Eldoret. Hitching is the only other way to get here, though banditry north of Lodwar is a serious problem. You can't get beyond Lokichokio without a police permit and unless you're an aid worker there is little reason to come here.

Places to Stay

Kate Camp and *Track Mark* are expat aid-worker oriented places with swimming pools. You'll end up paying around KSh 500 for a single room.

East of Lake Turkana

There are two main routes here. The first is the A2 highway from Nairobi to Marsabit, via Isiolo and Laisamis, and north from there to Moyale on the Ethiopian border. The other is from Nairobi to Maralal, via Gilgil, Nyahururu and Rumuruti and north from there to Loyangalani on Lake Turkana, via Maralal, Baragoi and South Horr. It's also possible to cross from Isiolo to Maralal. From Loyangalani you can make a loop all the way around the top of the Chalbi Desert to Marsabit via North Horr and Maikona. The tarmac ends at Rumuruti and Isiolo so after that you're travelling on rough murram or dirt roads which are are often corrugated and washed out after the rains.

ISIOLO
☎ 0165

Isiolo, where the tarmac ends, marks the frontier of north-eastern Kenya – a vast area of both forested and barren mountains, deserts and scrub, home to the Samburu, Rendille, Boran and Turkana peoples. It's a lively town with a good market and all the usual facilities. There are also bus connections to places north, east and south of Isiolo. If driving, beware of the numerous formidable speed bumps.

Information

Going north, Isiolo is the last place with a bank (Barclays – no ATM) until you get to either Maralal or Marsabit.

Likewise, there are no petrol stations north of here until you reach Maralal or Marsabit except at the Samburu Lodge (in Samburu National Reserve). This doesn't mean that petrol or diesel is totally unobtainable, it's just more difficult to get.

Travellers also need to stock up on food here, where there is more variety than anywhere else in the north. Be aware of the huge Muslim influence. Alcohol is prohibited in some hotels and women wearing shorts or short skirts may attract unwanted attention.

KENYA

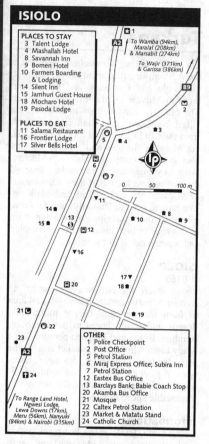

ISIOLO

PLACES TO STAY
3 Talent Lodge
4 Mashallah Hotel
8 Savannah Inn
9 Bomen Hotel
10 Farmers Boarding & Lodging
14 Silent Inn
15 Jamhuri Guest House
18 Mocharo Hotel
19 Pasoda Lodge

PLACES TO EAT
11 Salama Restaurant
16 Frontier Lodge
17 Silver Bells Hotel

To Wamba (94km), Maralal (208km) & Marsabit (274km)

To Wajir (371km) & Garissa (386km)

0   50   100 m

OTHER
1 Police Checkpoint
2 Post Office
5 Petrol Station
6 Miraj Express Office; Subira Inn
7 Petrol Station
12 Eastex Bus Office
13 Barclays Bank; Babie Coach Stop
20 Akamba Bus Office
21 Mosque
22 Caltex Petrol Station
23 Market & Matatu Stand
24 Catholic Church

To Range Land Hotel, Ngwesi Lodge, Lewa Downs (17km), Meru (56km), Nanyuki (84km) & Nairobi (315km)

Places to Stay – Budget

Campers should head to *Range Land Hotel* (☎ 2340) a few kilometres south of Isiolo on the main road (it's well signposted). There's a huge camping area (KSh 150 per person), a nice restaurant/bar set in extensive gardens and a few stone cottages (KSh 800 to KSh 1000 per person). It gets quite lively in the evenings at the weekend.

Jamhuri Guest House has been deservedly popular with travellers for many years and remains friendly and excellent value. Built around a courtyard, the rooms are clean, mosquito nets are provided and

the communal showers have hot water in the mornings. Singles/doubles cost KSh 120/200. Next door is a good cafe that serves snacks and chai masala.

Going up in price, there is *Pasoda Lodge* a clean and quiet place that offers doubles with bath for KSh 300. There are no singles. The hotel has its own restaurant and bar.

Another place to try is the tower block that is *Mashallah Hotel* (☎ 2142). It's scruffy but cheap and the top-floor rooms have great views. Self-contained rooms will cost you KSh 240/340 and rooms with shared bathroom are KSh 120/240.

The big and tidy *Mocharo Hotel* (☎ 2385) has rooms surrounding a courtyard that serves as secure parking. It's very clean and you get hot water in the mornings. Self-contained singles/doubles go for KSh 300/350. There is a cardphone outside.

Places to Stay – Mid-Range

There's only one mid-range hotel in Isiolo and that is *Bomen Hotel* (☎ 2225). This overrated three-storey hotel has 40 spacious but unremarkable rooms, reasonably decorated and furnished. Rates are KSh 900/1400 for singles/doubles with a toilet and hot shower, including breakfast, taxes and service charges. The hotel has its own bar and restaurant that serves good food at very reasonable prices. Guarded parking is available in the hotel compound. There's also a nyama choma bar. It's nothing special, so save your money and stay in Mocharo Hotel.

Places to Eat

Silver Bells Hotel next door to Mocharo Hotel is a good place for a feed (try the chicken curry), though probably the best cheapie in town is *Salama Restaurant* set just back from the main street (KSh 100 a throw). The restaurant at *Pasoda Lodge* is reasonable.

Frontier Lodge is something a bit different, thanks to the fluorescent paint and UV lights of the interior. Discos are held at the weekend and it does some reasonable food. Live bands sometimes play here.

For a minor splurge, go for lunch or dinner at *Bomen Hotel*.

Getting There & Away

Akamba operates two buses to Nairobi at 7.30 am and 7 pm daily, and two from Nairobi at 9 am and 7.30 pm. The journey takes about six hours and costs KSh 320. The buses travel via Nanyuki, Naro Moru and Thika. It's not a bad idea to book one day in advance. Eastex buses leave Isiolo for Nairobi at 7 am and head back to Isiolo at 1.30 pm from Seventh St in Nairobi. If you'd prefer the more comfortable Nissan minibuses, the fare is KSh 330. Regular matatus also head to Nanyuki (KSh 150) and Meru (KSh 100).

The Miraj Express (a big converted truck) leaves for Marsabit at 7.30 am on Tuesday, Thursday and Saturday, returning to Isiolo the day after. It costs KSh 500 and takes about seven hours. The booking office is in the Subira Inn on the main street and the bus is part of the convoy heading north. If you miss the bus and don't want to wait around, the alternative is to hitch a lift on a truck, which should cost you less than the bus, but can involve considerable legwork. Heading out to the police checkpoint at the end of the tarmac where the convoys heading north meet up is not always the best policy because the trucks are often full of paying passengers before they even leave town.

Getting a lift on a truck is the only way to get to Moyale on the Ethiopian border. The journey takes two days, so stock up with provisions. If you budget for KSh 800 you won't be too far off. If there has been any rain the road turns to mud and becomes impassable. The same arrangements apply to transport to Wajir and Mandera, northeast of Isiolo. This area is the domain of the *shifta* (Somali bandits, usually armed) and only those people with a specific reason (or a suicide wish) should contemplate travelling there. Each day at 8 am a convoy of vehicles headed for Wajir, Mandera or Garissa leaves the police checkpoint. They are mostly trucks and many will take passengers for a fee.

The Babie Coach leaves for Maralal (KSh 500) and Wamba (KSh 250) every day at around 1 pm from outside Barclays Bank.

Returning services leave Maralal at roughly the same time. The journey can take anywhere between five and eight hours. A matatu to Archer's Post reportedly costs KSh 100, but check it out locally.

SAMBURU, BUFFALO SPRINGS & SHABA NATIONAL RESERVES

Just north of Isiolo are three national reserves, Samburu, Buffalo Springs and Shaba, all of them along the banks of the Ewaso Ngiro River and covering an area of some 300 sq km. The terrain is scrub desert and open savannah plain, broken here and there by small rugged hills. Shaba is more hilly with springs and great rocky kopjes, replete with klipspringer and hyrax. The river, which is permanent, is the lifeline for all three parks and supports a wide variety of game. Specialities include Grevy's zebra, Somali ostrich and gerenuk. You are almost guaranteed close-range sightings of elephant, reticulated giraffe and various species of smaller gazelle in both Samburu and Buffalo Springs, but rhino were wiped out years ago. Game in Shaba is not as prolific, but the landscape is majestic and greater kudu and oryx can be seen, with cheetah, leopard and lion also present. There are some real monster crocs along the Ewaso Ngiro River.

If you're driving try and get a copy of the Survey of Kenya map, *Samburu & Buffalo Springs Game Reserves* (Survey of Kenya 85). The glossy *Samburu & Buffalo Springs and Shaba National Reserves* map published by Mount Kenya Sundries is widely available and wildly inaccurate.

It's not difficult to get around, but away from the main routes, roads are not well maintained (some are 4WD only) and the maze of tracks formed by wayward minibus drivers can get you lost. Signage within the parks is bad and reinvestment in all these parks is negligible.

Entry to Samburu and Buffalo Springs National Reserves is US$27 per person (US$10 for students and children) plus KSh 200 per vehicle per day (fewer than six seats) or KSh 500 per day (six to 12 seats). Tickets for Buffalo Springs and Samburu are interchangeable, but if you

KENYA

SAMBURU & BUFFALO SPRINGS NATIONAL RESERVES

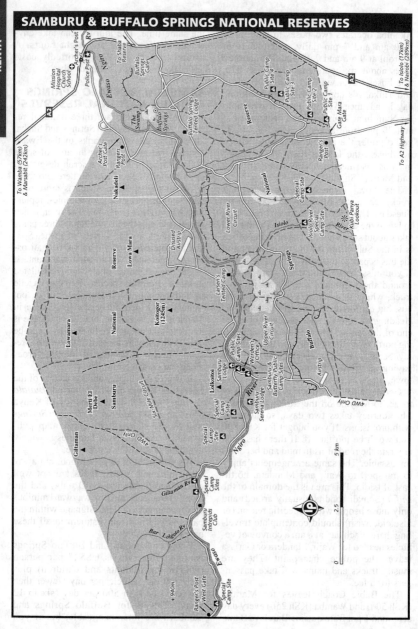

To Wamba (57km)
& Marsabit (242km)

To Isiolo (17km)
& Nairobi (289km)

To A2 Highway

Archer's Post

Ewaso Ngiro Rv

Mission Hospital
Church School

Police Post

To Shaba Reserve

Buffalo Springs Gate

Buffalo Springs Tented Lodge

Reserve

Public Camp Site 4

Public Camp Site 3

Public Camp Site 2

Public Camp Site 1

Gare Mara Gate

The Swamp

Buffalo Springs

Archer's Post Gate

Rangers Post

Nakadeli

Ranger's Post

National

Special Camp Site

Kudu Panya Lookout

Reserve

Lowa Mara

Disused Airstrip

Lower River Circuit

Isiolo

Springs

Isiolo River Special Camp Site

Special Camp Site

Lowamara

Kodogor (1245m)

Larsen's Tented Camp

National

Upper River Circuit

Buffalo

Airstrip

Reserve

Six-Mile Circuit

Public Camp Sites

Warden's Office

Loikoitoi

Samburu Lodge

Samburu & Butterfly Public Camp Sites

4WD Only

Merti El Debe

Samburu

Special Camp Site

Samburu River

Samburu Serena Lodge

Giltaman

Ngiro

Special Camp Site

4WD Only

Giltaman Rv

Special Camp Sites

Samburu Intrepids Club

Bar Lolgoto Rv

Rangr's Post West Gate

+ 940m

Ewaso Ngiro

Special Camp Site

0   2.5   5 km

also want to enter Shaba you pay again (US$15 and KSh 200 for vehicles with fewer than six seats).

After a number of brazen lodge hold-ups in Samburu National Reserve, security in all the parks has been considerably improved.

Places to Stay

Samburu Of all the public camp sites beside the Ewaso Ngiro River close to the park headquarters *Butterfly Camp Site* (KSh 440 per person) is the best, but facilities are minimal.

There are three top end lodges/tented camps and *Samburu Lodge* part of the Block Hotels chain (☎ 02-540780, fax 543 810, PO Box 47557, Nairobi) is cheapest and most popular. Singles/doubles with half board cost US$144/180 in the high season, dropping to US$58/116 in the low season. Prices are the same for simple rooms and cottages (which are far more pleasant). The lodge is the only place in the two parks with petrol for sale. Wildlife drives through the park can be organised at the lodge (US$125 per vehicle). Bird walks cost KSh 450.

Further east is *Larsens* a luxury tented camp also owned by Block Hotels. In the high season full board costs US$205/256 and US$326/240 for a suite. In the low season (9 April to 30 June) prices drop to US$80/160 and US$120/290. Children under seven are not allowed and everyone else is charged the full adult rate.

Samburu Intrepids Club (☎ 02-716628, fax 716457 in Nairobi, email prestigehotels@ form-net.com) further upstream on the northern side of the river is another luxury tented lodge. Full board costs US$142/215 in the high season, dropping to US$47/94 in the low season.

Buffalo Springs Four public *camp sites* (KSh 440 per person) are located close to the Gare Mara entrance gate, but security is not good. There are also a number of special *camp sites* along the Isiolo and Maji ya Chumvi Rivers further west (KSh 825 per person).

The wonderfully located *Buffalo Springs Tented Lodge* (☎ 0164-20784, 02-334510 in Nairobi) is stuck in a 1970s time warp and is probably closed – when we swung by we ended up loaning the depressed staff the battery from our vehicle so they could jump-start the main generator.

Samburu Serena Lodge (☎ 02-711077, fax 718103, email cro@serena.co.ke) is very pleasant. Cottages start at US$50/100 for singles/doubles (full board) in the low season, rising to US$110/150 in the high season, plus 29% tax.

Shaba The spectacular, almost over-the-top *Shaba Sarova Lodge* (☎ 02-713333, fax 715566, email reservations@sarova.co.ke) also sits on the Ewaso Ngiro River. It has a good pool, great service and excellent rooms. Singles/doubles with full board go for US$55/110 in the low season, rising to US$130/165 in the high season.

The best camp site is the splendid *Funan Camp Site* in the heart of the park on the way out to Shaba Gate. It's shaded by acacia trees, and a semi-permanent spring provides cool clean water and attracts game. It costs KSh 825 per person.

WAMBA

Wamba is essentially a one-street town off the Isiolo to Maralal road north of Samburu National Reserve. It's a sort of provincial headquarters for the surrounding area. There's precious little here for the traveller though it has quite a few well stocked dukas, a butchery, a big mission and a large police station, but no bank or electricity. The mission hospital here is excellent, easily the best in the north of Kenya, a fact worth remembering when travelling around the area.

Places to Stay

There's only one lodge in the village, *Saudia Lodge* which is at the back of the main street off to the right coming into town (signposted). Pleasant, clean singles/doubles cost KSh 250/325. You could probably camp at the mission where you may also be able to find a room if you're stuck.

KENYA

MARALAL
☎ 0368

Maralal is high up in the hills above the Loroghi Plateau (essentially a continuation of the Central Highlands), north of Nyahururu and Nanyuki and north-west of Isiolo, and connected to all these towns by gravel roads. Surrounding it is the Maralal National Sanctuary which is home to zebra, impala, eland, buffalo, hyena and warthog, all of which you often see from the road.

The town itself, while a regional headquarters, retains a decidedly frontier atmosphere. There's a sense of excitement blowing in the wind that frequently sweeps the plains and whips up the dust in this somewhat ramshackle, but very lively, township with its wide streets and wild-west-style verandas. In recent years the population has swelled considerably due to insecurity in the surrounding areas, though now that peace has been restored people are starting to leave.

People here are friendly, but soon after stepping off the matatu you'll find yourself surrounded by the so called Plastic Boys trying to sell everything from bangles to guiding services. After a while you start to feel like the pied piper.

The small supermarket and other dukas hold a good range of stock and there's regular bus transport to Isiolo and matatus to Baragoi. It's a bizarre but captivating place.

Information

Kenya Commercial Bank is open during normal banking hours and is the last bank going north. Outside of banking hours try Maralal Safari Lodge or Yare Safaris Club & Camp Site. Neither has great rates. The post office is open normal hours and you can make international calls here.

There are three petrol stations in town and you can be assured of getting what you need at regular prices. However, north of here you will find petrol only at Baragoi and Loyangalani (and then out of barrels). Mechanics can also be found.

Safaris & Treks

The hills and plains around Maralal make excellent walking country. About 22km north-east of Maralal and 5km west of Poror is **World's View**, one of the most captivating and beautiful view-points in Kenya. It's set in the middle of a sweeping escarpment and from here you can see across the Rift Valley

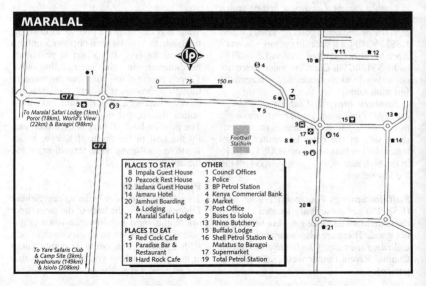

MARALAL

0   75   150 m

C77

●1

2

③3

To Maralal Safari Lodge (1km),
Poror (18km), World's View
(22km) & Baragoi (98km)

C77

To Yare Safaris Club
& Camp Site (3km),
Nyahururu (149km)
& Isiolo (208km)

▼11   ▲12

10 ▲

⊖ 4

7
6 ●   ☑
▼ 5

9 ▣
17 ☒   15 ☑
Football   8 ▲ ⊕16   13 ●
Stadium   18 ▼
19 ⊕   ▲14

20 ▲

▲ 21

PLACES TO STAY	OTHER
8 Impala Guest House	1 Council Offices
10 Peacock Rest House	2 Police
12 Jadana Guest House	3 BP Petrol Station
14 Jamaru Hotel	4 Kenya Commercial Bank
20 Jamhuri Boarding	6 Market
& Lodging	7 Post Office
21 Maralal Safari Lodge	9 Buses to Isiolo
	13 Rhino Butchery
PLACES TO EAT	15 Buffalo Lodge
5 Red Cock Cafe	16 Shell Petrol Station &
11 Paradise Bar &	Matatus to Baragoi
Restaurant	17 Supermarket
18 Hard Rock Cafe	19 Total Petrol Station

Maralal International Camel Derby

Inaugurated by Yare Safaris in 1990, this annual event takes place in late summer and attracts riders (amateur and professional) and spectators from the four corners of the earth, so you're likely to bump into some real characters up here. In the evening, the spectacle over, everyone retires to Yare Safaris Club & Camp Site for a long hard party sure to last until dawn.

Races start and finish outside Yare, a few kilometres south of Maralal, and are open to anyone. Amateurs pay an entry fee of KSh 500 (plus KSh 1000 for the camel and handler) and professionals pay KSh 1500. Applications for entry should be made to either the Maralal International Camel Derby (MICD) Secretariat, PO Box 281, Maralal; or Yare Safaris, PO Box 63006, Nairobi.

or walk down the escarpment to the valley floor. It costs KSh 100 to visit World's View and you can camp near the viewpoint. It's an excellent base for short treks though you must pay to cross local Samburu land (around KSh 300). There is the occasional matatu to Poror in the mornings and evenings or you can hire a taxi.

Regular camel safaris depart from Yare Safaris Club & Camp Site or you can hire guides and camels for independent treks. Organised treks, donkeys and guides are also available from Samburu Trails Trekking Safaris near Poror (see the Organised Safaris chapter).

Places to Stay – Budget
About 3km south of town is one of the best places to stay, *Yare Safaris Club & Camp Site* (☎/fax 2295 or 02-213445 in Nairobi, email travelkenya@iconnect.co.ke). You can camp (KSh 200 per person) or stay in self-contained wooden bandas. These are reasonable value at KSh 1020/1620 for singles/doubles, including breakfast. Soap and towels are provided and you'll get a bucket of hot water in the morning. Yare's facilities include a bar/lounge, games room and restaurant and nyama choma bar (on Wednesday and Saturday). The camp site has its own showers (cold) and toilets. Advance booking is essential during camel derby week held in the late summer (check locally for the exact dates).

A few kilometres before Poror and set in a wooded valley is *Samburu Trails Trekking Safaris* (☎/fax 32379). You can camp here for US$3.50 per tent and the farm

makes an excellent base from which to explore the surrounding area. Poror is about 18km from Maralal; 2km before the village the road turns left off the plateau and drops down to a stream. As it descends, a track on the left leads off to Samburu Trails Trekking Safaris (if you pass the dam and lake you have gone too far).

Because of the 'Plastic Boys', staying in Maralal itself can be a bit much, but if you are stopping for more than just one night there are a number of decent places to stay.

Good self-contained rooms are available at *Jamaru Hotel* (☎ 2215) for KSh 350/600 for singles/doubles. Cheaper rooms with shared facilities are also available. All rooms have mosquito nets, there's hot water and movies are shown in the evening.

The very clean *Peacock Rest House* (☎ 2068) behind Mama Sammy's Fashion Wear is great value. You'll pay KSh 150/300 for a room with shared facilities (hot showers). It's tidy and well run, the beds and linen are good and the owner can even arrange transfers from Nairobi.

Also worth a look is the new *Jadana Guest House* which has simple self-contained rooms (with mosquito nets) for KSh 300/600. There is a bar and butchery and it's considered to be one of the best places for nyama choma in Maralal. There is secure parking.

Places to Stay – Top End
The only top-end hotel in Maralal is *Maralal Safari Lodge* (☎ 2060, 02-211124 in Nairobi, PO Box 70, Maralal). The main building houses a restaurant, bar and souvenir shop, and there is a series of cottages.

It costs US$125/175 with full board. Meals are available to nonguests for KSh 250 (breakfast) and KSh 500 (lunch or dinner). The watering hole attracts a varied selection of wildlife right in front of the bar's veranda so you can watch the animals while sipping a cold beer. The lodge is about 1.5km from the centre of Maralal, off the road to Baragoi (signposted).

Places to Eat
The best place to eat is *Hard Rock Cafe* opposite the Shell station. The food is good and the staff are friendly and eager to please. On a good day the good-looking restaurant in front of *Jamaru Hotel* is also excellent. *Pop-In Cafe* can be recommended and *Red Cock Cafe* is a good place for a breakfast of chai and *mandazi*.

Entertainment
Green Bar is a good place for a drink in the evening. *Buffalo Lodge* is also popular and has two good bars – the one out the back, although the best, is essentially a pool hall.

Because of the insecurity of the region in the last few years the District Commissioner ordered the closure of Maralal's discos.

Getting There & Away
Minibuses ply the route between Maralal and Nyahururu via Rumuruti on a daily basis, usually in the morning and early afternoon. They cost KSh 250 and take four to five hours.

The Babie Coach departs from Nairobi for Maralal (KSh 500) and Wamba (KSh 250) daily at around 1 pm. Returning services leave Maralal the following day at roughly the same time from the matatu stand. The journey can take anywhere between five and eight hours.

The only other public transport leaving Maralal is north up to Baragoi by 4WD. There's usually one each day or two if there's enough demand. The cost varies but averages KSh 250 and the journey takes about three hours. You need to make inquiries in advance and preferably meet the driver. No one ever seems to know when they're leaving.

If you're heading further north to Lake Turkana, lifts on trucks are the only way (unless you are very lucky and hitch a ride with some 4WD tourist). Maralal is the best place to sort this out, because if you try hitching from Baragoi or South Horr you may find the trucks are already full. It's better to be stuck here for a couple of days rather than further north as there are more facilities and much of the transport passing through the northern towns will be full from Maralal onwards. The trip to Lake Turkana from Maralal costs around KSh 800 but you may have to negotiate. It takes 1½ days (you'll probably spend the night in South Horr).

All the buses and matatus leave from the dirt patch opposite the Shell petrol station.

RUMURUTI
About 18km north of this tiny town is *Bobong Camp Site* (☎ *035-61413, email kembu@net2000ke.com, PO Box 5, Rumuruti)*. At Bobong you can pick up one of the cheapest camel safaris in Kenya – KSh 750 per day for the hire of one camel and a handler (see the Organised Safaris chapter for more information). The camp site is also great value at KSh 200 per person. Simple bandas are also available for KSh 400 per person.

The camp is signposted from the main road (west) and sits on top of a small cliff. Take any matatu heading north or south between Maralal and Nyahururu and asked to be dropped at the sign. You'll probably have to hitch when you leave.

MATTHEWS RANGE
Matthews Range is north of Wamba, off the link road between Wamba and Baragoi via Parsaloi. Much of this area is thickly forested and supports rhino, elephant, lion, buffalo and numerous other species. The highest peak here rises to 2285m.

This is the true African bush experience. There is a move to turn the entire area into a game sanctuary – the mountains contain the largest free-ranging herd of rhino left in Kenya. The major initiative has come from the private sector, with the creation of the

Namunyak Wildlife Conservation Trust. This body (created thanks largely to the efforts of Ian Craig, Kinyanjui Lesenteria and the Lewa Wildlife Conservancy) has created a game sanctuary of 30,000 hectares in the mountains.

At the heart of the sanctuary is *Sarara Safari Camp*. Five luxury tents sleep 10 people and the concept is for visitors to rent the complete camp, which costs around US$300 per night on a self-catering basis, including camp staff (cooks, waiters, tent attendants, bush guide), exclusive use of camp facilities and camel-riding. The emphasis is on getting out and experiencing the bush on foot and the profits flow straight back to the local Samburu community. Book through Acacia Trails (☎/fax 02-446261) PO Box 41, Limuru. Getting here is tricky even with 4WD, as it's easy to get lost. Perhaps the best approach is from the Wamba to Parsaloi road. Just before Wamba you will get to a T-junction. Instead of going into Wamba, continue north and take the first obvious main track off to the right, several kilometres after the junction. It's important to get accurate directions and details of road conditions from Let's Go Travel (☎ 02-340331, fax 336890, email info@letsgosafari.com) in Nairobi before setting out.

Another luxury place is *Kitich Camp* where singles/doubles cost a whopping US$420/620. There is also a beautiful and cheap camp site. Contact Let's Go Travel in Nairobi to book, and check out the Web site at www.letsgosafari.com for a map.

BARAGOI

North of Maralal on the road towards Loyangalani is Baragoi, quite a substantial settlement and trading centre. Petrol can usually be bought here from a barrel – the local people will show you where to find it. The town seems to get rain when everywhere else is dry so the surroundings are quite green.

You'll find many people here willing to guide you on treks through the Suguta Valley all the way up to Lake Turkana. First you should get a good appraisal of the security situation, preferably from the police and army and then from people with inside knowledge such as bar owners and church workers.

Be careful not to take photographs in the town as it's supposedly forbidden. The local police are keen to enforce the rule and are not at all pleasant about it.

Places to Stay & Eat

A good place to pitch a tent is at the water-pumping station about 4km north of town. Take the road north towards South Horr. After a while you'll go through a small gully and then, a little further on, across a usually dry river bed. Take the next track on the right and follow this for about 1km. It will bring you to a concrete house and a fairly open patch of ground. This is the camp site. Facilities include toilets and showers and your tent will be guarded by Samburu *morani* (warrior). It costs KSh 200 per person per night. However, this is where all the locals come for their water so it's not very quiet or private. You may also be able to camp in the Farm Africa Compound in the middle of town.

Bowmen Hotel beside the post office is probably the best place to stay in town. It costs KSh 350/650 for a clean single/double with shared bathroom. It's the first building you come to when arriving in Baragoi from the south.

The best place to eat is a toss-up between *Hotel Mukhram* and *Wid-Wid Inn*. The Wid-Wid is on the north side of the main street. There's delicious meat stew and chapatis for dinner as well as pancakes, omelettes and tea for breakfast. Prices are very reasonable.

There are a few bars in town. *Bosnia Bar* is probably the best and has four reasonable rooms out the back (KSh 200). Also give *Sam Celia Joy Bar* a whirl. It's at the end of the main street going north.

LAKE TURKANA (THE JADE SEA)

Further north, the lushness of the Horr Valley gradually peters out until, finally, you reach the totally barren, shattered lava beds at the southern end of Lake Turkana. Top the ridge and there it is in front of you – the Jade Sea. It's a breathtaking sight – vast and yet apparently totally barren. You'll see nothing living here except a few brave, stunted thorn trees. The northern end of the lake isn't anywhere near as saline because it's fed by the Omo River from Ethiopia. At this point, most people abandon whatever vehicle they're in and plunge into the lake. If you do this, watch out for crocodiles.

On the eastern shore 100km north of Loyangalani is the wondrous Sibiloi National Park, the 'Cradle of Mankind'.

LOYANGALANI

A little further up the lakeshore and you are in Loyangalani – Turkana 'city'. There is an airstrip, post office, fishing station, luxury lodge, two camp sites, a Catholic Mission (which may reluctantly sell petrol at up to three times the price in Nairobi) and all of it surrounded by the yurt-like, stick and doum-palm dwellings of the Turkana tribespeople. Taking photographs of people or their houses here will attract 'fees'.

If you're an independent traveller and want to visit the village where the El-Molo tribe lives, ask the safari-truck drivers at the camp sites if they have room for you and agree on a price. Organised safaris to this part of Kenya usually include a trip to the El-Molo village. They're one of the smallest tribes in Africa and quite different from the Turkana. Tourism has also wrought inevitable changes in their lifestyle and you may feel that the whole thing has been thoroughly commercialised. You'll also pay handsomely for taking photographs.

Trips to Mt Kulal (forested) and Mt Porr (a well-known gold panning spot) can be arranged at Oasis Lodge but they're expensive. Locals may be able to sort out something similar, but you'll need to be well-equipped already.

Be aware that in the early evening the wind picks up tremendously and can be blowing at 60km/h by 8 pm. Storms also occur suddenly in this area so tie your tent down.

Places to Stay & Eat

El-Molo Camp is nothing more than a nice shaded camp site and a swimming pool fed from a hot spring. Camping will cost you KSh 200 and using the pool is another KSh 200. The bar and restaurant are long dead, but there is a big open banda providing shade and some basic toilets and showers. You may be able to get a beer at Oasis Lodge next door.

Luxurious *Oasis Lodge* has 15 double bungalows with private bathrooms and electricity (from the lodge's own generator) at US$130/200 for singles/doubles with full board. It's a beautiful place with two spring-fed swimming pools, ice-cold beer and a good view across the lake. If you are not staying but you want to use the facilities (bar and swimming pools), it's going to cost you KSh 300, and there are times when you won't even be allowed in. Book through Will Travel in Nairobi (☎ 02-503267, fax 501585, email willtravel@swiftkenya.com). You can hire boats here for trips out to South Island National Park. They cost KSh 2500 per hour and it's a two-hour return trip.

Outside the gates of Oasis Lodge is *Mosaretu Women's Group Camp Site*. You can pitch your tent here or stay in the traditional Turkana grass huts (which come complete with beds and mattresses) for KSh 200. The only drawback is the noise from the generator at Oasis Lodge nearby.

Out towards the Catholic Mission is *Mama Shanga* still the best house in town if you just want to flop down and sleep (KSh 200).

For places to eat try *Hilton Hotel* and *Cold Drink Hotel* on the main street.

Getting There & Away

There is no scheduled transport of any sort in or out of Loyangalani, so you need to be completely independent.

For the rich and/or famous, Oasis Lodge can arrange a light plane to the local airstrip.

Going north or north-east from here involves crossing the Chalbi Desert towards North Horr. It's fine in the dry season but can be treacherous after rain.

You also need to stop at every village you come across and ask for directions otherwise it's very easy to get lost. Don't assume that tyre tracks in the sand will lead you in the right direction.

Skull 1470

In the early 1970s, palaeontologist Richard Leakey made a significant fossil find on the shores of Lake Turkana. It was the discovery of a fossilised skull, which came to be known somewhat prosaically as 1470 (its Kenya Museum index number).

The almost complete, but fragmented, skull was thought to be from an early hominid. It was hoped that it would back up earlier fossil discoveries made by the Leakey family in the Olduvai Gorge in Tanzania in the 1960s. Initially these discoveries suggested the direct human ancestral line went back further than the one million years most people believed.

The pieces of the skull were painstakingly fitted together – a demanding task which kept two people fully occupied for more than six weeks. The completed jigsaw confirmed what they had suspected: here was an evolutionary sophisticated hominid, named *Homo habilis*, which was a direct ancestor of *Homo sapiens*. It was 2½ million years old.

Since then, other homo fossil finds have pushed the date back even further, but at the time, 1470 was a very important person.

SIBILOI NATIONAL PARK

This huge arid park on the eastern shore of Lake Turkana gives a fascinating insight into Kenya's prehistory and arid ecosystems. It was here that Dr Richard Leakey discovered the skull of a *Homo habilis* believed to be more than two million years old (see the boxed text 'Skull 1470'). More than 160 finds relating to the early hominids have been made here in the 'Cradle of Mankind'.

Three protected fossil sites remain in-situ although the heavy rains unearth more finds every year. It is strictly forbidden to remove any fossils as any future research could be compromised.

Tours of the park (KSh 6800 per vehicle) must be arranged in advance through the Public Relations Department at the National Museums of Kenya (☎ 02-742131 ext 201, fax 741424, email prnmk@africaonline.co.ke).

Write to PO Box 40658, Nairobi, and take a look at the Web site (www.museums.or.ke). A vehicle and a guide will be available when you arrive at the research base at Koobi Fora where you will also find some *bandas* (KSh 1000 per person per night) and a basic *camp site*.

It's ferociously hot here for most of the year, but June and July are the coolest months (December to March are the hottest). From May to September very strong winds blow from the south-east.

Park fees are US$15 for adults and US$5 for students and children.

Getting There & Away

The best way to get to Sibiloi is to fly, which means chartering a plane (see the Kenya Getting Around chapter). There are airstrips at KWS headquarters and Koobi Fora.

If you have a 4WD it's a three-day trip from Nairobi and the last real petrol station is in Maralal. After there you'll have to buy it in plastic containers from roadside dukas.

The best option for backpackers is to charter a motor canoe from Jade Sea Journeys (☎ 02-218336, fax 228107, email jadesea@africaonline.co.ke) which organises trips to Koobi Fora in Sibiloi National Park and Central Island from Kalekol on the western shore of Lake Turkana. A one-day trip to Central Island costs US$140 per boat (maximum 12 people) and US$220 for a two-day trip (maximum eight people). Two-day and three-day trips to Koobi Fora are US$540 and US$700 respectively per boat (maximum eight people). Bring all your own food, water and camping gear. Park fees cost extra.

MARSABIT

South of Maikona is Marsabit, where you are back in relative civilisation. The main attraction here is Marsabit National Park & Reserve, centred on Mt Marsabit (1702m).

The hills here are thickly forested and in stark contrast to the desert on all sides. Mist often envelopes them in the early morning and mosses hang from tree branches. The views from the telecommunications tower on the summit above town are magnificent in all directions. In fact, they're probably as spectacular as any of the views from Mt Kenya or Mt Kilimanjaro.

The entire area is peppered with extinct volcanoes and volcanic craters (called *gofs*).

Places to Stay & Eat

Probably the best option is *JJ Centre*. You can't possibly miss it as it's the biggest building in town and has singles/doubles for KSh 250/400.

Marsabit Highway Hotel is not as good and it costs KSh 250 for a double with shower and toilet. It's a large place and very clean. The hotel has its own bar/restaurant which is open from 11 am to 2 pm and 5 pm to midnight. There is a disco on Friday and Saturday nights.

Marsabit Tribespeople

One of the most memorable sights in Marsabit is that of the tribespeople thronging the streets and roads into town. Most noticeable are the Rendille, dressed in skins and with elaborate braided hairstyles and fantastic multicoloured beaded necklaces and bracelets. These people graze camels and, like the Samburu and Maasai, show little interest in adopting a more sedentary lifestyle, preferring to roam the deserts and only visiting the towns when necessary for trade. They are the major non-Muslim people in what is otherwise a largely Muslim area.

The other major tribes are the Boran and the Gabbra, both pastoralists who graze cattle rather than camels. They're allied to the Galla peoples of Ethiopia, from where they originated several hundred years ago. Many have abandoned their former transient lifestyle and settled down to more sedentary activities. In the process, there are many who have adopted Islam and the modes of dress of the Somalis with whom they trade and who have also migrated into the area. There are also quite a few Ethiopians in town as a result of that country's tragic and turbulent recent past.

The best place for tea, mandazi and snacks is *Bismillah Tea House* in front of the Catholic Technical School.

Getting There & Away

Mwingi buses run from Marsabit south to Isiolo. They supposedly run a couple of times a week depending on demand and breakdowns – be prepared for a wait. The cost is KSh 350 and the trip takes six hours. If Mwingi buses are not running then you'll have to arrange a lift with a truck, which costs a standard US$10 from Marsabit to Isiolo.

All vehicles, including buses travelling between Marsabit and Isiolo or Marsabit and Moyale, must travel in convoy to minimise the danger of attack from *shiftas* (bandits).

MARSABIT NATIONAL PARK & RESERVE

Marsabit National Park & Reserve is home to a wide variety of larger mammals including lion, leopard, cheetah, elephant, rhino, buffalo, warthog, Grevy's zebra, reticulated giraffe, hyena, Grant's gazelle, oryx, dik-dik and greater kudu. The area is thickly forested so you won't see much game unless you spend time here. Preferably camp at **Lake Paradise** on the crater floor of Gof Sokorte Guda – a ranger must be present while you stay here and it costs US$15 per person plus a KSh 5000 set-up fee. It's an enchanting place. Entry to the park, which is open from 6 am to 7.15 pm, costs US$15 per person (US$5 for students and children) plus KSh 200 for a vehicle.

There's a public *camp site* by the main gate (US$8); *Marsabit Lodge* is closed.

The Survey of Kenya map *Marsabit National Park & Reserve* is worth buying if you can find it in Nairobi.

For information on getting there and away see Getting There & Away in the Marsabit section.

MOYALE

Straddling the Kenyan-Ethiopian border, Moyale lies some 250km north of Marsabit across the Dida Galgalu Desert. It's a small town of sandy streets with a post office,

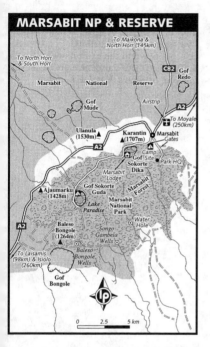

MARSABIT NP & RESERVE

Places to Stay & Eat

There are only three basic places to stay on the Kenyan side of Moyale. The best is *Hotel Medina* which costs KSh 100/160 for singles/doubles. It's clean, but like the other hotels it has no running water.

Barissah Hotel, which has the town's only bar, is nowhere near as good but it does offer reasonable food, the usual fare being meat stew and chapatis.

If the above two are full, head for the family-run *Bismillahi Boarding & Lodging* across from the Barissah and up behind the derelict Esso station. A bed here costs KSh 100 and facilities are absolutely minimal.

Kenyan shillings are acceptable when paying for meals and drinks.

Getting There & Away

Trucks between Isiolo and Moyale take two days and cost KSh 600 to KSh 1000. See the Isiolo section earlier in this chapter for details.

There are buses going north from the Ethiopian side of Moyale but they start at around dawn.

GARISSA

The only reason to come to Garissa is if you are taking the back route to Lamu from Nairobi via Garsen. There's nothing much to see or do here and the heat and humidity are unrelenting. However there is a bank, petrol stations, bars and a fair choice of places to stay. The only trouble with going via Garissa is getting there. As on the Malindi-Lamu run, most of the bus companies that used to service the town have pulled out because of the danger of shiftas and the state of the road.

bank, police station, bars, several shops and a small market area. Unlike those in Marsabit, the traditionally built houses here ensure that the interiors stay cool even when the outside temperature is 30°C and more.

The Ethiopian side of the town is larger and the facilities are much better, with sealed roads, electricity, a number of bars and small restaurants, a hotel, and a lively market area.

Recent security incidents have led to heightened tension in the area. The main problem is the conflict between the Oromo Liberation Front and the Ethiopian army which is spilling across the Kenyan border. In 1999 there were several skirmishes around Moyale, the border was closed and there were several incidents of land mines being laid on the surrounding roads. The security situation has improved, but seek local advice before travelling up to the border.

KENYA

Places to Stay & Eat

Perhaps the best place to stay for the night is *Safari Hotel* which offers relatively cheap, clean rooms with running water and reasonable food in the attached restaurant.

Garissa Government Guest House, a short distance out of town, is more expensive for rooms with bathroom and breakfast, but is worth the extra money. If both are full then there's also the more basic *Nile Lodging* or *Kenya Hotel & Lodging*.

The snowcapped peaks of Mt Kenya

A peaceful way to view the Kenyan countryside

Samburu National Reserve, Kenya

White rhinos graze in the shade of acacia trees at Lewa Downs in Kenya.

Winding down for the day on safari near Mt Meru in Tanzania.

Poachers beware! Tanzania

Wildebeest at Ngorongoro Crater, Tanzania

Towering baobab trees near Ndolelegi, Tanzania

Tanzania

Tanzania is East Africa's largest country and is also one of its most diverse, providing a home for more than 100 different ethnic groups, as well as some of the largest wildlife herds on the continent. It also has some of Africa's most spectacular topography, including the Great Rift Valley, Mt Kilimanjaro (the continent's highest peak) and the vast Serengeti plains. Offshore are idyllic islands ringed by beautiful palm-fringed beaches,

and Unguja (Zanzibar Island), with its exotic Stone Town. Topping it all off are Tanzanians themselves, who are known throughout the region for their warmth and openness.

Tanzania has a geological past spanning more than 300 million years. It holds archaeological treasures that include hominid fossils more than three million years old, and has a historical legacy that reaches from early tribal states through Julius Nyerere's

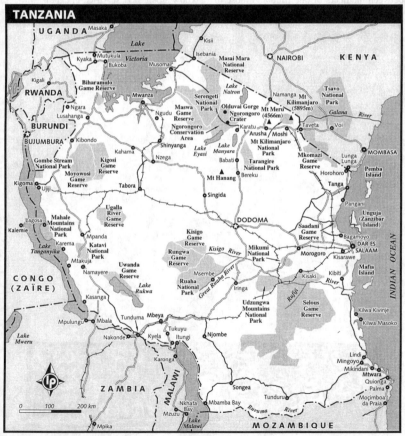

idealistic attempts at nation building, to recent steps towards multiparty democracy. It is a country of great natural wealth and beauty, where turquoise seas wash pristine coral reefs and vast plains are home to millions of hoofed animals. Its cool highland plateau is punctuated by the deep crevices of the Great Rift Valley, and its inland lakes glimmer with the reflected shadows of countless water birds.

There are over 100 different tribal groups in Tanzania, each with its own language and customs. Thus far, frictions arising from this diversity – between Muslims and Christians, between members of one tribe and those of another, between mainlanders and islanders – have been bridged by a shared experience of nationhood and by a common language (Swahili).

Tanzania is a land that for much of its history has been seen through the eyes of outsiders and it has only recently begun to define itself. It is a young nation forged around the ideals of community and family.

For travellers, apart from long distances and an undeveloped road network, Tanzania is one of the easier places on the continent to negotiate. It makes an ideal destination for those with some time who want to get to know a part of East Africa in depth.

Facts about Tanzania

HISTORY

Tanzania's early history dates back about 10,000 years to early hunter-gatherer communities living in the area south of the Olduvai Gorge. This period, as well as colonial era developments, are covered in the Facts about East Africa chapter.

Independence

The earliest seeds of Tanzanian independence can be traced to the Maji Maji rebellion of 1905 (see the boxed text 'The Maji Maji Rebellion' in The Southern Highlands chapter). During the decades following the rebellion, the nationalist movement gradually solidified. One of the main organisations during this time was the Tanganyika Africa Association (TAA), which served as a channel for grassroots resentment against colonial policies.

In 1953 the TAA elected Julius Nyerere as its president. Nyerere was a teacher, who had recently returned from studies in Europe, and one of only two Tanganyikans educated abroad at university level. Under his leadership, the TAA was quickly transformed into an effective political organisation. A new internal constitution was introduced on 7 July 1954 (an anniversary now celebrated as Saba Saba Day), and the TAA became the Tanganyika African National Union (TANU), which had as its slogan *'uhuru na umoja'* or 'freedom and unity'. Within a year, Nyerere had given up his teaching profession to devote himself full-time to leadership of TANU.

One of the first items on TANU's agenda was independence. In 1958 and 1959, TANU-supported candidates decisively won general legislative elections, and in 1959, the British colonial administrators agreed to the establishment of internal self-government, requesting Nyerere to be chief minister. On 9 December 1961 Tanganyika became independent, and on 9 December 1962 it was established as a republic with Julius Nyerere as its president.

TANZANIA AT A GLANCE

Area: approx 943,000 sq km
Population: 31 million
Population Growth Rate: 3%
Capital: Dodoma
Head of State: President Benjamin Mkapa
Official Languages: Swahili & English
Currency: Tanzanian shilling (TSh)
When to Go: late June & October

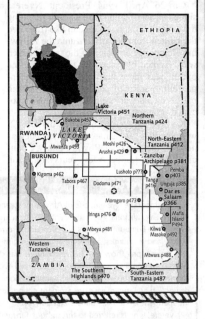

In the meantime on the Zanzibar archipelago, which had been a British protectorate since 1890, the main push for independence came from the radical Afro-Shirazi Party (ASP). Opposing the ASP were two minority parties, the Zanzibar & Pemba People's Party (ZPPP) and the sultanate-oriented Zanzibar Nationalist Party (ZNP), both of which were very strongly favoured by the British. As a result, at

Zanzibari independence in December 1963, it was the two minority parties which formed the first government.

This government did not last long. Within a month, a Ugandan immigrant named John Okello initiated a violent revolution against the ruling ZPPP-ZNP coalition which led to the toppling of the government and the sultan, and the massacre or expulsion of most of the islands' Arab population. The sultan was replaced by an entity known as the Zanzibar Revolutionary Council, which was comprised of ASP members and headed by Abeid Karume.

On 26 April 1964 President Nyerere signed an act of union with Karume, creating the United Republic of Tanganyika (renamed the United Republic of Tanzania the following October). Formation of the union, which was resented by many Zanzibaris from the outset, was motivated in part by the then-prevailing spirit of pan-Africanism, and in part as a cold war response to the ASP's socialist program.

Karume's government lasted until 1972, when he was assassinated and succeeded as head of the Zanzibar Revolutionary Council by Aboud Jumbe. A few years later, in an effort to subdue the ongoing unrest resulting from the merger of the islands with the mainland, Nyerere authorised formation of a one-party state and combined TANU and the ASP into a new party known as Chama Cha Mapinduzi (CCM, or Party of the Revolution). This merger, which was ratified in a new union constitution on 27 April 1977, marked the beginning of the CCM's dominance of Tanzanian politics which endures to this day.

Socialist Tanzania

Nyerere took the helm of a country that was economically foundering and politically fragile, its stability plagued in particular by the mainland's lack of control over the Zanzibar archipelago. Education had also been neglected, so that at independence there were said to be only 120 university graduates in the entire country.

This inauspicious beginning, and the problems it created, eventually led to the Arusha Declaration of 1967, which committed Tanzania to a policy of socialism and self-reliance *(ujamaa na kujitegemea)*. The cornerstone of this policy was the *ujamaa* (familyhood) village – an agricultural col-

Julius Nyerere

Julius Kambarage Nyerere, one of Africa's most renowned statesmen, was born in 1922 in Butiama, just west of Lake Victoria. After schooling in Tabora and Pugu and studies at Makerere College in Uganda, he went to Edinburgh University in Scotland. From 1949 to 1952 he pursued graduate studies there in history and economics, following which he returned to Tanganyika to begin a teaching profession.

It wasn't long, however, before Nyerere was drawn into politics. As president of the Tanganyika African National Union (TANU), he travelled within and outside of Tanzania advocating peaceful change, social equality and racial harmony. Soon his oratorical skills and political savvy earned him distinction as Tanganyika's pre-eminent nationalist spokesman, and by 1962, he was president of the independent United Republic of Tanganyika.

Nyerere, who is referred to throughout Tanzania as *Mwalimu*, the Swahili word for teacher, is well known internationally for his philosophy of socialism and self-reliance. He chose the term *ujamaa* (familyhood) to describe his program, which emphasised a blend of economic cooperation, racial and tribal harmony and moralistic self-sacrifice. While Nyerere's policies were a failure from an economic perspective, he gained widespread respect for his idealism, for his success in shaping a society which was politically stable and notably free of tribal rivalries, and for his contributions towards raising Tanzania's literacy rate. He also earned international acclaim for his commitment to pan-Africanism and for his regional engagement – an area where he was active until his death in October 1999.

Despite criticisms of his authoritarian style and economic policies, Nyerere was indisputably one of Africa's most influential leaders, and the person almost single-handedly responsible for putting Tan-

lective run along traditional African lines, with an emphasis on self-reliance. Basic goods and tools were to be held in common and shared among members, while each individual was obligated to work on the land. Nyerere's proposals for education were seen as an essential part of this scheme. They were designed to encourage cooperative endeavour, to promote social equality and responsibility, and to discourage any tendency towards intellectual arrogance among the educated. Additional aspects of the Arusha Declaration included nationalisation of the economy, and tax increases aimed at redistributing individual wealth.

In the early days of the ujamaa system, progressive farmers were encouraged to expand in the hope that other peasants would follow their example. This enriched those who were the recipients of state funds but resulted in little improvement in rural poverty. The approach was therefore abandoned in favour of direct state control. Between 1973 and 1978, 85% of Tanzania's rural population was resettled, often forcibly, into more than 7000 planned villages. These resettlements were aimed at modernisation of the agricultural sector and at making social services more accessible to rural dwellers. Yet, this new approach was also unsuccessful. The necessary finances exceeded the country's resources, and there was widespread resentment among large segments of the rural population towards compulsory resettlement. The government's authoritarian response to dissent further contributed to the discontent.

Tanzania's experiment in socialism and self-reliance was widely acclaimed in the days following independence. Despite the unpopularity of the ujamaa system, it marked a successful period of nation-building, and is credited with unifying the country, bridging ethnic and religious divisions, and expanding education and health care. Economically, however, the consensus is that it failed. Between 1978 and 1984, Tanzania's per capita income decreased by more than 30%, agricultural production became stagnant, the industrial sector ran at less than 50% of capacity, and virtually all economic incentives were eliminated. This decline was precipitated by a combination of factors, including the steep rise in oil prices during the 1970s, sharp drops in the value of major exports such as coffee and sisal, the

Julius Nyerere

SARAH JOLLY

zania on the world stage as one of the continent's major players. He has been widely acclaimed for his long-standing opposition to South Africa's apartheid system, and for his 1979 invasion of Uganda, which resulted in the deposition of the dictator Idi Amin Dada. In more recent years, Nyerere continued to be active as an elder statesman, taking a leading role in seeking a resolution of the Burundi crisis, and advocating increased African political and economic collaboration through multilateral organisations such as the Southern African Development Community (SADC) and the Common Market of Eastern and Southern African States (Comesa). Nyerere's promotion of a Tanzanian national identity and achievements in nation-building are among his greatest domestic legacies.

Nyerere wrote several books, including *Uhuru na Umoja* (Freedom and Unity) and *Uhuru na Ujamaa* (Freedom and Socialism). He also translated two Shakespeare plays, *The Merchant of Venice* and *Julius Caesar* into Swahili.

1977 break-up of the East African Community (an economic and customs union between Tanzania, Kenya and Uganda) and prolonged drought during the early 1980s. Tanzania's regional activism, particularly its involvement in deposing Idi Amin Dada in Uganda in 1979, was also a significant drain on government resources.

Multiparty Politics

Nyerere was re-elected to a fifth term as president in 1980. During the next few years, economic decline worsened and dissatisfaction with socialist policies grew. In 1985 Nyerere resigned, handing over power to Ali Hassan Mwinyi. Mwinyi tried to distance himself from Nyerere and his policies, and instituted an economic recovery program involving decreased government spending, price liberalisation and encouragement of foreign investment. Yet the pace of change remained slow, and Mwinyi's presidency was unpopular.

The fall of Communism in Europe at the beginning of the 1990s and increasing pressure from western donor nations accelerated the move towards multiparty politics. In 1991 a presidential commission published recommendations on the establishment of a multiparty system. In 1992, following a unanimous vote at an extraordinary sitting of the CCM, the constitution was amended to legalise opposition parties and a date was set for elections.

The first elections were held in October 1995 in an atmosphere of chaos. On the mainland, the CCM, under the leadership of Benjamin Mkapa, won 62% of the vote. Although the results were contested by the opposition, they were ultimately deemed to reflect the will of the people and were upheld.

On the Zanzibar archipelago, the voting for the Zanzibari presidency was universally denounced for its dishonesty. The opposition Civic United Front (CUF) candidate, Seif Shariff Hamad, is widely believed to have narrowly won the presidential seat. Yet the official results came out as 50.2% of the vote in favour of the CCM incumbent Salmin Amour, against 49.8% for Hamad. In the ensuing uproar, foreign development assistance was suspended and most expats working on the islands left. Negotiations moderated by the Commonwealth secretary-general to end the resulting stalemate concluded in June 1999 with an agreement between the CCM and CUF in which the CUF officially accepted the 1995 election results in return for reform of the Zanzibari electoral commission. The agreement – which has yet to be implemented – has had the effect of at least temporarily easing tensions, and has pushed the spectre of violence further to the background, although the balance that has been achieved is a delicate one.

The next presidential and legislative elections are scheduled for October 2000. While President Mkapa receives only muted approval from many Tanzanians on the street, his government has distinguished itself in the international community with its commitment to fight corruption, and with its steps towards financial austerity and reform. Mkapa's victory is further aided by the fact that there is no serious external contender for his seat; the opposition parties are in disarray and none can yet approach the national network or the resources of the CCM. The real action in the months leading up to the elections is likely to be within the CCM itself, as it determines whether Mkapa will continue at its helm, or whether another candidate will attempt to move to the forefront.

GEOGRAPHY

Tanzania is East Africa's largest country, with a total area of approximately 943,000 sq km, including 2640 sq km belonging to the Zanzibar archipelago.

Much of the mainland consists of a central highland plateau averaging between 900 and 1800m in altitude and situated between the eastern and western branches of the geological fault known as the Great Rift Valley. There is a narrow coastal strip varying in width from about 15 to 65km. In the north-west is the Lake Victoria basin. The main mountain ranges are grouped into a north-eastern section (the Eastern Arc) and a central and southern section (the Southern

Highlands or Southern Arc). There is also a belt of volcanic peaks in the centre of the country near the Ngorongoro Crater. Tanzania's (and Africa's) highest mountain is Mt Kilimanjaro (5896m). The lowest point in the country is the floor of Lake Tanganyika, which at 358m below sea level is also the lowest point in Africa.

The largest river is the Rufiji, which drains the Southern Highlands region and much of southern Tanzania. Other major rivers flowing into the Indian Ocean include the Ruvu, the Wami, the Pangani and the Ruvuma.

CLIMATE

Tanzania's climate displays marked regional differences due to the country's widely varying topography. In general, the coolest months are from June to October, and the warmest from December to March.

Along the coast and on offshore islands the climate is tropical, with relatively high humidity. Temperatures average between 27 and 29°C. On the central highland plateau, where climate is tempered by altitude, temperatures range from about 20 to 27°C during the cooler months of June to August, but can reach 30°C and higher between December and March.

Throughout much of the country, there are two rainy seasons, with the 'long' rains falling from mid-March to May, and the 'short' rains during November, December and sometimes into January. Rainfall varies from less than 500mm per year in some of central Tanzania's semi-arid areas to about 1500mm along the coast and more than 2000mm in mountainous areas of the northeast and south-west.

ECOLOGY & ENVIRONMENT

Tanzania has exceptionally rich and varied ecosystems. The forests of the Eastern Arc Mountains, which are among the most biodiverse in Africa, host numerous endemic plant and bird species. The country's inland lakes, notably Tanganyika and Nyasa, are also known for their biodiversity. Lake Tanganyika holds more than 200 different marine species, including numerous endemic

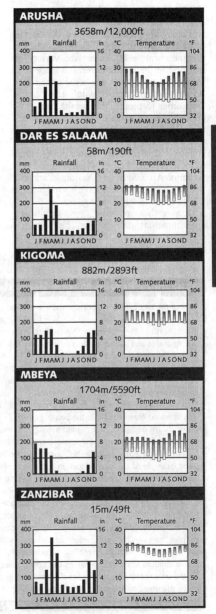

TANZANIA

cichlids, molluscs and crustaceans, and Lake Nyasa contains about 33% of the world's known cichlid species. Along the coast and around the offshore islands are pristine coral reefs and a wide variety of marine life, including several rare species. Tanzania's vast plains are home to some of Africa's largest herds of wildlife.

In order to protect this wealth, the government has set aside about 25% of Tanzania's land as protected parks, game and forest reserves, and has recently created the country's first national marine park. Three of these protected areas –Ngorongoro Conservation Area, Serengeti National Park and Selous Game Reserve – have been declared UNESCO World Heritage sites.

Despite these positive steps, significant environmental damage has already occurred in many areas. One of the most serious threats in coastal regions is dynamite fishing (see the boxed text 'Tanzania's Fragile Marine Ecosystems'). Inland, concerns include soil degradation and erosion, desertification and deforestation. In the national parks, poaching and inappropriate visitor use – especially in the northern circuit – threaten wildlife and ecosystems.

The best local contact for more in-depth information on environmental issues in the country is the Wildlife Conservation Society of Tanzania (☎ 051-112518, 112496, fax 124572, email wcst@costech.gn.apc.org), a membership organisation located on Garden St in Dar es Salaam. In addition to publishing the informative newsletter, *Miombo*, with features on environmental issues throughout the country, they also maintain a small library with information on national parks and game reserves. Staff are dedicated and knowledgeable.

World Wildlife Fund (☎ 051-75346, fax 75535) also has an informative office in Dar es Salaam.

Tanzania's Fragile Marine Ecosystems

One of the most serious threats to marine environments along Tanzania's coastline is dynamite fishing. Using dynamite, fishermen are able to pull in a large catch of fish within a very short time. Yet, in addition to killing all fish within a 15 to 20m radius, a dynamite blast also destroys most of the invertebrates and plankton upon which many fish feed, as well as damaging any hard coral near the area of the blast. As coral cover decreases, so too does the available space for fish to breed, rest and seek shelter from predators. As a result, areas that are subjected to frequent dynamite blasts soon begin to show marked reductions in fish abundance and diversity. The ability of coral reefs to recover from this type of damage is minimal.

In a few areas – for example, that encompassed by Mafia Island Marine Park (see the boxed text 'Mafia Island Marine Park' in the South-Eastern Tanzania chapter) – increased vigilance has resulted in significant decreases in dynamite fishing. Yet, much of the coastline still goes unpatrolled and unprotected. The problem is made more complex by the fact that in many cases it is not only local fishermen doing the blasting, but outsiders who have no direct stake in the local environment. A good example of this can be seen in the areas offshore from Kilwa Masoko and around the Songo Songo archipelago, where most dynamite fishing is carried out by fishermen from Dar es Salaam working for businessmen based in the capital.

Ultimately, a sustainable solution to the problem will require a combination of measures. In addition to more vigilant patrolling and police enforcement, and intensified community education initiatives, many conservation groups are now calling for more stringent regulation of dynamite supplies, or even the replacement of dynamite with an explosive which would not work in water. Other proposals include increasing accountability on the part of dynamite suppliers by permitting only a small number of companies to import, handle and use explosives; introducing stiff penalties for the unlicensed possession of explosives; and, implementing seize and destroy policies for all boats and equipment of fishermen caught dynamiting.

The best source of information on the marine resources of the Zanzibar archipelago is the Institute of Marine Sciences in Zanzibar Town on the seafront. For information on environmental issues relating to Lake Victoria, try the National Environmental Management Council; it's on the 3rd floor, Tancot building, Sokoine Ave (opposite Luther House) in Dar es Salaam.

FLORA & FAUNA
Flora
Approximately 33% of the Tanzanian mainland, predominantly in the south and west, is covered by miombo woodland. About 13 million hectares have been set aside as permanent forest reserves where small tree plantations have been established. In upland areas, notably in the Eastern Arc Mountain, are small but biologically significant areas of tropical rainforest that host most of Tanzania's endemic plant species, including *Celtis africana* (more commonly known as the Usambara or African violet). Much of the dry central highland plateau is covered with savanna, bushland and thickets, while grasslands cover the Serengeti plain and other areas that lack good drainage. The coastline is broken by extensive mangrove growth, especially at Rufiji River Delta and near the mouths of other major rivers.

Fauna
Tanzania's more than four million wild animals include representatives of 430 species and subspecies. Among the most common are zebra, elephant, wildebeest, buffalo, hippo, giraffe, antelope, dik-dik, gazelle, eland and kudu. There are also many predatory animals, including hyena, wild dog, lion and leopard, and bands of chimpanzee in Gombe Stream and Mahale Mountains national parks. In addition, Tanzania has about 25 types of reptiles or amphibians, including crocodile, 100 species of snake and numerous fish species.

The country hosts more than 1000 bird species, including a number of endemics such as Udzungwa forest partridge, Pemba green pigeon, Usambara weaver, South Pare white eye and Usambara eagle owl.

Endangered Species Endangered species include Uluguru bush shrike; hawksbill, green, olive ridley, and leatherback turtles; black rhino; and red Colobus monkey.

NATIONAL PARKS & GAME RESERVES
Tanzania's protected areas include 12 national parks, 14 game reserves and the Ngorongoro Conservation Area. The country's first marine park was recently gazetted, and there are protected marine reserves.

The country's national parks are managed by the Tanzania National Parks Authority or TANAPA (☎ 057-2371, 4082, fax 8216), PO Box 3134, Arusha. Gates at all parks are open from 6 am to 7 pm daily. Entry fees must be paid in hard currency, preferably in US dollars cash. All of the parks have camp sites, and usually simple *bandas* (thatched huts) or resthouses. Most also have more comfortable lodges or tented camps. In general, it is only the northern parks that have been extensively developed – in some cases, exploited. The situation in many of the southern parks is the opposite, and utilisation to date has been minimal. Although they are now beginning to see more visitors, overall the parks are quite rugged and remote, and you'll still have many areas to yourself.

Tanzania's game reserves fall under the jurisdiction of the Wildlife Division of the Ministry of Natural Resources and Tourism (☎ 051-866376, 866064), Ivory Room, Pugu Rd at Changombe Rd in Dar es Salaam. As with the national parks, entry fees (generally US$20) should be paid in US dollars. With the exception of Saadani, which has one permanent camp; Selous, which has tourist facilities in its northern sector; and Mkomazi, which has basic facilities, game reserves are undeveloped.

The Ministry of Natural Resources & Tourism's Division of Fisheries (☎ 051-116162, 116159, fax 110352, email fisheries@twiga.com), PO Box 2462, Dar es Salaam, oversees Tanzania's marine park and reserves. It's located on the 6th floor of Ardhi House, at the eastern end of Kivukoni Front in Dar es Salaam.

TANZANIA

TANZANIA

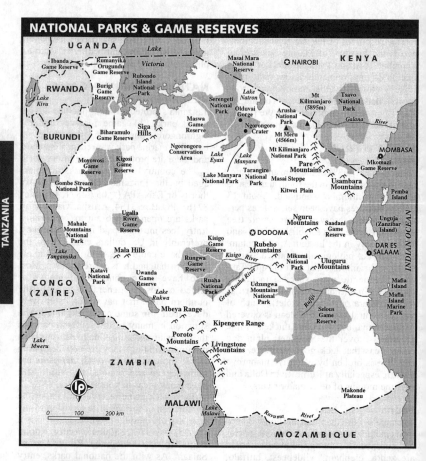

NATIONAL PARKS & GAME RESERVES

GOVERNMENT & POLITICS

Tanzania is a fledgling multiparty democracy. Executive power rests with the president and the ruling CCM party. Both the president and the vice president, as well as members of the unicameral National Assembly, are elected by direct popular vote for five-year terms. The prime minister, who functions as the head of the National Assembly, is appointed by the president. Cabinet members are selected by the president from among National Assembly members. Both the prime minister of Tanzania and the president of Zanzibar are vice presidents of the Republic of Tanzania.

Of the 275 seats in the National Assembly, 232 are elected from the mainland and the Zanzibar archipelago. An additional 37 are appointed seats for women, which are divided proportionally among the various political parties based on polling in individual constituencies. The remaining seats are elected by the Zanzibar House of Representatives. Opposition parties in Tanzania include the CUF, the National Convention for Construction and Reform (NCCR), the Chama Cha Demokrasia Na Maendeleo (CHADEMA) and the United Democratic Party.

The union government has jurisdiction over external affairs, defence, and external trade currency, while the Zanzibar government has jurisdiction over all nonunion matters.

Tanzania is divided into 25 administrative regions (which are further subdivided into districts), including 20 on the mainland, three on Unguja and two on Pemba.

ECONOMY

Agriculture is the mainstay of Tanzania's economy, employing about 80% of the workforce and accounting for about 60% of gross domestic product (GDP). Major commercial crops include coffee, tea, cotton, cashews, sisal and cloves; subsistence crops include rice, cassava, maize, millet and plantains. With the exception of sisal and tea, most agriculture is small-holder cash cropping.

Tourism, with an annual growth rate of more than 8%, is playing an increasingly important role in the economy, with growth constrained primarily by the country's underdeveloped infrastructure.

Other important sectors include mining, which represents about 7% of GDP, and industry (about 8% of GDP), although in comparison with other countries on the continent the industrial sector is considered weak. Tanzania's widely scattered mineral resources include nickel, iron, coal, gold and gemstones.

Tanzania's mid-term economic prospects are generally positive. Economic growth currently averages about 3.5% per year. Inflation, at about 13%, is well down from rates of a few years ago, but not yet at the targeted rate of less than 10%. Throughout much of the 1990s, the government pursued a course of trying to reverse the postindependence socialist policies of the Nyerere era. A major restructuring of state-owned enterprises has begun, including privatisation of more than 400 parastatals, although progress has been slower than initially anticipated.

Despite these improvements, servicing of Tanzania's US$8 billion external debt (close to half of which is multilateral debt) accounts for more than 33% of government expenditures, and the economy remains heavily dependent on outside donors. While the economic situation in Tanzania is far better than in many of Africa's war-torn or drought-afflicted nations (Tanzania was ranked 149th out of 174 countries on the UNDP Human Development Index in the late 1990s), daily life for many Tanzanians remains a struggle. Annual per capita income is estimated at US$260, and unemployment and underemployment are far more widespread than indicated statistically.

POPULATION & PEOPLE

Tanzania's population, estimated at about 31 million (including about 813,000 on the Zanzibar archipelago), is comprised of about 120 tribal groups, most of which are very small. About 95% of Tanzanians are of Bantu origin. The largest tribes include the Sukuma (about 13% of overall population), the Nyamwezi, the Makonde, the Haya and the Chagga. There are also small but economically significant Asian and Arabic populations, especially in Dar es Salaam, and a small European community. The three indigenous ethnic groups on the Zanzibar archipelago are the Hadimu, the Tumbatu and the Pemba. For more information on people of the region, see the special section 'Tribal Groups & Cultures'.

Tanzania is one of the least urbanised countries in sub-Saharan Africa. According to the most recent census (1988), urban dwellers constituted only 11.5% of all mainland Tanzanians, although the urban population is estimated to be growing at an annual average rate of 10%. In general, Tanzania is most densely populated around its perimeter, while settlement in the centre of the country is sparse. The average population growth rate for the Tanzanian mainland is about 3%; average life expectancy is 52 years.

EDUCATION

Tanzania's educational system is loosely modelled on that of the UK. There are seven years of primary school which, at least in theory, are compulsory, and four years of secondary school with an additional two

TANZANIA

years required for university entrance. Primary school instruction is in Swahili, while secondary level and university instruction is in English. While close to 70% of children obtain at least some primary schooling, only about 50% complete primary school, and less than 3% of these go on to finish secondary school. Cost is one factor: secondary school tuition rates, which average between TSh 80,000 and TSh 120,000 per year, pose hardships for many families.

Language is another barrier, as many students lack sufficient knowledge of English to carry out their course work at the secondary level. This leads to frustration and exacerbates the already dismal drop-out rate. Scarce government resources, shortages of qualified teachers, and insufficient facilities and supplies compound the problem. The situation is particularly bleak for girls, who constitute barely 25% of secondary school graduates (a figure which represents less than 5% of all Tanzanian women). Private schools – which were nationalised in the wake of the Arusha declaration – are again operating and are helping to redress the situation, but their geographical distribution is uneven.

Despite all this, literacy rates in Tanzania (which average about 70% for adults) are relatively high in comparison with those in many neighbouring countries. This is due in large part to the legacy of Julius Nyerere, who was convinced that the key to success for his philosophy of socialism and self-reliance lay in having an educated populace. During the early years of his presidency, he set aside 14% of the national budget for education, offered government assistance to villages to build their own schools, and made primary education free and compulsory.

By the late 1980s, Tanzania's literacy rate was one of the highest in Africa, although much of this initial momentum has since been lost.

ARTS
Music
Traditional musical instruments that you are likely to see include the *marimba*, which has metal strips of varying lengths that are plucked with the thumb; *kayamba* (shakers made with grain kernels); rattles and bells made of wood or iron; xylophones (also sometimes referred to as marimbas); *siwa* (horns), *tari* (tambourines); and *ngoma* (drums), which come in a wide variety of designs.

Modern Tanzanian music has been significantly influenced by Congalese (Zaïrean) jazz. One of the country's best-known musicians is Congalese (Zaïrean)-born Remmy Ongala ('Dr Remmy'), who, along with his Orchestre Super Matimila, has been one of the major forces in popularising music from the region beyond Africa's borders. Many of his songs (most of which are in Swahili) are commentaries on contemporary themes such as AIDS, poverty and hunger. The music, known locally as 'bongo beat', combines Caribbean influences with *soukous* (Congalese (Zaïrean) Lingala music). See The Zanzibar Archipelago chapter for information on *taarab* music.

Literature
One of Tanzania's most significant Swahili-language authors was Shaaban Robert (1909-62), who was born near Tanga and educated in Dar es Salaam. His works include the autobiographical *Maisha yangu*, and several collections of stories told in the form of traditional tales. Other well known Tanzanian authors of Swahili-language works include Muhammed Said Abdulla and Shafi Adam Shafi (both were born on Zanzibar Island), Joseph Mbele, and Ebrahim Hussein. Mbele wrote short stories, while Hussein is known primarily for his dramas and theatre pieces.

Contemporary Tanzanian authors of English-language works include Peter Palangyo *(Dying in the Sun* is one of his best known works), William Kamera (known for his poetry and for *Tales of the Wairaqw of Tanzania)*, and Tolowa Marti Mollel, who authored numerous short stories.

Painting
Tanzania's most well known school of painting is Tingatinga, which was begun in the 1960s by Edward Saidi Tingatinga, the

self-taught artist after whom it is named. Traditional Tingatinga paintings are composed in a square format, and generally feature colourful animal motifs against a monochrome background. One of the most distinctive characteristics of the style is its use of undiluted and often unmixed enamel and high-gloss paints which give the paintings their characteristic shiny appearance. A good place to see Tingatinga artists at work is Morogoro Stores in Dar es Salaam, where Edward Tingatinga's paintings were originally sold.

The Russian Cultural Centre in Dar es Salaam hosts frequent exhibitions of paintings by local artists.

Sculpture & Woodcarving

Among the major representatives of Tanzanian figurative art are the Makonde, who are renowned throughout East Africa for their original and often highly fanciful carvings. Authentic Makonde carvings are made from ebony wood. The most common include those with ujamaa motifs, and those known as *shetani*, which embody images from the spirit world. Ujamaa carvings are frequently designed as a totem pole or 'tree of life' containing from several to many interlaced human and animal figures, each of which is connected with and giving support to all of the others. One of the most well known of the original ujamaa-style carvers is Roberto Jacobo.

Carvings with shetani motifs are very abstract, often grotesque, and are designed to challenge the viewer to new interpretations while giving the carver's imagination free reign. The shetani style was first developed by an artist known as Samaki.

In contrast to the ujamaa and shetani motifs, which are relatively recent, earlier Makonde carvings generally depicted more traditional themes, often relating to various deities or rituals. Even today, the Makonde produce carvings of ordinary household objects such as bowls and walking sticks, although these are seldom seen for sale.

The major centres of Makonde carving in Tanzania are in the south-east on the Makonde Plateau, and in Dar es Salaam.

Cinema

Tanzania's tiny indigenous film industry received a major boost in 1998 with the opening of the first Zanzibar International Film Festival (ZIFF), held annually on Unguja (Zanzibar Island). The festival, which serves as a venue for artists from throughout East Africa and beyond, is one of East Africa's premier cultural events. One of last year's prize winners was the film *Maangamizi*, which was shot in Tanzania and co-directed by a Tanzanian, Martin M'hando (also known for his 1986 film *Women of Hope)*. In addition to screenings in Zanzibar Town, there are numerous activities elsewhere on Unguja, and on Pemba. For information on the festival, contact the ZIFF office (☎ 054-233408, fax 233406, email ziff@zanzibar.org), PO Box 3032, Zanzibar, which is in the Old Fort in Zanzibar Town. You also might like to check out the Web site at www.zanzibar.org/ziff.

SOCIETY & CONDUCT

As elsewhere in East Africa, politeness, respect and modesty are highly valued attributes in Tanzania's traditional society.

On Unguja and in some of the Muslim coastal areas, pay particular attention to modesty – especially in dress; many locals take offence at scantily clad westerners. For women, this means no sleeveless tops, and preferably slacks, skirts or at least knee-length shorts. For men, it means shirts and slacks or knee-length shorts. During Ramadan you can respect local sensibilities by not eating or drinking in public.

RELIGION

About 45% of Tanzanians are Christian and about 40% are Muslim. The remainder are adherents of traditional religions. There are also small communities of Hindus, Sikhs, and Ismaelis. Muslims have traditionally been concentrated along the coast, as well as in those inland towns that lined the old caravan routes. One of the areas of highest Christian concentration is in the north-east of the country around Moshi, which has been a centre of missionary activity since the mid-19th century.

TANZANIA

The population of the Zanzibar archipelago is almost exclusively Muslim, with a few tiny communities of Christians and Hindus.

LANGUAGE

Swahili (KiSwahili) and English are the official languages. While English is widely spoken in major towns, in smaller places and rural areas you'll need to know at least a few Swahili phrases. Outside cities and towns, far fewer people speak English than in comparable areas of Kenya.

In addition to Swahili there are also numerous other African languages spoken in Tanzania, a reflection of the country's ethnic diversity. The vast majority (about 95%) are Bantu languages, including Sukuma, Makonde, Haya, Ha, Gogo, and Yao. Other language groups represented include Nilotic (to which the Maasai language belongs), the Cushitic group, and Khoisan or 'click' languages.

See the Language chapter at the back of this book for a brief guide to Swahili and some useful words and phrases.

Facts for the Visitor

HIGHLIGHTS

Among Tanzania's most popular attractions are a trek up Mt Kilimanjaro, a safari to the wildlife-packed Ngorongoro Crater and trying to catch the annual wildebeest migration in the Serengeti. Additional drawcards include the country's many other national parks and game reserves; the Usambara and Pare mountains in the north-east, which offer good hiking and interesting culture; and Dar es Salaam, a colourful, bustling place with an interesting history.

Offshore are pristine coral reefs, rich and diverse marine life, and numerous idyllic islands. The largest of these are green and mysterious Pemba, and Unguja (Zanzibar Island) – East Africa's most famous Swahili city-state, with its mosques, winding alleyways, sultans' palaces and coral-sand beaches.

SUGGESTED ITINERARIES

Tanzania is a relatively easy country to negotiate. However, it's also a very large country; distances are long, and roads in many areas are in poor condition. If you try to compress too many things into a visit, you'll inevitably wind up disappointed and exhausted. It's far better to choose just one or two regions and concentrate on exploring them well.

One Week

Assuming that you will be arriving in Dar es Salaam, spend a day or two there getting oriented, perhaps a day at Mikumi National Park, and then the remainder of the week on Unguja, divided between Zanzibar Town and one of the beaches.

Two Weeks

With two weeks, you could expand this base a bit, staying longer on Unguja and adding on a few days hiking in the Usambaras or in Udzungwa Mountains National Park, or visiting Selous Game Reserve or Ruaha National Park.

Alternatively, head from Dar es Salaam towards Moshi and Arusha, spending a few days walking in the villages around Marangu and several days visiting one of the northern parks or the Ngorongoro Crater before heading to Unguja for the second week.

It would also be easy to spend two weeks alone on the Zanzibar archipelago – a week on Unguja, divided between Stone Town and the beaches, and a week on Pemba, exploring its many attractions.

Three Weeks

With three weeks, you could combine a week on the Zanzibar archipelago with two weeks on the mainland (see suggestions under One Week and Two Weeks) – or two weeks on the archipelago and one week on the mainland divided between Dar es Salaam, Bagamoyo and Mikumi National Park.

If you want to stay on the mainland, then three weeks would be ideal for making a small circuit through north-eastern and northern Tanzania, with stops in Dar es Salaam, Bagamoyo and Tanga before heading to the Usambara or Pare mountains for several days of hiking. Then continue on to Moshi and Arusha to visit Tarangire or Lake Manyara national parks or to arrange some village walks around Marangu.

Alternatively, you could head from Dar es Salaam south-westwards and take in the scenic Southern Highlands region, with stops en route in Morogoro, Mikumi, Udzungwa Mountains National Park, Iringa and Mbeya before exiting to Zambia or Malawi.

PLANNING
When to Go

The best time to visit Tanzania is between late June and October when the rains have finished and the air is coolest. However, this is also when hotels and park lodges are full and airfares most expensive. The second-best time is from late December to February or early March, just after the short rains and before the long rains, though temperatures will be higher (maximums around 30°C).

Budget travellers can save substantially on accommodation costs during the main rainy season from March until June, and you'll have many of the places to yourself. However, many secondary roads will be impassable and many areas of the country inaccessible. Some lodges and hotels also close during this period.

What Kind of Trip

Independent travel, involving a combination of public transport, organised safaris and occasional vehicle hire, is generally the most economical option in Tanzania and poses no particular problems in Tanzania other than requiring some time and patience. For those who prefer a more structured trip, or whose time is limited, tour companies abound. With the exception of parts of the south-east and of the Southern Highlands, you can find organised tours that go almost anywhere. This will usually be much more expensive than travelling on your own.

Trips can easily be planned around special interests. For example, you could combine hiking for a week or so with visits to nearby national parks, or combine a dive-based trip with exploration of historical sites along the coast or on the Zanzibar archipelago.

Maps

Maps of Tanzania are widely available in the USA, Europe and Australia, as well as in bookshops in Dar es Salaam, Arusha and in Zanzibar Town. One of the best is the *Nelles* map (1:1,500,000).

Topographical maps (1:50,000) are available from the Map Sales Office at the Surveys and Mapping Division on the corner of Kivukoni Front and Luthuli St in Dar es Salaam. Each sheet costs TSh 2500.

A good series of maps, hand drawn by Giovanni Tombazzi and marketed under the name MaCo (email maco@ark.eoltz.com), cover various areas of the country and are widely available in bookshops in Dar es Salaam, Arusha and Zanzibar Town for between TSh 2000 and TSh 5000.

For information on maps of towns and national parks, see the individual entries in other chapters.

What to Bring

You can buy almost anything you will need in Dar es Salaam or Arusha, except specialist trekking and sporting equipment. If you plan on doing trekking or a camping safari, you can save money and usually enjoy better quality by bringing your own sleeping bag and tent from home. It's often possible to sell these at the end of your trip to tour operators. Most places, including inexpensive guesthouses, have mosquito nets, but it doesn't hurt to carry your own for those times when none are available. If you plan on staying in budget accommodation, a sleeping sheet is also a good thing to bring along to lay over grubby linen.

In highland areas of the country you will need a lightweight jacket in the evenings; in some of the higher elevations along the Southern Highlands, in the Usambara and Pare mountains, and on the rim of the Ngorongoro Crater, a jacket or pullover is essential. Trekkers will need a full range of cold-weather clothing, which should be brought from home. There is a helpful section on this topic in Lonely Planet's *Trekking in East Africa*.

For more tips on what to bring, see Planning in the Regional Facts for the Visitor chapter.

RESPONSIBLE TOURISM

Tourism in Tanzania has experienced its most obvious detrimental impact on the heavily travelled 'northern circuit' around the wildlife-viewing areas of the Serengeti and Ngorongoro and on Mt Kilimanjaro (see the boxed text 'Tanzania's Overloaded Northern Circuit' in the Northern Tanzania chapter). Some coastal areas, in particular Unguja have also been hit pretty hard. See the boxed text 'Considerations for Responsible Diving' later in this chapter and the Regional Facts for the Visitor chapter for more information.

TOURIST OFFICES
Local Tourist Offices

The Tanzania Tourist Board's main tourist information office is in Dar es Salaam (see that chapter for details). There is also a branch office in Arusha; see the Northern Tanzania chapter for details.

Tourist Offices Abroad

In the UK, the Tanzania Tourist Board is represented by the Tanzania Trade Centre (☎ 020-7407 0566, fax 7403 2003, email director@tanzatrade.co.uk) at 80 Borough High St, London, SE1 1LL. In other countries, it is represented by Tanzanian embassies and high commissions (see the listings later in this chapter).

VISAS & DOCUMENTS
Visas

Visas are required by almost all visitors to Tanzania, except nationals of some Commonwealth countries; Canadian and British citizens require visas. The cost of a visa varies from US$10 to US$60, depending on nationality. Tourist visas are usually issued for a maximum of three months, although length of stay is determined at the border – one month is the norm.

It is best to obtain a visa before arrival. If you are unable to do so, visas are usually issued at Dar es Salaam international airport, Kilimanjaro international airport, Zanzibar airport, and at the Kenyan border crossing of Namanga. Entry regulations are constantly changing.

For up-to-date information, you should contact your nearest Tanzanian embassy or high commission.

Visa Extensions Application for a visa extension (assuming you have not already exceeded the three-month maximum) can be made at the immigration office in any of Tanzania's major towns and cities. There's no charge, and applications are generally processed on the same day; no photos are required.

Other Visas The following visas can be picked up in Tanzania:

Burundi A one-month single entry visa costs US$40, plus two photos and is usually ready the same day if you apply early. The Burundian consulate in Kigoma also issues one-month single entry visas.

Congo (Zaïre) The consulate in Kigoma issues one-month single entry visas for US$50, plus two photos. Allow up to a week for processing.

Kenya A one-month single entry visa costs between TSh 15,000 and TSh 32,500, depending on nationality. Visas are issued the same day if you apply early. Note that the USA, UK, Australia and many western European nationals no longer need visas for Kenya for visits of less than one month.

Malawi Citizens of the USA, UK and Germany do not require visas. For other nationalities, visas cost US$40, plus two photos, and are issued within 24 hours, or on the same day if you apply in the morning.

Mozambique A one-month single entry visa costs US$30, plus two photos and is usually ready within two days.

Rwanda Visas cost TSh 20,000, plus two photos and are ready in 48 to 72 hours.

Uganda A three-month single entry visa costs US$30, plus three photos, and is usually ready the same day if you apply in the morning.

Zambia A one-month single entry visa costs TSh 15,000 for most nationalities, plus two photos. Applications received in the morning will be processed the same day.

Driving Licence & Permits

If you plan on driving in Tanzania (including on Unguja), arrange an international driving permit before arrival. Otherwise, you will need to get a Tanzanian licence, available from the traffic police in major towns.

To bring a car into Tanzania from a neighbouring country, you'll need a completed C49 Customs Form (available at border crossings), as well as proof of insurance, vehicle registration papers, and a valid international driving permit.

International Health Card

Visitors must have an up-to-date health card showing proof of yellow fever vaccination.

EMBASSIES
Tanzanian Embassies

Tanzanian embassies in the region and around the world include the following:

Belgium (☎ 02-640 6500, fax 646 8026) 363 Ave Louise, 1050 Brussels
Canada (☎ 0613-232 1500, fax 232 5184) 50 Range Rd, Ottawa, Ontario KIN 8J4
France (☎ 33-01 53 70 63 70, fax 01 53 70 63 66) 13 Ave Raymond Poincare, 75116 Paris

TANZANIA

Germany (☎ 0228-358051, fax 358226) Theaterplatz 26, 53177, Bonn

Japan (☎ 03-425 4531, fax 425 7844) 21-9, Kamiyoga 4, Chome Setagaya-ku, Tokyo 158

Kenya (☎ 02-721742, fax 218269) Continental House, corner of Uhuru Hwy and Harambee Ave, Nairobi
(☎ 011-229595, fax 227077) Palli House, Nyerere Ave, Mombasa

Mozambique (☎ 01-490110) Ujamaa House, PO Box 4515, Maputo

Rwanda (☎ 07-76074) Ave Paul VI near Ave de Rusumo, Kigali

South Africa (☎ 012-323 9041, 342 4393 fax 323 9042) PO Box 56572, Arcadia 0007, Pretoria

Switzerland (☎ 022-731 8920, fax 732 8255) 47 Ave Blanc, CH-1201, Geneva

Uganda (☎ 041-256272, fax 242890) 6 Kagera Rd, PO Box 5750, Kampala

UK (☎ 020-7499 8951, fax 7491 9321) 43 Hertford St, London W1Y 8DB

USA (☎ 202-939 6125, fax 797 7408) 2139 R St, NW, Washington DC 20008

Zambia (☎ 01-253320, 227698) Ujamaa House, 5200 United Nations Ave, Lusaka

Note that there is no Tanzanian embassy in Malawi.

Tanzania is also represented by embassies or consulates in the following countries: Italy (Rome), Netherlands (The Hague) and Zimbabwe (Harare).

Embassies in Tanzania

Some useful foreign embassies in Dar es Salaam are listed below. For a more complete listing, check the telephone book or alternatively, one of the free tourist magazines available in Dar es Salaam. Australians needing assistance should contact the Canadian embassy.

Belgium (☎ 112688) 5 Ocean Rd, Upanga

Burundi (☎ 117615 in Kigoma, ☎ 0695 2865) Lugalo Rd, Upanga, behind Palm Beach Hotel. Open from 9 am to 3 pm.

Canada (☎ 112831) 38 Mirambo St

France (☎ 666021) Bagamoyo Rd

Germany (☎ 117409) 10th floor, NIC Life House, Samora Ave

India (☎ 117175) 11th floor, NIC Life House, Samora Ave

Ireland (☎ 666211) Msasani Rd just off Haile Selassie Rd and near the International School

Italy (☎ 115935) 316 Lugalo Rd, Upanga

Kenya (☎ 112811, fax 113098) 14th floor, NIC Life House, Samora Ave. Open from 9 am to 2.30 pm weekdays.

Malawi (☎ 113240) 6th floor, Wing A, NIC Life House Branch Bldg, Sokoine Drive. Open from 8 am to noon and 2 to 5 pm Monday to Friday.

Mozambique 25 Garden Ave. Open from 8.30 am to 4.30 pm weekdays.

Netherlands (☎ 118593) 2nd floor, ATC House, Ohio St at Garden Ave

Rwanda (☎ 130119) 32 Ali Hassan Mwinyi Rd, Upanga. Open from 8 am to 3 pm.

Uganda (☎ 117646) Extelecoms House, 7th floor, Samora Ave

UK (☎ 112953) Samora Ave, near Askari Monument

USA (☎ 666010) 140 Msese Rd, Kinondoni

Zambia (☎ 118481) 5/9 Sokoine Drive at Ohio St. Open for visa services from 9 to 11 am and 2 to 3 pm Monday, Wednesday and Friday.

Zimbabwe (☎ 116789) 6th floor, Wing C, NIC Life House Branch Bldg, Sokoine Drive. Open from 8.30 am to 1 pm and 2 to 4 pm Monday to Friday.

CUSTOMS

The export of shells, coral, ivory and turtle shells is illegal. You are permitted to export a maximum of TSh 2000 without declaration. There is no limit on the importation of foreign currency, although amounts over US$10,000 must be declared.

MONEY
Currency

The unit of currency is the Tanzanian shilling (TSh). There are bills of TSh 10,000, 5000, 1000, 500, 200 and 100, and coins of TSh 200, 100, 50, 20, 10, five and one shilling(s).

Exchange Rates

country	unit		shilling
Australia	A$1	=	Tsh 505
Canada	C$1	=	Tsh 539
euro	€1	=	Tsh 803
France	10FF	=	Tsh 1224
Germany	DM1	=	Tsh 410
Japan	¥100	=	Tsh 719
New Zealand	NZ$1	=	Tsh 406
UK	UK£1	=	Tsh 1276
USA	US$1	=	Tsh 798

Exchanging Money

You can change cash and travellers cheques with a minimum of hassle at banks or foreign exchange (forex) bureaus in all major towns and cities; rates and commissions vary, so it pays to shop around. Forex bureaus are usually quicker and less bureaucratic, although many smaller towns do not have them; banks often change cash only. For US dollars, forex rates are usually the same or slightly better than bank rates. For other foreign currency, bank rates are usually a bit higher than those at the forex bureaus.

Although they are seldom checked, save at least some of your exchange receipts in order to be able to change any remaining Tanzanian shillings back to hard currency on departure. You can do this at banks or foreign exchange bureaus in Dar es Salaam and major towns, and at the forex bureaus at Dar es Salaam international airport.

Officially, nonresidents must pay for lodging, park fees, air tickets and similar items with hard currency, although in practice many hotels and some airlines will waive this requirement and convert to Tanzanian shillings at the going rate. For organised treks and safaris you'll need US dollars.

Since liberalisation of currency laws, there is essentially no black market for foreign currency. You can assume that the frequent offers you'll receive on the street to change at high rates are a set-up.

Cash US dollars are the most convenient foreign currency, although other major currencies are accepted in larger towns.

Travellers Cheques Travellers cheques are widely accepted in major towns; exchange rates are generally slightly lower than for cash. If you pay park entry fees with travellers cheques, change is usually given in Tanzanian shillings. In smaller towns, banks often will not exchange travellers cheques; you will need cash.

At a few places, you'll be required to show your receipt when cashing travellers cheques. Rather than carrying the original together with your cheques, it's better to make a copy – most banks will accept this.

Credit Cards Credit cards are accepted by many top end hotels, some tour operators, and increasingly by mid-range establishments. Most places charge a commission ranging from 5 to 15%.

Dar es Salaam, Arusha and Zanzibar Town are the only places in Tanzania where you can get cash advances (in local currency) against Visa or MasterCard.

Costs

Local food, accommodation, markets and public transport are inexpensive. A meal of rice and sauce in a local restaurant usually costs about TSh 500 or less, while budget lodging ranges from TSh 1000 for something very basic to about TSh 8000 for a simple but fairly comfortable room.

If you stay only in budget accommodation, eat local food and travel via public transport, you should have no trouble keeping costs to about US$20 per day or less (not including safaris or other organised activities). In contrast, imported items, organised tours and tourist-class hotels can be very pricey – costs can easily exceed US$200 per person per day on organised safaris. Even on the lower end, organised safaris will be more expensive than in neighbouring Kenya, and will average at least close to US$100 a day.

Mid-range travellers seeking a degree of comfort and western-style meals in pleasant surroundings should plan on spending between US$20 and US$60 per day for lodging, and between TSh 6000 and TSh 10,000 for a full-course meal.

Unless otherwise noted, all prices listed in this book are for nonresidents. National parks, museums, ferries, many hotels, and other places often offer resident rates which can be significantly lower. If you have a resident card, always ask if special rates are available. In addition to making you eligible for reduced rates, a resident card also entitles you to pay all fees in Tanzanian shillings.

Tipping & Bargaining

General guidelines for tipping and bargaining are the same in Tanzania as in most

TANZANIA

other countries in the region. See Bargaining in the Regional Facts for the Visitor chapter. For treks and safaris, it's common practice to tip drivers, guides and porters if service has been good. For vehicle safaris, a rough guideline is to give an additional day's wage for every five days worked. Exceptional service deserves a higher than average tip, while substandard service would call for a lower tip or even no tip at all.

For treks, tipping rates will depend in part on where you are trekking. Porters on Mt Kilimanjaro – who are accustomed to large bonuses from high-rolling trekkers, and familiar with the high trekking fees on the mountain – can be quite aggressive in their demands. As a general guideline, tip about 10% of the total bill paid for the trek, divided between the guides and porters. On Mt Meru, tipping practices are more moderate. Average tips for a standard trek are about US$10 to US$15 for the guide, and around US$5 for each porter.

Taxes

While most hotels include Tanzania's 20% value added tax (VAT) in their quoted prices, some hotels and many restaurants do not. To avoid surprises, always ask whether taxes are included in the price you're quoted.

POST & COMMUNICATIONS
Post

Airmail postage to the USA and Australia costs from TSh 500 (TSh 400 to the UK); postcards cost TSh 400. Allow about two weeks for letters to arrive in Dar es Salaam from abroad and longer for those sent to smaller towns. Sending small parcels (non-valuable items only) is relatively reliable, although things occasionally tend to go missing.

There is a poste restante service in Dar es Salaam and in most major towns; it's usually fairly well organised. There's a charge of TSh 200 per received letter. Most post offices will hold mail indefinitely.

Telephone

You can make domestic and international calls from Tanzania Telecom offices in all major towns; the offices are invariably located near the post office. Local calls average TSh 200 for three minutes, with a three minute minimum charge. Domestic STD calls start at about TSh 600 for three minutes. International calls start at around US$4 per minute. Outside major towns, the international exchange is often unreliable. There are card phones in Dar es Salaam and many major towns.

There are also private telecommunications centres in Dar es Salaam and most larger towns, which are more expensive but generally more efficient. Hotels usually charge at least double the Tanzania Telecom rates.

For smaller towns with just one or two-digit telephone numbers, you will need to go through the operator. Cell phones are very common in Tanzania. The numbers are six digits, preceded by either 0811 or 0812, although the 0811 prefix is expected to change (see the boxed text 'Telephone System Changes'). Rates for dialling cell phone numbers are higher than those charged for dialling land lines.

Telephone System Changes

Over the next several years, Tanzania Telecom is planning an overhaul of telephone systems in several regions of the country, including the Kilimanjaro, Arusha, Morogoro and Mwanza regions. Telephone numbers in these areas – and possibly also regional dialling codes – are expected to change completely (not just by one or two digits either). No detailed information about the changes was available as this book was going to print, although both international and local telephone operators should be able to inform you of any changes to the regional dialling codes in Tanzania.

There were also rumours that the dialling code for all Mobitel numbers (Mobitel is one of the main cell phone providers in the country) would change sometime in early 2000 from 0811 to (probably) 0711, although this had not yet been confirmed as this book went to print.

Fax

Faxes can be sent and received from most Tanzania Telecom offices, and from private telecommunications offices. Rates at Tanzania Telecom average about TSh 2700 per minute to Europe and the USA.

Email & Internet Access

Internet access and email facilities are available in Dar es Salaam and most major towns. There are a few Internet cafes in Dar es Salaam. Elsewhere, Internet and email services are generally provided by top end hotels and computer and telecommunications centres. You'll find these in Dar es Salaam, Arusha, Zanzibar Town, Mwanza and several other places (see the individual town entries for more details). On the mainland, most places charge between TSh 1500 to TSh 3000 per half hour to access the Internet, and about TSh 500 to receive email; Internet charges are somewhat higher on Unguja.

INTERNET RESOURCES

The Tanzania Tourist Board has a Web site at www.tanzania-web.com/home2.htm. Other Tanzania-specific Web sites are listed throughout the Tanzania chapters.

BOOKS

See Books in the Regional Facts for the Visitor chapter for more information on books on East Africa.

Lonely Planet

If you plan on spending an extended period in Tanzania, it's well worth buying a copy of Lonely Planet's *Tanzania, Zanzibar & Pemba*, which covers both the mainland and the Zanzibar archipelago in considerably more depth.

Guidebooks

The *Tourist Guide to Tanzania* (1991) by Gratian Luhikula is one of the better local guides, with some useful background information on places of interest.

Globetrotter's *Tanzania Tourist Guide*, by long-time Tanzania resident Graham Mercer is full of interesting facts and historical tidbits.

Dar es Salaam: A Dozen Drives Around the City by Laura Sykes & Uma Waide contains many interesting details about the city's history and development and is recommended if you'll be spending an extended period there.

Zanzibar: An Essential Guide by Mame McCuthein gives a good overview of Zanzibar Town and other destinations on Unguja.

Travel

Ernest Hemingway's *The Snows of Kilimanjaro* is a short story in which Hemingway deals with some of the larger questions of life in an East African setting.

In the Shadow of Kilimanjaro: On Foot Across East Africa by Rick Ridgeway is another good travellers tale, which may get you in the mood for your travels in Tanzania.

History & Politics

Memoirs of an Arabian Princess by Emily Said-Ruete is the very readable autobiography of a Zanzibari princess who elopes with a German to Europe. In recalling her early life, Said-Ruete paints an intriguing historical portrait of Unguja in the days of the sultans. The book is widely available in Zanzibar Town.

General

Through a Window by Jane Goodall is a vivid portrayal of the author's research and life with the chimpanzees of Gombe Stream National Park.

African Voices, African Lives by Patricia Caplan focuses around village life on Mafia Island.

FILMS

Films shot at least in part in Tanzania include the 1951 classic *The African Queen*, starring Katharine Hepburn and Humphrey Bogart, and *Mogambo* (1953), with Clark Gable, Ava Gardner and Grace Kelly.

Numerous documentaries focusing on Tanzania's wildlife have been filmed on location, including *Africa: The Serengeti* (1994), which was shot in both Tanzania and Kenya, and focuses on the annual wildebeest migration.

TANZANIA

NEWSPAPERS & MAGAZINES

The *International Herald Tribune* and some international news magazines are available in Dar es Salaam and Arusha. Tanzanian English-language dailies include the *Guardian* and the *Daily News*.

RADIO & TV

Radio Tanzania, the government-aligned national station, broadcasts in both English and Swahili; Radio Tanzania Zanzibar broadcasts in Swahili only.

Televisions are common in larger towns and cities and almost all top end hotels have cable TV. Most local programming is in Swahili.

PHOTOGRAPHY & VIDEO
Film & Equipment

Print film is available in major towns, although selection is limited. A roll of 100 ASA 36 exposures will cost between TSh 2000 and TSh 3000. Faster speed film and (sometimes) slide film are available in Dar es Salaam and a few larger towns.

For developing, the Burhani chain is the best. The main shop in Dar es Salaam does very good work; quality is not as reliable in some of their other outlets. The cost of developing a role of 36 exposures ranges from about TSh 8000 in Dar es Salaam to TSh 5000 elsewhere.

For general tips on what equipment to bring along, see Photography & Video in the Regional Facts for the Visitor chapter. Whatever equipment you bring, it's important to have a bag that will protect it from dust, as dust seeps into everything if you're travelling on Tanzania's unpaved roads during the dry season.

Restrictions

Don't take photos of anything connected with the government or the military, including government offices, post offices, banks, ports, train stations and airports.

TIME

Time in Tanzania is GMT/UTC plus three hours. There is no daylight savings time adjustment.

ELECTRICITY

Tanzania uses 230V, 50 cycles, AC. Surges and troughs are not uncommon. Power cuts also occur with some frequency, particularly outside major towns, though they generally don't last very long.

Plugs and sockets vary but are usually the British three-square-pin or two-round-pin variety. Adapters are available in Tanzania.

WEIGHTS & MEASURES

Tanzania uses the metric system. Road distances are signposted in kilometres.

LAUNDRY

Most hotels, including budget places, can assist you with your laundry. Local rates are as low as TSh 100 to TSh 200 per piece. Mid-range and top end hotels often charge five to 10 times this amount.

If you want to wash your laundry yourself, most hotels will be happy to lend you a bucket and show you to a water tap. Small packets of laundry detergent are on sale in even the smallest towns for TSh 100.

DANGERS & ANNOYANCES

In general, Tanzania is a safe, hassle-free country. The main danger for most travellers is road accidents, particularly involving buses. See the Getting Around chapter for more on this. In terms of muggings and robberies, Tanzania is no worse than most other places, and can be a relief if you've recently been somewhere like Nairobi.

There have been sporadic occurrences of organised crime in some of the more remote areas near the Kenyan border, and in the Serengeti's Western Corridor, particularly during the low season. It's best to follow the advice of your embassy and tour operator when planning travel to these places.

See Dangers and Annoyances in The Zanzibar Archipelago and the Dar es Salaam chapters for more information.

LEGAL MATTERS

As in many areas of Africa, Tanzania's police – many of whom are underpaid and ill-equipped for their jobs – will generally be of little assistance in the event of an emergency. In some places, particularly on Unguja, they will all too often be in on the crime themselves. Nevertheless, if you are the victim of a crime, you should file a police report. While this is usually time consuming, most insurance companies require it before they will consider any compensation or reimbursement for your losses. If your passport is stolen, get a police report before trying to contact your embassy or going to immigration.

BUSINESS HOURS
Government offices are open from 7.30 am to 3.30 pm Monday to Friday. Business hours are from 8 am to 5 pm Monday to Friday and from 8.30 am to 1 pm Saturday; many shops close for an hour between noon and 2 pm, and on Friday afternoon for mosque services.

PUBLIC HOLIDAYS & SPECIAL EVENTS
Tanzanians observe the following public holidays:

New Year's Day 1 January
Zanzibar Revolution Day 12 January
CCM Foundation Day 5 February
Eid al Fitr (end of Ramadan)
Eid al Kebir (also called Eid al Haji); celebration of the sacrifice of Ismail, and an important time for pilgrimages to Mecca
Easter March/April – Good Friday, Holy Saturday and Easter Monday
Union Day 26 April
Labour Day 1 May
Maulidi (Mohammed's birthday)
Saba Saba (Peasants' Day) 7 July
Nane Nane (Farmers' Day) 8 August
Independence Day 9 December
Christmas Day 25 December
Boxing Day 26 December

The dates of Muslim holidays are based on the Islamic lunar calendar and are not fixed. In general, they fall about 11 days earlier each year.

For information on the Zanzibar International Film Festival and other festivals on Unguja, see this section in The Zanzibar Archipelago chapter.

ACTIVITIES
Boating & Kayaking
Local boat trips can be arranged anywhere along the coast or on Tanzania's offshore islands. Possibilities include trips in canoes among the mangrove swamps, or excursions to the many tiny islands off Pemba and Mafia Island. You'll need to bring along whatever food and water you require.

Tanzania offers some good kayaking possibilities for the adventurous, with the best places being along the coast and around offshore islands. You'll need to organise everything, including equipment, yourself; there are not yet any outfitters in Tanzania. A good source of information is Kayak Africa, which has a Web site at www.kayakafrica.co.za. See the Tanzania Getting Around chapter for details of dhow trips.

Cycling
In rural areas, cycling is one of the best ways of getting to know Tanzania. A good source of information is The International Bicycle Fund (email ibike@ibike.com), which organises cycling tours in Tanzania. See the Tanzania Getting Around chapter for more details on cycling in Tanzania. The Web site is www.ibike.org/bikeafrica

Diving & Snorkelling
Tanzania's coast and many of its offshore islands are edged with spectacular coral reefs, which offer superb diving and snorkelling opportunities. For information on dive outfitters, see Diving in the Dar es Salaam and The Zanzibar Archipelago chapters.

Hiking & Trekking
There is good hiking in the Usambara and Pare mountains in the north-east, around Tukuyu in the south-west, and in Udzungwa Mountains and Mahale Mountains national parks. The Uluguru mountains near Morogoro and the lower slopes of Mt Kilimanjaro near Marangu also offer many hikes and walks, as does the area around Iringa.

The main trekking destinations are Mt Kilimanjaro, Mt Meru and the Crater Highlands. For an overview of the possibilities, see the Northern Tanzania chapter. For

TANZANIA

Considerations for Responsible Diving

The popularity of diving is placing immense pressure on many sites (see also the boxed text 'Safety Guidelines for Diving' in the Zanzibar Archipelago chapter). Please consider the following tips in order to help preserve the ecology and beauty of the reefs:

- Do not use anchors on the reef, and take care not to ground boats on coral. Encourage dive operators and regulatory bodies to establish permanent moorings at popular dive sites.

- Avoid touching living marine organisms with your body or dragging equipment across the reef. Polyps can be damaged by even the gentlest contact. Never stand on corals, even if they look solid and robust. If you must hold on to the reef, only touch exposed rock or dead coral.

- Be conscious of your fins. Even without contact the surge from heavy fin strokes near the reef can damage delicate organisms. When treading water in shallow reef areas, take care not to kick up clouds of sand. Settling sand can easily smother the delicate organisms of the reef.

- Practice and maintain proper buoyancy control. Major damage can be done by divers descending too fast and colliding with the reef. Make sure you are correctly weighted and that your weight belt is positioned so that you stay horizontal. If you have not dived for a while, have a practice dive in a pool before taking to the reef. Be aware that buoyancy can change over the period of an extended trip: initially you may breathe harder and need more weight; a few days later you may breathe more easily and need less weight.

- Take great care in underwater caves. Spend as little time in them as possible as your air bubbles may get caught within the roof and thereby leave previously submerged organisms high and dry. Taking turns to inspect the interior of a small cave will lessen the chances of damaging contact.

- Resist the temptation to collect or buy corals or shells. Apart from the ecological damage and the fact that their export is illegal in Tanzania, taking home marine souvenirs depletes the beauty of a site and spoils the enjoyment of others. The same goes for marine archaeological sites (mainly shipwrecks). Respect their integrity; some sites are even protected from looting by law.

- Ensure that you take home all your rubbish and any litter you may find as well. Plastics in particular are a serious threat to marine life. Turtles can mistake plastic for jellyfish and eat it.

- Resist the temptation to feed fish. You may disturb their normal eating habits, encourage aggressive behaviour or feed them food that is detrimental to their health.

- Minimise your disturbance of marine animals. In particular, do not ride on the backs of turtles as this causes them great anxiety.

---

detailed information on routes in these and other areas, get a copy of Lonely Planet's *Trekking in East Africa*.

Safaris

Many travellers come to Tanzania to visit its national parks and game reserves, all of which offer an exceptional diversity of wildlife in spectacular natural settings. See the Safaris in Tanzania section in the Organised Safaris chapter for more information on different types of safaris and how to go about organising them.

LANGUAGE COURSES

Visitors interested in studying Swahili can contact the following:

ELCT Language & Orientation School (☎/fax 056-3173) PO Box 740, Morogoro, c/o Lutheran Junior Seminary

Institute of Swahili and Foreign Languages (☎ 054-230724) PO Box 882, Zanzibar, attn: Department of Swahili for Foreigners

KIU Ltd (☎ 051-851509, 0812-781160, fax 051-850503, email kiu@raha.com) PO Box 2345, Dar es Salaam, c/o Salvation Army Hostel

Maryknoll Language School PO Box 298, Musoma
Nyumba ya Sanaa (☎ 051-133960) Ohio St, next to Sheraton Hotel in Dar es Salaam; courses offered together with KIU Ltd

Swahili: A Complete Course for Beginners by Joan Russell, and an older edition of the same name by DV Perrott, provide a good start for those who want to study Swahili on their own. Both editions, as well as several other introductory Swahili books and some English-Swahili dictionaries are available in Dar es Salaam, Arusha and Zanzibar Town.

ACCOMMODATION
Camping
All of the national parks have established camp sites. 'Ordinary' camp sites have basic facilities, including toilets, fireplaces and often (though not always) a water source. Many of those in the crowded northern circuit parks are in poor condition, while those in the less visited parks can be quite pleasant. 'Special' camp sites are generally smaller than ordinary sites and usually have no facilities other than pit toilets. Unlike ordinary camp sites, they must be booked in advance. For either type of camp site, you will need to bring everything, including drinking water. Although you can purify water in some places, it's best not to count on this as the sources in many camp sites are very dirty.

Outside of the national parks, there are camping grounds in or near many major towns, although some of the sites leave a lot to be desired. Some hotels also allow camping on their grounds. There are, however, an increasing number of good private camp sites opening up in areas near national parks or along major overland routes, although these are still not widespread. Costs average between US$3 and US$5 per person per night.

If you plan on camping anywhere near a village, ask the village elders for permission first.

Guesthouses & Hostels
Almost every Tanzanian town of any size has at least one (usually very basic) guest-house. Larger towns will have several to choose from. Rates average from TSh 2000 to TSh 3000 per night. For those who like their peace and quiet, guesthouses without bars are usually the best choice. Most guest-houses offer shared facilities only, though some have rooms with a private bathroom; these will cost an additional TSh 1000 to TSh 2000. In many towns, water can be a problem during the dry season, particularly at less expensive places. Note that in Swahili, the word *hotel* (or *hoteli)* does not mean lodging, but rather food and drink only. If you are seeking accommodation, the more common term used is *guesti* or 'guesthouse'.

There are mission hostels and guesthouses all over Tanzania. While these are primarily for missionaries and aid organisation staff, they often have extra room available for independent travellers. In most cases, they are clean, safe, and very good value.

Hotels
All major towns have at least one mid-range hotel. Dar es Salaam, Arusha, Zanzibar Town, and several other centres also offer a good selection of top end accommodation. Most mid-range places have rooms with bathroom, and often also with air-con. Facilities are invariably somewhat faded but adequate. Prices range from US$20 to US$60 per person per night.

Top end hotels offer all the amenities you would expect for the price you will be paying – from US$60 to US$300 or more per person per night.

Homestays
Students spending extended periods in Tanzania studying Swahili frequently arrange to stay with local families. Costs are generally very reasonable; you will usually be expected to take your meals with the family. If you're interested in doing this, ask the staff at the language institute where you are studying.

FOOD
In Dar es Salaam and other major towns, there is a good selection of places to eat, ranging from local food stalls to western-style restaurants. The choice is more limited

in smaller towns and villages. The main meal is at midday; many places are closed in the evening.

Local Food

One of the most common local dishes is *ugali*, a staple made from maize or cassava flour and eaten with a sauce usually containing meat, fish, beans and/or greens. Good ugali is neither too dry nor too sticky; ask locals where to find the best. Rice and cooked plantains are also served frequently as staples; chips are ubiquitous in larger towns. Also very popular and available almost everywhere is *nyama choma* (grilled meat). On the coast and in the Zanzibar archipelago you'll find a wide range of traditional Swahili dishes based on seafood cooked in coconut.

Early in the mornings on Unguja and in many parts of the mainland, vendors sell *uji*, a thin, sweet porridge made from bean flour, as well as bread and hard-boiled eggs. Another street food you'll often see in the mornings is *vitambua*, small rice cakes vaguely resembling a tiny, very thick pancake. On Unguja, look for *mkate wa kumimina*, a bread made from a batter similar to that used for vitambua. Many regions of Tanzania, notably in the north-east around Tanga and near Lake Victoria, have fresh *mtindi* (also called *mtindi wa maziwa*), a cultured milk product similar to yoghurt.

Vegetarian

There is not much that is specifically billed as 'vegetarian', but there are many options and you can almost always find a basic beans and rice dish. In the capital and larger towns, the Indian restaurants are good places to try for vegetarian meals. Some tour operators are willing to cater to vegetarians, as well as other special dietary requests such as kosher or halaal.

Self-Catering

In general, a wide range of imported products is available in major towns, although the items are often expensive. Locally produced items, including dairy products, are very inexpensive.

In Dar es Salaam, there are several well stocked supermarkets, and in Arusha, Mwanza, and Zanzibar Town, there are numerous smaller grocery stores that sell a decent range of imported products such as processed cheese, peanut butter, crackers, cereals, and similar items.

DRINKS
Nonalcoholic Drinks

Sodas are available everywhere, usually cold; they cost about TSh 200 on the street. Fresh juices, including pineapple, sugar cane and orange, are also widely available and inexpensive.

Alcoholic Drinks

Mbege (banana beer) is a speciality of the Kilimanjaro area. In cashew growing areas, you will sometimes note a strong alcohol smell when passing through villages; it's usually from *gongo* (sometimes also called *nipa*), a distilled cashew drink which is illegal. The brewed version, *uraka*, is legal as is *konyagi*, the general term for local liquor. Local brews made from pawpaws are also common.

Safari and Kilimanjaro are the local beers. Kenyan, South African and German beers are also available. Beers cost between TSh 450 and TSh 600.

ENTERTAINMENT

Every town has a bar, except small places along the heavily Muslim coast. Dar es Salaam and Arusha have the best selection of nightclubs.

In Dar es Salaam, good-quality western films are shown at some of the cultural centres. Otherwise, at most theatres throughout the country you will find only B-grade westerns or Indian films.

In towns that see a lot of tourists, there are often performances of traditional dancing or drumming. Many hotels offer live music, generally on weekends.

SPECTATOR SPORTS

Soccer is the main spectator sport; no matter where you are on a Sunday afternoon, you are sure to find a match to watch.

SHOPPING

Tanzania has a good selection of local crafts, ranging from basketry and woodcarving to textiles and paintings. Craft centres and artists cooperatives in the capital and major towns often have good buys and prices are generally very reasonable (though bargain-ing is par for the course in most places, es-pecially those catering to tourists). Things to look for include Makonde carvings (best purchased in Mtwara or in Dar es Salaam), Tingatinga paintings (the best buys are in Dar es Salaam and Zanzibar Town) and tex-tiles (Zanzibar Town has some great buys).

Getting There & Away

For information on getting to Tanzania from outside East Africa, see the regional Getting There & Away chapter.

AIR

International flights to/from Tanzania are handled by Dar es Salaam international airport, Kilimanjaro international airport (situated between Arusha and Moshi) and Unguja (Zanzibar Island) airport. The airport in Mwanza handles some regional flights.

Departure Tax

The departure tax for regional and international flights from Tanzania is US$20, payable in US dollars. It's often included in the ticket price for international flights.

Burundi

Air Tanzania flies between Bujumbura and Dar es Salaam costing US$247/487 one way/return.

Kenya

There are five flights weekly between Dar es Salaam and Nairobi on Air Tanzania and four flights weekly on Kenya Airways. Both offer flights for US$150/300 one way/return. There are three flights weekly between Dar es Salaam and Mombasa on Air Tanzania (US$75 one way).

Air Kenya Aviation (☎ 02-501601, email resvns@airkenya.com) flies between Kilimanjaro international airport and Nairobi daily (US$135 one way). Precision Air offers a service between Kilimanjaro and Mombasa (US$127) if there is sufficient demand, which is infrequent.

Air Tanzania and Kenya Airways offer daily flights between Unguja (Zanzibar Island) and Nairobi (US$145/290) via Mombasa (US$66/132). It may be cheaper to fly to Mombasa and pick up a good deal on to Nairobi. Air Kenya Aviation occasionally runs special deals from Unguja to Nairobi.

RenAir/SkyLink fly twice weekly between Mwanza and Nairobi's Wilson airport (US$195).

Rwanda

Weekly flights on Air Tanzania connect Kigali with Dar es Salaam (US$225/300), Kilimanjaro (US$137/274) via Mwanza (US$123), and Unguja (US$268/300) via Kilimanjaro.

Uganda

There are flights about three times weekly between Entebbe and Dar es Salaam on Air Tanzania (via Kilimanjaro) and also Uganda Airlines (via Nairobi), and twice weekly on SA Alliance Air (direct). Each airline charges US$242/342 one way/return, while Air Tanzania charges US$195/390 to Kilimanjaro.

There are weekly flights with Air Tanzania between Entebbe and Unguja (Zanzibar Island) (US$386/564) via Mwanza (US$144/288). There are weekly flights between Entebbe and Mwanza with Eagle Air (US$100 one way).

LAND
Burundi

The border between Tanzania and Burundi has been officially reopened, though it is not often used by independent travellers due to the situation in Burundi and the ongoing refugee crisis in western Tanzania. The road between Kigoma and Lusahunga in particular is not considered safe at present for independent travellers; get a security update from your embassy before travelling in this region. The most commonly used crossing is at the Kobero bridge border crossing between Ngara (Tanzania) and Muyinga (Burundi).

In Tanzania, the road from Nzega (southwest of Shinyanga) to the Burundi border via Ngara is fairly good, though there is little public transport; hitching is the main option. From both Bukoba and Kigoma, the trip to Burundi via the Kobero bridge crossing is best done in stages via Lusahunga.

Kenya

The main route between Tanzania and Kenya is the tarmac road connecting Arusha and Nairobi via the border crossing at Namanga. There are also border crossings at Horohoro, north of Tanga; at Taveta/Holili, east of Moshi; at Illassit, north-east of Moshi; at Bologonya in the northern Serengeti; and at Isebania north of Musoma.

Mombasa Tawfiq/Takrim runs buses twice daily (several times weekly during the low season) between Dar es Salaam and Mombasa (TSh 9000, 10 to 11 hours). Buses depart Dar es Salaam at about 8.30 am and 2.30 pm. There are also daily buses between Tanga and Mombasa (TSh 3500, six hours plus extra time to complete border formalities).

There is a bus most days between Moshi and Mombasa (TSh 7500). Otherwise this trip can be done in stages if you want to do it the hard way (see Voi following).

Voi Minibuses run daily between Moshi and Holili on the border. From there you can hitch or walk (3km) to Taveta in Kenya, from where there is transport to Voi and on to Mombasa.

Nairobi Direct buses link Dar es Salaam with Nairobi several times daily (TSh 15,000, 12 to 14 hours). Buses depart Dar es Salaam between 6.30 and 9 am. Tawfiq has the most frequent service (daily departures at 7 and 8 am). Try to avoid changing money at the border as the rates are poor.

For travel between Arusha and Nairobi, the best option, and that used by most travellers, is one of the daily shuttles. These are comfortable 20-seater buses which cover the route in about five hours (from Arusha), including about half an hour to cross the border. The one-way fare between Arusha and Nairobi is US$25 (TSh 8000 for residents); between Moshi and Nairobi the fare is US$35 (TSh 13,000 for residents). With a little prodding, all the companies seem prepared to sell tickets to nonresidents for resident prices as long as you purchase the ticket directly with them rather than through a tour operator.

Shuttle bus companies include:

Davanu (☎ 055-53416, 057-53749) has departures daily at 8 am and 2 pm from Arusha. There are connections from Moshi daily at 11.30 am. The Arusha booking office is at the Novotel. The Moshi office is on the ground floor of Kahawa House near the CRDB bank on the clock tower roundabout.

Riverside (☎ 057-2639, 3916) has departures daily at 8 am and 2 pm from Arusha and at 10.30 pm from Moshi. In Arusha, book tickets at Riverside's office on Sokoine Rd. Pick-up points in Arusha are the Riverside office and the Novotel. In Moshi, the booking office and pick-up point are at New Livingstone Hotel. Many travellers complain that Riverside promises to drop them at their hotels in Nairobi, but just takes everyone to the New Stanley on arrival.

Regular buses also link Arusha and Nairobi daily (TSh 6000), but it's faster to take a shuttle. There are also share-taxis from Arusha bus station to the border (about TSh 2500), where you'll have to walk a few hundred metres and then pick up another vehicle on the other side (about US$6 to Nairobi).

Masai Mara There's no public transport along the route linking the northern Serengeti with Kenya's Masai Mara Game Reserve. You are permitted to cross in a private vehicle assuming you have the appropriate vehicle documentation. See Car & Motorcycle in the regional Getting Around chapter for details. You will have to pay park fees on both sides. If you need a visa for Kenya, you'll need to arrange that in advance as well.

Kisumu Minibuses run throughout the day between Mwanza and Musoma (TSh 2500). The first bus in either direction departs about 7 am. Some continue on to Isebania on the Kenyan border (TSh 3000 from Mwanza). Otherwise, there are frequent minibuses from Musoma to the border (TSh 1000) where you can change to Kenyan transport for Kisii and Kisumu.

Rwanda

Due to ongoing instability along the Tanzania-Burundi border just to the south, get an update on the latest security conditions before crossing overland between Rwanda and Tanzania or travelling in this region

Mwanza to Kigali The main crossing is at Rusumu Falls near Rusumu, south-west of Bukoba. The main junction on the Tanzanian side is Ngara, from where there is daily transport to the border. For details of air and road connections to Ngara, see Mwanza and Bukoba in the Lake Victoria chapter. At the border you'll need to change to Rwandan transport. Minibuses to Kigali cost RFr 1400 and take three hours.

Samma bus lines has a twice weekly direct service between Mwanza and Kigali (TSh 15,000).

Kigoma to Kigali Buses run at least twice weekly during the dry season from Kigoma to Lusahunga (TSh 7500) via Kasulu and Nyakanazi. Some buses go only as far as Nyakanazi (en route to Kahama and Mwanza), in which case you'll need to catch a minibus for the last leg between Nyakanazi and Lusahunga. The road between Kasulu and Lusahunga is in bad shape and can take several days. From Lusahunga, there is fairly regular traffic (minibus or hitching) to the border at Rusumu Falls.

Warning

There have been several instances of banditry along the road between Kasulu and Lusahunga, and the area isn't considered safe for independent travellers. Get a security update before travelling in this region.

Uganda

Direct The most commonly used border crossing is at Mutukula, north-west of Bukoba. Tawfiq runs buses at least three times weekly between Bukoba and Kampala, departing Bukoba at 7 am Tuesday, Thursday and Saturday and arriving in Kampala about 3 pm the next day (TSh 10,000). There are also minibuses most days between Bukoba and Mutukula (three to six hours), from where you need to walk a short distance over the border to catch Ugandan transport to Kyotera and Masaka. Due to improved road conditions it's possible to do the Masaka-Bukoba journey in one day, although not always in the wet season. From Masaka there is frequent transport to Kampala; plan on spending the night in Masaka.

The border crossing is not usually problematic. There's not much traffic along this route, although it's used by many overland companies. If you require a visa, have extra money handy (no photos are required).

There is also a crossing at Nkurungu, to the west of Mutukula, but the road is bad and little transport passes this way.

Via Kenya Tawfiq/Takrim run direct buses several times weekly between Dar es Salaam and Kampala via Arusha and Nairobi (TSh 36,000, 24 hours). Departures from Dar es Salaam are at 6.30 am, usually on Thursday and Saturday.

For details of the route from Mwanza via Kisumu (Kenya) see the Kenya Getting There & Away chapter.

SEA & LAKE
Departure Tax

For all boat and ferry services from Tanzanian ports there is a US$5 port tax (TSh 500 for residents).

Burundi

Ferry A weekly ferry service on the *MV Liemba* between Kigoma and Bujumbura was just resuming as this chapter was being researched. The boat is scheduled to depart Kigoma on Sunday about 6 pm, arriving in Bujumbura on Monday morning. Prices are US$30/25/20 for 1st/2nd/3rd class.

Tickets bought in Bujumbura and Mpulungu (Zambia) must be paid for in US dollars.

First class is relatively comfortable, with two reasonably clean bunks and a window. Second class cabins (four bunks) and 3rd class seating, however, are both poorly ventilated and uncomfortable. If you're going to travel 3rd class, it's more comfortable to find yourself deck space than to sit in the 3rd class seating section. Food is available on board and must be paid for in Tanzanian shillings, so bring enough money to cover this, but it's best to bring some supplements, as well as your own water.

For information on the MV *Liemba's* route between Mpulungu and Kigoma, see the regional Getting There & Away chapter. The boat no longer services Kalemie in Congo (Zaïre).

Lake Taxi & Matatu Your other option is to go from Kigoma to Kibirizi (about 3km north of Kigoma) by foot or minibus (see the Gombe Stream National Park Getting There & Away section in the Western Tanzania chapter). Small, motorised lake taxis depart Kibirizi daily except Sunday for Gombe Stream National Park (TSh 1000) and on to the Burundi border (TSh 2000). Once there, you'll need to walk a couple of kilometres to

the Burundi border crossing, and minibuses to Nyanza Lac and Bujumbura.

Kenya
On the coast, dhows sail sporadically between Mombasa and Unguja (Zanzibar) and Pemba islands. Allow plenty of time for journeys and bring all your own food and water. Ask at the port in Zanzibar Town or in Wete on Pemba for information about sailings.

At the time of research there was no ferry service on Lake Victoria between Tanzania and Kenya.

Uganda
On Sunday the MV *Victoria* departs Mwanza at 2 pm, arriving in Bukoba about 9 pm. It departs Bukoba at about 3 am on Monday and continues on to Port Bell, arriving Monday about 8 am. It departs Port Bell on Monday at 4pm, arriving back in Mwanza on Tuesday morning by about 11 am. It's a good trip and the fares are US$35/30 in 1st/2nd class sleepers and US$25/20 in 2nd/3rd class seats.

Getting Around

AIR
Domestic Air Services
There are two noncharter airlines operating domestic flights within Tanzania. Air Tanzania is the national carrier. The major private carrier is Precision Air. Service on both has improved markedly in recent times, although you can still expect cancellations and delays, particularly on Air Tanzania.

Charter airlines are also commonly used for domestic and regional travel, particularly for destinations not served by the two larger carriers. Prices can be reasonable if you have a group large enough to fill the plane (commonly either three or five-seaters). For charter flights to Unguja see Getting There & Away in the Stone Town section of the Zanzibar Archipelago chapter.

Nonresidents can pay for Air Tanzania flights in US dollars, Tanzanian shillings or with major credit cards (charged in US dollars at the current bank rate). Precision Air accepts US dollars cash and credit cards. Tanzanian shillings can sometimes also be used, converted at the going rate. Air Tanzania's rates are heavily subsidised, and are roughly equivalent to resident rates on Precision Air. Precision Air's nonresident rates, however, are significantly higher on almost all routes. Both Air Tanzania and Precision Air have offices in Dar es Salaam and other major towns. All tickets must be reconfirmed.

Air Tanzania operates flights between Dar es Salaam and Kilimanjaro international airport, midway between Arusha and Moshi, (TSh 51,000, daily), Mwanza (TSh 80,500, daily), Mtwara (TSh 57,000, three times weekly) and Unguja (TSh 22,500, five times weekly), and between Kilimanjaro international airport and Unguja (TSh 49,000, three times weekly) and Mwanza (TSh 55,000, twice weekly).

Precision Air services these same routes, and also flies to several additional destinations including Iringa, Mbeya, Mafia Island, Shinyanga and Ngara as well as to Arusha and Moshi airports. Some sample nonresident fares are: Dar es Salaam to Arusha/Mbeya (US$165), Arusha to Mwanza (US$145), Arusha to Unguja (US$165), Mwanza to Bukoba (US$65), Iringa to Mbeya (US$70).

Domestic Departure Tax
Domestic departure tax is TSh 3000 (US$4); it is often included in the ticket price.

BUS
Road Safety
Road accidents are probably your biggest safety risk while travelling in Tanzania, with speeding buses being among the worst offenders. Road conditions are poor and road users often very substandard. The situation can be even worse where road conditions are good, as buses and minibuses move along at dizzying speeds. The Dar es Salaam-Arusha highway is one of the most notorious stretches. In the wake of several fatal bus accidents in recent years, stricter speed controls have been introduced on some of the main roads and several bus companies have begun working to build a reputation for safety through the moderation of speed and vehicle maintenance, although there is still quite a lot of room left for improvement.

Buses are not permitted to drive at night in Tanzania. Although this rule is sometimes ignored, the last departure on any particular route will generally be timed so that the bus should reach its destination by evening (assuming that all goes well). For cross-border routes, departures are usually timed so that night driving will be done once outside of Tanzania.

On the northern routes (Dar es Salaam to Moshi and Arusha), Fresh ya Shamba is one of the better lines. On the southern routes (Dar es Salaam to Iringa and Mbeya), the best is Scandinavian. Ask locals which bus lines they recommend for other areas, or whether any competitors have started on these routes.

Bus Types & Reservations

For the major long-distance routes you'll generally have a choice of buses ranging from express to ordinary. Express buses are only marginally more expensive than ordinary buses, but are more comfortable, less crowded, and do not make as many stops en route. Other than on heavily travelled routes, it's generally not necessary to book in advance. Exceptions to this have been noted in the regional sections. Each bus line will have its own booking office at or near the bus station.

Most express buses depart on or close to schedule, so arrive in time to get your seat. Ordinary buses depart when full; no advance reservation is required although it's usually best to arrive well before departure if there will only be one bus going that day, in order to get a seat.

Most express buses have a compartment underneath for luggage. Otherwise, stow your backpack under your seat or in the front of the bus, where there is usually space near the driver.

Prices are more or less fixed, although for heavily travelled routes bus companies trying to fill their seats will often reduce prices to undercut their competitors.

If you want to go only a short stretch along a main route, express buses will generally drop you off, but you'll usually be required to pay the full fare to the next major destination.

MINIBUS & SHARE-TAXI

For shorter trips away from the main routes, the choice is generally between ordinary buses and minibuses (sometimes referred to as *dalla-dallas*, and equivalent to Kenyan *matatus*).

Like ordinary buses, minibuses and share-taxis leave when they are full; fares are fixed and journeys are almost always slow and uncomfortable (although share-taxis are a little faster than ordinary buses). Note that share-taxis of the type found in many areas of West Africa are relatively rare, except in the north near Arusha. See also the Local Transport section at the end of this chapter.

TRAIN

Tanzania has two train lines, which operate on different gauges: the TAZARA line links Dar es Salaam with Kapiri Mposhi in Zambia via Mbeya and Tunduma; the Tanzanian Railway Corporation's Central Line links Dar es Salaam with Kigoma and Mwanza via Morogoro, Dodoma and Tabora. A branch of the Central Line links Tabora with Mpanda; there is another spur between Dodoma and Singida. TAZARA is the more comfortable and efficient of the two lines.

While most travellers do not have any troubles, as with travel anywhere, it's best to keep an eye on your gear at all times, particularly in 3rd class. Even in 1st and 2nd class, make sure the window is jammed shut at night to avoid the possibility of someone entering when the train stops at stations. There's usually a piece of wood provided for this purpose, as the window locks often don't work.

Classes

There are three classes: 1st class (two or four-bed compartments); 2nd class sleeping (six-bed compartments); and 3rd class (seats only, varies from very crowded and basic to tolerable, depending on the train). Some trains also have a 2nd class sitting section, generally almost half the price of 2nd class sleeping, with comfortable seats, one seat per person. Men and women can only travel together in the sleeping sections if they book the entire compartment. Food is available on the trains (meals average about TSh 2500) and from vendors at the stations.

Reservations

Tickets for 1st and 2nd class should be reserved at least three to five days in advance, although occasionally you will be able to get a seat on the day of travel. It's not unheard of for railway staff to tell you all seats are full just to get a bribe from you. Depending on how good your interpersonal skills are and how badly you want the seat, you may have to arrange a small 'gift'.

Schedules & Costs

TAZARA The TAZARA line runs express and ordinary trains. Express trains depart

Dar es Salaam on Tuesday and Friday at 5.34 pm, arriving in Mbeya the following day at 1.10 pm. Ordinary trains depart Dar es Salaam on Monday, Thursday and Saturday at 11.25 am, arriving in Mbeya the following day at 12.24 pm. In the other direction, express trains depart Mbeya on Wednesday and Saturday at 12.11 pm, arriving in Dar es Salaam at 8.30 am the next day. Ordinary trains depart Mbeya on Tuesday, Friday and Sunday at 5 pm, arriving in Dar es Salaam about 6 pm the next day.

Fares to travel between Dar es Salaam & Mbeya are:

	1st	2nd	3rd
express	TSh 19,400	TSh 12,700	TSh 7600
ordinary	TSh 16,700	TSh 11,100	TSh 6700

For fares and schedules to and from Kapiri Mposhi, see Zambia in the Land section of the Regional Getting There & Away chapter. Note that fares on the TAZARA line were set to increase by about 15% within the lifetime of this book.

Central Line Central Line trains from Dar es Salaam to Kigoma and Mwanza depart on Sunday, Tuesday, Wednesday and Friday at 5 pm. The journey to both destinations normally takes between 36 and 40 hours, although it can sometimes take 50 hours or more. In the other direction, trains from Mwanza to Dar es Salaam depart on Sunday, Tuesday, Thursday and Friday at 6 pm; departures from Kigoma leave on the same days at 5 pm. If you're travelling between Mwanza and Kigoma, you'll need to spend at least one night in Tabora waiting for the connection.

Central Line has a helpful information centre (☎ 051-117833) at the TRC building on the corner of Railway St and Sokoine Drive in Dar es Salaam. It's open from 8 am to 1 pm and 2 to 5 pm weekdays, and from 8 am to 1 pm weekends and holidays.

CAR & MOTORCYCLE
About 20% of Tanzania's road network is paved. Many secondary roads are in poor condition at best and impassable during the rainy season. For most trips outside major towns you will need a 4WD; inquire with locals about road conditions before setting out.

While road accidents are probably your biggest safety risk travelling in Tanzania, you can possibly minimise the risks by being in your own vehicle or with a competent driver so speed can be controlled.

Tanzania follows the British keep-left traffic system. At roundabouts, traffic in the roundabout has the right of way. Avoid driving at night if possible. If you're not used to driving in Africa, watch out for pedestrians, children and animals on the road. Especially in rural areas remember that many people have only limited driving experience and are not aware of required braking distances and similar concepts; moderate your speed accordingly.

In towns, you'll see many street signs in Swahili: *barabara* (often abbreviated 'Br') means 'road', and *mtaa* (often abbreviated 'Mt') means 'street'. Thus Mtaa wa India or Mt India means 'India Street'.

Petrol costs about TSh 480 per litre in Dar es Salaam (TSh 380 for diesel), more inland and in remote areas.

Rental
Dar es Salaam There are numerous car rental agencies in Dar es Salaam. Most charge approximately the same prices, although local companies tend to be slightly cheaper than the international ones. For self-drive vehicles, daily rates start at about US$40 plus US$30 to US$40 for insurance, excluding fuel. For 4WDs, daily rates range from US$80 to US$130 per day, plus driver fees (US$15 to US$30 per day) and fuel. Most companies do not permit self-drive outside of Dar es Salaam and none are presently offering unlimited kilometres for trips outside Dar es Salaam. Avis offers a business drive package within Dar es Salaam. All agencies accept major credit cards.

Avis (☎ 051-861214, 0812-780981, fax 861212, email avis@raha.com) office on Pugu Rd at FK Motors, near the airport; (☎ 051-117050, 117132) booking desk at New Africa Hotel

Business Rent-a-Car (☎ 051-666693, email business@raha.com) office at Oysterbay Shopping Centre, Toure Drive, Msasani Peninsula; saloon cars and vans, town rentals only.

Europcar/InterRent (☎ 0811-786000, 325990, fax 326770, email europcar@raha.com) office at 2 Nelson Mandela Rd

Evergreen Car Rentals (☎ 051-182107, fax 183348, email evergreen@raha.com) office on Nyerere (Pugu) Rd, near Nkrumah St

Hertz (☎/fax 051-117753, email savtour@twiga.com) main office at the Sheraton, with a branch at Kilimanjaro Hotel

Tanzania Car Rentals (☎ 051-843036, 0811-601726, fax 844320) booking desks at New Africa Hotel and the airport

Outside Dar es Salaam You can rent vehicles in Arusha and Mwanza, although self-drive is generally not permitted. In other places, including Unguja, rentals with or without driver can often be arranged privately or through a travel agency or hotel. If you do rent in this manner, determine (in writing) before setting out exactly who bears responsibility for repairs.

BICYCLE
While main roads are generally not good for cycling (as there's often no shoulder and traffic moves dangerously fast), many of Tanzania's secondary roads are ideal. Even on main roads – with the exception of a few heavily travelled stretches – if you don't mind the occasional dive into the brush to escape an approaching vehicle, or the need to stay constantly alert, cycling can be fine and a fair number of travellers cover at least some of the country this way.

Distances are long enough in many areas, however, that you'll have to plan your food and water needs in advance and carry at least basic supplies – especially if you'll be travelling away from main routes. You'll also need to be self-sufficient with repairs and spare parts, including inner tubes. If you'll be doing extensive cycling, bring along a water filter and camping gear.

Mountain bikes are most suitable for Tanzania's terrain, and will give you more flexibility in setting your route. Standard touring bicycles are OK if you're planning

to stay on the tarmac. While simple single-speed bicycles can be rented in almost all towns (and sometimes even decent multi-speed mountain bikes), plan on bringing your own bicycle into the country if you will be riding extended distances. Good second-hand bicycles are only occasionally available from resident expatriates in Dar es Salaam or other major towns.

You can transport your bicycle on the roof of minibuses and ordinary large buses. There's also no problem and no additional cost to bring your bicycle on the Dar es Salaam to Unguja ferries or any of the lake ferries. Bicycles aren't permitted in national parks and game reserves.

HITCHING
In many of Tanzania's more remote areas your only transport option, unless you have your own vehicle, will be hitching a lift with truck drivers. Payment is generally expected, usually equivalent to or a bit less than what you would pay on a bus for the same journey, but it's best to clarify before getting in. A ride in the cabin usually costs about double the price of a lift on top of the load. To flag a vehicle down on the road, hold out your hand at about waist level and wave it up and down; the common western gesture of holding out one's thumb is not used in Tanzania.

Remember that as in any other part of the world, hitching is never entirely safe, and we don't recommend it. Travellers who decide to hitch should understand that they are taking a perhaps small but potentially serious risk. Hitching in pairs is obviously safer; hitching through less salubrious suburbs, especially at night, is asking for trouble.

BOAT
Ferry
Ferries operate on Lake Victoria, Lake Tanganyika and Lake Nyasa, as well as along the coast. In general, the ferries tend to be tolerable or even comfortable in 1st class, and overcrowded and uncomfortable in 2nd and 3rd class.

Lake Victoria's main ferry is the MV *Victoria*. See Getting There & Away in the Mwanza section of the Lake Victoria chapter.

The MV *Liemba* is the only passenger ferry operating on Lake Tanganyika. See Getting There & Away in the Kigoma section of the Western Tanzania chapter for schedule and fare information.

There is only one ferry operating on the Tanzanian side of Lake Nyasa. There is also a ferry service connecting Mbamba Bay in Tanzania with Nkhata Bay in Malawi. See Itungi in The Southern Highlands chapter, and Malawi in the Sea & Lake section of the Regional Getting There & Away chapter for details.

For ferry connections between Dar es Salaam, Unguja and Pemba see Getting There & Away in the Unguja (Zanzibar Island) section of The Zanzibar Archipelago chapter. For details of boats between Mtwara and Dar es Salaam see Getting There & Away in the Mtwara section of the South-Eastern Tanzania chapter.

Dhow

Dhows have sailed the coastal waters of Tanzania for centuries. Main routes include those connecting Unguja and Pemba with Dar es Salaam, Tanga, Bagamoyo and Mombasa, and those connecting Kilwa Masoko, Lindi and Mtwara with other coastal towns. Though now overshadowed by more modern ships, they still play an important role in local commerce. Many dhows are motorised, but it's still possible to find those that rely entirely on sail – dependent on wind and tide, they travel only when these variables are favourable.

Despite their romantic image, dhow journeys can be long, uncomfortable and risky. Following several accidents involving tourists, the Tanzanian government now prohibits foreigners on nonmotorised dhows, and on any dhows between Dar es Salaam and Unguja. Stricter controls for foreigners are also under consideration for the dhow trips to and from Pemba. As a result, boat captains are often unwilling to take you. If you do find one who is amenable, you'll need to bring all the food and water you will require. Journeys often last much longer than originally anticipated. Stories abound of trips that were supposed to take less than a day but that turned into two or three day ordeals. This said, sailing along under the moonlight with favourable breezes can be a great alternative to motorised travel.

If you do want to experience a dhow without the risks of a longer journey, consider hiring one for a sail of a few hours or half a day. Good places to arrange this include Kilwa Kivinje, Lindi and Mafia.

LOCAL TRANSPORT
Minibus & Taxi

Local routes are serviced by ordinary buses and, more commonly, by pick-ups and minibuses. Prices are fixed and very inexpensive. The vehicles make many stops and are invariably extremely overcrowded. Accidents are frequent, particularly in minibuses; many of these happen when the drivers race each other to an upcoming station in order to collect new passengers.

Taxis can be hired in all major towns and cities. The base rate for town trips is generally TSh 1000.

See also Minibuses & Share-Taxis earlier in this chapter.

Dar es Salaam

With a population of more than two million and an area of more than 1350 sq km, Dar es Salaam is Tanzania's major city, and capital in everything but name (Dodoma is the official capital). Yet, despite its size, Dar es Salaam is a pleasant place with a picturesque seaport, a vaguely oriental feel, and much of its colonial character still intact. While there's not too much to actually do, there are enough historical buildings, attractive nearby beaches, shops, and good restaurants – especially on the fast-developing Msasani Peninsula – to keep most visitors busy for at least several days.

HISTORY

Until the mid-19th century Dar es Salaam was just a small fishing village, one of many along the East African coast. In the 1860s Sultan Sayyid Majid of Zanzibar decided to develop the area's inland harbour into a port and trading centre, and named the site Dar es Salaam (Haven of Peace). No sooner had development of the harbour begun, than the sultan died and the town sunk again into anonymity, overshadowed by Bagamoyo, an important dhow port to the north.

It wasn't until the 1880s that Dar es Salaam assumed new significance as a seat for the German colonial government, which viewed Dar es Salaam's protected harbour as a better alternative for steamships than the dhow port in Bagamoyo. In 1891 the colonial administration was officially moved to Dar es Salaam from Bagamoyo. Since then Dar es Salaam has remained Tanzania's political and economic capital, although the legislature was transferred to Dodoma in 1973.

ORIENTATION

The city centre, with many banks, foreign exchange bureaus, shops and street vendors, runs along Samora Ave from the clock tower to the Askari Monument. North-west

Highlights

- Strolling through the streets of central Dar and enjoying the bustling harbour, colourful vending stalls and vibrant street life
- Spending an afternoon on Coco Beach or exploring other areas of the Msasani Peninsula
- Visiting Dar's many markets and craft shops

of Samora Ave, around India and Jamhuri Sts, is the Asian quarter, with many Indian merchants and traders. West of Mnazi Mmoja Park are the colourful areas of Kariakoo and Ilala.

On the other side of town, to the northeast of the Askari Monument, is a quiet area of tree-lined streets where you'll find the National Museum, Botanical Gardens and State House. Proceeding north from here along the coast, you first reach the upper-middle class section of Upanga and then, after crossing Selander Bridge, the fast developing diplomatic and upscale residential areas of Oyster Bay and Msasani.

Maps

The Gallery *Map of Dar es Salaam* has central Dar es Salaam on one side and the Msasani Peninsula on the other, as well as hotel and restaurant listings. It's available for TSh 4000 at shops around town, as well as at The Gallery on Gizenga St in Zanzibar Town.

The tiny *Dar es Salaam City Map* (1:25,000) is available at kiosks throughout Dar es Salaam for TSh 1500.

The Surveys & Mapping Division publishes a good street map *(Dar es Salaam City Map and Guide)* at a scale of 1:20,000, although few features are marked on it. It's available for TSh 5000 from the Map Sales Office at the Surveys & Mapping Division at Kivukoni Front and Luthuli Sts (open from 7.30 am to 3.30 pm Monday to Friday).

TANZANIA

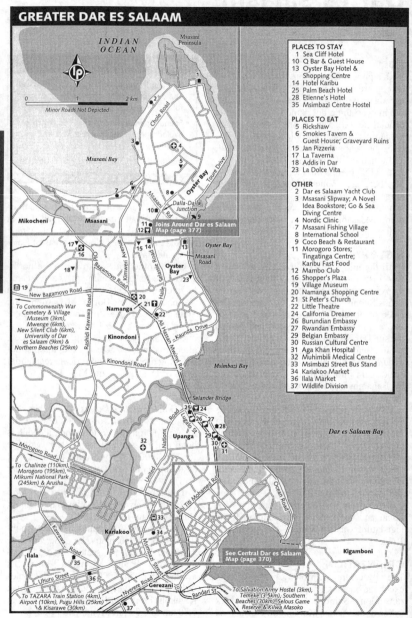

GREATER DAR ES SALAAM

INDIAN
OCEAN

Msasani
Peninsula

0   1   2 km

Minor Roads Not Depicted

Msasani Bay

Chole Road

Oyster Bay

Toure Drive

Msasani Bay

Dalla-Dalla
Junction

Mikocheni   Msasani

Joins Around Dar es Salaam
Map (page 377)

Oyster Bay

Msasani
Road

Oyster
Bay

Kimweri Avenue

Old Bagamoyo Road

Haile Selassie Road

New Bagamoyo Road

To Commonwealth War
Cemetery & Village
Museum (3km),
Mwenge (6km),
New Silent Club (6km),
University of Dar
es Salaam (9km) &
Northern Beaches (25km)

Rashidi Kawawa Road

Namanga

Kinondoni

Kinondoni Road

All Hassan Mwinyi Rd

Kaunda Drive

Msimbazi Bay

Selander Bridge

Dar es Salaam Bay

Morogoro Road

To Chalinze (110km),
Morogoro (195km),
Mikumi National Park
(245km) & Arusha

United Nations Road

Upanga

Lugalo St

Bibi Titi Mohamed Rd

Ocean Road

Kariakoo

Msimbazi Street

See Central Dar es Salaam
Map (page 370)

Kigamboni

Ilala

Uhuru Street

Kawawa Road

Gerezani

Nyerere Road

Bandari St

To TAZARA Train Station (4km),
Airport (10km), Pugu Hills (25km)
& Kisarawe (30km)

To Salvation Army Hostel (3km),
Temeke (3.5km), Southern
Beaches (30km), Selous Game
Reserve & Kilwa Masoko

PLACES TO STAY
1 Sea Cliff Hotel
10 Q Bar & Guest House
13 Oyster Bay Hotel &
   Shopping Centre
14 Hotel Karibu
25 Palm Beach Hotel
28 Etienne's Hotel
35 Msimbazi Centre Hostel

PLACES TO EAT
5 Rickshaw
6 Smokies Tavern &
   Guest House; Graveyard Ruins
15 Jan Pizzeria
17 La Taverna
18 Addis in Dar
23 La Dolce Vita

OTHER
2 Dar es Salaam Yacht Club
3 Msasani Slipway; A Novel
   Idea Bookstore; Go & Sea
   Diving Centre
4 Nordic Clinic
7 Msasani Fishing Village
8 International School
9 Coco Beach & Restaurant
11 Morogoro Stores;
   Tingatinga Centre;
   Karibu Fast Food
12 Mambo Club
16 Shopper's Plaza
19 Village Museum
20 Namanga Shopping Centre
21 St Peter's Church
22 Little Theatre
24 California Dreamer
26 Burundian Embassy
27 Rwandan Embassy
29 Belgian Embassy
30 Russian Cultural Centre
31 Aga Khan Hospital
32 Muhimbili Medical Centre
33 Msimbazi Street Bus Stand
34 Kariakoo Market
36 Ilala Market
37 Wildlife Division

TANZANIA

INFORMATION
Tourist Office
The Tanzania Tourist Board Information Centre (☎ 120373, 123491, email md@ ttb.ud.or.tz) is on Samora Ave just west of Zanaki St. It's open from 8 am to 4 pm Monday to Friday and 8.30 am to 12.30 pm Saturday. The office has free tourist maps of Tanzania, photocopied maps of Dar es Salaam and Zanzibar Town and some interesting leaflets.

Tourist Publications
The free bimonthly *Dar es Salaam Guide* contains a listing of diplomatic missions, hotel and restaurant advertisements, tide tables, airline schedules and other useful information. The monthly *What's Happening in Dar es Salaam* is similar. Both are available from the Tanzania Tourist Board Information Centre and from numerous hotels, restaurants, travel agencies and shops.

Immigration
The immigration office is on Ghana Ave west of Ohio St, and marked only in Swahili *(Wizara ya mambo ya ndani)*. It's open from 8 am to 1 pm Monday to Friday.

Money
Banking hours are from 8.30 am to 3 pm Monday to Friday and 8.30 am to noon Saturday. Banks offering foreign exchange include the National Bank of Commerce (NBC) on the corner of Azikiwe St and Sokoine Drive, CRDB on Azikiwe St opposite the main post office, and Greenland Bank, near the Askari Monument at Indira Ghandi Rd and Azikiwe St.

In addition to the banks, there are many foreign exchange (forex) bureaus scattered around the centre of Dar es Salaam, particularly along Samora Ave. They are generally less bureaucratic, and offer slightly better rates than banks. Most are open from 8 am to 5 pm Monday to Friday and on Saturday mornings. The foreign exchange bureau at the Sheraton Hotel offers lower rates but is open longer (from 8 am to 8 pm Monday to Saturday and 10 am to 1 pm Sunday and holidays).

You can withdraw cash (in Tanzanian shillings) from your Visa, MasterCard or EuroCard at Coastal Travels on Upanga Rd at a rate of US$1 to TSh 680. There's a TSh 2000 charge for telex fees and a withdrawal limit of US$500 per week. The office is open for credit card transactions from 9 am to 4 pm Monday to Friday and 9 am to noon Saturday.

American Express (Amex) is represented by Rickshaw Travels (☎ 115110), with offices at the Sheraton Hotel and on Upanga Rd. It does not give cash advances but issues US dollar travellers cheques if you use an Amex card.

Post
The main post office on Maktaba St is open from 8 am to 4.30 pm Monday to Friday and 9 am to noon Saturday.

Telephone & Fax
The cheapest place to make an international telephone call is at the Extelecoms House on Samora Ave (entrance on Bridge St). It's open from 7.30 am to midnight Monday to Friday, and 8.30 am to midnight weekends and holidays. Charges are TSh 2700 per minute for most intercontinental calls.

Faxes can be sent from the fax office at the Extelecoms House (open from 8.45 am to 11.45 am daily, TSh 2875 per minute for most international faxes), or from the EMS building next to the main post office (rate depends on destination). You can receive faxes at the Extelecoms House (fax 112752, 112754) for TSh 380 per page; incoming faxes are held indefinitely.

For both telephone calls and faxes, there are also many private communication centres; rates are more expensive than at the Extelecoms House but much cheaper than at hotels, where charges are often more than double the Extelecom rates. Card phones are scattered throughout Dar es Salaam, and phonecards, available at the Extelecoms House and at the main post office, can be used for international calls.

Email & Internet Access
There are communication centres scattered throughout central Dar es Salaam offering

TANZANIA

email services and Internet access; a few are listed here. The rates for Internet access averages around TSh 2000 to TSh 4000 per hour except at the Sheraton Hotel where it costs TSh 200 per minute.

Allyvay Secretarial Bureau YMCA compound, Upanga Rd
CyberTwiga above Coastal Travels, Upanga Rd
Management & Secretarial Services Sheraton Hotel
Printout@Slipway Msasani Slipway, opposite Melela Bustani
Ramniklal Chatrabhuj Ltd Internet Cafe corner of Kisutu and Zanaki Sts, near Libya St
The Work Station Computer & Email Centre Lehman Bldg, Mission St, just south of Samora Ave

Bookshops

A Novel Idea at Msasani Slipway has an excellent selection of books, and numerous maps as well. It's open from 10 am to 7 pm Monday to Saturday and from noon to 6 pm Sunday.

For older books, try some of the second-hand street stalls on and near Samora Ave.

Cultural Centres

Cultural centres in Dar es Salaam include:

Alliance Française (☎ 119415) Azikiwe St, opposite the main post office
American Cultural Center (☎ 117174) Bibi Titi Mohamed Rd
British Council (☎ 116574) Ohio St
Russian Cultural Centre (☎ 136578) corner of Ufukoni and Ocean Rds

Photography

Burhani at Shopper's Plaza in Msasani does good quality developing for around TSh 7500 for a roll of 36 exposures.

Medical Services

For medical emergencies, try the Nordic Clinic (☎ 601650, 0811-325569 for the 24-hour emergency line) in the Valhalla compound on the Msasani Peninsula.

For emergency evacuations, contact the Flying Doctors (☎ 116610, 115832 in Dar es Salaam for membership information, and ☎ 02-501280 or ☎ 501301 in Nairobi for evac-

uations). For further details, see Health in the Regional Facts for the Visitor chapter.

Emergency

The central police station (☎ 115507) and traffic police headquarters (☎ 111747) are on Sokoine Drive near the Tanzania Railways Corporation Central Line office. For the Msasani Peninsula, use the Oyster Bay Police (☎ 667332).

Dangers & Annoyances

Dar es Salaam is considered to be safer than many other places in the region, notably Nairobi. However, muggings and thefts do occur and visitors should take the usual precautions. The main danger during the day is pickpocketing which is rife, particularly at crowded markets and bus and train stations. If you go out at night, take a taxi rather than a *dalla-dalla* (city bus) and try to avoid travelling alone.

Walking or jogging alone along the path paralleling Ocean Rd is not recommended.

NATIONAL MUSEUM

The National Museum, open from 9.30 am to 6 pm daily, is next to the Botanical Gardens between Samora Ave and Sokoine Drive. It houses some important archaeological pieces, notably the fossil discoveries of *Zinjanthropus* from Olduvai Gorge, as well as small and somewhat scattered displays on a variety of other topics including the Shirazi civilisation of Kilwa and the German and British colonial periods. Entry costs TSh 1800.

VILLAGE MUSEUM

The open-air Village Museum, open from 9 am to 6 pm daily, is 10km from the city centre along New Bagamoyo Rd. It consists of a collection of authentically constructed dwellings from various parts of Tanzania, although it has suffered from neglect and rain damage and is fairly empty these days. Entry costs TSh 2000 (plus an additional TSh 2400 if you want to take photographs). *Ngoma* (drumming) shows are sometimes held here from 4 to 6 pm on weekends, and other cultural events are occasionally scheduled. Contact the Village Museum, the

Tanzania Tourist Board Information Centre or the National Museum for details about upcoming programs. To get here by public transport, take the Mwenge dalla-dalla from the New Posta transport stand and get off at Mikocheni by Makaburi St, near the Commonwealth War Cemetery (TSh 150).

MARKETS

Ilala market has a good selection of everything from fresh produce to textiles and pots and pans, and is favoured by locals as one of Dar es Salaam's best. Kariakoo market, between Mkunguni and Tandamuti Sts, is a bustling place with a large variety of fruit, fish, spices and vegetables. It's in a rough area, though – you'll need to watch your wallet.

The colourful fish market on Ocean Rd, near Kivukoni Front is best visited in the early morning, when it's at its busiest.

MSASANI

On the western side of the Msasani Peninsula, on the site of one of the oldest Arabic settlements along the Swahili coast, is the picturesque Msasani fishing village. Nearby, next to Smokies Tavern & Guest House, are ruins of what is said to be Dar es Salaam's oldest graveyard, dating back to the 17th century.

BIRD WALKS

The Wildlife Conservation Society of Tanzania (WCST, see Ecology & Environment in the Facts about Tanzania chapter) on Garden St has weekly bird walks (currently on Friday, meeting at WCST at about 7.30 am) to various places in and around Dar es Salaam. The walks are free and usually last between two and three hours.

BEACHES

The best beach in Dar es Salaam proper is at Oyster Bay, more commonly known as Coco Beach. It's popular with locals on weekends but you can only swim at high tide, so check the tide tables (see Local Publications earlier in this chapter) first. To get here by public transport, take the Masaki dalla-dalla from the New Posta transport stand in front of the

main post office and get off at Msasani Rd. From there, it's a 500m walk east. Taxis from the centre of town charge TSh 2000; for taxis back to town, walk to the dalla-dalla junction at Haile Selassie and Msasani Rds. There is parking at Coco Beach; refreshments and food are available on weekends at *Coco Beach Restaurant*.

For information on the beaches north and south of Dar es Salaam, see Around Dar es Salaam later in this chapter.

DIVING

Go & Sea Diving Centre (☎ 0812-784925), 200m south of the Msasani Slipway, offers excursions to the various dive sites near the city at prices comparable to the dive centres based at the northern beaches (see Around Dar es Salaam later in this chapter and the boxed text 'Considerations for Responsible Diving' in the Tanzania Facts for the Visitor chapter).

PLACES TO STAY – BUDGET
Camping

There is nowhere to camp in Dar es Salaam itself. The closest places are at Rungwe and Silver Sands, about 25km north of the city, or at Pugu Hills, about 25km south-west of central Dar es Salaam (see Around Dar es Salaam later in this chapter).

Hostels & Guesthouses

All of the following offer decent, reasonably clean budget accommodation.

The cheapest place to stay is the *YWCA* (☎ 122439, 0811-622707) on Maktaba St near the main post office, with simple singles/doubles for TSh 4000/6000 (TSh 10,000 for a double with bathroom); women and couples are accepted. The nearby *YMCA* (☎ 110833) on Upanga Rd has more expensive rooms with mosquito nets for TSh9000/11,000. The YMCA takes both men and women. Both Ys have canteens. The main drawback at both places is that some of the rooms get a lot of street noise.

Luther House Hostel (☎ 120734) near the junction of Sokoine Drive and Kivukoni Front has clean rooms with bathroom for TSh 12,000/15,000.

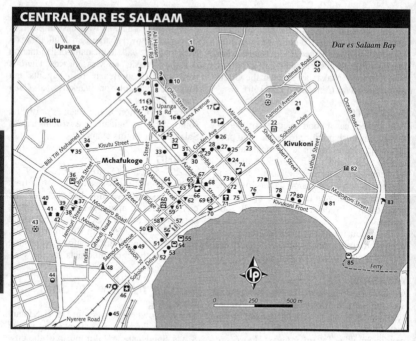

CENTRAL DAR ES SALAAM

South of town on Kilwa Rd near the stadium is ***Salvation Army Hostel*** (☎ 851509) with two-bed bungalows for TSh 4000 per bed. Running water is sometimes a problem but staff will help arrange a bucket. To get here, take the Temeke or Mtoni dalla-dalla from the New Posta transport stand (TSh 150) and ask to be dropped near the 'Jeshi'. There are several Temeke routes, so be sure the dalla-dalla is going via Kilwa Rd. A taxi from the centre will cost TSh 1500.

Msimbazi Centre Hostel (☎ 863508, 863204) west of town on Kawawa Rd has small but clean singles with bathroom for TSh 7800, and doubles from TSh 6400 (TSh 8200 with bathroom). To get here, take the Buguruni dalla-dalla from the Old Posta transport stand (TSh 150) and ask them to drop you at Msimbazi Centre. Taxis cost TSh 1500, more at night.

Q Bar & Guest House (☎ 0811-322119, 335374) in Msasani just off Haile Selassie Rd has a six bed 'backpacker room' with

bathroom for US$15 per bed. Rooms with bathroom, fridge and air-con are US$45/55.

Hotels
There are several decent hotels frequented by budget travellers near the Kisutu and Mnazi Mmoja bus stands.

Econo-Lodge (☎ 116048, fax 116053) on Band St just off Libya St has rooms with bathroom for TSh 10,000/15,000 (TSh 22,000 for a double with air-con). The nearby ***Safari Inn*** (☎ 138101, fax 116550) is a popular place with basic en suite rooms for TSh 6000/9600 (TSh 12,000 for a double with air-con).

Jambo Inn (☎ 114293) just around the corner on Libya St is similar with en suite rooms for TSh 6000/11,000 (TSh 18,000 for a double with air-con).

New Dar Guesthouse on Chagga St near the intersection of Morogoro Rd and Libya St, has basic but spacious rooms for TSh 4500/5000 with fans and shared baths.

CENTRAL DAR ES SALAAM

PLACES TO STAY
10 Sheraton Hotel
13 YMCA; Allyvay Secretarial Bureau
15 YWCA
31 Embassy Hotel
37 New Dar Guesthouse
39 Econo-Lodge; Safari Inn
40 Peacock Hotel
41 Hotel Starlight
42 Jambo Inn
68 New Africa Hotel; Shuttle Bus to Northern Beaches
72 Luther House Hostel; Swissair
77 Kilimanjaro Hotel

PLACES TO EAT
29 Street Food Vendors
35 The Cedars
38 Chef's Pride
52 Street Food Vendors
56 Blue Marlin
58 Sno-Cream
59 The Alcove
62 Salamander Coffee House
63 Burger Bite
64 Hard Rock Cafe; Club Bilicanas
75 Chinese Take-Away; NIC Life House Branch Building
76 Hotel & Tourism Training Institute

OTHER
1 Golf Course; Gymkhana Club
2 Hit Holidays Travel & Tours; UNICEF
3 Air India
4 Central Library
5 American Cultural Center

6 Air France; KLM; Kenya Airways
7 Raha Towers; Gulf Air; Alliance Air
8 Ethiopian Airlines; Southern Tanganyika Game Safaris & Tours
9 Nyumba ya Sanaa
11 Citibank; City Restaurant; Rickshaw Travels; American Airlines; Jet Air
12 Coastal Travels; CyberTwiga
14 St Alban's Anglican Church
16 Immigration
17 Canadian Embassy
18 Mozambican Embassy
19 Botanical Gardens
20 Ocean Road Hospital (closed)
21 Karimjee Hall
22 National Museum
23 NIC Life House (Main Building); Embassies of Germany, Kenya, Malawi & India
24 British Council
25 Aeroflot
26 Wildlife Conservation Society of Tanzania
27 Precision Air
28 Air Tanzania
30 Imalaseko Supermarket
32 Main Post Office; EMS Building; New Posta Local Transport Stand
33 Alliance Française
34 Ramniklal Chatrabhuj Ltd Internet Cafe
36 Kisutu Bus Stand
43 Mnazi Mmoja Park
44 Mnazi Mmoja Bus Stand

45 Traffic Police Headquarters
46 Central Police Station
47 Central Line Train Station
48 Clock Tower; Stesheni Transport Stand
49 The Work Station Computer & Email Centre
50 Tanzania Tourist Board Information Centre
51 National Shipping Agencies
53 MV Safari Booking Office
54 Flying Horse Ferry & Booking Office
55 Zanzibar Ferries & Booking Offices
57 St Joseph's Cathedral
60 Extelecoms House; Ugandan Embassy
61 Gogo Safaris
65 Greenland Bank
66 British High Commission
67 Askari Monument
69 National Bank of Commerce
70 Old Posta Local Transport Stand
71 Azania Front Lutheran Church
73 Tancot Building
74 Zambian High Commission
78 Ministry of Foreign Affairs; Ministry of Justice
79 Bureau of Statistics
80 Surveys & Mapping Division; Map Sales Office
81 Ardhi House; Division of Fisheries
82 State House
83 Tanganyika Beach Club
84 Fish Market
85 Ferry to Kigamboni

TANZANIA

Well out of the centre and just south-west of Selander Bridge on Ocean Rd is the pleasantly dilapidated *Etienne's Hotel*, which has rooms with fan and mosquito nets and for TSh 8000/10,000 (TSh 12,000 for a double with bathroom).

PLACES TO STAY – MID-RANGE
City Centre
Most mid-range places in the city centre, while fairly comfortable, tend to be dark, drab and overpriced.

The faded *Embassy Hotel* (☎ *117084, fax 112634*) on Garden Ave in the busy downtown area has singles/doubles from US$60/70 (US$70/80 with TV), including breakfast.

Peacock Hotel (☎ *114071*) opposite Mnazi Mmoja Park on busy Bibi Titi Mohamed Rd has rooms with TV, air-con and continental breakfast for US$60/70/105.

A few doors down is the similar *Hotel Starlight* (☎ *119387*). Rooms with air-con, TV and continental breakfast cost TSh 25,200/30,000.

The government-run *Kilimanjaro Hotel* (☎ *0811-332100*) off Kivukoni Front has been slated for renovation but was still running at the time of research. Rooms cost US$50/60, plus a 5% service charge.

Upanga & Msasani Peninsula

The mid-range accommodation situation improves markedly once you leave the city centre.

Popular *Palm Beach Hotel* (☎ *122931*) on Ali Hassan Mwinyi Rd has clean rooms for TSh 11,000/16,000 (TSh 19,500/ 26,000 with bathroom) including continental breakfast. There's also a restaurant here. It's a 25 minute walk from the city centre but it's better to take a taxi (TSh 1500).

Hotel Karibu (☎ *667761, fax 668254*) just off Haile Selassie Rd is also popular, with a swimming pool and rooms from US$80/90, including taxes and breakfast.

Smokies Tavern & Guest House (☎ *0811-337346, fax 601077, email smokies@twiga .com*) on the western edge of Msasani Peninsula has comfortable rooms for US$70/90, including breakfast and taxes. Rooms in the smaller Kaburini annex across the street are US$45/65. Discounts are available for longer stays; advance bookings are recommended.

PLACES TO STAY – TOP END
City Centre

New Africa Hotel (☎ *117050, fax 116731, email newafrica@cats-net.com*) has comfortable rooms from US$180/205, including buffet breakfast and all the amenities. It's on Azikiwe St, just south of Askari Monument.

Dar es Salaam's most expensive hotel is the *Sheraton* (☎ *112416, fax 113981, email dirsales@cats-net.com*) on Ohio St adjacent to the golf course and Gymkhana Club. Rooms start at US$240 (US$260 with breakfast), including use of a swimming pool, and fitness and business centres. Discounts are often available in the low season.

Msasani Peninsula

Sea Cliff Hotel (☎ *600380, fax 600476, email seacliff@tztechno.com*) overlooking the ocean at the tip of Msasani Peninsula has well equipped rooms from US$155/ 185, including breakfast and use of the fitness centre and swimming pool. Diving trips can be organised through White Sands Hotel (see Northern Beaches later in this chapter).

Oyster Bay Hotel (☎ *668062, fax 668631, email oysterbay-hotel@twiga.com*) on Toure Drive, opposite Oyster Bay Beach, has rooms from US$120/150, including continental breakfast. The hotel is OK, providing you don't mind what seems to be permanent scaffolding and construction.

All top end hotels accept credit cards.

PLACES TO EAT

Good places for street food include the stalls on Garden St diagonally opposite the Embassy Hotel, and the stalls along Kivukoni Front by the harbour.

For self-caterers, the best-stocked supermarket, with a large selection of imported items, is at Shopper's Plaza in Msasani. Downtown, the best option is *Imalaseko Supermarket* ('Farmer's Choice') on the corner of Pamba Rd and Garden St.

Melela Bustani outlet at the Msasani Slipway sells delectable home-made cheeses, cakes, breads and other items.

Another good place for home-made wheat breads, cheese and jams is *Fast Food Corner* at Oyster Bay Shopping Centre (closed Sunday).

For soft ice cream, the most popular place is *Sno-Cream* near Samora Ave on Mansfield St.

City Centre

Unless you will be dining at your hotel, keep in mind that most places in downtown Dar es Salaam are closed on Sunday.

There are many small restaurants and eateries in the city centre where you can buy a traditional African meal or Indian food for as little as TSh 600. The area south of Morogoro Rd and Mosque St is particularly good for inexpensive Indian food and takeaways.

The tiny *City Restaurant* tucked away next to Citibank on Upanga Rd has good local food at lunchtime for between TSh 700 and TSh 1000 (closed evenings and Sundays).

Moving up a step, there are many places along and near Samora Ave with chicken and chips, burgers and other fast food for between TSh 1000 and TSh 2500. One of the most popular is *Salamander Coffee House* on the corner of Samora Ave and Mkwepu St.

Opposite is **Burger Bite** with inexpensive pizzas, burgers, chicken and curries. This is one of the few places downtown that is open on Sundays.

Blue Marlin on Zanaki St near Sokoine Drive has a good selection of chicken dishes, omelettes and snacks.

Chef's Pride on Chagga St opposite New Dar Guesthouse serves good local food at reasonable prices, and is open on Sunday.

The best budget Chinese restaurant downtown is **Chinese Take-Away** on the ground floor of the NIC Life House Branch building, just off Kivukoni Front on Ohio St. Prices average about TSh 2000.

The Cedars on Bibi Titi Mohamed Rd serves snacks and Lebanese food.

Hotel & Tourism Training Institute previously Forodhani's on Kivukoni Front has a daily set western menu for about TSh 4000. Next door, local dishes are available for about TSh 1000.

The Alcove on Samora Ave has a decent selection of Indian vegetarian dishes from about TSh 3200 plus 20% tax. It's closed on Sunday.

New Africa Hotel and the **Sheraton** have good lunch buffets on weekdays (TSh 9500 at the New Africa, and TSh 12,000 at the Sheraton). Both hotels also have good a la carte restaurants (**Bandari Grill** and **Sawasdee Thai** at the New Africa, and **Serengeti** and **Raj** at the Sheraton).

Msasani Peninsula

The selection of budget options on Msasani Peninsula is more limited. For street food, the best places are in Masaki village or, on weekends, from vendors at Coco Beach. There are also local food places in Namanga, at the southern end of the peninsula.

Karibu Fast Food on Haile Selassie Rd near Morogoro Stores has good snacks and inexpensive fast food.

For vegetarian dishes (mostly southern Indian, Mughlai and Punjabi), try **Namaskar** at Shopper's Plaza; it's open from 10 am to 10 pm daily.

Smokies Tavern & Guest House has a popular buffet dinner on its rooftop terrace (see Entertainment later in this chapter).

La Dolce Vita on Toure Drive south of Oyster Bay Hotel has a pleasant setting and serves good Italian food and pizzas; it's closed Monday lunchtime.

Jan Pizzeria near Kimweri Ave also has good pizzas and takeaway service.

Europub to the west of Msasani Peninsula about 1km off Old Bagamoyo Rd offers good food including Mexican dishes, seafood and steaks. Meals average between TSh 4000 and TSh 8000.

La Taverna also west of the peninsula just beyond Shopper's Plaza on Old Bagamoyo Rd has Italian food, as well as some Chinese dishes.

Rickshaw off Haile Selassie Rd is good for Chinese food.

Amadeus Cafe at Oyster Bay Shopping Centre has crepes and other light meals.

For Ethiopian food, try **Addis in Dar** on Ursino St off Migombani St near the drive-in theatre by Shopper's Plaza; it's closed Sunday.

Azuma is a good Japanese restaurant at the Msasani Slipway; it's closed Monday.

Dhow Restaurant at the Sea Cliff Hotel (see Places to Stay – Top End earlier in this chapter) has expensive but good seafood and Indian meals. Reservations are required.

ENTERTAINMENT
Bars & Nightclubs

The rooftop terrace at **Smokies Tavern & Guest House** on Msasani Peninsula is the place on Thursday night if you want to meet other foreigners. There's a happy hour, a buffet dinner from 8 pm (TSh 8000 or TSh 6000 for residents of Smokies) and live music.

The nearby **Q Bar** (just off Haile Selassie Rd to the north of Hotel Karibu) is also popular, particularly on Friday and Saturday evenings.

Good places for dancing include **Club Bilicanas** (TSh 2500 entry on weekends) downtown adjoining Hard Rock Cafe; **California Dreamer** (TSh 5000 entry) on Ali Hassan Mwinyi Rd opposite Palm Beach Hotel; and **Mambo Club** on Haile Selassie Rd near Hotel Karibu. **New Silent Club** 10km out of town on Sam Nujoma Rd in Mwenge is favoured by locals.

TANZANIA

Traditional Music & Dance

Nyumba ya Sanaa (see Shopping later in this chapter) often has traditional dance performances on Friday evening.

Village Museum also has traditional drumming and dance performances (see Village Museum earlier in this chapter for further details).

Cinemas

British Council shows free films each Wednesday at 6.30 pm (general admission). *US Embassy Marine House* shows films once a week beginning at about 7.30 pm (TSh 1000, passport or photo identification required). There are also films on Tuesday evenings at the *Msasani Slipway* (TSh 1500).

Local theatres – for Indian or B-grade western films – include the *Avalon* on Zanaki St and the *Empire* on Azikiwe St.

SHOPPING
Shopping Centres

For upmarket mall-style shopping, try Shopper's Plaza on Old Bagamoyo Rd; Oyster Bay Shopping Centre at Oyster Bay Hotel on Toure Drive; The Arcade on Old Bagamoyo Rd; or the Msasani Slipway on the western side of the Msasani Peninsula.

Crafts & Souvenirs

There are numerous curio shops throughout central Dar es Salaam selling woodcarvings, batiks and other crafts, and galleries and boutiques selling more expensive works.

For Tingatinga motifs, try Tingatinga Centre (☎ 668075) at Morogoro Stores on Haile Selassie Rd. It's open from 7 am to 6 pm daily and you can watch the artists at work.

Nyumba ya Sanaa (House of Art) (☎ 133 960) is a conglomeration of nonprofit artists' cooperatives aimed at supporting young talent. It's next to Sheraton Hotel at the junction of Ohio St, Ali Hassan Mwinyi Rd and Bibi Titi Mohamed Rd. It's open from 8 am to 5 pm weekdays and 10 am to 4 pm weekends.

For woodcarvings, one of the best places is Mwenge, a few kilometres past the Village Museum off New Bagamoyo road. To get here, take the Mwenge dalla-dalla from the New Posta transport stand.

GETTING THERE & AWAY
Air

Dar es Salaam is the major international arrival point for flights from overseas and the main hub for domestic services.

The Dar es Salaam airport has two terminals. Most regularly scheduled domestic flights and all international flights depart from Terminal 2 (new terminal), while most flights on small planes and most air charters depart from Terminal 1 (old terminal), about 700m down the road past Terminal 2.

Airlines with offices in Dar es Salaam include the following:

Aeroflot (☎ 113332) Samora Ave, near Ohio St
Air France (☎ 116443) corner of Ali Hassan Mwinyi and Bibi Titi Mohamed Rds, near Citibank
Air India (☎ 152642) corner of Ali Hassan Mwinyi and Bibi Titi Mohamed Rds
Air Tanzania (☎ 110273, 110245) ATC Bldg, Ohio St
Alliance Air (handling South African Airways) (☎ 117044, email alliance@raha.com) Raha Towers, corner of Bibi Titi Mohamed and Upanga Rds
American Airlines & Jet Air (☎ 138798) Upanga Rd, next to Citibank
British Airways (☎ 113820) Sheraton Hotel, Ohio St
Dar Aviation (☎ 844158, 844168) Terminal 1, airport
Ethiopian Airlines (☎ 117063) corner of Ohio St and Upanga Rd
Gulf Air (☎ 137856) Raha Towers, corner of Bibi Titi Mohamed and Upanga Rds
Kenya Airways (☎ 119376) Upanga Rd, near Citibank
KLM (☎ 113336) same building as Kenya Airways
Precision Air (☎ 113036, email precisionair-dar@twiga.com) Ohio St, opposite Air Tanzania
Swissair (☎ 118870) Luther House, Sokoine Drive

Bus

There's no central bus station in Dar es Salaam; buses to various parts of the country leave from different areas as follows:

Kisutu (near Morogoro Rd and Libya St) Buses for Moshi, Arusha, Nairobi (Kenya), Uganda, Lindi and Mtwara

Mnazi Mmoja (on Bibi Titi Mohamed Rd near Uhuru and Lindi Sts, along the south-eastern side of Mnazi Mmoja Park) Buses for Tanga, Lushoto, Mombasa (Kenya), Iringa, Mbeya, Songea, Lake Nyasa, Malawi, Zambia and South Africa

Msimbazi St/Kariakoo (between Kariakoo market and Msimbazi St) Buses for Bagamoyo, Morogoro, Dodoma, Singida, Shinyanga, Mwanza

Temeke (about 5km south-west of the centre, just off Nelson Mandela Rd) Minibuses to Kilwa Masoko and Mloka (for Selous Game Reserve)

See individual town entries for details of fares and journey times. For information about direct buses between Dar es Salaam and destinations in Kenya, Uganda, Zambia, Malawi and South Africa, see the Tanzania Getting There & Away chapter.

Train

For information about the TAZARA line between Dar es Salaam and New Kapiri Mposhi in Zambia, see the regional Getting There & Away chapter. For details of Central Line trains between Dar es Salaam and Mwanza or Kigoma, see the Tanzania Getting Around chapter, and the Mwanza (Lake Victoria chapter) and Kigoma (Western Tanzania chapter) sections.

The TAZARA train station in Dar es Salaam (☎ 860344) is several kilometres from the town centre on the corner of Nyerere and Nelson Mandela Rds. The Tanzanian Railways Corporation (Central Line) office is near the port on the corner of Railway St and Sokoine Drive.

Boat

Commercial services connect Dar es Salaam with the Zanzibar archipelago, Tanga and Mtwara. For details of ferries connecting Dar es Salaam with Unguja and Pemba, see Getting There & Away in The Zanzibar Archipelago chapter. Booking offices for all ferries are on the seafront opposite St Joseph's cathedral.

To/From Tanga See Getting There & Away in the Stone Town section of The Zanzibar Archipelago chapter for ferry information between Dar es Salaam, Unguja and Tanga.

To/From Mtwara The MV *Safari*, the MV *Maendeleo* and the MV *Zahara* connect Dar es Salaam with Mtwara. See the Mtwara Getting There & Away section in the South-Eastern Tanzania chapter for details.

GETTING AROUND
To/From the Airport

Dar es Salaam airport is about 15km from the city centre. Dalla-dallas (marked U/Ndege) go there from the New Posta transport stand (TSh 150), and also from Kariakoo (ask for directions); in heavy traffic it can take more than one hour from either point.

Taxis to or from the airport cost TSh 5000 (more at night), although first quotes and citations of the 'official price' are often as high as TSh 10,000.

From the airport to town, there is a minibus 'shuttle' which meets many daytime arrivals, and will drop you at most hotels in the city centre (TSh 1000).

Bus

The minivans that serve as dalla-dallas usually have their first and last stops indicated in the front window. Fares for all destinations are between TSh 100 and TSh 200. The main terminals are:

New Posta Local Transport Stand Maktaba St, in front of the main post office
Old Posta Transport Stand Sokoine Drive, opposite the Azania Front Lutheran church
Stesheni Transport Stand near the clock tower

Dalla-dallas to the Temeke bus stand (TSh 150) leave from near the Central Line train station; ask for Temeke-Mwisho. For the TAZARA train station, take any dalla-dalla from either the New Posta or Old Posta transport stands heading to Vigunguti, U/Ndege (the airport) or Buguruni.

Car & Motorcycle

Most of the car rental agencies listed in the Tanzania Getting Around chapter have packages for self-drive rentals within Dar es Salaam. Avis also offers a special business drive package; a car with driver for 10

TANZANIA

hours per day costs US$65 including fuel, insurance and 100 free kilometres.

Taxi

Taxis have no meters and charge a standard TSh 1000 per journey inside the city centre. Slightly outside this area, they'll charge TSh 1500, and to Oyster Bay about TSh 2000. To the TAZARA train station, a taxi will cost between TSh 2000 and TSh 3000.

Good places to find taxis include Kivukoni Front near Mirambo St, at the small plaza in front of the National Bank of Commerce and opposite the Azania Front Lutheran church, and around the Askari Monument. On Msasani Peninsula, taxis frequently pass the intersection of Msasani and Haile Selassie Rds.

Around Dar es Salaam

PUGU HILLS

The attractive Pugu Hills area begins about 25km south-west of Dar es Salaam and extends past Kisarawe. The forest here – part of which has been gazetted as a protected reserve – hosts a variety of animal and birdlife including leopard, bushbabies, civets, and crowned eagles. The Wildlife Conservation Society of Tanzania (WCST) has established some hiking paths and is conducting several other projects targeted at reforestation and enhanced environmental protection. The area is also of interest from a historical perspective: several important mission stations were established here, and it is the site of Pugu secondary school – the mission school where Julius Nyerere worked as a teacher before entering into politics full-time. Despite their proximity to Dar es Salaam, many communities have remained quite conservative and traditional. If you do come out here, give particular thought to culturally responsible tourism (see Responsible Tourism in the Regional Facts for the Visitor chapter).

At the start of the Pugu Hills area, and about 25km from central Dar es Salaam, is

Pugu Hills (☎ 0812-780735, fax 051-112434, email kreamola@raha.com) a small place with camping possibilities, a pool, and a restaurant that serves up either lunch or dinner daily (TSh 5000). It's generally only open on weekends; if you're interested in coming during the week, you'll need to call in advance to make arrangements. There are some hiking paths nearby, including a short one hour walk which will take you to a lookout with good views over Dar es Salaam. Entry costs TSh 1000 per person (including children). Camping costs TSh 6000 per person including shower facilities; you'll need to bring your own tent. It's not designed to accommodate large groups or overland-style camping.

To get here, take the airport road southwest past the airport for roughly 10km until you reach the Agip petrol station in the village of Pugu Kajiungeni. Follow the main road to the left here for about 800m, and then turn right onto an unmarked dirt road. Continue another 200m where you will see another dirt road to the right. The Pugu Hills restaurant and camping area is at the end of this road. With public transport, take a dalla-dalla from central Dar es Salaam or the airport heading to Kisarawe, and get off at the Agip petrol station.

For further information on hiking paths elsewhere in the Pugu Hills area and on the *guesthouse* in Kisarawe, contact the Wildlife Conservation Society of Tanzania (see Ecology & Environment in the Facts about Tanzania chapter for details).

OFFSHORE ISLANDS

The islands of Bongoyo, Mbudya, Pangavini and Fungu Yasini off the coast of Dar es Salaam are popular diving and snorkelling sites, particularly Bongoyo and Mbudya islands. **Bongoyo Island Marine Reserve**, about 7km north of Dar es Salaam, has a nice beach, some short walking trails, and makes a pleasant day excursion. You can arrange a seafood meal with locals on the beach but you'll need to bring your own drinks. There is a boat to the island from the Msasani Slipway, which departs daily at 9.30 and 11.30 am and 1.30 and 3.30 pm, returning at 10.30

am and 12.30, 2.30 and 5 pm (TSh 5000 return); swimming here is not tide dependent as it is on the mainland beaches.

Mbudya Island, about 4km north of Bongoyo, is best reached from the beaches north of Dar es Salaam. It offers swimming and snorkelling, and numerous good dives in the surrounding waters. There are no facilities on the island.

NORTHERN BEACHES

About 25km north of Dar es Salaam and east of the Bagamoyo road are several beach resorts which are popular weekend getaways for Dar es Salaam's resident foreigners.

Diving & Snorkelling

Some of the resorts have dive centres that organise trips to Bongoyo, Mbudya and other offshore islands, as well as further afield, including to Mafia Island. Expect to pay approximately US$35 for a single dive (less with your own equipment), US$50 to US$60 for a double dive, US$230 to US$250 for a 10 dive package, and US$300 to US$350 for a four day certification course. (See the boxed text 'Considerations for Responsible Diving' in the Tanzania Facts for the Visitor chapter).

Blue Chip Diving (☎ 0811-325483, 0812-784408) PO Box 32185, Dar es Salaam; located at White Sands Hotel

Divemaxx (☎ 0811-329448, 328818, 051-650475, fax 051-650351, email divemaxx@hotmail.com) based at Bahari Beach Hotel, with a branch at Silver Sands Hotel

Sea Breeze Dive Centre (☎ 0812-783241, fax 0811-320714) PO Box 934, Dar es Salaam; based at Jangwani Sea Breeze Lodge

Silver Sands Scuba (☎ 650567, fax 0811-328086 or 329448) PO Box 9314, Dar es Salaam; located at Silver Sands Hotel, and under the same management as Divemaxx

Places to Stay

Camping There is camping at Silver Sands Hotel and at Rungwe Hotel. See later in this section for details.

Hotels Accommodation is listed from south to north. All prices include breakfast unless otherwise noted.

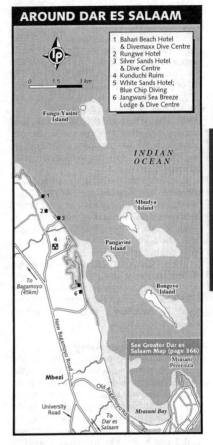

AROUND DAR ES SALAAM

1 Bahari Beach Hotel & Divemaxx Dive Centre
2 Rungwe Hotel
3 Silver Sands Hotel & Dive Centre
4 Kunduchi Ruins
5 White Sands Hotel; Blue Chip Diving
6 Jangwani Sea Breeze Lodge & Dive Centre

0   1.5   3 km

Fungu Yasini Island

INDIAN OCEAN

Mbudya Island

Pangavini Island

To Bagamoyo (45km)

Bongoyo Island

New Bagamoyo Road

See Greater Dar es Salaam Map (page 366)

Msasani Peninsula

Mbezi

Old Bagamoyo Rd

University Road

To Dar es Salaam

Msasani Bay

Jangwani Sea Breeze Lodge (☎ 647215, 0811-325908, fax 0811-320714, email jangwani@wilken-dsm.com) is a pleasant place with singles/doubles from US$88/108 plus 20% tax.

Next door is *White Sands Hotel* (☎ 116483, fax 118483, email wsandshtl@intafrica.com) with rooms for US$118/174; special weekend rates are also available. Both White Sands and Jangwani Sea Breeze Lodge are signposted on the same turn-off from New Bagamoyo Rd.

About 3km north of the turn-off for Jangwani and White Sands hotels is the turn-off for the popular *Silver Sands Beach Hotel* (☎ *650231, fax 650428, email silversands@ africaonline.co.tz)*. Camping costs US$3 per night (plus US$2 for car parking); you'll need your own tent. Comfortable rooms with fan cost from TSh 23,000/34,000 (from TSh 30,000/44,000 with air-con and from TSh 37,000/51,000 with an en suite bathroom). Meals cost an additional TSh 2000 to TSh 5500. The owners and dive centre operators are actively involved in protecting the off-shore reefs. Airport pick-ups can be arranged in advance, as can transfers to/from the Zanzibar ferries.

Further up the coastal road is the dilapidated but friendly *Rungwe Hotel (☎ 650295)* which has camping for TSh 1000 per person including a shower and accommodation in basic bungalows for TSh 10,000 per bungalow. There are cold drinks, and food can be arranged in advance.

The northernmost place is the upmarket *Bahari Beach Hotel (☎ 650352, fax 650 351)* with attractive accommodation for US$90 and a new dive centre (see Dive-maxx listing under Diving & Snorkelling earlier in this section).

Getting There & Away
Unless you have your own vehicle the best way to get to the northern beaches is via the shuttle bus which (usually) runs three times a day during the high season between the New Africa Hotel in Dar es Salaam and the Silver Sands and Bahari Beach hotels. Departures from the New Africa are at 9 am and 2 and 5 pm. The trip costs TSh 2000 one way and takes about an hour.

If the bus isn't running, the best option is to take a dalla-dalla from Kariakoo in Dar es Salaam to Mwenge (TSh 150, about 30 minutes) and then get a taxi from there to the beaches (TSh 3000 to TSh 4000). Alternatively, take a minibus from Dar es Salaam (Kariakoo) to Kunduchi Junction, where you may be able to find a taxi to the beaches (TSh 1500 to TSh 2000). Taxis from Dar es Salaam charge between TSh 10,000 and TSh 12,000 one way. In any case, don't walk – especially if you are alone – from Kunduchi Junction to the beaches (2 to 4km), as muggings along this stretch of road are frequent.

If you are driving, just follow the Bagamoyo road north. All the hotels are signposted to the right, beginning about 25km north of central Dar es Salaam.

SOUTHERN BEACHES
The coastline south of Dar es Salaam is attractive but for the most part undeveloped and difficult to access. For this reason it makes a pleasant alternative to the more crowded northern beaches.

Ras Kutani about 30km south of Dar es Salaam has cottage-style luxury accommodation for US$140 per person, full board, plus 20% tax. Windsurfing, snorkelling and sailing can be arranged. Book through Selous Safari Co (☎ 051-134802, fax 112 794, email selous@twiga.com) PO Box 1192, Dar es Salaam. Most guests fly in via charter aircraft (US$150 plus tax one way from Dar es Salaam for a three seater plane). You can also reach the resort by 4WD over a rough road via Mijimwema and Mbwamaji.

Amani Beach Club (☎/fax 0811-410 033, email abc@twiga.com, PO Box 1547, Dar es Salaam) also around 30km south of Dar es Salaam was scheduled to reopen in late 1999. Accommodation in 10 luxury cottages overlooking the sea costs US$275 per person sharing including full board. Access is via charter plane or 4WD. Diving and game fishing excursions can be arranged.

Zanzibar Archipelago

The lure of the 'spice islands' is legendary. From exotic Stone Town with its fascinating labyrinth of narrow streets, to palm-fringed beaches and pristine coral reefs, the archipelago is a complete change of pace from the mainland with which it is linked as part of the United Republic of Tanzania.

While Unguja (also called Zanzibar Island) gets most of the attention, the archipelago is also made up of Pemba to the north, plus numerous smaller islands and islets offshore. Mafia Island (which is geographically, but no longer politically, part of the archipelago) is covered in the South-Eastern Tanzania chapter.

Unguja's main attraction is Stone Town, with its whitewashed, coral-rag houses, quaint shops, bazaars, mosques, courtyards and squares. Another drawcard is its spectacular turquoise sea, abounding in marine life and beautiful coral formations and edged by fine, white sand beaches.

Pemba, in contrast, is seldom visited and one of the most laid-back places you will find in East Africa. It offers some beautiful beaches and offshore islands, a fascinating, largely undiscovered culture, and excellent diving.

HISTORY

Zanzibar's earliest residents were most likely Bantu-speaking peoples who made their way over from the mainland well over 2000 years ago. The islands had also been visited at a very early date by traders and sailors from Arabia. By the 10th century or earlier, Shirazi traders from Persia had

Highlights

- Exploring Stone Town with its exotic atmosphere, fascinating architecture and ancient rhythms
- Soaking up the 'coastal life' on the archipelago's enticing beaches with their rich marine life and superb diving and snorkelling
- Discovering the unknown corners and culture of the unique island of Pemba
- Enjoying a *taarab* concert or one of the archipelago's colourful festivals

begun to make their way to East Africa and had established settlements at several places in the region, including Pemba and perhaps also Unguja.

Trade between the archipelago and Arabia and the Persian Gulf reached its pinnacle between the 12th and 15th centuries. Zanzibar became a powerful city-state with trade links as far away as India and Asia. With the trade from the east also came Islam, and the Arabic architecture that still characterises Zanzibar today (see the boxed text 'Stone Town's Architecture' in this chapter).

With the arrival of the Portuguese in the early 16th century, this golden age on the archipelago came to an end, as first Unguja and then Pemba fell under Portuguese control. The era of Portuguese dominance did not last long, however. It was challenged first by the British, and then by Omani Arabs who in the mid-16th century attacked Portuguese strongholds on the archipelago. By the early 19th century, Oman had solidified its control over Zanzibar, which by this time had developed into a major commercial centre based primarily on trade in slaves and ivory. Caravans set out for the interior of the mainland, and trade reached such a pinnacle that the Sultan of Oman relocated his court from the Persian Gulf to Zanzibar.

Unguja vs Zanzibar

Unguja is the Swahili name and local term for Zanzibar Island. It is used in this text to distinguish the island from the Zanzibar archipelago (which also includes Pemba), as well as from Zanzibar Town.

TANZANIA

It was also during this time that clove plantations were established on Unguja and Pemba. By the mid-19th century, Zanzibar had become the world's largest producer of cloves and the largest slaving entrepôt along the coast. According to some estimates, nearly 50,000 slaves, drawn from as far away as Lake Tanganyika, passed through its market every year.

With the establishment of European protectorates in the late 18th century, the situation began to change. In 1798, Britain and Oman concluded a commercial treaty. As British interests in Zanzibar grew, so too did pressure for an end to the slave trade, which had been illegal in Britain since 1772. Beginning in 1845, the slave trade was limited to that between the archipelago and the mainland, and from 1873, all trade by sea was prohibited.

Meanwhile, Omani rule over Zanzibar was beginning to weaken and, in 1862, the sultanate was formally partitioned. Zanzibar became independent from Oman, with Omani sultans ruling under a British protectorate. This lasted until 10 December 1963 when independence was granted. In January 1964 the sultans were overthrown in a bloody revolution instigated by the Afro-Shirazi Party (ASP), which then assumed power. On 12 April 1964 Abeid Karume, president of the ASP, signed a declaration of unity with Tanganyika (mainland Tanzania) and the union, fragile from the outset, became known as the United Republic of Tanzania.

Karume was assassinated in 1972, and Aboud Jumbe assumed the presidency of Zanzibar until resigning in 1984. He was succeeded by Ali Hassan Mwinyi who ruled until becoming president of Tanzania in 1985. Mwinyi was followed by Abdul Wakil, whose unpopular term ended in 1990, when Salmin Amour, the current president, was elected.

Today, the two major parties on the archipelago are the Chama Cha Mapinduzu (CCM) and the opposition Civic United Front (CUF), which draws its primary support from Pemba. Tensions between the two peaked in the 1995 national elections, and have been simmering ever since. An agreement that was reached in June 1999 (see Multiparty Politics under History in the Facts about Tanzania chapter) has created at least a temporary hiatus, although many Pembans still feel marginalised and bitter. The general disregard displayed by the Unguja government towards the mainland has further clouded the atmosphere. While most observers do not believe the situation will deteriorate into outright violence, secessionist sentiment remains strong. For the moment, hopes are focused on implementation of the June 1999 accord as a first step towards levelling the playing field and paving the way for peaceful elections in October 2000.

CLIMATE
The long rains fall between March and May, and the short rains between October and December. Rain showers are also common during the dry seasons on both islands, especially on their western sides.

Temperatures on the archipelago average between 24 and 29°C year-round.

ECOLOGY & ENVIRONMENT
Today, only about 5% of the archipelago's original forest remains, primarily at Jozani on Unguja, and Ngezi and Msitu Mkuu on Pemba, all of which are protected reserves. There are also patches of primary forest on some of the islands offshore from Pemba.

Both Unguja and Pemba host several rare or endemic species, notably the red Colobus monkey on Unguja and the Pemba flying fox bat on Pemba.

Perhaps the archipelago's most obvious yet overlooked resource is its abundant and rich marine environment, which encompasses everything from coral sand beaches and mangrove ecosystems to delicate offshore coral reefs and a vast diversity of fish and other marine life. Unfortunately, this environment has suffered and continues to suffer degradation resulting from a number of threats, including destructive fishing practices, scanty government resources, over-exploitation, and rapid and inappropriate tourism development. Chumbe Island Marine Park provides an excellent example of how ecotourism could and should look if the maintenance of Zanzibar's fragile marine ecosystems is to be ensured for the future (see Chumbe Island later in this chapter).

VISAS & DOCUMENTS
You must have a valid Tanzanian visa to visit the archipelago. If you're coming from the mainland, you'll need to take care of immigration formalities again when you arrive in Zanzibar. The length of stay is determined on arrival; tourists are generally given one month. See this section in the Tanzania Facts for the Visitor chapter.

In addition to a visa, you'll also be required to show some proof of yellow fever vaccination.

PUBLIC HOLIDAYS & SPECIAL EVENTS
Festivals unique to Zanzibar include the Zanzibar Cultural Festival (held annually in mid-July), the Zanzibar International Film Festival (also in July), and Mwaka Kogwa (marking the Shirazi New Year). For information about the Cultural Festival, contact the Zanzibar Cultural Centre (☎/fax 232321, 0812-750969) PO Box 772, Zanzibar, at the Old Fort. For scheduling and other information about the film festival, contact the organisers (email ziff@zanzibar.org); their office is also at the Old Fort and the Web site is www.zanzibar.org/ziff. The date for Mwaka Kogwa varies; it will be on or about 24 July from 2000 to 2003. The best place to watch it is Makunduchi in the south-east of Unguja.

ACTIVITIES
Cycling
The archipelago is ideal for cycling, particularly Pemba. See Bicycle under the Getting Around sections for both Unguja and Pemba.

Diving & Snorkelling
The archipelago waters offer excellent diving and snorkelling, with dive sites for all abilities. See the boxed texts 'Considerations for Responsible Diving' in the Tanzania Facts for the Visitor chapter and 'Safety Guidelines for Diving' in this chapter.

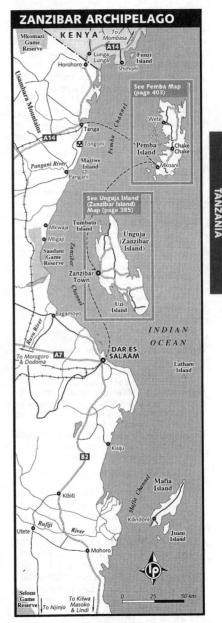

Some Unguja-based dive companies are listed below. Except at Cat-Diving Ltd (see details following), prices for noncustomised packages off Unguja average from US$35 for a single dive to about US$230 for a 10 dive package, including equipment. Night dives cost about US$45, and four-day certification courses cost around US$300. Most places give a discount of about 10% if you have your own equipment. Most also offer snorkelling trips and can arrange other water sports.

Cat-Diving Ltd (☎ 0812-781376, fax 054-231040, email inula@inula.co.tz) PO Box 3203, Zanzibar. A quality outfitter, and the only operation specialising in Pemba. Trips are customised, and based aboard the *Inula*, a 24m live-aboard sail and dive catamaran. Three-day all-inclusive packages off Pemba cost around US$540 per person (US$1080 for a seven day trip). There's also a 10 day standard package for US$1540, which circles the island, encompassing a full range of dive sites. Groups of between four and 10 people can be accommodated. Web site: www.inula.co.tz

East African Diving & Water Sports (☎/fax 0811-337453, 327747, email eadc@sbc.zenj.glcom.com) PO Box 2750, Zanzibar. Based at Amaan Bungalows (☎ 0811-335090) in Nungwi.

One Ocean/The Zanzibar Dive Centre (☎ 0812-750161, ☎/fax 0811-323091, email oneocean@twiga.com) PO Box 608, Zanzibar. Located under Africa House Hotel in Zanzibar Town.

Scuba Diving Adventure Afloat (☎ 0811-336454, fax 054-33080, email mcc@twiga.com) PO Box 3419. Based at Mtoni Marine Centre, 2km from Zanzibar Town.

Zanzibar Dive Adventures (☎/fax 054-232503) PO Box 2282. Located at Matemwe Bungalows (see Matemwe later in this chapter).

Fishing

There's good deep sea and game fishing off Zanzibar, especially in the Pemba channel. Some of the dive centres listed earlier, notably East African Diving & Water Sports, also (and incongruously) arrange charter fishing excursions. Otherwise, try contacting Mtoni Marine Centre (see Outside Zanzibar Town under Places to Stay – Mid-Range & Top End for details). Prices start from around US$25 per person per hour with a minimum of two people.

Safety Guidelines for Diving

Before embarking on a scuba diving, skin diving or snorkelling trip, carefully consider the following points to ensure a safe and enjoyable experience:

- Possess a current diving certification card from a recognised scuba diving instructional agency (if scuba diving).
- Be sure you are healthy and feel comfortable diving.
- Obtain reliable information about physical and environmental conditions at the dive site (eg, from a reputable local dive operation).
- Be aware of local laws, regulations and etiquette about marine life and the environment. See also the boxed text 'Considerations for Responsible Diving' in the Tanzania Facts for the Visitor chapter.
- Dive only at sites within your realm of experience; if available, engage the services of a competent, professionally trained dive instructor or dive master.
- Be aware that underwater conditions vary significantly from one region (or even site) to another. Seasonal changes can significantly alter any site and dive conditions. These differences influence the way divers dress for a dive and what diving techniques they use.
- Ask about the environmental characteristics that can affect your diving and how local trained divers deal with these considerations.

Spice Tours

While spices no longer dominate Zanzibar's economy as they once did, there are still numerous plantations in the centre of Unguja, which make an interesting visit if you've never seen cloves, vanilla or other spices in the wild. Most tour operators in Zanzibar Town organise tours that take in some plantations, as well as some of the ruins and other sights of historical interest.

Among the most popular spice tours are those given by Mr Mitu, whose office is signposted off Malawi Rd near Ciné Afrique in Zanzibar Town. They cost US$10 per person in a group of about 15, and include a lunch of local food. Tours depart at about 9.30 am.

LANGUAGE COURSES

The Institute of Swahili and Foreign Languages (see Language Courses in the Tanzania Facts for the Visitor chapter) is on Vuga Rd in Zanzibar Town. Rates are US$4 per hour or US$80 per week; books cost an extra US$4.

Unguja (Zanzibar Island)

☎ 054

ORIENTATION
Maps

The best is a hand-drawn map by MaCo, with a detailed map of Stone Town on one side, and Unguja on the other. It's on sale in many shops throughout Zanzibar Town for about TSh 2500.

The *Gallery Map of Zanzibar* also has Stone Town on one side and Unguja on the reverse, as well as hotel and restaurant listings. It's available in Zanzibar Town for TSh 2500.

The Zanzibar Tourist Corporation has a small but decent map, which is sold at many shops around town for TSh 1500 to TSh 2000.

INFORMATION
Tourist Offices

The Zanzibar Tourist Corporation or ZTC (☎ 231341) is at Livingstone House, 2km north of town on the Bububu road, with a branch office on Creek Rd in Malindi. It handles reservations for the government-run guesthouses in Bwejuu and Jambiani. Otherwise, its selection of tourist information is sparse.

Tourist Publications

The free bimonthly *Recommended in Zanzibar* has updated information on cultural events, transport timetables, tide tables, etc. It's available at restaurants, hotels and shops around Zanzibar Town.

The Swahili Coast, a glossy bimonthly widely available around Zanzibar Town for about TSh 2000, bills itself as 'the first international online travel magazine to promote coastal ecotourism in Tanzania'. It has some good photography, insightful articles on various aspects of Zanzibari culture, and reviews of books relating to the archipelago. Also check out its Web site at www.swahilicoast.com.

See Books in the Tanzania Facts for the Visitor chapter for titles of some local guidebooks.

Money

There are many foreign exchange bureaus in Zanzibar Town where you can change cash and travellers cheques with a minimum of hassle.

Mtoni Marine Centre is the agent for Visa and MasterCard. Their branch office next to the Zanzibar Serena Inn gives cash (Tanzanian shillings only) against these credit cards, as well as Eurocard, at a rate of US$1 to TSh 680 plus a TSh 2000 telex charge. There's a US$500 per week withdrawal limit.

The 20% value-added tax (VAT) is applicable on Unguja. Some hotels and restaurants include it in their quoted prices but many do not, so be sure to inquire.

Accommodation must be paid for in US dollars on Unguja. Although you'll sometimes be able to negotiate with budget hotels to make payment in Tanzanian shillings, almost all mid-range and top-end places require dollars. Changing Tanzanian shillings to dollars is no problem in foreign exchange bureaus on the island, although the rates are poor.

Post

The main post office with poste restante is east of the town centre near Amani Stadium. There's also a more convenient branch on Kenyatta Rd in Shangani.

Telephone

Telephone calls can be made from the post office in Shangani or from the telephones outside, as well as from the many efficient private telecommunications offices around Zanzibar Town (see Email & Internet Access following).

Zanzibar Telephone Number Changes

In 1999 all telephone numbers on Unguja and Pemba islands were changed from five to six digits. For all numbers in Zanzibar Town, and most numbers elsewhere on Unguja, simply add a '2' before the old five-digit number. For numbers on Pemba, add a '4' at the beginning of the old number.

A few numbers changed completely during the overhaul. Those included in this chapter have been updated. For others, you'll need to check with the telephone operator at Shangani Post Office in Zanzibar Town, or with Zanzibar Town travel agencies, who should have the new contacts for tourism-related entities.

Email & Internet Access

Some convenient email and Internet access places in Zanzibar Town are listed following. Most also offer general computer and telecommunications services. Prices average from TSh 3000 to TSh 5000 per half hour to access the Internet and about TSh 500 per page to receive email.

Asko Communications Centre Shangani St, next to the post office; open from 8.30 am to 8.30 pm daily

Institute for Computer Technology Hurumzi St; open until 10 pm weekdays

Internet Zanzibar ZAMEDIC Bldg, just off Vuga Rd; open from 8.30 am to 5.30 pm weekdays and 8 am to 1 pm Saturday

Travel Agencies

Travel agencies in Zanzibar Town that can help in arranging excursions on the island include:

Eco Tours & Travel (☎ 230514, fax 233476) PO Box 2731, office off Vuga Rd

Island Discovery Tours (☎ 233073, fax 231 373) PO Box 2243, office at Africa House Hotel (for information and accommodation on Pemba)

Madeira Tours & Safaris (☎ 230406, 0812-750289, email madeira@zanzinet.com) PO Box 251, office opposite Baghani House Hotel

Maha Travel & Tours Safaris (☎ 230029, 231729, fax 230016, email mahatravel@zanzinet.com), PO Box 1511, Vuga Rd

Marlin Tours & Safaris (☎/fax 232378, email marlin@zanzinet.com) PO Box 3435, Kenyatta Rd, Shangani

Sama Tours (☎ 233543, 0811-608576, fax 233 020, email next@zanzinet.com) Gizenga St

Tropical Tours (☎/fax 230868, 0811-339302) PO Box 325, Kenyatta Rd, opposite Mazson's Hotel

Zan Tours (☎ 233116, 233042, 0811-335832, fax 233116) Malawi Rd, opposite Ciné Afrique

Bookshops

The best selection of books by far is at The Gallery (☎ 232244, 0811-320644, email gallery@swahilicoast.com), PO Box 3181, on Gizenga St, which carries everything from coffee-table books on Zanzibar and Tanzania to historical works, travel guidebooks and more.

Photography

Print film is available in many shops on Unguja, though selection is often limited.

Medical Services

Dr Mario Mariani (☎ 233113 or 0812-750040 for the 24-hour emergency line) at the Zanzibar Medical & Diagnostic Centre (ZAMEDIC) comes highly recommended. His office is just off Vuga Rd near the Air Tanzania office.

Shamshu Pharmacy near the market is well stocked.

Dangers & Annoyances

While Unguja remains a relatively safe place, incidents of robberies, muggings and the like are increasing, especially within Zanzibar Town and along the beaches.

You should follow the normal precautions: avoid isolated areas, especially isolated stretches of beach, and keep your valuables out of view. Women can minimise hassles (and worse) by dressing appropriately. Avoid walking alone in Stone Town during the pre-dawn and dawn hours. If you go out at night in Zanzibar Town, it's best to take a taxi or walk in a group.

UNGUJA (ZANZIBAR ISLAND)

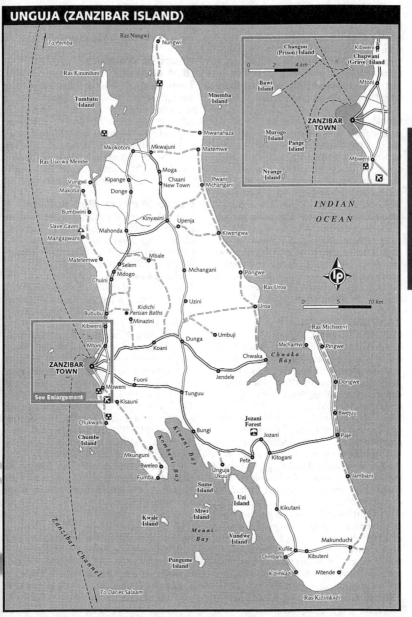

TANZANIA

As a rule, it's best to leave your valuables in a hotel safe, although it's not unheard of at some of the less reputable hotels for things from the safe to go missing as well. Should your passport be stolen, get a written report from the police. Upon presentation of this report, immigration will issue you a travel document that will get you back to the mainland.

Street Touts In Zanzibar Town you will undoubtedly come into contact with *papaasi* (street touts). These guides are not registered with the ZTC, and while some can be helpful, others can be aggressive and irritating (although thanks to a recent police crackdown, the problem isn't as bad as it was before). A polite but firm approach usually works best if you're being hassled.

If you're deciding whether to use the services of the papaasi, keep in mind that you have a better chance of getting a discount on your hotel room if you arrive without a papaasi, since the hotel can then give you the discount that would have been paid to the touts as commission.

ZANZIBAR TOWN (STONE TOWN)

The old Stone Town of Unguja is a fascinating place to wander around and get lost in, although you can't really get lost for too long because, sooner or later, you'll end up either on the seafront or on Creek Rd. Nevertheless, every twist and turn of the narrow alleyways will present you with something of interest – be it a school full of children chanting verses from the Quran, a beautiful old mansion with overhanging verandas, a shady square studded with huge old trees, a collection of quaint little hole-in-the-wall shops, or a group of women in *bui bui* (veils) sharing a joke and some local gossip.

Much of the fabric of this historic place has fallen into disrepair and you'll see a lot of crumbled and crumbling buildings as you walk around; however, fortunately, a determined effort is now being made to restore some of Stone Town's more important and historical architecture.

While a large part of the attraction of Stone Town is walking around and simply letting it unfold before you, it's worth putting in the effort to see some of its major features, which are described following.

House of Wonders (Beit el-Ajaib)

The Beit el-Ajaib, built in 1883, is one of the most prominent buildings in Stone Town. It was also one of the first buildings in East Africa to have electricity. In 1896 it was the target of a British naval bombardment. After it was rebuilt, Sultan Hamoud (1902-11) used the upper floor as a residential palace until his death. Later, it was used as the local political headquarters of the CCM.

Palace Museum (Beit al-Sahel)

This palace, on Mizingani Rd just north of the Beit el-Ajaib, served as the sultan's residence until 1964 when the dynasty was overthrown. Now, it is a museum devoted to the era of the Zanzibar sultanate.

The ground floor displays details of the formative period of the sultanate from 1828 to 1870, during which commercial treaties were signed between Zanzibar and the USA (1833), Britain (1839), France (1844) and the Hanseatic (Northern German) Republics (1859). The exhibits on the 2nd floor focus on the period of affluence from 1870 to 1896 during which modern amenities such as piped water and electricity were introduced to Zanzibar under Sultan Barghash. The 3rd floor consists of the modest living quarters of the last sultan, Khalifa bin Haroub (1911-60), and his two wives. Outside is the Makusurani graveyard where some of the sultans are buried.

It's open from 9 am to 6 pm Tuesday to Saturday and from 9 am to 3 pm on Sunday, Monday and public holidays. Entry costs TSh 2000.

Old Fort

Just south of the Beit el-Ajaib is the Old Fort. It's a massive, bastioned structure originally built around 1700 on the site of a Portuguese chapel by Omani Arabs as a defence against the Portuguese. In recent years, it has been partially renovated and now houses the Zanzibar Cultural Centre as well as the offices of the Zanzibar International Film Festival. Inside is an open-air theatre, which hosts frequent performances of local music and dance. There's also a small information centre, which has scheduling information for the performances, some craft shops, an art gallery, and the Neem Tree Cafe (see Places to Eat later in this section).

Anglican Cathedral & Old Slave Market

The Anglican cathedral, constructed in the 1870s by the Universities' Mission to Central Africa (UMCA), was the first in East Africa. It was built on the site of the old slave market, alongside Creek Rd, although nothing remains of the slave market today other than some holding cells under St Monica's Hostel next door. Services are still held at the cathedral on Sundays. For those wanting to visit during the week, there is a nominal entry fee, which includes a visit to the slave chambers.

St Joseph's Cathedral

The spires of St Joseph's Roman Catholic cathedral are one of the first sights travellers see when arriving at Unguja via ferry. Yet, the church is deceptively hard to find in the narrow confines of the adjacent streets. (If you get lost, the best thing to do is follow signs for Chit Chat restaurant, which is fairly well marked. The cathedral is opposite the restaurant.) The cathedral, which was designed by the French architect Beranger and built by French missionaries, celebrated its centenary in 1998. There's a brief summary of the mission's history just

Zanzibar's Slave Trade

While slavery has been practised in Africa throughout recorded history, its most significant expansion in East Africa came with the rise of Islam, which prohibits the enslavement of Muslims. Demands of European – primarily French – plantation holders on the islands of Réunion and Mauritius also contributed significantly to the trade, particularly during the second half of the 18th century.

Initially, slaves were taken from coastal regions, and then shipped to Arabia, Persia and the Indian Ocean islands. Many were shipped via Kilwa Kisiwani. As demand increased, traders made their way further inland, so that during the 18th and 19th centuries, slaves were being brought from as far away as Malawi and the Congo. By the 19th century, Zanzibar had eclipsed Kilwa Kisiwani as the major trading depot. According to some estimates, by the 1860s between 10,000 and 30,000 slaves were passing through Zanzibar's market each year. Overall, close to 600,000 slaves were sold through Zanzibar between 1830 and 1873, when a treaty with the British abolished the slave trade in the sultan's territories and closed down the Zanzibar slave market. While many of these slaves were shipped to Oman and elsewhere in the Middle East, others were kept to work on clove plantations in the Zanzibar archipelago.

Apart from the human horrors, the slave trade had significant effects on local life on the mainland. In some areas, particularly the sparsely populated and politically decentralised south, it led to increased inter-clan warfare as ruthless entrepreneurs from one tribe began to raid neighbouring tribes for slaves. In others, particularly in northern and central Tanzania, many scholars believe that the slave trade contributed to increased stratification of local society and resulted in altered settlement patterns. Another fundamental societal change was the gradual shift in the nature of chieftainship from a religiously based position to one resting on military power or wealth – both of which could be obtained through trade in slaves and other goods.

From a European perspective, the slave trade served as a major impetus for the initiation of missionary activity in East Africa, prompting the establishment of the first mission stations, as well as missionary penetration of the interior. After slavery was ended on Zanzibar, the Universities' Mission to Central Africa (UMCA) took over the slave market, and built the Anglican cathedral that still stands on the site today.

TANZANIA

Stone Town's Architecture

One of the most striking aspects of a visit to Stone Town is its fascinating architecture, which consists of a hybrid mixture displaying Arabic, Indian, European and African characteristics. Arabic buildings are often square, with two to three storeys, and have rooms lining the outer walls, allowing space for an inner courtyard and verandas. Indian buildings, also several storeys high, generally include a shop on the ground floor and living quarters above, with exposed and ornate facades decorated with railings and lacework balconies. The *baraza* – a stone bench facing into the street that serves as a focal point around which townspeople meet and chat – is a common feature of many houses.

Despite the beauty and historical value of Stone Town's architecture, and its integral value in Zanzibari life, many buildings have been allowed to disintegrate or become severely dilapidated over the years. One of the major factors in their demise has been water, which erodes the limestone foundations. Another culprit has been inherent design flaws, particularly flaws in roof design. Most original roofs in Stone Town are flat. This design works well in drier Arab countries such as Oman, but is unsuitable on Unguja due to heavier rainfall levels; the flat roofs trap water and exacerbate problems with dampness. While many flat roofs have been replaced with angled ones, this has often been done at the expense of preserving the adornments which traditionally decorated many of the buildings.

In 1982, following several deaths resulting from collapsed structures, the United Nations Centre for Human Settlements (the Habitat Fund) developed a plan focused on the preservation of Stone Town's architecture. The Stone Town Conservation and Development Authority (STCDA) was created and given responsibility for restoring the town's historic architecture. Following the creation of the STCDA, the government, which owned many of the buildings most in need of repair, began selling these properties to their occupants with the plan of channelling the proceeds into architectural restoration. International entities playing a role in Stone Town's restoration include the Aga Khan Trust for Culture, the European Union, SIDA (Swiss development agency), and the governments of Germany and Finland. Although much remains to be done, after almost two decades of work progress is now clearly visible, with about 600 buildings restored by 1999. Stone Town has recently been proposed as a possible contender for World Heritage status which, if granted, would enhance future architectural preservation efforts.

SARAH JOLLY

inside the entrance. If the front gate is closed, there is a second entrance via the small courtyard at the back.

Mosques
There are mosques scattered all around Zanzibar Town. The oldest one is the **Msikiti wa Balnara** (Malindi Minaret Mosque), originally built in 1831, enlarged in 1841 and extended again by Seyyid Ali bin Said in 1890. Others include the **Aga Khan Mosque** and the impressive **Ijumaa Mosque**. It's generally not permitted to enter any of the mosques because they're all in active use, although exceptions may be made if you are appropriately dressed.

Hamamni Persian Baths
These baths – the first public baths on Unguja – were built by Sultan Barghash in the late 19th century. They're no longer functioning, but you can still visit them. To get in, ask the caretaker across the alley to unlock the gate; there's a small entry charge.

Peace Memorial Museum (Beit el-Amani or Beit el-Salaam)
The larger of the two buildings that make up this museum presents a catalogued history of the island from its early days until independence. It contains Livingstone memorabilia, artefacts from the days of the Omani sultans and the British colonial period, drums used by the sultans, and a collection of old lithographs, maps and photographs dating from the 19th and early 20th centuries. The smaller building houses a decaying and apathetically displayed natural history collection specialising in butterflies and small animals.

The museum, near the junction of Kaunda and Creek Rds, is open daily except Sunday; entry costs TSh 500.

Livingstone House
Livingstone House, just north of the town centre along the Bububu road, was built around 1860, and was used as a base by many of the European missionaries and explorers prior to their journeys to the mainland. Missionary and explorer David Livingstone

Zanzibar's Carved Doors
A fascinating feature of Zanzibari architecture is the carved wooden door. There are over 500 remaining today in Stone Town, many of which are older than the houses in which they are set.

The door, which was often the first part of a house to be built, served as a symbol of the wealth and status of a household. While older (Arabic) doors generally have a square frame with a geometrical shape, 'newer' doors – many of which were built towards the end of the 19th century and incorporate Indian influences – often have semi-circular tops and intricate floral decorations.

Many doors are decorated with carvings of passages from the Quran. Other commonly seen motifs include images representing things desired in the household, such as a fish (expressing the hope for many children), chains (displaying the owner's wish for security), or the date tree (a symbol of prosperity). The lotus motif signifies regeneration and reproductive power, while the stylised backwards 'S' represents the smoke of frankincense and signifies wealth.

Some doors have large brass spikes, which are a tradition from India, where spikes protected doors from being battered down by elephants.

stayed here before setting off on his last expedition. Now it houses the main office of the Zanzibar Tourist Corporation. To get here, you can walk from town, or take a 'B' bus.

Old Dispensary
The Old Dispensary, on Mizingani Rd near the port, was built at the turn of the century by a wealthy Indian merchant. It has been renovated by the Aga Khan Charitable Trust, and now houses a few boutiques, craft shops and some displays of local artists' work.

Other Sights
The bustling **Darajani market** off Creek Rd has a wide assortment of items and is worth a visit.

TANZANIA

ZANZIBAR TOWN (STONE TOWN)

Zanzibar Channel

To Livingstone House &
Zanzibar Tourist Corporation
(2km), Mtoni Marine Centre
& Scuba Diving Adventure
Afloat (2km), Commission
for Natural Resources (5km),
Bububu & Fuji Beach (10km)
& Northern Beaches

Shangani

Gizenga Street

Baghani Street

Kenyatta

Mizingani Road

Malindi

Malindi Street

Creek Road

Mlandege Street

To
Mlandege Branch
CCM (600m) &
Chwaka & Uroa

Darajani Street

Kiponda St

Hurumzi St

See Enlargement

Gizenga

Street

Hamamni Street

Cathedral Street

Soko ya Muhogo Street

Cathedral Sreet

New Mkunazini Rd

Ng'ambo

To Amani Stadium,
Main Post Office,
Zanzibar Commission for
Tourism (3km), Jozani
Forest (35km), East
Coast Beaches,
Makunduchi &
Kizimkazi

Pipalwadi

Mkunazini Street

Vuga Road

Kaunda Road

Zanzibar

Channel

Museum

Mapinduzi Road

To Archives, Prison &
Kilimani (1km), Air Zanzibar
Office, Mbweni Ruins Hotel (5km),
Airport (6km) & Chukwani
Ruins (8km)

Forodhani Gardens (also called Jamituri Gardens), along the seafront opposite the Old Fort, is a popular gathering spot for locals in the evenings and a good place for inexpensive street food.

Diagonally opposite the Mnazi Mmoja hospital on Kaunda Rd is **Victoria Hall**, which housed the Legislative Council during the British era. The hall isn't open to the public but you can walk in the surrounding **gardens**; opposite is the State House (also closed to the public).

Places to Stay – Budget

Following are some of the more popular places listed in approximately ascending order of price. All room rates include breakfast. Many places offer reduced rates during the low season.

Bottoms Up Guest House off Hurumzi St has large but grubby singles/doubles with shared bath for US$10/20, and a noisy bar downstairs. Around the corner is *Hotel Clove* (☎ 232560) which has rooms with fridge, bath and fan from US$20/25.

Spice Inn near Hurumzi St and not far from the Clove has a lot of character but deteriorating facilities. Rooms with mosquito net, fan and bath cost US$28/46 (US$25/31 with shared bath).

Manch Lodge (☎ 231918) off Vuga Rd is a good place with decent rooms for US$10/20 (US$24 for a double with bath). The nearby *Haven Guest House* has rooms for US$10/20 (US$25 for a double with bath).

Florida Guest House (☎ 233136, fax 231828) on Vuga Rd, is a friendly place with rooms ranging from US$8 to $15 per person.

New Happy Lodge (☎ 231543) around the corner from Africa House Hotel has rooms with shared bath for US$10/20; there's also a noisy bar.

Riverman Hotel (☎/fax 233188) not far from the Anglican cathedral has well maintained rooms with shared facilities for US$10 per person; there's a pleasant breakfast room on the adjoining porch.

St Monica's Hostel (☎ 232484) off New Mkunazini Rd has large rooms with shared facilities for US$12/24 (US$28 for a single with bath and US$32 for a double, including air-con).

Garden Lodge (☎ 233298, fax 231619) on Kaunda Rd diagonally opposite the High Court has a tiny garden, friendly owners and good doubles for US$10 per person. Singles are also available for the same price but aren't as nice.

Just off Kaunda Rd in a pleasant part of town is *Victoria Guest House (☎ 232861)* which has large but dirty rooms for US$10 per person.

Kiponda Hotel (☎ 233052) near the waterfront has rooms for US$18/35 (US$45/55 for doubles/triples with bath) and a rooftop restaurant.

Malindi Guest House (☎ 230165, fax 233030, email riz@africaonline.co.tz, PO Box 609) near the port in Malindi is a well maintained place with good value singles/doubles/triples for US$15/30/45 (US$40 for a double with bath). It's best to make advance reservations as this place is generally heavily booked.

Malindi Lodge (☎ 232359) just around the corner from and not related to Malindi Guest House has clean, decent rooms for US$10/20. The lodge also runs the nearby *Malindi Annex* which has more basic accommodation for the same price.

Warere Guest House (☎ 231187) also near the port, gets good reviews from budget travellers. Rooms with fan, mosquito net and shared bath cost US$8/16.

Vuga Hotel (☎ 233613, fax 236532) near the Vuga police station has air-con rooms with bath for US$23/38, though you can sometimes negotiate better rates.

Karibu Inn (☎ 233058) in Shangani is a popular place with good rooms for US$15/25 (US$20/30 with bath and US$30/40 with air-con). Dorms for four, six and seven people cost US$10 per bed. The nearby *Coco de Mer Hotel (☎ 230852)* has a pleasant enough atmosphere, though the rooms are a bit cramped; rooms cost US$35/50.

The government-run *Zanzibar Hotel* near Chavda Hotel has interesting architecture but run-down rooms, which are overpriced at US$15/20.

Places to Stay – Mid-Range & Top End

Prices for the following places include breakfast. Low-season rates are generally available.

Baghani House Hotel (☎ 235654, fax 233030, email riz@africaonline.co.tz) just off Kenyatta Rd has lots of character and comfortable singles/doubles/suites costing US$45/50/60.

Shangani Hotel (☎/fax 233688) opposite Shangani post office has doubles/triples with TV, fridge, fan and air-con for US$65/80 (US$50 with shared bath), and a rooftop restaurant.

Hotel Marine (☎ 232088, fax 233082, email hotelmarine@africaonline.co.tz) is diagonally opposite the port entrance and has well equipped singles/doubles from US$45/50.

Mazson's Hotel (☎ 233694, fax 233695, email mazson@zanzinet.com) on Kenyatta Rd, has comfortable but somewhat stuffy rooms from US$45/60. There's a restaurant here.

Chavda Hotel (☎ 232115, fax 231931, email chavda@zanzinet.com) on Baghani St, has nice rooms with air-con, TV and phone for US$70/90. There's also a rooftop bar and a restaurant at ground level.

Emerson's & Green (☎ 230171, fax 231038, email emegre@zanzibar.org, 236 Hurumzi St) is a well established place full of character. Each room has its own individual decor, reminiscent of Unguja in its heyday; all are priced at US$125 per room. There's a restaurant on the roof with excellent meals and superb views of the harbour and town (see Places to Eat later in this section).

Nearby off Kiponda St is *Hotel International (☎ 233182, fax 230052)* which has comfortable rooms with TV and fridge from US$50.

Tembo House Hotel (☎ 233005, fax 233777, email tembo@raha.com) is on the seafront at one end of Shangani St and is popular with tour groups. Air-con rooms in both the new and old wings cost US$75/85. There's also a pool and a restaurant. No alcohol is served here.

CHRISTINE OSBORNE

Lutheran Church, Dar es Salaam, Tanzania

CHRISTINE OSBORNE

The golden sands of Zanzibar beach, Tanzania

DENNIS JOHNSON

The lush, green hills around Morogoro – one of Tanzania's most important agricultural areas

St Joseph's Cathedral, Stone Town, Tanzania

Old dispensary, Stone Town

High Court, Stone Town

Stone Town's Tembo House Hotel is full of character and charm.

Dhow Palace (☎ 233012, fax 233008, email dhowpalace@africaonline.co.tz) under the same management as Tembo House Hotel is tastefully furnished in old Unguja style. Rooms cost from US$55/70. It's just off Kenyatta Rd, next to Baghani House Hotel.

Zanzibar Serena Inn (☎ 232306, fax 233019, email zserena@zanzinet.com) has a beautiful setting by the water in the old Extelecoms House. Rooms with all amenities cost from US$195/290. Low-season, half-board and full-board rates are also available.

Outside Zanzibar Town *Mtoni Marine Centre* (☎/fax 250140, 0811-321381, email mmc@twiga.com) about 3km north of town just off the Bububu road has attractive beachfront grounds and comfortable air-con rooms from US$30 per double (from US$60 for suites or cottage-style accommodation). There's a dive shop here that can arrange excursions to Bawi and Prison islands.

Mbweni Ruins Hotel (☎ 235478, 0812-781877, fax 230536, email mbweni-ruins@twiga.com), about 5km south of town near the airport, is set in large, attractive gardens by the water. Accommodation will set you back US$160/220; discounts may be available in the low season and if you prepay. It's possible to swim here at high tide, and the hotel can arrange excursions to nearby islands. A free hotel shuttle runs several times daily to the Old Fort in town.

Places to Eat
The best place for cheap street food in the evenings is *Forodhani Gardens* where you can eat well for about TSh 500.

Blues part of the South African chain is a popular place with a good setting by the water at Forodhani Gardens, but the food is mediocre. Pizzas start at TSh 2800; pasta, seafood and grills from about TSh 4000.

Neem Tree Cafe at the Old Fort (Zanzibar Cultural Centre) serves good meals for about TSh 4500, as well as yoghurt.

1001 Nights Cafe near the Old Fort is usually deserted but the garden is relaxing. Curries and similar fare cost from TSh 3500 to TSh 4500.

Luis Yoghurt Parlour just off Kenyatta Rd is a pleasant place offering several freshly made menus of the day for about TSh 4000 plus excellent yoghurt, shakes and light Goan meals. It's open from 10 am to 2 pm and 6 to 10 pm Monday to Saturday.

Other places for good Goan cuisine include *Chit Chat* on Cathedral St (evenings only, closed Monday) and *Camlur's* on Kenyatta Rd (in the building where Freddie Mercury, lead singer of the rock group Queen, was born).

The French Alsatian-run *Fisherman Restaurant* opposite Tembo House Hotel has a pleasant atmosphere and a good selection of seafood dishes from TSh 4000.

Radha Food House is the best place for thalis and other vegetarian dishes. It's on the small street just before the tunnel at the end of Shangani St.

Dolphin Restaurant near the Shangani post office on Kenyatta Rd has slow service but inexpensive prices. The nearby *Namaste Indian Restaurant* formerly Luna Mare serves Indian, Chinese and seafood dishes for about TSh 3000 to TSh 5000.

Pagoda is Zanzibar Town's best Chinese restaurant. It's in Shangani opposite Africa House Hotel, and is open for lunch and dinner. There's a good business lunch special for TSh 3000.

Maharaja Restaurant on Kenyatta Rd not far from the High Court has good northern and southern Indian cuisine. Serving similar but less expensive food is *Sea View Indian Restaurant*. It's on the waterfront just north-east of the Old Customs House, on the 1st floor.

For authentic Zanzibari dishes, try *Sambusa Two Tables Restaurant* (☎ 231979) off Kaunda Rd near Victoria Hall & Gardens. Advance bookings are required.

Green Garden Restaurant not far from Haven Guest House serves inexpensive snacks and meals; it's closed Friday lunch.

Pichy's Pizza has pizzas from TSh 3000 and live music on weekends. It's on the waterfront just down from Forodhani Gardens.

Zanzibar Serena Inn (☎ 231015 for reservations) has a pasta lunch special from 11.30 am (3 pm on Sunday) for TSh 6000

TANZANIA

(see also Places to Stay – Mid-Range & Top End earlier in this section).

Dinner at the rooftop restaurant at **Emerson's & Green** is an experience not to be missed. The views over Stone Town at sunset are superb, and on Friday there is often traditional drum and dance performances. The fixed menu costs TSh 12,000; reservations are essential (see Places to Stay – Mid-Range & Top End).

Entertainment

Bars & Nightclubs *Livingstone Bar* at Baghani House Hotel is popular. The bar at *Africa House Hotel* has a good setting overlooking the sea, but is quite rundown these days.

For nightclubs, try *The Garage Club* on Shangani St, diagonally opposite Tembo House Hotel. It's open from Wednesday to Sunday.

Pichy's Pizza has live music on Friday and Saturday evenings.

Komba Disco at Bwawani Plaza Hotel, is very popular with locals. It's a good place to find DJ Cool Para (known for his *TAARAP* album, which mixed taarab and rap styles) and to hear East African Melody (see Traditional Music & Dance following), which plays there once weekly (currently on Tuesday, beginning at about 10 pm).

Traditional Music & Dance There are traditional dance and drumming performances several times weekly at the *Old Fort* (TSh 3000 for the performance; TSh 6000 for the performance and dinner).

Taarab, which combines African, Arabic and Indian influences, is Zanzibar's most well known form of traditional music. It is generally performed in clubs, and involves a high degree of audience participation; there is also always a singer involved. Themes usually centre around love, with many puns and double-meanings intertwined. Unguja's most famous taarab singers are Siti Binti Saad, who was the first taarab singer on the archipelago, and Bi Kidude, the first lady of taarab music, who helped popularise taarab clubs. For an introduction to taarab music, stop by the *Culture Musical Club* on Vuga Rd, which has rehearsals most evenings from about 7 pm (closed Sunday and Monday). *Akhwan Safaa*, in Malindi between Greenland Bank and the market off Creek Rd (ask locals to point the way) also has rehearsals several times a week from about 9.30 pm.

East African Melody – the most popular group by far on the Zanzibar archipelago – has built up enormous popularity among young Zanzibaris with its 'modern taarab'. This style expands taarab's traditional base with keyboards, guitars and synthesised sound, and incorporates lyrics more relevant to its younger audience. You can watch their rehearsals, which are held most evenings from 7 pm to 9 pm at the Mlandege Branch CCM building in Mlandege. Also check for their performances at Bwawani Plaza Hotel.

Shopping

There are craft dealers all over Zanzibar Town. A good place to start is Gizenga St, where you'll find all sorts of shops lining the road. The best of these is The Gallery, which has a wide selection of textiles, carvings, antiques, paintings, old photographs of Zanzibar Town and more.

Memories of Zanzibar on Kenyatta Rd is smaller and without The Gallery's atmosphere, but also good, with quality textiles, jewellery and other items.

Suraka Arts Studio on Gizenga St has a good selection of paintings by some enterprising and talented young Zanzibari artists. Some of the artists have set up a sidewalk studio just around the corner where you can watch them at work.

Mlandege St is a good place to look for cheap *kangas* (colourful cloths worn by many women); you can often find them for as little as TSh 1200.

Getting There & Away

Air Unguja is well connected with both Dar es Salaam (US$45 to US$55) and Arusha (US$165 to US$175) by daily flights. Airlines servicing these routes include Air Tanzania, Precision Air, Air Zanzibar (sporadic services) and Coastal Travels. Although flights are not cancelled or delayed nearly as often as they used to be, overbookings are frequent during the high season, so allow extra time if you have a connecting flight on the mainland.

Kenya Airways has daily flights to Mombasa, Kenya (US$61) and Nairobi, Kenya (US$160). For about the same price, Air Tanzania has twice weekly flights to Mombasa and twice weekly direct flights to Nairobi (weekly via Dar es Salaam). Coastal Travels has flights connecting Unguja with Selous Game Reserve (US$120, daily) and Ruaha National Park (US$300, three times weekly) (both in Tanzania).

Gulf Air flies three times weekly between Unguja and Muscat (Oman) via Dar es Salaam (US$512/745 one way/return).

Airline offices on Unguja include:

Air Tanzania (☎ 230297, 230213) office on Vuga Rd
Air Zanzibar (☎ 232512, 233098, fax 232512, email air@zanzibar.net) office on the airport road
Coastal Travels (☎/fax 233489, 0811-321381) office next to Zanzibar Serena Inn
Gulf Air (☎ 232824) office off Mizingani Rd
Kenya Airways (☎ 232041) office opposite Ijumaa Mosque, off Mizingani Rd
Precision Air (☎ 234521) office at Mazson's Hotel

Air Charter If you're in a group it can be fairly reasonable to charter a flight. Prices between Dar es Salaam and Unguja for a five seater plane are about US$300 one way. Charter operators include:

Air Zanzibar (see previous listing under Air)
Coastal Travels (see previous listing under Air)
Zan Air (☎ 233670, 233768, 0811-321061) office opposite Ciné Afrique; (232993, 0812-750476) at the airport

Train The TAZARA agent is at Riverman Hotel; a small section of seats is reserved for passengers booking in Unguja.

Ferry There are several boats that travel to/from Unguja. Services include the following: **to/from Dar es Salaam** Several daily ferries connect Dar es Salaam and Unguja. Most take about 1½ hours, though a few take much longer. In Dar es Salaam, all

ferry offices are on the waterfront opposite St Joseph's cathedral. In Unguja, all ferry offices are at or near the port.

For all boats, there is a US$5 port tax (in addition to the fares quoted below), which is normally collected when you purchase your ticket.

Azam Marine (☎ 233046, 0811-334347) Runs ferries three times daily between Dar es Salaam and Unguja. Departures from Dar es Salaam are at 8 am, 1.15 and 4 pm. Departures from Unguja are at 7 am, 1.30 and 4 pm. Tickets cost US$35/30 for 1st/2nd class. Travel time varies depending on which of their boats you take. Azam Marine's office is at the port.
Flying Horse (☎ 233031) This is the cheapest regularly scheduled ferry. Departures from Unguja are at 10 pm, arriving at Dar es Salaam at about 6 am (get to the dock early and head to the lounge at the front of the boat if you want a sleeping mat). From Dar es Salaam, departures are at 12.30 pm, arriving at Unguja about four hours later. Tickets cost US$10 one way. The Flying Horse office is at the port.
Maendeleo The MV *Maendeleo* runs sporadically between Dar es Salaam and Unguja. It's theoretically the least expensive option (less than US$5), but trying to get accurate information about departures is almost impossible. Inquire at the port.
Mega-Speed Liners (☎ 232423, 0811-326413) Mega-Speed's MS *Sepideh* goes five times weekly from Dar es Salaam to Unguja and on to Pemba, and back again. Departures from Dar es Salaam are at 7.30 am, arriving at Zanzibar Town at 9.15 am, and in Pemba at noon. Departures from Pemba are at 12.30 pm, and from Unguja at 4 pm, arriving in Dar es Salaam at 5.45 pm. Fares are US$20 between Dar es Salaam and Unguja, US$40 between Dar es Salaam and Pemba, and US$30 between Unguja and Pemba. There is no Unguja-Pemba run on Thursday and Sunday, and no Pemba-Unguja run on Wednesday and Saturday. The MS *Sepideh* also sails between Dar es Salaam and Tanga via Unguja and Pemba. Departures from Dar es Salaam are at 7.30 am on Wednesday and Saturday, arriving in Tanga at 2 pm. Going in the other direction, the boat departs on Thursday and Sunday at 10 am from Tanga, reaching Dar es Salaam at about 4 pm. Fares are US$65/40 in 1st/2nd class. Schedules for the *Sepideh* change frequently, so get an update from the Mega-Speed office once in Tanzania before planning your travels. All prices listed here are for the standard 'saloon' class. First-class tickets cost from US$5 to US$20, depending on the

route. Mega-Speed's booking office in Unguja is in the same building as Kenya Airways, just off Mizingani Rd near the seafront.

Sea Express (☎ 233002, 0811-340542) Departures from Dar es Salaam are at 8 and 10 am, noon, 2.30 and 4.30 pm; departures from Unguja are at 7 and 10 am, noon, 2.30 and 4.30 pm. The trip costs US$35/30 for 1st/2nd class and takes 1½ hours. Sea Express' office is at the port.

Sea Star (☎ 234768, 0812-789393) Has ferries from Unguja to Dar es Salaam at 8.15 and 10.15 am, 1 and 4.30 pm. From Dar es Salaam, departures are at 7.30 and 10 am, 2 and 4.30 pm. The trip costs US$30/25 for 1st/economy class and takes about 1½ to two hours. The office is at the port.

To/From Pemba There are connections between Unguja and Pemba five times weekly on Mega-Speed's *Sepideh*, twice weekly on Azam Marine's *Super Sea Bus III*, and sporadically on Azam Marine's *Serengeti*. See the previous listings under To/From Dar es Salaam and also see Getting There & Away in the Pemba section later in this chapter for information.

To/From Tanga See the listing for Mega-Speed Liners under Ferry on the previous page.

Dhow Dhows link Unguja and Pemba with Dar es Salaam, Tanga, Bagamoyo and Mombasa (Kenya). Foreigners are not permitted on dhows between Dar es Salaam and Unguja. If you want to try out one of the other routes, inquire at the beach near Tembo House Hotel in Zanzibar Town or in Mkoani or Wete on Pemba. Allow anywhere between 12 and 48 hours or more for dhow trips between the archipelago and the mainland, and plan on bringing all your own food and water. Also see Dhows in the Tanzania Getting Around section. See Changuu (Prison) Island later in this chapter for details of boat hire to Changuu.

Getting Around

To/From the Airport The U bus line connects Zanzibar Town with the airport (TSh 200); departures are from the corner opposite Mnazi Mmoja Hospital. Taxis cost about TSh 4000 to/from the airport.

Bus & Taxi Converted pick-ups (buses) link all major towns on the island. They are either lettered (for destinations around Zanzibar Town) or numbered (for destinations elsewhere on the island). Prices for town journeys are between TSh 100 and TSh 200. The maximum fare for destinations elsewhere on the island is TSh 1500; most routes cost about TSh 500.

Most numbered buses run only once a day, departing Zanzibar Town around noon and returning the next morning. Departures are from Darajani bus stand on Creek Rd, or from the market. Popular routes include:

A	Amani Stadium
B	Bububu
J	Jangombe
M	Magomeni
U	airport

No 2	Mangapwani and Bumbwini
No 6	Chwaka
No 9	Paje, and sometimes Jambiani and Bwejuu
No 10	Jozani
No 16	Nungwi
No 17	Kiwengwa

Taxis on Unguja don't have meters. Trips within town cost TSh 1000.

Car, Motorcycle & Moped Rental
Many travellers rent cars, mopeds or motorcycles on Unguja. In general, prices are reasonable and there are few hassles, although breakdowns are fairly common, as are moped accidents.

Before renting, you'll need either an international driving licence, or a licence from Zanzibar, Kenya, Uganda or South Africa. Zanzibari licences can be obtained at the traffic police office in Malindi on the corner near Greenland Bank. If you rent through a tour company, they'll assist you with this. If you don't have an international driving licence and haven't arranged a Zanzibari licence, you'll almost certainly wind up paying a fine or being at least temporarily detained.

Daily rates average around US$20 for a moped, US$25 for a motorcycle, and US$40 to US$50 for a Suzuki 4WD. You can arrange rentals through any of the tour companies, or on your own by the market (this is where many of the tour companies come anyway). If you're not mechanically minded, bring someone along with you who can be sure the motorcycle or vehicle you're renting is in reasonable condition, and try to take a test drive.

You're normally required to pay in full at the time of delivery for the number of days you will be keeping the vehicle. Don't pay any advance deposits before delivery of the vehicle.

Hired Vans Private minivans run daily to Nungwi and to the east coast beaches (TSh 3000, about 1½ hours to either destination). Book through any travel agent the day before you want to travel. The vans will pick you up at your hotel in Zanzibar Town between 8 and 9 am. Don't pay drivers in advance for the return trip as you'll likely see neither the driver nor your money again.

Bicycle You can rent bicycles through some tour companies, and by the market for between US$5 and US$7 per day.

Around Unguja (Zanzibar Island)

RUINS
There are a number of historical sites around Zanzibar Town. Many are included in the various spice tours of the island (see Spice Tours earlier in this chapter).

Mbweni & Chukwani
Mbweni is about 5km south of Zanzibar Town off the airport road. In the late 19th century the land here was owned by the Universities' Mission to Central Africa (UMCA) and used as a settlement for freed slaves. On the grounds of the Mbweni Ruins Hotel are the ruins of the UMCA's St Mary's School for Girls. About 5km further south are the remains of Chukwani palace (closed to the public), which was built in the late 19th century.

Maruhubi Palace
The Maruhubi palace, around 4km north of Zanzibar Town (and signposted off the Bububu road), was constructed by Sultan Barghash in 1882 to house his harem. In 1899 it was ravaged by fire. The remaining columns once supported a large upper-floor balcony as well as an overhead aqueduct.

The Persian Baths
The Persian Baths, 15km north-east of Zanzibar Town near Kidichi, were built in 1850 by Sultan Seyyid Said for his wife. They're in poor condition now. To get here, take the 'B' bus to Bububu, from where it's about a 5km walk east down an unpaved road.

Mangapwani Caves
The Mangapwani caves are located about 20km north of Zanzibar Town along the coast (now on the grounds of Mangapwani Beach Resort) and are best visited in conjunction with a spice tour. It's believed that they were used by slave traders to hide slaves after the trade was made illegal in the late 19th century.

BEACHES
There are some superb beaches on Unguja. Although many of them are becoming overcrowded and built-up (especially in parts of the east and north), they still offer a wonderful respite if you've been bumping along dusty roads on the mainland for any length of time.

Tides
Most of Unguja's beaches are subject to large tidal fluctuations and are swimmable only at high tide. At low tide, you may have to walk more than 20 minutes just to reach wading depth. An exception to this is Nungwi, where the tidal variations are not as great.

Tide tables are published in the free listings booklets *Recommended in Zanzibar*. Otherwise, they're sometimes available from the Institute of Marine Sciences on the waterfront in Zanzibar Town.

Bububu (Fuji Beach)

Fuji Beach, 10km north of town in Bububu ('B' bus), is the closest place to Zanzibar Town for swimming. It's located a few hundred metres off the main road down the dirt track heading west from the Bububu police station.

Bububu Beach Guest House (☎/fax 231110) has simple accommodation for US$10 per person. Otherwise, there's *Imani Beach Club* (☎ 0811-333731, fax 054-233939, PO Box 3248) with air-con singles/doubles for US$60/120.

Mangapwani

The only facility here is the new *Mangapwani Beach Resort*, under the same management as Zanzibar Serena Inn. It has a good restaurant by the water, which serves a three course prawn and lobster lunch for US$25. Snorkelling, windsurfing and other water sports can also be arranged. A hotel and golf course are planned for the near future. For reservations and additional information, contact Zanzibar Serena Inn (see Places to Stay earlier for details).

The resort is about 25km north of Zanzibar Town. Serena Inn runs a shuttle bus twice daily in both directions (US$25 return; book through Serena Inn). A shuttle boat should also be operating soon for the same price.

The village of Mangapwani itself is a pleasant place that sees few tourists, and is worth visiting for a couple of hours. If you decide to come up here via public transport, you'll most likely have to hitch back to Zanzibar Town.

Nungwi & Kendwa

Nungwi, at the northernmost tip of Unguja, is a large village and an important dhow-building centre. Although it has become completely overrun with tourists and insensitive development in recent years, you can still find a few quiet sections to the south-west and south-east of the main hotel area. From Zanzibar Town, take bus No 16 (TSh 600, four to six hours) from the market, or a private minivan (see Hired Vans earlier).

About 3km south-west of Nungwi along the beach is **Kendwa** village, which is a good spot if you're looking for somewhere more laid-back than Nungwi. You can walk to Kendwa from Nungwi at low tide in about 30 minutes. Alternatively, there are several daily boat taxis from Amaan Bungalows (see following) (TSh 1000 per person with a minimum of five people). To reach Kendwa by vehicle, take the unmarked, rough dirt road cutting sharply south-west off the main road into Nungwi; allow about 40 minutes.

Boats can be chartered here for Pemba, see Getting There & Away in the Pemba section later in this chapter.

Places to Stay & Eat There is a decent choice of both budget and top-end accommodation in Nungwi and Kendwa.

Morning Star Guest House and the similar *Ikibala Guest House* both in Nungwi village offer no-frills accommodation in private homes for US$8 per person. Neither place is anything special, except that you'll be mostly with locals rather than the tourist herds on the beach.

Ruma Guest House on the edge of Nungwi village and inland from the beach is an unattractive place with rooms around a concrete courtyard for US$10 per person.

Amaan Bungalows (☎ 0811-327747, fax 602747) run by East Africa Diving & Water Sports is a popular and hectic place set on the water just to the west of the cape. Comfortable cottages with fans and screens cost US$25/30 single/double (US$30/50 with bath). There's a restaurant, and you can rent bicycles (US$10 per day) as well as a full range of diving equipment.

The calmer *Baraka Bungalows* nearby has singles with shared facilities for US$15 (US$45/55 for doubles/triples with bath). Snorkelling equipment can be rented here.

On the quieter and more attractive eastern edge of the cape, the first place you reach coming from the north is *Mnarani Beach Cottages* (☎ 0811-334062, fax 233 440, email mnarani@cctz.com). Accommodation in comfortable bungalows costs US$50/70 for a single/double, including breakfast; half and full-board options are also available and credit cards are accepted.

Next is *Saheles* a pleasant place with doubles (no singles) from US$30 (US$45 with bath) and bungalows for US$45 per double. There are also simple *bandas* (thatched huts) overlooking the sea for US$8 per person, including rope beds and a shared bath. Book through Tabasam Arts & Crafts on Cathedral St in Zanzibar Town, just a few doors away from Chit Chat restaurant, or through a tour operator.

Ras Nungwi Beach Hotel (☎ *233767, fax 233098, email rasnungwi@zanzibar .net)* next door to Saheles has luxury accommodation from US$95 per person sharing, including full board (from US$110 in a chalet with sea views). Credit card payments are charged an additional 10%. There's also a PADI dive centre here.

White Sands at the northern end of the beach, has simple bandas for US$8 per person. *Amaan Annex* (☎/fax 0811-337543) several hundred metres south (run by Amaan Bungalows at Nungwi) has en suite accommodation priced the same as at Amaan Bungalows. There's a small dive centre here, and live music on Wednesday and Saturday evenings. Meals are available at both places.

Matemwe

Matemwe is a beautiful and quiet beach about 25km south-east of Nungwi, and reached via an unpaved road branching east off the main road by Mkwajuni.

Matemwe Bungalows (☎ *233789, fax 231342, PO Box 3275, Zanzibar)* is a relaxing place with simple but comfortable singles/doubles for US$80/130 (US$110/ 160 with bath), including full board; there's no electricity. Diving and snorkelling can be arranged. The owners have made great efforts to reduce the impact of their establishment on the local community, and have set up a variety of small-scale conservation projects aimed at building community support for and collaboration in conservation measures. The booking office is just a few kilometres north of Zanzibar Town, signposted on the Bububu road.

Kiwengwa

Kiwengwa, on the east coast, is set on a long, attractive beach, much of which is occupied by Italian-run resort hotels. Public transport (TSh 500, bus No 17) will drop you in the town centre.

Reef View (PO Box 3215) about 1.5km south of the main junction is a laid-back place with accommodation in bandas for US$10 per person, and a restaurant serving good meals (including vegetarian selections). There's snorkelling equipment and a boat for rent, and a small book exchange. To get here, you can walk from the town centre, or pay the bus driver about TSh 1000 extra to drop you off at Reef View. If you have trouble finding it, just ask locals to point the way to 'Haroub and Helen's place'.

North of the main junction are a string of upmarket resorts catering to Italian package tourists. All resort accommodation can be booked through tour operators in Zanzibar Town. Resorts include *Bravo Club* (☎ *0811- 339961, fax 333729)*, with full-board accommodation from US$140 per person, *Vera Club*, *Kiwengwa Club Village – Francorosso* and *Venta Club*.

Paradise Restaurant, just north of Francorosso, has simple bandas for about US$12 per person; meals can be arranged.

Further north is *The Shooting Star Restaurant & Lodge* (☎ *0811-335835)* which has inexpensive bandas, as well as cottage-style accommodation from about US$50 per person.

Uroa

Uroa is set on an attractive beach to the north of Chwaka Bay. *Zanzibar Safari Club* (☎/fax 0811-330345, PO Box 1561)* has comfortable accommodation from US$80 per person sharing, including half board.

The best access is from the south via Chwaka. The road to the north between Uroa and Kiwengwa is only passable in a 4WD.

Paje

Paje is the tiny village at the junction where the coastal road north to Bwejuu and south to Jambiani joins with the road from Zanzibar Town. (For information on Jozani

Forest – between Zanzibar Town and Paje – see Other Attractions later in this chapter).

Paje Ndame Village (☎ 0811-329535) has doubles with bath from US$25. Snorkelling and diving excursions can be arranged.

Paradise Beach Bungalows (fax 054-232327) is also a pleasant place; rooms with bath and mosquito net cost US$16/27. The owners also rent snorkelling equipment and bicycles.

Bwejuu to Pingwe

Bwejuu is about 3km north of Paje along a sand track. To get here from Zanzibar Town, take bus No 9 from the market to Paje, from where you'll have to walk or hitch a ride.

ZTC Resthouse has basic but decent accommodation for US$10 per double or US$20 for the whole bungalow (which sleeps up to five people). You'll need to book in advance through the tourist office at Livingstone House in Zanzibar Town. There are pans available if you want to cook, and supplies can be purchased in the village. Alternatively, the caretaker can shop and/or cook for you for a fee.

Next door is *Bwejuu Dere Beach Resort* (☎ 231047) with rooms for US$8 per person (US$10 with bath).

Further north, *Seven Seas Bungalows & Restaurant* has simple but clean rooms with bath for US$10 per person, and a restaurant.

Next up is *Palm Beach Inn* (☎ 232733, 0811-338553, fax 233886) with good singles/doubles for US$15/30 (including bath and mosquito nets), and a restaurant. The nearby *Jamal's Restaurant* has inexpensive meals.

Further north towards Dongwe are *Twisted Palm* offering beds for US$10 per person, and *Hammond's Guest House* about 2km from Bwejuu and set back from the beach with basic lodging for about US$7.

From here north to Pingwe, the only accommodation options are upmarket. *Sunrise Hotel & Restaurant* (☎/fax 0811-320206) has comfortable bungalow-style accommodation for US$60/70, and a good restaurant. It's about 3km north of Bwejuu.

The ritzy *Breezes Beach Club* (☎ 0811-326595, fax 333151, email breezes@africa online.co.tz) has rooms from US$90 per person sharing, including half board.

At the end of the peninsula are *Dongwe Blue Marlin* and *Karafuu Hotel Beach Resort* (☎ 0811-325157, fax 325670) with accommodation from US$160 per person. Both can be booked through tour operators in Zanzibar Town.

In addition to private minivans (see Hired Vans earlier in this section), there's usually a bus every morning from Bwejuu to Zanzibar Town. Otherwise, there are sporadic pick-ups throughout the day from the Paje intersection to Zanzibar Town (TSh 500).

Jambiani

Jambiani is popular with budget travellers, although there are some upmarket places too. From Zanzibar Town, take bus No 9 from the market, or a private minivan (see Hired Vans earlier). The places described below are listed in order from north to south.

ZTC Resthouse is set on the beach. Rates and booking information are the same as for ZTC resthouse in Bwejuu.

Annex of Imani Beach Lodge (☎/fax 233476) (no relation to Imani Beach Club north of Zanzibar Town) is a tiny place on the beach with simple accommodation for US$10 per person (US$30 for a double with bath). It also has a restaurant.

Oasis Inn has simple but acceptable singles/doubles for US$7/16, including mosquito nets, and shared bath.

East Coast Visitor's Inn (☎ 0811-333964) is popular with travellers. Rooms are US$20/30 (US$40 for a double with bath).

Also popular with travellers, *Jambiani Beach Hotel* has a concrete-block atmosphere, but the rooms are not bad. Rooms with bath are US$10/20. You can make bookings through Suna Tours (☎ 233597) in Zanzibar Town.

The upmarket *Sau Inn Hotel* (☎ 0811-340039, ☎/fax 0811-337440, email sau-inn@cats-net.com) has comfortable bungalow-style accommodation costingfor US$50/60, including breakfast. Half and full-board arrangements are possible, and fax and email services are available. You can also make bookings for this hotel through Zenith Tours (☎ 232320, fax 233973) in Zanzibar Town.

Kizimkazi

Kizimkazi is the site of a Shirazi **mosque** dating from the early 12th century. It is considered to be one of the oldest Islamic buildings on the East African coast, although much of what you see today is restorations carried out in the 1770s.

The area is also known for its **dolphins**, although with the large numbers of visitors, it's getting a bit overdone these days. You can arrange trips with tour operators in Zanzibar Town, or with local fishermen in Kizimkazi. Divemaxx (see Diving & Snorkelling under Northern Beaches in the Dar es Salaam section) also organises dolphin tours and diving trips to the area around Kizimkazi. Most travellers come here as a day trip but there is basic accommodation in Kizimkazi if you want to spend the night.

To get here from Zanzibar Town, take the No 10 bus towards Makunduchi, then transfer at Kufile to vehicles for Kizimkazi, or walk (5km). The mosque is about 2km north of the main section of town in Dimbani Village.

OFFSHORE ISLANDS
Changuu (Prison) Island

Changuu Island lies 4km north-west of Zanzibar Town. It was originally used to detain 'recalcitrant slaves' and later as a quarantine station. Today the island makes a pleasant day excursion from Unguja; the nearby reef is good for novice snorkelling.

Changuu is run by the Zanzibar Tourist Corporation, and there is a US$4 entry charge, though if you're spending the night on the island, you don't need to pay this fee.

Accommodation in basic bungalows costs US$12/20 for a single/double; book in advance through the ZTC's office at Livingstone House in Zanzibar Town. There's also a restaurant serving meals for about TSh 3000. Snorkelling equipment costs TSh 1000 per day.

Any of the Zanzibar Town tour operators can arrange an excursion to Changuu. Alternatively, fishing boats can be hired from the beach by the Tembo House Hotel or near Pichy's Pizza (TSh 12,000 to TSh 15,000 for a day trip) in Zanzibar Town.

Bawi Island

Bawi lies about 7km north-west of Zanzibar Town and about 4km south-west of Changuu Island. It offers a nice beach and good snorkelling. You'll need to bring equipment with you (hire it in Zanzibar Town or on Changuu). Fishing boats from Zanzibar Town can be hired for about TSh 15,000; the trip takes about 40 minutes. Various tour operators run day trips to Bawi with a stop en route at Changuu for TSh 12,000 to TSh 25,000 per person, usually including lunch.

Chapwani (Grave) Island

This tiny, privately owned island is 4km north of Zanzibar Town. There's a cemetery, a small beach and a few bungalows for overnight lodging. Make inquiries at tour operators in Zanzibar Town for details.

Mnemba Island

Privately owned Mnemba, north-east of Matemwe on the east coast, is surrounded by a coral reef that hosts an abundance of marine life. The only hotel is the exclusive *Mnemba Island Lodge*, run by Conservation Corporation Africa with booking offices in Kenya (☎ 02-441001, fax 750512, email conscorp@users.africaonline.co.ke) and Unguja (☎ 233110/7), the office is in a small alley between Zanzibar Serena Inn and Mazson's Hotel in Unguja). Luxury cottages costs US$500 per person per day, all inclusive. Access to Mnemba is restricted to hotel guests, although diving is permitted on the surrounding reef.

Chumbe Island

Chumbe, an uninhabited island 12km south of Zanzibar Town and covering an area of approximately 20 hectares, has an exceptional shallow-water coral reef along its western shore, which is noted for its diversity of corals and fish life. The reef was gazetted in 1994 as Zanzibar's first marine sanctuary by the Government of Zanzibar, and – together with the coral rag forest sanctuary on the island – is now administered as a private nature reserve (Chumbe Island Coral Park, or CHICOP).

The reef is in excellent condition, thanks to the fact that for decades, the island was part of a military zone and off-limits to locals and visitors. In addition to nearly 200 species of coral, the surrounding waters host about 370 species of fish. The island also provides a haven for green and hawksbill turtles, and has diverse birdlife with over 50 species recorded to date, including the endangered roseate tern.

Revenues generated from tourism on Chumbe are being used to subsidise a variety of conservation and education programs in the park. Current projects include establishment of a sanctuary for the rare Ader's duiker, and research into the rare nocturnal giant coconut crab. During low season, island excursions are provided free of charge to school children from Zanzibar Town.

Chumbe's exceptional environmental management programs have received widespread acclaim, including from the UN, and the park has been chosen to represent Tanzania at Expo 2000 as an example of sustainable management of a protected area.

While you can visit Chumbe as a day trip starting from the beach at the Mbweni Ruins Hotel (US$70 all inclusive), overnighting is encouraged in order to facilitate maintenance and appreciation of its environment. Comfortable accommodation in seven attractive ecobungalows – with well designed rainwater catchment systems, solar panels, compost toilets and more – costs from US$150 per person, including boat transfers, full board, drinks and activities.

Bookings for both day and overnight visits can be made through CHICOP (☎/fax 231040, 0811-601378, email chumbe.island@raha.com, chumbe@twiga.com) PO Box 3203, Zanzibar. There's also an informative Web site at www.xtra-micro.com/work/chumbe

OTHER ATTRACTIONS
Jozani Forest
Jozani Forest, 35km south-east of Zanzibar Town off the road to Paje, is the largest area of mature forest left on Unguja. It hosts populations of the rare red Colobus monkey, as well as Sykes monkeys, bushbabies, Ader's duikers, dassies, over 50 species of butterfly and about 40 species of bird. There's a nature trail in the forest, which takes about 45 minutes to walk. Guides are available at the information centre by the entrance gate. Entry (including a guide) costs US$10.

Despite what many tour operators say, when observing the monkeys it's important not to get too close – park staff recommend no closer than 3m. This is both for your safety and the safety of the animals. In addition to there being a risk of being bitten by the monkeys, there is considerable concern that if the monkeys were to catch a human illness it could spread and rapidly wipe out the already threatened population.

You can reach Jozani via bus No 9 or 10 (TSh 500), via chartered taxi, or with an organised tour from Zanzibar Town. The forest entrance is signposted on the main road.

Pemba

☎ 054

For much of its history, Pemba has been overshadowed by Unguja, its larger and more politically powerful neighbour to the south. Although the islands are only separated by about 50km of water, relatively few tourists make their way across the channel for a visit. Those who do, however, are seldom disappointed.

Unlike Unguja, which is flat and sandy, Pemba's terrain is hilly, fertile and heavily vegetated. In the old days of the Arab traders it was even referred to as al khuthera or 'the green island'. Throughout much of the period when the sultans of Zanzibar held sway over the East African coast, it was Pemba, with its extensive clove plantations and agricultural base that provided the economic foundation for the archipelago's dominance. Even today, cloves continue to be the mainstay of the island's economy, with between 75% and 80% of overall clove production on the archipelago coming from Pemba.

Pemba has also been long renowned for its voodoo and traditional healers, and the island still attracts people from throughout East Africa who are seeking cures or who want to learn the skills of the trade.

In addition to its rich history and traditions, Pemba is of interest to tourists for its wealth of natural resources ranging from beaches to mangrove ecosystems to natural forests. The coral reefs surrounding the island shelter a multitude of marine species and offer some superb diving.

The tourism industry on Pemba is in its infancy and infrastructure is for the most part fairly basic, although this is beginning to change. The main requirement for exploring the island is time, as there is little regular transport off the main routes.

HISTORY
Little is known about Pemba's original inhabitants, though it is believed that they migrated from the mainland, perhaps as early as several thousand years ago. The Shirazi presence on Pemba dates from at least the 9th or 10th century, and some 12th century Shirazi ruins at Ras Mkumbuu, north-west of Chake Chake, indicate that settlements were well established on Pemba by that time. The Portuguese attacked Pemba in the early 16th century and sought to subjugate its inhabitants by ravaging many towns and demanding tributes. Following a period of Portuguese dominance, various Omani groups gained ascendancy and governed the island until 1822. In 1890, Pemba, together with Unguja, became a British protectorate.

Following the Zanzibar revolution in 1964, President Karume closed Pemba to foreigners in an effort to contain antigovernment sentiment. The island remained closed until the 1980s, although even then the situation remained strained. Since the 1995 elections, Pembans have felt increasingly marginalised and frustrated. Away from main towns, illiteracy rates are as high as 95% in some areas and roads and other infrastructure have been badly neglected.

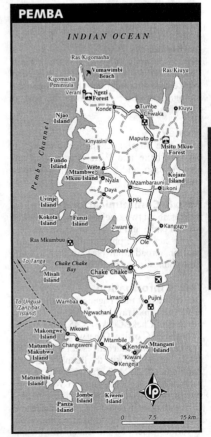

ORIENTATION
Maps
The only map of Pemba available on the island is the one put out by the Commission for Lands & Environment (1:100,000). The best place to look for it is at the tourist information office in Chake Chake.

INFORMATION
Tourist Offices
The Zanzibar Tourist Corporation's Pemba branch (☎ 452121) is located in Chake Chake next to the Hoteli ya Chake. It's worth stopping by to ask if any new hotels

have opened. The office can also assist in arranging car hire.

Immigration

If you are arriving in or departing from Pemba (to/from the mainland), you'll need to take care of immigration formalities. The immigration office is opposite the port in Mkoani.

Money

There are foreign exchange bureaus in Chake Chake and Wete where you can change cash and (sometimes) travellers cheques.

Post & Communications

It takes about two weeks to send a letter between Pemba and Europe or Australia.

You can make phone calls to the mainland or abroad from post offices or from card phones in the major towns.

Travel Information

One of the best travel agencies on the island is Partnership Travel & Tours; their main office is in Chake Chake (☎ 452278) across from the ZTC office. Otherwise, try Bachaa Travel & Tours, with offices at Le Tavern on the main road opposite the People's Bank of Zanzibar (☎ 457479, fax 452480, email bachaa@zanzinet.com), and in Wete opposite the post office (☎ 454136, fax 454138).

Guesthouses in Mkoani, Chake Chake and Wete can also be helpful in arranging visits to various places on the island. In Mkoani, staff at Jondeni Guest House (see Places to Stay & Eat under Mkoani later in this chapter) have gone to great lengths to gather information on all aspects of Pemba, and to make the island's numerous attractions accessible to visitors. They assist with arranging diving and snorkelling trips, excursions on local sailing boats, as well as land tours.

In Wete, the owner of Sharouk Guest House (see Places to Stay & Eat in the Wete section later) is friendly and extremely knowledgeable, and can assist with good excursions to Ngezi Forest, the Kigomasha Peninsula, offshore islands as well as to other destinations.

Medical Services

For dire emergencies, the Chinese-run government hospital in Mkoani is probably your best bet, although standards leave much to be desired.

ACCOMMODATION

There is no accommodation outside the main towns other than a few tourist resorts, although the number of these is beginning to expand. In Chake Chake, Wete and Mkoani there are government hotels and some guesthouses. Pemba has its own generators and main towns have electricity most days, although since one generator broke recently, power has been rationed. This shouldn't be a problem, though, once you've settled into the pace of life on Pemba and as long as you've got a room with good ventilation.

FOOD & DRINK

Guesthouses in the main towns prepare good meals, but in most cases you'll need to organise this well in advance.

Other than local brews (the most common being *nazi*, a fermented coconut wine), there is little alcohol available on the island. The best places to try for a beer are the government hotels or the police canteens in the main towns.

GETTING THERE & AWAY
Air

There are currently no commercial air services to Pemba, although Precision Air may begin a scheduled service in the near future. Zan Air (see Air Charter in the Getting There & Away section for Unguja earlier in this chapter) may also soon start a scheduled service.

Charter flights from Unguja cost from US$310 for a three seater plane and between US$450 and US$500 one way for a five seater. A one-way charter between Dar es Salaam and Pemba costs about US$700. For further details, contact one of the air charter operators listed under Getting There & Away in the Unguja section earlier in this chapter.

Bachaa Travel & Tours is the booking agent on Pemba for Gulf Air and Kenya Airways.

Boat

Mega-Speed's MS *Sepideh* sails five times weekly between Dar es Salaam and Pemba via Unguja, and twice weekly between Pemba and Tanga (note – frequent schedule cancellations and changes). For schedule and price information, see Getting There & Away in the Unguja section earlier in this chapter. On Tuesday and Friday, fares are reduced (by US$5 for nonresidents) on the Unguja-Pemba and Dar es Salaam-Pemba routes. Mega-Speed (☎ 456100 on Pemba) has booking offices in Mkoani, Chake Chake, and Wete. The *Sepideh's* Monday run seems to be particularly vulnerable to cancellations, since there are usually very few passengers (most locals wait until Tuesday, when fares are reduced).

Azam Marine's new *Super Sea Bus III* only goes twice weekly between Unguja and Pemba, but tends to be more reliable than the *Sepideh*. Currently it runs on Tuesday and Friday, departing Dar es Salaam at 7.30 am, departing Zanzibar Town at around 9.45 am and arriving in Pemba at about 11.45 am. Departures from Pemba are at 1 pm, reaching Zanzibar Town at 2.45 pm, and then on to Dar es Salaam. Fares are US$30/35 for economy/1st class (US$40/45 direct between Pemba and Dar es Salaam) plus US$5 port tax. Azam Marine's office is at the port.

The *Serehgeti*, also run by Azam Marine but crowded and not as comfortable as the *Super Sea Bus III*, is scheduled to sail between Unguja and Pemba on Tuesday and Thursday, departing Unguja at about 10 pm and arriving in Mkoani (Pemba) at about 6 am. The return departs Pemba at 10 am on Wednesday and Saturday, arriving in Unguja at about 4.30 pm. Actual sailings tend to be sporadic and vary with the season, so you'll need to inquire at the port. Tickets cost US$15 plus US$5 port tax.

The *Mapinduzi*, an uncomfortable boat that only sails sporadically, is currently out of service. When it's running, it costs TSh 4000/6500/8000 for 3rd/2nd/1st class plus US$5 port tax. It's well worth buying 1st class if you can afford it; deck seating is crowded and particularly uncomfortable.

For information and tickets on Pemba, inquire at the port in Mkoani. In Zanzibar Town, the office is on Mizingani Rd just after the Institute of Marine Sciences; look for an unmarked hole in the wall.

A new boat, the MV *Zahara*, is due to start services between Unguja and Pemba in the near future; inquire at the port in Mkoani or Zanzibar Town.

If you want to get to Pemba from Nungwi on the northern tip of Unguja, contact Lory (☎ 233056 or at the Fat Fish Bar in Nungwi), or inquire at Asko Communications Centre (see Email & Internet Access in the Unguja section earlier in this chapter). Charters can be arranged for about US$50 per person with a minimum of four people.

GETTING AROUND

Pemba is a small place and getting around is not too difficult provided that you have lots of time. Bus drivers are usually willing to take you to destinations off the main routes for an additional fee. Otherwise, there are sporadic pick-ups or other local transport. Cars and motorcycles can be hired in Chake Chake and sometimes in Wete, and the entire island is terrific if you're into cycling.

To/From Mkoani Port

Mega-Speed runs a shuttle bus from Chake Chake (TSh 500) and Wete (TSh 1000) to Mkoani connecting with the *Sepideh* departures. The buses leave from Wete about three hours before the *Sepideh's* scheduled departure time, and from Chake Chake approximately two hours before. In Wete, the main pick-up point is at Raha Tours & Travel, around the corner from the post office, and in Chake Chake it is in front of the Mega-Speed booking office at Partnership Travel & Tours. Otherwise, you'll have to take local transport to the port or hire a car in Chake Chake.

Bus

Pemba's major towns and several of the smaller ones are connected throughout the day by local buses. Prices for all destinations are about TSh 400 to TSh 500. The main lines are:

No 3	Mkoani to Chake Chake
No 6	Chake Chake to Wete via the 'old' road
No 24	Wete to Konde
No 34	Chake Chake to Wete via the 'new' (eastern) road
No 35	Chake Chake to Konde via the 'new' (eastern) road

Taxi & Car Rental

Pemba's taxi industry is in its infancy and there are only a few vehicles. However, in Chake Chake (and sometimes in Wete), you can arrange to hire a car, minivan or motorcycle for the day. Rates average from US$40 per day for a small Suzuki 4WD with driver, and about US$25 per day for motorcycles. Partnership Travel & Tours, the tourist office in Chake Chake, and guesthouses can assist with rentals.

Bicycle

Cycling is an excellent way to get around Pemba, although you'll need to bring your own bicycle unless you're content with one of the single-speeds available locally. Bicy-cle hire can be easily arranged through guesthouses in Mkoani, Chake Chake and Wete. Distances are relatively short and roads are not as heavily travelled as on the mainland. You'll need to come equipped with any spare parts you may need.

CHAKE CHAKE

Lively Chake Chake is Pemba's main town. Although it has been occupied for centuries, there is little architectural evidence remaining from its past other than the ruins of an 18th century fort, and some 12th century ruins at nearby Ras Mkumbuu. The town is set on a ridge overlooking Chake Chake Bay, and there is a small dhow port and fish market along the water.

While there isn't much of interest in Chake Chake itself, the town makes a good base for exploring Pemba and visiting **Misali Island**.

Information

The Pemba foreign exchange bureau opposite the ZTC office changes cash and travellers cheques. If they are closed or out of money, there's a branch of the People's Bank of Zanzibar just up the street.

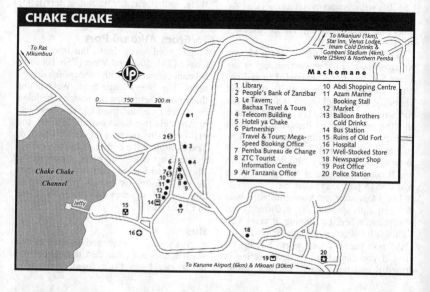

CHAKE CHAKE

To Mkanjuni (1km),
Star Inn, Venus Lodge,
Imam Cold Drinks &
Gombani Stadium (4km),
Wete (25km) & Northern Pemba

To Ras
Mkumbuu

Machomane

Chake Chake
Channel

Jetty

0   150   300 m

1 Library
2 People's Bank of Zanzibar
3 Le Tavern;
   Bachaa Travel & Tours
4 Telecom Building
5 Hoteli ya Chake
6 Partnership
   Travel & Tours; Mega-
   Speed Booking Office
7 Pemba Bureau de Change
8 ZTC Tourist
   Information Centre
9 Air Tanzania Office
10 Abdi Shopping Centre
11 Azam Marine
   Booking Stall
12 Market
13 Balloon Brothers
   Cold Drinks
14 Bus Station
15 Ruins of Old Fort
16 Hospital
17 Well-Stocked Store
18 Newspaper Shop
19 Post Office
20 Police Station

To Karume Airport (6km) & Mkoani (30km)

Misali Island

Tiny Misali Island, which is rumoured to be the site where the infamous Captain Kidd hid some of his treasure in the late 17th century, lies offshore from Chake Chake. In addition to its attractive beaches, the island provides a sea turtle nesting area and a haven for breeding sea birds. Along its western side are some notable coral reefs, which host a rich variety of marine life, including over 200 recorded species of fish. While there are no permanent settlements on Misali, it's in active use by local fishermen and there are several fishing camps.

In 1998 the island and surrounding coral reef were gazetted as the Misali Island Marine Conservation Area, which aims to maintain the island's ecosystems in harmony with ongoing usage by local fishermen. Both underwater and terrestrial nature trails have been established, and local guides are available.

Visits to the island can be arranged through Jondeni Guest House in Mkoani (see Places to Stay & Eat under Mkoani) or, more expensively, through tour operators on Unguja. There's a US$5 entry fee. A 'boat fee' of US$30 has been approved, although it wasn't yet being implemented as this book was being researched. Trips organised by Jondeni Guest House (including transport and lunch) cost US$25 plus the entry fee. Three-day, two-night packages from Zanzibar Town, including one day on Misali and one day on Pemba, cost about US$200 per person, all inclusive. Camping on the island is not permitted.

You can also reach the island on your own. Fishing boats can be hired to go over to Misali from the coast in the Mkanjuni area, about 1km north of Chake Chake on the Wete road. Expect to pay about TSh 35,000 for a return day-trip.

For more detailed information contact the Misali Island Conservation Association (☎/fax 054-454126, email micapemba@yahoo.com), PO Box 293, Chake Chake.

An email centre is supposed to open sometime during 2000 in Chake Chake. Check with Internet Zanzibar (see Email & Internet Access in the Unguja section) for an update.

Places to Stay & Eat

Hoteli ya Chake (☎ 452069) in the town centre has singles/doubles for US$15/25. It's fairly bleak but the rooms are large and reasonably clean. If you stay, you'll probably be the only one here.

The nicer *Le Tavern* (☎ 452660) on the main road and diagonally opposite the bank was just opening as this book was being researched. Rooms cost US$20 per person, including breakfast.

Star Inn (☎ 456042) about 4km north of town in Gombani (and opposite Gombani Stadium) has clean rooms with shared bath from US$15/30. It also has a restaurant.

Also in Gombani and about 300m down the road heading back towards Chake Chake, is *Venus Lodge* (☎ 452294) which has rooms

for US$20 with shared bath. Meals are available if you book well in advance. To get to Gombani, take any bus going north and ask them to drop you by the stadium.

Apart from the restaurants at Star Inn and Venus Lodge, there are several local food stalls in Chake Chake, and shops that sell basic supplies. For drinks, try *Balloon Brothers Cold Drinks* near the market.

Imam Cold Drinks just to the north of Star Inn has good, fresh *mtindi* (yoghurt).

Getting There & Away

Karume airport is about 6km east of Chake Chake. There's no regular bus service to the airport yet, though this should start once scheduled flights begin.

See the Pemba Getting Around section for information on local bus routes and car hire.

MKOANI

Mkoani is the southernmost of Pemba's main towns and its most important port,

TANZANIA

where ships from Unguja or elsewhere usually arrive. There is little to see here; most travellers stop here only briefly en route to/from Kiweni, Chake Chake or beyond.

Information

Despite signs you'll see on the road, there is no foreign exchange bureau in Mkoani.

Places to Stay & Eat

The best place to stay in Mkoani, and one of the most pleasant places on Pemba, is the recently re-opened *Jondeni Guest House* (☎ 456042, email pembablue@hotmail.com, PO Box 111, Mkoani); you can also book through Island Discovery Tours (☎ 233073, fax 231373) at Africa House in Zanzibar Town. The guesthouse is situated up on a hill about 800m from the port: go left out of the port past Mkoani Guest House, then bear right up the hill. A bed in a four-bed dorm costs US$8; singles cost US$15 (US$20 with bath); doubles cost US$10 per person (US$15 with bath); all rates include a full breakfast. There's a good restaurant, with great views and meals between TSh 3000 and TSh 4000. The shop sells basics, including both bottled and distilled water. Staff have a wealth of information on Pemba, and can arrange bicycle rentals, diving and snorkelling trips to Misali Island and offshore reefs, canoe trips through the mangroves, excursions to Chake Chake, Wete, and other destinations on the island, and more. They also offer free Swahili classes and guided walks around Mkoani.

Mkoani Guest House (☎ 456102), just to the north-east of the port, is a step down but is not bad. Rooms with shared bath cost US$10/20, and there's also a decent restaurant here.

The only other option is the usually empty government-run *Hoteli ya Mkoani* with rooms for US$15/25.

There are numerous places where you can find street-food stands in town and by the port.

Getting There & Away

See the Pemba Getting Around section for details of local transport. Jondeni Guest

House is the booking agent for the *Sepideh* ferry, which also has an office at the port. The bus station is about 200m east of the port, up the hill and just off the main road.

WETE

Wete is a pleasant town and a good base for exploring northern Pemba. It has the island's second most important port, through which much of its clove crop is exported. The picturesque road leading from Chake Chake to Wete via Ziwani passes villages, hillsides and many banana trees.

Information

You can change cash or travellers cheques at the Wete foreign exchange bureau on the main road.

Places to Stay & Eat

Hoteli ya Wete, just off the main road near the junction, is similar to the government-run hotels in Mkoani and Chake Chake, and charges the same prices.

Nearby is the friendly *Super Guest House* (☎ 454062) which has singles/doubles from US$8/18.

Sharouk Guest House (☎ 454386) at the western end of town is a good place with rooms for US$10/20 (US$25 for a double with bath). Meals are available with advance notice. The owner is very knowledgeable about Wete and the surrounding area, and can arrange bicycle rental and assist with excursions to Ngezi Forest, Vumawimbi beach and other nearby destinations.

For food, try *Green Garden Refreshments* at the western edge of Wete, which has a few outdoor tables on a tiny patio.

New Four Ways Restaurant just off the main road near the entrance to town also serves inexpensive meals.

Getting There & Away

For information on local bus routes see the Pemba Getting Around section.

Dhows sail frequently between Tanga and Wete for about TSh 4000, although captains are often unwilling to take foreigners. See the Boat section in the Tanzania Getting Around chapter.

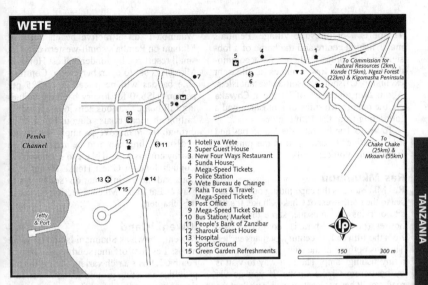

WETE

Pemba Channel

Jetty & Port

1 Hoteli ya Wete
2 Super Guest House
3 New Four Ways Restaurant
4 Sunda House;
  Mega-Speed Tickets
5 Police Station
6 Wete Bureau de Change
7 Raha Tours & Travel;
  Mega-Speed Tickets
8 Post Office
9 Mega-Speed Ticket Stall
10 Bus Station; Market
11 People's Bank of Zanzibar
12 Sharouk Guest House
13 Hospital
14 Sports Ground
15 Green Garden Refreshments

To Commission for Natural Resources (2km), Konde (15km), Ngezi Forest (22km) & Kigomasha Peninsula

To Chake Chake (25km) & Mkoani (55km)

0   150   300 m

TANZANIA

OTHER DESTINATIONS
Kigomasha Peninsula

The Kigomasha Peninsula in Pemba's north-western corner has several attractive beaches and a diving resort. It's also the site of the Ngezi Forest (see the Ngezi section following).

The nicest beach is **Vumawimbi** on the peninsula's east coast. Only the most basic provisions are available at the nearby village, so you'll have to bring your own food and drink. To get here, you can bicycle or try to hitch a ride from Manta Reef Lodge, to the west. Alternatively, Konde bus drivers are usually willing to take you out for an extra fee, although you'll need to make arrangements for the return. Car hire from Chake Chake will cost from about TSh 35,000 per day.

On the western side of the peninsula is **Verani Beach** and *Manta Reef Lodge*, which has cottage-style accommodation for US$160/260 a single/double, including full board. Discounts are often available during the low season. It's primarily a diving operation. Book through One Earth Diving in Mombasa (☎ 011-473914, fax 473462, email onearth@africaonline.co.ke) or through Part-

nership Travel & Tours in Chake Chake. The lodge is closed during May and often closes for other periods during the low season (and sometimes during the high season as well), so check first in Chake Chake before making your way up here. You can request someone from the lodge to pick you up at the ferry in Mkoani. Otherwise, take the No 35 bus to Konde, from where you'll have to arrange with the driver to take you on to Manta Reef Lodge.

Ngezi Forest

The small, dense forest at Ngezi is part of the much larger natural forest that once covered large areas of Pemba, and is the home of the Pemba flying fox bat (*Pteropus voeltzkowi*), which is endemic to the island. The forest is now a protected area and there is a small information centre, a short nature trail, and a US$5 entry fee.

Ngezi is north of Wete between Konde and Tondooni. To get here via public transport, take the bus to Konde, from where it's a 3 to 4km walk. Bus drivers are sometimes willing to drop you at the information centre for an additional TSh 1000 to TSh 2000.

Tumbe

Tumbe is a picturesque village, Pemba's major fishing centre and the home of a lobster fisheries project. There's no accommodation but the town makes a pleasant excursion. Offshore are some pleasant islets. About 2km south-east of Tumbe at **Chwaka** are the overgrown ruins of a mosque, and a fort dating from the 18th century.

To get to Tumbe, take the No 35 bus and ask the driver to drop you at the junction, from where you can walk.

Ras Mkumbuu

Ras Mkumbuu is the cape jutting out into the sea to the north-west of Chake Chake. It's the site of ruins of a mosque, some tombs and houses (possibly Shirazi) thought to date from the 14th or 15th century, perhaps earlier. There is nothing at the ruins now except for a tiny fishing camp. The best way to visit is by boat from Chake Chake. If you go via road, you'll have at least an hour's walk at the end; one section of the path often becomes submerged at high tide, so plan accordingly.

Pujini Ruins

About 10km south-east of Chake Chake at Pujini are the ruins of a town dating from about the 14th century. This was the seat of the infamous Mohammed bin Abdul Rahman who ruled on Pemba around the 15th century and was notorious for his cruelty. The ruins are in poor condition, and there's not much to see now.

There's no regular public transport to Pujini. The best way to get here is by bicycle. Car hire from Chake Chake costs about TSh 10,000 round-trip.

Waamba Beach

Waamba is an attractive beach north of Mkoani on Pemba's south-western coast. A small resort run by Jondeni Guest House in Mkoani is set to open here soon. Comfortable bandas will be priced at US$25 per person (US$50 for luxury bandas), including full board. Various activities, including sailing in local boats, dugout-canoe trips through the mangrove swamps, and diving and snorkelling can also be arranged. The nearby cove is a good place to see dolphins. Contact Jondeni Guest House for reservations and further information (see Places to Stay & Eat in the Mkoani section earlier in this chapter).

Kiweni Island

Kiweni, shown as Shamiani Island on some maps, lies just off the south-east coast of Pemba. It hosts a rich variety of birdlife and provides a nesting ground for some sea turtle colonies. It also offers some good snorkelling and diving.

The only place to stay is the relaxing *Kiweni Marine Resort* (☎ 051-600901, email pemba@intafrica.com, PO Box 215, Chake Chake). It's not officially open at this point due to funding difficulties but will sometimes take guests anyway for very negotiable prices. If you're in Zanzibar Town, ask around for Brian at Pichy's Pizza.

To get here, take any bus along the Mkoani-Chake Chake road to Mtambile junction. From Mtambile, you can find pick-ups or other transport to Kengeja, from where you'll have to walk a few kilometres to the water and then wait for a local boat over to Kiweni Island.

North-Eastern Tanzania

North-eastern Tanzania is one of the country's most enticing regions for travellers and one of its most diverse. Inland are the lush, forested Usambara and Pare mountains, which offer great hiking, beautiful scenery and fascinating culture. Along the coast are attractive beaches and Saadani, Tanzania's only seaside game reserve. For history buffs there is the former colonial capital of Bagamoyo and enough ruins to occupy several days.

Most attractions are fairly easily accessible from both Dar es Salaam and Arusha. While many secondary roads are in less than optimal condition, distances are not great and the local transport network is fairly good. If you have time to visit only one part of the country, the north-east would be a good choice.

BAGAMOYO
☎ 052

Bagamoyo was once one of the most important dhow ports along the East African coast and the terminus of the trade caravan route linking Lake Tanganyika with the sea. Many of the European explorers, including Burton and Stanley, began and ended their trips here.

From 1887 to 1891 Bagamoyo was the capital of German East Africa, and in 1888 it was the site of the first major uprising against the colonial government. Today, Bagamoyo is a sleepy place and most of its buildings are in an advanced state of decay. The beaches are attractive though, and enough interest remains to make it a good overnight excursion from Dar es Salaam.

Things to See & Do

Bagamoyo is a centre for dhow building; you can watch the **boat builders** at work near the port. There is also a colourful **fish market** with auctions most afternoons.

The small **museum** (open daily) at the Catholic mission north of town has interesting displays on the history of Bagamoyo and a section on some of the European ex-

plorers. On the same compound is the chapel where Livingstone's body was laid before being taken to Zanzibar Town en route to Westminster Abbey (see the boxed text 'David Livingstone').

Scattered around town are some **carved doors** and various buildings from the German colonial era, all in disrepair.

About 500m south of Bagamoyo along the road to Dar es Salaam is **Chuo cha Sanaa**, a well known theatre and arts college. When school is in session, there are sometimes performances of traditional dancing or drumming.

Still further south, about 5km from the town centre along the beach, are the overgrown and deserted **Kaole ruins**, which include the remains of a 13th-century mosque (one of the oldest on mainland Tanzania) and some gravestones estimated to date from the 15th century. To get here by foot, walk south along the beach for about 5kms past Kaole village into the mangrove swamps. Where the beach apparently ends, go a few hundred metres inland and look for the stone pillars. Only go in a group, and don't bring any valuables.

Places to Stay

Other than at the top end places, be prepared for an erratic water supply at many of Bagamoyo's hotels and guesthouses during the dry season.

TANZANIA

411

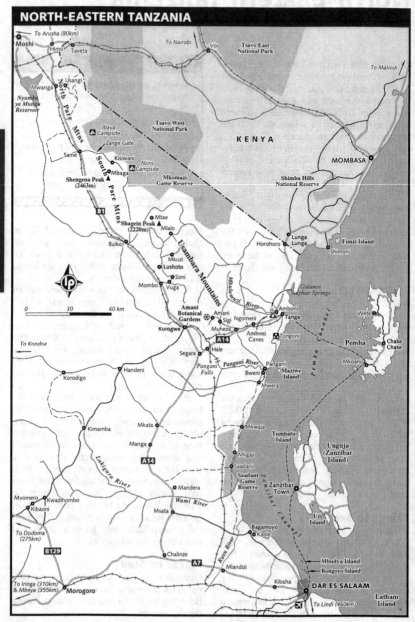

NORTH-EASTERN TANZANIA

0   30   60 km

To Arusha (80km)
Moshi
Himo   Taveta
To Nairobi   Voi   Tsavo East
National Park
To Malindi

Mwanga
Usangi

Nyumba
ya Mungu
Reservoir

Ibaya
Campsite
Zange Gate

Tsavo West
National Park

K E N Y A

Same   Kisiwani
Njiro
Mbaga   Campsite

Shengena Peak
(2463m)

Mkomazi
Game Reserve

MOMBASA

Shimba Hills
National Reserve

B1

South Pare Mts

North Pare Mts

Shagein Peak
(2220m)

Mtae
Mlalo

Funzi Island

Buiko

Mkuzi

Usambara Mountains

Lushoto

Lunga
Lunga   Shimoni

Mombo   Soni
Vuga

Amani
Botanical
Gardens

Amani
Sigi   Ngomeni

Horohoro

Galanos
Sulphur Springs

Amboni

Tanga

Korogwe   A14

Muheza
Amboni
Caves

Wete

To Kondoa

Segara   Hale

Tongoni

Pemha

Chake
Chake

Pangani
Falls

Pangani River

Pangani

Handeni

Bweni   Maziwe
Island

Mkoani

Korodigo

Mwera

Kimamba

Mkata

Manga

Mkwaja

Tumbatu
Island

Unguja
(Zanzibar
Island)

Mligaji

Saadani

Saadani
Game Reserve

Zanzibar
Town

Mvomero
Kwadihombo
Kibaoni

Mandera

Wami River

Msata

To Dodoma
(275km)

B129

Chalinze   A7

Bagamoyo
Kaole

Uzi
Island

To Iringa (310km)
& Mbeya (355km)   Morogoro

Mlandizi

Kibaha

Mbudya Island
Bongoyo Island

DAR ES SALAAM

To Lindi (460km)

Latham
Island

In the centre of town are several very grubby guesthouses, most of which are not recommended. The best is *Azania Guest House* on Majengo Rd, with basic but acceptable rooms for TSh 1500.

Most of the beach hotels are strung out along the 2km stretch of road leading north from the Catholic mission. All prices include breakfast. The first one you come to is the laid-back *Bagamoyo Beach Resort* (☎ 440083, 0811-322000, fax 440154) with decent singles/doubles for TSh 10,000/16,000 (TSh 21,000/24,000 with air-con and bathroom) and bungalows for TSh 7000 per person. Half-board and full-board options are also available.

Travellers Lodge (☎ 440077, fax 440 154) is the next along, with simple cottage-style accommodation for TSh 8000/10,000 (TSh 14,000/16,000 with bathroom and TSh 22,000/24,000 with air-con as well). Camping here costs TSh 1000 per person.

Paradise Holiday Resort (☎ 440136, 0811-335217, fax 440142, email paradise@ raha.com) a few hundred metres further north of Travellers Lodge has a pool and comfortable accommodation for US$50/65.

Just next door to the north of Paradise Holiday Resort is the luxurious, Italian-run *Livingstone Club* (☎ 440080, fax 440104, email livingstone@raha.com) which has rooms for US$120/150/210. Full-board rates are also available.

The German-owned *Badeco Beach Hotel* (☎ 440018, email 02132-70010@ t-online.de) is on the beach but at the southern end of town next to the German cemetery. It has comfortable rooms (all doubles) with bathroom and fan for TSh 16,000 (TSh 24,000 with air-con). There is also a

David Livingstone

Walking around Bagamoyo, you'll see numerous plaques and displays commemorating David Livingstone, the famous Scottish missionary-explorer. Livingstone, who was born in Scotland in 1813, first came to Africa in 1840 as a missionary and doctor with the London Missionary Society. After establishing a base in Bechuanaland (now Botswana), he set out to explore parts of the Kalahari Desert and the Zambezi River with the idea of opening up new areas for mission work and finding a navigable route into the interior. By the mid-1850s, he had made his way along the Zambezi to Victoria Falls, and had traversed the continent between Luanda (Angola) in the west and Quelimane (Mozambique) in the east. Between 1858 and 1864, he led an expedition along the Zambezi and Shire Rivers to southern Malawi and Lake Nyasa, parts of which he explored in great detail.

Livingstone's most well known expedition began in 1866, when he set off to find the source of the Nile River. After several years, during which time he was variously reported killed and missing, Livingstone was found by the Welsh-American journalist Henry Morton Stanley in Ujiji, on the shores of Lake Tanganyika. After greeting him with the famous words, 'Dr Livingstone, I presume?', Stanley attempted to persuade Livingstone – whose health was much weakened by this point – to return with him. Livingstone refused, and continued on with his search for the Nile until 1873, when he died in the village of Chitambo, south of Lake Bangweulu in Zambia. Two of his faithful followers, Chuma and Susi, cut out his heart and buried it under a tree. After preserving his body by drying and wrapping it, they set off on foot, carrying it more than 1000km across the continent to Bagamoyo, from where it was brought to Unguja (Zanzibar Island) and then shipped to England for burial in Westminster Abbey.

Although Livingstone never succeeded in finding the source of the Nile, his expeditions were widely reported in Europe. These accounts, together with his descriptions of the horrors of the slave trade, kindled European missionary and commercial interest in Africa and sparked the most active period of European involvement in the region. The founding of the well known Universities' Mission to Central Africa (UMCA) can be attributed to Livingstone, as can establishment of several other missionary organisations. And, within several months of his death, the slave market in Zanzibar Town was closed.

double with shared bath for TSh 10,000, and a triple with fan for TSh 20,000.

Places to Eat

The best place for local food is the small *canteen* near the museum. Plates of rice, meat and greens cost TSh 500. Look for the thatched *bandas* (thatched huts), or ask at the museum.

Otherwise, all of the hotels listed above have restaurants with prices on a par with their room rates.

Getting There & Away

Minibuses run throughout the day between Bagamoyo and Dar es Salaam (TSh 1000, three hours). In Dar es Salaam, departures are from Msimbazi St, opposite the petrol station; in Bagamoyo, departures are from near the market.

If you have your own vehicle, the best route from Dar es Salaam is via New Bagamoyo Rd (which soon joins Old Bagamoyo Rd), and is potholed or sand most of the way, although rehabilitation work is underway. You can also head west (only in a 4WD) from Bagamoyo to Msata, which is at the junction with the main road going to/from Tanga.

Dhows sail between Bagamoyo and Unguja (Zanzibar Island), though safety is an issue; if you want to try anyway, it can be arranged on the beach by the dhow port.

SAADANI GAME RESERVE

Saadani Game Reserve is on the coast about 70km north of Bagamoyo. It's a laid-back and relaxing place, where you can enjoy the beach and a good diversity of animals at the same time. The reserve is particularly noted for its birdlife; species you may see include fish eagles and lesser flamingos. Saadani's many animals include giraffe, buffalo, wildebeest, elephant, sable, crocodile and hippo.

Information

Entry to the reserve costs US$20 per day. In addition to relaxing on the beach and observing the birdlife, the main activities are walking safaris, wildlife drives and boat safaris on the Wami River. Boat safaris (US$30) can be arranged at the camp site (see Places to Stay following) or with residents of nearby Saadani village. Walking safaris booked through the camp cost US$15 per person (US$10 per person in a group of six) and half-day wildlife drives cost US$25.

Places to Stay

The best place and the only permanent camp site is *A Tent with a View*. Comfortable accommodation in tented en suite bandas along the beach costs US$85 per person, including full board. There's a treehouse at the camp, which is good for bird and wildlife viewing at the nearby water hole. Bookings can be made through A Tent with a View Safaris (☎ 0811-323318, fax 051-151106, email tentview@intafrica.com) PO Box 40525, Dar es Salaam. The Web site is www.saadani.com.

Getting There & Away

Air Charter flights can be arranged from Dar es Salaam and Unguja. A five seater plane from Unguja costs about US$300 one way. If you're travelling alone, check with A Tent With a View Safaris to see if they have any charter flights scheduled with extra seats.

Road A Tent with a View provides free road transport to/from Dar es Salaam three times weekly (minimum two people).

To get to Saadani from Dar es Salaam by car, the route is via Chalinze (on the Morogoro road), and then north to Mandera village (about 50km north of Chalinze on the Arusha highway). At Mandera, bear east along a newly upgraded road and continue for about 60km to Saadani. Allow four to five hours from Dar es Salaam.

Access is also possible from Pangani, across the Pangani River by ferry, then south via Mkwaja to the reserve's north gate at Mligaji. However, this road is very rough and seldom used, and is often impassable in the rainy season. The road just west of Bagamoyo which heads north to Saadani is not feasible as the Wami River ferry is almost always out of service.

Boat Local fishing boats sail between Saadani and Unguja. If you want to try this, it can be arranged with the fishermen at the beach near the Tembo House Hotel in Zanzibar Town. A better option, once it starts running, would be the scheduled dhow service being planned by A Tent with a View Safaris.

PANGANI

Pangani is a small town about 55km south of Tanga. During the late 19th century, it was a terminus of the caravan route from Lake Tanganyika, a major export point for slaves and ivory, and one of the largest ports between Bagamoyo and Mombasa.

Today, while there are still a few carved doorways and buildings from the German colonial era to be seen, the town is primarily of interest to those seeking somewhere to relax, and as a base for trips along the river or to nearby islands.

About 10km offshore from Pangani is **Maziwe Island**, which offers good snorkelling. Visits are only possible at low tide. Excursions can be arranged through the Tinga Tinga Resort (TSh 60,000 for a boat with a capacity of about 10 to 12 passengers). Alternatively, you can arrange transport with local dhow captains. There's no village on the island, so bring whatever food and drink you will need.

The scenic **Pangani River** hosts rich birdlife, as well as populations of crocodiles and other animals. Tinga Tinga Resort arranges good sunset cruises (TSh 5000 per person, five passengers minimum).

Places to Stay

The New River View Inn Restaurant & Lodge is a simple but clean place on the riverfront with singles/doubles for TSh 2000/4000. Despite the name, there's no food here.

Most travellers stay north of town, where there are several comfortable hotels. The most popular is *Tinga Tinga Resort (☎ Pangani 22 or 79)* which has doubles (no singles) for TSh 18,000 (TSh 5000 for each additional person), not including breakfast. Accommodation is in spacious bungalows with three beds. It's signposted just beyond the main junction on the coastal road, and about 2km north of the centre of town. The

owner can assist with organising snorkelling trips, river excursions, walking tours of Pangani and other activities.

Pangani Beach Resort (☎ Pangani 88) just south of Tinga Tinga Resort on the coastal road has comfortable air-con rooms for TSh 18,000/24,000 (plus TSh 1500/2000 for continental/full breakfast).

On the opposite side of the river on the beach is the comfortable *Emayani Beach Lodge (☎ 057-7182, 4222, email sss@yako.habari.co.tz, PO Box 111, Pangani)* with bungalow accommodation for US$60/75 (US$12 for children between six and 12 years, and free for children under six). Meals cost an additional US$5/12/12 for breakfast/lunch/dinner (half price for children between six and 12). There is an additional 5% service charge for accommodation and meals. Windsurfing, sailing and fishing can be arranged. To get here, you can either arrange a charter flight through Serengeti Select Safaris in Arusha (☎/fax 057-7182), or hire a boat from Pangani (either take the local ferry – which transports vehicles – or hire a boat through the Tinga Tinga Resort).

Places to Eat

For inexpensive local food, try *Central Restaurant* near the main square or *Pangadeco Bar & Lodge* at the beach end of the main street, about 50m through the coconut palms.

There is a good *restaurant* at Tinga Tinga Resort, which specialises in seafood meals.

Getting There & Away

Public transport stops at both the main junction (about 2km north of town) and also in the town centre. If you're going to Tinga Tinga Resort or Pangani Beach Resort, get out at the junction. Otherwise, stay on until the centre.

Minibuses run several times daily between Pangani and Muheza (TSh 500), from where you can get onward transport to Tanga, Korogwe and Lushoto. There's also a direct bus most days between Tanga and Pangani via Muheza (TSh 800, four to five hours). In the dry season there is occasional transport from Pangani to Tanga along the coastal road (TSh 800).

TANZANIA

If you're driving, the best way between Pangani and Tanga is via Muheza, rather than via the coastal road. Local boats (TSh 200) and a sporadic car ferry connect Pangani with Bweni, on the opposite riverbank. The road on the southern side of the river is only passable by 4WD in the dry season.

TANGA
☎ 053

Tanga is Tanzania's second largest seaport, and its third largest town behind Dar es Salaam and Mwanza. One of the main industries in the area is sisal. Despite its size, Tanga is a pleasant place with a sleepy, semicolonial atmosphere, and makes a good stop for those en route to or from Mombasa.

Things to See & Do

Tanga has several **parks**, including Jamhuri Park overlooking the harbour, and the park and cemetery surrounding the Askari Monument at the end of Sokoine St. Directly offshore is **Toten Island**, which has ruins of a mosque and some gravestones. Fishing boats on the western side of the harbour can take you over.

There are several interesting excursions in the nearby area, including to the Amani botanical gardens (see the Around Tanga section following).

Places to Stay

One of the cheapest places is *New Era Hotel* on Amboni Rd just off Makorongoro Rd. Grubby rooms are TSh 2500 for a single with shared bath and TSh 5000 for a double with private bathroom; the owner is often willing to negotiate. Camping on the cramped grounds is also permitted.

Makundi Guest House Annex is at the other end of town, about 1.5km north-west of the bus station. Clean singles/doubles with fan and mosquito net cost TSh 3000/3500 (TSh 4000 for a double with bathroom).

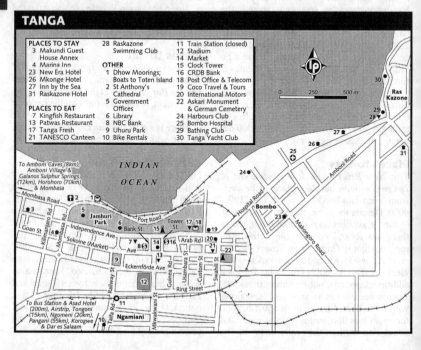

TANGA

PLACES TO STAY	28 Raskazone	11 Train Station (closed)
3 Makundi Guest House Annex	Swimming Club	12 Stadium
4 Marina Inn	**OTHER**	14 Market
23 New Era Hotel	1 Dhow Moorings;	15 Clock Tower
26 Mkonge Hotel	Boats to Toten Island	16 CRDB Bank
27 Inn by the Sea	2 St Anthony's	18 Post Office & Telecom
31 Raskazone Hotel	Cathedral	19 Coco Travel & Tours
	5 Government	20 International Motors
PLACES TO EAT	Offices	22 Askari Monument
7 Kingfish Restaurant	6 Library	& German Cemetery
13 Patwas Restaurant	8 NBC Bank	24 Harbours Club
17 Tanga Fresh	9 Uhuru Park	25 Bombo Hospital
21 TANESCO Canteen	10 Bike Rentals	29 Bathing Club
		30 Tanga Yacht Club

Asad Hotel, directly north of the bus station and the only high-rise building in the area, has doubles (no singles) for TSh 6000 (TSh 8000 with air-con).

For mid-range accommodation, try *Marina Inn (☎ 44362)* just west of the town centre on Goan Rd. It's a dark but decently maintained place with its own bar and restaurant, and air-con doubles (no singles) for TSh 8100, including continental breakfast.

At the other end of town overlooking the sea are several more attractive places. The first you reach is *Mkonge Hotel (☎ 44542)* on the eastern extension of Hospital Rd, with comfortable doubles (no singles) for US$50, including full breakfast.

Just beyond the Mkonge on the same road is *Inn by the Sea (☎ 44614)*. Good value air-con rooms facing the sea are TSh 10,000 (including continental breakfast); TSh 7000 for rooms with fan and no sea view.

The popular *Raskazone Hotel (☎/fax 43897)* is at the easternmost end of town and a few hundred metres inland. It has comfortable doubles (only) for TSh 15,000 (TSh 22,500 with air-con), including full breakfast. Ask about special 'backpacker' rates; camping can also be arranged.

Places to Eat
Kingfish Restaurant on Independence Ave is good for inexpensive meals.

Other budget places include the clean and cheap *TANESCO Canteen* on Sokoine St; the pricier *Food Palace*, also on Sokoine St (closed Monday evening); and *Patwas Restaurant* opposite the market.

Indian meals are available in the evening at *Raskazone Swimming Club* east of town along the water.

For fresh milk and yoghurt, try the *Tanga Fresh* outlet near the post office.

Getting There & Away
Bus Buses or minibuses run daily between Tanga and Dar es Salaam (TSh 3500, five hours), Lushoto (TSh 2500, three hours), Mombasa (TSh 3500, six hours plus border crossing time), Moshi (TSh 4200, five hours), Muheza (TSh 300, 45 minutes), and Pangani (TSh 800, four to five hours).

Boat Mega-Speed's *MS Sepideh* connects Tanga twice weekly with Dar es Salaam via Pemba and Unguja (see The Zanzibar Archipelago Getting There & Away section for details). Coco Travel & Tours (☎ 44131, fax 44132, email cocotravel@cats-net.com) in the Bandari building on Independence Ave is the Mega-Speed agent.

AROUND TANGA
Amani Botanical Gardens
The Amani gardens are west of Tanga in a beautiful area in the eastern Usambara Mountains, and are well worth a detour if you're in the area. After many years of neglect, the gardens and surrounding area have recently been gazetted as a nature reserve and rehabilitation work is underway. There are some good walks in the surrounding forest, and an extended series of guided trails around both Amani and Sigi (which lies about 10km below Amani) is planned for the near future. In addition to a large variety of plants, you may see several endemic bird species here, including the Nduk eagle owl, the Uluguru violet-backed, Amani and banded green sunbirds, and the green-headed oriole.

There are information centres at both Amani and Sigi. Alternatively, contact the East Usambara Catchment Forest Project office (☎ 053-43820) at the Finnida compound in Tanga. It's on the main Korogwe road, after the Total petrol station as you leave town.

Muheza is at the junction where the roads to Amani botanical gardens and to Pangani branch off the main Tanga highway. If you need to stay, there are local guesthouses in town. Otherwise, the grubby *Hotel Ambassador* on the main road has basic singles/doubles costing TSh 1800/2200 (TSh 3000/3600 with bathroom) and a *restaurant*.

Places to Stay & Eat There are two *resthouses* at Amani with accommodation for between TSh 6000 and TSh 10,000 per person; meals can be arranged with the caretaker. A six room *resthouse* is also being rehabilitated at Sigi and should be open soon.

Getting There & Away Amani is about 30km north-west of Muheza. Minibuses run several times daily between Muheza and Amani via Sigi; the road is very muddy in parts, particularly during the rainy season, so allow about three hours for the trip.

Amboni Caves

These limestone caves are located about 8km north-west of Tanga off the Tanga-Mombasa road. The best way to reach them is by bicycle from Tanga. Otherwise charter a taxi, or take a minibus heading to Amboni village and have the driver drop you at the turn-off for the caves. From here, it's about 2km on foot to Kiomoni village; the caves are nearby on the Mkulumuzi River. There's a TSh 1000 entry fee (TSh 500 for children).

About 4km north of the Amboni caves along the Tanga-Mombasa road at Amboni village are the **Galanos Sulphur Springs**. While the area is attractive, the springs aren't suitable for bathing. Minibuses from Tanga to Amboni village (TSh 400) run several times daily.

Tongoni Ruins

About 15km south of Tanga along the coastal road are the Tongoni ruins. These include the remains of a mosque and some graves estimated to date from the 14th or 15th century. There's no entry charge, although the caretaker appreciates a small donation.

KOROGWE

Korogwe's primary importance for travellers is as a transport junction. In the western part of town, known as New Korogwe, are the bus stand and several accommodation options. To the east is Old Korogwe with the train station (no passenger service).

Travellers Inn opposite the bus stand has clean doubles (no singles) with enormous bathtubs for TSh 5000, and a restaurant.

Usambara Mountains

The cool and beautiful Usambaras, part of the ancient Eastern Arc chain (see the boxed text 'The Eastern Arc Mountains'), are di-

The Eastern Arc Mountains

The Eastern Arc Mountains, which stretch in a crescent shape from the Taita Hills in southern Kenya down to Morogoro and the Southern Highlands, are estimated to be at least 100 million years old, with the stones that formed them being even older – perhaps as old as 600 million years. Thanks to their climatic isolation and stability, which has offered plant species a chance to develop during all these years, the mountains have an exceptional degree of biological diversity. They contain about one-third of Tanzania's flora and fauna species, including numerous endemics. Of the more than 2000 plant species that have been identified in the mountains, about one-quarter are endemic.

Over the past century, with the growth of logging interests, increasing population density, and a corresponding increase in the clearance of forest areas for small-scale farm plots, forest depletion has become a serious problem throughout the Eastern Arc. One of the most obvious and deleterious effects of this deforestation is erosion, which became so bad in parts of the western Usambara region in the early 1990s that entire villages had to be shifted to lower areas. Another less noticeable but just as serious concern is contamination of water resources. Villages in the Eastern Arc Mountains, as well as those in lower-lying coastal areas, depend on the maintenance of watershed areas for good quality water supplies. Diminished vegetation and forest cover at higher altitudes affect rainfall levels, erosion and ground water supplies. These in turn affect river flows, water quality and supply at lower levels.

vided into eastern and western ranges separated by a 4km-wide valley. The region has one of the highest degrees of biodiversity on the African continent. In addition to an impressive variety of plants, the mountains host a number of endemic and rare bird species, including the Usambara eagle owl, Kenrick's starling and the Usambara warbler. The Netherlands Development Organisation (SNV) and local residents have been working together to develop sources of livelihood that do not deplete the natural resources of the mountains. The main tribal groups in the Usambaras are the Sambaa, the Kilindi, the Zigua and the Mbugu.

For travellers, the mountains offer excellent hiking and birdwatching. The area around Lushoto in the western Usambaras is the most accessible. The best time to visit is from July to October, after the rains and when the air is at its clearest. Lonely Planet's *Trekking in East Africa* has more details.

The free tourist brochure, *Usambara View*, has helpful general information on the region. It's available at many hotels and from the tourist information offices in Lushoto, Dar es Salaam and Arusha. The Friends of Usambara Society can be contacted through the tourist information centre in Lushoto (☎ Lushoto 132) PO Box 151, Lushoto.

LUSHOTO

Lushoto is an attractive town set in a valley at about 1200m. It's the main centre in the western Usambaras and makes a good base for hikes into the surrounding hills. During the German colonial era, Lushoto (or Wilhelmstal as it was then known) was a favoured vacation spot for administrators and an important regional centre. At one point it was even slated to become the colonial capital.

Information

There's a good Tourist Information Centre (☎ Lushoto 132), PO Box 151, next to the bus station which can assist with arranging excursions and guides. Rates are TSh 6000 per group per day plus a TSh 1500 per person per day village development fee. For overnight trips, there is an additional TSh 4000 fee per group for the guide plus a TSh 2000 camping fee. You'll need to bring your own tent. The fees you pay for excursions go to support the conservation efforts of the SNV, which are being carried out within the framework of the West Usambara Cultural Tourism Program.

Hiking without a guide is not recommended as several muggings of lone travellers have been reported. When arranging a guide, be sure the one you hire is really from the information centre.

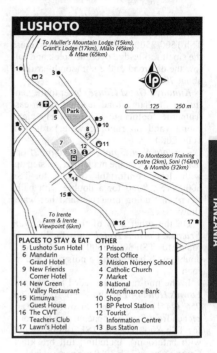

LUSHOTO

To Muller's Mountain Lodge (15km), Grant's Lodge (17km), Mlalo (45km) & Mtae (65km)

To Montessori Training Centre (2km), Soni (16km) & Mombo (32km)

To Irente Farm & Irente Viewpoint (6km)

0   125   250 m

PLACES TO STAY & EAT
5 Lushoto Sun Hotel
6 Mandarin Grand Hotel
9 New Friends Corner Hotel
14 New Green Valley Restaurant
15 Kimunya Guest House
16 The CWT Teachers Club
17 Lawn's Hotel

OTHER
1 Prison
2 Post Office
3 Mission Nursery School
4 Catholic Church
7 Market
8 National Microfinance Bank
10 Shop
11 BP Petrol Station
12 Tourist Information Centre
13 Bus Station

TANZANIA

Temperatures get very cool here in the evenings, especially around June, so bring a jacket.

Hiking

One of the most popular hikes from Lushoto is to **Irente Viewpoint**, approximately an hour's walk from Lushoto, which offers good views over the surrounding hills. En route and shortly before the viewpoint is the pleasant Irente Farm (see Places to Eat following). Camping is possible at the viewpoint.

Other possibilities include excursions to **Mlalo**, an attractive town about 45km north-east of Lushoto, and **Mtae**, with a beautiful cliff-top setting about 20km beyond Mlalo. Both places have simple guesthouses and many nearby hiking trails.

Places to Stay

There are numerous guesthouses in town, all basic. One of the better ones is *The CWT*

Teachers Club at the southern edge of town. Singles/doubles with shared bath are TSh 1500/2500. From the bus station, cross the small footbridge over the creek and follow the dirt road to the left (south-east) for about 700m.

Kimunya Guest House closer to the centre on the same road leading south-east from the footbridge has relatively clean rooms (and no running water) for TSh 1000/2000.

Lushoto Sun Hotel (☎ Lushoto 82) opposite the park on the main road is a step up, with clean, comfortable doubles for TSh 5000 (TSh 8000 for a double with bathroom), including breakfast and hot water showers.

On the other side of the park is *New Friends Corner Hotel* with fairly clean rooms for TSh 3000/5000 (TSh 6000 for a double with bathroom), a noisy bar and no food.

In the mid-range, the faded but pleasant *Lawn's Hotel (☎ Lushoto 5 or 66, or through 056-3445)* at the entrance to town as you approach from Soni has spacious, rustic rooms for TSh 8000/11,000 (TSh 14,000/18,000 with bathroom), including full breakfast. Camping costs TSh 2000 per person, including a hot shower and bathroom facilities.

Mandarin Grand Hotel, about 400m from the town centre (behind the Catholic church on the hill) has rooms for TSh 6000/7500.

The best places are about 15km north of Lushoto in the hilly area near Migambo village. The relaxing *Grant's Lodge (☎ 053-42491, fax 43628 for bookings)* is a rehabilitated colonial-era farmhouse with comfortable rooms costing TSh 30,000/60,000, including full board (and discounts for children).

Mullers Mountain Lodge (☎ Lushoto 134, PO Box 34, or through the BP petrol station in Lushoto) offers comfortable, good value accommodation in the main house or in self-contained cottages for TSh 14,000 per person, including breakfast. Lunch and dinner are an additional TSh 5000 each. Discounts are available for stays during the week (Monday to Thursday).

To get to these last two places from Lushoto, take a minibus heading to Mkuzi and ask the driver to drop you at the lodge turn-offs (signposted). Transport from Lushoto towards Mkuzi is in the afternoon; returning from the lodges, transport is in the mornings only. If you're walking or you have your own transport, take the road heading up to Magamba, turn right at the signposted junction and continue for about 7km to Migambo. Both places are signposted.

Places to Eat

New Green Valley Restaurant near the bus stand has inexpensive local food but somewhat lackadaisical service.

The *restaurant* at Lushoto Sun Hotel is better, with good meals for between TSh 600 and TSh 2500.

There are several places near Lushoto where you can buy fresh cheese and jam. The closest to town is *Montessori Training Centre* about 2km outside town off the road to Soni, down the hill to the right. Another place is *Irente Farm* where you can also get home-made bread and other delicacies, en route to Irente Viewpoint.

Getting There & Away

Buses run throughout the day between Lushoto and Mombo (TSh 500, one hour). There's also at least one minibus daily to/from Dar es Salaam (TSh 4000, nine hours) and Moshi (TSh 3000). To both Dar es Salaam and Moshi it's faster and more comfortable to take a minibus to Mombo and then get one of the larger buses running along the main highway; the big buses are often full so you may have to stand for most of the ride.

There's usually one bus daily between Lushoto and Mlalo (TSh 1000) and another between Lushoto and Mtae (TSh 1000). Departures from Lushoto are generally in the afternoon, returning early the next morning, which means that you will need to spend at least one night in Mlalo or Mtae if you are relying on public transport.

SONI

Tiny Soni lies about halfway along the Mombo-Lushoto road and offers some pleasant walks, including one to the top of Kwa Mungu Peak.

The best place to stay is *Soni Falls Hotel* (☎ *Soni 27*), a rustic place about 1km south-west of town on a small road on the side of the valley opposite the main road. Double rooms (no singles) cost TSh 9000, including breakfast.

Otherwise, the small *Hotel Kimalube* (☎ *Soni 10*) about 2km south-west of Soni on the main road has simple but clean singles/doubles with nets, shared bath and breakfast for TSh 2000/3500.

Minibuses from Soni to both Lushoto and Mombo costs TSh 300.

MOMBO

Mombo is the junction town at the foot of the Usambaras where the road to Lushoto branches off the main Dar es Salaam-Arusha highway. If you get stuck overnight here, the best option is *Midway Express* at the main junction, with basic but clean singles/doubles for TSh 1500/2000, and a restaurant.

Buses go throughout the day between Mombo and Lushoto (TSh 500). Dar es Salaam-Arusha buses will drop you at the junction; however, boarding these buses in Mombo can be difficult as they're almost always full. Minibuses run several times daily to both Moshi and Dar es Salaam.

Pare Mountains

The Pare Mountains, just to the north-west of the Usambaras, are also part of the Eastern Arc chain and, like the Usambaras, they are divided into two ranges – north and south. Although the Pare Mountains are not as accessible or developed for tourism as the Usambaras, they offer good village-based hiking and birdwatching. The main tribal group in the area are the Pare, also called the Asu.

Accommodation and food options throughout the Pares are fairly basic; for camping you'll need your own equipment. The best way to explore the mountains is to spend a night at Mwanga or Same getting organised, and then head up to either Us-angi or Mbaga. From each of these places there are several good hikes, ranging from half a day to three days or more in length. Guide fees for hikes from either Mbaga or Usangi are TSh 4000 per group per day or TSh 2000 for half a day, plus an overnight fee of TSh 2000 per group per day. There's an additional village development fee of TSh 2000 per person per day. Porters can be arranged for TSh 2000 per group per day. Camping in forest areas around the villages costs TSh 2500 per person.

More detailed information on tourism activities in the Pares is available from the SNV (Netherlands Development Organisation) Cultural Tourism Program (☎/fax 057-7515, email tourinfo@habari.co.tz) AICC/Serengeti Wing, Room 643 (PO Box 10455) Arusha.

The best time to visit the Pares is between July and November.

SAME

Same (SAH-may) is the main town in the southern Pares. Unlike Lushoto in the Usambaras, there is little tourist infrastructure here, and the town is more suitable as a starting point for excursions into the Pares than as a base. If you do want to stay a few days before heading into the villages, there are several walks into the hills behind town, though for most of the better destinations, you will need to take local transport at least part of the way.

Places to Stay & Eat

The best place to stay in Same is *Amani Lutheran Centre* near the market. Clean, good value singles/doubles are TSh 2000/3000 (TSh 3500 with bathroom); there's also a restaurant.

Kambeni Guest House opposite the bus stand has basic rooms for TSh 2000/2500 (TSh 3500 with bathroom).

For upmarket accommodation, try *Elephant Motel*, approximately 1km south-east of town on the main Dar es Salaam-Arusha highway. Comfortable rooms cost TSh 12,000/18,000, including breakfast. There's also a *restaurant* and a communal TV.

Getting There & Away

Minibuses connect Same with Dar es Salaam (TSh 5000), Moshi (TSh 1000) and Mombo (TSh 1500) several times daily. There's also daily local transport to Kisiwani (near Mkomazi Game Reserve), and on most days to Mbaga and other nearby hill villages.

MBAGA

Mbaga, about 30km south-east of Same next to the Mkomazi Game Reserve, is a good base for hikes deeper into the surrounding southern Pare Mountains and villages. You can also trek from here to the top of Shengena Peak (2463m), the highest in the Pares.

Hill-Top Tona Lodge (☎ 600158 or Same 156, PO Box 32 Mbaga-Same or PO Box 1592 Dar es Salaam) has simple but good accommodation for US$10 per person. Camping costs US$5 per person; bring along some water purification tablets. Lunch and dinner cost TSh 2500 but give advance notice. Sasa Kazi Hotel near the bus station in Same has additional information about the lodge and transport options to Mbaga.

There is transport most days from Same to Mbaga (about TSh 1000) via Kisiwani; the last bus departs Same about 2 pm.

MWANGA

Mwanga, about 50km north of Same on the Dar es Salaam-Arusha highway, is a good starting point for excursions into the northern Pares.

The best place to stay is *Rhino Hotel*, signposted about 2km out of town off the road to Usangi. Simple but decent rooms are TSh 5000.

There is daily transport linking Mwanga with Arusha, Moshi, Same and Usangi.

USANGI

Usangi, in the hills east of Mwanga, is the centre of the northern Pares and the best base for hiking in this area.

The main point of interest in town as far as hiking is concerned is *Lomwe Secondary School* which has been designated as a centre to assist travellers with finding guides and accommodation. There's also a *camp site* at the school with water, and *hostel accommodation* during school breaks (TSh 2000 per person for either option). Otherwise, there is a *guesthouse* in town near the Jumaa mosque with basic rooms for about TSh 3500; meals can be arranged.

Getting There & Away

There are several minibuses or pick-ups daily between Mwanga and Usangi. From Arusha, there is a minibus most days from the central bus station, departing in the morning (TSh 2500).

MKOMAZI GAME RESERVE

Mkomazi Game Reserve, north and east of the Pare Mountains on the Kenyan border, is contiguous with Tsavo National Park in Kenya. The reserve, which has essentially no tourist facilities, is known for its black rhino, which were introduced into the area from South Africa for breeding. Wild dogs have also been reintroduced into the area. Other animals include elephant, giraffe, zebra, antelope and numerous snakes; there is also a good diversity of birdlife.

Entry costs US$20 per day. To visit the black rhino, breeding area at Kisima, you'll need a special permit. These are issued at Zange Gate, the main entrance to the reserve, about 5km east of Same.

Places to Stay

There are three *camp sites* in the reserve, at Ibaya, Kisima and Njiro (US$20 per person). Ibaya, at the north-western end of the reserve, is the closest to Same (about 15km). Njiro is just south of Kisiwani village, near the road running along the reserve's south-western border. You'll need to bring all your own provisions.

Northern Tanzania

There are few areas of the continent that attract as much tourist attention as northern Tanzania. With snow-capped Mt Kilimanjaro, the wildlife-packed Ngorongoro Crater and the vast plains of the Serengeti, the region embodies what is for many quintessential Africa.

While these places are well worth visiting, the north also holds many other attractions. The area around Marangu, for example, offers some good walks and opportunities for getting to know the local culture. North of Arusha are small villages where you can experience the Maasai way of life. The remote Crater Highlands have some of Tanzania's most striking scenery and hold excellent hiking possibilities for the more adventurous. There are also some lesser-known national parks that are just as spectacular as the Serengeti, including serene Lake Manyara; Tarangire, with its high concentration of wildlife; and tiny but beautiful Arusha National Park.

Northern Tanzania is an accessible region; main roads are in good condition and the larger towns offer a range of accommodation and dining options. There's also direct air access from Europe and elsewhere in East Africa via Kilimanjaro international airport.

MOSHI
☎ 055

Moshi, a bustling town at the foot of Mt Kilimanjaro, is the home of the Chagga people and the centre of one of Tanzania's major coffee growing regions.

Most visitors use the town as a starting point for climbing Mt Kilimanjaro, although it's a pleasant place in its own right to relax for a few days. It also tends to be less expensive than nearby Arusha.

Information

Immigration Moshi immigration office (open from 7.30 am to 3.30 pm Monday to Friday) in Kibo House near the clock tower processes visa extensions while you wait.

Highlights

- Watching the sun rise from the top of Mt Kilimanjaro, Africa's highest mountain
- Climbing Mt Meru – pristine, dramatic and Tanzania's second-highest peak
- Exploring the remote, rugged and spectacular Crater Highlands
- Wildlife-viewing – superb opportunities in the region's many national parks and protected areas
- Learning about the colourful tribal groups, including the Maasai and the Chagga
- Village-based walking around Arusha, Moshi and Marangu

Money Foreign exchange bureaus include Key's Bureau de Change and Executive Bureau de Change, both on Boma Rd. The NBC and CRDB banks are both on the main circle by the clock tower.

Telephone & Fax You can make and receive international phone calls from the Coffee Shop (☎ 54843), listed under Places to Eat, or from the Telecom building.

Email & Internet Access If you want to send an email (TSh 2000/1000 per page to send/receive), try Kilimanjaro Information Technology (☎/fax 54182) in Technology House on Ghalla St.

Travel Agencies There are many travel agencies and tour operators based in Moshi which can assist with arranging climbs of Mt Kilimanjaro and excursions to the nearby national parks. The atmosphere isn't quite as cut-throat as in Arusha, although you'll still be frequently approached by street touts. Some reliable agencies are listed in the Organised Safaris chapter. For tips on choosing a tour operator, see the boxed text 'Warning' in the Organised Safaris chapter.

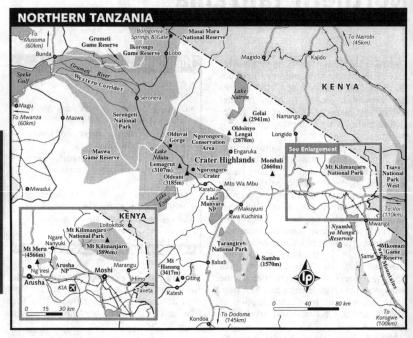

NORTHERN TANZANIA

Medical Services For emergencies go to the Kilimanjaro Christian Medical Centre (☎ 54377) about 3km from town on Sokoine Rd, although many foreign residents in Moshi prefer Nairobi for treatment.

Things to See & Do
Downtown Moshi makes for an interesting walk. The area around the market and Mawenzi Rd has a vaguely Asian flavour, with a Hindu temple, several mosques and many Indian traders.

A dip in the 25m **pool** at the YMCA costs TSh 2000 for nonresidents.

Machame, Umbwe and other towns above Moshi on Kilimanjaro's lower slopes are all linked by easy-to-follow footpaths which offer good **walks** through attractive terrain.

Places to Stay – Budget
Golden Shower Restaurant (see Places to Eat) allows camping for US$3 per person.

YMCA (☎ 51754) north of the clock tower on the roundabout between Kibo and Taifa Rds is a popular place with simple but clean singles/doubles with shared facilities for US$13/15. There's also a 25m pool, a dining room and a coffee bar.

KNCU Coffee Tree Hotel (☎ 55040) just east of the clock tower has basic rooms for TSh 7500/10,000 (TSh 5000 for a single with shared facilities and TSh 15,000 for a suite), and an inexpensive restaurant.

New Livingstone Hotel (☎/fax 55212) formerly the Moshi Hotel just to the west of the clock tower, has faded rooms for US$12/21 (US$36 for a double with bathroom), including breakfast.

Green Cottage Hostel is a private house about 1.5km north of the centre on Nkomo Rd. Small rooms go for US$10/15 (US$20 for a double with bathroom); there's no food available here.

In the downtown area near the market and bus stand are several places frequently

CHRISTINE OSBORNE

Brightly coloured *kangas* for sale, Tanzania

MARY FITZPATRICK

Ready for a sale at the Iringa market, Tanzania

MARY FITZPATRICK

Stone Town, on Tanzania's Zanzibar Island, is widely known for its flourishing local art scene.

The lunar-like landscape of Tanzania's only active volcano, Oldoinyo Lengai, offers superb trekking possibilities and spectacular views over the southern Rift Valley.

TANZANIA

The Chagga settlements containing traditional thatched houses usually
have a large network of hidden passageways and caverns underneath.

SARAH JOLLY

used by budget trekkers: **Kindoroko Hotel**
(☎ 54054, fax 54062, email kin doroko@
raha.com) on Mawenzi Rd has decent but
fairly small rooms for US$10/20, including
breakfast (US$20/25 with bathroom, TV
and refrigerator, and US$40 for a suite).

Hotel New Castle (☎ 53203) nearby, is not
as good. Mediocre rooms are US$10/15
(US$15/20 with bathroom), including break-
fast and hot water. Rooms on the upper floors
get noise from the rooftop bar.

Buffalo Hotel (☎ 50270) on Chagga St
behind Hotel New Castle has good doubles
for TSh 5000 (TSh 6000/7000 with private
bathroom).

Places to Stay – Mid-Range

Lutheran Uhuru Hostel (☎ 54084, fax
53518, email uhuruh@wilken.dsm.com)
about 3km north-west of the centre on the
road to Arusha has spotless singles/doubles
in attractive grounds from US$30/45 in-
cluding a buffet breakfast. There's also a
good restaurant. Taxis from town cost
TSh 1000.

Key's Hotel (☎ 52250, fax 50073, email
keys@form-net.com) on Uru Rd north-east
of the clock tower has been popular with
travellers for years. Comfortable rooms
cost US$40/50 (US$50/60 with air-con).
There's a substantial discount on room

prices for guests who book a Kilimanjaro
trek with the hotel. Downstairs are a restaurant and bar.

Philip Hotel (☎ 54746, fax 50456) is a
new place on Rindi Lane. Clean, comfortable rooms cost US$30/40/80.

Moshi Leopard Hotel (☎ 50884, fax
51261) on Market St near the bus stand has
modern rooms for US$30/40, including
continental breakfast.

Mountain Inn about 4km from town on
the Marangu road has rooms for US$35/ 45,
including breakfast. It's run by Shah Tours
and discounts are available for trekking and
safari clients. There's also a restaurant, a
garden and a mountain-climbing equipment
shop.

Places to Eat

Abbas Ali's Hot Bread Shop & Patisserie on
Boma Rd has wholegrain breads, cheese and
other home-made products. Directly opposite
is the fairly well stocked **Aleem's Grocery**.

Green Bamboo Restaurant at the Lutheran Uhuru Hostel has good *nyama
choma* (barbecued meat) and other grills for
about TSh 2000.

The Coffee Shop on Hill St one block
west of Mawenzi Rd is a great place with
good coffee, home-made breads, cakes and
light meals.

TANZANIA

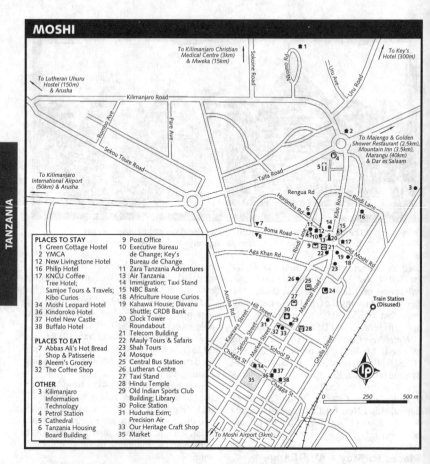

MOSHI

To Kilimanjaro Christian
Medical Centre (3km)
& Mweka (15km)

To Key's
Hotel (300m)

To Lutheran Uhuru
Hostel (150m)
& Arusha

Kilimanjaro Road

To Kilimanjaro
International Airport
(50km) & Arusha

To Majengo & Golden
Shower Restaurant (2.5km),
Mountain Inn (3.5km),
Marangu (40km)
& Dar es Salaam

Taifa Road

Rengua Rd

Boma Road

Aga Khan Rd

Old Moshi Rd

Train Station
(Disused)

To Moshi Airport (3km)

PLACES TO STAY
1 Green Cottage Hostel
2 YMCA
12 New Livingstone Hotel
16 Philip Hotel
17 KNCU Coffee
Tree Hotel;
Samjoe Tours & Travels;
Kibo Curios
34 Moshi Leopard Hotel
36 Kindoroko Hotel
37 Hotel New Castle
38 Buffalo Hotel

PLACES TO EAT
7 Abbas Ali's Hot Bread
Shop & Patisserie
8 Aleem's Grocery
32 The Coffee Shop

OTHER
3 Kilimanjaro
Information
Technology
4 Petrol Station
5 Cathedral
6 Tanzania Housing
Board Building

9 Post Office
10 Executive Bureau
de Change; Key's
Bureau de Change
11 Zara Tanzania Adventures
13 Air Tanzania
14 Immigration; Taxi Stand
15 NBC Bank
18 Africulture House Curios
19 Kahawa House; Davanu
Shuttle; CRDB Bank
20 Clock Tower
Roundabout
21 Telecom Building
22 Mauly Tours & Safaris
23 Shah Tours
24 Mosque
25 Central Bus Station
26 Lutheran Centre
27 Taxi Stand
28 Hindu Temple
29 Old Indian Sports Club
Building; Library
30 Police Station
31 Huduma Exim;
Precision Air
33 Our Heritage Craft Shop
35 Market

0   250   500 m

Golden Shower Restaurant north-east of
the centre on Taifa Rd has a pleasant garden
setting and good meals from TSh 3000.

Shopping
For crafts try Africulture House Curios
south-east of the KNCU building; Kibo Curios, in the central courtyard of KNCU; or
Our Heritage craft shop on Hill St.

Getting There & Away
Air Moshi is served by Kilimanjaro international airport, about 50km west of town
off the main Moshi-Arusha road. There is

also a small airport about 3km south-west
of the town centre along the extension of
Market St. Precision Air and Air Tanzania
have frequent flights to Dar es Salaam and
other destinations.

Air Tanzania's Moshi office (☎ 55205) is
next to the New Livingstone Hotel. The
Precision Air representative in Moshi is
Huduma Exim (☎ 53495) on Hill St.

Most flights depart from Kilimanjaro international airport, though some Precision
Air flights use Moshi airport. Check which
airport you'll be departing from when buying your ticket.

Bus Moshi's central bus station between Mawenzi Rd and Market St was temporarily closed for renovation when this book was researched. Until it reopens, all buses depart from the bus station in the Majengo area of town about 3km from the centre along the Marangu Rd. There are frequent minibuses to town; the best place to wait is near the main roundabout just down from the cathedral.

Most minibus shuttles that service the Nairobi-Arusha sector also continue on from Arusha to Moshi, though most of the regular buses do not. The main shuttle companies are Davanu, which leaves from the Davanu office on the clock tower roundabout, and Riverside (see the Land section of the Tanzania Getting There & Away chapter). Both companies require advance bookings.

Buses run throughout the day to Marangu (TSh 500, one hour) and Arusha (TSh 1000, one to 1½ hours). There are also daily direct buses to Dar es Salaam (TSh 6800, eight hours), departing throughout the morning from about 6 am.

Getting Around
To/From the Airport Air Tanzania runs a free shuttle between Moshi and Kilimanjaro international airport which connects with all flights. The shuttles leaves from the Air Tanzania office appromimately two hours before each scheduled flight departure time.

MARANGU
☎ 055
Marangu is a small, attractive town on the slopes of Mt Kilimanjaro about 35km north-east of Moshi. In addition to serving as a convenient overnight stop for those trekking on Mt Kilimanjaro's Marangu route, it also makes a good base for day and overnight hikes on Mt Kilimanjaro's lower slopes.

Travel Agencies
Most hotels in Marangu organise Kilimanjaro treks; some of the better ones are listed here.

Alpine Tours at Coffee Tree Camp Site Budget packages; village hiking around Marangu
Babylon Lodge Budget to mid-range packages
Capricorn Hotel Mid-range to more expensive packages; also organises day hikes along the lower section of the Marangu route
Marangu Hotel Mid-range to more expensive. The hotel also offers a no-frills 'hard way' option for budget-conscious travellers: US$170 plus park fees for a five-day Marangu climb. The hotel will take care of hut reservations and provide a guide with porter; you must provide food and equipment.

Places to Stay
Marangu Hotel (☎ 51307, fax 50639, email marangu@africaonline.co.ke, PO Box 40, Moshi) is the first hotel you reach coming from Moshi. It's good value with comfortable singles/doubles costing US$70/100, including breakfast and dinner, and camping

---

Yohani Kinyala Lauwo

The first Tanzanian to scale Kilimanjaro was Yohani Kinyala Lauwo. Lauwo, whose memory is still revered in his home town of Marangu, was only 18 in 1889 when he was appointed by Chief Marealle I to be the guide for Hans Meyer (the first westerner to reach Kibo). In those days, climbing the mountain was quite a different affair from what it is today: the route was not defined, climbing equipment was rudimentary at best, and wages were much lower. During his trek, Lauwo earned just one Tanzanian shilling a day.

Following the successful ascent with Meyer, Lauwo remained in Marangu where he spent much of the remainder of his life leading foreign trekkers up the mountain and training new guides. In 1989, at the 100th anniversary celebration of the first ascent of Kilimanjaro, Lauwo was the only person present who had been around at the time of the first ascent. Lauwo died in 1996 at the age of 125. His family still lives in Marangu.

for US$3 per person including hot showers. Rates are discounted if you join one of the hotel's fully equipped treks.

Kibo Hotel (☎/fax 51308, email kiboho tel@form-net.com) about 1.5km west of the main junction has decent but overpriced rooms for US$37/54, including breakfast and camping for US$6 per person with shower.

Babylon Lodge (☎ Marangu 5, fax 51 315) about 500m east of the main junction, offers simple but clean rooms for US$25/40, including breakfast.

Kilimanjaro Outpost (☎ Marangu 61, 057-8405, email outpost@ark.eoltz.com, PO Box 464, Marangu) has rooms for US$24/30, or it's US$13 for a dorm bed. The hotel can also assist with organising hikes around Marangu (TSh 5000 including lunch and guide for a trip to Marangu waterfalls).

Capricorn Hotel (☎/fax 51309, PO Box 938) about 3km from the junction is popular and upmarket with comfortable rooms for US$55 per person, including breakfast.

Coffee Tree Camp (☎ 50656, fax 50096, PO Box 835) is just beyond the Capricorn and about 700m east of the main road down a steep hill. Look for the turn-off just north of the Top-Kibo Grocery. Camping costs US$5 per person including hot and cold water and cooking facilities (fireplaces); you'll need to bring your own tent and food. The owner, who also runs Alpine Tours, is very knowledgeable about the Marangu area, and for reasonable prices can organise a variety of hikes in the surrounding area.

Getting There & Away

Minibuses run throughout the day between Marangu and Moshi (TSh 500). In Marangu they drop you at the main junction from where you can sometimes get a pick-up to the park gate (TSh 200, 5km).

ARUSHA
☎ 057

Arusha is one of Tanzania's most developed and fastest growing towns. It was the headquarters of the East African Community in the days when Tanzania, Kenya and Uganda were members of this economic and customs union. Today, Arusha is headquarters of the Tripartite Commission for East African Cooperation – a revived attempt at regional collaboration. It's also the site of the Tanzanian-moderated negotiations on Burundi, and the Rwanda genocide tribunal.

The town sits in lush countryside near the foot of Mt Meru (4566m) and enjoys a temperate climate throughout the year. Surrounding it are many coffee, wheat and maize estates tended by the Arusha and Meru people.

Arusha is the gateway to Serengeti, Lake Manyara, Tarangire and Arusha national parks. It is the safari capital of Tanzania. It's a good base for exploring the Crater Highlands and Ngorongoro Conservation Area.

Orientation

Arusha is divided by the small Naura river valley. To the east of the valley are most of the top end hotels, the post office, immigration, government buildings, safari companies, airline offices, craft shops and the Arusha International Conference Centre (AICC). Across the valley to the west are the commercial and industrial areas, the market, budget hotels and the bus station.

The AICC, where some tour companies mentioned in this section are located, is divided into three wings – the Serengeti wing to the west, the Kilimanjaro wing in the centre and the Ngorongoro wing to the east.

Maps MaCo puts out a good map of Arusha, available in shops around town for TSh 2500. Old photocopied town maps are available from the tourist information centre (free).

Information

Tourist Offices The Tanzania Tourist Board has a tourist information centre (☎ 3842, fax 8628, email ttb-info@yako.habari.co.tz) on Boma Rd just up from the post office. It's open 8 am to 4 pm weekdays and 8.30 am to 1 pm Saturday. It has some helpful information on Arusha, the nearby parks and other tourist sites in Tanzania as well as copies of a

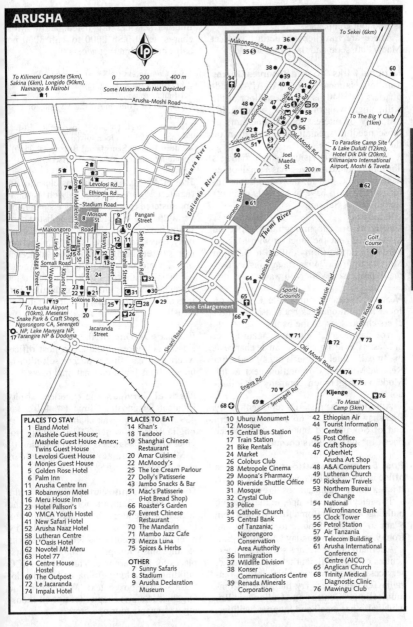

ARUSHA

PLACES TO STAY
1 Eland Motel
2 Mashele Guest House;
  Mashele Guest House Annex;
  Twins Guest House
3 Levolosi Guest House
4 Monjes Guest House
5 Golden Rose Hotel
6 Palm Inn
11 Arusha Centre Inn
13 Robannyson Motel
16 Meru House Inn
23 Hotel Pallson's
40 YMCA Youth Hostel
41 New Safari Hotel
52 Arusha Naaz Hotel
58 Lutheran Centre
60 L'Oasis Hotel
62 Novotel Mt Meru
63 Hotel 77
64 Centre House
  Hostel
69 The Outpost
72 Le Jacaranda
74 Impala Hotel

PLACES TO EAT
14 Khan's
18 Tandoor
19 Shanghai Chinese
  Restaurant
20 Amar Cuisine
22 McMoody's
25 The Ice Cream Parlour
27 Dolly's Patisserie
43 Jambo Snacks & Bar
51 Mac's Patisserie
  (Hot Bread Shop)
66 Roaster's Garden
67 Everest Chinese
  Restaurant
70 The Mandarin
71 Mambo Jazz Cafe
73 Mezza Luna
75 Spices & Herbs

OTHER
7 Sunny Safaris
8 Stadium
9 Arusha Declaration
  Museum

10 Uhuru Monument
12 Mosque
15 Central Bus Station
17 Train Station
21 Bike Rentals
24 Market
26 Colobus Club
28 Metropole Cinema
29 Moona's Pharmacy
30 Riverside Shuttle Office
31 Mosque
32 Crystal Club
33 Police
34 Catholic Church
35 Central Bank
  of Tanzania;
  Ngorongoro
  Conservation
  Area Authority
36 Immigration
37 Wildlife Division
38 Konser
  Communications Centre
39 Renada Minerals
  Corporation

42 Ethiopian Air
44 Tourist Information
  Centre
45 Post Office
46 Craft Shops
47 CyberNet;
  Arusha Art Shop
48 A&A Computers
49 Lutheran Church
50 Rickshaw Travels
53 Northern Bureau
  de Change
54 National
  Microfinance Bank
55 Clock Tower
56 Petrol Station
57 Air Tanzania
59 Telecom Building
61 Arusha International
  Conference
  Centre (AICC)
65 Anglican Church
68 Trinity Medical
  Diagnostic Clinic
76 Mawingu Club

'blacklist' of tour operators and a list of registered tour companies.

There are travellers' bulletin boards at Mac's Patisserie and the Outpost hotel.

National Parks & Game Reserves Offices
Tanzania National Parks (TANAPA) headquarters (☎ 8040) is on the 6th floor of the Kilimanjaro wing of the AICC building. It's primarily of interest to tour operators or those needing specialised information on the parks.

The Wildlife Division, which manages Tanzania's game reserves, has a small office near the AICC, but for more substantial information you'll have to go to its main office in Dar es Salaam.

Immigration The immigration office on Simeon Rd near the junction with Makongoro Rd is open from 7.30 am to 3.30 pm Monday to Friday. Visa extensions are normally processed while you wait.

Money Northern Bureau de Change on Joel Maeda St changes both cash and travellers cheques, as do the banks.

You can get cash advances against Visa or MasterCard from the bureau de change at the Impala Hotel (at bleak rates), and from Renada Minerals Corporation next to the Modern Refrigeration Company on Goliondoi Rd.

American Express is represented by Rickshaw Travels (☎ 6655) at the eastern end of Sokoine Rd but its Arusha office doesn't issue travellers cheques.

Post & Communications The main post office is on Boma Rd near the clock tower; it has a fairly organised poste restante.

The telephone exchange, in the Telecom building, is also on Boma Rd and open from 8 am to 10 pm Monday to Saturday and from 9 am to 8 pm Sunday and holidays.

Alternatively, there are several business centres offering efficient telephone and fax services at rates somewhat higher than Tanzania Telecom rates. Try the Konser Communications Centre on Goliondoi Rd, which also has email and Internet facilities.

A few other places providing email and Internet services are listed below. Most charge about TSh 2000 to TSh 3000 per half-hour for Internet access.

A&A Computers (☎ 8306) Goliondoi Rd
cyberBoma AICC Bldg, ground floor, Kilimanjaro wing
CyberNet (☎ 3149) in Arusha Art Shop on India St
Mac's Patissserie (☎ 3469) Sokoine Rd, just south-west of the clock tower
Modern Robots Secretarial Bureau (☎ 3550) Sokoine Rd, next to Mac's Patisserie

Travel Agencies Arusha has close to 100 registered tour operators as well as many unregistered companies. Only a small number of the reliable agents can be listed here. If you have doubts about a particular company, check before finalising your arrangements to see if they have an original licence (not a photocopy) from the Tourist Agents Licensing Authority (TALA). Refer to the Organised Safaris chapter for detailed listings of travel agencies and tour operators in Arusha.

Bookshops One of the better shops is Kase Bookstore opposite the post office, where you can find a decent selection of books about Tanzania's national parks.

Medical Services The excellent Trinity Medical Diagnostic Clinic (☎ 4401, fax 4392, email kfg@yako.habari.co.tz) at 35 Engira Rd, south-west of Old Moshi Rd, provides after-hours access for emergencies.

Moona's pharmacy on Sokoine Rd is well stocked.

Dangers & Annoyances Arusha is the worst place in Tanzania for street touts and slick tour operators. Such people prey on the gullibility of newly arrived travellers by offering them safaris and Kilimanjaro treks at ridiculously low prices. Among the worst places for touts are in and around the AICC building and along Boma and Goliondoi Rds. See the boxed text 'Warning' in the Organised Safaris chapter for tips on choosing a reputable tour operator.

Numerous muggings have been reported in the area between the Novotel and the AICC building; take a taxi here rather than walking.

Things to See & Do

The small **Arusha Declaration Museum** near the Uhuru monument on Makongoro Rd has a moderately interesting display on post-colonial Tanzanian history. It's affiliated with the National Museum in Dar es Salaam.

Other diversions include a colourful **market** in the town centre, and a **swimming pool** at the Novotel (TSh 1500 for nonguests).

Places to Stay – Budget

Camping *Masai Camp* about 3km from the centre on Old Moshi Rd is the best place. It costs US$3 per person including hot showers, and there's a restaurant and a bar.

Paradise Camp Site by Lake Duluti has a pleasant setting, with good birdwatching and walks nearby, but the camp site itself is run-down. The turn-off is on the Arusha-Moshi road, about 12km east of Arusha.

Guesthouses & Hotels The least expensive places are concentrated in the area east of Colonel Middleton Rd and north of the stadium. There are also many budget places closer to the central bus station.

Mashele Guest House is popular with budget travellers. Singles/doubles go for TSh 2000/3000, with shared bathroom. Continental/full breakfast is available for an additional TSh 1000/1500, and there's a restaurant. *Mashele Guest House Annex* next door is quieter with doubles for TSh 4000.

Twins Guest House has rooms for TSh 2000/3000, and *Levolosi* and *Monjes* guest houses both offer rooms for TSh 3000/3500. All have shared facilities.

Palm Inn (☎ 7430) to the west has clean doubles with mosquito nets for TSh 6000.

Robbanyson Motel on Kikuyu St has decent rooms with bathroom for TSh 5000 per person, and an inexpensive restaurant.

Arusha Centre Inn off Pangani St has reasonably clean rooms with bathroom for US$15/20.

Meru House Inn (☎ 7803, fax 8220) at the west end of Sokoine Rd is popular and has clean rooms for TSh 3500/4500 (TSh 7500 for a double with bathroom).

Arusha Naaz Hotel (☎/fax 2087) in the eastern end of town on Sokoine Rd has sterile but decent rooms for US$10/20 (US$20/25 with bathroom). There's a self-service snack bar downstairs for breakfast and lunch.

YMCA Youth Hostel (☎ 6907) on India St has tolerable rooms with shared facilities for US$13/15.

Lutheran Centre (☎ 8855) on Boma Rd near the post office has clean rooms for TSh 10,000/15,000, though it's often full.

Centre House Hostel on the grounds of Sekei Secondary School on Kanisa Rd is run by the Catholic diocese. Basic rooms with shared facilities cost TSh 4000/8000, including breakfast.

Places to Stay – Mid-Range

Outpost (☎ 3908, fax 8405, email outpost@ ark.eoltz.com) about 1km south-east of the clock tower on Serengeti Rd has good singles/doubles in a converted house and slightly run-down bungalows in the garden for US$24/30. There's also a five-bed dormitory room for US$13 per bed. Buffet dinner in the garden restaurant costs TSh 3700.

Jacaranda (☎ 6529, fax 8585, email jacaranda@cybernet.co.tz) nearby on the opposite side of Old Moshi Rd is a small but pleasant place, also in a converted house. Rooms cost US$40/45 (US$50/55 with bathroom), including breakfast.

Hotel 77 (☎ 3802) known locally by its Swahili name 'Hotel Saba Saba' has small but decent rooms for US$30/40. It's on the Moshi Rd about 400m north of the Impala Hotel.

Mezza Luna just south of Hotel 77 on Moshi Rd has a few rooms for US$35/45.

Hotel Pallson's (☎ 6411) is a good option in the busy downtown area near the market. Rooms with TV cost US$30/40 including continental breakfast. Credit card payments are charged an additional 10%.

Golden Rose Hotel (☎ 7959, fax 8862) opposite Sunny Safaris has comfortable rooms for US$36/48 plus 20% VAT, and a good restaurant with inexpensive local dishes. Credit card payments are charged an additional 10%.

New Safari Hotel (☎ 3261) on Boma Rd has reopened one wing and – in contrast with its run-down exterior – has surprisingly decent self-contained rooms for US$30/50 (suites US$70) and the Safari Grill Restaurant. Be prepared for some dust and scaffolding as construction is still underway.

Eland Motel (☎ 6892) north-west of town on the Arusha-Moshi road has comfortable rooms for US$40/50, including breakfast.

Places to Stay – Top End

Novotel Mt Meru (☎ 2711, fax 8503, email tahifin@yako.habari.co.tz, PO Box 877, Arusha) north-east of the centre off the Arusha-Moshi road has singles/doubles for US$116/145, including breakfast and use of the pool.

Impala Hotel (☎ 2962, fax 8220) at the junction of Moshi and Old Moshi Rds is also comfortable, with rooms for US$65/78, including breakfast.

Hotel Dik Dik (☎/fax 8110) well east of town on the lower slopes of Mt Meru has well appointed bungalow-style accommodation for US$141/212, including breakfast. It's signposted north of the Moshi road.

L'Oasis (☎/fax 7089) about 6km north-east of town in Sekei has comfortable rooms set in nice gardens for US$65/90 including breakfast. It's signposted about 1km off the main Moshi to Nairobi Rd; the turn-off is diagonally opposite the Novotel.

Places to Eat

Restaurants Popular with budget travellers is *Pizzarusha* opposite Mashele Guest House, which serves inexpensive meals.

Chick-King on the ground floor of the Serengeti wing of the AICC, has a patio grill serving nyama choma. This place also has inexpensive fast food.

Khan's is an auto spares store by day and a popular barbecue by night. It's on Mosque St next to Music Land Restaurant.

Jambo Snacks & Bar serves filling meals for less than TSh 2000.

Amar Cuisine off Sokoine Rd has a good variety of tandoori dishes for TSh 3500 and less, including vegetarian meals.

Arusha Chinese Restaurant on Sokoine Rd is inexpensive but mediocre. Most meals cost between TSh 2000 and TSh 2500.

Everest Chinese Restaurant on Old Moshi Rd has garden seating and good food and service. Meals range from TSh 1600 to TSh 4800, and there's a business lunch special for TSh 3200 to TSh 3500.

Roots at the Colobus Club has *tortillas*, *fajitas* and other Mexican dishes, as well as seafood and grills for about TSh 4000.

The Mandarin south-east of the centre on Serengeti Rd near the Outpost Hotel has a variety of Thai and Chinese dishes from TSh 3500 to TSh 6700.

Spices & Herbs on Old Moshi Rd around the corner from the Impala Hotel has a good selection of reasonably priced Ethiopian dishes and a pleasant atmosphere.

Roaster's Garden next to Everest Chinese Restaurant on Old Moshi Rd has nyama choma and rice for TSh 3000; it's not a bad place although service is slow.

Mezza Luna on Moshi Rd has a large Italian selection and outdoor seating.

Tandoor on Sokoine Rd has a good selection of Mughlai cuisine from TSh 3000; it's closed for Sunday lunch and all day Monday.

Shanghai Chinese Restaurant at the western end of Sokoine Rd, behind the Meru post office, has very good but pricey meals starting at TSh 4500 plus tax.

Cafes For burgers, pizzas and similar fare, try *McMoody's* (open from 10 am to 10 pm daily except Monday) on the corner of Sokoine Rd and Market St. Prices range between TSh 1300 and TSh 3000.

Dolly's Patisserie nearby on Jacaranda St has bread, pastries, yoghurt and other items.

Mac's Patisserie (Hot Bread Shop) on Sokoine Rd just down from the clock tower is a good place to meet other travellers. Coffee, soup, sandwiches and light meals are available at reasonable prices, and Internet/email services are available.

Cafe Bamboo near the Lutheran Centre on Boma Rd has sandwiches, coffee, home-made cakes and other snacks at reasonable prices (closed Sunday).

The Ice Cream Parlour is on Sokoine Rd at Jacaranda St.

Mambo Jazz Cafe has an all-day breakfast for TSh 3800, sandwiches, and a variety of Italian dishes from about TSh 2500. It's open from 8.30 am to 9.30 pm daily, except on Tuesday and Sunday when it closes at 5 pm.

On the Roof cafe and bar at the Colobus Club has sandwiches and other lunch fare from about TSh 1500.

Entertainment

Colobus Club off Sokoine Rd on Jacaranda St is the current hot spot, popular with both locals and foreigners. There's a disco on Friday and Saturday from 10 pm (TSh 3000), and the Roots bar is open daily from noon.

A good place to meet locals is the *Big Y Club* about 1km off the main Arusha-Moshi (Nairobi) road; the turn-off is diagonally opposite the Novotel. There's a breezy terrace upstairs and live Zaïrean music most evenings. Admission costs TSh 1000.

Other places include *Mawingu Club* on Old Moshi Rd in Kijenge; *Crystal Club* on Seth Benjamin Rd north of the Metropole Cinema; and the disco at *Hotel 77*. Admission charges are between TSh 1000 and TSh 1500; these places all get going after 10 pm.

Shopping

The small alley opposite Northern Bureau de Change is full of craft dealers; heavy bargaining is required here. There are several other craft shops nearby.

Getting There & Away

Air Arusha is serviced by two airports. Most flights use Kilimanjaro international airport, about halfway between Moshi and Arusha off the main highway. Many charters and some regularly scheduled routes use Arusha airport, about 10km from town on the Dodoma road.

Arusha is connected by scheduled flights with:

Dar es Salaam Air Tanzania TSh 66,000; Coastal Travels TSh 95,000; Precision Air US$165; all fares one-way; flights daily

Mombasa Precision Air US$127 one-way; flights about four times weekly but irregular

Mwanza Air Tanzania TSh 55,000; Precision Air TSh 95,000; all fares one-way; flights five times weekly

Nairobi Air Tanzania US$150 one-way; flights irregular

Seronera (Serengeti National Park) Precision Air US$135 one-way; flights twice weekly but irregular

Unguja (Zanzibar Island) Air Tanzania, Precision Air, Air Zanzibar and Coastal Travels fly daily for about the same fares as to Dar es Salaam. Precision Air and Coastal Travels have the most reliable flights to Unguja; Precision Air's daily flight is 'guaranteed' during the high season.

Airlines with offices in Arusha include:

Air Tanzania (☎ 3201) Boma Rd opposite the post office
Ethiopian Air (☎ 2013) Old Moshi Rd near the clock tower
Gulf Air (☎ 2871) Old Moshi Rd near the clock tower
KLM (☎ 8062, fax 4416) Boma Rd opposite the Telecom Bldg
Precision Air (☎ 2818, email precision@cybernet .co.tz) Ground floor, Ngorongoro wing, AICC

Bus Arusha is well connected by road in all directions. The Arusha central bus station has a reputation for being particularly chaotic, so watch your luggage here.

Dar es Salaam Express buses depart daily between 6 am and noon (TSh 12,500, nine hours). Fresh ya Shambaa is one of the better lines. There are also slower ordinary buses costing from TSh7800.
Dodoma Most transport goes via Chalinze (TSh 10,700). To go via Kondoa, you'll need to take a bus first to Babati (TSh 5000, five to eight hours), then find onward transport from there.
Moshi There are buses and minibuses throughout the day (TSh 1000, one hour).
Mwanza Most buses go via Nairobi, departing Arusha daily in the afternoon (TSh 18,000, 20 to 24 hours). During the dry season a bus goes once or twice weekly through the Serengeti via Seronera and Ikoma gates (TSh 25,000 plus park fees for Serengeti National Park and Ngorongoro Crater). Occasionally, buses take the route through the Serengeti's Western Corridor via Seronera and Ndabaka gates.

TANZANIA

Nairobi (Kenya) Between Arusha and Nairobi there's a choice of buses or minibus shuttles; all go through the border crossings without a change. Regular buses are cheaper but slower (TSh 5000, six to seven hours). For information on minibus services see the Tanzania Getting There & Away chapter.

Tanga There's usually at least one bus daily direct to Tanga (TSh 5200, six to eight hours).

Getting Around

To/From Kilimanjaro International Airport Air Tanzania has a free shuttle connecting with its arriving and departing flights. Departures are from the Air Tanzania office two hours before scheduled flight departure.

Taxis from town cost between TSh 15,000 and TSh 20,000, more at night.

To/From Arusha Airport Any bus heading out along the Dodoma road can drop you at the junction, from where you'll have to walk. Taxis from town charge between TSh 5000 and TSh 6000.

Precision Air runs a shuttle from its office at the AICC to Arusha airport, departing the AICC about 1½ hours before scheduled fight departures (TSh 1000 one way).

AROUND ARUSHA

Out of town are some good hikes which offer views of Arusha, Mt Kilimanjaro and Mt Meru. Sunny Safaris provides guides for day hikes to local Maasai villages for about US$15 per person for groups of four or more.

Several villages outside Arusha are sites for cultural tourism programs sponsored by the SNV (Netherlands Development Organisation). At **Ng'iresi** village, about 7km north of Arusha on the slopes of Mt Meru, you can visit local irrigation projects and do some light hiking.

Longido, about 90km north of Arusha, is the site of a weekly Maasai cattle market and the starting point for hikes on the slopes of Longido mountain.

In **Mkuru**, about 5km beyond Ngare Nanyuki village north of Momela gate of Arusha National Park, you can take camel safaris ranging from half a day to a week, or climb nearby Oldoinyo Landaree mountain.

For further information, contact SNV (☎/fax 057-7515, email tourinfo@habari.co.tz) or Room 643, Serengeti wing, AICC, PO Box 10455, Arusha.

About 20km west of Arusha along the Dodoma road is the **Meserani Snake Park**; admission costs US$5. There are several **craft outlets** along the main road near the snake park.

About 250km south-west of Arusha is the volcanic **Mt Hanang** (3417m), Tanzania's fourth-highest mountain and a good destination for rugged travellers. Although it's a bit time consuming to reach, its summit makes a good day or overnight trek. It's near an important grain-producing area inhabited by members of Tanzania's tiny Iraqw group, as well as by the Barabaig, a semi-nomadic people who have lost large areas of their traditional lands to large-scale wheat farms. The best contact for organising treks on Mt Hanang and visits to the surrounding area is IntoAfrica (☎ 0114-255 5610 in the UK or 02-350987 in Nairobi, email enquiry@intoafrica.co.uk). It's Web site is www.intoafrica.co.uk.

ARUSHA NATIONAL PARK

Although one of Tanzania's smallest parks, Arusha National Park is one of its most attractive and topographically varied. Its main features are Ngurdoto Crater, the Momela Lakes, and rugged Mt Meru (4566m), Tanzania's second-highest peak. The park's altitude, which varies from 1500m to over 4500m, has a variety of vegetation zones supporting numerous animal species; you're likely to see zebra, waterbuck, reedbuck, klipspringer, hippopotamus, buffalo, elephant, hyena, mongoose, dik-dik, warthog, baboon, and vervet and colobus monkeys. There are no lions however, and no rhinos due to poaching.

Ngurdoto Crater is surrounded by forest, while the actual crater floor is a swamp. To the west lies Serengeti Ndogo (Little Serengeti), an extensive area of open grassland and the only place in the park where herds of Burchell's zebra can be found.

The alkaline **Momela Lakes** attract a wide variety of wader birds, particularly flamin-

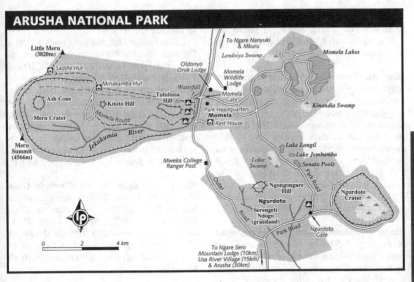

ARUSHA NATIONAL PARK

gos. The lakes are fed largely by underground streams; because of their varying mineral content each lake supports a different type of algae, giving each one a different colour. Birdlife also varies quite distinctly from one lake to another, even where the lakes are separated only by a narrow strip of land.

Mt Meru is a mixture of lush forest and bare rock with a spectacular crater.

While it's possible to see much of the park in a day, to appreciate the wildlife or do a walking safari you'll need to stay at least a night or two.

Information
Park entry fees for Arusha National Park and Tanzania's other northern parks are US$25 per person per day (US$5 for children between five and 16, free for children under five), plus a US$30 vehicle fee.

To walk in Arusha National Park you must be accompanied by an armed ranger (US$10, or US$15 for hikes on Mt Meru). While you can drive or walk around the Ngurdoto Crater rim, you're not allowed to walk down to the crater floor.

Park headquarters are by Momela gate, on the northern side of the park. There's a second entrance at Ngurdoto gate, on the south-eastern edge of the park. For information, camp site reservations or to arrange a guide, contact the senior park warden at park headquarters or through PO Box 3134, Arusha.

The booklet *Arusha National Park* put out by TANAPA contains a good summary of the history and geology of the area including descriptions of the flora and fauna found in the park. It's available at bookshops in Arusha and Dar es Salaam.

MaCo puts out a good map of the park, including trekking routes on Mt Meru. It's available in bookshops in Dar es Salaam and Arusha for TSh 5000.

Trekking on Mt Meru
Meru is a relatively obscure mountain, overshadowed by its more famous neighbour, Kilimanjaro. Yet its volcanic cone is spectacular and it's well worth a visit. A trek to the summit takes you through grassland and lush forest, followed by a dramatic walk along the knife edge of the crater rim. The fact that you'll meet few other people and have the place to yourself for most of the time makes it even more attractive.

Keep in mind that although Meru appears small when compared with Kilimanjaro, it's still a serious trek, and acclimatisation is important.

Momela Route The Momela route is the only route up Meru. It starts at Momela gate on the eastern side of the mountain and goes to the summit along the northern arm of the mountain's horseshoe crater. The route is steep but can be done comfortably in four days (three nights), although trekkers often do it in three days by combining stages 3 and 4. For a detailed description of the route, see Lonely Planet's *Trekking in East Africa*, which is highly recommended if you're contemplating a climb on Meru.

Stage 1: Momela Gate to Miriakamba Hut (10km, 4-5 hours, 1000m ascent) Two routes are available from Momela gate. The more interesting one is a track that goes through the forest towards the crater floor, and then steeply up to Miriakamba Hut. The second, shorter option is a path that climbs gradually through the grassland direct to Miriakamba; this makes a good descent route.

Stage 2: Miriakamba Hut to Saddle Hut (4km, 2-3 hours, 1050m ascent) From Miriakamba, the path climbs steeply up through pleasant glades to Topela Mbogo (Buffalo Swamp) and Mgongo Wa Tembo (Elephant Ridge), from where there are good views into the crater and up to the main cliffs below the summit. It then continues through some open grassy clearings and over several stream beds (usually dry) to Saddle Hut. There are good side trips from Saddle Hut to Little Meru (3820m) and to Rhino Point, both of which offer superb views of Kilimanjaro, as well as of Meru's Ash Cone.

Stage 3: Saddle Hut to Meru Summit & return (5km, 4-5 hours, 1000m ascent; plus 5km, 2-3 hours, 1000m descent) This stage, along a very narrow ridge between the outer slopes of the mountain and the sheer cliffs of the inner crater, is one of the most dramatic sections of trekking anywhere in East Africa. During the rainy season, ice and snow can occur on this section of the route, so take care.

From Saddle Hut, the path goes across a flat area, then steeply up through bushes before giving way to bare rock and ash. Rhino Point is marked by a cairn and a pile of bones. From Rhino Point, the path drops slightly before rising again to climb steeply around the edge of the rim over ash scree and bare rock patches. Meru Summit is reached after three to four hours.

Descent is via the same path around the rim, back to Saddle Hut (two to three hours).

Stage 4: Saddle Hut to Momela Gate (9km, 3-5½ hours, 2000m descent) From Saddle Hut, retrace your steps to Miriakamba (1½ to 2½ hours). From Miriakamba, you can return through the forest (2½ to three hours), or take the shorter route (1½ to 2½ hours) down the ridge directly to Momela gate.

Costs Organised treks on Mt Meru can be arranged with most travel agencies listed in the Organised Safaris chapter. For tips on choosing a reliable trekking company, see the boxed text 'Warning' in the Organised Safaris chapter. Rates for a four-day trip range from US$250 to US$500.

Organised treks are not obligatory, and you can do things quite easily on your own. For independent trekking, your costs will be primarily park entrance fees and hut fees.

Guides & Porters A guide is mandatory and can be arranged at Momela gate. The US$15 fee is paid to the national park (not directly to the guide). Unlike on Kilimanjaro, guides on Meru are rangers who are armed in case you meet some of the park's buffalo or elephant; they are not there primarily to show you the way (although they do know the route). While it's unlikely that an animal will have to be shot, you shouldn't underestimate the danger and walk too far away from your guide.

Porters, whose services are optional, are also available at Momela gate for US$6 per porter per day, though most trekkers go up Mt Meru with only a guide. This fee is paid at the gate and given to the porters after the trip. You'll also need to pay park entrance and hut fees for porters (US$3 per day, US$1.50 per night). Porters carry rucksacks weighing up to 15kg, not including their own food and clothing. Average tips for a standard Mt Meru trek are about US$10 to $US15 for the guide, and around US$15 for each porter.

Accommodation There are two well maintained bunkhouses (Miriakamba and Saddle huts) on the Momela route, conveniently spaced for a three- or four-day trek, so a tent isn't usually necessary. If you do camp, you'll pay the same fees anyway. The bunkhouses are large, and generally not full; check at the gate before starting.

Places to Stay

There are *camp sites* at Momela and at Ngurdoto; you'll need to bring all your own provisions. Camping costs US$20 per night at public camp sites and US$40 per night at special camp sites. There's also a basic *resthouse* near the Momela gate which accommodates up to five people (US$30 per person); book through the senior park warden.

Momela Wildlife Lodge (☎ 057-8104, fax 8264, PO Box 999, Arusha) just outside the park and north-east of Momela gate has pleasant singles/doubles for US$56/74, including breakfast. Half-board and full-board arrangements are also available.

Ngare Sero Mountain Lodge (☎ Usa River 38, fax 8690, PO Box 425, Arusha) at the foot of Mt Meru and 20km from Arusha on the Arusha-Moshi road is also comfortable. Full board costs US$150 per person, and there is trout-fishing in the nearby lake. To get here turn north off the Arusha-Moshi road at the sign for the Dik Dik Hotel, then follow the signs for Ngare Sero.

Getting There & Away

The Arusha National Park gate is about 35km from Arusha, and about 24km from the main Arusha-Moshi road. To reach here by public transport, take any bus running between Arusha and Moshi and get off at the park junction, 1km east of Usa River village (TSh 1000); look for signs for the park and for Ngare Nanyuki village. From Usa River, there are pick-ups most days which run to Ngare Nanyuki (TSh 2000), 10km beyond Momela gate; ask the driver to drop you at the park gate. About 1.5km from Usa River, the road north to the gate splits. On the western fork, or 'outer road', fees are not required for transit traffic. For the eastern 'park road', which runs through the park proper, fees are payable. The roads rejoin at Momela gate. Public transport takes the outer road.

Your other options are to hitch or walk (six to eight hours) the 24km from Usa River to Momela gate along the outer road. If you're staying at the Momela Wildlife Lodge, you can sometimes arrange transport with the minibus that brings staff from Arusha.

Alternatively, tour companies can provide transport to Momela gate (about US$100 per vehicle, divided between up to five passengers), or you can arrange a one-day safari to Arusha National Park (for slightly more) which drops you at Momela gate at the end.

Within the park itself, there's a good series of gravel roads and tracks leading to all the main features and viewing points. Most are suitable for all vehicles, though some of the tracks get slippery in the rainy season; a few tracks are suitable only for 4WDs.

MT KILIMANJARO NATIONAL PARK

At 5896m, snowcapped Mt Kilimanjaro is the highest peak in Africa and one of the continent's magnificent sights. From cultivated farmlands on the lower levels, Kilimanjaro rises through lush rainforest, alpine meadows and a barren lunar landscape to the twin summits of Kibo (the dome at the centre of the massif which dips inwards to form a crater) and Mawenzi (a group of jagged pinnacles on the eastern side).

The mountain lures several thousand trekkers each year. For most, the goal is Uhuru Peak, Kibo's highest point. The fact that, with the right preparation, you can

TANZANIA

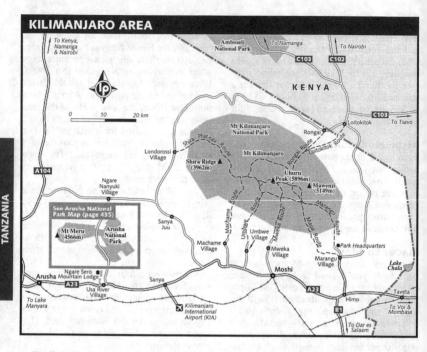

KILIMANJARO AREA

walk all the way to the summit without the need of ropes or technical climbing experience makes it even more attractive.

For detailed information on routes and other aspects of trekking on Kilimanjaro, Lonely Planet's *Trekking in East Africa* is highly recommended. Trekking on the mountain is also covered in-depth in Lonely Planet's *Tanzania, Zanzibar & Pemba*.

Information

Park entry fees for Mt Kilimanjaro National Park and Tanzania's other northern parks are US$25 per person per day (US$5 for children between five and 16, free for children under five), plus a US$30 vehicle fee. Huts cost US$50 per person per day, and there's a rescue fee of US$20 per person per trip. Park headquarters are located in Marangu (☎ Marangu 50).

The booklet *Kilimanjaro National Park* has interesting information on Kilimanjaro's history, flora and fauna. It's available

in bookshops in Arusha, Dar es Salaam and Unguja for about TSh 3000. Two good topographical maps are *Map & Guide to Kilimanjaro* by Andrew Wielochowski (1:75,000) and *Kilimanjaro Map & Guide* by Mark Savage (1:50,000).

Trekking on Mt Kilimanjaro

There are at least 10 trekking routes that begin on Kilimanjaro's lower slopes, but only three continue to the summit. The easiest and by far the most popular is the **Marangu route**. A trek on this route usually takes five days (four nights) up and back, although an extra night is recommended to help with the process of acclimatisation.

Other routes are more serious undertakings, usually taking six days. The **Machame route** has a gradual ascent before approaching the summit via the top section of the Mweka route. The **Umbwe route** is much steeper and a more direct way to the summit. Its upper section, which is often covered with snow and ice, is a serious undertaking. Trekkers on the Machame and Umbwe routes come down from the summit via the **Mweka route**, which is for descent only. Some Marangu treks also descend on the Mweka route.

Following is a brief overview of the Marangu route. For detailed descriptions of each stage, and of the other routes, see Lonely Planet's *Trekking in East Africa*.

Stage 1: Marangu Gate to Mandara Hut (7km, 4-5 hours, 700m ascent) This is an attractive path beginning at 1980m, ascending through a beautiful section of forest. From Mandara Hut you can visit Maundi Crater (two hours return), from where there are good views to the main peaks of Kibo and Mawenzi.

Stage 2: Mandara Hut to Horombo Hut (11km, 5-7 hours, 1000m ascent) Two parallel paths run through the forest and then through a zone of giant heather, meeting near the start of the open moorland. Although undulating and steep in places, the path is easy to follow all the way up to Horombo Hut (3700m). If you have time, you may prefer to spend two nights at Horombo to help acclimatisation.

Stage 3: Horombo Hut to Kibo Hut (10km, 5-7 hours, 1000m ascent) Two paths go from Horombo. The more gradually ascending western path is the most popular one. After passing the landmark Last Water point and crossing The Saddle, it joins with the steeper and rougher eastern path at Jiwe La Ukoyo (pointed rocks), from where it's another one to 1½ hours to Kibo Hut (4700m). Kibo Hut is more basic than Horombo and Mandara, and lacks a reliable water supply (water must be carried from Horombo or one of the Last Water points).

Stage 4: Kibo Hut to Uhuru Peak; plus descent to Horombo Hut (4km, 7-8½ hours, 1200m ascent; plus 14km, 4½-7 hours, 2200m descent) From Kibo Hut, the path zigzags up the scree to Hans Meyer Cave (5182m), where it becomes steeper and the walk is a slog. From Gillman's Point

(5680m), you'll have spectacular views over the plains, as well as down into the snow-filled crater and along the edge of the rim to Uhuru peak. From here to Uhuru is another two to 2½ hours. At Uhuru, there's a flagpole, a plaque inscribed with a quote of President Nyerere, and a sign to say you've reached the highest point in Africa.

It's usual to start this stage – the most strenuous part of the trek – shortly after midnight so as to see the sunrise (about 6 am) from the crater rim. Also, the scree slope up to Gillman's point and the snow on the path to Uhuru peak will still be frozen, which will make the walking safer and less tiring.

The return from Uhuru to Gillman's takes one to 1½ hours, and it's another easy two hours or less from there to Kibo Hut. From Kibo back to Horombo is two to three hours.

Stage 5: Horombo Hut to Marangu Gate (18km, 5-7 hours, 1900m descent) This final day retraces the route down to Marangu gate, with Mandara Hut at about the halfway point.

Costs All treks must be organised through a tour company; independent trekking is not allowed on Kilimanjaro. Companies organising treks are listed in the Moshi and Arusha sections earlier in this chapter. Standard five-day (four-night) treks up the Marangu route start from about US$400 to US$500, but at the bottom end of this range, it's likely that your hut will be double-booked, meals will be skimpy and porters will be desperate for tips. A more realistic budget would be between US$500 and $650 or more.

For budget treks on the Machame route, plan on spending anywhere from about US$650 at the lower end of the scale up to US$850 and more at the top end. When calculating your budget, remember that between US$300 and US$500 of the overall price goes to park fees.

Guides & Porters Guides and at least one porter (for the guide) are obligatory and are provided by your trekking company. All guides must be registered with the national park authorities, and should have permits showing this. Porters will carry bags weighing up to 15kg (not including their own food and clothing). Heavier bags will be carried for a negotiable extra fee.

For guidelines on tipping guides and porters see the Tipping & Bargaining section in the Tanzania Facts for the Visitor chapter.

Accommodation Accommodation on the Marangu route consists of three '*huts*' (actually groups of bunkhouses) spaced a day's walk apart. They are administered by the national park; overnight fees should be paid with your entrance fees. You can also *camp*, though you'll still have to pay the same overnight fees.

On the other routes there are no huts, so trekkers must camp.

Getting There & Away From Moshi there are minivans throughout the day to Marangu, from where you can sometimes find local transport to the park gate. Otherwise, it's a 5km walk from the main junction in Marangu.

LAKE MANYARA NATIONAL PARK

Among the main attractions of beautiful Lake Manyara National Park are rich birdlife, hippos and tree-climbing lions, which you can see at closer range here than at most other places. There are also a fair number of elephants although the population has been declining in recent years.

The park, which lies between 900 and 1800m above sea level, is bordered to the west by the dramatic western escarpment of the Rift Valley. To the east is the alkaline Lake Manyara which at certain times of year hosts thousands of flamingos, as well as a diversity of other bird life and a substantial hippo population. Depending on the season, about two-thirds of the park's total area of 330 sq km is covered by the lake.

Information

Park entry fees for Lake Manyara National Park and Tanzania's other northern parks are US$25 per person per day (US$5 for children between five and 16, free for children under five), plus a US$30 vehicle fee. For booking camp sites or for further information, contact the senior park warden (☎ Mto Wa Mbu 12) at PO Box 12, Mto Wa Mbu.

Lake Manyara National Park is a dated but useful booklet published by TANAPA; it's available in bookshops in Dar es Salaam, Unguja and Arusha.

MaCo produces a good map of the park; it's available at bookshops in Dar es Salaam and Arusha.

Places to Stay

There are *camp sites* and some simple bandas by the park entrance. You'll need to bring all your own provisions, although there is a good selection of basic foodstuffs available in Mto Wa Mbu village, about 3km east of the park gate on the main road to Arusha. There are also several tented camps and luxury lodges.

Kirurumu Luxury Tented Camp set on the escarpment about 12km from the park gate is a small, relaxing place with views of Lake Manyara in the distance. Full board costs about US$100 per person. Book through Hoopoe Adventure Tours (☎ 057-7011, fax 8226, email hoopoesafari@cyber net.co.tz, PO Box 2047, Arusha).

Lake Manyara Serena Lodge is to the south-west of Kirurumu, on the escarpment overlooking the Rift Valley. Rates are US$183/280 for luxury accommodation including all meals and amenities (US$138/210 between 1 April and 30 June). Book through Serena Hotels (☎ 057-4158, fax 4155, email serena@yako.habari.co.tz, PO Box 2551, Arusha).

Lake Manyara Lodge (☎ 057-4292, fax 8071) also has an attractive setting on the escarpment and luxurious accommodation. Half board costs US$135/186 per person.

Maji Moto Luxury Camp is run by Conservation Corporation Africa (☎ 02-441001, fax 750512, email conscorp@users.africa online.co.ke, PO Box 74957, Nairobi) and is 17km south-west of the park gate on the main road. Upmarket full board in one of 10 luxury cottages costs US$275 per person; the camp is closed during April and May.

Migunga Forest Camp 3km outside the park border has much simpler but decent tented half board for US$35 per person. Book through the Safari Company (☎ 057-3935, fax 8272, email sengo@habari.co.tz, PO Box 207, Arusha).

Mto Wa Mbu Village

Mto Wa Mbu (River of Mosquitoes) is just north of Lake Manyara and makes a good base for visiting the park.

There's an SNV cultural tourism program here. Contact SNV (☎/fax 057-7515, email tourinfo@habari.co.tz) in Rm 643, Serengeti wing, AICC, PO Box 10455, Arusha, for more information. Or ask at the Red Banana Cafe on the main road in Mto Wa Mbu.

Places to Stay & Eat You can camp at *Twiga Camp Site & Lodge (☎ Mto Wa Mbu 1)*. Book directly or through Parrot Tours (☎ 057-7850, 4th floor, Serengeti wing, AICC, Arusha). This place has camping for US$5 per person, and double rooms with bathroom and breakfast for US$20. There's hot water, cooking facilities and a restaurant. It's at the Arusha end of town, signposted just off the main road.

Jambo Camp Site & Lodge is slightly cheaper though not as nice. It's also signposted off the main road at the Arusha end of town.

Manyara Guest House, just off the main road to the right as you come into town from Arusha, has simple rooms with shared facilities for TSh 2000.

Red Banana Cafe has a few grubby rooms for TSh 1200/2400; food is available. It's on the main road diagonally opposite the market on the left when coming from Arusha.

Camp Vision signposted to the south of the main road has rooms (no camping) from about TSh 6000.

Holiday Fig Resort (☎ Mto Wa Mbu 2) is more upmarket, with modest but comfortable rooms for US$15/30, and camping for US$5 including showers. There's a small pool and nice grounds. It's signposted just to the north of the main road.

Getting There & Away

There's an airstrip just north of Lake Manyara for charter flights. Coastal Travels (see Travel Agencies in the Organised Safaris chapter) runs flights between Arusha and Lake Manyara (US$50 one way), connecting with flights from Dar es Salaam or Unguja.

The only road to Lake Manyara is to the north of the park, near Mto Wa Mbu. Most visitors come as part of an organised safari or with their own vehicles. While Mto Wa Mbu can be reached easily on public transport, hitching within the park is generally not feasible. Minibuses run daily between Mto Wa Mbu and Arusha.

Arrange car hire at Twiga Camp Site & Lodge (see Places to Stay & Eat). It costs US$120/$150 for a half/full day. Unless you're travelling in a group, this often becomes as expensive as an organised safari.

SERENGETI NATIONAL PARK

Serengeti, which covers 14,763 sq km and is adjacent to the Masai Mara National Reserve in Kenya, is Tanzania's largest national park. On its vast, treeless plains are several million hoofed animals, constantly on the move in search of fresh grassland. The wildebeest, of which there are up to two million, is the chief herbivore and also the main prey of large carnivores such as lions and hyenas.

The Serengeti is also famous for its lions, many of which have collars fitted with transmitters so their movements can be studied and their location tracked. The park is also known for its cheetah and large herds of giraffe.

Wildebeest Migration

One of the Serengeti's biggest attractions is the annual migration of wildebeest herds in search of better grazing. During the rainy season between March and May the herds are widely scattered over the southern section of the Serengeti and the Ngorongoro Conservation Area. These areas have few large rivers and streams and dry out quickly when the rains cease. When that happens the wildebeest concentrate on the few remaining green areas and gradually form huge herds which move north and west in search of food. At about the time the migration starts, the annual rut also begins – generally around June. For a few days at a time while the herds pause, bulls establish territories which they defend against rivals, and try to assemble as many females to mate with as they can. As soon as the rut is over, the females merge again and the herds continue their migration.

During the dry season (around July and August), the herds are in the western Serengeti. The famed river crossings usually occur around August as they continue moving north towards the Masai Mara National Reserve in Kenya to catch the short rains there. Around November, the wildebeest begin to move south again in time for calving, which begins at the start of the rainy season. If the rains come late, up to

80% of the calves may die from lack of food. If you're planning your trip around the migration, keep in mind that the actual time frame varies from year to year depending on the rains, and the actual viewing window can be short. Also remember that you may need to travel long distances within the park to reach the herds.

Information
Park entry fees for Serengeti National Park and Tanzania's other northern parks are US$25 per person per day (US$5 for children between five and 16, free for children

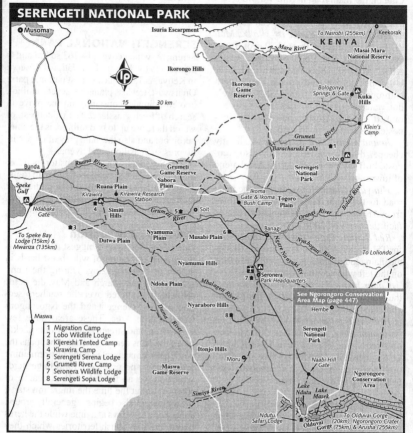

SERENGETI NATIONAL PARK

1 Migration Camp
2 Lobo Wildlife Lodge
3 Kijereshi Tented Camp
4 Kirawira Camp
5 Serengeti Serena Lodge
6 Grumeti River Camp
7 Seronera Wildlife Lodge
8 Serengeti Sopa Lodge

under five), plus a US$30 vehicle fee. Headquarters are located at Seronera, in the centre of the park.

The booklet *Serengeti National Park* put out by TANAPA has interesting information on the history and ecology of the park. It's available at bookshops in Arusha and Dar es Salaam. MaCo has a good map on the Serengeti, available in Arusha and Dar es Salaam and in some of the park lodges.

Those with a scientific interest in the Serengeti can contact the Serengeti Wildlife Research Institute (☎ 057-7677) in the Njiro Hill area of Arusha.

Binoculars are a good thing to bring to the Serengeti, because of its vast distances.

Activities
You can see the Serengeti via **balloon safari**. Hot air balloons holding up to 24 passengers take off daily at dawn from Seronera. The cost is US$375 per person, including a champagne breakfast after the two-hour flight. Book through Serengeti Balloon Safaris (☎ 057-8578, fax 8997, email balloons@habari.com.tz) at PO Box 12116, Arusha. Bookings must be made in advance. Credit cards are charged an additional 6%.

Places to Stay & Eat
Camping There are numerous *public camp sites* (US$20 per person) in the park, including those at Seronera, Kirawira, Ndabaka and Lobo. Facilities are minimal and some don't even have water, so you'll need to bring everything with you. Camp sites can be reserved by contacting the senior park warden (☎ 622852 for Seronera or 622029 for Ikoma) at PO Box 3134, Arusha.

There are also several *special camp sites* (US$40 per person) at Seronera, Kirawira, Lobo and Bologonya.

Lodges The lodges within the Serengeti all offer varying degrees of luxury.

Serengeti Serena Lodge offers singles/doubles with full board for US$183/280 (US$138/210 between 1 April and 30 June). Book with Serena Hotels (☎ 057-4158, fax 4155, email serena@yako.habari.co.tz, PO Box 2551, Arusha).

Serengeti Sopa Lodge offers half board for US$135 per person. Book through Sopa (☎ 057-6886, fax 8245, email sopa@africa online.co.tz, PO Box 1823, Arusha).

Seronera Wildlife Lodge in the centre of Serengeti and the *Lobo Wildlife Lodge* in the north-east have rooms for US$135/186 including half board. Book through Accor/Tahi (☎ 057-4292, fax 8071).

Tented Camps All of the following offer tented accommodation in attractive settings.

Migration Camp (☎ 057-2814, 051-114914, fax 057-8997, PO Box 12095, Arusha) overlooks the Grumeti River near Lobo. All-inclusive luxury accommodation costs US$228 per person.

Kirawira Camp about 90km west of Seronera near the Grumeti River has accommodation 'with a classic Victorian atmosphere' which costs US$425/677. Book through Serena Hotels (see details under Serengeti Serena Lodge earlier in this section). It's closed from mid-April to the end of May.

Grumeti River Camp is run by Conservation Corporation Africa (☎ 02-441001, fax 750512, email conscorp@users.africa online.co.ke, PO Box 74957, Nairobi). Full board in luxury tents will cost you US$275 per person; the camp is closed in April and May.

Ikoma Bush Camp 3km from Ikoma gate near the Western Corridor has simpler but decent facilities. Half board will set you back US$55 per person plus a village levy of US$10 per person. Book through the Safari Company (☎ 057-3935, fax 8272, email sengo@habari.co.tz, PO Box 207, Arusha).

Kijereshi Tented Camp (☎ 068-40139, PO Box 190, Mwanza) is in the Western Corridor about 15km east of the road between Mwanza and Musoma near Ramadi. Good, simple accommodation costs US$30 per person, including continental breakfast.

Getting There & Away
Air There's an airstrip at Seronera which handles frequent charter flights. Precision Air operates a scheduled flight between Arusha and

TANZANIA

Seronera (US$135) twice weekly, though it's sometimes cancelled.

Road Most vehicles enter at Naabi Hill gate at the south-eastern edge of the park on the road that runs through the Ngorongoro Conservation Area. From the gate, it's 45km to Seronera.

Alternatively, you can enter through the Western Corridor at Ndabaka gate, about 140km north-east of Mwanza and just south of the Western Corridor boundary, or at Ikoma gate ('Fort Ikoma'), about 30km north of Seronera and accessed via Bunda off the Mwanza-Musoma road. Both routes are often impassable in the rainy season. Bologonya gate, 10km from the Kenyan border, leads into the Masai Mara National Reserve. This route is also in poor condition. If you intend to cross the border, you'll need to arrange visas in advance.

The majority of travellers visit the Serengeti with an organised safari or with their own vehicle. For budget travellers the only other option for trying to get a glimpse of the animals is to take a bus or truck travelling between Arusha and Mwanza or Musoma via the Western Corridor route, although you'll still need to pay park fees. However, this is only possible in the dry season and you won't be able to stop at will to observe the wildlife. Although it's fairly easy to get to Ndabaka gate or Seronera by truck or public transport, efforts to hitch a lift from one of the lodges or camp sites inside the park are generally futile.

Tanzania's Overloaded Northern Circuit

According to the Tanzania Tourist Board, well over 100,000 people visit Serengeti National Park annually. The numbers are similar for Ngorongoro Crater. As these figures illustrate, tourism is big business in the north. Unfortunately, it has become such big business that the parks are beginning to suffer serious environmental damage.

Some of the problems arise from the sheer volume: with such large numbers of visitors, the parks are bound to suffer negative effects no matter what controls are implemented. Another aspect is the manner in which the parks are visited. 'Low-impact tourism' is often a meaningless term in these parts. Tour operators – scrambling for money and responding to demand – aim to attract as many clients as possible, and high-impact, quick in-and-out trips are standard practice in most of the northern parks. While many companies pay lip service to 'eco-friendly' ideals, there are relatively few that actually take the extra steps necessary to ensure that their safaris contribute to the well-being of the environment and of local communities.

If you decide to visit northern Tanzania's popular attractions, there are some steps you can take to ensure you will not be part of the problem. Book tours only with companies that make these measures a priority:

- One of the most important measures to take is to thoroughly research tour operators. Patronise only those that make environmental conservation a priority in fact as well as in word, and that collaborate with and assist local communities.

- Structure your trip so that you have the time and opportunity to get to know the locals who live in or near the areas you are visiting. Trekking and walking safaris are ideal in this respect.

- On treks and camping safaris, ensure that your rubbish is properly disposed of.

- Keep water sources clean.

- Use camping stoves rather than wood fires.

- Stay on established roads and paths.

- Practice respect in your behaviour. It's an important way of indicating that you value both the areas that you visit and their inhabitants, and can contribute to an overall atmosphere of respect for environment and culture.

TARANGIRE NATIONAL PARK

Tarangire is a beautiful area stretching south-east of Lake Manyara around the Tarangire River. During the dry season, it has one of the highest concentrations of wildlife of any of the country's parks. Large herds of zebra, wildebeest, hartebeest and elephant can be found here until October when the short wet season allows them to move on to lush new grasslands to the north-east. Eland, lesser kudu, gazelle, giraffe, waterbuck, impala and the occasional leopard or rhino can be seen at Tarangire year-round. The park is also good for birdwatching, with over three hundred different species recorded.

Since Tarangire National Park comprises less than 15% of the Tarangire ecosystem, its future is inextricably linked with that of the Maasai community lands adjacent to the park. In recognition of this fact, the Tarangire Wildlife Conservation Area (TWCA), which borders Tarangire to the north-east, was created to address the needs of local communities while at the same time promoting wildlife conservation projects in the area. Visitors can enjoy walking safaris and other nature activities here, while local villagers – who have set aside some of their land for the project – benefit directly from tourist revenues and remain involved in management of the conservation area. The best wildlife viewing in the conservation area is from late December, when first the wildebeest and zebras, followed in January by herds of elephant, move out of the park towards their breeding grounds along the east of the Rift Valley escarpment.

Information

Park entry fees for Tarangire National Park and Tanzania's other northern parks are US$25 per person per day (US$5 for children between five and 16, free for children under five), plus a US$30 vehicle fee. The senior park warden can be contacted at PO Box 3134, Arusha.

The TANAPA booklet *Tarangire National Park* has detailed information on Tarangire's flora, fauna and history. It's available at bookshops in Dar es Salaam,

Arusha and Unguja. MaCo puts out a Tarangire map available in Dar es Salaam and Arusha bookshops.

For information about the Tarangire Wildlife Conservation Area, contact the Tarangire Conservation Company (☎ 057-2814, fax 4199, PO Box 1215, Arusha) or Let's Go Travel in Arusha (see the Organised Safaris chapter for details).

Places to Stay & Eat

There are two public *camp sites* and six *special camp sites*. You'll need to bring all your own provisions, including water. Otherwise, there are several comfortable lodges and luxury camps.

Tarangire Sopa Lodge has half board for US$135 per person. Book through Sopa (☎ 057-6886, fax 8245, email sopa@africa online.co.tz, PO Box 1823, Arusha).

Tarangire Safari Lodge run by Serengeti Select Safaris (☎ 057-7182, PO Box 2703, Arusha) and set on a bluff overlooking the Tarangire River, has tented singles/doubles from US$55/65, and bungalows from US$60/75. Meals are US$5/12/15 for breakfast/lunch/dinner.

Oliver's Camp (☎ 057-4116, fax 8548, email olivers@habari.co.tz, PO Box 425, Arusha) just outside the park to the east offers exclusive luxury tented accommodation from US$300 per person. It's closed from 1 November to mid-December and from March to May.

Tamarind Camp Tarangire just outside the north-western corner of the park and about 20km from Makuyuni is a mobile luxury camp with comfortable tented accommodation with full board for US$98/ 155 plus 20% tax. It's closed from mid-April until early June. Book through Hoopoe Adventure Tours (☎ 057-7011, fax 8226, email hoopoe safari@cybernet.co.tz, Arusha).

Naitola Camp, to the north of the park gate, and about 1½ to two hours drive from Arusha, is the best base for walking safaris within the TWCA. Comfortable, environmentally appropriate accommodation costs US$180 per person including meals, foot safaris and day and night wildlife drives, but excluding transfers from Arusha and

TANZANIA

park fees if you plan on going into Tarangire. Book through Let's Go Travel in Arusha.

A luxury 16-bed lodge at the other end of the TWCA is currently under construction. Once this is open, foot safaris between the lodge and Naitola Camp will be possible, with fly-camps for overnight.

Getting There & Away

To visit Tarangire National Park you'll need to join an organised tour or use your own vehicle. The main gate is in the north-western corner of the park 5km south-east of Kwa Kuchinia.

Ngorongoro Conservation Area

The Ngorongoro Crater is just one part of a much larger area of interrelated ecosystems consisting of the Crater Highlands and vast stretches of plains, bush and woodland.

The entire Ngorongoro Conservation Area (NCA) covers about 8300 sq km and encompasses the Olduvai Gorge; the alkaline Ndutu and Masek lakes, which offer excellent wildlife viewing during the March to May rainy season (although Ndutu is actually just over the border in the Serengeti); and a string of volcanoes and collapsed volcanoes (often referred to as calderas), most of which are inactive.

Just outside the NCA's eastern boundary is the archaeologically important Engaruka, and along to the south is Lake Eyasi, home to the Hadzabe, descendants of one of Tanzania's original ethnic groups. To the northeast of the NCA on the Kenyan border is the beautiful Lake Natron.

Information

The NCA is under the jurisdiction of the Ngorongoro Conservation Area Authority (NCAA), which has its headquarters at Park Village at Ngorongoro Crater (☎ Ngorongoro Crater 6 or 7, PO Box 1, Ngorongoro Crater). You can also arrange guides (compulsory, $20 per day) and vehicle hire here

for Ngorongoro Crater and other areas of the NCA. Car hire costs about US$90/130 for a half/full day. The NCAA also has a branch office in Arusha near the Central Bank (☎ 057-6091, fax 3339, PO Box 776, Arusha).

For activities within the NCA you must pay an entry fee of US$25 per person (US$5 for children between five and 16 years old), plus US$30 per vehicle. Camping costs US$20 (US$5 for children) at regular camp sites and US$40 (US$10 for children) at special camp sites. There's an additional 'crater service' fee of US$10 to drive down into the Ngorongoro Crater. Increases in these fees were under discussion as this chapter was being researched, so check for an update in Arusha.

The booklet *Ngorongoro Conservation Area* put out by the Wildlife Conservation Society of Tanzania has detailed information about the different geographical zones within the NCA, plus sections on ecology and history. It's available at bookshops in Arusha and Dar es Salaam for about TSh 3000.

THE CRATER HIGHLANDS

The Crater Highlands, which lie to the west of Mt Meru and Mt Kilimanjaro and overlook the plains of the Serengeti, consist of an elevated range of volcanoes and calderas rising from the side of the Great Rift Valley and running along the eastern edge of the NCA. The peaks include Oldeani (3185m), Empakaai (3262m, also spelled Embagai), the active Oldoinyo Lengai (2878m), and of course Ngorongoro (2200m). Much of the area is remote and seldom visited, but it offers some of Tanzania's most rugged and unusual scenery as well as superb trekking. Most treks begin just north of Ngorongoro Crater and cross the highlands to finish at Ngare Sero near Lake Natron (about four days). An extra day is required for the ascent of Oldoinyo Lengai.

Because of the rugged terrain and wildlife, unaccompanied trekking in the Crater Highlands is not permitted. You'll need to arrange a vehicle, local guide and armed park ranger, as well as donkeys to carry supplies and water, and Maasai people

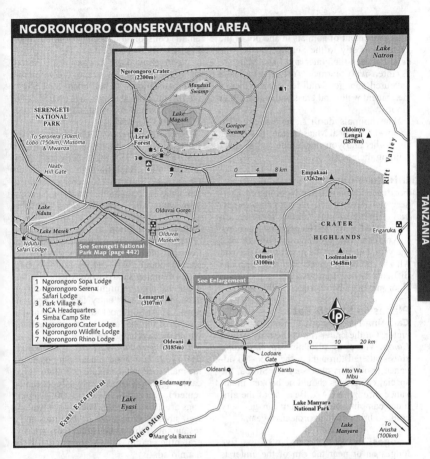

NGORONGORO CONSERVATION AREA

Ngorongoro Crater
(2200m)

Mandusi
Swamp

Lake
Magadi

Gorigor
Swamp

SERENGETI
NATIONAL
PARK

To Seronera (30km),
Lobo (150km), Musoma
& Mwanza

Leral
Forest

Naabi
Hill Gate

0   4   8 km

Lake
Ndutu

Lake Masek

Olduvai Gorge

Ndutu
Safari Lodge

See Serengeti National
Park Map (page 442)

Olduvai
Museum

1 Ngorongoro Sopa Lodge
2 Ngorongoro Serena
   Safari Lodge
3 Park Village &
   NCA Headquarters
4 Simba Camp Site
5 Ngorongoro Crater Lodge
6 Ngorongoro Wildlife Lodge
7 Ngorongoro Rhino Lodge

Lemagrut ▲
(3107m)

See Enlargement

Oldeani ▲
(3185m)

Lake
Natron

Oldoinyo
Lengai ▲
(2878m)

Rift Valley

Empakaai ▲
(3262m)

CRATER
HIGHLANDS

Engaruka

Olmoti
(3100m)

Loolmalasin ▲
(3648m)

0   10   20 km

Lodoare
Gate

Oldeani   Karatu

Mto Wa
Mbu

Endamagnay

Eyasi Escarpment

Lake
Eyasi

Kidero Mtns

Mang'ola Barazni

Lake Manyara
National Park

Lake
Manyara

To
Arusha
(100km)

TANZANIA

to look after the donkeys. Some of the travel agencies listed in the Organised Safaris chapter also arrange treks in the Crater Highlands. Costs (including entrance fees for the Ngorongoro Conservation Area) range from about US$80 per day at the bottom end to US$100 and up for better quality. Lonely Planet's *Trekking in East Africa* contains more detailed information, as well as route outlines and maps. MaCo's *Ngorongoro Conservation Area* map covers the area from Lake Eyasi to Oldoinyo Lengai.

There are no lodges in the highlands apart from the facilities at Ngorongoro Crater.

NGORONGORO CRATER

Ngorongoro Crater is one of Africa's best-known wildlife-viewing areas and one of Tanzania's most visited. At about 20km wide it's also one of the largest calderas in the world. Within its walls are a variety of animals and vegetation, including grasslands, swamps, forests, salt pans and a freshwater lake. You are likely to see lion, elephant, rhino, buffalo and many of the plains herbivores such as wildebeest, Thomson's gazelle, zebra and reedbuck, as well as thousands of flamingos wading in the shallows of Lake Magadi, the soda lake at the crater's base.

Despite its steep walls, there's considerable movement of animals in and out of the crater – mostly to the Serengeti, since the land between the crater and Lake Manyara is intensively farmed. Yet it remains a favoured spot for wildlife because there's permanent water and grassland on the crater floor.

The animals don't have the crater to themselves. Local Maasai tribes have grazing rights and you may come across them tending their cattle.

Information

For fee information, see Ngorongoro Conservation Area. If you intend to do commercial filming in the crater, there is an additional fee of US$100 per person per day.

You can visit Ngorongoro at any time of the year, but during the months of April and May it can be extremely wet and the roads difficult to negotiate. Access to the crater floor may also be restricted at this time.

Places to Stay & Eat

Camping There are no camp sites inside the crater. On the crater rim is the dirty *Simba Camp*. There are also nine *special camp sites* scattered throughout the park. No advance booking is necessary for Simba; the special camp sites should be booked in advance through NCAA. Because of the altitude, camping on the crater can get very cold, so bring enough protective gear.

Lodges The least expensive of the five lodges on or near the rim of the crater is *Ngorongoro Rhino Lodge (☎ Ngorongoro Crater 21, 057-4619, fax 3339, PO Box 16, Ngorongoro Crater)* which is run by the NCAA. There are no views of the crater but the rooms are simple and clean. Singles/doubles cost US$45/70 including breakfast.

Ngorongoro Wildlife Lodge on the edge of the crater rim has good views, and half board costs US$135/186. Book through Accor/Tahi (☎ 057-4292, fax 8071).

Ngorongoro Crater Lodge also has views of the crater and very upmarket accommodation for US$325 per person including your own butler. Book through Conservation Cor-

poration Africa (☎ 02-441001, fax 750512, email conscorp@users.africaonline.co.ke, PO Box 74957, Nairobi).

Ngorongoro Sopa Lodge on the eastern rim of the crater offers attractive, comfortable accommodation with half board for US$135 per person. Book through Sopa (☎ 057-6886, fax 8245, email sopa@africa online .co.tz, PO Box 1823, Arusha).

Ngorongoro Serena Safari Lodge on the western rim has luxurious full board for US$183/280 (US$138/210 between 1 April and 30 June). Book through Serena Hotels (☎ 057-4158, fax 4155, email serena@ yako.habari.co.tz) on the 6th floor, Ngorongoro wing, AICC (PO Box 2551), Arusha.

Karatu In addition to the lodges at the crater, there are several less expensive options outside the NCA in the nearby town of Karatu, about 20km east of Lodoare gate. Many camping safaris from Arusha use this place as an overnight stop in order to economise on park entry fees for Ngorongoro. There's a post office here and a branch of the National Microfinance Bank which will exchange cash.

Ngorongoro Safari Resort (☎ Karatu 59, 057-7102) is a good place, signposted on the main road in the middle of Karatu. It has camping for US$3 per person. Tents can be rented for an additional TSh 1000; sleeping bags are also available. There's hot water, a well stocked store, cooking facilities and a restaurant. If this place is full, there are several other camp sites signposted off the main road.

ECLT Lutheran Centre Hostel (☎ Karatu 55) has rooms for about TSh 12,000. It's just west of Ngorongoro Safari Resort, along the main road.

Gibbs Farm (☎ 057-6702, or Karatu 25, email ndutugibbs@marie.sasa.unep.no, PO Box 6084, Arusha or PO Box 2, Karatu) is upmarket and long-established, offering comfortable lodging for US$90/110. Good meals made with home-grown produce are available. It's signposted off the main road and closed during April and May.

Kifaru Lodge (☎ Karatu 20, ☎/fax 057-8908, PO Box 1187, Arusha) is another good place in a former farmhouse. Rooms cost US$90/112, including breakfast. It's about a 10 minute drive from Karatu.

Getting There & Away

The large white Ngorongoro Crater bus leaves daily from the main bus station in Arusha at about 9 am, reaching park headquarters at about 3 pm (TSh 3500). Ask the driver to drop you at Ngorongoro Rhino Lodge, from where you can arrange vehicle rental. You can also rent vehicles from the lodges around the crater rim or in Karatu, although rates are generally more expensive. Returning to Arusha, the bus departs from park headquarters at about 6.30 am; ask staff at the Rhino Lodge to show you the pick-up point.

If you're coming with your own vehicle, remember that only 4WDs are allowed down into the crater, except at certain times during the dry season when the authorities *may* allow conventional vehicles to enter. All roads into the crater, except the road from Sopa Lodge on the eastern side, are very steep, so if you are driving your own vehicle, make sure it can handle them.

Whether you are driving on your own or you're part of an organised tour, you'll need to take a park ranger with you (US$20 per day) and also pay the crater service fee of US$10 per vehicle.

OLDUVAI GORGE

The Olduvai Gorge is a canyon about 50km long and up to 90m deep which runs to the north-west of Ngorongoro Crater. Thanks to its unique geological history, in which layer upon layer of volcanic deposits were laid down in orderly sequence over a period of almost two million years, it provides remarkable documentation of ancient life.

The most famous of Olduvai's fossils is the 1.8 million-year-old ape-like skull known as *Australopithecus boisei*. Its discovery by Mary Leakey in 1959 gave rise to a heated debate about human evolution. The skull is often referred to as *zinjanthropus*, which means 'nutcracker man', referring to its large molars. In 1972, hominid (human-like) footprints estimated to be 3.7 million

years old were discovered at Laetoli, about 45km south of the Olduvai Gorge.

Based on these findings as well as other ancient fossils excavated in Kenya and Ethiopia, it has been posited that there were at least three hominid species in the region about two million years ago, including *Australopithecus boisei*, *Homo habilis* and *Homo erectus*. While *Australopithecus boisei* and *Homo habilis* appear to have died out (or in the case of *Homo habilis*, been absorbed by or evolved into *Homo erectus*), it is theorised that *Homo erectus* continued and evolved into *Homo sapiens*, or the modern human.

It's possible to go down into the gorge at certain times of the year to view the excavation sites (US$2 plus the US$25 entry fee for Ngorongoro Conservation Area). There's also a small museum on the site (usually open only during the dry season), which will be of interest primarily to those who are archaeologically inclined.

The gorge is about 45km from park headquarters off the road to Serengeti. To go into the gorge, you'll need to be accompanied by a guide, which can be arranged at the museum. The nearest accommodation is **Ndutu Safari Lodge** (☎ 057-6702, PO Box 6084, Arusha) on the border of Serengeti National Park at the western end of the gorge. Accommodation costs US$104/127, including breakfast.

ENGARUKA

Engaruka, on the eastern edge of the Ngorongoro Conservation Area, is a small village famous for the nearby ruins of a complex irrigation system with terraced stone housing sites estimated to be at least 500 years old. Scientists aren't sure of their origin, though some speculate they were built by ancestors of the Iraqw (Mbulu) people who live in the area today. To arrange visits and guided walks through the ruins, contact the SNV (☎/fax 057-7515, email tourinfo@habari.co.tz) at PO Box 10455, Arusha. Details of the SNV cultural tourism program are also available at the tourist information centre in Arusha.

Road access to Engaruka is via the village of Mto Wa Mbu along the Arusha road.

TANZANIA

From Mto Wa Mbu, it's another 60km further north along an unpaved road. Alternatively, you can hike from the Empakaai Crater, but you'll need a guide from the NCAA.

LAKE NATRON

Lake Natron, 25km north of Oldoinyo Lengai on the Kenyan border, is a 60km-long alkaline lake known for the huge flocks of flamingos that gather at certain parts of the lake at the end of the rainy season. To visit you'll need a 4WD.

Following a spate of attacks on tourist vehicles in the vicinity of the lake, security has been increased and tour operators are again taking groups to the area.

Lake Natron Camp at the south-western corner of the lake near the lake flats costs US$50 per person; full catering is possible, but you'll need to book in advance with the Safari Company (☎ 057-3935, fax 8272, email sengo@habari.co.tz) at PO Box 207, Arusha. Although the camp suffered considerable flood damage during 1998 and is a bit run-down, it's still an attractive place.

There's another more basic camp site in the area, but you'll need your own tents and provisions.

LAKE EYASI

Lake Eyasi is a salt lake lying at an altitude of about 1000m between the Eyasi escarpment in the north (an ancient fault line that is part of the Rift Valley system) and the Kidero mountains in the south. It's a hot, dry area, around which live the Hadzabe people (also known as Hadzapi or Tindiga), who are believed to have lived here for nearly 10,000 years. Today there are only a few hundred left. The lifestyle of the Hadzabe still centres around hunting and gathering traditions. Also in the area are the Iraqw (Mbulu), and the Maasai and various other groups.

Access to the lake is feasible only on foot. Arusha-based tour operators can arrange treks from Oldeani or other areas on the escarpment down to Lake Eyasi.

Lake Victoria

With an area of 68,800 sq km, Lake Victoria is the largest lake in Africa and the second largest freshwater lake in the world; about half of it lies in Tanzania. The surrounding region, while lagging behind many other areas of the country in terms of transportation and telecommunications, is one of Tanzania's fastest growing and most populous areas. Agriculture and fishing are the mainstays of the economy.

One of the main tourist attractions of Lake Victoria is the serene and beautiful Rubondo Island National Park, an excellent place for birdwatching and relaxing.

MWANZA
☎ 068

Mwanza is one of Tanzania's largest towns and the economic centre of the lake region.

It has numerous industries and a busy port that handles much of the cotton, tea and coffee grown in the fertile western part of the country. The surrounding area is also home to the Sukuma, Tanzania's largest tribe.

Mwanza makes a good base for a visit to Rubondo Island National Park, and in the dry season is a convenient starting point for

TANZANIA

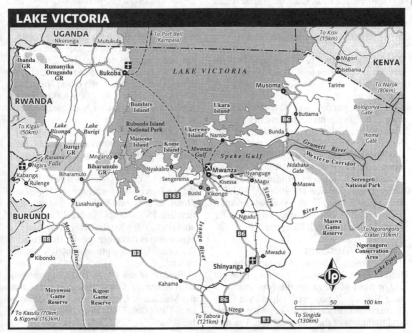

LAKE VICTORIA

451

a trip through the western Serengeti. It's also the major regional transit point for those travelling between other areas of Tanzania or to/from Rwanda or Uganda.

Orientation
On the western edge of town are the ferry docks, the clock tower, the local bus stand for transport to the airport, and several banks and shops. In the central and eastern sections of town are most shops, guesthouses, and mosques. On the eastern edge of town are the market and the main bus station, while the train station is to the south.

Information
Money Other than banks, there are several foreign exchange bureaus, including DBK Bureau de Change at Serengeti Services & Tours (see Travel Agencies following).

Post & Communications The Internet Cafe (☎ 500241, email cbcs@raha.com), at Computer Bureau & Commercial Services on Bantu St, charges TSh 1500/500 to send/receive an email. Internet links cost TSh 3000/5000 for 30 minutes/one hour.

Travel Agencies Travel agencies in town can assist with trips to Rubondo Island National Park, the western Serengeti and other destinations. They can also arrange car hire (TSh 15,000 per day, plus TSh 400 per kilometre, including fuel), and charter flights. Two agencies that are recommended are: Serengeti Services & Tours (☎ 500061, 0812-500567, fax 41210, email serengeti@mbio.net), PO Box 308, Mwanza, on Post St opposite the telecom building; and Fourways Travel Service (☎ 502620, 502273, fax 502502, email vinaysapra@hotmail.com), PO Box 990, Mwanza, on Station Rd near the junction with Kenyatta Rd.

Sukuma Museum
The open-air Sukuma Museum (also referred to as the Bujora Museum) is about 20km from Mwanza on the Musoma road near Kisessa. It was established by a Quebecois missionary and focuses on the culture and traditions of the Sukuma tribe. The mu-

seum also puts on occasional performances of traditional dance; inquire at travel agencies in town for schedule information. To get there, take a minibus from the market or from the stand near the Aga Khan Hospital to Kisessa, from where it's about a 15 minute walk. There is a nominal entry fee.

Saa Nane Game Reserve
The Saa Nane Game Reserve is on a tiny island just off Capri Point. There's a ranger and a small zoo but no food or lodging on the island. A boat departs daily at 11 am and 1, 3 and 5 pm from next to the Tilapia Hotel (TSh 700, 15 minutes); the last ferry back is at 5.15 pm. For further information, visit the reserve's office on Capri Point Rd, about 500m from the Tilapia Hotel.

Places to Stay – Budget & Mid-Range
You can camp on the grounds of *Sukuma Museum* (see earlier), which is well out of Mwanza along a rough road.

Inexpensive lodging in the town centre is at *Kishamapanda Guest House* (☎ 42523) on the corner of Uhuru and Kishamapanda Sts. Clean singles and en suite doubles with fan and mosquito net cost TSh 2500/ 4000. Adjoining the Kishamapanda is the slightly cheaper but grubbier *Geita Guest House* with rooms for about TSh 2000/3000. The entrance and reception for both guesthouses is at Geita Guest House.

Pamba Hostel (☎ 502697) on Station Rd has fairly clean rooms with shared bathroom for TSh 3600/5400, including continental breakfast.

North of the bus station across Nyerere Rd and over a footbridge is *Majukano Hotel*. Rooms with bathroom and mosquito nets are TSh 4800/6000; breakfast is available (extra). It's located a bit away from the centre and is therefore quieter than some of the other budget options, but it's nothing special.

Deluxe Hotel (☎ 500831) opposite the Kishamapanda Guest House is nicer than the Majukano. Clean rooms with bathroom cost TSh 6000/7200, including continental breakfast.

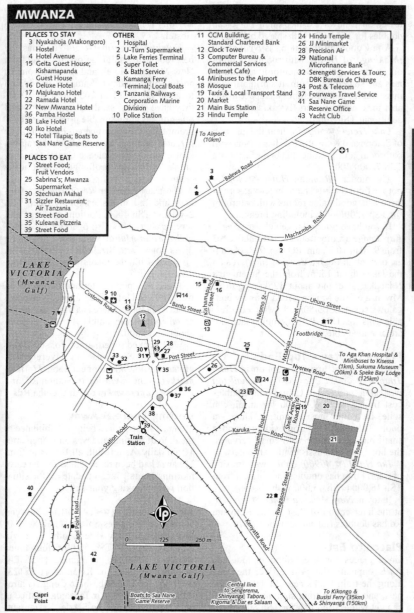

MWANZA

PLACES TO STAY
3 Nyakahoja (Makongoro) Hostel
4 Hotel Avenue
15 Geita Guest House; Kishamapanda Guest House
16 Deluxe Hotel
17 Majukano Hotel
22 Ramada Hotel
27 New Mwanza Hotel
36 Pamba Hostel
38 Lake Hotel
40 Iko Hotel
42 Hotel Tilapia; Boats to Saa Nane Game Reserve

PLACES TO EAT
7 Street Food; Fruit Vendors
25 Sabrina's; Mwanza Supermarket
30 Szechuan Mahal
31 Sizzler Restaurant; Air Tanzania
33 Street Food
35 Kuleana Pizzeria
39 Street Food

OTHER
1 Hospital
2 U-Turn Supermarket
5 Lake Ferries Terminal
6 Super Toilet & Bath Service
8 Kamanga Ferry Terminal; Local Boats
9 Tanzania Railways Corporation Marine Division
10 Police Station
11 CCM Building; Standard Chartered Bank
12 Clock Tower
13 Computer Bureau & Commercial Services (Internet Cafe)
14 Minibuses to the Airport
18 Mosque
19 Taxis & Local Transport Stand
20 Market
21 Main Bus Station
23 Hindu Temple
24 Hindu Temple
26 JJ Minimarket
28 Precision Air
29 National Microfinance Bank
32 Serengeti Services & Tours; DBK Bureau de Change
34 Post & Telecom
37 Fourways Travel Service
41 Saa Nane Game Reserve Office
43 Yacht Club

TANZANIA

Hotel Avenue about 1km from the clock tower on Balewa Rd has small but clean doubles for TSh 6000 with shared bathroom.

A few doors further along is *Nyakahoja (Makongoro) Hostel* with rooms (doubles only) for TSh 4000, including mosquito nets and shared bathroom. It's primarily for missionaries but sometimes has space available for other travellers. Breakfast costs an additional TSh 1000.

Lake Hotel (☎ 500658) near the junction of Station and Kenyatta Rds has rooms with bathroom and continental breakfast from TSh 7200/8400.

The modern *Ramada Hotel (☎ 40237)* not far from the bus stand on Rwagasore St has clean, good value rooms with bathroom for TSh 7800/9600, including breakfast.

If you have your own vehicle, try *Speke Bay Lodge* (radio frequency 4490.0 USB from 9.30 to 10.30 am, PO Box 953, Mwanza, or book through a travel agency). It's on the lake, about 15km from the Serengeti's Ndabaka Gate and about 125km north of Mwanza off the Musoma road. Luxury bungalows cost US$65/80/105, while comfortable tents cost US$19/28. Camping facilities are also available.

Places to Stay – Top End

Mwanza's most luxurious option is *Hotel Tilapia (☎ 500517, fax 500141, email tilapia@mbio.net)* east of Capri Point. Doubles cost from US$70 (US$100 for an air-con suite) including most amenities. There's a pool (TSh 4000 for nonresidents) and a small business centre with email services; the hotel can also assist with car rentals.

Iko Hotel (☎ 40900) on the western side of Capri Point has doubles (no singles) from TSh 15,000 (TSh 45,000 with air-con).

In town, *New Mwanza Hotel (☎ 501070)* at the intersection of Post St and Kenyatta Rd has doubles (no singles) for US$70.

Places to Eat

Good places for street food include the *stalls* opposite the post office, the area along the train tracks near the ferry terminals, and near the train station, where you can get whole fried fish for TSh 800.

You can also get inexpensive *local food* at Hotel Deluxe and the canteen at Pamba Hostel.

Kuleana Pizzeria (☎ 500765) has the best food in town. It is across the street from New Mwanza Hotel, and is open from 10 am to 8 pm Monday to Saturday. In addition to good pizzas (TSh 1000 to TSh 3000), they have salads, sandwiches, desserts and other dishes at reasonable prices. Service is prompt and the atmosphere is excellent. The pizzeria doubles as a vocational training centre run by the Kuleana Centre for Children's Rights, and profits go to benefit the centre.

The nearby *Sizzler Restaurant* has Chinese and Indian dishes for between TSh 2400 and TSh 4000. Portions are large and service is fast. It's also open for breakfast.

Szechuan Mahal Restaurant just a few doors down from Sizzler Restaurant serves up good Chinese meals averaging about TSh 3500.

There is a popular terrace *barbecue* on weekends at Hotel Tilapia; meals average about TSh 3000. There is a more expensive *restaurant* at the hotel with dishes from about TSh 5000.

Well stocked supermarkets for self-caterers include *Sabrina's* on Nyerere Rd, *Mwanza Supermarket* next door, *JJ Minimarket* on the extension of Station Rd, and *U-Turn Supermarket* on Machemba Rd.

Getting There & Away

Mwanza's airport was being rehabilitated at the time of writing, and was only open until 11 am daily. As a result, all flights to/from Mwanza had been rescheduled for the early morning hours. Get an update on the situation when booking your ticket.

Air Air Tanzania (☎ 40413) flies between Mwanza and Dar es Salaam (TSh 80,500, four times weekly direct, otherwise via Arusha), Arusha (TSh 55,000, four times weekly), Entebbe in Uganda (US$124, weekly), Kigali in Rwanda (US$123, weekly), and Lubumbashi in Congo (Zaïre) (US$275, weekly). Air Tanzania's office is on Kenyatta Rd next to Sizzler Restaurant.

Eagle Air also flies once weekly between Mwanza and Entebbe (US$100); book at any travel agency in Mwanza.

Precision Air (☎ 41688), opposite Air Tanzania's office, has flights between Mwanza and Dar es Salaam (US$205, three times weekly), Bukoba (US$65, daily), Arusha (US$145, three times weekly), Unguja (Zanzibar Island) (US$205, four times weekly), Ngara (US$95, twice weekly) and Shinyanga (US$60, five times weekly).

RenAir/SkyLink (☎ 562069, fax 560403) runs twice weekly flights connecting Mwanza and Nairobi (US$195 return). Book through Serengeti Services & Tours (see Travel Agencies earlier in this section.)

Bus Bus services to/from Mwanza include the following:

Lake Victoria Region Buses between Mwanza and Musoma run throughout the day (TSh 2500, six hours). The road is in poor condition for the first 35km to Nyanguge but there's good tarmac from there to over the border into Kenya.

There is a daily bus to Geita (TSh 2000) and on to Biharamulo (TSh 4500), where there are connections to Bukoba, Lusahunga and on to Ngara on the Rwanda/Burundi borders. There is a sporadic direct service between Mwanza and Bukoba but it's better to do the trip in stages. Roads are rough.

Samma and Lake Transport lines run twice weekly buses direct from Mwanza to Ngara (TSh 7000) and Rulenge (TSh 8000).

To Shinyanga, there are daily buses (TSh 3500, 5½ hours).

Other Destinations To Tabora, it's best to go via train. By road, take any bus heading to Nzega (TSh 6000), from where 4WDs run to Tabora (TSh 2000).

There are three routes from Mwanza to Arusha/Moshi and Dar es Salaam. The best is via Nairobi (TSh 25,000, approximately 30 hours to Dar es Salaam). Alternatively, there are sporadic buses during the dry season from Mwanza via the Ndabaka Gate and the Serengeti's Western Corridor to Moshi (TSh 19,000 to Moshi, plus park entrance

fees for the Serengeti and Ngorongoro Crater). At Moshi you'll need to change buses for Dar es Salaam. Depending on road conditions, some buses may alternatively go from Mwanza via Bunda to the Ikoma Gate, and then into the Serengeti from there. For information on the Serengeti routes, check with the Tanganyika Bus Service office at Mwanza's central bus station. Trucks also ply the Western Corridor route fairly regularly; ask around in Mwanza near the port if you want to find a ride this way.

The most unpleasant way to get to Dar es Salaam by bus is via Singida (TSh 19,000); allow at least three days.

The Saratoga bus line runs weekly between Mwanza and Kigoma (TSh 12,000) via Kahama and Shinyanga, departing at about 5 am and arriving the next day if you're lucky. To go to Kigoma via Biharamulo (TSh 12,000), your only option is Lake Transport, which has a weekly bus on Friday, departing at 5 am. Services are frequently interrupted or cancelled, especially during the rainy season.

See the Tanzania Getting There & Away chapter for details of buses to Kenya, Uganda, Rwanda and Burundi.

Train Mwanza is the terminus of a branch of the Central Line from Dar es Salaam. Trains depart Mwanza four times weekly (presently Sunday, Tuesday, Thursday and Friday) at about 6 pm for Tabora (TSh 11,900/8400/5300 for 1st/2nd sleeping/3rd class, 12 hours) and Dar es Salaam (TSh 44,600/32,600/12,300, 36 to 40 hours). Tickets for 1st and 2nd class should be booked at least several days in advance.

If you are heading to Kigoma, you must change trains at Tabora.

Boat Services to/from Mwanza include: Mwanza Gulf Two ferries ply the Mwanza Gulf, connecting Mwanza and Sengerema, Geita and other towns to the west. The more reliable is the Kamanga ferry, which docks at Mwanza port; it runs until 6 pm. The more southerly Busisi ferry operates (in theory) until 10 pm and connects with Kikongo, about 25km south of Mwanza.

Lake Victoria Mwanza is connected by ferry with Bukoba, with Port Bell (Kampala) in Uganda and with numerous islands in Lake Victoria, including Ukerewe. Possible expansion of services to Kampala and the introduction of a new ferry (planned for sometime in 2000) will likely result in changes to the schedules described here. For updated information, check at the port entrance, at the office of the Tanzania Railways Corporation Marine Division (next to the police station at the harbour), or with a travel agency in Mwanza.

Currently, the *MV Victoria* sails on Tuesday, Thursday and Sunday from Mwanza to Bukoba. Departures on Tuesday and Thursday are at 9 pm, arriving at about 6 am the next morning in Bukoba. The boat departs Bukoba on Wednesday and Friday evenings at about 9 pm, arriving back in Mwanza at about 6 am the next morning. On Sunday, the boat departs Mwanza at 2 pm, arriving in Bukoba at about 9 pm. It then continues on to Port Bell, arriving Monday at about 8 am. Departures from Bukoba are at about 3 am on Monday, and arriving in Mwanza at about 11 am on Tuesday morning. Fares between Mwanza and Bukoba are TSh 11,800/ 9300/6200 for 1st/2nd/3rd class. All fares are subject to an additional US$5 port tax.

The smaller and slower *MV Serengeti* also runs weekly between Mwanza and Bukoba, departing Mwanza at 3 pm on Saturday and arriving in Bukoba early Sunday morning. Departures from Bukoba are at 3 pm on Sunday, arriving in Mwanza early Monday morning. Fares are TSh 9400/6000/4600.

Mwanza is connected with Nansio on Ukerewe Island daily (TSh 2500/2000 for 2nd/3rd class; no 1st class) by the small *Clias* ferry.

The *Butiama*, an even smaller boat with deck class only, sails to Maisome Island on Wednesdays at about 3 pm (TSh 2800). To continue on to Rubondo Island National Park, you can arrange a boat pick-up with the park headquarters (see the Rubondo Island National Park section for contact details) or a travel agency in Mwanza.

Getting Around

To/From the Airport Mwanza's airport is about 10km north of town along a bad road. Taxis ask TSh 5000, but you can usually find one for TSh 3000 to TSh 4000.

Both Air Tanzania and Fourways Travel Service run a shuttle bus that meets most incoming flights (TSh 1500).

Minibuses to the airport (TSh 200) leave from the local bus station near the clock tower; allow an hour.

Bus & Taxi Local transport to towns north of Mwanza leaves from the bus stand near the clock tower. Transport to Kisessa and other destinations along the Musoma road leaves from the Bugando Hill stand near Aga Khan Hospital, south-east of the market, and from the stand opposite the market.

BUKOBA
☎ 066

Bukoba, home to the Haya people, is Tanzania's second largest port on Lake Victoria and a fairly popular overnight stop for travellers en route to or from Uganda or Rwanda. It's a small but bustling town with an attractive waterside setting.

Information

There are no foreign exchange bureaus in Bukoba. Travellers cheques can be changed at the NBC and sometimes at the CRDB.

Places to Stay

Nyumba ya Vijana, south-east of the telecom building, has basic but decent doubles for TSh 3000 with shared bathroom.

Kahawa Guest House, to the east of the market, is even cheaper, with doubles for TSh 2500 (TSh 3500 with bathroom).

ELCT Lutheran Centre (☎ 23121) on the airport road is good value and probably the best place to stay in town. Clean, comfortable singles/doubles cost TSh 6000/10,800, not including breakfast.

New Banana Hotel (☎ 20861) on Zamzam St about 400m from the bus station has decent rooms for TSh 6500/7500, including breakfast and bathroom (although there is sometimes no running water).

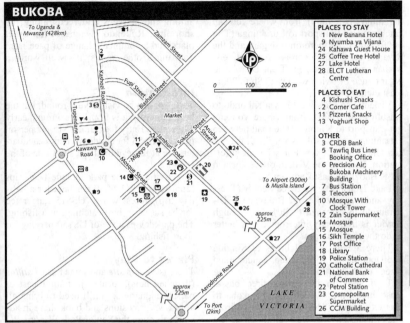

BUKOBA

To Uganda &
Mwanza (428km)

Zamzam Street

Fupi Street
Kashozi Road
Bushara Street

Market

Tupendane St.

Kawawa
Road

Mosque Street

Jamhuri Road

Sokoine Street

Arusha Street

Mgeyo St.

To Airport (300m)
& Musila Island

approx
225m

approx
225m

Aerodrome Road

To Port
(2km)

LAKE
VICTORIA

0   100   200 m

PLACES TO STAY
1 New Banana Hotel
9 Nyumba ya Vijana
24 Kahawa Guest House
25 Coffee Tree Hotel
27 Lake Hotel
28 ELCT Lutheran
   Centre

PLACES TO EAT
4 Kishushi Snacks
2 Corner Cafe
11 Pizzeria Snacks
13 Yoghurt Shop

OTHER
3 CRDB Bank
5 Tawfiq Bus Lines
   Booking Office
6 Precision Air;
   Bukoba Machinery
   Building
7 Bus Station
8 Telecom
10 Mosque With
   Clock Tower
12 Zain Supermarket
14 Mosque
15 Mosque
16 Sikh Temple
17 Post Office
18 Library
19 Police Station
20 Catholic Cathedral
21 National Bank
   of Commerce
22 Petrol Station
23 Cosmopolitan
   Supermarket
26 CCM Building

TANZANIA

The faded *Coffee Tree Hotel* (☎ 20412) on the main road leading to the lake has rooms for TSh 3600/4200 (TSh 7200 for a double with bathroom), including continental breakfast.

Lake Hotel (☎ 20237) at the edge of town overlooking the lake is the closest that Bukoba has to a luxury option. Somewhat dilapidated but comfortable rooms with bathroom are TSh 6500/8500 (TSh 4500 for a double with shared facilities), including continental breakfast. Camping is permitted for TSh 2500 per person, including shower facilities. Ask staff to show you the room where Katharine Hepburn and Humphrey Bogart stayed while filming *The African Queen*.

Places to Eat

Corner Cafe not far from the bus station is good for inexpensive local dishes and snacks.

Other places to try for inexpensive food include *Kishushi Snacks* on Tupendane St, and *Pizzeria Snacks* near the market.

New Banana Hotel has a decent *restaurant* serving reasonably priced local dishes.

For self-caterers, there are a few supermarkets with decent selections on Jamhuri Rd; the best two are *Zain Supermarket* and the *Cosmopolitan Supermarket* near the petrol station. Next door to Zain's is a small *shop* selling *mtindi* (a cultured milk product similar to yoghurt).

Getting There & Away

Air Precision Air flies daily between Mwanza and Bukoba (US$65). Their office (☎ 20545) is in the Bukoba Machinery building on Kawawa Rd. Flights from Bukoba to Dar es Salaam cost US$270 for nonresidents, via Mwanza and/or Arusha.

Bus Roads from Bukoba are in poor condition and most buses are in rough shape. Allow plenty of time for journeys. See the Tanzania Getting There & Away section for details of buses to/from Uganda.

Buses go several times weekly to Biharamulo (TSh 4000), from where you can catch onward transport to Lusahunga (TSh 1000), and from there on to Ngara and the Rwanda and Burundi borders. Alternatively, Vislam runs a direct bus from Bukoba to Ngara once or twice weekly (TSh 6000, at least eight hours).

Vislam also goes weekly via Kibondo to Kasulu (TSh 7500), from where you can get transport to Kigoma. The road between Lusahunga and Kasulu is very bad; the trip can take several days. For schedule information, check at the Vislam office, located off Kashozi Rd past Zamzam St.

Lake Transport goes twice weekly (Tuesday and Saturday) from Bukoba via Biharamulo to Mwanza (TSh 8000), though service is frequently interrupted; it's better to do the trip in stages.

There are occasional buses to Singida and Dodoma via Biharamulo, Kahama and Nzega (TSh 20,000).

Tawfiq/Takrim also runs a direct bus at least three times weekly from Bukoba to Dar es Salaam (TSh 34,000) via Nairobi and Arusha. The Tawfiq booking office is a block away from the bus station. It's best to book a day in advance.

Boat See the Mwanza Getting There & Away section for details of ferry service connecting Bukoba with Mwanza and Port Bell (Kampala).

RUBONDO ISLAND NATIONAL PARK

Rubondo Island National Park, in the southwestern corner of the lake, encompasses Rubondo Island as well as several smaller islands nearby. The park's main attraction is its rich and diverse birdlife. Close to 400 species have been identified including fish eagle, heron, stork, ibises and cormorant. In addition to the birds, there are many different types of butterflies, as well as populations of chimpanzee, hippo, crocodile, giraffe and even elephant (the latter were introduced several decades ago).

The island is also one of the few places in East Africa where you can observe the si-tatunga, an antelope that likes to hide among the marshes and reeds along the shoreline. Rubondo is a beautiful, quiet place and a complete change of pace from Tanzania's other parks; it's well worth a visit.

Information

The park can be visited year-round, but the best time to visit is from June through early November. Entry fees are US$15 per person per day (US$5 for children). Park headquarters are at Kageye on the eastern side of the island.

Activities in the park include boat trips (approximately US$50 per boat for a half-day trip), forest walks (US$15 ranger fee for half a day), birdwatching, and fishing. The park levies a fee of US$50 per day for sport fishing.

Places to Stay

There is a *camp site* and some basic *bandas* (thatched huts), located just south-east of park headquarters; you'll need to bring all your own provisions and book these in advance through the Senior Park Warden, PO Box 111, Geita. Alternatively, you can make arrangements through a Mwanza travel agency. Camping fees are US$20 (US$5 for children); accommodation in bandas is also about US$20.

The best option is the small and relaxing *Rubondo Island Camp*, overlooking the lake on the eastern side of the island. Comfortable, luxury tented accommodation costs US$160 per person sharing, including full board. Prices are reduced during the low season, and there are also significant discounts available for children. Book through Flycatcher Safaris Ltd (☎ 057-6963, fax 8261, email flycat@yako.habari.co.tz or flycat@swissonline.ch), 172 Serengeti Rd (PO Box 591), Arusha.

Getting There & Away

Air Charter flights from Mwanza can be arranged for around US$100 per person one way for a group of four people (US$360 for an entire five seater plane, US$250 for a three seater plane).

Assuming a minimum of four passengers, there are regular flights run by Northern Air, which operate twice weekly during the high season between Rubondo and Mwanza (US$100), Serengeti (Seronera or Kirawira) (US$175) and Arusha (US$280). For charter flight bookings, contact Flycatcher Safaris Ltd (see Places to Stay earlier). Alternatively, inquire with RenAir (office at the airport) or with travel agencies in Mwanza to see whether there is a charter flight with extra seats that you can join.

Boat For details of ferry connections between Mwanza and Rubondo, see the Mwanza Getting There & Away section earlier in this chapter.

Fishing boats generally don't enter into Rubondo. If you want to try arranging for a local boat to bring you over, it's a good idea to radio park headquarters in advance to inform them you'll be arriving this way.

The boat options will likely be more expensive than flying (US$150 to US$250 one way for the boat transfer depending on the pick-up point), and for both, you'll need to arrange the boat in advance. Fourways Travel Service in Mwanza and Flycatcher Safaris Ltd can assist with this and all other arrangements for a visit to Rubondo.

MUSOMA
☎ 068
Musoma is a quiet, pleasant town on the eastern shore of Lake Victoria and capital of the surrounding Mara region. About 45km south of Musoma is Butiama, the home town of Julius Nyerere.

Places to Stay & Eat
For budget travellers *Stigma Hotel* in the centre near the market has rooms for about TSh 5000.

Hotel Orange Tree near the lake on Kawawa St off Iringa St has decent rooms from about TSh 8000.

Though a bit faded, the *Peninsula Hotel* is Musoma's luxury lodging, with rooms for approximately TSh 25,000. It's about 2km from the centre on the Makoko road.

All of these places have *restaurants*.

Getting There & Away
Buses run throughout the day between Musoma and Mwanza (TSh 2500, six hours). The first bus departs in each direction at 7 am, the last at 3 pm. There are also frequent minibuses to the border (TSh 1000), where you can change to Kenyan transport to Kisii and Kisumu. The road from Musoma to the border and into Kenya is good tarmac.

There are no ferry connections from Musoma; to get to Mwanza, your only option is via road.

SHINYANGA
Shinyanga is south of the lake region in a gold mining area. There are several mediocre guesthouses in town. About 45km north-east of Shinyanga near Mwadui is the Williamson diamond mine, one of the world's largest, although production at the mine has been erratic over the past decade and its resources are believed to be almost depleted.

For transport details to/from Shinyanga, see the Mwanza Getting There & Away section earlier.

Western Tanzania

While remote from Dar es Salaam and lacking any sort of developed transport infrastructure, western Tanzania has numerous sites of interest for travellers. The seldom visited but beautiful Katavi and Mahale Mountains national parks are here, as is Jane Goodall's world-renowned chimpanzee research station at Gombe Stream National Park.

Tiny Ujiji, an important dhow-building centre, was the terminus of one of East Africa's most important caravan routes linking Lake Tanganyika with Bagamoyo and the sea. Lake Tanganyika itself – the world's longest and second deepest freshwater lake – is a useful transport route for those heading to or from northern Zambia.

KIGOMA
☎ 0695

Kigoma is a regional capital and the most important Tanzanian port on Lake Tanganyika. For much of its history it remained overshadowed by Ujiji to the south. It was only with the completion of the Central Line railway terminus in the early 20th century that the town gained regional significance. With the recent upheavals in nearby Congo (Zaïre), Rwanda and Burundi, the area around Kigoma has also become a major refugee centre (see the boxed text 'Refugees').

While there's little of interest in Kigoma itself, it's a pleasant place and a good base for visits to Gombe Stream and Mahale Mountains national parks and other locations along the lake.

Information

There are no foreign exchange bureaus in Kigoma. The NBC bank near the bus stand accepts travellers cheques.

Sunset Tours at Aqua Lodge (☎ 2586, fax 3707) PO Box 34, Kigoma, offers boat rental and can arrange visits to Gombe Stream and Mahale Mountains national parks.

Highlights

- Observing the chimpanzees at close range at Gombe Stream National Park
- Spending some time in the laid-back village of Ujiji
- Relaxing on the tranquil shores of Lake Tanganyika
- Visiting the remote and rugged Mahale Mountains National Park, or beautiful Katavi National Park

If you're in an emergency, the best hospital is the mission-run Kigoma Baptist Hospital (☎ 2241) near the airport.

Things to See & Do

About 4km south of town in Katonga is a **chimpanzee centre** for orphaned chimps, run by the Jane Goodall Institute. There are usually several in residence, many of whom have been recaptured from illegal traffickers. To get to the centre, take a minibus from the roundabout near the Tanzania Revenue Authority to Katonga (about a 30-minute ride) and then ask locals to show you the way. If you are driving, Katonga is to the right at the fork after the Kigoma Hilltop Hotel.

Also near Katonga is the small **Jacobsen's Beach** (TSh 2000 per day). Ask the bus driver to drop you at the turn-off for the beach, from where it's about a 15-minute walk; you'll need to ask locals for directions.

Places to Stay

The cheapest place is the *Community Centre* near the post office. Run by the Kigoma diocese, it has grubby singles/doubles and grubbier shared baths for TSh 1500/2000.

Kigoma Hotel on the main street, and *Lake View Hotel* diagonally opposite, are even worse, and also noisy. Both have rooms for about TSh 2200/2400.

About 2km from the centre, up the hill in the Mwanga section of town, are numerous

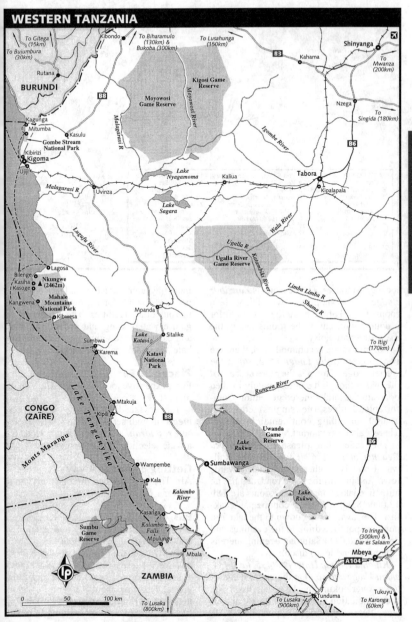

WESTERN TANZANIA

To Gitega (15km)
To Bujumbura (30km)

BURUNDI

Rutana

Kibondo

To Biharamulo (130km) & Bukoba (300km)

To Lusahunga (150km)

B3

Kahama

Shinyanga

To Mwanza (200km)

Kagunga
Mitumba
Kasulu
Gombe Stream National Park
Kibirizi
Kigoma
Ujiji

B8

Moyowosi Game Reserve

Kigosi Game Reserve

Malagarasi R

Moyowosi River

Nzega

To Singida (180km)

Malagarasi R

Uvinza

Lake Nyagamoma

Kaliua

Igombe River

Tabora

B6

Kipalapala

Lugufu River

Lake Sagara

Lagosa
Bilenge
Kasiha
Nkungwe (2462m)
Kasoge
Mahale Mountains National Park
Kangwena
Kibwesa

Ugalla R

Ugalla River Game Reserve

Wala River

Katumbiki River

Limba Limba R

Shama R

Mpanda

Lake Katavi
Sitalike

To Itigi (170km)

Sumbwa
Karema

Katavi National Park

Lake Tanganyika

CONGO (ZAÏRE)

Monts Marungu

Mtakuja
Kipili

B8

Rungwa River

Uwanda Game Reserve

Lake Rukwa

B6

Wampembe
Kala

Sumbawanga

Lake Rukwa

Kalambo River

Kasanga
Kalambo Falls
Mpulungu

Sumbu Game Reserve

Mbala

To Iringa (300km) & Dar es Salaam

Mbeya

A104

ZAMBIA

0   50   100 km

To Lusaka (800km)

To Lusaka (900km)

Tunduma

Tukuyu

To Karonga (60km)

TANZANIA

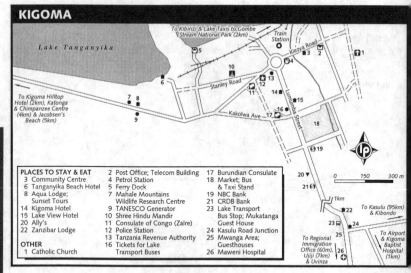

KIGOMA

PLACES TO STAY & EAT	2	Post Office; Telecom Building	17	Burundian Consulate
3	Community Centre	4	Petrol Station	18	Market; Bus
6	Tanganyika Beach Hotel	5	Ferry Dock		& Taxi Stand
8	Aqua Lodge;	7	Mahale Mountains	19	NBC Bank
	Sunset Tours		Wildlife Research Centre	21	CRDB Bank
14	Kigoma Hotel	9	TANESCO Generator	23	Lake Transport
15	Lake View Hotel	10	Shree Hindu Mandir		Bus Stop; Mukatanga
20	Ally's	11	Consulate of Congo (Zaïre)		Guest House
22	Zanzibar Lodge	12	Police Station	24	Kasulu Road Junction
		13	Tanzania Revenue Authority	25	Mwanga Area;
OTHER		16	Tickets for Lake		Guesthouses
1	Catholic Church		Transport Buses	26	Maweni Hospital

local guesthouses. The best one is *Zanzibar Lodge* on the main road, with fairly clean rooms from TSh 3000/4000 (TSh 5000 for a double with bath); the rooms facing the main street are noisy.

For mid-range accommodation, there are two choices. *Aqua Lodge (☎ 2586)* at the western edge of town is the more upscale of the two, although it's unfortunately located opposite the loud Tanesco generator. Comfortable doubles (no singles) cost TSh 18,000, including continental breakfast. There's also a restaurant.

The faded but pleasant *Tanganyika Beach Hotel (☎ 2694)* formerly the Railway Hotel is another 300m back towards town, and just off the same road, and has an attractive lakeshore setting. Rooms are TSh 12,000/18,000, including continental breakfast. The lawn sloping down to the lake is a popular spot for a drink in the evenings and on weekends. On Saturday evening there is a popular (and loud) disco.

Kigoma Hilltop Hotel (☎ 4435, fax 4434, email kht@raha.com) at the western end of town, overlooking the lake, has luxurious accommodation in cottages with TV and all amenities from US$51/72 plus 20% VAT,

including continental breakfast. There's a pool (TSh 2000 for nonresidents) and numerous other facilities. The hotel can organise water-skiing and parasailing trips, and excursions to Gombe Stream and Mahale Mountains national parks.

Places to Eat

For inexpensive local food, try *Ally's* on the main street.

Tanganyika Beach Hotel has decent *meals*, though service is slow. The expensive *restaurant* at Kigoma Hilltop Hotel has a wide selection of western dishes.

Getting There & Away

Air There is no commercial service to Kigoma.

Bus All roads in and out of Kigoma are very rough. Buses go daily to Kasulu (TSh 1500) and Kibondo (TSh 3000).

To Mwanza, the Saratoga line has a direct bus every Tuesday from Ujiji (TSh 12,000, at least 36 hours) via Kahama and Shinyanga, departing about 5.30 am. For bookings contact Khalfan Sood (☎ 3450) in Ujiji (it's the only two storey building in town).

To catch the bus in Kigoma, stand at the Kasulu road junction off the main road, although it's best to go to Ujiji (see Around Kigoma later) as the bus is often full by the time it reaches Kigoma.

Lake Transport has a weekly bus to Mwanza (via Biharamulo) on Friday (TSh 12,000), departing about 5 am from Mukatanga Guest House in the Mwanga section of Kigoma not far from Zanzibar Lodge, or from the Kasulu road junction. Book tickets at the Lake Transport 'office' opposite the market.

For Bukoba, you'll need to change buses at Lusahunga, or else travel to Kasulu and wait for the weekly Vislam bus. Allow several days for the trip, although it's sometimes faster.

Train The train departs Kigoma Sunday, Tuesday, Thursday and Friday at about 5 pm for Tabora (TSh 12,600/8900/5700, 1st/2nd/3rd class, 12 hours) and Dar es Salaam (TSh 45,200/33,100/12,500, 36 to 40 hours). To go north to Mwanza you'll need to change trains in Tabora. To go south to Mpanda you'll need to change trains in Kaliua. Book 1st and 2nd class tickets at least several days in advance.

Lake Ferries The MV *Liemba* departs Kigoma for Mpulungu in Zambia at 4 pm on Wednesday, servicing a number of ports on the Tanzanian lake shore along the way. An immigration officer is stationed at the Kigoma port for all arrivals and departures to/from Zambia. See Zambia in the Tanzania Getting There & Away chapter for further details.

A weekly ferry service was just resuming between Kigoma and Bujumbura (Burundi) as this chapter was being researched. The scheduled departure time from Kigoma is 6 pm on Sunday. See the Burundi Getting There & Away chapter for further details.

Lake Taxis Lake taxis are small, wooden boats, usually overcrowded with people and produce, that connect villages along the lake shore. They're very inexpensive but offer no creature comforts and usually no

Refugees

Under Julius Nyerere, Tanzania distinguished itself in Africa and in the world for its willingness to take in large numbers of refugees. During the 1970s and 1980s, thousands of people from Mozambique, South Africa, Rwanda, Burundi and Congo (Zaïre) found safe haven within the country's borders. In keeping with his *ujamaa* philosophy (see Socialist Tanzania under History in the Facts about Tanzania chapter), Nyerere also went to extraordinary lengths to provide these refugees with a dignified existence, in many cases offering land, housing and even citizenship. In 1983 he was honoured with the UNHCR's Nansen medal for these outstanding contributions.

During the 1990s, massive influxes of Rwandans fleeing the 1994 genocide in their country caused the security and environmental situations along Tanzania's western border to deteriorate. This, combined with changing political and economic trends (notably Tanzania's move to multiparty politics), led to a shift in the country's asylum policy. In 1995 Tanzania closed its border with Burundi (it's now open again) and announced that while it would continue to honour its humanitarian obligations it would not tolerate insecurity along its borders, nor the extensive environmental damage resulting from large refugee influxes. Despite this shift, Tanzania continues to host about 300,000 Burundian refugees, about 20,000 Congolese (Zaïrean) refugees, and an estimated 20,000 Rwandans (although the Rwandan refugee camps have been closed) – the largest concentration of refugees for any East African country. Most are in the Kigoma region, with a significant number also near Ngara in the Kagera region.

shade either. Lake taxis can be used to get to/from Gombe Stream National Park (see the Gombe Stream National Park section later for more details) and also Kagunga on the border with Burundi. The taxis don't stop at Kigoma itself but at Kibirizi village, just a few kilometres north of Kigoma along the train tracks.

AROUND KIGOMA
Ujiji

Ujiji, one of Africa's oldest market villages, was the main settlement in the region until the building of the Central Line railway terminus at Kigoma. It's also where the famous words, 'Dr Livingstone, I presume', were spoken by the explorer and journalist Henry Morton Stanley in 1871. The site where Stanley's encounter with Livingstone allegedly occurred (see the boxed text 'David Livingstone' in the North-Eastern Tanzania chapter) is set in a walled compound near an attractive garden. There's the inevitable plaque, as well as two mango trees said to have been grafted from the original tree growing there when the two men met. There is also a bleak museum housing a few pictures by local artists of Livingstone's time here. Entry is free but a small donation is welcome (especially if you have listened to the caretaker's historical presentation about Livingstone).

The site is signposted to the right of the main road (when coming from Kigoma), down the side street next to the Bin Tunia Restaurant – just ask for Livingstone and the bus driver will make sure you get off at the right place.

About 500m past the compound along the same street is Ujiji's small but picturesque beach and dhow port, with many local boat builders. Boat building is a thriving local industry, and fascinating to watch. The best day is Sunday when boats are brought ashore for repairs. No power tools are used – construction methods are the same as they were generations ago.

Places to Stay & Eat
Matunda Guest House on the main road has basic singles/doubles with mosquito net and common bath for TSh 700/1000.

For food, there are a few undistinguished local eateries along the main street.

Getting There & Away
Ujiji is about 8km south of Kigoma's centre. Local buses connect the two towns throughout the day costing TSh 200.

GOMBE STREAM NATIONAL PARK

With an area of only 52 sq km, Gombe Stream is Tanzania's smallest national park. It is also the site of the longest-running study of any wild animal population in the world and, for those interested in primates, a fascinating place.

The Gombe Stream area was gazetted as a game reserve in 1943. In 1960, the British researcher, Jane Goodall, arrived to begin a study of wild chimpanzees, and in 1968 Gombe was designated as a national park. Goodall's study is now in its fourth decade.

There are approximately 150 chimps in Gombe. They're well habituated, and you can sometimes get to within 5m of them. In addition to observing the chimps, visitors can swim in the lake or hike in Gombe's forest. Other animals you may see include colobus and vervet monkeys, bushbucks, baboons, bushpigs and a variety of birdlife.

Gombe Stream National Park is on the eastern shore of Lake Tanganyika, about 20km north of Kigoma.

Information
Entry fees are US$100 per person per day (US$20 for children aged five to 16). Guides cost US$20 per group. The park can be visited year-round.

The booklet *Gombe Stream National Park* put out by Tanapa is useful for background information. It's available in bookshops in Arusha and Dar es Salaam or from Tanapa headquarters in Arusha for about TSh 3000.

Places to Stay
The main place to stay is the *hostel* near park headquarters; the cost is US$10 per person per night. You can also *camp* on the beach for US$20. For either option you'll need to be self-sufficient, and bring all your own provisions from Kigoma. Bookings for the hostel should be made through Sunset Tours in Kigoma or through the senior park warden (PO Box 185, Kigoma).

Getting There & Away
The only way to reach Gombe is by boat. From Kigoma, take a minibus to Kibirizi, a

few kilometres north of Kigoma (TSh 200), or alternatively walk along the train tracks past the BP petrol station. From Kibirizi, motorised lake taxis go to Gombe daily except Sunday (TSh 1000, about three hours). You can also go to/from Gombe from Kagunga on the border with Burundi. When leaving Gombe, park staff can help you wave down a boat. Alternatively, you can arrange with a local fisher to charter out a whole boat for yourself, although this will be expensive.

Boats can also be chartered through Sunset Tours or the Kigoma Hilltop Hotel. Sunset Tours charges US$165 return per boat with a maximum of 15 passengers, plus a waiting fee of US$83 if you stay in Gombe overnight. Kigoma Hilltop Hotel charges US$300 per boat (10 passengers maximum) for a one night/two day visit to the park.

MAHALE MOUNTAINS NATIONAL PARK

Mahale is one of Tanzania's most remote parks and one of its most attractive. It's right on Lake Tanganyika, with the misty and rugged Mahale mountain range running down its centre. Like Gombe Stream to the north, Mahale is primarily a chimpanzee sanctuary, with a population of approximately 700 chimpanzees inside its boundaries. There are also a variety of other animals, including elephants, giraffes, zebras, buffalos and even some lions.

Information

Entry fees are US$50 per person (US$20 for children aged five to 16). Guide fees are US$20 per group (maximum six). Sunset Tours in Kigoma can assist with a radio call to park headquarters to let them know you will be arriving.

There are no roads in Mahale. The main way of exploring the park is by foot; boat trips along the lakeshore can also be arranged at the park headquarters. In Kigoma, you can obtain further information about the park through the Mahale Mountains Wildlife Research Centre (☎ 2072), PO Box 1053, Kigoma, which is in an unmarked white house next to Aqua Lodge.

The booklet *Gombe Stream National Park*, published by Tanapa, contains a small section on Mahale.

Places to Stay

There's a *camp site* near the park headquarters and a basic *resthouse* with cooking facilities in the park north of Kasiha. Camping costs US$20 per person per night and resthouse accommodation costs US$10 and should be booked through the senior park warden, PO Box 1374, Kigoma, or through Sunset Tours in Kigoma. For both you'll need to be self-sufficient and bring all your own provisions from Kigoma.

Alternatively, there is *Mahale Mountains Tented Camp* (☎ 0811-324341, 511443, email greystoke@luxurious.com) on Kangwena, to the south of the park headquarters. Information is also available through Greystoke Safaris in Kenya (☎ 02-502491, fax 502739, email bushhome@africaonline.co.ke) PO Box 56923, Nairobi. Comfortable accommodation costs US$295 per person, all inclusive. The camp is open between June and mid-October and from mid-December to mid-February.

Getting There & Away

Boat Mahale lies on Lake Tanganyika about 130km south of Kigoma. The MV *Liemba* stops at Lagosa (also called Mugambo), north of Mahale (TSh 7400/5400/2900 for 1st/2nd/3rd class, 10 to 12 hours from Kigoma). From Lagosa, you can hire a local boat to take you to park headquarters about two hours farther south, or arrange a pick-up in advance with park headquarters (US$50 per person, one way). Sometimes, you may be lucky enough to find park staff already at Lagosa who may be willing to give you a lift to the park in their boat for a reduced fee.

Alternatively, you can hire a boat through Sunset Tours in Kigoma (US$800 return, including two to three nights in the park).

Local boats also depart Ujiji twice a week (usually Tuesday and Friday) and sail down the coast towards Lagosa (TSh 3000, about 24 hours). Bring whatever food and water you may need.

TANZANIA

UVINZA

Salt production has long been the most important industry in Uvinza. To visit the Uvinza salt factory, you'll need to arrange a permit at the entry gate. For lodging, try *Sibuondo Guest House* in the centre of town, which has rooms for about TSh 3000.

Uvinza lies about two hours south-east of Kigoma along the Central Line railway. There's no regular public road transport between Uvinza and Kigoma. Trucks charge about TSh 2000 for a lift as far as Kasulu, from where there are daily minibuses to Kigoma (TSh 1500). Between Uvinza and Mpanda there are trucks a few times a week during the dry season (about TSh 4000, one to two days).

TABORA
☎ 062

Tabora was once one of the most significant trading centres along the old caravan route connecting Lake Tanganyika and Central Africa with Bagamoyo and the sea, and centre of the infamous slave trader Tippu Tib's empire. After the Central Line railway was constructed, it became the largest town in German East Africa.

Today, although Tabora gives the initial impression of being a bit of a dusty backwater, it still plays an important role as a transport junction as it's here that the Central Line branches for Mwanza and Kigoma. There are a few old houses in town dating back to Tippu Tib's era.

Things to See

About 6km out of town, via the Kipalapala road, is a tiny **museum** in a house where Livingstone lived. It contains some of the explorer's letters, a diary and other items. Entry is free, but a small donation is appreciated. Any bus heading that way can drop you off, or you can walk.

Places to Stay & Eat

Moravian Hostel has doubles with mosquito nets for TSh 2000. It's north-west of the centre, about 2.5km from the train station and past the market. There are no meals available.

Golden Eagle Hotel near the market, and *Hotel Wilca* off Boma Rd both have acceptable, reasonably priced rooms.

Top of the line is *Tabora Hotel* (☎ 4566) at the junction of Boma and Station Rds. Singles/doubles with bathroom and mosquito nets cost TSh 6000/9000. There's also a restaurant and satellite TV. If you're travelling via train from Mpanda, you'll arrive in Tabora at about 3 am. Many of the guesthouses and hotels will not admit you at that hour; one that will is Tabora Hotel.

The best place to eat is *Mayor's Restaurant & Ice Cream Parlour* just south of School St, which has good, inexpensive meals, fresh pineapple juice and ice cream.

Selfcaterers can try *Mr Sudra's store* off Lumumba St, close to the junction with Market St. Mr Sudra is a good source of information on Tabora and the surrounding area. *Cash & Carry Supermarket* on School St also has a decent selection.

Getting There & Away

Road Roads to and from Tabora are in poor condition. Most days 4WDs go north to Nzega from where you can get onward transport to Mwanza (see the Mwanza Getting There & Away section in the Lake Victoria chapter) or to Singida and on to Dodoma or Arusha. Allow several days for these journeys, and bring extra food, water and petrol if you are driving your own vehicle. To Kigoma, the only option is by train.

Train Tabora is the main Central Line junction for trains going north to Mwanza, west to Kigoma and south to Mpanda (via Kaliua).

Trains depart Tabora on Sunday, Tuesday, Wednesday and Friday at about 9.30 pm for Mwanza (TSh 11,700/7100/5300 for 1st/2nd/3rd class, 12 hours) and at about 8 pm on the same days for Kigoma (TSh 12,600/10,600/5700, 12 hours).

To Mpanda, departures are on Monday, Wednesday and Friday at about 9 pm (TSh 16,300/12,600/7500, 14 hours).

To Dar es Salaam, departures are on Sunday, Tuesday, Thursday and Friday at about 7.30 am (TSh 32,700/24,200/9200, 24 to 28 hours).

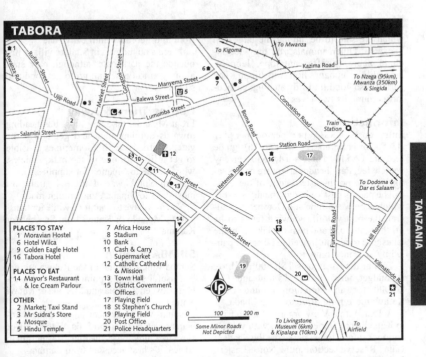

TABORA

To Mwanza
To Kigoma
Kazima Road
To Nzega (95km), Mwanza (350km) & Singida
Coronation Road
Mwanza Rd
Ruffia Street
Ujiji Road
Market Street
Gongoni Street
Manyema Street
Balewa Street
Lumumba Street
Salamini Street
Boma Road
Train Station
Station Road
To Dodoma & Dar es Salaam
Itetemia Road
Jamhuri Street
School Street
Fundikira Road
Hill Road
Killmatinde Rd

PLACES TO STAY	7 Africa House
1 Moravian Hostel	8 Stadium
6 Hotel Wilca	10 Bank
9 Golden Eagle Hotel	11 Cash & Carry
16 Tabora Hotel	Supermarket
	12 Catholic Cathedral
PLACES TO EAT	& Mission
14 Mayor's Restaurant	13 Town Hall
& Ice Cream Parlour	15 District Government
	Offices
OTHER	17 Playing Field
2 Market; Taxi Stand	18 St Stephen's Church
3 Mr Sudra's Store	19 Playing Field
4 Mosque	20 Post Office
5 Hindu Temple	21 Police Headquarters

0 100 200 m
Some Minor Roads Not Depicted
To Livingstone Museum (6km) & Kipalapa (10km)
To Airfield

TANZANIA

MPANDA

Mpanda is of interest mainly as a starting point for visits to Katavi National Park.

Most travellers stay at **Super City** in the centre of town; it's a bit of a brothel but tolerable. Doubles with mosquito net and bathroom cost TSh 4000. To get here from the train station, follow the tracks south to their end, then take the first left. There's also a newer *hotel* directly behind Super City, with clean en suite rooms for about TSh 6000.

Super City is the main place in town to eat; the food is OK but service is slow.

Getting There & Away

Bus Local buses to Katavi National Park and Sumbawanga (TSh 5000, 6½ hours) depart from in front of Super City. There's little traffic on the road towards Uvinza.

Train The train is the best option from Mpanda to Kigoma. Departures are Tuesday, Thursday and Saturday at 1 pm, arriv-

ing in Tabora about 3 am, where you'll need to disembark and wait for the connection to Kigoma. You can also wait for the connection at Kaliua. However, as there are few guesthouses and little to do here, most travellers continue on to Tabora. Fares from Mpanda to Dar es Salaam are TSh 43,300/31,800/12,000 for 1st/2nd/3rd class.

Boat The *MV Liemba* stops at Sumbwa or Karema, from where you can find transport to Mpanda and Katavi, though you may have to wait for a while. The road is in poor condition.

KATAVI NATIONAL PARK

Katavi, about 35km south-west of Mpanda, is one of Tanzania's most unspoiled and beautiful parks. You'll probably have the place to yourself, and are almost guaranteed to see animals, particularly around Lake Katavi in the northern section of the park and Lake Chada in the south-east.

Katavi is noted for its buffalo herds, which are said to be among the largest in Tanzania. Other animals you may see include zebra, giraffe, antelope, leopard, crocodile, elephant, lion and hippo. The park is also good for birdwatching, particularly around its two lakes.

Information

Entry costs US$15 per person per day (US$5 for children aged five to 16); guide fees are US$10. There's a US$30 per day vehicle fee. Park headquarters are near Sitalike, on the north-eastern edge of the park.

The park is best visited in the dry season, which is between June and October. In general, the best wildlife viewing tends to be off the main road and near the lakes. On the lakeshore road you'll need to be accompanied by an armed ranger.

Fuel at the park costs TSh 500 per litre, so budget between TSh 15,000 and TSh 20,000 for an excursion around Lake Katavi; more for a drive to Lake Chada.

A Tent With a View organises good trips to Katavi from Dar es Salaam, with vehicle and foot safaris in the park (see the Saadani Game Reserve section in the North-Eastern Tanzania chapter).

Places to Stay

Katavi's *Chief Nsalambo Camp Site* is in good condition. For those without a tent, there's also a well-situated *resthouse*. Camping costs US$20 per person per night (US$5 for children); for bookings at the resthouse contact the senior park warden (PO Box 89, Mpanda). Bring all your own provisions, including food and water (or purifying tablets).

Otherwise there is *Katavi Tented Camp* (☎ 0811-324341, 511443, email greystoke@ luxurious.com) with comfortable, luxury tented accommodation. Further information on this place is available from Greystoke Safaris in Kenya (☎ 02-502491, fax 502739, email bushhome@africaonline.co.ke) PO Box 56923, Nairobi. The camp is closed between mid-October and mid-December, and from mid-February until early June.

There's no lodging in Sitalike village just outside the park gate, although park staff allow you to come and go to get food and supplies.

Getting There & Away

From Mpanda, take any local bus heading towards Sumbawanga and get out at the gate. Alternatively, it's sometimes possible to get a lift with one of the park vehicles, which come to Mpanda for supplies.

From Sumbawanga there is transport most days to Mpanda via a rough road.

You may have to wait for a while for transport to Mpanda or Katavi from Sumbwa or Karema.

SUMBAWANGA

Sumbawanga, capital of the Rukwa region, is a useful stopping point for those travelling between Zambia and Mpanda or Katavi National Park.

South-west of Sumbawanga, on the Zambian border, is **Kalambo Falls**. With a drop of close to 250m, this is the highest waterfall in Africa; it's best accessed from Zambia.

Upendo View Hotel on Kiwelu Rd, near the market, has doubles for about TSh 5000. You can also get meals here, at *Sim's Restaurant* opposite, or at *Gloria's* on Maendeleo St just off Kiwelu Rd.

There's at least one bus daily between Sumbawanga and Mpanda (TSh 5000, 6½ hours). Direct buses also go several times a week to Mbeya (TSh 8000, at least 10 hours and longer during the rainy season); otherwise you'll need to transfer at Tunduma.

A bus bound for Sumbawanga (TSh 4000) sometimes meets the *MV Liemba* at Kasanga on Lake Tanganyika, but the best option between the two towns is usually a truck. The trip can take as long as eight hours, especially during the rainy season.

For details on onward travel to/from Zambia or Malawi, see the Tanzania Getting There & Away chapter.

The Southern Highlands

The Southern Highlands (also known as the Southern Arc Mountains) stretch from Morogoro in the east to Lake Nyasa and the Zambian border in the west. It's one of Tanzania's most pleasant and scenic regions, offering beautiful hill panoramas, good hiking, and a generally temperate climate.

While many travellers pass through the Southern Highlands en route to or from Malawi or Zambia, few stop along the way although there is much of interest. Facilities in most places are more than adequate and main routes are in generally good condition. For those seeking opportunities to hike, bike or just relax, the area is ideal.

DODOMA
☎ 061

Dodoma lies on the northern edge of the highlands and in the geographic centre of Tanzania, at a height of about 1100m. Since 1973, the town has been the country's official capital and headquarters of the ruling Chama Cha Mapinduzi (CCM) party, though the economic and political centre remains in Dar es Salaam.

There is not much reason for travellers to come to Dodoma. However, if you find yourself in the region, the town's agreeable climate and relaxed, friendly atmosphere make it a pleasant place to spend a few days.

Information
Dodoma is the headquarters of Mission Aviation Fellowship (☎ 354036), at the airfield just north of the town centre. In the case of a serious medical emergency, it may be able to offer evacuation assistance.

Water supply can be a problem in Dodoma, particularly during the dry season and especially at some of the cheaper hotels.

Dangers & Annoyances
Exercise caution when using a camera in and around Dodoma. Many of the buildings are considered government buildings, and photography is prohibited in most areas.

Highlights

- Exploring the vast and beautiful Ruaha National Park, which hosts one of the largest elephant populations in Africa
- Hiking in Udzungwa Mountains National Park, one of Tanzania's most beautiful wilderness areas
- Hunting for bargains in the colourful, abundant markets of Iringa and Songea
- Walking in the hill country around Lake Nyasa

TANZANIA

Things to See & Do
Overlooking Dodoma from the north-east, **Lion Rock** offers good views and makes a pleasant hike. Don't take any valuables up with you and go in a group if possible, as muggings are not uncommon. It's about a 45 minute walk to the top. To get to Lion Rock, ask any bus driver heading out on the Arusha road to drop you nearby, or take a taxi. Don't leave your vehicle unattended at the base. Although it's also enticing, the hill to the south-west of town near the prison is off limits for hiking.

Near Dodoma Hotel is a small geological **museum**, although it's in very substandard condition these days.

Dodoma is the centre of Tanzania's tiny wine industry, and there are **vineyards** throughout the surrounding area. If you are interested in visiting a wine cellar, a good place to start is the Tanganyika Vineyards Company, just out of town to the south of the Dar es Salaam road.

The area around Kolo, 180km north of Dodoma and just north of Kondoa, is known for its centuries-old **rock paintings**, which according to some theories were made by the Sandawe people who are distantly related to South Africa's San (Bushmen). Some of the paintings are thought to date back more than 3000 years, while others are probably not more than a few hundred years old.

THE SOUTHERN HIGHLANDS

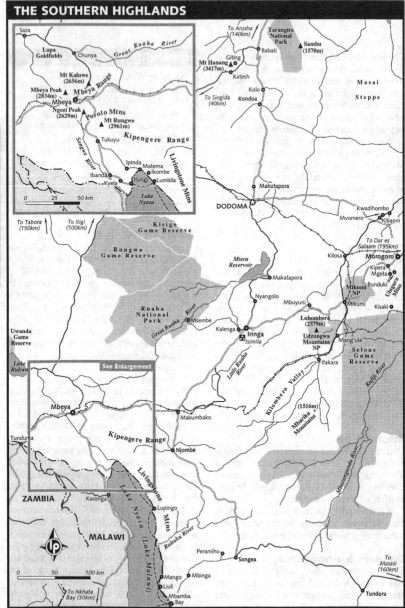

Places to Stay

For those on a tight budget, *Saxon Guest House* not far from the train station, has basic but acceptable singles/doubles for TSh 2000/2500.

In the centre of town in the grounds of the Anglican church is the *Christian Council of Tanzania (CCT) Compound* with basic rooms for TSh 5500/9000.

Dodoma Hotel (Railway Hotel) near the train station has faded rooms for TSh 12,000/18,000.

The best place to stay in Dodoma is the *Vocational Training Centre (☎ 324154)*.

Comfortable rooms are TSh 10,000/14,000 with fans, bathroom and breakfast. It's a couple of kilometres south-east of town, to the south of the Dar es Salaam road.

Nam Hotel in Area C is a step down, but has decent rooms for TSh 9000/12,000 (TSh 24,000 for a suite). To get here, take the second right after the airfield and follow the signs. It's a 30 minute walk from the centre.

Also in Area C is *Tiger Hotel & Restaurant* with acceptable rooms for TSh 6600/15,000 (though it sometimes operates as a bit of a brothel). Turn right immediately after the airfield, then left at the sign for the hotel.

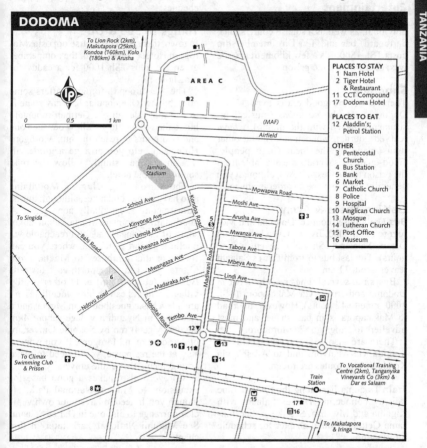

Places to Eat

All of the places listed under Places to Stay have *restaurants*. The best is the restaurant at the Vocational Training Centre, where good meals average TSh 4000; there's also a bar with TV. The restaurant at Nam Hotel is slightly cheaper, although not as good.

Allow plenty of time at Tiger Hotel & Restaurant, as meals sometimes take over an hour to arrive.

Aladdin's in the centre of town next to the petrol station on the main roundabout has soft ice cream. It's closed on Monday.

Entertainment

Climax Swimming Club has Dodoma's only pool, as well as a squash court, sauna, dartboard, bar and TV. Day membership costs TSh 1500. It's a few kilometres to the west of town past the prison.

Shopping

There are some good crafts available in Dodoma, notably *marimbas* (musical instruments played with the thumb), *vibuyu* (carved gourds), wooden stools, and other items made by the local Gogo people. Good-quality sisal crafts are available from the prison to the west of town, although you generally have to place an order in advance.

Getting There & Away

Bus Daily buses connect Dodoma and Morogoro (TSh 3000, five to seven hours) and Dar es Salaam (TSh 4500, seven to nine hours). The last bus to/from Dar es Salaam leaves about 11 am.

Buses run several times weekly between Dodoma and Iringa via Makatapora (TSh 4000, nine to 12 hours). However, the road to Makatapora is in bad shape, and most travellers to Iringa go via Morogoro.

There are also a few buses weekly to Singida via Manyoni and to Arusha via Kondoa. Both routes are rough.

Train Dodoma lies along the Central Line railway connecting Dar es Salaam with Kigoma and Mwanza. See the earlier Tanzania Getting Around chapter for schedule information.

MOROGORO
☎ 056

Morogoro is an attractive town set at the foot of the Uluguru Mountains. It's one of Tanzania's most important agricultural areas, and if you venture into the hills you will see numerous farm plots with all sorts of fruit and vegetables, as well as coffee and other crops.

Information

There are no foreign exchange bureaus in Morogoro. Both the CRDB and the National Microfinance Bank change travellers cheques.

Things to See & Do

In town, there is a **golf course** opposite Morogoro Hotel (TSh 6000 for the nonmember green fee, plus TSh 1000 for a caddy for nine holes).

The area around Morogoro offers some good **hiking**. One popular half-day route is to Morningside, an old German mountain hut to the south of town; allow between one and two hours to reach the hut. Morogoro Hotel can help you arrange a guide, although you can simply follow the road south from the hotel.

The surrounding **Uluguru Mountains** also have some good hikes, although tourist infrastructure is essentially nonexistent. A good starting point is Mgeta, about 25km south of the Iringa road, and reachable via public transport to Kipera, where you can find sporadic minibuses to Mgeta. From Mgeta, you can hike north-east towards Bunduki (about 10km) or to other nearby villages. Guides can be hired locally. There are a few basic guesthouses in Mgeta, and a resthouse in Nyandira village (about 4km beyond Mgeta) run by Sokoine University of Agriculture in Morogoro. If you want to stay at the resthouse, you'll need to make arrangements first at the university.

Morogoro also makes a good base for excursions to Mikumi National Park, although you'll need to have your own vehicle or arrange to hire one in Dar es Salaam. See Mikumi National Park later in this chapter.

MOROGORO

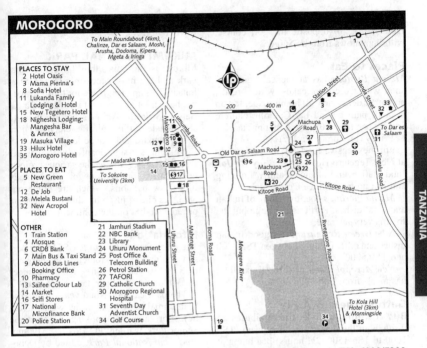

PLACES TO STAY
2 Hotel Oasis
3 Mama Pierina's
8 Sofia Hotel
11 Lukanda Family
   Lodging & Hotel
15 New Tegetero Hotel
18 Nighesha Lodging;
   Mangesha Bar
   & Annex
19 Masuka Village
33 Hilux Hotel
35 Morogoro Hotel

PLACES TO EAT
5 New Green
   Restaurant
12 De Job
28 Melela Bustani
32 New Acropol
   Hotel

OTHER
1 Train Station
4 Mosque
6 CRDB Bank
7 Main Bus & Taxi Stand
9 Abood Bus Lines
   Booking Office
10 Pharmacy
13 Saifee Colour Lab
14 Market
16 Seifi Stores
17 National
   Microfinance Bank
20 Police Station
21 Jamhuri Stadium
22 NBC Bank
23 Library
24 Uhuru Monument
25 Post Office &
   Telecom Building
26 Petrol Station
27 TAFORI
29 Catholic Church
30 Morogoro Regional
   Hospital
31 Seventh Day
   Adventist Church
34 Golf Course

TANZANIA

Places to Stay

A decent budget place is *Lukanda Family Lodging & Hotel* just around the corner from the Abood Bus Lines booking office. Doubles with shared bathroom will set you back TSh 2500. There are tiny singles with bathroom for TSh 3500 in a ground floor annexe.

Nighesha Lodging a couple of blocks south-west of the bus station is another place to try with basic singles for TSh 1500 and *Mangesha Bar & Annex* next door has small but clean doubles with mosquito nets and fan for TSh 3000 (TSh 3500 with bathroom), and a noisy bar.

New Tegetero Hotel on the main road just west of the bus stand is a step up. Noisy singles/doubles are TSh 4800/6000 (TSh 5400/6600 with bathroom), including continental breakfast.

Mama Pierina's (☎ 4640) off Machupa Rd has deteriorated but is still decent value for a mid-range place. Rooms with mosquito

nets, fan and bathroom are TSh 6000/7200, including breakfast.

Sofia Hotel (☎ 4847) on Mahenge St near the bus stand has rooms for TSh 6000/7000, including breakfast (TSh 9000/10,000 with bathroom).

Masuka Village (☎ 4774) is in a leafy area about 1km south of the main road. Its rooms are good value at TSh 7200 for a double with bathroom.

Kola Hill Hotel off the main road south of town has comfortable doubles costing about TSh 12,000 or about TSh 18,000 with air-con.

Two places frequented by business travellers are *Hotel Oasis (☎ 3535)* with comfortable rooms which cost TSh 25,000/30,000, including breakfast and *Hilux Hotel (☎ 3066)* with rooms from TSh 18,000 (TSh 22,000 in the new wing). The Oasis is next door to Mama Pierina's; the Hilux is on Old Dar es Salaam Rd, 300m past the Catholic church.

The most expensive option is **Morogoro Hotel** (☎ 3270) opposite the golf course, with bungalows from US$60/65.

Places to Eat

Melela Bustani has an upscale gourmet shop with ice cream, cakes, wine, breads, and other delicacies, all home-made. It's on a small path behind the Catholic church, and is open from 10 am to 5.30 pm Tuesday to Friday (to 1 pm Saturday).

For inexpensive food, try the **restaurant** at New Tegetero Hotel, or the tiny **De Job** food stall near Lukanda Family Lodging and just up from Saifee Colour Lab.

Mama Pierina's does a mixture of Italian and local dishes. Portions are large but the food is very average.

New Green Restaurant has good Indian dishes and other food for between TSh 2500 and TSh 5000.

New Acropol Hotel next to Hilux Hotel has meals from TSh 5000 or more.

Getting There & Away

Bus & Minibus Buses and minibuses go throughout the day to Dar es Salaam (TSh 1000 to TSh 1500, 3½ hours) beginning at 5.45 am. Try the Saddiq or Islam lines; Abood buses are the most frequent but have a reputation for unsafe driving.

There's at least one bus daily to Moshi and Arusha via Chalinze (TSh 4000, eight hours to Moshi, nine to 10 hours to Arusha), usually departing about 8 am.

To Dodoma, there are daily minibuses (TSh 3000, six to seven hours), and a large bus (Mbaraka line) every other day; departures are at 7 am. Otherwise, you can go to the main roundabout (known locally as the 'Msamvu keep-left'), about 5km from the centre and try to catch one of the Dar es Salaam to Dodoma buses there, though they are often full so you will probably have to stand. The buses stop about 200m down from the roundabout on the Dodoma road, usually arriving from Dar es Salaam between 8.30 and 9.30 am daily.

Train Morogoro lies on the Central Line connecting Dar es Salaam with Mwanza and Kigoma. To Dar es Salaam, it's faster to travel by bus.

MIKUMI NATIONAL PARK

Mikumi is Tanzania's third largest national park and the most accessible from Dar es Salaam. It's an ideal place for those who do not have a lot of time, but want to see a variety of wildlife. Animals you're likely to see include buffalo, giraffe, elephant, lion, zebra, leopard and crocodile.

Mikumi is a significant educational and research centre. Among the various projects being carried out is an ongoing field study of yellow baboons, which are numerous here. It's one of just a handful of long-term primate studies on the continent.

Information

The entry fee to Mikumi is US$15 per person per day (US$5 for children between five and 16 years old, free for those under five), plus a US$30 per day vehicle fee.

The park can be visited year-round. The best animal viewing is in the western section. For camp site bookings, contact the Senior Park Warden, PO Box 62, Mikumi.

Mikumi National Park, edited by Deborah Snellson and published by Tanzania National Parks Authority (TANAPA), is a dated but worthwhile booklet for those interested in detailed information on the park. It's available at bookshops in Dar es Salaam and Arusha for about TSh 3000.

Places to Stay

Inside the park are several **camp sites**; you'll need to bring a tent and all provisions. Camping costs US$20 per person per night (US$5 for children).

Mikumi Wildlife Camp has comfortable cottage-style accommodation for US$100 per person sharing, including full board. There is also dorm accommodation for US$50/37/30/25 per person in groups of two/three/four/five people, not including meals. Book with Oyster Bay Hotel (☎ 051-668062, fax 668631, email oysterbay-hotel@twiga.com, PO Box 2261, Dar es Salaam). Accommodation can be paid for in advance with credit card at Oyster Bay

Hotel; but credit cards are not accepted at the camp itself. The camp is just west of the main road, near the park entrance.

Mikumi Wildlife Lodge has rooms from about US$45, but is more run-down. Book through the park headquarters (see Information earlier) or any Dar es Salaam travel agent. The lodge is in the southern half of the park, about 3km east of the main road.

Vuma Hill Tented Camp (☎ 0811-338892, PO Box 40559, Dar es Salaam) in the southern half of the park has tented accommodation from US$125 per person, including half board.

In Mikumi town *Genesis Motel* about 1.5km from the main junction on the Dar es Salaam road has simple but inexpensive rooms. There are also decent rooms available for about TSh 6000 at the *guesthouse* behind Mikumi hospital.

Baobab Valley Campground (☎ 0812-785296, email snail79@hotmail.com) about 55km west of Mikumi and 20km east of Mbuyuni is a pleasant riverside place offering both catered and self-catered camping. There are self-contained chalets for those without tents. Overland groups are welcome. The camp site is signposted, and about 1km off the main road. To get there via public transport, take any local bus running between Iringa and Mikumi.

Getting There & Away

Although getting to the gate of Mikumi is easy via public transport (take any of the buses running along the Morogoro-Iringa road), there is no vehicle rental at the park. Efforts to hitch a ride are generally futile, so you'll need your own car. Allow about four hours driving time from Dar es Salaam.

Vehicle rental and tours of Mikumi are best arranged with a Dar es Salaam rental agency or tour operator. Coastal Travels has minivan service to Mikumi. A two-day safari costs TSh 200,000 for a group of up to seven, excluding accommodation, food and park fees.

UDZUNGWA MOUNTAINS NATIONAL PARK

Udzungwa Mountains National Park is a paradise for hikers and one of Tanzania's most beautiful wilderness areas. Its most striking feature, apart from its mountainous terrain, is its pristine and biologically diverse forest which hosts a variety of animal and plant species not found anywhere else in the world. Among its residents are six species of primates, including the rare Iringa red colobus and the Sange crested mangabey monkeys, as well as populations of elephant, buffalo, leopard and a rich variety of birdlife. The rare Udzungwa partridge is endemic to the area and has been sighted near the park's boundaries.

There are no roads in Udzungwa; instead, there are about four major and several lesser hiking paths winding through various sections of the park. Popular hikes include a short but steep half-day hike to the Sange Waterfalls, and a two-day climb to the top of Luhombero (2579m), Udzungwa's highest peak.

Information

Entry costs US$15 per person per day (US$5 for children aged between five and 16, and free for children under five).

The park is best visited between July and October. Hikes can be steep in parts and you must be accompanied by a guide (US$10). Both day and overnight hikes are possible; to visit the plateau where the best wildlife viewing is, you should allow two to three days.

The park headquarters is located in Mang'ula, 60km south of Mikumi town. For information, contact the Senior Park Warden (☎ Ifakara 24), Udzungwa Mountains National Park, PO Box 99, Mang'ula. Those with a research or scientific interest in Udzungwa can contact the Udzungwa Mountains National Park Monitoring Program (email bios@hotmail.com).

Places to Stay & Eat

There are three *camp sites* inside the park with fireplaces and a nearby stream. You'll need a tent and all your own supplies. It's US$20 per person per night for camping (US$5 for children).

Just outside the park in Mang'ula is *Twiga Guesthouse* (☎ Mang'ula 34 or 056-3357) with simple but decent singles/doubles with

TANZANIA

mosquito nets for TSh 2500/3500. It's about a five-minute walk from Twiga to the park headquarters.

Another five minutes walk down the road is *Udzungwa Mountain View Hotel*, with somewhat more luxurious rooms for TSh 9000 per person. You can also camp here for TSh 2000 per person.

Both hotels serve *simple meals*. Twiga Guesthouse also has a small shop stocking some basics, including mineral water. Basic supplies are available at Mwaya village, about 25 minutes on foot from the park headquarters. If you'll be staying for a while, it's not a bad idea to bring a supply of dried fruit and nuts with you as the diet available in Mang'ula is not particularly varied or vitamin-rich.

Getting There & Away

Bus In order to reach Udzungwa via public transport, you need to take any bus or minibus to Mikumi town, on the Morogoro to Iringa road. From the Mikumi junction, there are pick-ups and minibuses which run several times a day south to Mang'ula (TSh 700 to TSh 1000, three hours), on the Ifakara road.

Train For budget travellers, the easiest way to reach Udzungwa is via the TAZARA railway to Mang'ula, from where the park headquarters is about a 30-minute walk. Express trains don't stop in Mang'ula so you'll have to catch an ordinary train. The train from Dar es Salaam arrives in Mang'ula at about 8 pm.

IRINGA
☎ 064

Iringa is an attractive town set on a 1600m bluff overlooking the valley of the Little Ruaha River. It was initially built up by the Germans at the turn of the century as a bastion against the Hehe, the major tribal group in the surrounding area. Now Iringa is a district capital, and the centre of an important agricultural region. With its picturesque setting and pleasantly cool climate, it makes a good base for exploring the surrounding area.

Things to See & Do

Iringa has a well stocked market with all sorts of fruits and vegetables, as well as large, locally made **Iringa baskets**. Nearby, in front of the police station, is a **monument** to the Africans who fell during the Maji

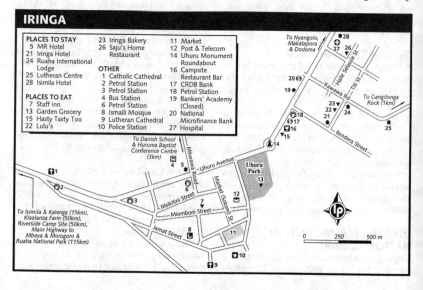

IRINGA

PLACES TO STAY	23 Iringa Bakery	11 Market
5 MR Hotel	26 Saju's Home	12 Post & Telecom
21 Iringa Hotel	Restaurant	14 Uhuru Monument
24 Ruaha International		Roundabout
Lodge	OTHER	16 Campsite
25 Lutheran Centre	1 Catholic Cathedral	Restaurant Bar
28 Isimila Hotel	2 Petrol Station	17 CRDB Bank
	3 Petrol Station	18 Petrol Station
PLACES TO EAT	4 Bus Station	19 Bankers' Academy
7 Staff Inn	6 Petrol Station	(Closed)
13 Garden Grocery	8 Ismaili Mosque	20 National
15 Hasty Tasty Too	9 Lutheran Cathedral	Microfinance Bank
22 Lulu's	10 Police Station	27 Hospital

To Nyangolo, Makatapora & Dodoma

To Gangilonga Rock (1km)

To Danish School & Huruma Baptist Conference Centre (3km)

To Isimila & Kalenga (15km), Kisolanza Farm (50km), Riverside Camp Site (50km), Main Highway to Mbeya & Morogoro & Ruaha National Park (115km)

Uhuru Park

Mwawa Road

Uhuru Avenue

Msikitini Street

Miomboni Street

Jamat Street

Market (Soroni) St

Bendera Street

Kawawa Rd

Haile Selassie St

Titi St

0   250   500 m

Maji rebellion between 1905 and 1907 (see the boxed text 'The Maji Maji Rebellion' later in this chapter).

The hills surrounding Iringa are ideal for **walking**. To the north-east of town is **Gangilonga Rock**, where Chief Mkwawa often used to meditate, and where he learned that the Germans were after him (see the boxed text 'Chief Mkwawa').

Places to Stay

Camping *Kisolanza Farm*, about 50km south-west of Iringa and about 1km off the main road to Mbeya, charges US$3 per person, including a hot shower.

Riverside Camp Site, about 50km north-east of Iringa and about 2km off the main road towards Morogoro, charges the same rates and also has hot showers. At both places, you'll need to bring your own food.

In Iringa, you can *camp* at the Huruma Baptist Conference Centre (see following).

Hotels & Guesthouses The *Lutheran Centre* (☎ 2286) at the end of Kawawa Rd has basic but clean singles/doubles at TSh 1700/2500 (TSh 3000 for a single with bathroom).

A small step up is *Ruaha International Lodge* (☎ 2746) on the corner of Kawawa Rd and Titi St with rooms for TSh 2500/4000 (TSh 3500/4500 with bathroom) and a disco on Friday and Saturday nights.

A good mid-range option is *Huruma Baptist Conference Centre* (☎ 2579) set in large grounds about 3km from the centre down Mkwawa Rd near the Danish school. It has comfortable, quiet rooms with bathroom for TSh 8500/12,000, including breakfast; other meals are available on request. Camping is TSh 4200 per person, including use of showers. Minibuses run down Mkwawa Rd every hour from the bus station.

Isimila Hotel at the northern end of town on the main road has comfortable rooms for TSh 6000/8000, including a continental breakfast.

Iringa Hotel (formerly the Railway Hotel) is situated one block north-east of the main road and a block south-east of Kawawa Rd has doubles (only) for TSh 10,000.

Chief Mkwawa

Mkwawa, chief of the Hehe and one of German colonialism's most vociferous resistors, is a legendary figure in Tanzanian history. Under his leadership during the second half of the 19th century, the Hehe became one of the most powerful tribes in central Tanzania. By the late 1880s they were threatening trade traffic along the caravan route from western Tanzania to Bagamoyo.

In 1891, after several attempts by Mkwawa to negotiate with the Germans were rejected, his men trounced the colonial troops in the infamous battle of Lugalo, just outside Iringa on the Mikumi road. The next year, Mkwawa's troops launched a damaging attack on a German fort at Kilosa, further to the east. The Germans placed a bounty on his head and initiated a counter attack in which Mkwawa's headquarters at Kalenga were taken. Mkwawa escaped, but later, in 1898, committed suicide rather than surrender to a contingent that had been sent after him. His head was cut off and the skull sent to Germany where it sat almost forgotten (though not by the Hehe) until it was returned to Kalenga in 1954.

In the centre of town on Mkwawa Rd next to the bus stand is the modern *MR Hotel* (☎ 2006, fax 2661) with good-value rooms with TV from TSh 15,000/18,000, and a restaurant.

Places to Eat

For inexpensive local food, try *Staff Inn* near the market, *Garden Grocery* in Uhuru Park or *Saju's Home Restaurant*, on Haile Selassie St at the northern end of town.

The popular *Hasty Tasty Too* on Uhuru Ave and open from 7.30 am to 8 pm daily has good breakfasts, yoghurt, shakes, and a variety of reasonably priced main dishes.

The Greek-owned *Lulu's* one block south-east of the main road near Kawawa Rd is a friendly place with a pleasant dining area and a varied menu selection. It's open from 8.30 am to 3 pm and 6.30 to 9 pm Monday to Saturday.

TANZANIA

Iringa Bakery next door to Lulu's has fresh rolls and bread.

Entertainment
Ruaha International Lodge (see Places to Stay earlier) has a popular *disco* on Friday and Saturday nights.

Campsite Restaurant near Hasty Tasty Too has a popular bar with dancing on weekends.

Getting There & Away
Precision Air runs flights three times weekly connecting Iringa with Dar es Salaam (US$105) and Mbeya (US$70), with connections to Arusha and Moshi. The airfield is about 12km north of town on the road to Dodoma.

Buses go every morning to Dar es Salaam (TSh 5000), Mbeya (TSh 4000) and Morogoro (TSh 3500). The best line is Scandinavian; book tickets a day in advance. The Morogoro to Mbeya highway bypasses Iringa town to the south-east. If you're having one of the Morogoro-Mbeya express buses drop you in Iringa, they'll let you off at the bus station on the highway; taxis from here to the main bus station in town charge about TSh 2000.

To Dodoma, there is a bus several times weekly via Nyangolo and Makatapora (TSh 4000, nine to 12 hours), though the road is rough and most travellers go via Morogoro.

AROUND IRINGA
Isimila Stone Age Site
About 15km outside Iringa off the Mbeya road is Isimila, where in the late 1950s archaeologists unearthed one of the most significant Stone Age finds ever identified. The tools found at the site are estimated at between 60,000 and 100,000 years old. Although the display itself is not particularly exciting, the area behind is attractive and many people come here on weekends for picnics. There's a TSh 500 entry fee.

Isimila is an easy ride on bicycle from Iringa. Otherwise, take a bus heading towards Tosamaganga (TSh 300) and ask to be dropped at the Isimila turn-off, from where it's about a 20-minute walk to the site. Taxis usually charge about TSh 5000 for the return trip.

Kalenga
About 15km from Iringa on the road heading to Ruaha National Park is the former Hehe capital of Kalenga. It was here that Chief Mkwawa had his administration until Kalenga fell to the Germans in the 1890s, and it was here that he committed suicide rather than succumb to the German forces. There is a small museum containing Mkwawa's skull and a few other relics from the era.

RUAHA NATIONAL PARK
Ruaha National Park is a vast wilderness area which hosts one of the largest elephant populations in Africa. In addition to the elephants, which are estimated to number at least 12,000, the park has large herds of buffalo, as well as Grant's gazelle, wild dog, ostrich, cheetah, and more than 450 bird species. It's also the only East African park where you can see greater and lesser kudu, as well as sable and roan antelopes. The Great Ruaha River flows through the eastern side of the park and is home to hippo, crocodile and many water birds.

With an area of almost 13,000 sq km, Ruaha National Park is Tanzania's second largest, and is part of an extended ecosystem that also encompasses the adjoining Rungwa and Kisigo game reserves. Large areas of Ruaha are unexplored, and one of the park's main attractions is its remoteness and isolation.

Due to Ruaha's vastness and character, you should set aside as much time as you can to visit; it's not a place to be discovered on a quick trip.

Information
Park fees cost US$15 (US$5 for children between five and 16 years old, free for those under five), plus a US$30 per day vehicle fee. The park headquarters is at Msembe; contact the Senior Park Warden, Ruaha National Park, PO Box 369, Iringa.

The park can be visited year-round, although during the rainy season from March to May, access to many areas becomes more

Endangered Elephants

In the mid-1980s, the situation for Ruaha National Park's elephants – as well as for those in many other parks in East Africa – looked bleak. Numbers were plummeting due to poaching, and no relief was in sight. Now the picture is much brighter. Since 1986, Ruaha's once dwindling population has more than doubled in number. An additional sign that the population is in recovery is the fact that about 25% of the park's estimated 12,000 elephants are two-years-old or less. Similar gains have been registered in other protected areas in Tanzania. Much of this progress has been attributed to the effects of a worldwide ban on ivory implemented in 1990 by the Convention on International Trade in Endangered Species (CITIES) following a vigorous campaign by conservation groups. An additional factor in Ruaha and elsewhere in Tanzania was Operation Uhai, an anti-poaching initiative of the Tanzanian government in collaboration with the military.

Maintaining these gains, however, will be difficult. In 1997 a decision was made to downgrade the CITIES ban for several African countries, permitting limited trade in ivory. Although Tanzania is not among these countries, many worry that the downgrade will simply set off poaching again throughout the continent; some claim detrimental effects are already noticeable.

Another problem is lack of resources. In large parks like Ruaha or Selous Game Reserve in the southeast, vast areas are often inaccessible to rangers, particularly during the rainy season, and poaching is difficult to control no matter how much money is available. Inadequate staff and facilities make things even more difficult. While hunting groups can be an important aid to anti-poaching efforts by monitoring the animals within their concessions, they generally only operate six months of the year. During the rainy season when they are not around, the way is open for poachers.

Entrenched interests complicate the picture. Between the elephants on Ruaha's plains and illegal ivory markets in Asia and elsewhere stand a variety of players including the poachers (often local villagers struggling to earn some money), ivory dealers, embassies, and government officials at the highest levels. The potential gains for all involved lead to ruthlessness, which complicates anti-poaching efforts even more: 1kg of ivory is worth about US$300 wholesale and rhino horn is valued at US$2000 per kilogram (or up to US$30,000 for a single horn).

Some argue that one way of promoting elephant conservation in the face of such constraints would be to loosen restrictions on the ivory trade even further. They contend that if trade is legalised but controlled, monies raised from ivory sales could be used to support conservation efforts benefiting both animals and local communities. The traded ivory itself would be gathered from culled elephants or from commercial hunting operations. Others counter such proposals by asserting that controls could never be made tight enough to prevent an increase in poaching.

difficult. Viewing wildlife is best during the dry season from June to October. The main activities are wildlife drives and short walks.

Places to Stay

There is a *camp site* near the park headquarters with *bandas* (thatched huts with wooden or earthen walls) or you can pitch your own tent. Camping costs US$20 per person per night (US$5 for children). You'll need to bring all your own food, and either have your own vehicle or arrange in advance for rental at the park headquarters.

Ruaha River Lodge about 15km inside the park gate has an attractive setting overlooking the river and accommodation is in comfortable stone bandas. The all-inclusive rate including two wildlife drives per day and airport transfers is US$200 per person (US$40 single supplement). The basic non-fly-in rate is US$100 per person, including full board. Wildlife drives cost about an extra US$30 per person for half a day. Bookings can be made through FoxTreks (*☎/fax 0811-327706, email fox@twiga.com, PO Box 10270, Dar es Salaam*) or through travel agents in Dar es Salaam.

Mwagusi Safari Camp is a select 16-bed, luxury tented camp beautifully situated on the Mwagusi Sand River, inside the park about 20km from the gate. Rates are US$275 per person, all inclusive. Bookings can be made through TropicAfrica in the UK (*☎/fax 020-8846 9363, email tropicafrica.uk@ virgin.net, 14 Castelnau, London SW13 9RU*).

Getting There & Away

Air Coastal Travels has scheduled flights three times weekly connecting Ruaha with Dar es Salaam and Unguja (Zanzibar Island, US$300 one way). It also runs flights three times weekly between Ruaha and Selous Game Reserve (US$270 one way).

Precision Air also runs three weekly flights connecting Iringa with Mbeya and Dar es Salaam, with connections to Arusha and Moshi (see Getting There & Away in the Iringa section). Both Mwagusi Safari Camp and Ruaha River Lodge can arrange airport transfers from Iringa (about US$180 per vehicle one way).

Road Ruaha is about 115km from Iringa. For budget transport, there are a few supply trucks which go several times a week from Iringa to the park headquarters. Ask around at the market for the schedule of the vehicles, or at Hasty Tasty Too (see Places to Eat in the Iringa section) for information. You'll have to make arrangements with the lodges or park headquarters in advance to be picked up at the gate, as well as for vehicle rental once in the park. Hitching a lift within Ruaha is usually not feasible.

MBEYA
☎ 065

Mbeya lies in a gap between the verdant Mbeya mountain range to the north and the Poroto Mountains to the south-east. It was founded in 1927 as a supply centre for the gold rush at Lupa, to the north.

Mbeya is a regional capital and an important transit point on the main road and rail routes connecting Tanzania with Zambia. It's also a convenient stop for travellers heading to or from Malawi via the Songwe River bridge. For those wishing to stay longer, there are many things to do in the surrounding region, especially if you enjoy hiking.

Information

There is one foreign exchange bureau in town, but it doesn't change travellers cheques; cash rates are about equivalent to those at the bank. NBC and the National Microfinance Bank both accept travellers cheques.

Dangers & Annoyances

As a major transport junction, Mbeya attracts a lot of transients, particularly in the area around the bus station. Take care with your luggage here and avoid walking alone through the small valley behind the station.

Places to Stay – Budget & Mid-Range

Out of town, the best budget lodging is at *Karibuni Centre* (*☎ 3035*) about 4km from the centre in Forest Area. It's run by Swiss missionaries and has clean doubles (only) for TSh 4000 (TSh 6000 with bathroom); meals are available. Minibuses to the centre pass nearby (TSh 100).

In town, the most popular budget lodging is *Moravian Hostel* (*☎ 3263*). Simple doubles with shared bathroom cost TSh 3600; there are no meals available. It's on Jacaranda Rd, about 600m from the market. Avoid walking along this road alone or after dark.

Warsame Guest House on Sisimba St near the market has singles/doubles for TSh 2000/3000, although there's nothing to recommend it except its central location.

Near the bus station, try *Nkwenzulu Hotel Number 1* (*☎ 2225*) which has rooms for TSh 6000/7200 (TSh 9600/ 10,800 with bathroom). It's opposite the bus stand and up the hill, and is not to be confused with the much grubbier Nkwenzulu Hotel Number 3 at the bottom of the hill.

On the other side of the valley is *Central Visitors Lodge* (*☎ 2507*) behind the bus station with doubles (only) for TSh 4800 (TSh 6000 with bathroom). For safety, to get here, it's best to take the longer route through town, rather than the more isolated shortcut behind the bus station.

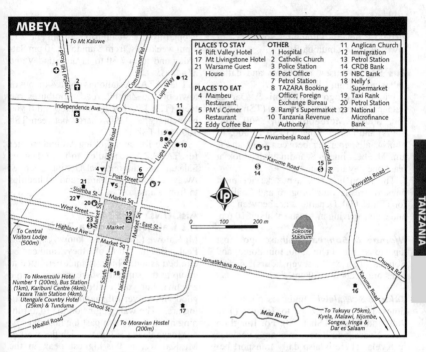

MBEYA

PLACES TO STAY
16 Rift Valley Hotel
17 Mt Livingstone Hotel
21 Warsame Guest House

PLACES TO EAT
4 Mambeu Restaurant
5 PM's Corner Restaurant
22 Eddy Coffee Bar

OTHER
1 Hospital
2 Catholic Church
3 Police Station
6 Post Office
7 Petrol Station
8 TAZARA Booking Office; Foreign Exchange Bureau
9 Ramji's Supermarket
10 Tanzania Revenue Authority
11 Anglican Church
12 Immigration
13 Petrol Station
14 CRDB Bank
15 NBC Bank
18 Nelly's Supermarket
19 Taxi Rank
20 Petrol Station
23 National Microfinance Bank

Rift Valley Hotel (☎ 4351) at the junction of Jamatikhana Rd and Lumumba Ave has better rooms from TSh 11,520/14,400.

Places to Stay – Top End

Central Mbeya's most 'luxurious' accommodation is the faded *Mt Livingstone Hotel* (☎ 3331) just off Jamatikhana Rd with rooms for US$40/60, including continental breakfast.

About 25km from Mbeya off the Zambia road is *Utengule Country Hotel* (☎/fax 4007, email utengule@twiga.com, PO Box 139, Mbeya) a comfortable lodge set among the hills and coffee plantations. Rooms cost from TSh 30,000 per person; special children's rates are available. The hotel has a pool, tennis and squash courts, and other facilities. Payment can be made in US dollars, South African rand, pounds sterling or Tanzanian shillings. To get here, you'll need your own vehicle. From Mbeya, take the Zambia road about 12km to Mbalizi. In the centre of Mbalizi take the first right; follow this road over a small bridge, go left at the fork, and then continue for 9km. The hotel is signposted to your right.

Places to Eat

Mbeya is not distinguished by its dining options. The best *local food* is at Karibuni Centre (see Places to Stay), which serves good, reasonably priced meals. The more expensive *restaurant* at Mt Livingstone Hotel has a fairly large selection.

In town by the market are several local food places. One of the better ones is *Eddy Coffee Bar* on Sisimba St. Others nearby include *Mambeu Restaurant* and *PM's Corner Restaurant*.

Self-caterers can try *Nelly's* supermarket on South St.

Getting There & Away

Air Precision Air has flights three times weekly connecting Mbeya with Iringa

(US$70) and Dar es Salaam (US$165). The airfield is several kilometres south-east of town, out on Lumumba Rd.

Bus Several buses, minibuses and dalla-dallas go to/from Mbeya.

Iringa, Morogoro, Mikumi & Dar es Salaam Buses go daily to Iringa (TSh 4000, four hours), Morogoro (TSh 8500, four hours) and Dar es Salaam (TSh 10,000, 11 hours), all departing between 6.30 and 7 am. The best line is Scandinavian. Book at least one day in advance.

The Hood line runs a bus service most days to Arusha via Morogoro and Chalinze for TSh 15,000. Departures are between 5.30 and 6 am, arriving in Arusha at about 10 pm.

Njombe & Songea Minibuses go most days to Njombe (TSh 3500, four hours) and Songea (TSh 5500, seven hours); departures are at about 5.30 am.

Tukuyu & Malawi Minibuses go several times daily from Mbeya to Tukuyu (TSh 700) and Kyela (TSh 1500). For Itungi on Lake Nyasa, you'll need to change vehicles in Kyela. There is also daily transport between Mbeya and the Malawi border, where you can pick up Malawian transport heading to Karonga and beyond.

There are also direct buses to Malawi. See the regional Getting There & Away chapter for details.

Zambia & Sumbawanga Minibuses go daily to Tunduma on the Zambian border (TSh 1500, two hours), where you can change to Zambian transport. There's also a direct bus a few times weekly between Mbeya and Lusaka (TSh 17,500).

A direct bus runs several times weekly to Sumbawanga (TSh 8000, at least 10 hours – longer during the rainy season); otherwise, you'll need to change at the junction before Tunduma.

Train Tickets for all classes can be booked at the TAZARA town booking office near the post office (open from 7.30 am to 3 pm weekdays, though it often closes early).

Otherwise, book at the station; the window is open from 7.30 am to 12.30 pm and 2 to 4 pm weekdays, from 8 am to 12.30 pm Saturday and from 7.30 to 11 am Sunday and holidays.

The TAZARA station is about 4km out of town on the Zambia road. Minibuses run there (TSh 150) but are often too full if you have luggage. Taxis charge between TSh 1000 and TSh 1500.

See the Tanzania Getting Around chapter for TAZARA schedules to/from Dar es Salaam. See the regional Getting There & Away chapter for fares and schedules to/from Zambia.

AROUND MBEYA
Mt Kaluwe & Mbeya Peak

Mt Kaluwe (2656m, also known as Loleza Peak), lies just north of Mbeya, and can be climbed as a day hike. It's not permitted to go up to the summit, where there is a large antenna, but you'll still be able to enjoy good views over Mbeya and the surrounding area. The walk begins on the road running north from town past the hospital.

Mbeya Peak (2834m), which lies west of Mt Kaluwe, is the highest peak in the Mbeya range. It's possible to climb it on a long day hike from Mbeya. The easiest way to reach the peak from town is by heading towards Mt Kaluwe and then following the ridge westwards for 7km.

Lake Rukwa & Uwanda Game Reserve

Lake Rukwa is a large salt lake notable for its diversity of water birds and its large crocodile population. Much of the lake and parts of the shoreline are protected within the boundaries of the Uwanda Game Reserve. As the lake has no outlet, its water level varies significantly between the rainy and dry seasons.

Visits to the lake and reserve are only practical with a 4WD, and even then access to the banks is difficult. The best approach is from Mbeya via Chunya and Saza to Ngomba on the lake shore (about 150km from Mbeya). There are no facilities at the lake, and very little en route.

TUKUYU
☎ 0658

Tukuyu is a small town set in the heart of a scenic area of hills and orchards near Lake Nyasa. While tourist facilities are minimal, the area is ideal for hiking (best from July to October) and Tukuyu makes a good base. Some possibilities include day hikes to the top of Mt Rungwe (2961m) or to the nearby volcanic Ngozi Peak (2629m). Guides can be arranged through Langboss Lodge (see Places to Stay & Eat following).

In this as yet little visited area, give particular thought to culturally responsible tourism (see Responsible Tourism in the Regional Facts about East Africa chapter).

Places to Stay & Eat

Most travellers stay at *Langboss Lodge* (☎ *2080*) about 1km east of the town centre. Basic singles/doubles are TSh 2000/3000 (TSh 4000 for a double with bathroom), and meals are available on request. The owner is knowledgeable about the surrounding area and helpful in arranging hikes and excursions.

Bombay Tea Room opposite the bank is good for inexpensive local food.

Getting There & Away

Transport runs several times a day from Tukuyu to Mbeya (TSh 700, one to 1½ hours) and Kyela (TSh 600, one hour) along a scenic, tarmac road.

Two roads connect Tukuyu with the northern end of Lake Nyasa. The main, tarmac road heads south and splits at Ibanda, with the western fork going to Songwe River bridge and into Malawi, and the eastern fork to Kyela and Itungi port. If you are going to Malawi you will have to change at Ibanda. For more details, see Malawi in the regional Getting There & Away chapter.

A secondary dirt road heads south-east from Tukuyu to Ipinda and then branches further eastwards towards Matema.

LAKE NYASA

Lake Nyasa (Lake Malawi) is Africa's third largest lake after Lake Victoria and Lake Tanganyika. It's bordered by Tanzania, Malawi and Mozambique. The Tanzanian side is rimmed to the east by the Livingstone Mountains, which form a beautiful backdrop. Few roads reach the towns strung out between the mountains and the shore along the lake's eastern side.

Places around the Tanzanian side of the lake through which travellers may pass include the following (listed from north-west to south-east).

Kyela

There's no reason to come to Kyela unless you arrive late at Itungi from Malawi and need somewhere to spend the night.

There are several basic, cheap guesthouses near the bus stand. One of the better ones is *Pattaya Hotel* with clean singles/doubles for TSh 4000/5000.

Minibuses run daily from Kyela to Tukuyu (TSh 600) and Mbeya (TSh 1500), and pick-ups run between Kyela and Itungi (TSh 200).

Itungi

Itungi, about 11km south-east of Kyela, is the main port for the Tanzanian Lake Nyasa ferry service. There is no accommodation; photography is forbidden. Pick-ups run sporadically to and from Kyela (TSh 200). The road to Itungi from Ibanda (at the junction with the paved main road) is in poor condition.

There are usually two ferries from Itungi servicing the villages along the Tanzanian side of Lake Nyasa, though the *MV Songea* (the larger of the two) is indefinitely out of service. The *MV Iringa* departs Itungi once weekly (presently on Thursday) at about 7.30 am, reaching Mbamba Bay by about noon on Friday and stopping en route at Lumbila, Lupingo, Liuli and several other villages. From Mbamba Bay, the boat crosses over to Nkhata Bay in Malawi (see the Regional Getting There & Away chapter for more details), then returns to Mbamba Bay, from where it departs Saturday to head back to Itungi. Tickets between Itungi and Mbamba Bay cost TSh 3240 (deck seating only). There's no restaurant on board.

If you are trying to coordinate road and boat travel, bus drivers in Mbeya (or those in Dar es Salaam who drive the Dar es Salaam-Mbeya route) sometimes have information on whether and when the Lake Nyasa ferries are running.

Matema

Attractive Matema beach is a popular place for swimming and relaxing; the water is considered to be bilharzia-free.

Lutheran Guest House has a generator and rooms for TSh 4800 to TSh 6000 per person, including breakfast. Other meals are also available. Before heading down, check with the Lutheran Mission in Tukuyu (just up from the market on the road to the NBC bank) to be sure space is available.

To get to Matema from Tukuyu via public transport, take a pick-up from the roundabout by the NBC bank to Ipinda, from where pick-ups run only very sporadically to Matema (35km). Chances for a lift are better on weekends. If you are heading to Matema in your own vehicle, the route is via Ipinda (not Kyela).

Mbamba Bay

Mbamba Bay is the southernmost Tanzanian port on Lake Nyasa. If you get stuck here waiting for transport, try *Mabugu Guest House* which has basic rooms for about TSh 1000. See Itungi earlier for details of ferry services between Mbamba Bay and Itungi port. See the regional Getting There & Away chapter for details of ferry connections with Nkhata Bay in Malawi.

If you are entering or leaving Tanzania via Mbamba Bay, you'll need to stop at the police station to take care of immigration formalities.

From Mbamba Bay, there are pick-ups to Mbinga (TSh 2000, four hours), from where you can catch a minibus on to Songea.

SONGEA

Songea, just over 1000m in altitude, is a bustling, pleasant place and capital of the surrounding Ruvuma region. The main ethnic group here are the Ngoni, who migrated into the area from South Africa during the 19th century, subduing many smaller tribes along the way.

The Maji Maji Rebellion

The Maji Maji rebellion began about the turn of the 20th century when German colonial administrators set about establishing enormous cotton plantations in the south-east and along the train line running from Dar es Salaam towards Morogoro. Most workers were recruited as forced labour and required to toil under miserable salary and living conditions. Anger at this harsh treatment and long-simmering resentment of colonial practices combined to ignite a powerful rebellion.

The first outbreak was in 1905 in the area around Kilwa, on the coast. Soon all of southern Tanzania was involved, from Kilwa and Lindi in the south-east to Songea near Lake Nyasa. Thousands died, both on the battlefield and due to the famine precipitated by the Germans' 'scorched earth' tactics, in which fields and grain silos in many villages were set on fire. Fatalities were undoubtedly exacerbated by a widespread belief among the Africans that enemy bullets would turn to water before killing them, and that their warriors would therefore not be harmed – hence the name Maji Maji (*maji* means water in Swahili).

By 1907, when the rebellion was finally suppressed, close to 100,000 people had lost their lives, large areas of the south were left devastated and barren, and malnutrition was widespread. Among the effects of the Maji Maji uprising were a temporary liberalisation of colonial rule and replacement of the military administration with a civilian government. More significantly, the uprising promoted development of a national identity among many ethnic groups and intensified anticolonial sentiments, kindling the movement towards independence.

Songea takes its name from one of the Ngoni's greatest chiefs who was killed following the Maji Maji rebellion (see the boxed text 'The Maji Maji Rebellion' on this page). In the town there's a monument dedicated to the Africans who lost their lives in the rebellion.

Places to Stay & Eat

OK Hotel opposite the Open University of Tanzania building has clean doubles from TSh 5000 and a restaurant.

De Luxe Guest House on the main road near the market is grubbier. Basic rooms cost about TSh 2000.

Getting There & Away

Buses run daily between Songea and Mbeya (TSh 5500, seven hours), with the first departure in either direction at about 6 am.

There is also a bus most days direct to Dar es Salaam (TSh 15,000, 14 hours), departing between 6 and 7 am in each direction.

To Mbamba Bay, buses go most days to Mbinga (TSh 2000, four hours), from where you can find sporadic transport to Mbamba Bay. There is occasional direct transport between Songea and Mbamba Bay during the dry season.

To get to Tunduru, see Getting There & Away in the Tunduru section following.

NJOMBE
☎ 0632

About 240km north of Songea is Njombe, a district capital and the centre of a productive agricultural region. The town lies at almost 2000m altitude and can get very chilly in the evenings. For accommodation, try *Mbalache Guest House* with basic but clean rooms for about TSh 2000, or *Lutheran Hostel*, also inexpensive.

Buses go daily from Njombe to Songea (TSh 3000, three to four hours) and to Makumbako, where you can get transport to

Mbeya. There's also a direct bus most days to Mbeya (TSh 3500, four hours).

TUNDURU

Tunduru is a dusty, bustling town about halfway between Songea and Masasi. It's in the centre of one of Tanzania's gemstone mining regions and has a bit of a 'wild west' feel to it. You'll need to spend at least one night here if travelling between Songea and Masasi.

The better guesthouses are at the westernmost end of town. There are plenty to chose from; all are around the same standard.

Also congregating at the western end of town are 4WDs to Songea.

Getting There & Away

It's best to reserve a seat for onward travel as soon as you arrive in Tunduru, as the vehicles fill up quickly.

The road from Tunduru in either direction is in very poor condition, particularly between Tunduru and Songea, and is often impassable during the rainy season. During the dry season, buses run several times a week between Tunduru and Masasi (12 hours). Between Tunduru and Songea, your only option for most of the year is by 4WD (TSh 10,000, 12 hours), which run a few times weekly, usually departing Tunduru between 3 and 4 am. If you are staying at a guesthouse near the 4WD 'station' you can usually arrange with a driver to wake you before departure. There is very little along the route; bring with you whatever food and water you will need.

South-Eastern Tanzania

South-eastern Tanzania is a beautiful region of open savanna and spectacular beaches. The continent's largest game reserve, the Selous, is here, as is Tanzania's first marine park, at Mafia Island. Inland, the Makonde Plateau is the home of Tanzania's famous woodcarvers, while at Kilwa Kisiwani on the coast are the ruins of one of East Africa's most important cities.

Despite these attractions, the south-east receives few visitors, and the region's undeveloped infrastructure – in particular the road network – means that journeys can be long and hard. While travellers seeking creature comforts may not enjoy themselves, those with an adventurous spirit, sufficient time and an openness to local customs, will find this unspoiled region to be one of Tanzania's most rewarding.

MTWARA
☎ 059

Mtwara, south-eastern Tanzania's major town, is a sprawling, friendly place in an attractive setting on Mtwara Bay. It was first developed after WWII by the British as part of their doomed East African Groundnut Scheme, a project aimed at alleviating the postwar shortage of plant oils through the implementation of large-scale groundnut production at various sites in the region. Following the failure of the scheme, Mtwara's port continued to serve as a regional export channel for cashew, sisal and other products, although development of the town itself came to a standstill.

In recent years, there has been a revival of interest in the tourism potential of Mtwara and the surrounding area. A few projects for hotel development and the rehabilitation of several historical buildings were under way at the time of research, and other projects were being discussed.

Orientation
Mtwara is loosely centred around a business and banking area to the north, near Tanu

and Uhuru roads, and the market and bus stand to the south, near the lively areas of Majengo and Chikongola. In the far northwest of town on the water is the Shangani Quarter where many of Mtwara's foreign residents live. East of here is the port.

Information
There are no foreign exchange bureaus in Mtwara. The NBC bank on Uhuru Rd changes travellers cheques and cash; the CRDB on Tanu Rd changes cash only.

Mtwara Colour Lab sells Kodak film and does a surprisingly decent job with film developing (TSh 90 per print plus a TSh 500 developing fee).

Things to See & Do
In town there's a well-stocked **market**, with an interesting traditional medicine section next to the main building. Much of Mtwara's fish comes from Msangamkuu on the other side of Mtwara Bay. The **ferry dock** and adjoining market are particularly colourful in the early morning and late afternoon. The **beach** in Shangani is popular on weekends.

Places to Stay
Nandope Hotel (☎ *333362*) just off Tanu Rd near the centre of town has simple but clean singles/doubles with fan, mosquito net and shared bath for TSh 2000/3000.

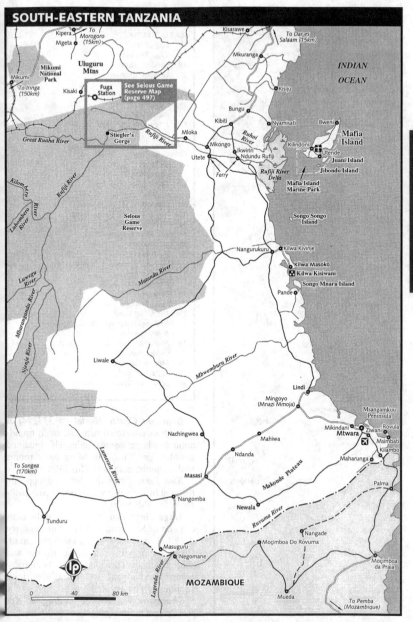

SOUTH-EASTERN TANZANIA

Kipera
Mgeta
To Morogoro (15km)
Kisarawe
To Dar es Salaam (15km)

INDIAN OCEAN

Mikumi National Park
Uluguru Mtns
Mkuranga

Mikumi
To Iringa (150km)
Kisaki
Fuga Station
See Selous Game Reserve Map (page 497)

Kisiju
Bungu
Kibiti
Ruhoi River
Nyamisati
Bweni
Mafia Island

Great Ruaha River
Stiegler's Gorge
Rufiji River
Mloka
Mkongo
Ikwirin
Ndundu Rufiji
Kilindoni
Utende
Juani Island

Rufiji River
Utete
Ferry
Rufiji River Delta
Jibondo Island

Kilombero River
Lahombero River

Mafia Island Marine Park

Selous Game Reserve

Songo Songo Island

Luwegu River

Matandu River

Nangurukuru
Kilwa Kivinje
Kilwa Masoko
Kilwa Kisiwani
Songo Mnara Island

Mbaranganda River

Pande

Njinjo River

Liwale
Mbwemburu River

Lindi
Mingoyo (Mnazi Mmoja)
Msangamkuu Peninsula

Nachingwea
Mahiwa
Mikindani
Ziwani
Mtwara
Rovula
Msimbati
Kilambo

Ndanda

To Songea (170km)
Masasi
Makonde Plateau
Maharunga

Lumesule River
Nangomba
Newala
Palma

Tunduru
Ruvuma River
Nangade

Masuguru
Moçimboa Do Rovuma

Lagenda River
Negomane
Moçimboa da Praia

MOZAMBIQUE

Mueda
To Pemba (Mozambique)

0   40   80 km

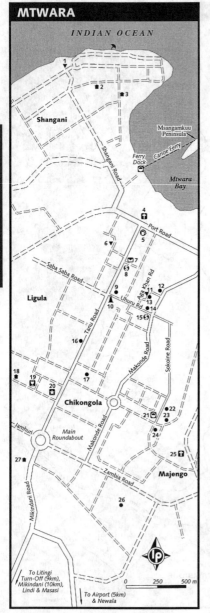

MTWARA

PLACES TO STAY
2 Finn Club
3 Tinga Tinga Inn
18 Nandope Hotel
27 Lutheran Centre Hostel

PLACES TO EAT
1 Safina Shop
6 Kwa Limo
11 Mtwara Deluxe Hotel

OTHER
4 Cathedral
5 BP Petrol Station
7 Post Office; Telecom
8 CRDB Bank
9 CCM Building
10 Monument
12 Bicycle Rental & Repair Stand
13 Maduka Makubwa (Big Square)
14 *MV Safari* Booking Office
15 NBC Bank
16 Air Tanzania;
   Tanzania Revenue Authority Building
17 Regional Block
   Administration Buildings
19 Bondeni Pub
20 Police Station
21 Bus & Taxi Stand
22 Booking Offices for *MV Maendeleo*
   & *MV Zahahra*
23 Market & Pick-Ups
   to Msimbati
24 Mtwara Colour Lab
25 St Paul's Church
26 Saba Saba Ground

Lutheran Centre Hostel (☎ 333294) at
the entrance to town near the main roundabout has large, comfortable, self-contained
doubles for TSh 8000. More basic rooms
with common bath cost TSh 3300/5800.

Kwa Limo down the dirt road opposite
the post office has grubby rooms with bathroom for TSh 5000.

Tinga Tinga Inn (☎ 333146) at the eastern end of Shangani and north of the ferry
dock is a cosy place with a small restaurant.
Clean rooms with fan, mosquito net and
shared bath are TSh 5000/7000. As at many
places in Shangani, water and electricity
supplies can be erratic here.

**Shangani Sea Breeze Loding & Re-
freshments** in Shangani about 500m west of

Safina Shop, has simple but relatively clean singles/doubles with nets and fans for TSh 5000/7000, including breakfast. Other meals can be arranged on request.

Finn Club (☎ 333020) in Shangani has small but spotless air-con rooms from TSh 8000/10,000, including breakfast. For bookings, contact Rural Integrated Project Support (RIPS) program housing office in the Finn Club compound. Priority is given to staff and aid workers. For a temporary membership of TSh 500 per day (TSh 1000 per day on weekends), you can use the restaurant, TV room, tennis and squash courts in the compound.

Litingi (☎ 333635) about 11km from town off Mikindani Rd is Mtwara's upmarket accommodation option, complete with its own generator (although you're likely to be the only guest). Doubles (no singles) with bathroom are TSh 15,000, including continental breakfast (TSh 24,000 for an air-con suite). To get there, follow the road to Mikindani for about 9km. Just before the Mikindani police station is a dirt track to the right (look for the sign for 'Makonde Beach Resort'); follow this for about 2km to Litingi. Taxis from Mtwara charge about TSh 4000. Otherwise, a minibus to Mikindani can drop you by the turn-off (TSh 200).

Places to Eat
Kwa Limo has pleasant *bandas* (thatched huts), and serves *nyama choma* (barbecued meat) and other local dishes for about TSh 1000. (See Places to Stay for details.)

Finn Club serves good meals for between TSh 2000 and TSh 3500 (plus the temporary membership fee – see Places to Stay).

Tinga Tinga Inn also has a restaurant; it's best to give advance notice.

The best dining in the town centre is at the *Mtwara Deluxe Hotel (☎ 333830)* on Aga Khan Rd. It's open from 7 am to 3 pm and 6 to 10 pm daily except Sunday, and has a good selection of Indian and other dishes from about TSh 2000.

The restaurant at *Litingi* (see Places to Stay) is also good. Meals cost TSh 3000 to TSh 5000.

For self-caterers, *Safina* in Shangani has the best selection of basics. In town, there

are several fairly well stocked shops along Uhuru Rd. For street food, try the *market* by the Msangamkuu ferry.

Entertainment
Popular places for a drink include *Bondeni Pub* near the police station and *Safina* and *Finn Club* in Shangani. *Litingi* operates a disco on Saturday nights (TSh 1000 admission for men), though it's fairly quiet these days.

Shopping
There's an excellent selection of Makonde woodcarvings at a small market held from 9 to 10.30 am each Wednesday in the grounds of St Paul's Church in Majengo. The vendors can show you to their nearby work space, where you can watch the carvers at work.

Getting There & Away
Air Air Tanzania flies three times weekly between Mtwara and Dar es Salaam (TSh 57,000 one way). The Air Tanzania office (☎ 333147, 333417) is on Tanu Rd.

There's a weekly charter flight (currently on Friday) between Mtwara and Pemba for US$170/300 one way/return. In Mtwara, inquire at the airport. In Pemba, book through Viatur Travel Agency (☎ 072-3431, fax 2249), Rua XII, No 312.

Bus Buses go daily to Lindi (TSh 1500, three to four hours), Masasi (TSh 2400, five to six hours) and Newala (TSh 2000, six to 10 hours). The post bus to Masasi leaves at 8 am. During the dry season, buses run at least several times weekly between Mtwara and Dar es Salaam (TSh 10,000, at least 24 hours); it's best to book a seat in advance. During much of the rainy season, the road to Dar es Salaam is closed.

The Rufiji River is bridged by two ferries, one at Ndundu and a smaller, less reliable one at Utete. Most buses cross at Ndundu. Both operate from 6.30 am to 6.30 pm, and neither operates during the rainy season. Bridge construction has begun midway between Ndundu and Utete, but completion is still several years away.

TANZANIA

To Mozambique, there's at least one pick-up daily (in the morning) going to the Tanzanian immigration post at Kilambo (TSh 2000). In the dry season, it continues on to within about 2km of the Ruvuma River, which you will need to cross with dugout canoe (TSh 1500). See Mozambique in the regional Getting There & Away chapter for more details.

Boat The *MV Maendeleo* sails between Mtwara and Dar es Salaam roughly twice a month; schedules are irregular (TSh 16,800/10,800/7300 for 1st/2nd (tourist)/3rd class). The Mtwara booking office (☎ 333307) is opposite the bus stand.

Africa Shipping Corporation's *MV Safari* is smaller, but sails more regularly, with runs about twice weekly between Mtwara and Dar es Salaam (TSh 8800/7800 for 1st/2nd class). There are no 1st class cabins – just an upper room with sofas; 2nd class is equivalent to deck seating. Schedules are posted at the ticket office in town opposite the NBC bank. Neither boat is comfortable and on both, the trip takes close to 24 hours. The *Safari* usually departs Mtwara at around 9 am; departures from Dar es Salaam are at about 8 am.

The large *MV Zahara* has just started sailing between Mtwara and Dar es Salaam for TSh 9000/8000 1st/2nd class, also taking 24 hours. The ticket office in Mtwara is opposite the bus stand.

To Mozambique, there is a small motorboat which travels occasionally between Mtwara and Moçimboa da Praia; inquire at the port for details. Local boats also sail from Mtwara to various destinations up and down the coast. If you're contemplating a trip, bring plenty of extra food and water and time your journey to go with the monsoon winds, which (roughly) blow north to south from about November to February and south to north from about April to September.

Getting Around
Taxis to/from Mtwara's airport (6km from the main roundabout) cost TSh 5000. Taxis (light blue) park at the bus stand; the cost for a town trip is TSh 1000.

Mtwara is very spread out, and the best way of getting around is by bicycle; these can be rented near the market, and at a small stand just east of the northern terminus of Aga Khan Rd.

AROUND MTWARA
Mikindani
Tiny but attractive Mikindani was previously an important dhow port and a terminus for trade caravans from Lake Nyasa. In the 19th century it served briefly as the headquarters of the German colonial government, and several buildings from this era remain.

Places to Stay & Eat *Hotel Mikindani* (☎ 059-334053, fax 333562, email njaya lodge@compuserve.com) has spotlessly clean rooms with common bathroom for TSh 10,000 per double (lower rates can usually be negotiated for singles). There's a good restaurant and bar with breezy bandas overlooking the water; meals cost between TSh 1500 and 3500. The hotel is a great place to relax if you've just made your way across southern Tanzania or arrived in the Mtwara area after a long bus journey from Dar es Salaam. Much of the road in between the two lodges (from Songea to Mikindani and Mtwara) is slated for upgrading as part of the Southern Corridor project to link Zambia with the sea. Renovations of the *Boma* (☎/fax 059-333875) are almost completed and it's set to open soon as a midrange hotel. For more information check out its Web site at www.mikindani.com.

Getting There & Away Mikindani is about 10km from Mtwara along a tarmac road, and an easy bike ride. Minibuses run between the two towns throughout the day (TSh 200).

Msangamkuu Peninsula
Msangamkuu Peninsula lies north and east of Mtwara town and, together with Msimbati and Mnazi Bay to the south, is earmarked to become part of the proposed Msangamkuu-Mnazi Bay Marine Park. The area to be covered by the park (which is still to be gazetted) stretches from the north-western side of

Msangamkuu Peninsula down to the Mozambique border. More than 400 marine species have been identified here to date. For travellers, the peninsula offers some beaches, and good diving and snorkelling to the north-west, near the village.

Camping on the peninsula isn't advised. Your best option is to arrange accommodation with one of the villagers. Fish and basic supplies are available in Msangamkuu village.

Dhows and canoes make the trip between the Shangani ferry dock and Msangamkuu Peninsula throughout the day (TSh 50); the trip takes about 15 minutes with favourable winds.

Msimbati

Msimbati, about 42km from Mtwara on Mnazi Bay, offers an attractive beach and good diving and snorkelling possibilities, although facilities are limited. About 7km beyond Msimbati town, along a sandy track (or along the beach at low tide), is the tiny village of **Rovula**. At the time of research, a small dive centre was about to open here, with accommodation and equipment rentals. Otherwise, the *CCM Guest House* just before the police station as you enter Msimbati town has basic rooms for about TSh 2000.

Getting There & Away Pick-ups and trucks from Mtwara depart sporadically from behind the market (TSh 1000). There is no regular public transport between Msimbati and Rovula.

MAKONDE PLATEAU

This plateau, much of which lies between 700 and 900m above sea level, is home to the Makonde people, famed throughout East Africa for their exotic ebony carvings.

Newala

Newala, a district capital and the main town on the plateau, is a bustling place with pleasantly cool temperatures and views over the Ruvuma Valley.

For accommodation, try *Sollo's Guest House* approximately 1km from town on the Masasi road. Otherwise, there are sev-

eral local guesthouses in town along the main road, including a decent *guesthouse* just behind the NBC bank.

Buses run daily from Newala to Mtwara (TSh 2000, six to 10 hours) and Masasi (TSh 1500, three hours).

Masasi

Masasi, which lies off the edge of the Makonde Plateau, is a district centre and transport hub. *Top Ten Guest House* about 1km east of the bus stand on the main road has basic but acceptable rooms for TSh 2000/3000. *Masasi Hotel* opposite the petrol station has similar rooms from TSh 4000. *Siraya* also near the petrol station is slightly more upmarket, with rooms going for TSh 7500.

Both Masasi Hotel and Siraya have simple *restaurants*. Otherwise, there are numerous *food stalls* near the market. If you're coming from Mtwara and are staying at any of these places, ask the bus driver to drop you off by the petrol station to avoid having to walk back into town from the bus stand (which is at the western end of town).

Minibuses run between Masasi and Mtwara throughout the day (TSh 2400, five to six hours); the last one in both directions leaves at about 2 pm.

LINDI

In its early days, Lindi was a terminus of the slave caravan route from Lake Nyasa, as well as being a regional colonial capital and the main town in south-eastern Tanzania. Today, a few carved doorways, ruins of an Arab tower, and the old German *boma* (village) are the only reminders of its more glorious past.

Apart from its history, the town's main feature is its attractive setting on palm-fringed Lindi Bay, which is still a busy dhow port.

Mtema Beach, about 6km from town off the airfield road, makes a pleasant excursion; keep an eye on your valuables.

Places to Stay & Eat

Nankolowa Guest House in the centre of town on Rutamba St, about 400m south-west of the market, has clean rooms with fans and mosquito nets for TSh 3000/3500, including breakfast. Other meals can be arranged.

The run-down *Coast Guest House* on the beach has grubby rooms for TSh 1200/1500.

Maji Maji Restaurant about 500m down from the CRDB bank has good local food for about TSh 500 per plate.

Getting There & Away
Commercial air services to Lindi have been suspended, but there's an airstrip for charter flights.

There's at least one bus daily to Mtwara (TSh 1500), and minivans throughout the day to Mingoyo junction (more commonly referred to as 'Mnazi Mmoja') where you can get transport to Masasi. There are also buses most mornings to Nangurukuru (TSh 4000, six to seven hours), from where you can get transport to Kilwa Masoko.

KILWA MASOKO
Kilwa Masoko (Kilwa of the Market), about halfway between Dar es Salaam and Mtwara, is of interest primarily as a base for visiting the ruins of the 15th century Arab settlement at nearby Kilwa Kisiwani.

The National Microfinance Bank changes cash only (no travellers cheques).

Places to Stay
The two better guesthouses in town are *Hilton Guest House* near the market and *Mjaka Enterprises Guest House & Hotel* on the main road. Both have acceptable rooms with fan and mosquito net for TSh 2000 (TSh 3000 with bathroom).

Places to Eat
Masasi's New Mnyalukolo Bar on the main road does good chicken and chips.

Both the *Hilton* and *Mjaka Enterprises Guest House & Hotel* have restaurants that do fish/chicken/meat with rice, although it is a rare day when you will have a selection of all three. There's good street food in the evenings in the area around the market.

Getting There & Away
Bus & Minibus Road access to Kilwa is cut off during the rainy season. During the

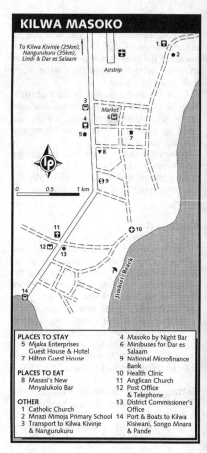

KILWA MASOKO

To Kilwa Kivinje (25km),
Nangurukuru (35km),
Lindi & Dar es Salaam

Airstrip

Market

Jimbizi Beach

0   0.5   1 km

PLACES TO STAY
5 Mjaka Enterprises
   Guest House & Hotel
7 Hilton Guest House

PLACES TO EAT
8 Masasi's New
   Mnyalukolo Bar

OTHER
1 Catholic Church
2 Mnazi Mmoja Primary School
3 Transport to Kilwa Kivinje
   & Nangurukuru

4 Masoko by Night Bar
6 Minibuses for Dar es
   Salaam
9 National Microfinance
   Bank
10 Health Clinic
11 Anglican Church
12 Post Office
   & Telephone
13 District Commissioner's
   Office
14 Port & Boats to Kilwa
   Kisiwani, Songo Mnara
   & Pande

dry season, minibuses run several times weekly between Kilwa Masoko and Dar es Salaam's Temeke bus stand (10 to 12 hours). Departures in either direction are at 6 am and the fare costs TSh 4500. It's a long, rough journey. Buses for Kilwa also sometimes leave from Kariakoo in Dar es Salaam. Buses from Kilwa to Dar es Salaam should be booked in advance; the ticket vendors are near the market.

Alternatively, from Dar es Salaam you can take a bus heading to Lindi or Mtwara and get out at Nangurukuru junction, from where you can get local transport to Kilwa

Kivinje (TSh 300) or Kilwa Masoko (TSh 500).

To go south from Kilwa, you'll have to go first to Nangurukuru, from where minibuses go most mornings to Lindi (TSh 4000, six to seven hours). From Lindi you can find onward transport towards Mtwara.

Boat Dhows from Kilwa ply the coast as far as Dar es Salaam. However, every year several boats capsize en route to Dar es Salaam and many captains are unwilling to take foreigners.

AROUND KILWA MASOKO
Kilwa Kisiwani
Kilwa Kisiwani (Kilwa on the Island) was once East Africa's most important trading centre. Today, the ruins of the settlement are considered to be one of the most significant groups of Swahili buildings on the East African coast. Despite their historical significance, the ruins are not well maintained and there are no tourist facilities. Because of this, and because it's so difficult to get to Kilwa, the ruins are likely to be attractive only to those with a particular interest in archaeology or East African history.

History Although the coast near Kilwa has been inhabited by humans for several thousand years, there were no significant settlements in the area until the end of the 10th century. In the early 13th century, trade links began to develop with Sofala, 1500km to the south in present-day Mozambique. Ultimately, Kilwa came to control Sofala and to dominate its lucrative gold trade, to become the most powerful trade centre along the East African coast.

In the late 15th century, Kilwa's fortunes began to decline. Sofala freed itself from the island's dominance, and in the early 16th century Kilwa came under the control of the Portuguese. It wasn't until more than 200 years later that Kilwa regained its independence and regained significance, this time as a trade entrepôt for slaves being shipped from the mainland to the islands of Mauritius, Réunion and Comoros. In the 1780s, Kilwa came under the control of the Sultan of Oman. By the mid-19th century, the town had completely declined and the local administration was relocated to Kilwa Kivinje.

Information To visit the ruins, you'll need to get a permit from the District Commissioner's office at Kilwa Masoko. There's no charge, and the permit is issued while you wait. Once at Kilwa Kisiwani, there is a local guide, although he speaks only minimal English and expects a fairly hefty TSh 1000 tip.

There are a few small villages on the island, but there's no accommodation.

The Ruins The ruins are in two groups. When approaching Kilwa Kisiwani, the first building you'll find is the Arabic **fort**, which was built in the early 19th century by Omani Arabs. To the south-west of the fort are the ruins of the **Great Mosque**, a few sections of which date to the late 13th century. Further south-west and behind the Great Mosque is a smaller **mosque**, which dates from the early 15th century and is considered the best preserved of the buildings at Kilwa. To the west of this mosque are the crumbling remains of the **Makutani**, which is a large walled enclosure in the centre of which lived some of the sultans of Kilwa.

About 1.5km from the fort along the coast is **Husuni Kubwa**, once a massive complex of buildings covering about one hectare and, together with the nearby **Husuni Ndogo**, the oldest of Kilwa's ruins. The complex, which is estimated to date from at least the 12th century, is largely overgrown. To get there, you can walk along the beach at low tide, or take the slightly longer inland route, for which you'll probably need a guide.

Getting There & Away Local boats go from the port at Kilwa Masoko to Kilwa Kisiwani whenever there are passengers (TSh 100, or TSh 1000 each way to charter your own boat). Tourists also have to pay a TSh 300 port fee. With a good wind, the trip takes about 20 minutes.

TANZANIA

Kilwa Kivinje

Kilwa Kivinje (Kilwa of the Casuarina Trees) is a tiny village with a small but attractive dhow port about 25km north of Kilwa Masoko. It served briefly as the regional capital during the mid-19th century following the decline of Kilwa Kisiwani. Most buildings from the era are in an advanced state of decay.

Kilwa Kivinje can be easily visited as a day trip from Kilwa Masoko. Accommodation options include *New Sudi Guest House* on the main road, *Savoye Guest House* by the dhow port, or *Four Ways Guest House* near the market. All have grubby single rooms (only) for TSh 1000, and all are equally basic. For meals, there are several food stalls in town.

Pick-ups run several times daily to Kilwa Masoko (TSh 500) and Nangurukuru (TSh 300). The minibus between Dar es Salaam and Kilwa Masoko also stops at Kilwa Kivinje (TSh 4000 from Kivinje to Dar es Salaam).

Offshore Islands

Songo Mnara Songo Mnara Island, which lies about 8km south of Kilwa Kisiwani, contains ruins at its northern end that are believed to date from the 14th and 15th centuries. On the western side of the island, at **Sanje Majoma**, are additional ruins dating from the same period. The small island of **Sanje ya Kati**, between Songo Mnara and Kilwa Masoko, has some lesser ruins of a third settlement, also believed to date from the same era.

There's no accommodation on Songo Mnara. To visit, you'll need permission from the District Commissioner's office in Kilwa Masoko.

A motorboat from Kilwa Masoko can be arranged through the District Commissioner's office (about TSh 30,000 return). Alternatively, there's a far cheaper motorised dhow that departs most mornings at about 6 am from Kilwa Masoko to Pande, and will stop on request at Songo Mnara. The boat returns to Kilwa Masoko the same day, departing Pande about 1 pm, and costs about TSh 3000.

Songo Songo Songo Songo Island, about 25km north-east of Kilwa Kivinje, is an ecologically important area for nesting sea turtles and marine birds. The island is also the site of a significant natural gas field.

To get here by sea, you'll have to go to Kilwa Kivinje and arrange a local boat there. As with all longer trips by dhow, be aware of safety considerations. The gas companies working on Songo Songo often have charter flights to the island from Dar es Salaam. Check with Dar es Salaam-based air charter operators to find out if there are any extra seats available.

MAFIA ISLAND

Mafia Island, which lies off the Rufiji River delta about 120km south of Dar es Salaam, was an important trading post from the 11th to 13th centuries when the Shirazis ruled much of the East African coastal area. After a lengthy period of decline, Mafia again began to flourish in the early 18th century as a trade centre linking Kilwa to the south with Unguja (Zanzibar Island) to the north.

Today, the island is better known as a resort for deep-sea fishing and scuba diving. It's a superb place for these activities, par-

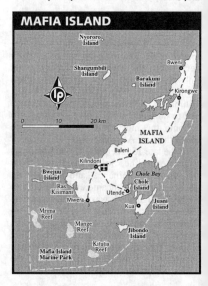

MAFIA ISLAND

ticularly as the 200m-deep trough running along the sea bed about 1km off Mafia's western shoreline is home to a vast number of aquatic species. The coral formations are best off the small islands scattered around Mafia, particularly the Kitutia Reef and other reefs around Juani and Jibondo islands close to Chole Bay.

Things to See & Do

Mafia's main attraction is its diverse and spectacular natural environment, which is now protected as part of Mafia Island Marine Park.

There are ruins on the island of **Juani**, principally those of five mosques dating from the 18th and 19th centuries. Offshore on tiny **Chole Island** are picturesque but overgrown ruins dating from the 19th century, and two short but interesting history/nature trails.

Places to Stay & Eat

For budget lodging, try *Lizu's* (☎ *051-116233 ext 96 in Dar es Salaam, or Mafia 96*) about a five-minute walk from the airfield in Kilindoni which has rooms for about TSh 5000.

There are several top end options. *Kinasi Lodge* (☎ *051-843501 in Dar es Salaam, fax 843495, email kinasi@int africa.com, PO Box 3052, Dar es Salaam*) overlooking Chole Bay has rooms from US$130 per person, including full board. Diving, snorkelling and fishing excursions can be arranged, as can diving certification courses.

Mafia Island Lodge, which is owned partly by the Tanzanian government and partly by the Accor/Tahi chain, has a good setting on Chole Bay, though its standards are a step down from those at the Kinasi. Rooms are US$147/210 a single/double with full board. Book through Accor/Tahi (☎ 057-4292, fax 8071, email tahi@yako .habari.co.tz).

The Italian-owned *Dolphin Island Pole Pole Bungalow Resort* (☎ *0811-372532, 051-843717, fax 051-116239 in Dar es Salaam, email archipelago@tanzania.org, PO Box 198, Mafia*) has two-bed luxury

Mafia Island Marine Park

Mafia Island Marine Park – Tanzania's first, and the largest marine park in the western Indian Ocean – encompasses an area of approximately 400 sq km around the southern end of Mafia Island and Chole Bay. Within its boundaries is a unique complex of estuarine, mangrove, coral reef and marine channel ecosystems, including the only natural forest on the island. It's a beautiful area with great biodiversity; close to 400 species of fish have been identified on the surrounding coral reefs.

Since its establishment in 1995, the park has registered several significant achievements, including a notable reduction in dynamite fishing on nearby reefs and increased community awareness of and support for conservation goals. However, many challenges remain. New restrictions on live coral mining and on small mesh nets are proving particularly unpopular with local residents. Many view coral as the only readily available building material they have, and fishing as their only way to earn a living. Park staff are now working with residents of the 10 villages within the park's boundaries (which have an estimated total population of between 15,000 and 17,000) to develop alternative livelihoods.

In addition to achieving its primary goals of protecting Mafia's ecosystems, conservationists are also hoping that the park will serve as a model and catalyst for the development of other marine parks and protected areas along the Tanzanian coast.

bungalows for US$120 per person (US$180 with private bathroom), including full board.

Emerson's On Chole (Chole Island) is a laid-back place with comfortable tented accommodation for US$40 per person, including full board; it's closed between April and May. Luxury tree houses are also planned to open soon from about US$100 a double, including full board. Book through Emerson's & Green on Unguja (☎ 054-230171, fax 231038, email emegre@zanzibar.org).

TANZANIA

All of these places can arrange fishing or diving and snorkelling trips. Most of them also include airfield transfers in their prices; verify when booking.

Getting There & Away

Air Dar Aviation (☎ 051-844095 in Dar es Salaam, 0811-406766) flies three times weekly between Dar es Salaam and Mafia Island (US$90 one way). Precision Air has flights four times weekly between Dar es Salaam and Mafia via Unguja (US$50), with connections to Arusha (US$180 between Arusha and Mafia). Kinasi Ltd (☎ 051-843501 in Dar es Salaam) provides an air charter service between Dar es Salaam and Mafia for guests of Kinasi Lodge.

Boat Dhows go to Mafia from numerous points along the coast, including Kisiju, about 45km south-east of Mkuranga off the Dar es Salaam to Kilwa road, and Nyamisati, about 45km south-east of Bungu, also off the Dar es Salaam-Kilwa road.

Getting Around

There's no regular public transport on Mafia. All the more expensive hotels arrange airfield pick-ups for their guests. Budget travellers can contact Mama Shirazi at Lizu's (see Places to Stay & Eat earlier) for assistance.

SELOUS GAME RESERVE

With an area of approximately 50,000 sq km, the Selous is Africa's largest game reserve and covers 5% of Tanzania's total land area. The reserve provides shelter for more than half of the country's elephants, as well as significant populations of buffalos, wild dogs, crocodiles and hippos, a rich variety of birdlife, and some of Tanzania's last remaining black rhinos.

One of the main features of the Selous is the huge **Rufiji River**, which has one of the largest water catchment areas in East Africa. In the northern end of the reserve, where the Great Ruaha River flows into the Rufiji, is **Stiegler's Gorge** (averaging 100m deep), named after a German explorer who was killed here by an elephant in 1907. Most of the safari camps and lodges are in this area.

Information

The entry fee for Selous is US$20 (US$5 for children between five and 15, free for children under five), plus a US$30 per day vehicle fee. Camping fees are US$20 per person (US$15 for children between five and 15, free for children under five).

The best times to visit are from June to October and January to February. Much of the reserve is inaccessible from late February to May during the heavy rains. The tourist camps close for at least part of this time, usually during April and May.

The booklet *Selous Game Reserve: A Guide to the Northern Sector* by Dr Rolf Baldus and put out by the Selous Conservation Program, is an great source of background information. It's available at bookshops in Arusha and Dar es Salaam, or from the Wildlife Division in Dar es Salaam. An expanded, updated version was due early in 2000.

In addition to wildlife drives, boat trips up the Rufiji River are offered by most of the camps; guided walking tours can also be arranged.

Places to Stay

All of the reserve's facilities are concentrated in the extreme northern end. There is a *camp site* close to Matambwe at the Beho Beho Bridge. You'll need to bring everything with you, including camping equipment, food and water.

Beho Beho Safari Camp on the Beho Beho River has accommodation in stone bandas for US$300 per person, all inclusive. Book through Oyster Bay Hotel (☎ 051-668062, fax 668631, email oysterbay-hotel@ twiga.com) PO Box 2261, Dar es Salaam.

The exclusive ***Mbuyuni Luxury Tented Camp*** on the Rufiji River charges US$275 per person, including full board. Book through Selous Safari Company (☎ 051-34802, fax 112794, email selous@twiga .com) PO Box 1192, Dar es Salaam.

Sand Rivers Selous (☎ 02-288 2521, fax 288 2728, email sand-rivers@twiga.com, PO Box 24133, Nairobi) also on the Rufiji River has accommodation in luxury cottages for US$365 per person sharing, in-

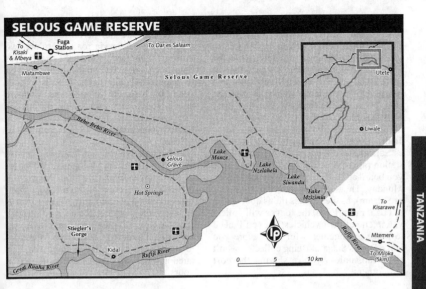

SELOUS GAME RESERVE

TANZANIA

cluding full board. Book directly or through a Dar es Salaam travel agent.

Rufiji River Camp also on the Rufiji has accommodation in luxury tents for US$230 per person, including full board. Book through Hippo Tours & Safaris (☎ 051-36860, fax 75165) PO Box 1658, Dar es Salaam; or through other Dar es Salaam tour operators.

Mbuyu Safari Camp on a tributary of the Rufiji with good views over the river has luxury tented accommodation for US$235 per person, including full board. Book through Southern Tanganyika Game Safaris & Tours (☎ 0812-781971, fax 051-111139, email stgs@twiga.com) PO Box 2341, Dar es Salaam.

All of the above prices include wildlife drives, boat trips or walking safaris. Less expensive accommodation-only prices are also available.

The new *Sable Mountain Lodge* about 10km from Kisaki on the north-western boundary of the Selous and just outside the reserve gate was just about to open at the time of research, and will be a good alternative if you're looking for something more affordable. Comfortable en suite accommo-dation costs US$85 per person per night, in-cluding full board; wildlife drives are US$25/45 per half/full day (minimum two people). Walking safaris and night wildlife drives can also be arranged, as can pick-ups from the airstrip and train station (disembark at Kisaki station, rather than Fuga). For foot safaris, you'll be able to save on entry fees, as they can be done outside the reserve gate in an adjacent area where there is still plenty of wildlife to see. Book through A Tent with a View Safaris (☎ 0811-323318, fax 051-151106, email tentview@intafrica.com).

Getting There & Away
Air Coastal Travels has daily flights to the Selous from Dar es Salaam (US$120) and Unguja (US$120), and three times weekly between the Selous and Ruaha National Park (US$270). All of the lodges arrange airfield transfers.

Bus & Minibus A minibus leaves daily at about 6 am from Dar es Salaam's Temeke bus stand to Mloka, about 10km from Mte-mere (TSh 3500, eight to nine hours). From Mloka, you can usually find a ride with a vehicle from the reserve for the remainder of the trip. Heading back to Dar es Salaam, buses depart Mloka between 5 and 6 am. There's no accommodation in Mloka, so you'll have to arrange something with the villagers. Before arriving, contact the reserve in advance to be sure there will be a rental vehicle available when you reach the gate. Trying to hitch a ride within the Selous isn't feasible.

Train To reach the Selous by train from Dar es Salaam, take the TAZARA line to Fuga station (approximately five hours). Be sure you board an 'ordinary' train (departures on Monday, Thursday and Saturday from Dar es Salaam), as the express trains do not stop at Fuga. From Fuga, the lodges will collect you in one of their vehicles, but you'll need to make arrangements for this before you leave Dar es Salaam. Being collected won't be cheap, unless you're sharing the cost with others.

Road You must have a 4WD in the Selous; motorcycles are not permitted in the reserve. To get here via road, there are two options. The first is to take the Dar es Salaam-Mkongo road via Kibiti and then on to Mtemere (250km). The road is in poor condition between Mkongo and Mtemere and is sometimes impassable during the rainy season. The last petrol station is in Kibiti. Allow about eight hours from Dar es Salaam.

Alternatively, you can go from Dar es Salaam to Kisaki via Morogoro and then on to Matambwe (350km). From Morogoro, drive in the direction of the teachers training college and then turn right towards Kisaki via a steep but scenic road through the Uluguru Mountains. The previously very rough stretch of road from Morogoro to Kisaki via Matombo is being rehabilitated and the trip now takes less than four hours.

Uganda

Uganda is one of the most beautiful countries in Africa, with fantastic natural scenery, half the world's remaining mountain gorilla population and some of the friendliest people you could hope to meet. However, Uganda's long string of tragedies since independence in 1962 has featured in the western media to such an extent that most people probably still regard the country as dangerously unstable and to be avoided.

The reality is vastly different. Stability has returned to most parts of the country. Kampala has returned to normal and is now the modern, bustling capital of Uganda with one of the fastest growing economies on the continent – the change has been quite astounding.

Before independence Uganda was a prosperous and cohesive country. Its great beauty led Winston Churchill to refer to it

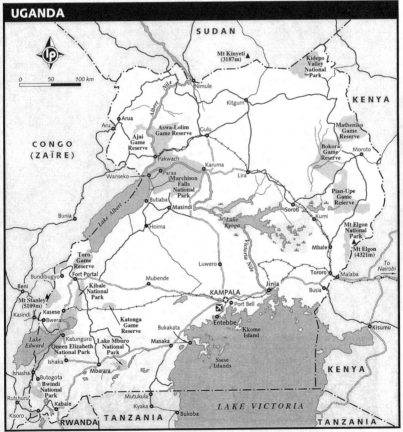

as the 'Pearl of Africa', but by early 1986 Uganda lay shattered and bankrupt, broken by tribal animosity, nepotism, military tyranny and politicians who had gone mad on power.

Yet despite the killings and disappearances, the brutality, fear and destruction of the past, Ugandans appear to have weathered the storm remarkably well. You will not meet a sullen, bitter or cowed people. Rather, though hard to believe, they are a smiling and friendly people with an openness absent in other places.

For the traveller, all this means that Uganda is a safe and friendly country to visit, although it is wise to take care when travelling in the north-east and in regions bordering Congo (Zaïre) and Rwanda.

The natural attractions are among the best in the region, and as tourism is still being re-established, you don't get the crowds found elsewhere.

It's a beautiful country with a great deal to offer, and sooner or later the tourist hordes will 'discover' it – make sure you get there before they do.

Facts about Uganda

HISTORY
For the story on Uganda's history in the years before independence, see the Facts about East Africa chapter.

Independence
Unlike Kenya and, to a lesser extent, Tanzania, Uganda never experienced a large influx of European settlers and the associated expropriation of land. Instead, tribespeople were encouraged to grow cash crops for export through their own cooperative groups. As a result, nationalist organisations sprouted much later than those in neighbouring countries, and when they did, it was on a tribal basis. So exclusive were some of these that when independence began to be discussed, the Buganda people even considered secession. By the mid-1950s, however, a Lango schoolteacher, Dr Milton Obote, managed to put together a loose coalition headed by the Uganda People's Congress (UCP), which led Uganda to independence in 1962 on the promise that the Buganda would have autonomy. The *kabaka* (king) was the new nation's president and Milton Obote was its prime minister.

It wasn't a particularly favourable time for Uganda to come to grips with independence. Civil wars were raging in neighbouring southern Sudan, Congo (Zaïre) and Rwanda, and refugees streamed into Uganda, adding to its problems. Also, it soon became obvious that Obote had no intention of sharing power with the kabaka. It meant that a confrontation was inevitable.

Obote moved fast, arresting several cabinet ministers and ordering his army chief of staff, Idi Amin, to storm the kabaka's palace. The raid resulted in the flight of the kabaka and his exile in London, where he died in 1969. Following this coup, Obote had himself made president, and the Bugandan monarchy was abolished, along with those of the kingdoms of Bunyoro, Ankole, Toro and Busoga. At the same time, Idi Amin's star was on the rise.

The Amin Years
Events started to go seriously wrong after that. Obote had his attorney general, Godfrey Binaisa (a Bugandan), rewrite the constitution to consolidate virtually all powers in the presidency. He then began to nationalise foreign assets.

In 1969 a scandal broke out over US$5 million in funds and weapons allocated to the Ministry of Defence that weren't accounted

UGANDA

for. An explanation was demanded from Amin. When it wasn't forthcoming, his deputy, Colonel Okoya, and some junior officers demanded his resignation. Shortly afterwards Okoya and his wife were shot dead in their Gulu home and rumours began to circulate about Amin's imminent arrest. It never came. Instead, when Obote left for Singapore in January 1971 to attend the Commonwealth Heads of Government Meeting (CHOGM), Amin staged a coup. The British, who had probably suffered most from Obote's nationalisation program, were among the first to recognise the new regime. Obote went into exile in Tanzania.

So began Uganda's first reign of terror. All political activities were quickly suspended and the army was empowered to shoot on sight anyone suspected of opposition to the regime. Over the next eight years an estimated 300,000 Ugandans lost their lives, often in horrifying ways: bludgeoned to death with sledgehammers and iron bars or tortured to death in prisons and police stations all over the country. Nile Mansions, next to the Conference Centre in Kampala, became particularly notorious. The screams of those who were being tortured or beaten to death there could often be heard around the clock for days on end. Prime targets of Amin's death squads were the Acholi and Lango tribes, who were decimated in waves of massacres. Whole villages were wiped out. Next, Amin turned on the professional classes; university professors and lecturers, doctors, cabinet ministers, lawyers, businesspeople and even military officers who might have posed a threat to Amin were dragged from their offices and shot or simply never seen again.

Also a target was the 70,000-strong Asian community. In 1972 they were given 90 days to leave the country with virtually nothing but the clothes they wore. Amin and his cronies grabbed the US$1000 million booty they were forced to leave behind and quickly squandered it on new toys for the army and frivolous luxury items. Amin then turned on the British and nationalised, without compensation, US$500 million worth of investments in tea plantations and other industries. Again the booty was squandered.

Meanwhile, the economy collapsed, industrial activity ground to a halt, hospitals and rural health clinics closed, roads cracked and became riddled with potholes, cities became garbage dumps and utilities fell apart. The prolific wildlife was machine-gunned by soldiers for meat, ivory and skins, and the tourist industry evaporated. The stream of refugees across the border became a flood.

Faced with chaos and an inflation rate that hit 1000%, Amin was forced to delegate more and more powers to the provincial governors, who became virtual warlords in their areas. Towards the end, the treasury was so bereft of funds that it was unable to pay the soldiers. At the same time, international condemnation of the sordid regime was strengthening daily as more and more news of massacres, torture and summary executions leaked out of the country.

About the only source of support for Amin at this time was Libya, under the increasingly idiosyncratic leadership of Colonel Gaddafi. Libya bailed out the Ugandan economy, supposedly in the name of Islamic brotherhood (Amin had conveniently become a Muslim by this stage), and began an intensive drive to equip the Ugandan forces with sophisticated weapons.

The rot had spread too far, however, and was way past the point where it could be arrested by a few million dollars in Libyan largesse. Faced with a restless army in which intertribal fighting had broken out, Amin was forced to seek a diversion. He chose a war with Tanzania, ostensibly to teach that country a lesson for supporting anti-Amin dissidents. It was his last major act of insanity and in it lay his downfall.

Post-Amin Chaos

On 30 October 1978 the Ugandan army rolled across north-western Tanzania virtually unopposed and annexed more than 1200 sq km of territory. Meanwhile, the air force bombed the Lake Victoria ports of Bukoba and Musoma. President Julius Nyerere ordered a full-scale counterattack, but it took months to mobilise his ill-equipped and poorly trained forces. By the following spring, however, he had managed to scrape together a 50,000-strong people's militia composed mainly of illiterate youngsters from the bush. This militia joined with the many exiled Ugandan liberation groups (united only in their determination to rid Uganda of Amin). The two armies met. East Africa's supposedly best equipped and best trained army threw down its weapons and fled and the Tanzanians pushed on into the heart of Uganda. Kampala fell without a fight, and by the end of April, organised resistance had effectively ceased. Amin fled to Libya, where he remained until Gaddafi threw him out following a shoot-out with Libyan soldiers. He now lives in Jeddah on a Saudi Arabian pension.

The Tanzanian action was criticised, somewhat half-heartedly, by the Organisation for African Unity (OAU), but it's probably true to say that most African countries breathed a sigh of relief to see the madman finally thrown out. All the same, Tanzania was forced to foot the entire war bill, estimated at US$500 million. This was a crushing blow for an already desperately poor country. No other country has ever made a contribution.

The rejoicing in Uganda was short-lived. The 12,000 or so Tanzanian soldiers who remained in the country, supposedly to assist with reconstruction and to maintain law and order, turned on the Ugandans as soon as their pay wasn't forthcoming. They took what they wanted from shops at gunpoint, hijacked trucks arriving from Kenya with international relief aid and slaughtered more wildlife.

Once again the country slid into chaos and gangs of armed bandits roamed the cities, killing and looting. Food supplies ran out and hospitals could no longer function. Nevertheless, thousands of exiled Ugandans began to answer the new president's call to return home and help with reconstruction.

Usefu Lule, a modest and unambitious man, was installed as president with Nyerere's blessing, but when he began speaking out against Nyerere, he was replaced by Godfrey Binaisa in Kampala, sparking riots supporting Lule in Kampala. Meanwhile, Obote bided his time in Dar es Salaam.

Binaisa quickly came under pressure to set a date for a general election and a return to civilian rule. Although this was done, he found himself at odds with other powerful members of the provisional government on ideological, constitutional and personal grounds – particularly over his insistence that the pre-Amin political parties not be allowed to contest the election.

The strongest criticism came from two senior members of the army, Tito Okello and David Ojok, both Obote supporters. Fearing a coup, Binaisa attempted to dismiss Ojok, who refused to step down and instead placed Binaisa under house arrest. The government was taken over by a military commission, which set the election for later that year. Obote returned from exile to an enthusiastic welcome in many parts of the country and swept to victory in an election that was blatantly rigged. Binaisa went into exile in the USA.

The honeymoon with Obote proved to be relatively short. Like Amin, Obote favoured certain tribes. Large numbers of civil servants and army and police commanders belonging to the tribes of the south were replaced with Obote supporters belonging to the tribes of the north. The State Research Bureau, a euphemism for the secret police, was re-established and the prisons began to fill once more. Obote was about to complete the destruction that Amin initiated. More and more reports of atrocities and killings leaked out of the country. Mass graves were unearthed that were unrelated to the Amin era. The press was muzzled and western journalists were expelled. It was obvious that Obote was once again attempting to achieve absolute power. Intertribal tension was on the rise, and in mid-1985 Obote was overthrown in a coup staged by the army under the leadership of Tito Okello.

The NRA Takeover

Okello was not the only opponent of Obote. Shortly after Obote became president for the second time, a guerrilla army opposed to his tribally biased government was formed in western Uganda. It was led by Yoweri Museveni, who had lived in exile in

Tanzania during Amin's reign and who had served as defence minister during the chaotic administrations of 1979 and 1980.

From a group of 27 grew a guerrilla force of about 20,000, many of them orphaned teenagers. In the early days, few gave the guerrillas, known as the National Resistance Army (NRA), much of a chance. Government troops made frequently murderous swoops across the Luwero Triangle (Museveni's original base), and artillery supplied by North Korea pounded areas where the guerrillas were thought to be hiding. Few people outside Uganda even knew of the existence of the NRA, due to Obote's success in muzzling the press and expelling journalists. At times it seemed that Museveni might give up the battle – he spent several months in London at one point – but his dedicated young lieutenants kept fighting.

The NRA was not a bunch of drunken thugs like Amin's and Obote's armies. New recruits were indoctrinated in the bush by political commissars and taught that they had to be the servants of the people, not their oppressors. Discipline was tough. Anyone who got badly out of line was executed. Museveni was determined that the army would never again disgrace Uganda. Also, a central thrust of the NRA was to win the hearts and minds of the people, who learnt to identify totally with the persecuted Bugandans in the infamous Luwero Triangle.

By the time Obote was ousted and Okello had taken over, the NRA controlled a large slice of western Uganda and was a power to be reckoned with. Recognising this, Okello attempted to arrange a truce so that the leaders from both sides could negotiate on sharing power. However, peace talks in Nairobi failed. Wisely, Museveni didn't trust a man who had been one of Obote's closest military aides for more than 15 years. Neither did he trust Okello's prime minister, Paulo Mwanga, who was formerly Obote's vice president and minister of defence. Also, Okello's army was notorious for its lack of discipline and brutality. Units of Amin's former army had even returned from exile in Congo (Zaïre) and Sudan, and joined with Okello.

What Museveni wanted was a clean sweep of the administration, the army and the police. He wanted corruption stamped out and those who had been involved in atrocities during the Amin and Obote regimes brought to trial. These demands were, of course, anathema to Okello, who was up to his neck in corruption and responsible for many atrocities.

The fighting continued in earnest, and by late January 1986 it was obvious that Okello's days were numbered. The surrender of 1600 government soldiers holed up in their barracks in the southern town of Mbarara, which was controlled by the NRA, brought the NRA to the outskirts of Kampala itself. With the morale of the government troops at a low ebb, the NRA launched an all-out offensive to take the capital. Okello's troops fled, almost without a fight, though not before looting whatever remained and carting it away in commandeered buses. It was a typical parting gesture, as was the gratuitous shooting-up of many Kampala high-rise offices.

During the following weeks, Okello's rabble were pursued and finally pushed north over the border into Sudan. The civil war was over, apart from a few mopping-up operations in the extreme north-west and in Karimoja Province. The long nightmare had finally ended.

Rebuilding

Despite Museveni's Marxist leanings (he had studied political science at Dar es Salaam University in the early 1970s and trained with the anti-Portuguese guerrillas in Mozambique), he has proved to be pragmatic since taking control. Despite the radical stand of many of his officers on certain issues, he appointed several arch-conservatives to his cabinet and made an effort to reassure the country's influential Catholic community.

In the late 1980s, peace agreements were negotiated with most of the guerrilla factions who had fought for Okello or Obote and were still active in the north and northeast. Under an amnesty offered to the rebels, as many as 40,000 had surrendered by 1988, and many were given jobs in the

NRA. In the north-west of the country, almost 300,000 Ugandans returned home from across the Sudanese border.

With the peace came optimism – services were restored, factories that had lain idle for years were again productive, agriculture was back on line, the main roads were resurfaced and the national parks' infrastructure was restored and revitalised. On the political front, all political parties were banned.

There was, however, still one thorn in Museveni's side: the refugee problem from neighbouring Rwanda. Western Uganda was saddled with some 250,000 Tutsi refugees who had fled Rwanda's intermittent tribal conflicts, and feeding and housing them was a severe drain on Ugandan resources. On several occasions Museveni tried hard to persuade Rwanda's President Habyarimana to set up a repatriation scheme, but to no avail. It seems Museveni's patience finally snapped, and in late 1990, Rwanda was invaded by a 5000-strong guerrilla force from western Uganda, which included NRA units and weaponry.

Evidence supports the contention that Museveni knew of preparations for the invasion, though he denies it. In any event, the rebels were thrown back across the border by the Rwandan army, assisted by troops from Belgium, France and Congo (Zaïre), and the ensuing witch-hunt of Tutsi inside Rwanda added to the number of refugees inside western Uganda. But the rebels were back in force shortly afterwards and by early 1993 were in control of around one-third of Rwanda, and finally came to power following the bloodbath of 1994.

The 1990s

The stability and rebuilding that came with President Museveni's coming to power in 1986 were followed in the 1990s with economic prosperity and unprecedented growth. For much of the decade, Uganda was the fastest growing economy in Africa, and has become a favourite among investors.

One of the keys to the success of the last few years was the decision to invite back the Asians who had been so unceremoniously evicted under Amin. As in Kenya, the Asians had a virtual monopoly on business and commerce. Without these people the economy was going nowhere fast, and it was clear to the pragmatic Museveni that Uganda needed them. They were, not surprisingly, very hesitant about returning, but assurances were given and kept, and property was and is still being given back to returned Asians or their descendants.

In 1993 a new draft constitution was adopted by the National Resistance Council (NRC). One surprising recommendation in the draft was that the country should adopt a system of 'no-party' politics for at least another five years, basically extending Museveni's National Resistance Movement (NRM) mandate for that period. However, given the potential for intertribal rivalry within a pluralist system, as history had shown, it was a sensible policy. Under the draft constitution, a Constituent Assembly was formed, and in 1994 elections for the assembly showed overwhelming support for the government. The only 'problem' area for the government was the north, where voters generally favoured anti-NRM candidates.

Also in 1993 the Bugandan monarchy was restored, but with no political power. This gave rise to concern among the Buganda that the existence of their tribal kingdom in the future would be threatened. In protest against the NRM government, they joined forces with the two main opposition groupings, former president Obote's Ugandan Peoples Congress (UPC) and the Democratic Party (DP), led by foreign affairs minister Dr Paulo Ssemogerere. In 1994 the Constituent Assembly voted to limit the kabaka's role to a purely ceremonial and traditional one.

Democratic 'no-party' elections were called for May 1996. Despite strong opposition from supporters of political parties the elections went ahead. The main candidates were Museveni and Ssemogerere, who had resigned as foreign minister in order to campaign. For all intents, it was still a party political election, between Museveni's NRM (officially a 'movement' and not a political party), and Ssemogerere, being supported by the former Democratic Party in alliance with the immensely unpopular (among the

UGANDA

Buganda) UPC. Museveni won a resounding victory, capturing almost 75% of the vote. The only area where Ssemogerere had any real support was in the anti-NRM north.

Uganda Today

Museveni's election carried with it great hope for the future, as many believed Uganda's success story could only improve with a genuine endorsement at the ballot box. However, Museveni's period as a democratically elected leader has been far less comfortable than his leadership period prior to the elections. The reasons for this are related to events both within Uganda and beyond its borders, in the civil wars of its neighbours. At home, one corruption scandal after another has blighted the administration, and while Museveni has maintained a clean pair of hands, some big heads have rolled in the meantime, including the president's half brother and former adviser, Salem Saleh. This has undermined the electorate's confidence in their government and given those calling for the formation of political parties new impetus in their drive for pluralism, as they argue it will lead to greater transparency in government.

And the debate about the formation of political parties has been dominating the agenda in the new parliament as the NRM seeks to delay a referendum on the issue, while proponents of pluralism argue that Uganda needs democracy. However, to drag the debate down to democracy, or a lack of it, is to misrepresent the situation, as the delicate balance of tribal representation in the NRM government has made it a lot more democratic than any previous Ugandan government, all of which have usually favoured one tribal group to the detriment of others.

The other dominant domestic concern has been the ongoing war against insurgents within the country. Both the Lord's Resistance Army (LRA) and the Allied Democratic Front (ADF) pose a threat to the people of Uganda. Supported by the Sudanese government in Khartoum, the LRA have been fighting a war in the north for well over a decade now, and have succeeded in nothing but killing villagers and brutalising children. The Ugandan army has largely succeeded in marginalising them in recent years, following the construction of a massive security fence along the border with Sudan that is regularly patrolled. And with Sudan slowly switching its arms and money to the ADF, it looks like time may be running out for the LRA.

Little is known about the ADF, who supports them and what they are fighting for. Rumours have linked them to Kinshasa and the Congo (Zaïre), but more likely their backing is coming from Sudan as the Khartoum government switches its allegiance away from the LRA. Like the LRA, one of their goals is an Islamic state, but this is more about securing guns and funds than a devotion to Allah. They have been waging a low intensity guerrilla war in and around the Ruwenzori Mountains for a number of years now. Their tactics are often brutal, and include decapitating victims and taking the heads back to bases in Congo (Zaïre).

It is not only these guerrilla outfits that destabilise Uganda's drive for development. The threat of the *Interahamwe*, the remnants of the Rwandan militia responsible for the 1994 genocide, remains very real, and exploded onto the world headlines when eight tourists were murdered in Bwindi National Park on 1 March 1999. These are desperate people with nowhere to go, and they will do whatever it takes to make their voice heard. There are currently anywhere between 1000 and 10,000 roaming around eastern Congo (Zaïre), depending whose estimates you believe, and their sole aim is to get back home and fight for a Hutu state. In the meantime they are content to make enemies of anyone who is perceived to stand in their way, including Uganda and its tourism industry. For more on the problem of the Interahamwe, see the boxed text 'The Interahamwe' in the Rwanda chapter.

However, it is not only internal instability that has undermined Uganda's determined drive for development – external instability has played its part as well. Uganda's time of growth and stability was matched only by a period of decline and conflict in some of the countries with which it shares borders. The genocide in Rwanda and Museveni's close association with Tutsi exiles resident in Uganda during the NRM war and subsequent period of rule, forced him to take sides in that conflict and this has had repercussions ever since. His former military commander Paul Kagame is now vice-president of Rwanda and the effective authority in that country. In allying himself with the Rwandan Patriotic Front (RPF), Museveni has tied the security of Uganda to the security of Rwanda and this has led him into war on more than one occasion for what are as much Rwanda's interests as Uganda's. Uganda found itself involved in a pan-African war ostensibly to ensure border security, but troops have since found themselves holed up in Kisangani, 700km from their borders, clashing with their Rwandan allies. For the full story on the mire that is Congo (Zaïre) and how it has affected both Uganda and Rwanda, see the boxed text 'Heart of Darkness' in the Facts about East Africa chapter.

The Future

Uganda is a country with much promise, but there are a number of tricky hurdles for it to overcome before it can fulfil its true potential. Firstly it needs to address the rampant corruption that is plaguing government, as this is rattling confidence among donors and the electorate, as well as choking development as earmarked funds disappear into deep pockets. This is already being addressed and Museveni seems very serious about stamping out malpractice in government, but it remains to be seen whether or not he can avoid alienating some influential individuals in government and the military in the process.

The debate about political parties looks set to dominate the domestic agenda for the next few years. The NRM are adamant that it is a bad idea to reintroduce parties at this stage as they argue it will simply turn back the clock to the bad old days when tribe was pitted against tribe. Proponents of democracy argue that the NRM have had long enough to run the country and that it is time to give parties a share in power. Whether or not multi-party politics returns to Uganda in

the near future very much depends on Museveni's personal ability to convince voters that it is too early to consider. However, at the same time, Uganda will no doubt be coming under international pressure to introduce a measure of democracy as donors seem to like a ballot or two here and there to legitimise their support of a particular government. What these same donors often fail to realise is that what works back home doesn't necessarily work in Africa. Western style democracy in areas bereft of western style nation states has wreaked havoc on politics in Africa, and in many ways Uganda's no-party system could serve as a model for the rest of the continent. However, the donors are the ones with the money so their will must eventually prevail, and of course, the donors are always right – as if Uganda could come up with a better solution than all the 'specialists'. If pluralism does return to Uganda, and it will probably have to eventually, it is to be hoped that a new generation of politicians brought up on the no-party system will form their parties based on policy not pedigree, although the sad truth is that lines will probably be drawn among tribes once again.

But real political stability is only possible if the government can bring to an end the insurgent campaigns within its borders and avoid costly and unnecessary involvement in events beyond its borders. If Uganda can negotiate a lasting peace with all its neighbours, that in turn should bring a rapid end to the capacity of rebel groups to destabilise the country. And with peace will come the biggest dividend of all – further development, and not just development for Kampala and the elite, but a genuine development in fields such as education and healthcare that takes the whole country forward together.

What is the greatest pity is that Uganda still has a massive image problem, as to most of the world it seems Uganda is synonymous with two things: Idi Amin and HIV/AIDS. Nevertheless, the future for Uganda and its people is brighter now than it has been for many, many years, if only those politicians can keep their egos under control.

UGANDA

UGANDA

GEOGRAPHY

Uganda has an area of 236,580 sq km, of which about 25% is fertile arable land capable of providing a surplus of food. Lake Victoria and the Victoria Nile, which flows through much of the country, together create one of the best-watered areas of Africa.

The land varies from semi-desert in the north-east to the lush and fertile shores of the lake, the Ruwenzori Mountains in the west and the beautiful, mountainous south-west.

The tropical heat is tempered by the altitude, which averages over 1000m.

CLIMATE

As most of Uganda is fairly flat, with mountains only in the extreme east (Mt Elgon), extreme west (the Ruwenzoris) and close to the Rwanda border, the bulk of the country enjoys the same tropical climate, with temperatures averaging about 26°C during the day and 16°C at night. The hottest months are from December to February, when the daytime range is 27 to 29°C.

The rainy seasons in the south are from April to May and October to November, the wettest month being April. In the north, the wet season is from April to October and the dry season is from November to March. During the wet seasons, the average rainfall is 175mm per month. Humidity is generally low outside the wet seasons.

ECOLOGY & ENVIRONMENT

With its relatively low population density and scarcity of wildlife (the latter courtesy of the decimation which occurred during the bad old days), Uganda lacks many of the environmental pressures faced by most other countries in the region. The absence of any notable numbers of tourists in the last 20 years means that the national parks and wilderness areas are generally in good shape, and conditions are ideal for the native wildlife to re-establish itself.

Uganda is therefore ideally placed to ensure that the environment remains in good condition. Programs are already in place for the responsible management of the national parks, and US Peace Corps volunteers can be found in most parks undertaking conser-

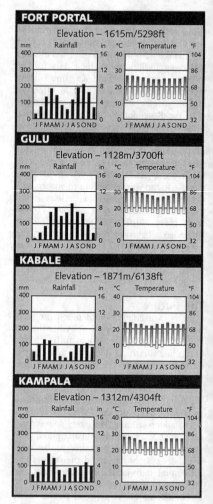

vation projects, such as building boardwalks and constructing walking paths.

Currently, the biggest environmental issues in Uganda are those of electricity supply and the dams required to fulfil demand, and the slow death of Lake Victoria, which must be urgently reversed as so many people depend on its resources for their livelihood. For more on the contentious issue of damming the Nile, see the boxed text 'Dammed if You Do, Damned if You Don't' in the Jinja section in the South-Eastern Uganda chapter. For the inside story on what's plaguing Lake Victoria, see the boxed text 'Water Hyacinth' in the Facts about East Africa chapter.

FAUNA

Uganda is home to more than half the world's mountain gorilla population, and viewing them in their natural environment is one of the most popular attractions for visitors to this country. For more information on these gentle creatures, their habitat, where to consider tracking them and the dos and don'ts once there see the special section 'The Mountain Gorillas of East Africa'.

Uganda is a fantastic country for birdlife, with more than 1000 species recorded in a country only the size of Britain. It is one of the best birding destinations in Africa (if not the world), and it is quite possible to see several hundred species during a two-week visit, with a keen eye, some binoculars and a field guide, of course. For birdwatchers coming to Uganda, the shoebill stork is one of the most sought after birds, but there are many other rare and interesting species to be seen throughout the country.

NATIONAL PARKS & RESERVES

Uganda's national parks and reserves are among the best in East Africa. While they may not be as stacked full of wildlife, neither are they as full of other visitors, which makes them very pleasant and relaxing places to visit. They also offer quite different experiences to those in neighbouring countries: viewing the mountain gorillas in Bwindi, the chimps in Kibale Forest, and the Nile's Murchison Falls are all highlights not to be missed.

While the low number of visitors is a great bonus, it's also a disadvantage in that the infrastructure in the parks is less developed – the luxury lodges and tented camps common in the parks of Kenya and Tanzania, for example, are few and far between here. Also, the organised safari options, especially for budget travellers, are much more limited. Despite this, many of the parks are relatively

easy to visit, and the rewards are ample for those who make the effort to get there.

Uganda Wildlife Authority (UWA; ☎ 041-346287, fax 346291, email uwahq@uol.co.ug) with its headquarters based just behind the Sheraton Hotel in Kampala, administers the national parks.

The UWA has a strict series of guidelines that should be observed by all visitors to the country's national parks:

- Do not camp or make campfires, except at official sites.
- Do not drive off the tracks.
- Do not disturb wildlife by sounding the car horn.
- Do not drive in the parks between 7.15 pm and 6.30 am.
- Do not bring dogs or other pets into the parks.
- Do not discard litter, burning cigarette ends or matches.
- Do not bring firearms or ammunition into the parks.
- Do not pick flowers or cut or destroy any vegetation.
- Do not exceed the parks' speed limit of 40km/h.

Overland trucks must pay particular attention to these rules, as ignoring them regularly has already led to trucks being banned from Queen Elizabeth National Park.

Park Fees

Uganda's park fees are fairly reasonable when compared with its bigger neighbours. However, it is the hidden extras that quickly add up and make visiting the national parks an expensive experience. Below are listed the fees that apply to all national parks; for more details on specific costs in individual national parks, see the relevant sections in other chapters. All prices are lower for Ugandan residents and much lower for Ugandan citizens.

Entry to Bwindi, Mgahinga, Murchison Falls and Queen Elizabeth costs US$15. For all other protected areas, the cost is US$7. For vehicles, a one-off entry payment is required. Motorcycles are charged US$20; minibuses, cars and pick-ups US$30; tour company vehicles US$100; and buses and trucks US$150. Transport hire within the parks is USh 2000 per kilometre for 4WDs, and USh 40,000 for the first hour on a boat (USh 15,000 for each additional hour).

However, separate prices apply for launch trips to Murchison Falls and along the Kazinga Channel in Queen Elizabeth. In the larger parks, rangers are available for wildlife drives and the charge is US$10 per vehicle for a half-day trip and US$15 for a full day.

Activities

See the Activities section in the Uganda Facts for the Visitor chapter for details of activities available in the various parks.

Accommodation

There is a wide range of accommodation available within Uganda's national parks, from simple camp sites with pit latrines and campfires, through *bandas* (thatched huts) with camp canteens to luxury tented camps and lodges with prices to match the facilities.

Camping in most national parks costs between USh 5000 and USh 10,000 per person per night, depending on facilities. Bandas are generally available for about USh 20,000 a double with shared facilities or USh 30,000

with bathroom. As for the luxury tented camps and lodges around Uganda, they charge anything from US$65 to US$200 per person per night full board, depending on the facilities and the time of year.

Accommodation charges do not include park entry fees, so many independent travellers opt to stay outside the national parks in nearby towns, guesthouses or camping grounds. Uganda Community Tourism Association (UCOTA) has a number of excellent community camping grounds around the country, including on the edges of Bwindi and Mgahinga and one at Kalinzu Forest near Queen Elizabeth National Park.

Access

Access is the big headache when it comes to visiting many of Uganda's protected areas. In order to visit many of the larger parks, it really helps to have your own vehicle, both for entry into the park and then exploring the park once inside. Even the smaller parks are not always easy to get to as transport to these remote, sparsely inhabited areas is irregular to say the least. Murchison Falls, Queen Elizabeth and Lake Mburo are all hard to reach and explore without transport, although with patience or good timing it can be done. Kidepo Valley and Bwindi are also tough to get to without transport, but once there, exploration is straightforward, Bwindi due to its size, and Kidepo Valley due to the fact that much of the wildlife is concentrated around the Apoka headquarters.

However, a number of the parks are much more simple to reach without your own transport and easily manageable on foot once there. These include Kibale Forest, Mgahinga and Mt Elgon.

In the long term, it is to be hoped that UWA wake up to the fact that they are losing revenue by not providing transport between park headquarters and nearby towns. It would not be that difficult to operate a daily shuttle between places like Masindi and Paraa (for Murchison Falls) and Katunguru and Mweya (for Queen Elizabeth) as there are park vehicles sitting idle in protected areas throughout Uganda.

UGANDA

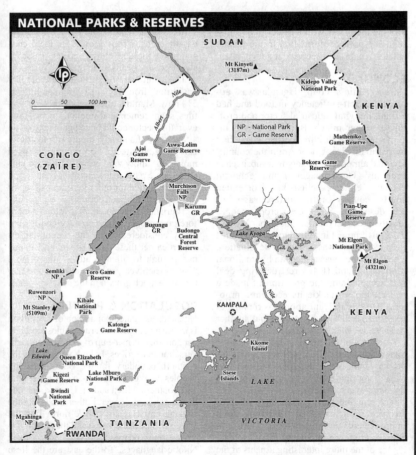

NATIONAL PARKS & RESERVES

SUDAN

Mt Kinyeti
(3187m)

Kidepo Valley
National Park

KENYA

NP - National Park
GR - Game Reserve

Matheniko
Game Reserve

CONGO
(ZAÏRE)

Ajai
Game
Reserve

Aswa-Lolim
Game Reserve

Nile

Albert

Bokora Game
Reserve

Murchison
Falls
NP

Karumu
GR

Pian-Upe
Game
Reserve

Bugungu
GR

Budongo
Central
Forest
Reserve

Lake Kyoga

Lake Albert

Mt Elgon
National Park

Semliki
NP

Toro Game
Reserve

Victoria

Mt Elgon
(4321m)

Nile

Ruwenzori
NP

Mt Stanley
(5109m)

Kibale
National
Park

KAMPALA

KENYA

Katonga
Game Reserve

Lake
Edward

Queen Elizabeth
National Park

Kkome
Island

Kigezi
Game Reserve

Lake Mburo
National Park

Ssese
Islands

LAKE

Bwindi
National
Park

Mgahinga
NP

RWANDA

TANZANIA

VICTORIA

UGANDA

GOVERNMENT & POLITICS

Uganda is a republic and a member of the Commonwealth. The president is head of state, the government and the armed forces. The governing 245-member Constituent Assembly has elected members, who, although standing as individuals, are affiliated with various political organisations (formerly parties), including the National Resistance Movement (NRM), the Uganda Patriotic Movement (UPM), Democratic Party (DP), Uganda People's Congress (UCP) and the Conservative Party. There are officially no political parties in the country, although this may change as there is a referendum on pluralism scheduled some time in the next few years. For the political history of Uganda since independence see the History section at the beginning of this chapter.

At the base of the NRM political administration are the local councils (formerly Resistance Committees), a village-based administration tool that is responsible for village matters. Council members can, in theory, be elected and pass through the system all the way to the Constituent Assembly. Apart from being a way to channel new faces into the political system, the councils provide the NRM with a direct line to disseminate policy information to the people and have improved security at a local level.

ECONOMY

Before Amin's coup, Uganda was approaching self-sufficiency in food and had a small but vital industrial sector and profitable copper mines. Boosting export income were the thriving coffee, sugar and tourist industries. Under Amin the country reverted almost completely to a subsistence economy. The managerial and technical elite was either expelled, killed or exiled and the country's infrastructure was virtually destroyed. Some cash crops made a tentative recovery under Obote, but Museveni's government inherited major problems.

In 1987 there was a massive devaluation, a new currency was issued, an International Monetary Fund (IMF) restructuring deal was accepted and the government made a real attempt to tackle its economic problems. Despite this, inflation was running at more than 100% within a year and another massive devaluation followed.

Uganda's problems stem from its almost total reliance on coffee, which accounts for the vast bulk of exports, plus the fact that 60% of foreign earnings is used to pay off the large overseas debt.

The remainder of the exchange reserves are spent on items aimed at bringing about improvements in the long term. Short-term benefits are few and poverty is widespread.

One of the more interesting aspects of the Ugandan economy is the barter system, whereby the country makes deals with foreign trading partners, exchanging goods (usually coffee) for much-needed imports. So far it has struck deals with Algeria, Cuba, the Czech and Slovak republics, Germany, Italy, Libya, North Korea and Rwanda.

Despite the obvious problems, the Ugandan economy is finally taking off again, and with growth of 10% in 1995, was the fastest growing in Africa for much of the decade.

Agriculture is the single most important component of the Ugandan economy. It accounts for 70% of gross domestic product (GDP) and employs 90% of the workforce. Coffee, sugar, cotton and tea are the main export crops. Crops grown for local consumption include maize, millet, cassava, sweet potato, beans and cereals.

The manufacturing sector's share of GDP has shrunk from 12% in 1970 to as little as 5% now. Manufactured goods include textiles, soap, cement and steel products. However, this sector could once again take off in a few years if a steady supply of electricity can be guaranteed. Foreign aid is used mostly to supply vital imported fuel, to purchase spare parts to get factories back to full production, and for other measures to repair the economic infrastructure.

Tourism has the potential to attract a lot of foreign currency to the country and is generally considered to be the second-largest export earner these days. However, Uganda has enough to offer to attract many more visitors each year, so this could be one sector to see much growth in the next few years.

POPULATION & PEOPLE

Uganda's estimated population of 22 million is increasing at the rapid rate of close to 2.5% per annum. It is made up of a complex and diverse range of tribes. Lake Kyoga forms the northern boundary for the Bantu-speaking peoples, who dominate much of east, central and Southern Africa and, in Uganda, include the Buganda and several other tribes like the Basoga and Bagisu. In the north live the Lango (near Lake Kyoga) and the Acholi (towards the Sudanese border), who speak Nilotic languages. To the east are the Iteso and Karamajong, who are related to the Maasai and who also speak Nilotic languages. Pygmies live in the forests of the west.

For more information about Uganda's people, see the special section 'Tribal Groups & Cultures'.

EDUCATION

The most recent figures show that out of the 3.5 million children of school-going age, only 1.7 million attend the around 8000 primary schools, and 250,000 students attend around 1000 secondary, technical and teacher-training schools. The main higher education institutions are Makerere University and Uganda Technical College, both in Kampala.

In 1996 Museveni pledged that the government would set up a secondary school in each of the 838 subdistricts of Uganda. Free primary education for the first four children in each family was scheduled to be introduced with the new school year beginning in January 1997. Literacy in Uganda currently stands at 48%.

SOCIETY & CONDUCT

Ugandans are very polite and friendly people and will often greet strangers on public transport or in rural areas. This is not just a simple 'hello' but also 'How are you?' or 'How is your family?' and the interest is genuine. Hence, in social situations it is always best to inquire after the well-being of whomever you are introduced to, rather than just a curt hello. See Society & Conduct in the Facts about East Africa chapter for more information.

RELIGION

While about two-thirds of the population are Christian, the remaining one-third still practise animism (a belief in the power of the natural world), and there's a small percentage who follow Islam. There were sizeable numbers of Sikhs and Hindus in the country until Asians were expelled in 1972, and many are now returning following a presidential invitation.

LANGUAGE

The official language is English, which most people can speak. The other major languages are Luganda and Swahili, though the latter isn't spoken much east of Kampala or in the capital, as most Ugandans associate it with the bad old days of Idi Amin when he tried to make it the national language. See the Language chapter at the end of the book for some useful words and phrases in Swahili.

UGANDA

Facts for the Visitor

HIGHLIGHTS

Without a doubt the main highlight of a trip to Uganda is tracking the mountain gorillas in the south-western rainforests, either at Bwindi or Mgahinga national parks. However, this is not all Uganda has to offer: the national parks of Murchison Falls and Queen Elizabeth are both worth a visit for their natural attractions, and the chimpanzees at Kibale Forest National Park, near Fort Portal, are also a big draw.

For those who want a much more physical adventure, there's great trekking on Mt Elgon on the Kenyan border; the mountain offers a very affordable alternative to Kilimanjaro if your budget won't stretch that far. Sadly, the Ruwenzoris – the legendary 'mountains of the moon', on the western border with Congo (Zaïre) – have been closed for several years due to landmines and the presence of rebels in the area, and look set to remain off limits for some time. For real adventure seekers, the white-water rafting at the Source of the Nile has become an increasingly popular adrenaline buzz.

Away from the challenge of rivers and mountains (and the rigours of tough travel), Uganda has some excellent spots for rest and recuperation. Lake Bunyoni, near Kabale in the far south-west, is fast emerging as the most popular place to relax – you can canoe around its many islands or just soak up the breathtaking scenery. And the Ssese Islands in Lake Victoria have always been a great place to chill out for a few days and let time pass you by. Out in the east, Sipi Falls is another beautiful location to explore, with some stunning views across the plains below and the opportunity to explore the base of Mt Elgon.

SUGGESTED ITINERARIES

As Uganda is a fairly compact country with a reasonably good infrastructure, it is relatively easy for the visitor to see many of its attractions in just a couple of weeks. When planning, however, it is worth bearing in mind the hold that Kampala can have on you – it really is a very pleasant city. Many visitors end up hanging around the capital for weeks, soaking up the nightlife.

One Week

Visitors with just a week usually restrict themselves to a gorilla visit in the southwest, with the possible option of a day or two's rest afterwards at beautiful Lake Bunyoni, and a visit to one of Uganda's two largest game parks, Murchison Falls or Queen Elizabeth. Another option is to forget about the game parks and instead take on the raging white waters at the Source of the Nile, then relax in Jinja for a day or two.

With ten days, it is possible to take on the itinerary above and consider adding an extra activity such as chimpanzee viewing at Lake Victoria or in the forests of Kibale or Budongo.

Two Weeks

Two weeks allows ample time to see the many attractions to the south and west. With your own transport it is just about possible to visit Murchison Falls, Kibale Forest, Queen Elizabeth, Bwindi or Mgahinga, Lake Bunyoni and Lake Mburo; however, you might find you've had enough of national parks before you are halfway through.

Another option on a circuit of this sort would be to visit the laid-back Ssese Islands on Lake Victoria. Without transport, you are realistically going to have to miss a few places as two weeks doesn't allow enough time for endlessly sitting on the side of roads. However, Kibale Forest, Queen Elizabeth, Mgahinga or Bwindi and Lake Bunyoni or the Ssese Islands is a pretty straightforward plan.

Three Weeks

With three weeks at your disposal, it is possible to start looking east at a number of attractions towards the Kenyan border. Sipi Falls is a beautiful waterfall located in the foothills of Mt Elgon, with some stunning views of the plains below and a number of easy walks nearby. For those that prefer more energetic walks, there is the option of climbing Mt Elgon, usually a five day trek, but possible in four days if you want to push it.

PLANNING
When to Go
The best time for a visit to Uganda is January and February and June to September, as the weather during these months is generally dry.

Maps
The best available map of Uganda is the Macmillan 1:1,350,000 *Uganda Traveller's Map*, which is available in bookshops in Kampala (USh 7000). It also has insets of the Murchison Falls and Queen Elizabeth national parks, and a street map of Kampala. Macmillan also has a separate foldout map of Kampala.

RESPONSIBLE TOURISM
There have been numerous reports of illegal gorilla trekking during the past few years. When permits are selling like hot cakes, tourists have been known to cut corners by bribing rangers into multiple visits each day. This is not only illegal, but also potentially life-threatening to this highly endangered species – it increases their stress levels, which in turn decreases their resistance to disease. Do not attempt to track illegally as you will be contributing to the demise of the mountain gorilla. For more information on this subject, see the special section 'The Mountain Gorillas of East Africa' at the end of the Uganda chapter.

TOURIST OFFICES
The Ugandan Tourist Board (UTB, ☎ 041-342196, fax 342188, email utb@starcom.co.ug) is in the IPS building, near the UK High Commission on Parliament Ave. The office is open from 8 am to 1 pm and 2 to 5 pm weekdays, and from 8.30 am to 12.30 pm Saturday.

There's a Uganda Community Tourism Association (UCOTA, ☎ 041-269982) office

in the Uganda Wildlife Authority (UWA) compound near the Sheraton Hotel.

VISAS & DOCUMENTS
Visas
Most non-African passport holders visiting Uganda require visas. Three-month single entry tourist visas cost US$30. If you are a student, this visa costs US$20, so it is worth having your ID handy for the embassy or border guards. Six month multiple-entry visas cost US$80. Two photos are required and the visas are issued within 24 hours, or possibly on the same day if you ask the embassy staff nicely enough. Visas are available at the border on entry for the same fee, though you probably won't need a photo.

Immigration, either at the airport or border crossings, may give you less than three months but the visa is renewable. If you want to avoid the hassle of getting it extended, be clear about how much time you want to spend in Uganda and they may give you more time.

Visa Extensions For visa extensions, pay a visit to the immigration office, which is now located on Jinja Rd, on the right-hand side, 300m past the roundabout after Centenary Park.

Other Visas Kampala is a good place for picking up visas to other countries as there are usually no queues at the various embassies. See under Foreign Embassies in Uganda following for the addresses of the various embassies.

Burundi If you apply in the morning, Burundian visas can be issued the same day. A one-month single-entry visa costs US$40.

Congo (Zaïre) A single/multiple-entry visa costs USh 45,000/70,000 for one month, USh 80,000/105,000 for two months and USh 115,000/135,000 for three months. Two photos are required and the visa is issued in 24 hours. However, at the time of writing, the embassy was temporarily closed due to the war between Ugandan-backed rebels and the Kinshasa government in Congo (Zaïre). If you plan to visit Congo (Zaïre) – extremely unwise at the time of writing – and it is still under rebel control, visas can be arranged on the border, costing anything from US$35 in Bukavu to US$60 at Goma.

UGANDA

Ethiopia Visas take at least 24 hours to process, often longer depending on your nationality. Visa costs range from US$28 for Africans to US$63 for most other nationalities.

Kenya If you apply before noon, the visa can usually be issued the same day. The cost is US$30 and two photos are required.

Rwanda One month multiple-entry-and-exit visas cost US$50 (the same for all nationalities), require two photos and are issued the same day if you apply in the morning. There are also two week single-entry visas available at the border for US$35.

Sudan The Sudanese embassy in Kampala has been closed for years due to the ongoing feud between the two countries over support for rebel movements in each other's territory.

Tanzania Visas are valid for three months, take 24 hours to issue and require two photos. However, if you take the application in early enough in the morning, they should be able to process the visa by 3 pm. Costs vary according to your nationality: French, USh 25,000; German, USh 10,000; UK and USA, USh 60,000; others are around USh 10,000 to USh 20,000.

Driving Licence

If you have an international driving licence, then you should bring it (although you really only need your local driving licence from home).

EMBASSIES
Ugandan Embassies

There are Ugandan embassies in the following places:

Belgium (☎ 02-762 5825, fax 763 0438) Ave de Tervuren 317, 450 Brussels

Canada (☎ 613-233 7797, fax 232 6689) 231 Cobourg St, Ottawa, Ontario KIN 8J2

Congo (Zaïre) (☎ 22740) 17 Ave Tombalbaye/Ave de Travailure, Kinshasa (☎ 336) BP 877, Goma

Denmark (☎ 3962 0966) Sofievej 15, DK 2900, Hellerup

Egypt (☎ 091-348 5975, fax 348 5980) 9 Midan El Messaha, Dokki, Cairo

Ethiopia (☎ 01-513531, fax 514355) Africa Ave H-18, K-36, N-31, Addis Ababa

France (☎ 01 47 27 46 80, fax 01 47 55 12 21) 13 Ave Raymond Poincare, 75116 Paris

Italy (☎/fax 06-322 5220) Via Ennio Quirino Visconti 8, 00193 Rome

Japan (☎ 03-3465 4552, fax 3465 4970) 39-15 Oyama-chi, Shibuya-ku, Tokyo 151

Kenya (☎ 02-330801, fax 330970, email ugahinrb@users.africaonline.co.ke) 4th floor, Uganda House, Baring Arcade, Kenyatta Ave, Nairobi

Rwanda (☎ 07-76495, fax 73551) Ave de la Paix, Kigali

South Africa (☎ 012-344 4100, fax 343 2809) Trafalgar Court, Apt 35B, 634 Park St, Arcadia 0083, Pretoria

Tanzania (☎ 051-117646) 7th floor, Extelecoms House, Samora Ave, Dar es Salaam

UK (☎ 020-8839 5783, fax 8839 8925) Uganda House, 58/59 Trafalgar Square, London WC2N 5DX

USA (☎ 202-726 0416, fax 726 1727) 5909 16th St NW, Washington DC 20011-2896

Embassies in Uganda

Foreign embassies in Kampala include the following:

Burundi (☎ 233674, fax 250990) 9 Roscoe Drive, Kololo. Open from 9 am to 1 pm and 2 to 6 pm weekdays.

Congo (Zaïre) (☎ 233777) 20 Philip Rd, Kololo. Closed at the time of writing.

Ethiopia (☎ 341885, fax 348340) Plot 3L, off Kira Rd. Open from 8.30 am to 12.30 pm and 2 to 5.30 pm weekdays.

France (☎ 242120, fax 241252) 9 Parliament Ave

Italy (☎ 241786, fax 250448) 11 Lourdel Rd, Nakasero

Kenya (☎ 258235, fax 267369) Nakasero Rd. Open from 8.30 am to 12.30 pm and 2 to 4.30 pm weekdays.

Netherlands (☎ 231859, fax 231861) Kisozi Complex, Nakasero Lane

Rwanda (☎ 244045) Plot 2, Nakaima Rd (next door to the Uganda Museum). Open from 8.30 am to 12.30 pm and 2.30 to 5 pm weekdays.

South Africa (☎ 343560, fax 348216) Plot 2b, Nakasero Hill Lane

Sudan (☎ 243518) Plot 21, Nakasero Rd. Closed at the time of writing.

Tanzania (☎ 256272, fax 242890) 6 Kagera Rd. Open from 9 am to 4 pm weekdays.

UK (☎ 257301, fax 257304) 10 Parliament Ave

USA (☎ 346841, fax 346840) 10 Parliament Ave, rear of UK High Commission Bldg

MONEY
Currency

The Ugandan shilling (USh) is a relatively stable currency and floats against the US dollar. It is also fully convertible (ie, you can buy Ugandan shillings with US dollars or US dollars with Ugandan shillings) at banks and foreign exchange bureaus.

Notes in circulation are USh 10,000, USh 5000, USh 1000, USh 500, USh 200, USh 100 and USh 50. Coins were introduced in late 1998 to underpin the economic stability Uganda has struggled to achieve. Denominations include USh 50, USh 100, USh 200 and USh 500.

Exchange Rates

country	unit		shilling
Australia	A$1	=	USh 943
Canada	C$1	=	USh 1029
euro	€1	=	USh 1475
France	10FF	=	USh 2249
Germany	DM1	=	USh 754
Japan	¥100	=	USh 1346
New Zealand	NZ$1	=	USh 735
UK	UK£1	=	USh 2400
USA	US$1	=	USh 1492

Exchanging Money

Cash The Ugandan shilling trades at whatever it's worth against the US dollar/UK pound and there's usually little fluctuation from day to day. However, as currency speculators prey on emerging market after emerging market, this might change in the future. Small US bills attract a much lower rate of exchange than US$50 and US$100 notes, so unless you don't mind losing as much as 20% of your money in a transaction, come with large bills. Barclays Bank is worth remembering as the one bank that exchanges at the same rate for all bills.

There is no black market. As a result, it doesn't really matter too much where you change your money, though the foreign exchange bureaus generally offer a slightly better rate than the banks. The trouble is that not every town has a foreign exchange bureau and, where one doesn't exist, the banks take advantage of this by giving lousy rates. Likewise, hotels give bad rates. The best bank rates are available at Crane Bank, which is represented in Kampala and Jinja. Elsewhere, you are usually stuck with Uganda Commercial Bank as the only choice.

You will find foreign exchange bureaus at both the Malaba and Busia border crossings (Uganda-Kenya border), Fort Portal, Jinja, Kabale, Kampala, Kasese, Kisoro, Masaka, Mbale and Mbarara. Elsewhere, plan ahead so you don't get caught short.

Travellers Cheques Travellers cheques can generally be exchanged at most banks in Uganda, but not necessarily at the foreign exchange bureaus. Rates offered are generally slightly lower than those advertised for cash. It is also possible to buy US dollar travellers cheques from Barclays Bank in Kampala for a small fee.

ATMs Barclays Bank is set to upgrade its ATMs to accept international credit cards, but at the time of writing there were no ATMs for non-Ugandan bank cards.

Credit Cards For credit-card advances, your only realistic option is Barclays Bank in Kampala, although in a fix you might be able to persuade an upmarket hotel to give you a cash advance against your card.

International Transfers Money transfers are actually more straightforward than you might imagine, even in the provinces, but are an expensive way to get your hands on cash. Western Union is quite well represented in major towns throughout the country; Cerudeb (☎ 041-345571), PO Box 166, Kyotera, Kampala, is the main agent.

Costs

Since the elimination of the black market and the introduction of foreign exchange bureaus, Uganda is now one of the more expensive countries in the region. Obviously, there are many ways of keeping costs to a minimum, but if you demand a reasonable level of comfort and facilities, you'll find your Ugandan notes diminishing at an alarming rate.

A budget hotel will cost you around USh 5000 to USh 10,000 for a double room, usually with a shared bathroom. Transport is cheap, as is food at a no-frills restaurant, but a splurge at a good eatery will cost you around USh 15,000 plus. National park entry fees are set at US$7 to US$15 per person per day, while camping costs vary from

UGANDA

USh 5000 to USh 10,000 per person. Foreign residents of Uganda pay somewhat less, and local Ugandans pay less again.

The cost of seeing the gorillas in Bwindi National Park is the local equivalent of US$250. At Mgahinga it's US$175, but that is likely to have risen to US$250 by the time you read this.

POST & COMMUNICATIONS
Post
The cost of sending a postcard or aerogram is USh 500 to Europe, USh 600 elsewhere; for a letter it's USh 600 and USh 700 per 10g, respectively. There is an efficient poste restante service at the main post office in Kampala.

Provincial post offices are reasonably reliable, and with the EMS Post Bus servicing a number of provincial capitals, it often only takes a day more than from Kampala. For a list of towns serviced by the EMS Post Bus, see Getting There & Away in the Kampala chapter.

Telephone
Telephone connections, both domestic and international, are pretty good, although not so reliable in the provinces. The provincial network is slowly being digitised, but you'll still need patience and understanding in smaller towns.

In most towns you'll come across card phones (yellow phone boxes) outside the post office. The blue phones can be used for national and international calls, and cards are available from the post office.

From public phone boxes international calls are charged at the rate of USh 3000 to USh 4000 per minute, and the highest denomination phone card is 100 units, costing USh 13,500 – clearly you're not meant to talk for too long!

In Kampala, Jinja, Mbale and Mbarara there's a much more effective option, the private operator called Starcom, and it has offices and card phones (green boxes) around the capital. Its charge is USh 3000 for one minute and cards come in 75 units or 150 units, costing USh 9000 and USh 17,500 respectively.

The country code for Uganda is ☎ 256. To make an international call from Uganda, dial ☎ 000. Directory inquiries is ☎ 901.

Fax
Fax charges are relatively cheap, at USh 1500 per page when sending from the GPO in Kampala; with Starcom it's USh 2500.

Email & Internet Access
Email and Internet access is very simple in Kampala and there are even a few flourishing Internet cafes. Access usually costs about USh 150 per minute. Beyond the capital, options dry up fast, although with the onward march of technology it won't be long before it spreads to the provinces. Jinja is currently the only other place you can access the Internet, but it is expensive because it involves a call to Kampala.

Basic email services are also available in Kabale, Mbale and at some of the upmarket lodges in national parks.

BOOKS
There are not many books that relate specifically to Uganda, but the following may be of interest.

Guidebooks
The Uganda Tourist Board (UTB) has published several excellent books covering wildlife and national parks in the country. For keen birdwatchers, *Where to Watch Birds In Uganda*, by Jonathan Rossouw and Marco Sacchi, is an absolute must; it covers every major birding area in the country, with a rundown on what to look out for and where. The book has some excellent photographs of some of Uganda's more than 1000 bird species and some good maps of the country's national parks. UTB have also produced a thoroughly professional guide to Murchison Falls National Park, which is useful if you're thinking of spending more than just a couple of days there.

If you want a guidebook for the coffee table, once your trip is over, one worth picking up is the *Spectrum Guide to Uganda*. Published by a photographic agency based in Nairobi, the book has plenty of nice shots as well as some useful information, although it is sometimes scant on nuts and bolts.

For more information on field guides to the wildlife and birdlife of East Africa, see the Regional Facts for the Visitor chapter.

History & Politics

The Last King of Scotland, by Giles Foden, is a must for every visitor planning a trip to Uganda. This best seller (1998) chronicles the experience of Idi Amin's personal doctor, as he slowly finds himself becoming confidante to the dictator. It is very much based on a true story and affords the reader a number of quirky insights into life in Uganda under Amin.

Uganda – From the Pages of Drum is an interesting compilation of articles, which appeared in the now defunct *Drum* magazine. These chronicle the rise of Idi Amin, the atrocities he committed, as well as Museveni's bush war and his coming to power. It is complete with photos and forms a powerful record of what the country went through.

Uganda Since Independence, by Phares Mutibwa, and *Uganda – Landmarks in Rebuilding a Nation*, by various authors, are both fairly dry accounts of the country's recent history.

Fong & the Indians, by Paul Theroux, is set in a fictional East African country that bears a remarkable likeness to Uganda. It is set in pre-civil war days and is at times both funny and bizarre as it details the life of a Chinese immigrant and his dealings with the Asians who control commerce in the country.

The Man With the Key Has Gone!, by Ian Clarke, is a recent account of the time spent in Uganda's Luwero Triangle district by a British doctor and his family. It is a lively read and the title refers to a problem that many a traveller may encounter in the provinces.

NEWSPAPERS & MAGAZINES

The pavements in Kampala are awash with printed matter. The daily *New Vision* is the government-owned newspaper. Unlike its equivalent in Tanzania, it's a good read, with plenty of African coverage, though less of other world events.

Much better for gutsy, analytical journalism is the *Monitor*, a daily paper that contains feature articles as well as better coverage of international news. However, it does have a tendency to exaggerate domestic turmoil in a desire to distance itself from the government.

The Kenyan daily, *Nation*, is available in the late morning as far west as Jinja. Also available is the weekly *East African*, which offers some solid regional news. Another regional publication, which is particularly useful for gaining a better insight into the turmoil that has engulfed Uganda's neighbours, is *The Link*. This publication deals with issues of politics and business in the Great Lakes region.

International magazines like *Time, Newsweek, New African* and *South* are also readily available, but dailies are harder to find; try the shop at the Sheraton Hotel in Kampala, Ban Cafe in Kampala for a free read or at Entebbe airport.

RADIO & TV

The government-run TV station is Uganda Television. In Kampala there's also a commercial station, Sanyu TV.

Radio Uganda broadcasts in English and other languages on AM frequencies.

Kampala has two commercial FM stations: the phenomenally popular Capital FM (91.3 MHz) and Radio Sanyu (88.2 MHz); both play western pop music.

PHOTOGRAPHY & VIDEO
Film & Equipment

Colour print film is widely available in Kampala (less so elsewhere) at prices similar to what you pay in Kenya. Expect to pay around USh 5000 for a 36 exposure colour print film. Slide film is much harder to find – it's safer to bring your own. For a wide selection of film, including slide and black & white, try Colour Chrome on Kampala Rd. This is also a reliable place to get your films developed as they process all the rafting shots taken by Adrift. The Star Photo Studio on Wilson Rd, Kampala, is another good place to find both print and slide film at prices better than you can find elsewhere.

UGANDA

Technical Tips

If you are hoping to get decent shots of the gorillas, then you are going to need fast film, but not too fast as the pictures will come out grainy; the best bet is to use ASA 400. And likewise for the wildlife in national parks, as you tend to see the most animals at dawn or dusk when there isn't so much light.

Restrictions

Although there are no official restrictions on photography, there is a certain amount of paranoia about photos being taken of anything that could be interpreted as spying (military and civilian infrastructure) or of poverty or deprivation. Most of the time there are no problems, but you should always ask permission before taking photos of people.

TIME

Uganda's time is GMT/UTC plus three hours.

ELECTRICITY

Power in Uganda is supposed to be 220V AC, but all the power cuts, surges and switch overs to generators mean you should take great care when using valuable electrical equipment. In most parts of Uganda, power cuts are commonplace. Even in Kampala, most of the suburbs have to go without electricity every other day, and the problem is likely to get worse before it gets better.

Most power points in Uganda take 13-amp three-pin square plugs such as those used in the UK.

WEIGHTS & MEASURES

Uganda uses the metric system.

LAUNDRY

Laundry services are available at hotels, guesthouses and camp sites throughout Uganda. It usually costs around USh 400 an item, although at upmarket hotels it's more like US$1 per piece.

DANGERS & ANNOYANCES

Even now, more than 13 years on from Museveni's rise to power, Uganda still has a lingering image as a dangerous and unstable country to visit. This is a great shame, as it is currently one of the more stable and less corrupt countries in the region, and also one of the safest – in Kenya, for instance, there is a far higher incidence of mugging and petty theft, things that are almost unheard of in Kampala.

Having said that, there are still some places where your safety cannot be guaranteed and due to the ongoing conflicts in many of Uganda's neighbours, it is hard to set in stone exactly what is safe and what is not. The north has long had a reputation for instability and there have been numerous attacks on villages and roads throughout the region. Definitely check on local security conditions before attempting to make an overland trip to Kidepo Valley National Park.

Security has worsened in the west due to the presence of rebels from the Allied Democratic Front (ADF – one of the most misleading names they could have come up with) in the Ruwenzori and Semliki national parks. For the time being they seem only capable of wantonly killing villagers who inhabit these areas, but they have made a few idle threats about targeting tourists in the future. As long as both national parks remain officially closed, give the area a wide berth – this is particularly important with regard to the Ruwenzoris as landmines have been laid there by both sides. Kibale Forest and nearby Fort Portal are generally considered safe, although always double-check this in Kampala before heading out.

As for the south-west, it is hard to be certain about the status of security in the aftermath of the Bwindi massacre. Bwindi now has a large military presence to ensure visitors are kept safe; Mgahinga also has some military, although nowhere near the extent of Bwindi. Most parts of the south-west can be visited safely, but do check the latest conditions if you are planning on visiting remote border regions such as Ishasha in Queen Elizabeth National Park.

The most important thing to remember about security is that there is absolutely no substitute for researching current conditions when you enter the country. Read newspapers, ask other travellers and hostels for the latest and check again locally once you are in the provinces. Things can change very quickly in Africa, for the better or worse, and it pays to be well informed.

LEGAL MATTERS

Most travellers are very unlikely to end up having a brush with the law. However, it should be remembered that marijuana is against the law in Uganda, so if you are a smoker be discreet, and when in Kampala be careful who you buy it from.

BUSINESS HOURS

Businesses in Uganda generally open between 8.30 am and 5.30 pm, with a break for lunch some time between noon and 2 pm. Most shops and banks do not break for lunch, but most banks close early at 3.30 pm.

PUBLIC HOLIDAYS

The following public holidays are observed in Uganda:

New Year's Day 1 January
NRM Anniversary Day 26 January
Women's Day 8 March
Easter March/April – Good Friday, Holy
   Saturday and Easter Monday
Labour Day 1 May
Martyrs' Day 3 June
Heroes Day 9 June
Independence Day 9 October
Christmas Day 25 December
Boxing Day 26 December

ACTIVITIES
Gorilla Tracking

This is one of the major reasons travellers come to Uganda. It's possible to track the mountain gorillas in Bwindi (US$250) and Mgahinga (US$175) national parks in the south-west, although bookings should be made in Kampala first. For more information on gorilla tracking, see the South-Western Uganda section and the special section 'The Mountain Gorillas of East Africa' at the end of the Uganda chapter.

Chimpanzee Trekking

Primate treks are a very popular activity in Uganda and there are several places where chimpanzee viewing is possible. Most popular of these are Budongo Forest Reserve (part of Murchison Falls National Park) and Kibale National Park. The chance of seeing chimps at both these parks is very high, as good as 85%, although this means nothing to visitors who fall into the 15% category of no shows. It is best to set aside two days for chimpanzee treks so if you draw a blank on the first day, you can try again a second time.

Kyambura Gorge, part of Queen Elizabeth National Park, is another excellent place to trek chimps as the gorge is truly stunning. Sightings here are not as certain as at Budongo and Kibale but the walk itself is enchanting. Semliki Valley Game Reserve (or Toro Game Reserve) also had a chimp habituation project underway at the time of writing.

However, in order to guarantee seeing chimpanzees, the sanctuary on Ngamba Island, Lake Victoria (near Entebbe) is the place to go as the chimps live in a semi-tame, protected environment.

Guided Walks

Guided walks are offered in many of the forested national parks and a number of smaller forest reserves throughout Uganda. The most popular of these are the chimpanzee-viewing walks (see earlier for more information); however, there are also a variety of other forest walks available at Bwindi, Kibale Forest and Mgahinga national parks, offering an opportunity to view some of Uganda's many birds and monkeys.

Beyond the national parks, there are some excellent walking trails in smaller community reserves around the country, particularly at the Bigodi Wetland Sanctuary, near Fort Portal, as well as at Mabira and Mpanga forest reserves, which are both found around Kampala and easy day trips from the capital.

At Lake Mburo National Park it's possible to undertake a walking safari with an armed ranger and have close encounters with hippo, buffalo and herds of zebra, particularly around watering holes in the dry season.

Most guided walks cost US$5 per person in national parks, or cheaper in community forest reserves.

UGANDA

Launch Trips

There are two famous launch trips on offer in Uganda – the journey up the Victoria Nile to the base of Murchison Falls, and the cruise along the Kazinga Channel in Queen Elizabeth National Park. Both of these trips offer the opportunity of viewing, at close quarters, hundreds of hippo, buffalo and often a few elephant. Although it is often more common to see predators such as lion and leopard along the banks of the Kazinga Channel, the Murchison Falls trip is ultimately more spectacular – the falls themselves are awesome, and there is a reasonable chance that bird-watchers will spot the elusive shoebill stork (see the boxed text 'Stalking the Shoebill' in the Facts about Uganda chapter).

Mountain Climbing

The two main opportunities for mountain climbing in Uganda are the Ruwenzoris and Mt Elgon. The Ruwenzoris offer one of the most challenging mountain experiences in Africa, but unfortunately still remained closed to tourists at the time of writing due to the presence of rebels and landmines. However, Mt Elgon is an excellent mountain to climb, and somewhat easier than the Ruwenzoris. A five-day trek costs US$90, making it a very affordable option.

It is also possible to climb two of the three volcanoes at Mgahinga National Park – Mt Muhavura and Mt Gahinga. These are both day climbs and each costs US$30 per person. The views towards Rwanda and Congo (Zaïre) are spectacular.

Trekking

Uganda has always had a strong attraction among the dedicated trekking fraternity, mainly for the opportunities presented by the Ruwenzori Mountains in the west and Mt Elgon in the east. Both are national parks in pristine condition, although the Ruwenzoris are likely to remain closed for the foreseeable future; see the Uganda National Parks & Reserves chapter for more detailed information.

White-Water Rafting

Only in Uganda is it possible to raft the source of the mighty Nile River, and the water here is very big, with four Grade Five rapids waiting for the brave.

The trips are operated by two companies, Adrift and Nile River Explorers, and can be booked in Kampala (see that chapter). For all the juicy details on life on the river, see the White-Water Rafting in the Jinja section of the South-Eastern Uganda chapter.

Wildlife Drives

There are four national parks in Uganda that offer the opportunity for wildlife drives: Murchison Falls, Queen Elizabeth, Kidepo Valley and Lake Mburo. The greatest variety of wildlife is to be seen on a drive through Queen Elizabeth as it has the largest number of species of any park in Uganda; however, Murchison Falls, north of the Nile, has a good selection of wildlife. At both these parks, you should see elephant, buffalo, bushbuck and kob; and although it's not so easy to spot predators, with a bit of luck you might also see lion and leopard.

In Kidepo Valley, much of the wildlife is found within a short walking distance of the Apoka rest camp, so organised wildlife drives aren't so necessary. However, to have an opportunity of spotting cheetah or giraffe, you may need to venture farther afield.

As Lake Mburo is the only savanna environment in Uganda where you can undertake guided walks with an armed ranger, many people don't bother with wildlife drives. It's also usually possible to see the large herds of zebra, for which it is famous, as you drive into the park.

Sport Fishing

The Victoria Nile is a favoured habitat of the massive Nile perch, some weighing more than 100kg. Sport fishing permits are available for US$50 per day.

Caving

For information on caving near Mgahinga National Park, see the South-Western Uganda chapter.

WORK

It is not that easy for the casual tourist to pick up work in Uganda, especially as the popular money-earner, English teaching, is not much in demand. There are plenty of nongovernmental organisations in Uganda, but most of these recruit highly skilled locals or professionals from their base countries. The one possibility for work in Uganda is in the tourism sector, particularly if tourism continues to grow; however, the jobs will still be few and far between, so it's probably best to save your CV for somewhere else.

ACCOMMODATION
Camping
There are enough opportunities for camping in Uganda that it's worth considering carrying a tent. There are a few private camp sites but most are found in the national parks, and the facilities are basic. The cost of camping is usually between USh 5000 and USh 10,000 per person per day, plus the national park entry fee (from US$7 to US$15 per person per day). When it comes to camping at some of the smaller national parks, it is possible to use camping grounds just outside the park boundaries, thus saving on the park entry fee.

Hotels
Hotels range from the fleapit to the five star, although at the moment the former far outnumber the latter. As tourism and commerce pick up, so does the construction of new hotels and lodges. Currently, upmarket hotels are limited to Kampala; elsewhere the best you'll find are no more than about three-star quality.

The same applies to the lodges in the national parks – this is not Kenya. Again, things are gradually improving, and a number of sophisticated operations have opened their doors (or tent flaps) for business.

At the other end of the scale, you can count on all small towns having at least one basic lodge. These are cheap but you'll need a fairly strong constitution.

FOOD
Local food is much the same as what you find in Kenya, except that in Uganda *ugali* (maize meal) is called *posho*, and is far less popular than *matoke* (mashed plantains).

Fastfood is not well entrenched in the country, so away from the relatively cosmopolitan Kampala, you'll only have the choice of good, cheap local food, or expensive western food from the upmarket hotels and lodges.

Vegetarians will find themselves reasonably well catered for, although as most local dishes are meat-based there is little choice – posho and matoke and the occasional Indian dishes are about the limit.

DRINKS
Nonalcoholic Drinks
Soft drinks (sodas) are everywhere, the most popular being Fanta, Pepsi and Coca-Cola (ho hum). Prices range from USh 400 in local stores to about USh 1000 in decent restaurants.

Alcoholic Drinks
Like all East Africans, Ugandans love their beer, and mercifully, unlike their counterparts in Kenya, they don't have a fetish for drinking the stuff warm – if a town has electricity you can be sure it will have a fridge, and this will have beer in it!

Uganda Breweries and Nile Breweries are the two local companies, and they produce similar, unexciting but quite drinkable lagers. Bell is a light beer and renowned for its 'Great night, good morning' advertising campaign. Nile Special is substantially stronger at 5.6% and known for its irritating radio jingles that dominate the airwaves of local stations. For the brave or stupid, there is also Chairman's ESB, a potent brew at 7.2%. You'll also find South African Castle beer, which is brewed locally.

Bottled local beer costs from USh 1000 to USh 2000 a bottle, depending on where you're drinking. Imported beers are available in Kampala but are more expensive than the local juice.

Waragi is the local millet-based alcohol and is relatively safe, although it can knock you around and give you a mean hangover. It is a little like gin and goes down well with a splash of tonic. In its undistilled form, it is known as *kasezi bong* and would probably send you blind if you drank enough of it.

ENTERTAINMENT

Nightlife in Uganda is fairly low-key, with Kampala, the rocking capital, being the one exception. In Kampala there are nightclubs and discos, some of which have live music. Many of them rage on well into the night, and Al's Bar (see Entertainment in the Kampala chapter) will generally stay open until daybreak every night. Kampala is also the place to find a cinema or two.

Away from the capital, things are much quieter. You'll always be able to find somewhere to have a drink in the evening, but there's very little action. The larger provincial towns usually have a disco, but these are more about drinking than dancing, or drinking then trying to dance.

SPECTATOR SPORTS

The most popular sport in Uganda, as in most of Africa, is football and it is possible to watch regular matches at the Nakivubo Stadium, opposite the new taxi park in Kampala. There is a domestic league with matches held most weekends, and every month or so there's an international game involving Uganda's national team, 'The Kobs'.

Boxing is also quite popular in Uganda and bouts are occasionally held in Kampala, although nothing like the 'Rumble in the Jungle' in Kinshasa back in 1974.

Rallying is another popular spectator sport and several East African rallies include Uganda on their circuit.

Look out for sporting events in the listings sections of Uganda's daily newspapers.

SHOPPING

While Uganda lacks the shopping opportunities found in countries such as Kenya and Zimbabwe, it does have a few interesting crafts to look out for and a lot of pieces imported from Congo (Zaïre), now that tourism has temporarily ceased to exist over there.

Kampala has the best selection of things to buy in Uganda (see the Kampala chapter for details); elsewhere the opportunities dry up fast.

Getting There & Away

For information on getting to Uganda from outside East Africa, see the regional Getting There & Away chapter.

AIR

Few travellers enter Uganda by air because most of the discounted air fares available in Europe and North America use Nairobi (Kenya) as the gateway to East Africa. However, discounted fares are now available in Kampala, so an increasing number of tourists are flying out of Entebbe (Kampala's international airport). With Nairobi's reputation for crime ever worsening, Entebbe has an excellent opportunity to stake its claim as a regional hub and an increasing number of airlines are flying here.

Departure Tax

There is a departure tax of US$20 on all international flights from Entebbe, payable when you buy your ticket. This may also be paid in Ugandan shillings.

Burundi

SA Alliance Express and Uganda Airlines fly between Entebbe and Bujumbura. Tickets cost US$123/246 one way/return with SA Alliance Express, but one way costs more with Uganda Airlines (US$148/235). There are also flights between Entebbe and Bujumbura with City Connexion Airlines (US$148/271 one way/return).

Kenya

If you intend flying between Entebbe and Nairobi, try and book at least a few days in advance, as flights are sometimes heavily subscribed. Flights cost US$138/276 one way/return and take about 1½ hours. Flights are operated by Kenya Airways and Uganda Airlines.

Rwanda

There are regular flights between Entebbe and Kigali with SA Alliance Express and Uganda Airlines. Both companies charge US$123/246 one way/return. However, Uganda Airlines often has some promotional one-month return fares available for about US$180 and SA Alliance Express has a similar deal for US$210.

Tanzania

There are connections between Entebbe and Dar es Salaam (US$242/342 one way/return) with Air Tanzania via Arusha's Kilimanjaro international airport (US$195/ 390), SA Alliance Air (direct) and Uganda Airlines (via Nairobi).

Air Tanzania also flies between Entebbe and Mwanza (US$144/288) and Unguja (Zanzibar Island) (US$386/564). There are weekly flights between Entebbe and Mwanza with Eagle Air (US$100 one way).

LAND
Kenya

The two main border crossings that most overland travellers use are Malaba and Busia, with Malaba being by far the more commonly used. You would probably use Busia only if you were coming from Jinja or Kampala and wanted to go directly to Kisumu, bypassing Tororo.

Bus Akamba (☎ 041-222501) operates four direct buses between Kampala and Nairobi daily. The executive class buses cost USh 20,000, depart at 7 am and 3 pm, and take about 12 to 14 hours. Akamba also has its daily Royal service, which is real luxury with large seats similar to 1st class in an aircraft. There are only three in each row! Tickets cost USh 38,000, and the price includes a meal at the halfway point (Eldoret). The overnight service arrives in Nairobi in the early hours of the morning but nobody gets off the bus until daylight – the bus driver will not let you off for your own safety! The Akamba office in Kampala is on Dewinton St.

Takrim (☎ 041-349411) also has a daily service to Nairobi for USh 14,000, which departs Kampala at 4 pm, arriving at daybreak. The office is just opposite Tourist Hotel, near the old taxi park. The advantage of this service is that you don't have to sit on the bus waiting for daylight.

Tawfiq (☎ 041-344275) has daily services to Nairobi, departing at 3 pm and arriving 14 hours later. The price is very reasonable at USh 12,000 and the office is located near the new taxi park in Old Kampala. This service continues on to Mombasa and you can buy a ticket through to the Kenyan coast from Kampala for USh 20,000.

Mawingo also operates daily buses at 3 pm. Fares are substantially cheaper than Akamba's (USh 12,000 from Kampala), but the buses are more crowded and take up to 15 hours. The depot in Kampala is right by the old taxi park.

Another increasingly popular option among independent travellers is the Kampala-Nairobi shuttle service operated by Jaguar Tours & Camping Safaris. It is a small, comfortable minibus that makes the run from Kampala on Monday, Wednesday and Friday for USh 40,000 per person at 7 am. The fares includes lunch. This service is usually a lot faster than the big buses as it doesn't stop and immigration formalities are quicker. You can book a place on the shuttle through Backpackers Hostel (☎ 041-272012) in Kampala; or email jaguar@nbnet.co.ke to contact the company directly.

Doing the journey in stages, there are frequent minibuses between Malaba and Kampala (USh 5000, three hours) or Jinja (USh 4000, two hours) until late afternoon. There are also frequent minibuses between Tororo and Malaba which cost USh 500 and take less than one hour.

The Ugandan and Kenyan border crossings are about 1km from each other at Malaba and you can walk or take a *boda-boda* (bicycle-taxi).

On the Kenyan side there are daily buses between Malaba and Nairobi with various companies, departing at about 7.30 pm and arriving at about 5.30 am the next day. The fare with Akamba is KSh 450. If you prefer to travel by day there are plenty of matatus between Malaba and Bungoma which take

about 45 minutes. If you stay in Bungoma overnight there are plenty of cheap hotels to choose from. From Bungoma there are several buses daily to Nairobi which leave at about 8 am and arrive about 5 pm the same day.

Taking a vehicle through this border crossing is fairly straightforward and doesn't take more than an hour or so.

The other crossing between Kenya and Uganda is via Busia, which is further south. Akamba has direct buses on the route between Kampala and Kisumu. There are frequent minibuses between Jinja and Busia (USh 3500) and matatus between Busia and Kisumu.

Train All Ugandan passenger train services were suspended at the time of writing, but they may someday resume. For this reason, the following information may be useful.

Departure from Kampala was at 4 pm on Wednesday, arriving in Nairobi at 2.40 pm on Thursday, and the fare was USh 57,850/35,300 in 1st/2nd class.

Rwanda
There are two main crossing points: between Kabale and Kigali via Katuna, and between Kisoro and Ruhengeri via Cyanika.

Kabale to Kigali Between Kabale to Kigali there are many minibuses daily which cost USh 7000 and take about two hours (not including immigration formalities and army roadblocks). These are only supposed to take 14 passengers but sometimes they squeeze in a few more. Expect a delay at the

> **WARNING**
>
> Crossing into Rwanda by land at the Katuna border, south of Kabale, has been safe and straightforward for several years now. However, the same cannot always be said for the Cyanika crossing between Kisoro and Ruhengeri, as Rwandan *Interahamwe* rebels occasionally manage to infiltrate this north-west region of Rwanda. Check conditions carefully in Kampala or Kisoro or at Ruhengeri or Kigali before deciding to use this border.

border while time-wasting immigration officials examine your passport minutely. It takes about 45 minutes to get through the two border crossings. There are two military checkpoints between the border and Kigali where your baggage will be searched.

There are also Ugandan buses that do the run between Kabale and Kigali leaving Kabale at 7 am, taking about two hours. The cost is the same as the minibuses.

For those in a hurry to get between Kampala and Kigali, there's a daily bus that leaves Kampala at 7.30 am. These buses are operated by Jaguar Tours and Happy Trails (both in Kampala), cost USh 15,000 and take about 10 hours.

Kisoro to Ruhengeri From Kisoro to Ruhengeri via Cyanika the road is in pretty good shape these days. At the time of writing, rebel activity and ambushes had ceased along this route, but the area remains potentially volatile. Check current security conditions in Kisoro or Kampala or in Ruhengeri or Kigali on the Rwandan side before crossing this way.

Tanzania
Direct The most commonly used direct route between Uganda and Tanzania is on the west side of Lake Victoria between Bukoba and Masaka, at Mutukula. Road conditions have improved considerably over the last few years, so it's possible to do the journey from Masaka to Bukoba in one day, although not always in the wet season. From Kampala to Masaka costs USh 2500 by minibus or bus. There are taxis from Masaka to Kyotera (USh 1500, 45 minutes) plus several daily pick-ups from there to the border at Mutukula (USh 1500, one hour), which go when full. The border crossings are easy and there are moneychangers on the Tanzanian side, though they give a lousy rate. The border crossings are right next to each other. There's also a basic place to stay and eat on the Tanzanian side.

From the border, a daily bus goes to Bukoba early in the morning and also at 5 pm (TSh 3000, about six hours) over variable roads. If the bus has departed before

you arrive at the border, your only option is to hitch (not easy, as there's little traffic) or stay overnight. South of the border, there's a checkpoint in Bunazi where you're obliged to stop and have your passport checked.

There is another border crossing at Nkurungu, which is to the west of Mutukula, but the road is bad and little transport passes this way.

Via Kenya There are direct buses running between Kampala and Tanzania via Kenya. Tawfiq has buses from Kampala to Dar es Salaam (USh 35,000, 25 hours) via Arusha (USh 27,000). These depart on Tuesday, Thursday, Friday and Saturday.

Takrim also offers bus services to Dar es Salaam (USh 37,000) via Arusha (USh 30,000) and Moshi (USh 32,000). These leave four times a week from Kampala, but Monday is the only through-bus while the others may stop in Nairobi if there aren't enough prebooked tickets sold. Takrim also has a weekly service that goes all the way to Malawi for USh 105,000.

Akamba also offers services to Dar es Salaam, but charges more at USh 46,000.

For details of the route from Mwanza via Kisumu (Kenya) see the Kenya Getting There & Away chapter.

> ## WARNING
> ! We strongly advise against crossing by land into Congo (Zaïre) from East Africa as there was a civil war going on there at the time of writing involving troops from as many as nine countries.
>
> There are also armed members of the *Interahamwe* (Hutu militia in Rwanda) roaming this part of Congo (Zaïre) and they have been known to target tourists.

LAKE
Tanzania
There's a regular service on Lake Victoria between Port Bell (near Kampala) and Mwanza (Tanzania) via Bukoba (Tanzania) provided by the *MV Victoria*, a modern boat

UGANDA

brought in to replace the *MV Bukoba*, which sank in 1996 with the tragic loss of more than 600 lives.

The ferry departs from Port Bell on Monday at 4 pm and arrives in Mwanza by about 11 am the following day. It's a good trip and costs US$30/25 in 1st/2nd class sleepers and US$20/15 in 2nd/3rd class seats. There is a US$5 port tax on all tickets.

To transport motor vehicles the cost is US$80 or TSh 50,000. The boat has capacity for just five vehicles, so it is advisable to book some time in advance.

Tickets should be booked the morning of the day of departure at the Port Bell port gate (☎ 041-221336). This is going to involve a taxi trip, unless you want to hang around all day until the ferry leaves.

Getting Around

AIR

Uganda Airlines is the national carrier, but offers no scheduled internal flights.

However, there are several smaller airlines offering both scheduled and charter flights. Eagle Uganda (☎ 041-344292, fax 344501) offers flights throughout the country. Destinations include Kisoro (for Mgahinga National Park), Kasese, Arua, Gulu, Moyo and Nebbi. Other private operators (such as Bel Air, CEI Aviation and Take Air) offer charter services to destinations such as Murchison Falls National Park and Kidepo Valley National Park.

BUS

Normal buses connect the major towns on a daily basis. They're cheaper than taxis but travel just as fast. They are much slower overall, however, because they stop a great deal to pick up and drop off passengers. From Kampala, they have no fixed departure times as they leave only when full. From Kampala, there will be at least one bus per day to most towns, the first one leaving any time after 6.30 am. However, from provincial destinations, they tend to have scheduled departure times.

EMS Post Buses

In addition to the normal private buses, there are also the EMS Post minibuses. These travel from Kampala to all the major centres daily. They cost less than a normal bus or taxi, and they are safe and stop much less frequently. Bookings can be made in advance; do this the day before at the town's post office.

See the Kampala Getting There & Away section for details of routes, schedules and prices.

MINIBUS & TAXI

Uganda is the land of share minibuses (known as taxis or matatus), and there's never any shortage of them. Fares are fixed and vehicles leave when full. Unlike Kenya, where the concept of 'full' has no meaning, travel by taxi in Uganda is relatively civilised, even though many drivers are speed maniacs who go much too fast to leave any leeway for emergencies. Luckily, traffic density on Ugandan roads is much lower than on Kenyan roads, so accidents are much less frequent. The only time you are likely to experience overcrowding is when you are a fair distance away from urban centres. The travellers' routes most likely to be overcrowded are the road to Sipi Falls from Mbale and the road to Kibale Forest National Park from Fort Portal.

There are also saloon car taxis throughout the country, known commonly as specials. These can be chartered around the capital, between cities and into national parks, but are more expensive than minibuses. However, they can be a cheap alternative to hiring a car if you are prepared to bargain hard and cover the driver's food and accommodation as you go.

TRAIN

There are two main railway lines in Uganda. The first starts at Tororo and runs west all the way to Kasese via Jinja and Kampala. The other line runs from Tororo north-west to Pakwach via Mbale, Soroti, Lira and Gulu. However, all passenger services have been suspended indefinitely and staff at Kampala train station don't seem too convinced that they will ever start again.

CAR & 4WD

There's a pretty good system of sealed roads between most major population centres in the southern part of the country, and work is well in hand on the roads to Gulu and Fort Portal.

It is pointless to talk of which particular roads are good and which are bad as it changes rapidly from year to year. Uganda has two wet seasons, which means the roads take a serious pounding from the elements, and surfaces deteriorate rapidly. Roads that are good this year are bad the next and good again, if repaired, the year after. When travelling on sealed roads, it is necessary to have your wits about you as large potholes often loom out of nowhere.

The network of dirt roads varies widely depending on whether it is the wet or dry season. In the dry season, dirt roads are very, very dusty and you'll end up choking behind trucks and taxis, while covering the local population in a fine layer of orange dust. In the wet season, a number of the dirt roads become muddy mires and may be passable only in a 4WD vehicle. If you are travelling around Uganda in the wet season, always ask about the latest road conditions before setting off on a journey.

What are totally missing in Uganda are road signs. There are hardly any, even outside major towns. Unless you know where you're going, it's possible to get hopelessly lost.

Carrying a map is one suggestion, but you'll also need a compass, since there are no decent large-scale maps. Getting out of the vehicle and talking to local people is obviously the best idea, but sometimes they don't know the way either!

What is good in Uganda is road safety. All the main roads you're likely to use are sealed and traffic volume is minimal, the main danger being excessive speed.

Fuel Costs

Fuel is horrifically expensive. Petrol costs about USh 1150 per litre; diesel is only a couple of hundred shillings cheaper. In the provinces, fuel can cost as much as USh 1300 per litre.

Rental

Uganda's vehicle hire industry, unlike Kenya's, is in its infancy and there are few options. Avis (☎ 041-347280, fax 347277) has its main office in the United Assurance building on Kimathi Ave, Kampala; it also has an office at Entebbe airport. Its rates including insurance, VAT and 100 free kilometres for a small car/4WD are US$132/212 for two days and US$623/1061 for a week; extra kilometres are charged at US$0.30/0.50. Simple daily hire charges

are US$40/70 plus US$20/25 for insurance and US$0.30/0.50 per kilometre. Drivers can be hired for US$10 per day.

Hertz (☎ 041-347191, fax 347192) has an office in the new Telecommunications Tower. All-inclusive rates, including insurance and 150 free kilometres per day, are US$78 per day for a small car and US$163 per day for a modern 4WD. However, these high rates are apparently 'negotiable'. Excess kilometres are charged at US$0.20 for a small car, US$0.50 for a 4WD.

Phoenix Cars (☎ 041-236096, fax 23 6097) is another good bet. It charges US$45 per day for a small car, with 100 free kilometres per day and US$0.25 per kilometre thereafter. A Suzuki Vitara 4WD costs US$75 per day (US$0.30 each excess kilometre), and a Landrover will cost US$120 per day (US$0.40 each excess kilometre).

Also worth trying is City Cars (☎ 041-232335, fax 232338, email citycars@star com.co.ug) at Baumann House, Parliament Ave. It has Suzuki 4WDs for rent, as well as camping gear.

A cheaper option is to rent a vehicle from one of the smaller local operators. A good company is Nile Safaris (☎/fax 041-345092) at Farmers House (next to the UK High Commission), Parliament Ave, Kampala. Its rates are very reasonable and include a driver. For a small car/4WD (including 100 free kilometres), you're looking at USh 45,000/75,000 per day, with extra kilometres charged at USh 300/350.

Another cheap option is to negotiate a comprehensive price with a 'special hire' taxi in Kampala. You have to bargain hard, but can come up with a surprisingly reasonable price. You may be able to negotiate something around USh 40,000 a day, excluding fuel and driver's accommodation and food.

HITCHING

Without your own transport, hitching is virtually obligatory in some situations, such as getting into national parks where there's no public transport. Most of the lifts you get will be on trucks, usually on top of the load at the back, which can be a very pleasant way to travel, though sun protection is a must. Free lifts on trucks are the exception rather than the rule, so ask before you get on.

Other sources for lifts are game wardens and rangers who work in the parks, international aid workers, missionaries, businesspeople and the occasional diplomat, but you may have to wait a long time in some places before anyone comes along. See the Getting Around East Africa chapter for more information on hitching in the region.

BOAT
Lake Victoria Ferries
There are very limited opportunities for travel by boat on Lake Victoria, the only options being the various methods of getting to the Ssese Islands from Bukakata (east of Masaka) and Kasenyi (a 30-minute taxi ride from Kampala). See Ssese Islands in the South-Western Uganda chapter for details.

LOCAL TRANSPORT
Kampala has a local share-taxi network, as well as 'special hire' taxis for private trips. Elsewhere you'll have to rely on bicycle-taxis (known locally as *boda-bodas*, as they originally shuttled people between border posts) or, in places such as Kampala and Fort Portal, on motorcycle taxis.

ORGANISED TOURS
For information on organised tours, see the Organised Safaris chapter.

UGANDA

Kampala

☎ 041

Kampala is a vibrant and confident city, in stark contrast to the battered shell that emerged from the last civil war. Modern buildings have gone up all over the city and old, dilapidated ones are slowly being renovated. And it is not only the buildings that are looking in better shape; there is a confidence about Kampala residents today which is infectious and the nightlife in the city has become something to savour.

The capital suffered a great deal during the years of civil strife following Idi Amin's defeat at the hands of the Tanzanian army in 1979. The turmoil only ended with the victory of Yoweri Museveni's National Resistance Army in early 1986.

Unless you've had previous experience of upheavals like these, it's hard to believe the amount of gratuitous destruction and looting that went on: office blocks and government offices had the bulk of their windows shattered; the buildings were riddled with rifle fire; plumbing and electrical fittings and telephone receivers were ripped from walls; buses were shot at and abandoned; and stores were looted of everything.

In the period since Museveni's victory, the city has transformed from a looted shell to a thriving, modern place befitting the capital of one of the most rapidly developing countries in Africa – the electricity works (in the city centre at least), water comes out of the taps and the shops and markets are once again well stocked. These days Kampala even has casinos, nightclubs and decent restaurants. The fact that many Asians have returned has certainly given business and commerce in Kampala a major boost.

The best thing about Kampala, though (and this is in stark contrast to Nairobi), is that it's quite safe to walk around at any time of the day or night in virtually any part of the city. You would be very unlucky to get mugged here – the city is green and attractive, and the people are very friendly – it's a great place.

Highlights

- Sample the vibrant nightlife of one of the continent's safer capitals
- Explore Entebbe's botanical gardens, bursting with tropical flora
- Take a step into Buganda history at the Kasubi Tombs
- Head down to the Musicians Club 1989 for an African jam session

ORIENTATION

Kampala is said to be built on seven hills, though you'll probably spend most of your time on just one of them – Nakasero, in the city centre. The top half of this hill is a type of garden city, with wide, quiet avenues lined with flowering trees and large, detached houses behind imposing fences and hedges. Here you'll find many of the embassies, international aid organisations, top end hotels, wealthy homes, the high court and government buildings.

Between Nakasero and the lower part of the city is Kampala's main thoroughfare – Kampala Rd (which turns into Jinja Rd at one end and Bombo Rd at the other). On this road are the main banks, the post and telecommunications office, the train station and a few hotels and restaurants.

Below Kampala Rd, towards the bottom of the valley, are heaps of shops and small businesses, budget hotels and restaurants, the market, the immense temples of the Asian Hindu community, and the bus station and taxi parks. It's a completely different world to that on the top side of Kampala Rd. Here there are congested streets thronging with people, battered old cars and minibuses, lottery ticket sellers, impromptu street markets and pavement stalls offering everything from rubber stamps to radio repairs. There are hawkers, newspaper sellers, hustlers, and one of the most mind-boggling and seemingly chaotic taxi parks you're ever likely to see.

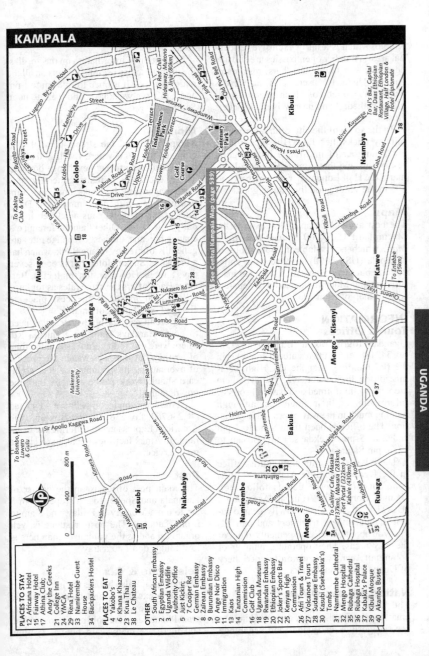

KAMPALA

See Central Kampala Map (page 535)

UGANDA

PLACES TO STAY
12 Africana Hotel
15 Fairway Hotel
17 Athina Club;
21 Andy the Greeks
24 College Inn
   YMCA
29 Rena Hotel
33 Namirembe Guest
   House
34 Backpackers Hostel

PLACES TO EAT
4 Yakobo's
6 Khana Khazana
8 Krua Thai
38 Le Chateau

OTHER
1 South African Embassy
2 Egyptian Embassy
3 Uganda Wildlife
   Authority Office
5 Just Kickin'
7 Crooper Rd
7 German Embassy
8 Zairean Embassy
9 Burundian Embassy
10 Ange Noir Disco
11 Immigration
13 Kaos
14 Tanzanian High
   Commission
16 Golf Club
18 Uganda Museum
19 Rwandan Embassy
20 Ethiopian Embassy
22 Joker's Sports Bar
25 Kenyan High
   Commission
26 Afri Tours & Travel
27 Volcanoes Tours
28 Sudanese Embassy
30 Kasubi (Ssekabaka's)
   Tombs
31 Namirembe Cathedral
32 Mengo Hospital
35 Rubaga Cathedral
36 Rubaga Hospital
37 Kabaka's Palace
38 Kibuli Mosque
40 Akamba Buses

To the east, across the golf course, is Kololo, which is a fairly exclusive residential area. A number of embassies are situated here, as are a few hotels, bars, restaurants and the Uganda Museum. To the west is Namirembe, on top of which stands the Anglican cathedral and nearby is Backpackers Hostel.

To the south of the city centre, across the railway tracks, lies Tank Hill, where there are a number of mid-range hotels, good restaurants and that famous Kampala landmark, the Half London bar, to which everyone in search of good live music goes.

Maps

The best available map of Kampala is the Macmillan 1:1,350,000 *Uganda Traveller's Map*, which is available in bookshops in Kampala (USh 7000). It covers the entire country but there's a useful street map inset of Kampala. Macmillan also has a separate foldout map of Kampala.

INFORMATION
Tourist Offices

Ugandan Tourist Board (UTB; ☎ 342196, fax 342188, email utb@starcom.co.ug) is in the IPS building, near the UK High Commission on Parliament Ave. The staff here are very well informed and have all sorts of information at their fingertips, although nothing much in the way of printed information. The office is open from 8 am to 1 pm and 2 to 5 pm weekdays, and 8.30 am to 12.30 pm Saturday.

There is also a community tourist office in the Uganda Wildlife Authority (UWA) compound (see more details following). Uganda Community Tourism Association (UCOTA, ☎ 269982) is heavily geared towards independent travellers and can advise you about travel arrangements to out of the way areas. They operate a number of community campgrounds on the periphery of Uganda's national parks.

National Parks Office

The UWA office (☎ 346287, fax 346291, email uwahq@uol.co.ug), does bookings to see the gorillas in Bwindi and Mgahinga national parks. It is just behind the Sheraton Hotel.

In addition to information on the gorillas, the office also has useful handouts on all the national parks. It is open from 8 am to 1 pm and 2 to 5 pm weekdays, and 9 am to noon Saturday.

Money

Kampala Rd and the streets parallel to it going up the hill is where you'll find all the banks and many foreign exchange bureaus. These exchange bureaus generally stay open longer than the banks, and offer competitive rates with no commission. Daily rates at the main bureaus are listed in the daily *New Vision*. Other than the foreign exchange bureaus, the best exchange rates are generally offered by Crane Bank, which has a branch at Speke Hotel that is open seven days a week. However, for small bills, Barclays Bank offers the same rates as for large bills which makes it the best place to change US$20 notes or smaller.

For credit card cash advances, you need to go to Barclays Bank on Kampala Rd. There were no credit card ATMs at the time of writing, but Barclays was in the process of overhauling its machines so your credit card should work in the wall by the time you read this.

At the Sheraton Hotel is Express Uganda (☎ 236767, fax 236769) PO Box 353, the American Express agent, offering the usual range of Amex facilities, including a clients mail service.

Post

The main post office is on the corner of Kampala and Speke Rds. It's open from 8 am to 6 pm Monday to Friday, and 8 am to 2 pm Saturday. The poste restante is well organised and as the volume of mail here is low, things don't go astray.

Telephone & Fax

The post office also houses the international telephone exchange, and there are public phones where you can ring and fax overseas. Phone cards are sold at the post office, and there are many card phones (yellow phone boxes) around town. Fax services are cheap from the post office, at about USh 1500 a page, but the bureaucracy involved in sending one can be frustrating, as you need to visit at least three counters.

For overseas and long-distance phone calls it's much cheaper to use Starcom offices around town. From their offices you can make direct phone-card calls. Starcom has a number of phone boxes around town (green boxes), but only the ones in its offices or at hotels are set up for international calls. Starcom offices are open from 7.30 am to 9 pm Monday to Saturday, and 9 am to 4 pm Sunday.

International faxes are more expensive from Starcom at about USh 3000 a page, but if you are in a hurry to communicate, it is quicker than the post office.

Email & Internet Access

Email and Internet services have sprung up all over town in recent years. There are even a few fully blown Internet cafes where cyber junkies can get their regular fix. One of the most popular is Cyber World Cafe, in the Park Royal Arcade opposite Hotel Equatoria. Access here is USh 150 a minute, but if you are staying around Kampala a while, it is worth considering membership (USh 6000) as access charges drop to USh 100 a minute. Also found in the Park Royal Arcade is Uganda Online, a smaller operation.

The Dome Cyberspace is at the opposite end of town on Jinja Rd. This is a nicely designed, spacious cafe with more than 10 terminals. Access here is also USh 150 a minute, although there is a discount of USh 600 if you pay for an hour.

One place that is slightly cheaper than the competition is Prime Telecentre on Kampala Rd, which offers a wide range of telecommunications services, including Internet access for USh 7000 an hour.

Other places that offer Internet access include Backpackers Hostel (USh 150 per minute), Red Chili Hideaway (US$6 per hour), and mid-range and top end hotels around town.

Sending standard emails is about USh 1000 from most places around town.

Travel Agencies

Delmira Travel (☎ 235494, 231927, email delmira@imul.com) on Hill Rd has a good reputation. For airline tickets, Speedwing Travel Bureau (☎ 231052, fax 231053) on Kimathi Ave is pretty reliable. A reliable agent is Afri Tours & Travel Ltd (☎ 232306, fax 232307), Lumumba Rd on Nakasero Hill.

For information on tour operators offering tours and safaris in Uganda, see the Organised Safari Tours chapter.

Bookshops

For English-language publications, one of the best places is the Aristoc Booklex shop on the corner of Kampala Rd and Colville St. Their shelves are filled to capacity with books and maps for Uganda and East Africa, novels and educational texts. Also worth a look is the Uganda Bookshop around the corner on Colville St.

Camera Shops

Colour Chrome, at 54 Kampala Rd, is a reliable outfit for developing film. It can also arrange passport photos in a couple of hours. For cheap film there are lots of shops along Wilson Rd, and these places can also do passport photos in about one hour. There are also quite a number of instant photo booths around town if you are in a hurry.

Cultural Centres

Alliance Française is located on the 1st floor of the National Theatre near the parliament buildings.

The British Council (members only) is in the IPS building on Parliament Ave.

Medical & Emergency Services

The best place to get treatment in Kampala is International Medical Centre (☎ 341291, 075-741291, fax 342608, email iclark@ infocom.co.ug) in the Kampala Pentecostal Church building, opposite Hotel Equatoria. Run by Dr Ian Clarke, it offers a wide range of professional medical services, including dependable malaria smears. It is open 24 hours and operates an ambulance service in an emergency.

UGANDA

Another good option is The Surgery (☎/fax 256003, email stockley@imul.com) based at the UK High Commission. Opening hours are 8 am to 6 pm weekdays, 9 am to 1 pm Saturdays and 10 am to noon Sundays. There is a 24 hour emergency number as well: ☎ 075-756003.

For emergency police assistance, dial ☎ 999.

Dangers & Annoyances

Kampala is a safe city as far as capitals in Africa go and there is no need to be paranoid when out late at night. However, from time to time incidents do happen, like anywhere in the world, so it pays not to have all your valuables on you in poorly lit areas at night. The only area in Kampala in which you should take care late at night is around the taxi parks, as pickpockets operate here.

There have been other security concerns in Kampala in recent years with terrorist campaigns coming to the capital. There was a spate of bomb attacks on nightspots and public places during 1998 and early 1999, but the ringleaders were captured. However, this does mean that security at government buildings, embassies, bars and nightclubs is extremely tight. However, you get used to the searches pretty quickly, and remember, it is for your own safety.

Beggars are a common sight in central Kampala, but they are not very persistent. However, if you do get plagued, try and be patient as there isn't much of a social security system in Uganda so they have no fallback except to beg. There are also lots of children around the city asking for sponsorship for schooling, often claiming to be refugees from Sudan or Somalia. While some of the cases may be genuine, locals say that many are bogus and just begging for their parents. Others say that waving the paper in your face is simply a diversion for a spot of sneak theft, so keep your eyes open.

One final annoyance in Kampala is that taxi drivers have a tendency to run out of petrol at the most inconvenient times. Drivers often have the bare minimum of fuel in their tank so that if the car gets stolen it won't get far. Daft though it sounds, it is no joke, and often they miscalculate how much they have left and don't make it to the nearest garage – make sure you get in a cab at the top of a hill!

The Naked Truth About Crime in Kampala

Some of Africa's capitals are notorious for muggings and robberies, but Kampala has never been one of them. Nearby Nairobi has a terrible reputation and Dar es Salaam is hardly safe, but in Kampala you can generally walk the streets day or night without fear. At last the reasons have been exposed and you may not believe it. In many African cities, thieves are dealt with through mob justice and lynchings are not uncommon throughout the continent. However, Ugandans have opted for something a little less final and a little more humiliating, stripping thieves down to their 'Adam suits' or ripping all their clothes off in public.

Several cases of these mob strips are reported each day in Kampala's newspapers and even a few women have fallen victim to this instant justice. Officially the police are trying to discourage this practice as they feel that mob justice often fails to discriminate between the guilty and innocent.

But most Kampala citizens feel that it is the police who fail to discriminate between the guilty and the innocent in the capital, and that many of the police are themselves thieves. If they are not soliciting bribes of some sort from the public, then a number of officers have been known to turn to a little pickpocketing themselves. However, police chiefs down play corruption in the force, one officer on the record as saying: 'The police are like your buttocks, you only notice their importance when you have a boil on them.' Just how many policemen have proverbial boils on their buttocks remains to be seen, but if some of them don't change their thieving ways, Kampalans may just start exchanging their uniforms for their 'Adam suits'.

UGANDA MUSEUM

The Uganda Museum on Kira Rd is open from 10 am to 6 pm Monday to Saturday and from 3 to 6 pm Sunday. Entry costs USh 2000 (USh 500 for children). It hasn't had much investment in recent years so it looks pretty mothballed these days. It has some good ethnological exhibits covering hunting, agriculture, war, religion and *juju*, as well as archaeological and natural history displays. Perhaps its most interesting feature is a collection of traditional musical instruments, which you're allowed to play.

A booklet for sale here, *Kasubi Tombs*, describes the history of the Buganda and the royal palace enclosure on the hill above Mengo.

There's also an office of the East African Wildlife Society at the museum, open from 10 am to noon on Monday, Wednesday and Friday.

To get here, catch a Kamjokya share-taxi from the old taxi park (USh 200).

KASUBI TOMBS

Also well worth a look are the Kasubi Tombs (also known as Ssekabaka's Tombs) on Kasubi Hill just off Masiro Rd which were first built in 1881. Here you will find the huge traditional reed and bark cloth buildings of the *kabakas* (kings) of the Buganda people. The group of buildings contains the tombs of Muteesa I, his son Mwanga, Sir Daudi Chwa II, and his son Edward Muteesa II, father of the current kabaka Ronald Mutebi. He died in London in 1969, three years after being deposed by Obote. The tombs are taken care of by the Ganda clans.

The Kasubi Tombs are open daily from 8 am to 6 pm, including Sunday and holidays; the entry fee is USh 3000. Remove your shoes before entering the main building. You can get to the tombs by share-taxi, either from the old taxi park in the city centre (ask for Hoima Rd) or from the junction of Bombo and Makerere Hill Rds. The share-taxis you want are the ones that terminate at the market at the junction of Hoima and Masiro Rds. The tombs are a few hundred metres walk up the hill from here (signposted).

BUILDINGS OF THE BUGANDA KINGDOM

Kampala has always been the heartland of the Buganda kingdom and within the capital are found a number of their impressive administrative centres and royal buildings. Most of these are located in and around Mengo and include the Kabaka's palace, inside a vast walled enclosure, the Buganda parliament, located at the end of a ceremonial driveway leading from the palace and the Buganda Court of Justice, now the location for Uganda's National Court. Backpackers Hostel has an organised tour that takes in these locations. See Organised Tours following for details.

RELIGIOUS BUILDINGS

Also worth a visit are the four main religious buildings in Kampala: the gleaming white Kibuli Mosque dominating Kibuli Hill on the other side of the train station from Nakasero Hill; the huge Roman Catholic Rubaga Cathedral on Rubaga Hill; the Namirembe Anglican Cathedral (where the congregation is called to worship by the beating of drums); and the enormous Hindu temple in the city centre.

ACTIVITIES
White-Water Rafting

Day trips on the Victoria Nile near Jinja are operated by Adrift and Nile River Explorers, and the river has four Class 5 rapids, making it as big a challenge as the more popular Zambezi River at Victoria Falls in Zimbabwe.

The cost with Adrift is US$95 including transport from Kampala, lunch and beers. They also offer half-day and two-day trips. Bookings can be made either through Adrift (☎ 268670, 075-707668, fax 241245, email adrift@starcom.co.ug) or Backpackers Hostel (☎/fax 272012, email backpackers@ in focom.co.ug).

Nile River Explorers (☎ 043-120236, fax 121322, email rafting@starcom.co.ug) is based in Jinja and offers shorter day trips for US$65.

For details on each operator and the big, big waters of the Nile, see White-Water

Rafting under Jinja in the South-Eastern Uganda chapter.

Lake Victoria

There are a variety of activities available on Lake Victoria, including boating, fishing and horse riding. For more details on these options, see the Around Kampala section at the end of this chapter.

ORGANISED TOURS

As Kampala has few major tourist attractions, it is not really worth arranging an organised tour of the city. However, Backpackers Hostel (☎/fax 272012, email back packers@infocom.co.ug) offers an interesting minibus tour of all the important buildings of the Buganda Kingdom in the capital.

PLACES TO STAY

Accommodation in Kampala is not that cheap if you want anything with a modicum of comfort and a bathroom.

Places to Stay – Budget

Most travellers opt to stay at the excellent Backpackers Hostel or the newer Red Chili Hideaway as the cheap hotels are mostly near the noisy bus station and taxi parks.

Camping Campers have a choice of three places in Kampala: the YMCA, Backpackers and Red Chili. See following for details.

Hostels The most popular place is *Backpackers Hostel (☎/fax 272012, email back packers@infocom.co.ug)* about a 10-minute share-taxi ride out of the centre at Kalema Rd, Lunguja, not far from the landmark Namirembe Cathedral. It's quiet and relaxed, the staff are friendly and the bar has recently been renovated giving it a much fresher feel. Camping costs USh 3500 per person, or there are basic beds for USh 5000 in a dorm, or USh 11,000 for a double room. *Bandas* (thatched-roof huts) cost USh 15,000 and there is also a self-contained double for USh 20,000. There are basic cooking facilities, but inexpensive, good set meals and burgers are also available. To get there, take a Natete

share-taxi from the new taxi park (USh 400 uphill, but only USh 200 back to town!); there's a sign on a pole in the middle of the park – you can just ask for the Backpackers. The hostel also has a minibus that meets the Akamba bus and the Port Bell ferry.

A newer place is *Red Chili Hideaway (☎ 223903)* up in Bugolobi district about 7km out on the road to Port Bell. It has camping for USh 3500, dorm beds for USh 5000 and small doubles for USh 12,000. There are also nice two-bedroom cottages with lounge, bathroom and kitchen facilities. There is decent food available, a bar and a pool table. On Sunday nights Red Chili has a very reasonable barbecue, open to all. To get there, take a minibus from the new taxi park to Bugolobi for USh 400 and get off at the Colgate factory. There are free pick ups and drop offs for the Port Bell ferry.

YMCA (☎ 230804) is on Buganda Rd, about 15-minutes walk from the city centre. You can camp here for USh 2000 but you won't get much privacy, as the site is on a playing field which fronts onto busy Kampala Rd (Bombo Rd). In the building itself, you can sleep on the floor on a mattress for USh 2000. It's inconvenient staying here as you must leave by 7 am each day, as it's used as a school on weekdays. The showers are erratic and the toilets could do with a good scrub.

There is also a *YWCA (☎ 242024, fax 241519)* but rates are significantly higher. Rooms with bathroom are US$40, those with shared bathroom cost US$30.

Hotels The budget hotels are all in the busy part of town near the taxi parks and bus station. There's a large choice these days, but all offer the same standard so choosing where to stay is more a question of a thousand shillings or a bathroom here and there. However, one or two stand out as offering better value than others.

Arguably the best deal in this part of town is newly refurbished *L'Hotel Fiancee (☎ 345015)*. It is very clean and airy, with a small restaurant and free tea. Singles/doubles with attached bathroom are USh 12,000/15,000, making it very good value.

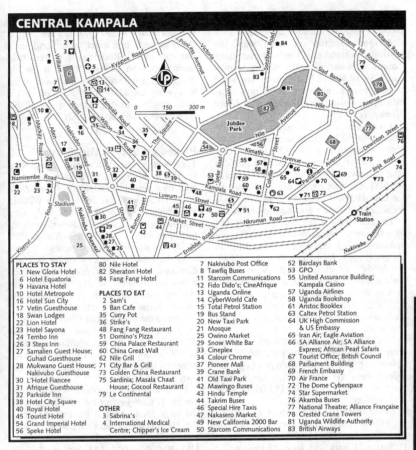

CENTRAL KAMPALA

0   150   300 m

PLACES TO STAY	80 Nile Hotel	7 Nakivubo Post Office	52 Barclays Bank
1 New Gloria Hotel	82 Sheraton Hotel	8 Tawfiq Buses	53 GPO
6 Hotel Equatoria	84 Fang Fang Hotel	11 Starcom Communications	55 United Assurance Building;
9 Havana Hotel		12 Fido Dido's; CineAfrique	Kampala Casino
10 Hotel Metropole	PLACES TO EAT	13 Uganda Online	57 Uganda Airlines
16 Hotel Sun City	2 Sam's	14 CyberWorld Cafe	58 Uganda Bookshop
17 Vetin Guesthouse	5 Ban Cafe	15 Total Petrol Station	61 Aristoc Booklex
18 Swan Lodges	35 Curry Pot	19 Bus Stand	63 Caltex Petrol Station
22 Lion Hotel	36 Strike's	20 New Taxi Park	64 UK High Commission
23 Hotel Sayona	48 Fang Fang Restaurant	21 Mosque	& US Embassy
24 Tembo Inn	51 Domino's Pizza	25 Owino Market	65 Iran Air; Eagle Aviation
26 3 Steps Inn	59 China Palace Restaurant	29 Snow White Bar	66 SA Alliance Air; SA Alliance
27 Samalien Guest House;	60 China Great Wall	33 Cineplex	Express; African Pearl Safaris
Guhad Guesthouse	62 Nile Grill	34 Colour Chrome	67 Tourist Office; British Council
28 Mukwano Guest House;	71 City Bar & Grill	37 Pioneer Mall	68 Parliament Building
Nakivubo Guesthouse	73 Golden China Restaurant	39 Crane Bank	69 French Embassy
30 L'Hotel Fiancee	75 Sardinia; Masala Chaat	41 Old Taxi Park	70 Air France
31 Afrique Guesthouse	House; Gocool Restaurant	42 Mawingo Buses	72 The Dome Cyberspace
32 Parkside Inn	79 Le Continental	43 Hindu Temple	74 SA Supermarket
38 Hotel City Square		44 Takrim Buses	76 Akamba Buses
40 Royal Hotel	OTHER	46 Special Hire Taxis	77 National Theatre; Alliance Française
45 Tourist Hotel	3 Sabrina's	47 Nakasero Market	78 Crested Crane Towers
54 Grand Imperial Hotel	4 International Medical	49 New California 2000 Bar	81 Uganda Wildlife Authority
56 Speke Hotel	Centre; Chipper's Ice Cream	50 Starcom Communications	83 British Airways

UGANDA

One of the best places is the friendly ***Mukwano Guest House*** (☎ 232248) on Nakivubo Place, opposite the busy Owino Market. This place, around since 1963, is cleaned daily, sheets are also changed daily and there's hot water in the showers. Dorm beds are USh 5000 (four-bed), singles/doubles with shared bathroom are USh 10,000/12,000 and rooms with bathroom go for USh 15,000/18,000.

Nakivubo Guesthouse (☎ 259088) next door is another decent option offering self-contained rooms for USh 10,000/15,000. There's hot water, a rooftop restaurant and international telephone services.

A few doors on is ***Samalien Guest House*** (☎ 245737) which is clean and OK although the welcome is not exactly overpowering. It's also a little more expensive at USh 12,000/15,000 for rooms with shared bathroom and USh 20,000 for doubles with attached bathroom. This place has a good restaurant out the back with cold beers.

Another couple of doors along is ***Guhad Guesthouse*** (☎ 342182) which has basic rooms with shared hot water bathroom for USh 8000/12,000.

Further along again, towards Entebbe Rd, is *3 Steps Inn* (☎ 244539) another basic but reasonable guesthouse with rooms for USh 10,000/14,000 with shared bathroom.

Afrique Guesthouse overlooks the bustling bus stand so it's noisier than most. Rooms with shared hot water bathrooms cost USh 10,000/13,000. Nearby are some similar places including *Midcity Guesthouse*, *Gateway Guesthouse* and *Hotel Metropole*.

There are a couple more reasonable places near the bus stand and new taxi park. *Vetin Guesthouse* (☎ 349031) has rooms for USh 8000/10,000 with shared bathroom (shared between three rooms). *Swan Lodges* (☎ 348836) offers rooms with no bathroom for USh 10,000/15,000. Both rates include breakfast and there's also secure parking.

The other budget guesthouses in this part of town are spread across roads leading up to Kampala Rd, but none of them inspire. Best of these is *Hotel Sun City* (☎ 345542, fax 236541) which has singles with shared bathroom for USh 10,000, and singles/doubles with attached bathroom for USh 15,000/20,000. The hotel employs friendly staff, has hot water and contains a small restaurant.

The other cheapies aren't up to much around here. *Parkside Inn* (☎ 230816) involves negotiating a labyrinth just to get inside. Rooms with shared bathroom and no hot water cost USh 10,000/15,000, making it overpriced.

Royal Hotel is a little further up the hill, opposite the old taxi park and has large double rooms for USh 15,000 and singles for USh 10,000, both with shared bathroom.

Heading out of town on the Namirembe Rd are a couple of prominent places. *Tembo Inn* (☎ 344240) is a rambling and run-down place with rooms for USh 10,000/15,000 with shared bathroom. The rooms aren't great, but there is a good local restaurant and a lively bar downstairs.

A little further up the hill is *Hotel Sayona* which has singles with shared bathroom for USh 12,000 and doubles with bathroom for USh 15,000. The rooms are fairly spartan, but they do claim to provide 24-hour room service and their motto is 'Our guest is our king'.

At the top of this range is *Namirembe Guest House* (☎ 272071). It's set in spacious grounds in a quiet suburb and has a range of rooms. Rooms with shared bathroom cost USh 14,400/19,200 in the old wing; rooms with attached bathroom in the new wing are USh 16,800/21,000. It's a pleasant place to stay. Meals are available for USh 4600 (breakfast), USh 5750 (lunch) and USh 6900 (dinner).

Places to Stay – Mid-Range

There's very little choice in this range. Reasonably good value in the city centre, at least by Kampala standards, is *New Gloria Hotel* (☎ 257790, fax 269616) on William St. It's a small place that has recently been renovated, and has a cafe. Rooms with attached bathroom cost USh 25,000/45,000/50,000 for singles/doubles/triples.

In the heart of the city centre is *Hotel City Square* (☎ 256257, fax 251440) which offers rooms for USh 35,000/45,000, including breakfast. All rooms are clean and include bathroom, TV and telephone.

West of the centre, *Rena Hotel* (☎ 272336) on Namirembe Rd is good value, at USh 17,500/25,000 with shared bathroom or USh 25,000/36,000 with private bathroom. All prices include breakfast, and the hotel has its own bar and restaurant.

Far better, but a 15-minute walk from the centre, is *College Inn* (☎ 531994) just off the large roundabout at the top of Bombo Rd. Here you can get a single/double with attached bathroom, including breakfast, for USh 30,000/50,000. The staff are friendly and the food in the restaurant is good.

Lion Hotel (☎ 233934, fax 343682, email sekalala@imul.com) is a clean and modern hotel, just above the new taxi park at 18 Namirembe Rd. It doesn't necessarily impress from the outside, but the rooms are well appointed and reasonably priced. It costs USh 35,000/45,000, including bathroom, TV and telephone.

Tourist Hotel (☎ 251471, fax 251473, email tourist@swiftuganda.com) has recently reopened after refurbishment and offers top end standards at mid-range prices. It overlooks the lively Nakasero Market in the heart of the city and has singles ranging from US$25 to US$30, doubles for US$35 to US$40, all with spotless bathroom, TV and telephone. Breakfast is US$5. This is one of the best value places in town for those who want a little more comfort, but don't want to pay international prices.

Havana Hotel (☎ 343532, fax 343533, email Havana@starcom.co.ug) overlooks the busy new taxi park and offers a range of rooms, catering mainly to business travellers. Rooms will set you back USh 43,785/52,650 with shared bathroom, USh 52,650/64,350 with attached bathroom. With air-con, the price escalates to USh 76,050/93,600, but it is generally an unnecessary luxury with Kampala's cool nights. All prices include breakfast.

One final option at the top of this price range is *Fang Fang Hotel (☎ 235828, fax 250422)* just below the Sheraton Hotel on Ssezibwa Rd. Rooms are modern, clean and well appointed and cost US$45/50, including breakfast. This is very good value when compared with some of the top end hotels, which charge twice as much for the same quality room. There is also a good restaurant here, part of the Fang Fang chain, and it has slightly lower prices than the city centre branch.

Places to Stay – Top End

Although most of the accommodation in this price bracket is quoted in hard currency (US dollars), you can pay your bill in local or foreign currency. However, unless you are on an organised tour or a business account, it is worth checking out the best mid-range places, like the Tourist or Fang Fang hotels, as they offer similar comfort at significantly lower prices. Most of the prices quoted below exclude VAT of 17% and service charges of 5%.

Very popular is *Speke Hotel (☎ 259221, fax 235345)* on Nile Ave. It has plenty of character and atmosphere. Most of the rooms have attached bathrooms and are spacious, and the majority have a TV and balcony. It's good value at US$55/65, US$65/70 with air-con, including breakfast. The terrace bar is a popular meeting place,

and there's a snack bar/coffee shop and a good Indian restaurant.

Fairway Hotel (☎ 259571, fax 234160) on Kafu Rd, near the golf course, is another option. It's recently been refurbished, and rooms cost US$76/96, including tax. The hotel has two open-air restaurants – one Indian, the other *nyama choma*, and, perhaps more importantly, a swimming pool.

Africana Hotel (☎ 348080, fax 348090, email africana@starcom.co.ug) is a relatively new outfit, on the east side of Centenary Park. Rooms start at US$70/85, with a US$5 surcharge for air-con. The hotel includes a health club and offers free temporary membership to the nearby golf course.

North-east of here, on Kololo Hill, is *Athina Club (☎ 241428)* on Windsor Crescent. This is a reasonable place to stay, with lots of atmosphere. Rooms with attached bathroom (with hot water) and full board cost US$65/80. Nonguests can also eat here, but Andy the Greeks, tucked away behind, is a better option.

Further out beyond Kololo is *Kabira Club (☎ 543481, fax 541257, email kabira@starcom.co.ug)* a hotel and residential complex that is quite popular with expats. Facilities here include a bar and restaurant, a swimming pool and tennis courts. Many of the rooms are overpriced, starting at US$46/58 with shared bathroom and US$58/75 with attached bathroom. Some of the cottages are quite nice and include a kitchen. All rates include breakfast and a free laundry service.

On Tank Hill, to the south-east, *Hotel Diplomate (☎ 347625, fax 347655)* is a reasonable place but forget about staying here unless you have your own transport, as it's near the top of the hill and some distance from a share-taxi route. The views, however, are excellent. The hotel has a good range of rooms from US$66/78 including breakfast and taxes. The staff are very friendly, there's a bar, a restaurant and even a video library.

In the centre of town are two recently opened places, both of which were shot-up hulks from the bad old days. *Hotel Equatoria (☎ 250780, fax 250146)* has quite decent rooms, most with a small balcony with views. There's also a small swimming pool and several good restaurants. The cost is US$79/89, or US$109/119 with air-con, both including breakfast.

Grand Imperial Hotel (☎ 250681, fax 250606) is plush but smaller and more intimate than the Sheraton, and has very good facilities, including a very small swimming pool, bars, a cafe and restaurants. At US$140/160 it's hardly cheap – but reasonable value for a five-star hotel.

At the very top end of this scale are two large hotels on Nakasero Hill. *Sheraton Hotel (☎ 244590, fax 256696, email res 410_kampala@ittsheraton.com)* on Ternan Ave just above Speke Hotel is in Jubilee Park (which is open to the public in daylight hours but closes at 7 pm). It has all the facilities you'd expect of a Sheraton hotel, including swimming pool, tennis and squash courts, several restaurants and bars, and a shopping precinct. There's live music in the enclosed bar every night and in the open-air bar on Sunday afternoon and evening (no charge for entry; nonguests welcome). Rooms with breakfast cost US$208/228 without air-con, plus tax. With air-con, the price rises to US$230/250.

Cheaper than the Sheraton is *Nile Hotel (☎ 235900, fax 259130, email nileh@imul.com)* adjacent to the Uganda International Conference Centre on Nile Ave. It has all the usual facilities, including a pool, and offers rooms for US$110/140, including breakfast; taxes cost extra. It's quite often fully booked when there is a conference in progress.

PLACES TO EAT

The cheapest places to eat in Kampala are the ubiquitous takeaways that dot the city centre. It is impossible to recommend any in particular as they are fairly standard outfits, offering dishes such as chicken, meat, sausages, fish and chips, as well as samosas and chapatis. Prices are the same whether you eat in or takeaway and range from USh 1000 to USh 3000 for a meal. Look out for the takeaway signs sticking out of buildings all over the city.

It is worth noting that quite a lot of the better restaurants in Kampala are closed on Sundays or Mondays, so check in advance to avoid disappointment.

Restaurants

Kampala is packed with quality restaurants, ensuring you will never go hungry.

Ugandan Surprisingly, one of the best deals in town is to be found at *Kampala Casino* on Kimathi Ave. On Thursday evenings they put on a Ugandan buffet, and at USh 7500 this is great value. If you haven't tried local food this is a good opportunity, and there's live music while you eat. You do, of course, need to be reasonably smartly dressed to get in here.

Chinese There are a surprising number of Chinese restaurants in Kampala, but some are better than others. One of the best is *Chopsticks* at Hotel Equatoria, which has a huge menu of Chinese food and a few Thai and Vietnamese choices thrown in for good measure. Main dishes cost about USh 7000. They often have promotional menus available such as five courses for USh 10,000.

Fang Fang is another popular place in the Greenland Bank building on Kampala Rd. There's a good selection of popular Chinese dishes and you can eat well for about USh 10,000. Popular specialities include shark's fin soup for USh 6000 and fried crispy prawns with ginger and garlic.

Well regarded is *China Palace Restaurant* on the 1st floor of the high-rise office building on Pilkington St (signposted, though inadequately, on the ground floor). Main dishes cost from USh 5000 to USh 7000. It's open Tuesday to Sunday for lunch and dinner. Also reasonable is the long-running *China Great Wall* on Kampala Rd up from and on the opposite side of the road to Nile Grill. It's open from noon to 11 pm daily.

Continental An excellent restaurant for quality steaks is *Le Chateau* out on Gaba Rd. This place is also home to the Quality Cuts Butchery where many expats pick up their meat. A great meal can be had for about USh 20,000 and this is a very popular restaurant with well-to-do Ugandans. They have an excellent menu of continental cuisine and if you are looking to spoil yourself, this is arguably the location. For lovers of fine French cuisine, the menu even includes frog's legs and snails.

Yakobo's is one of the best places in town for a steak. The meat melts under the knife and comes with a variety of sauces and butters. There's also a selection of European dishes and you can expect to spend about USh 15,000 to USh 20,000 a meal with drinks. It is closed on Sunday.

Near Yakobo's are a couple of restaurants with versatile menus of popular European food. The somewhat uninspiringly named *7 Cooper Rd* (after its location), but hence easy to find, has a solid menu of meat, fish and a number of vegetarian dishes. They also offer a salad bar that is popular during lunch-times, mainly with expats. It is closed on Sunday.

Also here is *The Crocodile* an attractively designed cafe-bar with reasonable food, although sometimes the prices are as ambitious as the cooking. It stays open Sunday, so often gets busy at the end of the weekend.

Despite its somewhat formidable reputation as an expensive place, Sheraton Hotel offers reasonable western-style food for around USh 10,000 at its *Victoria Restaurant*. You might also want to check out the buffet breakfast at the Sheraton – for USh 14,000, you can tuck into a mind-boggling array of food as often as you like. You won't need lunch when you've finished.

Also reasonable value are the buffet meals at *Lion Bar* (separate from the main building but in the same grounds as Lion Hotel). The all-you-can-eat buffet meals are particularly good value.

An excellent place serving French Congolese dishes is *Le Continental* near the UNDP headquarters on the north side of Nakasero Hill. Dishes are meat-oriented but are very nicely done and good value at about USh 7000.

Ethiopian For African cuisine of a different type, try *Daas Ethiopian Restaurant* on Gaba Rd, just before the turn-off to Kabal-

agala. The food here is very good and the service attentive. Dishes will cost you USh 4500 to USh 6000 and include spiced beef with cottage cheese and spinach, and goat curry.

Fasika is another decent Ethiopian restaurant in Kabalagala, just over the road from the ever-popular Capital Bar. The menu here is similar to that at Daas and includes some tasty chicken dishes and a sort of Ethiopian answer to a thali with a little bit of everything. Most dishes are between USh 5000 and USh 7000.

Another Ethiopian place in the same area as Fasika is *Ethiopian Village* which also offers very good food at reasonable prices.

Greek For Greek food, the best place to go is *Andy the Greek's* on Windsor Crescent in Kololo. Tucked away at the back of the Athina Club, it is run by Anglo-Greek Cypriots, so you know the food is authentic. The menu includes all the Greek favourites such as stuffed *dolmades*, deep fried aubergine and the ever-popular dips of *houmous*, *taramosalata* and *tzatziki*. You're looking at USh 20,000 for a decent meal including a glass of wine. It's open for lunch and dinner. The bar here is a popular stop with expats on the road to a hangover at the weekend.

Indian *Haandi* is a classy restaurant in Equatorial Hotel, which offers some excellent Indian meals. The presentation and service are impeccable and large, tasty curries cost from USh 7000 to USh 10,000. The house vegetarian *masala* is excellent, as are the *tilapia* curries. You can eat and drink very well for about USh 20,000 per person.

Khana Khazana in a large villa on Acacia Ave in Kololo is regarded by many expat residents as the best Indian restaurant in Kampala. It is very expensive, but the food is fantastic. You are looking at about USh 30,000 or more for a reasonable spread, but it is worth it.

Maharaja is another well regarded Indian restaurant at Speke Hotel and prices are a little cheaper than the two best places in town, but then the food is not quite in the same class.

UGANDA

For something a little cheaper, there are many alternatives. On the lower part of Kampala Rd, towards the train station, is the smart *City Bar & Grill*. This is a very popular lunch-time hang-out, and serves excellent tandoori and other Indian dishes, as well as western meals such as steak. Prices are in the USh 5000 to USh 7500 range, and there's also a full-sized snooker table and bar.

Another good value *restaurant* is the Indian place above Munchies in Hotel Equatoria. There's an extensive menu of curries for about USh 5000 and a host of lunch-time specials like cheap and filling *thalis*.

For a cheap Indian meal try *Masala Chaat House* on Dewinton Rd, opposite the National Theatre. This is a popular little place that serves vegetarian thali meals for USh 4500, and other vegetarian and non-vegetarian dishes. It also has a wide selection of tasty masala *dosas* and other southern Indian food.

Just a few doors down is *Gocool Restaurant*, with main dishes for USh 2500 to USh 3200, and Gujarati thali meals costing USh 4800.

Another popular restaurant is *Curry Pot*, on Kampala Rd. It offers good stews for USh 3000 to USh 5000, but hardly anything in the way of curries rather curiously. They have quite a good breakfast deal if you are looking for a cooked breakfast for about USh 3500.

Italian *Mamba Point* on Akii Bua Rd Nakasero Hill, is authentic as many of the ingredients are imported from Italy. They have a wide range of tasty pastas and pizzas and you can eat well for about USh 15,000.

Other Italian restaurants worth considering are *Mama Mia* in Speke Hotel, and *La Trattoria* in Hotel Equatoria. Mama Mia specialises in pizzas and ice cream and a small pizza, just about enough for a meal, is about USh 7000. La Trattoria has a wide range of Italian meals available at surprisingly reasonable prices. Main dishes are about USh 8000 and you can eat a decent meal with wine for not much more than USh 14,000.

Thai Thai food has finally come to Kampala in the form of *Krua Thai* a family-run restaurant up in Nakasero Hill. The menu is very good, however, if you are used to Thai food in Thailand, you might want to tell them to spice it up, as they tone down the chillies on many dishes. Most meals are about USh 7000 and more.

Cafes & Grills

If you are staying at Backpackers Hostel, it is worth venturing up the hill towards Mengo to sample the local *food stalls* that set up here each night. It doesn't get cooking until about 8 pm, but once they do, the food is very cheap and filling. For USh 1000, you can get a heaped plate of *matoke*, Irish potatoes, groundnut sauce, beans, greens, and meat or fish.

If you're staying near the YMCA, there are a couple of cheap local restaurants by the roundabout, such as *Ploughmans Cafe*, or you can eat at the YMCA's own *canteen*. There's also *College Inn* which has good meals of roast chicken or steak and chips at very reasonable prices.

If you're staying in the taxi park area, the choice is limited. Best is the tiny *City Restaurant* in the small group of shops on the southern side of the old taxi park. Here you can get a good egg and tea breakfast for USh 1000, and other basic meals for about USh 2000. There are a couple of other places in this group of shops, including *Fresh Corner* a takeaway fast food place. There are a host of cheap restaurants around the edge of the new taxi park.

As Kampala continues to develop, a cafe culture is emerging. Most residents reckon that the best coffee in the city is to be found at *Ban Cafe* which has two outlets in Kampala one opposite the Park Royal shopping arcade and another in Grand Imperial Hotel. There is a good selection of freshly ground coffee for USh 1000 to USh 2000, fresh juices and shakes at slightly higher prices and some tasty cakes. Sandwiches and salads are about USh 5000, making it a popular stop for lunch. It also has a selection of recent international newspapers floating about on the counter.

If you want to get out of the city centre, try *Gallery Cafe* which is 2km along Masaka Rd from Entebbe Rd not far from Natete. The gallery itself is worth a look (see Shopping following for more details), and you can sit on the front veranda and enjoy a pleasant lunch chosen from a small eclectic menu. Dishes cost from USh 5000.

A popular city centre meeting place on Kampala Rd is *Nile Grill*. It's not the cheapest place to go but is popular with expatriate aid workers and well-to-do locals. Outside there are tables with umbrellas. The food is expensive and not that great, but if you're hanging out for a steak or roast chicken, it's one place to head for. Many people come here for just a coffee or a beer. It's open from 9 am to 10 pm Monday to Saturday and 9 am to 9 pm Sunday. There's occasionally live music here on Saturday night.

Further afield, a very popular place with good food is *Half London* on Gaba Rd. It offers a range of grills and western-style food and the service is good. You're looking at about USh 8000 for a meal. But it's not just a place to eat; the bar is one of *the* places to go in the evenings among young people. For more details see under Live Music in the Entertainment section.

Sardinia on Dewinton St is also well regarded for a decent meal. It serves a range of grills for about USh 8000 and puts on a Saturday lunch-time Chinese menu.

Ice Cream
Ice cream is very popular in Kampala and a number of ice cream parlours have sprung up throughout the city. The best ice cream in town is found at *Le Chateau* restaurant on Gaba Rd, but the location is inconvenient for a casual treat. In the city centre, *Mama Mia's* at Speke Hotel has very good imported ice cream, but the flavours are very rich.

Chipper's is very popular, and they have a couple of branches, one on Kampala Rd and another in Kabalagala. They have scoop, whip and sundaes. Another good place in the centre of town is *Fido Dido's*, also on Kampala Rd. *Blitz* has a good range of imported ice creams like Mars and Walls. It's not far from Fido Dido's.

ENTERTAINMENT
Nightlife in Kampala is something to relish these days, with a host of decent bars and clubs throughout the city. There is generally something happening in the city on most nights of the week, although Friday and Saturdays are definitely the big nights out.

Bars
There are plenty of good African bars around town. One good cheap place is *Snow White Bar* a rooftop place opposite L'Hotel Fiancee down near the Owino Market. This is a great place in the evening as you can look over the balcony at the chaos below. It's a very popular place among travellers staying in this area.

The best bar around the taxi parks is the rooftop bar in *Afrique Guesthouse*. The drinks here are cheap and the views of the madness below are incredible to behold around evening rush hour. If you are here during the day, keep an eye on the bus park below as the touts perform a veritable 'pantomime meets Bruce Lee' in trying to attract passengers. And if there is a football match on in Nakivubo Stadium, this is a place from which to watch it on the cheap.

A good locals' bar if you are staying at Backpackers Hostel in Natete is *Maggie's Bar* near Mengo Hospital. They have cheap drinks and a pool table and it often stays open pretty late.

In town is the more sophisticated *Sabrina's* just a short walk west from Hotel Equatoria on Bombo Rd. It has a small, popular bar at the front, and out the back has a huge stage and cinema screen where sometimes there's live music, karaoke and movies.

Just Kickin is a sports bar up in the Kololo district. It is very popular with expats so the atmosphere can feel a bit incestuous at times, but it is always lively at weekends. It is a good spot to watch the big games of the sporting world.

Al's Bar is legendary in Kampala. This is the one place in town that you can be guaranteed to find some people propping up the bar into the wee hours of the morning. It gets very busy at weekends and attracts a regular crowd of expats, Ugandans and a fair number of prostitutes. They have two pool tables, but you have to wait a while to get a game. Drinks are reasonably priced and it is not uncommon for this bar to be open until dawn. It's next door to the Half London (see Live Music following) on Gaba Rd. You can take minibuses here until about 11 pm from the old taxi park, costing USh 500. Special hire taxis from the centre cost anything from USh 3000 to USh 7000 depending on your negotiating skills and how drunk you are by the time you leave.

In a similar vein to Al's is *Capital Bar* in Kababalagala. This place is heaving at weekends and has its fair share of hookers, but most of them troop off to Al's by the early hours.

Kaos is part bar, part nightclub, part bakery (!?!) and an excellent place to be, particularly on Friday nights when a good chunk of Kampala's beautiful people seem to turn up. It is a huge place with an indoor bar and dance floor, an outdoor dance floor and stage and enough pool tables to keep even a hustler happy. Drinks are reasonably priced and it goes on until late into the night. Sometimes there's a nominal entry charge of USh 2000, particularly on Fridays.

A relative newcomer on the nightlife scene is *On the Rocks* at Speke Hotel. This has a covered bar and a huge outdoor area and thrives in the dry season. It remains to be seen what will happen when the big rains come, as the amount of people frequenting this place on Fridays and Saturdays simply won't fit into the bar. It is very popular at weekends and is usually jamming between midnight and 4 am.

Discos & Nightclubs

Several of the bars have a nightclub feel to them in the early hours of the morning and it is not unusual to see dancing at Al's Bar and On the Rocks. Kaos has a big dance floor, but it fills up fast on Fridays.

One of the cheapest and most informal nightclubs, where there's always a good crowd, is *New California 2000 Bar* on Luwum St. There's usually live music here, and a small entry fee is charged.

There are a couple of discos out in the industrial area of town, just off Jinja Rd, east of the two main roundabouts. Both places play a lot of swing and house and locals dance late into the night. Perhaps the most popular disco is *Ange Noir* (pronounced locally as 'Angenoa'). Everyone knows it but it's not signposted on the main road. It's open from 9 pm to 5 am nightly. On Wednesday and Thursday nights women pay only USh 1000.

Club Silk is in the same street and is a similar sort of club that is very popular with locals. Entry charges vary from night to night.

Viper Room is something of a nightclub for the elite located in Hotel Equatoria. Entry is USh 5000 and up depending on the night.

Live Music

Half London (on Gaba Rd below Tank Hill) is a very popular place for live music any night of the week, but especially from Thursday to Sunday. It's partially open-air, partially enclosed, the crowd is mixed, the bar is friendly and boisterous and the beers are normal price. The music is a great introduction to the best the region has to offer and this place is about as close to a must as it gets in Kampala. Get here early at weekends if you want a table or the luxury of parking anywhere within 500m of the joint. You can get share-taxis here (USh 500) until about 10.30 pm from the old taxi park (just ask for Half London); later in the evening you'll need to take a special hire taxi.

Musicians Club 1989 upstairs at the National Theatre meets every Monday night for informal jam sessions. It's definitely worth the time if you are in town on a Monday. Drinks are reasonably cheap and the place fills up with Ugandans letting off steam after a Monday back at work. Sessions start at about 7 pm and go on until around 10 pm, and entry is free.

Quite a few of the upmarket hotels have live bands over the weekend, including Fairway Hotel, Hotel Equatoria, Sheraton Hotel and Nile Hotel. Sabrina's also has a live group from Congo (Zaïre) on Fridays called Stone Band. These guys can really move and usually get the crowd dancing.

If you want to catch Uganda's number one group, Afrigo Band, they often play at *House of Entertainment* which is near Crested Crane Towers. However, to be sure of catching live music while in Kampala, check out Friday's listings page in the *New Vision* newspaper.

Theatre & Dance

If you're interested in traditional dance and music, check out the Ndere Troupe. It's composed of members of the many ethnic groups in Uganda and has gained international acclaim in Europe and North America. The troupe performs fairly regularly in Kampala; contact the booking office at the National Theatre to see if any performances are coming up. *The National Theatre* hosts a range of productions; call in for details.

Cinema

There are now two cinemas in Kampala. The best is *Cineplex* on Wilson Rd, which shows Hollywood movies, and occasionally something with a little more backbone from elsewhere. Shows at 7 and 9.30 pm cost USh 5000 and there are also cheaper shows during the day at 2 (USh 3500) and 4.30 pm (USh 4500).

CineAfrique is on Kampala Rd and shows an eclectic mix of Hollywood, Bollywood and European arthouse films.

Casino

Kampala Casino on Kimathi Ave is open from 2 pm until late daily. There's the usual range of gaming tables, good meals (see Places to Eat), live music, and free beer if you're playing on the tables. No shorts or scruffy gear is allowed here.

More casinos have been opening up regularly in Kampala so avid gamblers should have no trouble finding somewhere to part with their money.

SHOPPING

With such a fledgling tourism industry, Kampala doesn't have a huge range of shops selling crafts and other items of interest.

Behind the National Theatre is the Uganda Arts & Crafts Village, which consists of a number of stalls selling handicrafts such as caneware, wood carvings and small trinkets from around the country at quite reasonable prices. It is open from 9 am to 7 pm Monday to Saturday, and 10 am to 4 pm Sunday.

The Pioneer Mall shopping centre on Kampala Rd has a number of fairly swish boutique-type clothes shops, with prices to match.

On Bombo Rd, not far south from the YMCA, is Uganda Crafts, a nonprofit shop selling a wide variety of crafts, including goods made from leather, wood and cane, and there's a good little open-air cafe.

Gallery Cafe, out on the Masaka Rd, 2km from Entebbe Rd, is one of the best sources of contemporary crafts (ceramics, fabrics, sculpture) and paintings. It's also a great lunch spot (see Places to Eat). To get there by public transport, take a Natete share-taxi from the old taxi park, and get off just after it passes the large Uganda Railways locomotives workshop on the left; the gallery is on the right.

There are a couple of gift shops up in Kololo, near Just Kickin. Just Lookin has a few local items, but is mainly a sort of exiled gift shop from home. Nicer is Cassava Republic, next door to Yakobo's restaurant. Here they sell attractive batiks, decorative furnishings and T-shirts. Prices are relatively high for Uganda, but the quality is good.

Markets

Owino Market is the busiest in Kampala and sprawls around the Nakivubo Stadium, near the taxi parks. Here you can find all sorts of goods for sale, but it is most popular with travellers for its wide range of second-hand clothes from Europe and the USA.

Nakasero Market is Kampala's most famous market and is just below Kampala Rd. It is divided into two areas, one partially covered, where produce is sold, and another located in an attractive old building where hardware, clothes and even a few tourist items are on sale.

UGANDA

GETTING THERE & AWAY
Air
The following airlines run scheduled flights to the international airport at Entebbe:

Air France (☎ 342907, fax 342995) 3 Parliament Ave
Air India (☎ 230600, fax 340605) Grand Imperial Arcade
Air Tanzania (☎ 234631, 234673) United Assurance Bldg, Kimathi Ave
Alliance Air (☎ 344011, fax 344534) 13/15 Kimathi Ave
British Airways (☎ 247414, fax 259181) Centre Court, Plot 4, Ternan Ave
Eagle Uganda (☎ 344292, fax 344501) Kimathi Ave
EgyptAir (☎ 233960, fax 236567) Grand Imperial Hotel
Ethiopian Airlines (☎ 254796, 254797) United Assurance Bldg, Kimathi Ave
Gulf Air (☎ 343190, fax 230526) United Assurance Bldg, Kimathi Ave
Inter Air Uganda (☎ 255508) Grand Imperial Arcade
Iran Air (☎ 255502, fax 344122) just off Kimathi Ave
Kenya Airways (☎ 344304, 256506) United Assurance Bldg, Kimathi Ave
Sabena (☎ 234201, fax 342790) Sheraton Hotel
Uganda Airlines (☎ 232990, fax 257279) Colville St

Bus
Within Uganda The main bus stand is on the corner of Allen Rd and Luwum St, below Kampala Rd. It's a busy place with daily buses to every main town in the country. Most buses leave in the morning, so make enquiries the day before so you can get there early for a decent seat.

To Butogota (for Bwindi National Park), there is one departure at 6 am daily with Silverline; the trip takes most of the day and costs USh 14,000. There are daily buses to Kabale (many companies, USh 10,000, six hours) via Masaka and Mbarara; three daily to Kasese (Safe Journey, USh 10,000, eight hours); daily to Masindi (USh 6000, three hours); and two daily to Fort Portal (USh 8000, six hours). For further details, see the individual entries on each town.

EMS Post Buses EMS Post Buses depart at 8 am daily from the main post office on Kampala Rd for Kabale (USh 9000) via Masaka (USh 4000, two hours) and Mbarara (USh 6000, four hours); Fort Portal (USh 9000, 10 hours) via Mbarara (USh 6000) and Kasese (USh 8000, eight hours); Hoima (USh 8000, six hours) via Masindi (USh 6000, four hours); and Soroti (USh 8000, seven hours) via Jinja (USh 1500), Tororo (USh 5000, four hours), Mbale (USh 6000, five hours) and Kumi (USh 7000, six hours). There is also a direct bus to Fort Portal via Mubende, which takes just four hours.

The post buses are an excellent way to travel, and bookings should be made at the post office a day or so in advance. From originating provincial towns to Kampala, they depart the post offices a little earlier at about 6.30 am. Tickets and reservations should be made at the main post office in town.

Outside Uganda For daily buses to Nairobi, Akamba has its office on Dewinton Rd on the eastern edge of the city centre, Mawingo has its office just on the uphill side (Burton St) of the new taxi park, Takrim is located opposite Tourist Hotel above the old taxi park and Tawfiq is just above the new taxi park in Old Kampala. Akamba also have a service to Kisumu in Kenya.

Takrim and Tawfiq also offer services to Arusha and Dar es Salaam from Kampala. Direct buses to Kigali (Rwanda) depart daily from the main bus station.

See the Uganda Getting There & Away chapter for details and prices of international services.

Minibus Kampala has two taxi parks for minibuses. Although on first appearance these places seem chaotic, they are in fact highly organised and minibuses for a particular destination always leave from the same place within each park. Both parks serve destinations within Kampala and around the country. The old taxi park, on the triangle formed by Burton, Luwum and South Sts, is the bigger of the two and serves all parts of the city and country to the east; the new taxi park services destinations west and north.

As with buses, there are share-taxis to all major parts of the country, including Jinja

(USh 2000, one hour), Mbale (USh 7000, three hours), Malaba (USh 5000, two hours), Masindi (USh 7000, three hours), Fort Portal (USh 8000, six hours), Kabale (USh 10,000, six hours), Masaka (USh 3000, two hours) and Mbarara (USh 7000, four hours).

Train
All passenger trains had ceased operating at the time of writing, which is probably a blessing in disguise as they were so painfully slow and uncomfortable.

Ferry
From Kampala's Port Bell, there used to be ferries to the Ssese Islands (Kalangala) twice a week, but these have been suspended indefinitely. The best way to the islands now is from Masaka, although you can still catch fishing boats from Kasenyi (near Entebbe). Unfortunately these are small, leave in the afternoon and so travel in the dark, and are generally none too safe. See the Ssese Islands section in the South-Western Uganda chapter for more details.

Mwanza (Tanzania) The weekly ferry which connects Port Bell with Mwanza leave Port Bell at 4 pm on Monday. Tickets should be bought by the morning of the day of departure from the port gate at Port Bell. Share-taxis to Port Bell leave from the old taxi park in Kampala. See the Uganda Getting There & Away chapter for full details.

GETTING AROUND
To/From the Airport
The international airport is at Entebbe, 35km from Kampala. There are share-taxis between Kampala (old taxi park) and Entebbe town (USh 1000), and then you can catch another share-taxi from there to the airport (3km, USh 500 per person or USh 2000 for the vehicle). A special hire taxi from Kampala to Entebbe airport costs about USh 30,000.

Minibus
The ubiquitous white minibus taxis leave from the two taxi parks and fan out all over the city. They are cheap, quick and leave every few minutes to most destinations in the city. To find the minibus taxi you want, simply ask around at the taxi parks – people are generally very helpful.

Special Hire
In Kampala itself, there are plenty of 'special hire' taxis, all clearly marked with black and white chequers.

Good places to find them in the centre are outside the taxi parks, around Nakasero Market, at the upper end of Colville St and outside the Pioneer Mall on Kampala Rd. A standard short-distance fare is about USh 2500. Negotiate a price for longer distances, including waiting time if that's what you want.

Around Kampala

ENTEBBE
☎ 041
Entebbe is an attractive, verdant town located on the shores of Lake Victoria. It is home to the Botanical Gardens, which offer a nice escape from the hustle and bustle of life in Kampala, and Entebbe Wildlife Education Centre which is more than just a zoo. It is also the location of Uganda's international airport and can be a convenient place to spend a night or two when arriving late or departing early by plane.

Information
Money There is a branch of Uganda Commercial Bank on Kampala Rd where you can change cash and travellers cheques. There are also foreign exchange desks at Entebbe international airport and the town's top end hotels.

Post & Communications The post office has international telephone and fax services, and there are also card phones and a small post office at the airport.

Entebbe phone numbers were all recently changed and the district code of 042 dropped, making them Kampala numbers. Five digit numbers that used to begin with a 2 are now six digit numbers beginning with 34.

Entebbe Botanical Gardens

The botanical gardens are worth visiting if you have half a day available. Laid out in 1898 by A Whyte, the first curator, they're along the lakeshore between the sailing club and the centre of Entebbe. Locals claim that some of the Johnny Weismuller Tarzan films were made here, although you aren't going to see any chimps like Cheetah here today. Even if you're not particularly enthusiastic about botany, there are some interesting, unusual trees and shrubs and the gardens are fairly well maintained. There is quite a variety of bird species found in the gardens and for arachnophobics, there is a spider walk, and there are a lot of big ones clinging to their webs. The gardens are a lovely spot for a picnic on a sunny day.

Entry costs USh 200 per person, USh 1000 for a car, USh 2000 for a camera and USh 5000 for a video camera, but there isn't a great deal to film.

Entebbe Wildlife Education Centre

The Uganda Wildlife Education Centre is not far from the botanical gardens. Formerly little more than a small zoo, it has been revamped with a grant from USAID

and is now worth a visit if you are in Entebbe. The animals here are mostly recovered from poachers and traffickers and are housed in reasonable conditions. Entry costs USh 2000.

Entebbe Beach Resort

This is a large lakeshore resort that is very quiet during the week, but at weekends becomes packed with Ugandan families escaping the capital for a picnic. There is a weekend charge of USh 3000 to enter the complex, but this doesn't include access to the swimming pool, which costs an additional USh 5000. There is also a restaurant here and some outdoor bars.

Places to Stay

Entebbe has almost nothing in the way of cheap accommodation to offer, but some tourists end up staying here as it is near the airport.

It is possible to pitch a tent at *Entebbe Beach Resort* but the price is a little unreasonable at USh 10,000 per person per night.

There are no budget hotels in Entebbe, but there are some good mid-range options if you are willing to part with some more

Hijacking Entebbe's Reputation

Entebbe would probably be one of the world's more obscure airports were it not for an infamous hijack that took place in June 1976. A Lufthansa plane was hijacked in a combined operation involving Palestinian and German terrorists and the pilot was forced to land at Entebbe. After releasing all non-Israeli hostages, the terrorists demanded the release of prisoners held in Israeli jails, and money, in return for the remaining captives.

Idi Amin offered his services as mediator between the hijackers and the Israeli government, but immediately set about stalling a solution. His sympathies for the Arab cause were widely publicised and he had already expelled Israeli military advisers from the country some years earlier. This made him a less than ideal mediator and the Israelis decided to apply their own solution to the problem.

They launched a surprise raid, with help from the German and Kenyan authorities, which saw Israeli paratroopers land a plane on the runway and drive out of it in a Presidential Mercedes, thus duping the hijackers into believing it was Idi Amin returning from negotiations. Almost all the hostages were freed and the hijackers shot dead in a clinical operation. This caused much embarrassment to Idi Amin as he had been flouncing about attempting to engineer his own peculiar settlement. In retaliation, he broke off relations with Kenya, signalling the death-knell of the already moribund East African Community. One of the Israeli hostages, Dora Bloch, who had been taken to hospital after choking on her food was never seen again, presumably killed in retaliation for Amin's humiliation.

The old airport building is no longer used as a newer airport has since been completed. However, it may be possible to visit the old building if you clear it with airport security staff first.

shillings. **Sophie's Motel** (☎ 340885, fax 340139) is set a little way off the road to the airport and is clearly signposted. Single/ doubles with bathroom cost USh 35,000/ 45,000, and small cottages with better facilities are USh 65,000. One reader described staying here as rather like staying with your favourite aunt, as the owner Christine is very friendly.

The other mid-range choice in town is **Entebbe Flight Motel** (☎ 340812, fax 340 241) just beyond the Windsor Lake Victoria Hotel on the road to the airport. They have slightly more basic but comfortable rooms available for USh 35,000/45,000, including breakfast.

There are two top end places in town. **Imperial Botanical Beach Hotel** (☎ 340800, fax 340832) is on the shores of Lake Victoria. International standard rooms cost US$95/112 plus taxes. Beers and soft drinks are available, as well as meals and snacks. There was a swimming pool under construction at the time of writing.

The other top-end option is **Windsor Lake Victoria Hotel** (☎ 340645, fax 340 404) which has rooms for US$95/120 (including breakfast), plus 22% taxes. There's a swimming pool, bars and restaurants. Nonguests can use the pool for USh 5000, redeemable against snacks or drinks, making this a very good deal. It's a very popular place among the well heeled for a meal and drinks on the weekend.

Another upmarket hotel midway between Entebbe and Kampala on the shores of Lake Victoria is **Ranch on the Lake** (☎ 200147, fax 200148) with rooms for US$70/100. There are also villas for US$100 for one person, US$140 for two people and US$200 for four people. All rates are inclusive of breakfast, but not taxes. It is a peaceful location, but very out the way unless you have your own transport.

Places to Eat

When it comes to food in Entebbe, most people eat at one of the hotels listed in Places to Stay. Entebbe Flight Hotel has a wider range of meals than Sophie's Motel. Windsor Lake Victoria Hotel has a massive selection of menus, encompassing Chinese, Indian, Italian and American (burgers and fries etc) food. Most dishes are between USh 6000 and USh 10,000.

However, there is a pretty good alternative in the form of **China Garden Restaurant**. It serves some tasty Far Eastern fare for about USh 6000 to USh 10,000 a dish. It is on Kampala Rd, not far from Uganda Commercial Bank.

Getting There & Away

Minibuses run between Entebbe and Kampala throughout the day. It costs USh 1000 for the trip and they run from the new taxi park in Kampala.

Getting Around

To/From the Airport To get out to the airport from Entebbe, take a share-taxi (USh 500) or charter the entire cab for USh 2000.

LAKE VICTORIA
Ngamba Island Chimpanzee Sanctuary

There is a chimpanzee sanctuary located on Ngamba Island in Lake Victoria, which is becoming a popular day trip for tourists staying in Kampala. The chimps here can be viewed at very close range during feeding times, at 11 am and 3 pm. There are more than 20 chimps and they are free to wander about the forested island. The island is 23km from Entebbe.

Trips out to visit the chimpanzees have to be arranged in advance with tour companies in Kampala. G & C Tours (☎ 321479, 077-502155, email gctours@imul.com) based in Entebbe has a speedboat and a slower, local boat which make the trip. The slow boat costs US$50 per person for between five and eight people; more than 10 and the price drops to US$30. This journey takes up to two hours. On the speedboat, it costs US$50 per person with more than four people, US$200 for the boat with fewer, taking about one hour.

Semliki Safaris (☎ 259700, email gwg@ swiftuganda.com) also offer boat trips out to Ngamba Island by speedboat. The boat departs from Munyonyo marina near Gaba.

UGANDA

Both these companies also offer trips combining fishing for Nile perch (see following) on Lake Victoria with a visit to the chimps.

Fishing Trips
Semliki Safaris and G&C Tours offer fishing trips on Lake Victoria, the quarry being the gigantic Nile perch, specimens of which often come in at more than 100kg. Prices for an all day trip, including lunch, start at about US$100 per person for a small group and rise as numbers drop.

Horse Riding
Horse riding around the Lake Victoria area of Kampala is available through Speke Equestrian Centre (☎ 259221), located at Munyonyo marina, near Gaba. There are a variety of treks available from just one hour to all day.

The African Queen
One of the actual boats used in the making of *The African Queen* has been fully refurbished and is available for cruises on Lake Victoria. To take a cruise costs US$20, or US$30 with lunch or dinner.

The owners also run a small *camp site* on the shores of the lake. Full board accommodation costs US$65 per person per night. For further details on *The African Queen*, call ☎ 075-723672 or ☎ 077-505407.

MABIRA FOREST RESERVE
This large, attractive forest reserve is one of the more convenient places to see some of Uganda's myriad bird species as it is home to more than 300 species. Monkeys are also easily spotted, but of the bigger animals possibly present such as leopard, little is seen. There is a well established trail system here that offers access to pristine forest and birdlife. There is a charge of US$6 per 24 hours spent in the reserve.

There is an attractive community *camping ground* here, which has camping for USh 3000 per person per night, bandas for USh 10,000/15,000 for singles/doubles and USh 20,000 for three or more people. The staff here can also prepare food for about USh 3000. It is a great place to escape the traffic and noise of Kampala.

To get here just jump on a minibus travelling between Kampala and Jinja and get off when you see the signpost for the reserve. It lies about 20km outside Jinja.

MPANGA FOREST RESERVE
Mpanga Forest Reserve, about 37km southwest of Kampala on the road to Masaka, is another little getaway if the rigours, or nightlife, of the capital become too much for you. This is a young forest, little more than 50 years old, as it was used as a tropical research institute, but the sheer size of the trees attest to the progress that can be made with well managed reforestation programs.

This reserve is well known for its many butterflies (181 species) and birds (141 species), and a number of clearly marked paths have been cut out of the thick undergrowth to enable closer viewing. There are also red tailed monkeys around. Entry to the reserve costs USh 3000.

A VSO volunteer has established a small inexpensive *camp site* here, where you can pitch a tent for USh 3000 per person per night, or you can stay in a banda for USh 10,000 per night. Food should be available but take your own just in case.

To get here, take a minibus from the new taxi park in Kampala to Mpigi for USh 1200 and then a *boda-boda* (bicycle-taxi) on to Mpanga for USh 500. Alternatively take a bus or minibus heading to Masaka (USh 2500) and ask to get off at Mpanga.

THE EQUATOR
Uganda is one of only 10 countries in the world through which the equator passes and this has led to the usual monument and souvenir shops that spring up in destinations from Ecuador to Indonesia. The equator crosses the Kampala to Masaka road at a point 78km south of the capital. There are two cement circles marking the line and it isn't such a bad spot for a photo opportunity, although it is altogether more convenient with your own transport.

To get here from Kampala, jump on a Masaka bus and minibus and hope to pay USh 2000, although it is likely they will charge the full Masaka fare of USh 2500.

UGANDA

South-Eastern Uganda

JINJA
☎ 043

Jinja lies on the shores of Lake Victoria and is a major market centre for southern and eastern Uganda. It is an interesting little place with much Indian-influenced architecture reflecting the days when the town had a sizeable Asian community. Many Asians have returned to reclaim their businesses and properties in recent years, having been forced to leave during the Amin years, and since their return the town has once again prospered. There is a host of spacious mansions in various states of repair, surrounded by extensive lawns, overlooking the lake along Nile Crescent, adjacent to the town's golf course. Jinja did not suffer as badly as many other towns during the last civil war and so does not wear the same cloak of dereliction. According to local residents, Okello's retreating troops were told in no uncertain terms that they were not welcome.

While there is not a lot to do here, it is a comfortable base for white-water rafting, and the source of the Nile is something to behold when you consider how far the water has to travel on its journey to the Mediterranean through Sudan and Egypt.

Coming from Kampala, the Owen Falls Dam forms a spectacular gateway to the town: as you coast across the top, look down on the raging river below. The dam supplies Uganda with the bulk of its electricity, or doesn't supply it with much electricity, depending on which way you look at it. An extension is currently nearing completion.

Orientation
Although Jinja is a major step down from Uganda's capital in terms of the number of people living here, it is quite spread out and so getting your bearings away from the centre can take time. The centre of town is built on a simple grid system. Main St is the commercial strip and includes the post office, at its southern extremity, and most of

Highlights

- Ride the grade five rapids at the source of the Nile – they eat people for breakfast
- Take a hike up Mt Elgon, one of the region's highest mountains, with cliffs, caves, gorges and waterfalls
- Relax at Sipi Falls, one of the most peaceful, idyllic spots in Uganda

the banks, shops and cafes. The taxi park and bus station are a few blocks east of the northern end of Main St. Although the centre is easily negotiable on foot, it is a fair walk from other spots in town. However, boda-bodas (bicycle-taxis) will pedal you around quite cheaply.

Information
Tourist Office There is no government tourist office in Jinja, but the Tourist Centre on Main St is helpful, although it is primarily a private business.

Money There are several banks that change cash and travellers cheques, including Allied Bank and Crane Bank. They are all open on weekdays and Saturday morning. There are also a few foreign exchange bureaus along Main St that stay open a little later than the banks.

Post & Communications The main post office is on the corner of Main St and Bell Ave and offers the usual postal and communication services. Starcom operates a small branch in a shipping container on Main St. It may look basic, but includes international telephone and fax services. All Jinja numbers recently had a 1 placed in front so if you are trying to contact someone in Jinja and the number has only five digits, add a 1.

Email and Internet services are available in Jinja, but access is painfully expensive as

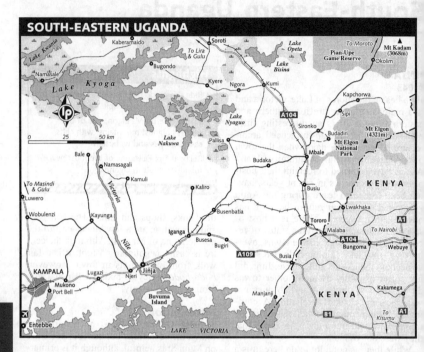

SOUTH-EASTERN UGANDA

it involves a call to Kampala because there is no local server. Source Cafe on Main St charges USh 1000 for the first email message and USh 100 for each message after that, and they serve the best coffee in town. Explorers Backpackers charges the same, convenient if you are staying there. Both outfits charge USh 500 a minute for Internet access – ouch!

Source of the Nile
The source of the Nile is promoted as one of Jinja's premier drawcards and tourists are bussed in from Kampala to marvel at the start of this mighty river, but the reality is that there is very little to see. Before the building of the Owen Falls Dam, this was the site of the Ripon Falls, where the Nile left Lake Victoria on its long journey to the Mediterranean. The falls were inundated by the waters of the dam, but you can still make out where they used to be from the turbulence in the river.

The area was recently sponsored by Bell Breweries so everything has been painted yellow and red in keeping with the corporate image. It is pretty garish, but at least you can get a cold drink under the shade of some trees. There is a large plaque telling you all about the 'discovery' of the source by John Speke, although many Africans contend that their ancestors knew this was the Nile's source long before the white man found out.

You can take boat rides on the river from here. Locals will charge around USh 10,000, but for something a little more organised try the nearby Speke's Sporting Bar, which offers hour-long cruises at 10.30 am and 12.30 and 3.30 pm, and sunset cruises at 5.30 and 6.30 pm, all costing USh 15,000.

White-Water Rafting
The source of the Nile is one of the most spectacular white-water rafting destinations in the world and for many visitors to Uganda a rafting trip is the highlight of their visit.

There are two companies offering exhilaration without compromise: international operator Adrift (☎ 041-268670, fax 341245, email adrift@starcom.co.ug) and local outfit Nile River Explorers (☎ 120236, fax 121 322, email rafting@starcom.co.ug). There is no love lost between the two, so depending on whom you talk with, you will hear good and bad stories about both.

Adrift runs a choice of three trips on the Nile, the most popular being the full-day option, which costs US$95 including transport, lunch and beer on the journey home. This is the trip to take if you like big water as the Adrift gang takes on the Big Four, all monster grade five rapids, including Itanda (Bad Place). Adrift has a shorter trip which is cheaper at US$65, but it includes only two of the Big Four rapids. For rafting addicts, Adrift has a two-day trip that includes camping out on an island and a gentler second day meandering past villages. But addiction comes at a price and that is a hefty US$230. Adrift picks up punters in Kampala from both the Backpackers Hostel and the Sheraton Hotel and drops you back there in the evening if you are not staying in Jinja.

Nile River Explorers is a cheaper option, charging just US$65 for a full day's rafting, but as their rafts are smaller and lighter, they are unable to take on the biggest water, and hug the edges on the grade fives. However, the bumps and jumps will feel just as big because your raft is that bit smaller. Nile offers a second day of rafting at just US$30 for repeat offenders.

Both operators accept credit cards and you can also book trips through guesthouses and hotels in Kampala. Adrift and Nile River Explorers both have camping grounds at Bujagali Falls; see that entry later in this chapter for details. It is possible that both outfits will end up going under, literally, if the proposed dam at Bujagali Falls goes ahead – see the boxed text 'Dammed if You Do, Damned if You Don't' later in this chapter for more details.

Gandhi's Shrine
Near the Source of the Nile Plaque is a small memorial garden commemorating

Gandhi in Uganda?

It comes as something of a surprise to find a statue commemorating Mahatma Gandhi (or more precisely, the scattering of his ashes) at a Hindu temple near Jinja.

It seems that on Gandhi's death in 1948, his ashes were divided up and sent to many locations around the world to be scattered – and some ended up in the Nile River in Uganda. There were also some that ended up in a bank vault in India and were only released in 1997 following a lengthy custody dispute.

Mahatma Gandhi, the centrepiece of which is a bronze bust donated by the Indian government. This area is becoming quite a pilgrimage site for Ugandan Indians as this is one of the places where Gandhi's ashes were scattered. So Gandhi was rafting the Nile long before Adrift came to town.

Nile Brewery
For those consuming litres of Nile Special in Kampala, this alternative 'Source of the Nile' makes a lively day out, and includes the obligatory free beer. Free guided tours take place on Tuesday and Thursday. If enough people turn up, they may show you around on another day of the week. There is a small souvenir shop where you can buy T-shirts, bottle openers and the like. It is certainly a more original brewery visit than one to the Heineken brewery in Amsterdam.

Jinja Club
Part of Jinja Golf Club, the club offers the only public swimming pool in Jinja, tennis, squash, a nine-hole golf course and snooker. There is also a bar that is popular with Swedish dam workers and a small restaurant with reasonably priced meals. Swimming costs USh 5000 per day; tennis, squash and snooker are USh 3000 per session; and two rounds of golf is USh 10,000, plus USh 2000 for caddie fees.

Places to Stay – Budget
For campers, there are two excellent camp sites out at Bujagali Falls. See the Bujagali

UGANDA

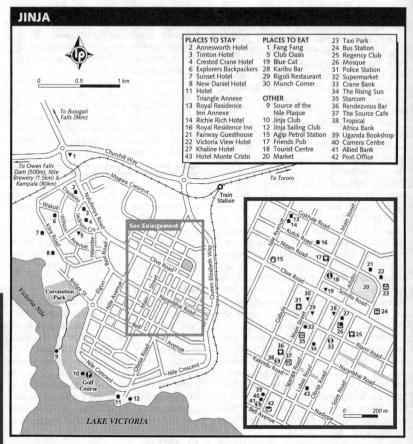

JINJA

PLACES TO STAY	PLACES TO EAT	23 Taxi Park
2 Annesworth Hotel	1 Fang Fang	24 Bus Station
3 Timton Hotel	5 Club Oasis	25 Regency Club
4 Crested Crane Hotel	19 Blue Cat	26 Mosque
6 Explorers Backpackers	28 Karibu Bar	31 Police Station
7 Sunset Hotel	29 Rigoli Restaurant	32 Supermarket
8 New Daniel Hotel	30 Munch Corner	33 Crane Bank
11 Hotel		34 The Rising Sun
Triangle Annexe	OTHER	35 Starcom
13 Royal Residence	9 Source of the	36 Rendezvous Bar
Inn Annexe	Nile Plaque	37 The Source Cafe
14 Richie Rich Hotel	10 Jinja Club	38 Tropical
16 Royal Residence Inn	12 Jinja Sailing Club	Africa Bank
21 Fairway Guesthouse	15 Agip Petrol Station	39 Uganda Bookshop
22 Victoria View Hotel	17 Friends Pub	40 Camera Centre
27 Khaline Hotel	18 Tourist Centre	41 Allied Bank
43 Hotel Monte Cristo	20 Market	42 Post Office

Falls entry later in this chapter for details. A pleasant option for campers in town is **Timton Hotel** which has an attractive garden where you can pitch your tent for just USh 3000. See Places to Stay – Mid-Range for details of the Timton.

The most popular guesthouse in town is **Explorers Backpackers** (☎ 120236, fax 121 322, email rafting@starcom.co.ug, 41 Wilson Ave) a budget crashpad run by Nile River Explorers. It has dorm beds for US$5, double rooms at US$15 or you can pitch a tent for just US$3. There is a cheap bar and the obligatory pool table, and it also offers

email facilities. It can get pretty loud when a truck or two comes through, but it all adds to the atmosphere. It accepts credit cards for raft bookings, so you can lump your accommodation in with this if you are short of cash.

There are quite a few other cheap guesthouses spread throughout Jinja, but many of these cater solely for students studying in Jinja. The best option is **Victoria View Hotel** (☎ 121363) although its name is purely wishful thinking. Like many of Jinja's hotels, the place is sleepy, but the 30 self-contained rooms are a reasonable deal at USh 8000. This place is conveniently located near the taxi park.

Just up the road is *Fairway Guesthouse* (☎ 121784) which offers musty singles/doubles for USh 8000/10,000 though it isn't as clean as the Victoria View. It has a cheap restaurant downstairs, however, and this is a good option for breakfast.

One other cheap option is *Hotel Monte Cristo* down on the southern end of Lubas Rd. Downstairs is a lively bar and restaurant, and upstairs it offers pretty grungy rooms for USh 7000.

Places to Stay – Mid-Range

There is a whole host of mid-range hotels in Jinja catering to dam construction workers, but these are often fully booked. However, there still seem to be far more beds than visitors in this quiet town so don't be afraid to ask for a discount.

Cheapest in this category is *Khaline Hotel* (☎ 121209) on Lubas Rd near the market. It has basic singles/doubles with bathroom for USh 10,000/15,000, but it's nothing special compared with the budget hotels.

Royal Residence Inn (☎ 120152) on Kutch Rd used to be known as Bellevue Hotel, and has long been a favourite with NGOs. It offers singles/doubles for USh 15,000/20,000 with attached bathroom and hot water. It also operates an annexe on Nile Ave with similar charges.

Next door to this annexe is *Richie Rich Hotel* with standard rooms for USh 15,000/20,000. There is a little bar downstairs and a pool room.

If you are willing to spend a little more, then *Timton Hotel* (☎ 120278) is a friendly little family place set in attractive gardens. Singles/doubles cost USh 17,000/30,000 and a suite costs USh 50,000, all with breakfast and attached bathroom. There are telephones in the rooms for receiving calls, and a small restaurant.

Annesworth Hotel (☎ 120086) in the same area is similar in style to Timton Hotel, with rooms at USh 20,000/30,000, including breakfast.

Along Kiira Rd above Lake Victoria is *New Daniel Hotel* (☎ 121633, fax 121322) with rooms for US$25/35 and suites for US$40 to US$50. These prices are quite high given the mothballed feel to the rooms, but the friendly owner maintains that they are negotiable.

Crested Crane Hotel & Tourism Training Centre (☎ 121954, fax 121515) is owned by the Ministry of Tourism and has been around for years. As the name suggests, the Ministry uses it to train staff in the tourism industry, but fear not, trainees are not let loose on the hotel itself. Well appointed singles/doubles cost USh 41,250/47,500 and large executive suites cost an even USh 100,000; all rates include breakfast. There are a couple of bars and some pool tables downstairs.

Places to Stay – Top End

There are a couple of hotels that just about rate as top end, although the rating is more for the prices than for the facilities. *Sunset Hotel* (☎ 120115, fax 121322) has a mind-boggling array of rooms available with options like TV and air-con. Basic singles/doubles cost USh 35,000/55,000, rising to USh 75,000 for a double with all the trimmings. It also offers suites for USh 95,000. These rates include breakfast. This place often fills up with dam workers, so it may be worth booking ahead to be sure of a room. It overlooks the Nile, making the bar here a great place for a sunset drink.

A relative newcomer on the Jinja scene is *Hotel Triangle Annex* (☎ 122098, fax 122099), also known as Hotel Triangle at the Source of the Nile (not to be confused with the cheaper Hotel Triangle) which sits above Lake Victoria near the golf course. It offers a large number of clean, modern rooms and more are under construction. Singles/doubles cost USh 50,000/60,000, or USh 70,000 a double for an executive room, which is larger than the standard. In practice, ground floor rooms are USh 50,000, those upstairs with a better view are USh 60,000 and executive rooms are Ush 70,000. It has a great location, but unfortunately the building itself is pretty unattractive with no thought given to traditional design.

UGANDA

Places to Eat

The choice of restaurants in Jinja is nothing like that in Kampala, but there are a few spots worth checking out if you are in town for a few days. There are a couple of reasonable Indian restaurants in town, but nothing like the level of subcontinent food you would expect from a town with such a large Asian population. *Munch Corner* does the standard selection of *dosas* (a type of Indian savoury pancake) and curries for anything from USh 2000 to USh 4000. A newer place is *Rangoli Restaurant* on Main St, which has an extensive menu of Indian dishes. Large *thalis* (mixed curry selection including rice and poppadoms) are Ush 4500 with meat, Ush 3500 for vegetarian.

For African staples, there are a lot of little places serving chicken, beans, rice and so on at pretty low prices. *Karibu Bar* has a lively atmosphere and a reasonably wide menu, and *Blue Cat* also pulls a healthy local crowd, although more often for the beer than the food.

Some of the mid-range hotels also have small restaurants. The menus are normally pretty eclectic and the prices reasonable. Best of the lot is probably the restaurant at *Royal Residence Inn* on Kutch Rd, but *Timton Hotel* has a much more tranquil location.

There are several decent restaurants in town if you want to spend nearer to USh 10,000 than USh 1000. For pizzas and a few basic pastas, head to *Club Oasis* near Explorers Backpackers and the Crested Crane. The pizzas are good as an Italian taught the staff how to make them; they range from about USh 6500 to USh 8500.

There is also a good selection of Italian food available at *Sunset Hotel* because the owners learnt to cook for an Italian construction team staying here. Prices are about USh 6000 a plate. It also provides pretty good Chinese food and a very popular Sunday buffet that costs around USh 10,000. It's a great place to while away a Sunday watching life at the source of the Nile.

For the best Chinese food you need to head out of town to *Fang Fang* on the Kampala roundabout. The food here is highly rated and you can eat a good spread

with a drink or two for around US$10. There is another branch of this popular establishment in Kampala.

Entertainment

There is not a lot of it, particularly if you are coming from Kampala. However, coming from Nairobi, you might consider it entertainment just being able to walk the streets at night without being mugged.

Although it seems that many a year has gone by since any boating happened here, *Jinja Sailing Club* is well maintained and has some lush lawns that run right up to the edge of the lake. This is one of the best spots in town to sip a cold drink and watch the sun go down across the lake. It has a good menu as well, which makes it a popular place for lunch and dinner, particularly Sunday lunch. The club is just below the Hotel Triangle Annex, a 20-minute walk from the centre of town or a quicker boda-boda ride.

In town, there is a nightclub near the bus station called *Regency Club*. It is open all week and has heaps of promotions to encourage you to enter.

Speke's Sporting Bar is worth checking out for an evening beer. It has perhaps the best location of any bar in Jinja, nestled on the river near the Source of the Nile Plaque. It is built entirely from wood and has a series of walkways running along the edge of the river. It serves a good range of food and a whole host of drinks. To get here take a boda-boda to the Source of the Nile Plaque and head upriver a short way. It is quite a descent to the riverbank from the side of the road, so watch out on a dark, wet night after a few ales.

A popular haunt in the centre of town is the Austrian-run *Amadeus*. This bar attracts a pretty reasonable mix of locals and expats, although drink prices are a little more Kampala than Jinja. On Friday night it has a tasty set evening meal for around US$5.

The best thing about bars in Jinja is that most of them are very close together. For those who like a beer or two, Main St offers an excellent strip for a bar crawl, as every shopfront seems to be a bar by night.

Getting There & Away

Bus The road between Jinja and Kampala is 80km of solid tarmac so the trip takes little more than one hour by minibus or bus. Minibuses from Kampala leave from the new taxi park and cost USh 2000. Coaster buses are slightly cheaper at USh 1500 and probably slightly safer because of their size. However, they take longer to fill up.

There are minibuses from Jinja to the Kenyan border at either Malaba (USh 4000) or Busia (USh 3500). If you are heading to Mbale for Sipi Falls or Mt Elgon, they cost USh 5000.

Ferry Ugandan Railways ferries operate between Jinja and Mwanza in Tanzania, but they don't take passengers. To get to Mwanza by ferry, you'll have to take the MV *Victoria* from Port Bell. See the Uganda Getting There and Away chapter for details.

Getting Around

The centre of Jinja is compact enough to wander about on foot. However, if you are heading to the source of the Nile, the Owen Falls Dam or the Nile Brewery, you might be advised to take a boda-boda. These cost between USh 500 and USh 1000, depending on your negotiating skills.

AROUND JINJA
Bujagali Falls

Bujagali Falls are more like a series of large rapids, but the location is very beautiful, and popular with locals on weekends. There is a picnic spot just below the falls where you can get cold drinks and snacks. It is likely that increasing numbers of travellers will end up staying in this area if they are rafting, as both operators have camp sites out here.

Ugandans take a peculiar delight in watching local men throw themselves into the top of the falls with nothing more than a plastic jerrycan, sealed with an avocado, to keep them alive. Each to their own and all that, but this is a seriously dangerous practice. Should they lose their grip, they are dead, and several people go this way each year. Surely this is taking risking one's life to make a living to extremes, and it should not be encouraged by tourists. Save your USh 5000 for something else, or give the guys USh 5000 not to chuck themselves in, as they probably have families to look after.

Places to Stay *Nile River Explorers* has a camp site above the falls which doesn't look much from the road, just a field really, but when you venture into the site itself you will find terraces for camping all the way down to the riverbank. The showers look out over the river, which can make a wash more interesting than usual. Camping costs US$3 and there are drinks and food for sale.

At the falls themselves is *Speke Camp Site* which Adrift uses as a base for rafting. It is an attractive site with camping and *bandas* (thatched huts) available, and a small restaurant and bar area that fills up on weekends. It costs USh 3000 per person per night to camp, USh 5000 for a dorm bed in a banda, USh 7000 per person in a twin banda and USh 16,000 for a secluded double banda. All bandas have a great location, set among coffee plantations that overlook the falls. If you are coming just for the day, there is an entry charge of USh 2000 per person. The only downside to this beautiful location is that it may be inundated in a few years if the Bujagali Falls Dam is constructed (see the boxed text 'Dammed if You Do, Damned if You Don't' later in this chapter).

Getting There & Away Bujagali Falls are about 9km from Jinja. To get here, head north-west out of town and go straight ahead at the roundabout by Fang Fang. Follow this bumpy road and you will come to a large signpost directing you left along a 1km road to the falls. Adrift plans to run an irregular shuttle in and out of town, so this could be one way to get here. Otherwise you'll need to find a minibus heading out that way (USh 500) or charter a special taxi for about USh 5000.

Mabira Forest Reserve

For details on this lush forest reserve about 20km outside Jinja, see the Around Kampala section in the Kampala chapter.

TORORO

☎ 045

In the very eastern part of Uganda, not far from the border with Kenya, is Tororo. It must have looked particularly beautiful once, with its flowering trees, and it had a substantial Asian community, as the two large Hindu temples suggest. These days, however, there's little of interest and the town wears a cloak of dereliction. Its only redeeming feature is the intriguing, forest-covered volcanic plug that rises up abruptly

Dammed if You Do, Damned if You Don't

No visitor who spends more than a few days in Uganda can fail to notice that the country has power problems, serious power problems. Uganda's shortage of electricity generating capacity is compounded by the fact that it exports 30MW of its 183MW total to Kenya and smaller amounts to both Tanzania and Rwanda. While it may seem ridiculous for a country that keeps its own citizens in the dark to be selling power to its neighbours, the fault lies not with the Ugandans but with the British colonial authorities who set up the agreement back in 1954 when Owen Falls Dam was completed.

The Owen Falls Dam was built at a time when rock'n'roll was yet to be invented, the Mini was yet to hit the road, Winston Churchill was still in Downing St and Hungary was the best football team in the world. Now it doesn't take a musician, mechanic, politician or footballer to tell you that was a long time ago, and things have moved on since then. Unfortunately, Uganda's power supply has not, partly because of the terrible upheavals of the 1970s and 1980s and partly because the government did nothing to address the problem before it reached crisis point. All over Uganda, load-shedding (a handy euphemism for turning off the power in a town or district) takes place every other day, even in Jinja, where the dam is located. While this remains little more than an inconvenience for most Ugandans, it is an impediment to the redevelopment of a solid manufacturing base, as without power it is hard for factories to operate.

An extension to the Owen Falls Dam is currently nearing completion, although extension is rather a misleading term as eventually the original dam will have to be shut down and filled with concrete as it is structurally unsound. And to make matters worse, right now it is the only thing holding back the waters of Lake Victoria, because the rock shelf that created the Ripon Falls was blasted away to ensure a smooth flow of water into the dam's turbines. Lake Victoria has a surface area of 69,599 sq km; multiply that by a depth of 15m and you have one hell of a lot of water. It could make for the ultimate white-water rafting trip, all the way to the Mediterranean probably, but for the people of northern and southern Sudan, it would be like emptying a swimming pool on an ants' nest. So the 'extension' will soon be a replacement, but in the meantime two turbines of 40MW will be installed with an option on a further three as funding becomes available.

However, this capacity will still not be enough as demand is constantly growing as the population increases. The private sector has proposed two more dams for hydroelectric power projects, both on the Nile: a US$500 million, 250MW station at Bujagali Falls near Jinja and a US$167 million, 100MW station at Karuma Falls near Murchison Falls.

There is a fair amount of opposition to the project at Bujagali, not only because the land is considered sacred by local people, but because it will wipe out several of the rapids used by the rafting companies, possibly putting them out of business.

The project at Karuma would have less of an environmental impact because the plan is to channel water underground rather than build a huge concrete dam, but this plan has less government support than the Bujagali proposal.

So the government and the private sector are attempting to address the problem of power in Uganda. However, by the time one of these proposed projects is completed, demand will have risen yet again and even more power will be needed to light up the lives of the average Ugandan.

from the plain at the back of the town. The views from the top are well worth the climb.

For travellers, Tororo is a place to stop and rest on the way to Mbale, Mt Elgon and points further north and north-west, although the accommodation options are much better in Mbale.

Information

There is a branch of the Uganda Commercial Bank in town, but no obvious foreign exchange bureaus. The post office offers international telephone and fax services.

Places to Stay & Eat

The only dirt cheap place worth considering is *Tororo Christian Guesthouse* diagonally opposite the Total petrol station on Mbale Rd. It's clean and friendly and costs USh 4500/6000 for singles/doubles.

The clean and friendly *Coop Hotel* charges USh 7000/10,000. Bucket showers are available and the toilets are kept clean (trivia lovers will be thrilled to know that the cisterns are genuine cast-iron Shanks, 'Made in England'). The hotel has its own bar and restaurant, which serves a standard African menu.

Similar is *Safeway Hotel*, which charges USh 7000/9000. Unfortunately, it doesn't have an attached supermarket of the same name.

Slightly smarter than these places is *Deluxe Guesthouse* which offers single rooms with shared facilities for USh 8000 and doubles with private bathroom costing USh 12,000.

The best hotel in the centre of town is *Crystal Hotel* which has clean doubles (no singles) for USh 15,000. The generator here is good news for those on the 1st floor, who get electricity, but it doesn't seem to have the output to make it to the 2nd floor. There's a restaurant, which serves good meals, and a bar.

On the outskirts of town on the road to Malaba is *Rock Hotel* a large old place set in attractive gardens. Rooms here are USh 20,000/30,000, including bathroom and breakfast. There is a certain charm about the place, even though the location is not so convenient.

If you're not eating at your hotel, there is decent food available at *St Peter's College*. Basically, it's a canteen, but the meals are good and prices reasonable. You could also try *New Safari Hotel* on the corner of Mbale and Uhuru Rds.

Getting There & Away

A minibus to Kampala costs USh 6000 and takes about three to four hours. The short ride to Malaba on the Kenyan border costs USh 1000, and to Mbale the cost is USh 1500.

MBALE
☎ 045

In stark contrast to Tororo, Mbale is a thriving provincial city with plenty of activity and well maintained facilities. It enjoys a superb setting at the base of Mt Elgon, and makes an excellent base for expeditions to the mountain from the Ugandan side. It's also a good base for visits to Sipi Falls, the country's most beautiful falls and the ones you will frequently see featured on posters promoting Uganda. Mbale is definitely one of Uganda's nicer towns.

TORORO

To Mbale (45km)

Oguc Street

Uhuru Road

Mbale Road

Station Road

To Tororo Christian Guest House (400m) & Kampala (205km)

To Golf Course, Rock Hotel & Malaba (15km)

To Train Station (700m)

0   100   200 m

1 Municipal Offices
2 Esso Petrol Station
3 Hindu Temple
4 St Peter's College
5 Deluxe Guesthouse
6 Market
7 Safeway Hotel
8 New Safari Hotel
9 Coop Hotel
10 Uganda Commercial Bank
11 Post Office
12 Crystal Hotel
13 Hindu Temple
14 Shell Petrol Station
15 Bus & Matatu Stand
16 Agip Petrol Station

UGANDA

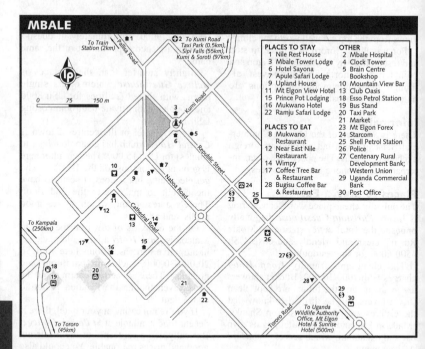

MBALE

PLACES TO STAY	OTHER
1 Nile Rest House	2 Mbale Hospital
3 Mbale Tower Lodge	4 Clock Tower
6 Hotel Sayona	5 Brain Centre
7 Apule Safari Lodge	Bookshop
9 Upland House	10 Mountain View Bar
11 Mt Elgon View Hotel	13 Club Oasis
15 Prince Pot Lodging	18 Esso Petrol Station
16 Mukwano Hotel	19 Bus Stand
22 Ramju Safari Lodge	20 Taxi Park
	21 Market
PLACES TO EAT	23 Mt Elgon Forex
8 Mukwano	24 Starcom
Restaurant	25 Shell Petrol Station
12 Near East Nile	26 Police
Restaurant	27 Centenary Rural
14 Wimpy	Development Bank;
17 Coffee Tree Bar	Western Union
& Restaurant	29 Uganda Commercial
28 Bugisu Coffee Bar	Bank
& Restaurant	30 Post Office

Information

There are several banks in town, including Uganda Commercial Bank and Centenary Rural Development Bank. There are also a couple of foreign exchange bureaus in the centre.

The post office has international telephone and fax services, but it has some competition from Starcom, which has an office in an old shipping container, with cheaper and more reliable international telephone services.

For information on climbing Mt Elgon, visit the Uganda Wildlife Authority office near Mt Elgon Hotel (not to be confused with the Mt Elgon View Hotel). It is open every day from 8 am to 5 pm, and the staff here can help you organise your trip. For details on climbing Mt Elgon, see the Mt Elgon National Park section later in this chapter.

Places to Stay – Budget

One of the best places around Mbale is *Salem Mbale* (☎ 077-505595) a guesthouse some distance out of town that supports local projects such as childcare and a health centre in Nakaloke district. All profits go towards these community projects so your money is going to a good cause. Camping costs USh 2000 and a dorm bed is just USh 4000. It also offers double rooms with partly shared facilities for USh 15,000 and doubles with bathroom for USh 25,000. Many of these rooms are in attractive bandas. It also offers reasonable meals and refreshments. To get here, take a minibus to Nakaloke (USh 500) and then a boda-boda to the guesthouse for about USh 300 (although you are more likely to end up paying USh 500).

The cheapest accommodation in town is not that great. The pick of the very meagre bunch is *Mbale Tower Lodge* because it is slap bang in the middle of town, overlooking the clock tower. Plain singles cost USh 5000 or USh 6500, depending on size, and doubles are USh 8000.

UGANDA

Nile Rest House has been around a while and charges USh 5000/6000 for singles/doubles with attached bathrooms, which is pretty good value, but it has a neglected feel. Another cheap option is *Prince Pot Lodging* which charges USh 6000/8000.

Somewhat more salubrious is *Upland House* in the centre of town. Spartan but reasonably clean rooms go for USh 9000/12,000 and there's hot water in the communal bathroom.

Apule Safari Lodge offers what it bills as executive accommodation, although it is doubtful that many corporations would rate it as such. Rooms cost USh 8000/12,000 with private bathroom. Each room is named after one of Uganda's many lakes.

Ramju Safari Lodge is a big hotel near the market, but its prices are slightly steep for what it offers, at USh 10,000/12,000.

Best of all in this range is the recently refurbished *Mukwano Hotel* with singles/doubles with attached bathroom for USh 10,000/15,000 most with a small balcony overlooking the street. It's kept very clean, and there's hot water in the showers and friendly staff. The hotel has its own bar and restaurant on the ground floor.

Another good choice is the friendly *Hotel Sayona* overlooking the clock tower. It offers a variety of rooms with prices ranging from USh 7000 a single to USh 14,000 a double, all with shared bath and hot water.

Places to Stay – Mid-Range

Mt Elgon View Hotel is Mbale's only option in this price range, although the rooms and service are not necessarily a significant improvement on the cheaper lodgings in town. And the name (not to be confused with the Mt Elgon Hotel) is more than optimistic as there is little chance of seeing Mt Elgon from the centre of town. Large double rooms with shared bathroom cost USh 15,000 and doubles with private bathroom cost USh 20,000. There is an attractive restaurant and the hotel has a friendly feel to it.

Places to Stay – Top End

Mt Elgon Hotel (☎ 33454) is a relic from the time of the British. It has seen better days,

but it's still comfortable and the rooms are very spacious. Singles/doubles with attached bathroom cost USh 35,000/40,000 including breakfast and taxes. It's in a very quiet part of Mbale, surrounded by its own grounds, with guarded parking out the front. The bar is a popular social spot in the evenings with guests, local project workers and businesspeople. The staff are friendly and helpful.

Nearby is a new hotel called *Sunrise Inn* which has prices on a par with the Mt Elgon but its rooms are much smarter. However, it lacks the atmosphere of the Mt Elgon Hotel.

Places to Eat

Most of the cheap hotels have their own simple restaurants, or you can get cheap local food at *Mukwano Restaurant*, which has a couple of branches in town. Another popular place is *Near East Nile Restaurant*, which serves local food and greasy-spoon standards.

For snacks and coffee, try *Bugisu Coffee Bar & Restaurant* near the post office. It's popular with office workers at lunch-time. There's also a *Wimpy* which has some kitsch advertising posters from decades gone by. The menu is not exactly authentic Wimpy cuisine, but many would consider this a blessing. It does, however, offer inexpensive burgers, along with omelettes and Ugandan dishes.

Slightly more expensive, but still good value, *Coffee Tree Bar & Restaurant* offers meals from USh 2000. There's a choice of Ugandan dishes and western-style meals. The open-air terrace bar that overlooks the street is a popular place for a cold beer or two.

More expensive are the restaurants at *Mt Elgon Hotel* and *Sunrise Inn* but they have a much better selection of food. For USh 5000 you can eat pretty well.

Entertainment

There are some reasonable local bars in Mbale, including the upstairs *Mountain View Bar* which is pretty popular most nights.

The nearest thing you'll get to a night-club in Mbale is the disco held at *Coffee*

UGANDA

Tree on Saturday night. *Club Oasis* on Cathedral Rd is basically a place where people come to talk. The best thing about it is the deep, upholstered lounge suites.

Getting There & Away

There are frequent minibuses to Tororo (USh 1500), Jinja (USh 5000) and Kampala (USh 6000), as well as to Soroti (USh 2500). The taxi park is small but fairly chaotic – just ask around. Next to it is the bus stand, where you can find buses to Jinja and Kampala and the occasional one to Soroti. Destinations are posted in the front window.

For Sipi Falls (USh 3000) and Budadiri (USh 1000), you need to go to the Kumi Rd taxi park. Services are less frequent to these smaller places.

For travel around town, there are plenty of boda-bodas. The fare to the Mt Elgon Hotel or the Uganda Wildlife Authority office is USh 200.

MT ELGON NATIONAL PARK

This is one of the most recently created of Uganda's national parks and encompasses the upper regions of Mt Elgon up to the Kenyan border.

The mountain is said to have one of the largest surface areas of any extinct volcano in the world and is peppered with cliffs, caves, gorges and waterfalls. Wagagai is the highest peak at 4321m. The views from the higher reaches across the wide plains are among the most spectacular in Uganda. The upper slopes are clothed in tropical montane forest, while above this a vast tract of alpine moorland extends over the caldera, a collapsed crater covering some 40 sq km at the top of the mountain.

Trekking

Tourism on Mt Elgon is still in its infancy, so you need to be resourceful, patient, self-sufficient and not expect well-worn paths such as those you find on Mt Kenya and Kilimanjaro. You obviously need your own camping and cooking equipment, your own food, appropriate clothing and a guide. Don't attempt to trek without a guide, as it is forbidden.

Warning

Mt Elgon is a big, wild mountain. Even the established trekking routes are sometimes hard to follow, especially on the peaks and higher slopes, where rain, hail and thick mists are not uncommon, even in the dry season. Temperatures drop below freezing most nights. Guides may not be familiar with every part of the mountain, so if you're going off the established routes you should know how to use your compass, and have good gear and at least one day's extra food. If you go out for a day walk, take adequate clothing. This might sound a bit over the top, but Mt Elgon is exhilarating precisely because it can be serious, and you can only enjoy it fully if you're properly equipped.

Altitude sickness can also be a problem on the higher parts of Mt Elgon. It is advisable not to drive straight up to one of the roadheads and start walking immediately, as this does not give you time to acclimatise.

The best time to climb the mountain is from December to March, but the seasons are unpredictable and it can rain at any time.

Trekking on Mt Elgon costs US$90 for up to five days, including park entry fees. On top of this you must pay US$10 a day for the services of a guide. Porters are optional and cost US$8 per day. These prices cover food for the guide and porters.

The Uganda Wildlife Authority (UWA) office in Mbale can help with any information you might need about trekking on the mountain, as can the park headquarters at Budadiri. You can pay park fees at the these offices, as well as arrange guides and porters, and find information on accommodation and routes. Guides can also be found at *Wagagai Hotel* in Budadiri, 30km north-east of Mbale. Singles/doubles at the Wagagai will cost you USh 5000/8000; you can camp for USh 4000.

Sasa River Trail So far, there are three established camp sites along the Sasa River Trail, the usual route to the summit. Give yourself a minimum of three days to do this trek and five if you want to reach Jackson's Summit, Wagagai and Suam Gorge.

From Budadiri, which is considered the trailhead, a road leads to Bugitimwa, then it's about three hours walk to the forest. Almost as soon as you enter the forest, you reach Mudangi cliffs, which are scaled via 'ladders' (piles of branches). From the top, the trail is well defined and less steep. About a 30 minute walk up this path is bamboo forest and a further 30-minutes across the other side of the Sasa River brings you to the first camp site. Getting across the river involves boulder-hopping or wading knee-deep through fast-flowing water, depending on the season.

The camp site is marked by a well used fireplace and there are enclosed toilets and a rubbish pit. If it's still early in the day when you get here, you have the option of continuing another two hours further up the trail to stay at the next camp site, some 300m to the left of the trail near the Environmental Task Force Hut.

The next part of the trail goes up to the top of the forest and into the heathland, where there's another possible camp site close to a small cave (about three hours beyond the first camp site). The moorland is studded with giant senecio (groundsel) and you'll often see duikers bounding through the long grass and lammergeier vultures overhead.

A further three hours brings you to a split in the path just before the caldera. The left fork leads directly into the caldera and the hot springs at the head of the Suam Gorge. The right fork leads to Jackson's Summit via Jackson's Pool. The latter path crosses a permanent stream, and there is a possible camp site if you wish to stay up here.

Jackson's Summit and Wagagai can be reached in a minimum of 14½ hours allowing for a comfortable return to the second camp site in good light. The return journey from the second camp site back to the road can be done in five to six hours.

If you're heading over the border into Kenya via Suam Gorge (not officially open to foreigners but still possible), you can stay at **Kabyoyon Farm** about 8km off the main road and signposted but you need to bring your own food if you turn up unexpectedly.

Getting There & Away
There are regular, if infrequent, taxis to Budadiri from Mbale (USh 1000). Between Mbale and Kampala there are frequent minibuses (USh 7000).

SIPI FALLS
Sipi Falls is a truly beautiful sight, and it's well worth making the effort to get here. The falls are about 55km north of Mbale, in the foothills of Mt Elgon and not far from the town of Kapchorwe. Not only are the falls spectacular; so are the views of Mt Elgon above them, and the wide plains of eastern and northern Uganda disappearing into the distance below. There are some excellent walks on a network of well maintained local trails and beautiful scenery in every direction. It is easy enough just to ramble off on your own, but all the lodges and camp sites in the area offer guided walks for a small fee. These include short walks around the falls area itself and longer walks up to the tree line at the base of Mt Elgon. It is worth spending a night or two in this peaceful and pretty place.

Places to Stay
Accommodation options have improved immensely in the past few years and there are some very tasteful camps to suit all budgets.

Two small camps cater to independent travellers. **The Crow's Nest** offers some breathtaking views of the falls, being located on a hilltop across the valley. The camp was originally established by Peace Corps volunteers and the cabins are attractively constructed in Scandinavian style. Camping here costs USh 3500 per person, while tents and sleeping bags are available for hire at USh 3000 and USh 1000 respectively. Dorm beds cost USh 6500, and attractive cabins with shared facilities are USh 15,000. Cabin accommodation prices include morning tea and coffee, and the buildings have some great views over Sipi Falls. There is a small restaurant and bar with inexpensive food from USh 1000, including pancakes, eggs and African staples.

The newer of the backpacker operations is **Moses' Camp Site** an attractive camping

UGANDA

ground set among flourishing flower gardens. Camping costs USh 3000 per person and there are a couple of small bandas available for USh 5000 per bed. The views from some of the camping areas are excellent and the staff are very friendly. There is a basic restaurant serving local meals, and drinks are available.

Elgon Maasai Hotel used to be the only choice in town, but doesn't see many visitors these days because of the better competition. Single rooms are USh 7000 with shared bathroom, while doubles with bathroom cost USh 10,000. It has a small restaurant and bar.

Sipi Falls Rest Camp run by Volcanoes tour company is an upscale resort offering accommodation in well-appointed bandas. The old house here was used as a residence by the last British governor of Uganda, and certainly has an authentic colonial look to it. Prices are a big leap from the other places around Sipi Falls, but a lot of business comes from clients on tour packages. Prices range from US$60 for a single room in the old rest house to US$80 per person in a triple banda and US$100 in a double banda. These prices cover full board including three-course lunch and dinner. Nonresidents can eat here for USh 10,000 for set meals.

There is also a bar and games room in the compound.

Getting There & Away

Minibuses run between Mbale and Sipi Falls daily for USh 3000. Unless you arrive at Mbale's Kumi Rd taxi park early, you may have to wait some time for the minibus to fill up, so be patient. Minibuses returning to Mbale from Kapchorwe often come through Sipi full so you may have to do a two-stage journey to get out, first by truck to Kamu for USh 500 and then by minibus to Mbale for USh 2000, sneakily saving USh 500 in the process. If you are in a group, you may want to consider hiring a taxi to take you up here if it is late in the day.

The road was in poor shape at the time of writing, but plans are afoot to grade it and, some time in the next couple of years, to surface it. Currently it takes about 1½ hours to reach the Sipi trading centre from Mbale. The road on to Kapchorwe and the Kenyan border at Sumi is very poor, but this long stretch is also slated for improvements. This could become a scenic and relaxing way to travel between Kenya and Uganda in future, as it offers stunning views of the Elgon massif above and the plains of Karimojaland below.

South-Western Uganda

FORT PORTAL
☎ 0493

Fort Portal, a green, pleasant and quiet town at the north-eastern end of the Ruwenzori Mountains, is the centre of a verdant tea-growing area and the provincial headquarters for Kabarole District. The town is also the base from which to explore Kibale Forest National Park, the beautiful crater lakes in the area and the Semliki Valley (hot springs and Pygmy villages). It's an area of Uganda well worth checking out, so set aside a week or so to make the most of it.

Information

Money There is a branch of Uganda Commercial Bank, but its rates are not particularly good. The Moons foreign exchange bureau is across the road from Wooden Hotel, but it's very unreliable and seems to be closed more than it's open.

Post & Communications The post office has international telephone services, but as the connection is analogue, it is not always good. There is a telephone office behind the main building where staff can connect you worldwide via Kampala, although you will have to be patient while they arrange it.

Travel Agencies Kabarole Tours (☎ 22182, fax 22636) signposted behind the Esso petrol station is an excellent tour agency and information bureau covering all the area's places of interest. The staff are very friendly and helpful, and tour prices are very reasonable, as long as you have a group to share the cost. It offers departures to the Semliki Valley, Lake Nkuruba and Queen Elizabeth National Park, and a combined walking/driving tour to hot springs towards Kasese. Kabarole can also organise bicycle day trips in the area, which cost USh 5000 and include a map and suggested itinerary. If you don't have much time and want to make the most of the area, these people can help you to do so. The office is open daily from 8 am to 6 pm.

Places to Stay – Budget

The best choice in this price range is *Continental Hotel (☎ 22450)* right in the centre of town. It offers clean singles/doubles with shared facilities for USh 7000/10,000 and additional doubles with bathroom for USh 20,000. It has a small restaurant downstairs, where they also show films each night. It is better to get a room upstairs if you want an early night.

If money is more important than comfort, there is a whole string of super-cheapies along Lugard Rd. They are all much of a muchness, with rooms at USh 3500/5000. Places include *Tropical Lodge*, *California Lodge*, *Economic Lodge* and *Christian Guesthouse*.

Next door to the Tropical is the slightly better *New Linda Lodge (☎ 22937)* which offers singles/doubles at USh 5500/7500.

Close to the cheapies, *Wooden Hotel (☎ 22034)* has been around for years. It offers quite a decent selection of rooms. Those with shared bathroom cost USh 6000/8500, while it's USh 8500/13,500 with private bathroom (hot water is delivered to your room in a bucket). The hotel has a bar and restaurant with decor that could have been inspired by a visit to a New Orleans brothel. A sign at the

UGANDA

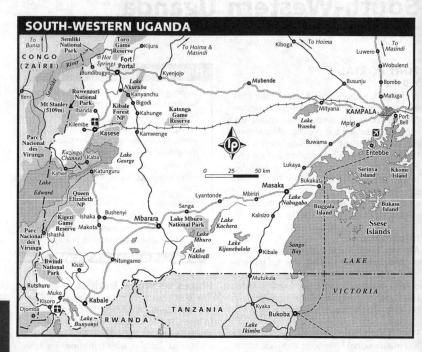

SOUTH-WESTERN UGANDA

entrance to the bar warns that patrons wearing caps or slippers will not be admitted!

Overlooking the taxi park is ***Kakuru Guesthouse*** which offers basic rooms for USh 5000/8000. It might get noisy in the morning with all the taxis revving up for business. There is a very good restaurant here, however, called Cedric's.

Places to Stay – Mid-Range

The best place in town is the very pleasant ***Ruwenzori View Guest House*** (☎ *22102*) run by an Anglo-Dutch couple. It's just a small place, signposted off Toro Rd, with a rural aspect and good views of the mountains. Well appointed, attractive singles/doubles with bathroom cost USh 27,000/35,000, including breakfast. Other meals (both local and western) are available.

Mountains of the Moon Hotel (☎ *22513*) on the hill above the town is also OK. The rooms are nothing special, but the main building is obviously a colonial relic and

has lots of atmosphere, with open fires and polished floors in the lounge. Rooms with bathroom, including breakfast, cost USh 25,000/40,000. There's a bar and restaurant, and you can eat on the veranda.

Places to Eat

One of the best restaurants in town is ***The Gardens*** tucked away in the Pepsi factory on the way to the Post Office. It has a varied menu with some good Indian staples, including a filling vegetable curry, and all of the *mochomo* (barbecued meat) you could imagine, and some you perhaps couldn't. Prices run from USh 3000 to USh 6000 a meal and it gets busy in the evening.

Another decent place to get a meal is ***Cedric's*** in Kakuru Guesthouse near the taxi park. Cedrics offers a mainly Indian menu, with large biryianis and curries for about USh 4000. It may not be entirely planned, but the place seems to be making the first moves towards Italianised Indian food, as some of the food tastes of parmesan; it's better than it sounds.

There's good, reasonably priced food at the *restaurant* at Wooden Hotel (if you can see what you're eating and if they have anything on the menu available).

It's also worth checking out *Tree Shades Restaurant* opposite the Esso petrol station. Good, solid local meals are served here for about USh 1500 to USh 2500. This is a good place for breakfast, with huge juices. However, a word of warning: do not be disappointed if you can't get your eggs the way you want them – we were told that the scrambled eggs lady had not arrived yet!

For those wanting to buy their own provisions, there are a couple of good supermarkets in town, *Andrew Brothers Stores* and *Nina's Grocery*. You can find pretty much any food supplies you might desire in these places.

Entertainment

There are not many riveting places to go for a drink in Fort Portal. Most of the bars have turned into dreary video parlours where no one talks to anyone else. On weekends there's live music until late in the *bar* at Wooden Hotel, and a disco that rocks until morning. Cedric's also has a lively *disco* on Saturday night.

Getting There & Away

There are daily Post Bus services connecting Fort Portal and Kampala; one direct and the other via Kasese and Mbarara. For details on these services, see Getting There & Away in the Kampala chapter.

From the bus stand at the western end of Babitha Rd things are more predictable. There's a daily bus to Kabale (USh 10,000, via Kasese) at about 6 am, and departures for Kampala (USh 8000) at 7 and 10 am.

The taxi park is on Kahinju Rd, near the junction with Lugard Rd. As elsewhere, there's no schedule so you just hang around until they're full, but there are fairly frequent departures to Hoima (USh 6000), Kasese (USh 3000) and Kampala (USh 8000).

Local share-taxis (pick-ups) to Kamwenge (for Kibale Forest National Park) and

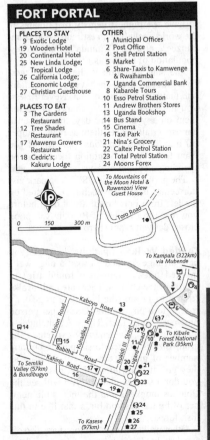

FORT PORTAL

PLACES TO STAY	OTHER
9 Exotic Lodge	1 Municipal Offices
19 Wooden Hotel	2 Post Office
20 Continental Hotel	4 Shell Petrol Station
25 New Linda Lodge;	5 Market
Tropical Lodge	6 Share-Taxis to Kamwenge
26 California Lodge;	& Rwaihamba
Economic Lodge	7 Uganda Commercial Bank
27 Christian Guesthouse	8 Kabarole Tours
	10 Esso Petrol Station
PLACES TO EAT	11 Andrew Brothers Stores
3 The Gardens	13 Uganda Bookshop
Restaurant	14 Bus Stand
12 Tree Shades	15 Cinema
Restaurant	16 Taxi Park
17 Mawenu Growers	21 Nina's Grocery
Restaurant	22 Caltex Petrol Station
18 Cedric's;	23 Total Petrol Station
Kakuru Lodge	24 Moons Forex

Rwaihamba (for Lake Nkuruba) leave from the intersection near where the main road crosses the river. There's not a lot of traffic, but there are usually a few share-taxis each day. Monday and Thursday are market days in Rwaihamba so there are plenty then.

AROUND FORT PORTAL
Kibale Forest National Park

Set at an altitude of 1200m, this 560 sq km national park, 35km south-east of Fort Portal, is home to chimpanzee, baboon, red and white Colobus monkey, and larger mammals such as bushbuck, sitatunga, duiker, civet, buffalo and forest elephant. It is said to have the highest density of primates in the world, including an estimated 600 chimpanzees, and has Uganda's third-largest population of elephants.

The star attraction is the **chimpanzees**, five groups of which have been partially habituated to human contact. Nevertheless, you have only an 80% chance of seeing them on any particular day, though you'll almost certainly hear them as they scamper off into the bush on your approach. If you want to be sure of sighting them, plan on spending a couple of days here.

The park entry fee is US$7. The park visitor centre is at Kanyanchu, signposted on the left from Fort Portal about 6km before you reach the village of Bigodi. Reception closes daily at 6 pm sharp.

Guided Walks At park headquarters you can arrange guided walks along well-marked tracks (3 to 5km round trip) in search of the chimps. There are daily walks from 8 to 11 am (the best time to go) and from 3 to 6 pm, costing US$10 per person plus park entry fees. The price includes a guide, but a tip is generally expected. The group size is limited to six people but any number of groups can set off, as long as they go off in different directions. Even if you don't see the chimps, you will see the Colobus monkeys and the incredible number of butterflies and birds that live in this lush forest.

Other walks through the forest are also offered daily. These hikes can be geared towards those with a particular interest in the more than 300 species of birds in the park. Forest hikes cost just USh 6000 and can take anything from five to eight hours depending on how much you want to see. Night hikes are also possible, to view the four species of nocturnal primate that live in the forest, also for USh 6000. Longer walks of several days can be arranged on demand. There are plans to offer de-nesting walks to see the chimps waking up and starting the day.

Places to Stay & Eat You can *camp* at the park headquarters for USh 5000 per person.

Facilities include water, firewood, toilets and showers. There are also some comfortable and clean *bandas* (thatched-roof huts) available for USh 10,000/15,000 a single/double. They are some of the nicest bandas found in Uganda's national parks. There are plans to construct some treehouses for guests to use. The great little restaurant here is run by a Bigodi women's group, and tasty, cheap meals are available daily, although it is best to give some notice. All proceeds go to the local community and there is a small shop here with some basic supplies.

If you don't want to camp at park headquarters, there are a few alternatives not so far away. Charles Lubega runs *Safari Hotel*, which is in Nkingo village, about 6km from the park headquarters towards Bigodi village. Here there are rooms for USh 4000, including a free laundry service and free tea, or you can camp for USh 2000. You can also get excellent, tasty meals if you order in advance, as Charles used to be a chef in Kampala. It is generally considered to be a very friendly place to stay, but take care of your valuables because the rooms aren't all that secure.

Mantana Safaris (☎ 041-320152, fax 321 522) runs a luxury tented camp in Kibale Forest National Park. Full board costs US$137/220.

See also the other entries in the Around Fort Portal section for more accommodation options nearby.

Getting There & Away Share-taxis to Kamwenge from Fort Portal pass the park visitor centre (USh 2000) and continue to Bigodi (USh 2500). However, drivers may try and charge you USh 1000 for your bag if it takes up a lot of space, as they like to play sardines on this route. Alternatively, you can charter a minibus from Kabarole Tours in Fort Portal (USh 25,000 one-way shared by up to seven people), or arrange to have them collect you and take you back to Fort Portal for the same price.

The gravel road between Fort Portal and Bigodi is in excellent condition, apart from one or two rough patches, and in your own vehicle it should take no more than one hour.

Bigodi Wetland Sanctuary

This wetland sanctuary, established to protect the Magombe Swamp, is a haven for birds, butterflies and a number of primates. The guided walks through this sanctuary have been developed with the aim of assisting community development projects in the Kibale area, so the project deserves support. Many of the guides have a good knowledge of birdlife in the sanctuary and are also adept at spotting elusive primates from a distance. Guided walks are offered at the sanctuary entrance at 8 am and 3 pm. They take about three hours and cost US$6.

For accommodation, *Mucusu* at the back of Bigodi village is run by David Nyamuganya and his wife. This cosy, friendly place costs USh 3000/6000 for singles/doubles including breakfast. Excellent, tasty food is available if ordered in advance. The communal bathroom facilities are clean, bucket hot water is available and the prices include laundry.

Bigodi Wetland Sanctuary is just off the road between Fort Portal and Kamwenge, about 5km south-east of Kanyanchu. For Getting There & Away details, see Kibale Forest National Park earlier in this section.

The Crater Lakes

The landscape south of Fort Portal is dotted with picturesque crater lakes, all of which offer great walking and exploration options. There are several accommodation options throughout the area, although further south they dry up fast. Most of the lodges and guesthouses can help out with suggestions on walks and activities in the area. Kabarole Tours in Fort Portal organise tours to the area.

Walking is not the only activity available. Cycling is also a pleasant option as the roads wind their way around these beautiful lakes, which are believed to be bilharzia free, although that doesn't mean they're hippo and crocodile free – check with locals before plunging into the waters.

Also in this area is **Mahoma Waterfall**, small but attractive and a great spot for a natural power-shower.

Lake Nkuruba Lake Nkuruba, 25km south of Fort Portal, is a stunning crater lake. There are good walking opportunities from the camp site here, including a one-hour trek to Lake Nyabikere, from where you can continue to Rweteera and Kibale Forest National Park or Bigodi.

Places to Stay & Eat For a few days of relaxation, *Lake Nkuruba Community Camp Site* at the lake is quite basic, but the welcome is warm and the setting is ideal. There are three areas in which to camp, one at the lakeshore, with the others higher up the hillside with views of the surrounding landscape. It costs USh 3000 per person to camp, and there are tents for hire for USh 1000. There is also a beautiful lakeshore banda, available for USh 15,000. If you're coming on a day trip from Fort Portal you can pay USh 1000 to use the facilities, which include a cooking shelter and bush shower.

Cheap vegetarian meals are available (order in advance) and bread is also baked here. You can also get limited supplies from the village of Rwaihamba, a short distance away.

Getting There & Away Share-taxis from Fort Portal to Kasenda or Rwaihamba pass Lake Nkuruba (USh 1000), which is signposted on the left just before Rwaihamba. At least three vehicles a day do the trip, and on Monday and Thursday (market days in Rwaihamba) there's plenty of traffic.

Lake Nyabikere This lake is another beautiful and tranquil spot and lies just off the road to Kibale Forest National Park. It is often used by travellers as a base for chimpanzee treks in the park. There are dugout canoes available from CVK Resort for exploring the lake.

Places To Stay & Eat A major banda and camping operation, *CVK Resort* (☎ 0493-22305) is about 15km north-west from Kibale Forest National Park's Kanyanchu camp. There is a whole host of sleeping options at various prices ranging from USh 3000 to camp, USh 4000 for a bare banda, USh 6000 for a mattress in a banda, and USh 13,000/25,000 for a furnished single/

double banda, including breakfast. There is also a restaurant here, but prices are quite high compared with Fort Portal.

Just a short way north along the road is the signpost for *Rweetera Safari Park & Tourist Camping Centre* a community camp site with views of the lake. Camping costs US$3 per person and food is available with advance notice, although basic supplies are also available at the nearby Rweetera village. The centre offers walks around the natural attractions of the area, although at US$10 and up, these are more like Uganda Wildlife Authority prices than those of a community project.

Lake Nyinambuga This lake is located south of Lake Nkuruba and near the Mahoma Waterfall. Perched above the lake is *Ndali Lodge (☎ 0493-22636, 041-235494)* a luxurious camp offering accommodation in well appointed cottages set around a large central lodge. The setting is breathtaking and access to nearby attractions is straightforward. However, such surroundings do not come cheap and it costs about US$140 for a cottage with full board.

Semliki Valley

Many visitors to Fort Portal make a day trip (at least) to the Semliki Valley and to **Bundibugyo** on the other side of the Ruwenzoris. However, at the time of writing, this area is off-limits to tourists because of acts of terror committed by the misnamed Allied Democratic Front (ADF). Many locals have been murdered in this campaign of systematic violence and until the army gets the situation under control, Semliki National Park will remain closed and visitors should keep their distance. However, the Toro (Semliki Valley) Game Reserve is still safe and visits can be arranged.

The main attractions in the valley are the hot springs near Sempaya in the Semliki National Park and the Batwa pygmy villages near the village of Ntandi in the forest a few kilometres before Bundibugyo. However, the best part of this trip is the magnificent views over the rainforest and savannah of the Semliki Valley and into Congo (Zaïre).

Unfortunately the pygmy villagers have gone the way of those in eastern Congo

(Zaïre) and are now seriously commercialised, their culture for sale, and in all it's a depressing proposition. Still, the tourists roll in day after day, allowing themselves to be harassed and fleeced. If you insist on going, the 'official' charge for a visit to their village is USh 1500 per person, but you'll be lucky to get away with paying less than three times that amount and the pressure to buy rubbish is enervating.

However, in many ways, it is only this commercialisation process that ensures the survival of the pygmies as a distinct ethnic group within Uganda. The Batwa have always been at the bottom of the social pile in Uganda and are in some respects the forgotten people of the jungles. With much of their natural territory already turned over to forested national parks such as Bwindi, they have found it very hard to adapt to life in modern Uganda. Ironically it is tourism that has allowed them a way to be proud of their identity and culture, and make a bit of money from it at the same time.

The other 'attraction' is the hot springs. At least you won't get hassled here but the place is very much a let-down. This is not Bogoria National Park (Kenya) and it's worlds away from the geysers of Rotorua (New Zealand) and Iceland. There is a walking trail around the springs.

Places to Stay & Eat At the Semliki National Park headquarters at Ntandi there's a basic site where you can *camp* for USh 5000 per person.

Near the toll station, there's a simple *hotel* where you can stay the night for USh 3000 a double. You can also stay at one of the two *bandas* run by Morence Mpora (☎ 22245) at Kichwamba/Nyankuku, on the way to Bundibugyo. Morence has been offering accommodation for years now in an effort to help finance the orphanage he runs. The charge, in principle, is meant to be by donation, but in practice US$10 per person is expected for the banda and three meals a day. Just ask the taxi driver to drop you off at the right place – it's near the Kichwamba Technical College.

If you find yourself in Bundibugyo (the local administrative centre) and need to stay the night, there's *Moonlight Hotel* which costs USh 5000 per person, or *Union Guest House*.

Getting There & Away There are irregular share-taxis and pick-ups between Fort Portal and Bundibugyo, and these are a cheap way to go if you don't mind staying a night or two out of town. To get to the park headquarters from Fort Portal costs about USh 3000 and to Bundibugyo USh 5000. Hitching isn't easy as there is not all that much traffic.

The most straightforward way to get to the Semliki Valley is to go on one of Kabarole Tours' full-day excursions (USh 60,000 shared between up to four people). Alternatively, hire a car and driver for the day. This will cost much the same.

Toro (Semliki Valley) Game Reserve

Often referred to on maps as Toro Game Reserve, this was once one of the best-stocked wildlife parks in Africa. It was the first gazetted game reserve in Uganda and by the 1960s was one of the most popular parks in East Africa. However, the years of civil war took their toll and the Tanzanians went home with truckloads of dead bushmeat. Now wildlife is slowly starting to recover and there are plans to reintroduce some lost species. Currently you can expect to encounter kob, bushbuck, buffalo, elephant and Colobus monkey. A number of lions have also recently returned to the reserve, most likely refugees from the conflict in Congo (Zaïre), and leopard are sighted quite regularly. For birdwatchers, there is a range of species found within the park, including the elusive shoebill stork on the shores of Lake Albert. A chimpanzee habituation project is underway in the reserve, offering yet another activity for visitors. It costs US$7 per person.

Places To Stay & Eat Unfortunately it is not possible to camp in the reserve which rather limits options for the independent traveller. However, it is possible to stay in nearby villages on the shores of Lake Albert.

For those with a healthy budget, there is an attractive lodge here, *Semliki Safari Lodge*

(π/fax 041-259700, email gwg@swiftugan da.com). Luxury tents set under thatched bandas have Persian carpets and bathrooms with regular hot water. However, the best thing about the lodge is the main building, set under a huge eaved roof with plush furnishings, Congolese crafts and a restaurant for guests. But such opulence doesn't come cheap: full board costs US$150 per person.

Wildlife drives, chimp trekking and boat excursions on Lake Albert can be arranged through the lodge. The wildlife drives include the daunting option of an adventure in a dense forest of bamboo, where you may encounter buffalo and elephant. Visibility is no more than about 5m, so the chances of a charge or stand-off are very real.

Getting There & Away Most visitors arrive by light aircraft from Kampala as part of an all-inclusive package. However, it is possible to make your own way here by road from Fort Portal, a bumpy journey taking about two hours. First take the road for Bundibugyo and then fork right at Karagutu, 30km down the valley. Another 25km of rough track brings you to the lodge. It can just about be done in a regular car, but not in the wet season.

KASESE
π 0483
Kasese is at the western end of Uganda's railway line, for what it's worth, and the base from which to organise a trip into the Ruwenzori Mountains or Queen Elizabeth National Park. There's no other reason to visit, however – it's a very small, hot, dusty, quiet town in a relatively infertile and lightly populated area, and it wears an air of permanent torpor. However, it was once important to the economy because of the nearby copper mines at Kilembe (copper was Uganda's third most important export during the 1970s), though these are now closed. Until the Ruwenzoris reopen for tourism, this town is unlikely to see many visitors.

Information
There's a foreign exchange bureau on the ground floor of the Saad Hotel but it's not

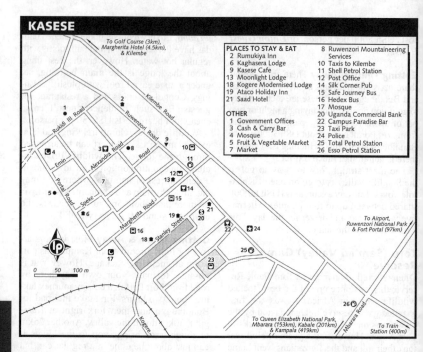

KASESE

PLACES TO STAY & EAT	8	Ruwenzori Mountaineering
2 Rumukiya Inn		Services
6 Kaghasera Lodge	10	Taxis to Kilembe
9 Kasese Cafe	11	Shell Petrol Station
13 Moonlight Lodge	12	Post Office
18 Kogere Modernised Lodge	14	Silk Corner Pub
19 Ataco Holiday Inn	15	Safe Journey Bus
21 Saad Hotel	16	Hedex Bus
	17	Mosque
OTHER	20	Uganda Commercial Bank
1 Government Offices	22	Campus Paradise Bar
3 Cash & Carry Bar	23	Taxi Park
4 Mosque	24	Police
5 Fruit & Vegetable Market	25	Total Petrol Station
7 Market	26	Esso Petrol Station

always open. Nearby is a branch of the Uganda Commercial Bank.

The post office has an international phone, but it is unreliable.

Ruwenzori Mountaineering Services, or RMS (☎ 44115) PO Box 33, Kasese, has an information and booking office on Alexandra Rd. It is open daily. This is where you would make arrangements for trekking or climbing the Ruwenzoris (see Ruwenzori National Park for more details). However, whether or not this operation will still be running when the Ruwenzoris eventually reopen is anyone's guess.

Things to See & Do

Kasese has no attractions but if you have half a day to kill, hire a bicycle and cycle the 13km to the old **copper mine** at Kilembe for an interesting diversion. It is a long gradual uphill climb, which makes for hard work on the way there but it's great fun on the way back! You can sometimes get a tour of the

surface remnants (crushers, concentrators, separators etc) free of charge but you're not allowed underground. The manager of your hotel should be able to arrange bicycle hire. You can call in for a cold beer en route at Margherita Hotel, 4.5km from Kasese.

Places to Stay – Budget

Rumukiya Inn on Ruwenzori Rd is a fairly new place and it claims to 'maximumly serve'. As with most hotels in Kasese, the rooms are set around a little courtyard, and cost USh 4000/6000 with shared bathroom, or there's one double room with private bathroom for USh 8000.

Also good, and very similar to the Rumukiya, is *Kogere Modernised Lodge* on Stanley St. Rooms at this little place all have shared bathrooms, and cost USh 4000/5000. This is good value as they are clean and comfortable.

There are a number of other cheapies around town, including *Moonlight Lodge* which is pretty reasonable with rooms at USh 5000, and **Kaghasera Lodge** but the Kaghasera doesn't seem to want to rent rooms these days.

Ataco Holiday Inn has slightly better rooms than the other hotels, but at higher prices. Singles/doubles with shared bathroom cost USh 7000/11,000. It has a fairly lively bar.

Places to Stay – Mid-Range
Saad Hotel (☎ 44139) on Ruwenzori Rd used to be a popular place, and many people who climbed the Ruwenzoris stayed here for rest and recreation both before and after the climb. However, with the mountains closed to tourists, there is little business in town and the rooms now seem optimistically overpriced. However, the staff are very friendly and the rooms are OK. Basic doubles with bathroom in the old wing cost USh 23,400, including breakfast. In the new wing, you get carpet and air-con thrown in for USh 35,100, including breakfast. The hotel has a good restaurant downstairs, with all the usual staples, but no alcohol as the owners are Muslim.

Places to Stay – Top End
Margherita Hotel (☎ 44015) 4.5km out of town on the road up to Kilembe has singles/doubles including breakfast for USh 36,000/54,000. It also has more-expensive chalets available for that extra bit of privacy. The hotel is on a beautiful site looking out towards the Ruwenzoris on one side and the golf course on the other, surrounded by flowering trees. The restaurant serves reasonable food for about USh 7000 for main courses.

Places to Eat
There are several inexpensive restaurants around the taxi park and market where you can get traditional staples like meat stews, *matoke* (plantains), beans and rice. For breakfast the **grocery store** next to Ataco Holiday Inn will rustle up an omelette, tea and bread for a few hundred shillings.

Otherwise, the **restaurant** at Saad Hotel is about the best option. There's a good se-

lection of dishes, the food is tasty and the staff are friendly. You're looking at USh 2500 for a main course.

Kasese Cafe also has a reasonable menu of cheap, standard food, as does **Moonlight Lodge**.

Entertainment
Half of the buildings in Kasese seem to be bars these days, suggesting the townsfolk are hoping to drink their way out of the current malaise. The liveliest **bar** for a cold beer is at Ataco Holiday Inn, which attracts a good crowd every lunch-time and evening. The front veranda is a great place to hang out in the heat of the day. It basically stays open until the last person wants to go home. Other reasonable bars include **Silk Corner Pub** and **Campus Paradise Bar**.

Getting There & Away
Air Eagle Aviation operates flights between Kampala and Kasese, via Kisoro, on Wednesday, Friday and Sunday. Tickets cost US$85/170 one way/return.

Bus The Post Bus runs from Kampala to Kasese daily, via Mbarara. For details of this service, see the Getting There & Away entry in the Kampala chapter.

There are daily buses in both directions between Kasese and Kampala via Mbarara (USh 10,000, about 8 hours). The hopefully named Safe Journey company, with its offices on Margherita Rd, has departures at 6, 8 and 11 am.

There's also a daily bus in both directions between Fort Portal and Kabale via Kasese and Mbarara. It starts from Fort Portal at 6 am, arriving in Kasese at about 8 am. It then continues on to Kabale, taking about six hours. The fare from Kasese to Kabale is USh 10,000. The last part of the journey south crosses a mountain pass from which, weather permitting, you'll be rewarded with spectacular views to the west of the volcanoes along the Uganda-Rwanda border.

Share-Taxi There are frequent share-taxis to Fort Portal (USh 3000, one hour) and Mbarara (USh 4000).

UGANDA

Getting to Queen Elizabeth National Park is straightforward. Catch a Mbarara share-taxi and ask for the national park entrance, which is signposted on the left just before the village of Katunguru. From here you'll have to hitch into the park, but you may have to wait a couple of hours for a lift.

RUWENZORI NATIONAL PARK

The legendary, mist-covered Ruwenzori Mountains on Uganda's western border with Congo (Zaïre) used to be almost as popular with travellers as Kilimanjaro and Mt Kenya but they are definitely harder to climb. They have a well deserved reputation for being very wet at times. This was best summed up by a comment on the wall of Bujuku hut: 'Jesus came here to learn how to walk on water. After five days, anyone could do it'. Take warm, waterproof clothing.

The mountain range, which is not volcanic, stretches for about 100km. At its centre are several mountains which are permanently snow and glacier-covered: Mt Speke (Vittorio Emmanuele is its highest peak at 4890m); Mt Baker (Edward is its highest peak at 4843m); Mt Gessi (Iolanda, 4715m); Mt Emin (4791m); and Mt Luigi di Savoia (4627m). The three highest peaks in the range are Margherita (5109m), Alexandria (5083m) and Albert (5087m), all on Mt Stanley.

> ### WARNING
>
> Trekking in the Ruwenzori Mountains was suspended in late 1996 because of the activities of Allied Democratic Front (ADF) rebels in the area. The area has remained closed since and is unsafe for tourists, so do not attempt to go up there illegally. It may reopen some time during the life of this book, but even if the Ugandan army can flush the rebels out of the mountains, there is still the major problem of land mines to be dealt with. It is likely to be some time before the Mountains of the Moon are back on the trekking map of East Africa.

Trekking

Five days is the absolute minimum for a trek through the range, but seven or eight days is better, with one or two days at the top huts. The best times to trek are from late December to the end of February, and mid-June to mid-August, when there's less rain. Even at these times, the higher reaches are often enveloped in mist, though this generally clears for a short time each day.

With heavy USAID investment, many improvements have been made to the walking tracks as well as the huts. The huts have essentials such as kitchens, walls and roofs (which they lacked not long ago) and there's a wooden pathway over the bog and bridges over the larger rivers. All this has been done to lessen the impact of walkers on the fragile environment.

If you want to reach one of the main summits you need to have some mountaineering experience. The routes to the peaks on Mts Stanley and Baker all cross snow and glaciers, and require the use of ice-axe, ropes and crampons, plus a competent guide. In the right conditions, the summit of

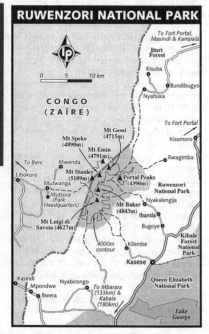

RUWENZORI NATIONAL PARK

Mt Speke is an easier proposition but it still requires some mountain experience.

Books & Maps Before attempting a trek in the Ruwenzori Range, it's strongly recommended that you obtain a copy of *Ruwenzori – Map & Guide* by Andrew Wielochowski. This is an excellent large-scale contour map of the mountains, with all the main trails, huts and camp sites marked (as well as other features).

On the reverse side of the map are detailed descriptions of the various possible treks as well as sections on history, flora and fauna, weather and climate, necessary equipment, useful contacts, costs and advice in the event of an accident. It's for sale in most Kampala bookshops.

Lonely Planet's *Trekking in East Africa* is useful for those requiring more details on trekking in the Ruwenzoris.

Food & Equipment Prepare for your Ruwenzoris trek in Kasese, where you'll find a reasonable selection of food and equipment as well as the office of Ruwenzori Mountaineering Services, or RMS (☎ 0483-44115) PO Box 33, Kasese, on Alexandra Rd. The RMS office organises bookings, guides and porters, hires equipment and arranges transport to the trailhead at Ibanda/Nyakalengija, off the Kasese-Fort Portal road.

The RMS also controls all the facilities on the mountain. You'll save nothing by attempting to do it all yourself, since a guide and porter are compulsory for anything other than a short day-walk and there's nowhere else to hire equipment in Kasese. That doesn't mean that there's no flexibility.

As far as your own food is concerned, be warned that the variety of food available in the two 'supermarkets' and the market in Kasese is limited. This is not Kampala. If there's anything you particularly want to eat on the trek or you have any special requirements, bring these items with you. Don't assume you can buy them in Kasese. You'll need a camp cooker of some description as fires are banned in the park. Kerosene and methylated spirits are readily available in Kasese.

No special equipment is required for a trek if you don't go onto the ice or snow, but whatever you bring, make sure it's warm and waterproof and that you have a decent pair of boots. Joggers are definitely not recommended – your feet will get soaked walking through the bogs, making you cold and miserable all day.

A waterproof jacket is an essential item, as it's almost impossible to stay dry in these mountains. Waterproof trousers (or at least a waterproof covering) are advisable. Your extra clothing, sleeping bag and perishable food should be wrapped in strong plastic bags to protect them from water. A small day-pack is useful if porters are going to be carrying the bulk of your equipment.

Since night temperatures often drop below zero, you'll need a good sleeping bag, an insulating sleeping mat and suitable warm clothing. This should include a warm hat (up to 30% of body heat is lost through your head).

Don't forget insect repellent, maximum protection sunscreen, sunglasses, a torch (flashlight), water bottle, first-aid kit, cutlery and a cup.

Equipment Hire The RMS has the following equipment for hire in Kasese:

item	cost (USh per trek)
closed-cell mat	5000
crampons	5000
gaiters	5000
ice-axe	5000
raincoat	5000
rope	10,000
rubber boots	5000
sleeping bag	10,000
trekking boots	5000

Guides, Porters & Fees There are plans to standardise fees when the park re-opens. The idea is to charge US$250 for a seven-day trek, plus extra for guides, porters and transport. However, the following fees were charged before closure, and are included in case the Uganda Wildlife Authority (UWA) changes its mind. There are standard fees for everything you need. Park entry fees are USh 15,000 for one day, USh 30,000 for two to

Ruwenzori Mountain Services Trekking Packages

trek	duration		cost per person (Ush)	
	days	(1 person)	(2 to 3 people)	(4 to 6 people)
Nyabitaba (travelling solo)	1	31,200	23,700	21,900
Nyabitaba (porter & guide)	2	64,600	52,000	46,000
John Mate Camp	3	147,000	102,300	91,100
Bujuku (3rd Camp)	5	203,200	134,400	117,200
Circuit	7	246,700	162,200	141,100

Note that you can only travel solo for a trek of one day or less. All rates include everything except your own food.

five days, with extra days at USh 5000, plus a one-off USh 10,000 rescue fee. There's also a USh 10,000 per day service fee which includes use of the RMS huts – you can reduce the fee by USh 5000 per day by using your own tent, but this is discouraged.

To the above you must add the cost of porters (USh 4000 per stage) and guides (USh 4700) plus food for these people (USh 1800 each per day), transport to and from the trailhead (USh 10,000 return) and fuel (USh 10,000 per day). See the boxed text for a list of the standard all-inclusive packages offered by RMS. A porter can carry 22kg, which comprises 10kg of his own gear and 12kg of the trekker's.

Note that guides' and porters' fees are per *stage* not per day. The stages are: Ibanda/Nyakalengija to Nyabitaba; Nyabitaba to John Mate; John Mate to Bujuku; Bujuku to Kitandara (or to Irene Lakes, Speke Peak or Margherita); Elena Hut to Margherita; Kitandara to Guy Yeoman (or to Baker or Lugigi); Guy Yeoman to Nyabitaba; and Nyabitaba to Ibanda/Nyakalengija. If you walk two stages in the day, you have to pay for two stages.

Remember that if you want a good trip, befriend your guide and porters. These people are drawn from the Bakonjo, a hardy but friendly mountain people, most of whom have Biblical names. They'll be staying in rock shelters overnight while you stay in the huts or in your own tent, so be generous with small handouts and give a decent tip at the end of the journey.

Altitude Sickness Be aware of the dangers of Acute Mountain Sickness (AMS). In extreme cases it can be fatal. Altitude sickness usually becomes noticeable above 3000m and is a sign of your body adjusting to lower oxygen levels. Mild symptoms include headaches, mild nausea and a slight loss of coordination. Symptoms of severe altitude sickness include abnormal speech and behaviour, severe nausea and headaches, a marked loss of coordination and persistent coughing spasms. When any combination of these severe symptoms occurs, the afflicted person should immediately descend 300 to 1000m. When trekking, such a descent may even have to take place at night.

There are no known indicators as to who might suffer from altitude sickness (fitness, age and previous altitude experience all seem to be irrelevant), and the only cure is an immediate descent to lower altitudes.

The Trails Ibanda or Nyakalengija is the starting point for a trek in the Ruwenzoris. There are two basic trails up the mountain starting from here which will take you between the peaks of Mt Baker and Mt Stanley. They both have the same approach as far as Nyabitaba Hut on the first day. After that you can go either clockwise or anticlockwise between the peaks. There are quite a few other minor trails, both up the mountain and across the top to Mutwanga in Congo (Zaïre) – the border essentially crosses the peaks, although crossing the frontier this way is illegal.

The following description applies to the clockwise route (the anticlockwise route is the reverse).

Day 1 Nyakalengija to Nyabitaba Hut (2650m), the first stage, is a fairly easy walk taking four to five hours.

Day 2 From Nyabitaba Hut, you can take either the old route to Guy Yeoman Hut (3450m, five to six hours) or the new safer route (seven hours). Along the new route, you also have the choice of staying at Kuruguta Hut/camp site (2940m). The route takes you through tropical vegetation, over two minor streams, across the Mahoma River and finally up the side of a steep valley to the ridge on which the hut is situated.

Day 3 From Guy Yeoman Hut, you pass through a bog to the Kabamba rock shelter (3450m) and waterfall, then trek via the Bujongolo rock shelter and the Freshfield Pass (4215m) to the Kitandara Hut (3990m). This takes about seven hours. The hut is picturesquely situated on the shore of the lake of the same name.

Day 4 This is possibly the most interesting part of the trek. After leaving the twin Kitandara lakes, you climb over boulders at the foot of Mt Baker on the one side and the glaciers of Savoia and Elena on the other. From here you cross Scott Elliot Pass (4372m) and proceed down to Bujuku Hut (3900m). The walk takes about four hours. If you intend to scale Mt Stanley, on the other hand, you head for Elena Hut (4547m), in which case both you and your guide and porters will need appropriate equipment to deal with ice and snow.

Day 5 Assuming you don't scale Mt Stanley, the trek from Bujuku Hut to John Mate Hut (3350m) is all downhill. The walk takes about five hours. En route you pass Bigo Hut (3400m), where you have the option of taking a difficult track north leading to Mt Gessi, Mt Emin and Lac de la Lune via a series of bogs. There are also three bogs between Bujuku Hut and John Mate Hut, but

it's here you'll come across stands of giant heather, groundsel and bamboo. Should you decide to spend the night at Bigo Hut, it sleeps up to 12 people and there is room for tents.

Day 6 From John Mate Hut, it's downhill again along a rough track to Nyabitaba (about five hours).

Day 7 The final stage is the return to Nyakalengija and onward travel to Kasese.

Organised Treks If it's your time rather than your money that is limited, you can have all the necessary arrangements made for you by a safari company.

QUEEN ELIZABETH NATIONAL PARK

This park covers almost 2000 sq km, bordered to the north by the Ruwenzori Mountains and to the west by Lake Edward.

The Queen Elizabeth National Park was once a magnificent place to visit, with its great herds of elephant, buffalo, kob, waterbuck, hippo and topi. But like Murchison Falls National Park, most of its wildlife was wiped out by the retreating troops of Amin and Okello and by the Tanzanian army, which occupied the country after Amin's demise. They all did their ivory-hunting, trophy-hunting best. Although the animal numbers are slowly recovering, there's still not that much wildlife in the park compared with parks in Tanzania and Kenya, apart from gazelle, buffalo, hippo, a few small herds of elephant, and the occasional lion. But it's worth a visit just to see the hippos and the birds, and there are also opportunities for walking and viewing chimpanzees.

Information

The main Katunguru gate is on the Mbarara to Kasese road near the small village of Katunguru, where the road crosses the Kazinga Channel. From here it's 6km along a track that follows the channel to **Mweya** in the north-west of the park, where most of the tourism activity is based. A much less visited area is that around **Ishasha**, in the southern

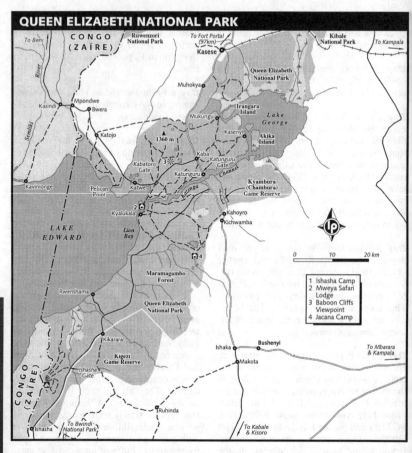

QUEEN ELIZABETH NATIONAL PARK

1 Ishasha Camp
2 Mweya Safari Lodge
3 Baboon Cliffs Viewpoint
4 Jacana Camp

part of the park on the border with Congo (Zaïre). The lions in this area are famous for their habit of climbing trees, and the setting is superb. The track between Katunguru and Ishasha cuts right through the park, but it's in pretty poor shape these days as hundreds of aid convoys have thundered down this way taking supplies to Congo (Zaïre). It is impassable for much of the wet season. However, in the dry season, it offers a convenient way to combine a visit to Bwindi with Queen Elizabeth National Park.

The Maramagambo Forest in the south-eastern section of the park has recently been

opened for limited tourism, and now sports a small tourism centre, camp site and up-market lodge.

Entry to the park costs US$15 per day. The price for a car is USh 5000 or US$30, depending on whether the car is registered as local or foreign.

Kazinga Channel Launch Trip

Almost every visitor takes a launch trip up the Kazinga Channel to see the thousands of hippos and the pelicans. If you're lucky you will also catch sight of one of the elephant herds and very occasionally see a lion or leopard. The two-hour trip costs US$20 per person or US$120 for the whole boat. There are trips at 9 am (the best time) and 11 am, and at 3 and 5 pm. Bookings can be made at Mweya Safari Lodge, and the trips leave from just below the lodge.

Kyambura Gorge Walking Safari

In the eastern corner of the park is the beautiful Kyambura (Chambura) Gorge, and walking safaris can be arranged at the small ranger post here. The gorge is home to a variety of primates, including chimpanzee, and these are often seen on the walking safaris, which last from three to five hours and cost US$30 per person; children under 15 years are not permitted. Bookings can be made at Mweya Safari Lodge or Jacana Camp, or most times you can just show up.

Wildlife Drives

There is a small network of trails around Mweya Safari Lodge and Katunguru gate. North of the road to Katwe there are some stunning craters within the park. Baboon Cliffs is a viewpoint that gives excellent views over the surrounding area. Over in Kyambura Game Reserve, there are also some salt lakes which attract flamingos in huge numbers.

Forest Walks

In the south-eastern section of the park, guided forest walks are available in the Maramagambo Forest, great if you enjoy birdwatching. They cost US$5 for half a day and US$7.50 for a whole day.

Walks can also be arranged in Kalinzu Forest, which is a cheaper option as it lies outside the national park boundary. It contains numerous bird species, 381 at the last count, several types of primate, including the rare L'Hoest monkey, and many varieties of butterfly. Guided walks here cost USh 5000 during the day and USh 6000 at night.

Places to Stay & Eat

Mweya Many of the places to stay are on the Mweya Peninsula close to Mweya Safari Lodge. The cheapest option is to camp at *Students' Camp* which costs USh 10,000 per

person. It's a reasonable site but has no shade. Hippos wander through at night. If you don't have a tent, you can get a dorm bed for USh 10,000, although it is often booked out by large groups of Ugandan students.

A good deal more expensive is the *Ecology Institute* where you can get a clean and comfortable double room with shared bathroom for USh 20,000 per person. The shared bathrooms seem to be subject to insect infestation at night, however, so take sandals if on a toilet run.

Top notch is *Mweya Safari Lodge* (☎ 041-255992, fax 255277) which has a stunning position on the raised peninsula with excellent views over Lake Edward to Katwe and Congo (Zaïre) and in the other direction along the Kazinga Channel. Sitting on the terrace with a cold drink at sunset is perfect. The lodge has recently changed hands and is undergoing a US$4 million refurbishment by the Madhvani Group, so things may have changed dramatically by now – or be in the process of changing. At the time of writing it was very comfortable, with single/double rooms for US$65/84 with bathroom and breakfast. During the week the place is almost deserted but it gets busy on weekends. Watch out for the mongoose which come scampering across the lawns in the late afternoon; at night, hippos browse across the lawns, so watch what you're walking into! A return fare of US$50 between Kampala and Mweya by minibus is available to guests without their own transport.

Tembo Canteen at Students' Camp is where the safari drivers hang out, and decent meals are served here for USh 3000, but you need to order in advance. There are also basic food supplies available in a shop nearby. Good lunches and dinners are available for reasonable prices at the *restaurant* at Mweya Safari Lodge (USh 12,000 for the excellent buffet dinner) which is open to all.

Katunguru Just outside the main gate to the park in the village of Katunguru is a small, inexpensive *hotel* which has rooms for USh 5000/8000. There is also a small *restaurant* here. This is a good place to stay if you want to avoid the national park fees.

UGANDA

Ishasha In the southern part of the park there are *bandas* at the Ishasha ranger station, which cost USh 15,000/20,000 for singles/doubles, or you can camp for USh 10,000.

Kalinzu Forest There is accommodation available in Kalinzu Forest Reserve. *Camping* costs USh 2500 per person per night or USh 4000 for two nights. On top of this you must pay an entry fee to the reserve of USh 6000 for one day or USh 9000 for two days, but this is a lot cheaper than the charge for Queen Elizabeth National Park. Community projects in villages around the park receive 40% of the entry fees.

To get here, turn off the Kasese road at Butare village and after 10km you come to the Kalinzu ecotourism site. In the wet season you will need a 4WD to get here.

Maramagambo Forest The *camp site* here is set right at the foot of the Kichwamba Escarpment, and as yet sees few visitors. Access is direct from the highway.

Jacana Camp is operated by Inns of Uganda (☎ 041-255388, fax 233992). It is a furnished luxury tented camp with splendid views over some crater lakes in the Queen Elizabeth National Park. Full board costs US$135/180 for singles/doubles. This is a lovely spot to stay if you have the funds.

Getting There & Away
Any vehicle travelling between Kampala and Kasese passes through Katunguru. There are regular minibuses from Katunguru to Kasese (USh 1500, one hour) and Mbarara (USh 4000, two hours). Hitching out of the park from Mweya is easy – just stand by the barrier at Mweya Safari Lodge. Better still, make arrangements the night before at the lodge.

For Maramagambo Forest, get off the bus or share-taxi at the village of Ndekye, south of Katunguru, from where a 10km path leads through small villages to Maramagambo (also known locally as Nyamusingiri). Ask locals for directions.

The road from Katunguru to the village of Ishasha cuts through the park and passes Ishasha gate. Although you don't need to pay any park entry fees to travel along this road,

you'll be fined USh 100,000 if you're caught venturing off it and into the park. At Ishasha, you can cross into Congo (Zaïre), or head south for Butogota and Bwindi National Park; it takes around five hours to drive from Bwindi to Mweya in the dry season.

BWINDI NATIONAL PARK
Bwindi is one of Uganda's most recently created national parks, and is in the southwest of the country, very close to the Congo (Zaïre) border. Formerly known as the Impenetrable Forest, the park, which covers 331 sq km, encompasses one of the last remaining habitats of the mountain gorilla, and is where half of the surviving mountain gorillas in the world live – an estimated 320 individuals. Because of problems in Rwanda and eastern Congo (Zaïre), Bwindi has become the main place in East Africa for seeing the mountain gorillas.

However, since March 1999, Bwindi has been known to the world for all the wrong reasons. The kidnap and subsequent murder of eight tourists here made headline news around the world. In the light of this dreadful incident, gorilla bookings nose-dived and security was upgraded significantly. There is now a large, invisible army presence down here and it is arguably safer to visit than it ever was before the massacre. However, it pays to check in Kampala for the latest situation at Bwindi.

A major conservation effort has been going on here for a number of years to protect the gorillas' habitat. As a result, en-

---

Warning

Bwindi is generally considered safe, as security has been beefed up considerably in the aftermath of the terrible attack on tourists on 1 March 1999. However, it is wise to check the latest situation in Kampala before heading this way.

There have also been disturbing reports of illegal gorilla visits at Bwindi, potentially endangering the lives of these rare creatures by increasing their stress level, thereby reducing their immunity to disease. For more information on responsible gorilla tracking, see the special section 'The Mountain Gorillas of East Africa'.

croachment on the montane forest by cultivators has been stopped, poaching has ceased and the gorilla families have been gradually habituated to human contact.

Gorillas are not the only animals to have benefited from this project. The park contains about 20 elephants, at least 10 species of primate (including chimpanzee, Colobus monkey and baboon), duiker and bushbuck and the rare giant forest hog, as well as a host of bird and insect species. It is one of the richest areas in Africa for flora and fauna.

For birdwatchers it is one of the most exciting destinations in the country, with more than 350 species of bird. These include 23 of the 24 Albertine rift endemics and several endangered species, including the African green broadbill, but it might not be easy to see many birds because of the density of their habitat.

The park headquarters is at Buhoma on the northern edge of the park. The gorilla visits start from here and this is where you'll find the only accommodation. Be aware that this area is rainforest, and not surprisingly it rains a hell of a lot – be prepared.

Entry to the park is US$15 per day. Vehicles entry is free but vehicles cannot proceed beyond the park headquarters.

Tracking the Gorillas

The gorillas in Bwindi are fairly used to human contact, and sometimes you don't have to walk more than 10 minutes from the park headquarters at Buhoma to find them. There are two families here that have been habituated.

Once you finally join a tracking group, the chances of finding the gorillas are excellent. The time you actually spend with the gorillas once you find them is limited to one hour, and not a minute more.

Group numbers for gorilla tracking are limited to six people, and unfortunately demand generally far exceeds supply. However, the massacre here in 1999 changed all this and for much of the rest of the year it was possible just to turn up at the park and pay on the day. But with tourism slowly recovering, it won't be long before it is business as usual. The big safari companies often book blocks of places months in advance, meaning that for the individual visitor, it can be difficult to get a confirmed place. All bookings must be made through the Uganda Wildlife Authority (UWA) office in Kampala (☎ 041-346287, fax 346 291, email uwahq@ uol.co.ug), although staff will often tell you that there are no vacancies for months. Be persistent, and if necessary, turn up at the park and see if there are any no-shows.

Gorilla-tracking permits cost US$250 (in addition to the park entry fee), payable in hard currency (any major foreign currency) or Ugandan shillings. The trips leave at 8.30 am each day, and you have to report to park headquarters 30 minutes before that. Note that children under 15 years old are not permitted to track the gorillas, and anyone with a cold or other illness is likewise excluded. Do not try and feign good health if you are unwell as you could be endangering these rare creatures' lives. A full refund is given to anyone who withdraws because of ill health.

For more information on the mountain gorillas, their habitat and where to track them, see the special section 'The Mountain Gorillas of East Africa'.

Forest Walks

The park headquarters at Buhoma has a beautiful setting, and there are three walks in the area which are well worth doing. Two of them are in the park, and the third is outside. For the walks inside the park, the cost is USh 30,000 (in addition to the park entry fee) and a ranger accompanies all walkers.

The **Waterfall Trail** takes you to a 33m waterfall on the Munyaga River. It's a fairly strenuous walk that takes about three hours for the round trip.

The **Muzabijiro Loop Trail** gives excellent views south to the Virunga volcanoes and the western Rift Valley in Congo (Zaïre), weather permitting. It also takes about three hours.

Lastly there's the **Munyaga River Trail**, an easy half-hour walk in the vicinity of the park headquarters, but actually outside the park.

Places to Stay & Eat

Buhoma The cheapest option is *Buhoma Community Campground* which is right by the park headquarters. It has a beautiful setting and you can camp here for USh 5000 per person. There are also four-bed bandas, which cost USh 7000 per person or USh 25,000 for the whole banda. These are very basic, but sheets and blankets are supplied and there's hot water by the bucket.

Also in this area is *Buhoma Homestead* a private set-up owned and run by African Pearl Safaris (☎ 041-233566, fax 235770) in Kampala. This is a very pleasant and well run place, and the communal evening candlelit meal is very convivial. Most of the people who stay here are African Pearl clients, but others can stay for US$65 for full board. Advance bookings are essential.

There are also a couple of *luxury camps* in Buhoma, but they both closed in the aftermath of the Bwindi massacre. However, both looked set to re-open at the time of writing. Mantana Safaris (☎ 041-320152, fax 321522) charge US$137/220 for singles/doubles with full board, while the Abercrombie & Kent camp charges US$80 per person for bed and breakfast. However, both places are often full of tour package clients when gorilla permits are fully booked.

There are plans underway for more camp sites to be set up near Buhoma.

Across the track from the community camping ground is *H&P Canteen* where you can get filling local meals for USh 3500 for dinner and USh 2000 for breakfast although they must be ordered in advance. Primus beer from Congo (Zaïre) is also available (USh 2000).

Butogota The only accommodation in town is *Butogota Travellers Inn*, a modest place with clean rooms at USh 4000/6000. This is where the bus to and from Kampala terminates.

Getting There & Away
Butogota is the nearest village to Buhoma and the closest you can get to the park by public transport. Without your own transport it's too far from the park to use as a base for gorilla tracking, but many travellers spend a night here en route from Kabale or Kampala before walking or hitching the 17km to Buhoma the next day, and visiting the gorillas the day after. Otherwise you can hire a pick-up (USh 20,000 to USh 30,000) or a motorcycle (USh 15,000) to take you. There's also an immigration office at Butogota and a border crossing nearby to Rutshuru in Congo (Zaïre) – that is, when the civil war ends.

There is a direct Silverline bus daily in each direction between Kampala and Butogota, which goes via Kisizi. It leaves Kampala sometime after 6 am, arriving in Butogota around 6 pm; the fare is USh 14,000.

The other alternative is the irregular pick-ups and share-taxis that connect Kabale and Butogota; there are plenty of these on Tuesday and Friday. If you can find one, the fare is USh 6000, and you can usually persuade the driver to continue on to the park for an additional USh 6000 per person. If there is nothing from Kabale to Butogota, take a Kihihi share-taxi as far as Kanyantorogo, from where you can pick up the bus as it comes through from Kampala.

By private vehicle the better route is via Kabale as you stay on the bitumen a lot longer. The turn-off to Bwindi/Buhoma is signposted off the road to Kisoro, and the trip from Kabale takes around four hours. It's a very scenic road through mountainous rainforest.

KABALE
☎ 0486
Kabale is in the Kigeza area, which tourist brochures are fond of dubbing the 'Switzerland of Africa', although you'll be lucky to see volcanoes in Switzerland. Nevertheless, this south-western corner of Uganda is certainly very beautiful, with its intensively cultivated and terraced hills, forests and lakes. It offers breathtaking views of the Virunga chain of volcanoes from the summits of various passes such as the one just before you drop down into Kabale on the road from Mbarara, and also from the Kanaba Gap, 60km from Kabale on the road to Kisoro. There are also tea-growing estates all the way from Kabale to the Rwandan border at Katuna.

Although the town of Kabale itself is nothing special, it is a convenient base from

Uganda's Sipi Falls at the foothills of Mt Elgon

NICK RAY

Looking down from Kibale-Kisoro Rd, Uganda

DAVID WALL

Uganda's awesome Murchison Falls is possibly the most powerful natural surge of water on earth.

DAVID WALL

Transport in East Africa can be as chaotic or as simple as you like. In Uganda you can take your chances at a crowded bus park in Kampala (top) or use pedal power like this banana seller (bottom) in Fort Portal.

DENNIS JOHNSON

GREG ELMS

which to explore some superb hiking country and the area is honeycombed with tracks and paths, trading centres and farms. It is also the gateway to Lake Bunyonyi, fast becoming the most popular place in Uganda for travellers to rest and relax for a few days. It's a good base for trips to the gorillas at Mgahinga and Bwindi.

Kabale is Uganda's highest town (about 2000m) and turns cool at night, so have warm clothes handy. Water pressure in town is intermittent at best, so you may want to check that water is likely to come out of the pipes before you strip off under a shower on a cold evening.

Information

Tourist Office The Uganda Wildlife Authority maintains an office in the main street, but as the staff cannot actually book gorilla trips here, and are not in direct contact with either Bwindi or Mgahinga, there's very little they can do for you, apart

from tell you how many permits are already booked for which day. It's probably best to try the office in Kisoro instead.

Money There are several foreign exchange bureaus in Kabale, including the banks near the post office and in the Highland Hotel, but rates are generally poor. The best rates are to be found at the National Bank of Uganda, where they are almost the same as in Kampala.

Post & Communications The post office has international phone and fax services and the connection is reasonably reliable as it is already digitised.

There is also a business centre attached to Highland Hotel from where you can make international calls and send faxes. It charges USh 2000 to send an email and USh 500 a page to receive one. The email address for receiving is highland@imul.com. Internet access is slow and expensive.

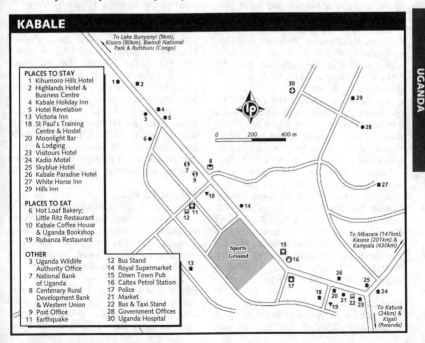

KABALE

To Lake Bunyonyi (9km),
Kisoro (80km), Bwindi National
Park & Rutshuru (Congo)

UGANDA

PLACES TO STAY
1 Kihumoro Hills Hotel
2 Highlands Hotel &
  Business Centre
4 Kabale Holiday Inn
5 Hotel Revelation
13 Victoria Inn
18 St Paul's Training
  Centre & Hostel
20 Moonlight Bar
  & Lodging
23 Visitours Hotel
24 Kadio Motel
25 Skyblue Hotel
26 Kabale Paradise Hotel
27 White Horse Inn
29 Hills Inn

PLACES TO EAT
6 Hot Loaf Bakery;
  Little Ritz Restaurant
10 Kabale Coffee House
  & Uganda Bookshop
19 Rubanza Restaurant

OTHER
3 Uganda Wildlife
  Authority Office
7 National Bank
  of Uganda
8 Centenary Rural
  Development Bank
  & Western Union
9 Post Office
11 Earthquake

12 Bus Stand
14 Royal Supermarket
15 Down Town Pub
16 Caltex Petrol Station
17 Police
21 Market
22 Bus & Taxi Stand
28 Government Offices
30 Uganda Hospital

0   200   400 m

Sports
Ground

To Mbarara (147km),
Kasese (201km) &
Kampala (430km)

To Katuna
(24km) &
Kigali
(Rwanda)

Places to Stay – Budget

There is a good range of budget accommodation in Kabale, with two particularly popular places near the bus and taxi stand.

The first is *Visitours Hotel* (☎ 22239) part of which is divided into units of three rooms which share a bathroom, a toilet and a small lounge. It is not the world's most salubrious hotel, but it is cheap at USh 2500/5000 for singles/doubles. The rooms don't look too secure so be sensible with your valuables. The hotel has an excellent restaurant and there's an attractive upstairs veranda overlooking the street.

The other good option, but somewhat more expensive, is *Skyblue Hotel* (☎ 22 154) which has very clean rooms with towel and soap provided and bucket hot water on request. The service is excellent, but can feel a little over the top for the money you pay. It costs USh 7000/10,000. Some rooms are bigger and better than others so ask to see a couple before you decide. Arguably the best option is to stay at Skyblue and eat at Visitours, getting the best of both worlds.

There are plenty of other bargains about the town. Next door to the Skyblue is *Skyline Hotel* (☎ 24071) which has basic rooms with a shared bathroom for USh 6000/8000. There is also a small, inexpensive restaurant here.

A good choice is *Kadio Motel* (☎ 23558) just before the Katuna road, which offers a selection of rooms starting at USh 5000/ 7000 with a shared bathroom. It also has doubles with a balcony at the front of the hotel for USh 12,000 and mini-suites for USh 15,000.

Elsewhere there is a host of optimistically named guesthouses and lodges that don't quite live up to the image the names convey. *Kabale Paradise Hotel* is pretty bad with some cell-like singles for USh 4000. *Hotel Revelation* is certainly not: rooms are USh 6000/10,000. Finally there is *Kabale Holiday Inn* with basic rooms for USh 5000/7000 – it is unlikely to become affiliated with the international chain in the near future.

Places to Stay – Mid-Range

The most popular place in this price range is *Highland Hotel* (☎ 22175). The staff

here are very friendly and helpful, but some rooms are better than others. It costs USh 14,000 for a single room with a shared bathroom, or USh 27,000 with bathroom; breakfast is included. However, most rooms feel a little musty these days. Towel and soap are provided and there's hot water in the showers if the plumbing is intact. The big plus about this hotel is its excellent restaurant and the very popular bar. There is also a handy business centre attached to the hotel (see Post & Communications earlier for more details).

Along similar lines is the airy *Victoria Inn* (☎ 22134), which offers comfortable singles/doubles with bathroom for USh 17,000/25,000. A light breakfast (tea and bread) is included. The hotel has its own bar and restaurant and the staff are friendly.

Places to Stay – Top End

Kabale's most famous hotel is *White Horse Inn* (☎ 23336, fax 23717) up on the hill overlooking the town. It's a very attractive place, but its design definitely owes something to another era. The hotel offers singles/doubles for USh 45,900/63,240, including breakfast. It also has some large suites for USh 85,000. The hotel has a bar and restaurant. You should be able to negotiate a discount on these prices as long as tourists remain thin on the ground.

Hills Inn (☎ 24442, fax 24443) is a newer place, not far from the White Horse, with modern rooms for USh 45,000/65,000 including breakfast. There is a small restaurant with a decent enough menu. The hotel is signposted from the town centre.

Places to Eat

You can find a good cheap *breakfast* at Visitours Hotel or Skyblue Motel. Visitours has an excellent, inexpensive menu including large curries and a tasty guacamole and chapati. Skyblue's menu is more expensive, but includes some reasonable steaks.

Hot Loaf Bakery has great cakes for USh 500, and it also offers fresh bread, pizzas and tasty samosas. This makes it a good stop for breakfast and a useful place to pick up some snacks for a long road journey.

UGANDA

One of the best restaurants in town is the new *Little Ritz Restaurant* above the Hot Loaf Bakery. This place has an eclectic menu of western and African dishes for about USh 4000. It is also a good option for the 'BEST' breakfast – baked beans, egg, sausages and tomatoes.

Good value also is the *restaurant* at Highland Hotel. It costs about USh 2000 to USh 4000 for a main course but it's well worth it, assuming they have what you want to eat (fish is frequently not available). You have the choice here of eating in the enclosed restaurant or in the partially open-air bar area with a log fire to warm your cockles.

For a real splurge, but not necessarily better food, go to the *restaurant* at White Horse Inn, which has a pleasant garden setting. Expect to pay about USh 5000 to USh 6000 for a main course.

Entertainment
Kabale isn't the dance capital of Africa, but it is home to *Earthquake* the local disco that is rumoured to make the earth move under your feet. It only really rocks at weekends, but goes on into the small hours and attracts a healthy provincial crowd of drunkards and hookers. It regularly goes mobile and takes the sound system to places like White Horse Inn and Lake Bunyonyi.

Getting There & Away
Bus The Post Bus operates between Kabale and Kampala daily. For details of the service, see Getting There & Away in the Kampala chapter.

There are numerous daily buses to Kampala, which take about six hours and cost USh 10,000. To Fort Portal, there's a daily bus via Mbarara and Kasese at 7 am (USh 10,000, about eight hours).

Minibus The daily minibuses between Kabale and Kisoro cost USh 5000/6000 to/from the Congo (Zaïre) border, and take up to three hours. There are scheduled departures to Kisoro at 10 am and 4 pm. Otherwise, they go when full, and 'full' means just that! Most of them are dangerously overloaded but the ride, over a very dusty

road, is absolutely magnificent and the views are superb. The minibuses depart from next to Visitours Hotel.

There are also regular departures for Kampala (USh 10,000) which go via Mbarara (USh 5000).

For Bwindi National Park there are a couple of vehicles heading to Butogota on Tuesday and Friday, and they should cost USh 6000. It's a slow but highly scenic journey, and once you get to Butogota, you should be able to persuade the driver to carry on to park headquarters for about USh 6000 a person.

For details about Lake Bunyonyi, see Getting There & Away in the following Around Kabale section.

There are also direct minibuses to Kigali (Rwanda) from the bus stand next to the market. See the Uganda Getting There & Away chapter for details.

AROUND KABALE
Lake Bunyonyi
This famous beauty spot over the ridge to the west of Kabale is fast overtaking the Ssese Islands as *the* place for travellers to chill out on a long trip through Uganda. It's a large and irregularly shaped lake with a number of islands, and the surrounding hillsides are intensively cultivated. The area is great for trips on the lake, cycling or hiking.

Things To See & Do There are endless opportunities for activities in the Lake Bunyonyi region. Many of the villagers, and several of the guesthouses and camp sites, have boats and you shouldn't have any difficulty arranging a trip on the lake. **Canoeing** is also a popular activity and dugouts can be rented from most of the camps. Charges are pretty reasonable, but you might need to practise for a while before heading off on an ambitious trip around the islands as many tourists end up going round and round in circles, doing what's known locally as the *muzungu* corkscrew.

There are endless walking opportunities in the area and for those who want a challenge, you can boat across the lake before trekking down to Kisoro. **Guided walks** are very popular and these can be easily arranged through Jasper's Campsite. However, if you want an easy-going amble along the shores of the lake, it is straightforward enough to find your own way.

Mountain bikes can be hired from Bunyonyi Overland Camp and are a great way to get along the lakeshore. You can also hire fishing gear here, although there are very few fish in the lake.

Further on, **Kyevu market** is held every Wednesday and Saturday, drawing villagers from all over the region. It is a long way from most of the camps around the lake, and involves a three-hour trip by dugout. However, most of the camps should be able to fix you up with an oarsman to help out, or you could charter a motorboat. However, the people out here are pretty shy so be sensitive with your camera. There are also a number of Batwa villages in this part of the region and if you can link up with a friendly guide at the market, you might be able to arrange a visit to a Batwa community.

Nearer to the camps is **Punishment Island**, located midway between Bushara and Njuyera islands; so named because it was once the place where unmarried pregnant women were dumped to die. And tragically most of them did die in trying to swim for shore, because they usually didn't have the stamina to make it. It is easy to spot as it has just one small tree in the centre.

Places to Stay & Eat Lake Bunyonyi looks set to take off as one of Uganda's most popular destinations. There has been a mushrooming of camp sites and guesthouses in the area during the past few years.

There are two very popular places for backpackers, both of which are great places to stay. *Bunyonyi Overland Camp (☎ 0486-23741, fax 23742, email highland@imul .com)* is on the mainland and is very popular with overland companies. It offers some great facilities and a whole range of options for accommodation. Camping is USh 2000 per person, renting a tent is USh 4000 (bedding USh 1000 extra), furnished double tents are USh 16,000 and singles/doubles are USh 10,000/20,000. The camp boasts arguably the best toilets in Uganda, hot water in the morning and evening and a restaurant. There is plenty of open space to lose yourself if it is busy, there is a small swimming pier, and kayaks and mountain bikes are available for rent.

Jasper's Campsite is particularly popular with independent travellers. Located on Itambira Island, this is a community development project run to raise funds for the local Bwama primary school. There is a range of accommodation options, starting with camping for USh 2500 per person, dorm beds for USh 3500, single rooms for USh 4500 and a classy little house with a breezy veranda for USh 10,000. Prices include free tea all day. Good, hearty meals are available and there is a relaxed little bar where you can kick back and while away the day. Other facilities include solar-heated showers, board games and dugout canoes to explore the lake. To get to Jasper's, take a canoe from the mainland, which should cost no more than USh 1000 to charter.

There are a couple of other cheap options around the lake, but they see very few guests. *Kyahugye Island Resort* is on the island of the same name, but has very few facilities. It costs USh 3000 to pitch your own tent and USh 5000/10,000 for a spartan tent for one/two people. There are basic washing facilities, but no food, so if you do decide you want to do the wilderness thing this might be the place to do it. It has the feel of somewhere that needs an injection of imagination or money.

Over on Njuyera Island, in British missionary Stanley Sharp's old place, is the small *Church of Uganda Guesthouse*. It is quite run-down, but offers basic rooms for USh 2500 per person. Most travellers who want the island life make for Jasper's.

Moving upmarket, *Bushara Island Camp (☎ 0486-22447)* is a community project run by the Church of Uganda. You can camp here for US$3, or there are permanent furnished tents at US$25. There is a good restaurant here with pizzas, crayfish dishes and desserts like caramelised bananas and crepes. It has a good selection of wines, but no beer. It's a fair walk from the camping area to the restaurant. There's also a snack bar, picnic area, outdoor barbecue and volleyball court. A dugout canoe across to the island from the end of the road from Kabale costs USh 1000, but if you organise things in Kabale, you are more likely to be put on the motorised boat, which will cost USh 8000.

Far Out Island Camp is the most sophisticated place to stay in the Lake Bunyonyi area. Set up by Swedes, all the buildings have a homely 'log cabin' feel to them and the small island is a great place to relax for a few days after some hard travelling around the country. Accommodation is in tents with three beds in each and a nearby shared bathroom with regular hot water. Prices are US$35 per person including breakfast, US$45 per person for half board or US$60 for full board. The bar and restaurant is a pleasant place to relax over a beer with great views across the lake. Even if it isn't in your budget to stay here, it is definitely worth popping over by dugout to take a beer with the larger-than-life host, Niklas.

A couple more options that are likely to open during the life of this book include *Lake Bunyonyi Resort* a striking property on the shores of the lake and under renovation by the team that runs Backpackers Hostel in Kampala. Idi Amin once used it as a holiday home, having confiscated it from a minister who was executed early in the regime. Until UEB's electrification program reaches Lake Bunyonyi, this is also the only place with power – not that the UEB is much good at supplying regular power anyway.

Just before Bunyonyi Overland Camp is *Bamboo Resort* where several bandas are nearing completion, although they look more suited to a prison camp than a holiday camp.

Getting There & Away To get to Lake Bunyonyi, you can take a minibus (USh 500, Monday and Friday only), or hitch or walk (about 9km from Kabale). Otherwise you can get a lift from the Highland Hotel at 9.30 am or 4.30 pm (USh 2500), returning to Kabale at 10 am or 5 pm. You can also charter a special taxi between a few of you for USh 8000.

The access road for Bunyonyi from Kabale is off to the left about 1km past the Highlands Hotel on the road to Kisoro. If you're walking, you can take a shortcut by heading straight uphill alongside the stream just past the small dams, but it is a long way with a pack.

KISORO

Kisoro is at the extreme south-western tip of the country on the Ugandan side of the Virunga Mountains, across from Ruhengeri in Rwanda. As a town it has absolutely nothing to recommend it; the main draw for travellers is as a base from which to visit the gorillas in Mgahinga National Park to the south or the gorillas at Djomba just over the border to the west in Congo (Zaïre). However, on a clear day, the views of the Virunga chain of volcanoes from this dusty little town are fantastic.

Information

There are a couple of foreign exchange places in Kisoro. Uganda Commercial Bank exchanges travellers cheques at better rates than in Kabale. If Djomba is open again, bear in mind that the Congolese prefer cash payment in Ugandan shillings or US dollars.

The post office offers the only telephone link with the rest of Uganda, but for international links you are likely to have to go to Kabale.

The Uganda Wildlife Authority (UWA) office is on the main road in the centre of town, and it's here you should inquire about the gorillas at Mgahinga and arrange for transport to take you there. The office is open daily from 8 am to 12.30 pm and 2 to 5 pm. You can also pay for your gorilla permits here if you have just turned up with no reservation.

Kisoro occasionally runs out of petrol, the whole town that is, so if you are coming from Kabale in your own transport, fill up.

Things To See & Do

Apart from the nearby gorillas, there is a good range of activities available in the Kisoro area, including **trekking** the volcanoes in Mgahinga National Park and **cave**

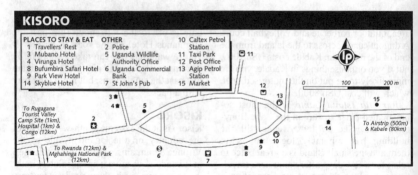

KISORO

PLACES TO STAY & EAT	OTHER	10	Caltex Petrol
1 Travellers' Rest	2 Police		Station
3 Mubano Hotel	5 Uganda Wildlife	11	Taxi Park
4 Virunga Hotel	Authority Office	12	Post Office
8 Bufumbira Safari Hotel	6 Uganda Commercial	13	Agip Petrol
9 Park View Hotel	Bank		Station
14 Skyblue Hotel	7 St John's Pub	15	Market

To Rugagana
Tourist Valley
Camp Site (1km),
Hospital (1km) &
Congo (12km)

To Rwanda (12km) &
Mghahinga National Park
(12km)

To Airstrip (500m)
& Kabale (80km)

0   100   200 m

exploration near the park (see the Mgahinga National Park section later in this chapter).

Another interesting option is to take a **snake safari** to Lake Mutanda. Trips to see the large pythons at the lake can be arranged through Rugagana Campsite. It costs about US$20 to charter the minibus plus some money for the guides.

Places to Stay

Rugagana Tourist Valley Campsite is very popular with overland trucks and, in the past, you could often find a bunch of them here waiting for permits for Mgahinga or Djomba. However, in the aftermath of the Bwindi and Djomba incidents, business has been slow, making this a quiet retreat where you can camp for USh 2500 per person or rent a tent for USh 5000. Meals are available for USh 3000 and there is a decent bar area and satellite TV.

In Kisoro itself, there are a few cheap places if you are looking to save money. *Bufumbira Safari Hotel* and *Park View Hotel* are near each other and offer pretty much the same, with singles/doubles at USh 3000/6000. These are no-frills set-ups with just a couple of beds in each room and shared bathrooms. Both places have cheap little restaurants offering various combinations of *matoke* and *ugali*.

Probably the best place to stay in Kisoro is *Virunga Hotel* which has doubles for USh 10,000 with shared bathroom and USh 20,000 with private bathroom. There is a cheap menu of basic African dishes available.

Another decent hotel is *Skyblue Hotel* and if you have seen the one in Kabale, you know what to expect. Rooms are clean, service is impeccable and facilities are shared. Rooms cost USh 8000/12,000. It also offers reasonable food at the restaurant.

Mubano Hotel used to be a good place to stay, but as the owner is an MP in Kampala these days, he seems to have little time to uphold standards in his hotel. The rooms are looking more than a little mothballed, but are quite cheap at USh 10,000 for a small room with bathroom, or USh 13,000 for what amounts to a mini-suite with shared facilities. The hotel has a restaurant and bar, but no electricity or running water.

Moving rapidly upmarket, *Travellers' Rest* has recently been refurbished by the Volcanoes tour company. This is a hotel with a history: it was set up by the so-called father of gorilla tourism, Walter Baumgartel, and Dian Fossey visited often. However, such history and heritage don't come cheap in the modern world. Half board is US$55 per person, while full board is US$65. The price for residents of East Africa is cheaper at USh 40,000/50,000. The rooms are attractive and simple, and the showers hot and rewarding after the dusty drive from Kabale. There is also a restaurant, and the bar is a good place to take a nightcap on a cold evening, with its open fire and abundance of spirits and liquors.

See also Places to Stay in the Mgahinga National Park section later in this chapter, for two places outside the park which offer superb views of the Virungas.

Places to Eat

There is not a great deal choice in town and most visitors usually end up eating at the hotel or guesthouse in which they are staying. The most reasonable *restaurants* are those at Skyblue Hotel, which offers meals from USh 3000 to USh 5000, and Virunga Hotel, which offers cheap African food.

The *restaurant* at Travellers' Rest is worth considering if you want to treat yourself to better surroundings. Three-course meals are available for USh 10,000 and main courses at USh 5000.

If you are looking for life in Kisoro, generally you might as well forget it. However, *St John's Pub* is a lively little spot in the middle of town. It has a pool table, darts and a selection of cheap drinks.

Getting There & Away

Air Eagle Aviation has flights between Kampala and Kisoro on Wednesday, Friday and Sunday. Flights can be a handy option for those who want to trek to see the gorillas, but have little time to spare for the long bus ride. Tickets cost US$85/170 one way/return.

Bus & Minibus There's a direct bus between Kampala and Kisoro daily, leaving Kampala sometime after 7 am (USh 14,000). It passes through Kabale about noon if you want to pick it up there (USh 4000).

Between Kabale and Kisoro there are frequent daily minibuses, which depart when full and cost USh 5000 (see the Kabale section earlier in this chapter for more details). These take from two to three hours depending on the season. There are also two scheduled departures at 7 am and 1 pm. Coming from Kabale, these minibuses continue on a further 12km to the Congolese border at Bunagana (USh 500). The only onward public transport from there to Rutshuru is on Friday. The rest of the time you'll have to hitch, and there's very little traffic.

The Rwandan border south of Kisoro at Cyanika is open, but the road is in poor condition on the Ugandan side. As for the Rwanda side, you need to check security conditions carefully before travelling this way as there have been fighting and am-

bushes on and off over the last few years. It's better to go via Katuna (Gatuna) from Kabale. See the Uganda Getting There & Away chapter for full details of the routes into Rwanda and Congo (Zaïre).

LAKE MUTANDA

This is a beautiful lake set against the towering backdrop of the Virunga volcanoes. It lies 14km north of Kisoro and is a nice area for walking.

Large pythons nest in the lake region and you can observe them at close quarters if you wish, although bearing in mind their girth, you may want to keep a sensible distance (see Things to See & Do in the Kisoro section earlier in this chapter for more details).

Mgahinga Safari Lodge sits on the shores of this natural wilderness. It is an upmarket operation with tented chalets available for about US$140 per person with full board. At the time of writing, it was up for sale, but prices will most likely stay the same.

MGAHINGA NATIONAL PARK

Mgahinga National Park is tucked away in the far south-western corner of the country. It covers just 34 sq km and the tropical rainforest is another mountain gorilla habitat. The park is contiguous with the Parc National des Volcans in Rwanda, and the Parc National des Virungas in Congo (Zaïre).

UGANDA

Warning

There were isolated security problems in the Mgahinga National Park during the second half of the 1990s, due to its proximity to the Congo (Zaïre) and Rwandan borders. Check with the Uganda Wildlife Authority (UWA) office in Kampala, Kabale or Kisoro before planning a visit to this park.

There have also been disturbing reports of illegal gorilla visits at Mgahinga, potentially endangering the lives of these rare creatures by increasing their stress level, thereby reducing their immunity to disease. For more information on responsible gorilla tracking, see the special section 'The Mountain Gorillas of East Africa'.

The three together form the Virunga Conservation Area, which covers 420 sq km, and is home to an estimated half of the world's mountain gorilla population of about 640 animals (the other half are found in Bwindi National Park).

As at Bwindi, it is possible to track gorillas here, but it is less convenient as the gorillas have a tendency to duck across the mountains into Rwanda or Congo (Zaïre). As a result, fewer people visit the gorillas here, instead opting for the more reliable choices of Bwindi or Djomba, across the border in Congo (Zaïre) – if the border crossing is open.

There is just one group of gorillas habituated to visitors at Mgahinga and it has nine members, including two silverbacks. It can take longer to locate the gorillas here than at Bwindi, but the going is not as hard as in the 'impenetrable forest'. Mgahinga is certainly a spectacular location to trek the mountain gorillas, and the backdrop of the Virunga volcanoes is something straight out of *Gorillas in the Mist*.

Three volcanoes loom large over the park headquarters: Muhavura, Gahinga and Sabinyo. Muhavura has a crater lake at its summit and is the highest point in the park, at 4127m.

The park headquarters is about 15km from Kisoro at Ntebeko Camp, and entry to the park costs US$15 per day.

Tracking the Gorillas

A group of six people heads out from the park headquarters at 8 am each day to track the gorillas. Reservations for the trips are best made at the Uganda Wildlife Authority (UWA) head office in Kampala (☎ 041-346287, fax 346291, email uwahq@uol.co.ug), and the cost is US$175. This price is likely to rise to US$250 sometime soon. You can also make arrangements and cash payments at the UWA office in Kisoro; this way you can find out if the gorillas are in Uganda or taking a vacation across the border. You need to check in at the booking office in Kisoro (near the Virunga Hotel) by 5 pm on the day before your trip and pay your fee. There are no stand-by places available

at Mgahinga, but it is generally much easier to get a confirmed booking, as tour companies don't tend to book blocks of permits here.

Trekking

Two of the three volcanoes in the park (Mt Muhavura at 4127m and Mt Gahinga at 3437m) can be climbed for US$30 per person including a ranger/guide. There's also a 13km nature trail (USh 6000 per group plus USh 6000 per person) which gives you a chance to spot some of the more than 100 species of bird found in the park, including the Ruwenzori turacao and the scarlet-tufted malachite sunbird.

There are also a number of trekking options available in the area that skirts the edges of the national park, saving you the US$15 entry fee. The best person to contact about these is Sheeba, who can sometimes be found at the community camp just outside the park headquarters.

Caving

The Garama Cave is about 2km from the park headquarters (outside the park boundary) and visits cost USh 6000 per group plus USh 6000 per person. Bring a torch (flashlight), or rent one for USh 2000.

There is also a cave outside the park which is bigger than the Garama Cave. Staff at the community camp can arrange to take you there for about USh 1000 per person, or more if you are alone.

Places to Stay & Eat

There is basic *camping* (USh 5000) at the park headquarters but you need to be fully equipped as only water and firewood are available.

Also at the main gate is the excellent *Arnajambere Iwacu Community Campground* which costs USh 5000 in your own tent or USh 5000 in a dorm, and USh 10,000 for a double banda. It also offers some larger bandas that can sleep up to four people for USh 20,000. The camp site offers fine views of the Virungas. There is a small canteen and the proceeds are pumped back into the local community.

There is also an upmarket camp located just outside the park, operated by Volcanoes tour company. *Mt Gahinga Rest Camp* has a stunning location at the foot of the brooding volcanoes. Accommodation is in well-appointed but not exactly luxurious bandas, and safari tents. The bandas cost US$140/220 for singles/doubles with full board. The tents cost US$100/160, also with full board.

The only other options are 15km away in Kisoro (see that section earlier in this chapter for details).

Getting There & Away

There is no transport along the rough 15km track between Kisoro and the park headquarters; without your own vehicle you can walk (about three hours) or hope for a lift (although there's very little traffic). However, the best way to get out to the park is to radio Sheeba or the management at the community camping ground from the UWA office in Kisoro and pay USh 10,000 each way for a ride. Local pick-ups from Kisoro cost USh 20,000 (USh 30,000 in the wet season), or you can occasionally get lifts with national parks vehicles for USh 15,000.

DJOMBA

Djomba is across the border in Congo (Zaïre), on the slopes of Muside and Sabinyo volcanoes. To see the gorillas, you must be at the departure point by 8 am to pay the fee and be allocated to a group. The fee includes a compulsory guide and an armed ranger, both of whom will expect a tip from each person at the end (US$2 is about average but many tip more).

There are two families of gorillas here, known as the Marcel family (23 animals) and the Oscar family (11 animals). The guides can usually find their allotted group of gorillas within an hour or two, sometimes less.

Note that gorilla viewing fees *must* be paid in hard currency, and everything else here has to be paid for in hard currency or in Ugandan shillings. Congos may be accepted but the old Mobuto notes never were.

WARNING

! In August 1998, four tourists were kidnapped at Djomba while attempting to track the gorillas; one was released, but three were still missing at the time of writing, presumed dead. Djomba has remained closed ever since.

The civil war going on in Congo (Zaïre) involves troops from as many as nine countries. Armed members of the *Interahamwe* roam this region and they have been known to target tourists.

Because of the possibility that peace will eventually return to this region and Djomba will reopen, we include the following information. However, should you hear that Djomba is once again open and safe to visit, check the information very carefully in Uganda with as many sources as possible, as it is a very volatile part of the world.

Places to Stay & Eat

There's an excellent *hut* at the park headquarters, containing two dorms with four beds in each (good value at US$2 per bed). Clean sheets are provided and there's an earth toilet outside. There's also ample *camping* space with water and toilet. Camping costs US$1 per tent (if the money is collected – often it's not). If you're not cooking your own food, you can buy very tasty home-cooked *meals* at the park headquarters.

If you have camping equipment, you can *camp* free by the border at Bunagana (Uganda) outside the Ugandan immigration post. The people here are very friendly and will keep an eye on your tent while you're away at Djomba. Bring food with you. Drinks (beer and soft drinks) are available at the border – local youths will arrange all this for you. You'd have to make a very early start to get to the park headquarters by 8 am.

There's also the possibility of staying at the *Catholic Mission* in Bunagana or at the *American Baptist Mission* at Rwanguba, 5km uphill from Bunagana, but neither is very welcoming towards travellers.

UGANDA

Getting There & Away
You need a Congolese visa to visit Djomba *unless* you are only going to visit the gorillas and then return to Uganda the same day. In this case, immigration will charge you US$50, retain your passport and allow you to go to Djomba. When you return, you get your passport back. This is cheaper than buying a tourist visa (US$75 for one month, single-entry). Re-entry into Uganda costs US$20 or US$25, depending on your nationality, unless you already have a multiple-entry visa.

At Bunagana, you'll be met by local children and youths who will offer to guide you to the park headquarters at Djomba and/or carry your bags. Don't pass up their services or you'll get lost in the maze of farms and paths along the way. The usual tip is around US$3. The 7km, gradual uphill walk to the park headquarters should take you about two hours.

If you intend to head further into Congo (Zaïre), the only public transport to Rutshuru is on Friday. The rest of the time you'll have to hitch, and there's very little traffic.

MBARARA
☎ 0485
The main town between Masaka and Kabale, Mbarara suffered a great deal during the war to oust Idi Amin but now bears few scars of those times. It's a very spread-out town, but pleasant with a good range of facilities, and it's a useful place to stay overnight between destinations.

Safariland is a place almost beyond words, a surreal resort located in a valley just below the university. It is a sprawling wooden building which owes something to African architecture and something to Hans Christian Andersen, an overactive imagination or some strong drugs. Within the complex are several bars, a restaurant, coffee shop and amphitheatre. The river valley in which the resort is located supports myriad birdlife and is said to be home to hippos in the wet season.

Information
There are several foreign exchange places along the main road. The best bet is probably Nile Bank Forex.

The post office has international telephones and there is a Starcom office housed in a container; look for the huge dish on the roof.

Places to Stay – Budget
There isn't quite the range of cheap, basic guesthouses you find in other provincial towns. *Camping* is available at both University Inn and the kitsch resort, Safariland. For more details see Places to Stay – Mid-Range.

Hotel Plaza has simple singles/doubles with shared bathroom for USh 5000/10,000.

Another reasonably priced place is *Buhumuriro Guesthouse* which has a flat rate of USh 10,000 for all rooms with attached bathroom. There is an international telephone outside.

A good place in this price range is *Mayoba Inn* (☎ 21161) on the main road. It has singles/doubles with shared bathroom for USh 7500/9000, or USh 12,000/14,000 with private bathroom. The hotel has its own bar and restaurant.

Places to Stay – Mid-Range
Up in price but close to the centre of town is *Pelikan Hotel* (☎ 21100) which is quiet and costs USh 15,000 for a room with shared facilities, USh 25,000/35,000 for singles/doubles with private facilities and a whopping USh 50,000 for so-called suites, which aren't much value. There's a bar and restaurant and credit cards are accepted. These prices are a little high for what you get.

A good-value establishment is *University Inn* (☎ 20334) at the south-western end of town. It's a friendly place and rarely full, and offers doubles (no singles) with bathroom, including breakfast, for USh 18,000. You can also camp in the grounds here for Ush 5000. There's a bar and restaurant.

Safariland (☎ 21692, 041-258359 in *Kampala*) is an amazing place (see the Mbarara introductory section for more details). Built in the early 1990s, it has recently been taken over by a Kampala tour operator who hopes to turn it into a regular stop for overland trucks. Camping here costs USh 2000 per person. The rooms are

MBARARA

To Masaka (146km)
& Kampala (283km)

0   125   250 m

To Police Station, Lake
View Hotel, Rwizi Arch
Hotel, University Inn,
Safariland (4km), Kabale
(147km) & Kasese (153km)

PLACES TO STAY	4 Nile Bank Forex
1 Agip Motel	6 Dee's Pub
3 Mayoba Inn	7 Taxi Park
5 Hotel Plaza	8 Market
11 Classic Hotel	9 Gold Trust Bank
17 Buhumuniro Guesthouse	10 Lucky Supermarket
21 Pelikan Hotel	12 Market
	13 Uganda Bookshop
PLACES TO EAT	15 Centenary Rural
14 Mbarara Coffee Shop	Development Bank;
18 Little Rock Cafe	Western Union
22 Friends Corner	16 Uganda
23 Western Hotel	Commercial Bank
	19 Post Office
OTHER	20 Shell Petrol Station
2 Total Petrol Station	24 All in One Pub

substantially more expensive and not such good value at US$30/40. It is easy to get lost here after a few beers, so take care to remember your way out if you hope to see your tent or room again.

Places to Stay – Top End

There has been something of a building boom in Mbarara when it comes to upmarket hotels, so don't be afraid to negotiate a discount if you're looking for some comfort. All rates include breakfast.

Mbarara's top hotel was long the modern *Lake View Hotel* (☎ 21398, fax 21399) on the outskirts of town off the road to Kasese. It's sited in front of a tiny artificial lake (more like a small dam) and has 70 bedrooms, all with bathroom, hot and cold running water, colour TV, video and telephone. Increased competition now means it costs USh 40,000/60,000 for singles/doubles, which is very good value. The hotel has its own swimming pool, sauna, bar and restaurant.

Speaking of the competition, it comes from three directions. *Classic Hotel* (☎/fax 20609) is a spotless place in the centre of town, offering rooms with bathroom, TV and telephone for USh 35,000/45,000. This is really good value for the standard of rooms.

Agip Motel (☎ 21615, fax 20575) is on the road to Masaka, unsurprisingly located near the Agip petrol station. It offers well appointed rooms for USh 60,000/80,000. There are also some large but expensive suites available for USh 140,000. The hotel has an á la carte restaurant, sports bar and conference facilities.

There's *Rwizi Arch Hotel* (☎ 20821, fax 20402) just off the road to Kasese. This is perhaps the most luxurious place of all, but has the prices to match. Rooms with all the trimmings cost US$60/75 and executive rooms are US$80. The hotel has a very good restaurant.

Places to Eat

For good, cheap, filling local dishes, try *Western Hotel* or *Friends Corner* in the centre of town, where you can get meals for about USh 1500.

Mbarara Coffee Shop has an excellent menu of pastas, curries and African standards for USh 3000 to USh 5000, and inexpensive sandwiches and cakes. It is very popular with locals and offers exemplary service.

Up in price somewhat, all the mid-range and top end hotels have *restaurants* which serve reasonably good food. Probably the best value is University Inn, with main dishes from USh 1500 to USh 2500, but for a splurge, try *Mariza Restaurant* at the Lake View Hotel, or Rwizi Arch Hotel, which has one of the most varied menus you are likely

UGANDA

to see in provincial Uganda, including pasta, meat and fish from USh 5000 to USh 7000 and desserts such as creme caramel.

If you have your own transport, it is worth calling in to Safariland for a *snack* or a drink. Without transport, you are looking at a long walk.

Getting There & Away

There are frequent buses and share-taxis from Mbarara to Kampala (USh 7000, four hours), Masaka (USh 2500), Kabale (USh 4000, two hours) and Kasese (USh 4000). There are also EMS Post buses running this route (see the earlier Kampala chapter for more information).

For Queen Elizabeth National Park, catch a Kasese-bound share-taxi and ask to get off at Katunguru (USh 3000), from where you'll need to hitch into the park.

LAKE MBURO NATIONAL PARK

Between Mbarara and Masaka and covering an area of 260 sq km, this national park is mainly savanna with scattered acacia trees. There are five lakes here, the largest of which is Lake Mburo. Created in 1982, the park features some of the rarer animals in Uganda, such as impala, eland, roan antelope, reedbuck, klipspringer and topi, as well as zebra, buffalo and hippo.

Adjacent to the park are the ranches of people of the Bahima tribe, who herd the famed long-horned Ankole cattle which are a common sight. This is one of the parks you're allowed to walk through (accompanied by a ranger), or you can go on wildlife drives. There are canoes, either paddled (USh 10,000) or outboard-driven (USh 30,000), available on Lake Mburo, although the motorboat was out of action at the time of writing.

Entry to the park costs US$7 per person per day.

Places to Stay

There are three *camp sites* in the park (USh 10,000 per person), or you can stay at the park headquarters at *Rwonyo Rest Camp* which has single, double and four-bed bandas with bedding, mosquito nets and bath-

room facilities. They cost USh 10,000/ 15,000/20,000 for singles/doubles/ triples. Relatively expensive meals are available here or you can cater for yourself. Fishermen sell fresh fish from the lake each morning. There's no electricity or refrigeration but kerosene lanterns, pit toilets and warm bucket showers are available.

Mantana Lake Mburo is a luxury tented camp on the edge of the park, run by Mantana Safaris (☎ 041-321522, fax 320152) in Kampala. Singles/doubles cost US$137/220 with full board. Meals are taken under the roof of a central bar and restaurant.

Getting There & Away

There are three possible ways into the park from the main Masaka-Mbarara road, but if you are hoping to hitch into the park or arrange a special taxi or *boda-boda* (bicycle-taxi) it is best to use the route from Sanga. It's possible to hitch lifts with the irregular but accommodating park vehicles from the main road. If you're taking your own vehicle, a 4WD is recommended, but the trip is possible in a 2WD car during the dry season.

Coming from Kampala, the first turn-off for the park is 13km after Lyantonde. If you have your own vehicle, it is easier to take this first turn-off. The second turn-off is at Sanga, 24km after Lyantonde, or 50km before Mbarara.

MASAKA
☎ 0481

In 1979 Masaka was trashed by the Tanzanian army in the closing stages of the war that ousted Idi Amin. A lot of rebuilding has taken place since then, but the scars are still visible and even now the potholes in the streets are definitely something to behold! There's very little to do in Masaka, and for most travellers it's just an overnight stop en route to the Ssese Islands in Lake Victoria or south into Tanzania. Masaka has a museum, but it's closed.

Information

There are banks in town where you can change money including a venerable looking branch of the Uganda Commercial Bank.

MASAKA

0   250   500 m

To Mbarara
(146km)

To Masaka
Backpackers
(4km) & Bukoba
(Tanzania)

Kampala Road

To Bukakata
(36km) &
Kampala
(137km)

OTHER
1 Masaka Sports Club
5 Bank of Uganda
6 Esso Petrol Station
7 Agip Petrol Station
8 Bus Stand
9 Peugeot Taxis
10 Taxi Park
12 Taxi Park
13 Post Office
14 Uganda
    Commercial Bank
15 Greenland Forex
16 Shell Petrol Station
17 Immigration
18 Museum
19 Hindu Temple
20 Police
21 Market
22 Mosque
23 High School

PLACES TO STAY & EAT
2 Hotel Brovad
3 Laston Hotel
4 Tropic Touch
11 Victoria End Guesthouse
24 Hotel La Nova

The post office offers international telephone and fax services.

Places to Stay

There's very little choice of hotels in Masaka (most were destroyed in the war). *Victoria End Guest House* costs USh 6000/8000 for singles/doubles and is good value given the lack of competition. The restaurant here has good meals.

About 4km south of town, and just off the road to the Tanzanian border, is *Masaka Backpackers* (☎ 21288, fax 20514). Here you can camp for USh 3000, take a bed in a dorm for USh 3500, or get a room for USh 5000. The owner is very friendly and helpful. To get here from Masaka, take a Kirimya share-taxi for USh 500, get off at Kasanvu and follow the signs from there.

In the middle range, there's a choice of three hotels, all of which are very pleasant. The cheapest is *Hotel La Nova* (☎ 21520), which is popular with aid workers. All the

rooms have bathrooms and cost USh 20,000/23,000, including breakfast. The staff are very pleasant and there's a bar, restaurant and guarded parking.

Somewhat more expensive is *Laston Hotel* (☎ 20309), in the north-east of town, which has singles with bathrooms for USh 20,800. Twin-bedded rooms are USh 30,000, while doubles go for USh 39,000. This is a very well managed hotel, spotlessly clean and with friendly staff. There are several open-air terraces and balconies where you can eat and drink, as well as an indoor bar and restaurant.

The latest place in town is *Hotel Brovad* (☎ 21455, fax 20997) which is near the Laston and offers a selection of clean, modern, well appointed rooms for USh 32,800/56,200/72,200, including breakfast. All rooms have bathroom, TV, fridge and phone.

Places to Eat

There isn't exactly a wealth of decent places to eat in Masaka. Most people end up eating at one of the hotels mentioned above. However, one restaurant stands out as a cut above the rest: *Tropic Touch*. This is an Indian-run restaurant offering a good selection of subcontinental cuisine and some continental favourites as well. Prices are more like those in Kampala, but then so is the food. Most dishes start at USh 5000.

Elgin Inn restaurant at Victoria End Guest House has good meals for USh 1500. Meals at the Laston Hotel are good value and cost, on average, about USh 6000. There is a good *restaurant* downstairs at the Hotel Brovad which has a large á la carte menu and a cheaper snack menu.

Getting There & Away

Buses and minibuses run frequently to Kampala (USh 2500) and Mbarara (USh 2500) and less frequently to Kabale.

Bukakata (from where boats leave for the Ssese Islands) is 36km east of Masaka along a *murram* (dirt) road, which is in reasonable shape except for a rough 10km stretch close to Masaka. There are infrequent and very crowded minibuses between the turn-off at Nyendo (about 3km on the

UGANDA

Kampala side of Masaka) and Bukakata (USh 1500).

Getting to Bukakata in your own transport can be an exercise in frustration, as there are no signposts whatsoever and the only people who seem to know the way are other drivers. Basically, you head downhill (east) out of Masaka centre, cross over the river bridge and then turn right (where there's a sign for the Church of Uganda Holiday & Conference Centre). From here you go straight across the first junction and then turn left at the next T-junction.

Masaka is also the starting point for crossing into Tanzania via the Kagera salient and Bukoba. See the Uganda Getting There & Away chapter for details.

AROUND MASAKA
Lake Nabugabo
Lake Nabugabo is a small, attractive lake, separated from its much bigger sister by a small strip of forest. The advantage it holds over Lake Victoria is that the water is cleaner and apparently free from bilharzia. The *Church of Uganda Resort* is located on the lakeshore and camping costs USh 3000 per person. Dorm beds cost USh 5000, double bandas are USh 15,000 and the large family bandas with their own lounge and bathroom are USh 25,000. Good meals here cost about USh 3000, but alcohol is not available.

Getting here is not so straightforward as it is 4km off the road between Masaka and Bukakata. If you don't mind walking the last 4km, just get on a minibus to Bukakata and ask to get off when you see the sign, about 15km from Masaka. If you don't like the idea of walking, then negotiate with a special hire taxi in Masaka, which you might be able to get for USh 10,000 if you bargain well.

SSESE ISLANDS
This group of 84 islands lies off the north-western shore of Lake Victoria, east of Masaka and south of Entebbe. The islands are connected to the mainland by ferries from Bukakata to Luku and fishing boats from Kasenyi to Kalangala.

The islands offer an interesting and refreshingly different facet of Uganda which is worth exploring, but don't come here looking for 'action' – this is rest and recreation time. Unlike the mainland, these islands escaped the ravages of the civil wars and so remain largely unspoiled. The people, known as the Basese, form a distinct tribal group, with their own language, culture and folklore. They are primarily fishermen, and farmers of coffee, sweet potato, cassava, yams and bananas. As you might expect, fish forms a major part of their diet.

Most islanders are members of one or other of the various Christian sects. A minority are Muslims. Communities are tightly knit and there are no dangers associated with wandering around the islands on foot. In fact, this is the best way to see them.

The main islands of Buggala, Bufumira, Bukasa, Bubeke and Kkome are hilly and, where not cultivated, are forested with a wide variety of trees. Animals you're likely to come across include various species of monkey, hippo, crocodile and many different types of bird, but there are no large predators, other than crocodiles.

Many spots afford beautiful views over the lake and across to the other islands. You'll have no problems persuading the fishermen to take you out on their boats. Swimming is also possible off most of the islands, as long as you observe the usual precaution about avoiding reedy areas (where the snails that carry the bilharzia parasite live).

All up, you're looking at a very mellow and peaceful time on these islands. There is a plentiful variety of food and, although they are becoming increasingly popular, the islands are far from overrun with visitors.

Information
The main town on the islands is Kalangala on Buggala island. It's the administrative centre, with a post office which has telephone connections to Kampala, and a branch of the Uganda Commercial Bank. However, bring all the cash you need because getting money changed is very difficult on the Ssese Islands.

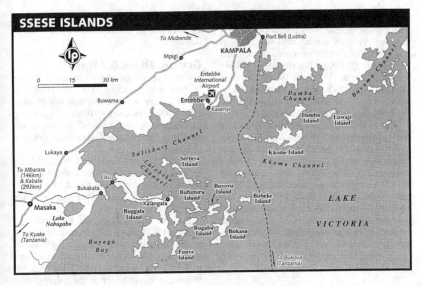

SSESE ISLANDS

To Mubende
Port Bell (Luzira)
KAMPALA
Mpigi
To Mbarara (146km) & Kabale (293km)
Entebbe International Airport
Buwama
Entebbe
Kasenyi
0   15   30 km
Damba Channel
Buyuma Channel
Damba Island
Luwaji Island
Kkome Island
Kkome Channel
Lukaya
Salisbury Channel
Serinya Island
Liku
Bukakata
Lulohoka Channel
Kalangala
Buggala Island
Bufumira Island
Buyovu Island
Bubeke Island
LAKE
Masaka
Lake Nabugabo
VICTORIA
To Kyaka (Tanzania)
Buyaga Bay
Bugaba Island
Bukasa Island
Funve Island
To Bukova (Tanzania)

Places to Stay & Eat

Buggala Island The most popular place on the island is **Hornbill Camp Site** about 15-minutes walk from Kalangala. Camping costs USh 2500, a dorm bed is USh 3500 and single/double bandas cost USh 4500/12,500. The doubles have attached bathroom. There's a selection of filling meals available at the camp site from USh 2000 to USh 4000. The people who run this place are very friendly, and it's a fun place to stay, although rumours are circulating that it may be sold to a tour operator in Kampala who will upgrade it considerably.

Another option is **PTA Andronico's Lodge** (☎ 0481-255646) owned by Mr PT Andronico Ssemakula a schoolteacher who speaks fluent English. A bed here in rather scruffy rooms costs USh 5000, while doubles are USh 8000 and meals cost USh 2000. Camping is possible (USh 1500) although there's not much space. Beers and soft drinks are also available and you can rent bicycles. Andronico is a real local character – a local eccentric, some might say, who has met the Pope. He has a habit of writing PTA on everything in his house, which suggests he is worried about theft,

but if you ask him why, there is a more complicated explanation. The lodge is signposted from town.

Panorama Camping Safaris is another camp site and lodge in Kalangala. It has been well set up, with camping in among the rainforest at USh 2000, and a number of bandas at USh 15,000 with shared bathroom, or USh 30,000 with private bathroom. Excellent meals are available (around USh 3000 to USh 4000) and the service is good and very friendly. You can arrange hot showers on request and have both a generator and lanterns at night. To find the place, walk down to the lake opposite the post office and look for the place with red-roofed stone huts.

In Liku, about 500m from where the Bukakata ferry docks, is **Scorpion Lodge** a pleasant place with rooms at USh 3000/7000 or you can camp for USh 1500. It also does decent meals (about USh 1800) and you can hire bikes here.

There are also a couple of upmarket resorts. **Ssese Palm Beach** (☎ 077-503315) has an attractive location near the water and a variety of accommodation options to suit most budgets. It is possible to camp here for

US$5 per person. The resort also offers its own executive tents with beds for US$20. It has two types of bandas available: executive and royal. Executive rooms cost US$25 per person, US$30 with breakfast or US$45 with full board. The prices for royal rooms are US$35, US$40 and US$55 respectively. However, if it is quiet, you might want to try and bargain a bit on the prices.

Top of the range in the Ssese Islands is **Ssese Islands Club** (☎ 041-231385) which offers wooden cabins set in a forest near Bugwanya beach. No camping is allowed here, but it does offer tented camps for US$55 per person, while cabins are US$65 per person. Rates include full board. The club has hot water on demand and a generator for lighting at night. The restaurant, which is open to nonguests, offers an expensive menu of European dishes for lunch and dinner. You are looking at USh 10,000 to USh 15,000 for a set meal.

Bukasa Island The only cheap place on Bukasa island is **Father Christopher's Guesthouse** run by the friendly Father Christopher and his wife Maria. Accommodation in the house costs USh 5000 per person in small rooms and camping is possible for USh 2000 per person. Facilities are quite basic, but hot water can be arranged with notice. Likewise, if you want to eat there, it is best to tell them in advance as they'll need to pick up supplies. Overlooking one of the biggest bays on the island, this is a very friendly place to stay as Father Christopher loves a yarn.

There is a lodge of sorts in the shape of **Bukasa Guesthouse** (☎ 041-247943). This place was formerly a lot cheaper and known as Agnes' Guesthouse. Full board is available for USh 75,000 per person. It has solar powered lighting and a generator for the fridges and hot water. The owner has some ambitious plans for developing the island, including luxury beachside bungalows and an airstrip sometime in the future. The guesthouse also has a powerboat, which can be used as transport to and from the island.

It costs USh 300,000 to charter the boat for up to 15 people and takes about 1½ hours to Kasenyi.

Getting There & Away

There is an irregular air service to the islands run by Mission Aviation Fellowship (MAF). It has a small seaplane and charges USh 35,000 one way. When the airstrip planned for Bukasa island is developed, there may be regular flights from Entebbe to Bukasa.

Boats (fishing boats and outboard canoes) go to the islands from the mainland points of Bukakata (35km east of Masaka) and Kasenyi (a 35-minute minibus ride from Kampala).

See the Masaka section for details of transport to Bukakata. From Bukakata there are outboard canoes that ferry people across to Liku (USh 1000), from where pick-ups make the trip to Kalangala (USh 1000). Vehicles can safely be left at the police station in Bukakata for a small fee. If you are using this ferry with your own vehicle, you will have to pay between USh 5000 and USh 10,000 for the crossing, depending on the size of the vehicle.

For boats to Buggala and Bukasa islands from Kampala, take a minibus from the old taxi park to Kasenyi for USh 1000. It should only be a 35-minute journey, but it is best to leave Kampala no later than 2.30 pm in case of heavy traffic – always a possibility in the capital. There is no pier in Kasenyi so you have to pay someone to take you out to the boat on their shoulders! This costs about USh 500 for you and USh 500 for your bag. Watch out for your valuables here as there are a lot of people milling about. The boat for Bukasa leaves at around 4 pm daily except Sunday (USh 4000) and arrives at around 7 pm. Boats for Kalangala (Buggala) leave at the same time and so arrive in the dark, often as late as 11 pm, and cost USh 5000. As these boats travel in the dark and have little in the way of safety equipment, it may be preferable to take the short ride from Bukakata.

Northern Uganda

For all practical purposes the northern part of Uganda is virtually a separate country from the southern part. Politically it has been isolated from the south, and it is one of the few black marks against President Museveni's otherwise excellent record that he has failed to reconcile the north and deal with the rebels.

For travellers the main focus of interest is the western part of the region, where the Murchison Falls National Park and the Lake Albert area are well worth exploring.

For those with a thirst for real adventure, there is the overland journey to Kidepo Valley National Park, straight through the heart of Karamojaland, home to the Karamojong people. These are a tough tribe of cattle herders and they have managed to resist control from outsiders, black or white, for centuries now. Keep in mind that this journey should not be undertaken lightly as there are potential security risks with all the cattle-rustling and banditry that take place in the north-east.

For detailed information on Mt Elgon National Park see the earlier South-Eastern Uganda chapter.

MASINDI
☎ 0465

Masindi is a small, easy-going provincial headquarters, and is the last town of any substance on the way to Murchison Falls. It's a good place to stock up on provisions.

Information

There is a branch of Uganda Commercial Bank but it has no foreign exchange facilities, so bring cash with you.

Warning

The overall security picture in the north has improved considerably in the last few years, as the Ugandan authorities have constructed a huge fence along the border with Sudan and a regularly patrolled road runs alongside it. This has significantly reduced incursions by the Lord's Resistance Army (LRA), and has severed supply lines for those fighters in Uganda itself. However, it is still a volatile region – unless you have a good reason for visiting much of the north, it is probably best to give it a miss. There have been incidents on the roads between Arua and Gulu, and between Gulu and Lira. The road from Soroti to Tororo in the south is considered safe.

Pay attention to developments in Karamojaland in the north-east as groups of local cattle herders, the Karamojong, have been known to ambush highway travellers. There is often fighting among the Karamojong themselves, and to make matters more complicated, large numbers of Turkana tribesmen from Kenya often cross the border looking to steal cattle – this attracts the attention of the Ugandan army. Sometimes it becomes too dangerous to travel to Moroto by road from Soroti because of fighting between the Karamoja, the Turkana and the Ugandan army. Check the latest security conditions with reliable sources in Kampala before setting out, and check local security conditions at every town or village along the way, because trouble is often not far away in Karamojaland.

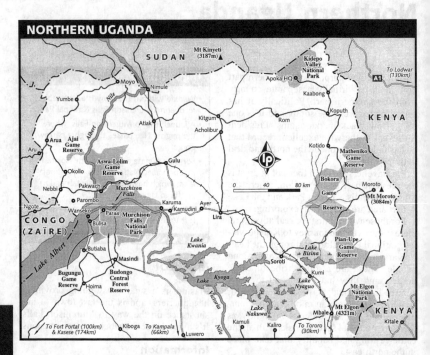

NORTHERN UGANDA

The post office has international telephone and fax services, but the lines are not that reliable.

The Uganda Wildlife Authority (UWA) office may be able to assist with transport into and around the park.

Places to Stay & Eat

Pick of the handful of cheapies is *Executive Lodge* which is close to the taxi rank. Large singles/doubles with shared bath cost USh 3500/5000; soap and towel are provided. They can also fix you up with local food here; stew and *matoke* (mashed plantains) is USh 1500. Another cheap guesthouse worth considering is *Tot Lodge* with simple rooms for USh 3500/7000.

Also reasonable is the modern *Hotel Aribas* on the main road a short walk from the taxi rank. The rooms are set around a concrete courtyard and cost USh 5000/8000 with shared bath. Hot water is available by the bucket.

Regarded by expats as the best place to stay is *Alinda Guesthouse* (☎ 20482) near Hotel Aribas. Singles with shared facilities cost USh 7000; doubles with attached bath cost USh 18,000; while rooms with three beds cost USh 20,000. All rooms are clean and all rates include breakfast.

There are a few places around the market. *New Paradise Lodge* has reasonably clean rooms from USh 6000/12,000 with shared bath, rising to USh 17,000 with attached bath; all rates include a light breakfast. *Karibuni Guesthouse* is a similar operation. Rooms cost USh 7000/10,000 with shared bath, while larger self-contained doubles cost USh 20,000. All rates include breakfast, which is taken in the large open-air bar area. *Buma Hotel* overlooks the market and offers well-priced rooms with attached bath for USh 10,000/16,000.

Masindi's most venerable hotel, and a great place to stay, is the creaking old

Masindi Hotel (fax 20411). It was originally built by the East African Railways Corporation in the 1920s and has barely changed since. The rooms in the original building have the atmosphere; those in the 'new' wing (which is probably at least 40 years old!) are more comfortable. Singles/doubles cost USh 16,500/26,500; suites cost USh 55,000, including breakfast. There's a good bar and restaurant and it is a convenient lunch-time stop on the way to or from the park as it is right next to the turn-off. Meals are pretty good and cost about USh 4500. The hotel is in the northern part of town, about 1km from the taxi rank.

A popular spot for a meal is *Travellers' Corner Restaurant* near the post office, which caters to western tastes and has slightly higher prices to match – main courses are around USh 3000 to USh 4500. They have some of the best sausages you are likely to find outside Kampala.

There are also good, inexpensive restaurants at many of the cheaper lodges mentioned above. For food with a minor Indian twist, try *Curry Pot* which has a few curries available in the USh 2000 to USh 3000 range.

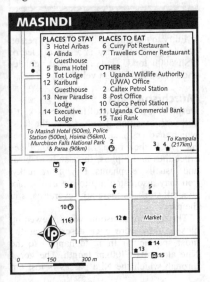

MASINDI

PLACES TO STAY	PLACES TO EAT
3 Hotel Aribas	6 Curry Pot Restaurant
4 Alinda Guesthouse	7 Travellers Corner Restaurant
5 Buma Hotel	**OTHER**
9 Tot Lodge	1 Uganda Wildlife Authority (UWA) Office
12 Karibuni Guesthouse	2 Caltex Petrol Station
13 New Paradise Lodge	8 Post Office
14 Executive Lodge	10 Gapco Petrol Station
	11 Uganda Commercial Bank
	15 Taxi Rank

To Masindi Hotel (500m), Police Station (500m), Hoima (56km), Murchison Falls National Park & Paraa (90km)

To Kampala (217km)

Market

0   150   300 m

Getting There & Away

Minibuses between Kampala and Masindi (Ush 7000, three hours) travel throughout the day. There are also irregular departures to Hoima (USh 3000, one hour), Bulisa (USh 4000), Wanseko (USh 5000) and Butiaba (USh 5000, usually one daily in the morning).

Buses between Kampala and Wanseko pass through Masindi (Ush 6000 between Kampala and Masindi). These currently run on a daily basis, but may run less often if the Gulu-Arua road becomes safe to use again (see Getting There & Away in the Murchison Falls National Park section).

For hitching to Paraa, check at the UWA office to see if any national parks vehicles are around; you may be able to get a ride with them. Otherwise, inquire at Travellers' Corner Restaurant and Masindi Hotel for hitching opportunities, as these are popular rest stops.

HOIMA

Hoima is not a town with a great deal to offer the casual visitor, but some travellers do end up spending a night here when taking the dirt road between Fort Portal and Murchison Falls National Park. Hoima is also a useful starting point for a back route (and cheaper way) into the national park via Lake Albert.

Bring cash to this town as there are no banks or foreign exchange bureaus.

Places To Stay & Eat

In the centre of town, the best budget choice is *Classic Inn* where basic singles/doubles with mosquito nets and shared facilities cost USh 5000/8000. There is also a good inexpensive restaurant and bar out front where locals gather to quaff an ale or two at night. There is a sign saying 'no idlers allowed', which is probably aimed more at Ugandans than backpackers. Another cheap option in town is *Hoima Inn* with similarly basic rooms for USh 4000/8000.

Moving upmarket, although hardly in leaps and bounds, is *Nsamo Hotel* which has clean self-contained rooms for USh 10,000/15,000. It serves food but not alcohol; for drinks, Classic Inn is close by.

UGANDA

The newly opened *Call Inn Pub* has rooms with shared facilities costing USh 12,000/13,000, including breakfast. This is a good place to hang out in the evening as it has a restaurant, bar and pool table.

Getting There & Away
The road from Fort Portal is reasonable, if dusty in the dry season, but is hard work in the wet season. Minibuses cost USh 6000 and the trip takes about four to five hours.

The road from Masindi is a short but uncomfortable stretch, although improvements are being made. Minibuses cost USh 3000 and the trip takes one hour.

Minibuses run to Butiaba (Ush 4000, two hours), an atmospheric fishing port on Lake Albert. The last leg of the journey is spectacular (see the Lake Albert section later in this chapter).

MURCHISON FALLS NATIONAL PARK
This is the largest park in Uganda. Sir Samuel Baker named the Murchison Falls in honour of a president of the Royal Geographic Society and the park was subsequently named after the falls. The Victoria Nile flows through it on its way to Lake Albert. It used to be one of Africa's best national parks; during the 1960s, as many as 12 launches a day would buzz up the river to the falls, filled with eager tourists.

The park also used to contain some of the largest concentrations of wildlife in Uganda, including as many as 15,000 elephants. Unfortunately, poachers and troops, both armed with automatic weapons, wiped out practically all wildlife, except the more numerous (or less sought after) herd species. There are now no rhinos and only a few groups of lions, but you can see good numbers of elephant, Ugandan kob (antelope), buffalo, hippo and crocodile.

Wildlife drives usually take place on the north bank of the Victoria Nile, in the area between Paraa and Lake Albert. There is very little wildlife south of the river, and driving in from Masindi you might be forgiven for thinking you are on a vegetarian safari.

When a Disaster Isn't
Although it seems like sacrilege to say it, the mass slaughter of wildlife that took place in Murchison Falls National Park was in fact a good thing from an ecological viewpoint. Before Idi Amin's regime, the park was carrying many more animals (particularly elephants, with herds of more than 500 commonly seen) than it could sustain. The elephants alone, which numbered more than 15,000, chomped their way through 1.4 million *tonnes* of vegetation each year! Add to this the 26,000 buffalo, plus herds of hartebeest, kob and hippo, and the scale of the ecological problem can be appreciated.

The wiping out of most of the large animals has given the environment here a breather, and while it was obviously a major disaster from a wildlife point of view, it means that the park's ecology is now in excellent condition and the animals are once again on the increase. The concentrations of game are still low, however, so don't come to Murchison expecting animals everywhere. Aerial surveys taken in 1995 estimated there were 200 elephant, 1000 buffalo and around 10,000 hartebeest and kob in the park.

Entry to the park costs US$15 per person per day; vehicle entry is a one-off fee of USh 5000 for Uganda-registered vehicles and US$30 for foreign vehicles.

Murchison Falls
Despite the lack of wildlife in the park, it's still worth visiting if only to see the falls, which involves a superb ride up the Victoria Nile to their base. En route you'll see crocodiles and hippos, thousands of birds and, usually, elephants. If you are lucky, you may also catch a glimpse of the rare shoebill stork, as there are several pairs in the park.

The falls are awesome when viewed up close – they were once described as the most spectacular thing to happen to the Nile along its 6700km length. The gorge through which the Nile passes is just 6m

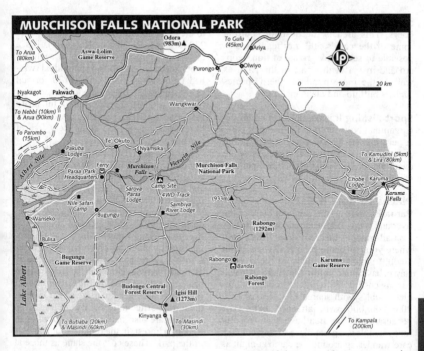

MURCHISON FALLS NATIONAL PARK

wide, making this possibly the most powerful natural surge of water found anywhere in the world.

There's an old ranger station here, which is staffed by local people who sell soft drinks and will guide you around for a small fee. There's also a picnic area with shaded bandas and a basic camp site with pit toilets. Hopefully, a more sophisticated camping ground will be developed here with bandas, as it is a great place to spend the night (although not for sleepwalkers perhaps).

You can also visit the falls by vehicle. A rough track leads off from the main access track 24km south of Paraa, and from here it's about a 30-minute drive. 2WD is OK but take care.

Activities

Launch Trip The three-hour launch trip from Paraa up to the base of the falls operates daily at 9 am and 2 pm if there's enough demand. The cost is USh 10,000 per person if there are 10 or more people, with a minimum charge of USh 100,000 for the whole boat. On weekends there's a good chance of finding other people to share the cost with; on weekdays you may have to cough up the entire USh 100,000.

If you take the morning launch up the river, it is possible to ask the captain to let you off at a trailhead for the slippery walk up to the top of the falls. He can then pick you up later if there is an afternoon launch. This is also a good way for backpackers to get to the camping ground at the top of the falls, where you can camp overnight before returning to Paraa the next day.

Wildlife Drives Wildlife drives are possible on the north bank of the Victoria Nile (see Getting Around at the end of this section for details on ferry times and prices). The best circuit for wildlife is the Buligi Circuit, which includes the Buligi, Victoria Nile, Queen and Albert Nile tracks. This

606 Northern Uganda – Murchison Falls National Park

covers at least 120km and takes four to five hours. This area is the best for spotting some of the park's 500 giraffe. It is also possible to see a few groups of lion, leopard and hyena in this part of the park, as well as the more numerous herd species such as buffalo and elephant.

Sport Fishing It is possible to fish for the gargantuan Nile perch in the national park. A permit costs US$50 per day or US$300 per year. You will also need a boat; these are available for USh 180,000/300,000 per half day/full day.

Places to Stay & Eat

Paraa Paraa is on the southern bank of the river and is the park headquarters. As well as a small village, there's *Paraa Rest Camp* where you can camp on a grassy site (USh 10,000) with limited views of the river or stay in basic but comfortable mud and thatch bandas costing USh 10,000/15,000 for singles/doubles with shared facilities, or USh 20,000/30,000 with attached bath. The restaurant and bar area have been recently renovated. It is a great place to stay but take care wandering around the camp at night as lions sometime roam the area and are often found just below the ridge towards the river.

Sarova Paraa Lodge across the river was bombed, burnt and looted years ago, but has recently been completely refurbished by Sarova Hotels (☎ 041-251215, fax 251209 in Kampala). It has a superb location with views up the river towards the falls and some excellent facilities, including a bar in a swimming pool overlooking the Victoria Nile. Low-season prices for full board are US$161 (single occupancy) and US$199 (double occupancy). In high season, prices go through the roof, at US$220/275.

Elsewhere in the Park At the head of the falls there is a *camp site* with a very nice position right on the river, although you'll definitely need a 4WD to get to the best sites on the river's edge. You'll also need to be self-sufficient as there are no supplies of any sort, and the only facilities are a pit toilet. Camping costs USh 5000.

Just off the main track, beside the turn-off to the falls is *Sambiya River Lodge* (☎ 041-232306, fax 232307 in Kampala). It's a modern, comfortable lodge in a secluded spot. Accommodation is in individual twin-bed units, which cost US$90/130 for full board singles/doubles in the low season and as much as US$140 per person for full board in high season. It's a very nice place and, unlike Paraa, this area is completely free of mosquitoes.

North of the river are two old lodges: *Pakuba Lodge* which is very close to the Albert Nile in the western part of the park and *Chobe Lodge* on the Victoria Nile in the far east of the park. Pakuba Lodge is a massive, empty old place put up by Idi Amin during the 1970s. The location is fantastic, overlooking the Albert Nile, but the building is pretty much beyond repair these days. Chobe Lodge has apparently been earmarked for redevelopment so may reopen some time during the lifetime of this book. Inquire at park headquarters at Paraa or at the tourist office in Kampala.

There are also national parks *bandas* in Rabongo Forest, in the remote southern part of the park. These cost the same as those at Paraa.

Outside the Park Arguably the nicest place to stay actually lies outside the park's western boundary, between Bugungu gate and Lake Albert. *Nile Safari Camp* (☎ 041-258273, fax 233992) has an unrivalled position high up on the south bank of the Victoria Nile with sweeping views over the water. Accommodation is in comfortable permanent tents, each with attached bath, balcony and chairs with river view. There's also a bar and dining area. Comfort doesn't come cheap at US$129/174 for singles/doubles with full board. The well signposted turn-off to the camp is 15km from Bulisa (on Lake Albert), and 4.5km from Bugungu Gate; it's then a further 11.5km along a rough track.

Getting There & Away

From Masindi there is the choice of the direct northern route or the longer but more scenic route, which heads west to Lake Albert and then enters the park via the western Bugungu gate. You could make it a round trip, entering via one route and leaving by the other. Both routes go through Budongo Central Forest Reserve, a recommended stopover (see that section later in this chapter).

Getting from Masindi directly to Paraa by public transport is not possible, but you can charter a minibus to take you all the way for around USh 100,000 (not a cheap option unless you happen to be part of a football team).

From Masindi the only scheduled public transport is buses and taxis to Wanseko on Lake Albert. These run daily, and are popular because local people from the Arua region in the north-west are currently travelling to Kampala via the lake rather than via Gulu, because of security problems along the Arua to Gulu road. You can either go as far as Bulisa for USh 6000 and then negotiate for a *boda-boda* (bicycle taxi) to take you to Paraa for around USh 10,000, or go to Wanseko for USh 7000 and then negotiate with the minibus driver to take you to Paraa for about USh 40,000. Bulisa is the obvious option for solo travellers, but if you have a group, it is worth carrying on to Wanseko.

The best chance of hitching a lift is with the park vehicles that come from Masindi a few times a week. On weekends there's a good chance of getting a lift with other tourists from Masindi (see Getting There & Away in the Masindi section earlier in this chapter). Getting out of the park is much easier in this respect as you can find out where vehicles are heading to and book yourself a ride.

The other option is to go on an organised safari from Kampala. All the safari companies offer trips to Murchison Falls (see the Organised Safaris chapter for details).

Getting Around
Land Tracks within the park are generally well maintained, and a 2WD vehicle with good ground clearance should have little trouble. However, the tracks can be treacherous in the wet season. There are also some

nasty bumps where drainage channels have been built, so look out for concrete culverts on the side of the road and slow down.

Fuel is available on the north side of the Victoria Nile at Paraa, but it's more expensive than in Masindi.

Ferry & Speedboat The vehicle ferry (a motorised barge) crosses the river at Paraa. It operates to a schedule but breakdowns are not uncommon and you may have to wait for a few hours. The crossings take just a few minutes, and are scheduled at 7, 9 and 11 am, noon, and 2, 4 and 6 pm. The fare is USh 1500 for passengers, a hefty USh 10,000 each way for passenger vehicles and USh 60,000 for overland trucks. Unscheduled crossings cost more again.

You can take a speedboat across at any time for USh 5000 return per person.

All ferry and speedboat fees are payable at the park headquarters near the ferry landing.

BUDONGO CENTRAL FOREST RESERVE
Budongo Forest is right on the road to Murchison Falls, just to the south of the park, and is a great place to stop and have a guided walk through the dense virgin tropical forest. The main attractions are the numerous primates (see Chimpanzee Trekking in the Uganda Facts for the Visitor chapter), the prolific birdlife and the huge mahogany trees that dominate the forest in this area.

The forest's 'Royal Mile' is thought by many to offer the best birdwatching in the whole of Uganda. There are more than 350 species found here including several types of kingfishers, hornbills and eagles. At dusk, it is possible to view bat hawks.

Two areas have been put aside for chimpanzee habituation and viewing. **Kaniyo Pabidi** is on the main Masindi to Paraa road, 29km north of Masindi and actually inside the southern boundary of Murchison Falls National Park (note that you will have to pay the US$15 entry fee for the park). **Busingiro** is 40km west of Masindi on the road that connects Masindi with the national park via Lake Albert.

UGANDA

At both places guided walks (with a guide and an armed ranger) take place every day at 7.30 am (US$6) and 2 pm (US$4), and there's an additional US$4 entry fee. There are no minimum numbers and the walks last anything from one to three hours.

It's possible to camp at both places for USh 10,000 per person. The *camp sites* are pretty reasonable, with pit toilets and hot showers. *Bandas* are also available for USh 15,000/USh 20,000 for single/double occupancy with shared facilities. There are information centres at both these places.

Kaniyo Pabidi is not served by regular public transport. Busingiro is on the route used by buses and minibuses heading for Wanseko (see Getting There & Away in the Murchison Falls National Park section earlier in this chapter).

LAKE ALBERT

Lake Albert is part of the Great Rift Valley system that extends from the Middle East to Mozambique, and since 1894 has formed part of the border between Uganda and Congo (Zaïre). The first European to spot the lake was the British explorer Sir Samuel Baker in 1864, who named it after Albert, prince consort of Great Britain.

The people who live by the lake make their living from fishing its waters, and a visit to one of these fishing villages along the eastern shore makes an interesting diversion. The approach for the turn-off for the fishing village of **Butiaba** on the eastern shore is spectacular as you wind down the Albertine Escarpment, with sweeping views of the lake and the Blue Mountains of Congo (Zaïre) in the distance. The village itself is small, and judging by some of the old buildings, had its share of Asian traders. It was from here that the East African Railways Corporation used to run river steamers up to Fajao at the base of Murchison Falls. If you visit the old port, you can still see some majestic old boats slowly decaying in the lake's waters. If you have any desire to go wreck diving in Uganda, forget it, as there are crocodiles around.

The best time to visit is in the late morning when the fishing catch is brought ashore

from the small fishing boats – huge Nile perch weighing in excess of 50kg are quite common.

While there is no formal accommodation in the village, you could probably find someone willing to put you up for a day or two, but be sure not to abuse local hospitality. However, there may be a camping ground and banda operation up and running by the time you read this, as there are plans to encourage visitors to the sandy beaches nearby.

GULU

Gulu is the largest town in the north of the country. About 30km north of Gulu at Patiko is Baker's Fort, built by the British in the 1870s as a base from which to suppress the slave trade.

Places to Stay & Eat

A good, cheap place and excellent value is *Church of Uganda Guesthouse*. Also excellent value is *Uganda Red Cross Society* which has a couple of cheap rooms where travellers can stay. Other places recommended by readers include *New Gulu Restaurant* in Pakwach Rd and *Luxxor Lodge* opposite the truck park.

The top hotel is *Acholi Inn*. It has standard singles/doubles with attached bath for USh 25,000/35,000.

Getting There & Away

Buses and minibuses go between Kampala and Gulu. The road is good bitumen most of the way and the buses absolutely fly along here, doing the trip in around four hours. It costs USh 10,000, but you might be able to bargain down to USh 9000.

Gulu is on the railway line that connects Pakwach with Tororo in the south-east, but passenger services were suspended some years ago because of security problems.

ARUA

Few travellers ever make it up this way, but Arua has a large population of aid workers, as it is the distribution centre for relief efforts in war-ravaged southern Sudan. This means there are also a large number of Sudanese and Congolese refugees living in tented camps on the outskirts of town, which is a pretty sorry sight if you have never seen these kind of hardships before. However, the market is very lively as it attracts people from all over the region.

Rhino Inn is popular with aid workers based here. Clean singles/doubles with attached bath cost USh 25,000/35,000. The restaurant is reasonable.

There are daily buses from Kampala to Arua for USh 20,000 but it is a very long direct journey of about 12 hours. It is possible to break the journey in Gulu or Pakwach.

SOROTI

Few travellers find themselves staying overnight in Soroti, which is a pleasant, if dull, town. The town boasts some attractive Asian architecture, as it was once an important business centre. Like Tororo to the south-east, it has a curious volcanic plug poking skywards on the edge of town from which there are fine views of the surrounding countryside.

Be aware that the north-east is an unstable region – see the boxed text 'Warning' earlier in this chapter.

Places to Stay & Eat

There are a number of cheap dives around the town's central square and these charge about USh 5000 for a basic room. There is also the pleasant *Soroti Hotel* on the edge of town, which is set among verdant gardens. Singles/doubles with attached bath cost USh 20,000/30,000.

Getting There & Away

Minibuses run between Mbale and Soroti (USh 2500, two hours) on the sealed road. From Kampala, there are direct buses departing daily (after 7 am) for USh 10,000. The EMS Post bus also makes a daily run from the capital; see Getting There & Away in the Kampala chapter for details.

For those feeling adventurous or with their own transport, there is also a dirt road west to Lira and beyond to Murchison Falls National Park. The minibus to Lira costs USh 3000.

Minibuses also travel the dirt road north to Moroto (USh 6000, four hours).

MOROTO

Moroto is a small district capital with a real frontier feel, as it is the gateway to the wilds of Karamojaland to the north. Most of the inhabitants of the town are Karamoja, but this is not obvious as they have forsaken traditional tribal dress, or rather lack of it, and now wear the same clothes as other Ugandans.

Be aware that the town suffers from chronic water shortages and electricity is available only between 7 and 11 pm.

If you are heading north on the overland route to Kidepo Valley National Park, then this is the last real centre for supplies, so stock up.

Places to Stay & Eat

For a cheap bed, try *Guluna Lodge* which has plain rooms with a fan and mosquito nets for USh 5000.

A more expensive option is the dilapidated *Moroto Hotel* a leftover from the days of the British protectorate. Rooms here cost USh 30,000, which would be fair enough if things like water and electricity were reliable, but it seems a little steep today. There is a reasonable restaurant, however.

Getting There & Away

The most convenient way to get to Moroto from Kampala is by direct bus. Gateway runs daily services from the bus park in Kampala (USh 14,000, 11 hours) departing after 7 am.

Do not take the direct road between Mbale and Moroto as it is considered unsafe and ambushes are common – always go via Soroti as it is both safer and faster (see the boxed text 'Warning' earlier in this chapter). From Soroti, minibuses cost USh 6000 and take about four hours on a dirt road.

MOROTO TO KIDEPO VALLEY NATIONAL PARK

The next stop on the journey north is **Kotido**, a 'wild east' town where the Karamajong dress in traditional clothes, or lack of them, and AK-47s are as common as walking sticks and blankets. A daily bus leaves Moroto for Kotido at 5 pm (1½ hours). In Kotido, *Airport Lodge* is a reasonable place to stay with rooms for USh 7000.

The next leg of the journey sees you bidding goodbye to civilisation, although some would say that happened on leaving Kampala. From Kotido, there are daily pick-ups leaving early in the morning for **Kaabong** (USh 4000, 1½ hours) along a pretty bad road. Should you get stuck in Kaabong you could stay at *Karimajong Lodge*.

The final leg of the journey involves chartering a vehicle from Kaabong to the Kidepo Valley National Park headquarters at **Apoka** or jumping on an irregular pick-up to **Karenga** and getting off at the Apoka fork, just 2km from the headquarters. Chartering a vehicle is expensive, probably around USh 40,000 or so depending on your bargaining skills, so if you have the time (which you obviously do if you have come this far by public transport already!) then catch the pick-up to Karenga.

Doing the journey in reverse is a little easier as the rangers at Kidepo know when the pick-ups between Karenga and Kaabong are passing by.

KIDEPO VALLEY NATIONAL PARK

This hidden valley in the extreme north-east of the country, along the border with Sudan, is considered by many to offer the most stunning scenery of any national park in Uganda. Surrounded by mountains, the park covers 1440 sq km and is notable for a number of animals that are found nowhere else in Uganda, including cheetah, ostrich and bat-eared fox. There are also large concentrations of elephant, zebra, buffalo and bushbuck, and a healthy number of predators including lion, leopard and hyena.

This is an unstable region and caution should be taken when travelling overland here – see the boxed text 'Warning' earlier in this chapter.

A place worth looking out for, although you'll have no chance of finding a bed these days, is *Grand Katurum Lodge* constructed during Idi Amin's regime. It never really saw any guests as his domestic policies weren't exactly consistent with tourism growth. However, it occupies a fantastic location, built into a huge rock bluff that overlooks the Narus Valley and Mt Lotuke in Sudan.

Apoka Rest Camp has camping for Ush 10,000 and bandas for USh 20,000.

THE MOUNTAIN GORILLAS OF EAST AFRICA

There can be few experiences in the world more memorable and magical than an encounter with the mountain gorillas of East Africa. As the father of gorilla conservation George Schaller once wrote: 'No one who looks into a gorilla's eyes – intelligent, gentle, vulnerable – can remain unchanged, for the gap between ape and human vanishes, we know that the gorilla still lives within us.' There are thought to be just 600 mountain gorillas *(Gorilla beringei)* left in the world today, all found in a small area of East Africa straddling the borders of Uganda, Rwanda and Congo (Zaïre).

Relations between humans and gorillas haven't always been fraternal. For centuries, gorillas were considered fearsome and aggressive, and it was only this century we learned they are gentle and vegetarian.

The first mountain gorillas were discovered in 1902, when a German officer, Oscar von Beringe, shot two on the slopes of Mt Sabinyo (in Mgahinga National Park), giving his name to the subspecies. Hunting the gorillas became a popular pastime until one hunter, Carl Akeley, decided that something must be done to preserve the population of these magnificent creatures, and in 1925 he persuaded the Belgian government to create Africa's first protected area, Albert National Park. However, over the years, agriculture and administrative division reduced the size of this protected area and poaching reduced the number of gorillas.

The first scientific study of the mountain gorillas in the Virunga volcanoes area was undertaken by George Schaller in 1959. His work was continued by Dian Fossey from 1967 and her story has been made into a film, *Gorillas in the Mist*. Fossey took a very confrontational attitude towards local people living around Parc Nacional des Volcans, and her uncompromising stance on poaching led to her murder in 1985.

Despite Fossey's scepticism of tourism, by the late 1960s gorilla tracking had already become popular in Congo (Zaïre), and by 1978, gorilla tourism was also being promoted in Rwanda with tremendous results for the local economy. At the same time, the local population was educated as to the importance of the animals and the habitat in which they lived. By the late 1980s, gorilla tourism was an important source of income for Rwanda, and the gorillas had become a symbol of national pride. Uganda was slow to realise the potential of promoting its gorillas; however, because of political instability in neighbouring Rwanda and Congo (Zaïre), by the late 1990s it was the most popular country to track the gorillas.

Gorilla tourism today stands at a crossroads. All three countries where the remaining gorillas live have a history of instability that makes it hard for international conservation organisations to operate with any certainty. The International Gorilla Conservation Programme (IGCP) and the Dian Fossey Gorilla Foundation (DFGF) have tried to promote sustainable practices to encourage the active participation of local communities in conservation, and this has played a large part in ensuring the gorillas'

Top: Gorillas maintain a strong family unit in groups of various sizes. (Photo: Jason Edwards)

survival during turbulent times. However, many of the local communities around these protected areas are bitter, as they're aware of the money flowing in from visitors, with very little of it coming to them.

The Ugandan authorities pioneered a program to give 10% of gorilla revenue to the local communities around Bwindi and Mgahinga national parks; however, after the initial fanfare, the amount was quietly trimmed back to 10% of park entrance fees, not 10% of gorilla-tracking fees, which is the difference between US$1.50 and US$25 per visitor! Unless the local communities have more of an incentive to protect these beautiful creatures, the future of the gorillas will never be secure.

Visitor numbers to Bwindi and Mgahinga are rapidly recovering after the attack on tourists at Bwindi in March 1999. Rwanda has once again opened Parc Nacional des Volcans and visitors will no doubt begin to trickle back, especially as permits become more difficult to obtain in Uganda. The gorilla sanctuaries in Congo (Zaïre) remain closed because of the protracted civil war there, but with peace talks staggering on across the continent and the area under firm rebel control, there were whispers of them reopening during 2000.

The most important development for the future of gorilla tourism could be a plan under discussion to create a tri-national protected area under a single administration, which would market the gorillas internationally. Booking procedures would be streamlined and the income pooled, with the possibility of a visa and a gorilla-tracking permit being obtainable together. This might help Rwanda and Congo (Zaïre) to overcome their stigma as dangerous and unstable places.

THE GORILLAS

Gorillas used to inhabit a swathe of land that cut across Central Africa, but the ice age diminished the forests and divided the gorillas into three groups – the western lowland gorilla, the eastern lowland gorilla and the mountain gorilla. Mountain gorillas are now found only in two small pop-

Left: The male silverback dictates the movements of his group each day, deciding when to rest and eat.
(Photo: Jason Edwards)

ulations of about 300 each in the forests of Bwindi and on the slopes of the Virunga volcanoes. There is no doubt that mountain gorillas are a very rare species, as there is just one for every 10 million people on earth.

Mountain gorillas are distinguished from their lowland relatives by longer hair, a broader chest and a wider jaw. Although the gorillas in Bwindi are less shaggy than those of the Virunga volcanoes (which first led some scientists to believe they were of the lowland species), it is now widely accepted that they are also mountain gorillas.

Lifestyle

Gorillas are vegetarians and their diet consists mainly of bamboo shoots, giant thistles and wild celery, all of which contain a lot of water, and allow the gorillas to survive without drinking for long periods of time. Gorillas spend about 30% of their day feeding, 30% moving and foraging, and the remainder resting. They spend most of their time on the ground, moving around on all fours, but stand up to reach for food.

The silverback dictates movements for the day and at night each gorilla makes its own nest. Nests are only used once. Gorillas aren't big movers and will usually only travel about 1km a day.

Families

Gorillas generally live in family groups of varying sizes, usually including one or two older silverback males, younger black-back males, females and infants. Most groups contain between 10 and 15 gorillas but in Rwanda there are groups of more than 30.

There are strong bonds between individuals in a gorilla family and status is usually linked to age. Silverbacks are at the top of the hierarchy, followed by females with infants or ties to the silverbacks, then black-backs and other females.

Conflict

Gorillas are placid and serious confrontations are rare, although violence can flare if there is a challenge for supremacy between silverbacks. Conflicts are mostly kept to shows of strength and vocal disputes.

Conflict between groups is also uncommon, as gorillas are not territorial. However, ranges can often overlap and if two groups meet, there is usually a lot of display and bravado on the part of silverbacks, including mock charges. Often the whole group joins in and it is at this point that young adult females may choose to switch allegiance.

If gorillas do fight, injuries can be very serious as these animals have long canine teeth. If a male is driven from a group by another silverback, it is likely the new leader will kill all the young infants to establish his mating rights.

Communication

Gorillas communicate in a variety of ways, including facial expressions, gestures and calls. Adult males use barks and roars during confrontations or to coordinate the movement of their gorilla groups to a different area. Postures and gestures form an important element of intimidation and it is often possible for a clash to be diffused by a display of teeth-baring, stiff-legging, lunging and charging. And if all this fails, a terrifying scream is enough to deter most outsiders.

Friendly communication is an important part of group bonding and includes grunts of pleasure, particularly associated with food and foraging. Upon finding food, gorillas will grunt or bark to alert other members of the group. Grooming is not as common as among other primates.

Biology

Gorillas are the largest primates in the world and adult males weigh as much as 200kg. Females are about half this size. Mountain gorillas are the largest of the three gorilla species, although the largest gorilla ever recorded was an eastern lowland male.

Male gorillas reach maturity between eight and 15 years, while females reach sexual maturity at about eight years. Conception is possible for about three days each month and once a female has conceived, she spends most of her life pregnant or nursing.

The duration of pregnancy is about 8½ months. Newborn infants are highly dependent on adults and a young infant will rarely leave its mother's arms during its first six months. Initially, the infant clings to the front of its mother, but gradually it spends more time on her back.

In its second year, a young gorilla begins to interact with other members of the group and starts to feed itself. Infant gorillas and silverbacks often form a bond and it is not uncommon for a silverback to adopt an infant if its mother dies. This distinguishes gorillas from other primates, where child-rearing duties are left to females.

From about three years old, young gorillas become quite independent, and build their own nests. However, not all gorillas make it to adulthood, with 30% dying before the age of six.

Left: A newborn infant gorilla will rarely leave mother's arms during th first six months. (Photo: Jason Edwards)

WHERE TO TRACK THE GORILLAS

For many visitors to East Africa, a gorilla visit is the largest expenditure they make in the region. It is worth putting some thought into where to visit them, not only for the experience but for security as well.

Warning

Over the last few years there have been numerous reports emerging from Uganda of illegal gorilla visits. Usually this takes the form of tourists bribing rangers into taking them into the mountains to view the gorillas during the afternoon. However, it is not unknown for rangers to approach tourists, particularly if business is booming and there are simply no gorilla permits available.

It is easy to understand a visitor being tempted to jump at this opportunity, as the gorillas may represent the highlight of their trip, but no one should resort to illegal means to see these endangered animals.

Illegal gorilla visits increase the animals' stress levels, which reduces the gorilla's immunity to disease and could lead to the gradual demise of the species. The threat of increased stress levels should not be underestimated, considering three out of 10 gorillas die before adulthood.

Illegal gorilla tracking needs to be stopped before it threatens the survival of the mountain gorillas, and the only way it can be stopped is if tourists play by the rules. If you are offered the chance to track the gorillas illegally, don't take it as doing so may contribute to the death of a gorilla somewhere down the line.

Uganda

Bwindi National Park

In recent years Bwindi has become the number-one place to track the mountain gorillas. Its popularity and reputation took a plunge after the murder of eight tourists here in March 1999; however, security has since been considerably beefed up and tourists are again returning in numbers.

It can be very difficult to get permits for Bwindi as there are only 12 available per day and tour operators book most of them months in advance. A gorilla permit costs US$250, plus US$15 park entry fee.

This is a dense forest (hence its other name, the Impenetrable Forest), so tracking the gorillas can be quite hard work. Fortunately, the gorillas are known to occasionally venture very close to the Buhoma headquarters, so tracking them can also be easy. There are two mountain gorilla groups habituated to human contact at Bwindi. Fast film or push-processing is necessary for good photographic results, as it is darker in the forests of Bwindi than at the Virunga volcanoes.

Security was prioritised in the aftermath of the Bwindi attack and there is now a considerable military presence, although visitors will not find it noticeable. The park's proximity to Congo (Zaïre) means that the Ugandan government cannot relax its guard and fail its visitors as it did in March 1999. Although the access roads to Bwindi are poor and a 4WD is preferable, the trip can be done in a car. See the Bwindi National Park section in the South-Western Uganda chapter for more information.

Mgahinga National Park

Mgahinga takes in parts of the Virunga volcanoes, which span the borders of Uganda, Rwanda and Congo (Zaïre). Before the Bwindi attack, this was a popular stop for overland trucks as permits could not be prebooked. Gorillas are not guaranteed here, as they occasionally duck across the border into Congo (Zaïre).

When business is back in full flow, you'll have to be very patient getting a permit; you may have to wait for more than a week. There is only one family habituated to visitors at Mgahinga and a permit to see them costs US$175, although it will have probably risen to US$250 by the time you read this. There is also a US$15 park entry fee.

Security at Mgahinga has been generally good but its proximity to unstable areas of East Africa means that there is always the possibility of some unforeseen incident. There is an army presence down here, though it's not as large as at Bwindi. Mgahinga is more accessible than Bwindi, particularly if you don't have your own transport – you can take the bus to Kisoro and proceed from there. See the Mgahinga National Park section in the South-Western Uganda chapter for more information.

Rwanda

Parc Nacional des Volcans

This was *the* place to view the mountain gorillas during the 1980s, but the combination of civil war, genocide and armed rebels kept it off the travel map for much of the 1990s. The park reopened in July 1999.

This park is where Dian Fossey was based and where the film about her work was made. If you want the most authentic gorilla experience, some say this is the place to come, as the towering volcanoes form a breathtaking backdrop. Unfortunately for Rwanda, potential visitors are more likely to associate the country with genocide than with gorillas, making it an uncomfortable destination for the average tourist.

There are 18 gorilla permits available each day and it is likely to remain pretty easy to get one for the next couple of years at least. The cost is US$250, including entry to the park. If you are visiting from Uganda, you also have to factor in the cost of a visa (US$35).

Security at the park is actually very tight. A foreign-trained elite military unit guards the park, which is closed to visitors if there is so much as a footprint out of place. As long as the park remains open, it is arguably the safest place to visit the gorillas, but there is always the possibility that rebels will infiltrate the north-east, forcing its closure. Access is quite straightforward from Ruhengeri. For more information, see the Parc Nacional des Volcans section in the Rwanda chapter.

The highlight of a trip to Uganda, Rwanda or Congo (Zaïre) is undoubtedly an encounter with the endangered mountain gorillas of East Africa.

Some of Africa's best inland beaches can be found at Lake Kivu in Rwanda.

Want a lift? Bicycle-taxis in Rwanda

The 3711m-high Visoke volcano, Rwanda

Wooden carvings at a central Kigali craft market, Rwanda.

Rwanda

Rwanda is a beautiful yet brutalised country, known for the wrong reasons. It's a land of endless mountains, breathtaking views and home to some of the world's few remaining mountain gorillas. However, Rwanda has become etched into the consciousness of the late 20th century as the focus of one of the world's most horrific attempts at genocide. What happened here in 1994 is beyond belief.

Following the shooting down of an aircraft carrying the president (and also the president of Burundi), half a nation went on the rampage. Within just three to four months, up to one million people were dead, hacked to death with *pangas* (machetes), shot through the head or butchered with anything on hand. In addition, up to two million people fled their homes and lived as refugees along the border regions of neighbouring countries.

Before the outrages in 1994, many travellers used to come to Rwanda to visit the beautiful Parc Nacional des Volcans in the north, where the borders of Rwanda, Uganda and Congo (Zaïre) meet. The thickly forested slopes are one of the last remaining sanctuaries of the mountain gorilla. This endangered species, too, suffered in the civil war, losing quite a few of its dwindling numbers. However, you can now once again visit two of the family groups, and travellers are starting to trickle back.

Rwanda has shown itself to be an unstable country over the past few decades so it is imperative that you check the latest security conditions before contemplating a visit. This is Africa and events can unfold very fast. It is probably easiest to pick up reliable information in Kampala.

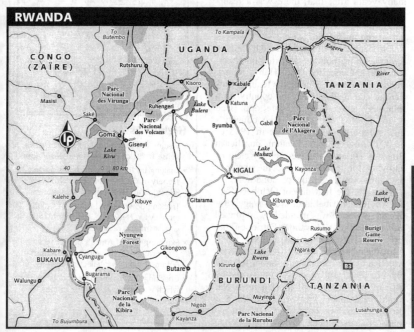

RWANDA

Facts about Rwanda

HISTORY

For the background on Rwanda's history prior to independence in 1962, see the Facts about East Africa chapter.

Independence

When independence was granted in 1962, it brought the Hutu majority to power under Prime Minister Gregoire Kayibanda. However, certain sections of the Tutsi were unwilling to accept the loss of their privileged position and formed guerrilla groups that mounted raids on Hutu communities, thus provoking further Hutu reprisals. In the fresh round of bloodshed that followed, thousands more Tutsi were killed and tens of thousands of their fellow tribespeople fled to Uganda and Burundi.

Although intertribal tensions eased for many years after that, there was a resurgence of anti-Tutsi feeling in 1972 when tens of thousands of Hutu tribespeople were massacred in Burundi.

The slaughter reignited the old hatreds in Rwanda and prompted the army commander, Major General Juvenal Habyarimana, to oust Kayibanda. During his tenure of office he managed to keep the country on a relatively even keel, despite depressed prices for tea and coffee (the country's major exports) and an influx in 1988 of 50,000 refugees from the ethnic conflict in Burundi. He also managed to stay clear of applying for IMF loans and the austerity measures that are a usual precondition.

Then, on the first day of October 1990, the whole intertribal issue was savagely reopened. Rwanda was invaded by 5000 well armed rebels of the Rwandan Patriotic Front (RPF), a Tutsi-dominated military front, from their bases in western Uganda. They were led by Paul Kagame, a former security chief of the Ugandan army, and assisted by officers and soldiers of the Ugandan National Resistance Army (NRA). All hell broke loose. Two days later, at Habyarimana's request, France, Belgium and Congo

RWANDA AT A GLANCE

Area: 26,338 sq km
Population: 9.5 million
Population Growth Rate: 2.1%
Capital: Kigali
Head of State: President Pasteur Bizimungu
Official Languages: Kinyarwanda, French & English
Currency: Rwandan franc (RFr)
When to Go: Anytime but mid-March to mid-May when the long rains set in

Highlights

- Visiting the rare mountain gorillas in the dense forest of Parc Nacional des Volcans

- Soaking up the sun, sand and stunning scenery at Gisenyi, on Lake Kivu, Rwanda's answer to the Mediterranean

- Tracking down huge troupes of Colobus monkeys in Nyungwe, the country's largest tropical rainforest

- Exploring one of Africa's best ethnographical and archaeological museums in Butare, Rwanda's intellectual capital

- Checking out the nightlife in Kigali, which is slowly regaining its former reputation

(Zaïre) flew in troops to help the Rwandan army repulse the rebels.

With this support assured, the Rwandan army went on a rampage against the Tutsi and any Hutu 'suspected' of having collaborated with the rebels. Thousands were shot or hacked to death and countless others indiscriminately arrested, herded into football stadia or police stations and left there without food or water for days. Many died. Those that could, fled to Uganda. Congolese (Zaïrean) troops, likewise, joined in the carnage.

President Museveni of Uganda was accused of having encouraged the rebels and supplying them with equipment. The accusations were denied but it's inconceivable that Museveni was totally unaware of the preparations that were going on, and it was also common knowledge that Uganda was keen to see the repatriation of the 250,000 Tutsi refugees based in western Uganda.

The setback for the RPF was only temporary, however. It invaded again in 1991, this time better armed and prepared. The government forces were thrown back over a large area of northern Rwanda, and by early 1993 the RPF was within 25km of Kigali. At this point a ceasefire was cobbled together and the warring parties brought to the negotiating table in Arusha (Tanzania).

The negotiations stalled several weeks later and hostilities were renewed. French troops were flown in, ostensibly to protect foreign nationals in Kigali, but they were accused by the RPF of assisting the Rwandan army. The accusations were denied but TV footage of their activities didn't quite confirm their denials. Meanwhile, with morale in the Rwandan army at a low ebb, the RPF launched an all-out offensive. Habyarimana attempted to contain this by calling a conference of regional presidents to which the RPF was invited. Power sharing was part of the agenda. Habyarimana came away from this conference in April 1994 with somewhat less than he would have liked (and Museveni of Uganda was less than supportive) but just as his light jet was about to land at Kigali airport on the way home it was shot down by a surface-to-air missile. Both he and his colleague, the president of Burundi, died in the crash. It will probably never be known who fired the missile (there are several theories) but this event unleashed one of the 20th century's worst explosions of bloodletting.

The Genocide

Habyarimana's Hutu political and military supporters decided at that point to activate what amounted to a 'final solution' to the Tutsi 'problem' by exterminating them. It was clearly all pre-planned and the principal player among those in favour of this course of action was the army commander, Colonel Theoneste Bagosora, who had been in charge of training the Hutu Interahamwe militias in Kigali before the shoot-down. (For more information on the Interahamwe, see the boxed text in this section.) One of his first acts was to direct the army to kill the 'moderate' Hutu prime minister, Agathe Uwilingiyimana, and 10 Belgian UN peacekeepers. The killing of the UN peacekeepers prompted Belgium to withdraw all of its troops – precisely what Bagosora had calculated – and the way was then open for the genocide to begin in earnest.

Rwandan army and Interahamwe death squads ranged at will over the countryside killing, looting and burning, and roadblocks were set up in every town and city. Every day thousands of Tutsi and any Hutu suspected of sympathising with them or their plight were butchered on the spot. The streets of Kigali were littered with dismembered corpses and the stench of rotting flesh was everywhere. Those who attempted to take refuge in religious missions or churches did so in vain and, in some cases, it was the nuns and priests themselves who betrayed the fugitives to the death squads. Any mission that refused the death squads access was simply blown apart. But perhaps the most shocking part of the tragedy was the enthusiasm with which ordinary Hutu – men, women and even children as young as 10 years old – joined in the carnage.

It's probably true to say that a large number of Hutu who took part in the massacre were caught up in a tide of blind hatred, fear

RWANDA

and peer pressure, but there's no doubt whatsoever that it was inspired, controlled and promoted by the Rwandan army and Interahamwe under the direction of their political and military leaders. Yet the carnage also proved to be their nemesis. While up to one million people were being butchered – mainly Tutsi but also many so-called 'moderate' Hutu – the RPF pressed on with its campaign and with increasing speed pushed the Rwandan army and the Interahamwe militias out of the country into Congo (Zaïre) and Burundi. The massacre finally ended with the RPF in firm control of the country but with some two million of the country's population huddled in refugee camps over the border in Congo (Zaïre), Burundi and Tanzania.

The Aftermath

Of course, that is far from the end of the story. Within a year of the RPF victory, a legal commission was set up in Arusha to try those accused of involvement in the genocide; Rwandan prisons are still overflowing with suspects (including women and youths). However, many of the main perpetrators of the genocide – the Interahamwe and former senior army officers – fled into exile out of the reach of the long arm of the RPF.

Some went to Kenya where they enjoyed the protection of President Moi who refuses to hand them over. This has created severe tensions between Kenya and Rwanda and led to the breaking of diplomatic relations. Others, including Colonel Theoneste Bagosora, the alleged architect of the genocide, and Ferdinand Nahimana, the director of the notorious Radio Milles Collines, which actively encouraged Hutu to butcher Tutsi, fled to Cameroon where they enjoyed the protection of that country's security boss, John Fochive. However when Fochive was sacked by the newly elected president of Cameroon, Paul Biya, the Rwandan exiles were arrested. Cameroon has since sent a number of prominent Rwandans associated with the genocide to Arusha for trial.

Of more importance though were the activities of the Interahamwe and former army

The Interahamwe

The Interahamwe are known to the world as the militia responsible for the deaths of as many as one million Tutsi and moderate Hutu during the genocide of 1994. More recently, the Interahamwe again made headline news on 1 March 1999 with the murder of eight tourists in Bwindi National Park, in south-western Uganda.

Formed in the early 1990s, the militia were unleashed on a defenceless population in April 1994 and embarked on their reign of terror. They fled the country with the arrival of the Rwanda Patriotic Front (RPF) in Kigali, but their campaign of terror did not end there.

Since 1994, the fortunes of the Interahamwe have risen and fallen, but they remain a genuine threat to the stability of Rwanda. Following their ignominious retreat into eastern Congo (Zaïre), they formed an alliance with the former Rwandan army (FAR) to control the refugee camps there through a combination of intimidation and violence. Control of the camps gave them control of the aid coming into the camps, which in turn they could use to exchange for weapons with the Congo (Zaïre) armed forces (FAZ) loyal to Mobutu, the then Congo (Zaïrean) president. This helped make them a very real threat to north-west Rwanda and attacks began to multiply.

The RPF government in Rwanda felt that Mobutu was not doing anywhere near enough to bring the situation under control and mounted an invasion to flush the rebels out. This was a great success, sending the Interahamwe scattering throughout the country, and formed the basis of what became Rwandan government policy to overthrow Mobutu and replace him with someone (Laurent Kabila) more amenable to Rwandan security concerns.

However, while the Rwandans and Ugandans were busy kingmaking with Kabila, the Interahamwe began to establish contacts with other Hutu dissident groups in the region, notably those

personnel in the refugee camps of Congo (Zaïre) and Tanzania. Determined to continue their fight against the RPF, they cynically manipulated the situation in the camps to their advantage by spreading the fear among the refugees that if they returned to Rwanda they would be killed. When Congo (Zaïre) and Tanzania began to demand the repatriation of the refugees, the grip of the Interahamwe on the camps was so complete that few dared move. Even when the UN made a valiant effort to persuade the refugees to return home, they succeeded only in scratching the surface and then gave up.

However, what concerned the RPF most was that the Interahamwe used the refugee camps as staging posts for raids into Rwanda, with the complicity of the Congolese (Zaïrean) army. Congo (Zaïre) was warned by Rwanda that if these raids did not stop, the consequences would be dire. The raids continued and the RPF mounted a lightning two-day campaign into Congo (Zaïre) and targeted one of the main refugee camps north of Goma. Tens of thousands

fled further west into the bush along with the Interahamwe but many others took the opportunity to return home to Rwanda.

Several months after this, events in eastern Congo (Zaïre) totally changed the picture. In October 1996, a new guerrilla movement known as the Alliance of Democratic Forces for the Liberation of Congo/ Zaïre, led by Laurent Kabila, suddenly emerged. Composed largely of Banyamulenge (ethnic Tutsi born in Congo [Zaïre]) who had been dispossessed and disenfranchised by the Congolese government), they swept through eastern Congo (Zaïre) and, by December, were in control of every town and city in the region.

The Congolese (Zaïrean) army retreated west in disarray towards Kisangani, looting and pillaging as they went. They were joined by their allies, the Interahamwe and former Rwandan army personnel.

The grip of the Interahamwe on the refugee camps had been broken. Hundreds of thousands of refugees began streaming back into Rwanda, not only from Congo

The Interahamwe

from Burundi. And with the overthrow of Mobutu came new recruits in the shape of FAZ troops, who blamed Banyamulenge (Tutsi from the east) for their loss of power.

The Interahamwe found themselves with new contacts for arms supplies and a new constituency to spread their message of hate. The Interahamwe alone may be nothing but a bunch of stateless thugs seeking to avoid the clutches of Rwandan justice, but together with the FAR, the FAZ, the Mai Mai and Burundian Hutu, they became a dangerous political force with a militant agenda.

Radio Television Libre des Milles Collines played a major role in spreading the message of hate that inflamed the genocide in Rwanda. Once again radio is playing a role in the ongoing conflict between Hutu and Tutsi with the broadcasts of Voix du Patriote in Kivu Province, which call on the local population to ensure 'the visitors (Tutsi) return to their home'. 'The country has been sold to the Tutsi' is a regular theme and Tutsi are described as Ethiopians and Egyptians. Radio proved a powerful tool in 1994 and could prove so again in the future.

There is very little chance that the Interahamwe will ever again find the opportunity to finish off the genocide they began in Rwanda. However, they will continue to threaten the livelihoods of the Rwandan people who are slowly trying to put the pieces of their lives back together after the nightmare that visited their country in 1994. They are a dangerous and dedicated group with nowhere to call home. Stateless and hated, they are condemned to wander the jungles of Congo (Zaïre), avoiding the armies of Rwanda, Burundi and Uganda that are hunting them down. They are desperate people as the events at Bwindi proved and until they can be brought out of the jungles in which they hide, they will continue to destabilise not just Rwanda, but all the countries in the Great Lakes region.

RWANDA

(Zaïre) but also from Tanzania. The government has been slowly resettling these refugees during the past few years, mostly in newly built villages located throughout the country. Much of Parc Nacional de l'Akagera was given over to this 'villagisation' program and much of the north-west is also being slowly resettled.

Rwanda Today

Rwanda has done a remarkable job of getting back onto its feet and has achieved an astonishing level of safety and security in a remarkably short space of time, albeit with considerable help from a rather guilty international community. You can walk around in safety again without having to climb over dismembered bodies in the streets and deal with panga-wielding thugs. All the same, not everyone is happy with the RPF government and rebels remain a threat to the stability of the country.

Both the country's geography and demography, however, make it hard to predict whether this period of stability will last. The war in Congo (Zaïre) is not simply a war about who controls the mineral resources of that vast country, but in microcosm, it is a war about which tribe controls which area of the Great Lakes region. Many old wounds in the area have been re-opened by manipulative individuals seeking to strengthen their agenda. Militant Hutu, be they the remnants of the Interahamwe or the Rwandan army, have stirred up populations into a frenzy of anti-Tutsi hatred that has transformed the Hutu-Tutsi problem into a regional issue rather than a national one. For more on the war in Congo (Zaïre) and Rwanda's involvement, see the boxed text 'Heart of Darkness' in the Facts about East Africa chapter.

However, needless to say, Rwanda is at the heart of an unstable region and its problems have to a great extent been responsible for destabilising the countries around the Great Lakes. As long as it can keep the problem exported to Congo (Zaïre), Rwanda will remain safe, but whether that is possible or not depends very much on a settlement to the war there and border security – Rwanda's justification for interfering in Congolese (Zaïrean) affairs in the first place.

When it comes to demography, Rwanda is home to two distinct tribes, the Hutu and the Tutsi, and the former outnumber the latter by a margin of more than four to one. The RPF government may be a national unity government with a number of Hutu representatives but by many it is viewed as a Tutsi government ruling over a predominantly Hutu country. However, the RPF government has done an impressive job of promoting reconciliation and restoring trust between the two communities. This is no small achievement after the horrors that were inflicted on the Tutsi community during the genocide of 1994. It would have been all too easy for the RPF to embark on a campaign of revenge and reprisal, but instead the government is attempting to build a society with a place for everyone, regardless of background. Rwanda today is a peaceful country, but sadly history shows it may not last.

It is to be hoped that as and when a peace settlement is negotiated in Congo (Zaïre), one of its central platforms will be the disarming of the Rwandese militias roaming the countryside there. Until they are disarmed and held accountable for their actions, they will continue to pose a threat to stability and progress in Rwanda and the region, and continue to push the tribal issue to the forefront of people's minds. Rwanda is enjoying the most success and stability it has had for a long time, but the fundamental divisions that have precipitated so much bloodshed in the past remain. Unless a wider solution to the Hutu-Tutsi problem in the Great Lakes region is sought, the population can never be certain that peace is here to stay, as events nearby will have the potential to ignite Rwanda once again.

What is potentially more dangerous is a repetition of what happened in Rwanda in Burundi. Intertribal tension there has reached a crisis point with somewhere around 200,000 (estimates vary from 50,000 to 500,000) people having been killed in clashes over the last seven years. If it were to explode, the whole region would, once again, be sucked into the vortex.

GEOGRAPHY

Rwanda is one of the world's most densely populated countries. To feed the people, almost every available piece of land is under cultivation, except for parts of the Akagera (along the border with Tanzania) and the higher slopes of the volcanoes. Since most of the country is mountainous, this involves a good deal of terracing. The banded hillsides are similar to those in Nepal or the Philippines. Tea plantations take up considerable areas of land.

In terms of statistics, Rwanda's mountainous terrain occupies 26,338 sq km. Land use is about 35% arable, 20% pasture and 11% forest.

CLIMATE

The average day temperature is 30°C with a possible maximum of 34°C, except in the highlands, where the day range is 12° to 15°C. There are four discernible seasons: the long rains from mid-March to mid-May, the long dry from mid-May to mid-October, the short rains from mid-October to mid-December and the short dry from mid-December to mid-March.

It rains more frequently and heavily in the north-east, where volcanoes are covered by rainforest. The summit of Karisimbi (4507m), the highest of these volcanoes, is often covered with sleet or snow.

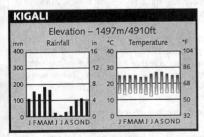

ECOLOGY & ENVIRONMENT

The most serious problem confronting Rwanda today is soil erosion resulting from overuse of the land. The terracing system in the country is fairly anarchic, unlike in Bali or Vietnam, and the lack of coordinated water management has wiped out much of the topsoil on the slopes. This is potentially catastrophic for a country with too many people in too small a space, as it points to a serious food scarcity problem in the future. Perhaps it is time to send some of the overpaid nongovernmental organisations (NGOs) home and bring out some Vietnamese to save the land for future generations.

FLORA & FAUNA

Rwanda shares much of the flora and fauna of its larger neighbours in the region. For more information on the rare mountain gorillas of Parc Nacional des Virunga or the Colobus monkey of Ngungwe Forest see the Facts about East Africa chapter and 'The Mountain Gorillas of East Africa' special section.

GOVERNMENT & POLITICS

The head of state of the Rwandan Patriotic Front (RPF) government is President Pasteur Bizimungu but the real power in Rwanda is wielded by the vice president and defence minister, Paul Kagame, who is also head of the RPF.

There is a Constituent Assembly composed of both Tutsi and Hutu members and while it enjoys certain powers in formulating policy and acting on that, the army retains overriding influence. There are good reasons for that, the main one being the continuing threat of invasion by forces linked to the ousted regime.

ECONOMY

The economy is agriculturally based, with coffee by far the largest export, accounting for about 75% of export income. Tungsten, tin, pyrethrum and tea are also important, although the tin industry is in a state of paralysis following the forced liquidation of the state mining company after the collapse of the International Tin Agreement in 1985.

The country is a major recipient of international aid, particularly from the UN, Japan, Belgium, Germany and the UK.

Agriculture is the main employer and export earner, contributing about 40% of GDP. The principal food crops include plantain, sweet potato, beans, cassava, sorghum and maize.

The manufacturing sector accounts for nearly 20% of GDP. Local produce includes cigarettes, soap, plastics and textiles.

A privatisation program has been under way since 1996 and of the original 64 enterprises originally earmarked, about one-third have already been sold off. However, the big names, such as Rwandatel and Electrogaz, are yet to be tackled.

Inflation is running at 10% per annum, while real GDP growth is about 8%.

POPULATION & PEOPLE

The population stands at about 9.5 million, which gives Rwanda one of the highest population densities of any country in Africa.

Almost all of the two million refugees who were living in Congo (Zaïre), Burundi, Tanzania and elsewhere have now returned to Rwanda; virtually the only ones who haven't are those who had some involvement in the genocide of 1994 and are roaming the Great Lakes region terrorising local populations.

EDUCATION

The Ministry of Education has set a target of universal primary education by 2005. However, this is a very ambitious target as many teachers were killed and a number of schools and colleges destroyed during the genocide. Only about 30% of current teachers are actually qualified, and there are only 2000 primary schools, 300 secondary schools and one university in the whole country. Illiteracy runs as high as 50%.

RELIGION

About 65% of the population are Christians of various sects, a further 25% follow tribal religions, often with a dash of Christianity, and the remaining 10% are Muslims.

LANGUAGE

The national language is Kinyarwanda. The official languages are Kinyarwanda, French and English. Kinyarwanda is the medium of school instruction at primary level, and French is used at secondary level (only 8% of the population reach secondary level).

The Slow Hand of Justice

Following a shaky start, the International Criminal Tribunal for Rwanda (www.un.org/law/rwanda or www.inter-media.org/) has begun to net some major suspects with help from authorities in Cameroon and Kenya. Ironically it was these very countries that first harboured Kigali's most wanted, frustrating the Rwandese authorities in their attempts to seek justice. The tribunal was established in Arusha in 1995 with the intention of bringing those responsible for the genocide in Rwanda to justice. The UN Security Council has also called for an inquiry into the UN's role during the genocide.

The tribunal has had much success in tracking down many of the former ministers of the interim cabinet that presided over the country during the genocide. In February 1999, Casimir Bizimunga, foreign minister and health minister under the Habyarimana regime and in office throughout the genocide, was arrested in Nairobi and transferred to the ICTR soon after. The Cameroonian authorities, who have arrested many of the suspects now awaiting trial by the ICTR, handed over three more prominent former ministers in April.

While almost all the leading interim government figures that ruled during the genocide are included in the list of 35 suspects awaiting trial in Arusha, the tribunal has been much less successful in getting its hands on members of the Interahamwe militia, directly responsible for most of the atrocities committed in Rwanda. The trial of Interahamwe leader Georges Rutaganda began in March 1997 and is dragging on, lacking direction. He has conceded to being a shareholder in Radio TV Libre Mille Collines, the station responsible for whipping up the population into a frenzy of anti-Tutsi feeling with its propaganda broadcasts, but this is unimpressive evidence given he is the only member of the Interahamwe leadership standing trial.

RWANDA

Little English is spoken beyond Kigali, but Swahili can be useful in some areas. See the Language chapter at the back of this book for some useful Swahili words and phrases.

Facts for the Visitor

HIGHLIGHTS

It's hard to talk about 'highlights' in Rwanda after the recent genocide. Yet the butchery took place in a country that is scenically beautiful. There are thickly forested **volcanic mountains** along the entire border with Uganda and Congo (Zaïre) to the north, which are the home of the endangered **mountain gorillas**. Many of these family groups had previously been habituated to human contact and thousands of overseas visitors had the unique experience of spending some time in their presence. Incredibly, they're still there, despite the artillery battles that engulfed the mountains, but their numbers have, regrettably, been depleted. With relative peace having been re-established,

you can now visit these remarkable animals once again. This is *the* highlight of a visit to Rwanda. For more information see 'The Mountain Gorillas of East Africa' special section.

Trekking the volcanoes was, for the intrepid, as equal a buzz but required a high degree of resilience. They're a tough climb and discomfort is the name of the game. Unfortunately, access is currently prohibited.

The **Parc Nacional de l'Akagera** used to be awash with wildlife of every description but civil wars and bad management have resulted in serious depletion. However, the stunning **Nyungwe Forest** has fared somewhat better and is home to many species of primate, including huge troupes of Colobus monkeys.

And for beach bums who thought their luck was out, there are some of Africa's best inland beaches on the shores of **Lake Kivu**. Both Gisenyi and Kibuye have white sand and water sports, and fantastic views across the beautiful waters to the mountains of Congo (Zaïre) beyond.

The Slow Hand of Justice

Back in Rwanda, the prisons are still overflowing with genocide suspects. Prison numbers are thought to be around 122,000, and many of these prisoners are seen all over the country in their pink uniforms, helping on civil works programs. Security may look lax, but that is because the prisoners have little motivation to escape as lynch mobs would kill them in a second.

There are three categories of prisoner in Rwanda: category one suspects are those who planned and orchestrated the genocide; category two prisoners are those who oversaw massacres and failed to prevent them when in a position to do so; and category three are those who killed or looted during the genocide. Most prisoners are category three, but evidence against them is mainly hearsay, hence the government has revived the *gacaca*, a traditional tribunal headed by village elders, to speed up the process. However, it looks to be a long time before Rwanda is through with its process of justice.

Elsewhere, the Catholic Bishop of Gikongoro, Augustin Misago, was arrested in April 1999 and charged with genocide. This has pitted state against church in a country where the majority of the population is Catholic. Several priests have already been sentenced to death in Rwanda for involvement in genocide and the Vatican has publicly accepted that some church officials aided and abetted the genocide. However, never before has such a senior figure been implicated and this could create further embarrassment for the church, already badly tainted by its involvement in the genocide. The church itself has resisted calls for an internal inquiry into its conduct during the genocide.

The quest for justice in Rwanda looks set to be a long one and will cast a long shadow over the country's attempts to make a new start. Justice is a necessary part of reconciliation, but remains a principle rather than priority as the country simply has too many cases to deal with and too many other problems to worry about.

RWANDA

SUGGESTED ITINERARIES

Rwanda is such a compact country that to talk in terms of specific itineraries is unnecessary. For those with just 10 days in the country, it is possible to cover most of the attractions. It is straightforward enough to do a loop south through Butare, Nyungwe Forest to Cyangugu and then charter a speedboat north through Kibuye to Gisenyi. From here it is a short distance to Ruhengeri and the mountain gorillas and then another short hop to Kigali.

If you only have a week or less, it is probably best to concentrate on the north-west and visit just Kigali, Ruhengeri and Gisenyi.

For those with two weeks or more, you can do the above and also relax at a couple of the beaches on Lake Kivu and consider making a trip to Parc Nacional de l'Akagera, although there is not much wildlife here these days; or take in one or two of the genocide memorials, which although extremely disturbing, are a chilling and educational reminder of the evil that visited this land. The two most famous of these memorials are found at Nyamata and Ntarama, both within an hour's drive of Kigali.

PLANNING

For details about planning your trip, and what to bring, see the Planning section in the Regional Facts for the Visitor chapter.

When to Go

With the infrastructure in such reasonable shape, it doesn't matter too much when you visit Rwanda. However, if you don't like rain, you may want to avoid the long rains of mid-March to mid-May.

Maps

It is hard to get hold of decent maps of Rwanda before getting to the country. Most visitors make do with a map of East Africa. Once in Kigali, you can purchase slightly out-of-date maps of Rwanda, Kigali and the national parks from the tourist office and Libraire Caritas.

What to Bring

See the Regional Facts for the Visitor chapter for details on what to bring to Rwanda.

Bear in mind that many of the tourist attractions are at high altitude so you need to bring a sweater and a waterproof jacket.

TOURIST OFFICES

The tourist office, Office Rwandais du Tourisme et des Parcs Nationaux (ORTPN; ☎ 070-76514) in Kigali is open from 8 am to 5 pm Monday to Friday, and Saturday mornings. Its main function is to take bookings for the gorillas. There is very little in the way of printed information or maps, though it does have a list of current prices for the mid-range and top end hotels around the country.

VISAS & DOCUMENTS

Visas

Visas are required by everyone except nationals of Germany and the USA. Avoid applying for your visa outside East Africa, as this often involves a lot of red tape. They cost US$50 in most countries, require two photos, allow a one-month stay and generally take 24 hours to issue, though you can sometimes get them the same day if you get your application in first thing in the morning. When applying, you do not have to show an onward ticket or 'sufficient funds'.

When applying for a visa, request a double-entry or multiple-entry visa, especially if you intend to re-enter Rwanda from Congo (Zaïre) or Burundi. There's no extra cost and it gives you flexibility. The main reason for this is that one of the routes between Bukavu in Congo (Zaïre), and Bujumbura in Burundi, is a road which passes through Rwanda, and for this you will need a Rwandan visa, even though you have no intention of getting off the bus, truck or car. There are alternatives to this route, so a Rwandan visa is not absolutely essential.

Most of the few travellers visiting Rwanda, however, get their visa on arrival at the border. The 15-day visit visa costs US$35 and takes 10 minutes to issue.

Those driving their own vehicles are required to buy a permit at the border, which costs US$76.

Visa Extensions Both tourist and transit visas can be extended in the capital, Kigali, at

MININTER (Ministère de l'Intérieur; ☎ 070-85856) in the Kacyiru district, about 7km north-east of the city centre. Extensions take one to two days to issue, cost RFr 3000 and you can get up to three months. Visas cannot be extended in Ruhengeri even though there's an immigration office there.

Other Visas If you want to get visas to neighbouring countries while you're in Rwanda, take note of the following (see Embassies in Rwanda later in this section for the addresses):

Burundi Visas cost US$40 for one month single entry. Visas are available at the border but you're strongly advised not to travel through northern Burundi as this area of the country is not under the control of the central government.
Congo (Zaïre) At the time of writing visas were no longer issued for travel to Kinshasa as the embassy is closed. However, for land crossings to Eastern Congo (Zaïre), currently under Rwandan-backed rebel control, you can get one-month visas at Bukavu for US$35; at Goma it will cost you US$60 for some unknown reason.
Kenya Visas cost US$30 or the equivalent in local currency, require two photographs and are issued the same day if you apply before 11.30 am. No onward tickets or minimum funds are asked for. If the Rwandan embassy in Nairobi is closed then this embassy will probably also be closed.
Tanzania Visas require two photos and generally take 24 hours to issue. The cost depends on your nationality (see the Tanzania Facts for the Visitor chapter for details).
Uganda Visas cost US$30, require two photos and are issued in 24 hours. However, it is far easier to get them at the border.

EMBASSIES
Rwandan Embassies
There are Rwandan embassies in Brussels (Belgium), Ottawa (Canada), Cairo (Egypt), Addis Ababa (Ethiopia), Paris (France), Bonn (Germany), Abidjan (Ivory Coast), Tokyo (Japan), London (UK) and Washington DC (USA).

In East Africa, visas can be obtained from the following Rwandan embassies:

Burundi (☎ 26865) 24 Ave du Zaïre, Bujumbura

Kenya (☎ 02-240563, fax 336365) 12th floor, International House, Mama Ngina St, Nairobi
Tanzania (☎ 051-130119) 32 Ali Mwinyi Rd, Upanga, Dar es Salaam
Uganda (☎ 041-244045) Plot 2, Nakaima Rd, Kampala

There are no Rwandan consulates at either Bukavu or Goma in eastern Congo (Zaïre), so it's advisable to get your visa in Kinshasa (or elsewhere) if you're coming from the west – that's assuming that the Rwandan embassy re-opens as and when peace comes to Congo (Zaïre). On the other hand, 15-day Rwandan visas are available at the border for US$35.

Embassies in Rwanda
Kigali, the capital of Rwanda, is a small city, and most foreign embassies are within easy walking distance of the centre. The telephone code for Kigali is ☎ 070.

Belgium (☎ 75551) Ave de la Paix
Burundi (☎ 73465) Rue de Ntaruka off Ave de Rusumo
Congo (Zaïre) (☎ 75327) Rue Député Kamuzinzi. Closed at the time of writing.
France (☎ 75225) Ave Paul VI
Kenya (☎ 82774, fax 86234) Rue Kadyiro, near Hôtel Umubano, Kacyiru. Open from 8.30 am to noon and 2 to 4.30 pm Monday to Friday.
Tanzania (☎ 76074) Ave Paul VI, near Ave de Rusumo. Open from 9 am to 2 pm Monday to Friday.
Uganda (☎ 76495, fax 73551) Ave de la Paix
UK (☎ 84098, fax 82044) BP 576
USA (☎ 75602, fax 72128) Blvd de la Republique

CUSTOMS
Rwanda has standard customs allowances of the 200 cigarettes and 1L of spirits type you find internationally.

MONEY
Currency
The unit of currency is the Rwandan franc (RFr). It's divided into 100 centimes, but it's unlikely you'll come across these. Notes come in 100, 500, 1000 and 5000 denominations. Coins come in 1, 5, 10, 20 and 50.

RWANDA

Exchange Rates

country	unit		franc
Australia	A$1	=	RFr 214
Canada	C$1	=	RFr 234
Euro	€1	=	RFr 335
France	10FF	=	RFr 511
Germany	DM1	=	RFr 171
Japan	¥100	=	RFr 310
New Zealand	NZ$1	=	RFr 167
UK	UK£1	=	RFr 546
USA	US$1	=	RFr 340

Foreign exchange bureau rates and street transaction rates are US$1 = RFr 370 for large bills and RFr 340 for small bills but they only take cash – no travellers cheques.

Exchanging Money

It is definitely best to come with US dollars cash to Rwanda, as rates for travellers cheques and other currencies are significantly lower.

The banking sector has pretty much returned to normal after virtually all the banks were shot up, looted and trashed during the genocide. There are a number of banks open in Kigali, but some can be very slow at dealing with currency exchange.

There are also banks open again in Butare, Cyangugu, Gisenyi, Gitarama and Ruhengeri. However, these are generally only branches of Banque Commerciale de Rwanda and Banque de Kigali. Banque de Kigali is best avoided in the provinces as service takes forever and they demand ludicrously high commissions for both cash and travellers cheque exchanges.

In addition to the banks, there are several foreign exchange bureaus in Kigali, mainly around the post office. Another option is to change cash on the street or in shops, and you sometimes find you are offered slightly higher rates than elsewhere, particularly for non-US dollar currencies.

Credit cards are generally accepted only in relatively expensive hotels and restaurants in places such as Kigali and Gisenyi. You can make cash withdrawals against credit cards at Banque de Kigali and Banque Commerciale de Rwanda in the capital, but minus a commission and a lot of your time. There are no ATMs in the country.

Costs

Rwanda is a pretty expensive country because of the large number of expatriates and NGOs here. Being landlocked, a lot of export earnings are spent importing food, drink and transport requirements for the expatriates. As a budget traveller, you will be hard-pressed to live cheaply, even if you stay in mission hostels. It's difficult to exist on a Kenyan, Tanzanian or Ugandan budget, and student cards are only useful to get into the national parks at a discount.

Transport (by minibus) and food in roadside restaurants cost much the same as in the rest of East Africa, so long as you don't want meat with your meal. Meat will just about double the price. Anything on which culinary expertise has been lavished will be expensive.

Tipping & Bargaining

Tipping is common in the cities these days due to the large international presence. As in many parts of the developing world, Rwandan salaries are low and a tip of about RFr 50 to RFr 100 for good service will be appreciated.

Bargaining is necessary in some situations, but generally when it comes to shops and travel, prices are fixed. It is definitely worth haggling if you are buying souvenirs on the street in Kigali, as they will want to overcharge you.

POST & COMMUNICATIONS
Postal Rates

Overseas postal rates for postcards are RFr 115 for Africa, RFr 150 for Europe and North America and RFr 200 elsewhere. Airmail letters are RFr 175, RFr 215 and RFr 265 respectively.

Receiving Mail

There is a poste restante facility at the post office in Kigali. See the Kigali section for details.

Telephone & Fax

International calls are relatively expensive at RFr 700 to RFr 900 per minute to most countries including the UK and Australia.

Fax charges are the same per minute. There are few telephone area codes in Rwanda, but Kigali is ☎ 070 and Butare ☎ 032.

Email & Internet Access
Email and Internet access in Rwanda is basically limited to Kigali for the general public. See the Kigali chapter for details, but be warned that access and connections are unreliable.

BOOKS
For an in-depth appraisal of the Rwandan tragedy read *The Rwanda Crisis – History of a Genocide* by Gerard Prunier, written in English by a French historian; and *Rwanda & Genocide* by Alain Destexhe, a Belgian senator and former secretary general of Médecins sans Frontières.

Gorillas in the Mist is an account by Dian Fossey of her time spent among the gorillas of the Parc Nacional des Volcans, and is definitely worth reading before you track the gorillas.

NEWSPAPERS & MAGAZINES
The local press has yet to recover from the civil war and there's nothing much currently available. You can purchase imported newspapers, mainly from Uganda, such as *New Vision*. They can be purchased at top-end hotels. *The Link* is an informative magazine covering the Great Lakes region and is the best source for gaining a greater understanding of exactly what is going on in Rwanda and its turbulent neighbours.

RADIO
There are two AM and five FM radio stations, which generally broadcast in either Kinyarwanda or French. There are also programs in Swahili and English.

PHOTOGRAPHY
Bring plenty of film with you, as it is very expensive here and the choice is extremely limited – usually only 64 ASA and 100 ASA colour negative film and then only in places like Kigali and Gisenyi. Slide film is almost impossible to obtain. If you buy film, check the expiry dates carefully.

Be extremely careful wherever you take photos in Rwanda as the authorities are very sensitive about what you are allowed to shoot. Always ask before you take a photograph of anything or anybody other than landscapes.

To take photos of the gorillas in the Parc Nacional des Volcans, you will need high-speed film. It's often very dark in the jungle where they live, so normal film will produce very disappointing results when developed. Use 400 ASA and consider getting it pushed one stop if conditions are particularly dark. Buy it before you get to Rwanda.

TIME
Rwanda time is GMT/UTC plus two hours.

ELECTRICITY
The electricity supply is 220V AC. The power supply is pretty good in most of the major urban centres, a novelty if you have come from Uganda.

WEIGHTS & MEASURES
Rwanda uses the metric system.

LAUNDRY
Laundry services are generally only available through hotels in Rwanda and are quite expensive. If you are on a tight budget, do it yourself or ask a staff member if they are able to do a private wash, so to speak.

TOILETS
Toilets are very reasonable in the urban centres of Rwanda. Many are sit down flush, and those that aren't are clean long drops. In remote areas, however, expect things to be pretty basic.

WOMEN TRAVELLERS
Although Rwanda is a safe place in which to travel, there are a few concerns for women travellers. In general women will find that they encounter far fewer hassles from men than on the coast of Kenya, although it is wise not to travel alone in remote areas.

RWANDA

DANGERS & ANNOYANCES

It is imperative that you check security conditions within Rwanda before entering the country as it is in a very unstable area of the world. At the time of writing the country was pretty safe, but security concerns in the north-west can never be underestimated and there were reports that some Interahamwe rebels had re-entered the country and were ambushing along the Ruhengeri to Gisenyi road. The most important thing to remember about security is that there is absolutely no substitute for researching current conditions before you arrive and when you are in the country. Read newspapers, ask other travellers and hostels for the latest and check again locally once you are in the provinces. Things can change very fast in Africa, for the better or worse, and it pays to be well informed.

Urban Rwanda is now one of the safer places to be in this region of Africa, but in Kigali, like any capital, you should take care around unlit areas at night.

Out in the countryside, do not walk along anything other than a well used track; you may step on a land mine, although most have now been cleared by international demining organisations.

Never take photographs of anything connected with the government or the military (post offices, banks, bridges, border crossings, barracks, prisons, dams etc). Your film and maybe your equipment will be confiscated. In fact take care of where you point your camera anywhere in the country, as most Rwandans are very sensitive to who and what you are snapping.

The most common annoyance is the roadblocks on all of the main roads. You must stop at these and your baggage will be searched along with the vehicle you are in. The soldiers will also want to check your passport.

BUSINESS HOURS

Normal business hours are from 8 am to 12.30 pm and 2.30 to 5.30 pm Monday to Friday.

Many shops and offices tend to be closed between 1 and 5 July.

PUBLIC HOLIDAYS & SPECIAL EVENTS

Rwanda observes the following public holidays:

New Year's Day 1 January
Democracy Day 8 January
Easter March/April – Good Friday, Holy Saturday and Easter Monday
Labour Day 1 May
Ascension Thursday May
Whit Monday May
National Day 1 July
Peace & National Unity Day 5 July
Harvest Festival 1 August
Assumption 15 August
Culture Day 8 September
Kamarampaka Day 25 September
Armed Forces Day 26 October
All Saints' Day 1 November
Christmas Day 25 December

WORK

With all the international money sloshing around Rwanda, you could be forgiven for thinking it would be easy to pick up work here. However, it is not, as most international organisations recruit professionals back home. However, if you are considering looking for work, you must secure a work permit from a Rwandan embassy before you enter the country. They cost more than US$300.

ACCOMMODATION
Camping

Camping in the Parc Nacional des Volcans is prohibited due to sporadic rebel activity. The only regular camp site in the country is at Ngungwe Forest, but you may be able to camp at some of the missions around the country if you ask.

Hostels

Dorm accommodation at the mission hostels costs RFr 500 to RFr 1000 per night without food. A private double room at the hostels costs from RFr 2000 to RFr 4000 per night.

Mission hostels seem to attract an exceptionally conscientious type of manager who takes the old adage 'cleanliness is next to godliness' fairly seriously. You might not get hot water but your bed and room will be spotless. The one catch with mission hostels is that they're often full, particularly on weekends or in places where there is only one mission hostel in town. Also, the door is usually closed at 10 pm (or earlier).

Hotels

Compared with mission hostels, hotels are considerably more expensive and rarely worth the extra amount, especially at the budget end, where they are often none too clean. There are, of course, exceptions but not many.

The top end hotels are much the same as their counterparts elsewhere in Africa. The difference in Rwanda is that many of them are semipermanently full of expatriates working for various NGOs and the UN agencies, so advance booking by telephone is a very good idea.

FOOD & DRINK

African fare in Rwanda is very similar to that in Kenya and prices are reasonable. (See the Food section in Kenya Facts for the Visitor.) You'll find *tilapia*, which is Nile perch, and *wat* and *injera* are a staple Ethiopian dish. There's also a wide variety of continental food available and some of it is excellently prepared and presented but it is considerably more expensive than local fare.

Soft drinks (sodas) and the local beers, Primus and Mulzig, are available everywhere as is the local firewater, *konyagi*, but wines (both South African and European) are generally only available in the more expensive restaurants and hotels.

ENTERTAINMENT

Bars

Rwandans love their beer and love drinking it in their bars. There are lively local joints all over the country, most serving cold beers. Prices are very reasonable. For a bit more sophistication, Kigali is the only option and many of the most popular bars are also nightclubs. At these places, a full range of drinks is available, but at much higher prices.

Nightclubs

These are pretty much confined to Kigali and are most popular at weekends. Some stay open as late as 5 am, and attract a mixed crowd of locals, expats and women of the night.

Traditional Dance

Traditional dance displays can be arranged at the National Museum in Butare – see that entry for details.

Festivals and ceremonies in Rwanda are often accompanied by music, punctuated by the sound of a beating drum.

SHOPPING

Rwanda produces some attractive handicrafts, but the lack of tourists in the country has kept development of souvenir shops to a minimum. Work to look out for includes basketry, batik, drums and statuary. There is also a lot of Zaïrean (Congolese) craft available, including the ever-popular masks. The easiest place to find articles for sale is in the centre of Kigali or at the National Museum in Butare.

RWANDA

Getting There & Away

You can enter Rwanda by air or road; there are no railways, apart from the international gravy train. Lake ferries are suspended at present.

For information on getting to Rwanda from outside East Africa, see the regional Getting There & Away chapter.

AIR

International airlines flying into Rwanda include Air Burundi, Air France, Air Tanzania, Cameroon Airlines (CCA), Ethiopian Airlines, Kenya Airways, Rwanda Airlines, SA Alliance Express (Rwanda's flag carrier), Sabena and Uganda Airlines. SA Alliance Express is the most efficient operation for regional flights.

Air tickets bought in Rwanda for international flights are relatively expensive and compare poorly with what is on offer in Nairobi. You can pay for them in local currency.

Compulsory Certificates

Cholera vaccination certificates are compulsory for entry or exit by air, as are yellow fever certificates. If entering overland, the check is cursory but officials sometimes ask about it.

Departure Tax

There is a departure tax of US$20 or RFr 700 but only locals can pay in francs.

Burundi

Air Burundi, Rwanda Airlines, SA Alliance Express and Uganda Airlines fly to Bujumbura. Prices are pretty uniform at US$85/170 one way/return. SA Alliance Express are the most reliable option.

Kenya

SA Alliance Express flies to Nairobi three times a week for US$206/412 one-way/return fare. Promotional fares are more like US$150/250. Kenya Airways also flies three times a week, for US$206/250. Rwanda Airlines flies once a week via Bujumbura and charges US$175/250.

Tanzania

Air Tanzania flies from Kigali to Unguja (Zanzibar) (US$268/300) via Mwanza (US$123), Kilimanjaro (US$137/274) and Dar es Salaam (US$228/300) once a week on Sunday.

Uganda

SA Alliance Express flies between Kigali and Entebbe for US$123/246 one way/return. Promotional one-month returns are available for US$210. Uganda Airlines also flies between Kigali and Entebbe for the same prices, but its one-month return fares are cheaper at US$180.

LAND

Rwanda shares borders with Burundi, Congo (Zaïre), Tanzania and Uganda. The land crossings into Burundi and Tanzania may not be safe to use because of the presence of armed Burundian rebels along the border area. Check the latest conditions before passing this way.

WARNING

At the time of writing, it was dangerous to cross the Rwandan border into Burundi as the northern part of Burundi is out of the control of the central Burundi government. We do not recommend it. The information in this section is provided in the event that the situation changes.

Burundi

Kigali to Bujumbura via Butare The main crossing point between Rwanda and Burundi is via Butare and Kayanza, on the Kigali to Bujumbura road. The road is sealed all the way. Share-taxis do the trip daily leaving at 8 am (RFr 2000, five hours).

Titanic Express (☎ 71089) runs buses between Kigali and Bujumbura. They cost

RFr 5000 and depart at 9 am on Monday, Wednesday and Friday from Kigali, and at 9 am on Tuesday, Thursday and Saturday from Bujumbura. The journey takes about six hours.

Eagle operates a daily bus service between Kigali and Bujumbura that costs about RFr 4000.

WARNING

!

We strongly advise against crossing by land into Congo (Zaïre) from East Africa as there was a civil war going on there at the time of writing, involving troops from as many as nine countries. There were also armed members of the *Interahamwe* roaming this part of Congo (Zaïre) and they have been known to target tourists. However, because of the possibility that peace will eventually return to this region, we include the following information.

Cyangugu to Bujumbura This route goes via Congo (Zaïre). Cyangugu is the actual border crossing but Kamembe is the town and transport centre. From Kamembe, minibuses make the 15-minute ride to the Congo (Zaïre) border for RFr 100. It is an easy border crossing in that you can walk between the two posts. From the Ruzizi border crossing, it's a 3km walk or taxi ride to Bukavu in Congo (Zaïre). From Bukavu take a minibus to Uvira in Congo (Zaïre). These buses go through both Rwanda and Congo (Zaïre) before terminating in Uvira. From there, you'll need to take another minibus or taxi across the border to Bujumbura. It's a good, sealed road.

You *may* need a Rwandan transit visa to make this journey or, better still, a re-entry visa, and you will definitely need a dual or multiple-entry visa for Congo (Zaïre).

Tanzania
Kigali to Mwanza From Kigali, take a minibus to Rusumo, the last Rwandan town before the border (RFr 1000, three hours), and then a pick-up truck from there across the border to Ngara. Two types of buses service the route between Ngara and

Mwanza: weekly minibuses operated by Samma Bus Co in Mwanza (TSh 6000, about 12 hours); and twice weekly normal-sized Isuzu buses operated by Tanganyika Bus Service in Mwanza (TSh 6000, about 12 hours). It's a good road part of the way but there are some very rough sections. Samma also operates a direct service twice weekly between Kigali and Mwanza (TSh 15,000).

Kigali to Kigoma From the border at Rusumo, take a share-taxi to Benaco (TSh 1500, including an armed escort). At Benaco there's *Silent Night Guest House* at TSh 3000 for a double. A minibus from Benaco to Nyakanazi (just to the south of Lusahunga) takes 1¼ hours and costs TSh 4000. There is little traffic from Nyakanazi to Kigoma, but aid vehicles driven by locals are pressed into service and are a comfortable and easy way to travel. In share-taxis Nyakanazi to Kibondo costs about TSh 3000 (three hours), Kibondo to Kisulu is TSh 4000 (3½ hours) and Kisulu to Kigoma is TSh 3000 (2½ hours).

Uganda
There are two main crossing points you could try: between Kigali and Kabale via Katuna, and between Ruhengeri and Kisoro via Cyanika.

Kigali to Kabale From Kigali to Kabale there are many minibuses daily which take about two hours (not including border formalities and army roadblocks); the last minibus leaves Kigali at 1 pm. Normal Ugandan buses leave Kigali for Kabale daily at 6.30 am. Several private Kampala-based buses operate daily between Kigali and Kampala (about RFr 4000, 10 hours).

Ruhengeri to Kisoro From Ruhengeri to Kisoro via Cyanika the road is in pretty good shape these days. At the time of writing, rebel activity and ambushes had ceased along this route, but the area remains potentially volatile. Check current security conditions in Ruhengeri or Kigali before crossing this way.

RWANDA

Getting Around

AIR

Internal flights are available with Rwanda Airlines. Flights to Cyangugu and Gisenyi from Kigali cost US$80/160 one way/return, although there are often discounts on these stiff prices. Air Rwanda no longer has any aircraft so is unable to offer any flights.

BUS

Rwanda has an excellent road system, mainly due to massive injections of foreign aid. The only unsealed roads are those to Kibuye, on the shore of Lake Kivu, and some smaller stretches around the country.

You'll find plenty of well-maintained, modern minibuses serving all the main routes. Between dawn and about 3 pm, at the bus stand in any town, you can almost always find one going your way. Destinations are displayed in the front window and the fares are fixed (ask other passengers if you're not sure). However, if you get stuck somewhere late in the afternoon, you are going to pay top price for the privilege of getting out.

Minibuses leave when full, and this means when all the seats are occupied (unlike in Kenya and Tanzania, where most of the time they won't leave until you can't breathe for the people sitting on your lap and jamming the aisle). They are, however, more cramped than Uganda as they put four to a seat, not three. You should not be charged for baggage. Many minibuses have decent sound systems, so you might hear some good African music that isn't ear-splitting.

There are also modern government buses (many of them bearing the Japan-Rwanda assistance program logo) on quite a few routes. These are cheaper than minibuses but take longer and are far less frequent.

Whichever form of transport you take you must be prepared for military checkpoints. These vary in number depending on where you're going, but at each you'll be required to get off the vehicle and allow the soldiers to examine your luggage. Other than the time it takes, there's no hassle.

Warning

Petrol prices almost doubled overnight during the second half of 1999. The following day minibus fares shot up in response, but the government intervened forcing companies to hold their regular prices. It remains to be seen what will eventually be agreed upon, but do not be surprised if the fares you are quoted are higher than shown in this chapter. Ask locals what they are paying before boarding the bus.

CAR

Car hire isn't well established in Rwanda, so you'll have difficulty finding something. They're basically only available in Kigali and Ruhengeri. Inquire at travel agencies in Kigali; many can provide cars for around US$50 per day and up. The ORTPN tourist office that can put you in touch with a Range Rover or Land Cruiser (eight seats) for around US$120 per day. All hire cars come with a driver.

HITCHING

Hitching around Rwanda is relatively easy because of the prodigious number of non-governmental organisation (NGO) vehicles on the roads. Drivers will rarely ask you to pay for a lift. Women who decide to hitch should realise that accepting a lift from long-distance truck drivers is unwise but the NGOs are otherwise OK.

If you're looking for lifts on trucks from Kigali to Uganda, Kenya, Burundi or Congo (Zaïre), go to MAGERWA (short for Magasins Généraux de Rwanda) in the Gikondo suburb, about 3km from the centre of Kigali. Take your pick from the scores of trucks at the customs clearance depot. To get there, head down the Blvd de l'OUA and turn right when you see the sign. It's sometimes possible to find a free lift all the way to Mombasa, but usually it's a matter of negotiating a fare with the driver. Remember, travellers who decide to hitch should understand that they are taking a small but potentially serious risk.

BOAT

Before the latest civil war, there used to be ferries on Lake Kivu that connected the

Rwandan ports of Cyangugu, Kirambo, Kibuye and Gisenyi but these are still suspended at present. There are irregular cargo boats going up and down the lake, mainly to and from the Primus brewery in Gisenyi, but these are slow. There is also a charter speedboat between these ports, but you pay for speed.

LOCAL TRANSPORT
Taxi-Motor
Most towns are compact enough to get around on foot, but where you need transport, the taxi-motor is a good bet. It's just a motorcycle and you ride on the back. The driver can usually sling your pack across the petrol tank and they generally drive pretty safely, though of course there's no helmet for the passenger.

Taxi
These are only really necessary in Kigali. See the Kigali section for details.

ORGANISED TOURS
Organised tours are individually customised and tend be on the very expensive side. For a list of up-to-date operators check with the ORTPN office. There is a long-established agent at the Hôtel des Diplomates (☎ 070-75111) and the agency at the Okapi Hotel (☎ 070-74169, fax 74413) is also usually reliable.

Kigali

☎ 070

The national tourist organisation used to describe Rwanda as the 'Land of Eternal Spring'. Kigali, the capital, still lives up to this description to a large extent. Built on a ridge and extending down into the valley floors on either side, it's a small and attractive city with an incredible variety of flowering trees and shrubs. From various points on the ridge, there are superb views over the intensively cultivated and terraced countryside. The mountains and hills seem to stretch forever and the abundant rainfall keeps them a lush green.

Unfortunately, there was quite a lot of damage done to the city during the latest civil war and a number of buildings lie in partial or total ruin, though a lot of rehabilitation work has been done and continues to be done. All the same, the scars can be seen everywhere. The banks and the post office are back in normal operation, as is the transport system.

Information
Tourist Offices The national tourist office, Office Rwandais du Tourisme et des Parcs Nationaux (ORTPN; ☎ 76514) BP 905, is on Place de l'Indépendance, around the corner from the post office (PTT). It's open from 8 am to 5 pm Monday to Friday, and Saturday mornings. The office has a few leaflets (in French and English) about the mountain gorillas, but little else. Staff here simply aren't used to dealing with tourists so can seem pretty hopeless; be patient and you should be able to find out what you need to know. Reservations must be made here to see the mountain gorillas in the Parc Nacional des Volcans. You may have trouble if you can't speak French.

The cost for a gorilla visit is US$250 per person, which includes a gorilla permit, the park entry fee as well as two guides and two armed guards per group. See the Parc Nacional des Volcans section later in this chapter for more details.

If you are planning to go to the Parc Nacional de l'Akagera, purchase a map here, as they are not available within the national park. Park entry fees for Akagera can be paid here or at a travel agency. They cannot be paid on arrival at the park.

Money Banks in the capital include: Banque de Kigali; Banque á la Confiance d'Or; Banque National de Rwanda; Banque Populaire Rwandaise; and the Banque de Commerce, de Developement et de l'Industrie. For cash transactions they are best avoided.

For travellers cheques, all banks offer significantly lower rates than for cash on the street. For credit card cash advances, Banque Commerciale de Rwanda and Banque de Kigali are the only options.

Post & Communications The poste restante is quite well organised and staff will let you look through the logbook of letters, so it's unlikely that you'll miss anything sent to you for collection, including parcels. There's a small charge for each letter collected. The post office is open from 8 am to 5 pm Monday to Friday, and Saturday 8 am to 4 pm.

The telephone office is also here and is open the same hours. This is the cheapest place to make telephone calls in the capital. There are also a whole host of telecommunications kiosks near the post office that are open for longer, but charge a little more.

Email & Internet Access Access is pretty thin on the ground in Kigali and the connection is very bad, although there are rumours of a couple of Internet cafes opening up some time. At the time of writing, there are only really two places; Matcom, at the rear of the Ethiopian Airlines building next door to the US embassy, and the business centre at Hôtel des Milles Collines. Access is RFr 2000 for an hour at Matcom, while it is a hefty RFr 1000 for 15 minutes at the hotel business centre. It is sometimes very hard to get a line, and disconnections are regular, so be patient.

Bookshops There are a few bookshops in Kigali, selling mainly French-language publications. The best is probably Librairie Caritas, Ave du Commerce.

Camping Goods The so-called 'disposable' Campingaz cartridges can be bought at the Rwanda Petrolgaz shop below the market, or at the Janmohammed Store, Rue du Travail. As with most things in Rwanda, they're not cheap.

Emergency The police in Kigali can be contacted on ☎ 82459 (day) and ☎ 75117 (night).

The best hospital in Kigali is the South African-operated Netcare King Faycal Hospital (☎ 82421, 83203) in Kacyiru, out near the Hôtel Windsor Umubano. Prices are high but so are standards, so this is the best

place to get treatment. Some of the embassies also have medical attaches who offer services through private practices.

There is an international dentist based in Kigali at Adventist Dental Clinic (☎ 82431) also found out near the Hôtel Windsor Umubano.

Activities

If you're feeling energetic or need a workout, go to the sports centre on Ave du Rugunga where there are facilities for swimming, tennis, golf and horse riding. On weekdays the entrance fee is RFr 500 plus RFr 2000 for the use of any one facility. At the weekend the charge is RFr 1000 entry plus RFr 2000 for the use of any one facility.

Places to Stay

Finding accommodation is not a great problem, but advance telephone reservations are recommended where possible.

Places to Stay – Budget

Mission Hostels The cheapest place is *Hôme d'Accueil Nazareth*, Blvd de l'OUA, behind Église St Famille, which has dorms with 15 bunk beds at RFr 500 per bed. Facilities are primitive – a basic toilet and a tap. It's really only for those on desperation row, as its main function is as a home for the poor and needy.

The *guesthouse* at the Église Épiscopale au Rwanda (☎ 76340, 32 Ave Paul VI) is much better but not very popular, mainly because it's a long way from the city centre (really only an option if you have transport or are prepared to walk 30 minutes from the city centre). The rooms are clean, bright and plentiful, so you should always be able to find accommodation. There are cold showers and a large laundry area. The gate closes at 10 pm and there's no check-in after 9 pm.

Hotels *Kigali Hotel* (☎/fax 71384) tucked behind the mosque on the road to Nyamirambo is by far the best deal in Kigali. Large, clean rooms with TV, telephone and bathroom cost just RFr 5000/7000 for singles/doubles. If you like getting cosy, it is RFr 2500 per extra person.

KIGALI

PLACES TO STAY
1 Okapi Hotel
4 Hôtel Panafrique
12 Hôme d'Accueil Nazareth
18 Auberge d'Accueil
22 Motel Le Garni du Centre
23 Hôtel des Milles Collines
37 Hôtel Gloria
40 Hôtel Isimbi
53 Hôtel Kiyovu
64 Hôtel des Diplomates

PLACES TO EAT
2 Restaurant Pacifique
13 Kingfisher
14 Addis Ethopian Restaurant
17 The Crescendo
21 Aux Caprices du Palais
28 Pilipili; Nile Grill
31 Les Palmares
35 Serena Restaurant
36 Janmohammed Store
38 Eden Garden
42 Le Glaçon
45 L'Oasis
47 La Sierra
48 Beijing Chinese Restaurant
49 Caiman Bar & Restaurant
51 West End Restaurant
52 Le Colibri
63 Jali Club
66 Carpe Diem Restaurant
67 Le Joker Restaurant

OTHER
3 Air Burundi; Rwanda Airlines
5 Alirwanda Supermarket
6 Punctual Taxi
7 Bus Stand
8 Trans Express 2000; Titanic Express
9 Motor Taxi Park
10 Taxi Park
11 Burundi Embassy
15 New Cadillac
16 Carwash
20 Banque de Commerce, de Developement et de l'Industrie
24 Tourist Office (ORTPN)
25 Place de l'Indépendence
26 Post Office
27 PetroRwanda
29 Athenee Supermarket
30 Masjid Medina Mosque
32 Bel Air Bar
33 Rwanda Petrolgaz
34 Market
39 Fotolab
41 Librairie Caritas
43 Banque de Kigali
44 Kenya Airways
46 Banque á la Confiance d'Or; Nord Sud Travel Agency
50 Banque Commerciale de Rwanda
54 Zanzeebar
55 Congo Embassy (temporarily closed)
56 Uganda Airlines
57 US Embassy; USIS
58 Air France
59 Ethiopian Airlines; Matcom Internet
60 Air Rwanda
61 Belgian Embassy
62 Ugandan Embassy
65 French Embassy

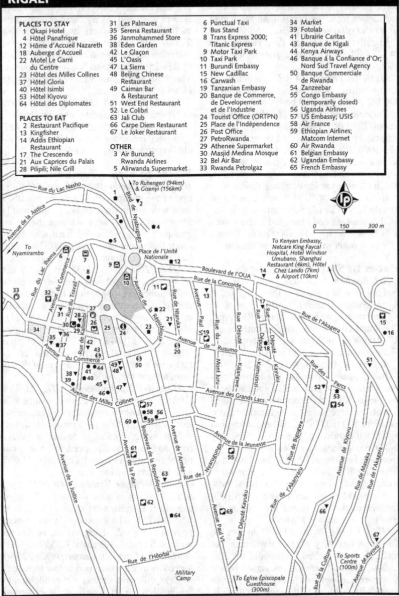

RWANDA

There are a couple of other reasonable hotels on the road to Nyamirambo, but they are further from the centre than the Kigali Hotel and offer less comfort.

The first is *Auberge de Nyamirambo* (☎ 72879) which offers rooms for RFr 5000/6000.

Motel la Vedette (☎ 73575) nearby is pretty similar with rooms going at RFr 4000/6000 with shared bathrooms.

Closer to central Kigali *Hôtel Panafrique* just off Blvd de Nyabugogo has doubles (no singles) with bathroom (cold water only) for RFr 5000. It's OK and the rooms are large but it's seen better days. Upstairs there's a popular bar and restaurant, with a pool table, which offers great views over Kigali.

Hôtel Gloria (☎ 71957) on the corner of Rue du Travail and Ave du Commerce is better. It's pleasant and clean and offers rooms with bathroom for RFr 6000/8000. There's only cold water in the showers at present.

Places to Stay – Mid-Range

Hotel Baobab (☎ 75633, fax 71048) is probably the best value in this range but it is somewhat inconveniently located in Nyamirambo, near the Stade Regional. Clean and comfortable singles/doubles are RFr 10,000/13,000 and are well appointed. There is also an excellent restaurant here.

Auberge d'Accueil (☎ 76779, fax 78919, 2 Rue Député Kayuku) at the Église Presbytérienne au Rwanda is also good value in this range. It's been completely refurbished and offers large rooms with attached bathroom for RFr 10,000/12,000 including hot water in the showers. The staff are friendly and it has a restaurant where you can get breakfast for around RFr 1000 and lunch or dinner for RFr 2000. The auberge is a 15-minute downhill walk from the bus stand.

Other mid-range hotels within striking distance of the city centre are thin on the ground, but there are a couple.

Hôtel Isimbi (☎/fax 75109) on Rue de Kalisimbi has very clean rooms with hot water in the attached bathrooms for RFr 15,000/18,000. There's a restaurant with a good menu, as well as a large bar/TV lounge downstairs, but both of these are pretty dull.

Hôtel Kiyovu (☎ 75106, 6 Ave de Kiyovu) is about the same price. It's in an attractive area of town and is very clean. Rooms with bathrooms (hot water) are RFr 15,000/24,000. The restaurant here offers a good selection of continental dishes for RFr 2000 to RFr 2500, plus there's a bar/TV lounge. The doubles are poor value compared with Hôtel Isimbi.

Hôtel La Mise (☎ 73869) out on the road to Nyamirambo is slightly cheaper than the above centrally located hotels. It has well appointed rooms for RFr 10,000/15,000, including attached hot-water bathroom.

Places to Stay – Top End

Hôtel Chez Lando (☎ 84328, fax 84380) is one of the cheapest in this range but it's a long way out in the Remera suburb and is not an option for those without their own transport. Singles/doubles here with bathroom (hot water) are US$60/90. The hotel has its own restaurant, bar and nightclub.

Okapi Hotel (☎ 76765, fax 74413) not far from the Hôtel Panafrique is a new place and another cheaper option. It has a bewildering variety of rooms and prices, but all are spotlessly clean and include TV, telephone, bathroom and breakfast. Singles range from US$60 to US$85, doubles from US$80 to US$100. There is a good restaurant here with a healthy selection of dishes from around the world.

Hôtel des Diplomates (☎ 75111, 43 Blvd de la Révolution) in the town centre is a large but pleasant hotel with a reasonable restaurant (RFr 3000 for a meal). However, it is showing signs of wear and tear these days and looks in dire need of an international investor. It costs RFr 24,000/31,000 with breakfast included.

Hôtel Windsor Umubano (☎ 82176, fax 82178) is a long way out in the Kacyiru suburb. It is quite a bit more expensive at US$103/113. The hotel has a swimming pool and a good, if expensive, restaurant with buffet meals for about US$17.

Motel Le Garni du Centre (☎/fax 72654) tucked away on a side road below Hôtel des Milles Collines is another recent addition to the hotel scene in Kigali. It is an atmospheric little operation, altogether more European than most of the competition. Attractive rooms with TV, fridge, telephone and bathroom cost RFr 30,000/40,000, including a buffet breakfast. All rooms are built around the swimming pool, which is much less hectic than the big hotel pools.

Hôtel des Milles Collines (☎ 76531, fax 76541) on Ave de la République is at the top end of the range. It has rooms for US$155/165 including breakfast. Facilities include a swimming pool and restaurant (about RFr 5000 for a meal). Use of the hotel swimming pool costs RFr 2000 for nonguests, and is a popular place to relax at weekends.

Places to Eat

Restaurants There are several good places to get a cheap feed in the centre of Kigali.

Les Palmares on Rue du Travail is one of the cheapest. It has kebabs for RFr 150 until 11 pm and cheap Primus beer (RFr 300).

Restaurant Pacifique on Blvd de Nyabugogo offers good African fare for RFr 500 until 9 pm.

Pilipili on Rue de Kalisimbi has a good African buffet lunch at RFr 600 to RFr 1000 and is open from 7.30 am until around 8 pm. Next door and identical in every respect is *Nile Grill*.

Serena Restaurant on Ave du Commerce opposite the market, is another good choice. It offers African dishes for RFr 600 to RFr 800 and is open from 7 am to 4 pm.

Carpe Diem Restaurant on Ave de Kiyovu is further afield. It serves a mixture of African and French dishes. Kebabs are RFr 600 and steaks RFr 1500. The restaurant is open from 9 am to 5 pm daily.

L'Oasis on Ave de la Paix probably can't be beaten for snacks. It has good pies for RFr 300 as well as ice cream and fruit juices. It's open between 7.30 am and 9 pm.

Le Glaçon on Rue de Kalisimbi is similar. It is basically an ice-cream parlour but also offers snacks and milkshakes and is open from 8 am to 8 pm.

One of the best value restaurants is at *Hotel Baobab* a long way out of town in Nyamirambo. It offers a great selection of dishes, most at around RFr 2000, including steaks, fish and some pretty good pizzas.

A similar selection of French/Italian dishes, including steaks, chicken and spaghetti, can be found at *Hôtel Panafrique* on Blvd de Nyabugogo for about RFr 3000. However, the food seems relatively expensive these days as the place feels more like a youth club than a restaurant.

West End Restaurant is the place to go on Rue de l'Akagera for a very good African buffet as well as some continental dishes priced between RFr 1200 and RFr 2500. It is open between noon and 10 pm.

Eden Garden on Rue de Kalisimbi has been a great place to eat for many years with its bamboo decor and informal ambience. It's open from 7 am to 10 pm daily and offers very good French steaks, chicken and tilapia with chips and salad for an average price of about RFr 2000.

On Blvd de la Révolution *Caiman* is Kigali's answer to fastfood, with a bar and restaurant offering sandwiches for RFr 500, and burgers, pizzas and pastas for about RFr 1500 to RFr 2000. It is popular with the work crowd as it is bang in the middle of things.

The Crescendo on Rue Député Kayaku has a standard European menu with salads for about RFr 1000, and steaks for RFr 2500 but is quite popular with locals during the day.

Jali Club a small garden restaurant in the grounds of a villa is down in the heart of the diplomatic quarter. The ambience is pleasant and it offers three-course set meals for RFr 3000 (lunch) and RFr 4000 for dinner.

Top of the line in terms of French cuisine are: *Kingfisher* on Rue du Mont Juru which has dishes for RFr 4000 and is open from 11 am to 2 pm and 5 to 11 pm daily except Tuesday; and *Aux Caprices du Palais* on Rue de Ntaruka which is excellent but considerably more expensive – US$30 to US$40 per person without wine. It is open from noon to 2 pm and 6 to 10 pm daily except Monday.

Le Colibri opposite Hôtel Kiyovu is the place to go to try some good Italian food. It has a range of authentic pizzas, some well dressed salads and some tasty ice cream to wind things up.

RWANDA

Hellenique is the place to go for Greek food, but be warned: it's quite a way from the centre, will cost you a minimum of RFr 4000 and the portions are small.

Addis Ethiopian Restaurant on Blvd de l'OUA is an excellent choice for something different. It serves excellent goat and chicken dishes along with wat and injera for RFr 1500 to RFr 2000. It's open from 10 am to 10 pm and also has a pleasant terrace bar.

La Sierra is one of the best Indian restaurants but it has a limited menu. It offers a buffet lunch for RFr 3000 and dinner for RFr 3500. It's open from noon to 2 pm and 7 to 9.30 pm daily except Sunday. It's a popular place to eat and also for afternoon drinks.

Beijing Chinese Restaurant on Blvd de la Révolution isn't too bad but it's expensive and the quality doesn't really justify its prices – RFr 3000 plus rice. It's open from noon to 3 pm and 6 to 11 pm daily.

Shanghai Restaurant is a better Chinese place but it is a long way out from the centre towards Hôtel Windsor Umubano. It has a reasonable selection of dishes for RFr 3000, but portions are pretty healthy.

Le Joker is in a similar bracket but it's quite a distance from the centre at the junction of Rue de l'Akagera and Ave de Kiyovu. It serves oriental dishes as well as steaks for about RFr 3000. It's open from noon to 3 pm and 6 to 11 pm daily except Tuesday.

Self-Catering Travellers who want to self-cater or who are planning a safari will find most of the things they'll need at *Alirwanda Supermarket*, Ave du Commerce, close to the bus stand. Another good supermarket is *Athenee* just west of the main post office on Rue de Kalisimbi.

Entertainment

Bars Apart from all the nightclubs, which many people frequent as bars as opposed to dance venues, there's *Nile Grill* on Rue de Kalisimbi next to the Pilipili Restaurant. This has a popular terrace bar where people congregate for a drink and to people-watch.

The beers are cheap costing around RFr 350 each.

Bel Air Bar is a popular local bar on Rue de Commerce with some great views over the centre of town. Beers are cheap and there is an inexpensive buffet. However, watch the stairs carefully on the way home if you have had your fair share of Primus beer, they are really steep!

The *restaurant* at Hôtel Baobab is a great place to go for a beer if you want a bit of privacy or you are catching up with people you haven't seen for a while.

Le Piano at Hôtel Windsor Umubano is another popular bar. It attracts a large expat crowd at weekends.

The *swimming pool* at Hôtel des Milles Collines ends up serving as the city's most popular daytime bar at weekends, as half the expats in the city are relaxing in the gardens.

Zanzeebar near Hôtel Kiyovu is the most popular late-night haunt in town. It gets going some time after 10 pm and stays open late. It is a cool place to sink the drinks that will eventually and inevitably carry you on to a nightclub. Drinks are expensive, but you pay for the atmosphere as much as anything.

Nightclubs *New Cadillac* not far from the centre of Kigali in the Kimikurure district is the most popular nightclub in town. It is a large, partly open-air venue that plays a mixture of high-life, *soukous* (Congalese [Zaïrean] Lingala music) and western tunes most nights from 5 pm. There's a cover charge of RFr 1500 on Friday and Saturday nights, and the beer is quite expensive (RFr 1000 for Primus) but it is cold. It doesn't really pick up until after midnight, but once it does, it really rocks. Concerts are often held here to promote local Rwandan talent.

Carwash not far from New Cadillac is both a bar and, rather bizarrely, a carwash. Rwandans drop their cars off for a clean and give their throat a bit of a clean out with Primus. It is a lot cheaper to drink here than in New Cadillac, so many people stop off at Carwash to wet their whistle on the way to the nightclub.

Maxim's is a new nightclub at Hôtel Windsor Umubano. This is a worthwhile stop when New Cadillac thins out. It is quite a sight for Kigali and easily the equal of hotel nightclubs in the west. Drinks are expensive and it closes about 5 am.

Getting There & Away
Air Airline offices in Kigali include Air Burundi (☎ 77103), Air France (☎ 75566, fax 74452), Air Tanzania (☎ 73079, fax 72231), Cameroon Airlines (☎ 75492, fax 78135), Ethiopian Airlines (☎ 75045), Kenya Airways (☎ 77972, fax 76426), Rwanda Airlines (☎ 77103, fax 77669), SA Alliance Express (☎ 77777, fax 74452), Sabena (☎ 75290, fax 73082) and Uganda Airlines (☎ 78332, fax 73031). See the Getting There & Away and Getting Around sections earlier in this chapter for information on services to/from Kigali.

Bus Minibuses run from the main bus stand to towns all over Rwanda, including Butare (RFr 800, two hours), Cyangugu (RFr 1500, five hours), Gitarama (RFr 500, one hour), Katuna (RFr 1000, two hours), Kibuye (RFr 800), Ruhengeri (RFr 600, two hours), Rusumu (RFr 1000, three hours) and Gisenyi (RFr 1000, four hours). These minibuses leave daily, all day, when full, except at weekends when they tend to dry up between 2 and 3 pm. All you have to do is turn up and tell someone where you're going. See the respective town entries for further details.

Punctual Taxi and Trans Express 2000 run buses between Kigali and Butare (see Getting There & Away in the Butare section later in this chapter for details).

Getting Around
To/From the Airport The Gregoire Kayibanda international airport is at Kanombe, 12km from the city centre. A taxi costs about RFr 3000, but you can get there more cheaply by taking a direct minibus from the bus stand (RFr 100).

Taxi A taxi fare within the city centre costs, on average, RFr 1000 to RFr 1500, more if you're going out to the suburbs.

Western Rwanda

CYANGUGU
At the southern end of Lake Kivu and close to Bukavu in Congo (Zaïre), Cyangugu is an attractively positioned town on the lakeshore. Kamembe, a few kilometres from the border, is the main town and transport centre and an important location for the processing of tea and cotton. Nearby is the Nyungwe Forest, home for elephant, buffalo, leopard, chimpanzee and many other mammals and birds.

The **waterfalls** of the Rusizi River and the **hot springs** of Nyakabuye are near here.

WARNING

! There are certain parts of Lake Kivu where it is very dangerous to swim, as volcanic gases are released continuously from the lake bed and, in the absence of wind, tend to collect on the surface of the lake. Quite a few people have been asphyxiated as a result. Make inquiries or watch where the local people swim and you'll probably be safe.

Places to Stay & Eat
Hôme St François at the border is convenient if you're heading to or coming from Congo (Zaïre). It's friendly, spotlessly clean and offers reasonably priced singles (RFr 1400 and RFr 2000), doubles (RFr 2300 and RFr 3450) and triples (RFr 3450). The only problem is that couples may be separated. The meals are excellent and very good value.

Mission Pentecoste with great views over the lake is similar.

Muli Peace Guesthouse on the hill between the airport and port is another religious guesthouse, but somewhat more expensive. Clean singles/doubles are RFr 3000/5000. The shared bathrooms are clean, plentiful and have hot water. There are pretty impressive views from here across the lake to Bukavu.

There are a couple of hotels in Cyangugu that offer a little more comfort. Cheapest is *Hotel Kivu* (☎ 61414) right next to the border. Double rooms cost RFr 5000 with bathroom and balcony, while there are also a couple of larger double rooms with a bath that cost RFr 7000.

Hotel des Chutes is the smartest place in town and offers rooms for RFr 8000 and RFr 10,000. The cheaper rooms have attached bathroom with hot water, while the more expensive ones have balconies with views and satellite TV. Located above the port, there are great views across the lake. There is also a very good restaurant here with a range of European cuisine available for RFr 2000 and up.

Black & White and *La Jeunesse* around the market in Kamembe both offer good Rwandan food for RFr 300 to RFr 600.

Restaurant La Saveur in Kamembe is more expensive and service here is very slow.

Getting There & Away
Bus Minibuses between Cyangugu and Kamembe cost RFr 100. From Kamembe to Butare minibuses cost RFr 1200 and take about three hours. This road is incredibly spectacular in parts and passes through the superb Nyungwe rainforest, where you are likely to see troupes of monkeys playing by the side of the road. You can also get direct minibuses to Kigali for RFr 1500.

Boat Passenger ferry services connecting Cyangugu with Kibuye and Gisenyi across Lake Kivu are currently suspended. However, you may be able to persuade a cargo barge to take you up the lake, but be warned: they are slow and leave very early. There is also a speedboat available for charter. See the Kibuye and Gisenyi sections for more details.

KIBUYE
A small town about halfway along Lake Kivu, Kibuye has an excellent beach and water sports facilities. It's a pleasant place to relax for a few days. If coming here by road from Gisenyi, try not to miss **Les Chutes de Ndaba**, a waterfall at Ndaba. It's more than 100m high.

Places to Stay
The missions that used to offer budget accommodation here were destroyed during the civil war. That leaves *Guest House Kibuye* (☎ 68554, 083-00954) on the lakeshore as the only place to stay. It's relatively expensive (RFr 5900/8000 for singles/doubles), but you can camp in the grounds cheaply. The guesthouse has a good outdoor bar, with cold beers at the usual price, and a diving board that anyone can use.

Places to Eat
Restaurant Nouveauté and *Restaurant Moderne* are both cheap places at the eastern edge of town. They have the same menu (goat stew, beans, rice, potatoes, omelettes) and you can eat well for RFr 500 to RFr 800. They also offer cold beers and soft drinks.

Getting There & Away
From Kigali, the road is partly sealed and minibuses cost RFr 800. Getting between Kibuye and either Cyangugu or Gisenyi is pretty difficult without your own vehicle as share-taxis and buses are very infrequent. Friday is generally the best day for getting in and out, but otherwise you are looking at chartering a vehicle and that will be expensive.

Contact the guesthouse in Kibuye to charter a speedboat north to Gisenyi or south to Cyangugu. Expect to pay about US$100 for the boat in either direction.

GISENYI
Gisenyi is a resort town for rich Rwandans and expatriate workers. Their beautifully landscaped villas, plush hotels and clubs take up virtually all the Lake Kivu frontage and are quite a contrast to the African township on the hillside above.

For those with the money, there's a wide variety of water sports available, plus nightclubs and restaurants. For those without, there are magnificent views over Lake Kivu and, looking north-west, the 3470m-high volcano of Nyiragongo. Swimming and sunbathing on the sandy beach are also free. It's a pleasant town to stay in but is, as you might expect, expensive, especially if you want some action.

Information

Visas & Embassies There is no Congo (Zaïre) consulate here, but you can get a visa on the border if crossing to Goma (inadvisable at the time of writing, due to the intractable civil war).

Money Banque Commerciale de Rwanda is near the market and Banque de Kigali is near the Hôtel Izuba-Méridien.

Things to See & Do

Gisenyi is home to the **Primus Brewery**, the factory responsible for churning out all those huge bottles of lager found all over Rwanda. It is possible to arrange a tour of the brewery, located about 7km out of town along a lovely lakeshore road. The tour is free and may include free beer, but keep your cameras well out of sight, as they are very sensitive about photographs.

Places to Stay – Budget

Most travellers used to stay at the Mission Presbytérienne's *Centre d'Accueil* (☎ 40522) about 100m from the market and bus stand and after being trashed during the civil war, it is now fully operational again. Dorm beds are RFr 500, including hot-water showers. Rooms are expensive at RFr 4000, but are clean and include a bathroom. There is an inexpensive restaurant here offering breakfast for RFr 400. There is also a little craft shop selling handmade cards and toys to raise money for local womens' groups.

Another religion, another option, is found at *Centre d'Acceuil St Francois Xavier* between the market and lakefront. Dorm beds here, which turn into giant tacos as the springs are like trampolines, are RFr 800 and there is no hot water. There are fewer beds to a room than at the Mission Presbytérienne.

There are a couple of other cheap options near the bus station.

Umoja House of Gisenyi is hardly inspiring, but offers cheap rooms with shower inside, toilet outside, for RFr 2000.

L'Auberge de Gisenyi had recently been gutted by fire at the time of writing, but may well have re-opened by now and has reasonable rooms.

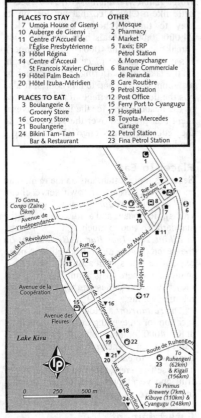

GISENYI

PLACES TO STAY	OTHER
7 Umoja House of Gisenyi	1 Mosque
10 Auberge de Gisenyi	2 Pharmacy
11 Centre d'Accueil de	4 Market
l'Église Presbytérienne	5 Taxis; ERP
13 Hôtel Régina	Petrol Station
14 Centre d'Acceuil	& Moneychanger
St Francois Xavier; Church	6 Banque Commerciale
19 Hôtel Palm Beach	de Rwanda
20 Hôtel Izuba-Méridien	8 Gare Routière
	9 Petrol Station
PLACES TO EAT	12 Post Office
3 Boulangerie &	15 Ferry Port to Cyangugu
Grocery Store	17 Hospital
16 Grocery Store	18 Toyota-Mercedes
21 Boulangerie	Garage
24 Bikini Tam-Tam	22 Petrol Station
Bar & Restaurant	23 Fina Petrol Station

Places to Stay – Mid-Range

Hôtel Palm Beach and *Hôtel Régina* (☎ 085-02226) the two leading mid-range hotels in Gisenyi are both on Ave de la Coopération, the palm-shaded lakeshore drive. The Régina is a pleasant colonial-era building complete with attractive gardens. It has single rooms with shared bathroom for RFr 4600, or with bathroom for RFr 6900 and doubles for RFr 9200. The Hôtel Palm Beach is a newer establishment and charges RFr 6500/10,000 for a single/double with bathroom (there's hot water in the showers).

Places to Stay – Top End

Hôtel Izuba-Méridien (☎ *61319*) feels a little like a Club Med that got lost on its way to the Seychelles and costs RFr 24,000/30,000. Meals here are RFr 2000 (breakfast) and RFr 4000 (lunch or dinner). It's a very pleasant place to stay and right on the lakeshore, offering facilities such as a swimming pool and tennis courts. It also has the dubious privilege of having served as the headquarters for the interim government that presided over the genocide – so they could flee into Congo when things got too hot.

Places to Eat

Several simple restaurants on the main road in the African part of town serve cheap meals (usually *matoke* (mashed green bananas), rice, beans and a little meat), but the standard isn't up to much.

Bikini Tam-Tam Bar & Restaurant on the beach on Ave de la Production is more expensive but still reasonably priced. A main course here costs about RFr 1000 and they have some tables on the sand for a romantic evening.

The *restaurant* at Hôtel Régina is a nice location for an evening meal, but not cheap at RFr 4000 for three courses. It's still worth calling in for a cheap Primus, even if you don't want to eat here.

For self-caterers, there's a wide variety of fruit and vegetables available at the main market.

Entertainment

Hôtel Palm Beach's bar is very popular with locals most nights and has a pool table and reasonable music.

Bikini Tam-Tam Bar & Restaurant is the only other place you'll find any action at present. It draws a small crowd weekdays, and holds the town's only disco on Saturday. Perhaps it will one day be the location for Rwanda's first full moon party, as it certainly has the setting.

Getting There & Away

Air Rwanda Airlines offers flights to Gisenyi from Kigali for US$80/160 one way/return. This is also the way to get to Goma in Congo (Zaïre) from Kigali by air.

Bus A bus from Ruhengeri to Gisenyi takes about two hours (RFr 500). It's a beautiful journey through upland forest and villages and there are panoramic views of Lake Kivu as you descend into Gisenyi.

Minibuses between Kigali and Gisenyi take about four hours and cost RFr 1000. There is only infrequent public transport between Gisenyi and Kibuye. To cross the border into Congo (Zaïre) – see the Getting There & Away section earlier in this chapter.

Boat All passenger ferries across Lake Kivu to other Rwandan ports are currently suspended. However, there are irregular cargo boats plying the lake and there are always beer-laden boats departing the Primus factory, 7km out of town. It might be worth making inquiries a few days in advance.

There is also a speedboat available for charters to Kibuye and Cyangugu. Telephone ☎ 083-00954 a day or two in advance and expect to pay about US$150 for the boat.

RUHENGERI

Most travellers come to Ruhengeri on their way to the Parc Nacional des Volcans, which is where the Rwandan mountain gorillas live.

It's a small town with two army barracks, a very busy hospital and some magnificent views of the volcanoes to the north and west – Karisimbi, Visoke, Mikeno, Muside, Sabinyo, Gahinga and Muhabura.

Forget any ideas you may have about climbing the hill (Nyamagumba) near the post office, as it's a military area and access is prohibited.

Information

There are two banks in Ruhengeri, Banque Commerciale de Rwanda near the market and Banque de Kigali, near Hôtel Muhabura. As usual, you are best off steering clear of Banque de Kigali's exorbitant commissions.

The post office is back in its prewar location. It's open Monday to Friday from 8 am to noon and 2 to 4 pm. The telephone ex-

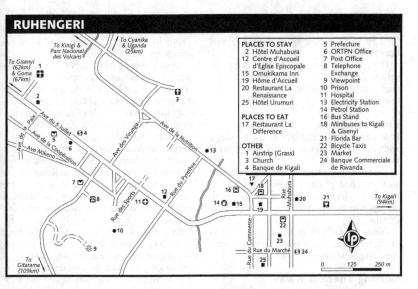

RUHENGERI

PLACES TO STAY
2 Hôtel Muhabura
12 Centre d'Accueil
d'Eglise Episcopale
15 Omukikama Inn
19 Hôme d'Accueil
20 Restaurant La
Renaissance
25 Hôtel Urumuri

PLACES TO EAT
17 Restaurant La
Difference

OTHER
1 Airstrip (Grass)
3 Church
4 Banque de Kigali
5 Prefecture
6 ORTPN Office
7 Post Office
8 Telephone
Exchange
9 Viewpoint
10 Prison
11 Hospital
13 Electricity Station
14 Petrol Station
16 Bus Stand
18 Minibuses to Kigali
& Gisenyi
21 Florida Bar
22 Bicycle Taxis
23 Market
24 Banque Commerciale
de Rwanda

change is in the building opposite the post office. Rates are the same as those in Kigali.

For details about visiting the mountain gorillas, see the Parc Nacional des Volcans section following.

Places to Stay

Centre d'Accueil d'Eglise Episcopale is on the north-west corner of Rue du Pyrethre and Ave du 5 Juillet. It's clean and has dorm beds for RFr 1000 (six bunk beds in two rooms) and singles/doubles for RFr 1500/3000. The communal showers have hot water and the toilets are clean. There's a restaurant with meals for RFr 1500 but you need to order food in advance.

There are no-nonsense *rooms* with shared bathroom at Restaurant La Renaissance, Rue Muhabura, for RFr 2000.

Hôme d'Accueil, Ave du 5 Juillet, in the town centre, has eight small rooms and charges RFr 3000/3500 with your own bathroom, although there's no hot water. Other than that, it's OK.

Omukikama Inn near the minibus park on Ave du 5 Juillet is another similar place. It has singles with shared bathroom for RFr 2000 and doubles with attached bathroom for RFr 4000. It's clean and secure but has only cold water in the showers.

Hôtel Urumuri (☎ 46704) down a small side street off Rue du Marché is a move up in comfort but hardly in price. It is very clean and pleasant and offers rooms with bathroom (hot water) for RFr 3500/4000.

Hôtel Muhabura (☎ 71511) near the ORTPN office is Ruhengeri's best hotel. It offers large, clean, airy rooms with bathroom and hot water for RFr 4950/7150. Only one blanket is provided so you may need a sleeping bag in the winter months.

Places to Eat

Restaurant La Difference on Ave de la Nutrition (a suitable location!) is the cheapest of the African eateries.

Restaurant La Renaissance (see under Places to Stay) is another cheap place. It has great kebabs and steak and is open from noon to 10 pm. Brochettes are just RFr 100 and Primus beer is an unbeatable RFr 250.

Near the market, *Hôtel Urumuri* has an outdoor area where you can get good meals of chicken or spaghetti (RFr 500 to RFr 800) from 7 am until evening – if they don't run out. It also has very cold beers.

RWANDA

Hôtel Muhabura's food is also reasonable value – two large brochettes with chips for RFr 800 – plus they have cold Primus beer for RFr 300.

If you are putting your own meal together, there's a good variety of meat, fish, fruit and vegetables at the market in the town centre.

Entertainment

Ruhengeri is a quiet place in the evenings and you won't find much open after around 10 pm.

Restaurant La Renaissance and *Florida Bar* are good places to go if you want to meet some local people after dinner. Both are open until 9 or 10 pm and have cheap Primus.

Hôtel Muhabura is the place to go to meet international movers and shakers spending their large allowances.

Getting There & Away

From Kigali, minibuses take about two hours and cost RFr 600. The road ascends and descends magnificently over the intensively cultivated mountains. From Cyanika, on the Rwanda-Uganda border, minibuses to Ruhengeri cost RFr 300. From Gisenyi, on the Rwanda-Congo (Zaïre) border, they cost RFr 500 for the two hour trip.

Getting Around

There are no taxis in Ruhengeri but there are *boda-bodas* (bicycle-taxis) if you don't want to walk. A typical fare from the bus stand to the Hôtel Muhabura is RFr 100. Motorcycle taxis are also available but they are pretty optimistic with their prices.

Bicycles are for hire near the market, but at RFr 800 per day, they're not that cheap.

PARC NACIONAL DES VOLCANS

This area along the border with Congo (Zaïre) and Uganda has to be one of the most beautiful sights in Africa. There is a chain of no less than seven volcanoes, one of them (Karisimbi) more than 4500m high.

But it's not just the mountains that attract travellers. On the bamboo and rainforest-covered slopes is one of the last remaining sanctuaries of the mountain gorilla *(Gorilla beringei)*. These animals were studied in depth by George Schaller and, more recently, by Dian Fossey.

Fossey spent the best part of 13 years living at a remote camp high up on the slopes of Visoke in order to study the gorillas and to habituate them to human contact. She'd probably still be there now had she not been murdered in December 1985, most likely by poachers with whom she had made herself very unpopular. Without her tenacious efforts to have poaching stamped out, there possibly wouldn't be any gorillas left in Rwanda.

Fossey's account of her years with the gorillas and her battle with the poachers and government officials, *Gorillas in the Mist*, makes fascinating reading. Pick up a copy before coming here. Her story has also been made into a film of the same name, and following its success, the tourism industry in the country boomed for a while, until fighting between the government and the RPF put the area out of bounds to tourists. Things have been on and off since then, but at the time of writing it was safe to visit.

It remains to be seen what will happen to the four known groups of gorillas that survive but, during the early part of the latest civil war, these mountains were the focus of intense fighting that included artillery duels. This was hardly conducive to good gorilla-human relationships and it was reported that at least seven of the gorillas had met their end – probably by the hands of soldiers greedy for 'trophies'.

It isn't just poaching or soldiers, however, that threaten the gorillas. Also clawing away at their existence is local pressure for grazing and agricultural land, and the European Community's pyrethrum project – daisy-like flowers processed into a natural insecticide. This project was responsible in 1969 for reducing the size of the park by more than 8900 hectares – almost half its area! The park now covers only 0.5% of the total land area of Rwanda.

The park only re-opened to visitors in July 1999, after being forced to close for two years due to the presence of armed and dangerous Interahamwe rebels in the area.

PARC NACIONAL DES VOLCANS

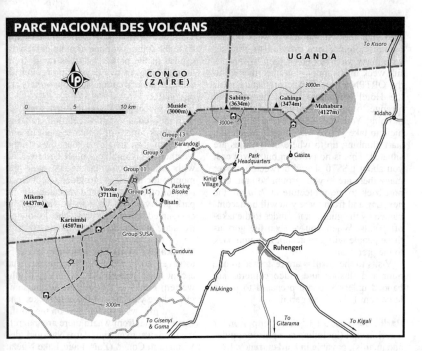

This means booking procedures and logistics are still slowly being ironed out and may be subject to change. Find out what you can in Kampala before heading south.

Visiting the Gorillas

As with visiting the gorillas in Uganda and Congo (Zaïre), many travellers rate a visit to these beautiful creatures as one of the highlights of their trip to Africa. It isn't, however, a joy ride. The guides can generally find the gorillas within one to four hours of starting out, but this often involves a lot of strenuous effort scrambling through dense vegetation up steep, muddy hillsides, sometimes to more than 3000m. It also rains a lot in this area. If you don't have the right footwear and clothing, you're in for a hard time.

An encounter with a silverback male gorilla at close quarters can also be a hair-raising experience if you've only ever seen large wild animals in the safety of a zoo. Despite their size, however, they're remarkably nonaggressive animals, entirely vegetarian, and are usually quite safe to be around. For most people, it's a magical encounter.

There are four gorilla groups you can visit, including the Susa group, which has 35 members. Numbers of people allowed to visit either of the groups varies, but is no more than eight people at any one time, and may be just six.

Reservations To see any group, you must make advance reservations at the tourist office in Kigali, Office Rwandais du Tourisme et des Parcs Nationaux (ORTPN; ☎ 070-76514) Place de l'Indepéndance, BP 905. These used to be hard to get in the days before the genocide but there's no longer any pressure so you're virtually guaranteed a booking on any day you name. However, if you don't have a booking, you can also just turn up in Ruhengeri and pay in cash at the ORTPN the day before you want to trek. Children under 15 cannot visit the gorillas.

RWANDA

Having made a booking in Kigali and paid your fees (supposedly a week before, but this might prove difficult to enforce, with many visitors not wanting to spend a full week in Rwanda), you must then go to the ORTPN office (in the prefecture, near the Hôtel Muhabura) in Ruhengeri and arrange to see the gorillas the following morning. You will also have to arrange a vehicle to take you to the point at which you start climbing up to where the gorillas are situated. This is no problem but it will cost you about US$70 shared between however many there are in your group. You must report back to the prefecture at 7.30 am the next day and from there you will be accompanied by the guards and guides to the take-off points. When you've seen the gorillas these people will also accompany you back to the prefecture.

Visits to the gorillas are restricted to one hour and flashes and video cameras are banned unless you are prepared to pay a large sum for a video permit!

Park Fees Fees are US$250 per person for a gorilla visit (including compulsory guides and guards), payable in hard currency. Resident foreigners can pay the equivalent in local currency. Porters are also available but you pay extra for this service. The guides, guards and any porters will expect a tip (between US$2 and US$5 each depending on the quality of the service) at the end.

WARNING

! Other than to visit the gorillas, climbing the volcanoes is prohibited at present. There are good reasons for this, the main two being the inability of the government to guarantee your safety from armed rebels and the very real possibility of stepping on a land mine. The government is justifiably concerned about the adverse publicity that a maimed or dead tourist would attract in the western media.

Some day, the mines will be cleared and you'll be allowed to climb the mountains again so, just in case this becomes possible, we're including a description of the possible climbs.

Trekking the Volcanoes

There are several possibilities for trekking up to the summits of one or more of the volcanoes in the park. The treks range from several hours to two days or more. For all these, a guide is compulsory but porters are optional.

The ascents take you through some remarkable changes of vegetation, ranging from thick forests of bamboo, giant lobelia or hagenia on to alpine meadows. If the weather is favourable, you'll be rewarded with some spectacular views over the mountain chain. It is forbidden to cut down trees or otherwise damage vegetation in the park and you can only make fires in the designated camping areas. The following treks are among the more popular:

Visoke (3711m) The return trip takes six to seven hours from Parking Bisoke. The ascent takes you up the very steep southwestern flanks of the volcano to the summit, where you can see the crater lake. The descent follows a rough track on the northwestern side, from where there are magnificent views over the Parc National des Virunga in Congo (Zaïre) and Lake Ngezi.

Lake Ngezi (about 3000m) The return trip takes three to four hours from Parking Bisoke. This is one of the easiest of the treks, and if you get there at the right time of the day, you may see a variety of animals coming to drink.

Karisimbi (4507m) The return trip takes two days. The track follows the saddle between Visoke and Karisimbi and then ascends the north-western flank of the latter. Some five hours after beginning the trek, you arrive at a metal hut, which is where you stay for the night (the hut keys are available at Parking Bisoke). The rocky and sometimes snow-covered summit is a further two to four hours walk through alpine vegetation. You descend the mountain the following day. To do this trek, you need plenty of warm clothing and a very good sleeping bag. It gets very cold, especially at the metal hut, which is on a bleak shoulder of the mountain at about 3660m.

The wind whips through, frequently with fog, so you don't get much warmth from the sun.

Sabinyo (3634m) The return trip takes five to six hours from the park headquarters at Kinigi. The track ascends the south-eastern face of the volcano, ending up with a rough scramble over steep lava beds along a very narrow path. There's a metal hut just before the start of the lava beds.

Gahinga (3474m) & Muhabura (4127m) The return trip takes two days from Gasiza. The summit of the first volcano is reached after a climb of about four hours along a track that passes through a swampy saddle between the two mountains. There is a metal hut here, which offers a modicum of shelter, but it's in a bad state of repair. The trip to the summit of Muhabura takes about four hours from the saddle.

Getting There & Away
The access point for the national park is Ruhengeri. Minibuses between Kigali and Ruhengeri take about two hours and cost RFr 600.

Southern Rwanda

BUTARE
☎ 032
Butare is the intellectual centre of Rwanda, and it's here that you'll find the National University, the National Institute of Scientific Research and the excellent National Museum.

In the surrounding area are several craft centres, such as **Gihindamuyaga** (10km) and **Gishamvu** (12km). If you're thinking of buying anything at these places, look first at the quality and prices of what's for sale at the National Museum shop and the handicrafts shop opposite Hotel Ibis.

Those interested in trees should visit the **Arboretum de Ruhande**.

Information
There are branches of Banque Commerciale de Rwanda, Banque de Commerce, de De-velopment et de l'Industrie and Banque de Kigali. For foreign exchange purposes, you are best off dealing with Banque Commerciale de Rwanda.

The post office has postal services, but no telephones. For domestic and international calls try the shops opposite Hotel Ibis.

National Museum
This huge museum was opened in 1989 and is probably the best museum in East Africa. It's certainly the most amazing building in the country. A gift from Belgium to commemorate 25 years of independence, it's well worth a visit for its ethnological and archaeological displays. The museum is open from 2.30 to 4.30 pm Monday, from 9 to 11.30 am and 2.30 to 4.30 pm Tuesday to Friday, from 2 to 5 pm Saturday, and from 9 am to noon and 2 to 5 pm Sunday. Entry is RFr 300, or RFr 200 if you have a student card. It's about 2km north of the centre, past the minibus stand. It is probably best to take a boda-boda for RFr 100 or hitch a pick-up.

Traditional Dance
There is a traditional Rwandan dance troupe based in Butare and the show is spectacular. The dance originated in neighbouring Burundi and is done in full costume, to the accompanying rhythm of drums. Performances can be organised through the National Museum and cost RFr 10,000 for up to five people and then rises by RFr 2000 for every additional five people. This is pretty good value if you are in a group as you can also take photographs, although video is not allowed. At weekends, prices rise by 25% and for an evening performance you are charged 50% more.

In practice, you can turn up and arrange a performance within 45 minutes, but in reality you are better off telephoning ahead and confirming the dancers are in town. Phone ☎ 32136 to make a booking.

Places to Stay – Budget
Procure d'Acceuil is a very attractive building surrounded by flower gardens. Clean singles/doubles with shared bathroom are RFr 2500/4000.

RWANDA

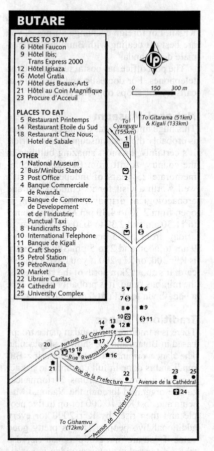

BUTARE

PLACES TO STAY
6   Hôtel Faucon
9   Hôtel Ibis;
    Trans Express 2000
12 Hôtel Igisaza
16 Motel Gratia
17 Hôtel des Beaux-Arts
21 Hôtel au Coin Magnifique
23 Procure d'Acceuil

PLACES TO EAT
5   Restaurant Printemps
14 Restaurant Etoile du Sud
18 Restaurant Chez Nous;
    Hotel de Sabale

OTHER
1   National Museum
2   Bus/Minibus Stand
3   Post Office
4   Banque Commerciale
    de Rwanda
7   Banque de Commerce,
    de Developement
    et de l'Industrie;
    Punctual Taxi
8   Handicrafts Shop
10 International Telephone
11 Banque de Kigali
13 Craft Shops
19 Petrol Station
19 PetroRwanda
20 Market
22 Libraire Caritas
24 Cathedral
25 University Complex

0   150   300 m

To Cyangugu (155km)
To Gitarama (51km) & Kigali (133km)

Avenue du Commerce
Rue Rwamamba
Rue de la Prefecture
Avenue de la Cathédral
Avenue de l'Université

To Gishamvu (12km)

Hôtel de Sabale tucked away behind Restaurant Chez Nous is the other cheap place to stay. It is RFr 2500 for one or two people and facilities are shared. It is not the cleanest of places but at least staff are friendly.

Places to Stay – Mid-Range
Motel Gratia (☎ 30278) on Rue Rwamamba is a cosy little place to stay. It offers singles/doubles set around a small garden costing RFr 4000/4500. Rooms are clean and furnished and hot water is available on request.

Hôtel au Coin Magnifique near the market seems a little overpriced with rooms for RFr 3000/5000.

Hôtel Igisaza is similar, but rooms are RFr 3500, including a large bathroom.

Hôtel des Beaux-Arts (☎ 30584) about 300m on the left (south side) of Ave du Commerce just past Rue Rwamamba is the only other place in this category. Single rooms cost RFr 5000, while doubles cost RFr 7000 to RFr 8000. All rooms include hot-water bathrooms. The hotel is attractively laid out with local products and there is a handicrafts shop where you can purchase what you see on the walls.

Places to Stay – Top End
There are two contending operations for title of top hotel in town.

Hôtel Ibis (☎/fax 32160) charges RFr 12,650/14,400 for singles/doubles with bathroom, including breakfast. The staff are very friendly and helpful here. It also has a good terrace bar that serves drinks and snacks.

Hôtel Faucon (☎ 32061) nearby, provides the competition with big rooms costing RFr 11,500/15,000. Rooms come with a bathroom, satellite TV and seating area, and breakfast is included. There is not much to choose between them really, but the TV could swing it for some.

Places to Eat
Restaurant Chez Nous near the market has good local food, with a RFr 500 buffet.

Restaurant Etoile du Sud also offers a menu of local fare, and has a nice balcony overlooking the bustling road below.

Restaurant Printemps next to the Punctual Taxi office is more sophisticated. It has a daily buffet for about RFr 1000 and up depending on what meats and fish you opt for.

More expensive are the restaurants at the hotels in town, but the menus include a great deal more variety.

Motel Gratia has the best-value tucker, with a set meal for RFr 1000 each night and cheap breakfasts.

Hotel Ibis's food is good with a selection of meats and fish for about RFr 2000 and an excellent *salade composée* for RFr 800.

RWANDA

The best food in town is at *Hôtel Faucon* which has a large menu of European dishes African specialities and pizzas for about RFr 3000. It also has a set menu for RFr 3000 and some tasty looking desserts for RFr 1000 and up.

Entertainment

For a university town, there is surprisingly little going on in Butare. Most drinkers tend to gather at the *bars* of the posh hotels in town, and there is even a weekend *nightclub* at Hotel Faucon.

Getting There & Away

Bus There are two bus companies operating between Butare and Kigali: Punctual Taxi (Kigali ☎ 070-77768) and Trans Express 2000 (Butare ☎ 32160, Kigali ☎ 070-78486). Punctual Taxi departs at 7 and 10 am, 1 and 4 pm and Trans Express 2000 leave at 15 minutes past the same hours. Both companies charge RFr 1000 and it is wise to book a day in advance. Punctual Taxi has bigger buses.

Minibus The bus stand is just a patch of dirt about 1km north of the town centre, by the stadium. Arriving minibuses often drop you in the centre of town, but when leaving, you have to get yourself to the bus stand. Bodabodas abound, so this is not a problem.

To Kigali, minibuses cost RFr 800 and take about two hours. To Kamembe (close to Cyangugu), it's RFr 1200 and takes about three hours. The road is spectacular in parts and passes through the Nyungwe Forest, which contains some amazing virgin rainforest between Uwinka and Kiutabe.

There are also minibuses to the Burundi border but there's not much point going there at present as the north of Burundi is out of the control of the central government, and is therefore dangerous. If the border becomes safe, see the Getting There & Away section earlier for details.

NYUNGWE FOREST CONSERVATION PROJECT

Despite not being a national park, the Nyungwe Forest ranks among Rwanda's foremost attractions. One of the largest protected montane rainforests in Africa, it covers 970 sq km and offers superb scenery overlooking the forest and Lake Kivu as well as views to the north of the distant volcanoes of the Parc Nacional des Virunga.

The project began in 1988 and has been sponsored by the American Peace Corps, the New York Zoological Society and the Rwandan government. The project aims to promote tourism in an ecologically sound way while also studying the ecology of the forest and educating local people about its value.

The main attraction is the guided tours to view large groups of black-and-white Colobus monkeys (up to 300 in each troupe). The lush, green valleys also offer outstanding hiking across 20km of well maintained trails passing through enormous stands of hardwoods, under waterfalls and through a large marsh. There are about 270 species of tree, 50 species of mammal, 275 species of bird and an astonishing variety of orchids and butterflies.

The guided tours depart from the project headquarters at Uwinka three times daily, at 8 and 11 am and 2 pm. An information centre is also at the headquarters. The tours cost RFr 2000 per person and you should expect to walk for about an hour. Sturdy shoes, binoculars and rain gear are advisable.

Another guided tour (RFr 1500 per person) goes to the Kamiranzovu Marsh, where the area's six remaining elephants reside in the forest.

In addition to the tours, there are six other trails, ranging from 1 to 9km in length, along which you're free to hike without a guide.

Places to Stay

There are nine *camp sites* at the Uwinka headquarters but you must bring everything you need – tent, sleeping bag, cooking equipment, water, food and warm clothes (the nights are cold at 2400m and frost is not uncommon). There is nothing here other than toilets, charcoal and wood. Camping fees are RFr 2000 per person per night, but this includes visits to the forest trails as well. Uwinka sits on a ridge overlooking the forest and offers impressive views in all directions.

RWANDA

There's a **camp site** at Karamba about 14km towards Cyangugu from Uwinka.

Plans are being made to connect the existing trails with other camp sites enabling those who prefer backpacking to take two to three-day treks in the forest. The nearest towns for provisions are Cyangugu and Butare.

Getting There & Away

The Nyungwe Forest lies between Butare and Cyangugu. Minibuses leave from Kigali and Butare to Kamembe throughout the day (and from there you can catch a minibus to Cyangugu). The Uwinka headquarters is just past the 90km post and is marked by a board on which a black-and-white Colobus monkey is painted. The trip from Kigali takes between four and five hours.

From Cyangugu, take a minibus towards Butare and get off at Uwinka, which is just past the 54km post. The journey takes about one hour.

Eastern Rwanda

PARC NACIONAL DE L'AKAGERA

Created in 1934 and covering an area of 2500 sq km, l'Akagera used to be one of the least visited but most interesting wildlife parks in Africa. However, with the massive numbers of refugees who have returned to Rwanda in the last few years, as much as two-thirds of the park has been resettled with new villages. This human presence has also led many of the animals in the remaining sector to take a holiday in Tanzania. So a visit to this park might well prove to be a vegetarian safari these days.

There are, however, three distinct environments in the remainder of the park. Some parts of the park are covered with treeless savanna, but there is an immense swampy area about 95km long and between 2 and 20km wide along the border with Tanzania. This area contains six lakes and numerous islands, some of which are covered with savanna, others with forest.

There is a chain of low mountains (from 1618 to 1825m high) that stretches through much of the length of the park. The vegetation here is variable, ranging from short grasses on the summits to wooded savanna and dense thickets of xerophilious (adapted to a dry habitat) forest on the flanks of the park.

The best time to visit is during the dry season (mid-May to mid-September). November and April are the wettest months.

Tsetse flies can be bad in the north and east, but you could be bothered by the odd one anywhere in the park, so bring a fly swat and/or a good insect repellent.

Hiring a guide is a waste of money. You won't find any more animals with a guide than you will without. All you need is a map of the park, your eyes and a pair of binoculars. Park maps, for sale at the tourist office in Kigali, are remarkably accurate despite the way they appear – you can't buy these at the park. A wildlife handbook is also a useful thing to have.

Take all your own food, drinking and washing water, and fuel. It's best to assume you won't be able to get these in the park.

Park entry fees are RFr 3500 per person (RFr 1200 for students and children between the ages of seven and 18 years), plus RFr 1600 for a car, RFr 2200 for a jeep or RFr 2400 for a minibus or truck. A guide costs RFr 500 per day and a fishing licence costs RFr 1500 per day. You need to pay your park entry fees before you get there, either at a travel agency or at the tourist office in Kigali.

Places to Stay

Camping is not allowed inside the park. The only place that is open is **Hôtel Akagera** which is very expensive. It sits on the top of a hill and commands excellent views. A boat trip on the lake is recommended, as it's cheap and there are plenty of birds to be seen.

Getting There & Away

The problem with getting to Akagera is you need to have your own transport or join an organised safari. Safaris do not, as in Kenya and Tanzania, cater to budget travellers.

The only feasible entry into the park at present is via Nyamiyaga, about 16km from the sealed road going through Kayonza. This road will take you through to Hôtel Akagera.

Burundi

Burundi is a small and beautiful mountainous country. Sandwiched between Tanzania, Rwanda and Congo (Zaïre), there are magnificent views over Lake Tanganyika.

Burundi has had a stormy history of tribal wars and factional struggles between its ruling families. This has been further complicated in recent times by colonisation, first by the Germans and later by the Belgians. Since independence in 1962, intertribal tensions have boiled over on numerous occasions leading to the deaths of tens of thousands of people. That is happening all over again right now and as many as several hundred thousand people may have lost their lives since civil war erupted in 1993.

Burundi is one of the most densely populated countries on earth, with 180 people per sq km. Despite this, there are very few urban

WARNING

We strongly suggest you keep your eye on developments in Burundi before contemplating a visit. There has been a civil war here for the past two years and until the situation is resolved travellers should stay away. The violence doesn't usually affect foreigners, but you'd hardly want to be around if anything happened. You wouldn't be the first innocent bystander to be taken hostage or shot for some political motive.

As this edition of *East Africa* was researched, Burundi was dangerous. We were only able to do first-hand research on Bujumbura.

centres. The only towns of any size are the capital, Bujumbura, and Gitega. Most people live in family compounds known as *rugos*.

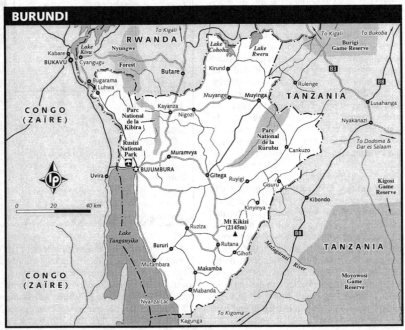

Facts about Burundi

HISTORY

For an insight into events in Burundi prior to independence from colonial rule, see the Facts about East Africa chapter.

Independence

In the 1950s, a nationalist organisation based on unity between the tribes was founded under the leadership of the *mwami's* (king's) eldest son, Prince Rwagasore. However, in the lead-up to independence, the prince was assassinated with the connivance of the colonial authorities, who feared their commercial interests would be threatened if he came to power.

Despite this setback, when independence was granted in 1962, challenges were raised to the concentration of power in Tutsi hands (the ethnic minority) and it appeared that the country would have a majority government. This had already happened in Rwanda, where a similar tribal imbalance existed.

Yet in the 1964 elections, even though Hutu candidates attracted a majority of votes, the mwami refused to appoint a Hutu prime minister. Hutu frustration boiled over a year later in an attempted coup staged by Hutu military officers and political figures. Though the attempt failed, it led to the flight of the mwami into exile in Switzerland. He was replaced by a Tutsi military junta. A wholesale purge of Hutu from the army and the bureaucracy followed, but in 1972 another large-scale revolt resulted in more than 1000 Tutsi killed.

The military junta responded to this challenge with what amounted to selective genocide. Any Hutu with wealth, a formal education or a government job was rooted out and murdered, often in the most horrifying way. Certainly there were few bullets used, and convoys of army trucks full of the mutilated bodies of Hutu rumbled through the streets of Bujumbura for days on end, initially even in broad daylight. Many Hutu were taken from their homes at night, while others received summonses to police stations.

BURUNDI AT A GLANCE

Area: 27,835 sq km
Population: 6.8 million
Population Growth Rate: 2.6%
Capital: Bujumbura
Head of State: President Pierre Buyoya
Official Languages: Kirundi & French
Currency: Burundi franc (BFr)
When to Go: May to October

Highlights

- Bujumbura, nestled at the top of Lake Tanganyika, has some of the region's best little eateries
- Les Tambourinaires, one of the most exciting drumming and dance troops in Africa
- The novelty of being one of the few tourists in the country

It is hard to believe how subservient the Hutu had become to their Tutsi overlords. Even the most uninformed peasant was aware of what was occurring. After three months 200,000 Hutu had been killed and 100,000 had fled to Tanzania, Rwanda and Congo (Zaïre). Neither the Christian missions inside the country nor the international community raised any protest against this carnage. Indeed, while it was in full swing, an official of the Organization of African Unity (OAU) is on record as having visited Bujumbura to congratulate President Michel Micombero on the orderly way the country was being run.

The Bagaza Years

In 1976, Jean-Baptiste Bagaza came to power in a bloodless coup, and in 1979 formed the Union pour le Progrès National (UPRONA), ruling with a central committee and small politburo. As part of a so-called democratisation program, elections in 1982 saw candidates (mostly Tutsi and all approved by UPRONA) voted into the National Assembly. The elections gave the Hutu a modicum of power, limited by the fact that they have only ever held about 25% of government ministries.

During the Bagaza years, there were some half-hearted attempts by the government to remove some of the main causes of intertribal conflict, but these were mostly cosmetic. The army and the bureaucracy remained under Tutsi domination, with the Hutu confined to menial jobs, agriculture and cattle raising. The government even vetoed international aid when it suspected this might be used to educate or enrich the Hutu, and thus sow seeds of discontent.

In 1985 the government tried to lessen the influence of the Catholic Church, which it believed was sympathetic to the Hutu majority. Its fears of a church-organised Hutu revolt were heightened by the fact that in Rwanda, Hutu were in power. Priests were put on trial and some missionaries were expelled from the country.

Bagaza was toppled in September 1987 in a bloodless coup led by his cousin, Major Pierre Buyoya. The new regime did a reasonable job of mending fences between the government and the Catholic Church/international aid agencies. It also attempted to address the causes of intertribal tensions yet again by gradually bringing Hutu representatives back into positions of power in the government. However, there was a renewed outbreak of intertribal violence in the north of the country in August 1988. As in previous clashes of this nature, the violence was unbelievable. Depending on which figures you believe, somewhere between 4000 and 24,000 people were massacred and thousands more fled into Rwanda.

The 1990s

Then, in 1992, Buyoya bowed to international pressure and announced that multi-party elections would be held the following year. For a time, it seemed that reason might prevail over the endless cycle of bloodletting. However, it was not to be.

Although peaceful elections were duly held in June 1993, which brought a Hutu-dominated government to power headed by Melchior Ndadaye (also a Hutu), a dissident army faction, led by Colonel Sylvestre Ningaba, staged a bloody coup in late October, and assassinated the president along with several prominent ministers. The coup failed when army generals disowned the plotters but, in the chaos which followed the assassination, thousands of people were massacred in intertribal fighting and an estimated 400,000 refugees fled to Rwanda. Surviving members of the government, who had holed up in the French embassy in Bujumbura, were able to reassert some degree of control several days later with the help of French soldiers and troops that remained loyal to the government.

Yet it was not until February the following year that things had cooled sufficiently for Cyprien Ntaryamira to be sworn in as the new president. Ntaryamira, a Hutu, was chosen as part of a compromise deal between the government and the opposition, part of which was the allocation of 40% of government posts to the opposition. Once again, the future looked bright, but it was an illusory new dawn.

On 6 April 1994, Ntaryamira was killed along with President Habyarimana of Rwanda when the plane in which they were travelling together was shot down as it was about to land at Rwanda's Kigali airport. While this was the spark that ignited genocide in Rwanda, Burundi remained relatively calm

BURUNDI

and Sylvestre Ntibantunganya was immediately appointed as interim president.

Unfortunately, it was just another window-dressing stand-off. Neither Hutu militias nor the Tutsi-dominated army passed up the opportunity to go on the offensive. No war was actually declared but at least 100,000 people were killed in clashes between mid-1994 and mid-1996, most of them in counter-reprisals. The Burundian army retained nominal control of Bujumbura and much of the centre and south of the country, but quickly lost control of the northern part to the Hutu militias.

On 25 July 1996, Buyoya, the former president, carried out a successful coup and took over as the country's president with the support of the army. Former Tanzanian president Julius Nyerere, mediator in the Burundian peace talks, called for an imposition of sanctions against the Buyoya regime. These were internationally accepted and included a ban on all international flights. Burundi was very isolated and the civil war dragged on.

The whole sanctions issue was deeply divisive in the region and pushed the Burundian government into a position of non-cooperation with the Tanzanian mediators, as the only people that really seemed to benefit from the policy were the well connected Tanzanians who were awarded contracts to supply basic commodities such as oil.

The sanctions drama essentially froze peace talks between the Burundian government and Hutu rebels. Sanctions were finally lifted at the start of 1999. Still, the civil war drags on throughout Burundi and it is not uncommon to hear gunfire in the hills around Bujumbura at night. The future is far from bright as the capital is essentially a Tutsi city these days, while the vast majority of peasants in the countryside are Hutu. Neither side appears willing to ease towards cooperation. However, Nelson Mandela was appointed as mediator in the peace talks at the end of 1999 following the death of Julius Nyerere, and this has raised hopes in some quarters that he will be able to work his magic on a deeply divided society.

GEOGRAPHY
Burundi occupies a mountainous 27,835 sq km. The capital, Bujumbura, is on the north-eastern tip of Lake Tanganyika.

CLIMATE
Burundi has a variable climate. The lower land around Lake Tanganyika is hot and humid, with temperatures around 30°C. In the more mountainous north, the average temperature is around 20°C. The rainy season lasts from October to May, with a brief dry spell in December and January.

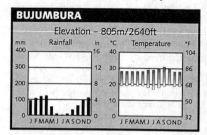

GOVERNMENT & POLITICS
Following multiparty elections in June 1993, the Burundi Democratic Front (FRODEBU) came to power with some 71% of the vote compared to some 26% garnered by the previous ruling party, UPRONA. This gave the Hutu a majority of deputies in the National Assembly (65 out of a total of 81). The president, Sylvestre Ntibantunganya, a Hutu, was ousted in the July 1996 coup led by Pierre Buyoya, a Tutsi. International sanctions placed on Burundi to force Buyoya to step down or stage elections were subsequently lifted in 1999. No date has yet been set for elections as peace negotiations have failed to produce a settlement.

ECONOMY
Burundi's economy is predominantly agricultural, with coffee, the main commercial crop, accounting for 65% of export income. Recently attempts have been made to encourage development of the noncoffee sector in an effort to diversify the economy. Consequently, the production of tea has increased greatly in the past few years.

Agriculture accounts for more than 50% of gross domestic product (GDP) and employs about 85% of the workforce. Apart from coffee and tea, cash crops include cotton, palm oil and tobacco. Subsistence crops (which occupy most of the cultivated land) include cassava, bananas, sweet potatoes, maize and sorghum.

The manufacturing sector, based in Bujumbura, accounts for 15% of GDP, with output including cigarettes, glass, textiles, cement, oxygen and processed coffee.

Wood is used to meet most energy needs at the village level. Major energy needs are met through oil imports from the Persian Gulf and electricity from Congo (Zaïre).

The country's balance of trade deficit is alarming and Burundi is heavily dependent on foreign aid from Belgium, France, Germany and international donor organisations. Its debt repayments consume some 44% of export earnings. Inflation is running at about 10%.

POPULATION & PEOPLE
The population of 6.8 million is about 15% Tutsi and 85% Hutu.

ARTS
Burundi is famous for its athletic and acrobatic forms of dance. Les Tambourinaires du Burundi are the country's most famous troupe and have performed in cities such as Berlin and New York. Their performances are a high-adrenalin mix of drumming and dancing that drown the audience in a wave of sound and movement.

The *Intore* is another form of dance, practised in the north-east and famous for its warrior-like qualities. However, it is not easy to arrange to see these dances as the civil war has reduced the tourism industry to rubble. The best hope is the chance of a performance at one of Bujumbura's leading hotels. Otherwise, contact the tourist office in Bujumbura and see if it can help.

RELIGION
The majority of the population are Christians of various sects. Muslims are a significant minority.

LANGUAGE
The official languages are Kirundi and French, and Swahili is also useful. Outside Bujumbura, few people speak English. See the Language chapter at the back of this book for some useful Swahili words and phrases.

Facts for the Visitor

PLANNING
For details about planning your trip and what to bring, see the Planning section in the Regional Facts for the Visitor chapter.

VISAS & DOCUMENTS
Visas
Visas are required by all visitors to Burundi. Transit visas cost US$10 and a one-month tourist visa costs US$40. You will need two photos and can generally get your visa the same day, if you apply early enough in the morning.

There's no extra charge for requesting a multiple-entry visa, so if there's any chance you could need one, get it now rather than later.

For some reason, certain Burundi embassies (Nairobi in Kenya and Kigali in Rwanda are two) will not issue visas, telling you to get them at the border. Visas are still available from the embassy in Kampala (Uganda) and the consulates in Kigoma (Tanzania) and Bukavu in Congo (Zaïre).

Tourist visas can be extended at the immigration office in Bujumbura on Blvd de l'UPRONA. Extensions cost BFr 10,000 per month and take 24 hours to issue. Apply early in the morning, as it's very busy in the afternoon.

Other Visas If you need visas for neighbouring countries, this is the deal:

Congo (Zaïre) The Kinshasa government maintains an embassy in Bujumbura. Single transit visas cost BFr 17,000, double transit visas are BFr 34,000. One-month tourist visas are BFr 28,000, and BFr 44,500 for multiple entry. Three-month visas cost BFr 72,500 and BFr 83,500 respectively. Visas are issued in 24 hours.

BURUNDI

Rwanda A one-month multiple-entry visa costs US$50, requires two photos and is issued in 24 hours. Two-week, single-entry visas are available at the border.

EMBASSIES
Burundi Embassies
In the region, there are Burundi embassies in:

Congo (Zaïre) SINELAC Bldg, top floor, 184 Ave du Président Mobutu, Bukavu. Also in Kinshasa.

Kenya (☎ 02-575113, fax 219005) Development House, Moi Ave, PO Box 44439, Nairobi

Rwanda (☎ 07-73465) Rue de Ntaruka off Ave de Rusumo, Kigali

Tanzania (☎ 051-117615, 0695-2865 in Kigoma) Lugalo Rd, Upanga, behind Palm Beach Hotel

Uganda (☎ 041-233674, fax 250990) 9 Roscoe Drive, Kololo, Kampala

Elsewhere in Africa there are Burundi embassies in Addis Ababa (Ethiopia), Algiers (Algeria), Cairo (Egypt) and Tripoli (Libya).

Outside Africa, there are Burundi embassies in Beijing (People's Republic of China), Bonn (Germany), Brussels (Belgium), Bucharest (Romania), Geneva (Switzerland), Moscow (Russia), Ottawa (Canada), Paris (France) and Washington DC (USA).

Embassies in Burundi
Embassies in Bujumbura include:

Congo (Zaïre) Ave du Zaïre. Open from 8.30 am to noon Monday to Friday.

Rwanda (☎ 26865) 24 Ave du Zaïre. Open from 8 am to 4 pm Monday to Friday.

Other countries that have embassies in Burundi include Belgium (☎ 233641), France (☎ 251484), Germany (☎ 415729) and the USA (☎ 223454).

MONEY
Currency
The unit of currency, the Burundi franc (BFr), is divided into 100 centimes, which you're unlikely to come across. Notes in circulation are BFr 5000, BFr 1000, BFr 500, BFr 100, BFr 50 and BFr 10. The only coins are BFr 5 and BFr 1.

Exchange Rates
The exchange value of the Burundi franc fluctuates according to the international currency market, depending particularly on the value of the US dollar and the French franc, and devaluations are not uncommon.

country	unit		franc
Australia	A$1	=	BFr 397
Canada	C$1	=	BFr 433
euro	€1	=	BFr 620
France	10FF	=	BFr 945
Germany	DM1	=	BFr 317
Japan	¥100	=	BFr 568
UK	UK£1	=	BFr 1010
USA	US$1	=	BFr 628

Changing Money
Bring US dollars cash with you to Burundi, as banks exchange money at the official rate, which is half the street rate.

Commission rates for changing travellers cheques are bad news at most banks – some charge up to 7%. Banque de la République du Burundi is the best place, as it charges only a small commission and may even change small amounts of US dollar travellers cheques to cash dollars, which could save you being penalised by the official exchange rate. You can also change travellers cheques at one of the large hotels in Bujumbura (Novotel or Source du Nil). The rates are below the banks, and there's no commission.

There's an open black market in Bujumbura. Dealers hang around near the Dmitri supermarket and the market. Rates vary according to the official exchange rate and the amount you want to change (large bills are preferred). At the time of writing, the street rate was double the bank rate.

Tanzanian shillings can be bought here, which is handy if you're going to Kigoma.

At the border crossing between Uvira in Congo (Zaïre) and Bujumbura, you'll run into a lot of moneychangers. Their rates are quite reasonable, as long as you know the current street rates for the Burundi franc.

Costs
Burundi once had a reputation as an expensive place to visit. However, the economy

took a serious pounding during the imposition of international sanctions and the currency has dived. Burundi is now a relatively inexpensive place to visit and if you spend a little more than elsewhere in the region, you will find you get very good value for money.

Hotel rooms can be found for as little as BFr 3000 in the suburbs of the capital; in the centre you are looking at more like BFr 6000 and up, but the rooms are often huge, with plenty of character. Besides Bujumbura city centre, meals can usually be found at a fair price and transport costs are about the same as in Rwanda.

POST & COMMUNICATIONS
Post
The postal service is reasonably efficient, but the poste restante service at the main post office (PTT) in Bujumbura is poorly organised. Make sure you check not only the pile for your surname but also those for any other possible combinations or spellings. The post office is open from 8 am to noon and 2 to 4 pm Monday to Friday and 8 to 11 am Saturday.

Telephone & Fax
Rates for international telephone calls are quite reasonable, as long as the Burundi franc remains weak. Phonecards are available from the telecommunications office behind the post office. A 220 unit card costs BFr 5000 (US$5) and should last about four minutes for an international call. Cards also come in 20 units (BFr 600), 50 units (BFr 1590) and 120 units (BFr 2400). Fax charges are also reasonable at about BFr 1500 per page.

There are no area codes in Burundi.

Email & Internet Access
Internet services in Burundi aren't bad, and private access is generally much easier than in Rwanda. However, public access is a problem, as there are almost no places to get online. Bujumbura offers the only opportunity.

NEWSPAPERS
The main newspaper is the French-language daily, *Le Rénouveau du Burundi*. It's under strict government control.

RADIO
Local radio stations broadcast in Kirundi, French and Swahili. There are some broadcasts in English on the local FM station (98.10 MHz). It also plays African music.

TIME
The time in Burundi is GMT/UTC plus two hours.

ELECTRICITY
Power supply in Burundi is 220V AC.

DANGERS & ANNOYANCES
Burundi is embroiled in civil war, so it pays to check the security situation in the provinces carefully before entering the country by land or travelling to the provinces. Locals may undertake dangerous journeys as a matter of course, but are often unable to assess the risk for a foreigner.

Kigali or Kigoma are probably the easiest places to pick up reliable information on events in Burundi. Bujumbura, however, is fairly safe these days, although it is sensible to avoid walking the roads between the docks and the centre of town at night.

PUBLIC HOLIDAYS
Burundians observe the following public holidays:

New Year's Day 1 January
Easter March/April – Good Friday, Holy
  Saturday and Easter Monday
Labour Day 1 May
National Day 1 July
Feast of the Assumption 15 August
National Holiday 18 September
National Holiday 13 October
All Saints' Day 1 November
Christmas Day 25 December

Getting There & Away

You can enter Burundi by air, road or lake ferry. There are no railways.

For information on getting to Burundi from outside East Africa, see the regional Getting There & Away chapter.

AIR

The sanctions placed on Burundi from 1996 until 1999 included a flight embargo. A number of airlines that used to fly to Bujumbura have not resumed their services. At the time of writing, there were no direct flights to Europe.

International airlines servicing Burundi include Air Burundi, Air Tanzania, Cameroon Air, City Connexion Airlines (CCA), Ethiopian Airlines, Kenya Airways, Rwanda Airlines, SA Alliance Express and Uganda Airlines.

Departure Tax

Burundi's international departure tax is somewhat disturbing at US$30, but then perhaps the government is trying to make up for lost revenue after a three-year flight embargo.

Kenya

Air Burundi, Kenya Airways and SA Alliance Express fly between Nairobi and Bujumbura. Flights with Air Burundi cost US$200 one way and US$275 for a three-week return.

Rwanda

Air Burundi, CCA and SA Alliance Express fly between Kigali and Bujumbura. Tickets cost US$110/195 one way/return. SA Alliance Express is the safer option.

Tanzania

Air Tanzania offers Dar es Salaam for US$247/487 one way/return.

Uganda

There are flights between Entebbe and Bujumbura with CCA (US$148/271 one way/return), SA Alliance Express (US$123/246) and Uganda Airlines (US$148/235). CCA is the only airline to fly direct.

LAND
Rwanda

Bujumbura to Kigali via Butare Although this is the most direct route between Bujumbura and Kigali, you are seriously warned not to take it.

> **WARNING**
>
> ! At the time of writing, it is dangerous to cross the Rwandan border into Burundi as the northern part of Burundi is out of the control of the central Burundi government. We do not recommend it. The information in this section is provided in the event that the situation changes.

The unnervingly named Titanic Express (☎ 211288) has buses to Kigali on Tuesday, Thursday and Saturday for BFr 10,000, departing at 9 am and taking about six hours. They return to Burundi on Monday, Wednesday and Friday.

Eagle (☎ 242080) operates a daily service to Kigali departing at 9 am (BFr 10,000, about six hours).

Bujumbura to Cyangugu Possibly a safer way between Burundi and Rwanda is a taxi from Bujumbura to the border with Congo (Zaïre) and another from there to Uvira in Congo (Zaïre). Take a minibus from there to Bukavu. The road goes back into Rwanda part of the way (but not through Cyangugu) before re-entering Congo (Zaïre) so you'll need a multiple-entry Rwandan visa and a multiple-entry Congolese (Zaïrean) visa. Rwandan transit visas are available at the border if you don't have a multiple-entry visa. From Bukavu, take a minibus across the border to Kamembe (near Cyangugu).

> **WARNING**
>
> ! We strongly advise against crossing by land into Congo (Zaïre) from East Africa as there is a civil war going on there at the time of writing, involving troops from as many as nine countries. There are also armed members of the *Interahamwe* roaming this part of Congo (Zaïre) and they have been known to target tourists. However, because of the possibility that peace will eventually return to this region, we include the following information.

Tanzania

The border between Tanzania and Burundi is officially open, though it is not often used by independent travellers because of the situation in Burundi and the ongoing refugee situation in western Tanzania; get an update on the security situation from your embassy before travelling in this region. The most commonly used crossing is at the Kobero bridge border crossing between Ngara (Tanzania) and Muyinga (Burundi).

In Tanzania, the road from Nzega (south-west of Shinyanga) to the Burundi border via Ngara is fairly good, though there is little public transport; hitching is the main option. From both Bukoba and Kigoma, the trip to Burundi via the Kobero Bridge crossing is best done in stages via Lusahunga.

LAKE
Tanzania
The two routes available between Bujumbura and Kigoma (Tanzania) both use Lake Tanganyika at different points. The direct route is on the venerable MV *Liemba*. However, a more interesting route is via Nyanza Lac and Gombe Stream National Park, the chimpanzee sanctuary across the border in Tanzania.

Ferry Weekly ferry service on the MV *Liemba* between Bujumbura and Kigoma was just resuming as this chapter was being researched. Prices are set at US$30/25/20 for 1st/2nd/3rd class. In addition, port fees of BFr 1500 are payable upon boarding in Bujumbura. Tickets for the ferry can be bought from Air Tanzania (☎ 224904, fax 223601), Immeuble Old East, Place de l'Independence.

Food is available on board and must be paid for in Tanzanian shillings, so bring enough money to cover this, but it's best to bring some supplements, as well as your own water. First class is relatively comfortable, with two reasonably clean bunks and a window. Second class cabins (four bunks) and 3rd class seating, however, are both poorly ventilated and uncomfortable. If you're going to travel 3rd class, it's more comfortable to find yourself deck space than to sit in the 3rd class seating section.

Tickets purchased in Mpulungu (Zambia) and in Bujumbura must be paid for in US dollars.

For information on the MV *Liemba's* route between Mpulungu and Kigoma, see the regional Getting There & Away chapter. The boat no longer services Kalemie in Congo (Zaïre).

Lake Taxi & Matatu The alternative to the MV *Liemba* is to travel partly by minibus and partly by lake taxi between Bujumbura and Kigoma, via the Tanzanian border village of Kagunga and the Gombe Stream National Park. The national park is primarily a chimpanzee sanctuary and is well worth a visit, but it does cost US$100 entry fee plus US$20 for accommodation. If you can't afford this, then simply stay on the lake taxi, which will take you all the way to Kigoma.

From Bujumbura, minibuses go daily to Nyanza Lac (BFr 2500). You must go through immigration here; the office is about 1km from the town centre towards the lake. After that you take a minibus (BFr 400) to the Burundi border crossing. From this post to the Tanzanian border crossing at Kagunga, it's a 2km walk along a narrow track.

From Kagunga, there are lake taxis to Kigoma (actually to Kibirizi, about 3km north of Kigoma), which cost TSh 2000, leave some time before dawn and take most of the day. The taxis call at Gombe Stream (about halfway), where you can get off if you like. The fare to Gombe Stream costs TSh 1000, as is the fare from there to Kigoma.

The lake taxis are small wooden boats that are almost always overcrowded not only with people but with their produce, and they offer absolutely no creature comforts whatsoever. They're good fun when the weather is on your side, though if there's a squall on the lake, you may be in for a rough journey. If you have a choice then try to board a boat with a cover, as it gets stinking hot out on the lake in the middle of the day. These lake taxis do not operate on Sundays.

BURUNDI

Getting Around

AIR

Air Burundi, the national airline, does not have regular internal flights.

BUS

As in Rwanda, most of the major routes are sealed. Most of the vehicles available are modern, Japanese minibuses. They are not overcrowded and are cheaper than share-taxis. Destinations are displayed in the front window and vehicles depart when full. You can usually find one heading in your direction any day between early morning and early afternoon at the *gare routière* (bus stand) in any town or city.

Government OTRACO buses serve the area around Bujumbura.

Bujumbura

Sprawling up the mountainside on the north-eastern tip of Lake Tanganyika, Bujumbura overlooks the vast wall of mountains in Congo (Zaïre) on the other side of the lake. The Burundi capital is a mixture of grandiose colonial town planning (wide boulevards and imposing public buildings) and dusty crowded suburbs like those which surround many African cities. It's also one of the most important ports on Lake Tanganyika.

Like Kigali in Rwanda, Bujumbura has a big expatriate population of international aid organisation workers, medicos, missionaries and businesspeople. Even Libya's Colonel Gaddafi has made his mark here, in the form of the large and beautifully conceived Islamic Cultural Centre and mosque, which must have cost a small fortune. There is also a pleasant botanical surprise: like many places along Lake Tanganyika, Bujumbura sports coconut palms – most unusual at well over 1000km from the sea.

Parts of Bujumbura have a slightly sleazy atmosphere and it is certainly not the friendliest place in the world. You are advised not to walk along Ave de la Plage between the Cercle Nautique restaurant and the port, even during the day, as there have been reports of muggings. Rue des Swahilis, in the same area, should be avoided for the same reason. You should also avoid Kamenge, on the hill. Army personnel will want to know why you're there and will assume you are up to no good. Possession of a camera will guarantee you a hard time.

Information

Tourist Offices There are two tourist offices in Bujumbura, one for information and another for souvenirs. For information, it is necessary to visit Office National du Tourisme (☎ 222202) on Ave des Euphorbes, near the cathedral. It has some basic maps of Burundi, pocket-sized guidebooks in English and French and friendly staff, who are eager as they get so few visitors these days. The office is open from 7.30 am to noon and 2 to 4.30 pm Monday to Friday.

The tourist office gift shop on Blvd de l'UPRONA is a useful place to scout out prices before heading to a craft market. It sells mainly woodcarvings and basketry, but also has just about the cheapest postcards available in Bujumbura.

Post & Communications The main post office is in the city centre on the corner of Blvd Lumumba and Ave du Commerce. The international telephone service is housed in the same building. Both are open from 8 am to noon and 2 to 4 pm Monday to Friday and 8 to 11 am Saturday.

Email & Internet Access It is not easy to find online access in Bujumbura, but Ku Nama (☎ 210176) may be able to get you connected. It is a restaurant and business centre that charges BFr 1000 for 30 minutes to use a computer and BFr 50 per minute for Internet access.

Cultural Centres The American Cultural Center on Chaussée Prince Rwagasore screens video news from the USA from 5.15 pm Monday to Friday. Its library is open from 2 to 8 pm Monday to Friday, as well as from 9 am to noon Tuesday and Thursday. Alliance Française is across the road and has similar services and facilities.

BURUNDI

BUJUMBURA

PLACES TO STAY
1 Hôtel Albatross
2 Karibu Hôtel;
  Hôtel Le Metropole
5 Hôtel Source du Nil
8 Hôtel Le Doyen
9 Novotel
12 Hôtel Burundi Palace;
   Dong Fang Restaurant;
   Le Pichet
19 Hôtel de L'Amitie
25 Hôtel Nikamor
44 New Tourist Hôtel
52 Hôtel Tanganyika
55 Hôtel Safari Gate

PLACES TO EAT
4 Restaurant Chez Laurent
13 Aux Délices Restaurant
16 Restaurant Pizza Oasis
20 Restaurant Au Chalet D'Or;
   Sicoop Petrol Station
21 Café D'Azur; Au Paradis
34 Kappa
35 Kasuku Restaurant

36 Boulangerie-Pâtisserie
   Trianon
54 Cercle Nautique

OTHER
3 Banque Burundaise pour le
  Commerce et l'Investissement
6 Stadium
7 Handicrafts Market
10 Air Tanzania
11 Taxis
14 Alliance Française
15 Ethiopian Airlines
17 Tourist Office Gift Shop
18 Polyclinique Saint Jean
22 Rwanda Embassy
23 Congo (Zaïre) Embassy
24 Dimitri Supermarket
26 Eagle Transport
27 Ku Nama
28 Chez Marc
29 Banque Commerciale du
   Burundi; US Embassy
30 Market; Minibuses
31 Post Office; Telephone Centre

32 Sabena
33 Banque du Crédit de
   Bujumbura
37 Air Burundi
38 American Cultural Center
39 Air Tanzania
   (MV Liemba Bookings);
   Kenya Airways
40 Mosque
41 DHL; Galerie Alexandre
42 CCA
43 BP Petrol Station
45 Belgian Embassy
46 L'Archipel
47 SA Alliance Express;
   Uganda Airlines;
   Le Petit Suisse
48 Banque de la République
   du Burundi
49 Cathedral
50 Tourist Office
   (Information)
51 La Reine
53 Musée Vivant;
   Parc des Reptiles

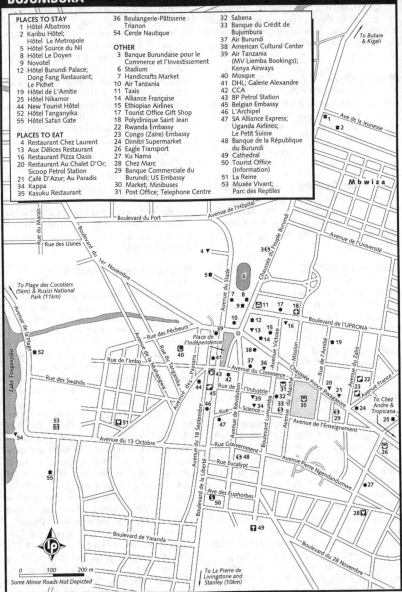

BURUNDI

The Islamic Cultural Centre and mosque is a beautiful building near Place de l'Indépendence. Paid for by the Libyan government, it is worth visiting. Sometimes there are public performances by dance troupes, drummers and singers.

Musée Vivant

This is a reconstructed traditional Burundian village on Ave du 13 Octobre with basket, pottery, drum and photographic displays. Occasionally there are traditional drum shows. Entry costs BFr 200 (BFr 50 for students) and the museum is open from 9 am to noon and 2.30 to 5 pm daily except Monday.

Musée de Géologie du Burundi

Opposite the reptile park, the geology museum is dusty and run-down but has a good collection of fossils. Entry is free. The museum is open from 7 am to noon and 2 to 5 pm weekdays.

Parc des Reptiles

Adjacent to the Musée Vivant, this park (☎ 25374) exhibits just what you might expect. Entry costs BFr 500 but the park is only open from 2 to 4 pm on Saturday, or by appointment during the rest of the week.

Swimming Pool

Nonguests can use the swimming pool at Hôtel Source du Nil for BFr 1500.

Places to Stay – Budget

During the mid-1990s, the ongoing conflict between Hutu and Tutsi came to the suburbs of the capital itself. Many of Bujumbura's cheapest hotels were forced to close and several never re-opened. However, there are a few very cheap places to stay if you don't mind being a short distance from the city centre.

The cheapest hotels are generally in the Mbwiza suburb north of the centre. The disadvantage of this part of town is that it is not the safest place at night so you may find taxi fares adding up later in the evening.

An old-timer in this area is *Hôtel Albatross* (☎ 229182) on the corner of Chaussée du Peuple Burundi and Ave de la Jeunesse.

It has single rooms for BFr 4500, doubles for BFr 5000 and some rooms with air-con for BFr 6000. The rooms have an air of decay, rather like the hotel, but it is cheap.

One block south are a couple of even cheaper places, although they are often full. *Karibu Hotel* (☎ 228264) is built in Rwandan style around a small courtyard. It offers singles/doubles for BFr 3000/4000 with shared bathroom, and also has cheap meals at BFr 700 for lunch or dinner. Almost next door is *Hôtel Le Metropole* with all rooms at BFr 3500, including a basic bathroom, but little French is spoken here.

New Tourist Hôtel (☎ 241483) is much more centrally located, just off Place de l'Indépendence. It offers rooms for BFr 6000/7000. The rooms are cavernous and include bathrooms that would be rented out as cell-like rooms in other parts of Africa. It is reasonable value but the whole place has an air of neglect.

Places to Stay – Mid-Range

The cheapest place in this category in the city centre is *Hôtel Burundi Palace* (☎ 222920, fax 223670) full of character with a good range of rooms. The cheapest single rooms start at BFr 7500/8500/9000, depending on size. Huge doubles start at BFr 10,000 and rise to BFr 14,000 with fan, BFr 16,000 with air-con. Most of these doubles are more like suites and include regal bathrooms with porcelain bidets and hot water. All rates include breakfast.

A similar sort of place is *Hôtel de l'Amitié* (☎ 226195, fax 219127, Rue de l'Amitié) which offers another bewildering array of rooms. Singles start at BFr 8000 and doubles at BFr 12,000. If you want a little more comfort, there are well appointed doubles with TV and fridge for BFr 18,000. All rooms are clean and comfortable and include towel and soap. The hotel has its own restaurant but the food is nothing special.

If you want to be down near Lake Tanganyika, the new *Hôtel Safari Gate* (☎ 214 779, fax 214780) is an excellent place to stay. Owned by the genial Colonel François, all rooms are BFr 12,500 and include a small balcony and hot-water bathroom. Set in an old colonial building just a few hundred metres from the lakeshore, this is definitely a relaxing place to stay if you have your own transport. There is also a restaurant and terrace bar here with fantastic views across the lake towards the mountains of Congo (Zaïre).

A little more expensive is **Hôtel Le Doyen** (*☎ 224378, fax 214986, Ave du Stade*) a splendid colonial-style building set in beautiful grounds. All rooms have mosquito nets, and soap and towel are provided. Rooms with twin beds but shared showers and toilets cost BFr 5000 a double, or there are double rooms with attached bathroom for BFr 8000. There are also vast air-con doubles with attached bathroom for BFr 16,000. Though this appears to be no more expensive than the other mid-range hotels, foreigners are charged in US dollars at the official rate, and this makes rooms about US$10/15/30 respectively. The hotel has a good restaurant but it's not cheap. Nonguests can also eat and drink here, and the garden bar is popular in the evening.

Places to Stay – Top End
There are several top end hotels in Bujumbura and they all have one thing in common: they prefer payment in US dollars.

Novotel (*☎ 222600, fax 222692, Chaussée du Peuple Burundi*) is the best hotel in Bujumbura and has all the facilities you would expect in a hotel belonging to this chain, including a swimming pool and gym. As elsewhere in the world, it's expensive at US$105/110 a single/double.

Hôtel Source du Nil (*☎ 225222, fax 225205*) off Ave du Stade is another large, luxurious hotel with facilities such as a swimming pool and tennis courts. Rooms here are very reasonable for Africans at BFr 31,000 for a townside room and BFr 35,700 for a lakeshore room, but others must pay in US dollars at official rates, pushing the prices to more like US$60/70.

Hôtel Nikamor (*☎ 223886, fax 211604*) has risen from the ashes of its predecessor Hôtel Residence, but with a whole different level of service and tariffs. Double rooms are US$50 plus BFr 3000 for a TV and BFr

5000 for an extra bed. Large attractive apartments are US$70, or US$90 with aircon. These include an office, bathroom and fridge. All rooms are tastefully decorated with local handicrafts, making it arguably a better choice than its larger, sterile competitors. There is also a good restaurant here and a small tavern for evening drinks.

Places to Eat
Restaurants There are some excellent European restaurants in Bujumbura, but you have to be prepared to pay prices that are a little more European as well. However, at the time of writing, dining out was pretty cheap, as most restaurants were yet to raise prices in response to the weak exchange rate.

Au Chalet d'Or is an excellent little continental restaurant opposite the minibus stand in the centre of town. It has a huge menu with filling breakfasts available for about BFr 2000 and inexpensive main courses such as *salanga* (fish), steaks and pizzas, all at between BFr 3000 and BFr 5000. The service is good and the staff is friendly.

Le Pichet offers a similar menu, but with a better outdoor setting. It is next door to the Hôtel Burundi Palace and the terrace is very popular with well-to-do beer drinkers come evening.

Tucked away under the Hôtel Burundi Palace is *Dong Fang* Bujumbura's only Chinese restaurant. The menu here includes a wide range of Chinese favourites, with most main courses costing from BFr 5000 to BFr 8000. Vegetarian dishes are cheaper at around BFr 4000.

For those wanting the best in European cuisine, there are some very sophisticated establishments around the city. *Kasuku* which is housed in an attractive villa on Rue de l'Industrie has a wide range of sauced-up steaks, impressive pastas and crisp salads. The service and setting are stylish, but the prices are relatively high at BFr 6000 and more for a main course. The only strange thing about this restaurant is the pet antelope here, which looks a little lost. Perhaps they plan to include game on the menu in future.

The city's two most celebrated restaurants are arguably *Chez Andre* and *Tropicana* both housed in large modern villas on the eastern extreme of Chaussée Prince Rwagasore. Residents claim the food is better at Chez Andre, but at either place you'll get fine food and a selection of fine wines. Expect to pay BFr 10,000 and more for food and drink.

For some Italian food, you could do worse than try *Restaurant Pizza Oasis* on the corner of Ave Victoire and Blvd de l'UPRONA. This place has been around for an eternity and offers good pizzas and pastas for around BFr 5000 and more.

Worth a visit, but not necessarily for a meal, is *Cercle Nautique* on the lakeshore at the end of Ave du 13 Octobre. It has regular barbecues, including fresh fish. It's a great place to sip a cold beer even if you don't want to eat and you might be entertained by the occasional hippo. The Cercle is open from 5 pm daily except Tuesday, and from 11 am on Sunday. It's popular with local expats.

Cafes One of the best places in town for breakfast is *Kappa* on Rue Science which is extremely popular with local office workers between 8 and 9 am. It sells cheap coffee and pastries so you can get a basic breakfast for as little as BFr 500.

Another popular place for breakfast is *Boulangerie-Pâtisserie Trianon* on Ave du Commerce. It has excellent croissants and omelettes, and also inexpensive drinking yoghurt. A tasty ham and cheese croissant is about BFr 700.

One more cafe worth checking out is *Café d'Azur* which does good coffee and cakes. Next door is *Au Paradis* video shop, which doubles as a fast-food snack bar with cheap burgers, sandwiches and fruit juices.

For good snacks and main meals *Aux Délices* is popular though the main attraction seems to be the video rather than the food. Meals are from BFr 2000 to BFr 3000 and snacks range from BFr 1000 to BFr 2000. The service is not exactly fast as the waiters also find the video interesting.

Self-Catering For those looking to prepare their own food, Bujumbura is a surprising

treat, with many luxury imports available at reasonable prices. *Dmitri supermarket* on Chaussée Prince Rwagasore is the best in town, with a huge wine selection, cheese from all over Europe and even French favourites such as spicy *saucisson*. It is open from 8 am to 12.30 pm and 3 to 6.30 pm Monday to Friday, plus Saturday morning. The *central market* has a good selection of fruit and vegetables, while the city's bakeries have some excellent fresh bread.

Entertainment

Bujumbura has been suffering a curfew for a number of years now and this has dampened the reputation for freewheelin' that the city once enjoyed. The curfew is currently midnight, but if you have a vehicle it is not so rigidly enforced. Some of the nightclubs operate 'lock-ins' at the weekend where you have to decide just before midnight whether to go hard or go home.

There is a reasonable choice of bars in Bujumbura, although most of them are primarily restaurants. *Botanika* is pretty popular with Bujumbura's beautiful people and students. Located near the tourist office gift shop on Blvd de l'UPRONA, it is open every day except Wednesday.

L'Archipel on Blvd de la Liberté is a large restaurant, but also a fairly popular spot for a drink come darkness.

Le Petit Suisse on Rue Science is really an ice cream parlour, but has somehow developed a reputation as a bit of a pick-up joint, so some folks head there at night for a beer.

One of Bujumbura's most popular institutions is the amateur bar, a sort of private house and garden that opens its doors and sells beer. Residents love to park their cars in the garden, set up a little table and have a sort of lager picnic. *Chez Marc* very much fits this bill, but only sells imported beer making it kind of expensive. *La Reine* just off Ave du 13 Octobre is cheaper as it serves local brews such as Primus and Amstel.

For a bar with a great view, it is worth trying out the terrace of *Hôtel Safari Gate* (see Places to Stay), but more popular is the nearby *Cercle Nautique* (see Places to Eat).

Casa Nova down near the lakeshore by Hôtel Safari Gate is pretty popular at weekends and plays a lot of Congolese (Zaïrean) tunes.

Shopping

Burundi was never exactly famous for its locally produced handicrafts and the civil war has hardly improved things. However, a lot of excellent work makes its way across the border from Congo (Zaïre) and can be picked up very cheaply in Bujumbura.

The best place to shop is in the small craft market just to the north of Hôtel Le Doyen on Ave du Stade. You have to haggle furiously to get a good price, but there are some bargains to be found. As well as an assortment of masks from Congo (Zaïre) and Tanzania, it also sells carvings of all shapes and sizes, cheap jewellery and mobiles.

Getting There & Away

Air There are no real discounts on the scheduled air fares offered by the airlines themselves. The Air Burundi office on Ave du Commerce is able to book tickets for all airlines, so it's a useful first stop in the search for a ticket.

The following airlines have scheduled flights to Bujumbura:

Air Burundi (☎ 223460, fax 223452) Ave du Commerce
Air Tanzania (☎ 224904, fax 223601) Immeuble Old East Bldg, Place de l'Indépendence
CCA (☎ 241364, fax 241365) Ave du Commerce
Ethiopian Airlines (☎ 226820) Ave Victoire
Kenya Airways (☎ 223542, fax 221484) Immeuble Old East Bldg, Place de l'Indépendence
Uganda Airlines (☎ 217788) Blvd de la Liberté

Bus There are two bus companies operating services between Kigali (Rwanda) and Bujumbura. Titanic Express (☎ 211288) has buses to Kigali on Tuesday, Thursday and Saturday for BFr 10,000, departing at 9 am and taking about six hours. Buses return to Burundi on alternate days.

Eagle (☎ 242080) operates a daily bus service to Kigali that costs BFr 10,000, departing at 9 am and taking about six hours.

Car Rental If you're thinking of hiring a car, ask at Hôtel Le Doyen (see Places to Stay). The staff may be able to link you up with a vehicle. Otherwise try the tourist office.

AROUND BUJUMBURA

Beaches

The most popular beach around Bujumbura is Plage des Cocotiers (Coconut Beach), about 5km north-west of the city centre. It gets quite busy at weekends and on a sunny day you could be forgiven for thinking you were on the Mediterranean.

Another popular beach is even nearer to the city, just in front of Hôtel Tanganyika, but the water here may not be so clean, as it is also near the docks.

Resha Beach, about one hour south of the capital, used to be the most popular beach in the country, but was taken over by the military and access is currently forbidden.

Rusizi National Park

The most accessible of Burundi's national park, Rusizi is just 15km outside Bujumbura. It is a wetland environment and provides a habitat for hippo, sitatunga (antelope) and a wide variety of birds. Entry is just BFr 1000 for tourists, BFr 500 for residents, surely one of the cheapest national parks in the region.

La Pierre de Livingstone and Stanley

This large rock is alleged to mark the spot where the infamous 'Dr Livingstone, I presume?' encounter took place between Livingstone and Stanley. There is some ancient graffiti marking the date as 25 November 1871. The rock is at Mugere, about 10km south of the capital.

Around Burundi

GITEGA

Gitega is the second largest town in Burundi and is home to the **National Museum**. Although small, the museum is well worth a visit and is very educational. Entry is free. There might be a folklore performance – ask if Les Tambourinaires are playing. They usually play at Gishola, about 10km away, on the last Sunday of every month.

A good day trip from Gitega is to the **Chutes de la Kagera**, near Rutana. These waterfalls are spectacular in the wet season (October to January) but there's no public transport there, so you'll have to hitch.

Places to Stay & Eat

Mission Catholique has a huge guesthouse and is probably the best place to inquire for budget accommodation. You should be able to get a bed here for BFr 2000 to BFr 4000.

A good place to eat is *Foyer Culturel*, which does good, cheap food but has slow service. For a splurge, the *Pakistani restaurant* in the town centre is excellent value. *Zanzibar* is a good place for a cold beer.

Getting There & Away

Gitega is just more than an hour's drive from Bujumbura and minibuses make the run for BFr 1500 throughout the day. As with all road journeys in Burundi, it is worth checking the security situation before travelling.

KAYANZA

Kayanza is on the road north to Kigali, near the Rwandan border. It has a good market on Monday, Wednesday and Saturday.

The missions won't take guests, so stay at *Auberge de Kayanza*, which costs BFr 3000 a double.

Minibuses from Bujumbura cost BFr 2000 and take about two hours.

KILEMBA

The principal attraction here is the **Kibabi Hot Springs**, 16km from town. There are several pools of differing temperatures, the main one hovering at around 100°C. A little further uphill is a waterfall, and another deep pool where it's safe to swim.

Do You Trust your Sources?

Uganda has long laid claim to the source of the mighty Nile River. However, more than 70 years after John Hanning Speke named the Ripon Falls at Jinja in modern-day Uganda as the source of the Nile, German explorer Burckhard Waldecker discovered an alternative source way up in the mountains of Burundi. High up on the summit of Mt Kikizi (2145m), near the commune of Rotovu, is the southernmost source of the Nile, marked by a small pyramid. Unfortunately for the Burundian tourist authorities, the water table has dropped in recent years so the water now has to be coaxed out of the ground through a pipe, hardly as dramatic as the raging river near Jinja.

However, there is little doubt that this insignificant-looking little spring is important, as not only did Waldecker claim it as the source of the Nile, but also as the source of the enormous Congo River that eventually spills into the Atlantic, thousands of kilometres away. That said, it seems fair to say that if a natural leak of this small size can be considered a realistic contender, then there must be hundreds of ground springs all over the region that might justly claim the same.

Sadly, some might say gladly, the civil war has made this area of the country unsafe to visit. However, in the event security improves, you can stay at the Mission Catholique in Rutana, 7km away.

Most people stay at *Swedish Pentecostal Mission* which has a very good guesthouse. A bed in the dormitory costs BFr 1500. Private rooms with a shower and toilet and the use of a fully equipped kitchen cost BFr 4000 per person.

Language

Although Swahili may initially seem a bit daunting, its structure is fairly regular, and its pronunciation is uncomplicated. You'll soon discover that just a handful of basic words will rapidly break down barriers between you and the many people you meet on your travels in East Africa.

If your time is limited, concentrate first on the greetings and then on numbers (very useful when negotiating with market vendors, taxi drivers etc). The words and phrases included in this chapter will help get you started; if you'd like a more comprehensive guide to the language get a copy of Lonely Planet's excellent 2nd edition *Swahili phrasebook*.

'Standard' Swahili is the language spoken in Zanzibar, although many other variants or dialects can be found throughout East Africa. Written Swahili, the language used in newspapers, textbooks and literature, usually conforms to the coastal standards. This language guide uses the standard variety as it should be more universally understood. If words are used which are specific to any one country they are noted in brackets.

Pronunciation

Perhaps the easiest part of learning Swahili is the pronunciation. Every letter gets pronounced, unless it's part of the consonant combinations discussed in the 'Consonants' section below. If a letter is written twice, it is pronounced twice – or rather, gets extended into two syllables. For example, *mzee* (respected elder) has three syllables: *m-ZE-e* (note that the 'm' is a separate syllable, and that the double 'e' indicates that the vowel sound is lengthened).

Word stress in Swahili almost always falls on the second-to-last syllable.

Vowels

Correct pronunciation of vowels is the key to making yourself understood in Swahili. If the following guidelines don't work for you, listen closely to how Swahili speakers pronounce their words and spend some time practising. There's also a useful audio pronunciation guide available on the World Wide Web at: http://www.yale.edu/swahili/sound/pronunce.htm

Remember that when two vowels appear next to each other, each must be pronounced in turn. For example, *kawaida* (usual) is pronounced *ka-wa-EE-da*.

a	as in 'calm' (*dada*, 'sister')
e	as the 'a' in 'may' (*wewe*, 'you')
i	as the 'e' in 'me' (*sisi*, 'we')
o	as in 'go' (*moja*, 'one')
u	as the 'o' in 'to' (*duka*, 'store')

Consonants

r	Swahili speakers make only a slight distinction between **r** and **l**; try using a light 'd' where you read 'r' and you'll be pretty close.
dh	as 'th' in 'this' (*dhambi*, 'sin')
th	as 'th' in 'thing' (*thelathini*, 'thirty')
ny	as the 'ni' in 'onion' (*nyasi*, 'grass')
ng'	as in 'singer' (*ng'ombe*, 'cow'); practise by trying to use the 'ng' sound at the beginning of a word
gh	a guttural sound, similar to the *ch* in Scottish *loch* (*ghali,* 'expensive')
g	as in 'get' (*gari*, 'car')
ch	as in 'church' (*chakula*, 'food')

Greetings & Civilities

Hello.	*Salama/Jambo.*
How are you?	*Hujambo?*
I'm fine.	*Sijambo.* (response)
How are you?	*Habari?*
Good.	*Nzuri.* (response)

There is also a respectful greeting used for addressing elders: *Shikamoo*. The reply is *Marahaba*.

Goodbye.	*Kwa heri.*
Yes.	*Ndiyo.*
No.	*Hapana.*

Please. (if asking a big favour) — *Tafadhali.*

Thank you (very much). — *Asante (sana).*

Excuse me. — *Samahani.*

Can you help me, please? — *Tafadhali, naomba msaada.*

What's your name? — *Jina lako nani?/ Unaitwa nani?*

My name is ... — *Jina langu ni .../ Naitwa ...*

Where are you from? — *Unatoka wapi?/ Kwenu ni wapi?*

I'm from ... — *Natokea .../Kwetu ni ...*

Maybe. — *Labda/Pengine.*

OK. — *Sawa.*

May I take a picture? — *Naomba kupiga picha.*

Language Difficulties

Do you speak English/Swahili? — *Unasema Kiingereza/ Kiswahili?*

I don't speak English/Swahili. — *Sisemi Kiingereza/ Kiswahili.*

Do you understand? — *Unaelewa?*

I understand. — *Naelewa.*

I don't understand. — *Sielewi.*

Please speak slowly. — *Tafadhali sema pole pole.*

Please repeat that. — *Tafadhali sema tena.*

How do you say ... in Swahili? — *Unasemaje ... kwa Kiswahili?*

Getting Around

(Remember to always exchange greetings before asking for help or information.)

What time is the ... leaving? — *... inaondoka saa ngapi?*

bus — *basi*

minibus — *dalla dalla* (Tanz) *matatu* (Kenya)

plane — *ndege*

train — *treni/gari la moshi*

Is there a bus going to ...? — *Kuna basi ya ...?*

What time will we arrive? — *Tutafika saa ngapi?*

I'd like to buy a ticket. — *Nataka kununua tikiti.*

How much per person? — *Ni bei gani kwa kila mtu?*

I'd like to make a reservation to ... — *Nataka kufanya buking kwenda ...*

Please tell me when the bus arrives in ... — *Basi ikifika ..., tafadhali unijulishe.*

I want to get off here. — *Nitashuka hapa.*

Drop me off! — *Shusha!*

Stop! — *Simama!*

Where is the ...? — *... ni wapi?*

airport — *uwanja wa ndege*

bus station — *stesheni ya basi*

bus stop — *bas stendi*

taxi stand — *stendi ya teksi*

train station — *stesheni ya treni*

1st class — *daraja la kwanza*

2nd class — *daraja la pili*

3rd class — *daraja la tatu*

ship — *meli*

dhow (traditional sailing boat) — *dhau*

small wooden boat with motor — *mashua*

Where do we get on the boat? — *Tupande meli wapi?*

What time does the boat leave/arrive? — *Meli inaondoka/ inafika saa ngapi?*

I'd like to hire a ... — *Nataka kukodi ...*

bicycle — *baisikeli*

car — *gari*

motorcycle — *pikipiki*

row boat — *mtumbwi*

Directions

Excuse me, I'm looking for ... — *Tafadhali, natafuta ...*

I want to go to ... — *Nataka kwenda ...*

Is it near? — *Ni karibu?*

Signs

HATARI	DANGER
IMEFUNGWA	CLOSED
IMEFUNGULIWA	OPEN
MAHALI PA KUINGIA	ENTRANCE
MAHALI PA KUTOKA	EXIT
HAIRUHUSIWI KUINGIA	NO ENTRY
USIVUTE SIGARA	NO SMOKING
MAELEZO	INFORMATION
SIMAMA	STOP
CHOO; MSALANI	TOILETS
WANAWAKE	WOMEN
WANAUME	MEN

Is it far?	*Ni mbali?*
How many kilometres from here?	*Ni kilomita ngapi kutoka hapa?*
Turn around.	*Kata/Geuka.*
Turn back.	*Rudi nyuma.*
Turn/Go …	*Kata/Pita/Chukua …*
left	*kushoto*
right	*kulia*
straight ahead	*moja kwa moja*
there	*huko*
over there	*pale*
next to	*jirani/karibu na*
map	*ramani*
north	*kaskazini*
south	*kusini*
east	*mashariki*
west	*magharibi*

Around Town

Where is the …?	*… ni wapi?*
beach	*baharini/ufukwe*
bank	*benki*
church	*kanisa*
… embassy	*ubalozi wa …*
market	*soko*
mosque	*msikiti*
museum	*makumbusho*
park (gardens)	*bustani*

police station	*kituo cha polisi*
post office	*posta*
river	*mto*
tourist office	*ofisi ya watalii*
Is (the post office) open?	*(Posta) imefunguliwa?*
I want to change some money.	*Nataka kubadilisha pesa.*
cheque	*hundi ya benki*
currency	*hela/pesa*
telephone centre	*mahali pa kupiga simu*
I'd like to make a phone call.	*Nataka kupiga simu.*
Is there a phone near here?	*Je, kuna simu karibu na hapa?*

Accommodation

guesthouse	*gesti*
hotel	*hoteli* (note: *hoteli* also means restaurant)
Excuse me, is there a hotel nearby?	*Samahani, kuna hoteli hapa karibuni?*
Do you have a room?	*Je, kuna nafasi ya chumba hapa?*
I want a … room.	*Ninataka chumba …*
ordinary	*cha kawaida*
cheaper	*cha bei rahisi*
larger	*kikubwa zaidi*
smaller	*kidogo zaidi*
quieter	*ambacho hakuna kelele*
Is there (a) …?	*Je, kuna …?*
air conditioning	*AC*
bath	*bafu*
electricity	*umeme*
fan	*feni*
key	*ufunguo*
hot water	*maji ya moto*
toilet	*choo*
telephone	*simu*
How much is it per …?	*Ni bei gani kwa …?*
person	*kila mtu*
night	*usiku*
week	*wiki*

I'll stay for two/ three nights.	*Nitakaa kwa usiku mbili/tatu.*	OK, I'll take it.	*Haya, nakubali.*
Can I look at the room?	*Ningependa kutazama chumba.*	I'm just looking.	*Naangalia/ Natazama tu.*
Do you have any other rooms?	*Kuna vyumba vingine?*	I want one/two.	*Nataka moja/mbili.*
		I want a larger ...	*Nataka ... kubwa zaidi.*
I need (a) ...	*Ninahitaji ...*	I want a smaller ...	*Nataka ... ndogo zaidi.*
blanket	*blanketi*	battery	*betri*
mosquito coils	*dawa ya mbu*	insect repellent	*dawa ya kuzuia mbuu*
mosquito net	*chandalua*	razor	*wembe*
pillow	*mto*	sanitary napkins	*Kotex*
sheet/sheets	*shuka/mashuka*	soap	*sabuni*
soap	*sabuni*	suntan lotion	*dawa ya kukinga jua*
toilet paper	*karatasi ya choo*	tampons	*OB/Tampax*
towel	*tauli*	toothbrush	*mswaki*
		toothpaste	*dawa ya meno/Kolgeti*
bed	*kitanda*	water purifier	*chombo cha kusafishia maji*
bedroom	*chumba cha kulala*		
breakfast	*chai cha asubuhi*	a little	*kidogo*
lights	*taa*	a lot	*nyingi*
room/rooms	*chumba/vyumba*	enough	*bas/inatosha*
		too much/many	*mno*

Shopping

Is there a store near here?	*Je, kuna duka hapa jirani?*
Where can I buy ...?	*Naweza kununua ... wapi?*

Where is a ...?	*... ni wapi?*
bakery	*duka la mkate*
barber	*kinyozi*
bookshop	*duka la vitabu*
butcher	*duka la nyama*
chemist/drugstore	*duka la dawa*
clothes shop	*duka la nguo*
fruitshop	*duka la matunda*
vegetable shop	*duka la mboga*
general store/shop	*duka/kioski*
market	*soko*

How much is it?	*Bei gani?*
That's very expensive.	*Ghali sana.*
Is there a cheaper one?	*Kuna nyingine ambayo siyo ghali?*
Can you lower the price?	*Tafadhali, upunguze bei.*
It's a fair price.	*Ni bei nzuri/nafuu.*

cheap	*rahisi*
(too) expensive	*ghali (mno)*

Health

Where can I find a (good) ...?	*Naweza kupata ... (mzuri) wapi?*
dentist	*daktari wa meno*
doctor	*daktari/mganga*
hospital	*hospitali*
medical centre	*matibabu*

I'm sick.	*Niko mgonjwa.*
My friend is sick.	*Rafiki yangu ni mgonjwa.*
I need a doctor.	*Nataka kuona daktari.*
It hurts here.	*Naumwa hapa.*
I've been vaccinated.	*Nimechanjwa.*
I feel dizzy.	*Nasikia/Nasihi kizun guzungu.*
I feel nauseous.	*Nataka kutapika.*
I've been vomiting.	*Nina tapika.*
I'm pregnant.	*Nina mimba.*

diarrhoea	*harisha/hara/endesha*
fever	*homa*
headache	*umwa kichwa*
malaria	*maleria*
nausea	*tapika*

rabies	*nimeumwa na mbwa wa kichaa*
stomachache	*umwa tumbo*
toothache	*jino linaniuma*
virus	*kirus/virus* (pl)
vomiting	*tapika*

I'm allergic to ...	*Nina aleji ya ...*
antibiotics	*antibayotiki*
penicillin	*penesilini*

I'm on medication for ...	*Nakunywa dawa ya ...*
asthma	*ugonjwa wa pumu*
diabetes	*dayabeti*
epilepsy	*epilepsi*

aspirin	*aspirini/panadol/ dawa ya kichwa*
condom	*kondom*
contraceptive pill	*kuzuia mimba*
medicine	*dawa*
pill	*kidonge/vidonge* (pl)

Emergencies

Help!	*Nisaidie!Jamaani!*
It's an emergency.	*Ni jambo la haraka.*
Call a doctor!	*Muite daktari!*
Call the police!	*Muite polisi!*
Fire!	*Moto!*
I'm ill.	*Naumwa.*
I've been robbed!	*Nimeibiwa!*
Go away!	*Toka!*
Leave me alone!	*Niache!/ Usinisumbue!*
I'm lost.	*Nimepotea.*

Time, Days & Numbers

What time is it?	*Ni saa ngapi?*
It's ... o'clock.	*Ni saa ...*
half past	*na nusu*
quarter past	*na robo*
quarter to	*kasa robo*
minute	*dakika*

today	*leo*
tomorrow	*kesho*
yesterday	*jana*
now	*sasa*
soon	*sasa hivi*
later	*baadaye*
always	*kila wakati*
every day	*kila siku*
day(s)	*siku*
week(s)	*wiki*

Saturday	*Jumamosi*
Sunday	*Jumapili*
Monday	*Jumatatu*
Tuesday	*Jumanne*
Wednesday	*Jumatano*
Thursday	*Alhamisi*
Friday	*Ijumaa*

0	*sifuri*
1	*moja*
2	*mbili*
3	*tatu*
4	*nne*
5	*tano*
6	*sita*
7	*saba*
8	*nane*
9	*tisa*
10	*kumi*
11	*kumi na moja* (lit: ten-and-one)
12	*kumi na mbili*
20	*ishirini*
21	*ishirini na moja* (lit: twenty-and-one)
22	*ishirini na mbili*
30	*thelathini*
40	*arobaini*
50	*hamsini*
60	*sitini*
70	*sabini*
80	*themanini*
90	*tisini*
100	*mia* or *mia moja*
200	*mia mbili* (lit: hundred-two)
300	*mia tatu*
1000	*elfu*
100,000	*laki*

one million	*milioni*
half	*nusu*

FOOD & DRINK
Basics

I'm vegetarian.	*Nakula mboga tu.*
I don't eat meat.	*Mimi sili nyama.*
Is there a restaurant near here?	*Je, kuna hoteli ya chakula hapo jirani?*
Do you serve food here?	*Mnauza chakula hapa?*
I'd like …	*Nataka …*

water	*maji (ya moto)*
drinking water	*maji ya kunywa*
mineral water	*maji safi*
milk	*maziwa*
(fruit) juice	*jusi/maji (ya matunda)*
soda/soft drink	*soda*
beer	*bia (baridi)*
ice	*barafu*
spirits	*pombe kali*
wine	*mvinyo*

boiled	*ya kuchemka*
bread	*mkate*
butter	*siagi*
cup	*kikombe*
curry	*mchuzi*
egg(s)	*yai (mayai)*
food	*chakula*
fork	*uma*
fried	*kaanga*
glass	*glasi*
hot/cold	*ya moto/baridi*
hot (spicy)	*hoho*
Indian bread	*chapati*
knife	*kisu*
napkin	*kitambaa*
pepper	*pilipili*
plate	*sahani*
raw	*mbichi*
ripe	*mbivu*
roast	*choma*
salt	*chumvi*
sauce	*mchuzi*
soup	*supu*
sugar	*sukari*
sweet	*tamu*
table	*mesa*
teaspoon	*kijiko*
yoghurt	*maziwalala*

Vegetables & Grains

aubergine	*biringani*
cabbage	*kabichi*
capsicum	*pilipili baridi*
carrots	*karoti*
cassava	*muhogo*
garlic	*vitunguu saumu*
kidney beans	*maharagwe*
lettuce	*salad*
maize-meal porridge	*ugali, posho*
mashed plantains	*matoke*
onions	*vitunguu*
plantains	*ndzi*
potatoes	*viazi*
rice	*wali*
spinach (boiled)	*sukuma wiki*
tomatoes	*nyana*
vegetables	*mboga*
vegetable stew	*mboga*

Meat & Fish

beef	*nyama ya ngombe*
crab	*kaa*
fish	*samaki*
kebabs	*mushkaki*
lobster	*kamba*
meat	*nyama*
meat stew	*karanga*
mutton, goat	*nyama ya mbuzi*
pork	*nyama ya nguruwe*
squid	*ngisi*
steak	*steki*

Fruit

banana	*ndizi*
coconut (green)	*dafu*
coconut (ripe)	*nazi*
custard apples	*stafeli*
dates	*tende*
fruit	*matunda*
grapefruit	*madanzi*
guava	*pera*
lemon	*limau*
lime	*ndimu*
mango	*embe*
orange	*chungwa*
papaya	*papai*
passionfruit	*pasheni*
pineapple	*nanasi*
sugar cane	*muwa*
(water)melon	*tikiti (maji)*

Glossary

The following is a list of words and acronyms you are likely to come across when in East Africa. For a more complete glossary of food terms, see the Language chapter.

askari – security guard, watchman

banda – thatched-roof hut with wooden or earthen walls; also simple wooden and stone-built accommodation
boda-boda – bicycle-taxi
boma – village
bui-bui – black cover-all garment worn by Islamic women outside the home

CCM – Chama Cha Mapinduzi, ruling political party in Tanzania
chai – tea, but also a bribe
chakula – food
chang'a – dangerous home-made alcoholic brew containing methyl alcohol
choo – toilet (pronounced as 'cho')
CITES – UN Convention on International Trade in Endangered Species

dalla-dalla – Tanzanian minibus
dhow – ancient Arabic sailing vessel
dudu – a small insect or bug; a creepy crawly
duka – small shop or kiosk selling household basics

forex – foreign exchange bureau
fundi – repair man/woman (eg, clothing, building trades, cars etc); also an expert

gacaca – traditional tribunal headed by village elders

Ghai – the Kikuyu god

hakuna matata – no problem. Watch out – there often is!
harambee – the concept of community self-help, voluntary fund-raising. A cornerstone of Jomo Kenyatta's ideology.

hatari – danger
hoteli – basic local eatery; 'restaurant' in Swahili

Interahamwe – Hutu militia in Rwanda

jinga! – crazy! (also used as an adjective)
jua kali – literally, 'hot sun'; usually an outdoor vehicle repair shop or market.

kabaka – king (Uganda)
kanga – printed cotton wrapround incorporating a Swahili proverb. Worn by many women both inside and outside the home.
kikoi – printed cotton wrap-around traditionally worn by men
kiondas – woven baskets
kitu kidogo – 'a little something', a bribe
KWS – Kenya Wildlife Service

lugga – dry river bed, mainly in northern Kenya

makonde – wood carving
makuti – thatched roof made of palm leaves, mainly on the coast
malaya – prostitute
manamba – matatu tout, often a veritable style guru and all-round dude
mandazi – semisweet, flat doughnut
manyatta – Maasai or Samburu livestock camp often surrounded by a circle of thorn bushes
marimbas – musical instruments played with the thumb
matatu – Kenyan minibus with megadecibel sound system, seemingly unlimited carrying capacity and two speeds – stationary and flat out
matoke – mashed plantains (green bananas)
miraa – bundles of leafy twigs and shoots that are chewed as a stimulant and appetite-suppressant
moran – Maasai or Samburu warrior (pl *morani*)

murram – dirt or part-gravelled road
mwami – king (Rwanda and Burundi)
mwananchi – worker of any kind but usually agricultural (pl *wananchi*, which is also used to refer to 'the people')
mwizi – a thief
mzee – an old person or respected elder
mzee kipara – 'mosquito airport' (bald man)
mzungu – white person (pl *wazungu*)

NRA – National Resistance Army (Uganda)
NRM – National Resistance Movement (Uganda)
nyama choma – barbecued meat, often goat
Nyayo – 'footsteps'. One of the cornerstones of Moi's political ideology. In other words, to follow in the footsteps of Kenyatta.

panga – machete, carried by many people in the East African countryside and often by thieves in the cities
parking boys – unemployed youths or young men who will help park a vehicle and guard it while the owner is absent
pesa – money

RMS – Ruwenzori Mountaineering Services (Uganda)
RPF – Rwandan Patriotic Front

safari – 'journey' in Swahili
shamba – small farm or plot of land
shifta – bandit
shilingi – money

taarab – music that combines African, Arabic and Indian influences; popular on Unguja
taka taka – rubbish
TANAPA – Tanzania National Parks Authority
taxi – minibus (Uganda)
tilapia – Nile perch
TTC – Tanzania Tourist Corporation

Uhuru – freedom or independence
Unguja – Zanzibar Island (Tanzania)
UWA – Uganda Wildlife Authority

vibuyu – carved gourds

waragi – Ugandan millet-based alcohol
Watutsi – plural of Tutsi

LONELY PLANET

Lonely Planet Journeys

JOURNEYS is a unique collection of travel writing – published by the company that understands travel better than anyone else. It is a series for anyone who has ever experienced – or dreamed of – the magical moment when they encountered a strange culture or saw a place for the first time. They are tales to read while you're planning a trip, while you're on the road or while you're in an armchair in front of a fire.

These outstanding titles explore our planet through the eyes of a diverse group of international writers. JOURNEYS books catch the spirit of a place, illuminate a culture, recount a crazy adventure or introduce a fascinating way of life. They always entertain, and always enrich the experience of travel.

MALI BLUES
Traveling to an African Beat
Lieve Joris (translated by Sam Garrett)
Drought, rebel uprisings, ethnic conflict: these are the predominant images of West Africa. But as Lieve Joris travels in Senegal, Mauritania and Mali, she meets survivors, fascinating individuals charting new ways of living between tradition and modernity. With her remarkable gift for drawing out people's stories, Joris brilliantly captures the rhythms of a world that refuses to give in.

THE GATES OF DAMASCUS
Lieve Joris (translated by Sam Garrett)
This best-selling book is a beautifully drawn portrait of day-to-day life in modern Syria. Through her intimate contact with local people, Lieve Joris draws us into the fascinating world that lies behind the gates of Damascus. Hala's husband is a political prisoner, jailed for his opposition to the Assad regime; through the author's friendship with Hala we see how Syrian politics impacts on the lives of ordinary people.

SONGS TO AN AFRICAN SUNSET
A Zimbabwean Story
Sekai Nzenza-Shand
Songs to an African Sunset braids vividly personal stories into an intimate picture of contemporary Zimbabwe. Returning to her family's village after many years in the west, Sekai Nzenza-Shand discovers a world where ancestor worship, polygamy and witchcraft still govern the rhythms of daily life – and where drought, deforestation and AIDS have wrought devastating changes. With insight and affection, she explores a culture torn between respect for the old ways and the irresistible pull of the new.

THE RAINBIRD
A Central African Journey
Jan Brokken (translated by Sam Garrett)
Following in the footsteps of famous Europeans such as Albert Schweitzer and HM Stanley, Jan Brokken journeyed to Gabon in central Africa. *The Rainbird* brilliantly chronicles the encounter between Africa and Europe as it was acted out on a side-street of history in a kaleidoscope of adventures and anecdotes. A compelling, immensely readable account of the author's own travels in one of the most remote and mysterious regions of Africa.

LONELY PLANET

Guides by Region

Lonely Planet is known worldwide for publishing practical, reliable and no-nonsense travel information in our guides and on our Web site. The Lonely Planet list covers just about every accessible part of the world. Currently there are thirteen series: travel guides, shoestring guides, walking guides, city guides, phrasebooks, audio packs, city maps, travel atlases, diving & snorkeling guides, restaurant guides, first-time travel guides, healthy travel and travel literature.

AFRICA Africa on a shoestring • Africa – the South • Arabic (Egyptian) phrasebook • Arabic (Moroccan) phrasebook • Cairo • Cape Town • Cape Town city map • Central Africa • East Africa • Egypt • Egypt travel atlas • Ethiopian (Amharic) phrasebook • The Gambia & Senegal • Healthy Travel Africa • Kenya • Kenya travel atlas • Malawi, Mozambique & Zambia • Morocco • North Africa • Read This First Africa • South Africa, Lesotho & Swaziland • South Africa, Lesotho & Swaziland travel atlas • Swahili phrasebook • Tanzania, Zanzibar & Pemba • Trekking in East Africa • Tunisia • West Africa • Zimbabwe, Botswana & Namibia • Zimbabwe, Botswana & Nambia Travel Atlas • World Food Morocco

Travel Literature: The Rainbird: A Central African Journey • Songs to an African Sunset: A Zimbabwean Story • Mali Blues: Traveling to an African Beat

AUSTRALIA & THE PACIFIC Auckland • Australia • Australian phrasebook • Bushwalking in Australia • Bushwalking in Papua New Guinea • Fiji • Fijian phrasebook • Healthy Travel Australia, NZ and the Pacific • Islands of Australia's Great Barrier Reef • Melbourne • Melbourne city map • Micronesia • New Caledonia • New South Wales & the ACT • New Zealand • Northern Territory • Outback Australia • Out To Eat – Melbourne • Out to Eat – Sydney • Papua New Guinea • Pidgin phrasebook • Queensland • Rarotonga & the Cook Islands • Samoa • Solomon Islands • South Australia • South Pacific • South Pacific Languages phrasebook • Sydney • Sydney city map • Sydney Condensed • Tahiti & French Polynesia • Tasmania • Tonga • Tramping in New Zealand • Vanuatu • Victoria • Western Australia

Travel Literature: Islands in the Clouds • Kiwi Tracks: A New Zealand Journey • Sean & David's Long Drive

CENTRAL AMERICA & THE CARIBBEAN Bahamas, Turks & Caicos • Bermuda • Central America on a shoestring • Costa Rica • Cuba • Dominican Republic & Haiti • Eastern Caribbean • Guatemala, Belize & Yucatán: La Ruta Maya • Jamaica • Mexico • Mexico City • Panama • Puerto Rico • Read This First Central & South America • World Food Mexico

Travel Literature: Green Dreams: Travels in Central America

EUROPE Amsterdam • Amsterdam city map • Andalucía • Austria • Baltic States phrasebook • Barcelona • Berlin • Berlin city map • Britain • British phrasebook • Brussels, Bruges & Antwerp • Budapest city map • Canary Islands • Central Europe • Central Europe phrasebook • Corfu & Ionians • Corsica • Crete • Crete Condensed • Croatia • Cyprus • Czech & Slovak Republics • Denmark • Dublin • Eastern Europe • Eastern Europe phrasebook • Edinburgh • Estonia, Latvia & Lithuania • Europe on a shoestring • Finland • Florence • France • French phrasebook • Germany • German phrasebook • Greece • Greek Islands • Greek phrasebook • Hungary • Iceland, Greenland & the Faroe Islands • Istanbul City Map • Ireland • Italian phrasebook • Italy • Krakow •Lisbon • London • London city map • London Condensed • Mediterranean Europe • Mediterranean Europe phrasebook • Munich • Norway • Paris • Paris city map • Paris Condensed • Poland • Portugal • Portugese phrasebook • Portugal travel atlas • Prague • Prague city map • Provence & the Côte d'Azur • Romania & Moldova • Rome • Russia, Ukraine & Belarus • Russian phrasebook • Scandinavian & Baltic Europe • Scandinavian Europe phrasebook • Scotland • Slovenia • Spain • Spanish phrasebook • St Petersburg • Switzerland • Trekking in Spain • Ukrainian phrasebook • Venice • Vienna • Walking in Britain • Walking in Ireland • Walking in Italy • Walking in Spain • Walking in Switzerland • Western Europe • Western Europe phrasebook • World Food Italy • World Food Spain

Travel Literature: The Olive Grove: Travels in Greece

INDIAN SUBCONTINENT Bangladesh • Bengali phrasebook • Bhutan • Delhi • Goa • Hindi & Urdu phrasebook • India • India & Bangladesh travel atlas • Indian Himalaya • Karakoram Highway • Kerala • Mumbai (Bombay) • Nepal • Nepali phrasebook • Pakistan • Rajasthan • Read This First: Asia & India • South India • Sri Lanka • Sri Lanka phrasebook • Trekking in the Indian Himalaya • Trekking in the Karakoram & Hindukush • Trekking in the Nepal Himalaya

Travel Literature: In Rajasthan • Shopping for Buddhas • The Age Of Kali

LONELY PLANET

Mail Order

Lonely Planet products are distributed worldwide. They are also available by mail order from Lonely Planet, so if you have difficulty finding a title please write to us. North and South American residents should write to 150 Linden St, Oakland, CA 94607, USA; European and African residents should write to 10a Spring Place, London NW5 3BH, UK; and residents of other countries to PO Box 617, Hawthorn, Victoria 3122, Australia.

ISLANDS OF THE INDIAN OCEAN Madagascar & Comoros • Maldives • Mauritius, Réunion & Seychelles

MIDDLE EAST & CENTRAL ASIA Arab Gulf States • Central Asia • Central Asia phrasebook • Dubai • Hebrew phrasebook • Iran • Israel & the Palestinian Territories • Israel & the Palestinian Territories travel atlas • Istanbul • Istanbul to Cairo • Jerusalem • Jerusalem City Map • Jordan & Syria • Jordan, Syria & Lebanon travel atlas • Lebanon • Middle East on a shoestring • Syria • Turkey • Turkey travel atlas • Turkish phrasebook • Yemen
Travel Literature: The Gates of Damascus • Kingdom of the Film Stars: Journey into Jordan • Black on Black: Iran Revisited

NORTH AMERICA Alaska • Backpacking in Alaska • Baja California • California & Nevada • California Condensed • Canada • Chicago • Chicago city map • Deep South • Florida • Hawaii • Honolulu • Las Vegas • Los Angeles • Miami • New England • New Orleans • New York City • New York city map • New York Condensed • New York, New Jersey & Pennsylvania • Oahu • Pacific Northwest USA • Puerto Rico • Rocky Mountain • San Francisco • San Francisco city map • Seattle • Southwest USA • Texas • USA • USA phrasebook • Vancouver • Washington, DC & the Capital Region • Washington DC city map
Travel Literature: Drive Thru America

NORTH-EAST ASIA Beijing • Cantonese phrasebook • China • Hong Kong • Hong Kong city map • Hong Kong, Macau & Guangzhou • Japan • Japanese phrasebook • Japanese audio pack • Korea • Korean phrasebook • Kyoto • Mandarin phrasebook • Mongolia • Mongolian phrasebook • North-East Asia on a shoestring • Seoul • South-West China • Taiwan • Tibet • Tibetan phrasebook • Tokyo
Travel Literature: Lost Japan • In Xanadu

SOUTH AMERICA Argentina, Uruguay & Paraguay • Bolivia • Brazil • Brazilian phrasebook • Buenos Aires • Chile & Easter Island • Chile & Easter Island travel atlas • Colombia • Ecuador & the Galapagos Islands • Healthy Travel Central & South America • Latin American Spanish phrasebook • Peru •Quechua phrasebook • Rio de Janeiro • Rio de Janeiro city map • South America on a shoestring • Trekking in the Patagonian Andes • Venezuela
Travel Literature: Full Circle: A South American Journey

SOUTH-EAST ASIA Bali & Lombok • Bangkok • Bangkok city map • Burmese phrasebook • Cambodia • Hanoi • Healthy Travel Asia & India • Hill Tribes phrasebook • Ho Chi Minh City • Indonesia • Indonesia's Eastern Islands • Indonesian phrasebook • Indonesian audio pack • Jakarta • Java • Laos • Lao phrasebook • Laos travel atlas • Malay phrasebook • Malaysia, Singapore & Brunei • Myanmar (Burma) • Philippines • Pilipino (Tagalog) phrasebook • Read This First Asia & India • Singapore • South-East Asia on a shoestring • South-East Asia phrasebook • Thailand • Thailand's Islands & Beaches • Thailand travel atlas • Thai phrasebook • Thai audio pack • Vietnam • Vietnamese phrasebook • Vietnam travel atlas • World Food Thailand • World Food Vietnam

ALSO AVAILABLE: Antarctica • The Arctic • Brief Encounters: Stories of Love, Sex & Travel • Chasing Rickshaws • Lonely Planet Unpacked • Not the Only Planet: Travel Stories from Science Fiction • Sacred India • Travel with Children • Traveller's Tales

Index

Abbreviations

B – Burundi   R – Rwanda   U – Uganda
K – Kenya   T – Tanzania

Text

A

Aberdare National Park (K) 268-9, **268**
accommodation 75, *see also* individual country entries
activities, *see* individual entries
Adzungwa Mountains National Park (T) 475-6
Aga Khan Mosque (T) 389
air travel
   to/from Burundi 660-2
   to/from East Africa 78-82
   to/from Kenya 146
   to/from Rwanda 632
   to/from Tanzania 356
   to/from Uganda 525
   within Burundi 662
   within East Africa 86
   within Kenya 150
   within Rwanda 634
   within Tanzania 360
   within Uganda 529
Akamba (K) 36
Amani Botanical Gardens (T) 417-18
Amboni Caves (T) 418
Amboseli National Park (K) 186-7, **186**
Amin, Idi (U) 501-2
Anglican Cathedral (T) 387
Apoka (U) 610
Arabuko-Sokoke Forest Reserve (K) 216
architecture 226, 388
arts 27-30, *see also* individual entries
Arua (U) 608-9
Aruba Dam (K) 239
Arusha (T) 428-34, **429**
   entertainment 433
   getting around 434
   getting there & away 433-4
   places to eat 432-3
   places to stay 431-2
   safety 430-1
Arusha Declaration Museum (T) 431

Arusha National Park (T) 434-7, **435**

B

Baden-Powell Museum 267
Bagamoyo (T) 411-14
Bagaza, Jean-Baptiste (B) 655
Bagisu (U) 46
balloon safaris 141
Baragoi (K) 323
bargaining 54
Basoga (U) 46
Bawi Island (T) 401-2
beaches
   Burundi 667
   Kenya 141, 209, 232-4
   Tanzania 369, 377-8, 397-401, 409, 410, 460, 491, 493
   Uganda 550
Beit al-Sahel (T), *see* Palace Museum
Beit el-Ajaib (T), *see* House of Wonders
Bigodi Wetland Sanctuary (U) 571
Bio Ken Snake Farm & Laboratory (K) 213
birdwatching 256, 257, 509
boat travel
   to/from Burundi 661-2
   to/from East Africa 85
   to/from Kenya 149
   to/from Tanzania 358-9
   to/from Uganda 527-8
   within East Africa 88
   within Kenya 155
   within Rwanda 634-5
   within Tanzania 363-4
   within Uganda 531
Bomas of Kenya, The (K) 181
Bongoyo Island (T) 376-7
Bongoyo Island Marine Reserve (T) 376-7
books, *see also* individual country entries
   flora & fauna 56
   health 61

history 56
literature 29-30, 129-30
Lonely Planet 55-6
travel 56
border crossings
   Burundi 660-2
   Kenya 146-9
   Rwanda 632-4
   Tanzania 356-8
   Uganda 525-7
Bububu (T) 398
Budongo Central Forest Reserve (U) 607-8
Buffalo Springs National Reserve (K) 317-19, **318**
Buganda (U) 20, 46
Buganda Kingdom, Buildings of the (U) 537
Buggala Island (U) 599-600
Bujagali Falls (U) 559
Bujumbura (B) 662-7, **663**
   entertainment 666-7
   getting there & away 667
   places to eat 665-6
   places to stay 664-5
   shopping 667
Bukasa Island (U) 600
Bukoba (T) 456-8, **457**
Bundibugyo (U) 572
Burundi 653-68, **653**
   embassies 658
   getting around 662
   getting there & away 659-61
   history 654-6
   holidays 659
   Internet services 659
   money 658-9
   postal services 659
   safety 659
   telephone services 659
   visas 657-8
bus travel
   to/from Burundi 660-1
   to/from East Africa 82-5
   to/from Kenya 146-9
   to/from Rwanda 632-3
   to/from Tanzania 356-8

Bold indicates maps.

Bold indicates maps.

Boxed Text

Bold indicates maps.

MAP LEGEND

CITY ROUTES

Freeway .... Freeway	Street .... Street	Unsealed Road	Stepped Street
Highway .... Primary Road	Lane .... Lane	One Way Street	Tunnel
Road .... Secondary Road	On/Off Ramp	Pedestrian Street	Footbridge

HYDROGRAPHY

.... River, Creek — Dry Lake; Salt Lake
.... Lake — Spring; Rapids
Waterfalls

TRANSPORT ROUTES & STATIONS

.... Train — Walking Trail
.... Ferry — Walking Tour
Path

REGIONAL ROUTES

.... Tollway, Freeway — Secondary Road
.... Primary Road — Minor Road

BOUNDARIES

.... International — Disputed
.... State — Fortified Wall
Cliff

AREA FEATURES

.... Building	.... Market	Beach	.... Campus
.... Park, Gardens	.... Sports Ground	Cemetery	.... Plaza

POPULATION SYMBOLS

✪ **CAPITAL** .... National Capital	● **CITY** .... City	● Village ....Village
◉ **CAPITAL** .... State Capital	● **Town** ....Town	.... Urban Area

MAP SYMBOLS

★ ....Place to Stay	▼ ....Place to Eat	● ....Point of Interest
Airfield; Airport	Embassy	Museum	Shopping Centre
Bank	Golf Course	National Park	Stately Home
Bus Stop/Terminal	Hospital	Parking	Taxis
Camp	Hut	Petrol	Telephone
Caravan Park	Internet Cafe	Police Station	Temple
Cave	Lookout	Post Office	Tomb
Church	Monument	Pub or Bar	Tourist Information
Cinema	Mosque	Ruins	Transport

Note: not all symbols displayed above appear in this book

LONELY PLANET OFFICES

Australia
PO Box 617, Hawthorn, Victoria 3122
☎ 03 9819 1877 fax 03 9819 6459
email: talk2us@lonelyplanet.com.au

UK
10a Spring Place, London NW5 3BH
☎ 020 7428 4800 fax 020 7428 4828
email: go@lonelyplanet.co.uk

USA
150 Linden St, Oakland, CA 94607
☎ 510 893 8555 TOLL FREE: 800 275 8555
fax 510 893 8572
email: info@lonelyplanet.com

France
1 rue du Dahomey, 75011 Paris
☎ 01 55 25 33 00 fax 01 55 25 33 01
email: bip@lonelyplanet.fr
www.lonelyplanet.fr

World Wide Web: www.lonelyplanet.com *or* AOL keyword: lp
Lonely Planet Images: lpi@lonelyplanet.com.au